Julia Hoydis
Risk and the English Novel

Buchreihe der Anglia/ ANGLIA Book Series

Edited by
Lucia Kornexl, Ursula Lenker, Martin Middeke,
Gabriele Rippl, Daniel Stein, Hubert Zapf

Advisory Board
Laurel Brinton, Philip Durkin, Olga Fischer, Susan Irvine,
Andrew James Johnston, Christopher A. Jones, Terttu Nevalainen,
Derek Attridge, Elisabeth Bronfen, Ursula K. Heise, Verena Lobsien,
Laura Marcus, J. Hillis Miller, Martin Puchner

Volume 66

Julia Hoydis

Risk and the English Novel

From Defoe to McEwan

DE GRUYTER

ISBN 978-3-11-076597-7
e-ISBN (PDF) 978-3-11-061541-8
e-ISBN (EPUB) 978-3-11-061556-2
ISSN 0340-5435

Library of Congress Control Number 2019945308

Bibliographic information published by the Deutsche Nationalbibliothek
The Deutsche Nationalbibliothek lists this publication in the Deutsche Nationalbibliografie; detailed bibliographic data are available on the Internet at http://dnb.dnb.de.

© 2021 Walter de Gruyter GmbH, Berlin/Boston
This volume is text- and page-identical with the hardback published in 2019.
Printing and binding: CPI books GmbH, Leck

www.degruyter.com

Contents

Introduction: Risk Theory and Narrative Fiction – An Interdisciplinary Overview —— 1

Part I Survival Against the Odds: The Rise of Risk in the 18th-century Novel

1 **Calculating a New View of Life** —— 43
1.1 Probability, Chance, and the Spirit of Quantification —— 43
1.2 A Projecting Age: Speculation, Credit, Gambling —— 53
1.3 Realism, Uncertainties, and the Early Novel —— 61

2 **Defoe and his Protagonists at Large in the Risk Society** —— 71
2.1 Calculations of Survival and Fear: *Robinson Crusoe* —— 71
2.2 Risk Management and Human Behaviour in Times of Crisis: *A Journal of the Plague Year* —— 98
2.3 Marriage, Crime, and the Hazards of Women: *Moll Flanders* —— 118
2.4 Possession, Paranoia, and the Risk of the Past: *Roxana, The Fortunate Mistress* —— 131

3 **Swift, Smollett, Sterne, and Walpole: Fears of Masculinity and Parodies of Calculation** —— 147
3.1 Of Man's Control by Speculation and Fear: *Gulliver's Travels* —— 147
3.2 Risky Games and the Disorder of Passion: *Roderick Random* —— 162
3.3 Individualism, Parental Anxiety, and Fears of Destruction: *Tristram Shandy* —— 178
3.4 Overwhelming Fears and Struggles for Authority: *The Castle of Otranto* —— 201

4 **Picturing Female Youth at Risk: *Camilla*** —— 217

Part II Out of the Ordinary: The Gamble of Life in the 19th-century Novel

5	**Old and New Concerns** —— 253
5.1	Cinderella 'At Sea': *Persuasion* —— 253
5.2	The Risk of Our Creation: *Frankenstein, or the Modern Prometheus* —— 270

6	**Precariousness, Accidents, and Divisions** —— 286
6.1	Industrial Novels and the Victorian Risk Society —— 286
6.2	Suffering From Unmanageable Risk: *Mary Barton* —— 301
6.3	The Danger of Power Relations: *Shirley* —— 310
6.4	No Way Out of Coketown: *Hard Times* —— 320
6.5	Dealing with Change and Loss: *North and South* —— 329

7	**Epic Tales of Ambition and Speculation** —— 339
7.1	New Money and Marriage Plots —— 339
7.2	More Losses than Gains: *The Way We Live Now* —— 345
7.3	Gambling for Self and Happiness: *Daniel Deronda* —— 363

8	**The Dangers of Human Nature and the Struggle Between the Sexes** —— 381
8.1	The Female Body as Risk: *Tess of the d'Urbervilles* —— 381
8.2	'An Irrevocable Oath is Risky': Marriage and Death in *Jude the Obscure* —— 400
8.3	Drowning in Modern Life: *The Whirlpool* —— 416

Part III Crisis and Contingency: Threats to Humanity in the 20th- and 21st-century Novel

9	**A Sense of Endings** —— 433
9.1	'Madness or Despair': *The Secret Agent* —— 433
9.2	'Panic and Emptiness': *Howards End* —— 451
9.3	Ordinary Apocalypse: *Coming Up For Air* —— 467

10	**Gendered Routines of Risk-Taking** —— 483
10.1	'If You Don't Weaken': *Saturday Night and Sunday Morning* —— 483
10.2	Illusions of Safe Space: *The Swimming-Pool Library* —— 501

11	**Running Out of Time** —— 520
11.1	Posthumans Coming of Age: *Never Let Me Go* —— 520
11.2	The Ticking Bomb of Denial and Inertia: *Solar* —— 537

12	**Domestic (In)securities** —— 555
12.1	'Or you can be happy if you dare': *Saturday* —— 555
12.2	'The bullet of an ordinary life': *Arlington Park* —— 571

Epilogue —— 587

Works Cited —— 596
        Primary Works —— 596
        Secondary Sources —— 600

Subject Index —— 655

Index of Persons —— 663

Introduction

Risk Theory and Narrative Fiction – An Interdisciplinary Overview

If one consults etymological dictionaries, the origins of 'risk' are judged to be somewhat hazy but traceable back to denoting the danger of running a ship against rocks unseen in the water while trying to navigate among cliffs.[1] Thus the beginnings of risk, as most (Western) theoretical-historical accounts of the term agree, lie at sea, referencing the hazard of voyaging in uncharted waters and the uncertain outcome of mercantile adventures and trade, and affirm the ocean's symbolic significance as a realm of danger and an original focal point of discourses of uncertainty. Risk is firmly tied to emerging concepts of probability and insurance. There is also agreement on the time horizon, which situates the origins of risk as a scientific and popular concept in the mid-17th century, from thenceforth it gains rapid momentum in the 18th, is fully implemented and institutionalized in society in the course of the 19th, and reaches popular and interdisciplinary academic currency in the late 20th century. At the beginning of the third millennium, it has taken on global proportions, and alongside semantically related notions such as fear and precarity seems to be everywhere. Still, what is lacking to date, despite important book-length contributions by Bernstein (1998) and a vast number of sociological studies[2], is, as Jens Zinn observes, "a systematic reconstruction of the historical development of the semantic of risk" (Zinn 2010: 113). This is a gap the present study seeks to close, at least partially, while specifically relating the rise of risk to the development of the English novel from its beginnings in the early 18th century to the present. As such, the diachronic analysis, which consists of twenty-nine case studies of British fictions from Daniel Defoe to Ian McEwan, is situated in the field of studies of the novel and of literature and science studies and pursues its interdisciplinary focus through close narratological analysis and a perspective

---

[1] A typical entry for 'risk' reads thus: "The ultimate origins of *risk* have never been satisfactorily explained. English acquired it via French *risqué* from Italian *risco*, a derivative of the verb *riscare* 'run into danger,' but there speculation takes over. One persistant theory is that its ancestral meaning is 'sail dangerously close to rocks,' and attempts have been made to link it with Greek *rhíza* 'cliff' and Latin *resegare* 'cut off short' (from the notion of coastal rocks being 'cut off sharply' or 'sheer')" (Ayto 1990: 446; original emphasis). See also Klein (1967: 1350) and Skeat (1963: 520).

[2] See, for example, Adams (1995), Arnoldi (2009), Bonß (1995), Gardner (2008), Haltaufderheide (2015), and Wilkinson (2010).

informed by new historicism and cultural studies. For the discursive nature of risk – as a fictional, social construct – inevitably transcends the realm of literature and literary production.

A study of fictional literature suggests new insights into the pervasiveness of risk in its various manifestations. To this day, the research of risk scholars and professionals alike is highly diverse and, one might dare saying, inconclusive. Though risk has gained general prominence as a salient category of social self-reflection, it is constituted differently in different theoretical fields and discourses (see Knights and Vurdubakis 1993: 730; Banse 1996: 70). It has diverging and sometimes even opposing meanings and objects of inquiry in disciplines such as technical risk analysis, economics, political science, sociology, medicine, law, psychology, philosophy, and literary studies. To give one example: A traditional definition of risk in economics and insurance literature hinges on Frank H. Knight's distinction between risk and uncertainty, the latter allowing no numerical prediction and determination.[3] This clear-cut binary has, of course, proven to be difficult to uphold in theory and practice and called forth justified criticism about a lack of clarity what "measurable" uncertainty, i.e. risk, means in different contexts (see Haltaufderheide 2015: 146–147). Moreover, this widely debated distinction[4] is used inconsistently or even in direct opposition in sociological approaches to risk, e.g. Knight's uncertainties are precisely what scholars prescribing to Ulrich Beck's risk society theory or Foucault's governmentality approach call risks. In recent years there is even a general reversal of Knight's definition with risk having come to refer to "that which cannot be calculated and that therefore is uncertain" (Arnoldi 2009: 24).

Each scientific community or branch of research ultimately has its own – but by no means inherently clear – understanding of risk and concepts used interchangeably or in opposition, such as uncertainty, contingency, chance, hazard, and danger. Several of these are outlined further and contrasted in the following brief survey, revealing the need to broaden, integrate, and historicize sociological-cultural concepts of risk. In addition, it shows the value of applying risk as an analytical frame to a diachronic corpus of realist fictional texts which fruit-

---

[3] Knight writes: "It will appear that a *measurable* uncertainty, or 'risk' proper, [...] is so far different from an *unmeasurable* one that it is not in effect an uncertainty at all" ([1921] 2002: 19–20; original emphasis).

[4] Arnoldi, while acknowledging that the distinction between risk and uncertainty is an important one, argues that "it is constantly conflated, not so much analytically but because potential dangers can involve both risk and uncertainty and because risk and uncertainty can have similar consequences" (2009: 183). On the recent popularity of the concept of uncertainty see Nowotny (2016).

fully moves the study of risk in the English novel beyond its to date customary confinement to speculative postmodernist and dystopian disaster narratives. The analysis in the present study, however, consciously refrains from drawing any clear semantic lines between risk and closely interrelated concepts,[5] for it purports that ultimately more important is risk's function as an anthropocentric means of conceptualising and dealing with the perceived uncertainty of the future and of exploring and managing "the tension between the vision of stability and predictability and a precarious and uncertain world" (Knights and Vurdubakis 1993: 730).

Approaching risk as an object of study, one faces the task of trying to differentiate between partially contrasting and overlapping risk discourses which are usually either driven by formal-normative or cultural-sociological concerns, pursue either action- or system-oriented perspectives, and can be probabilistic-technical, economic, anthropological-political, psychological-cognitive or sociological-philosophical in orientation. Thus, though undoubtedly intuitively understandable, risk is not self-explanatory and its ubiquity has not lead to greater clarity but rather the opposite, as Wolfgang Bonß (1995: 29–30) for example has noted. One finds many other voices that affirm risk's multi-facetedness:[6] "Risk comes in many forms. [...] The list is as long as there are adjectives to apply to behavior in the face of uncertainty" (Adams 1995: 21); "there is no universal set of characteristics for describing risk" (Slovic 1997: 284); "There is little that is precise about the use of the term risk. [...] No definition [...] can exhaust the meaning and usage of the risk concept" (Furedi 2005: 17); "Risk is an ineliminable part of human existence. [...] there are as many 'kinds of risks' as there are kinds of negativities in human affairs" (Rescher 1983: 9).

The lamented fuzziness of the term risk seems to lie in the fact that there is only consistency or agreement to be found about two aspects: The first is hardly satisfactory from an analytical point of view, but opens it particularly for literary analysis and affirms the necessity to integrate different approaches

---

5 One can follow Niklas Luhmann's argument on the semantic confusion and overlap in this context: "In the largely English-language literatue the words risk, hazard, and danger are available and are usually employed almost synonymously" (1993: 22).

6 See especially David Garland's summary: "Today's accounts of risk are remarkable for their multiplicity and for the variety of senses they give to the term. Risk is a calculation. Risk is a commodity. Risk is a capital. Risk is a technique of government. Risk is objective and scientifically knowable. Risk is subjective and socially constructed. Risk is a problem, a threat, a source of insecurity. Risk is a pleasure, a thrill, a source of profit and freedom. Risk is the means whereby we colonize and control the future. 'Risk society' is our modern world spinning out of control" (2003: 49).

and to seek a transcending meaning and patterns of risk beyond narrow, schematic sociological categories. For as the examples cited above illustrate, one hardly finds a study of risk which does not open with a declaration of the impossibility to define risk and the acknowledgment that it remains unclear and is being stretched over a wide "range of social activities, practices and experiences" (Mythen and Walklate 2006: 1), despite of or due to the rapidly increasing currency of the term's use in contemporary culture since the 1980s and the avalanche of writing and debate produced in the wake of Ulrich Beck's first formulation of the 'risk society' thesis.[7] As Bob Heyman sums up, the "ubiquity of risk-thinking in modern cultures challenges definitional efforts", while its "[d]efinitional absence stands in sharp contrast to extended usage in every sphere of modern life" (Heyman 2012: 606; 605). The second concerns the paradoxical nature of risk as something between fact and fiction, between reality and constructed imagination. Risk furthermore entails in equal measures a rational, probable and objective estimation and reference of existing uncertainties and course of future events and an emotional, subjective component that risk analysts and policy makers across various fields continue to struggle with and to account for. Referring originally neutrally to the objective estimations of possible events, because the predominately (and nowadays often exclusively) negative association with danger and loss rather than gains is only shaped in the course of the 19th century (see Douglas 1990: 3; Lupton 1999b: 8), risk comprises affective responses such as concern, fear, and thrill besides statistical probabilities. To talk about risk, as an anthropocentric concept, inevitably implies a self-conscious subject capable of perceiving it, of making and judging decisions and anticipating the future (see Bonß 1995: 37; Schmitz-Emans 2013: 843). Denoting above all a perceived relationship between human beings and the world, risk is marked by its crucial focus on human agency (see Mizruchi 2010: 111; Garland 2003: 51) but, not without paradox for a scientific term, begins in the realm where knowledge and certainty end.

According to the editors of the *Handbook of Risk Theory*, one of the most comprehensive overviews of interdisciplinary risk research to date, one central shared characteristic of risk emerges among the diversity of topics and approaches, namely that "risk involves statistics as much as ethics and social values" (Roser et al. 2012: 23). As an important token in a society's self-understanding of its relation to nature, forms of knowledge, governing ethical, social and scientific paradigms, the concept of risk always combines a descriptive and

---

[7] See Ulrich Beck's *Risk Society: Towards a New Modernity* ([1986] 1992) and his many publications on the subject since.

normative side (see Renn 1992: 56; Thompson 1986: 285). However, while this underlines plausibly both risk's universal strategic, instrumental use and its constructedness, derived from specific historical and cultural conditions and practices of social organization (through statistiscal measurements, calculations, mediations of risk via different media etc.), what remains a constant in all risk concepts, but also a difficulty – primarily in the sciences dedicated to empirical research –, is risk's status in-between reality and unreality, that is mere possibility, or, fiction. John Adams explains how risk only exists "in the minds of people" (Adams 1995: 30), as anticipations formed as behaviour-guiding principles in the present, based on projecting experience from the past into the future. As an inherently relational category, risk expresses perceived relationships between self and world, emerging out of context-depending conventions and shared meanings. Asa Boholm emphazises this point, saying that

> what is or what is not considered a 'risk' depends to a large extent on other things. Social relationships, power relations and hierarchies, cultural beliefs, trust in institutions and science, knowledge, experiencce, discourses, practices and collective memories all shape notions about risk or safety. (Boholm 2003: 175)

This, in turn, implies that risk cannot be severed from (collective, individual) perception. Rather than debating its ontological status, the focus needs to be placed on risk's ethical and epistemological qualities and functions. To borrow David Garland's suggestive words: "If our orientation towards life's dangers were suddenly to shift from active concern to fatalistic acceptance, our world would be no less hazardous but the risk society would disappear" (Garland 2003: 52). Instead of a reality in itself, risk has to be understood as a means of seeing and interpreting the world, of attempting to create a calculable order and sequences of events. With risk and risk-taking appearing as human strategies to assign significance to life,[8] risk discourses are relational world and self-descriptions. They reflect assessments and projections as well as retrospective interpretations of varying concepts of uncertainty. These, as Monika Schmitz-Emans (2013: 845; 844; 837) underlines, intersect with theories of free will and rationality, knowledge and belief. Inevitably conveyed through calculations and narratives, risk entails the desire to control the future, to search for causality by identifying regularities, possibilities, and responsibilities, i.e. consequences and culprits.

---

[8] For this argument see, e.g., Dean (1999: 131), Ericson and Doyle (2003: 8), Ewald (1991: 199), Garland (2003: 49), and Tulloch and Lupton (2003: 19).

According to philosophical definitions,[9] risk can refer to an event which may or may not occur, to its cause, to the probability and statistical expectation value of its occurrence, or simply to any decision made under condition of known probabilties (see Hansson 2011). Other meanings exist, varying yet again between normative vs descriptive approaches. In most philosophical studies of risk, however, the focus clearly lies on the practical study of making explicit the ethical judgments inherent in risk analysis, about the values, justice, acceptability, in other words, how one determines who or what is worth risking when. Similarly, in parts of sociological and economic theory, risk evaluation and management is understood as part of wider theories of decision-making and rationality in choice and action (see Rescher 1983: 5).[10] While aspects of investigation concern levels of risk thresholds and acceptability of degrees of uncertainty, central is also consent, i.e. the difference between imposed and voluntary risk and risk-taking (e.g. in public decision-making about health and safety). Informed by the empirically-derived fact that people's attitudes towards risk differ vastly and inevitably transcend any 'rational' cost-benefit analyses, philosophy and sociology, in contrast to economic theory which tends to focus only on the decision maker and issues of liability, engage more with the complexity of the question of human behaviour and agency in the face of uncertainty (see Hansson 2013: 19; Rehmann-Sutter 1998: 129–130), the latter being, of course, also what is explored and negotiated in fictional narratives.

In sociological discourse, risk has become dominant especially in the last three to four decades and has led to a vast number of empirical and theoretical studies.[11] The literature can broadly be divided according to perspectives on risk perception, assessment, and management, which prioritise either investigating what is considered a risk or what is done in the name of risk. While the development of human society is inseparable from risk, reasons for the booming attraction of social scientists to the concept lie in its dominance in public media and in central questions such as how human behaviour and society are governed by risk and what its social, political, cultural dimensions are. The interest is typically dual, i.e. a micro and macro one, looking at the role of the state and its

---

9 See especially Hansson's study *Ethics of Risk. Ethical Analysis in an Uncertain World* (2013); see also Hansson (1989; 1999; 2011), Altham (1984), Lewens (2007), MacLean (1985), Rehmann-Sutter (1998), Teuber (1990), J. Thompson (1985), and P. Thompson (1986).
10 Still, Hansson (2013: 1) notes, risk and uncertainty are comparatively rarely considered in moral philosophy although they are an intrinsic part of decision making.
11 There are numerous studies which summarize the field, for example Boyne (2003). An accessible and comprehensive volume is Jens O. Zinn's *Social Theories of Risk and Uncertainty: An Introduction* (2008a).

measures of calculating and maintaining the security of the social body and at the individual and its lifestyle choices, risk-taking or aversion. Main areas of concern being economics, health care, crime, and environmentalism, typical kinds of risks analysed include financial collapse, pandemics, terrorism, pollution, and environmental disaster (see Arnoldi 2009: 5).

Since the 1980s, three major theoretical perspectives of risk have emerged and impacted on interdisciplinary understandings of risk: The Risk-Society approach (Beck, Giddens), the Systems Theory or Governmentality approach (Foucault, Luhmann), and the cultural approach (Douglas, Wildavsky, Slovic). These have developed and diversified from the original concern with technical-scientific issues of risk management and supplemented initially dominant rational-actor-models of behaviour with approaches allowing for the complexity of risk responses and their embeddedness in psychological and socio-cultural, as well as political and historical factors. To different degrees, they also all seek to grapple with risk's ambivalent ontological status between reality and constructedness.

Sociological Approaches (I): Risk Society

A main disciplinary difference between economic theory, sociology and anthropology lies in the general evaluation of risk as a category: the first views risk as necessary, calculabe, enabling and mainly positive; the latter sees risks as largely incalculable and humans as creatures who need safety and clarity and cannot tolerate uncertainty in too great degrees (see Turner 1994: 170). A turning point and trigger in the history of risk research is therefore the proclaimed rise of uncertainty and incalculable, unmanageable human-made risks from the cold-war period onwards. Many theorists characterize this era of 'postmodern', 'late', 'second', or 'reflexive' modernity through its ambivalence, uncertainty, and fragmentation (Bauman 1991; Giddens 1991). Most notably perhaps Zygmunt Bauman has described modernity as a state of constant flux and liquidity, which erodes all solids (referring here to social structures more than to beliefs and certainties as in the earlier stages of modernity).[12] While the changing experience of time and space is crucial for perceiving modernity as liquid, emphasizing dissolution, acceleration and speed (see Rosa 2012), and ambivalence is mainly experienced as a disorienting disorder, Bauman argues that order (predictability) and

---

[12] See Bauman's *Modernity and Ambivalence* (1991), *Liquid Modernity* (2000), *Liquid Love* (2003), and *Liquid Times* (2007).

chaos (uncertainty) appear, in fact, as *"modern* twins" (Bauman 1991: 4; original emphasis). Both categories, which merge in the category of risk, also only exist in retrospective or anticipatory reflection. The sociological interest in risk is closely connceted to theories such as Bauman's and others about processes of globalization, and reflexive, i.e. radicalized modernization which cause "more risks, bigger risks, unheard-of risks" (Bauman 1991: 272). For Anthony Giddens, "[t]o live in the universe of high modernity is to live in an environment of chance and risk" (Giddens 1991: 109; see Giddens 1998: 26), while for Ulrich Beck "being at global risk is the human condition at the beginning of the twenty-first century" (Beck 2006: 330).

Beck first put forth the conviction that modern science has produced risks beyond human control in *Risk Society* (1992), arguably one of the most influential works of European social analysis in the late 20th century, originally published as *Risikogesellschaft* in German in 1986 and written in the wake of disasters such as Chernobyl, Bhopal, and Three Mile Island. His idea of the "risk society" portrays risks as overwhelmingly negative and contains the main argument about the intertwining of reflexive modernization and risk. Later updating his thesis to *World Risk Society* (1996) to include global dangers, decisive for Beck is society's preoccupation with risks it has itself produced, i.e. manufactured uncertainties. The global risks share three further important features, de-localization, incalculableness, and non-compensability (Beck 2009: 294; Beck 2006: 336). They are dangers produced by human civilization which cannot be insured, delimited and controlled in space or time.

There are close parallels between Beck and Giddens's work on risk and reflexive modernization. Both argue that a rising distrust in the authority of science, i.e. the belief that scientific advance equals an advance of security, leads to science widely being perceived as relative to knowledge and as a source of danger rather than as a saving grace. According to Giddens (1999), it is this scepticism towards science which characterizes reflexive modernity. Generally, reflexivity means that modernity becomes more complex and advances in intensity. Thus it turns self-destructive and self-endangering, producing the conditions of the global risk society which replace the industrial society of first, or 'simple', modernity. It forces people to deal with uncertainty on an unprecedented scale (see Beck 1994: 7) because in this less controllable world individuals are also forced to make more and more choices. Although Beck notes, at least in passing, that "calculating risks is part of the master narrative of first modernity" (Beck 2002b: 41), he emphasises the rise of global, uncontrollable risks in late modernity. Agreeing on much with Beck, Giddens displays slightly more historical awareness. Admitting that risk has a much longer connection to (first) modernity which can be traced back centuries,[13] he still argues that it assumes new importance at the turn of the 20th to the 21st century (Giddens 2000: 43), claiming that: "Our age is not more dangerous – not more risky – than those of earlier generations, but the balance of risks and dangers has shifted" (2000: 52).

It needs stressing that both Giddens and Beck are, in fact, focused on the link between risk and collective and individual responsibility, tied to the central ethical question "how do we wish to live?" (Beck 1992: 28; Beck 2002: 215; see Giddens 1999: 5; Giddens 1998), which assumes urgency in the face of an understanding of risk as having come to mean "the threat of self-destruction of all life on Earth" (Beck 1992: 21). The risk society thesis is inseparable from its specific historical context, a time which saw several instances of environmental havoc on a global scale, clearly attributable to processes of technological modernization.[14] This leads Beck and his followers to the strong emphasis that humanity has reached a period of global disasters beyond its control (see Wilkinson 2010: 45), and that drastic actions need to be taken. For despite its obvious apocalyptic pessimism, Beck's world risk society is at its heart a theory of socio-political resistance with a somewhat utopian kernel, sustained by an underlying appeal for cosmopolitan action induced by humanity's shared awareness of the globality of risks and survival as a common goal. While obviously disregarding any specificities, heterogeneities, and the historicity of the term, risk for Beck maintains a quality of eye-opening potential rather than paralyzing fear (see Beck 1998: 20), an aspect that makes his approach appear strategic, and markedly different from others, more schematic ones. He claims that "it is irrelevant whether we live in a world which is in fact or in some sense 'objectively' safer than all other worlds; if destruction and disasters are anticipated, then that produces a compulsion to act" (Beck 2006: 332); "Global risk has the power to tear away the facades of organized irresponsibility" (2006: 339). Although he admits that "global risks are per se unequally distributed" (Beck 2002b: 42), the World Risk Society, for Beck, is a cosmopolitan society, integrated by an overwhelming sense of "globally shared collective future crisis" (Beck 2002c: 27). Limiting his analysis across his various publications to three main kinds of catastrophic risks,

---

13 In *Runaway World* (2000) Giddens affirms the origins of risk in 16th and 17th century, its connection with seafaring and travel, which then assumes temporal connotations and comes to represent a broad spectrum of chance and uncertainty, reflecting modern society's emerging orientation towards the future, as "territory to be conquered or colonized" (Giddens 2000: 40).

14 This refers in particular to the post-Chernobyl climate and the rise of the Green movement in Germany in the 1980s. See Robert Dingwall, who describes Beck's *Risk Society* as a "a profoundly German book" (Dingwall 1999: 475) that needs to be understood within its specific temporal and local context.

environmental, terrorist, and economic, the global risk society, he argues, needs to tackle national and global security and risks such as "global warming, immigration, poison in the food chain and organized crime" (Beck 2002a: 116) through transnational cooperation.

The above already suggests why one should not seek in the risk society thesis a general, widely applicable theory of risk that holds up to deeper social, cultural and historical reflection. However, one can agree with critics such as Wolfgang Bonß (1995: 14; 11) who still credit Beck for linking risk and theory of modernity and pushing risk on the world stage of academic and popular discussion. A perhaps inevitable downside of the wide appeal of catchphrases such as the "risk society", written on a rather generalizing level, is their rudimentary, sketchy quality and inherent Eurocentrism (cf. Campell and Currie 2006: 162).[15] A reason why Beck's has proven more popular than any other risk theory to date is its dramatic "*Nostradamuslich* quality" (Alexander and Smith 1996: 259; original emphasis). As Alexander and Smith point out: "Risk Society translates the rich and suggestive mythology of technological discourse into the empirical categories of social science" Alexander and Smith 1996: 26). It is Beck's rhetoric, the prophetic use of idioms such as "living on the volcano of civilization" (Beck 1992: 17), the title of the first chapter in *Risk Society*, which appears as a translation of "a cosmology of mysterious all-embracing threats – into a modern and only superficially secular form" (Alexander and Smith 1996: 260) and attracts interest in and outside academic circles.

But there are undoubtedly several argumentative and theoretical problems which are hard to ignore, especially from the perspective of a literary and cultural critic. These are only mentioned briefly, as the wider debates within sociology have little relevance here and the existing literature on the subject is vast.[16] Scanning through the body of Beck's publications, his understanding of modernization is, harshly spoken, Eurocentric, ahistorical, and disregards issues of gender, ethnicity and class, while the concept of risks is narrow and exclusively neg-

---

[15] Despite the hype of the "risk society" thesis, the theoretical engagement, the in-depth academic discussion is lacking behind, especially in literary circles; Beck remains among the most cited authors, but references to the risk society are usually reduced to mere name-dropping (see Bonß 1996: 165).

[16] For strong criticism of Beck's theory see Campell and Currie (2006) and Elliott (2002). For critical reflection of Beck's theoretical grounding and assumptions inherent in 'reflexive modernization' and 'risk society' see Lash, Szerszynski and Wynne (1996), and Adam, Beck and Van Loon (2000); for the lacking consideration of impact of factors such as gender, age, class, ethnicity, nationality, levels of education and access to knowledge, see, e.g., Alexander (1996), Lupton (1999b), and Beck, Bonß and Lau (2003).

ative (see Baker and Simon 2002: 20). Lacking focus on diversity and motivations, let alone, the pleasures of risk-taking,[17] Beck's risk society fails to account for the reality that modernization and 'global' risks affect different people differently and refuse sweeping homogenization into unilateral process or grand narratives such as the risk soceity (see Adams 1995: 182; Tulloch 2008: 153; Tulloch and Lupton 2003: 39); this, however is a charge that applies to other social theories as well as to Beck's.[18] Though he modifies many problematic assumptions from one of this many essays to the next, making it difficult to pinpoint definitions or claims, one frequently finds troubling statements such as that "the earth has become an ejector seat that no longer recognizes any distinctions between rich and poor, black and white, north and south or east and west" (Beck 1992: 36), which hardly need further commentary other than that risk and global crisis are employed as unifying categories which gloss over realities of inequality, oppression and poverty and ignore the concentrations and dynamics of capitalism.[19] For Beck, risks "display an equalizing effect" (Beck 1992: 35) that goes as far as making class disappear. But as various critics have rightly emphazised, judged from a Western cultural perspective, we still live in an unequal rather than unsafe society (see Tulloch 2008: 160; Elliott 2002: 303). In addition, Beck's definition of risk as "a systematic way of dealing with hazards and insecurities introduced by modernization itself" (Beck 1992: 21) makes no distinction between risk and risk perception and adheres to a problematic division between supposedly 'objective' expert and subjective lay perceptions of risk.[20]

To conclude the discussion of the risk society, one can agree that Beck develops important and fascinating lines of thought, but fails to explore them in detail and complexity, missing a broader historical dimension, as Mark Lacy (2002: 59)

---

17 According to Kelly Hannah-Moffat and Pat O' Malley, "for the risk society thesis, risk's diversity of forms is of no great importance, and not a salient subject of theorizing within the approach" (2007: 13). On these aspects see instead Tulloch and Lupton (2003); Lupton and Tulloch (2002), Hannah-Moffat and O'Malley (2007).
18 See Iain Wilkinson's argument: "Social theories of risk society almost invariably incorporate generalizing accounts of dominant modes of social consciousness and feeling. Indeed, I would be inclined to suggest that the overall coherence and logic of the majority of theoretical works on this topic rest extensively upon crude idealizations of our social subjectivity. For example, writers such as Beck [...] can be seen to elaborate in the broadest terms on the dynamics of social change by reflecting upon the possible social and political implications of a particular representation of risk consciousness" (Wilkinson 2006: 37).
19 See Slavoj Žižek's criticism of the unacknowledged logic of capitalism in Beck's risk society thesis, which he sees as both too general and too particular and, above all, glossing over the capitalist market economy as a key risk-generating factor (Žižek 2008: 439).
20 See, e.g., Brian Wynne (1996: 44–83) on the "expert-lay knowledge divide".

suggests, and, as Anthony Elliott adds, fails to grasp hermeneutical, aesthetic, psychological dimensions in a social-theoretical frame of reference (see Elliott 2002: 300). From the perspective of a literary-cultural critic, he also ignores postmodernity, in the sense that it was not only new technological risks since the cold-war period which led to the undermining of belief in the master narratives of science and progress. Furthermore, throughout his writing on the subject, Beck's epistemological understanding and semantic use of risk is rather inconsistent and ambivalent (see Zinn 2010: 114). For example, Beck has tried to distinguish older "dangers" and "threats" from new "risks", as incalculable, uninsurable, and man-made, "manufactured uncertainties". He defines risk as a modern concept that "presupposes human decisions, humanly made futures (probability, technology, modernization)" (Beck 2009: 293); but this classification, hinging on a implified distinction according to calculability and controllabilty, immediately collapse when one draws historical comparisons. Still, it is hard to completely defute the claim, as John Adams notes, that science and technology have created new risks, "although the distinction between the fears and anxieties of preindustrial societies and those of the modern world may not be as sharp as Beck suggests" (Adams 1995: 180; see 179). Ultimately, the main argument for the limitations of Beck's risk society thesis is its exclusive contemporaneity which has been challenged by many critical voices.[21] Failing to engage with older theories of risk and uncertainty, Beck's criteria and characteristics of 'modern' risks hardly hold up to historical scrutiny over the last three centuries, in particular from an interdisciplinary vantage point. Risk, as a social category and concern for individual and government emerged much earlier than the late 20th century. As Mitchell Dean sums up: "It is clear that the genealogy of risk is much more complex than the theory of risk society allows. Risk and its techniques are plural and heterogeneous and its significance cannot be exhausted by a narrative of a shift from a quantitative calculation of risk to the globalization of incalculable risks" (Dean 1999: 145). And lastly, while the human distrust and fear of science cannot be seen as a development of the late modernity, neither can assumptions such as the following hold up to closer diachronic scrutiny: "Even the traditions of marriage and the family are becoming dependent on decision-making, and with all their contradictions must be experienced as personal risks" (Beck 1994: 14). Taking a cue from the criticism of Beck's risk society, it is aspects such as decisons concerning familial and

---

[21] For criticism of the argument that the human obsession with risk only begins in the late 20th century, see Bonß (1996: 174–175), Ericson and Doyle (2003: 13), Dingwall (1999), and Taylor-Gooby and Zinn (2006: 4).

romantic relationships and attitudes towards science which the present study strives to show as continuous risk perceptions over the last three centuries; these are supplemented by a focus on differences caused by the impact of class and gender identities.

Sociological Approaches (II): Governmentality

Regarding risk, most theorists agree upon the significance of the issues of power and control, trust and observation, in particular those that belong to the so-called Systems Theory or Governmentality approach. It is based on Foucault's concept of governmentality – a neologism for "government rationality" – which sees modern societies governed through a bureaucratic, disciplinary apparatus instilling a sense of risk and morality in the individual and society as a collective, through employing circulations "among the alternating registers of security, danger, anxiety, and fear" (Ericson and Doyle 2003: 113).[22] According to the historical genealogies and lines of thought Foucault develops in *The Birth of the Clinic*, *Discipline and Punish* and continues in *Security, Territory, Population*, risk appears as a category strategically imbricated in "regimes of government" (Dean 1999: 131), seeking control of the social body via surveillance, measurement and the collection of data, especially from the turn of the 18th to the 19th century onwards. It is related closely to the concept of biopower, first introduced in *The History of Sexuality* and presented in Foucault's later lecture series on *The Birth of Biopolitics*, employed to refer to regulatory mechanisms for controlling risk of health and heredity in the population.[23]

Governmentality theorists, in the wider sense, are scholars such as Mitchell Dean, Richard Doyle, Aaron Erickson, François Ewald, Ian Hacking, Pat O'Malley, and Nikolas Rose (see Arnoldi 2009: 53). At the heart of their approaches lies the concern with the usage and conception of risk, focused, for example, on insurance and precaution (Ewald 1991; 2002), chance and probability (Hacking 1975; 1990), and the nexus between risk and morality (Doyle and Erickson 2003), with a dominant focus on the 19th century. As Colin Gordon outlines in his introduction to *The Foucault Effect: Studies in Governmentality*, it is then

---

22 See Burchell, et al.'s *The Foucault Effect: Studies in Governmentality* (1991). The classic essay in this volume is Foucault's "Governmentality" (87–104). See also Japp and Kusche (2008).
23 See Foucault's *The Birth of Biopolitics* (2010); Morton and Bygrave's *Foucault in an Age of Terror* (2008); Cisney and Morar's *Biopower: Foucault and Beyond* (2016); in the latter volume see especially the chapters by Hacking, "Biopower and the Avalanche of Printed Numbers" (65–81), and Rabinow and Rose, "Biopower Today" (297–325).

that risk becomes "a kind of omnivorous encyclopaedizing principle for the objectification of possible experience – not only of the hazards of personal life and private venture, but also of the common venture of society" (Gordon 1991: 39). Governmentality theorists, as Rigakos and Hadden argue, thus "tend to privilege a version of history which locates a particular type of probabilistic thinking in the early 19th century" (Rigakos and Hadden 2001: 63).[24] More importantly, they place the spotlight on "the modern epistemic relationship between people and their representation as 'data' or populations to be managed and controlled" (2001: 73), as individuals and members of a particular class, which serves clear ideological purposes in the historical evolution of the surveillance state and the instrumentalization of power and knowledge. It emphasizes the importance of bureaucracy as a "highly rationalized mode of information gathering and administrative control" (Dandeker 1990: 2). The disciplinary social paradigm is linked to a continually extended range of prediction and control and emerging institutional risk management, through techniques of identifying transgressions, panoptic technologies of observation, and statistical classification of (ab)normalities (see Rigakos and Law 2009: 83). This leads, for example, to the categorization of certain groups of the population as "risks", usually those near the bottom of the social ladder. Aside from the perception of the poor as the 'dangerous' class, Robert Castel describes a decisive shift towards the risk embodied in the mentally ill, because the modern ideology of risk prevention which "plays on the alternate registers of fear and security, inducing a delirium of rationality, an absolute reign of calculative reason" (Castel 1991: 289; see 284) is extended to fields such as medicine and psychiatry.

The paradigm of security is inseparable from the imperative of prevention. While uncertainty, through the language of risk, is put in a new scientific light, it also becomes connected to rights and duties, as François Ewald (2002; 1993; 1991) has shown. Another important development is therefore the institutionalization of insurance as a moral and political technology. Pat O'Malley explains, "Better understood as *prudentialism*, it is a technology of governance that removes the key conception of regulating individuals by collectivist risk management, and throws back upon the individual the responsibility for managing risk" (O'Malley 1996: 197). The idea of the prudent subject and the duty to be 'well and safe', the responsibility for one's own risk prevention and management (see 1996: 200–203), is historically conditioned and shifts the conception of risk. It

---

[24] The position of Rigakos and Hadden presents an exception because it explicitly links risk to 17th-century English capitalism. They argue: "Our understanding of 'risk society' and treatment of risk discourse in the 17th century is identical to that of *fin de siècle* risk sociology" (Rigakos and Hadden 2001: 65; original emphasis).

becomes socially inscribed in relations between people, rather than those between man and (hostile) nature. While it is extended to apply to human beings and their relations, dispositions, behaviour, it becomes a moral and social obligation to manage risk and to take precautions. As Ewald underlines: "The age of the security societies was dawning. A new order was born, with its own way of conceptualizing relations between the whole and the part, the individual and society, good and evil. [...] The way was thus open for the universalization of the notion of risk" (Ewald 1993: 227; see 226). As the opposite of security, in the emerging capitalist welfare-state, risk is applied to all social ills, but also affirms the idea of human life as an enterprise which continuously requires the individual to make provisions for preservation and reproduction of its own capital. As strategies of managing uncertainty, the language and technologies of risk are adopted as primary techniques of government in the Foucauldian sense, set to realize the ideal of objectifying and controlling the future and shielding citizens from harm (see Gordon 1991: 20; Ewald 1991: 219).

While Niklas Luhmann's systemic distinction between danger and risk remains in many ways even more rudimentary and fuzzy as Beck's (cf. Bonß 1996: 166 ff), he usefully emphasizes the discursive nature of risk, which must be communicated and framed through notions of cause, consequence, structures of time and language, and its multi-dimensionality, combining temporal, imaginative, and social aspects: "The outside world itself knows no risks, for it knows neither distinctions, nor expectations, nor evaluations, nor probabilities – *unless self-produced by observer systems in the environment of other systems*" (Luhmann 1993: 6; original emphasis). According to Luhmann (1993: 42), risk evaluation is always dependent on the present, but also often takes place in retrospect, dependent on whether loss has occurred or not. With evaluations of risk shifting in the course of time, there is no correct, objective vantage point; the horizons of past, present and future intersect in the concept of risk which itself reflects in the shifting of these temporal horizons. This is why it is interesting to explore its depiction in fictional representation, considering for instance Robinson Crusoe's changing feelings of risk and safety over his lonely decades on the same island, or the risk of Anne's rejection or acceptance of Captain Wentworth in *Persuasion* which she sees completely differently seven years later. Luhmann also usefully points towards the need to broaden the perception of risk from technological and medical risk, and he suggests to include marital relations, "and in a later period informal intimate relations" because "failure makes its appearance in partnerships as a risk to be weighed up beforehand" (Luhmann 1993: 45).

Thus there are several important cues one can take from systems theory and the governmentality approach for the study of risk in narrative fiction. In comparison to Beck's approach, a governmental analysis of risk reveals the function of risk as a means of organising reality, society and behaviour. It highlights the function of risk as a strategy of government and the construction of risk mentalities. Understanding risk and security as central elements of knowledge, power, and domination makes them appear as interpretive rather than factual realities, representing specific ways "in which aspects of reality can be conceptualized and rendered controllable" (Zinn and Taylor-Gooby 2006a: 45). It exposes "how the world and existing problematisations are *made into risks*, what effects this form of ordering entails upon populations" (Aradau and van Munster 2007: 15; my emphasis); or as Kelly Hannah-Moffat and Pat O'Malley put it, it shows how fears, threats and hazards are *coded* "as 'risks'" (Hannah-Moffat and O'Malley 2007: 15).

Sociological Approaches (III): Cultural Theory and Risk as Feelings

Whereas economists usually focus on risk in relation to rational choice, action and assessments, social theorists and anthropologists have long been concerned with the issues of affect, trust and the cultural framing of risk; recently these approaches have received new input and traction from psychology and media studies. Placing the main focus on how people perceive and respond to risk is referred to as the "cultural turn" in risk research, related to the wider turn to culture in the humanities (see Zinn and Taylor-Gooby 2006b: 68; Zinn 2008b: 16). Cultural theories of risk place emphasis on the embeddedness of risk and fear/dread in the sociocultural background and everyday life. Traditions, beliefs, emotions and trust are seen to stand in direct relation to risk, because they step in whenever knowledge is limited and influence the individual's worldview (religion, ideology) and its attitude towards institutions (state, family), abstract systems (money, economy, medicine, science), or other people. As such psychology and sociology have established what Luhmann called a "countermove" (Luhmann 1993: 1) to the idea that people calculate and act rationally when faced with risk; in fact, individual risk behaviour often deviates from the predictions and prescriptions of statisticians and so-called risk expert opinions. 'Lay' risk perception, though of course influenced by a myriad of external factors such as medial representation, appears as largely irrational and does not reflect the 'realities' of risk. Otherwise people would need to worry about heart disease much more than about terrorism; there are often huge discrepancies between people's fears and the 'real' probabilities of an event happening.[25] With empiri-

---

25 See also Freudenburg (1996).

cal research pointing towards worldview and cultural patterns having a strong influence on risk perception, theorists such as Mary Douglas, Karl Dake, Scott Lash, Deborah Lupton, Steve Rayner, John Tulloch, and Aaron Wildavsky [26] have emphasized the aesthetic, affective and cultural aspects of risk. Setting different accents, they all argue that what is needed is turning away from the obsession with rationalization and cognitive reflection, with security and technicalization, and instead a stronger grounding in aesthetic reflexivity, symbolic practice and identity politics.[27]

In the history of risk theory, the works by anthropologist Mary Douglas take a foundational place. The crossing of borders being traditionally associated with the risk of contamination (of ideas of moral goodness with evil, of propriety with taboos, of notions of Self/community with dangerous Others), her focus on risk developed out of her work on culturally conditioned notions of purity and the dangers of pollution and transgression.[28] Generally, Douglas's cultural focus is closely linked to issues of identity and alterity. Her interest lies in revealing how perceptions of danger and explanations of misfortunes are politicized, how interests and ideology pollute risk perceptions (Douglas 1992: 11). Douglas describes how political vocabularies of accountability and moral responsibility are infused with the language of risk and transcend the scientific assessment of probabilities. While notions of sin and taboo function to protect the order of a specific community, perceived dangers give insight into a community's (or society's, nation's) principles of border-drawing, exclusion, and stigmatization (Douglas 1992: 34–36).[29] For Douglas, risk is a pseudo term, employed to give 'danger' the rational, scientific veneer, "the pretension of a possible precise calculation" (1992: 25). It serves as a mechanism of social control and rhetorical strategy that allocates praise and blame; it allows various scenarios, not always explainable in terms of actual physical danger, to be rewritten in terms of threats of transgression. While this creates a parallel to governmentality theory, Douglas argues for the opposite as Beck in the sense that people are not united by risk awareness but divided by the sense of dangers (see Douglas 1990: 13). As Iain

---

[26] See Dake (1992), Lash (2000), Rayner (1992), and Tulloch (2008).
[27] However, from the perspective of literary criticism, the term "cultural theory" or "cultural approach" to risk bears little resemblance to the meaning of the term in Cultural Studies (see Heise 2002a: 79).
[28] See Douglas's study *Purity and Danger: An Analysis of the Concept of Pollution and Taboo.* ([1966] 2002); and the essay "Risk as a Forensic Resource" (1990). Her main books on risk are *Risk and Blame* (1992), and, written with Aaron B. Wildavsky, *Risk and Culture* (1983).
[29] According to Douglas and Wildavsky (1983: 37–38), many of these fears are associated with sexuality.

Wilkinson explains, throughout her writings, she also "advises that although our technology may be new, humanity has always conceived itself to be courting catastrophe in face of an uncertain future" (Wilkinson 2001: 3).

While the question of the acceptance or rejection of risks was first raised in a groundbreaking essay by Chauncey Starr 1969 in which he famously asked about the relation between social values, risk and safety: "How safe is safe enough?" (Starr 1969: 1233),[30] in *Risk and Culture* (1983) Douglas and Wildavsky also start from the question how risk perceptions and behaviour reflect values and how dangers are disregarded or selected for attention. They develop a rather rigid structural framework of risk types and selection that needs not be drawn out in detail here, but the underlying assumption is relevant. The so-called 'grid-group' model of different cultural responses to risk ('grid' referring to the degree of autonomy, 'group' to the perceived degree of incorporation), consists of differnet types forming distinct cultural groups. Whether an individual can be classified as entrepreneurial, egalitarian, bureaucratic, fatalistic, hierarchist, or autonomous determines his/her view whether risks should be taken or avoided. Each individual is seen to have a preferred way of life, and to act to protect this life style which determines the risks taken and rejected; these are further categorized into socio-political risks (e.g. violenec, dangers emanating from the social structure), economic risks, and natural risks (including ecological and technological risks).

Douglas and Wildavsky argue that each form of sociality "has its own typical risk portfolio. Common values lead to common fears (and, by implication, to a common agreement not to fear other things)" (Douglas and Wildavsky 1983: 8). As such, their cultural approach to risk integrates moral judgements about living with personal preferences and empirical judgments what the world is like: "We moderns can do a lot of politicizing merely by our selection of dangers" (1983: 30; see 10). Of the same opinion are Dan Kahan et al., who write: "In selecting some risks for attention and dismissing others as unimportant, individuals are, effectively, advancing one culturally partisan vision of the ideal society over others" (Kahan et al. 2007: 496).

Taking variance in risk perception as a leading question, cultural theories of risk reveal normative complexities and relate the issue descriptively to the realm of everyday life. Common ground exists in the understanding of risks in terms of

---

30 See also Rayner and Cantor's essay "How Fair is Safe Enough? The Cultural Approach to Societal Technology Choice" (1987).

"*orienting dispositions*" (Dake 1991: 63; original emphasis; see Slovic 1997: 295);[31] the link to individual identity, and the cultural and psychological "framing", i.e. the subjective process of risk perception/selection and decision-making (see Tversky 1990; Tversky and Kahneman 1981). Other influential approaches, propagated, above all, by the works of Paul Slovic (1987; 1997; 2010) include the conception of "risk as feelings", which seeks to account for the complex intertwining of reason and emotion guiding human behaviour, and the "psychometric paradigm",[32] a "framework that assumes risk is subjectively defined by individuals who may be influenced by a wide array of psychological, social, institutional and cultural factors" (Slovic 2010: xxv). Meanwhile the so-called social amplification of risk framework (SARF),[33] set out to explore risk's "rippling effects" (Kasperson 1988: 187) across time and space, asking how varying perceptions of the same risks can occur, or how minor risks can cause major public concern or the opposite, e.g. through processes of habituation, deliberate ignoring, dramatization and distortion through media, and the differences between expert and lay interpretations of risk. Though the results of empirical psychological studies in the field are hardly conclusive in the sense of allowing for wider generalization, agreement exists about the finding that there is no such thing as a 'risk-taking' or 'risk-averse' personality/individual, but that risk assessment and behaviour is always dependent on the specific case and circumstances, and adapted coherently to fit and defend particular worldviews (see Dake 1992: 24). Influenced by factors such as economics (put simply, the rich fear different than the poor), cultural biases, trust in ideologies and institutions, individuals, as Dake and Wildavsky sum up, "perceive a variety of risks in a manner that supports their way of life" (Dake and Wildavsky1990: 57).

A frequent result from psychological studies investigating how people reason about risk is that humans do rather poorly as far as rational reasoning is concerned and risk-cost-benefit analyses are awash with irrationalities (see Gibbard 1985: 94). Research also demonstrates that mathematical procedures in turn fail to calculate or incorporate the impact of human behaviour *as risk* (cf. Dacu-

---

[31] See Dake's article "Orienting Dispositions in the Perception of Risk – An Analysis of Contemporary Worldviews and Cultural Biases" (1991); and Dake and Wildavsky's "Theories of Risk Perception: Who Fears What and Why?" (1990).
[32] On Risk as feelings, and the nexus risk-value-emotions see Slovic (1987: 281; and 1997), Kunreuther and Slovic (1996), Slovic et al. (2010), Loewenstein, Weber, Hsee and Welch (2001), and, especially, Slovic's *The Feeling of Risk* (2010). The latter volume offers a summary of the extension of risk research in the early 21st century and an overview of the various approaches, also including reprints of famous articles in the field.
[33] See J.X. Kasperson et al. (1988), R.E. Kasperson et al. (2003).

nha-Castelle 1996: 143). The conundrum lies in the discrepancy between humans' self-perception as rational creatures and their actual decisions, largely based on feelings, which impacts on the political-social issue of controlling the masses. Transcending narrow probabilistic, economic, and other sociological approaches, cultural-psychological perspectives on risk affirm its complexity through the emphasis on the connection between risk and emotion, thus blurring boundaries between notions of rational/irrational and accurate/biased risk perceptions.[34]

While the 'reality' of risk has been debated from various angles and to varying degrees, all different approaches outlined above acknowledge risk's duality and see it having a grounding as real life threats and dangers, but also being firmly "embedded in the discursive context of an anxiety-ridden society" (Rigakos and Law 2009: 95), "discursively constructed in everyday life with reference to the mass media, individual experience and biography, local memory, moral convictions, and personal judgements" (Zinn and Taylor-Gooby 2006b: 60); even Ulrich Beck is forced to admit that "without symbolic forms, without mass media, etc., risks are nothing all" (Beck 2006: 332). To some extent, risks only become real through/as fictions, which is why the study of novels offers a rich archive for some of the central questions of cultural risk research: "What are the narratives, epistemologies, discourse, rhetorical moves, choices of 'rational arguments' and courses of action which people use to organize 'risk' as a cultural concept? What kinds of risks do they choose to take or avoid, and why?" (Tulloch and Lupton 2003: 11).

Risk and the Novel

A literary study of risk as the present one occupies a fruitful analytical middle ground which strives to integrate the subjective, psychologically constructed notion of risk prevalent in sociological cultural theory, the systemic function of risk as a means of discursive and technical social control, and the realism of the rationalist notions of risk inherent in economic and scientific-technical approaches. Focusing on risk as a narrative construction that spans the realms of fact and fiction, of rationality and irrationality, crucial questions concern the perceptions of other oppositions such as causality/contingency and agency/

---

[34] See Lupton and Tulloch's argument that risk-taking "is far more complex than is suggested in the traditional social scientific literature. It may be based just as much on knowledge [...] as on ignorance" (2002: 123).

determinism. The temporal dimension is another important aspect, because as Peter Bernstein reminds us, "Risk and time are opposite sides of the same coin, for if there were no tomorrow there would be no risk" (Bernstein 1998: 15). Fictional narratives usually present an ordering of time (real or imagined, linear or dislinear), and especially the novel, due to its form and scope, offers an interesting ground of study for the perception and the management of risk. According to Laura Russell and Austin S. Babrow risk can be examined as: "(a) located in the flux among the past, present, and future; (b) exemplified in the exigencies of human agency; (c) realized through processes of selection; and (d) conceived primarily through narrative constructions" (Russell and Babrow 2011: 244–245). All four dimensions merge when examining risk in the novel. Emphasizing the narrative quality of risk, Russell and Babrow argue further that risk is constituted and signified through storied explanations, evaluations and expectations of "uncertain experiences through time;" "risk takes shape through the forms of narrative we construct" (2011: 240; 239) as a conceptual and experiential phenomenon. What makes a risk suitable and fascinating topic to explore through fictional narrative are the discrepancies between knowledge and emotion, calculation and hope or dread, rationality and irrationality, fact and fiction, norm and exception. Another reason is, simply, that risk perception makes for good storytelling (Gardner 2008: 160–187). It creates suspense and threads of causality, and thus moves plots forward: "One crosses boundaries when taking risks, moving from one space to another. It is risk-taking that impels movement and progression" (Tulloch and Lupton 2003: 33).

Risk can be related to a wider frame of investigation which has received thorough attention in narratology since the 1980s. This concerns the link to ethical criticism and conceiving of storytelling as an intrinsically human means of constructing meaning, orientation, coherence and thus dealing with uncertainty and randomness. According to David Carr, "Life can be regarded as a constant effort, even a struggle, to maintain or restore narrative coherence in the face of an ever-threatening, impeding chaos at all levels" (Carr 1986: 91). Risk appears as an integral part of (self-)narration, it allows for the sublimation of accidents, chances and fears into storied lives (cf. 1986: 97). Risk (perception), if understood as as probilistic and evaluative orientation, can be (and is continually) formulated for past, present and future, and it both deconstructs narratives, through its intrinsic link to uncertainty, and continually leads to the creation of new ones. This opinion is shared by Babrow, Kline and Rawlins: "Every probabilistic and evaluative thread, particularly when woven hastily, fitfully, in anguish or uncertainty, is both the substance of a given narrative as well as the material of its unraveling and the fiber out of which new stories are spun" (Babrow, Kline, and Rawlins 2005: 49–50; see 36). Another point of linkage is to studies such as Brian Richardson's *Unlikely Stories: Causality and the Nature of Modern Narrative* in which he shows cause as one of the most fundamental aspects in the world of fiction. There are various subdivisions of causal agency, such as probability, fortune, determinism, chance, coincidence etc., which, like risk, can be considered ideological valences inscribed with different notions of fate and agency. Richardson argues that "important literary deployments of causation need to be juxtaposed with corresponding developments in philosophical discourse: it is no coincidence that the role of chance becomes prominent in fiction at the same time that theories of probability begin to emerge" (Richardson 1997: 14). Although my study is not per se concerned with the study of (im)probabilities and the distinction between "natural" and "unnatural" (risk) narratives, i.e. scenarios that could exist or not exist in the real world (see Alber 2014), which would also be an interesting project, the focus lies on risk as variant in the system of causation governing fictional worlds and its intersection with scientific and philosophical developments as postulated by Richardson.

The rise of the English novel is tied to the emergence of secular modernity and risk. The ability to 'tame' and make prognoses about events and the future comes into being at the same time as narrative emplotments of the perceived (un)predictability of life. The rise of risk is embedded in wider discourses of shifting or retreating notions of probability, chance, fate, luck, providence and determinism that captures intellectual-scientific debates at the heart of the foundation of modern society and the attempts to increase stability and security via measurability. Interestingly, around the same time that Beck first publishes his *Risk Society*, one finds "signs that the concept of probability is coming to be recognized as among the central and inescapable topics for intellectual history" (Newsom 1988: 7) in other disciplines, including literary studies.[35] While wide interest in the idea was initially generated through theorists such as Foucault, e.g. in *Discipline and Punish*, systematic studies such as Hacking's did much to lay important groundwork on the matter.[36]

Though the term risk exists in European languages since the 14th century, it rapidly gains prominence from the mid-17th century onwards. Although there have undoubtedly been significant changes in the perception and the management of risk, this fact forms an entry point for the critique motivating the present study, namely the idea introduced by sociologists such as Beck and frequently perpetuated in public discourse that the awareness of risk only begins to matter

---

35 See especially Robert Newsom's *A Likely Story: Probability and Play in Fiction* (1988) and Douglas Lane Patey's *Probability and Literary Form* (1984).
36 See Hacking's *The Emergence of Probability* (1975) and *The Taming of Chance* (1990).

in the later 20th century and constitutes a new phase of modernity.[37] In fact, the "risk society" emerges together with the novel, the genre dedicated to plotting time and causality, coincidences and calamities while negotiating individual consciousness, characters' motives, fears and hopes. According to Jesse Molesworth, risk is "implicated in the very notion of plot" (Molesworth 2010: 116) in the early novel. Arguing from a more transhistorical perspective, one can see the novel as a form of fictional writing inseparably tied to the perception of risk because it generally relies, as Gillian Beer argues, "upon the drive of anxiety and hope, on the pleasures of prediction and hypothesis" (Beer 1984: 185). Significantly, Beer, writing about 19th-century realist fiction, adds that the reader is usually made to experience the future "covertly converted into retrospect. The future we are about to read has already been inscribed by author and experienced by characters" (1984: 185). This is one of the reasons for focusing mainly, notwithstanding a few borderline cases such as Swift's *Gulliver's Travels* and Ishiguro's *Never Let Me Go*, on realist novels and not on speculative fictions.

Aside from science historical accounts, the present study takes a cue from readings of 18th century fiction such as Thomas M. Kavanagh's *Enlightenment and the Shadows of Chance* (1993) and Jesse Molesworth's *Chance and the Eighteenth-Century Novel: Realism, Probability, Magic* (2010) and argues that the scientization of the world beginning in the Enlightenment and further related, decisive developments such as capitalism and changing formations of individual and society, which are all reflected and negotiated in the early novel, are linked through the emerging category of risk. Kavanagh speaks in this context of "a fundamental congruence, perhaps even a monadic harmony" (1993: 107) between the rise of the novel and a science of probability as cultural phenomena. Particularly in the last two decades several scholars have approached the study of the novel and topics such as chance, probability, gambling, or contingency and dedicated book-lengths studies[38] to it, as well as essays too numerous and varied in

---

37 In the afterword to her book on gambling and 18th-century fiction Jessica Richard also briefly criticizes Beck's popular theory of the emergence of the "risk society", which takes the fact that people have to live with man-made risk on an unprecedented scale as "a uniquely modern moment in human history" (Richard 2011: 169) and argues instead for structural parallels between the (contemporary) risk society and the 18th-culture of gambling (170). Although she refers to capitalism, rather than risk, Richard's study emphazises the similarities between the 18th and 21st centuries, saying that the attraction of gambling and speculation surely have not decreased and that the tension between chance and control still characterizes human behaviour and politics.

38 Kavanagh's *Enlightenment and the Shadows of Chance* (1993) is a ground-breaking study in the field of literature, the early novel, and probability theory, although the readings are examples only of French literature. Rüdiger Campe's *The Game of Probability* (2012) offers a compa-

scope to list with any claim of comprehensiveness. While these critical works implicitly refer to risk-related topics, and form important points of departure for my study, with the exception of Molesworth (2010) few, however, mention, let alone theorize risk as a category in its own right.[39] While risk has found increasing interest in many disciplines, Anglophone literary criticism is only relatively slowly picking up on this trend, and, coming mainly from American studies scholars, furthermore tends to focus its investigations on contemporary speculative 'disaster' fiction and novels dealing with environmental destruction.[40]

---

rative reading of German and English novels. On the English novel, see Jesse Molesworth's *Chance and the Eighteenth-Century Novel* (2010), and Jessica Richard's *The Romance of Gambling in the Eighteenth-Century British Novel* (2011). See also the collection edited by Paula Backscheider, *Probability, Time, and Space in Eighteenth-Century Literature* (1979), and the theoretical chapters in Newsom (1988). The following studies focus on the modern, i.e. 20th century novel, but also contain useful theory parts which construct historical and/or general arguments about the relation between chance and fiction: Leland Monk's *Standard Deviations: Chance and the Modern British Novel* (1993) and Julia Jordan's *Chance and the Modern British Novel* (2010).

39 Generally, it is noteworthy that 'risk' is rarely to never included as a conceptual entry in the indexes of books. This changes, however, significantly in publications after 2010. Molesworth (2010) is perhaps the most important recent study with points of linkage to my approach and analysis. While chance is his main focus, the book contains an extensive bibliography on probability theory and fiction in the 18th century and throughout his study, Molesworth engages with the "principal architects in a modern view of risk", i.e. Pascal, Bernoulli, de Moivre, Thomas Bayes, Edmund Hoyle (2010: 12).

40 Signs of the rising interest in risk in (Anglophone and German) literary studies are the interdisciplinary DFG symposium "Literatur als Wagnis/Literature as Risk", held at the Villa Vigoni in 2011, and the American studies conference "The Shaping Power of Risk: Literature – Culture – Environment", held at the University of Bayreuth in 2012, as well as the steadily growing number of publications on the subject. Examples of edited collections include the proceedings from the 2011 DFG symposium (see Monika Schmitz-Emans et al. 2013), however, the textual examples are mainly taken from German contemporary literature and the dual focus on literature *as* risk is not relevant. See also Paul Crosthwaite's *Criticism, Crisis, and Contemporary Narrative: Textual Horizons in an Age of Global Risk* (2011a); and Gil and Wulf's *Hazardous Future: Disaster, Representation and the Assessment of Risk* (2015). The latter volume, though exclusively focusing on the contemporary, offers a transcultural perspective and offers a view of diverse medial representations (prose, art installations, and film) of risk. See also Grabher and Bahn-Coblans's *The Self at Risk in English Literatures and Other Landscapes* (1999), which offers one of the rarer literary case studies of risk in texts other than postmodern American or German novels, though the main focus is selfhood, not risk. A different contribution is Elaine Freedgood's *Victorian Writing about Risk: Imagining a Safe England in a Dangerous World* (2000); it deals with a variety of 19th-century (non-canonical, popular, non-fiction) writing covering risk topics and activities such as Alpine mountaineering, political economy, sanitary reform, balloon flight, and colonial exploration in Africa. Finally, see essay-length studies such as Fücker and Schimank (2015).

This is largely due to the agenda of the pioneering literary critic in the field, Ursula K. Heise, whose writings on risk and fiction are strongly informed by ecocriticism.[41] Her critical focus and criteria for selecting texts are maintained in several later studies by Susan L. Mizruchi, Sylvia Mayer and others,[42] with frequently cited primary works including texts by Don DeLillo and Richard Powers. Taking her theoretical cue from the strong link between sociological writings on risk, such as Beck's risk society thesis, and environmentalist concerns,[43] Heise is one of the first to link the exploration of narrative form to the expression of uncertainties preoccupying the global risk society such as environmental pollution and nuclear threats. In order "to denote various cultural representations of environmental hazards" (Mizruchi 2010: 118), she reads contemporary fictions with reference to what Lawrence Buell has termed "toxic discourse" (see 2001: 30–55). Her main aim being an ecocritically-oriented study of culture which, she claims, needs to incorporate perceptions of ecological and technological risk, in *Sense of Place and Sense of Planet* Heise emphazises how "the idea of a coming 'world risk society' has recently emerged as one of the most important ways of imagining global connectedness" (Heise 2008: 12). But elsewhere, in her argument that the ongoing "constitution of risk within specific socio-cultural fields" since the 1970s establishes an interdisciplinary bridge to the concerns of literary criticism (Heise 2002: 762), she also puts forth an idea which suggests a much wider applicability with regard to the motif of risk in narratives. She says that

> a focus on the notion of risk as a literary theme can substantially sharpen and shift standard interpretations of some contemporary texts and, on the other hand, [...] a consideration of risk and the kind of narrative articulation it requires has potentially important implications for the analysis of narrative form. (2002: 747)

Crosthwaite (2010) and McGurl (2010) both relate sociological risk theory to an analysis of modernist and contemporary fictions.

41 See Heise's seminal study *Sense of Place and Sense of Planet* (2008) and her articles "Risk and Narrative at Love Canal" (2002a), "Toxins, Drugs, and Global Systems: Risk and Narrative in the Contemporary Novel" (2002b), "Die Zeitlichkeit des Risikos im amerikanischen Roman der Postmoderne" (2002c), and "Cultures of Risk and the Aesthetic of Uncertainty" (2009).
42 See Mizruchi's "Risk Theory and the Contemporary American Novel" (2010), Mayer's "Science in the World Risk Society: Risk, the Novel, and Global Climate Change" (2016), Mayer and Weik von Mossner's *The Anticipation of Catastrophe. Environmental Risk in North American Literature and Culture* (2014), and Wegener's *Risk and Speculation in Millennial Fictions of the North American Pacific Rim* (2014).
43 For the strong link between risk theory and ecology see, e. g., Lash, Szerszynski, and Wynne (1996), Strydom (2002), and Löfstedt and Frewer (1998).

Though she mainly limits her analysis to postmodern and highly experimental literary forms, like hyper-texts, which are employed to capture the uncertainties of the global risk society, Heise suggests that interpreting plot patterns, metaphors and characterization in different genres (such as detective fiction, the gothic, the pastoral, Bildungsroman, tragedy, and epic) can be illuminating and show how different narrative templates make risk scenarios intelligible to the reader (see Heise 2008: 139; 2002: 762).[44] Although her list of genres suggests a vast body of possible texts for investigation and she does not give any concrete examples, her argument points towards multiple ways and forms for the intersection of risk analysis and literary criticism beyond contemporary literature and ecocriticism. Aside from this, Heise identifies a still-existing scholarly desideratum, namely that "the entire field of risk theory, such an important interdisciplinary area in the social sciences, is for the most part unknown to literary and cultural scholars" (Heise 2008: 122).[45] Risk theorists in turn have to date given little notice to fictional narratives and their role in shaping risk perceptions (see 2008: 137). I agree with Heise that, as risk analysis has long transformed from a specialized field to a prominent topic in public and academic awareness, interdisciplinary risk theory has much to gain from the kind of in-depth analyses of cultural practices, metaphors, plot patterns etc. offered by literary criticism, not least because any research on risk perception must be carried out at the intersection of culture, science and society that defines 'risk' itself and thus, beyond its technical definitions, "include complex cognitive, affective, social, and cultural processes without which it cannot be conceived, defined, or investigated" (Heise 2008: 131; 136; see 2002c: 762). Several critics have since affirmed this view, for instance, Paul Crosthwaite when he writes that "many of the most visible and influential 'stories' of risk in contemporary culture take the very form – fictional narrative – that literary and cultural critics are often most adept and practiced at analyzing" (Crosthwaite 2011b: 5), or Mizruchi, who emphazises that "beholden to ethical and affective considerations as it is to scientific ones, the phenomenon of risk seems especially suited to fictional representation" (Mizruchi 2010: 119).

---

44 Applying Heise's theory to reading McEwan's *Solar*, Evi Zemanek (2012: 52) adds satire to Heise's list of risk modes.
45 Mizruchi, who focuses on contemporary American culture's preoccupation with the prospect of disasters (e. g. economic collapse, illness, nuclear war, terrorist attack, environmental destruction) in her reading of writers such as Don DeLillo, Richard Powers, Richard Russo, Cormac McCarthy, and Kiran Desai, also underlines that the study of risk, "fairly advanced in other fields, it is still new in literary studies" (2010: 111).

Considering the existing critical studies, a focus on British literature, and especially one beyond contemporary texts, seems to be both fruitful and necessary in order to balance the field. There exist to date only a handful of articles and book chapters dealing with risk in the English novel. While I engage with these readings in the individual fictional case studies, they usually tend to disregard wider critical contexts, or misinterpret them, as Michael Jonik does in his reading of *The Secret Agent*. Though he falsely asserts that probabilistic thinking only emerged at the turn from 19th to the 20th century, his following observation about risk and the novel is useful and points towards a wider temporal frame of exploration as it is pursued in my study. Jonik argues that

> despite the manifold ways in which the novel has been read as a form of social critique, there has been comparatively little work explicitly devoted to its relationship with risk. If current conceptions of our global 'risk society' are not merely responses to contemporary exigencies, but have complex and deeply rooted histories, the question emerges concerning *how we might reconsider the [...] novel not only as a chronicle of the struggles of individual characters and communities, but as a varied archive of risk* [...]. (Jonik 2014: 21; my emphasis)

Outline of Study

Tracing a shared evolution of risk perception and management and the English novel over roughly three hundred years, this study proceeds in chronological order and is subdivided into three main parts. As laid out in detail in the introductory parts of Part I, "Survival Against the Odds: The Rise of Risk in the 18th-century Novel" (1.1–1.3) the concept of risk appears as a decisive feature of modernity and human consciousness since the Enlightenment and has a shaping impact on society, and the understanding of what constitutes knowledge, belief, certainty, and, above all, the secularized understanding of human agency and the control over nature. In *Against the Gods: The Remarkable Story of Risk* Peter Bernstein opens his historical account of the emergence of risk with an axiom that is also a central point of departure for this study: "The revolutionary idea that defines the boundary between modern times and the past is the mastery of risk: the notion that the future is more than a whim of the gods and that men and women are not passive before nature" (Bernstein 1998: 1). This reiterates the connection between risk, secularism, and human agency, because if, as Ortwin Renn reminds us, "the future is either predetermined or independent of present human activities, the term risk makes no sense" (Renn 1992: 56). Central pillars of Enlightenment thought, rational choice, measure, the weighing of alternatives and the calculation of a future which was conceived as uncertain, yet at same time lying within the mastering power of human will and offering potential losses and gains, pushed aside the belief in divine providence. New questions of responsibility, orientation and action all cluster around the notion of risk, because if people did no longer perceive themselves to be "at the mercy of impersonal deities and random chance, they could no longer remain passive in the face of an unknown future" (Bernstein 1998: 20). In the realm of risk-*taking* this includes the pushing of boundaries[46] and focusing the human passion for gambling into progress-oriented growth in the field of economy and technology. On the other hand, this is paralleled by a growth of activities of increasing risk-*aversion*, e.g. insurance. Generally, the new spirit and fascination with speculation branched out in these two opposing directions: the new financial system, with its fascination for the stock market, global economy, credit and speculation, and, at the other end of the risk-taking spectrum, the desire for safety and insurance. Gerda Reith explains how Europe through the rise of mercantile capitalism from the 17th century onwards entered a tumultuous period of radical economic changes, shaped by a distinctly speculative nature which "saw the emergence of an entrepreneurial, risk-taking milieu, the birth of modern science, of individualism, and of many of our contemporary institutions and ideas" (Reith 1999: 26) and encouraged the speculative branching out into the paradoxical longing and fascination with both risk-taking and risk-aversion (see Hacking 1975: 4; Patey 1992: 23).

Tools to interpret uncertainty have always existed and notions of risk and disaster were integrated in cultural systems which attributed causality and responsibility long before the upcoming of mathematical theories of probability, which is seen to originate in a famous exchange of letters between Blaise Pascal and Pierre de Fermat in 1654 about the chances of winning in a game of dice. But, while science and technology gain importance as means to realize man's desire for control over nature and the future, it is the new Enlightenment idea of the self-determining subject and the beginning scientization of uncertainty which distinguish the emerging modern concept of risk from pre-modern uncertainty concepts such as catastrophe or fortune.[47] The foundations for the math-

---

[46] Boundaries can be understood literally here, because spatial expansion, i.e. the formation of Britain's empire, is inseparable from the changing worldview and the emergence of risk-consciousness. The history of the colonial project of overseas expansion and its relation to Britain's economic development is well known. There would not have been an Industrial (and probably no financial) revolution of the same scale without England's colonial ventures (cf. Landes 1969: 37).

[47] See T.J. Clark, who writes: "Pre-modern social orderings were not 'predictable.' [...] Pre-modern natural disasters were not experienced as risk. They were fury or fate. The very idea of natural disaster is a modern one, an invention of actuaries, aiming to objectify a previous congeries

ematical tools and the social institutions of risk management that shape the world today are laid at the end of the 17th and the beginning of the 18th century. In mathematics, this refers centrally to probability theory,[48] in philosophy to the renegotiation of absolute 'truth' vs. 'probable' opinion and empiricism,[49] in economics to the rise of capitalism and its instruments such as the free market and the banking system, stock-trading, and the insurance business. It is also the time when speculation, accounting and forecasting start to become 'national' preoccupations.[50]

Throughout the 18th century, the novel takes on the task of negotiating probability, and exploring the tension between the increasingly dominant rational, secular outlook and persisting superstitions and beliefs in the ordering force of divine providence. This raises general questions about knowledge, human agency, and world order. Robert Newson stresses this aspect, saying that

> the novel has from its beginnings been animated in major ways by questions of evidence and the desire for secure knowledge in the face of life's uncertainty. Consider the probabilistic echoes of such words as *fortune, adventure, hazard, providence, expectation, surprise* as well as the really vast and commonplace vocabulary having to do with probable inference or interpretation and including such words as *hope, doubt, belief, supposition, wonder*, and so on. (Newsom 1988: 184; original emphasis)

---

of terrors" (1999: 11); Ewald affirms that "To calculate a risk is to master time, to discipline the future. To conduct one's life is the manner of an enterprise indeed begins in the eighteenth century" (1991: 207). For studies of risk perception and the societal management from a historical perspective, see Gallant's *Risk and Survival in Ancient Greece* (1991) and W.C. Clark's essay "Witches, Floods, and Wonder Drugs: Historical Perspectives on Risk Management" (1980).

48 For a survey of the history and the dominance of probability theory in contemporary life and society see: Dacunha-Castelle's *Spiele des Zufalls* (1997), Gigerenzer et al.'s *The Empire of Chance* (1989), Daston's essay "The Domestication of Risk: Mathematical Probability and Insurance, 1650–1830" (1987), and Kendall and Plackett's *Studies in the History of Statistics and Probability* (1978). For historical summaries with a special focus on literature and culture see Molesworth (2010: 65ff) and Kavanagh (1993: 9–28).

49 See Shapiro (1983) for a summary of the changes in scientific discourse in different domains (philosophy, history, law, religion), highlighting how literary and linguistic attitudes and productions in 17th century Britain were related to the contemporary concern with truth, the search for a rhetorical accuracy, and the communication of facts. The desire to improve scientific and philosophical communication is also connected to shifting notions of authority and plausibility/probability.

50 See Hacking, who explains the success of the mathematical concept of probability: "No public decision, no risk analysis, no environmental impact, no military strategy can be conducted without decision theory couched in terms of probabilities. [...] Our public fears are endlessly debated in terms of probabilities: [...] This imperialism of probabilities could occur only as the world itself became numerical" (1990: 4–5).

The genre reflects the impact of credit, colonial expansion and science and the hopes and fears connected to it. Decisive is the consciousness, displayed by the protagonists of the early novel, of human agency and the need to act and calculate the possible consequences of the actions of oneself and of others, an awareness of the strong incalculable force of random accidents and calamities and the need to come up with explanatory patterns when experiencing the limits of knowledge or belief.

The spirit of this "projecting age"[51] is captured nowhere better than in Defoe's personal life and writings, which are the first fictions under scrutiny in chapter 2. The South Sea Bubble had just burst and England was both afraid of and fascinated by the potential of financial speculation. Gambling, lotteries, the growing insurance business, the climate at the beginning of the 18th century, was shaped by an increasing awareness of personal and collective (national) risk; debt and bankruptcy being the fears of ruin on the horizon. In terms of other disasters, London still had not forgotten the two catastrophes, which followed suit half a century earlier, the plague epidemic of 1664/5 and the Great London Fire of 1666. The fear of both these destructions beyond human control still ruminated strongly in people's minds; it finds reflection in Defoe's *A Journal of the Plague Year*, chronicling the narrator's personal and the city's official strategies of disease risk management. Aside from the struggle for survival against the (pseudo-statistically calculated) odds, always narrated in retrospect while keeping up the pretence of a 'cautionary' tale, the growing spirit of individualism and capitalism shapes the plots and characterization of the protagonists in *Robinson Crusoe*, *Moll Flanders*, and *Roxana, The Fortunate Mistress*. The characters demonstrate the risk-taking intrinsic to capitalist consciousness and an emerging 18th-century risk society as "a future-oriented society where having the skills and the means to invest in the future, to approach and apprehend the future strategically, with discipline, foresight and care, is richly rewarded" (Arnoldi 2009: 184). The possibilities of taking control of one's future and fortune which are realized through a mix of cunning and coincidence, are counterbalanced by various fears which often border on paranoia, e.g. Crusoe's anxieties of being attacked by cannibals, Moll and Roxana's fear of having their identity and criminal money-making schemes discovered. Though the protagonists in all four novels are at some point confronted with existential risks to their own life, and otherwise largely engaged in anxiously calculating the growth and loss of their possessions, for Defoe's female characters, there are the added hazards that

---

51 The expression is used in the 'Author's Introduction' of Defoe's *Essay on Projects* (1697: 21); cf. also Gigerenzer et al. (1989: 25).

come with femininity, marriage and motherhood. Moll and Roxana each have to risk manage a series of husbands, lovers, pregnancies and children, which brings them repeatedly close to ruin. Defoe's novels celebrate survival, lucky escapes and spectacular gains, while also highlighting the particularly precarious situation of women in 18th-century society, moreover, they serve as illustration of a whole gamut of risk running from financial ruin, disease, colonialist ventures abroad, travel, dealing with strangers, to the marriage market, and life in the city.

Chapter 3 looks at Jonathan Swift's *Gulliver's Travels*, Tobias Smollett's *Roderick Random*, Laurence Sterne's *Tristram Shandy*, and Horace Walpole's *The Castle of Otranto*, all fictions which display fears of masculinity and, to different degrees, present parodies of rational risk calculations. These texts are chosen as examples for the early to mid-18th-century novel which "offers a rich field where play, chance, risk, and determinism were displayed and worked out" (O'Brien 2011: 293). In particular *Gulliver's Travels* and *Tristram Shandy* engage explicitly in satirical form with the "l'esprit géométrique" – "the quantifying spirit" (Heilbron 1990: 2) of the century, which refers to the growing human passion to order, systematize, measure and calculate.[52] Taking the form of fantastic travel narrative, stories of picaresque and maritime adventures, or Gothic tale, the fictions in this chapter thematize the advance of science and questions of truth and empiricism, linked to the experience of contingency and threats to male identity. They include issues of national and class identity (*Gulliver's Travels*, *Roderick Random*) as well as personal fears of legitimacy (*Tristram Shandy*, *The Castle of Otranto*).

Concluding the discussion of the 18th-century novel, in chapter 4 Frances Burney's study of the risks of female (mis)conduct at the turn of the century are the focus of a reading of her epic novel *Camilla*. In contrast to Moll Flanders, who always fears "having no Friend in the World to trust" (MF 103) even more than without a husband or money, in *Camilla*, the social and familial networks, which should in theory offer support and stability, are shown to be fraught with danger and even function as isolating principles. While the women struggling for survival in Defoe's novels are self-assured women, in Burney they are sheltered, impressionable young girls who run the risk of losing their most precious possessions, their good reputation and looks. Meanwhile the male characters are equally conflicted in seeking to risk-manage their financial and romantic futures;

---

52 See Frängsmyr, Heilbron and Rider's *The Quantifying Spirit of the 18th Century* (1990); see also Rousseau and Porter's *The Ferment of Knowledge* (1980).

negotiating the pitfalls of disclosing or withholding one's feelings the novel presents courtship, for both sexes, as a precarious gamble for happiness.

One can observe a development throughout the 18th-century novel, starting from a more positive and very subjective approach to risk-taking, dominated by a spirit of adventure and will to survive. This is slowly supplemented and eventually pushed aside by more satirical narrations and intellectualizations of the spirit of quantification and rationality. A concern with the power and destructive potential of human passion and a development towards a stronger desire for risk-aversion and security characterizes many of the later novels of the century. From the solitary adventures of Defoe's Robinson Crusoe to Burney's Camilla, who is struggling to adhere to the expectations society has of 'female youth', all texts illustrate the effects of the institutionalization of risk, probability theory, and the increasingly "stochastized view of life" (see Davis and Hersh 1986). Taking *Camilla* as example, the fictions at the end of the century also bear testimony to the fact that "what began as an ethics of the individual freed from the weight of the past subordinated itself to the far more oppressive ideologies of the probable and the normal" (Kavanagh 1993: 25). While these questions and the negotiation of oppressing ideals of normalcy, deviation and transgression become more important in the Victorian novel, 18th-century fiction captures from the beginning the main effect of probabilistic discourse and theory, namely the provision of the individual "with the tools necessary to quantify and carefully measure the array of alternatives before them and thus to ensure what seemed to be the ultimate rationality of their actions" (Kavanagh 1993: 21); these ideals of rationality are also often satirized in the Augustan novel. Furthermore, while all fictions demonstrate how what was considered "reasonable or certain in the 17th and 18th centuries was intimately bound up with questions of probability and risk, in contexts ranging from law to morality, economics to public health" (Rider 1990: 385), the focus is placed on the individual and its struggles. Societal concerns play a role, but remain in the background. Regarding the perception and management of risk, this also reflects the fact that risk is not yet firmly institutionalized. In contrast to the 19th century, insurance, and bankruptcy are still mainly personal, private matters, rather than those of families, social groups, or even nations. This changes in the Industrial novel of the 19th-century.

Part II, "Out of the Ordinary: The Gamble of Life in the 19th-century Novel", begins with a reading of Jane Austen's *Persuasion* alongside Mary Shelley's *Frankenstein, or the Modern Prometheus* (chapter 5). While Austen's novel continues the concern with the risk of taking insufficient or misguided precautions in matters of the heart and of acting or not acting at the wrong time, set against a political background, Shelly's text pioneers staging the risk of posthuman creation and scientific as well as personal responsibility. Chapter 6 then turns to the Industrial novel of the 1840s and 50s, focusing on four examples, Elizabeth Gaskell's *Mary Barton* and *North and South*, Charlotte Brontë's *Shirley*, and Charles Dickens' *Hard Times*. The novels are read with a focus on precariousness, accidents, and social and gender divisions, relating them to the emerging Victorian risk society marked by a great concern with statistics, insurance and questions of personal liberty. Juxtaposing working-class suffering with the sense of threat working-class agency poses to the security of the other classes, the texts negotiate the violent impact of class conflict, change and loss, as well as possibilities of reconciliation and compensation.

This is followed by the analysis of two high-Victorian novels in chapter 7, Anthony Trollope's *The Way We Live Now* and George Eliot's *Daniel Deronda*. These epic multi-stranded narratives weave intricate plots of largely failed and betrayed ambitions and speculations; they demonstrate how risky gambles shape the money and marriage plots, which also take on a darker quality and are ripe with the risk of violence and psychological and physical abuse. Through the villain in Trollope's biting satire, the strange foreign banker Melmotte, and, in Eliot's novel, Gwendolen's disastrous marriage to the ominous Grandcourt, and Daniel Deronda, the idealistic eponymous hero, who eventually discovers his Jewishness and his destiny, both texts engage with the risks of trusting strangers and one's own feelings and judgment. The struggle between the sexes and the fight between rationality and the emotional, and instinctual sides of human nature is also at the heart of the three fictions discussed in chapter 8, Thomas Hardy's tragic novels of rural provincial life, *Tess of the d'Urbervilles* and *Jude the Obscure,* and George Gissing's equally dark exploration of life in the destructive vortex of fin-de-siècle London, *The Whirlpool*. The reading of *Tess* focuses on the depiction of the female body and the fallen woman as risks, while the destructive force of Christian marriage laws and risks of hereditary 'flaws' and nervous disease play a central role in *Jude* and *The Whirlpool*.

In the course of the 19th century the modern concept of society emerges, and with it the idea and practice of insurance, itself to a large extent a statistical construct which entails numerical sub-categories that increasingly form "the basis for individual and collective identity" (Porter 1995: 42; 37). Statistical data allow not only for comparing measures of profitability, e. g. in education or the work place. In the sense of Foucault's notion of governmentality, numbers give direction to bureaucratic policies; they create norms, deviations, and standards for judgment in a vast array of different fields, such as sexuality, and they render individuals, above all, governable. During the Victorian era, the statistical rule of numbers, in team with Darwinian evolutionary biology, lead to an oppressive discourse shaped by standards of progression, normalcy and deviation, which is taken up and criticized harshly, for instance, by writers like Charles Dickens, George Eliot, and Thomas Hardy.[53] Main development in terms of risk perception are the shift from anxiety about coming from or being associated with the wrong family to hereditary risk, the shift from subjective to institutionalized objective notions of probability, and increasing fears of sexual-moral transgression and deviancy. By the end of the century, the fear of God is fully equalled or replaced by the fear of (human) nature. One can also observe a change in the dominant understanding of risk from something an individual voluntarily faces or enters in, to a sense of risk as a condition humans are largely involuntarily subjected to, which gained currency from the mid-19th century onwards (cf. Choi 2001: 586). Furthermore, as Amartya Sen argues using the example of Defoe's Robinson Crusoe as the isolated individual *per excellence* (Sen 1985: 158; original emphasis), there is a historical shift in the evaluation of risk from individual to community, from isolated risk-taking that does not affect others and hence does not complicate the right to take personal risks, to the question how an individual's behaviour might endanger the safety of a whole family or community. For example, the reckless speculations of Trollope's Melmotte in *The Way We Live Now* ruinously involve a vast number of characters.

There are, however, also continuities. Aside from the risks of losing one's money and possessions, which, if anything, only increase in importance, in particular for the female characters the risky adventure remains more often than not limited courtship and the encounter with society and its forms of deceptions and manipulations. Ultimately, as Winfried Fluck argues, "The risk the heroine of the realist novel of manners takes is [...] marriage" (Fluck 1999: 82; see 75). While the characters demonstrate the link between risk behaviour and identity construction, formal and informal principles of social surveillance also play a significant role. For both sexes, the central risk remains choosing an individual course of action, a career path, or a marriage partner, "that may turn out well or badly, or one that will change one's life in [an] unpredictable way" (MacLean 1985: 29).

The final Part III, "Crisis and Contingency: Threats to Humanity in the 20th- and 21st-century Novel", traces the anxieties induced by the experience of man-made mass destruction and the reach of technology on an unprecedented scale, as well as societal changes that allow for greater freedom and individuality and which return the risk rhetoric, to some extent, from society to the individual, but also show an emergent global consciousness and sense of precarity. Not unexpected, perhaps, this part begins with a reading of "A Sense of Endings" (chap-

---

[53] On this aspect see Porter (1995: 77–78) and Hacking (1990). On the impact on social statistics on the shaping of collective and individual identity see also Rose (1998; 1999).

ter 9), looking at risk perception in the period from the turn of the century up until WW2 through readings of Joseph Conrad's *The Secret Agent,* E.M. Forster's *Howards End,* and George Orwell's *Coming Up For Air.* Conrad's novel, which can be considered as one of the first sophisticated fictional texts that places the theme of terrorism and the threat of foreign invasion centre stage, also deals with (pseudo)-scientific fears of degeneracy and energetic decline. At the heart of the narrative, however, lies Winnie Verloc's tragically failed risk management of her brother Stevie through entrusting him in the care of her corrupt husband. The plot of *Howards End,* Forster's 'condition-of-England' novel, negotiates conflicting Edwardian ideas of humanist altruism and social Darwinism and explores the risks of seeking connections across lines of class and gender. While the threat of the destruction of England's rural idyll looms in the background, the theme of the apocalyptic dimensions of modernity is fully realized in *Coming Up For Air.* Orwell's clumsy every-man George Bowling, who assumes the role of a prophetic doomsday cryer, still haunted by memories of one war while already foreseeing the mass destruction and the nightmares of fascism involved in the next, is denied both the return to his risk-free rural childhood idyll and a lasting escape from his oppressive lower middle-class existence.

In chapter 10, the focus is on gendered routines of risk-taking in two postwar novels, Alan Sillitoe's *Saturday Night and Sunday Morning* and Alan Hollinghurst's *The Swimming-Pool Library,* revealing the connection between the experience of temporality, risk behaviour and masculine identity – heterosexual and queer. Both texts engage with questions of class consciousness and conflicts and issues of trust and relationships. They furthermore explore the consequences of leisure time filled almost exclusively with physical, reckless behaviour and sexuality as central means of male identity construction, as well as a means of escape from larger political and social risks, e.g. the looming threat of the cold war (in Sillitoe) and the advent of the AIDS crisis (in Hollinghurst). Risk-taking is largely connoted positively by both protagonists, Arthur Seaton and Will Beckwith, who in different ways believe in their exceptional abilities, such as strength, cunning, beauty and athleticism, and are accustomed to win against other, weaker men, or always, however narrowly, beat the odds. But both eventually suffer a violent physical encounter, which shakes the belief in their own luck and invincibility to the core, at least temporarily. This chapter deals with some issues related to voluntary risk-taking and masculinity that have also found interest in sociological risk research as the so-called "white male effect",[54] a risk behaviour and fearlessness specifically attributable to a certain group,

---

54 See, e.g, Finucane et al. (2000), Kahan et al. (2007), and Palmer (2003).

and, at least to some extent, "edgework" theory,[55] which explores the phenomenon of deliberate (high) risk-seeking through activities such as extreme sports, or sex and is also often connected to drug use and alcohol. According to edgework theory, functions of deliberate risk-taking are seeking an experience that allows rebellion against constraints, a sense of spontaneity and anarchic self-actualization (Lyng 1990: 864; 878). Though their described risk behaviour would not meet the extreme standards set in empirical studies by edgework theorists, these motivations can be applied to the protagonists in *Saturday Night and Sunday Morning* and *The Swimming-Pool Library*.

Chapter 11 turns to post-millennial fictions that thematize specific fears and risks related to science and (the end of) humanity, Kazuo Ishiguro's *Never Let Me Go* and Ian McEwan's *Solar*. The motif of time plays again a significant role, taking the form of a nostalgic, traumatic awareness of inevitably being too late to save anyone in Ishiguro's text, and of running out of time while trying to ignore disaster until the very last moment in McEwan's. Dealing with cloning (*Never Let Me Go*) and climate change (*Solar*) both are narrative case studies of man-made, essentially catastrophic risks that fall into Beck's contemporary risk society, and can potentially destroy the individual, humanity and the planet. While Ishiguro's novel allows for an ambivalent exploration of posthuman identity, *Solar* presents a satirical study of male ego and disastrous risk management, affected by vanity, inertia and denial.

Finally, chapter 12 reads another fiction by McEwan, his post-9/11 'condition of England' novel *Saturday,* alongside Rachel Cusk's bleak feminist exploration of marriage and motherhood in English suburbia, *Arlington Park*. Both texts are in a sense concerned more with security than risk and give insight into the psyche of main characters which lead sheltered and privileged lives. Both novels, which can be categorized as variations of Woolf's *Mrs Dalloway* as well as "neo-modernist glocal novels" (Latham 2015: 137), negotiate the risk of (global) terrorism and local, personal, domestic insecurities and vulnerabilities, such as aging and the passing of time, and the pitfalls of regret that come with choosing an 'ordinary' existence. While *Saturday* also thematizes the old links between risk and hereditary disease and fears of class conflict, *Arlington Park* tackles the reiterative experience of femininity as risk.

The selection of fictions in this study traces the ways in which risk, its perception and management, is an integral part of novelistic narration. Special attention is being paid as to how it informs characterization and plot development, how its shapes the texts on the level of language (e.g. the use of typical

---

[55] See Lyng (1990) and Lyng and Matthews (2007).

risk rhetoric and metaphors), and how the fictions reflect their socio-cultural, political, and scientific contexts in regards to it. The decision to focus mainly on major canonical novels was made deliberately in order to show the centrality of risk as a category for narrative analysis and how it can usefully supplement or reorient existing readings of the individual texts. I also consider the continued interest and currency of most of these novels, in other words "their very 'canonicity'" (Crosthwaite 2010: 333), itself to be born partially, if not largely, of their projections of risk, of presents and futures defined by uncertainty and instability. Furthermore, without claiming to offer any kind of comprehensive overview, a main aim is to relate the histories of risk and the English novel and reveal their intrinsic link. The selection of texts is, as any must be, a subjective and incomplete one. It tells a particular 'new' history of risk and the novel, which does suggest the inclusion and study of many further examples, but, as I believe, does nonetheless hold up to generalization and serves to illustrate a wider context. With risk offering a potentially endless field of study, exclusions had to be made in order to plausibly show the evolution and continuity of risk perception across time. The first one, already mentioned above, concerns genre and narrative mode: For reasons of comparability, but mainly to dissociate the category risk from the limited application to apocalyptic and environmental disaster fiction, the majority of texts can be considered realist, and belongs to genres such as adventure and travel narrative, satire, the picaresque, the Bildungsroman, and the condition-of-England novel. A small group of speculative fictions (*Frankenstein*, *Gulliver's Travels*, *The Castle of Otranto*, and *Never Let Me Go*) is included for reasons of topicality and canonicity. These examples also do not violate the specific form of secular risk perception that distinguishes them from more generic science fiction, which according to Heise "articulates quite clear-cut distinctions between good and evil, desirable and undesirable futures", relying "on a different mode of projecting the future than theories of risk, which tend to emphasize persistent uncertainties, unintended consequences, and necessary trade-offs" (Heise 2008: 141).

What I am also not interested in presently is the power and function of literature to inspire action in the 'real' world, i.e. explore if and how fictions can influence risk behaviour, or in engaging with the topic of literature (of writing and reading novels) *as risk*. The last analytical caveat concerns the locality of the chosen textual examples. According to Maurie Cohen, any study of the cultural absorption of science needs a specific, historically informed context and makes generalizing difficult (Cohen 1999: 173). Taking into account that risk discourse and theorizing is "inevitably confounded by 'Zeitgeist'" (Zinn 2008b: 3), and thus always both "historical and local" (Tulloch and Lupton 2003: 1), I chose to focus on British fictions and thus avoid conflating differences, in particular in the development of science, and of a scientifically-derived, social and cultural conception such as risk, in different national contexts. It is furthermore important to acknowledge the specific social stratum that shapes the novel as a genre, namely the middle class, using it also as the vantage point for depicting or comparatively assessing different social risk perceptions. As a result, though some of the fictions deal with 'existential' risks, i.e. those posing basic, actual threats to the characters' survival, the majority of risks negotiated in the texts also reflects the following observation about the current preoccupation with risk in interdisciplinary research: It is tied to "one particular approach to contingency which draws on probabilistic reasoning and the metaphor of randomness. *It is found primarily in rich, science-based countries whose citizens can afford to invest the required resources into precaution*" (Heyman 2012: 603; my emphasis).

Considering what Deborah Lupton first stated as a surprising phenomenon nearly twenty years ago, namely that there (still) has been comparatively "little interaction between areas of inquiry such as media and cultural studies, the sociology of the body, postcolonial theory and gender theory and sociocultural theories of risk" (Lupton 1999b: 6), this study goes some way to remedy this,[56] in particular with regards to gender studies.[57] Generally, literary scholarship can illustrate how gendered mappings of risk consciousness operate in different areas and how "gendered knowledges inform risk practices" (Hannah-Moffat and O'Malley 2007: 26). Gender and risk are in a way mutually constitutive, with gendered norms and configurations of inequality being related to expectations about risk behaviour and public displays of fear and courage. There is also the crucial perception of gender and sexuality as risk. Particularly in the 19th century novel women are often seen as posing risks to men, connected also to the historically-conditioned link between risk, gender, criminalization; furthermore

---

[56] A gap that certainly needs addressing in research is the study of risk in fictional narratives from a postcolonial critical perspective and Anglophone fictions from outside of Britain; however, these are not included here for the reasons given above.

[57] Much of sociological research has ignored the complexities of the nexus of risk and gender (and still does) (see Hannah-Moffat and O'Malley 2007: 5–6). While in Beck's risk society gender gets 'collapsed' into women, in most other empirical studies of risk and gender the focus is usually placed on the differences in the acceptance of technological, environmental, financial or health risks, operating from the premise that women show a generally lower risk preference. On the so-called "gender gap" in risk perception, see e.g. Bord and O'Connor (1997) and Flynn, Slovic and Mertz (1994); on gender and technological/environmental risk, see Davidson and Freudenburg (1996) and Cutter, Tiefenbacher and Solecki (1992); on crime, risk and gender, see Chan and Rigakos (2002); on gender and risk behaviour in financial decision making see Powell and Ansic (1997). One of the few volumes exclusively dealing with risk and gender is Hannah-Moffat and O'Malley (2007).

many aspects of marriage and motherhood are interpreted through risk. Though a majority of the texts is written by male authors, questions of gender identity and relations are an important point of focus in all readings. The nexus between risk and femininity that is opened up in Defoe's *Moll Flanders* and *Roxana* reverberates through many of the Victorian fictions, such as Hardy's *Tess*, as well as 21st-century novels like *Arlington Park*. Meanwhile the intersections between masculinity and risk are explored in the novels by Sterne, Smollett, Swift, and Walpole (chapter 3), and those by Sillitoe and Hollinghurst (chapter 10). Further recurring topics and points of linkage between the texts include decline plots and the perceived dangerousness of specific activities or situations (e. g. speculation, gambling, loss of control), places (e. g. London as a "riskscape"[58], as well as the contrast between city and country), parts of the population (e. g. strangers and foreigners, the poor, women), and of unpredictable passions and irrational behaviour. Although external risks such as environmental risks play a role, of special importance are what Tulloch and Lupton call "intimate risks" (Tulloch and Lupton 2003: 23), those associated with love, marriage, and relationships as risky undertakings (emotionally, physically, economically, psychologically, socially), and "embodied risk" (2003: 25), that is physical, financial or health risks which most people perceive as an intrinsic part of their lives. Tracing (dis)continuities in risk perception in novels from Defoe to McEwan, the study highlights the preoccupation with hazards, safety and the control of the future, and how characters deal with uncertainties through developing their own and socially constructed 'logics' of risk, which oscillate between rational calculation and emotion and an enabling spirit of adventure and a destructive sense of danger.

---

58 Heise (2002a: 97) borrows the term 'riskscapes' from geographer Susan L. Cutter to refer to hazardous landscapes that emerge in the later 20th century out of changing relations between environment, technology, and society. Mehnert (2014) employs 'riskscapes' in her study of climate change fiction, adding it conceptually to the five interconnected dimensions ('scapes') of the deterritorialized state developed in Arjun Appadurai's *Modernity At Large* (1996).

Part I **Survival Against the Odds: The Rise of Risk in the 18th-century Novel**

1 Calculating a New View of Life

1.1 Probability, Chance, and the Spirit of Quantification

Many semantically interrelated terms like chance, hazard, danger, adventure, and probability cluster around a notion of 'risk.' Despite the fact that each of these comes with its own historical and theoretical complexity and provides sufficient material for a study in itself, scholarly agreement exists that around 1665 a conception of risk is born, which links – at least partially – all of these terms. Gerda Reith describes it as follows:

> It is at this point that we also see the emergence of the notion of risk, in both its senses of 'danger, exposure to peril' and the more specific 'chance or hazard' of commercial loss in the case of insured property. Both these connotations appeared in the seventeenth century, from the Anglo-French risqué; the first instance of the term being cited in 1661 as 'Risqué – peril, jeopardy, danger, hazard, chance' (in Oxford English Dictionary 1989, vol. 13, p. 987). Slightly later the sense of risk as something linked with commercial exploits was made explicit. (Reith 1999: 27)

Etymologically, most words related to the semantic cluster of 'risk' do stem from games of chance. Considered to be almost as old as humankind,[1] in ancient Greece and Egypt chance games of dice were "referred to as 'hazard', from *al zahr*, the Arabic word for dice" (Bernstein 1998: 13).[2] From the 12th century onwards, as Thomas Kavanagh explains, "Hazard came to designate the very idea of risk, peril, or any menacing situation beyond human control. It is that meaning which, in the English 'hazard', as well as in the Italian *azzardo* and the Spanish *azar*, has prevailed in all European languages except French" (Kavanagh 1993: 3). Meanwhile, the emergence of the term 'probability' can be traced back to the ancient Greek *eikos*, defined by Socrates as "likeness to truth" (Popper 1963: 236–37; Bernstein 1998: 16), a meaning clearly preserved in the German *Wahrscheinlichkeit* – as that which is 'seemingly true.'[3] But the term acquired its

---

[1] See F.N. David's *Games, Gods and Gambling* (1998) and Gerda Reith's *The Age of Chance* (1999).
[2] The Latin *aleatorius*, also referring to games of dice, has been preserved in the adjective *aleatory*, commonly used to describe events with uncertain outcome (cf. Bernstein 1998: 47 f).
[3] See Karl Popper (1963). See also Rüdiger Campe's *The Game of Probability* (2012). Campe (2012: 8–9) points out that while the term 'probability' always implies a reference to a notion of 'reality', the German 'Wahrscheinli chkeit' makes no distinction between probability (in the mathematical quantifiable sense of probability theory) and verisimilitude (as "appearance of truth" as an aesthetic concept, artistic representation). Generally, I am not concerned with ver-

mathematical meaning and significance relevant in the present context only in the mid-17th century.

Regarding the etymology of the term 'risk' itself, it is derived from the Greek 'risco'/'rhiza' ("root, ledge, reef") and the early Italian 'risicare' ("to dare"), which underlines the elements of danger, choice and action also inherent in the Latin 'riscare' – meaning "to sail around a reef" – thus referring to a dangerous activity which has the potential of causing loss and connoting the uncertain outcome rather negatively (see Bernstein 1998: 8; Dacunha-Castelle 1997: 128; Wolf 2010: 67). The earliest official use of the term 'risk' is in the context of venturing into a dangerous sea, risking shipwreck in order to achieve financial gain. Thus, the sea appears as the original realm of risk. From the 14th century onwards, 'rischio and 'rischiare' was commonly used among Italian merchants to refer to the putting of money in a maritime trading contract (see Münkler 2010: 19; Wolf 2010: 55; Bonß 1995: 132–34). With the expansion of global trade, the shipping of goods became increasingly important and a practice of maritime insurance, which entailed both a betting on the safe arrival of cargo and compensation in the event of its loss, was established and flourished during the late 15th and 16th centuries in Central Europe (see Gigerenzer et al. 1989: 2; Ewald 1991: 199; O'Brien 2011: 293). This also shows how, from its beginnings, the concept of risk combines contradictory impulses, namely commercial rational reasoning, a calculation of potential losses and gains, the desire to provide security in the case of loss, and the thrill of adventure, i.e. courageously risking the sea voyage. As Herfried Münkler explains, "man kann sagen, dass die bindende Kraft des ritterlichen Ideals durch die Flexibilität des kaufmännischen Kalküls abgelöst wird. Was für den fahrenden Ritter Gefahr und Bedrohung, das ist für den Fernhandelskaufmann das Risiko" (Münkler 2010: 20). In other words, 'ad-ventura' (the advent of luck, chance) was increasingly applied as expression in a business context, referencing financial rather than romantic risk, a semantic shift which manifested itself in the course of the 17th century.[4] In addition to this, the idea of 'fortune' changed generally, not just in the realm of business. Gradually, Fortuna was no longer seen as the ruling Goddess over human fate, which lead to what Burckardt Wolf describes in this context as a new "Allegorie des Wagnisses" (Wolf 2010: 53), and the evolution of a "neuzeitlichen Glücksstrebens" (2009: 54), meaning that human relationships (e.g. love, business) were gradually and actively aiming at security and safety while at the

---

isimilitude in the sense of narrative/fictional probability but with the mathematical-conceptual implications of the term which transcend the textual level. For studies of literary probability ('likeness') in relation to probability theory see Patey (1984) and Newsom (1988).

4 See Michael Nerlich's *Abenteuer oder das verlorene Selbstverständnis der* Moderne (1997).

same time accepting the danger of the unknown, the uncertain outcome in order to gain something. The future became a realm open to the realization of desire, improvement, and man's own shaping of happiness.

Writing about historical consciousness and the changes characterizing modernity, Reinhart Koselleck introduced the distinction between "Erfahrungsraum" (realm of experience) and "Erwartungshorizont" (horizon of expectation) which usefully highlights in the present context the centrality of the shifting relationships between past, present and future and the spirit of calculation, expansion, and the attempt to predict and master the unknown. Koselleck argues that these two categories suitably express the sense of historical time, capture the perceived temporal connections between past-present-future and are utilized to guide actions in the political sphere and in individual social interaction (Koselleck 1979: 353). They are mutually dependent categories and centrally based on the element of rational reflection, i.e. "Erwartung", for Koselleck, clearly transcends "hope", while "Erfahrung" goes beyond "memory". Characteristic of a modern consciousness is the emphasis on "Erwartung", which can be subjective or collective, but always takes place in the present and is directed towards the "Not Yet" ("Noch-Nicht"), focusing on the theoretically calculable and venturing beyond the experienced or even allowing for randomness. Before the advent of Enlightenment thought, Christian doctrine had clearly limited human expectations and ordered the relation between past and future, maintaining a gaze directed more equally in both directions and eliminating notions of the 'random' or the 'coincidental.'[5] The well-known paradigm shift of the Enlightenment described by Koselleck relates the emerging secular consciousness to an increasing orientation towards the future. The new ideology based on (linear) progress opens up the future as "Erwartungsraum", partially accessible via human prognostics and utilizing past experiences to calculate them.[6] Furthermore, the future is perceived to approach with increasing speed, and entails the advance into the unknown, into new territories (e.g. with regard to localities and technologies). In tune with many other theorists who have stressed the speed and 'liquidity' of modernity (e.g. Bauman 2007; 2000; Berman 1982), Koselleck also takes

---

5 See Koselleck (1979: 361). F.N. David also stresses that Christianity did a lot to hinder and reject the concept of the random. As long as the belief in God's all-controlling will and man's ignorance about the divine design and nature of things was intact, here was no reason and motivation to look for any rules to predict and thus master the uncertainty of future events (1998: 26).
6 Although Koselleck argues that prophecy was increasingly replaced by rational prognosis, he takes care to stress that the shift was, of course, a gradual one. He also refers to the characteristic bizarre duality of 18th-century thought, which constructs the approach of the (unknown) future often with an ideological mix of divine prophecy and rational calculation (1979: 28; 33).

the changing, flexible connections, the erosion of distance between "Erwartungshorizont" and "Erfahrungsraum", as a decisive element shaping modernity. The increasing speed necessitates constant renegotiations between expectation and experience.[7] And risk, although not mentioned by Koselleck, is a central perception that emerges from these reflections.

Another factor stressed by Koselleck is the idea of constant progress in the sense of gradual perfection and improvement. He argues that only from the age of Enlightenment onwards, "die ganze Geschichte als ein Prozeß andauernder und zunehmender Vervollkommnung begriffen werden [konnte], der, trotz aller Rückfälle und Umwege, schließlich von den Menschen selber zu planen und zu vollstrecken sei" (1979: 363). "Progress" thus functions as a qualitative and temporal category directly linking experience and expectation and introducing a 'progressive' difference between past and future. Claiming that this leads to the phenomenon that the difference between expectation and experience has to be bridged constantly anew and with increasing speed in order to be able to orient oneself, and to live and act, Koselleck sees this asymmetry between expectation and experience as a specific result of the 'modern' world view.

J.H. Plumb, who has given what can still be considered as a valid and accessible portrayal of 18th-century culture in England (see Plumb 1978 and 1982) also stresses a fascination with expectancy for the future and the manipulation of nature as integral parts of man's "acceptance of modernity" (Plumb 1982: 335). Springing from the intersecting beliefs in science, progress and human control and agency, "improvement" appears indeed as one of the key terms of 18th-century culture, as many critics have noted.[8] As Keith Thomas has shown in great

---

[7] A good example of late 20th/early 21st -century Western culture is the frequent consultation of 'experts' in public media whenever crises (e.g. terror, natural disasters, accidents) occur. The experts are often forced to comment on events apparently nobody did see coming, and which clearly transcend the realm of current knowledge and experience.

[8] Cf. Clarence J. Glacken's magisterial study *Traces on the Rhodian Shore* (1990). It provides a detailed history of ideas and the changing relationship between nature/culture, religion and environment up to 18th century. On the influence of Francis Bacon and man's growing awareness of the power over nature see especially chapter 10 "Growing Consciousness of the Control of Nature" (461–496). For other accounts of the development of scientific thought in Britain and the socio-cultural implications, see Mathias (1972); Inkster (1983). Landes's *The Unbound Prometheus* (1969) offers a historical account of the Industrial Revolution, yet presents it as a linear story of advance and progress; John Henry's "Scientific Revolution in England" (1992) offers a more nuanced study of the development of science in England, tracing the simultaneous rise of scientific and philosophical empiricism. Henry argues that in this regard England, where the Puritan Revolution went hand in hand with a scientific one, developed differently in comparison to the rest of Europe (cf. Henry 1992: 182).

detail, due to the decline of old magical beliefs, triggered by the rise of science and leading to a new ideology of self-help, "the period saw the emergence of a new faith in the potentialities of human initiative" (Thomas 1991: 792; 797). Left with having to calculate and face the possible consequences of their actions, a human need arose for new methods and tools to measure these.

As Jesse Molesworth's claim that this "point has been made so many times, and the evidence is so overwhelming, that it is hardly worth retracing in full" (2010: 62) is somewhat justified, a brief sketching of the context may suffice here:

> Within Europe between roughly 1600 and 1800, a universe governed by particular Providence was threatened and ultimately weakened by a universe governed by statistical laws and odds. Simply put, the reason for why things happen – ordinary things like the fall of a dice, the death of a person due to disease, or the sudden onrush of a rainstorm – changed. (2010: 62)

Although games and notions of chance date back to antiquity and have fascinated people for centuries, historians of science and mathematicians agree that it was not before the mid-17th century that any systematic attempts of calculating chance(s) were made. To be more precise, the birth of probability theory is usually tied to the year 1654, to an exchange of letters about predicting the odds in a game of chance between the French mathematics Blaise Pascal, Chevalier de Méré, and Pierre de Fermat.[9] Gerd Gigerenzer et al. describe this important founding moment as follows:

> In July of 1654 Blaise Pascal wrote to Pierre Fermat about a gambling problem which came to be known as the Problem of Points: Two players are interrupted in the midst of a game of chance, with the score uneven at that point. How should the stake be divided? The ensuing correspondence between the two French mathematicians counts as the founding document of mathematical probability, even though it was not the first attempt to treat games of chance mathematically [...]. Some years later, Pascal included among his *Pensées* an imaginary wager designed to convert sporting libertines: no matter how small we make the odds of God's existence, the pay-off is infinite; infinite bliss for the saved, and infinite misery for the damned. Under such conditions; Pascal argued that rational self-interest dictates that we sacrifice our certain but merely finite worldly pleasures to the uncertain but infinite prospect of salvation [...]. These two famous Pascal manuscripts, the one mathematical and the other philosophical, reveal the double root of the mathematical theory of probability. It emerged at the crux of two important intellectual movements of the seventeenth-cen-

---

9 See Keith Devlin's *The Unfinished Game: Pascal, Fermat, and the Seventeenth-Century Letter that Made the World Modern* (2008). Cf. also Bernstein (1998: 58–72); and chapter 8 "Fermat and Pascal" in David (1998: 70–97); the extensive appendix to David's study (1998: 229–267) contains, e.g., the letters between Pascal and Fermat (from 1654–1660), as well as excerpts from Abraham de Moivre's *Doctrine of Chances* (1756).

tury: a pragmatic rationality that abandoned traditional ideas of certainty; and a sustained and remarkably fruitful attempt to apply mathematics to new domains of experience. (Gigerenzer et al. 1989: 1)

While there is agreement among the prominent theorists on the history of probability, Ian Hacking, Lorraine Daston, Gerd Gigerenzer and others, about the "probabilistic revolution" which took place from the 1660s onwards,[10] all grapple with the question why this did not happen sooner, why it took so long for a systematic mathematical study of probability to develop if, in theory, the tools and ideas had existed for centuries. This is a debate which need not be replicated in full,[11] but one of the most frequently given answers to this question sustains a crucial point in the argument: the need simply was not there. As long as the orientation of the future was sufficiently and authoritatively provided by means of and the belief in oracles, divine providence, superstition etc., people did neither dare nor have to come up with their own predictions. Consequently, the decline of providential thinking brought a 'taming of chance' (Hacking) on the one hand because speculation about good/bad fortunes was gradually replaced by (mathematical) calculation, yet the interest in apparently random patterns also brought a greater awareness of chance as a category: "Now it was no longer understood with reference to notions of divine providence and the will of the gods but in the language of science – probability, odds, and statistics" (Reith 1999: 10). Still, the new science was considered to provide far from absolute clarity and could, above all, only offer descriptive value of patterns of regularities, rather than predict the outcome of specific cases. As Gottfried Wilhelm Leibniz, one of the first philosophers to engage with probability theory,

---

[10] Cf. in particular Hacking's important studies (1975; 1990); also Issac Todhunter's *A History of the Mathematical Theory of Probability from the Time of Pascal to that of Laplace* (1865), which remains an authoritative survey on the subject (cf. Hacking 1975: 1); see also Lorenz Krüger, Lorraine Daston and Michael Heidelberger's *The Probabilistic Revolution Vol. I* (1987).

[11] Daston emphasizes that risk-taking was not unheard of before the advent of mathematical probability, and that, in fact, maritime insurance, annuities, and gambling were practiced long before. Yet people's approach to risk could "hardly be described as statistical or probabilistic" (1987: 239; 238). The appendix of Patey's study (1984: 266 ff) contains a detailed summary of the debate why the 1660s where the turning point in mathematical history and why the tools for probabilistic calculation had not been developed earlier. Newson argues that around 1660 'probability' was put on a new mathematical basis, although already Aristotle had theorized a concept of probability (1988: 6), while David comments on the fact that already Cicero (in *De Divinatione*, Book I and II), engages in questions of accident, luck fortune, and a surprising secular notion of chance (1998: 21; 24). Cf. also Reith (1999: 24 ff), Davis and Hersh (1986), and Hacking (1975: 11 ff) for a survey of the parallel developments in the field of probability theory taking place across Europe.

expresses it aptly in a letter to Jacob Bernoulli[12] in 1703: "Nature has established patterns originating in the return of events, but *only for the most part*" (cited in Bernstein 1998: 329; my emphasis).

Generally, if prior to the mid-17th century probability and mathematics of randomness were part of an "absent family of ideas" (Hacking 1975: 1; cf. Reith 1999: 20), this changed rapidly. Regarding mathematical problems of chance Hacking points out: "No one could solve them until about 1660, and then everyone could" (1975: 5). The famous discovery made by Pascal and Fermat was evolved by Bernoulli, Arnauld and others, and culminated in the Port Royal *Logic*, often considered as a founding text which also used gaming in order to represent epistemic probability.[13] Whereas the early probabilists were thus mainly concerned with the analysis of chance games, the field quickly moved on to more serious calculations of expectancies, such as life expectancy and tables of birth, disease, and mortality. This led to a changing meaning of probability, Lorraine Daston argues, as it started to transcend the prediction of regularities of games of chance towards controllability and prognostics in the field of early statistics, which required a legally binding degree of certainty and proof, for instance in insurance contracts.

A standard work for 18th century mathematicians and an example of the application of probability theory to the issue of mortality is Abraham De Moivre's 1725 *Treatise of the Annuities of Lives* (see Daston 1987: 242), published just a few years after Daniel Defoe, himself a collector of bills of mortality and highly interested in the subject and their accuracy, had fictionalized material from an early ground-breaking study of mortality in his *A Journal of the Plague Year* (1722): John Graunt's *Natural and Political Observations Mentioned in a Following*

---

12 Probabilist Jakob Bernoulli is especially known for writing *Ars Conjectandi* ('The Art of Conjecturing') in 1713. Many theorists acknowledge Bernoulli's paper as one of the first studies of the psychology of risk, as it raised basic questions about the acceptability of risk-taking vs. risk-aversion and the relation between probability, value, and utility which concerns scientists of risk today (cf. Bernstein 1998: 110 ff; and Hacking 1975). For more details see, e.g., chapter 13 "James Bernoulli and 'Ars Conjectandi'" in David (1998: 130–139).

13 Cf. Antoine Arnauld and Pierre Nicole's *Logic, or, The Art of Thinking being the Port-Royal logic* ([1662] 1850). J.M. Keynes writes about the *The Port Royal Logic* that these pages present for the first time "the logic of probability in the modern manner" (Keynes 1921: 80; see Patey 1984: 52). Other important studies appearing at the time and who all apply probability theory to the analysis of card games are Christiaan Huygens *De Ratiociniis in aleae ludo* (1657), later included in Pierre Rémond de Montmort *Essai d'analyse de jeux de hazard* (1708); the third and revised edition (1756) of Abraham de Moivre's *The Doctrine of Chances: or, a method for calculating the probabilities of events in play* (first edition 1718) is also widely considered as the "first modern book on probability theory" (David 1998: 171).

Index and Made upon the Bills of Mortality (1662), which is based on a sampling of births and deaths in London over six decades (1604–1661). Apart from giving numbers and reasons of deaths in each year, Graunt's pioneering work gives the first estimate of London's population, and captures the prevalent anxieties about public health at the time.[14] F.N. David describes his achievements thus: "Graunt, then, was the first Englishman to calculate empirical probabilities on any scale;" "He gave impetus to the collection of vital statistics, to life-tables, to insurance; he illustrates as none other of his time and race that the empirical approach of the English to probability was not through the gaming table but through the raw material of experience" (David 1998: 109; 103).[15] David refers to the often stated fact that the British – unlike the French, Dutch, Italians, or Germans – made no significant theoretical contribution to probability theory, their research was generally more practically oriented, yet it prepared the way for the institutionalization of statistics in the 19th century (cf. Reith 1999: 31).

Regarding the rise of statistics, the next important development is Abraham de Moivre's "normal curve" in the second edition of *The Doctrine of Chances* (1739), now commonly known as the '*bell curve*', which set the pattern for determining the structure of normal distribution and standard deviation, and which build the foundation for the quantification of risk and the emerging related sciences based on ideas of normalcy, and the 'mean.' Over the course of the next century and a half, the new understanding of the world based on the calculus of probability, the normal curve, and the 'law of large numbers', developed "first by Jakob Bernoulli in 1713 and most completely by Poisson in 1835" (Kava-

---

[14] Applying today's standards, Graunt's study would obviously count as unrepresentative and unreliable, as it contained more guess work than proper statistics and suffered from incomplete data, e.g. giving the cause of a person's death but not the age (cf. Bernstein 1998: 74–75; Daston 1987: 241). The only available data for Graunt were the parish registers which provided the first collections of quantitative data related to life and death; the issuing of weekly bills of mortality actually first became a common practice in England in 1538, due to injunctions made by Thomas Cromwell in order to get information regarding the plague epidemics. See also the chapter "Bills of Mortality" in David (1998: 98–109)

[15] Following Graunt's work, Edmund Halley published a collection of life tables in his *Transactions* (1693), which would provide a basis of data insurance companies and the government would rely on for almost a century. Cf. the chapter "Mathematics and Life Insurance" in Carl B. Cone's. *Torchbearer of Freedom* (1952: 37–51). Cone provides background on 18th century British mathematics, focussing on the life of the philosopher, preacher, and actuary Richard Price, who had a keen interest in statistics and studies of mortality and build on the works of Graunt and Halley.

nagh 1993: 16),[16] took over many central aspects of life and played a decisive role in developing the relation between individual, society, and nation. The notion of the 'probable' and the 'normal' had, of course, far-reaching influence on ethics and politics, bringing a newly comparative understanding of the self (in relation to others) and setting 'universal', or rather 'average', standards of health, money, education, or happiness.

It is an interesting contradiction that a "stochastized" view of the world means, on the one hand, an acknowledgment and perception of chance, and randomness as "real, objective and fundamental aspect[s] of the world" (Davis and Hersh 1986: 18).[17] On the other hand, the emerging theory of probability and risk aims at a control of chance, seeks to master it by formulating laws and regularities of chance processes and increasingly by establishing means of insurance against all odds. If especially insurance appears as the ultimate "domestication of risk", there is still a paradox inherent in the attempt to regularize hazard, because the whole process is still related to and applies laws derived from gambling (see Daston 1987: 248). It is important to note the shift in the public perception of what was considered as 'truth', 'evidence' or 'high' science in this context.[18] Before the emergence of probability theory, "science was about causes, not chance" (Gigerenzer et al. 1989: xiii). The rise of risk and probability theory appears thus based on a complex linkage of both elements. Whereas in pre-Enlightenment thought and science it would have been considered blasphemy to consider an "uncaused" event, chance, increasingly separated from 'fortune', becomes a distinct category, while the search for causality and calculability continues to soar.[19] The reality of chance posed a threat to the Enlightenment ideal of order and predictability, the newly secularized world was fragile to the extent that the absence of the divine created a void which could either be filled with an optimistic blown-up belief in human rationality and the certainty of control and calculability, or "an antithetical vision of the world as ruled by the uncontrollable forces of chance and hazard" (Kavanagh 1993: 5). The early novel is primarily concerned with negotiating these tensions.

---

16 A summary is given in "The Law of Great Numbers" in Keynes's *A Treatise on Probability* (1921: 332–336).
17 'Etymologically, 'stochastic' is derived from the Greek 'stochos' ("to guess, aim at").
18 See Hacking (1975) and Steven Shapin's *A Social History of Truth* (1994).
19 Cf. Jordan (2010: 5). Yet it is still a long way to the acceptance of chance as an ontological category in its own right; as many critics in their historical studies of chance have noted, it is not till the 20th century that chance was granted a place as a central constituent of the universe (see Reith 1999: 11; Molesworth 2010).

Relevant is also the relation between the era's decline of a belief in fortune and the consequences for the human emotions of "uncertainty, hope and fear", Lorraine Daston has examined, referring centrally to Hume's theory of passions developed in *A Treatise of Human Nature* (1739/40) (Daston 1994b: 27; 34 ff).[20] She explains that these passions (re)gained significance because probability and uncertainty were now put on a partially rational basis, conceived as relative degrees of knowledge. Yet, they were distinctly seen to operate on the borderline between reason and emotion. In fact, Hume's famous statement that: "Reason is, and ought to be the slave of the passions, and can never pretend any other office than to serve and obey them" (Hume 2003: 295; Book II. Part iii, section 3), contains some central insight into the psychology of risk perception (without theorizing the concept).[21] Hume argues that rational reasoning (e.g. in mathematics or empirical science) has been limited to no effect on human emotion ('the passions'); in comparison, probable reasoning is significant only in so far as it focuses on the human aversion to pain or loss and the inclination to pleasure onto things, events etc., that are perceived to be causally related to them. Hume describes the human experience of probability and the weighing alternatives in the face of uncertainty thus:

> Probability arises from an opposition of contrary chances or causes, by which the mind is not allow'd to fix on either side, but is incessantly toast from one to another, and at one moment is determin'd to consider an object as existent, and at another as the contrary. The imagination or understanding, call it which you please, fluctuates betwixt the opposite views; and tho' perhaps it may be oftner turn'd to the one side and the other, 'tis impossible for it, by reason of the opposition of causes or chances, to rest on either. (Hume 2003: 313; Book II, Part iii, Section 9)

He makes a strong case for the inseparable influence of 'unsteady' passions, irrational emotions such as hope and fear, on the consideration of decisions and the mental process of calculation. For Hume, as Daston puts it, "to appeal to prob-

---

[20] Daston (1994a and 1994b) presents a historical study of the concepts of calculation in the Enlightenment as an issue that concerned not only mathematicians, but writers and philosophers, as even moral sentiments were seen as subject to and forms of calculations. Locke and Hume are perhaps the most prominent representatives of thinkers who made inquiries into human nature, and the origins and limits of knowledge, and their philosophical queries are considered today to be part of psychology as well as of epistemology and science (see 1994a: 191).
[21] Hume's *Treatise of Human Nature* contains reflections on knowledge and probability (Book I, Part III) and on the passions and the human will (Book II, Part III). Hume is mainly concerned with a theory of moral philosophy which questions the subordination of the human emotions to rational thinking.

abilities in the explication of hope and fear is to mingle reason with the passions" (Daston 1994b: 35; 37). This highlights a striking tension at the heart of the construction of risk that keeps complicating (objective) risk measurement and management until today. The fact that the passions of uncertainty, i.e. hope and fear, are to some extent resistant to reasoning by (mathematical) probability (1994b: 39), is demonstrated, for instance, in Defoe's fictions and a reoccurring topic in many narratives since. Defoe's protagonists are also good examples of the fact that most active 'practitioners' of risk at this time, partaking in the new boom of financial speculation, were very willing to ignore any mathematical theory of risk, which was instead calculated somewhat intuitively,[22] while the focus was on the individual interest in schemes and potential profits.

1.2 A Projecting Age: Speculation, Credit, Gambling

Apart from a general striving for 'improvement', in historical-cultural summaries the 18th century is usually also characterized by a pervasive sense of risk and crisis. London is seen as the metropolitan centre, fraught with anxieties – about crime, disease, poverty, debt – and the tensions between excess, danger and opportunity: "There was an edge to life in the eighteenth century which is hard for us to recapture. In every class there is the same taut neurotic quality – the fantastic gambling and drinking, the riots, brutality and violence, and everywhere and always a constant sense of death" (Plumb 1978: 95; 12–15).[23] The coming or going of war contributed to the general atmosphere of unpredictability and disaster proneness; a second major "erratic influence" on 18th-century economy and public consciousness were financial crises (Hoppit 1987: 130).[24]

---

[22] The point made by many critics is that despite the rise of probability theory and mathematic knowledge about the calculation of probabilities and regularities, there was only a slow acceptance of these rules, and that it had no influence on the fascination with gambling and speculation. The reorientation towards the statistic 'average" in public decision-making with regard to risk was a slow process because "accepting the mathematical theory of risk required a profound change in beliefs" (Gigerenzer et al. 1989: 26). See Daston (1987), and Richard (2011: 13).
[23] On the role of London as a marketplace metropolis see Sussman's *Consuming Anxieties* (2000).
[24] See Hoppit (1986) and his *Risk and Failure in English Business* (1987). Telling the story of the rise of capitalism, Hoppit highlights the failures and bankruptcies, rather than economic opportunities and investments; he also identifies a strong desire for security, fear of failure and risk-aversion existing alongside the spirit of capitalist venture (1987: 16–17). He also argues that the experience of being at war heightened a sense of instability in the population, causing a need

Occurring with almost regular frequency, the crises seemed, in John Brewer's words, "just as arbitrary and cruel as a death, flood or plague" (Brewer 1982: 212). When writing about the evolution of finance and capitalism in the early 18th century many scholars comment on the closeness of the atmosphere to that of our time and draw parallels to the climate of the late 20th and early 21st century.[25] For instance, Laura Brown writes: "The early eighteenth century was the first age to live the immediate intensity of credit, loans, discounts, shares, futures, national debt, deficit spending, and the fascinating fluctuations of stock exchange in a way directly comparable to our own" (Brown 2001: 97).[26] Similarly, Ian Baucom emphasizes the era's "speculative finance culture", which originated in a context of a mix of "new actuarial science", "novelized critical imaginary" and which "our own hyperfinancialized 'present' inherits from this eighteenth-century 'past'" (Baucom 2005: 41). Julian Hoppit describes especially the second decade of the 18th century as a key moment of financial crises on a national scale caused by a series of dangerous speculations and bursting investment bubbles: "During those ten years England was racked by political instability, war, financial innovation at the public and corporate levels, speculative manias, a massive recoinage and a financial crises of some magnitude" (Hoppit 1990: 308).

A very brief summary of the 'Financial Revolution' in Britain must suffice here. It is the era of the foundation of the South Sea Company, Lloyd's of London, the Bank of England, and the London Stock Exchange. In other words, Britain saw the emergence of the banking and credit system,[27] the rise of joint-stock companies and overseas trade, and of an insurance industry, competent not just to render manageable the risks of global commerce, but to insure against all sorts of threats: "Underwriters were willing to write insurance policies against almost any kind of risk, including [...] house-breaking, highway robbery, death by gin-drinking, the death of horses, and 'assurance of female chastity'" (Bern-

---

for insurance: "Certainty was eroded, confidence ebbed and the prospect of stability vanished" (1987: 129).

25 Landes singles out the status of England at the time with regard to the development of the financial system and the people's fascination with "wealth and commerce, collectively and individually" (1969: 66), and claims that in "no country in Europe in the eighteenth century was the financial structure so advanced and the public so habituated to paper instruments as in Britain" (74–75). Therefore, English fiction generally provides an exceptional textual base to look for negotiation of these discourses and an emerging sense of financial risk.
26 See also Barbara Maria Stafford's essay "The Eighteenth Century at the End of Modernity" (1995).
27 For an introduction see Dickson's *The Financial Revolution in England* (1967).

stein 1998: 90; cf. Baucom 2005: 38).²⁸ The simultaneous development of the insurance and the deposit and credit banking system expresses the spirit of individualism and self-help, the interest in property, and the belief in the potential of a collective management of risk and control of the future (cf. Thomas 1991: 779; Reith 1999: 27). Yet, the new financial system, resting on institutions such as the Bank of England, founded in 1695, was still largely unregulated and dangerously unstable. While national debt was generally mounting, bankruptcies were also a frequent occurrence. Furthermore, the new pillars of the financial system, credit and paper money, captured the national imagination and sparked hopes and fears, yet were perceived as having an unreal, somewhat 'fictional' quality. Writers and journalists such as Defoe were at the forefront of shaping the discourse and narrative of credit and speculation at the beginning of the century.²⁹

> This experience of credit and debt pervaded English life in this period, bringing with it an immediate sense of fluctuation, instability, and change, and enforcing at the same time a vital excursion into the realm of the imagination. As Defoe himself concludes, trade is a mysterious force, shaped not by the rules of logic, coherence, or order but by the 'Power of the Imagination' to create a world of its own outside those rules. (Brown 2001: 101)

As many critics have noted, in public discourse trade and credit were often referred to using metaphors of the sea, evoking risk, fluidity, limitlessness, and the possibility of drowning.³⁰ *Lady Credit*, Defoe's symbolic figure of the seductive

---

28 Insurance played a crucial role in Britain's turn-of-the-century financial revolution and its practice had taken on concrete forms by the 1720s. On 18th-century trade and the development of insurance practices see Cockerell and Green's *The British Insurance Business* (1994) and Clarke's *Betting on Lives* (1999); see also O'Brien (2011), and Pearson's *Insuring the Industrial Revolution* (2004). For a transatlantic perspective, see Eric Wertheimer's *Underwriting: The Poetics of Insurance in America, 1722–1872* (2006).
29 The literature on the topic is, of course, vast. See, for instance, Brantlinger's *Fictions of State* (1996); Ingrassia's *Authorship, Commerce and Gender in Eighteenth-Century England* (1998); Poovey's *Genres of the Credit Economy* (2008), Schaffer (1989), Scheuermann's *Her Bread to Earn: Women, Money, and Society from Defoe to Austen* (1993), Sherman's *Finance and Fictionality in the Early Eighteenth Century* (1996), and Thompson's *Models of Value* (1996).
30 For instance, in *The Complete English Tradesman* (1726), often taken as one of the first English business manuals, Defoe speaks repeatedly of "the great ocean of business" (33; Chapt. II), and compares a tradesman, who does not keep accounts and is lured by profits, to "a ship at sea, steered without a helm" (30; Chapt.1); meanwhile he defines a "safe tradesman" as someone who averts risks and "goes in the road of his business without launching into *unknown oceans*; and content is neither led by ambition or avarice, and neither covets to be greater nor richer by such *uncertain and hazardous attempts*" (p. 78; Chapt. VI; my emphasis). For an analysis of *The Complete English Tradesman* which Defoe tries to "craft as a model for how to prosecute high-

Goddess ruling over the nation's finances, which he introduced in the *Review*, adds to this imagery and had a strong influence on shaping the public imagination of credit and economy, capturing the duality of fascination and fear, which was also, in this case, clearly gendered and linked to femininity. Laura Brown sums up this aspect saying: "Among these representations of modern trade, oceans and rivers, storms and hysteria, fancy and the female figure intersect in a *complicated evocation of risk, loss, uncertainty, volatility, value, prosperity, modern finance, and historical change*" (Brown 2001: 96; my emphasis). Lady Credit's career "as the imaginative embodiment of paper money in all its forms" (Baucom 2005: 81) reached a peak in 1720, the year of the South Sea Bubble.[31]

The bursting of the South Sea Bubble and the ensuing crisis, which resulted in the 1721 Bubble Act that put a stop to the foundation of joint-stock companies, is commonly recognized as "England's first modern financial disaster" (Sussman 2012: 67). It is the first experience of the risks of financial speculation on a grand scale and had a lasting effect on society and the attitude towards credit; it also features prominently in the literary imagination of the decade. Sandra Sherman puts it thus: "The contingency of a world configured by credit inspired plays, poetry, and cautionary tracts [...]. The Bubble became a metonym of greed and corruption, played out against a speculative frenzy in which hundreds of lesser bubbles competed for capital and gulled the unwary" (Sherman 1996: 23).[32] In fact, interesting parallels exist between the new print and writing culture, national debt and paper credit; they all rely on an imaginative selling of the 'future' as a construction clients, citizens and readers – however temporary – have to place their belief and trust in. Thus newly dependent on a mortgaging of a (secular) future, one can observe a paradigm shift in society towards "living to an increasing degree by speculation and by credit: that is to say, by men's expectations of one another's capacity for future action and performance" (Pocock 1985: 98).

---

risk endeavor" and as "a practical manual for business people" and Defoe's use of the sea as a metaphor for the risk of trade, see Cohen (2010: 65f).

31 On Defoe's Lady Credit and her symbolic power as the "Nation's Mistress", see Baucom (2005: 80–112), Backscheider (1981), Brown (2001: 95–132), O'Brien (1996); also Sherman (1996: 14–54).

32 Cf. Plumb (1978: 26); Hoppit (1990: 306). For background and details on the South Sea Bubble see Carswell's *The South Sea Bubble* (1960) and Hoppit (1986). A shorter summary can be found in Hentzi (1993b); see also Ingrassia's chapter "Women, Credit and the South Sea Bubble" in *Authorship, Commerce and Gender in Eighteenth-Century England* (1998: 17–39).

Paper credit and speculation also suddenly provided the unique chance of rapidly changing one's personal situation, and hence possessed the same appeal as gambling; generally it triggered a new awareness of the fluidity of identity because circumstance were seen to be able to change drastically within short spans of time.[33] Furthermore, credit, like trust, reputation, and the assessment of character, centrally depend upon belief. Mary Poovey emphasises that all the notions connected to the thematic cluster of "credit, credibility, credentials, and credulity" are essentially based on "people's willingness (or need) to believe" and fuses political, economic, and psychological mechanisms (Poovey 1998: 27).[34] Similarly arguing that the concept of "credit" is central to the dynamics of 18th-century culture and society, Thomas Kavanagh explains how "[c]redit had to do, not with any dogma anchored in the past, but with a belief in the future, a belief in what one thought would happen but of which one could never be certain. *Anticipating an uncertain future, credit was defined by the twin emotions hope and fear*" (Kavanagh 1993: 69; my emphasis).

Both Poovey and Kavanagh draw attention to the psychological implications of the concept of 'credit' from a theoretical point of view and underline the inherent duality of emotions and risk. In pamphlets and literary works of the time, we find an awareness of credit as having become an inevitable and necessary part of the world and the organization of a capitalist society, but also a reflection of a new 'immaterial' source of anxiety. To consider only two, but telling and well-known examples, Defoe writes in *An Essay Upon Public Credit*:

> CREDIT is a Consequence, not a Cause; the Effect of a Substance, not a Substance; 'tis the Sun-shine, not the Sun; the quickening SOMETHING, Call it what you will, that gives Life to Trade, gives Being to the Branches and Moisture to the Root; 'tis the Oil of the Wheel, the Marrow in the Bones, the Blood in the Veins, and the Spirits in the Heart of all Negoce, Trade, Cash, and Commerce in the World. ([1710] 1840: 69)

A more negative and satirical view is expressed in the following lines from Alexander Pope's "Epistle to Bathurst" (1744):

> Blest paper-credit! Last and best supply!
> That lends Corruption lighter wings to fly!
> Gold imp'd by thee, can compass hardest things,
> Can pocket States, can fetch or carry Kings;

---

[33] Regarding 18th-century culture and the performativity of identity see Wahrman's *The Making of the Modern* Self (2004).
[34] On "credit" as a part of character "probability" see O'Brien (1996: 603f); also Lynch's *The Economy of Character* (1998).

> A single leaf shall waft an Army o'er,
> Or ship off Senates to a distant Shore;
> A leaf, like Sibyl's, scatter to and fro
> Our fates and fortunes, as the winds shall blow:
> Money brought new uneasiness
> ([1744] 2007. ll. 69–75)

Generally, credit becomes a symbol of the instability of a secular, man-ordered world and its risks; it brings new power-balances, hopes and dangers. It systematically establishes what many scholars describe as a new "double economy" of trust and capital (cf. Baucom 2005: 64). For instance, in order to accept a bill of exchange people had to calculate and take a dual risk concerning, firstly, the monetary value and, secondly, the trustworthiness of the creditor. The novel assumes an important function in the illustration of the emerging nexus between credit and credibility and the testing of beliefs and character. Often, we find dual plot lines that link the risk of a loss of credit (money) to a loss of reputation and social identity. Questions of judgment and choice becoming all-important, personal relations are also perceived as risky and run the gamut from 'lucky' chance encounters to disasters resulting from putting trust in strangers and misjudgements of character. While these issues are at the centre of Defoe's *Roxana*, who, despite her increasing paranoia maintains an adventurous approach to speculation, the risks connected to loosing personal 'credibility', reputation and virtue, are even more pronounced in Burney's *Camilla*, a text which foreshadows the topical preoccupation with social order, status, and the dangerous sides of risk-taking and transgression in the 19th-century novel.

Many 18th-century novels deal with epistemological questions regarding the status of knowledge and the distinction between 'facts' and 'fictions;'[35] they also reflect the central contradictions of an era which saw the surge of rational calculation and mathematics coincide with a booming of chance and speculation. Jesse Molesworth points out how "the century that would promote a mathematician, Isaac Newton, to godlike status [...] was simultaneously the century that would elevate the state lottery (established in 1694) to its modern form as an indispensable form of government revenue, financing enormous projects like the building of Westminster bridge and the British Library" (2010: 9). The paradoxical development with regard to the management and institutionalization of risk is most strikingly reflected in the contemporary regulations and attitudes towards gambling. Although gambling gained a bad reputation and

---

[35] Most studies of 18th-century fiction engage with this aspect (see fn. 58). Cf. Davis's *Factual Fictions* (1983) and Mayer's *History and the Early English Novel* (1997).

1.2 A Projecting Age: Speculation, Credit, Gambling — 59

became synonymous with the ills of capitalist speculation after the South Sea Bubble and other stock-jobbing scandals in the first half of the 18th century, Europe, and here in particular England, Holland, and France, were swept by a "lottery craze" (Daston 1987: 244) and gambling generally continued to have an unbroken attraction.[36] On the one hand, this testifies to people's growing acceptance and adjustment to risk; together the public credit system, the stock-market and the lottery certainly contributed to rooting gambling within society (see Richard 2011: 29; Molesworth 2010: 24).[37] Unsurprisingly, gamblers occur in most 18th-century and 19th-century novels and it is interesting to relate the appeal of gambling to the narrative construction and characteristics of the novel genre and plots which similarly reflect the "tension between chance and control, between an unknowable and a predictable outcome" (Richard 2011: 3). While Jessica Richard rightly stresses the early novels' ambivalence resulting from the increasing attempt to represent life with probability but still integrate chance events (2011: 7), Jesse Molesworth relates the element of "fantasy" inherent in gambling and or playing the lottery, the imminent possibility of a drastic change of personal circumstances, to the human "quest for plot" (2010: 23) and explains further that

> the point remains that gambling entices, at bottom, through the very offer of plot – the creation of risk rather than its minimization. To gamble is to fictionalize oneself in precisely the same narrative of triumph and failure offered to the basketball players, to discover a plot within a series of events that is ultimately plotless; the point is neither to win nor to lose, but to risk winning or losing. (2010: 89–90)

In her historical-sociological study of gambling, Gerda Reith also takes the fact that the struggle with uncertainty and unknown outcomes of actions is intrinsic to human culture and a modern worldview as a point of departure.[38] Stressing

---

[36] Cf. also Gigerenzer et al. (1989: 19) and Miers (1989: 118). The gambling 'boom' in Britain reached a new height during the Restoration. Queen Anne's gaming act of 1710 thought to regulate gambling, which was later outlawed completely by George II. On the legislation and public opinion of gaming, see especially Miers (1989). Many writers and artists of the time take up the public's fascination with gambling. Examples are Defoe's harsh satire on contemporary gambling practices, *The Gamester: A Benefit-Ticket for all that are concern'd in the Lotteries* (1719), William Hogarth painting "The Lottery" (1721), or Henry Fielding's opera-play "The Lottery: A Farce" (1732). Cf. also Molesworth (2010: 56) and Kavanagh (1993: 119).
[37] On the historical context, the founding of the lottery system and the growing national debt based on lotteries cf. Richard (2011: 18ff); a good and detailed account is also given in the first chapter "Fortune's Fools: the novel and the lottery fantasy" in Molesworth (2010: 19–54).
[38] Gerda Reith's *The Age of Chance* opens with the remark that: "One of the most striking features to emerge from a cursory glance at the phenomenon is its almost universal prevalence

the universal appeal of gambling, Reith analyses the psychology of gambling, the belief system constructed by gamblers as a coping mechanism which falls back on the belief in magic and luck on purpose (rather than out of ignorance) and describes it as "an order of knowledge which works to make sense of an environment of chance, and, furthermore, to provide individuals with an efficacious basis for action while in it. It is here that the dynamic of gambling itself – the tension between uncertainty and order, chance and meaning – is to be found" (Reith 1999: 12).

Appearing on the one hand as the antithesis to the Enlightenment's pursuit of reason, gambling reflects the era's obsession with speculation; furthermore the psychological mechanisms involved in the activity of gambling also go a long way in explaining why the rise of mathematical probability theory did not minimize the appeal of gambling, as many scholars have noted (with more or less surprise).[39] The ideological mix operating in the minds of gamblers, oscillating between rational-scientific calculation and magical/religious thought is found in many early novels, for instance in the conjectures of Defoe's *Robinson Crusoe*. The figure of the gambler, striving to make sense of and master uncertainty, exemplifies the paradoxical struggle and desire for human control and the belief in some higher power predetermining the game and thus 'ordering' the world. On these grounds Gerda Reith considers the pursuit of play to show

---

throughout history and across cultures: it unites peoples as diverse as the ancient Greeks and the North American Indians with the inhabitants of modern western societies" (1999: 1).

39 Reith argues that the fact that gamblers tend to ignore the 'realistic' insights of probability theory and expect to win in the midst of catastrophic losses or 'against all odds', springs from a notion of "luck" as a sort of magical, illusionary control over the game, which suggest a very human characteristic, the desire for order and causality: "Few concepts are as alien to human thought as the notion of pure chance – [...]. Probability theory – the apologist of secularized chance – is equally alien. Probability creates order out of randomness, but not for the gambler" (1999: 157). She argues further that the belief in forces such "luck, omens, fate and destiny" becomes for the gambler an epistemological order "which works to make sense of the gambling environment in a way that the scientific explanation of probability theory does not. The latter does not really 'explain' the situation any more effectively – it cannot advise on what will happen next or how to act" (1999: 180–81). For an historical argument and debate of the inconsistency between theory and practice see, for instance, the pamphlet *The Gamester* (1719), attributed to Defoe, in which he expressed the opinion that the new mathematical tools of probability theory would soon erase games of chance, like dice, cards etc. The prediction that irrational 'passions' such as hope and fear might soon be controlled by applying laws of reason was a typical idea at the time (Molesworth 2010: 55; 57–58), yet, as time has shown, this has not happened; people kept gambling despite the growing mathematical knowledge about the odds of the game. For details see chapter 2: "Two Predictions on the Fate of Gambling and Probability Theory" in Molesworth (2010: 55–99); also Daston (1994b).

"a fundamental fact of human existence, for, along with the image of homo ludens, homo faber and homo economicus, the sphere of human activity also embraces homo aleator: man the gambler" (Reith 1999: 184).[40] Generally, games of risk-taking, e.g. financial speculation or gambling, can be described as games of extremes which follow one main rule, namely the rapid change between hope and fear. The attraction of gambling and the fact that gambling calls forth existential human fears and desires has fascinated many writers to the present day.[41] For instance, Georges Bataille writes: "A part of human life escapes from work and attains freedom. It is the part of play that admits the control of reason, but within the limits of reason, determines brief possibilities of a leap beyond its limits. This is the game that, like a catastrophe, is fascinating, that permits a glimpse, positively, of the dizzying seductiveness of chance" (Bataille 2011: 63). Similarly, Walter Benjamin, in his "Notes on Gambling", describes the psychological aspect and the fascination thus:

> [...] one should note the factor of danger, which is the most important factor in gambling, alongside pleasure (the pleasure of betting on the right number): it arises not so much from the threat of losing as from that of not winning. [...] gambling generates by want of experiment the lightning-quick process of stimulation at the moment of danger, the marginal case in which presence of mind becomes divination – that is to say, one of the highest, rarest moments in life. (Benjamin 1999: 298)

Just from these two examples it becomes clear how the perception and taking of risks, here captured in the metaphor and activity of gambling, is intrinsically narrative, combines rationality and irrationality, and, perhaps most importantly, presents a means to assert human identity and agency while highlighting their contingency.

1.3 Realism, Uncertainties, and the Early Novel

So far it has been stressed that the 18th century, often referred to as the 'Age of Reason', is also the 'age of speculation' and the 'age of probabilities', descriptions which affirm the importance of rational reasoning, but also modify its claim for absoluteness with regard to knowledge or truth. In order to form and accommodate a cultural-scientific conception of risk, the paradigm shift towards

---

[40] See the classic studies of the subject, Roger Callois's *Man, Plays and Games* ([1958] 2001) and Johan Huizinga's *Homo* Ludens (1956).
[41] It has inspired countless novels, among them works of world literature such as Fyodor Dostoevsky's *The Gambler* (1867).

a probabilistic worldview outlined above is crucial.⁴² Obviously, probability theory and the novel both have roots reaching further back than the turn of the 17th to the 18th century, yet they clearly 'rise' at the same time.⁴³ By the time Defoe publishes his first fictions, probability theory is recognized as an established discipline, and the category of risk has begun to shape public perception and imagination, while increasingly influencing individual and political decision-making.⁴⁴

Generally, if one wants to argue that the developments in the field of probability theory (both in science and philosophy) actually necessitate and are inseparable from the rise of the novel, Thomas Kavanagh in particular was one of the first critics to suggest plausible points to support this argument and claimed: "The triumph of probability theory and the rise of the novel were part of a single shift in our understanding of the world and of how we represent our place within it" (1993: ix). He explicitly relates this to the uncertainties and ambivalent attitudes towards Enlightenment rationality and the persistence and experience of chance, in other words, to the difficulty to grasp the coexistence of calculability and randomness. The novel, he argues,

> more than any other literary genre, reflects this ambiguity of the eighteenth century's attitude toward chance. The novel of that period always tells two stories. On the one hand, it speaks of a deterministic universe in which actions are followed by reactions. On the other, it tells the story of how, within that predictability, the chance event may at any moment redefine the individual's place within the world's apparently ordered sequences of cause and effect. (Kavanagh 1993: 108)

---

42 Campe affirms its significance: "This 'probabilistic revolution,' [...] was not merely a revolution that changed our idea of society and nature. Indeed, with statistics, the doctrine of chances, and the form of the modern novel, it brought our modern ideas of society and nature into existence in the first place" (2012: 2–3).
43 See Ian Watt's classic study *The Rise of the* Novel (1987), Michael McKeon's *The Origins of the English Novel* (1987) and John Paul Hunter's *Before Novels* (1990a). For an accessible summary of the rise of the novel studies and the criticism of the early novel from different perspectives see Backscheider and Ingrassia (2009: 1–17). Other recent studies include Charlotte Sussman's *Eighteenth-Century English Literature* (2012), Brean Hammond and Shaun Regan's *Making the Novel* (2006), and Patrick Parrinder's *Nation and Novel* (2006). For gender-critical approaches to the novel see Nancy Armstrong's *Desire and Domestic Fiction* (1987), Margaret Anne Doody's *The True Story of the Novel* (1997), and Helen Moglen's *The Trauma of Gender: A Feminist Theory of the English Novel* (2001).
44 Cf. Hacking's temporal argument that the "story of the emergence of probability comes to an end with the publication of *Ars conjectandi*" in 1711 and that soon after "the mathematics of probability was recognized as an independent discipline in its own right" (1975: 166).

Whether one wants to go as far Kavanagh, who considers the development of probability to be "the most important mutation of human thought since Aristotle" (1993: 21), in any case, it had an undeniably strong impact and correlates with the other, much-theorized developments which shape the context of the early novel: secularism, capitalism, (in particular middle-class) individualism, ordinary ('average') people, and domesticity. It also finds reflection in some of the early novel's defining formal and narrative characteristics: realism, a concern with circumstantial description and evidence, and with questions of trust, credibility, and certainty.

The novel's interest in the depiction of causality is reflected prominently in the language of 18th-century fiction and the employment of what Christian Thorne calls a "Machiavellian vocabulary" (2003: 325), i.e. the prominence of words like fortune, virtue, prudence. Fortune refers generally to (good/bad) circumstances and chance events, but most frequently to economic developments or situations where there is a perceived risk of gains and losses. Paradoxically, fortune appears both beyond control and within man's reach and becomes a concept evoked when causality fails: "When eighteenth-century characters cannot name causes, or when they mean to emphasize the implacable complexity of those causes, they invoke fortune. [...] *Fortune* names the lack of transparency" (Thorne 2003: 326). Julia Jordan underlines this aspect, arguing that the concept of fate or fortune comes to be recognized as a secular pattern: "Fate may still exist, but its now an internalized force, coming humanistically enough, from ourselves, rather than from God" (Jordan 2010: 14).

The novel, as many critics have noted, is the genre which strongly reflects the evolving capitalism and the related socio-economic shifts of the era, which includes renegotiation of questions of value(s), of (acceptable) losses and gains and the ethics of gambling and trade (cf. Richard 2011; also Poovey 2008; Thompson 1996; Raven 1992). While Atlantic trade, capitalism, wartime economy, new forms of credit and consumerism shape public culture and society, these changes also necessitate the formation of ethical codes, laws and forms of linguistic and artistic expression suited to deal with them. The search for a new rhetoric of 'factuality', the emphasis on precision and experience, had an impact in many disciplines; the stylistic goal of the accurate description (of things, environment, people) and the illusion of matters of 'fact' and reliable testimony were reflected in the era's new and popular literary forms, like the novel, travel narratives and the newspaper. In particular Defoe and Swift are representatives of these new kinds of writing.[45]

---

[45] Cf. Barbara J. Shapiro (1983: 228–232; 262ff); also John Bender (1998), who also focuses on

Generally, the developing 18th-century novel takes up many tensions and testifies, perhaps, to one 'fact' most clearly: the more conventionalized, straightforward providential narratives of the 17th century do no longer hold.[46] The novel's scope and flexible form allows writers (and readers) to pursue multiple narrative strands, and to depict a plurality of perspectives, locations and temporalities, which also includes the fascination with the emerging "capitalism in all its incalculable complexity" (Richard 2011: 44; also 17). Terry Eagleton explains the particular linkage as follows: "Commerce is nervous of disruptions and upheavals, just like the novel. Like the novel, too, it is all a matter of plot, of establishing connections between far-flung elements and drawing them into an elaborate yet orderly whole" (Eagleton 2003: 191). Money is often a large component of the plot, e.g. money's relation to marriage comes up almost obsessively in the 18th-century's novels, and this hardly decreases in the 19th century. Many texts are fraught with anxieties about marriage and finance, representing the close, well-documented, intersection of the domestic and the economic. Adding to the perceived element of realism in the texts, we find many characters primarily concerned with risk and survival and with managing the odds in both areas:

> The figures who populate eighteenth-century novels need money, which they may find, lose, inherit, earn, steal, beg, borrow, or be given. Their counterparts in romance require neither money nor, apparently, food. The novel's characters hire coaches, which may leak or overturn or collide with obstacles. They concern themselves with love, but also with survival. They make minor mistakes as well as catastrophic ones. More often than not they fight duels or battles, they stop at inns or attend balls. In short, they do things that ordinary readers would recognize and understand. (Spacks 2006: 13)

Related to this is the function of characters in the early novel. According to James Thompson, "they model ordinary lives, and therefore *they are about expectations: what one can reasonably expect to happen in these circumstances*" (1996: 11; my emphasis). While both economic and novelistic discourses appear to mediate reality, these arguments affirm again that risk, tied to the perception of expectation and circumstances, is an inseparable part of the emerging genre and the depicted experience of life. So one can even argue that "[b]y extending

---

the 18th-century novel as a narrative realm for linking science ('facts') and fiction and seeking to validate new knowledge by setting it in opposition to other, older forms of belief.

46 For summaries of the social and literary changes from 1700 onwards see, for instance, Thorne (2003) and Braudy (1981). On poetry in comparison to prose fiction see Jackson's *The Probable and the Marvelous* (1978). For a general study of religious providence in contrast to a secular-scientific worldview and the notion of coincidence, see Pollard's *Zufall und Vorsehung* (1960).

the illusion of plot to ordinary people, the novel was simultaneously extending the invitation to risk" (Molesworth 2010: 39).[47]

Generally, the mediation of risk and the epistemological and ethical questions of agency vs. predetermination or exposition to 'higher' forces, transcend, of course, the economic realm. In particular the question of how much control the hero/heroine has is frequently addressed in theoretical debates of the genre. For instance, George Lukács writes about the psychological and causal depiction of the protagonist and his/her actions in the novel that, in contrast to other genres, "the life of a person with such a soul becomes an uninterrupted series of adventures which he himself has chosen" (Lukács 1971: 99). As a consequence, Terry Eagleton sees the novel as a "posttragic" genre, because, for him, the realism of the novel "is marked by a concern with causation that is untragically exculpatory" (MacPherson 2010: 7).[48] According to this view, tragedy disappears with the rise of empiricism and secularism; in the narratives there is now always the potential for the human protagonists to save their own lives or to redeem themselves, to intervene, calculate the odds, consider evidence before judgment etc. Emphasizing the broader relation between narrative, realism, ethics and psychology here,[49] the construction of risk is situated at the intersection of knowledge, control and human choice and relations. In her study of 18th-century fiction, Sandra MacPherson takes a critical approach to the novel informed by legal studies, feminist scholarship and consensus theory, saying that the novel, above all, contains and reflects the changing attitudes about "persons and their connections to others" (MacPherson 2010: 20). Without going into any detail about the many legal changes taking place at the time, it is noteworthy

---

47 Patricia Spacks underlines that the early novel's concern with "ordinary people" does not mean "realism" in the literal sense, rather it does refer to a concern with psychological experience and complexity, varying degrees of depicting social details and generally with the portrayal of "actuality" (cf. 2006: 2–3).

48 See Eagleton's *Sweet Violence: The Idea of the Tragic* (2003: 178–201); this phase, according to Eagleton, lasts until the late 19th century, because he sees Thomas Hardy, Joseph Conrad, or Henry James as distinct writers of tragedy. See also Macpherson's *Harm's Way: Tragic Responsibility and the Novel Form* (2010).

49 Cf. also Bernard Williams (1993). Focusing on Greek tragedy, Williams investigates the question of the origin of the ethics and the ideas of causality, strict liability, and human responsibility for actions even if they are unintentional. He argues that already in ancient Greece life could not be separated into things one does intentionally and things that "merely happen to one", an insight onto which the modern insurance system is based (1993: 70). Macpherson, commenting on Williams's approach, writes that "the tragic principle that persons must accept responsibility for things they could not avoid doing is at the very heart of ethics" (2010: 17).

that the notion of risk irrevocably enters personal and business relationships, such as marriage, loans etc., and that questions of trust and responsibility become increasingly important, 'man-made' issues.

To refer to Ian Watt's well-known (and, despite some disputes, still valid) argument, formal realism, as a defining characteristic, or, as a "set of narrative procedures" of the novel genre, reflects the philosophical realism of the age, the spirit of individualism, the rising middle-class, the growth of literacy, and the "circumstantial view of life" (Watt 1987: 32). One can see a direct relation between the formal realism of the early novel and the manifestos of probability theory, such as the Port Royal *Logic*, as both rely on circumstantial evidence in order to arrive at 'true' reports and seek to induce causality (cf. Newsom 1988: 87 ff).[50] Regarding this aspect, Paul Korshin argues that before the 18th century the notion of probability (here mainly in the sense of trustworthiness) of character was of little concern. Whereas one can argue that the concept generally made characterization 'modern' in our sense, both probability theory and narrative construction of plot and character in the early novel are closely related to conjecture and circumstantial evidence, as the description of psychological motives and situations gain importance (Korshin 1979: 64). For example, in particular the era's popular genre of criminal biography calls for circumstantial evidence, and the evaluation of guilt and responsibility. Indeed, a main function and appeal of the novel is the element of implied causality, for it "promised a greater understanding and mastery of life's apparently random events" (Kavanagh 1993: 117). The narrative aim to "tell the truth",[51] to provide orientation and lend causality to disasters (personal, natural, financial etc.), appear to spring from and reflect, alongside epistemological questions and problems of "faith", a deep "cultural crisis in attitudes circling around the relation between the external social world and the moral state of the individual" (McKeon 1987: 20).

In this context, it is interesting to consider that in his well-known study *Before Novels* John Paul Hunter gives a list of characteristic features of the novel, listing "Credibility and probability" among the features which make the genre "novel", yet he also claims that many of the early fictions noticeably chal-

---

[50] Bender sees shared traits between scientific experimentation, the deduction of speculative knowledge, and fiction because they are similarly concerned with "world making and sense making" (1998: 15).
[51] Particularly in a post-1660 context, Mark Knights (2005: 3) argues, considering the climate of religious and scientific debates, civil war, political suspicions etc., questions of how to detect lies and deceptions, and of how to judge (mis)representations and negotiate various conflicting truths claims assumed urgency in many areas.

lenge probabilities.⁵² The novel, Hunter writes, "in spite of its strong commitment to credibility and probability, is full of incidents that do not admit of a quick and easy rational explanation" (1990a: 32).⁵³ But the idea of plausibility is still central to the novel, and it moreover reflects a loyalty to "a modern 'scientific' conception of the world in which immutable physical laws operate" (1990a: 33). One the other hand, exceptional events, the fantastic, and 'in-credible' coincidences are by no means absent from the early novel, which suggests that it also takes on another important function, namely, forming a fictional counterbalance to the new paradigm of rationality and secularity: "It was as if the scientific explanation thrust upon early eighteenth-century readers threatened to make their world too predictable, and in their fiction they sought some evidence that it would not be so" (Hunter 1990a: 34). Similarly, Molesworth argues for seeing the early novel not just as expression of realism and secular worldview but as "seeking to heal the rift between the magical and the secular worldviews" (Molesworth 2010: 2).⁵⁴ As in the early novel many plots rely indeed heavily on coincidences, Hunter emphasizes that one has to notice the novel's engagement with "the unusual, the uncertain, and the unexplainable" and its function to seek to narratively "satisfy, in a context of scientific order, the itch for news and new things that are strange and surprising" (Hunter 1990a: 35).

This does not only show the origins of the genre but also links it to the modern concepts of risk and uncertainty, and to the attempts at prediction and achieving safety in the emerging risk society. The early novels are full of fears, of violence, loss, poverty, disease, full of wounds of war and love, social scandals and isolation. A recurring central fear is of the individual making the wrong choices. What aids the depiction of risk is the focus on the solitary individual and the array of weighing options and epistemological questions the novel engages in. Concerning narrative perspective, the first-person narrative appears especially suitable and relevant from a formal point of view, because it is a

---

52 This is one of the reasons why Hunter criticizes Watt's argument of the novel's realism as being "non-sensical" (cf. 1990a: 23f). Without agreeing with this criticism, Hunter's point is nonetheless relevant here.
53 One of the examples Hunter gives here is from Defoe's *Robinson Crusoe:* "What are the odds that in the middle of an island one solitary footprint will suddenly be visible, with no others anywhere nearby?" (Hunter 1990a: 32). This scene is discussed in chapter 2.1 as one of the first instances of risk-consciousness in the novel.
54 For this debate, which is a very wide and fundamental one, see Cynthia Wall Sundberg's *The Prose of Things* (2006), Jane Bennett's *The Enchantment of Modern Life* (2001), and Bruno Latour's *We Have Never Been Modern* (1991).

form which specifically allows for inner reflection and questioning. This aspect is particularly relevant for the reading of Defoe's fictions.[55]

The selection of primary texts in this chapter is, like any, subjective and carefully chosen to best fit the specific focus. While some of the most canonized 18th century novels and authors are included for this reason, the exclusion of works of Henry Fielding and Samuel Richardson and of novels like *Tom Jones*, *Joseph Andrews*, *Pamela* or *Clarissa* perhaps calls for a brief commentary. As pointed out in the introduction, the over-arching focus of this study is a broad diachronic one, which necessitates exemplary close readings rather than aiming for any sort of comprehensiveness. Many of the earlier novels by female authors such as Eliza Haywood's *Love in Excess: Or, the Fatal Inquiry* (1719/20) have been disregarded due to style or subject matter. Generally, the typical amatory plots are full of fears, sensations and surprises, but contain little 'reflection' or calculation by the characters and narrative constructions of risk-perception and management in the sense relevant here.[56] Sure enough, adventures and accidents are also found in many sensationalist fictions as well as in Fielding and Richardson's novels, as are debts, gambling, risky passions and the all-important question of who to trust. Yet, whereas we find many similar elements on the level of plot, style, and narrative techniques (e.g. coincidences, precarious situations, picaresque journeys, 'risky' encounters, or satire), and often a by no means lacking critical approach towards Enlightenment thought and the influence of science, a providential authority is still more firmly in place, giving a character like Tom Jones or Clarissa Harlowe a less secular and 'probabilistic' outlook on life than Robinson Crusoe, Roxana, or Tristram Shandy.

What sets apart Fielding's novels in particular is the providential design and structure of his fictions and the staging of the 'marvellous', which has been thoroughly analysed in criticism, and which is noticeably stronger and more palpable than in Defoe, Swift, or Sterne.[57] For instance, as Melvyn New writes about

---

55 See also Ermath (1981).
56 In their study of the early novel, Hammond and Ragan comment on the comparatively bad quality of "the love centered or 'amatory' fiction" (2006: 8) by writers like Aphra Behn, Delarivier Manley, Eliza Haywood, and Penelope Aubin. Social issues and the new ideology of calculation are certainly negotiated more prominently and with more innovation by novelists like Defoe. Hammond and Ragan argue that love and desire are the main topic in novels such as Haywood's *Love in Excess*, causing the reader to focus on questions of suspense and "what happens next? Who will seduce whom? What duels might ensue?", while "Defoe's text, by contrast, [...] had much to say about some of the most important aspects of contemporary cultural life" (2006: 27).
57 The literature on Fielding is vast; for critical studies offering a good analysis of Fielding's attitude towards science and religion and his belief in universal/particular providence see, for instance, Damrosch's *God's Plot and Man's Stories* (1985), Kalpakgian's *The Marvellous in Field-*

Tom Jones, Fielding may often undercut the classical structure of romance, yet "he never abandoned [...] [its] God-sustained world" (New 1976: 242).[58] Agreement exists that signs of providential design are persistent in Fielding's literary oeuvre, and that although it reveals an increasing consciousness of the cruelty of fate and of 'bad' fortune, the author held onto a belief in providence till the end of his life (Rawson 1972: 67). Fielding's writings display awareness of life's unpredictabilities and of harsh realities beyond human control, but they maintain a firm sense of structure and order, especially if seen in contrast to the much more 'chaotic' plots of Smollett or Sterne. Richard Rosengarten, in his nuanced study of the providential view of life in Fielding's fictions,[59] points out the centrality of the narrative perspective in this context. Typically, 18th-century fiction is told in retrospection, relating things that happened in the past and giving much room to elaborating on the "circumstantial chain" of events. Still, a first-person narration (as Defoe's) maintains a sense of future-orientation, because within the story the reader is made to retrace the narrator's process of decision-making, i.e. with the calculation and anticipation of events, as well as with their explanation in hindsight. Apart from not deconstructing providence to the same extent as some other contemporary fictions,[60] Fielding's novels, due to their length and complexity, and especially Fielding's narrative voice, would deserve a close reading in a different and more comparatively-oriented context to do justice to the notions of order, contingency and human agency inherent in them, but this clearly goes beyond the scope of the present study. This also applies to Richardson's fictions, which also lack any 'mathematical' dimension of probability, although one might argue, that no other novelist has immortalized a tragic heroine who is 'at risk' for pretty much the entire narrative better than Richardson his Clarissa Harlowe.[61] Also in *Sir Charles Grandison* we find reflections of financial risks and games of chance and, as Jessica Richard has shown, a marked rejection of gambling, or rather, an ethical, risk-

---

ing's *Novels* (1981), Rawson's *Henry Fielding and the Augustan Ideal under Stress* (1972), and Rosengarten's *Henry Fielding and the Narration of Providence* (2000).
58 Cf. Melvyn New's essay "The Grease of God" (1976).
59 It is important to stress that for Fielding and his contemporaries there was "unmistakable consensus [about] the idea that providence is no longer a matter of easy, or at least ready, attribution" (Rosengarten 2000: 4), yet, as Rosengarten argues, in Fielding's work the 'will' to belief is stronger.
60 See, e.g., Poovey's comparison of Richardson and Fielding in "Journeys from this World to the Next: The Providential Promise in Clarissa and Tom Jones" (1976).
61 Other novels with a distinctly providential world-view such as Sara Scott's *Millenium Hall* (1762) have been excluded for the same reason.

averse stance which values control over chance (Richard 2011: 34).[62] While one can observe a turn away from God's ordering hand in Richardson's novels in so far, that the focus is placed on individual psychological needs, the epistolary form also makes it harder to analyse the fictions comparatively from a formal perspective.

---

[62] However, the text shows a typical condemnation of gambling and a critique of a dominant conception of masculinity defined by thrill-seeking, gambling, or horse racing, which persists in the 19th-century novel. Richard's reading points to the interesting and crucial gendering of risk-behaviour and characters transgressions of gender expectations, often phrased in terms of risk that are central in my readings of Burney's *Camilla* and the Victorian novels.

2 Defoe and his Protagonists at Large in the Risk Society

2.1 Calculations of Survival and Fear: *Robinson Crusoe*

Making a claim about the rise of novel and the rise of modern (risk) society is bound to face the difficult task of having to choose a beginning. I certainly do not want to enter what has aptly been called the "wild goose chase" (Hammond and Ragan 2006: 9) about what should be considered as the first English novel,[1] nor the extensive debates about the beginning of modernity, which varies, of course, depending on whatever one takes the term to mean.[2] The present argument is that the first writer whose life and fictions demonstrate a preoccupation with and a, in many instances, masterly management of risk is Daniel Defoe.[3] His writings show both the characteristics of the novel genre and a strong concern with the new ideas and projects constituting 'modernity' as outlined in the previous chapters. The author captures, above all, the ambivalence and emerging plurality of world views and the 'fluid' moving between positions by constructing "a fictive world neither Christian nor secular, but in transition between the

---

[1] Patricia Meyer Spacks in *Novel Beginnings: Experiments in Eighteenth-Century English Fiction* (2006) argues that setting the beginning of the novel around 1700 is rather arbitrary, but still begins her study with Defoe's *Robinson Crusoe*; she also refers to Eliza Haywood's *Love in Excess*, published in the same year. Other lines of tradition start before Defoe in the second half of 17th century, or go back as far as the Puritan and rogue prose of the 1450s, as Patrick Parrinder's *Nation and Novel* (2006) does; Brean Hammond and Shawn Regan (2006) begin with William Congreve and Aphra Behn. For the general debate and evolutionary history of the genre, see also John Paul Hunters' *Before Novels* (1990a). In particular some feminist scholars make a case for Aphra Behn's *Oroonoko, or the History of the Royal Slave* (1688) as being the first English novel, rather than Defoe's *Robinson Crusoe*. For this argument see, e.g., the introduction to Sandra Macpherson's study *Harms Way* (2010), in which she refers to the increasing frequency with which *Oroonoko* is taken to be the first realist novel. Still, as Oliver Lindner observes, despite all debates and recent re-evaluations of the traditional canon and many necessary inclusions, especially of female writers, "Defoe is still widely perceived as the author whose works of fiction initiated the discourse of the novel in English literature" (2010: 9).
[2] Helpful, I think, is MacPherson's comment that even if "modernity is moved forward and backward along a scale of historical temporality, [...] the contours of modernity, its characteristic transcendence of status remain the same" (2010: 33).
[3] For introductions to Defoe's life and works see John Martin's *Beyond* Belief (2006), Maximilian E. Novak's magisterial study *Daniel Defoe* (2001) and John A. Richetti's *The Life of Daniel Defoe* (2005); Oliver Lindner's *Matters of Blood* (2010) contains an extensive bibliography and offers a survey of Defoe scholarship in the introduction.

two" (New 1976: 241; 240). Agreeing with the many critics who see this combination of conflicting visions as the characteristic tension shaping Defoe's writing, his plots and his characters strongly underline the element of human choice, the need for calculation of potential losses and gains, the use of 'rational', scientific methods for doing so, but also the need for consoling re-orientation if the calculation fails. Hence we find Defoe's characters' beliefs oscillating between economic self-sufficiency, opportunism and a longing for, or fear of, divine providential order.[4] Either way, they illustrate the fact that providence in 18th-century fiction was increasingly "psychologized", signalling a distance from God, who is mainly being called upon when the individual experiences a loss of control (see Faller 1993: 114). In Defoe's fictions one sees the author still consciously playing with the options offered by providential order; we find patterns of reward and punishment, lucky coincidences and second chances, but no consistent belief system.[5] With God's foresight becoming just one possibility among many, a typical mechanism in the early novel, and one that applies especially to Defoe's first-person narrators, is that "[w]ithout providence, the longing for order can be satisfied either with progress or with paranoia" (Braudy 1981: 622). Characters like Moll, Robinson Crusoe, and Roxana all show the relentless striving for profit teamed with paranoia as the two main forces that guide their behaviour and also give coherence to the narration of their lives. This is reflected in the paradoxical quality and structural design of Defoe's writings which Leopold Damrosch describes as the author taking on the role of "inventor of plot who pretends that his plot was planted by the Almighty" (Damrosch 1985: 5).[6] This also causes the many ironies in the narratives that illustrate the retaining of old providential frameworks, but as shattered hold-ups. All in all, Defoe certainly "restores the relationship between men and God to a proper disequilibrium" (Faller 1993: 122).

---

4 Cf. Ilse Vickers's *Defoe and the New Sciences* (1996). Showing Defoe as an ardent follower of Baconian science and the spirit of experimental empiricism, Vickers argues mainly that Defoe's writings testify to the fact that he saw no incompatibility between the new sciences and Christian faith.
5 For an analysis of Defoe's novels and the characters' complicated relationship with Providence, see Lincoln B. Faller's *Crime and Defoe* (1993). Faller specifically links the discussion of providence to the popular genre of criminal autobiography and the contemporary fascination with crime.
6 In *God's Plot, Man's Stories*, Leopold Damrosch sees the 18th-century novel generally preoccupied with negotiating tensions between secularism and Christianity (1985: 2).

With regard to risk, G. Starr's well-known analysis of Defoe's use of casuistry[7] is interesting because it highlights Defoe's favouring of a somewhat flexible moral outlook which circumvents the rigidity of any one system and utilizes, depending on the 'case', i.e. the circumstances, more than one tradition (Starr 1971: vii). At the same time, the detailed reflection of the particular situation, captured in the main narrative method of extensive circumstantial description, constructs risk as a category for weighing options and evaluating behaviour. Starr observes further that the 'plotting' by Defoe in his texts often consists of a series of episodes that present instances of individual problem-solving in the face of crisis, and are linked by the continual overall struggle and achievement of survival, without a necessarily coherent master-plan. The inherent fragmentation of the texts, the consideration of psychological factors and circumstances of the protagonists, which according to Starr reflect a casuistical conception of life, can also be viewed as distinctly 'modern.' Although the focus is here not on the ethical orientation of Defoe's narratives, casuistry shares with risk perception and management the dependence on experience and the inevitable link to choice and action, and responsibility.

Born in 1660, Defoe witnessed the time when probability theory was born as well as crucial disasters such as the Great London Plague (1665) and the Great London Fire (1666). Generally, London featured strongly as a risk-scape in the public imagination of the time and it also occurs as a setting in Defoe's fictions, for instance in *Moll Flanders* and *Journal of the Plague Year*, in the sense that Charlotte Sussman's stresses in her summary of the climate and status of the 18th-century metropolis:

> For the people of eighteenth-century England, and of the world beyond, London was an awe-inspiring, and sometimes terrifying, phenomenon. [...] Complicated new financial structures – stock markets, insurance companies, joint-stock companies – flourished there. [...] eighteenth-century London was also filthy and dangerous, crisscrossed by open sewers and traversed by the polluted Thames, afflicted by both disease and crime. [...] London as the Renaissance had known it disappeared in 1665 and 1666 in the wake of an epidemic of bubonic plague, closely followed by the Great Fire of London. The plague year of 1665 killed almost one in six Londoners, about 80,000 people. The subsequent fire, in September 1666, destroyed nearly four-fifths of the medieval city, razing more than 373 acres in the city itself and leaving 100,000 people homeless. (Sussman 2012: 63)

---

[7] Casuistry can be defined as a part of ethics which "rests on the axiom that 'circumstances alter cases' – the principle that every ethical problem must be approached on its own terms and decided on its own merits; rhetoric, on the principle that every occasion demands its own mode of expression" (Starr 1971: 7). See also James Chandler (1998).

Apart from memorable natural disasters or accidents like these, it is well known that during his career as a writer, journalist, and merchant Defoe experienced the dual nature of risk, the thrills of financial speculation as well as the reality of spectacular loss and bankruptcy.[8] He personally invested in many maritime trading projects, losing fortunes in "one absurd scam after another" (Skwire 2008: 22). Consequently, he was jailed for debt at least seven times, and died hiding from his creditors in 1731. Throughout his life he displayed a keen interest in many risk-related topics, such as credit, insurance, pensions, and actuarial science and he held a number of government jobs related to taxes and lotteries. In addition to many pamphlets warning of the dangers of credit and stock-jobbing,[9] Defoe's *An Essay Upon Projects* (1697) explicitly deals with all of these issues, as well as elaborating on the topic of maritime insurance and friendly societies.[10] Actuary Daniel Skwire explains that Defoe's discussions and ideas in the text indeed "reveal a surprisingly deep understanding of the principles of risk and insurance" (Skwire 2008: 24) from today's perspective. Despite the fact that Defoe was not a mathematician and it is only possible to speculate about his exact degree of knowledge about, for instance, probability theory or the calculation of life expectancy, Skwire praises Defoe's visionary ideas for pension schemes saying that his "ambitious project was not so different in concept from its modern counterparts" (2008: 26).

While many of his earlier essays and pamphlets deal with 'projects' such as assurance, liability, national debt, the condition of the poor, natural disasters, or the precarious situation of children and women, Defoe's first novel was writ-

---

[8] Damrosch comments on Defoe's "rocky career as capitalist and speculator" (1985: 189). The intertwining of speculation and gambling on one side, and the instinct for safety and insurance on the other, is very pronounced in Defoe's writings and can be seen in connection to his own risk biography. On this topic see also Bram Dijsktra's *Defoe and Economics* (1987), and Novak's *Economics and the Fiction of Daniel Defoe* (1976). In *Finance and Fictionality in the Early Eighteenth Century* (1996); Sandra Sherman (1996: 14–54) gives a detailed account of Defoe's his writings surrounding the South Sea Bubble, and his ambivalent attitude towards risk-taking and capitalism, focusing on Defoe's reflections in the *Review* 1710–1711. See also Novak (2001: 402ff) for details about Defoe's personal experience with debt and his ideas on trade. For Defoe's interest in colonialist overseas schemes as a source of new wealth see Lindner (2010).
[9] See, for instance, Defoe's *Essay on Public Credit* (1710) or the pamphlet *The Villainy of Stock-Jobbers* (1701).
[10] In the *Essay upon Projects* Defoe is furthermore concerned with education and the situation of widows and the provision of women in general. His ideas of pension schemes relate to his central project of seeking to eliminate poverty in England, while taking into account mortality rates; the text also reveals Defoe's interest in enterprise liability. Later Defoe's novel *Roxana* takes up the topic explicitly and includes many calculations of taxes, interest rates, or insurance schemes.

ten "during the great financial crisis which began with the failure of Walpole's Sinking Fund in 1717 and ended with the burst of the South Sea Bubble in August 1720" (Schaffer 1989: 14). Having had personal investments in the scheme, Defoe is usually considered as one of the early "prophets of the eventual downfall of the South Sea Company" (Novak 1976: 14), which he attacked in various pamphlets prior to the bursting of the bubble. A conservative at heart, Defoe liked to flirt with speculation, but remained firmly committed to the higher goal of national financial stability and economic security for the poor. The year that saw the publication of *Robinson Crusoe* also brought, in many ways, the first national experience of financial risk-taking. Gary Hentzi writes: "From the first 'money subscription' or sale of shares on 14 August until the collapse of South Sea Company stock at the end of August, England was absorbed in a financial enterprise that increasingly became both a source of feverish hopes and the focus of widespread suspicions" (Hentzi 1993b: 32). Written in the aftermath of the South Sea Bubble, all of Defoe's later novels represent the instability of their time of production and embody, to borrow Hentzi's words again, "some of the most pressing contradictions of their age" (1993b: 38), including the criticism and fascination of financial gambling, the apprehension of national debt and individual bankruptcy.

Sandra Sherman is one of the many critics who argue that Defoe's fictions are centrally about the cultural anxiety and the ambivalent engagement with credit.[11] While many of Defoe's protagonists are famously obsessed with capital and property, the author shows it as contingent and in the texts an individual's worth can disintegrate from one moment to next (see Sherman 1996: 7; 11). With property comes the risk of its loss and Defoe's fiction reflect a topical preoccupation with property which Wolfgang Schmidgen sees as a central shaping force in the public imagination in Britain in the 18th century (Schmidgen 2002a: 10). The texts also engage explicitly with shifts in social order and ideology which allow for entrepreneurial spirit and success, survival skills and accumulation of wealth and property as measures of social status, instead of 'born' associations such as rank, family, and connections. Regarding these aspects, Defoe's novels appear as psychological studies of risk-management, which deal with the human instinct of self-preservation, often in potentially life-threatening situations, e.g. dislocation, hunger, disease, and poverty, which are shown as integral parts of human experience. The various enemies and threats imag-

---

11 Though Defoe was central in shaping the contemporary discourse on credit through his numerous essays, pamphlets and novels, he was not the first writer to engage with these topics. Cf., for instance: Courtney Beth Beggs's dissertation *Risky Business: The Discourse of Credit and Early Modern Female Playwrights before Defoe* (2010).

ined by Defoe and his characters, whether they are visible (e.g. cannibals) or invisible (e.g. the plague), contribute to the complex fictionalization of psychological nightmares; yet it is clearly the economic struggle for survival which features most prominently. Maximilian Novak says: "All the heroes and heroines are motivated by a fear of poverty and by its accompanying trait, avarice. To the facts of poverty they react with courage and ingenuity, preferring to survive through illegal and sinful means rather than to perish through despair" (Novak 1976: 10; 92; 2001: 560). Novak also argues that Defoe transforms the traditional *picaro* into a realistic hero/heroine, for whom survival is an important problem, yet success is not always guaranteed (1976: 67), despite the often spectacular gains, lucky escapes and turns of fortune.

Before proceeding to a closer reading of four of Defoe's novels, it is noteworthy that "all of Defoe's fictions depend heavily on risk-seeking behavior, as their subtitles highlight" (Molesworth 2010: 38). The subtitles typically allude to the various 'adventures' and the serial interchanging of 'fortunes' and 'misfortunes' which make up the plots. The guiding questions, continuously contemplated by the protagonists are what will happen next, to themselves and to their possessions. In this sense, Defoe's protagonists exemplify the attempt to try to conjecture and quantify uncertainty, and appear as characteristics displays of the new consciousness brought on by the probabilistic theories of Bernoulli and others. Furthermore, they rely on speculation in order to survive, Robinson Crusoe, e.g., by predicting the weather and time to harvest his precious crop, Moll by playing the marriage game and her later career as a master thief, while Roxana does nothing but calculate the best way to secure her wealth and is later driven into paranoia by speculating about Susan's possible revelation of her 'true' identity; H.F., the narrator in *Journal of the Plague Year*, relies on statistical description of disease and tables of mortality to calculate his chances of survival in the city. At the centre of Defoe's works we find illustrations of many of the pervasive fears and risks of today's society: poverty, disease, financial speculation, marriage, and moral depravity. To sum up the relevance of Defoe's fictions in the context of shaping the early risk society:

> As a measure of anxieties that cut across the realms of religion and morality, psychology and economics, Defoe's novels speak to us in a voice that has only become more insistent over the intervening centuries. It is, finally, this aspect of his writing – its ability to anticipate something of the modern world's fundamental instability – that continues to claims our attention [...]. these novels reflect the beginnings of an uneasiness that is now a permanent feature of modern life. (Hentzi 1993b: 42)

To embark on a 'new' analysis of Defoe's *Robinson Crusoe* (1719) is, of course, a daunting undertaking, as is sorting through the vast existing and still growing body of criticism of the novel. Recent studies of Defoe's fictions, such as Oliver Lindner's (2010), offer a good summary of the state and history of criticism of the author, while classic magisterial studies of Defoe's life and works like Maximilian Novak's (1976; 2001) still have validity. The main, well-known divide in the criticism of Defoe's first novel exists between the scholarly branch which takes the novel mainly as spiritual autobiography, stressing the elements of Protestant ethics, providence, and conversion, and the other camp which emphasizes the strong economic orientation of the text and sees Crusoe as the first capitalist subject in English fiction.[12] Then there have been the, in my eyes convincing, attempts to unite these aspects.[13] Equally important are the more recent readings of the text from a postcolonial vantage point that focus on the text's imperialist rhetoric and the notions of race and otherness.[14] A reading concentrating on the construction of risk in the narrative usefully links the three approaches.

As a writer, Defoe engaged with questions of risk on many levels. First of all, *Robinson Crusoe*, like *Journal of the Plague Year*, testifies to the author's "fascination with the power of natural catastrophes" (Hentzi 1993a: 419). With storms and shipwrecks being central to the narrative, the plot can be summed up as follows: "*Robinson Crusoe*, after all, is the story of an unsuccessful merchant sailor who suffers losses at sea" (Skwire 2008: 26). As the introductory part of this chapter has shown, the beginnings of risk lie at sea and are connected to travel and trade, their imaginative appeal, their dangers and spectacular chances of loss and gain. So it does make sense to begin the close readings with a story of maritime adventures.[15] The glossary to the novel in the Penguin Classics edi-

---

12 A summary of this debate shall not be replicated here. For an accessible overview of the history of criticism of the novel see Paul Baines (2007). Regarding the many studies focusing on the novel in relation to economics and capitalism, it is interesting to keep in mind that it is often read in context with Adam Smith's *Wealth of Nations*, which was not published until sixty years later (see Lewis 2000: 42). Nonetheless, *Robinson Crusoe* and *Journal of the Plague Year* have to be considered as Enlightenment texts that "count everything" and "underscore the relationship between the reflex of calculation and the interests of an expanding commercial class" (Hentzi 1993: 422).
13 This includes most of the earlier major critics such as Novak, Richetti, Watt, or McKeon.
14 Numerous postcolonial readings have appeared in the last two decades: See Edward Said's influential reading in *Culture and Imperialism* (1994) and Peter Hulme's *Colonial Encounters* (1992: 175–222). See also Carey (2009), Ellis (1996), Dharwadker (1998), Flynn (2000), Nechtman (2010), Schmidgen (2002a), Turley (2004), and Lindner (2010).
15 Campe also mentions that the central plot incident refers directly to the beginnings of probability theory: "Survival chances in the wake of a shipwreck also cite both cases in which the theory of games of chance first hit upon statistical material: marine insurance and annuities" (2012: 182).

tion lists the following meaning for "all adventures" in the text: "great risk, all risk" (RC 283),[16] which is interesting to consider with regard to the novel's full title: "The Life and Strange Surprising Adventures of Robinson Crusoe of York, Mariner". Margaret Cohen identifies "the maritime picaresque" (2010: 60) as a new subgenre that becomes popular in the 1720s–1740s,[17] and subsumes *Robinson Crusoe* under this category of texts, which represent the era's height of the fascination with the "adventure of global seafaring" (2010: 62).[18] In her reading, Cohen explicitly places Defoe's work in a context of risk-taking, while critically engaging with the prominence of the economic readings of the novel:

> The ideological work of *Robinson Crusoe*, for critics who read it as a fable of *homo economicus*, is to vindicate the power of bourgeois ratio, exorcising the risk intrinsic to capitalist profit by banishing it to an early moment in capitalist exploitation. [...]. Risk is no longer a stage on the way to a more rational, moderate form of capitalist behavior modeled by the reformed sinner. Rather, high-risk activities are endemic to the capitalist pursuit of profit, and the problem becomes how to undertake them with the best chance of success. [...] How to succeed in high-risk speculation was a problem that preoccupied Defoe from the first work of his career as a writer [...] published just one year before the South Sea Bubble of 1720. (2010: 63)

In the novel, the young Crusoe receives an education as a sailor and a merchant and learns how to profit from high-risk speculation in overseas trade. Thus, he undergoes a transformation from "a sinning prodigal into a hardworking, calculating entrepreneur" (Cohen 2010: 61). Although he develops attachments to his possessions and, with growing age and wealth, starts to strive for security and stability, like Swift's Gulliver, Crusoe struggles to give up travelling and settle down permanently. As the course of the plot and in particular the ending shows,

---

16 This is true for the Penguin and Arcturus editions of *Robinson Crusoe*. The glossary of the Oxford edition does not include an entry for *adventure*. The term *risk* itself occurs twice in the original text; *adventure* altogether 53 times; semantically related terms like *danger, hazard, apprehension, misfortune* etc. are frequent, as the selected excerpts from the narrative show.
17 Cf. Defoe's essay *The Storm: Or, a Collection of the most Remarkable Casualties and Disasters which happened'd in the Late Dreadful Tempest both by Sea and Land* (1704). The fascination with the sea and the forces of nature, which are often used metaphorically in relation to business and speculation, has been mentioned in chapter 1.1. By the way, Cohen rightly draws attention to the fact that the metaphorical links between maritime imagery and capitalist risk persist in literature and popular culture until today (2010: 66).
18 *Robinson Crusoe*, Cohen argues, triggered a wave of maritime adventure fiction in the 1720–1740s on both sides of the channel (2010: 88). Furthermore, she points out that: "In mariners' accounts of the early modern era, 'strange' and 'surprising' are synonyms for remarkable dangers" (2010: 67). The word used today to describe Crusoe's "strange" adventures and the many "remarkable occurrences" would probably be "extreme".

after every rescue and return home, he ventures out into the world again, which signifies his persisting fascination with risk. With reference to the economic readings of the narrative, Crusoe's 'capitalist' preoccupation with calculating profits, seeking to prevent losses, mastering dangers, but constantly seeking 'improvement' of his situation, all appear as attempts of risk-management. In this regard, Crusoe's character unites the two streaks of being the capitalist owner of his resources with the combinatorial gambling of the entrepreneur "in creative and risk-taking configurations" (Lewis 2000: 35). Peter Hulme draws attention to an interesting aspect in this context.[19] He explains that the term 'adventure(r)' needs careful historical contextualization, because it carries ideological weight and has undergone significant semantic changes. In existence ca. since the 12th century, it originally meant investor, or "merchant adventurer", basically referring to anyone involved in overseas trade. At Defoe's time, that changed to "adventure capitalist", linking the world of financial speculation and Atlantic trade and sea-faring, with risk being the common element. Therefore, Defoe "could endow Robinson Crusoe with something of the heroism of the adventurer who risked life and limb as well as capital, therefore, adventitiously, providing a link between the Elizabethan era and the true age of adventure in the second half of the nineteenth century" (Hulme 1992: 184).

Apart from adventure and economic risk, the novel can also be described as "the strange story of the industrious man on the island who spends his days listing his provisions and walling himself deeper into his isolation against a danger that fails to materialize for twenty years" (Davis 1983: 154). This draws attention to the element of paranoia. Among the critics who implicitly refer to the prominence of fear in *Robinson Crusoe* is Helen Moglen, who says that the text, "which is ordinarily read as formal realism's founding fiction, reveals in its fantastic subtext an obsessive, claustral, appropriative, and hunted subjectivity" (Moglen 2001: 11). The narrative, in fact, gives a strikingly complex insight into the psychology of human fear and risk perception, which is one of the aspects that make this text the first modern novel. Crusoe's calculations, even if not convincing at all from a mathematical point of view, still reveal a lot of 'truths' when read against contemporary psychological studies of risk and human behaviour.

---

19 Hulme's essay is one of the earlier post-colonial attempts to "return the text to the Caribbean" (1992: 182) and furthermore relates the novel to another financial speculation disaster prior to the South Sea Bubble fiasco, namely the failure of the Darien project in 1699, an attempt to build a Scottish colony in Central America. See Hulme's argument also for the links between the rise of adventure stories set outside of Europe and the rise of overseas colonial investments (1992: 183).

Several recent studies have approached the novel from angles which highlight elements and concepts such as maritime speculation (Cohen 2010), accident (Hamilton 2007), and probability theory (Campe 2012), which all point towards the prominence of risk.[20] Engaging with these critical readings, the analysis focuses especially on the novel's beginning, the famous 'discovery of the footprint'-scene, and Crusoe's calculations throughout the plot in order to show his psychological as well a physical management of risk and how it surfaces as a narrative construct. Defoe's protagonist, who is described in the beginning as a man with a "competent Knowledge of the Mathematicks" (RC 17), is above all engaged in calculating the odds of this survival on the island and approaches and narrates all dangers, hopes and fears – be it loosing provisions or gaining stock, the weather, harvesting, or encountering cannibals – using a pervasive rhetoric of risk, even if the awareness of being "safe" or in "danger" often comes in hindsight and his calculations freely combine rational (i.e. pseudo-mathematical) and irrational (e.g. bibliomancy) methods.

A first-person confessional narrative, Robinson Crusoe, born in York as the third son of a middle-class merchant, begins the account of his life and adventures by revealing his risk-loving nature. He is driven by the desire to go to sea, much against the will and warnings of his father, who is aware of the dangers of a sea-faring life and advocates instead the security and stability of the "middle station" (RC 12). This refers to the balanced, risk-free state of his own class and home, with not too much to lose or gain, in other words, to "the just standard of true felicity, when he prayed to have neither poverty or riches" (RC 12). Robinson's father explicitly describes this state as the safest, because "the calamities of life were shared among the upper and lower part of mankind; [...] the middle station had the fewest disasters" (RC 12). Furthermore, his father sees adventure-seeking as inappropriate and condemns it on moral grounds; this attitude is characteristic of middle-class-consciousness according to which any sort of gambling or thrill-seeking was "associated with loss of self-control and detachment from the laws of cause and effect and was disparaged as an indulgence befitting a reprehensible aristocracy" (Hamilton 2007: 138). The middle station, however, has no attraction for young Crusoe. At some level, this rebellion surely appears as a father-son conflict (cf. Frick 1988: 120), because Crusoe junior rejects the law career his father has intended for him. Ignoring all warnings, or rather, "without any consideration of circumstances or consequences" (RC 15), he voyages out.

---

20 See Hamilton's reading of *Robinson Crusoe* (2007: 129–160); see also the chapter in Campe (2012: 172–194), and Cohen (2010: 59–98). Cohen's study is one of few recent studies that actually list 'risk' on the index. An important earlier essay is Paul K. Alkon's "The Odds Against Friday: Defoe, Bayes, and Inverse Probability" (1979).

Thus the misfortunes begin. He encounters his first storm at sea, which leaves him, retrospectively looking at his 18-year-old self, "dreadfully frightened" (RC 18). Added to this is the ruthless behavior of his shipmates: "I was in tenfold more horror of mind [...] the terror of the storm, put me into such a condition, that I can by no words describe it. But the worst was not come yet" (RC 19). The narrative conveys a strong sense of danger, although, as is typical for Defoe's narrators, Crusoe speaks from a position of safety, telling tales of past risks, successfully managed, and dangerous situations he has escaped. He gets through his first shipwreck, after which he contemplates in his characteristic manner the possible alternative choices and muses: "Had I now had the sense to have gone back to have gone home" (RC 21). As he voluntarily makes the decision to travel onwards, this statement reveals already a central tension within the narrative. Crusoe's account continuously wavers between references to divine providence or human agency as guiding his actions. In parts, the novel reads almost like an ironic portrayal of a strong human will hiding behind religious exculpations of responsibility. This becomes clear, for instance, in the ambivalence of the narrator's presentation of the choice of "going home" as something far beyond his power:

> 'But my ill fate pushed me on now with an obstinacy that nothing could resist; and though I had several times loud calls from my reason and my more composed judgment to go home; yet I had no power to do it. I know not what to call this, nor will I urge, that it is a secret over-ruling decree that hurries us on to be the instruments of our own destruction, even though it be before us, and that we rush upon it with our eyes open.' (RC 21)

The passage presents Crusoe's state, a triumph of passion and risk-seeking over reason, as conscious, yet curiously passive. Particularly in the first part of the narrative, Defoe portrays him as a victim of his desire for adventure, as he is clearly no victim of circumstances or driven to his journey out of necessity. Frequently Crusoe receives warnings by older men to "not tempt Providence" (RC 22), yet he laments: "[...] it was always my fate to choose for the worst" (RC 23). This again highlights the interesting mix of belief in predetermination and his own decision-making capacities. Tempted by the chance to make money and see the world, he ventures out to sea again. The narrative relates a number of successful adventures and financial gains, showing Crusoe's development into a shrewd sailor and merchant. After surviving pirate attacks and two years of captivity in Morocco, Crusoe settles on a sugar plantation in Brazil. After a while, all dangers and hardships are forgotten and he builds a comfortable, secure life for himself, yet the minute he realizes that, he comments: "I might as well have stayed at home" (RC 39), still apparently valuing thrill over stability. He is tempted by an opportunity presented by the captain to secure this left-behind stock in England and send it via Portugal to add to his fortune in Brazil. The captain's speech illustrates the calculation of the risks of the enterprise and shows the attempt to split the danger by a process of 'empirical' testing, as he says to Crusoe that

> 'since human affairs are all subject to change and disasters, I would have you give orders but for one hundred pound sterling, which you say is half your stock, and let the hazard be run for the first; so that if it comes safe, you may order the rest the same way; and if it miscarry, you may have the other half to have recourse to for your supply.' (RC 40)

After four years of living in safety, Crusoe decides to leave the Brazil planation. In contrast to his earlier voyages, he now has significantly more to lose and the concern for his properties causes his need for risk-management: "In short, I took all possible precaution to preserve my effects, and keep up my plantation;" (RC 43), before he embarks on another sea voyage, "attended with all its common hazards" (RC 44). This journey ends, of course, with another storm and shipwreck.

With the contemplation of risk running through the narrative, besides the constant mental battling of chances, fears and hopes, this episode highlights another important trigger of feelings of danger, the human distress in the face of the unknown. When Crusoe and the other sailors approach the shore in a small boat, he captures their shared feelings thus:

> 'What the shore was, whether rock or sand, whether steep or shoal, we knew not; the only hope that could rationally give us the least shadow of expectation, was, if we might happen into some bay or gulf, or the mouth of some river, where by great chance we might have run our boat in, or got under the lee of the land, and perhaps made smooth water. But there was nothing of this appeared; but as we made nearer and nearer the shore, the land looked more frightful than the sea.' (RC 46–47)

Crusoe finally ends up on the island alone, at this moment feeling "free from danger" and having made it "safe on shore" (RC 48). But the initial joy soon gives way to an overwhelming feeling of being at risk, when he realizes that he is utterly defenseless:

> 'I had a dreadful deliverance; for I was wet, had no clothes to shift me, nor anything either to eat or drink to comfort me; neither did I see any prospect before me but that of perishing with hunger or being devoured by wild beasts; and that which was particularly afflicting to me was, that I had no weapon, either to hunt and kill any creature for my sustenance, or to defend myself against any other creature that might desire to kill me for theirs.' (RC 50)

To remedy the situation, he builds a raft and ventures to the shipwreck to secure valuable provisions, yet this time he is driven to the risky act by necessity rather than thrill-seeking, because the "hope of furnishing myself with necessaries, encouraged me to go beyond what I should have been able to have done upon another occasion" (RC 52). The narrative contains many examples for this behavioural motivation. Crusoe's exploration of the island is driven by the main goal of finding a safe place:

> 'My next work was to view the country, and seek a proper place for my habitation, and where to stow my goods *to secure them from whatever might happen.* Where I was, I yet knew not; whether on the continent or on an island; whether inhabited or not inhabited; *whether in danger of wild beasts or not.*' (RC 55; my emphasis).

The quote underlines Crusoe's awareness of his situation and his means of managing the risks, e.g. here using weapons against wild animals. But it also shows his lack of orientation and knowledge about the environment, which adds to the feeling of being at risk. His fears eventually give way to a feeling of safety, which is caused by a sense of 'knowing the place.' Crusoe recounts how, initially, he was scared of everything: "I was afraid to lie down on the ground, not knowing but some wild beast might devour me, though, as I afterwards found, there was really no need for those fears" (RC 56), in other words, there were not half the risks he imagined. Throughout the novel Crusoe's fears change according to situations and his priorities; the minute he has managed one, another one crops up. Hamilton comments on this aspect saying that Crusoe, characteristic for "anyone engaged in a survival struggle, [...] becomes preoccupied by necessities" (Hamilton 2007: 139). Part of the psychological depth of the narrative is showing the constant ranking of risks and adjustment of their perception. For example, the minute he has achieved getting as much as possible out of the ship and has conquered the fear of losing irreplaceable valuables, such as arms and ammunition, and he says: "My thoughts were now wholly employed about securing myself against either savages, if any should appear, or wild beasts, if any were on the island" (RC 60). Later in the novel, Crusoe's increasing paranoia and the fear of another human presence on the island eclipses again the 'household' fears of securing his supplies:

> 'I confess that these anxieties, these constant dangers I lived in, and the concern that was now upon me, put an end to all invention, [...] I had the care of my safety more now upon my hands than that of my food. I cared not to drive a nail, or chop a stick of wood now, for fear the noise I might make should be heard: much less would I fire a gun for the same reason: and above all I was intolerably uneasy at making any fire, lest the smoke, which is visible at a great distance in the day, should betray me.' (RC 167)

In Crusoe's long descriptions of building his fortress, most interesting is the emphasis he places on it constituting a risk-free zone.[21] Although in hindsight he considers some of his fear and danger-management as unnecessary, he is engrossed in his own risk narrative, "and so I was completely fenced in and fortified, as I thought, from all the world, and consequently slept secure in the night, which otherwise I could not have done; though, as it appeared afterwards, there was no need of all this caution from the enemies that I apprehended danger from" (RC 61). While he is lying secure, surrounded by his provisions, including the precious supply of gun powder, a thunder storm sets off another contemplation of risk: "Oh, my powder! My very heart sank within me when I thought that, at one blast, all my powder might be destroyed; on which, not my defence only, but the providing my food, as I thought, entirely depended" (RC 62). In this manner, the narrative runs on, relating a string of experiences of imagined or real dangers, finding means of protection, moments of feeling safe before the perception of the next danger or possible loss.

As several critics have noted, Crusoe makes frequent use of 'statistical' speculations about the odds of events and his own luck or misfortune. For example, after he manages to secure the supplies from the ship, he reflects, "what would have been my case if it had not happened, *Which was an hundred thousand to one*, that the ship floated from the place where she first struck and was driven so near the shore that I had time to get all these things out of her" (RC 65; my emphasis). Like H.F.'s narration about mortality rates and the spread of disease in *Journal of the Plague Year*, Crusoe's account shows a fascination with the new science, yet probability theory still has little practical value within the narrative and no 'actual' probabilities are given. Rather, they appear somewhat arbitrary or intuitively based on a kind of 'implied probability', which, as Paul Alkon points out, was characteristic of people's experience at the time. The awareness of mathematical probability was undeniable, yet despite a growing technical sense of how odds can be calculated, people were also aware that "life is not like a card-game, a lottery, or even two stacked decks" (Alkon 1979: 52).[22] Therefore, Alkon justly notices that Defoe's use of terms like "risk" or "expectation"

---

21 Later, in Crusoe's 23rd year of residence on the island, a cave far in the woods becomes his new safety-ground and hiding place from the savages.
22 Alkon alludes here to the fact that Abraham Moivre's influential *Doctrine of Chances* had been published the year before Defoe's *Robinson Crusoe*. He writes further: "At the point where mathematical theories of probability begin to assume their distinctly modern character of scientific rigor, they also diverge from ready application to the ordinary events of life. Insofar as readers become more aware of mathematical concepts, their elusiveness also becomes more apparent" (1979: 52).

throughout the novel is slightly inconsistent, creative, and does not conform to a strictly scientific application. The reader never learns exactly – in the sense of receiving any 'plausible' data – how Crusoe works out the odds "that it is ten thousand to one against the footprint being discovered, more than a thousand to one against survival on the mainland, and a hundred thousand to one against the wreck floating close enough for salvage" (1979: 40). This suggests that the calculations serve another purpose. Defoe's narrative appears as a literary illustration of the imaginative aspects of probabilistic thinking and, although Alkon does not mention this aspect, it highlights the psychological function of risk calculation as means of orientation and survival. Campe implies this element, when he says that Crusoe's calculation presents "a reflection of the hero in a story narrated by himself, but it is no maxim for acting" (Campe 2012: 177).[23] The frequent temporal division between observation, reflection and action, appears to be for Crusoe a deliberate means to resist falling into the paralyzing passivity of despair because if he were to make a truly 'realistic' calculation in his situation, one can argue, he could reasonably only come with a "frightening balance" (2012: 178).[24] One can also see Defoe's peppering of Crusoe's account of his life on the island with somewhat spectacular calculations of chances as a narrative device to create suspense.

Throughout the novel, all deliberations aid to create a sense of exception for Crusoe and are only measured against a vague idea of the 'normal', expected course of events. The focus is very much on the exemplary, single individual

---

23 The main, interesting point made by Campe is that risk calculation, in a sense of applying 'actual' mathematical probability, only occurs in the third part of *Robinson Crusoe*, where the calculation also precedes and determines the action. He argues for a development in the sense of seeing Crusoe growing "able to follow the reflective view of probability and calculation in and for his own actions" (2012: 185), but only reaching this state in the final chapters. In his analysis, Campe focuses on three dangers-rescue scenarios in the novel, which present clear instances of calculations of probabilities. First, Crusoe getting all his supplies undamaged from the shipwreck; second, his escape from the savages; third, after leaving the island, surviving the confrontation with the wolves in the French mountains (2012: 187–188). This episode is often neglected in criticism and Campe usefully draws attention to it. Yet one can wonder if it presents really an impartial, 'rational' description of the situation, as Crusoe compares the danger encountered here dramatically to all his previous experiences: "For my part, I was never so sensible of danger in my life; for, seeing above three hundred devils come roaring and open-mouthed to devour us, and having nothing to shelter us or retreat to, I gave myself over for lost; and, as it was, I believe I shall never care to cross those mountains again: I think I would much rather go a thousand leagues by sea, though I was sure to meet with a storm once a-week" (RC 277).
24 Considering Crusoe's general mind-set, it is significant that at the beginning of his journal he refers to "this dismal, unfortunate island, which I called 'The Island of Despair' (RC 73).

fighting the odds. Apart from the reflection on the (im)probability of events *after* they have occurred, Crusoe's calculations include projections into the future, concerned with both short-term and long-term risks. He starts keeping a calendar, makes pro/con lists, keeps meticulous accounts in his diary, which mainly function as tools of risk-management, supporting attempt to objectify fears by collecting data and being able to compare individual situations: "I drew up the state of my affairs in writing, […] as to deliver my thoughts from daily poring over them, and afflicting my mind; […], that I might have something to distinguish my case from worse; and I stated very impartially, like debtor and creditor, the comforts I enjoyed against the miseries I suffered" (RC 68). With regard to the role and evolution of book-keeping Mary Poovey explains that since the mid-17th century: "British efforts to formulate new 'sciences' of wealth and society have been pervaded by the metaphor of bookkeeping", which "constituted one of the earliest systems to privilege both things in themselves […] and a formal system of writing numbers that transformed representations of these things into usable facts" (Poovey 1998: 29). The psychological function of Crusoe's bookkeeping and the collection of circumstantial evidence shows that the dimension of risk management is central to his presentation as the first *homo economicus*.

The description of Crusoe's spiritual awakening and his (re)turn to a belief in divine providence contains a central insight into the human psyche: people tend to be more pious and turn to prayer in situations of crisis and despair, i.e. when things are perceived to be beyond their own control or when confronted with the violent forces of nature. The earthquake, which makes Crusoe shake with the "fear of being swallowed up alive" (RC 83) and costs him his sleep, is an example of this; afterwards he readily admits that "though nothing could be more terrible in its nature, or more immediately directing to the invisible Power which alone directs such things, yet no sooner was the first fright over, but the impression it had made, went off also" (RC 89). Later he falls ill with fever and is plagued by terrible nightmares, which trigger reflections of the horrors of divine punishment. While praying, he also evaluates his turning to God as a helpless voicing of anxieties: "I cannot say they were either a prayer attended with desires or with hopes: it was rather the voice of mere fright and distress. My thoughts were confused, the convictions great upon my mind, and the horror of dying in such a miserable condition raised vapours into my head with the mere apprehensions" (RC 90). In the following famous scene, the still delirious Crusoe finds a Bible in a cupboard, opens it at random, and begins to read it, which he describes as stumbling across "a cure, both for soul and body" (RC 92). In his own causal construction of events, this is presented as the beginning of his (re)turn to belief and spiritual guidance, giving him a new order and relieving him from fear and the experience of hopelessness and contingency.

Amongst other critics, Ross Hamilton (2007: 143) reads Crusoe's conversion as not convincing, and argues that his outlook remains a secular one at heart and that his belief in some sort of providential design tends to waver once he is out of danger and no longer needs to fight despair. Walter Frick (1988) takes a similar view and emphasizes that the narrative oscillates between an unresolved dichotomy of contingency and providence, individualism and conformity to norms.[25] He also states that Robinson's religious insights are always only temporary, and that his so-called conversion is, in fact, mainly a secular one (Frick 1988: 110; 138). Considering in particular Crusoe's increasing concern with safety and protecting his possessions and securing economic growth, he seems to convert indeed to the commercial, middle-class ways of his father, accepting the benefits of order, and of caring for his stock and provisions. He clearly adopts a Protestant ethics of work and rationality, while his logic is based entirely on avoiding coincidences as much as possible and trying to find security in life, which many critics see as him ultimately striving towards a capitalist bourgeois existence. Another point is interesting to consider in this context. Both Hamilton and Campe have referred to Crusoe's conversion in connection to Pascal's famous wager about betting on the improbability of God's existence. Hamilton explains: "Crusoe takes his presence on the island to be a statistical improbability [...] and calculates the odds of his survival. This detail emphasises the fact that the structure of this tale, which ostensibly transforms an atheist into a believer in God's providence, enacts Pascal's argument that in uncertain circumstances, religious belief is worth the wager" (2007: 137). Meanwhile Campe says that the novel illustrates Pascal's wager in the sense that Crusoe comes to realize that losing the faith in God is a high price to pay and constitutes the most significant loss one can risk in the gamble for certainty and knowledge. In the novel, Crusoe utters what reads indeed like a clear variation of Pascal's apologetic wager: "if I had all the world, and should lose the favour and blessing of God, there would be no comparison to the loss" (RC 111).

Crusoe continues to empirically assess nature and his surroundings with regard to risks and in the process uses his experiences in the years on the island as barometers for measuring dangers comparatively. For instance, he judges the different seasonal rains and their potentially hazardous impact onto his health,

---

[25] As Fricke's study is written in German, it has not really been received in Anglo-American criticism. However, it is an interesting comparative study, which seeks to investigate the mutual dependencies between the erosion of a traditional, theological-metaphysical grounded worldview as a result of secularization tendencies and the structural and semantic changes in the development of the genre of the novel.

noticing how "the rain which came in the dry season was almost always accompanied with such storms, so I found that rain was much more dangerous than the rain which fell in September and October" (RC 97). He also observes the weather closely because unexpected climatic change poses as a threat to his calculation of harvests. Following Weber's theory of the 'disenchantment' of the world as a central marker of modernity,[26] Gilbert Germain emphasizes that "humankind is driven by a transhistorical imperative to extend its power over nature in order to better secure its chances for survival. The species instinct for self-preservation, [...] manifests itself in the desire to control those variable and contingent natural processes that pose a threat to human safety" (Germain 193: 29). While the impulse for survival is surely as old as the origin of the species, the means and power to achieve this control and to guarantee survival have shifted, with science occupying the dominant place rather than magic or other practices. Defoe's Crusoe is the first fictional character to embody this imperative and to show the management of various risks and the struggle for safety and survival as a human preoccupation. In his island microcosm he presents another important idea and activity which is developing in 18th-century thought, the belief in man's role as the modifier of nature. This, of course, also has implications for the conception of risk based on man's relationship with nature and the perceived amount of control. As Clarence Glacken (1996: 664–706) has demonstrated, the debate about man's place in nature is deeply tied to questions of belief, determinism, and world order. Seeking to take control over nature, man aimed at increasing his own numbers and populating the globe, furthermore, he aimed at multiplying domesticated plants and animals. Robinson Crusoe is the first man in fiction to strive to change nature. Constantly battling against nature, and demonstrating how man takes possession of it by cultivation, Crusoe is successful in his endeavour.

In the process of measuring his needs for food against his growing stock of corn, barley, and rice, he concludes that he has more than is necessary to sustain mere survival in the present. Yet his orientation is a long-term one. Based on past experiences and in order to feel secure, he takes precautions against possible risks such as bad harvests or losing supplies in a storm and "resolved for the future to have two or three years' corn beforehand; so that, *whatever might come*, I might not perish for want of bread" (RC 150; my emphasis). His reflections constantly cluster around judging his circumstances as being either fortunate or bad

---

26 Max Weber refers explicitly to the "Entzauberung der Welt" ("disenchantment of the world") in his essay "Science as Vocation" ([1922] 1991). See also Jane Bennett's *The Enchantment of Modern Life* (2001).

and hopeless, always depending on the situation and on the perceived presence or absence of dangers. Repeatedly he expresses the opinion that his condition is blessed and cursed at the same time and even concludes at one point that, he, strangely enough, has ended up in an almost risk-free place:

> 'I could hardly have named a place in the uninhabitable part of the world where I could have been cast more to my advantage; a place where, as I had no society, which was my affliction on one hand, so I found no ravenous beasts, no furious wolves or tigers, to threaten my life; no venomous creatures, or poisons, which I might feed on to my hurt; no savages to murder and devour me [...].' (RC 128)

All the while still hoping for an escape from the island, it becomes obvious that the more secure and competent, i.e. knowledgeable, in the managing of risks he grows, the more the idea of leaving the island and being unable to return to it is conceived as a threat and potential loss, rather than posing a risk he is willing to take in order to 'gain' the return to mainland civilization. After many years of living quite comfortably on the island, Crusoe ventures out onto the sea in order to surround it by boat. Seeing the island from a distance, and nearly being carried away by the strong currents, he is overcome by the following sensation: "It is scarcely possible to imagine the consternation I was now in, being driven from my beloved island (for so it appeared to me now to be) into the wide ocean, almost two leagues, and in the utmost despair of ever recovering it again" (RC 134). Although he safely reaches the shore again, the experience of the danger haunts him for a long time. Despite his strong desire to get his boat to the other side of the island, he carefully weighs his options and decides on a risk-averse strategy, in other words, he does not undertake the journey again.

> 'As to the east side of the island, which I had gone round, I knew well enough there was no venturing that way; my very heart would shrink, and my very blood run chill, but to think of it; and as to the other side of the island, I did not know how it might be there; but supposing the current ran with the same force against the shore at the east as it passed by it on the other, I *might run the same risk* of being driven down the stream, and carried by the island, as I had been before of being carried away from it: so with these thoughts, I contented myself to be without any boat, [...].' (RC 137; my emphasis)

This reflection is proto-typical for Crusoe's perception of and dealing with risk. Even though he has settled in this instance on avoiding risk, he considers various means of potentially minimizing the danger of failure and conquering nature after all. One solution, Crusoe deduces rationally, would be gathering more knowledge about the situation, i.e. closely observing the sea and its currents for a prolonged period of time. Nonetheless, his emotions interfere with his plans and he abandons it in favour of an altogether less risky one:

> '[...] *I had such terror upon my spirits at the remembrance of the danger I had been in, that I could not think of it again with any patience, but, on the contrary, I took up another resolution, which was more safe, though more laborious* – and this was, that I would build, or rather make, me another periagua or canoe, and so have one for one side of the island, and one for the other.' (RC 145, my emphasis)

Throughout the novel, Defoe's protagonist shows both risk-taking and risk-averse tendencies. On the island, he generally tries to avoid any circumstances that could produce feelings of unfamiliarity, confusion and uncertainty, usually at least for as long as the imprint of such a situation is still fresh in his memory. Yet Crusoe soon encounters precisely such an event which puts him "out of his knowledge" (see RC 147). The climactic scene of Crusoe's discovery of the singular footprint on the beach is a striking illustration of one the narrative's central structural devices, and shows how any new event or information challenges him rationally and emotionally, causing fear and unsettlement, speculation, and triggering action and a readjustment of behaviour. This well-known moment, presenting a pivotal point with regard to risk perception, is worth quoting at length:

> 'It happened one day, about noon, going towards my boat, I was exceedingly surprised with the print of a man's naked foot on the shore, which was very plain to be seen on the sand. [...]. I listened, I looked round me, but I could hear nothing, nor see anything; I went up to a rising ground to look farther; I went up the shore and down the shore, but it was all one; I could see no other impression but that one. I went to it again to see if there were any more, and to observe if it might not be my fancy; but there was no room for that, for there was exactly the print of a foot – toes, heel, and every part of a foot. How it came thither I knew not, nor could I in the least imagine; but after innumerable fluttering thoughts, like a man perfectly confused and out of myself, I came home to my fortification, not feeling, as we say, the ground I went on, but terrified to the last degree, looking behind me at every two or three steps, mistaking every bush and tree, and fancying every stump at a distance to be a man. Nor is it possible to describe how many various shapes my affrighted imagination represented things to me in, how many wild ideas were found every moment in my fancy [...].' (RC 147–148)

At this moment Crusoe's world order is disturbed; his knowledge and rational faculties prove insufficient, all attempts at gathering visual evidence fail him. Instead, his imagination and feelings of terror take over. The episode brings a change in the narrative intensity and constitutes a major "turning point" in Crusoe's life (see Schmidgen 2002a: 35; Alkon 1979: 30). Suddenly new possibilities lie before him and trigger feverish speculations, while at the same time all measures of explanation and applying probabilities fall short. The footprint poses threats on different levels and confronts him with practical as well as philosophical problems, which becomes obvious when looking closely at the rhetoric used by Crusoe and the string of epistemological questions: "The footprint does just this: it reveals the fragile basis of Crusoe's 'Knowledge'" (Schaffer 1989: 28; see Cohen 2010: 78). Despite his fear, the irony does not escape him that after years of isolation and want for signs of human society, "I should now tremble at the very apprehensions of seeing a man, and was ready to sink into the ground at but the shadow or silent appearance of a man having set his foot in the island" (RC 151). The theme of solitude as safety, which is endangered and disrupted by others occurs frequently in Defoe's fictions, e.g. the threat of contagion running through *Journal of the Plague Year*, or Roxana's paranoia of discovery. At the same time, Crusoe has nobody to consult and struggles in his isolation to control his fearful imagination:

> 'In the middle of these cogitations, apprehensions, and reflections, it came into my thought one day, that all this might be a mere chimera of my own; and that this foot might be the print of my own foot, when I came on shore from my boat. This cheered me up a little too, and I began to persuade myself it was all a delusion, [...].' (RC 152)

As his elaborate reflections demonstrate, his sense of safety is shaken and risk has, irrevocably, entered his perception of the environment, although the only alteration is a single footprint. Ultimately, "the entire landscape is transformed from a state of benign, if empty, familiarity into a kind of sinister no-man's land, teeming with unseen threats" (Hentzi 1993a: 423). Despite all attempts to rationalize his fears, he now notices "with what fear I went forward, how often I looked behind me, how I was ready, every now and then, to lay down my basket, and run for my life" (RC 152). His reaction illustrates the rational and irrational components of risk-perception and shows it as a concept integral to his view of his world. Shortly after this episode comes the clearest formulation of the discrepancy between the objective and subjective sides of risk. For Crusoe the feeling of being 'at risk' is harder to bear than exposal to actual danger: "Oh, what ridiculous resolution men take when possessed with fear! [...] fear of danger is often a thousand times more terrifying than danger itself when apparent to the eyes; and we find the burden of anxiety greater, by much, than the evil which we are anxious about" (RC 153). Like many of Defoe's later first-person narrators, Crusoe here offers a complex psychological insight into the operations of human fear.

The incident with the footprint occurs after 15 years of relatively safe residence, and all the odds point against any immediate danger, yet all Crusoe's fears from when first coming on the island, are rekindled. So he does not rest until he has taken the precaution of building an additional fence. Later he realizes that all his actions and calculations have been clouded by fear. Nonetheless, as Peter Hulme argues convincingly,

> The time between the discovery of the footprint and the arrival of the cannibals is the period of greatest anxiety for Crusoe, the period in which, one might say, his notion of self is most under threat; the period which turns to almost unbearable intensity the screw of the paradox that what makes solitude so frightening is that you might not be alone, until, in the firing of the gun, you reach that other paradox that the fear of being eaten is dependent on the absence of the cannibals. (Hulme 1992: 201)

After falling back into a state of feeling relatively safe, he suddenly spots the cannibals on the beach, which, interestingly, causes fantasies of (colonial) violence rather than fear. Although soon again restored to his former calmness, he continues to dream of killing the 'savages.' These considerations and religious justifications are more than dubious from an ethical and interesting particularly from a postcolonial point of view. Crusoe says: " [...] I was convinced now many ways, that I was perfectly out of my duty, when I was laying all my bloody schemes for the destruction of innocent creatures" (RC 164).

Most critics nowadays acknowledge that the interest in British colonization noticeably sparked the plot of *Robinson Crusoe* and that the novel is "impossible to understand outside the context of Britain's conquest of the New World" (Sussman 2012: 244; cf. Novak 2001: 547; Hentzi 1993a: 434). Edward Said, who voiced one of the earliest criticisms of the novel as aiding the formation of imperial attitudes so inseparably bound to economic relations and capitalist interests, writes: "Robinson Crusoe is virtually unthinkable without the colonizing mission that permits him to create a new world of his own in the distant reaches of the African, Pacific, and Atlantic wilderness" (Said 1994: 75). While claiming that the imperial perspective has been neglected in studies of the early novel, – a criticism which does not hold anymore to the same extent it did in in the early 1990s – Said singles out *Robinson Crusoe* as the 18th-century narrative most concerned with "the act of accumulating riches and territories abroad" (1994: 83). Furthermore, in the education of Friday, Crusoe obviously propagates the 'civilizing' values of Christianity and Western social hierarchical order, continuing on to establish his rule over his own kingdom on the island.

In Carey's postcolonial reading of the novel, a main question is whether Friday should be considered as a voluntary or a coerced slave. Either way, the bond between the two men, despite the obvious master-servant hierarchy, is one of companionship and is built on shared fear and the will to survive. The most relevant part of Carey's analysis is the detailed historical account given about the European fear of cannibalism, which can be considered to be largely imaginary, contradicting evidence of the cultural practices of the native peoples in any of the British colonies, and particularly in the Caribbean.[27] Similarly, Schmidgen (2002a) argues that Crusoe's fear of cannibalism remains a challenge to criticism if one tries to place it in a 'factual' historical context. One fact one can deduce, however, is that cannibalism appears mainly as a risk created by cultural translation and colonialist rhetoric, symbolizing the fear of barbarity and otherness and functioning as a made-up justification of the civilizing mission masking the colonial enterprise. Therefore, representations of cannibalism occur frequently in literature of the period, typically evoking "an ancient form of terror and a method for reinforcing cultural difference" (Sussman 2000: 14). Considering the imaginary, or rather 'fictional', quality of the fear of cannibalism, it is striking that Crusoe lives on the island for over two decades without witnessing it; yet the minute he has 'evidence' of any other human presence, he becomes manically afraid of it. Lindner, who sees Robinson Crusoe as a novel which "is first and foremost concerned with aspects of colonial violence" (Lindner 2010: 14), plausibly relates the plot to the political climate of the time and the risks felt on a national level, including above all the fear of invasion by enemies from outside, across the channel, and of rebellion and economic instability.

As this brief survey shows, many critics have noticed that Crusoe reacts to the footprint with "a disproportionate fit of anxiety and an imagination spinning out of control" (Schmidgen 2002a: 35). The emphasis on irrationality and emotion is decisive. Hulme also stresses the unreal nature of his fear, existing even prior to the discovery of the footprint and argues that the "persistence of Crusoe's fear which proves to be psychotic inasmuch as it constantly disavows all contradictory evidence. [...] The issue is not Crusoe's initial fear of the cannibals, [...] it is rather his unswerving adherence to this fear despite the evidence that confronts him" (Hulme 1992: 193–194).[28] Obviously, the scary element is the intrusion into his space of an unknown presence, and Crusoe deduced that the footprint, as it cannot belong to "the Devil" (RC 150), must belong to the next best thing, i.e. a monster or savage. The fear of the savages dictates his actions

---

[27] Carey's main example is New Zealand and historical 'records' of Maori cannibalism in the 18th century.
[28] In this context, Hulme stresses a point about the debate of Defoe's realism. While it is surely justified to apply the stylistic label of narrative realism to the novel, it does not present an accurate portrayal of the Caribbean (cf. 1992: 185). He argues further that Defoe's is a kind of realism with mythic undertones feeding on colonial ideology comparable to Shakespeare's *The Tempest*. The narrative details "have demonstrably less to do with the historic world of the mid-seventeenth-century Caribbean than they do with primary stuff of colonialist ideology – the European hero's lonely first steps into the void of savagery" (1992: 186).

from now on and furthermore marks a change in his construction of identity. Suddenly he starts to draw borders between self/other and mine/yours in a literal way, rushing to build a stronger fence. Above all, the footprint appears to him as a sign of transgression and signals that his self and his space are vulnerable to violation by others.[29] Moreover, his reaction shows, Schmidgen argues, that the scene "presents the cultural assumptions that would congeal into the notion of terra nullius in a state of deep cultural and ideological uncertainty;" the narrative shows how the perception of an apparently 'vacant', territory can be transformed into an "unnatural, frightening condition from the perspective of a culture that treated possession as an unproblematic social given" (Schmidgen 2002a: 34). Whereas the fear and threat of invasion is a theme that runs through the narrative, it is significant that Crusoe encounters the footprint on the beach, near the threshold to the open sea. According to Alain Corbin, the seaside has inspired horror since antiquity, carrying various symbolic connotations of disorder, abyss, and misfortune.[30] With the ocean constituting the prime loci of risk, the beach is perceived as an instable, dangerous border zone, bearing the possibility of dangerous encounters with monsters or the forces of nature. For Corbin, Defoe's novel typifies a narrative rendering of the seashore as a site of danger:

> Here the beach is the scene only of the disasters whose marks its still bears: the ship ripped apart and smashed against the coastal reefs. [...]. This is were cannibals indulge in their orgies, as Robinson watches, fascinated, a voyeur threatened by the animality of collective rejoicing. It is from the shore that danger menaces the womb-like shelter which the hero has lovingly built for himself; [...]. (Corbin 1994: 15)

It is indeed remarkable that in the whole novel, Crusoe stays away from the shore as much as possible; when he goes near it, he either nearly drowns, as in the episode with his small boat or he watches in horror, first the footprint and later the savages. Typically, the risk of savages is one Crusoe thinks he "ought to have considered well before" (RC 120), yet only after he has seen

---

[29] The theme of the fear of transgression and of the erasure of borders is related to deep cultural anxieties and feelings of being at risk. At least in this moment, Crusoe appears as tormented as Roxana.
[30] See Corbin's *The Lure of the Sea* (1994). The main argument of Corbin's study is not relevant here, but it is a useful source on the socio-cultural fascination with the sea. Corbin links the progress in oceanography from the 1660s onwards to the disappearing belief in Satan, arguing that the ocean, as a huge unknown ground of danger slowly became conquerable, turning the seaside from a site of fear and danger into an attraction and 'cure' for elite society from the mid-18th century onwards.

them, does he reflect: "That if I once came into their Power, *I should run a Hazard more than a thousand to one of being killed, and perhaps of being eaten*; for I had heard that the People of the Caribbean Coast were cannibals, or Man-eaters" (RC 120; my emphasis)

As shown above, Crusoe ponders on possible outcomes of situations retrospectively and his calculations of risk often take place after the immediate danger is over. They do not always function as guides to action in a decision-making process, but rather support the reinterpretation of events, typically into signs of the incredibility of his survival. Therefore he often looks back on events and considers himself 'lucky.' The belief and the hope that rescue is possible are integral to Crusoe's survival and sustain his morale and this is where a strong providential element comes in. Throughout the novel, Crusoe's attitude shows the curious mix of old and new worldviews. Concerning this aspect, Alkon points out that the Christian tradition has a different temporal orientation with regard to probabilistic reasoning than a secular doctrine of chances because it is more oriented towards the past; at the same time the scientific question of "inverse probability" was harshly debated at the time of Defoe, for instance by Hume and Locke and later by Thomas Bayes (cf. Alkon 1979: 37–38). Negotiating these philosophical-scientific tensions, *Robinson Crusoe* first captures in a nutshell what Rüdiger Campe describes as a characteristic feature of the genre: "Modern novels are narratives of danger that are no longer actual, but only repeat and reflect on the contingency of survival" (Campe 2012: 189).

Despite the huge time gaps in the narrative, the individual episodes connect to form a coherent picture. As narrator, Crusoe's aim is to explain his survival on the island as plausibly as possible and to relate the conquering of the odds and his risk-management to himself as much as to the implied audience. The episodes in the novel follow a clear pattern; expressed in the most basic form it consists of a problem-solving process, i.e. a remarkable, startling occurrence, Crusoe's perception of a danger (to himself, his possessions, his plans) and the finding of a remedy. Hence, in these causal sequences Crusoe embodies the Baconian spirit of empirical observation and experiment, of the mode of learning by trial and error (cf. Vickers 1996: 4; Cohen 2010: 68). Or, as another critic puts it, "Defoe endows his character with relentlessly practical responses colored by his own understanding of contemporary scientific inquiry" (Hamilton 2007: 139).[31] Margaret Cohen underlines the importance of the psychological

---

31 Hamilton elaborates in a footnote (fn 17; 2007: 139) that Defoe has Crusoe's island experience begin in September 1659, the year prior to the foundation of the Royal Society. Crusoe's experimental trials are not satirized, like in Swift's portrayal of the academy in Laputa in *Gulliver's*

aspect and says that the novel accurately portrays reactions of human beings under extreme stress, forced into a process of questioning and solution-finding in order to survive (Cohen 2010: 79). It is noteworthy that the narrative always evaluates happiness as a state of no-danger, e.g. "I began to be very well contented with the life I led, if it might but have been secured from the dread of savages" (RC 172).

As a study of human consciousness, the narrative contains two main insights into the psychological implications of risk perception. Firstly, that the anticipation of danger is often far worse than having to deal with a calamity. Secondly, that risk as a category of judgment of an event, is highly subjective and dependant on perspective and tied to memories, experiences, beliefs and changing with new or fading evidence. As such it has rather little to do with "reality", and the same event can be perceived as danger or deliverance. For instance, on the occasion of the boat of men stranding on his island, he says: "Thus what is one man's safety, is another man's destruction" (RC 176). This view becomes obvious in a moment when Crusoe takes stock of his life. He underlines the fact that the awareness of risk, devoid of an actually encountered danger, can destroy a man's peace, which is what happened to him in the footprint episode:

> 'I ran over the whole history of my life in miniature, [...], I was comparing the happy posture of my affairs in the first years of my habitation here, *with the life of anxiety, fear, and care which I had lived in ever since I had seen the print of a foot in the sand*. Not that I did not believe the savages had frequented the island even all the while, and might have been several hundreds of them at times on shore there; but *I had never known it, and was incapable of any apprehensions about it; my satisfaction was perfect, though my danger was the same, and I was as happy in not knowing my danger as if I had never really been exposed to it.*' (RC 184; my emphasis)

This statement is soon followed by what appears as a central explicit standpoint taken by Defoe on the function of the belief in divine providence in opposition to scientific, secular knowledge. Using a typical Enlightenment metaphor, it emphasizes the link between the conception of risk and knowledge as the "seeing" of things, while feeling safe is equated with ignorance. Additionally, the quote reads as an ironic commentary on man's expulsion from paradise:

> 'How infinitely good that Providence is, which has provided, in its government of mankind, such narrow bounds to his sight and knowledge of things; and *though he walks in the midst*

Travels, but rather testify to Defoe's fascination with invention and experimentation. See Hamilton also for a reading of Crusoe's dependence on interpreting various events as 'accidents', such as English barley growing near his camp.

of so many thousand dangers, the sight of which, if discovered to him, would distract his mind and sink his spirits, he is kept serene and calm, by having the events of things hid from his eyes [...].' (RC 184; my emphasis)

With the arrival and 'domestication' of Friday commence Crusoe's happiest years on the island. Having company makes possible a new sort of risk-management and attack, and with united force Crusoe and Friday kill the tribe of savages and rescue their prisoners, among them Friday's father. While Crusoe settles into his new role of ruler over people as well as territory, he observes how the men, having newly arrived on the island, are scared of everything, making him remember his own arrival nearly three decades ago. He notices again how any feelings of danger and safety are dependent on the degree of knowledge about a situation: "so these three poor desolate men knew nothing how certain of deliverance, [...] and how effectually and ready they were in a condition of safety, at the same time that they thought themselves lost" (RC 232). Furthermore, he observes that a feeling of being at risk can operate without any concrete content, because the men "were full of apprehensions of danger, [...] though they could not tell what the danger was they had to fear neither" (RC 242). However, with regard to himself and Friday and their habituation to the island, Crusoe boasts to the captain that "men in our circumstances were past the operation of fear" (RC 240), which seemingly contradicts most of his previous narrative, yet holds true in comparison to the others. After his return to England, he is confronted with new fears and questions of risk-management, of how to secure his wealth and who to trust, problems at the heart of another novel, Defoe's Roxana. Crusoe ends his life account with a description of his wealth, happiness and stability, but not without a final affirmation of his risk-taking nature: "Any one would think that in this state of complicated good fortune I was past running any more hazards – and so, indeed, I had been, if other circumstances had concurred; but I was inured to a wandering life" (RC 278). As has been frequently noted, Defoe constructs Crusoe's narrative as a warning, yet as a capitalist success story. It is futile to speculate if risking the hazards of a life at sea and leaving the security first of his home in England and then of the plantation in Brazil were worth it; they are presented as inevitable and necessary for his development, both spiritually and economically. Defoe's first novel presents a complex illustration of human psychology and risk. Being a study of an individual human consciousness, risk is perceived in the narrative without the mediation of knowledgeable experts or society, while the focus is on the subjective and strategic intertwining of rational deduction and belief in the calculation of probabilities in order to assign meaning to life and to motivate survival skills. Situated between realism and allegory, *Robinson Crusoe* thus "narrates the odds of holding onto life in the face of constant danger in the adventure that is life itself" (Campe 2012: 175).

2.2 Risk Management and Human Behaviour in Times of Crisis: *A Journal of the Plague Year*

Within the criticism of Defoe's fictions, *A Journal of the Plague Year* (1722) is the text that has attracted the most explicit readings for risk. A testimony to Defoe's fascination for natural disasters, the text captures "a time of such danger, [...] of a national infection" (JPY 37).[32] Opening in September 1664, when first rumours of the plague reach London, the narrative focuses on the portrayal of the metropolis as a site of disease, danger, and poverty. The first-person narrator, H.F., describes the changing appearance of the city: "though some parts were not yet overwhelmed, yet all looked deeply concerned; and as we saw it apparently coming on, so everyone looked on himself and his family as in the utmost danger" (JPY 18). Quickly, the atmosphere of danger reaches almost apocalyptic dimensions, as people imagine nothing less than that they are "doomed to be destroyed from the face of the earth, and that all that would be found in it would perish with it" (JPY 21). Shaped by the "continuous proximity of death" (Mäkikalli 2007: 119), the *Journal* presents, perhaps, Defoe's most literal staging of the isolated individual's fight for survival under hostile conditions (cf. also Steel 1981: 94), which culminates in the narrator's final outcry "yet I alive!" (JPY 280). Furthermore, in this historical-fictional account of the terrible plague year of 1664/65, Defoe writes against the rise of a doctrine of managing crisis by impersonal statistics and reducing people's lives to numerical entries in bills of mortality. The account of the plague, while also engaging in detail with the various speculations of causes and cures of the disease and the measures of managing the risk, is turned by Defoe "into a study of human nature; *he reminds us that the plague was not a set of statistics but a sum of individual tragedies*" (JPY xi; my emphasis), as David Johnson notes in his introduction to the novel. The text also presents a striking study of human behaviour and the psychological aspects of dealing with the threat of death in a plague-ridden city.

Published in 1722 but set in the mid-1660s, Defoe's *Journal* links two time frames. Most critics see the narrative as written by the author in order to combat

---

32 For example, in the essay *The Storm* Defoe fictionalized another natural disaster, the great storm which hit the south of England in November 1703, and which Aino Mäkikalli, arguably, refers to as "most dramatic natural disaster of Defoe's lifetime" (2007: 117).

a contemporary threat, namely the spread of the plague from Marseilles across the channel, rumours of which reached London in the early 1720s, after the disease had virtually been absent from England for almost half a century. Part of Defoe's political agenda was to alert the population to the new risk and popularize the support of the Quarantine Act, and prior to the *Journal* he wrote several articles and pamphlets warning against a plague epidemic, such as the tractate *Due Preparations for the Plague, as well for Soul as Body etc.* (1721). Defoe's writings belong to a number of texts at the time motivated by "public concern about the disease" (Mayer 1990: 531) and the *Journal* presents a narrative reaction to a public scare, as well as an early literary engagement with the mediation of risk through public discourse, rumours, and official channels. Defoe's chosen retrospective frame illustrates the phenomenon that people in times of crisis frequently tend to look back to older crises; revisiting past disasters is a strategy to affirm survival and evoke some sort of knowledge and orientation when faced with helplessness in the present. Thus the *Journal* is both an allegory of current problems and a critical engagement with risk management in the plague year of 1665. From today's scientific-medical perspective, Defoe's account of the plague is, of course, entirely fictional and incorrect. Although the psychological aspects and the descriptions are accurate, the main lack of knowledge in the text is the fact that the bubonic plague is transmitted by flies and rats. A central source of confusion and fear in the text are the various theories about the origin and spread of the disease, as the narrator notes repeatedly: "But from the whole I found that the nature of this contagion was such that it was impossible to discover it at all, or to prevent its spreading from one to another by any human skill" (JPY 203). While the over-arching narrative is undoubtedly one of risk, Defoe's text sceptically contrasts different belief systems and explanatory patterns and their efficacy in times of crisis.

From a 21st-century perspective, the narrative possesses a striking appeal and offers valid insight into human reactions to life-threatening events beyond man's understanding and control; generally Defoe's reflections and the characters' reactions in the *Journal* do not differ much from fictional works about super viruses or nuclear accidents, the ultimate risk scenarios of today. Barbara Leavy shares this view, saying: "This image of a plague-ridden city unable to cope with a disease and its outcome undoubtedly provides the Journal with much of its contemporary significance" (1992: 30). The *Journal* is a didactic-descriptive text, full of encyclopaedic detail, and peppered with anecdotes and opinions. Despite giving a plethora of numbers and details, the narrator often struggles for words trying to make a chaotic disaster-scenario visible: "it is impossible to say anything that is able to give a true idea of it to those who did not see it, other than this, that it was indeed very, very, very dreadful, and such as no tongue can express" (JPY 68).

Defoe's narrator, H.F., modelled on the author's uncle Henry Foe, a saddler living in London (see Novak 2001: 605), is characterized by his scepticism. Like many of Defoe's other protagonists, he is isolated and set apart from the community, yet moving among them. Throughout the narrative he raises a series of questions about the disease: "How did the plague begin? Could it have been anticipated? What was God's role in it? How was it spread? Was there any way to prevent or avoid it? What was the best way to treat it? Did it help to shut up houses?" (Starr 1971: 57). All these are vital questions in the process of calculating and managing the risk the plague poses to London's population. The narrative, however, focuses more on the difficult process of choosing between conflicting ideas and solutions, rather than suggesting any definite answers. Through his narrator Defoe strategically employs different explanatory "lenses", religious or scientific and shows the pitfalls and comforts of both. Consequently, the narrator often contradicts himself, and appears morally-spiritually confused. The wavering of his religious thoughts and his general uncertainty are triggered by the confrontation with a phenomenon that defies comprehension. The metaphysical questions raised by the narrator include: What is miraculous or providential? What is pre-determined in nature, what is chance? Are death and survival arbitrary? With a marked tension between fear and control, chaos and order shaping the narrative, the *Journal* appears as Defoe's "deepest ideological fiction", and due to its inherently sceptical outlook, comes "as close as Defoe ever does to advocating (albeit vicariously) avowed uncertainty" (Brantlinger 1996: 154; 155).

The complexity and ambivalence of the text is mirrored in its form, and countless scholars have engaged with the *Journal*'s status as a work *sui generis*.[33] Possible generic descriptions of the *Journal* include "an authentic history, a novel, a historical novel, a fictional history, a spiritual autobiography, an allegory, am authoritative medical record, an original example of literary realism, a romance, a true narrative, a false narrative", while the narrator uses a gamut of material running from "personal reminiscences, parish records, official decrees produced verbatim, magical diagrams, medical opinions, verses, and even an episode that looks very much like an act from a play" (Rambuss 1989: 115–16). Summarizing the changing reception of the text over the years, Robert Mayer explains that at the time of its publication it was understood as a "genuine

---

33 See Richetti (1992: 295) and especially Mayer (1990; 1997). Mayer gives an overview of the *Journal*'s reception in criticism over nearly three centuries and argues for its hybrid form between history and novel.

memoir" of the plague year of 1665, later considered as a "historical novel", while some prominent critics, like Richetti (1992), have referred to it as a "pseudo-history", due to its containing difficult implications about truth and accuracy of facts (Mayer 1990: 533; 540; 542).[34] However, in the present context the debate of the text's genre, narrative techniques and focus, is only relevant with regard to the individual and collective/public construction of risk; it highlights the status of risk perception in-between objective evidence and subjective fears, hopes, and beliefs, sustained as much by fictions as by reality. Defoe's text, above all, illustrates how a 'reality' of risk emerges out of a fusion of irrational emotions and rational calculations.

The genre debate aside, the existing criticism of the novel can roughly be divided into two major lines of inquiry. One stresses the textual struggle of the representation of suffering and death, and the portrayed impossibility of mastering the disease. The other focuses on the text's didacticism and sees it mainly concerned with the imposition of order, as Isabel Karremann sums up: "This line of interpretation sees the Journal as an exercise in the ordering power of man, with the plague serving as a kind of stage on which the cultural techniques of ordering – surveillance, distinction, meaning-making language – are successfully displayed" (Karremann 2011: 31).[35]

One aspect critics agree on is that the novel is characterized by its uniting of contradictions. This is also the case with the narrator. The reader receives little to no information about the character whose voice controls the narrative (cf. Leavy 1992: 37). Much like Christopher Isherwood's famous camera 'I' in *Goodbye to Berlin*, H.F. is mainly observing and recording details and impressions, thus assuming a stance that simultaneously claims subjective and objective authority.[36] Throughout the narrative, as Richard Rambuss points out, "the 'I' of emotional spiritual testimony regularly gives way to the 'I' of empirical observation. This is especially so when H.F. is speculating about the modes of contagion. [...] the very colourlessness of H.F.'s account seems to testify to its scientific validity"

---

[34] Regarding the vexed question of the text's historicity, one can agree with Mayer, who says: "Poised at the border between two discourses, the *Journal* warns us to be wary of dismissing the possibility of there being such things as fictional facts – fictive statements that genuinely refer to historical reality" (1990: 549).
[35] See Rambuss (1989); also Novak (2001; 1977), Brooks (1992), Juengel (1995), Fass Leavy (1992), and Womersley (2005).
[36] According to Healy, there are two main strands of tradition in plague writing. Firstly, mythological accounts seeking to 'explain' the affliction by calling on the natural/supernatural divide, and, secondly, eyewitness accounts, which give details about symptoms and describe the "effect of the epidemic on society in visual and moral terms" (Healy 2001: 62). Defoe clearly adheres to the latter, yet also uses elements of the first.

(Rambuss 1989: 125). H.F. inhabits what John Richetti calls the "contemplative edge" (1992: 295) of inherently hostile, dangerous surroundings, and, like Moll, Crusoe or Roxana, he transforms them into an arena for self-expression. However, a main difference is the much smaller temporal scope of the *Journal*. H.F.'s narrative covers barely a year, rather than a whole lifetime, and he is much more passive.

It is furthermore interesting to see the *Journal* and its narrator in relation to the media representation of risk and society's changing understanding of what constituted 'facts' in a situation perceived as crisis. Less concerned with assessing his individual life in retrospect and offering 'warnings' to the reader, H.F. assumes the role of the observing commentator in the narrative present, thus taking on "a new social position – that of the expert" (Poovey 1998: 15). And while some critics claim that it is precisely the narrator's "intensity of the focus" (Zimmerman 1992: 294) that makes this text a novel, more relevant are approaches relating the narrative perspective employed by Defoe to one of the most important scientific discoveries of the time, the microscope. Although Defoe does not play with perspective and size the way Swift does in *Gulliver's Travels*, we also find numerous narrative "close-ups". Isabel Karremann argues along these lines saying that "the composition principle of the Journal could be described as taking a close look at the plague through a microscope with different lenses. Depending on which lens is chosen – the religious, the moral, the scientific, or the economic – different 'shapes' emerge" (Karremann 2011: 42). In this sense, Defoe's narrator also embodies Hobbes' "naked and calculating citizen",[37] preoccupied with the sorting of true from false facts and aware that knowledge is a guarantee of power and control.

Defoe's account of the plague illustrates the intrinsic relation between questions of epistemology and those of social order. It has often been noted, through the narrative voice Defoe presents a mix of belief in science (medicine, statistics) and providential intervention in the world's natural design, showing the characteristic ambivalence that also shapes *Robinson Crusoe:* "But when I am speaking of the plague as a distemper arising from natural causes, we must consider it as it was really propagated by natural means; nor is it all the less a judgment for its being under the conduct of human causes and effects" (JPY 219). The difference here is a much greater textual hybridity; furthermore the narrator's reflections transcend matters of individual fate and concern wider social-political issues, as well as expressing scepticism and addressing metaphysical questions. The

---

[37] The reference here is to Hobbes' account of the new political subject in the *Leviathan*; see Latour (1991: 28); also Poovey (1998: 20).

text's distinctly historical dimension is important because it captures a specific traumatic moment and an experience of a disaster deeply ingrained in London's memory, like the other great fear of the century, fire. The attitudes towards the disease portrayed by Defoe appear as accurate reflection of the prevailing beliefs of the time. Natural disasters were often regarded as having a "moral cause" (Thomas 1991: 108), i.e. being punishments for sins. With good health equally being perceived as God-given, the consequence was distrust in doctors and man-made remedies. But despite the element of devoted Christianity in the text, the narrator displays a firm trust in man's ability to control that shows a clear progression from mid-17th-century to early 18th-century thought. In fact, this temporal-ideological split created by Defoe accounts for the central ambiguities and oppositions in the *Journal*, as David Brooks explains: "But, in the 1660s modern civilization had not yet developed its powers. The Baconian philosophy of mastering Nature by understanding it was more an ideal than a reality. When the Plague strikes, natural philosophy is tested, and fails. For a brief period, the Middle Ages and the modern world interpenetrate each other" (Brooks 1992: 176). The narrative is shaped by this tension and the interpenetration between science and religion as the "two dominant yet incompatible explanatory contexts for the plague" (Karremann 2011: 40). The traditional religious view which sees the disease as a "terrible judgment upon the whole nation" (JPL 17) which simply has to be endured is opposed by secular-sceptic views that struggle equally to convert into a meaningful pattern the forceful experience of the arbitrariness of deaths and suffering, but focus on natural chains of causality and look for active human intervention (i.e. preventative measures, containment, treatment etc.). Like other modern accounts of disease, Defoe's narrative also shows the failure of rational thought in the face of disaster adding another layer of horror to the experience (cf. Brodsley 1992: 21). However, the connection established in the text between people's spiritual and physical health remains a strong one. Even if one does not read the text as predominantly religious, it is concerned with moral decay and disease also metaphorically.

The one critic who has explicitly linked the text to a modern notion of risk, Jesse Molesworth, returns to a crucial question which has, in different forms, concerned many readers over the years, namely why the narrator, whose "reasoning, seen through the focus of statistical analysis, is far more progressive and coherent than normally allowed" (Molesworth 2010: 112), chooses to remain in London, rather than flee from the plague-ridden city.[38] On the one hand, this

---

[38] See Molesworth (2010: 104–115), who also argues that the narrator's remaining in London is just a necessary authorial means to stage an eye-witness report of the plague; but other than that

does seem to run counter to his portrayal as a not overtly courageous, risk-averse character, because as a reporter of the deadly disease he commits "some of the most risk-seeking acts imaginable: he wanders the streets frequently during the plague's peak" (2010: 113 – 14).[39] Yet, on the other hand, he appears in a way paralysed by his own desire to judge the 'rationality' of such an action, i. e. he is unsure of what really constitutes the safest measure. Like Isherwood's camera 'I', Christopher, Defoe's H.F. ends up staying nearly fatally long in a hostile city.[40] While critics like Molesworth stress the inconsistency or even implausibility of the narrator's behaviour, Everett Zimmerman underlines the narrator's uncertainty and diminishing trust in authorities as the main influencing factors:

> He includes himself among the confused populace in the opening pages, and then tells us of his own morally ambiguous decision to remain in London. As H.F. presents the multitude of details about the plague year, we can see his confusion and anxiety reflected in his manner of narration. The numbers, the lists, the incidents are somehow expected to fix the truth, but the truth is evasive. (Zimmerman 1992: 288)

The narrator's decision not to leave the city marks the beginning of the *Journal*. Together with his elder brother H.F. tries to assess the risks of the situation and although they consult all available data (news, rumours, mortality bills) on the plague, this process is not really conclusive and leads his brother, who fears above all for his life, to leave the city, and H.F., who fears above all for his business, to stay. The narrator justifies his reasoning as follows: "that I would trust God with my safety and health, was the strongest repulse to my pretensions of losing my trade and my goods", while his brother asks him whether it is "not reasonable that you should trust God with the chance or risk of losing your trade, as that you should stay in so eminent a point of danger, and trust Him with your

---

it appears is a paradoxical move for a character so conscious of risk. Similarly, David Brooks comments on the fact that the narrator risking his life by wandering the streets seems foolish, but ultimately sees him weighing financial against health hazards, and consequently subordinates "the risk to his life to the risk to his property" (1992: 177; 183).

39 Although her focus is on notions of legal liability, McPherson draws attention to the story of the waterman in *A Journal of the Plague Year* as another example of extremely risky male behaviour. She argues that the man's "decision to allow H. F. on board when he has scrupulously avoided human contact registers as uncharacteristically risky – negligent, even, given how closely the welfare of others is tied to his own" (2010: 41).

40 Isherwood's novel is set in Berlin at the time of Hitler's rise to power and chronicles the changes and the upcoming fascism, which make the place increasingly dangerous for a foreigner and homosexual like Isherwood's alter-ego narrator Christopher.

life" (JPY 10).⁴¹ H.F. also tries to base his decision on the proclaimed origin of the disease, which leads again to inclusive contemplations, and reveals his falling back on belief only in the face of a lack of scientific answers: "It immediately followed in my thoughts, that *if it really was from God* that I should stay" (JPY 11–12; my emphasis).⁴² Furthermore, like Robinson Crusoe, he bases his decision on an act of random determination via bibliomancy, using the words of Psalm 91 as justification to act against his own counsel – and against the common belief that "the best preparation for the plague was to run away from it" (JPY 10). Throughout the narrative, H.F. is conscious of the risk he runs and tries to take all possible measures of protection. At the same time, as he readily admits to himself, he is also driven by a certain recklessness and curiosity, which gets the better of his precautionary impulses: "But though I confined my family, I could not prevail upon my unsatisfied curiosity to stay within entirely myself; and though I generally came frighted and terrified home, yet I could not restrain" (JPY 90–91). The fact that the narrator ventures out again and again into the midst of the infected bodies, suggests that he is not without a certain voyeuristic interest in the spectacle of the disease and he seemingly shows a belief in his own invincibility (cf. Karremann 2008: 96). John Bender sums up the narrator's contradictory risk-behaviour thus: "H.F: the compulsive walker and watcher; H.F. the man who believes himself providentially sheltered yet tries to shut himself up to gain safety; H.F. the reluctant examiner; H.F. the social projector and reformer" (Bender 1987: 79). Taking all aspects into account, the inconsistency of the narrator's behaviour appears clearly less as implausibility from the side of the author, but gives insight into the mix of rational calculation and emotions operating in the human perception and management of risk. H.F. sees his own risk-behaviour replicated around him by people who discuss all options and dangers, only to then "run all hazards, and that in it they hope to be preserved" (JPY 69). The narrator's confessional observations reveal another psychological truth. Not only do people sometimes act against better judgment, but also

---

41 Campe writes about the narrator and his family's decision-making process: "They at first only read in the tables that chance and risk exist. Chance and risk do not have any calculable values; they simply show that a situation of decision and probabilities is at hand. [...] A new increase in the mortality numbers then splits up the parallels between economic survival and the chances of survival in the name of God" (2012: 230).

42 Etymologically, 'plague' is derived from the Latin 'plaga', meaning "a stroke, a blow, a wound" (OED; cited in Healy 2001: 55). Having strong biblical connotations, historically it was often seen as sent by God as a sudden punishment, leaving visible (or sometimes invisible) marks on the victims/sinners.

only fresh impressions of imminent danger are strong enough to influence behaviour.

> 'When I had been out, and met with such terrible things as these I have talked of, I say I repented my rashness in venturing to abide in town. I wished often that I had not taken upon me to stay, but had gone away with my brother and his family. Terrified by those frightful objects, I would retire home sometimes and resolve to go out no more; and perhaps I would keep those resolutions for three or four days, [...].' (JPY 85–86)

Arguing more on a structural level, one can agree with Molesworth, who writes: "Even the least miraculous of Defoe's fictions, *A Journal of the Plague Year*, the archetypal plot of risk averseness, in the end reveals itself to be particularly risk-seeking" (2010: 129).[43]

Several critics have focused on the connection between the plague and the financial crises at the time of the *Journal*'s publication, arguing that Defoe engages with a duality of contemporary threats in this narrative, furthermore tying it to metaphysical questions and a moral discourse about the punishment of human 'sinful' behaviour, greed, and decadence, as he also does in *Roxana*.[44] Pat Rogers comments upon interesting similarities in the public discursive mediation of the crises:

> 'It soon became evident that the vocabulary of sickness was widely felt to be the most appropriate for the effects of the Bubble. Words such as disease, distraction, distemper, medicine, recovery, and so on, are in regular employ. Sometimes from the imagery used

---

[43] Molesworth distinguishes *A Journal of the Plague Year* explicitly from *Moll Flanders* and *Robinson Crusoe*, emphasizing that 18th-century fiction is full of incidents which present "statistical miracles (the sailor who survives the shipwreck; the serving maid who marries her master; the orphan whose revealed parentage brings a fortune);" he writes further that "the novel has never relinquished its bias toward the 1 out of 1,001 blip" (2010: 129). He also draws attention to a central tension. Comparing the accounts of Crusoe and H.F., with regards to the odds of survival, he argues that both narrators "create interpretative frameworks that tend to dismiss these statistical operations of chance: if there exists some cosmological lottery, then both Crusoe and H.F. comfort themselves with the knowledge that God is the lottery master. [...] Nevertheless, both Crusoe and H.F. are absolutely fascinated with odds and likelihoods" (2010: 100–102).
[44] Novak makes this point explicitly, writing about *A Journal of the Plague Year*: "The chaos Defoe really had in mind was that of 1721. And the cause of that chaos was not merely the fear of the plague in Provence but also the awareness of the 'plague of avarice' that had ruled England and much of Europe for a number of years" (1977: 244). The impact of the Bubble crisis on public awareness and perception of risk has been outlined in detail in the previous chapter and will not be the point of focus here. For a close reading of the interlinking of the two catastrophes in public discourse and many interesting parallels see Rogers (1985).

it is hard to know whether a newspaper story concerns the plague, the financial collapse, or both'. (Rogers 1985: 155)

Without pursuing the overlap of crises in historical detail, some general observations of the structural parallels are important. Defoe's *Journal* (whether read literally or metaphorically) has to be considered as a "masterly study of a community *in extremis*" (Rogers 1985: 166), or of "a city in crisis" (Novak 2001: 606). Throughout cultural history, plague discourse, Margret Healy explains, "is a very good indicator of a period's particular social tensions" (Healy 2001: 94), and Defoe's *Journal* is an example of this. Clearly both the plague and the credit system sparked the fearful imagination of the public, confronting humans with situations beyond their control and only vague ideas about counter-measures, causes and effects. In the novel, the narrator tries his best to monitor the disease and grasp it epistemologically in order to gain some sort of control, for instance, he follows the mortality figures "with grim precision" (Rogers 1985: 161), in a similar vein as one would follow the rise and fall of stocks. Yet, despite all observation, the disease and the credit system prove to defy clear expression and understanding. Stressing the analogies between literature, public discourse and disease at the time, David Steel (1981: 106) sees a similar fear of the spreading of dangerous new ideas and disease. Seen to propagate by 'oral' contagion (rumours etc.), both develop from a catching start via a feverish climax to a (fatal) decline, also reflected in the structure of Defoe's narrative. Paula McDowell emphasizes this connection, saying: "At times of crisis, the scope for unfounded stories is immense, and H.F. explores in detail how rumours originate, function, and spread. [...] Oral rumours are themselves a kind of plague, for they make a bad situation worse" (McDowell 2006: 100).[45]

The narrative situation of Defoe's *Journal* is a good illustration of what Susan Gilman (1988) describes as a main function of literature and art about illness, namely to capture projections of the human fear of collapse and, at the same time, to produce a safe distance, a boundary between representation and the disease. Through this projection, the fear of dissolution is located externally and rendered more manageable, a strategy Defoe's narrator H.F. employs from the

---

[45] McDowell, who reads the whole text as paying testimony to a significant media shift from oral to print culture in the 17th century, argues that the reliability of both oral rumours and printed news is questioned in the novel, much like the opposition of science and divine providence. Part of the narrator's struggle is "to reject mere oral 'Stories' in favor of empirical evidence and written records" (2006: 103); furthermore, while the *Journal* opens with a rumour about the disease, oral street culture becomes almost extinct when the plague reaches its height and written, statistical representation make up a large part of the narrative.

start. Gilman's notion of the boundary already highlights the central binary distinction, between sick/healthy, polluted/pure, inherent in the process of representing disease. Any attempt of prevention or management of disease depends on identification according to those categories, i.e. helping those in danger, and protecting the others (or, most commonly, the narrating 'self') from contagion. Chaos erupts if classification according to this binary is difficult or even impossible. In Defoe's *Journal* people die suddenly on the streets without showing any outward signs of the disease. Perhaps the most shocking, fear-provoking insights for both narrator (and readers) is this invisibility, or rather disguise, of the disease, complicating any attempts to tell the infected from the healthy, a mechanism which also shapes a lot of public reactions to contemporary diseases like AIDS (see Leavy 1992: 27; Karremann 2011: 38f).

> 'Now it was impossible to know these people, nor did they sometimes, as I have said, know themselves to be infected. These were the people that so often dropped down and fainted in the streets; [...] other times they would go about till they had the very tokens come out upon them, and yet not know it, and would die in an hour or two after they came home, but be well as long as they were abroad. These were the dangerous people; these were the people of whom the well people ought to have been afraid; but then, on the other side, it was impossible to know them.' (JPY 216)

The plague thus defies calculability and control, and assumes the status in public perception as "an undetectable enemy, whose movements cannot be plotted" (Brooks 1992: 171). Hence the majority of people see no other solution than to run away from it, a reaction of panic which can be found in many contemporary art works on the threat of disease, e.g. in films like Steven Soderbergh's *Contagion* (2011).

The process of (fearful) 'othering' is a decisive mechanism not just in identity construction but also in dealing with disease. Throughout her study, Gilman focuses on the aspect of power and construction of self/other, and she describes how humans tend to equate falling ill with a "real loss of control that results in our becoming the Other whom we have feared" (1988: 2). At the same time, the mere confrontation with illness reveals and tests an individual/or a societies' perceived inner order and strength: "How we see the diseased, the mad, the polluting is a reflex of our own sense of control and the limits inherent in that sense of control" (1988: 3). Drawing borders between the randomness and chaos of illness is crucial to preserve a sense of order and stability. Gilman stresses that humans have a constant sense of the precariousness of life, as she puts it, "we are all at risk all of the time" (1988: 6), and hence desperately try to control our fears, of which the fear of illness is a prominent one. H.F.'s narrative in Defoe's *Journal* can be read as an exercise in controlling fear, by writing, gathering evidence, sampling cases, and constantly drawing boundaries between the sick 'others' and his healthy self. [46]

Representations of the plague are inseparable from cultural anxieties and invariably show confusion and a questioning of authorities in a time of crisis.[47] The plague is also a classic metaphor for transgression and the fear of pollution by/and otherness. From an anthropological vantage point, Mary Douglas has identified mechanisms that are integral to human societies and concern notions of purity/pollution and danger which are applicable to Defoe's plague narrative. Often blame is placed on 'polluted' persons who are perceived as having crossed a line and now posing a risk to others. Moreover, the judgment depends on an ideal of clear structures (social, scientific, cosmic) without which a conception of pollution or transgression is not feasible (Douglas 1991: 12). Disease, or any

---

[46] See Healy's *Fictions of Disease in Early Modern England* (2001) and Steel (1981). The main focus of Healy's study is on Renaissance drama, poetry, and pamphlets. However, the social-political functions of plague writing she identifies are also applicable to Defoe's *Journal*. Due to its rapid spread, and mortality, the plague was the most terrible and feared disease during the Tudor and Stuart reigns. As a consequence, in time of plague, survival assumed an urgency that made all questions of social decorum irrelevant. Throughout history, "Plague thus comes to represent the ultimate horror, that of both individual and social disintegration: only those two competing scourges, famine and war, match its effects. Ideas about social decay, disorder and instability are thus encoded in the word 'plague'" (Healy 2001: 62). Also emphasizing the plague's role in Western (cultural) history, Steel writes: "The most virulent and fearsome of diseases that Europe has known is bubonic plague. […] More consistently than any other illness it has seized the creative imagination of writers from the medieval period to the twentieth century" (1981: 88–89).

[47] See also Thomas (1991: 9ff) on the mystery surrounding the disease and the various beliefs about its spread and cure. Generally, the speculations and uncertainties surrounding disease were often referred to in 18th-century fiction and sometimes heavily satirized, for instance, in Henry Fielding's *A Journey From This World to the Next* (1743), where the narrator's voice, speaking from beyond the grave, gives an account of how the fear of smallpox and contagion shapes social encounters. The following conversation ensues between two passengers journeying in a carriage to the other world: "Perhaps, sir", said I, "you died of that distemper, which therefore made so strong an impression on you". – "No, sir", answered he, "I never had it in my life; but the continual and dreadful apprehension it kept me so long under cannot, I see, be so immediately eradicated. You must know, sir, I avoided coming to London for thirty years together, for fear of the smallpox, till the most urgent business brought me thither about five days ago. I was so dreadfully afraid of this disease that I refused the second night of my arrival to sup with a friend whose wife had recovered of it several months before, and the same evening got a surfeit by eating too many mussels, which brought me into this good company" (Fielding 2006: 10–11). Apart from the idea that smallpox can be transmitted via eating seafood, the satire in the episode rest also on an understanding of the contagious nature of smallpox in which fear seemed to take on the role of causative agent, an idea which can also be found in Defoe's *Journal*, where people sometimes die of "sheer terror" of the plague.

other agent of disorder, is perceived as "destructive to existing patterns; also that it has potentiality. It symbolizes both danger and power" (1991: 1). Douglas thus draws attention to the attraction of the border zone – the zone between safety and contagion H.F. hovers on throughout the entire narrative – that evokes notions of risk and power. As theorists like Douglas or Foucault, who also writes that "the image of the plague stands for all forms of confusion and disorder" (Foucault 1995: 199), have shown, notions of pollution, danger and taboo are deeply entrenched in the formation of cultural regimes of order, including hygiene, social classification, or disease management.[48] Generally, a confrontation with the 'low' and the 'filthy' triggers disgust and calls forth acts of exclusion. Defoe's narrative demonstrates, long before any anthropological theories of culture and pollution, how "a system and subject position are in a state of crisis when impunities rupture these boundaries, when the continuity of the system is threatened by what are viewed as 'contaminants'" (Juengel 1995: 139–40). Adding to this, the narrative's intertextuality and straddling of the borders of various genres and discourses also represents this aspect on a formal level and ruptures any "fantasy of wholeness" (Gilman 1988: 5) a reader or spectator might have. H.F.'s account of the plague reveals how any attempt of representing disease faces a breaking of clear-cut boundaries and brings a struggle to maintain binary images of sick/healthy and order/disorder.

Several critics, most noticeably Stephen Gregg (1999; 2009) and Isabel Karremann (2008; 2011) have read the text focusing on early 18th-century gender identities and anxiety. Arguing, in a sense, for manliness being 'at risk' in the narrative, Gregg analyzes the question what kind of character and (gender) behaviour can survive or rescue the nation as a major concern in the text, saying that Defoe ultimately advocates an ideal of rationality as basis for "godly manliness" (Gregg 2009: 104), which, and this is Gregg's implication, triumphs over madness, superstition, hypochondria, and irrationality, which are all commonly associated with femininity.[49] One can generally agree with Gregg that the text depicts identities at a time of crisis and shows how men react to the "fear of annihilation" (2009: 92). However, while Defoe tests ideas and coping strategies and risk management on various levels, no stable role or strategy emerges. And H.F., despite all his scepticism and interest in science and statistics, is an ambivalent portrayal of what Gregg calls "the rationality of the godly man" (2009:

---

[48] See Douglas (1991) and Foucault (1994; 1995).
[49] However, in terms of assessing the contrast between superior clear-thinking males vs. the panic-stricken women in the text, it is, of course, important to stress that the reader only gets H.F.'s subjective, biased descriptions of people and events.

107), because, like Crusoe, he is torn and observes how rationality fails in times of existential crisis.

Karremann also focuses on manliness as a precarious quality, which is found and lost in the fight against the disease. Her analysis ascertains the relevance of the notion of risk (perception/management) for the construction of gender identity, although she does not mention this explicitly. She argues that the mediation of gender identity in the text depends on a notion of masculinity as guarantee for social order. Defoe's narrative juxtaposes notions of courage, piousness, blind faith, and rational worldview. All fail in the confrontation with the plague and disrupt the stability of traditional male leadership ideals, leaving the question which group of men is best suited to sustain order, i.e. the magistrate, the clergy, the physicians, or brave individuals. Karremann rightly points out: "Their rational world-view is repeatedly presented as a safeguard against the dangerous superstition and headless panic of those who fall prey to quacks, charlatans, and their useless remedies, [...] the manly ideal embraces an active courage and an ethos of self-help" (2011: 35).

Besides gender issues, both Gregg and Karremann's readings are sensitive to the differences of class and the precarious situation of the poor in the text. While the poor present a burden to the 'stronger' middle and upper classes (cf. Gregg 1999: 151), in particular the urban merchant class H.F. belongs to is characterized by an "ability and willingness to carry out an effective plague management" which sets them apart from "the egoistic, irresponsible nobility on the one hand and the dangerously reckless poor on the other" (Karremann 2011: 35). The narrator comments on the latter aspect repeatedly in his account:

> 'It must be confessed that though the plague was chiefly among the poor, yet were the poor the most venturous and fearless of it, and went about their employment with a sort of brutal courage; I must call it so, for it was founded neither on religion nor prudence; scarce did they use any caution, but ran into any business which they could get employment in, though it was the most hazardous. Such was that of tending the sick, watching houses shut up, carrying infected persons to the pest-house, and, which was still worse, carrying the dead away to their graves.' (JPY 101)

Many critics have noted that Defoe's *Journal* is an exceptional text due to its "concentration on the life of the poor such as never had been attempted before" (Novak 1977: 243). The narrative captures the democratization of the city on the one hand; the shared experience of living with the risk of imminent death, yet also shows how the disease, while crossing and erasing certain thresholds, is distinctly class-bound. Like Ulrich Beck in his depiction of late 20th-century risk society, Defoe highlights how the confrontation with risk is shared through the disastrous effect on people's imagination. But the effects are often distributed unequally. The above quote furthermore serves as an example of the risk rhetoric employed by the narrator throughout the *Journal* and shows his ambivalent attitude towards the poor. While he is compassionately aware that precaution is a luxury not everybody can afford, e. g. the poor are forced to go to the market to get supplies, or cannot leave the city, he also criticizes their folly and ignorance which leads to behaviour which endangers others. But the narrative juxtaposes this with numerous examples of human pity, sacrifice and sympathy for others brought forth by the extremity of the condition, which presents a confrontation with alterity on many levels. This becomes clear in H.F.'s reflection: "Another plague year would reconcile all these differences; a close conversing with death, or with diseases that threaten death, would scum off the gall from our tempers, remove the animosities among us, and bring us to see with differing eyes than those which we looked on things with before" (JPY 199).

As argued above, historically the plague was commonly thought of as a disease of the poor and frequently associated with moral depravity. This perception also caused a lack of interest in investigating the medical-naturalistic causes and possible cures of a disease, for instance, from the side of the physicians of the Royal College of Physicians (see Thomas 1991: 790). Apart from this class-related explanation of a lack of knowledge regarding the plague, the theories of its contagion and measures to contain it were not neutral either and often followed an ulterior political agenda. According to Foucault, "the plague gave rise to disciplinary projects. [...] it called for multiple separations, individualizing distributions, an organization in depth of surveillance and control" (Foucault 1995: 198).[50] Especially important in this regard is the control, or rather minimizing the visibility of the disease, e. g. by clearing the corpses from the streets, burying the dead at night, shutting up houses and other quarantine measures, and by increasing the presence of police on the street.[51]

Although H.F. congratulates the city magistrates on some decisions, he condemns most of the official risk management as ineffectual. If he had previously acknowledged "that London may be a pattern to all the cities in the world for the good government and the excellent order that was everywhere kept, even in the time of the most violent infection" (JPY 177), when the epidemic reaches its height, people "began to break into that excellent order of which I have spo-

---

50 Healy writes about the measures against the plague discussed in 17th-century London that, "the fears many of the governors expressed about disorder were exaggerated, unjustified and possibly even part of a rhetorical strategy to win the support of the 'middling sort' for punitive legislation against the poor" (2001: 95–96).
51 For a longer discussion of Foucault in this context and the measures taken to document the chaos and to reach some sort of comprehension, see Karremann (2008: 59–61).

ken so much" (JPY 201); e.g. the increasing numbers of corpses are buried during the day and the plague generally becomes more and more visible, heightening people's sense of risk. Of all the 'methods' employed against the disease, the 'shutting up' of houses presents one of the most heavily debated, and is explicitly criticized by H.F. He holds the magistrate responsible for miscalculating its effects; "the shutting up of houses was in no wise to be depended upon. [...]; *for whoever considers all the particulars in such cases* must acknowledge, and we cannot doubt but the severity of those confinements made many people desperate, and *made them run out of their houses at all hazards*" (JPY 60; my emphasis).

The reason why all policies to control fail is, of course, that the real way the plague is spread is unknown. H.F. rejects many scientific theories, e.g. the miasma theory, which was prominent at the time, and believes the disease to be caused by a bad, infectious cloud of air and goes as far as to say that he considers these theories "the effect of manifest ignorance and enthusiasm; likewise the opinion of others, who talk of infection being carried on by the air only, by carrying with it vast numbers of insects and invisible creatures, who enter into the body with the breath, or even at the pores with the air" (JPY 84–85). His account documents the numerous popular superstitions and misconceptions surrounding the plague. Recurringly, the narrator explicitly distances himself from the "common people" and their "almost universal melancholy apprehensions" (JPY 23). With an undeniably ironic undertone H.F. comments on the upsurge of astrologers and fortune-tellers on the street, who try to predict the development of the plague, for instance by relating it to the sight of a comet in the sky. Defoe's narrative also highlights the profitable side of the business with risk and people's fear. The desire to know and control the future, in particular when faced with randomness and death, drives people, as H.F. complainingly notes, "ignorant and stupid in their reflections" to "conjurers and witches, and all sorts of deceivers, to know what should become of them (who fed their fears, and kept them always alarmed and awake on purpose to delude them and pick their pockets)" (JPY 33). However, with the deaths from the plague reaching new heights, all "what they called cunning-men, conjurers, and the like", disappear, and as the narrator sardonically points out: "But now they were silent; many of them went to their long home, not able to foretell their own fate or to calculate their own nativities" (JPY 202). As he does the astrologers, H.F. dismisses many medical professionals, or those acting as ones, as incompetent. Questioning measures and authorities, the narrator is in a state of deep uncertainty.[52] His constant weighing of opinions and alternatives against each other is reflected in his rhetoric, e.g. in the frequent use of conjunctions like 'yet", however', 'still', or 'nonetheless'.[53] But the narrator also formulates is own stand point and suggests political-social measures against the plague, some of which are illusionary, like a mass evacuation of the city's poor.

Mary Poovey lists Defoe among the early "champions of statistics" (1998: 13). The growing fascination with 'facts' and numbers as the most neutral, accurate form of representation, is very pronounced in Defoe's writing and in the *Journal* he takes it further than any other 18th-century author. Although it is the 19th century that Poovey identifies as the time when numbers came to assume their cultural–scientific authority and acquired a status beyond the necessity for any interpretation – which is what she refers to as the historical evolution of "modern fact" (1998: xii) – the distinct function of numbers, charts and their narrative commentary she outlines is applicable to Defoe's early text. It employs the inclusion of figures in Poovey's sense, seeking to "simultaneously describe discrete particulars *and* contribute to systematic knowledge" (ibid; original emphasis).[54] Defoe inserts tables of mortality, taken from John Graunt's *Natural and Political Observations* (1662), into his narrative, thus placing evidence in front of the reader in a very specific visual and journalistic way. These tables of mortality force the readers to distinguish between fact and fiction within the narrative and they visualize the presence of statistical probability. Interestingly, the plague mortality tables from John Graunt are cited in the narrative by Defoe without reference, yet they "establish the fundamental epistemic implication of evidential representation" (Campe 2012: 229). But rather than concrete, reliable data narrator and reader get only a sense of the rise and fall of deaths from it; however,

---

[52] Brodsley identifies a typical characteristic of disease narratives, reading Defoe alongside other plague narratives by Boccaccio, Camus, Paul Monette, or Randy Shilts. While Brodsley's particular focus is on parallels between historical and contemporary disease narratives, she argues: "Plague was not fully understood in the eighteenth century. AIDS is not fully understood now" (1992: 18).

[53] See Starr (1971: 51; 69–71). Starr's reading of Defoe's *Journal* offers an analysis of how the tension between certainty and uncertainty is constructed through the language, for instance through the frequent juxtaposition of words like "indeed", "no doubts", etc.

[54] In *A History of Modern Fact*, Poovey investigates questions such as: For what purpose did people start to count? What were the social and institutional functions of numbers and calculations? How did numbers acquire the impartiality and their connotation of transparency that makes them the basis for any epistemological study today? (1998: 5). The answers to these complex questions are, of course, all related to the attempts to represent uncertainty in a somewhat concrete way and to give it an air of objectivity, processes which are at the heart of the evolving risk industry and insurance business.

if one looks at any article dealing with 'risk assessment' today, Defoe's methodology and the construction of his text appears strikingly modern. The narrator detects various errors in the mortality charts and expresses his mistrust in their accuracy:

> 'for now for about nine weeks together there died near a thousand a day, one day with another, even by the account of the weekly bills, which yet, I have reason to be assured, never gave a full account, by many thousands; the confusion being such, and the carts working in the dark when they carried the dead, that in some places no account at all was kept, but they worked on, the clerks and sextons [...] not knowing what number they carried.' (JPY 111)

Many examples like the above could be given from the text, until the narrator arrives at his final verdict and his "settled opinion that they never could come at any just account of the numbers [...] all this confirms what I have said above of the uncertainty of the bills of mortality" (JPY 215). While this does not compare to any present-day criticism of statistical data, the reflections of Defoe's narrator give insights into the methodological problems in the early stages of the field of statistics. Daston explains how "for most of the eighteenth century the statistics of choice dealt with human mortality. Therefore, any account of the mathematical theory of risk in this period must begin with why, when, and how contemporaries kept track of death" (Daston 1988: 126; see Kavanagh 1993: 27). Apart from capturing a stage in the rise of statistical data in society, the numbers fulfil another function in the text. The narrator turns to them with a mix of fascination and horror, asserting his own survival against the growing odds, but also uses the scientific distance as consolation, because, as Kavanagh writes, references to probability theory generally help to avert the eyes "from that most terrifying gamble of all – our own death" (Kavanagh 1993: 28). Steel takes a similar view, saying that in Defoe's *Journal* "the backbone of the story is not provided by dramatic incident or descriptions, but by numbers" (Steel 1981: 93). Arguing for the contrary, Molesworth claims that the "*Journal's* emphasis on numbers, statistics, and inferences acts as little more than an alibi for its ultimate allegiance to H. F.'s curiosity, his synonym for risk-seeking behavior" (Molesworth 2010: 116). The narrative allows for both kinds of readings. But by intersecting numerous personal stories and anecdotes with the mortality charts and through H.F.'s commentary of them, Defoe seeks to humanize the statistics. For instance, in his interpretation of tables of infant mortality, H.F. strongly appeals to the reader's sympathy:

> 'As to those who were with child, we have seen some calculation made; 291 women dead in child-bed in nine weeks, out of one-third part of the number of whom there usually died in

that time but eighty-four of the same disaster. Let the reader calculate the proportion. There is no room to doubt but the misery of those that gave suck was in proportion as great. Our bills of mortality could give but little light in this [...].' (JPY 133)

By drawing attention to the examples of pregnant women and breast-feeding mothers as "one of the most deplorable cases in all the present calamity" (JPY 131), as in Moll Flanders, and to some extend in Roxana, Defoe reveals a concern with the situation of women and their risks, which are perceived as much greater than those of men, as they are not tied to children in the same way.

Apart from trying to insert a human face, emotions and doubts into numerical representations, the narrative reveals their limitations. A crucial incident is the narrator's risky trip to the nightly churchyard where he witnesses the burial of carts of plague bodies. The sight of the mountain of corpses puts him in a state of shock. The confrontation with the vastness of dead bodies is an experience literally beyond words. Much later in the novel, when the crisis reaches its climax, H.F. again refers to it as defying numerical as well as narrative representation: "when the violent rage of the distemper in September came upon us, it drove us *out of all measures. Men did then no more die by tale and by number.* They might put out a weekly bill, and call them seven or eight thousand, or what they pleased; 'tis certain they died by heaps, and were buried by heaps, that is to say, without account" (JPY 267; my emphasis).

The analysis has focused on Defoe's *Journal* as a study of risk management and of the interaction between intellect and affect in people's reaction to crisis. Illustrating the complexity and contradictions of human risk behaviour, the narrator continuously observes and judges people's actions as mechanisms of fear, noting "a thousand unaccountable things they would do in the violence of their fright" (JPY 116). These include, for instance, the fleeing of people onto ships on the river, where, as the narrator comments, "they had certainly the safest retreat of any people whatsoever; but the distress was such that people ran on board, in their fright, without bread to eat" (JPY 129). Another observation which recurs through H.F.'s account is that the situation calls forth egoism and the instinct of self-preservation which override altruism or compassion: "It is not, indeed, to be wondered at: for the danger of immediate death to ourselves took away all bowels of love, all concern for one another" (JPY 130–131). This selfishness extends, or rather turns into, carelessness once despair takes over, once an individual's fight against the risk of infection is lost: "And indeed when men are once come to a condition to abandon themselves, and be unconcerned for the safety or at the danger of themselves, it cannot be so much wondered that they should be careless of the safety of other people" (JPY 174). Many of the anecdotes in the narrative highlight the fact that the disease turns human contact into risk. An often-cited example is the story of the women apparently murdered by the kiss of a stranger in the street. The episode also shows how human fear and imagination can be almost as powerful as 'real' infection. Revealing his characteristic underlying scepticism and the willingness to resists the general panic and search for 'rational' explanations, H.F. tells the story thus:

> 'A poor, unhappy gentlewoman, a substantial citizens wife, was (if the story is true) murdered by one of these creatures in Aldergate Street, or that way. He was going along the street, raving mad, to be sure, and singing; the people only said he was drunk, but himself said he had the plague upon him, which, it seems was true; and meeting this gentlewoman, he would kiss her. [...] he caught hold of her, and pulled her down also, getting up first, mastered her, and kissed her; and which was worst of all, when he had done, told her he had the plague, and why should not she have it as well as he? [...] when she heard him say he had the plague, she screamed out and fell down into a swoon, or in a fit, which, though she recovered a little, yet killed her in a very few days, and I never heard whether she had the plague or not.' (JPY 180)

Another common behaviour, the irony of which does not escape the narrator, is people going to church to pray for protection, while ignoring the risk this activity in itself poses: "they come to the churches without the least caution, and crowded together, as if their lives were of no consequence" (JPY 198). Yet the sum of "unaccountable" actions also refer to the narrator's own risk-behaviour, who after his many wanderings around the city, always returns home "*where I could not but consider with thankfulness the risk I had run*" (JPY 72; my emphasis). H.F.'s account is sensitive to the propagation as well as to the sustaining of fear, highlighting the role of story-telling, medial representation and risk perception. On the other hand, it shows how fear subsides with habituation, even if the 'reality' of the danger has not changed. Whereas people, "upon the first fright of the infection, [...] shunned one another, and fled from one another's houses and from the city", they later "made no more of the plague than of ordinary fever" (JPY 254). The conception of risk is shown to possess a distinctly fictional quality, like a story that is no longer told, it fades from people's minds, or like a story that is told too often, it fails to excite.[55] Moreover, the narrative shows the inseparable fusion of rational and emotional calculations. While the narrator shakes his head at people's lack of caution, rumour of a decrease of the infection causes masses of Londoners to return to the city; "they flocked to town without fear or forecast [...]. It was indeed surprising to see it, for though there died still from

---

[55] Brodsley argues along these lines: "Hence, 250 years before the AIDS epidemic, Defoe understood that public health education achieves its purpose not through logic but through passion" (1992: 12).

1000 to 1800 a week, yet the people flocked to town as if all had been well" (JPY 256–57). From today's perspective, Defoe's *A Journal of the Plague Year* is amazing in its insight into human nature and has great validity as a literary study of the construction of risk and humans dealing with a situation of crisis. Above all, with all its complex paradoxes and inconsistences, it testifies to the fact that: "Nobody can account for the possession of fear when it takes hold of the mind" (JPY 272).

2.3 Marriage, Crime, and the Hazards of Women: *Moll Flanders*

Moll Flanders (1722) and *Roxana* are often categorized as Defoe's "domestic novels" (Lindner 2010: 245), though this label is only fitting in direct contrast to the author's other fictions. The narrative follows Moll's life from her early youth through her five marriages in the first part, and chronicles her career and rise to a master-thief in the second. Written again as a first person narrative, this time Defoe presents the account of the life of a woman, "well known in the Records, or Registers at Newgate, and in the Old-Baily" (MF 7). The beginning implies an idea of self-perpetuating history and underlines the importance of family relations, because Moll is born in prison as the daughter of a woman, a whore and thief, who was exiled to America for stealing bread to feed her small child. Thus abandoned as an infant, Moll is first raised by gypsies before catching a 'lucky' break and being taken in by a wealthy middle-class family. In characteristic manner, Defoe introduces a number of serious political and social issues – e.g. about child-care, education – into what sets out to be a rather sensational plot from the start and creates a distinct atmosphere of risk. Like many of Defoe's other protagonists, Moll is placed in harsh, exceptional circumstances, and the narrative poses questions "about human nature in extreme form" (Starr 1971: 136). With reference to *Robinson Crusoe*, Moll is usually seen as the first female character that embodies Defoe's tradesman mentalities and as the first "economic woman", her main capital being her beauty as well as her cunning. The novel features a female heroine, who is actively seeking and successfully managing risks. It combines domestic anxieties with the new speculative spirit of the time and captures the fear and fascination of it by showing both positive and negative possibilities and outcomes, i.e. moral corruption vs. remaking identities and overcoming dire circumstances.

The preface promises a novel full of "excellent Warnings in such Cases to be more present to ourselves in sudden Surprizes of every Sort" (MF 5) and calls for attentiveness and shrewdness of people, who are otherwise at risk of falling prey to the exploits of criminals like Moll, who "in her Depredations upon Mankind stand as so many warnings to honest People to beware of them, intimating to them by what Methods innocent People are drawn in, plunder'd and robb'd, and by Consequences how to avoid them" (MF 5). Striving for an air of (biographical) reality, Defoe's narrative fictionalizes his experiences with London's criminal underworld and seeks to raise the ethical and risk-awareness of the reader in a humorous way. For the ultimate goal of his heroine is not the upholding of morality, but rather surviving in the world to the best of her ability, without getting caught by the authorities. R.T. Jones explains: "Moll's warnings, it seems, have more to do with the wisdom of the streets and with the advisability of keeping on the right side of the law if one can, and covering one's traces if one can't, than with Christian virtue" (MF ix). Generally, the novel displays an "incongruity between crime and punishment" (Chaber 1982: 215); and the law has seemingly little implications for Moll's risk perception or moral judgment. Throughout the novel, her pleasure about her gains and good fortune clearly overrules penitence. Like Roxana, she is from a young age repeatedly put into situations "where virtue and survival seem at odds" (Scheuermann 1993: 35), or, as another critic puts it, "Ultimately, Moll's narrative subordinates moral instruction to a more practical purpose: lessons in survival" (Swaminathan 2003: 206). Indeed, Defoe's narrative puts forth a rather radical notion of conduct as survival strategy or risk management,[56] for example Moll, like Roxana, abandons her children. And, one can only agree with G.A. Starr that Moll's character presents a complicated convergence of fears and desires, set against the limitations of her background and the existing social order, which render difficult any "clear-cut choices on her part (and clear-cut evaluations on ours)" (Starr 1971: 148).

A main focus of the novel is the exploration of women's precarious lives and limitation of choices. In contrast to men who "play the Game all into their own Hands" (MF 17), women are utterly dependent on them in all financial matters. In the beginning, Moll expresses the awareness that even if a woman does have qualities like "Beauty, Birth, Breeding, Wit, Sense, Manners, Modesty" (MF 17), without money, "she's no Body" (MF 17). Characterized by her beauty and sex appeal, a crucial aspect driving the plot action is Moll's ambition "to be among Gentlewomen" (MF 13). Her education and circumstances foster this

---

[56] Carol Houlihan Flynn reads *Moll Flanders* alongside Defoe's conduct manuals and argues that Defoe's fictional realities often clash with the actual ones: "When Defoe, the author of conduct manuals, demands self-control and moral management, he presupposes a domestic life of stability and substance safe from arbitrary intrusions from invisible hands. [...] His novelistic domestic economies, however, reveal a terrible instability" (1987: 84).

desire. However, the typical female upbringing she receives leaves her unfit for any profession – other than prostitution and thievery, as the author seems to critically imply. Comparing herself to other women, Moll asserts her sense of self-worth and the value of her good looks early on. At the same time, she is conscious of the risk connected to knowing her own beauty: "But that which I was too vain of, was my Ruin, or rather my vanity was the Cause of it" (MF 16). While Moll never shows her fear or despair, it takes her some time to learn the painful lesson that "marriage is not as good a safeguard as money" (Scheuermann 1993: 16). Through the first part of the narrative she tries again and again to achieve security in the conventional and socially acceptable way, yet each new husband sooner or later brings a form of ruin or abandonment. In fact, Moll experiences all the hardships and contingencies connected to marriage, with her husbands dying, going bankrupt, or disappearing. Adding to this, although the first part focuses on domestic life, Moll is presented a being alone and lacking an "adequate social safety net" (Faller 1993: 208), that is the support of family, friends, or other contacts and acquaintances.

Her first misfortune is her amorous entanglement with the two brothers, which is also her painful introduction to the risky game of sexual relations. Supposed to marry one brother, she loses her virtue to the other, who keeps her as a mistress but has no inclination of marrying her, bringing her dangerously close to losing all social standing. Commenting on her young inexperienced self, Moll explains that she was unaware of the consequences of her decision and acted out of passion and naivety: "I gave up myself to a readiness of being ruined without the least concern" (MF 21); "for from this Day, [...] I had nothing of Value left to recommend me, either to God's Blessing, or Man's Assistance" (MF 23). Courageously, Moll then decides to be true to her heart and tells her first lover: "I had much rather [...] be your whore than your Brothers Wife" (MF 32). Afterwards, she falls seriously ill with fever. During her convalescence, her lover begs her not to stand in the way of her own safety, offering her money and urging her to marry his brother. In her lovesick state, Moll suddenly becomes aware of the high risk she is running: "I began to see a Danger that I was in, which I had not consider'd of before, and that was of being drop'd by both of them, and left alone in the World to shift for myself" (MF 45). To avert this worst-case scenario, Moll enters into her first marriage, which leaves her a widow with two children after just five years. No longer a naïve girl but a woman with some means, she has lots of admirers, yet she is now acutely aware of the rules and risks of giving herself to a man: "I had been trick'd once by that Cheat call'd Love, but the Game was over; I was resolved now to be Married or Nothing, and to be well Married or not at all" (MF 47).

Her downward spiral begins with her second marriage to her Draper husband and her misjudgement of his character. Unable to handle finances, he drives the family into bankruptcy and ends up being jailed for debt. He breaks out and escapes to France. With the disappearance of this husband, Moll's situation is again a precarious one: "I had a Husband, and no Husband, and I could not pretend to Marry again, tho' I knew well enough my Husband would never see England any more" (MF 50). In particular throughout the first part of the novel Moll's reflections constantly circle around the economic gains and risks of love and sexual relations. Marriage is perceived as a game of chance consisting of trying to bet on a man's character, risking high-stakes in the process. While she herself errs in judgment and loses a number of times in this gamble, Moll condemns the unfair rules of the marriage market in general. In the narrative she employs a striking metaphor to express the risks of harm peculiar to women in the marriage market:

> 'the Women have ten Thousand times the more Reason to be wary and backward, by how much *the hazard of being betray'd is the greater*; and would the Ladies consider this, and act the wary Part, they would discover every Cheat that offer'd; [...] As for Women that do not think their own Safety worth their Thought, that impatient of their present States, resolve as they call it to take the first good Christian that comes, that run into Matrimony, as *a Horse rushes into the Battle*, I can say nothing to them, but this, that they are a Sort of Ladies that are to be pray'd for among the rest of distemper'd People, and to me they look like People *that venture their whole Estates in a Lottery where is a Hundred Thousand Blanks to one Prize*.' (MF 59; my emphasis)

Much has been written on Moll's economic rhetoric and the close relation between marriage and money in the novel.[57] Defoe's use of metaphors ('a lottery', 'a horse rushing into battle')[58] underlines both choice and randomness and raises the crucial questions of power and control in this context. A women's choice of husband is compared to a risky manoeuvre with should be based on conscious, clear calculations if not, possibly, best be avoided all together. Moll's reference to entering into matrimony as taking "a Leap in the Dark" (MF 59) leaves little doubt about her view. But she is also conscious of the double-edged situation of women, as not getting married is equally perceived as a

---

[57] See Chaber (1982), Erickson (1986), Kibbie (1995), Pollak (1989), and Scheuermann (1987; 1993).
[58] The image of a horse rushing into battle also occurs in Defoe's tract on *Conjugal Lewdness* (1727: 32–33); cf. also Chaber (1982: 218). For an analysis of the author's attitude towards marriage with reference to his conduct manuals and didactic tracts, such as *The Family Instructor* (1715) or *The Complete English Gentleman* (1728–729), see Richetti (1982).

social danger. Therefore, Moll vehemently argues another case for careful deliberation, instead of making rushed, emotional decisions, and she presents her own calculations of the probabilities of a 'safe' marriage thus:

> 'Tis nothing but lack of Courage, the fear of not being Marry'd at all, and of that frightful State of Life, call'd an old Maid; of which I have a Story to tell by itself: this I say, is the Woman's Snare; but *would the Ladies once but get above that Fear and manage rightly, they would more certainly avoid it by standing their Ground*, [...]: In a word, there is no Woman, Deformity, or lost Reputation excepted, *but if she manages well, may be Marry'd safely one time or other; but if she precipitates herself, it is ten Thousand to one but she is undone.*' (MF 59–60; my emphasis)

A majority of the existing criticism focuses on the novel's concern with and revealing of society's restrictiveness towards women, and Moll's "Matrimonial Whoredom" (Novak 1976: 88). The commercialization of marriage and relationships certainly are at the core of the novel. Amongst others, David Blewett has emphasized that Defoe was writing at an "important moment in the history of marriage in England" (1981: 77) and set out to criticize the (forced or accepted) practice of putting financial security before love.[59] Well documented are the era's changes in the social structure, the emergence of the nuclear family and notions of domesticity, "with its physical isolation and social instability, [which] made a woman's fate more precariously dependent than ever on her husband's" (Chaber 1982: 218; cf. Watt 1987: 139–140). Consequently, the choice of marriage partner forms the central hazard in the first part of the narrative.[60] Defoe thoroughly deconstructs the notion of marriage as a "safe harbour" and shows the precariousness of women's dependency on the exclusively male management of its institutional hazards. Among the legal and social inequalities at the time, were for example, Chaber explains, that although "such institutions as joint-stock companies began to emerge during this period to ease the risks of trade, nothing was done for deserted or widowed wives" (1982: 218).

The men in *Moll Flanders* are portrayed for the most part as incompetent, inconsiderate, or criminal, either endangering women with their behaviour or at least failing to protect them. This supports the underlying idea that drives a lot of the plot-action, namely that "a woman's money is safest in her own hands" (Scheuermann 1993: 21). In this context it is important to consider that

---

[59] Blewett (1981) and many other critics have stressed the author's role as moralist writing about family life, as is demonstrated in Defoe's pamphlets such as *Conjugal Lewdness, or Matrimonial Whoredom* (1727).
[60] The topic is developed further in the Victorian novel, but on a more emotional, psychological level.

economic discourse was gendered differently at the time of Defoe. While nowadays, as for instance the public discourse about the global 2008 financial crisis has shown, highly speculative, reckless behaviour is widely associated with masculinity, in the 18th century it was femininity that was linked to notions of speculation and insatiableness.[61] In the novel the strong association of money and sexuality is reflected in the prominent theme of prostitution. Yet there is another crucial aspect to the relation between risk and gender established in the narrative and this gendered distinction has persisted over time. Defining the lack of equality and the differentiation between the sexes in terms of risk, Susan Sontag writes: "'Masculinity' is identified with competence, autonomy, risk-taking, independence, rationality; 'femininity' is identified with incompetence, helplessness, irrationality, passivity, noncompetitiveness, being nice" (Sontag 1983: 181). Referring to this distinction, Chaber notes that this "patriarchal identification" of masculinity with risk-taking and competence "is apparently as unsatisfactory to Defoe as it is to Susan Sontag" (Chaber 1982: 221). Arguing along similar lines Mona Scheuermann emphasizes that in comparison to other male authors of his time Defoe believed "equally in the self-made woman" (Scheuermann 1993: 12). While being generally at risk from rape, bad marriages, or poverty, Defoe's female characters are typically capable, active, and intelligent, displaying little interest in traditional courtship and valuing their (financial) independence above anything. Especially Moll is noticeably less fragile than other famous 18th-century heroines like Richardson's Clarissa; and although Defoe in *Moll Flanders*, as well as in *Roxana*, claims to be telling a "cautionary tale", Scheuermann righty points out, "the cautions he makes weigh heavily against acceptance of victimization" (1993: 12; 8). Although it might be a stretch to call Defoe a feminist writer, he acknowledges and highlights the precarious realities of women, with regard to child-care, poverty, and the dependence on the unpredictability of a husband's decisions. According to Scheuermann, what Defoe shares with feminist writers such as Mary Wollstonecraft is that the danger of the heroine is never cushioned by the fact that, potentially, she can always go home to her wealthy family. In Defoe's fictions money is made rather than inherited, which contributes to a specific risk-scape and a dynamic flux of loss and gain,

---

[61] See Kibbie (1995: 1025–26). The feminized imagery and the "allegorical figures of disorder – unstable 'goddesses' like Credit, Fortune, Luxury" (Ingrassia 1998: 27) have been referred to in chapter 1.1. Defoe's novels and protagonists like Moll and Roxana capture women's new involvement in the business world and active pursuit of pleasure and wealth. The text illustrates the seductive potential and new chances of women's advance in the unchartered territories of finance and trade, which caused, of course, anxiety in society, and new regulations and restrictions soon followed.

which is very different, for instance, from later novels like Burney's *Camilla*. In Defoe's writing, other than friends and connections, only money appears as a "hedge against disaster" (Scheuermann 1987: 316; see Swaminathan 2003: 192), and as a means of protection and guarantee of freedom, whereas marriage is shown as utterly instable, and in Moll's case, even the seemingly perfect union, her third marriage, bears a most horrible danger, i.e. incest.

This third marriage comes about by Moll deceiving a man into thinking her a rich widow, "one of the most dangerous Steps a Woman can take, and in which she runs the most hazard of being ill us'd afterwards" (MF 66). She follows this husband, a sea captain, to Virginia, where her new mother-in-law receives her. The odd turn of events, the coincidence of this woman being her own exiled convict mother, turns Moll's situation of new-found stability and happiness upside-down. In this episode Moll comes closest to real tragedy. Finding herself incestuously married to her own brother, and having borne him three children, Moll is confronted with an impossible and dangerous scenario she does not know how to handle and one which certainly requires some rather unusual risk management. Living more or less in denial for three years, she only tells her husband the truth when he threatens to put her in a madhouse due to her obvious mental distress and her refusal to sleep with him. The underlying threat is the destruction of the nuclear family. After telling her husband-brother the truth, he attempts suicide and finally dies, after which Moll returns to England. The episode highlights several important aspects. Firstly, the marriage to her brother transgresses sexual codes and norms and renders the imperatives of moral conduct books ironically irrelevant because the world is shown to be full of improbable coincidences (cf. Houlihan Flynn 1987: 84–85). Secondly, whereas all of Defoe's novels mediate threats, a recurring motif is the danger of sexual encounters that bear the risk of harm and "social death", i.e. loss of reputation, illegitimate pregnancy and ruin.[62] Thirdly, the incest motif reveals another lurking danger which comes from not knowing one's own family or where one belongs, a theme that is illustrated in even darker colours in *Roxana*. In addition, it is significant that the episode takes place in the colonies. Without focusing on this aspect in detail, on the one hand America appears as a relatively safe space of freedom and possibility in Defoe's writing; on the other hand many of the ultimate transgressions in the novels, the risks which are perceived as

---

[62] See Lindner's argument that sex scenes in Defoe's fiction are often rendered with descriptive violence, showing the coercion or endangerment of the woman. In *Moll Flanders* he sees an explicit connection between the use of a military rhetoric (e.g. words like "attack", "conquered" etc.), sexual violence and danger (e.g. Moll's husband threatening her with the madhouse after she refuses him in the bedroom (2010: 248–249).

deeply threatening to the human self and the order of society, are encountered in the colonies, and are thus displaced 'elsewhere' far away from England, e. g. cannibalism in *Robinson Crusoe*, or the incest in *Moll Flanders*. Sussman argues along these lines saying that "those seemingly untrammeled and anarchic spaces present Moll with greater dangers than the autonomy and freedom of early eighteenth-century London" (Sussman 2012: 77). It certainly shows that the portrayal of risks and crimes in fiction is never devoid of deep cultural and political implications.

The thematic link of sex and money is carried further through the narrative. After her return to England, Moll takes up residence in Bath and soon embarks on a new profitable affair. After nursing her married lover through a prolonged illness, he makes Moll "a Present of Fifty Guineas for my Care, and, as he call'd it, for hazarding my Life to save his" (MF 89). Yet while living as a kept woman and despite being financially secure, Moll "wanted nothing but to be a Wife, which however could no be in this case" (MF 92). The narrative always returns to Moll's worst fear, poverty, which is presented as the motivational force behind many of her decisions. For instance, on her reasons for embarking on this immoral affair, she comments as follows: "But as Poverty brought me into it, so fear of Poverty kept me in it" (MF 94). This existential threat is a constant presence in Moll's life, looming in the background, sometimes closer or further away. Another fear and problem which preoccupies Moll recurrently in this first part of the novel is having no one to turn to for protection and advice, which she perceives to be a dangerous state particularly for a woman: "I had no Body to whom I could in confidence [...] depend upon for their Secresie and Fidelity"; "if a Woman has no Friend to Communicate her Affairs to, and to advise and assist her, 'tis ten to one but she is undone; nay, and the more money she has, the more Danger she is in of being wrong'd and deceiv'd" (MF 100). The ideas of making wrong decisions, of letting her guard down for a moment, and of possibly losing money cause Moll "great Distress" (MF 101). She constantly feels at risk and does not know whom to trust. Furthermore, on the new institutions designed for the managing of finances, like banks, stocks, and "such things, I look'd upon it as unsafe; that if they were lost my Money was lost, and then I was undone; and on the other hand I might be robb'd, and perhaps murder'd in a strange place [...] and what to do I knew not" (MF 102). It is a bank clerk who later becomes her fifth husband, the only one she dares to trust with her affairs. Yet before this comes another brief marital interlude with Moll's Lancashire husband; possibly the only relationship in the novel based on instant attraction and some sort of emotional connection. But this fourth marriage is also based on a double deceit, as both marry the other in the belief of getting a fortune. Once the truth is revealed Moll says:

"I saw nothing before us but Ruin" (MF 115), and the couple splits up after just a short time together. Finding herself again alone and pregnant, Moll returns to London, having no place or friend to turn to in her condition. Mother Midnight, governess, shrewd businesswoman and mistress of a whorehouse, offers her a safe haven for her lie-in. The meeting of Moll and Mother Midnight constitutes the main event that changes Moll's life and the turn of events. Srividhya Swaminathan draws attention to an important point, saying that rather than as a "a series of relationships with men or as a *solitary* struggle for survival", Moll's narrative should be "read as an alternative conduct manual, one that explores the options available to women in unstable, often desperate circumstances" (Swaminathan 2003: 186). It is gender solidarity, not her autonomy and the solitary instinct to survive which ultimately gets her through the misfortunes, not least because Moll falls out of two systems of social order, family and marriage. Without necessarily agreeing with an over-emphasis of the portrayal of sisterhood, because Moll, like Defoe's other protagonists is forced to act 'alone' for a large part of the narrative and this impression is reinforced by the first-person perspective, there is certainly a contrast regarding the relations between the sexes. As argued above, men endanger women (e.g. by exploitation, abuse, mismanagement), and it is other women who are crucial to the survival of their own sex. The "female support system" Swaminathan focuses on in her analysis (2003: 194) emphasizes the portrayal of successful collective female risk-management in the narrative. Women like Mother Midnight can be seen to provide the basic infrastructure to guarantee survival: offering shelter during a pregnancy out of wedlock, taking care of child-birth, later finding a place for the children, arranging contacts, providing job opportunities and valuable advice and friendship. The fact that Mother Midnight runs her whole business 'underground' highlights the dramatic inequalities between men and women in society. With especially pregnancy reoccurring as a "visible" danger in Moll's life, which limits her mobility and options, the only chances are to be found by hiding and evading the gaze of the public. However, with regard to Moll's safety, Mother Midnight has another, almost ironic function, because she fosters her criminal behaviour. With the experience of risk being a strong bond between the two women, Mother Midnight teaches Moll how to be "safe" in the business of thievery, i.e. how to avoid the threat of Newgate, how to best dispose of stolen goods, how to switch costumes and identities, and all other technicalities of the trade. Becoming literally partners in crime, the two women share risks as well as caring for each other's well-being. And this bond certainly lasts longer than Moll's typical marriage; in the final part of the narrative the governess steps in to secure Moll's escape and future in the colonies of New England.

Many critics have noted that the risk for unwanted children, and the burden and danger of pregnancies and childcare for women's health and social situation is a prominent topic for Defoe. Sandra MacPherson puts it bluntly: "One has the sense reading Defoe's work that [...] [t]o be a woman is to be engaged in an undertaking – reproduction – so dangerous that one is never delivered of its burdens: the burden of care and the corresponding burden of liability. (MacPherson 2010: 47). After the birth in Mother Midnight's establishment, Moll gives up her child because she is unable to care for it and voices her strong opinion that to neglect children "is to Murther them" (MF 135). Finding herself free again, she agrees to marry her bank clerk because "I was in no condition now to say no; I had no reason now to run any more such hazards" (MF 140). Again Moll enters into a relationship out of purely economic considerations. The metaphor she uses to express her feeling of security in this marriage employs classic risk rhetoric: "Now I seem'd landed in a safe Harbour, after the Stormy Voyage of Life past was at an end" (MF 146). This state lasts five years before Moll is ruined by the death of the bank clerk and faces poverty again. This time Moll, who is by now well into middle age, embarks on her criminal career rather than on seeking another marriage.

In the second part of the novel, Defoe constructs London as a dangerous ground, a site of crime and adventure. Lindner sees the metropolis in *Moll Flanders* "delineated as a space of violence", highlighting the contemporary discourse and the anxieties about rising crime rates in the city (2010: 253; 259). It forms the background for Moll's career as thief, con woman and prostitute; or if one wants to take a different view on the matter, the city is both precarious ground for women but also a space in which identities and histories can be remade and fortunes be changed. Defoe captures this two-sidedness of the city in the narrative, of London as a site of opportunities and rapid economic expansion, and of a prospering criminal underworld (cf. Sussman 2012: 69). Defoe's London epitomizes the 18th century risk-scape. While the setting in this function can also be found, for instance in Smollett's *Roderick Random*, it reoccurs in many of Defoe's fictions, where London is either the site of the deadly encounter with the plague, or a ground for ruinous encounters with strangers. In particular the plots of *Moll* and *Roxana* exemplify Defoe's "mistrust of the urban unknown" (Schaffer 1989: 23). In marked contrast to the rigidity of society and its representation in the Victorian novel, particularly early and mid-18th century fiction, of which Defoe is taken as a typical representative, often shows a more fluid urban society lacking clear-cut borders, and strict administrative control, which poses both chances and dangers for the individual (see Richetti 1988).

Moll adjusts quickly to London's criminal underworld and her new high-risk profession and proves to be exceptionally talented at it. This is presented, in her own account, as largely due to the fact that she approaches her dangerous activities with careful calculations rather than instinct. Mona Scheuermann goes as far as to stress an element of risk-aversion in Moll's behaviour and describes her as a "careful survivor", who takes an "approach to thieving [which] is, then, thoroughly businesslike: she determines to earn the greatest rewards with the least risk" (1987: 312; 313). While Moll strives to maintain as much control as possible and shows little scruples, she is shocked by her own action in the famous scene when she robs a child's necklace and thinks of killing the child so it will not betray her. But as usual, Moll manages to quickly get her fear and emotions under control. The narrative tells of a series of "many Adventures after this" (MF 151), which all end well for Moll, despite the "daily dread" (MF 152) of being caught. The catalyst of Moll's rise to professional thief, and, as argued above, her competent risk-manager, is Mother Midnight, who "conquer'd all my Modesty, and all my Fears" (MF 156).

As in *Robinson Crusoe*, Defoe has his heroine repeatedly lament her misguided actions, but without any sign of trying to change them; the course of events is presented as inevitable, despite Moll's undeniably strong will and agency. Her criminal life consists of a mix of thrills and fears. Hearing the numerous stories about other thieves who ended up in prison, Moll cries: "And O! cou'd I have but taken warning by their Disasters, I had been happy still, for I was yet free, and had nothing brought against me: but it could not be, my Measure was not yet fill'd up" (MF 158). Once she has managed to sustain a living for herself, Moll does not stop and is also overcome by the desire for more. She is now increasingly torn between the greatest possible gains and minimizing the rising danger. Every narrow escape frightens her for a while, but only for as long as the memory of the danger is fresh in her mind does she decide on a more risk-averse strategy. With the narrative providing insights into the mind of a female risk-taker, Moll is shown to live in a tension between the enjoyable thrill of her existence and managing to live independently, and the fears and burden to assure her own safety. She expresses this clearly saying that apart from "horrible Apprehensions", "I liv'd very comfortably indeed, (the secret Anxiety of my mind excepted)" (MF 170). Thus rising to fame in thievery, Moll maintains for a long time a perfect balance of risk-taking: "I grew the greatest Artist of my time, and work'd myself out of every Danger with such Dexterity, [...] I always got off, tho' many times in the extreamest Danger" (MF 166). The danger of being known leads her to assume a new identity and she takes on the name of Moll Flanders. Her risk-management furthermore comprises a number of rather playful episodes of cross-dressing and numerous costumes changes and other deceptions.

It is interesting that Moll only appears in full control as long as she is working alone; like Crusoe, she is used to fighting and fending for herself and associates company, at least in certain situations, with danger. The quote below illustrates her conscious assessment of danger, safety and her trust in her own skills:

> 'I had the best luck when I ventur'd by my self; and so indeed I had, for I was seldom in any Danger when I was by my self, or if I was, I got out of it with more Dexterity than when I was entangled with the dull Measures of other people, who had perhaps less forecast, and were more rash and impatient than I, for tho' I had as much Courage to venture as any of them, yet I used more caution before I undertook a thing [...].' (MF 171)

Defoe's novel is a study of crime and circumstances, not just of the motivations and the questions of (moral) responsibility, but also of learning to live with dangers. Immunity to risk, born out of necessity and poverty, the narrative seems to imply, bears above all a spiritual risk, as Defoe has Moll say: "when once we are harden'd in Crime, no Fear can affect us, no Example give us any warning" (MF 171). Moll maintains caution and perceptiveness to risk and does not appear to become hardened by her criminal life to such an extent that she stops being afraid. She continues to be extremely careful to protect her identity and never lets her history, or name, become known to others: "[...] this weariness was my safety upon all these Occasions" (MF 172).

Nonetheless, the development of the narrative conveys a sense of inevitable doom and downfall; Moll comes closer and closer to being caught each time. She tries to calm her growing fear by comparing her own situation to others facing worse dangers, like beggars, prostitutes, or less skilful robbers; "at least I was for no such terrible Risques as those" (MF 197). Despite her cautionary instincts, Moll has also "always most Courage when I was in most danger" (MF 209), and that gets her out of a number of a few impossible situations where a more cowardly inclined personality would have faltered. The narrative relates a further series of lucky escapes, with Moll always coming "off with flying Colours, tho' from an Affair, in which I was at the very brink of Destruction" (MF 211). However, eventually Moll does get caught and is carried to Newgate. Although the prison is described as "an Emblem of Hell itself" (MF 212), it soon becomes a place of relative comfort and safety. Moll's unbreakable spirit of survival is perhaps most obvious in this episode. She forces herself to become accustomed to Newgate, a habitat not of her own choice, like Crusoe's island, and even gains a position of power inside due to her charms and reputation: "All my terrifying Thoughts were past, the Horrors of the Place were become Familiar, and I felt no more uneasiness [...]; in a Word, I was become a meer Newgate-Bird" (MF 216).

Defoe's novel portrays a prison culture radically different from later centuries. In the 1700s, Christopher Dandeker explains, prisons were places for "passing through the wheels of justice [rather] than places of punishment", and demonstrate the fact that 18th-century society is still a largely "unpoliced society. [...] In addition, the relations between the prison and the outside world were highly permeable" (Dandeker 1990: 134).[63] In Newgate Moll demonstrates her rational head most clearly. She proves capable of manipulating her way out of it, admittedly largely aided by the lucky coincidence of being reunited with her Lancashire husband. Telling each other their life stories, Moll's first reaction to her husband's plan to save her is the reply that "it was a Risque too great, not worth his running the hazard of, and for a Life not worth his saving; 'twas no matter for that he said, it was a Life worth all the World to him" (MF 231). Nonetheless, the couple starts calculating their options and the "probability of Success" (MF 235) of restoring their fortunes; they end up supporting each other in their trials and prepare for exile together. They appear to be well matched indeed, and Defoe seems to make an implicit argument for the success of a marriage only when based on equality and shared sins and desires. It is a typical irony of Defoe that he includes here the brief hint that Moll's husband is an even better criminal and has lived through more risky situations, for he has Moll comment: "I have observ'd that the Account of his Life, would have made a much more pleasing History" (MF 236). Aided by Mother Midnight, they board the ship into exile with as many of their stored-away riches and possessions as they can carry. Bargaining with the captain on their voyage, they avert their fate of being sold as slaves and arrive free and safe in Virginia. However, like Crusoe, after some time Moll shows a "certain irritable restlessness. She cannot stay secure in Virginia but must venture out again, back alone across the ocean" (Faller 1993: 127) and so ends the life story with a return to England.

The experience of change and risks and her own abilities to master them, is intrinsic to Moll's character and development in the novel. The moral of her story

---

63 See also John Bender's *Imagining the Penitentiary* (1987) and Christopher Dandeker's *Surveillance, Power and Modernity* (1990). Bender emphasizes that the 18th-century prison signified chaos and arbitrariness, rather than the institutionalization of law and order. In this sense the Newgate experience of Moll and Defoe's account of her time there "outlines the cultural significance of the old prisons. Their filth, their dangerousness, their mysterious randomness, their carnival subculture, their absorption of the divine and otherworldly imagery of hell into a secular and social context all point to their provision of transformational experience on privileged ground where both festivity and profound danger are structurally central" (1987: 47). In Smollett's *Roderick Random* prison fulfills a similar function as in Defoe's novel; it is a place much feared, yet also a place for passing through, a meeting place, rather than a severe punishment; and carnivalesque elements feature again strongly in the description. This radically changes, however, within the next century. For instance in Elizabeth Gaskell's *Mary Barton*, and in other Industrial novels, prisons are no longer presented as places for 'lucky' chance meetings and escapes, but as dark, final, and ruinous places of isolation.

is an ambivalent one. Although "this Account of my Life is for the sake of the just Moral of every part of it, and for Instruction, Caution, Warning and Improvement to every Reader" (MF 253), it ends with Moll admiring her own good fortune and the life and wealth she built for herself against all odds and by a shrewd management of dangers. Various interpretations of the novel's ending are possible. For instance, Leon Faller suggests that: "A punished Moll is a warning, a saved Moll an encouragement, and an exhausted Moll an admonition not to leave off repenting too long" (Faller 1993: 127). More relevant is the emphasis on the negotiation of human control vs. the experience of randomness and contingency. Above all, R.T. Jones puts it aptly: "Moll is presented as lucky, and the overriding moral law of the world she lives in is that you can never tell how anything will turn out" (MF vii). As a text, *Moll Flanders* offers psychological insight into the problems of judgment of action and conflicts of conscience, all the while it shows the world to be ruled by luck and cunning rather than virtue. Meanwhile the heroine's development from being involuntarily put 'at risk' to an active control and even being a risk to others, is presented as an act of successful emancipation.

2.4 Possession, Paranoia, and the Risk of the Past: *Roxana, The Fortunate Mistress*

Often referred to as Defoe's "strange last novel" (Blewett 1982: 9) and the only tragedy among his fictions, *Roxana* (1724) picks up many thematic strands from the previous works, including the strong economic orientation of the plot and the concern with the situation of women in society. It takes the portrayal of risk and human relations, the suffering springing from ties of blood, marriage, obligation, or loyalty to extremes. *Roxana* is a chronicle of both surveillance and scandal, capturing the political fears of the time, of trans-national conspiracy, as well as of financial speculation and sexual transgressions, which are intertwined in the narrative.[64] Consequently, the novel adheres to a dark and claustrophobic feel throughout, which gains momentum in the last part. The heroine is always conscious of the risk of exposure, that is, after she has managed and averted the initial threat of poverty. As especially psychoanalytical readings of the novel have shown,[65] *Roxana* is essentially a story of increasing paranoia, featuring a heroine who desperately seeks safety and material wealth, trying to disguise

---

64 On surveillance and anxiety in this context, see Aravamudan (1996).
65 See Terry Castle (1995); also Hentzi (1991: 188–190).

her past and to protect her reputation. While Roxana aspires to financial security, this later becomes the source of uncertainty and results in a constant feeling of being at risk. She is obsessed with maintaining control of her wealth, causing any relationship, especially marriage, to be perceived as a risky co-dependence. Implicit in the novel's subtitle is an association of Roxana's feminine identity and her talent for accumulating wealth with "*fortuna*, with risk, adventure, a sort of erotic piracy" (Thorne 2003: 335; original emphasis).[66] Despite her luck in financial matters, Defoe's "fortunate mistress"[67] is in fact a character haunted by her choices, always torn between freedom and extreme limitations. It is her own daughter Susan, abandoned years ago by Roxana in dire straits, who comes back to haunt her and endangers the security of the life and identity she has built for herself.[68] The fears of exposure and of the loss of her assets are the risks preoccupying Roxana and her faithful maid. Amy, an instrumental character and arguably the one who "preserves Roxana's security" (Castle 1995: 53), mainly functions as Roxana's risk manager, guarding her increasing wealth, organizing the surveillance of her brewer husband, and finally murdering Susan.

Throughout her first-person narrative, Roxana displays the same insight as Robinson Crusoe that the perception of danger is often worse than the actual confrontation with it. Particularly in Roxana's case, her "life is her punishment and her story Defoe's expression of his tragic vision of the human lot" (Blewett 1982: 24). Over and over, the narrative presents Roxana's feelings of being at risk. To some extent Defoe seeks to portray her as a typical example of a virtuous woman corrupted by circumstances. As for Moll, beauty, intelligence, and business instinct is Roxana's capital and she has to manage her own ambition and her limited agency in a world of men. She makes a number of decisions in order to manage her situation and to gain financial independence which turn

---

[66] Christian Thorne sees causality as an important preoccupation in the early novel, yet argues that it is always counterbalanced by chance and fortune. He writes: "We can say that at least three modes of storytelling vie for priority in the eighteenth century, often in the same pages: providence, fortune, and causality. [...] Fortune, in this scheme, is a skeptical term. It suggests that the forms of knowledge generally thought proper to narrative are not, in fact, obtainable" (2003: 341). Defoe's fiction exemplifies such a skeptical use of fortune.

[67] Roxana presents the most typical fictional embodiment of Defoe's *Lady Credit*, and a distinctly gendered nexus between femininity, credit, and prostitution is created in the text. For wider discussions of this aspect, see Baucom (2005), Backscheider (1981), Brown (2001), O'Brien (1996), and chapter 2.1 above.

[68] Defoe's chosen subtitle draws attention to Roxana's many identities and the theme of fortune: "The Fortune Mistress or, a History of the Life and Vast Variety of Fortunes of Mademoiselle de Beleau, afterwards called the Countess de Wintelsheim in Germany Being the Person known by the Name of the Lady Roxana in the time of Charles II".

out to increase her feelings of risk later on and cost her peace of mind. The main choices in this regard are the abandonment of her children, lying about the disappearance of the jewels after her husband is murdered, and the misguided handling of the situation after seeing Susan again. Each decision is either born out of fear, or by the desire to increase her wealth, thus always related to a perception of risk.

The novel is often read as a cautionary tale of moral degradation, and, in the predominantly economic readings, as a criticism of luxury and avarice.[69] The confrontation of trade and morality, in other words, the new ethical questions posed by capitalism that are a major concern of Defoe, are also at the centre of *Roxana* (see Dijkstra 1987: xi). In contrast to Moll, Roxana is very quickly rich enough to sustain a comfortable living and rises to a life of high-rank prostitution, deceit and luxury, rather than one of underground criminality and thievery. This also means that exculpation by necessity and circumstances does not work long for Roxana, although her narrative implies that the traumatic memories of the initial hardship she experiences after her first marriage shape her for life. This is reflected in Roxana's famous morally charged self-questioning of her behaviour: "*What was I a Whore for now?*" (RFM 243; original emphasis), and repetitions of this question occur over several pages in the narrative.

Even if Roxana is a morally indecisive – or even questionable – character, she is shrewd and self-assured in financial matters (see Scheuermann 1987: 314). Indeed, Defoe's eponymous heroine manages financial transactions across European country lines with ease. For this reason critics like Bram Dijkstra have argued that the narrative appears as a study of the challenges of securing and maintaining wealth across borders, and as an allegory of international trade and investments, while local questions are of lesser interest.[70] James Thompson explicitly connects Roxana's transformations and the frequent switching of locations or appearances to the exchange of money and the fluidity of the credit and trading system. As "Banknotes and bills of exchange are the chief instruments that do not indeed tell of their origins" (Thompson 1996: 89), they also symbolize

---

[69] *Roxana* has been taken as a criticism of the extravagance and hedonism of the Restoration court of Charles II. For a summary of the novel's critical reception, see Novak (2001: 617 f). Bram Dijkstra (1987) presents a detailed reading of the novel in relation to Defoe's economic-political pamphlets, arguing that *Roxana* resembles more a case study than a novel, and illustrates Defoe's view on trade and its risks.

[70] While the precarious situation of London's poor is more of a preoccupation in *A Journal of the Plague Year*, the theme of investment in the New World of the Americas does also play a noticeable role in *Moll Flanders* and *Robinson Crusoe*, although the texts maintain a stronger focus on one locality, i.e. Moll's London and Crusoe's island.

flux and defy clear identification. This anonymity equals safety, for instance, the jewels, which are in contrast clearly traceable and connected to an owner, time, and place, present a risk for Roxana's identity and are only made 'safe' by being converted into bills of exchange. The allegorical relation between the system of trade and Roxana's identity shows both the fascination of the exotic, dynamic transformation and the fear for security and stability.

In *Roxana*, as in many of Defoe's texts, the acquisition of wealth is firmly tied to anxieties and fears of its loss. While the specific dangers vary from text to text, including theft, exploitation, and loss by accident, natural disaster, or being cheated by a partner, James Thompson refers to this motif as a "frame of hazard" or "frame of peril" which is "ubiquitous in Defoe's fiction" (Thompson 1996: 95; 117). Roxana's frame consists of the obsession with finding agents she can trust her money with and she also considers marriage either as a threat or as means to secure her treasures. Eventually, she learns the same lesson as Moll, namely "that the only means of minimizing risk and maximizing security is mastery of the credit system" (1996: 97). But one can observe a distinct difference between Moll and Roxana, as Patrick Brantlinger does, with regard to their attitudes towards risk: "Moll's implication in chance distinguishes her from Roxana. Roxana plays chess, calculating and responding. She fears the random. Moll plays dice" (Brantlinger 1996: 157).

It is interesting to focus again on Defoe's 'realistic' view of human character. Ambition and egotism are presented as an integral part of human behaviour, irrespective of gender or class, and the inherent moral criticism is complex and transcends binary oppositions, e. g. such as laudable altruism vs. evil selfishness. Particularly avarice does not appear to have an exclusively negative meaning for Defoe, yet business-sense and self-interest can pose risks in so far that it "might drive an otherwise perfectly competent businessman into foolish gambles for quick gain which were likely to backfire and ruin him" (Dijkstra 1987: 171). As his characters Moll, Crusoe, and Roxana show, the author constructs speculation as an integral part of human nature and has his protagonists profit from risky undertakings. On the other side, he continuously propagates caution as well as 'moral' constraints in trade.[71]

---

[71] For instance, Defoe writes in *The Complete English Tradesman* (1726): "The Tradesman, as he is never out of the Danger of a Blow to his Credit... the higher his Leap, the greater his Fall; the more his Adventure, the more Danger of his Miscarriage". (CET, II, 16–17; 18). Countless more examples of similar rhetoric could be given from *The Villainy of Stock-Jobbers Detected* (1701), or from the many other pamphlets, such as *The Anatomy of Exchange Alley* (1719). Thompson gives a good summary of Defoe's other non-fictions and the portrayal of the fears and dangers

Besides the idea of losing her wealth, the highest risks for Roxana are the loss of her cover identity and reputation; essential to her feeling of 'safety' is keeping a tight grip over what others know about her past. Verona Kelly comments almost laconically that "if any moral is encoded in Roxana's memoirs, it is that those who control their histories can make a bundle" (Kelly 1993: 143). However, her almost desperate desire for respectability and social/financial security, pushed forth by flirts with luxury and greed, trap her and put her at risk. In comparison to Defoe's other protagonists, Roxana paradoxically appears the least free, the least in control and the most guilt-ridden. Her freedom seems the most precarious (cf. Faller 1993: 114–15 Houlihan Flynn 1987: 90), although she is never threatened immediately (e.g. by prison, cannibals, or disease) and accumulates the greatest fortune. Furthermore, of all of Defoe's characters, it is Roxana, rather than Robinson Crusoe, who illustrates the perils of solitude and isolation most powerfully. Roxana is a cosmopolitan character, moving through cultures and adapting to various different languages (English, French, Dutch, Italian), locations, social spheres, and, one might add, men with apparent ease. Yet she remains alienated and while her attempts at mimicry are often presented by Defoe with a pinch of satirical humour, for instance in the famous episode of her dance in her Turkish costume, she never really belongs anywhere. Intimacy generally presents a threat for Roxana. Throughout her changing of life-styles, cities, clothes and men, Amy is her only constant. Despite adopting multiple identities and names, she feels always at risk of discovery, her traveling is not liberty, but she appears condemned to movement and flexibility in order to feel safe.

According to Richetti, Roxana is finally "undone by a retelling of her story in which its details have a force and meaning she cannot control" (Richetti 1982: 35), referring to Susan's retelling of her episode with the Turkish dress. Susan is so dangerous precisely because she undoes Roxana's shield of protection and is not willing to stop until she has uncovered her mother's secret history. Ironically, this story which originally captures a moment of triumph, sexual manipulation and playfulness of disguise, now becomes a danger and a reminder that disguise has long turned into necessity. In the narrative Roxana describes the fearful situation of listening to Susan's story as follows:

> 'her Talk made me dreadfully uneasie and the more when the Captain's Wife mentioned but the name of Roxana. What my Face might do towards betraying me I knew not, because I cou'd not see myself, but my Heart beat as if it wou'd have jump'd out of my Mouth,

---

of trade and credit (cf. 1996: 126–129). However, in his plausible economic reading, Thompson, like many other critics, refers repeatedly to risk, but without theorizing it explicitly as a category.

and my Passion was so great, that for want of Vent I thought I shou'd have burst. [...]; I durst not leave the Room by any means, for then she wou'd have told all the Story in my Absence, and I shou'd have been perpetually uneasy to know what she had said or had not said; so that, in a word, I was oblig'd to sit and hear her tell all the Story of Roxana, that is to say, of myself, and not know at the same time whether she was in earnest or in jest; whether she knew me or no, or, in short, whether I was to be expos'd or not expos'd.' (RFM 331)

Concerning Defoe's portrayal of gender roles and relations, in *Roxana* another woman noticeably embodies the ultimate, final risk that drives Roxana and Amy over the edge. Yet in the beginning, men endanger their situation. Roxana describes her first husband, the brewer, as "the Foundation of my Ruin" (RFM 39) and as "a weak, empty-headed, untaught Creature" (RFM 40). Furthermore, she comments that she has committed the worst mistake by marrying an incompetent man, because: "be any thing, be even an Old maid, the worst of nature's Curses, rather than take up with a Fool" (RFM 40). Through four years of marriage Roxana suffers the characteristic impotence of a wife, having no access to money, and, smart as she is, she has to stand back and see her foolish husband lose it all. The downfall, she assesses shrewdly, finally comes when the inheritance from his father is added to his capital: "[...] for he had no Genius to Business; he had no knowledge of Accounts" (RFM 42). In contrast to her husband, Roxana is aware of the risk of mismanaging their funds and "foresaw the Consequence of this" (RFM 42). Yet while her husband goes hunting every day and ignores the mounting risk of poverty, Roxana sees her "Ruin hastening on, without any possible Way to prevent it" (RFM 43). With imminent bankruptcy upon the family, her husband disappears and leaves Roxana and five children to starve, a traumatic experience which is the motor behind all her future decisions, leading to the slow build-up of Roxana's later tragedy. As in *Moll Flanders*, a focus point of the narrative is the concern with the disadvantageous position of women in comparison to men's freedom. Like Moll, Roxana tries the limited socially conventional and accepted way of women to support themselves, that is, marriage, but later finds that she can much better realize her idea of security and control over her money alone. In both novels Defoe draws attention to the precarious lives of women with children, who cannot simply escape responsibility and face poverty. Her utter lack of connections worsens Roxana's situation, like Moll, she is desperate because: "I had not a Friend of my own left in the World", and she perceives her condition as "the most deplorable that Words can express" (RFM 46). To save her children from starvation, Roxana gives them away to a relative. This protective, if selfish, measure will come back to haunt her.

2.4 Roxana, The Fortunate Mistress — 137

Also in this novel Defoe justifies actions with necessity, showing, for instance, how poverty stretches the limits of Christian morality to extremes. Amy comments: "Poverty is the strongest Incentive; a Temptation, against which no Virtue is powerful enough to stand out" (RFM 61). Meanwhile her mistress sees that high morals standards are luxuries they can no longer afford: "I think Honesty is out of the Question, when Starving is the Case" (RFM 62). The only option for Roxana at this point is "but to be a Whore" (RFM 62), a decision that leads Amy to affirm her unbreakable loyalty to her mistress: "I will starve for your sake, I will be a Whore, or anything, for your sake" (RFM 62). This declaration is soon enough put to the test in one of the most controversial and shocking scenes when Roxana forces Amy to go to bed with the rich lover she herself has taken. The two women, like Moll and Mother Midnight, share all risks and secrets, especially those related to the realms of money and sexuality; eventually Amy ends up pregnant by Roxana's lover. The two women also share the exaggerated perception of risk in the final part of the narrative and end up being caught inside the same bubble of paranoia, yet react very differently to it. The scene of Amy's forced intercourse signifies a distinct notion of precariousness, which enters the scene never really to depart again and which defines their relationship early on. Reading the scene essentially as Amy's corruption by Roxana, in Terry Castle's opinion the scene introduces the specific dynamic between the two women. While Roxana is hierarchically superior, she is also more anxious and lethargic, leaving Amy to often act as a force of Roxana's mind and body (Castle 1995: 46–48).[72]

Soon after this scene Roxana moves to Paris to live with the rich jeweler merchant. One day, he has to go to Versailles to see if a royal client will get a foreign bill accepted, planning to carry a case of very expensive jewels with him, as he usually does when meeting with potential buyers. The ensuing discussion between him and Roxana illustrates the perception of the risk involved in the trip; reluctantly he agrees to her idea to leave the case at home in order to avoid robbery:

> 'I hope there's no danger', said he, 'seeing I have nothing about me of any value; and therefore, lest I should, take that too', says he, and gives me his gold watch, and a rich diamond which he had in a ring and always wore on his finger. [...]
> 'Well, but, my dear', says I, 'you make me more uneasy now than before, for if you appre-

---

[72] Novak takes a more moralizing view of the episode. He discusses *Roxana* as a novel of "moral decay" (1966: 446), and stresses the fact that Roxana is the only of Defoe's characters who forces 'evil' upon another character and commits an act which is condemnable as sin (1966: 450; 453).

hend no danger, why do you use this caution? and if you apprehend there is danger, why do you go at all?' [...] 'There is no danger', says he, 'if I do not stay late, and I do not design to do so.' (RFM 86–87)

Nonetheless, Roxana continues to be very afraid, and has premonitions of a disaster: "I had a strange terror upon my mind about his going, [...] "My dear", said I, "I am frighted to death; you shall not go; depend upon it, some mischief will befall you" (RFM 87–88). Yet he ignores her warnings, is promptly robbed on the highway, and killed by the enraged robbers who fail to find any valuables on him. Ironically, the narrative shows a precaution taken to be the very cause for his death; at least this is Roxana's interpretation. She feels that she triggered his death in some way and although her premonitions and anxiety seem strangely exaggerated, the outcome renders the scene highly ambivalent for the reader. For instance, Sandra MacPherson comments: "Yet in this moment Roxana does not so much foresee as help to bring about the death of her husband" (2010: 2). Despite feeling pangs of guilt for giving, in this case fatal, advice, the jeweler's misfortune presents a chance for Roxana. At the inquest she confirms the loss of the jewels, as rumour on the streets has it, although they remain well hidden in her chest of drawers. Suddenly in possession of a fortune and in need of an identity and story that will protect her, Roxana sets out to present herself from now on as "The Pretty Widow of Poictou" (RFM 93), one of many changes of biography, appearance, and location to come. She then strikes up an affair with the Prince her jeweler merchant went to see in Versailles the day of his death.

Her account of events always returns to the risk of women and their relations with men, be they rich or poor. Unlike her first crucial decision, Roxana is now conscious that she has no real ethical excuse, as she did not act out of a situation of poverty but relative financial security. Yet, she is always haunted by the memories of her miserable situation, and these reflections, for instance after she sees a beggar women on the street, appear as apologetic insertions regarding her behaviour: "I, that knew what this Carcass of mine had been but a few Years before, how overwhelm'd with grief, drown'd in Tears, frighted with the Prospect of Beggary, and surrounded with rags and Fatherless Children" (RFM 110). Apart from poverty, the narrative refers to the greater risk of women in comparison to men due to pregnancy and childbirth. When Roxana finds herself pregnant by the prince and has to plan her delivery, she also has to manage her married lovers' risk of exposure. Convincing him that she has to go into hiding, as anything else "would be a great Risque on his Side" (RFM 113), the narrative offers a bitter reflection of the gendered imbalance of the situation. Not only do men not have to face the dangers to life and health by going through childbirth, moreover,

"Great men are indeed delivered from the burden of their natural children, or bastards, as to their maintenance" (RFM 116). Defoe highlights the facts that illegitimacy poses a risk for both mother and child and that starvation is often the only option, or the even more drastic solution "of seeing the poor infant packed off with a piece of money to some of those she-butchers who take children off their hands, as 'tis called—that is to say, starve 'em and, in a word, murder 'em" (RFM 116).

At this point in the plot, the central theme of chase and surveillance is introduced when Roxana sees her first husband again in London, who is now a Gendarme in the French army. According to Roxana's perception, the encounter threatens her whole existence.[73] Seeking to control the potential danger, Roxana and Amy hire a spy to keep track of the brewer's whereabouts. Roxana's reflections of the situation are representative of the rhetoric of calculating options and minimizing risks that makes up large parts of the narrative:

> 'Amy and I had several consultations then upon the main question, namely, *how to be sure never to chop upon him again by chance and so be surprised into a discovery, which would have been a fatal discovery indeed.* Amy proposed that we should take care always to know where the Gendarmes were quartered, and thereby effectually avoid them; and this was one way. [...] I found out a fellow who was completely qualified for the work of a spy (for France has plenty of such people). This man I employed to be a constant and particular attendant upon his person and motions, and he was especially employed and ordered to haunt him as a ghost, that he should scarce let him be ever out of his sight.' (RFM 131; my emphasis)

Doing everything in her power to make herself feel safe, Roxana nonetheless feels pursued by the "Spectre, or even the Devil" of her former husband (RFM 132). In addition to this, Roxana's fear of loss and being ruined increases, although the immediate threat of poverty has long been averted. She is dominated by the "frightful Thought" (RFM 137) that something might happen to Amy, her solely trusted person. Unable to confer about her worries and financial matters with others, especially men, she struggles with having to disguise her wealth. Furthermore, like Moll, Roxana judges the men in her life on their business sense and is wary of their lacking abilities. Travelling through Italy with the prince confronts her with the problem of where and how to deposit her wealth. While the prince suggests a "risky, and worse, unproductive solution" (Dijkstra 1987: 41), Roxana keeps her jewels locked up in an iron chest guarded by Amy, and always assures herself via Amy's "Accounts, that everything was very safe, and that was very much to my Satisfaction" (RFM 142). When the ill-

---

[73] The laws of marriage at the time did not allow women to remarry legally even if a husband had not been heard of in years (see RFM 127).

ness of the Prince's wife brings an end to her royal affair, Roxana's immediate reaction is devoid of emotions, focused only on cushioning her separation by preparing for all eventualities, "that I shou'd fall as softly as I cou'd" (RFM 134).

Her main, recurring problem is the risk of trust, for instance, the task of finding a suitable merchant to help her turn her jewels into cash. Preparing for her move from France to England via Amsterdam, Roxana sees "no remedy but that I must trust somebody" (RFM 149). Yet when she later shows the jewels to the merchant Amy recommended, she immediately realizes her miscalculation and the danger of the situation: "As soon as the Jew saw the Jewels, I saw my Folly, and it was ten Thousand to one but I had been ruin'd and perhaps put to Death in as cruel a Manner as possible;" (RFM 150). After a narrow escape Roxana is caught in a storm crossing the channel. Typically, this natural disaster is perceived by her as a form of punishment for her wickedness, much like Robinson and Moll, who also tend to lament their wretched lives only when things go wrong. Roxana recollects the situation thus:

> 'the Sea went Mountains high, and the Noise of the Water was as frightful to us, as the Sight of the Waves; nor was any Land to be seen, nor did the Seamen know whereabout they were; at last, to our great joy, they made Land, which was in England, and on the Coast of Suffolk; and the Ship being in the utmost Distress, they ran for the Shore, at all Hazards, and with great Difficulty, got into Harwich, where they were safe, as to the Danger of Death [...].' (RFM 165)

Although the Dutch merchant she flees from later becomes Roxana's "guide into the world of the latest forms of capital management" (Dijkstra 1987: 43), she is fiercely determined to keep her independence and resist the temptation of a partnership or emotional attachment which she has long started to consider potentially dangerous. At various points in the novel Roxana reflects on the financial status and security of a wife in comparison to a mistress and from after the death of her first husband onwards, all of Roxana's decisions with regard to marriage, or rather her refusal of it, are ruled by calculations of financial security and risk. Making what reads like a strong plea for the equality of the sexes (see RFM 187), Roxana criticizes women's customary fear of the "trouble" of having to deal with managing property, while the real grounds for fear and apprehension lie elsewhere: "I thought it was far safer for the Sex not to be afraid of the Trouble, but to be really afraid of their money; that if no-body was trusted, no-body wou'd be deceiv'd; and the Staff in their own Hands, was the best Security in the World" (RFM 193). However, turning down the proposal from the Dutch merchant is not an easy decision and Roxana is scared by the merchant's uncanny predictions of what will happen to her as a single woman. Relating her thoughts by employing the metaphor of risk at sea, Roxana assesses the ironic ambivalence of marriage, which is usually thought to present a "safe harbor", despite posing so many risks for women. This becomes obvious in her reflection of her life: "I call'd myself a thousand Fools, for casting myself upon a Life of Scandal and Hazard; when after the Shipwreck of Virtue, Honour, and Principle, and failing at the utmost Risque in the stormy Seas of Crime, and abdominable Levity, I had a safe Harbour presented, and no Heart to cast-Anchor in it" (RFM 202). Nonetheless, soon afterwards Roxana affirms her strength and determination not to rely on male support or to submit to male control and says: "I was resolv'd it shou'd not be made worse by the Sex; and seeing Liberty seem'd to be the Men's Property, I wou'd be a *Man-Woman*; for I was born free, I wou'd die so" (RFM 212; original emphasis).

Regarding the issue of gender and risk management in Defoe's narrative, two aspects are crucial. The correlation established between a lack of knowledge, lack of control and the risk of financial loss, because inexperience, and a lack of consideration, are presented as inevitable sources of disaster. In addition, an understanding of the value of female beauty and sexuality teamed with a detached control over emotion and personal relationships. The novel shows Roxana's development "from a Lady of Pleasure, [into] a Woman of Business, and of great Business too" (RFM 169) and portrays women as shrewd risk-takers actively fighting for survival rather than as passive victims. Moreover, despite stereotypical attributes like beauty, female characters like Moll or Roxana have strict control over their passions and desires, and, in fact, never display them explicitly. The novel also takes up Defoe's theme of portraying marriage as prone to the same risks of loss as any commercial deal. In *Roxana*, we find the same argument as in *Moll* that marriage offers little safety, or rather that "the unmarried woman with money has the most security of any woman" (Scheuermann 1993: 48). As an author, Defoe appears to be quite pessimistic about domesticity because the nuclear family is presented as a locus of risk rather than stability: "Nowhere in his fiction does Defoe suggest that the home can be a safe harbor, a haven in a heartless world; the best one can hope for is to keep one's treasure intact" (Thompson 1996: 122). As Richetti argues, Roxana never manages to escape the oppressive burden of the "triad of sex, marriage, and the family" (Richetti 1982: 35). In marked contrast to Moll, she is never liberated from these ties or manages to twist them in her favour by 'having it all' in the end.

When reaching her fifties Roxana starts to inquire about her children, driven by the wish to better their situation, if necessary. This endeavour, which leads to the discovery of her daughter Susan, proves to be Roxana's riskiest move yet and it endangers the facade she has securely kept over the past decades. With her fears of exposure mounting, Roxana contemplates another change of identity and a move from one end of the town to the other, with her sole confidant Amy telling her to change "if was possible, your very Face" (RFM 251). Eventually, she settles on the Quaker dress as the perfect disguise; yet she still never feels safe for longer than a brief moment at a time. With increasing frequency and intensity, Roxana mentions the risk of public discovery of her courtesan past, the possibility that "all the Story of Roxana, and the Balls, shou'd come out" (RFM 286). At the same time, in her isolation, as she shuts herself off from social life and interaction almost completely, she is at the mercy of her own dark imagination. Due to a lack of new information, her personal risk scenario spirals out of proportion and her "State of Uncertainty" (RFM 280) has little basis on any calculations of probabilities. Her feverish mental disorder, bordering on paranoia, does not go unnoticed by Amy and the Dutch merchant, but they are unable to help her. It is interesting to see that Roxana's 'madness' seems to be induced by the vexation of freedom of choice as well as guilt. She is overwhelmed by her fear of her past and the task of risk management in the present; she constantly worries about having made the wrong decisions, both in terms of financial and personal safety.

Significantly, she always returns to the metaphorical comparison of her life to the risks of sea voyages and trade. After finally giving in to another marriage and accepting the Dutch merchant, she reflects on her new state of social propriety and says: "I was like a Passenger coming back from the Indies, who having, after many Years Fatigues and Hurry in Business, gotten a good Estate, with innumerable Difficulties and Hazards, is arriv'd safe at London with all his Effects, and has the Pleasure of saying, he shall never venture upon the Seas any-more" (RFM 287–288). But her stocktaking of her situation, as she is left even richer by her marriage, leaves her with a happiness that is only temporary and precarious due to the inability to shake off her past and guilt which maintain a poisonous presence. While the narrative describes her increasingly melancholic state – lack of sleep and appetite, her being haunted by nightmares etc. – it builds toward a claustrophobic climax. Roxana encounters Susan, "this impertinent Girl, who was now my Plague" (RFM 349), on board of a ferry to France, one of a series of events presented as 'accidents' and aiding to the sense of danger closing in. Stuck in the captain's cabin, Roxana struggles to maintain her composure:

> 'I was in the utmost Extremity between so many particular Circumstances as lay upon me, for I was to conceal my Disorder from every-body, at the utmost Peril, and at the same time expected every-body wou'd discern it. I was to expect she wou'd discover that she knew me, and yet was by all means possible to prevent it; [...].' (RFM 324)

After this episode follows a brief period of relative safety before Susan reappears on the scene, causing Roxana to feel that "in a word, the Clouds began to thicken about me, and I had Allarms on every side" (RFM 344). Keeping her only friend besides Amy, the Quaker lady, in the dark about the danger she is in, Roxana tries to gain some sort of control over the situation by carefully censoring what she tells to whom, e.g.: "if she [Susan] came, she [the Quaker lady] did not know where I was gone, she desir'd I wou'd not let her know; and to make her Ignorance the more absolutely safe to herself, and likewise to me, I allow'd her to say, that she heard us talk of going to Newmarket, &c" (RFM 350). But despite all schemes and efforts, Roxana feels pursued by Susan: "*I was safe no-where*, [...] she haunted me like an Evil Spirit" (RFM 358; my emphasis). At least Roxana appears to be more in control, and less angry and passionate than Amy, "who was next door to stark-mad about her" (RFM 358). After the following disappearance of Amy and Roxana's suspicion of her crime she is tormented to the extent that she can no longer sleep, yet later excuses Amy's deed and acknowledges her part in it by saying that "all the Fault she was guilty of, was owing to her Excess of Care for my Safety" (RFM 365).

Characteristically for Defoe's writing, a majority of *Roxana* consists of an internal dialogue the heroine has with herself (and the implied reader) about risks, gains, and losses. However, it presents a clear increase of insecurity and perceived risk, and takes a distinctly negative turn. Throughout the narrative "Defoe goes to some pains to create a sense of apparent security" (Hume 1982: 382), which is then invariably shattered. The minute everything is well and ordered, Roxana starts to feel paranoid, she never trusts her good fortune, although she always relies on it, like Crusoe and Moll do. Agreeing with the critics who see the novel being concerned with moral instruction, it, above all, presents a psychological study of the interaction of guilt and fear and with regard to the conception of risk, removes it quite far from any rational calculations.[74] Roxana's punishment is the complete erosion of feelings of safety and community for her; she is trapped and isolated by her possessions and her guilty conscience. Terry Castle even sees Roxana's development in the final part of the novel as a case-study of hysteria and argues: "Roxana's anxiety that she will be found out by her daughter seems far to exceed the stated reason for her

---

[74] According to G. Starr, one of the critics who interpret the heroine's state in ethical terms, in Roxana's account Defoe seeks to stress, "how necessary and inseparable a Companion, Fear is to Guilt" (quoted from Defoe's *The Life of Colonel Jack*). For an analysis and numerous examples and variations of this idea in Defoe's nonfictional writings, see G. Starr (1971: 178, especially fn. 20).

fear – [...] this anxiety – which becomes almost unbearable to read about – is a consequence of her abbreviated psychic development" (Castle 1995: 53). Sandra MacPherson takes another view by drawing attention to the fact that in contrast to the exculpatory possibility offered by Catholicism, Protestantism is based on strict liability from which there is no escape. In this sense, Roxana is haunted by the claims of the children she has neglected, embodied by Susan.[75] Reading Defoe's novel against the legal developments and changes of liability at the time, MacPherson argues that the text consequently pursues "a project of blame not exculpation" (2010: 13). Undoubtedly, Defoe's narrative engages with the complexity and ambivalence of notions of causality, responsibility, or coincidence, and it raises a number of ethical questions such as the complicity of Roxana in Amy's murder, the question of her agency and control.[76] As a narrative, *Roxana* is distinctly ordered in temporal-causal sequence, not providential design, and all questions of determination of action are less a matter of providence than being "reformulated as private anxiety – as psychology or smarting conscience" (Thorne 2003: 338). Regarding the specific nature of Roxana's fear, Terry Castle suggests an interesting difference to H.F. in *A Journal of the Plague Year*. While he decides to stay and face the risks in the city, Roxana is always on

---

[75] Sill sets out to investigate the 'reality' of the threat posed by Susan, e.g. by establishing the ages of Roxana's children form the dates and clues given in the novel and describes the possibility of her being the long lost daughter as an "error" (2000: 264–66). Still, both Roxana and Amy perceive Susan as a risk and try to 'manage' it. And even if Susan's claim has no grounding in 'reality', Sill admits, the narrative construction of risk actually assumes more prominence: " [...] it is a study of the power of anger, fear, and doubt to infect a mind, pathogenize the reasoning process, and erode the integrity of the subject" (2000: 263).

[76] Many of Defoe's novels are obsessed with choices, responsibilities, options, and the outcome of human actions. While the question of Defoe's use of providence has received detailed attention in criticism, other, related questions of accidental harm, responsibility for (un)intended action or unforeseeable consequences, have not, as MacPherson says and furthermore claims: "Defoe uses the law – in particular a newly refined doctrine of agency making masters vicariously liable for the acts of their servants – to reimagine and revalue providentialism as a tragic ethos, one that connects us to and makes us responsible for the strangeness of our acts and the strangeness of others" (2010: 13). A central question raised in the novel is about the reach and beginning of ethical responsibility, e.g. if Roxana can be a "cause" of events, such as the death of the jeweler or Amy's murder, even when she is not acting. And can people be held responsible for 'projecting' their wishes onto others or for wishing 'accidents' to happen? This question is also taken up by George Eliot in *Daniel Deronda* in Gwendolyn Harlowe's guilty collapse after 'wishing' her husband Grandcourt's death in the boat accident. Furthermore, Roxana presents herself and Amy in her account as having fallen victims to the devil. Amy's role as a "diabolic agent" and the question whether she is more villain than victim has been analysed, for instance, by Snow (1976).

the run (Castle 1995: 54). Furthermore, all her risk-management only makes things worse, and not just with regard to her own perception of security. As a risk-taker, Roxana ventures far beyond securing her mere survival. Yet in contrast to Moll, Roxana lacks the ability to shake off her own moral standards and although she shares the pleasure in disguise, speculation, and manipulation, Roxana does not thrive on risk-taking, as Moll does, but cannot control her fears. While both characters are skilled at fighting the odds and the hardships of their early lives, gaining immense wealth in the process, what survives of Roxana "is an empty shell" (Sill 2000: 270).

Many critics have expressed dissatisfaction about the novel's abrupt ending and a felt lack of authorial control (see R. Hulme 1982). Defoe, after getting so close into Roxana's mind and portraying her anxieties, seemingly struggles to bring his narrative to an end, at least to one which is equally acceptable from a moral, political, or from a genre-convention point of view.[77] The ending does, however, break with any remaining ideal of safety or stability, because there is a definite hint of new dangers for Roxana. Defoe is obviously torn between showing his heroine at risk and her survival strategies at the same time. While making a strong claim for female strength and business skills, the ending suggests that Roxana ultimately fails to protect herself and her possessions, although the reader is not told if it is finally her past which destroys her. Houlihan Flynn plausibly interprets the ending as signifying the heroine's struggle to navigate through the time's sexual economy and contradictory moral discourse concerning women's situation in society. As such, Defoe's conclusion "emphasizes the impossibility of attaining enough domestic security to make possible the ideological fictions of correct conduct" (Houlihan Flynn 1987: 88–89). More recently Lindner has made the interesting point that by linking femininity to crime, "in

---

[77] According to Verona Kelly, Roxana simply "grows wealthier and guiltier until the novel rather than its heroine suddenly comes to what critics have agreed is a bad end" (Kelly 1993: 140), i.e until the final short paragraph informing the reader about the calamities befalling Roxana and the loss of all her wealth. Meanwhile Novak argues that Defoe feels he has to punish his heroine in the end for her two economic sins, luxury and avarice, but does so without actually describing the loss of her wealth. Thus, he takes it as a strategic ending, rather than a plausible one (Novak 1976: 139; 134). Meanwhile Sill also sees Defoe, as a Puritan writer, obliged to present a final punishment of his heroine in order to be coherent with the form of a moral parable (Sill 2000: 262). However, Sill rightly stresses that "the conclusion of the book depicts not a spiritual but a mental deterioration brought on by the murder of her child" (2000: 263). From a psychological point of view, Roxana appears to be already punished enough, because Defoe focuses on her paranoia and mental torments in the whole last part of the narrative, while the ending itself appears just like an add-on, providing conventional closure.

*Roxan*a and in *Moll Flanders* the protagonists themselves, as women, are a dangerous Other that threatens bourgeois society from within" (Lindner 2010: 268). Leaving the judgement of Roxana's crimes up to the reader, by linking psychological insight with sensationalist plots Defoe certainly exploits some of the fascination and "moral panic around the violent criminal" (2010: 269) at the time, adding it to his complex imaginative portrayal of early 18th-century risk society.

3 Swift, Smollett, Sterne, and Walpole: Fears of Masculinity and Parodies of Calculation

3.1 Of Man's Control by Speculation and Fear: *Gulliver's Travels*

After it became publicly known that the author of the scandal-causing text *A Tale of a Tub* (1704) was the Anglo-Irishman Jonathan Swift, Allan Ingram writes, this "inevitably attached a reputation for danger, for risk-taking, and unpredictability to his name" (Ingram 2012: 17). According to Irvin Ehrenpreis, during his writing career Swift saw himself in the tradition of other political-utopian writers such as Thomas Moore and "liked to imagine he was [...] devoting his life to preserve a people on the edge of ruin" (Ehrenpreis 1983: 187). The surgeon and dean Swift, who produced his best-known work *Gulliver's Travels* (1726) at nearly sixty years of age, maintained in his writings a harsh, almost self-destructively critical satirist perspective on contemporary social issues, developments in science, economics, and politics, and human vices and follies. *Gulliver's Travels* remains one of the most eminent works of English literature today precisely for the reason that the text offers insight into many concerns of the early 18th-century but also presents an enduring, 'universal' study of human nature. Any reader of Swift's text, Herman J. Real argues, "will have to account for its allegorical nature one way or another", and he also underlines that allegory, as a "figure of indeterminacy", typically introduces "an element of hermeneutic instability, if not arbitrariness, into critical discourse" (Real 2001a: 81). In other words, it calls for the reader's interpretation even more than other text types. The history of reception of Swift's novel shows that its allegorical structure has been read either predominantly 'historical', focusing on the depiction of political-scientific history in the text, or 'ahistorical', stressing its universal significance and topicalities which transcend the historical-cultural context and references to real personas, institutions or events.[1] Arguing for ambiguity, or rather a 'historico-universal' approach (Real 2001a: 82) seems to be, as in so many cases, a plausible solution. While it is not easy (and perhaps less relevant) to try and pinpoint what stands for who or what in the narrative, and Swift certainly "delighted in polysemous enigmas, not in one-dimensional allegories" (Zach 1993: 98), one

---

[1] For historical-political criticism, see, e.g., Arthur E. Case's *Four Essays on Gulliver's Travels* (1958) and Irvin Ehrenpreis's *Swift. The Man, His Works, and the Age. Vol. I–III* (1964–1983); for the contrasting position, Frederic P. Lock's *The Politics of Gulliver's Travels* (1980).

also cannot ignore a fact which applies to 18th-century texts in particular, namely that "literature then was so aggressively devoted to present events and issues" (Hunter 2003: 219). *Gulliver's Travels* exemplifies how science, economic entrepreneurship, and imperialism dominate early 18th-century thought and politics. Reflecting a perception of the world as bizarre and instable, the focus of my reading is on Swift's satirical depiction and engagement with the speculative empiricism of the 'projecting age', and man's behaviour and opinions, influenced as much by reason as by passions. The text takes up questions about the dangers and difficulties of inter-cultural communication, dislocation, of (mis)perceptions, and dealing with otherness. Consequently, fear is an important controlling principle in the narrative. David McNeil, who focuses on Swift's criticism of Tory politics and depiction and justification of warfare in the novel, argues that it presents "a statement on how naturally humankind capitulates to international fear and suspicion. Although Gulliver points to pride as the most deplorable human passion, *fear clearly dominates the action of the Travels*" (McNeil 1990: 74; my emphasis). His argument can be broadened to include new fears and risks induced by scientific experiments and observation. This is most obvious in Gulliver's encounter with the fearful Laputians and the 'projectors' in the Academy of Lagado in book III. Gulliver's voyages present different case studies, not just of politics and science, but of how humans react to difference and the 'unknown', to challenges to (self-)perception, and, most importantly, how they deal with risk and fear. In all cases, this is shown to produce rather grotesque results.

Written in a style which is indeed best characterized as "grotesque realism" (Nicholson 1994: 118), the narrative has raised questions of categorisation and interpretation on all possible levels. It makes use of and satirizes many generic traditions and affiliations, most notably travel literature. It also parodies the obsession with subjectivity and objective, empirical observation, "not only of travel narratives per se but also of a larger developing class of first-person fictional narratives that make extraordinary claims for the importance of the contemporary, [...] the significance of the individual, and the imperialistic possibilities of the human mind" (Hunter 1990b: 69). In other words, it parodies the emerging novel genre and early popular 'classics' like Defoe's fictions. As far as the 'travel' aspect is concerned, the text, first entitled "Travels into Several Remote Nations of the World", provides no accurate data, neither anthropological nor geographical, about places or people. Yet it illustrates an important function of popular travel narratives at the time, J. Paul Hunter explains, by "implicitly challenging English notions of normativity and offering a glittering array of possibilities about otherness in all its forms" (Hunter 2003: 222f). It violates the teleological design of traditional travel accounts; instead of progression, learning and improvement, we find merely a repetition of structure. The formal frame narrative of Gulliver venturing out to sea is repeated in each of the four parts, sustaining the questioning of the human capability for progress and (self)development on the content level.

Although the genre(s) of *Gulliver's Travels*, as well as in particular the objects and addressees of the author's satire and the narrative's 'realism', have been heavily disputed, it is still not ill-described as a tale of travel across the seas and adventures in 'foreign' lands.[2] Other possible classifications of the text include, of course, satire, allegory, fable, scientific discourse, philosophical treatise, picaresque or utopian novel (see Real 2001: 96). The picaresque element is most interesting, the sense of the lone individual making its way through a world full of odd encounters and threats of various sorts, which also marks Smollett's *Roderick Random*. Also worth considering are the parallels to Defoe's *Robinson Crusoe*. Gulliver shares with Crusoe a thrill-seeking nature and, "Having been condemned by nature and fortune to an active and restless life" (GT 83), he time and again leaves the safety of his native country behind for the uncertainty of foreign shores. While the chapter headings in all four parts frequently allude to the "The Author's dangerous voyage" (e. g. IV, Chapt. 11), they also prepare the reader that, despite all accidents and adventures, the "Author" always "gets safe on shore", or "returns safe to his native country" (e. g. I, Chapt. 1; Chapt. 8). Swift's narrator, the "author", speaks like Defoe's narrators from a position of safety (if not sanity), telling his story in retrospective. He presents a detached account, dominated by observation, and recorded debates and reflection.

In addition to featuring a protagonist who survives shipwreck, pirate attacks, and prolonged stays on strange islands, Swift's narrative shows other similarities to Defoe's first novel.[3] Its context of production, the aftermath of the South Sea Bubble, and the topics of speculation, debt, and imperialism, are hard to ignore, not least because "two of Gulliver's four voyages take him to the 'South Sea'"

---

[2] On the debate of genre see Smith (1990a) and, on the subject of the picaresque, Novak (1990); see also Hunter (2003), and Real (2001b).

[3] Especially the opening and the final part of *Gulliver's Travels* have been read as a parody of Defoe's *Crusoe* (cf. Hunter 2003: 224; Hammond and Ragan 2006: 81). Both Gulliver and Crusoe participate in sea faring, trading, and in systems of acquisition and exchange. Nicholson even sees a direct link between the two texts, or rather a development from the accumulation of possessions to the reflection on it: "Gulliver's originary status and nature as economic man has not always received the attention it deserves. [...] the suggestion that *Gulliver's Travels* begins where *Robinson Crusoe* ends; enquiring and reflecting where the others rest content to act and possess, is to the point" (1994: 94).

(Brantlinger 1996: 67).⁴ The fascination with speculation in all areas and fears induced by the new credit system inform large parts of the narrative.⁵ But Swift's attitude towards the 'Bubble'–mania and the new commercialism differs from Defoe's, as he perceives the new class of "moneyed" men and interest as a threat to the predominant old, "landed" ruling class (see Kelly 2003: 128; Duncan 2012) and anxieties of change dominate over the thrill of possibilities. Patrick Brantlinger explains further that:

> Swift's fantasy points toward incoherence, insanity, and the loss of a secure future; Defoe's novels are individualistic success stories. For most of Defoe's main characters [...], the future turns out to be better, more prosperous and also more stable, than the stormy seas of the past through which they have navigated. For Swift, credit (and the future) is near-allied to madness [...]. (Brantlinger 1996: 75)

While Defoe was certainly not uncritical towards the credit system, he embraces risk, where Swift (mostly) rejects it. The fears staged in Defoe's fictions concern the question of how to survive or to increase and secure 'new' wealth; Swift's fears the question of how to maintain order and ethics in society. Rather than focusing on the individual's chances and dangers of access and control over money, Swift, who had also invested and lost money in the South Sea Company, fears the moral impact of credit on Britain's 'value' system, an instability brought on by an order of corruption and gambling, and by a greedy individualism perpetuating into the ruling class and thus the whole nation. Although Swift shared Defoe's social concerns with the condition of the poor,⁶ in criticism he is generally considered much more of a traditionalist. Yet things are more complicated, because while Swift's narrator seemingly values stability and order, he also con-

---

4 Arthur E. Case emphasizes the importance of the historical context and suggests that "quite possibly we may date the conception of Gulliver early in that fall, when the significance of the South sea debacle was becoming evident" (1958: 107). Similarly, Pat Rogers writes that Swift's text looks "at the doings of speculators, engineers, inventors, and company promoters. Gulliver's Travels may have entered the history of ideas, thanks mainly to the Houyhnhnms and Yahoos. But it derives not just from a course of philosophic reading, but from a lively engagement in contemporary life, and a ready exposure to the popular news-stories of the day" (1985: 25).
5 For a general survey of Swift's body of economic writing, see Kelly (2003). For criticism which places the narrative in the context of the South Sea Bubble, see Nicholson (1994), Brantlinger (1996), and Duncan (2012).
6 Swift was, of course, concerned with the condition of poor in Ireland for which his well-known *A Modest Proposal for Preventing the Children of Poor People in Ireland, from being a Burden to their Parents* (1729) is the best example. Kelly describes the pamphlet as a reflection of "Swift's overwhelming despair at the failure of contemporary economic wisdom to offer any solution to Ireland's problems" (2003: 140).

stantly abandons his family for the lure of travel and adventure.[7] Interestingly, both Defoe and Swift utilize a shipwreck in their narratives, an event that references the original context in which the notion of risk emerged, and "an obvious metaphor for the general insecurities and disasters that beset economic man (and woman) and that imperil the nation ship of state" (Brantlinger 1996: 85). But while Swift reflects on similar themes as Defoe, a marked difference lies in their attitudes towards the British mission to conquer and 'civilize' foreign lands. Where Defoe puts forth a traditional view of the civilized/savage divide, and his Crusoe excels at becoming 'King' of his island, Swift rather "casts a cold eye on the motives and consequences of colonialism" (Todd 2003: 372).[8]

The novel sets the stage for the other texts under scrutiny in this chapter in numerous ways. The narrative perspective is a distinctly subjective and indisputably male one. Female characters play a less relevant role in comparison to the male protagonist and narrator, who is also, like Sterne's Tristram, highly unreliable. In fact, both Gulliver's integrity and the security of the narration itself are constantly undermined, and the uncertainties insinuated by Swift's narrative are

---

[7] Emphasising the radical anxiety expressed by Swift about altered practices, about the conflict between landed and moneyed interests, Nicholson writes: "In a sequence of narratives where Gulliver repeatedly leaves terra firma for the sea we read multiply ironic and compromised meditations on the historical transition from a morality founded on real property to one founded on capital liquidity, mobile property and the shifting vanities and fantasies of a new possessing class" (1994: 122).

[8] This issue can only be touched upon briefly here. Especially the last chapter of the novel is usually the focus of postcolonial readings, as Gulliver there gives what can rightly be considered as "one of the most pointed and all-encompassing critiques of colonialism to be found in early eighteenth-century literature" (Sussman 2000: 50). In the face of the British 'enslavement' of Ireland, Swift, being Anglo-Irish, suffered from a sense of guilt and conflicting solidarities, finding himself in a "schizophrenic" position for most of his life. Frequently attacking a system of exploitation that also benefitted him, he has often been described as being of a "divided mind" regarding the issues of national identity and colonialism, or as even as an "anti-colonial colonialist" (cf. Zach 1993: 96–97). I agree with Wolfgang Zach's argument that *Gulliver's Travels*, which firmly reasserts the spirit of liberty and anticolonialism, cannot be fully understood without Swift's troubled and conflicted loyalties. For example, we find clear condemnations of colonial oppression on the one hand in the episode of the tyrannical rule of the Flying Island over the people in Balnibarbi, or in the end of book IV. Yet Gulliver also idealizes his Houyhnhnm master's 'rational' rule over the passion-driven Yahoos. Throughout the narrative Swift uproots the chance to make generalizations about human nature, including the rigidity of categories like the 'civilized/savage' divide, and complicates judgment or justification of dominance of one race over another. Instead, Dennis Todd argues, he locates "contempt and cruelty everywhere, he finds that they spring from our certainty: certainty about our own superiority, certainty about our rightness, and, of course, certainty about what constitutes human nature itself" (2003: 376). On the subject of Swift and colonialism see also Hawes (1991).

of various kinds, discursive, mental, and physical. Gulliver is full of a naïve gullibility, pride and self-confidence. Although he does not develop, learn, or change, he is mainly distinguished by his curiosity, which is never abated by the memory of any of his past misfortunes (cf. Hunter 2003: 226; Nicholson 1994: 109; Real 2001: 98).

The narrative shows an almost obsessive concern with observation, with seeing and being seen.[9] With the faculty of vision being considered to be the most important and instructive of all senses in the age of Enlightenment empiricism, it is significant that "Lemeul Gulliver is perhaps the first bespectacled hero in English literature" (Rogers 1985: 1; 4) and himself characterized by weak eye sight. Thoroughly questioning the certainties derived from empirical observation, and playing with the juxtaposition of various transformations of scales and reversals of perspective which produces comic as well as disorienting effects, the narrative suggests that moral certainty is even harder to come by than 'sensibly' derived knowledge. Characteristic of the early novel, Swift's narrative displays elements such as a minute description of things and reflects cultural changes such empirical analysis and new technological ways of seeing, enabled, e.g. by the invention of the microscope. Through Gulliver's compulsive travels Swift also shows the dangerous side of modern empiricism, an over-curiosity, which produces insights which do not really benefit anybody. Furthermore, the narrative questions the possibility of a detached point of view and raises questions about 'just' standards for comparative analysis.[10]

Considering Gulliver's original scientific background – being a surgeon – he has a surprising and distinct air of naiveté about him. Also, he is never seen to practice his medical craft in the novel and his professional knowledge is shown as having clear limits, or even being altogether useless.[11] Significantly, he only encounters species and types of humans to which his expertise fails to apply; either the potential patients are too small, too big, or fall in the realm of veterinary science. The first voyage takes Gulliver to Lilliput, a world of miniature. The Lilliputians perceive the giant Gulliver initially as a risk and tie him to the

---

9 Rogers (1985: 7) draws attention to the many verbs denoting the activity of observation, which shape and control the narrative. In fact, the word 'observation' (including variations) occurs over 140 times in the novel.
10 The topic is relevant especially with regard to cross-cultural comparison and 18th-century theories of travel and measures of the European advance of civilization. For example, it was a firm 18th century belief that travel in space also meant travel in time, thus making the 'Others' encountered in foreign lands earlier ('backward') versions of themselves (cf. Fox 1998: 210–211)
11 On this subject see Allan Ingram's essay "Doctor at Sea: Gulliver and Medical Perception" (2013).

ground. But throughout his stay on the island, Gulliver notes how: "The natives came by degree to be less apprehensive of any danger from me" (GT 31), despite the fact that he could still extinguish them with a single careless footstep. The inhabitants of the state of Lilliput, often considered as an allegory representing England, come up with complicated calculations in order to determine Gulliver's food supply; "asking a friend at court how they came to fix on that determinate number, he told me that his Majesty's mathematicians, having taken the height of my body by the help of a quadrant, and finding it to exceed theirs in the proportion of twelve to one, they concluded from the similarity of their bodies, that mine must contain at least 1728 of theirs" (GT 39). This highlights the Lilliputians' reliance on empirical measures in order to deal with the stranger, as well as Gulliver's outsized difference. In order to repay them, he becomes actively involved in the long-standing controversy between Lilliput and Blefuscu about the correct 'end' of opening boiled eggs. He aids the king of Lilliput to attack Blefuscu by functioning as a giant war weapon: "I was ready, with the hazard of my life, to defend his person and state against all invaders" (GT 45). David McNeil argues about the depiction oft he Lilliputians: "Although we may recognize universal human fear and suspicion in their military precautions, everything Lilliputian seems somehow ludicrous simply because of its inconsequentiality [...] Swift exaggerates this pettiness, in accordance with the basic technique of the grotesque" (McNeil 1990: 66).[12] While Gulliver's support in this war is most welcome and secures the Lilliputians' victory against their enemies, it is ironically another attempt of Gulliver to try and 'save' the king from an accident, which leads to his fall from grace. He extinguishes a fire in the palace by urinating on the building which in turn ignites the anger of the Lilliputians, leading to an intrigue against Gulliver and his eventual flight from Lilliput.

All the 'nations' Gulliver visits cause him to reflect on matters of government, questions of war and peace, and the authority and moral character necessary to rule. For example, in his critical comparison of Lilliputian vs. British politics, he says:

> [...] the mistakes committed by ignorance in a virtuous disposition, would never be of such fatal consequence to the public weal, as the practices of a man whose inclinations led him to be corrupt [....]. In like manner, the disbelief of a Divine Providence renders a man

---

[12] On the topic of war in Gulliver's Travels see David McNeil's *The Grotesque Depiction of War and the Military in Eighteenth-Century English Fiction* (1990: 54–83). The final argument that "Swift was exceptional in his awareness of how fear and mechanical art could distort human conflict, and how history exaggerated the importance, if not the relentlessness, of military events" (1990: 83) is especially relevant.

uncapable of holding any public station; for, since kings avow themselves to be the deputies of Providence, the Lilliputians think nothing can be more absurd than for a prince to employ such men as disown the authority under which he acts. (GT 56)

Characteristically, he employs a rhetoric that equals a morally unfit government with high danger; moreover he satirizes the paradoxical tension caused by a loss of faith in divine providence and the persisting belief in the 'divine' hierarchical order of society.

Gulliver's second voyage takes him to Brobdingnag and brings a complete reversal of perspective. He boards the ship *Adventure*, soon caught in "a very fierce storm; the sea broke strange and dangerous" (GT 84). The storm leaves Gulliver stranded on an island, where he realizes that not just are the proportions of Lilliput reversed, but most crucially his own experience of power hierarchies. Suddenly he is at risk from other people, instead of being a threat to them. Hiding in the grass and watching the giant inhabitants of Brobdingnag, he "was struck with the utmost fear and astonishment" (GT 86). This also causes him to reflect on the fact that his own actions and judgments have put him in this situation and neither accidents, nor higher forces. He is also filled with a new perception of the Lilliputians:

> In this terrible agitation of mind I could not forebear thinking of Lilliput, whose inhabitants looked upon me as the greatest prodigy that ever appeared in the world; [...] I reflected what a mortification it must prove to me to appear as inconsiderable in this nation as one single Lilliputian would be among us. But this I conceived was to be the least of my misfortunes: for as human creatures are observed to be more savage and cruel in proportion to their bulk, what could I expect but to be a morsel in the mouth of the first among these enormous barbarians that should happen to seize me? (GT 111–12)

While he gains the valuable insight "that nothing is great or little otherwise than by comparison" (GT 112), Gulliver is constantly afraid during his stay at the palace where he is kept as a precious toy and source of amusement.[13] This does not go unnoticed by the Queen, who, unable to comprehend Gulliver's fearfulness and the precariousness of his state of "littleless", which exposes him "to several ridiculous and troublesome accidents" (GT 120), asks him "whether the people of my country were as great cowards as myself" (GT 113). Gulliver is nearly crashed by apples and hail corns, or falls into holes in the ground, but soon

---

[13] The scholars of Brobdingnag declare Gulliver to be a freak and joke of nature, a 'Lusus Naturae'. In this episode Swift engages also with the century's fascination with monstrosity and spectacle and the public exhibition of dwarfs etc. For a more detailed account of this, see, e.g., Fox (1998: 202–204).

"a more dangerous accident happened to me in the same garden" (GT 121). Gulliver is seized by a spaniel dog and only narrowly escapes death. All animals are potentially lethal dangers, besides dogs and frogs, "the greatest danger I ever underwent in that kingdom was from a monkey" (GT 127). He is also at risk when entertaining the royal family with his tricks, or gets dropped from dangerous heights, or into cream bowls.[14] Gulliver spends two years in the country, displayed and exploited like a slave by his giant masters. His escape from Brobdingnag is one of the most dramatic scenes. When Gulliver is finally allowed to go, he is provided with a house-sized box as a vessel of transportation. The box is picked up by a bird, but soon dropped into ocean. Gulliver, who thought himself safe inside the box, "began to perceive the woeful condition I was in" (GT 150). Calculating his slim chances of escape, he consequently wishes "every moment to be my last" (GT 152). After being finally rescued by a ship, he is haunted for a while by dreams of "the dangers I had escaped" (GT 155).

However, these memories do not last long, and after only a short stay with his wife and children Gulliver in book III journeys to Laputa, the Flying Island, whose inhabitants are obsessed with two things, arithmetic and music. Gulliver soon notices that the minds of some of the Laputians, called the "flappers", "are so taken up with intense speculations, that they neither can speak, nor attend to the discourses of others, without being roused by some external taction upon the organs of speech and hearing" (GT 172). This section satirizes the contemporary obsession with theoretical and new scientific knowledge, expanding so rapidly at the time. Its pursuit is shown to only lead to more confusion and less sympathy for others. An example of the lack of practicality and the mis-appliance of the inhabitants preoccupation with mathematics is the tailor taking Gulliver's measurements for a new set of clothes: "He first took my altitude by quadrant, and then with a rule and compasses described the dimensions and outline of my whole body, all which he entered upon paper, and in six days brought my clothes very ill made, and quite out of shape, by happening to mistake a figure in the calculation" (GT 175). Despite the use of fancy instruments, the result is literally ill fitting. Clearly, the object of criticism is the favouring of theory over practice,

---

14 Real is one the few critics who has tried to analyse the 'meaning' of Gulliver's series of misfortunes and accidents in Brobdingnag in detail; the episode is usually ignored in criticism. Real reads the accidents politically, for instance he dissects the cultural-historical connotations of the frog and the monkey and identifies them as references to threats to British rule by the Dutch and the Earls of Kildare (2001a: 83–84). This is less relevant in the present context; the accidents are significant, however, in underlining that the experience of fear and confrontation with the fears of others is a structuring principle of the narrative and the obvious reversal of perspective between book I and book II also relates to the depiction of the feeling of being at risk.

and the pursuit of scientific 'advance', which does nothing to improve the living conditions of the majority of people, but distracts the government from pressing concerns of the state: "Their houses are very ill built, the walls bevil, without one right angle in any apartment, and this defect ariseth from the contempt they bear to practical geometry, which they despise as vulgar and mechanic, those instructions they give being too refined for the intellectuals of their workmen, which occasions perpetual mistakes" (GT 176). In fact, the preoccupation with theory is not just unproductive, but appears downright ruinous in Gulliver's eyes. Furthermore, the Laputians are described as being "under continual disquietudes, never enjoying a minute's peace of mind; and their disturbances proceed from causes which very little affect the rest of mortals. Their apprehensions arise from several changes they dread in the celestial bodies" (GT 178). The Laputians' knowledge brings fear rather than greater clarity or stability, and a majority of their time is spent on the calculation of pending doom. They are, for instance, terribly afraid of comets and the movement of stars and the sun in the sky, which they observe with telescopes. It leads them to prognostics of apocalyptic scenarios such as that of the next comet,

> which they have calculated for one and thirty years hence, will probably destroy us. For if in its perihelion it should approach within a certain degree of the sun (as by their calculations they have reason to dread) it will conceive a degree of heat ten thousand times more intense than that of red-hot glowing iron; [...] if the earth should pass at the distance of one hundred thousand miles from the nucleus or main body of the comet, it must in its passage be set on fire, and reduced to ashes. (GT 178)

As a consequence, Gulliver notes how the people are completely robbed of any quality of life, dominated by (unlikely) risk perceptions and

> so perpetually alarmed with the apprehensions of these, and the like impending dangers, that they can neither sleep quietly in their beds, nor have any relish for the common pleasures and amusements of life. When they meet an acquaintance in the morning, the first question is about the sun's health, how *he* looked at his setting and rising, and what hopes they have to avoid the stroke of the approaching comet. (GT 178; my emphasis)

The male pronoun used by Gulliver denotes a striking gender difference he becomes aware of: The obsession with calculating dangers is an exclusively masculine preoccupation. Meanwhile the women engage in flirtations and generally "act with too much ease and security; for the husband is always so rapt in speculation" (GT 179). On these grounds, Gulliver is soon glad to leave Laputa, and its people, "so abstracted and involved in speculation, that I never met with such disagreeable companions" (GT 190). Particularly from a contemporary reader's perspective, Swift's narrative rings with a prophetic quality and reads like a satire of an over-apprehensive risk society, immobilized by a calculation of dangers as a result of their overly-scientific minds. This adds another dimension to the timeless appeal of Swift's satire. Stephan Haller, although arguing in a different disciplinary context, underlines the connection between the early 18th-century and our present-day perception and management in his reading of Swift. He sees a great topicality of Swift's description of Laputa as an illustration of the difficulties of judging risk and the necessity of precaution. Accordingly, Swift pokes

> fun at those who are in a perpetual state of anxiety over potential doom. The cloud-dwelling Laputians were incessant doomsayers – [...] We are in much the same position today. We also have predictions of a catastrophic end to our environment and our ways of life and are greeted daily with discussions of potential environmental disaster. Swift suggests that the Laputians wasted their energies worrying about threats that were not well enough founded to justify their reaction to them. (2000: 176)

The fearful Laputians also employ risk as a principle of government, not in the abstract Foucauldian notion of inducing fear via bureaucracy and surveillance, but by direct threat. They use their floating island, which keeps them safe from outside intrusion, as a means to exercise power over the people of Balnibarbi on the ground beneath, and to restore them to obedience, either by simply obstructing sun and rain or, in more serious cases, by dropping the island onto them. Yet this manoeuvre bears high risks for the Laputians themselves and is therefore not executed "unless upon the utmost necessity. For, if the town intended to be destroyed should have in it any tall rocks, [...], a sudden fall might endanger the bottom or under surface of the island" (GT 186).

Critics usually perceive the Laputa episode to contain two types of satirist material, scientific and political ideas and events. For example, Robert Fitzgerald interprets Swift's Flying Island as an illustration of the idea of sovereignty, of rule "from above", and a critique of tyranny, which has only brute force and fear to set against the threat of a rebellion "from below" (Fitzgerald 1988: 223). He also reads the sun and the comets feared by the Laputians as political symbols for the fear of the monarch (sun) and omens of public disaster (comet). However far one wants to trace the political symbolism, it is a plausible argument that Swift's narrative plays with the thought of contemporary philosophers and scientists like Hobbes who acknowledge "fear as central to their thinking: the fear of the anarchy and chaos that follows the breakdown of order" (1988: 224).[15] Regarding the scientific context, the Laputians are depicted as learned

---

15 Fitzgerald reads the Lagado episode explicitly as Swift's exploration of forms of government

people yet more afraid than their superstitious ancestors, and their fears are rooted profoundly in contemporary science. General developments in astronomy, like Newton's theories of gravity and planetary movements, received public attention in the early 18th century. According to Nicholson and Mohler, Swift's depiction of the Laputians' fear about a comet reducing the earth to ashes refers to something real, which would not have escaped Swift's contemporary audience, Halley's comet, "the first comet whose period of return was definitely predicted with resultant great excitement both to literary and to scientific imagination" (Nicholson and Mohler 1937: 312). Both scientific and political implications of the metaphor cluster around the notion of risk and imply the threat of a loss of order, or even destruction. It also shows the intertwining of scientific risk perception and politics; it reveals the power of fear, be it perpetuated by the rulers from 'above' or by learned 'experts.'

Gulliver's account of his visit to the grand "Academy of Projectors" (GT 194) in Lagado, wholly dedicated to the "advancers of speculative learning" (GT 199) is often read as Swift's ironic portrayal of the Royal Society, and their (mis)direction of efforts, values, and resources.[16] The Lagado academy is engaged in risky and pointless experiments, like extracting sunlight from a cucumber, turning human waste back into food, or that of a "great physician" (GT 199) who tries to cure disease by blowing wind into a dog's anus. The projects also include a basic computer, or randomization machine,[17] ideas to economize human communication by having people carry all items needed to signify objects and ideas around with them, and many others.[18] As Gulliver observes, these people "fell into schemes of putting all arts, sciences, languages, and mechanics upon a new foot" (GT 194), and sought "new rules for and methods of agriculture and building, and new instruments and tools for all trades and manufacturers" (GT 194). Therefore, some critics see Swift's depiction of the projects in the Grand Academy closer to business schemes and crazy ideas which "were everywhere during the Bubble mania" (Rogers 1985: 19; see Nicholson 1994: 100; Duncan 2012: 13),

---

and ideas of a 'just' commonwealth. He relates the sun-comet symbolism to the Whigs and the threat of Protestant succession (1988: 225).

16 In a much cited essay, Nicholson and Mohler (1937) have argued that Swift borrowed from very discernible sources in this episode and that the inspiration for the Flying Island and the Grand Academy came from contemporary science and publications such as the Philosophical Transactions of the Royal Society. For this argument see also Nicholson (1994: 99), Smith (1990b), and Fox (1998).

17 See Eric A. Weiss's "Jonathan Swift's Computing Invention" (1985).

18 On the cultivation of the experimental spirit and the creation of new laboratories by the Royal Society from the mid-17th century, which set goals which were, perhaps, too ambitious, see Shapin and Schaffer (1985: 339 f).

than to experiments of the Royal Society. As Rogers argues, the contemporary notions of "projects" and "projector" were powerful ones, but "had very little semantic relation to academic science" (1985: 19). Gulliver's criticism of the new "enterprising spirit" and the disregard of "the old forms" (GT 194) in the episode support the argument that the 'projectors' he encounters in Lagado are referential to the activities of contemporary stockjobbers.[19] Speculation is pursued to absurd extremes, but "none of these projects are yet brought to perfection, and in the mean time, the whole country lies miserably waste, [...] the people without food or shelter. By all of which, instead of being discouraged, they are fifty times more violently bent upon prosecuting their schemes, driven equally on by hope and despair" (GT 194). If one wants to place the satirical focus on financial, entrepreneurial, or scientific speculation, in either case "Swift's imaginative exploration of speculative initiatives brings the risk which they entailed into acute recognition" (Duncan 2012: 14).

When Gulliver encounters the Struldbrugs, he initially envies them for their freedom from man's greatest fear, "being born exempt from that universal calamity of human nature, have their minds free and disengaged, without the weight and depression of spirits caused by the continual apprehensions of death!" (GT 227). Interestingly, part of the many inconsistencies in the opinion about science in Swift's narrative is Gulliver's dream of what he would do with immortality, namely utilizing the time to acquire scientific knowledge in order to make predictions and accurate calculations, especially in the arena of politics, ultimately aiming to preserve the moral state of the nation:

> I would carefully record every action and event of consequence, that happened in the public, [...] I would exactly set down the several changes in customs, language, fashions of dress, diet, and diversions. [...] These *struldbrugs* and I would mutually communicate our observations [...] giving perpetual warning and instruction to mankind; which, added to the strong influence of our own example, would probably prevent that continual degeneracy of human nature so justly complained of in all ages. (GT 229–230)[20]

---

19 See Nicholson's suggestion that "Exchange Alley would be the appropriate neighbourhood for siting Lagado because the cultural matrix of Gulliver's travels was the projecting society Swift knew" (1994: 100). Rogers also sees a clear evocation of the Bubble era in Swift's satire, rather than of Royal Academy of Science experiments, arguing that the latter were activities of a relatively secluded, elitist group of people: "Its cultural matrix can be defined as the Age of Projectors – a bustling, uncerebral world of entrepreneurs and inventors. [...] Swift, I shall argue, meant to site Lagado nearer Exchange Alley than Gresham College" (1985: 12).
20 Like Defoe in *A Journal of the Plague Year*, Swift takes up the topic of demographics and the calculation of life expectancies in this episode.

Gulliver displays a firm belief in the advance of science as part of the future, because during a prolonged life, he imagines that he should live to see "the discovery of the longitude, the perpetual motion, the universal medicine, and many other great inventions, brought to the utmost perfection" (GT 230). In fact, he dreams of an active participation in the age of speculation: "What wonderful discoveries should we make in astronomy, by outliving and confirming our own predictions; by observing the progress and return of comets [...]" (GT 230). But regarding this dream, Gulliver soon comes to realize the miseries of eternal life, as the Struldbrugs "had not only all the follies and infirmities of other older men, but many more which arose from the dreadful prospect of never dying" (GT 232). In this part of the narrative Swift, by this time in his life increasingly conscious of bodily decay and his own dwindling strength, takes up the theme of the fear of old age and physical and mental loss, concerns which also feature prominently in Sterne's *Tristram Shandy*. The Struldbrugs suffer from aches and pains, social isolation and disappearing memory. Thus, as J. Paul Hunter comments, Swift includes into the account of the Struldbrugs, "virtually every mortal anxiety except the fear of mortality itself" (2003: 234).

After another brief spell of domestic life in England, Gulliver admits that he is still incapable of learning "the lesson of knowing when I was well" (GT 243) and sails out again as captain of the *Adventure*. This stay is the one that causes Gulliver's hatred of his own race. In the country of the Houyhnhnms, he sees the deficiencies of man in contrast to the ruling class of horses, creatures capable of pure rationality and whose name means "the perfection of nature" (GT 259). Gulliver's many prolonged conversations with his Houyhnhnm master about England and his own 'race' give satirical insight into the irrational, passion-side of risk-taking as intrinsic to human nature.[21] This contrasts with the Houyhnhnms, who, being purely rational, fail to grasp the concept and condemn the running of hazards and the taking of chances (which is, of course, the standpoint any extreme rationalist would have to take). This becomes clear in Gulliver's report of his last voyage when he was commander of the ship and

> had about fifty *yahoos* under me, many of which died at sea, and I was forced to supply them by others picked out from several nations; that our ship was twice in danger of being sunk, the first time by a great storm, and the second by striking against a rock.

---

[21] Gulliver's stay among the Houyhnhnms and the Yahoos is the part of the narrative that has inspired the most critical debate. The majority of it concerns the questions of Swift's attitude towards human nature, either stressing Swift's dark satire, tragedy, and the shock element in the so-called 'hard' schools of interpretation, or a more benevolent didacticism, compromise, and comedy in the 'soft' school approaches. See Clifford (1974).

> Here my master interposed, by asking me, how I could persuade strangers, out of different countries, to venture with me, after the losses I had sustained, and the hazards I had run? I said, they were fellows of desperate fortunes, [...]; none of these durst return to their native countries, for fear of being hanged, or of starving in a jail; [....]. (GT 268)

Gulliver's narrative implies that desperation and dissatisfaction with one's current state motivate the taking of dangers. He furthermore struggles to explain to the leader of the horses the existence of diseases or the concept of doctors and cures. It forces him to admit that a lot of suffering is self-inflicted by people's irrational behaviour:

> I told him we fed on a thousand things which operated contrary to each other; that we ate when we were not hungry, and drank without the provocation of thirst; [...] many other diseases, were propagated from father to son; so that great numbers came into the world with complicated maladies upon them; that it would be endless to give him a catalogue of all diseases incident to human bodies, for they would not be fewer than five or six hundred, spread over every limb and joint – [...]. (GT 279–280)

To this, he adds a harsh criticism of his own profession, saying that the human race is subject to as many real as imaginary diseases and that the doctors are mainly distinguished by "their skill at prognostics, wherein they seldom fail; their predictions in real diseases, when they rise to any degree of malignity, generally portending death, which is always in their power, when recovery is not" (GT 281).

When the master has to judge in how far Gulliver's poses a threat to the Houyhnhnms, he is aware of his bad dispositions and belonging to a corrupt, war-faring species, but concludes, "however, it is happy that the shame is greater than the danger" (GT 272). But still Gulliver's account of his own people and their similarities to the Yahoos causes the Houyhnhnms master some uneasiness and he no longer perceive them as ignorant, yet innocent, but sees them instead as dangerously corruptible and prone to evil, be it out of desperation or temptation. The Yahoos' unmasked greed and interest in money is one of the characteristics which lead Gulliver to see uncanny parallels with his fellow humans. Main differences between humans/Yahoos and the naturally virtuous Houyhnhnms are that the latter do not have a conception of evil, and are furthermore incapable of muddling the clarity of their decisions with desires, opinions, or of diluting rational reasoning with debates of opinion. For them, Gulliver admiringly states, reason is not "[...] discoloured, by passion and interest. I remember it was with extreme difficulty that I could bring my master to understand the meaning of the word opinion [...] controversies, wranglings, disputes, and positiveness, in false or dubious propositions, are evils unknown among the Houyhnhnms" (GT 295–296).

Therefore, Gulliver's beloved horse-master cannot comprehend how credit and speculation can inform the basis of a society, and "he would laugh that a creature pretending to reason should value itself upon the knowledge of other peoples conjectures, and in things where that knowledge, if it were certain, could be of no use" (GT 296). This attitude, of course, also completely excludes a concept of risk. Without judging the rationality of any of the fears portrayed in the narrative, one can only agree with Colin Nicholson's point that "Swift's literary technique invokes a lost integrity of discourse to produce an anxiety of orientation, a dislocating indeterminacy to which Gulliver and his first readers are subjected much as we are" (1994: 111). However, Swift undeniably imagined Houyhnhnm-land as the utopian ideal of a safe, completely risk-free society, and not just because the concept itself is unfeasible for the inhabitants. In a society of 'purely' rational creatures, all evils and dangers of human society, mental and physical, the passions, risky ventures, criminals schemes, motivated by freed and other disturbing emotions would be gone. Among the Houyhnhnms, Gulliver tells the reader:

> I enjoyed perfect health of body, and tranquillity of mind; [...] I wanted no fence against fraud or oppression: here was neither physician to destroy my body, nor lawyer to ruin my fortune; no informer to watch my words and actions, or forge accusations against me for hire: here were no gibers, censurers, backbiters, pickpockets, highwaymen, housebreakers, attorneys, bawds, buffoons, gamesters, politicians, wits, splenetics, tedious talkers, controvertists, ravishers, murderers, robbers [...]. (GT 306)

3.2 Risky Games and the Disorder of Passion: *Roderick Random*

Often described as episodic and somewhat eclectic, Smollett's fictions are not always included in the grand canon of the 18th century novel and remain marginalized in comparison to the works of Defoe, Fielding or Richardson.[22] Displaying a lack of formal design and structural sophistication on the one hand, and of experimentalism on the other, Smollett's works still employ formulas of the earlier romance to a larger extend than those of some of his contemporaries and

---

[22] John Skinner admits that Smollett only "has a limited appeal" (1996: 9) within 18th century studies, and has been neglected in comparison to his contemporaries. See also Adamson (1989: 12) and Beasley (1998: 36).

many seem to owe more to accidental accumulation than to constructive design.²³ In his introduction to Smollett's first novel, W.H. Hodges claims that "the varied and lively episodes in the many changes and chances of his hero's fortunes make it possible to read his *Roderick* literally at random" (1964: xiii). Yet, as many critics, most prominently perhaps Paul-Gabriel Boucé (1976), have argued, Smollett's *The Adventures of Roderick Random* (1748) achieves some coherence through the consistent pursuit of the relation between adventure and morality in the text.²⁴

Referring to chance and risk already in the eponymous hero's name,²⁵ the plot is full of coincidences and hazards of all sorts, which take place in settings typical for the 18th-century novel, i.e. on the road, at inns, at sea, on battle fields, in the labyrinth of the metropolitan city, and in prison (cf. Bunn 1981: 456). While one can see in the protagonist's name a suggestion of "not only the arbitrary twists of fortune to which the hero is exposed, but also a corresponding lack of pattern in his adventures: Random the man, and random his narrative" (Skinner 1996: 209), other critics have rightly modified this claim and seen chance itself as a main structuring principle in the narrative. For instance, Jerry Beasley writes, "from moment to moment, scene to scene, episode to episode; causality, most often unintelligible in its specific workings, goes by the name of Chance or Fortune" (1998: 39). Although Smollett does not develop any full theory of randomness in the narrative, or include philosophical reflections on causality or chance like Laurence Sterne in *Tristram Shandy*, he still captures a major cultural anxiety and presents "a narrative imaging of randomness as an epistemological

---

23 See Skinner (1996: 9–30) for a summary of the reception history of Smollett's first novel. He argues that *Roderick Random*, published a year before *Tom Jones*, has been unjustly criticized and measured against the 'novel' standard set by Fielding's monumental work. An example of such a negative comparison of the two works is Leopold Damrosch's comment that Smollett's novel is "an utterly un-Aristotelian work that looks back to Elizabethan rogue narratives, puts its unlovable hero through a series of disasters and recoveries that are as random as the title suggests, and ends by conferring wealth, a wife, and a long-lost father he has done nothing to deserve" (1985: 286).
24 According to Boucé, adventure in the novel "has an educative function on the physical, intellectual and moral plane;" he also underlines the structuring force of the struggle of good vs. evil (1976: 123; 142–43).
25 The names of Smollett's protagonists often bear connotations to the activity of travelling, like Peregrine Pickle, or Ferdinand Count Fathom, with Ferdinand referring etymologically to the Old German words, '*fardi*' ('journey') and '*nathi*' ('venture or risk') (see Skinner 1996: 209). With the exception of Humphry Clinker, all his fictions furthermore deal with the protagonist's 'adventures'. Interestingly, in Johnson's *Dictionary* of 1755, the contemporary meaning of the term 'adventure' is defined as "an accident; a chance; a hazard; an event of which we have no direction" (cited in Adamson 1989: 242).

position" (Beasley 1998: 72). Stressing a different angle on this subject, according to W.H. Hodges,

> the structure of his story, for it cannot be said to possess a plot, is therefore consciously derived from the Picaresque school of writers [....]. Smollett intends to provide us with a novel depicting crowded hours of adventurous life by sea and land, in the tavern or the gambling-den, and introducing in almost bewildering succession types of all sorts and conditions of men (Hodges 1964: ix)

The novel functions as an illustration of chance and, through Roderick's series of misfortunes and coincidences, shows how the picaresque tradition, based on the rogue heroe's encounters with chance and his drifting through time and space, embraces a particular line of thought, namely the "emergent eighteenth-century epistemology based upon minute accidents within large populations – that is probability theory" (Bunn 1981: 453).[26] Besides satire, romance, and autobiography, the critical genre parameters of the picaresque are most commonly applied to *Roderick Random*, a narrative that situates Smollett in a line of tradition with writers such as Cervantes, Swift, or Defoe. Recently, Margaret Cohen (2010) has argued that *Roderick Random* falls into a specific subgenre, the maritime picaresque, which comprises picaresque novels in which large sections are set at sea. This is worth considering insofar that the 'sea chapters' are typically considered to be the most memorable in the whole novel (see Beasley 1998: 62; Lewis 2003: 33). This point is underlined by Hodges who sees the special value of Smollett's debut novel in the fact that the reader encounters "for the first time in 'true' fiction, a new set of characters taken from the quarter-decks and forecastles of His Majesty's ships. Neither Defoe nor Swift nor Fielding had the first hand-experi-

---

[26] While Bunn draws attention to the fact that patterns of repeated accidents occur in many 18th century novels (1981: 467), he sees Smollett's text and Roderick's journey and struggle for fixity (of place, social position, professional identity) in particular as an illustration of probability, randomness and a new scepticism about structures of cause-effect. By the mid-18th century, urban population had grown so large that it became possible to 'vanish' in the crowd, therefore, Bunn claims, the text also illustrates an early sense of "statistical anonymity" (456). Reading the novel alongside Hume's *Enquiry*, published in the same year, he argues: "Questions of randomness, accident, or improbable event, and the anonymity of large numbers render certainty about personal identity a matter of conjecture rather than confidence. Statistical inquiry and probability theory enter eighteenth-century epistemology at the same time as Hume's philosophical quandary about personal identity being hopelessly mixed with the apparent randomness of a sequence of events in time" (457). However, the picaresque fiction in general reveals a particular world view which calls for the negotiation of concepts such as chance, fortune, choice, necessity, luck, contingency, determinism.

ence of the Navy, essential for the task;" thus *Roderick Random* triggered a "public taste for sea fiction" (1964: xiii; x).

As is the case with many 18th-century writers and their works, it is difficult to "escape the autobiographical dimension" (Skinner 1996: 64) with Smollett, and in particular Roderick Random has called forth autobiographically-oriented criticism.[27] Emphasizing the author's connection to risk in this life and profession, John O'Brien writes:

> Smollett is a promising example of someone who had close contact with the aleatory, in areas where careful assessment of risk was a life or death question. Smollett was trained as a physician, a job that in the eighteenth century even more than now relied on reading physical signs and assessing the probabilities that they indicated various types of illness; in the absence of modern clinical testing, the interpretation of signs – an art of weighing probabilities – was all that Smollett or any eighteenth-century physician had to go on. And, to add an extra layer to his experience with the aleatory, Smollett was for a time naval surgeon, serving as a surgeon's mate in the British navy for about two years. That is, he spent time at sea, the site where chance, fortune, was imagined to have its greatest sway, the place of greatest risk. (2011: 293–294) [28]

Set in the 1730s and 40s, the narrative tells the life story of Roderick Random, son of a Scottish gentleman and a lower-class woman, who dies soon after his birth. After the subsequent disappearance of his father, and shunned by the rest of his paternal family, Random has to endure hardship from childhood and can only rely on the occasional support of his maternal uncle, Tom Bowling, a sailor, who opens Roderick's way into the life of travel and sea-faring adventures which take him to London, Bath, France, the Caribbean, West Africa and South America. Together with his loyal companion Hugh Strap, Roderick tries various schemes and professions in order to gain the financial means to

---

[27] In criticism there is a marked tendency to read Roderick Random with a strong autobiographical focus, although Smollett himself tried to oppose such readings directly after publication in various letters and in an "Apologue" to the 1760 edition of the text. In a letter to an American admirer, he writes: "The only similitude between the circumstances of my own fortune and those I have attributed to Roderick Random consists in my being born of a reputable family in Scotland, in my being bred a surgeon, and having served as a surgeon's mate on board of a man of war during the expedition to Cartagena. The low situations in which I have exhibited Roderick I never experienced in my person" (cited in Lewis 2003: 10). For details on the autobiographical speculation, which has haunted the novel and for the partially strong support available in Smollett's letters to back up the correspondence between the young author and his protagonist, see Skinner (1996: 40; 47) and Paul-Gabriel Boucé (1976: 40–67).

[28] An informative biography of Smollett is Lewis (2003). Other useful studies of Smollett and the historical context include Jones (2011) and Brack (2007). On the state of Smollett criticism and the contemporary reception of the novel, see L. Kelly (1995).

reclaim his position in society. These include fortune-hunting by attracting rich heiresses, being a naval surgeon, a soldier, a footman, or an apothecary, and generally switching identities as readily as locations. In the narrative, Roderick explains it thus: "If one scheme of life should not succeed, I could have recourse to another, and so to a third, veering about to a thousand different shifts, according to the emergencies of my fate, without forfeiting the dignity of my character beyond a power of retrieving it, or subjecting myself wholly to the caprice and barbarity of the world" (RR 141). Examples of this spirit run through the novel. Although acting mainly impulsively, his choice of schemes and professions are presented with an ironic mix of spontaneity, desperate necessity, and thoughtful calculation. For example, Roderick says: "Having, therefore, maturely weighed the circumstances *pro* and *con*, I signified my consent, and was admitted into the regiment of Picardy, said to be the oldest corps in Europe" (RR 243); a while later, he reflects on a number of options as follows:

> When I thought of turning merchant, the smallness of our stock, and the risk of seas, enemies, and markets, deterred me from that scheme. If I should settle as a surgeon in my own country, I would find the business already overstocked; or, if I pretended to set up in England, must labour under want of friends and powerful opposition, obstacles insurmountable by the most shining merit: neither should I succeed in my endeavours to rise in the state, inasmuch as I could neither flatter nor pimp for courtiers, nor prostitute my pen in defence of a wicked and contemptible administration. (RR 253)

He then decides to try this luck again by attracting a rich lady, but once more fails in this efforts and, "Baffled hitherto in my matrimonial schemes, I began to question my talents for the science of fortune-hunting, and to bend my thoughts towards some employment under the government" (RR 303). The episodic plot consists of a series of failures of Roderick's schemes, until he is finally rescued by a stroke of good luck when he is happily reunited with his now wealthy father in Argentina. After inheriting sufficient funds from him, Roderick is finally able to return home to Scotland, take up his position as a gentleman, and marry his beloved Narcissa without the consent of her guardian brother.

The plot and the ending are foreshadowed in the beginning of the narrative, which opens with a dream Roderick's mother had during her pregnancy: "She dreamed she was delivered of a tennis-ball, which the devil (who, to her great surprise, acted the part of the midwife) struck so forcibly with a racket, that it disappeared in an instant; [....] when all of a sudden, she beheld it return with equal violence, and enter the earth beneath her feet, whence immediately sprung up a goodly tree covered with blossoms" (RR 9). A highland sage interprets this to Roderick's parents as a sign that "their first-born would be a great traveller; that he would undergo many dangers and difficulties, and at last return to his native land, where he would flourish in happiness and reputation" (RR 9). Despite its proclaimed 'randomness', the novel thus has a discernible circular structure. A function of Roderick's mother's dream, which appears like a satire on the force of Providence, is to reassure the reader of the fate of the hero, and to create suspense, which is, however, "of an intellectual nature and not purely an emotional thrill. The certainty that the hero's life will be saved, whatever the danger that threatens him, only heightens the dramatic interest" (Boucé 1976: 105). There is another dimension to the comparison between the course of the hero's life and the forceful bouncing-back of a tennis ball. The metaphor introduces the element of physicality and violent action, and relates also to the telling name of Smollett's protagonist.[29] James Bunn stresses this point, saying:

> When we think of the word 'random,' we usually mean 'at random'; but the time-tested root of 'random' always involves violent action: to ride, to run, to drive, to strike with extreme force. [...] we may construe Smollett as being quite literally correct in creating a character named Random whose ruling passion is to strike back, as does Roderick, with physical violence. (Bunn 1981: 466)

In fact, physical threats and violence are predominant from the beginning. A large part of Roderick's education consists of experiencing the arbitrariness of punishments, cruelty, and physical force as the only way to solve conflicts and assert authority. This is particularly obvious in the duel scenes. Despite being wounded, Roderick feels only relief and pride afterwards: "Now that the danger was past, I was very well pleased with what had happened, hoping that it would soon become known, and, consequently, dignify my character not a little in this place" (RR 361). The description of the duel itself, as the ultimate symbol of gentlemanly courage and tradition, turns it into a farce and exposes the uncontrollability and irrationality of the event, motivated merely by passion and the desire for revenge. Also the attachment between Roderick and his "faithful sidekick" (Beasley 1998: 54) is formed by Hugh Strap having saved Roderick's life once, "at the risk of his own; and often fathered offences that I had committed, for which he suffered severely, rather than I should feel the weight of the punishment I deserved" (RR 24). Central to the behavioural pattern and characterization of Roderick are paradoxical feelings of persecution, unjust accusation, neglect, and abandonment, "together with its corollary, the overwhelming desire for

---

29 Rivka Swenson sees the choice of name as part of Smollett's typological characterization and a symbolic reference to Roderick's life as just one among many other travelling Scotsmen at the time (2011: 1983).

revenge" (Skinner 1996: 22; 56).[30] He grows up being in competition against a world, which is "constantly elbowing him out of the way" (Braudy 1981: 623). Young Roderick's self-assessment of his situation is symptomatic in this regard:

> As I was now capable of reflection, I began to consider my precarious situation; that I was utterly abandoned by those whose duty it was to protect me; and that my sole dependence was on the generosity of one man [his uncle], who was not only exposed by his profession to continual dangers, which might one day deprive me of him forever; but also, no doubt, subject to those vicissitudes of disposition which a change of fortune usually creates, [....]. (RR 27)

Soon afterwards, Roderick embarks on this first journey into the world; throughout his following adventures, he frequently states that he is "deserted to all horrors of extreme want" (RR 33), or "in danger of perishing by want" (RR 216). About a quarter into the narrative, Roderick finds himself:

> by the inequity of mankind, in a much more deplorable condition than ever: for though I had been formerly as poor, [...] at present my good name was lost, my money gone, my friends were alienated, my body was infected by a distemper contracted in the course of an amour, and my faithful Strap, who alone could yield me pity and assistance, absent I knew not where. (RR 119)

As mentioned above, with regard to risk, Smollett's protagonist spends little time calculating and considering circumstances and rather acts impulsively. Jerry Beasley emphasizes this point saying that Smollett "did not make his hero a reflective fellow; Roderick shows almost no interest in drawing connections among the many episodes recounted from his memory [...]. He initiates little in his life; instead, people and events happen to him" (1998: 40). Similarly, Phillip Stevick writes: "There are no alternatives to anything he does, either in his own mind or in ours. There is no particular play of consequences, nor are there any rewards" (1971: 114). This suggests a link between the narrative's formal construction, i.e. the fragmented, episodic structure, which lacks causal coherence, and the eponymous hero, who is incapable of the kind of inner reflection which the next novel under scrutiny in this chapter, Sterne's *Tristram Shandy*, takes to parodist extremes. However, Roderick is very aware of the dangers of losing one's reputation, of misjudging the character of strangers and acquaintances, and of the very basic dangers springing from want of food, shelter, the support of family and friends, and, of course, financial means. But in Roderick's first person

---

[30] Boucé notes that "revenge" is a key word particularly in the first half of the narrative (1976: 106).

account risk is constructed mainly from the outside. The reader, by contrast, quickly realizes what continuously puts his life and happiness at risk: pride and passion for vengeance, paired with a certain naiveté of the world.

Surviving adventures, hardships, and risk-taking are construed as necessary parts of Roderick's rite of passage. In contrast to Gulliver or Robinson Crusoe, Roderick has to travel, and only returns to his home country once circumstances allow him to do so in what he considers 'a creditable way' (RR 208). According to Michael McKeon, the driving force in the novel is the hero's "status inconsistency" (1987: 17). Throughout his apparently random journeys, Roderick struggles to achieve the stability and means of the gentleman-status of his birth. Yet he seeks to restore the order he so desperately wants by employing courage rather than calculation. As an inexperienced, rather angry young man, he continuously gets caught up in battles of pride, leaving all reason behind. His main problem is to control his temper. Moreover, he is stubborn, does not really learn from his experiences and continues to trust appearances, which gets him into trouble more than once. Most good advice, usually given by older men, comes too late. An example is Roderick's mistake to trust an apparently friendly stranger during a stay at the Bedford Coffee-house:

> He was no sooner gone than the old gentleman took me aside, and said, he was sorry to see me so intimate with that fellow, who was one of the most graceless rakes about town, [...] and setting a lewd example of all manner of wickedness; and that, unless I were on my guard, he would strip me in a short time both of my money and reputation. I thanked him for his information, and promised to conduct myself accordingly, wishing, however, his caution had been a few hours more early, by which means I might have saved five guineas. (RR 287)

Like its narrator, Smollett's novel does not explain or theorize but shows by example. It illustrates the unpredictability of life and of people in particular. The greatest danger for Roderick comes from his own behaviour and that of others. While Smollett's fictions negotiate general questions about chance and determination, they also suggest, O'Brien writes, "that people constitute a greater risk than do physical objects, or at least that a person runs no less a risk attempting to ensure against the unpredictability of human actions as against the chanciness of the material world" (2011: 294).

The danger and difficulty of judging appearances and the struggle to gain control over one's passions are the main moral themes in the narrative and constitute Roderick's 'education', which he has to master before he can achieve balance and stability. With the duel scenes being symptomatic for the pattern of "physical escalation" (McNeil 1990: 104), which furthermore includes the battle scenes on board the ship, and various brawls, or robberies, the narrative establishes a psychological connection between hurt pride and masculine rage. Any confrontation with differences leads to physical violence. In this regard, the tension between the risk management typically chosen by the narrator and the proposed 'moral' of the text is very clear. The protagonist embodies pride, passion, and the desire for power and advance as driving forces in human society. The conflicts between reason and instinct being an ancient topic in philosophical discussions of human nature, Smollett illustrates this tension on his protagonist, but the exploration of psychology never turns openly didactic. As a violent emotion, Roderick's pride is a risk to himself and to others. According to William Adamson (1989), the novel almost equals pride with a sort of 'madness', in the sense of a dangerous condition of 'disorder'. Interestingly, Adamson emphasizes two psychological aspects in Roderick's characterization that relate to his risk-taking: Firstly, that "the prospect of not reaching the heady heights of social success frightens him", and secondly, that "Roderick's vanity is so strong that it even overrides material considerations, which indicates his inability to look beyond the moment and consider the possible consequences of his heated actions" (Adamson 1989: 120). Throughout the narrative, Roderick's desires and temper impair his judgment and make him vulnerable.

Like many of Defoe's protagonists, Roderick is obsessed with economic progress and struggles to survive in a society prone to corruption, deceit, and violence. Such a depiction of the world is typical of the picaresque genre, challenging the hero to find survival tactics and still preserve his moral integrity against all odds. Regarding the matter of finding means of survival, Phillip Stevick stresses the element of picaresque play and games, which are in Roderick's case motivated by a pattern of "humiliation and revenge, provocation and response, challenge and defense" (Stevick 1971: 115; see McNeil 1990: 85).[31] Roderick's attitude towards gambling is interesting in this context. While Roderick's actions seem instinctual and random, rather than calculated, risk is a constant presence. Throughout the novel, lucky periods intersect with disastrous ones, which creates a noticeable structure of gain-loss-regain. After every setback, Roderick typically begins "to deliberate with myself in what manner I should attempt to retrieve the movables I had so foolishly lost" (RR 310). Although he says of himself "I was not much inclined to gaming" (RR 76), he cannot resists the offer to engage in various games of chance, be it cards, dice or roulette, when he is desperate. Once started, he often fails to control himself,

---

[31] Games of a (typically male) picaresque hero usually consist of trying to be quicker and cleverer than the authorities or villain characters, typically involving fraud, disguise, trickery; yet he is never in danger of excess or being corrupted by play, and he always plays for a higher end.

for instance, at the card-table, Roderick and Hugh "were very soon stripped of all our gains" (RR 76) and are afterwards told by an older gentleman: "But what in the name of goodness could provoke you to tempt your fate so long? It is always a maxim with gamesters to pursue success as far as it will go, and to stop whenever fortune shifts about. You are a young man, and your passions too impetuous; you must learn to govern them better" (RR 77). This advice contains the novel's themes in a nutshell. Roderick looks "upon the gaming-table as a certain resource for a gentleman in want" (RR 318); it is typically the last resource when no other is readily available. For example, after not hearing from Narcissa for a while, and having lost hope to ever win her against the other suitors, he decides

> in a fit of despair, to risk all I had at the gaming table, with a view of acquiring a fortune sufficient to render me independent for life; or of plunging myself into such a state of misery, as would effectually crush every ambitious hope that now tortured my imagination. Actuated by this fatal resolution, I engaged in play, and, after some turns of fortune found myself, at the end of three days, worth a thousand pounds; but it was not my intention to stop there, for which cause I kept Strap ignorant of my success, and continued my career until I was reduced to five guineas [...]. (RR 363)

Rivka Swenson (2011: 1987) approaches the theme of loss and gain in the narrative from another angle, arguing that it relates to a pattern of alienation and restoration/reunion, tied to the displacement from Scotland, which bears chances of loss and gain for the protagonist, and the ultimate goal being the restoration of order and the stability of a homeland and family. As often noted in criticism, the topics of national identity and the mid-century tensions between England and Scotland feature prominently in Smollett's novel. Prejudices, questions of trust, belonging and superiority, which contribute to a felt lack of sympathies between the two nations, shape Roderick's adventures as a traveling Scot and are often connected to a heightened sense of being at risk, especially during his stay in London.[32] Upon his and Strap's arrival in the city, Roderick notes that "we have not been in London eight and forty hours, and I believe we have met with eight and forty thousand misfortunes. – We have been jeered, reproached, buffeted, pissed upon, and at last stripped of our money; and I suppose by and by we shall be stripped of our skins" (RR 78). Similar to the portrayal in Defoe's fictions, London is depicted as the centre of corruption, danger, and depravity.

---

32 See Gottlieb (2007), who argues that *Roderick Random* testifies to Smollett's own experiences of struggling for assimilation in English metropolitan society. He analyses the novel with a focus on the depiction of Anglo-Scottish relations and notions of (trans)national unity or conflict. See also Swenson, who explores the theme of travelling Scots and Scottish exile in a wider political context, and argues that Smollett's text "expresses a complicated patriotism" (2011: 178).

Roderick experiences in London a system of bribery and arbitrary gratification, which reinforces his felt lack of control over his circumstances and makes him conclude, "that surely London is the devil's drawing-room" (RR 100). Furthermore, there is a noticeable aggression against outsiders, and foreigners, because at the time, John Skinner explains, "Underneath a characteristic English xenophobia, however, there lurked more substantial economic fears: Scots took jobs from the English" (1996: 50). Resentment and hostility are palpable on both sides. From the beginning, Roderick displays a fervent patriotism and acknowledges his loyalties clearly: "My prejudice in favour of my country was so strong that I could not bear to see anybody belonging to it in distress" (RR 114). This attitude is shared by his fellow Scotsman Strap, who first scolds Roderick for lending money to a stranger in the city and running the risk of never getting it back, but then says: "if you are sure he is a Scotchman, I believe you are safe" (RR 83).

Having been in London for a while, Roderick sees no other options for him than the military and becomes a surgeon's mate on a Navy ship, fighting in the war of the British against the Spanish in the New World. The chapters 24–37 set on board the ships present a satirical commentary on the bad administration, the inefficiency, and the mix of absurdity and cruelty of the Royal Navy; after all "there was scarce any body on board, who understood the pointing of a gun" (RR 182).[33] Recording the horrors of battle, illness, and death, they create a notion of the 18th-century warship as a "floating concentration camp" (Lewis 2003: 33). It is also the section in the narrative in which Roderick comes very close to death, and more than once comments on the deplorable conditions on board: "It would be tedious and disagreeable to describe the fate of very miserable object that suffered by the inhumanity and ignorance of the captain and surgeon, who so wantonly sacrificed the lives of their fellow creatures" (RR 162). Therefore, David McNeal mentions that the naval episode "dwells on the theme of human self-destruction" (1990: 91). Revealing Smollett's medical knowledge, this section also engages with the various health risks and issues of disease, hygiene, mortality, and medical treatment on board.[34] But, above all, it exposes

---

[33] For details of life in the Navy at the time and Smollett's experience of the Cartagena expedition and the dire and perilous conditions on board see Lewis (2003: 22–50).
[34] Elevating the text to the status of a "medical classic", Wendy More claims: "For the most vivid account of 18th century naval surgery, nothing beats Tobias Smollett's comic novel *The Adventures of Roderick Random*", because "Smollett ridiculed blundering physicians" and highlighted the effects of "tropical diseases under a beating sun, with poor provisions and filthy conditions" (Moore 2011: 591). The fact that "Roderick only survives by refusing all medicine" (ibid) is obviously particularly amusing to medical professionals. See also Chilton (2011), who inves-

the authoritarian structure of the Navy, the risks of either abuses of power or discrimination and exploitation that requires from the sailors all the strength and cunning they can muster simply in order to survive. As Boucé explains: "The life of an individual depends on the convenience of stupid and barbarous despots. [...] Roderick is exposed in his turn, at the peril of his life, to the bloody and futile horror of a pointless naval battle" (1976: 113).

Although in particular the description of the Cartagena expedition has at its heart a criticism of militarism and the meaninglessness of warfare, characteristically for Smollett's narrative, this section also satirizes fears and situations of danger. For example, initially Roderick is scared of sleeping in a hammock on deck: "it was some time before I could prevail upon myself to trust my carcass at such a distance from the ground, in a narrow bed, out of which I imagined I should be apt, on the least motion in my sleep, to tumble down at the hazard of breaking my bones" (RR 156). After being appointed surgeon's third mate on the *Thunder,* Roderick proudly notes: "I was an officer, resolved to maintain the dignity of my station against all opposition or affronts" (RR 158), a statement which shows again his constant expectation of being threatened and his readiness to fight. Soon enough, he gets into a box fight with midshipman Crampley, because the latter made a derogatory remark about Scotland. Nearly killing Crampley, Roderick wins the fight and, as a consequence gains the fearful respect of the crew. After this episode, Crampley continuously tries to manoeuvre Roderick into danger, for example by calling him to dress wounds on the open deck during a battle. Displaying his typical pride, Roderick "was resolved to convince my rival that I was no more afraid than he of exposing myself to danger. With this view I provided myself with dressings, and followed him immediately to the quarter-deck, through a most infernal scene of slaughter, fire, smoke, and uproar" (RR 185).

Roderick harshly criticizes all military or medical decisions made by the people in charge as "guesswork" (RR 184). Thus he continues to make enemies on board, most importantly the chief surgeon Mackshane, who shows little concern for the sick and wounded and reacts with malice and jealousy to Roderick's contradictions of his medical knowledge and ordered procedures, e. g.: "With this view he asked if we would undertake to cure the leg at our peril – that is, be answerable for the consequence" (RR 167). The "inhuman disregard" criticized by Roderick mainly concerns the surgeon's lacking care for the wounded: "Their wounds and stumps being neglected, contracted filth and putrefaction,

---

tigates Smollett's first printed prose works *Thomsonus Redivivus* (1746) and *Don Ricardo Honeywater Vindicated* (1748) as documentations of the author's contribution to medical literature.

and millions of maggots were hatched amidst the corruption off their sores" (RR 188–189).[35] But it extends to other instances of unnecessary malpractice on board, for example, starving the sailors despite sufficient supplies and allowing them no water but copious amounts of pure brandy in the morning. Roderick notes,

> this fast must, I suppose, have been enjoined [...] with a view to mortify them into a contempt of life, that they might thereby become more resolute and regardless of danger. How simply, then do those people argue, who ascribe the mortality among us to our bad provision and want of water; and affirm that a great many valuable lives might have been saved, if the useless transports had been employed in fetching fresh stock, turtle, fruit, and other refreshments from Jamaica, and other adjacent islands. (RR 187–188)

His account furthermore reveals the hazard of the military operations, ordered from afar by the British government, the sending of too few troops into dangerous battles, which they are destined to lose, without any concern for the waste of human lives involved.

> But surely our governors had their reasons for so doing [...] Perhaps they were loth to risk their best troops on such desperate service; or the colonel and field officers of the old corps, who, generally speaking, enjoyed their commissions as sinecures or pensions, for some domestic services tendered to the court, for some domestic services refused to embark in such a dangerous and precarious undertaking, for which refusal, no doubt, they are much to be commended. (RR 182)

However, things get worse for Roderick and he comes close to losing his own life twice. Together with the captain, the surgeon Mackshane stops at nothing to try and complete his vengeance against Roderick. Thus he ends up being taking prisoner and chained on deck during a bombardment because he is reported to be a spy for the Spanish. Roderick's emotional account of fearing for his life and watching his fellow mates die around him reads thus: "I could contain myself no longer, [...] I redoubled my cries, which were drowned in the noise of the battle; and finding myself disregarded, lost all patience and became frantic" (RR 170). In this scene, Roderick experiences a moment of intense terror; he is denied any physical movement or action and cannot relieve his own suffering or that of those around him; all he has left is language. Beasley points out: "Roderick fires off words like shots, as though they could kill what he condemns

---

[35] On Smollett's characterization of Mackshane, see McNeil's comment: "Military surgeons throughout the eighteenth century were generally considered to be little more than butchers who hacked in haste – granted they did not work in ideal circumstances – and whom men feared almost as much as they did the enemy" (1990: 92).

and fears. But they cannot" (1998: 64). After surviving this episode, Roderick falls seriously ill with the "bilious fever" (RR 191). For weeks, he has seen the effects and conditions of the rows of sick men lying cramped together under deck, "breathing nothing but a noisome atmosphere of the morbid steams exhaling from their own excrements and diseased bodies" (RR 149). Therefore, now that he finds himself "threatened with the symptoms of this terrible distemper" (RR 191), he decides to lie on the more open middle deck, and additionally refuses all medication. Roderick survives the fever, saved by a mix of empirical observation, medical knowledge and trusting his instincts. On the prospect of returning to England, he is relieved to leave the dangerous grounds of Jamaica behind and considers his lucky escape: "I felt excessive pleasure in finding myself out of sight of that fatal island, which has been the grave of so many Europeans" (RR 208).[36]

Generally, the naval episodes present an exception with regard to Roderick's consciousness and management of risk in the narrative. His professional knowledge is obvious and brings a rare rational clarity to his calculations, he here proves to be capable of reflecting on causes and effects, as well as of learning from experience. This includes his many correct diagnoses and hints at possible cures for the most pressing ills on board, such as more fresh air, food, and better hygiene. It is also illustrated during his second engagement on board of a ship. Upon his arrival in New Spain, Roderick says:

> Being arrived in the warm latitudes, I ordered (with the captain's consent) the whole ship's company to be blooded and purged, myself undergoing the same evacuation, in order to prevent those dangerous fevers to which northern constitutions are subject in hot climates; and I have reason to believe, that this precaution was not unserviceable, for we lost but one sailor during our whole passage to the coast. (RR 400)

Nonetheless, as far as Roderick's challenge to conquer his passions, to master more self-control, and to achieve some financial security, the prerequisites for entering the safe haven of domestic bliss with Narcissa, is concerned there is little to no development. Roderick recurrently ends up in a situation almost identical to the one shortly after he left home:

> I found myself alone in a desolate place, stripped of my clothes, money, watch, buckles, and everything but my shoes, stockings, breeches, and shirt. [...] I cursed the hour of my birth, the parents that gave me being, the sea that did not swallow me up, [...] the villainy

---

36 At the time of Smollett, the Caribbean was considered as a famously dangerous climate and dreaded area for Europeans, bearing the risk of infection with all kinds of fevers and other diseases (see Lewis 2003: 47).

of those who had left me in that miserable condition; and, in the ecstasy of despair, resolved to lie still where I was, and perish. (RR 211)

The only change is that he has become better equipped and shrewd at dealing with mankind, and he has acquired a thorough first-hand experience of his uncle's wise observation that "life was a voyage in which we must expect to meet with all weathers" (RR 233).

But the love of Narcissa is instrumental to aid Roderick in his struggle and has a strong influence on him; "the remembrance of my charming Narcissa was a continual check upon my conscience [...] and perhaps contributed to the bad success of my scheme, by controlling my raptures and condemning my design" (RR 294).[37] He is always in danger of straying from the right path when his romantic feelings are overcome by other passions. On such occasions, "my pride soared beyond all reason and description; I lost all remembrance of the gentle Narcissa" (RR 300). Part of Smollett's satire is that Roderick tries at all costs to keep his customary life-style from his 'ideal' woman. Not contemplating any alteration of his behaviour, he only fears detection and the ruin of his reputation and the image Narcissa has of him; he is always keen to "run no risk of being discovered by Narcissa, in a state of brutal degeneracy" (RR 346). With his feelings for Narcissa come further risks for Roderick, mainly the acute fear of losing her to another man. Although he courts other rich ladies and never avoids any flirtation, he fears for Narcissa's constancy and is so "tortured with jealousy" (RR 351) that any rumour to the contrary brings Roderick's passions into disarray. But he is reassured when he learns from her maid that Narcissa has meanwhile been informed of Roderick's lack of means and still loves him, saved by the news from "a world of confusion and anxiety" (RR 355). When Roderick finally declares his feelings to Narcissa, he portrays his love of her as a soothing, protective shield: "[...] it has lived unimpaired in the midst of numberless cares, and animated me against a thousand dangers and calamities" (RR 340). In the dramatic final part of the narrative, it is all or nothing for Roderick who must retrieve Narcissa, "or perish" (RR 363). He blindly decides to risk seeing her, despite all warnings and the fact that Narcissa, after her return from Bath, is under strict prison-like surveillance from her brother and not allowed any visitors.

---

37 Many critics have commented on the role of Narcissa as a catalyst for the rescue and transformation of Roderick, functioning as an emblem and "projection of his deep desire for beauty, tranquillity, and stasis" (Beasley 1998: 47; see Swenson 2011: 190). Yet, in turn, she does rarely speak or present a fully-fledged character in the novel, instead she is reduced to the status of idealized womanhood. See also Gottlieb (2007: 71).

Right to the end, he continues to impatiently fear for his love, and is full of apprehensions of Narcissa having been unfaithful or coming to any physical harm. Regarding the depiction of gender stereotypes in the novel, despite all his displays of masculine courage, Roderick is one of the most instable and almost feminized characters, constantly put at risk by this violent imaginations and uncontrolled outbursts of emotions. Although the novel is in many ways very conservative and maintains some typical elements of 18th-century misogyny, as Johnson (2011: 208) points out, the treatment of the theme of passion exceeds traditional gender boundaries at the same time. Taking a slightly different view, Boucé (1976: 121) reads Roderick's passionate feelings, of "ecstasy", being "madly in love", or "frantic", as uncontrolled outbursts, which merely imply his immaturity. In contrast, Narcissa is the embodiment of constancy, composure, gentleness, and beauty. This idealized image of femininity is ironically contrasted with Narcissa's aunt, a woman dishevelled in appearance and prone to bouts of madness, "sometimes fancying herself an animal, sometimes a piece of furniture, during which conceited transformations it was very dangerous to come near her, especially when she represented a beast" (RR 222). Narcissa's characterization, however, is based on a traditional paradox, she needs to be captivating enough to render Roderick's attraction to her credible, yet she has to be silent and restrained and plain enough to fulfil the requirements of appropriate feminine behaviour.[38] She is almost devoid of emotions, other than passionately declaring her constancy and love for Roderick at regular intervals and despite the long periods of Roderick's absence.

Scotland and Narcissa have a similar function in the narrative, staying largely in the background, yet they are passionately desired, and once Roderick returns to them, all is well, and he has arrived in an idyllic, stable, risk-free environment. The narrative's concluding paragraph paints a picture of untainted bliss and compensation for all bad fortune in the past:

> If there be such a thing as true happiness on earth, I enjoy it. The impetuous transports of my passion are now settled and mellowed into endearing fondness and tranquillity of love, rooted by that intimate connection and interchange of hearts which nought but virtuous wedlock can produce. Fortune seems determined to make ample amends for her former cruelty; (RR 427–428)

---

[38] See Johnson's criticism of the novel's predominant, stereotypical image of femininity as "beautiful, compliant, and vacuous" (2011: 202), which is likely to make any modern critic cringe, and the even harsher comment that *Roderick Random* is a "deeply misogynistic text that presents sex as sport and women as trophies" (204).

Moreover, Roderick awaits the birth of his first child as "something to crown my felicity" (RR 428). Thus the novel ends with a homecoming, a reunion of father and son, husband and bride, and a pregnancy to ensure the family lineage. Smollett's final depiction of "Arcadian bliss" (Skinner 1996: 210) has been criticized as a mere gesture towards romance convention.[39] It reconciles the protagonist to safety, society and order, forming a marked contrast to the rebellion, dangers, and chaos of the rest of the narrative. But while the pregnant Narcissa and the fulfilment of the opening dream of Roderick's mother epitomize status, love, but also cyclical repetition, the exaggerated order of the final pages appears almost mythically removed from reality, affirming by contrast the randomness of the rest of the plot. The ending presents an ideal of continuity and a risk-free state set against a reality of instability and threats. However one wants to read Roderick's agency or his capacity for change in the novel, Smollett's interrogation of providential intervention and his portrayal of Roderick are presented with heavy satire. As James Bunn puts it, "the forced contrivance of the ending reminds one sceptically that the vitality of this novel is in its syncretic gatherings of people far from home: adventuring, gaming, cheating, warring, where randomness and metonymy now seem the provenance of culture" (Bunn 1981: 469). The narrative, via a final deus-ex-machina resolution, presents fortune, stability and moral improvement as the culmination of Roderick's random adventures. Yet, Margret Cohen suggests, "Following *Roderick Random*, the maritime adventure novel will yield in the second half of the eighteenth century to novels set on land about the pleasures and desires of civil society" (Cohen 2010: 98). However, these are no less risky, as the reading of Sterne and Walpole shows.

3.3 Individualism, Parental Anxiety, and Fears of Destruction: *Tristram Shandy*

Laurence Sterne, an Irish priest living in Yorkshire, struggled with his health throughout his life. He wrote the nine volumes of *The Life and Opinions of Tristram Shandy* between 1759 and 1767 while his body was rapidly deteriorating, which is why many critics see a distinct sense of a "race with death" (Damrosch

---

39 The final chapters have been criticized for racing towards order and restoration via a heavy reliance "on easy romance convention" (Beasley 1998: 69), culminating in a "reactionary" ending to a novel which is ultimately "about restoration, not development" (Swenson 2011: 1988). The ending is generally seen as abrupt and unmotivated. While Roderick does undergo what Boucé calls "a certain evolution" towards self-control and maturity, the resolution remains "somewhat marred by clumsiness and improbability" (1976: 124).

1985: 294) in the narrative, and argue that Sterne and his narrator apparently share a fear of time running out before they can finish their story (see Bloom and Bloom 1988: 507; Erickson 1986: 201).[40] Roy Porter also emphasizes the reflection of Sterne's preoccupation with his medical condition and calamities,[41] and draws attention to the author's dedication of the text to William Pitt in which Sterne acknowledges his "constant endeavour to fence against the infirmities of ill health, and other evils of life, by mirth" (TS 33). In other words, while "mishap, and mayhem, disease and death scar the novel" (Porter 1989: 62), and the "book seems written under the influence of anxiety, and the anxiety is of more than one kind" (Hunter 1989: 180), its author tries to set a kind of humour against it; he seeks to banish an overwhelming sense of being at risk by ridiculing calculations and chasing narrative fixity. The text, which reflects the Augustan tradition of scepticism and learned wit,[42] is nowadays often considered as a postmodern text *avant la lettre*.[43] It tells essentially a "cock-and-bull

---

40 Taking a closely biographical view of Sterne's novel, Bloom and Bloom see the defiance of death as strong motif in the text in which "[d]eath looms as the capricious adversary, to be faced with a mixture of defiance and optimism" (1988: 500).
41 Roy Porter explains: "*Tristram Shandy* was the testament of a dying man, whose 'leaky bellows' had fallen victim to consumption. [...] All but one of his children were stillborn or died shortly after, and his sole surviving daughter, Lydia, languished with asthma and probably epilepsy" (1989: 62). Arguing that the history of the body and illness is generally a neglected area in literary criticism, Porter's point of departure is that "the fundamental question of how people dealt with embodied existence, their fusion of vitality and mortality, remains little understood because the importance of health and sickness to our forebears has never been adequately addressed" (1989: 61). A lot has certainly been done and written since, yet with regard to Sterne's novel, the medical aspect remains comparatively underrepresented in criticism. See Porter's essay for a detailed analysis of the signs of illness and references to consumption in the text, as well as of Sterne's attitude towards psychiatry.
42 In criticism, Sterne is often placed in a line of tradition reaching back to Rabelais and Burton's *Anatomy of Melancholy* (see Ricks 1985: 11). Parallels are often drawn between Sterne and Swift, both clergymen and satirists. The text's inherent anti-dogmatism as a reflection of 18th-century thought is interesting to consider as the main counter-argument against the often proclaimed 'postmodernity' of the novel: "The satiric reduction of system-builders in Burton, Swift and Sterne is more than a conflict between the comic and the scientific; it is a product of, and a response to, an intellectual movement that had its birth in the crisis of the Reformation" (Parnell 1994: 227).
43 Numerous sources could be given here. For instance, Damrosch describes *Tristram Shandy* as the "eighteenth-century work that most anticipates the modern world" (1985: 289). More recently, Sussman mentions the fact that Sterne is often referred as "the first postmodern writer" or, at the very least, as a "precursor" introducing narrative techniques now considered as hallmarks of postmodern writing. However, it is important to note, as Sussman does, that the explosion of novels published in the second half of the 18th century might have sparked the need for

story",[44] and is famously "odd" – as Dr Johnson called it in 1776,[45] full of mockery and countless digressions. The text's supposed order or disorder, its status as an unusual and chaotic or as typical, highly controlled and structured text has been a matter of critical debate for centuries.[46] Whichever stand one chooses to take, it is hard to disagree with W.C. Booth's description of the novel's structure, contradicting the opinion of some of the text's earliest reviewers who claimed that it defied any attempt of giving a plot summary:[47]

> The chaos is all of his own making. Sterne and the reader are always aware of the existence of a clear, simple chronology of events that could be told in a hundred pages without difficulty. We have, in fact, only two simple story threads: Tristram's conception, birth, naming, circumcision, and breeching, and uncle Toby's courtship of the Widow Wadman. The two are juggled adroitly throughout the nine volumes [...]. (Booth 1961: 231)[48]

---

experimentation and self-conscious narratives in order to get noticed by the audience (Sussman 2012: 131). On the perceived anachronism of the text see also Thomas Keymer's *Sterne, the Moderns and the Novel* (2010).

44 A cock-and-bull story is "idiomatically, a tale of nonsense, one that purports to convey meaning but has no truth in it" (Spacks 2006: 268). Marshall Brown, tracing back the meaning of a cock-and-bull story to Boccaccio's *Decameron*, describes it as "a rambling, shapeless narrative (1991: 287).

45 On March 21, 1776, Samuel Johnson famously and wrongly predicted the longevity of Tristram Shandy: "Nothing odd will do long" (in: Boswell and Waingrow 1994: 197).

46 Opinions have been very divided: In *Aspects of the Novel*, E.M. Forster famously commented on the plot and structure of Tristram Shandy thus: "Obviously a god is hidden in Tristram Shandy, his name is Muddle, and some readers cannot accept him" (2000: 164). More recently, Jo Alyson Parker wrote: "Sterne, in effect, gives us a chaotic text – globally determined, locally unpredictable" (1997: 111); Julia Jordan has called the novel a "haphazard and disordered masterpiece" (2010: 16). Well-known is also Victor Shklovsky's counter-argument that Sterne's text is simply of a different order and possesses a distinct structure and scheme of organization, which make *Tristram Shandy* "the most typical novel of world literature" (1968: 89). According to Shklovsky, unity is achieved by recurring motives and time-shifts, which follow intentional laws, like in an abstract, at a first glance distorted-looking painting: "The novel's characteristic trait is precisely the unusualness of the pattern of deployment often even of its typical elements" (1968: 87; 67). Arguing along similar lines, Eric Rothstein even claims: "To read Tristram as Sterne's novel is to read a controlled book" (1975: 77). Various other structuring themes will be discussed in this chapter, a predominant obviously being the depiction of risk and anxiety.

47 For example, one contemporary reviewer wrote about *Tristram Shandy:* "This is a humorous performance, of which we are unable to convey any distinct idea to our readers" (*Critical Review* 9, January 1760: 73; cited in Howes 1974: 52); see also Ross (2001: 13).

48 In *The Rhetoric of Fiction*, W.C. Booth gives a still valid analysis of the unity of the novel. He approaches the question of narrative unity with regard to three dominant traditions and narrative conventions, "the comic novel exploded; the sugar-coated collection of philosophical essays, and the miscellaneous satire" (1961: 224). Another device which gives the story coherence

The novel can be described as a highly idiosyncratic narrative that reflects the unpredictability of the human mind. Like many other novelists of the time, Sterne utilizes many different narrative conventions, but ultimately writes "a comic epic of narcissism, an epic of extraordinary self-awareness" (Spacks 2006: 263; 258). According to John Paul Hunter, 18th-century novels typically "dwell at length on a relatively short amount of time in which choices are made and patterns are set, although others explore over a longer haul the consequences of youthful determination or lack of it" (Hunter 1990a: 95). While the novels of Defoe or Smollett cover decades in the life of a character, others, like Burney's *Camilla*, focus on a short crucial time span of decision-making of the protagonists. *Tristram Shandy* ironizes both types of plot structures, dramatizing and stretching out non-events over time, always implying dramatic consequences of actions and developments, which are either extremely sudden, disastrous, or fail to materialize altogether. For instance, the narrator often announces what will happen in the next chapter, while then digressing onto another issue; a typical example reads thus: "What were the consequences, and what was Yorick's catastrophe thereupon, you will read in the next chapter" (TS 56).

For Terry Eagleton, this aspect makes *Tristram Shandy* a typical modern novel, as he considers the genre in comparison to the epic to be "inherently untragic": "What rules now is less fate than human agency, less codes of honour than social conventions. Work and home, not court, church and state, become the primary settings, and high politics yields to the intrigues of everyday life" (Eagleton 2003: 178; 180). In other words, the focus on the prosaic, the private, and the ordinary contradicts any real tragic action.[49] *Tristram Shandy* takes the narration of trivialities in Eagleton's sense to extremes, and despite the narrator's efforts to present his observations as meaningful and of gravest importance, he and his attempts drown "in the great ocean of irrelevancies" (2003: 181). It also captures the shift from matters of cosmic destiny to questions of routine, causality and mere survival; moreover the novel's fragmented temporality and the focus on flux and process creates a bulwark against any sort of perception of a 'finite' tragedy (2003: 186–187). Sterne's text substitutes grandeur, dan-

---

is the presence of Tristram as a dramatized, unreliable narrator, the first in a long tradition in fiction (1961: 222; 238).

49 Regarding the aspect of the novel's untragic quality, Rosenblum draws an interesting comparison between Tristram and Oedipus: "The flattened nose is a mark no less fateful than the maimed foot of Oedipus. [...] to read this novel is to be instructed in the art of noticing coincidences. Not the gross and melodramatic kind that have become so familiar in the old plots: a man murders his father at a place where three roads meet and marries a princess who is his mother. Sterne's coincidences, [are] neither so spectacular nor so sinister" (1977: 243).

ger, and tragedy by the pettiness of accident, subjective risk perception and the general precariousness of life. In contrast to many earlier novels, especially Defoe's, it also highlights and adds a distinctly emotional dimension of risk perception.

A recurring motif is the struggle against what Stuart Sim has called "the metaphysics of catastrophe" (1990: 120) in the novel. Tristram himself tells the reader: "What is the life of man! Is it not to shift from side to side?– from sorrow to sorrow?– to button up one cause of vexation! – and unbutton another!" (TS 331). The process of the creation of Tristram is shown as a risky, accident-prone endeavour. Significantly, all the accidents happening to Tristram – his conception, birth, naming, and circumcision – concern crucial identity-shaping events. But although Tristram has to suffer from the various miscalculations by his parents and other guardians, he is not the only vulnerable character; rather, as Bloom and Bloom put it, "everyone whose life touches upon his appears to be at risk" (1988: 499).

When focusing on the anxieties and methods of sceptical calculation in the novel, the reflections and constructions of time and chance are important, as they in turn are linked to the major risk that clouds Tristram's consciousness, the anxiety about his own parentage and masculinity, a topic, which generally gained prominence in the novel in the second half of the 18th century. The threat of illegitimacy, of approaching death, of meaninglessness and unpredictabilities are all risks which directly and intimately concern the narrator's life and person, rather than, as so often in Defoe's fictions, society as a whole or a character's possessions. Tristram tries to fight his anxieties through writing, for him the only available means of constructing causality and achieving a sense of validity and permanence. In Sterne's text, the individual is reduced to state of ontological insecurity, and a lot is at stake, the intermingled matters of fertility, life, death and the continuity and straightness of (male) lines. Like in *Roderick Random*, masculinity is at risk while women remain comparatively out of focus, or rather lurk as the unspoken challenge to male supremacy in the background,[50] as does another threat to human life, war, which is presented indirectly and mainly portrayed as a game in the novel.[51]

---

50 On apprehensions about sexuality and legitimacy running through the narrative see Brown (1991: 293), Doody (1997: 446), and Parker (1997: 106). Many critics have taken a negative stand and criticized the derogatory portrayal or marginalization of women in the text, while others have defended Sterne against this charge. For a summary of the male-centred reception of the text and the debate of chauvinist vs. feminist criticism of the book see Pesso-Miquel (2004: 41f) and Motooka (1998: 180f). For feminist readings, the treatment of sexuality, and analysis

In contrast to Swift or Defoe's fictions, Sterne's first-person narrator does not speak from a distance and with the wisdom of a character decades removed from the turmoil of his own youth. He is highly self-conscious and less concerned with the morality of his story than with actually piecing it together. This process assumes a matter of urgency and he constantly draws attention to his rapidly declining health, in particular in the last three volumes where he says, for example: "– and feel my want of powers. It is one comfort at least to me, that I lost some fourscore ounces of blood this week in a most uncritical fever which attacked me at the beginning of this chapter; so that I have still some hopes remaining, it may be more in the serous or globular parts of the blood, than in the subtle aura of the brain– " (TS 598). Above all, the narrative shows the fragility of human existence; moreover it reveals the inevitable partiality of comprehension, leaving a huge gap to be filled with speculation and attempts to create meaning and control. Underlining the necessity of narration on the one hand, the novel ridicules a number of disciplines thought to produce knowledge and security about the world on the other, including psychology, medicine, law, science, history, and religion (see Hammond and Ragan 2006: 169). Although there are notable parallels and both novels show the paradoxes and absurdities of science, *Tristram Shandy* differs from *Gulliver's Travels* in so far that Sterne does not take his criticism to the extremes Swift does, for instance, in the depiction of the experiments in the Academy of Lagado. Sterne's text nonetheless playfully deconstructs both religious and scientific master-narratives of his time.

The opening moment of the plot relates to a popular idea in 17th- and 18th-century thought, the debate about in what ways an embryo is shaped by or at its moment of conception and the theory of the "homunculus"; and many critics see it as a reflection of Sterne's interest in speculations about embryology.[52] According to Erickson, birth and sex are generally often presented as 'fatal' in

---

of the (neglected) women in the novel, see, for instance: Dennis W. Allen (1985), Leigh A. Ehlers (1981), Ruth Marie Faurot (1970), and Juliet McMaster (1989).

51 On this topic see the chapter "Sterne: Military Veterans and 'humours'" in McNeil (1990: 144–167). It analyses war as a central structural motif in the text and argues that it contains a number of victims of war, e.g. Uncle Toby, Corporeal Trim, LeFevre. McNeil sees in particular Toby's strange wound and Tristram's accident with the window sash as symbolic representation for "the danger that war poses to the human species" (1990: 159).

52 Originally "homunculus" means "little man" in Latin; the term is typically used in debates about embryology. See especially Louis A. Landa's essay "The Shandean Homunculus" (1963).

18th century literature,[53] but Sterne gives particular weight to the risks and fears connected to issues of conception and child-birth, employing a protagonist who is "afflicted with anxiety even before he is born" (Erickson 1986: 258), and showing the "Tristram homunculus" to exist in a "womb of anxious speculation" (1986: 205). As the narrator puts it: "Tristram's Misfortunes began nine months before he came into the world" (TS 37) and he clearly laments his parents' lack of caution and calculation of all probabilities concerning his conception:

> I wish either my father or my mother, or indeed both of them, as they were in duty both equally bound to it, had minded what they were about when they begot me; had they duly consider'd how much depended upon what they were then doing; – that not only the production of a rational Being was concerned in it, [...] – Had they duly weighed and considered all this, and proceeded accordingly; – I am verily persuaded I should have made a quite different figure in the world, from that, in which the readers is likely to see me. (TS 35)

What the novel shows perhaps most crucially is the human thought process of association and how the continuous wandering of the mind can produce folly, and peril. While the narrator tells the reader that with his conception there was nothing less at stake than the "production of a rational Being", his mother distracts his father at the crucial coital moment by reminding him to wind the clock..[54] Significantly, a symbol of accuracy and measurement is evoked to bring confusion and disorder, meanwhile Tristram blames his mother's lack of mental focus as the real misfortune of the scene,

> which, in a great measure, fell upon myself, and the effects of which I fear I shall carry with me to my grave; namely, that from an unhappy association of ideas which have no connection in nature, it so fell out at length, that my poor mother could never hear the said clock wound up, – but the thoughts of some other things unavoidably popped into her head – & vice versa [...]. (TS 39)

As a symbol, the clock introduces the role of temporality, and the disrupted course of events in a narrative in which nothing runs like clockwork.[55] The scene is a satirical illustration of the new mechanical world view, in the sense

---

53 Erickson writes on the subject of infant mortality in the 18th century: "Every age is an age of anxiety. The period 1720–1750, however, [...], might be called in England 'the age of mortality' – only one out of four children born in London survived" (1986: xi).
54 On this aspect see Hunter (1989), Vanderbeke (2006), and Motooka (1998).
55 The whole novel has often been read "as a battle with time" (Booth 1961: 233). See also Laura Brown who writes about Sterne and Tristram: "Seeking to master time, he begins the novel like a man, calculating and reckoning" (Brown 1991: 290).

that Shapin and Schaffer describe it: "In the root metaphor of the mechanical philosophy, nature was like a clock: man could be certain of the hour shown by its hands" (Shapin and Schaffer 1985: 24). Parker interprets it even as a sign of Sterne's deliberate resistance to Newtonian science and determinism as one of the "grand narratives" of the 18th century (Parker 1997: 103).[56] Newtonian science is based on a premise of predictability, causality and linear progression of events; yet such an order is disturbed right at the beginning, violating both scientific and novelistic principles. *Tristram Shandy*, Parker explains, thus deviates from the typical course of 18th-century novels, "which move forward with deterministic inevitability to their culminations in marriage or death", and "serves as an implicit demonstration of the fact that linear causality is an inadequate model for the complex workings of the mind, reminding us that the great explanative 'narrative' put forward under the Newtonian paradigm leaves the human element out of the equation" (Parker 1997: 107; 103).

The establishment of probability theory gave rise to philosophical debates, notably Hume's sceptical problem, the question about induction and knowledge about future, and the argument that human expectations are based on habit and lack objective justification. These questions shape the context of *Tristram Shandy*, as many critics have noted, while the mathematical outlook on life, in particular the centre piece of Newtonian science, that is the laws of gravity, plays another significant role. Hacking explains:

> Gravitation was the greatest discovery and the greatest mystery of the age. The initial successes of seventeenth century science had relied on 'mechanical' explanation. Gravitational force changed all that. [....] the laws of gravity are merely devices for computation, prediction, and description of constant regularities. They do not state the efficient causes by which bodies attract each other; they are merely constant conjunctions based on experience. [...]. Like gravity, the laws of chance are 'merely descriptive.' The causes lie in divine energy. (Hacking 1975: 172–173).

Science was gaining in explanatory power, but still required a similar quantity of belief as religious faith, as it also could not explain, or rather, predict, everything. Like the doctrine of chances, laws of gravity could capture certain patterns and regularities but not infuse all events with causal meaning. The plot of Sterne's *Tristram Shandy* literally illustrates the workings and meanings of chance, as the "falling of things", e.g. in the chestnut incident or Tristram's

---

[56] Although a wider debate of this aspect is beyond scope, Sterne's novel can be considered postmodern in this sense and doubts the explanatory potential and totality of authority of the new rising God, science, as well as grappling with the dwindling authority of the old one, divine providence.

accidental circumcision.[57] Therefore, Sigurd Burckhardt (1961) sees a very "literal" order at work in the narrative, the gravitational force of everything spiralling downwards. Furthermore, all falling things have a tendency to always land on or near the genitals, e.g. rocks, sash windows, chestnuts, toy bullets etc.[58] Another structuring device related to the laws of gravity is the elliptical avoidance of linearity, as indeed not a single chapter and hardly a sentence in the novel "runs straight" (Burckhardt 1961: 80).[59] Meanwhile Paul J. Hunter also sees an inevitable downward drive to "toward disorder and disaster" (Hunter 1989: 182) in the text, and Stuart Sim, taking an anachronistic approach, reads it against the background of postmodern physics. He describes the landscape of *Tristram Shandy* as "a world that is in its very essence discontinuous, catastrophic, non-rectifiable, and paradoxical" (Sim 1996: 109). This atmosphere is aptly captured by Walter Shandy's lamentation half way through the novel: "Unhappy Tristram! [...] What one misfortune or disaster in the book of embryotic evils, that could unmechanize thy frame, or entangle thy filaments! Which has not fallen upon thy head, or ever though camest into the world − what evils in thy passage into it! − what evils since! −" (TS 295).

As shown above, Sterne's novel testifies to the 18th-century fascination with mathematics and the popularity of scientific images and metaphors in cultural discourse, with measuring time, with physical laws, and minute empirical observation of events; moreover it consciously parodies the premise which forms the basis for all scientific and technological advance, an intelligible communicability of experience and a transmission of knowledge. It demonstrates the two contradictory impulses, a new awareness of chance and a deterministic, scientific approach which both had a decisive impact on the individual's perception of the world, as Kavanagh explains:

> To choose science was to elect an understanding of the individual's role as one of participation in a struggle to fathom, describe, and explicate the laws governing a rigorously determined physical and social universe. To choose chance was to choose to understand

---

57 Etymologically 'chance' derives from the Latin verb 'cadere', meaning 'to fall', and the noun 'cadentia', usually defined as "the falling out or happening of events", (Reith 1999: 14; see Jordan 2010: 6), which is still very visible in the German "Zufall".
58 Brown also mentions "the book's downward tendency" (1991: 277) as an ordering principle, while Parker goes a step further and argues that al lot of the imagery in the novel is graphically and dynamically constructed and can be read through "the lens of chaos theory" (1997: 102).
59 However, one may wonder if gravity appears in the text as a symbol for an inevitable scientific law that humans cannot escape, thus providing a very specific certainty in the midst of uncertainty.

the individual as a singular, isolated consciousness within a world of disorder and unpredictability shared with other, equally limited consciousnesses. (Kavanagh 1993: 5)

As narrator, Tristram employs a very curious notion of fortune, showing strange, incomprehensible causes triggering chains of events, yet always implying that there is a possible means of prevention or interference, and seeking to account responsibilities. It is clearly the human mind which designs action and then uses notions like "misfortunes" as a means of retrospective narrative explanation. About his relation with fortune, Tristram says, "the ungracious Duchess has pelted me with a set of as pitiful misadventures and cross accidents as ever small Hero sustained" (TS 40). The classic providential rhetoric is employed ironically by Sterne and conveys a perception of a world full of risks and randomness. In the beginning, the narrator finds himself "brought into this scurvy and disastrous world of ours" (TS 40). Much later, in a chapter telling entitled "Vexation upon vexation", he offers what reads like a stock-taking of his life saying: "I think [I find] myself inexcusable, for blaming Fortune so often as I have done, for pelting me all my life long, [...] surely, if I have any cause to be angry with her, 'tis that she has not sent me great ones—a score of good cursed, bouncing losses, would have been as good as a pension to me" (TS 494).

Tristram's birth is the second major plot incident and risky undertaking following his conception. Beforehand, his parents discuss the various options, e. g. whether to have a doctor present at the delivery. While Mrs Shandy prefers an experienced midwife, Mr Shandy tries to consider all facts and the dangers involved for mother and child:

> These facts, though they had their weight, yet did not altogether satisfy some few scruples and uneasiness which hung upon my father's spirits in relation to this choice. – To say nothing of the natural workings of humanity and justice, – or of the yearnings of parental and connubial love, all which prompted him to leave as little to hazard as possible in a case of this kind; [...]. (TS 72)

Another issue in the long parental discussion is whether the lie-in should be in London or at Shandy Hall. Tristram's father fears the latter option. Yet these specific fears are immediately mixed up with the feelings about the political situation; as usual his risk assessment digresses into a myriad of facts and facets.

> There was little danger, he would say, of losing our liberties by French politics or French invasions; – nor was he so much in pain of a consumption from the mass of corrupted matter and ulcerated humours in our constitution, – which he hopes was not so bad as it was imagined; – but he verily feared, that in some violent push, we should go off, all at once, in a state-apoplexy; – and then he would say, The Lord have mercy upon us all. (TS 73–74)

In the novel Walter Shandy is described as "a philosopher in grain, – speculative, – systematical" (TS 81). At the same time: "There was that infinitude of oddities in him, and of chances along with it, by which handle he would take a thing, – it baffled, Sir, all calculations"; "his road lay so very far on one side, from that wherein most men travelled" (TS 374–375). His character is inherently paradoxical. Despite his proclaimed love of rational reasoning and the collection of factual knowledge, his is also inclined towards superstition and his attitude often shows a high degree of emotion and irrationality. This becomes obvious, for instance, in the process of naming his son. The correlation between a person's fate, identity and name, implying an enormous risk of making the wrong choice at a person's birth, is just one of Mr Shandy's "many odd opinions" (TS 79). And of all possible names Tristram is the worst; "he had the lowest and most contemptible opinion of it of anything in the world" (TS 81). Yet by the accidental misremembering of the maid who passes on the chosen name at the baptizing, this is what his son comes to be called. At this point little Tristram has already had his nose crushed by Doctor Slop's delivery. Prior to this, the men actually had discussed the statistics and new-borns' risks of deformity: "it so happened that, in 49 instances out of 50, the said head was compressed and moulded into the shape of an oblong conical piece of dough" (TS 164). But as with all characters, during their often joint attempts at managing risks, there "was no remedy against some evils which neither he nor she foresaw" (TS 177). Significantly, Tristram's nose is damaged while the men are distracted by discussion.

Walter's constant philosophical discussions and calculations continuously distract him from reality, his real anxieties and emotions. He finds solace in the project of writing the *Tristra-paedia*, supposedly for the benefit of his son's education but just as much to order his own scattered thoughts after the loss of one son and the failure to protect and successfully shape the young life of the other. Tristram describes his father's perception of life as a gamble against calamities thus: "I was my father's last stake– he had lost my brother Bobby entirely, – he had lost, by his own computation, full three-fourths of me– that is, he had been unfortunate in his three first great casts for me– my geniture, my nose, and name, – there was but this one left;" (TS 366). Walter's desperate efforts at dogmatic control, the only one left to him, culminate, in his tour de force project, the *Tristra-paedia*, which, according to David Mazella: "Like all of Walter's schemes, [...] is an attempt to control a future outcome, via abstract systems of knowledge and speculation, which can only be understood retrospectively" (Mazella 1999: 165). It is an example of the fact that all characters, in their own ways, are deeply absorbed in managing the future, and shows that a notion of risk is firmly implanted in each of the their world views, although all attempt at precautions, like Walter's are rendered futile and absurd. Furthermore, in the novel Walter is described as "a great MOTIVE-MONGER, and consequently a very dangerous person for a man to sit by" (TS 440). For Mazella, Sterne depicts a fear of moral error through Walter's character: "Walter Shandy – failed father, philosopher, and (especially educator) – embodies the risks, though not mortal risks, of knowledge as interpretation" (Mazella 1999: 173). Sterne shared a notion of the risk of erroneous interpretation with other authors of his time, based on a normativity and monologism of texts, which the modern novel, as a dialogic text in Bakhtin's sense, defies, and which is illustrated particularly through Tristram's father.[60]

Many theorists and historians of science see the 18th-century characterized by an awakening encyclopaedism and spirit of quantification and, due to the rapid expansion of knowledge, desire for order. However, as Gunnar Broberg explains, the two desires cancel each other out, to some extent, as knowledge seemed to become infinite and a complete cataloguing increasingly difficult: "If 'encyclopaedia' means 'the circle of knowledge,' the circle was broken during the latter part of the 18th century" (Broberg 1990: 46). Sterne's narrative appears as a symbolic rendering of the broken circle of certainties, linearity, and completeness. It illustrates, via Walter Shandy's failed monumental *Tristra-paedia* and through Tristram's many aborted narrative strands how the struggle for causality in the face of an overwhelming plurality of opinions, leads only to an imploding result and a non-climatic ending, signifying the "epistemological shake-up of the early Enlightenment" (1990: 46).

Sterne's novel is often read with contextual reference to David Hume's *Treatise of Human Nature* (1739) and John Locke's *An Essay Concerning Human Understanding* (1689/90), two founding philosophical texts in the field of epistemology and the questioning of the correspondence between sensory impressions, ideas and reality.[61] Dealing with comprehension and the construction and reach of human knowledge, both texts are precursors in the field of the empiricism, human psychology and the study of emotion. Furthermore, at the centre of mid-17th to mid-18th-century discussions, linking mathematics and phi-

---

60 See Mazella (1999), who focuses on the relation between characterization in the text and moral pedagogy. His notion of 'moral risk' is mainly directed at the reader, and therefore less relevant here.
61 Thomas Keymer says: "Locke's account of human psychology and language as vexed by obscurity and instability has long been recognized as an important context for Tristram Shandy" (2002: 174). For a good summary of scholarship on Hume and Locke in connection with Sterne see the bibliographical notes in Norton (2006). See also Lupton (2003), Moglen (2001: 88), and Hamilton (2007: 152).

losophy, are questions of certainty of absolute truth in relation to partial truth, probabilities and opinions. In his *Essay*, Locke famously writes, "[God] has afforded us only the twilight, as I may so say, of Probability, [...] that state of mediocrity and probationership he has been pleased to place us in".[62] The quote implies a Platonic scale from lightness to darkness, from impression and opinions, over probability's "twilight", to absolute truth. Later Hume introduces a similar central distinction in his study between knowledge and probability. In 18th-century attempts to differentiate degrees of knowledge, the creation of new forms of mathematical certainty and calculation of probabilities (see chapter 1.1) were, in fact, set against a background of increasing scepticism. Ian Hacking describes the abandonment of *scientia* in favour of *opinio*, which generally meant that empiricists increasingly claimed that probability was all that was possible as far as physical knowledge was concerned (Hacking 1975: 185).[63] With the increasing acceptance of statistical, empirical data in society and on human decision-making, an important change took place regarding the acceptance of opinions. Hacking describes this paradigm shift as a gradual substitution of rational demonstration and causes with "constant conjunction and lawlike regularity" (1975: 182). There are repeated references to Locke in the text, e.g. the narrator notes how "Endless is the Search of Truth" (TS 110). Most importantly, the fact that Sterne's novel is entitled *The Life and Opinions of Tristram Shandy*, highlights the fascination and increasing weight given to opinions and the debates surrounding them, but also signals a break from the earlier novelistic formula "The Life and Adventures of..." (see Hammond and Ragan 2006: 165; Hamilton 2007: 159), by moving away from the spectacular plots to focus on the workings of the mind of the protagonist, which is in fact, all the reader gets in this novel. Laura Brown writes: "Previous autobiography had always separated life and opinions, but here they come close to merging in a book whose subject is Tristram's conceptions" (Brown 1991: 268). While Sterne's novel presents a narrator who states: "I have undertaken, you see, to write not only my life, but my opinions also" (TS 41), this focuses the attention on the inevitable subjectivity and on the mental battles and adventures of the human mind rather than on physical ones in the outer world.

---

[62] See Book IV, "Of Knowledge and Opinion", in Locke's *Essay* (2008: 422).
[63] Shapin and Schaffer write: "English experimentalisms of the mid-seventeenth century and afterwards increasingly took the view that all that could be expected of physical knowledge was 'probability,' thus breaking down the radical distinction between 'knowledge' and 'opinion.' [...] By the adoption of a probabilistic view of knowledge one could attain to an appropriate certainty and aim to secure legitimate assent to knowledge claims" (1985: 24). See also Shapiro (1983) and Patey (1984: 27ff).

All men in the novel are presented as quixotic characters, and suffer from their involuntary associations, causing many comedic moments, yet also isolating each character. Communication is made nearly impossible, as Sterne places the emphasis on showing how individuals perceive the world differently. Therefore the text appears as an empirical demonstration of idiosyncrasy (see Deporte 1974: 133; Motooka 1998: 174). Many critics have traced this aspect back to the influence of Lockean theories about the fallibility of individual human judgment. For instance, Ross Hamilton, who reads Sterne's text as a narrative mapping of the mental processes of the Shandy family, argues: "Sterne adapted Locke's theory of accidental association to show the irrational aspects of communication. [...] By applying this idea at face value, Sterne suggested that associations confuse communication. He considered them subjective phenomena that isolate one person's understanding from that of another" (Hamilton 2007: 156). Additionally, the narrative highlights the subjectivity of notions of temporal sequence and duration which are derived as categories of the human mind, and which are a recurring topic of Shandean discussion: "I would remind him, that the idea of duration and of its simple modes, is got merely from the train and succession of our ideas" (TS 122). Throughout, Sterne's novel displays a deep scepticism about language's potential to convey "truth" via words; and a strategy of Tristram is to always offer multiple possible explanations and opinions.[64] Christina Lupton speaks in this context of "Sterne's epistemological risk-taking", as an unsettling uprooting of language in relation to other areas of certainty (Lupton 2003: 105). Drawing on Hume in her reading, she says that Sterne, while showing that language can never give 'real' clarity, uses a double-edged strategy by writing a metafictional novel (rather than philosophical treatise) and thus, "uses this forum to stage a 'safe' but dialectical version of the skeptic's debate. Here, as a work of fiction *Tristram Shandy* denies knowledge both of the status of a problem at all and the possibility of resolution" (2003: 113).

The portrayal of the various hobbyhorses reflects dominant theories in 17- and 18th-century psychology about the imagination and passion, which can control a man's mind, leading to an obsession with only one or two thoughts.[65] In the novel, Tristram notes: "When a man gives himself up to the government of a ruling passion, – or, in other words, when his Hobby-Horse grows headstrong, farewell cool reason and fair discretion!" (TS 113). The novel also tests perceptions of oddities and eccentricities against an idea of normality; like in Swift's *Gulliver* all judgement is shown as subjective and relational. Michael Deporte

---

[64] See Parnell (1994) and Parker (2010).
[65] See especially Michael Deporte's *Nightmares and Hobbyhorses* (1977).

draws attention to another aspect important with regard to the hobbyhorses, linking it to the mediation of risk and the topic of war in the novel. The hobbyhorses offer a helpful escapism and compensation for physical inabilities; they provide structure and a sense of purpose to men like Toby, traumatized by war, and Walter, haunted by marital problems, loss, and parental anxieties. In this sense, "The hobbyhorsism of Toby and Walter is not merely tolerated, it is shown to be necessary for their survival" (Deporte 1974: 152). This aspect is indicative of the 'modernity' of Sterne's text. The characterization displays an understanding of human beings as a totality, of an inseparable connection between body and mind, between physical and mental states. Roy Porter emphasizes the reflection of Sterne's awareness "of the new physiological importance of the nerves, organisation, sensitivity and sexuality" (Porter 1989: 78; 69). While the hobby-horses symbolize radical individuality on the one hand, they also create a sense of 'universal', shared oddity and symbolize a necessary, orientating function. As Eric Rothstein puts it: "Each [man], obviously, has his hobbyhorse, a system of reference that interprets facts and defines priorities in his mental world" (Rothstein 1975: 64).

Whereas the narrator claims that his only urgency is to present a sense of coherence to the reader, the narrative constantly disrupts causality and the novel offers perhaps as its only certainty that there is no security about beginnings, middle, and endings, and about how people will behave. The notion that the human mind itself poses the greatest risk to mankind is introduced from the beginning. Interestingly, this idea has been confirmed in modern psychological risk research and concerns in particular the question of how accidents happen, and thus how they can possibly be predicted and prevented. Yet, as theorists agree, the one thing that cannot be calculated and thus be insured, is the human mind and the decisions of a single individual.[66]

Sterne's narrator is preoccupied with attempting to find causality and deal with what is perceived as 'accidents'. To only briefly consider the distinction between 'accident' and chance', whereas chance is usually understood as "general causelessness" in the perception of an event, accident refers only to the absence of "an immediate cause", i.e in the sense of 'coincidence', the simultaneous occurrence of two seemingly unrelated events.[67] According to Mario Bunge, "Both deterministic and indeterministic metaphysics define chance in

---

[66] A classic study which makes this argument is Charles Perrow's *Normal Accidents* (1984).
[67] One can argue that is the individual's perception which turns a contingency into a coincidence: "In other words, coincidence in *Tristram Shandy* is a name for those contingencies in which somebody is interested" (Rosenblum 1977: 241); or as Julia Jordan writes: "coincidence is, in one sense after all, just randomness that has been brought to our attention" (2010: 8).

3.3 Individualism, Parental Anxiety, and Fears of Destruction: *Tristram Shandy*

a negative way: the accidental is that which is not necessary, or that which is not ordered" (Bunge 1951: 215).[68] *Tristram Shandy* illustrates not only the negative workings of chance in this way, because the countless little accidents are never 'lucky" ones but usually harm or disorient the characters, but also shows how mankind actively produces notions of contingency in the perception of events. Applying Bunge's definition, the narrator's attempts to chronicle his own coming into the world demonstrate the typically human struggle of a continuous back-and-forth between chance and causality: "But man does no only know and produce casual chains, but also contingent events. For every chance he defeats he creates other accidents. Thereby the progress of learning and of mastering nature and life does not bring with it the quantitative reduction but the qualitative modification of the domain of chance" (Bunge 1951: 221). In his analysis of the novel Hamilton employs the Aristotelian distinction of accidental vs. necessary qualities mentioned by Bunge above, referring to the first as the changing, contingent site of individual identity (of persons or objects). He argues that *Tristram Shandy*: "In both context and form, [...] represents the operations of countless contingencies. Like *Tom Jones*, it begins with accidents of birth, but it conspicuously lacks the order that Fielding imposed upon his narrative" (Hamilton 2007: 151).

Sterne's characters are engaged in various processes of trying to secure things and meanings, for instance, Uncle Toby the patterns of war, Walter his son's future, and Tristram his sense of origin and self. Meanwhile they are all challenged by the constant impact of accidents. Generally, Sterne domesticates accidents by showing them as "details of everyday life, such as the buzzing of a fly, a hot chestnut rolling from a tabletop, or an absent-minded turn of phrase" (Hamilton 2007: 152); however they all influence the accidental qualities of Tristram's own existence. Therefore, Hamilton points out, Sterne "gives accidents unprecedented power" (2007: 152). Significantly, the narrator describes himself in the beginning as the "Sport of small accidents, Tristram Shandy! that thou art, and ever will be!" (TS 179). In the Shandean world, man has little to no control over the circumstances, which as the narrative painfully shows, are forceful determinations and impossible to control. As Parson Yorick, the protagonist in Sterne's *A Sentimental Journey* says: "I am governed by circumstances – I cannot govern them" (SJ 53). The characters' attempts at precaution or controlling events

---

[68] For a still valid definition of chance and an understanding of the concept from antiquity onwards, see Bunge (1951). He defines contingency as an event which is accidental, that is "when it may or may not be", furthermore "contingent is all that cannot be predicted with certainty" (1951: 223), regardless of whether this is due to an absence of causal law or merely man's ignorance and lacking precision of circumstances. See also Reith (1999) and Jordan (2010).

often backfire and produce exactly the opposite of the desired result, for instance with Tristram's naming. The characters grapple with complicated questions of responsibility and agency, guilt and blame, e.g. after Tristram's injury by the window sash: "When Susannah told the corporal the misadventure of the sash, with all the circumstances which attended the murder of me, – (as she called it,) – [....], – Trim's conscience told him he was as much to blame as Susannah, –" (TS 370). The life portrayed by Sterne is indeed "a confused muddle of intent and accident" (McNeil 1990: 161). Furthermore, with all the little crude explanations the reader is constantly given by Tristram serving to increase the readers' awareness of the importance of circumstances, the narrator presents himself as the unwilling, helpless victim and product of them. The result of his attempts to describe the accidents, which have shaped his existence, is a satirical demonstration of the perceived influence of external events and chains of causality on human life.

Sterne employs a narrator, who is obsessed with circumstantiality, in all its anti-climactic, distractive and digressive details, and thus takes the task of giving the reader a sense of what Frank Kermode referred to as "contingent reality" (2000: 131), the rendering of circumstances any novelist has to do justice to, to satirical extremes. In the author's endless regressions one can see a mix between the "circumstantial method" of Defoe and the scepticism of judging human nature and the psychological angst we find in Gothic novels or Burney's fictions – perhaps even a foreshadowing of the modern uncertainty of narrative which comes much later.

The topical struggle between a sense of contingency and explanatory forces, the question of how people make their orders, constitutes the great appeal and validity of Sterne's novel in a postmodern context, or rather as what links the mid-18th to the late 20th century. The reader of Sterne's text is certainly confronted with more contingency than in most other 18th-or 19th-century novels; however, the narrative also continuously offers explanation for it. The narrative illustrates the process of meaning-making, less concerned with how the world works, but how individuals perceive it to be, and Michael Rosenblum adds: "For Tristram contingency is surprisingly dry and geometric; it is not an affliction but a challenge. Wherever he casts his gaze the human meanings multiply" (Rosenblum 1977: 246).[69] The incident with Phutatorius and the hot chestnut is a good exam-

---

[69] See Rosenblum's argument: "As a clergyman, Sterne may have been concerned with the designs of the divine Geometrician, but as a novelist his great resource is the shakier designs that men trace. Contingency, that state of affairs which Sterne seems to attribute to the world, is also that state of affairs which will most challenge men as they go about the task of constructing their orders" (1977: 245).

ple of this and shows various different perceptions and conjectures about the cause and meaning of the 'accident'. It takes place at the dinner hosted by Walter, Toby, and Yorick for the local church authorities; at stake is the possibility of renaming baby Tristram, i.e. reversing time and the damage done by his accidental baptism. However, the discussion at the table is disturbed by a falling hot chestnut, which penetrates Phutatorius' clothes and hurts his leg, because he has forgotten to firmly tie his breeches. Brian Norton gives an insightful and detailed reading of the scene, taking Phutatorius' untied breeches as an illustration of the "characters' never-ending struggles to shield themselves from external evils" (Norton 2006: 408).

Regarding the narrative's treatment of chance, it is interesting to relate the novel briefly to one of Sterne's sermons, on "Time and Chance".[70] It is an exegesis of the opening line from Ecclesiastes IX. II, "but time and chance happeneth to them all", which is repeated over and over in the sermon. Apart from this humbling reference to the democratizing, inescapable, and forceful effects of time and chance on every human, Sterne seeks to downsize the belief in human control and agency: "The histories of the lives and fortunes of men are full of instances of this nature, – where favourable times and lucky accidents have done for them, what wisdom or skill could not" (Sterne 1768: 12). He emphasizes man's limited grasp of causality, saying: "That things are carried on in this world, sometimes so contrary to all our reasonings, and the seeming probabilities of success, – [...] that the most likely causes disappoint and fail of producing for us the effect which we wished and naturally expected from them" (9). Expounding on the human experience that "there was so much of lottery in this life" (13), Sterne's carefully constructed argument seeks to present divine providence as the only possible "other cause" interfering with human affairs (14). Yet Sterne's rhetoric is also clearly based on a secular, mathematical understanding of the world, "where events have run counter to all probabilities" (15). He gives an interesting definition of chance as the human term to describe events, which "fall out quite contrary both to our intentions and our hopes" (16). Thus chance is inseparable from an experienced lack of causality and control. Interestingly, he concludes his sermon by referring to "this great and fundamental doctrine of a providence; the belief of which is of such consequence to us, as to be the great support and comfort of our lives" (23). This comforting belief is shattered in his novel which also contains a whole "Chapter on Chances",

---

70 See Sterne's *The Sermons of Mr Yorick Vol. II* (1768: 7–23), and Marjorie S. David's introduction to *The Sermons of Mr. Yorick by Laurence Sterne* (1973: 7–25) for the parallels between Sterne's fictions and his sermons.

according to Jesse Molesworth, "perhaps the most famous fictional meditation on chance authored in the eighteenth century" (Molesworth 2010: 193). It reads, in fact, like a disrupted attempt of Tristram's father and Uncle Toby of calculating the risks of the accidents of Tristram's birth and naming. The narrator renders it as follows:

> What a chapter of chances, said my father, [...] – what a long chapter of chances do the events of this world lay open to us! Take pen and ink in hand, brother Toby, and calculate it fairly! – I know no more of calculation than this baluster, said my uncle Toby (striking short of it with his crutch, and hitting my father a desperate blow souse upon his shinbone)– 'Twas a hundred to one – cried my uncle Toby – I thought, quoth my father, /rubbing his shin) you had known nothing of calculations, brother Toby. 'Tis a mere chance, said my uncle Toby– Then it adds one to the chapter – replied my father. (TS 281)

Tristram's narrative circles around mysterious incidents, always implying that someone should or will be able to tell why, when and how they happened; for example: "But whether that was the case or not the case; – or whether the snapping of my father's tobacco-pipe so critically, happened through accident or anger, – will be seen in due time" (TS 120). Furthermore, statements like the following occur again and again: "The moment could not be without cause. I'm lost. I can make nothing of it" (TS 275); "as all the world knows, that no effect in nature can be produced without a cause", (TS 520); "–'twas a matter of contingency, which might happen, or not, just as chance ordered it" (TS 541). Tristram always measures his descriptions against a notion of the 'normal' course of events; concluding that it usually "seems to run opposite to the natural workings of causes and effects" (TS 519). And the only recurring insight presented to the reader is that "we live among riddles and mysteries– [...]; and even the clearest and most exalted understandings amongst us find ourselves puzzled and at a loss in almost every cranny of nature's works" (TS 292). Julia Jordan, who sees chance as a central organizing principle of the novel, argues that the narrative accumulates "comically improbable chance events", which create an ironic pattern or rather "tissue of contingency that starts to look a lot like fate" (Jordan 2010: 16).[71] Another aspect of Sterne's depiction of chance needs stressing. By narrativizing accidents, his narrator tries to regulate them and to convert "accident to incident, causeless to caused", "not because it is simpler to do so, but because the consequences of not doing so are too terrifying" (Molesworth

---

[71] See Jordan (2010: 2–3). Although Jordan focuses mostly on 20th-century novels, she underlines the importance of *Tristram Shandy* as an early text, which reflects a significant change regarding the perception of chance and employs a new aesthetic that seeks to reflect contingency and uncertainty.

2010: 205; original emphasis; see Damrosch 1985: 292). Sterne's fictional demonstration of the ability of the human imagination to render chance occurrences meaningful reveals the motivation behind this activity, namely the banishing of a feeling of risk and lack of control.

The novel illustrates the potential of perception and opinions to be more tormenting than reality, especially if a control of that reality is beyond reach. For the title pages of the first two volumes of *Tristram Shandy*, Sterne borrows a motto from the late Stoic Epictetus' *Enchiridion:* "Men are disturbed, not by Things, but by the Principles and Notions, which they form concerning Things. Death, for instance, is not terrible, else it would have appeared so to Socrates. But the terror consists in our notion of death that it is terrible".[72] The quote highlights the power of imagination, and one can see a direct rendering of it in the beginning of volume 7 where the narrator admits that his fear of dying is actually worse than this terminal illness: "I never seriously think upon the mode and manner of this great catastrophe, which generally takes up and torments my thoughts as much as the catastrophe itself" (TS 470). It is possible to see the whole novel as a desperate exercising of control over personal impressions contrasted with the presentation of external circumstances, which are beyond human control.

A lot of criticism of *Tristram Shandy* stresses the aspect of play in the novel.[73] The motif applies on many levels, a dominant being, of course, the stylistic one, i.e Sterne's playful merging of metaphors, stories, topics and registers, as well as the intersection of different temporalities. Patricia Spacks describes a function of Tristram's language games thus: "Language betrays. By playing with it Tristram declares not his authenticity but his precarious power, shared by all writers: to control temporarily what ultimately evades human mastery" (Spacks 1976: 146). Specifically, Tristram evades a 'clear' telling of his family's history while seeking narrative control over his own life and origin. This aspect further-

---

[72] Translation from the Latin by Elizabeth Carter (1759); cited in Bloom and Bloom (1988: 500); also in Norton (2006: 409). See Norton for a more detailed analysis of the phrase in the context of Stoicism; he offers a useful interpretation of the motto in relation to the text: "From the Stoic point of view, however, his gap between subject and object is less an epistemological obstacle than an ethical boon [...] founded on a rigorous distinction between the internal workings of the mind and external reality, between what is 'up to us' and what is beyond our control. Stoic imperturbability – the state of being beyond the reach of contingency and external evils – is predicated on the idea that only what is in our power can fundamentally affect our well-being" (2006: 411).

[73] See, e.g., Alter (1968), Burckhardt (1961), Lanham (1973), Rothstein (1975), and also Brown (1991: 263).

more allows a comparison to the rhetorical tradition of debating and the competitive struggle for philosophical-argumentative dominance. According to Robert Lanham, the game of debating seeks momentary persuasion, not definite results. As it can always be begun anew, all results can only be considered intermediary ones (Lanham 1975: 45).[74] This sheds light on the narrator's persona and on the circular structure of the narrative, which are concerned with side-stepping the (fearful) truth and evasion of determination, of keeping options open and avoiding fixation just as well as direct physical confrontation. Yet the risk involved here is not the obvious one of winning or losing against an opponent, but the struggle with time and death.

The various hobbyhorses of the male characters are interesting to consider in this context. A point of linkage between the different games (linguistic, philosophical, war etc.) in the novel is the question of the governing role of chance vs. the individual's mastery of the game. McNeil analyses the men's games in the novel, especially Uncle Toby's miniature battlefields, in connection to an underlying military theme, and also considers them as grotesque representations, fitting the novel's catalogue of "ludicrous-fearful dualities" (1990: 150). In this sense, Toby's hobbyhorse is both absurd game and reminder of the battle as the origin of his mysterious yet crippling wound. "The wound is as horrific as Sterne could have made it – a piece of a parapet breaks off and hits Toby in the groin, crushing his hip bone and confining him to his room for four years (McNeil 1990: 153–154). Toby's wound, like Tristram's accidents, is shown as petty, grotesque and deeply unheroic. However, the game element, as Peter Stevick also argues, highlights Toby's struggle to infuse the senselessness of war with meaning (1969: 173). It is part of Sterne's satire to reduce the threat and destructiveness of war to the depiction of the miniature games and unspeakable wounds. Nonetheless, in Sterne's novel, as well as in Swift and Smollett's, war and physical harm are a constant presence, and masculinity is shown to be under threat both at home and abroad.

Arguably the main subject of Sterne's cock-and-bull story is the timing of conception, and it connects the opening and ending chapters. The novel ends with a reference to the impotence of the bull, the main concern of Obadiah's calculations; in the beginning Tristram struggles to calculate the exact moment of his own conception from all circumstantial evidence he can possible line up. Collecting details and speculations about 'family' traits like the famous Shandy nose, the one question Tristram never dares to ask is about his own difference.

---

74 Although Lanham's study *Tristram Shandy: Games of Pleasure* briefly refers to probability theory and games of chance (1973: 38), it does so without reflecting on the element of risk.

3.3 Individualism, Parental Anxiety, and Fears of Destruction: *Tristram Shandy* — 199

According to Marshall Brown, Tristram "never names his real fear, but he hints unmistakably at it" (1991: 291). Over the years, various critics have focussed on the hints of Tristram's illegitimacy in the text.[75] Considering the fact that Tristram tries to present the first Sunday night in March as the moment of his conception, "beyond all possibility of doubt" (TS 39), they all argue that there are signs that Mrs Shandy might have been already pregnant then, because Tristram was born on 5 November, 1718, a mere eight months after the only possible day Walter could have impregnated Mrs Shandy. Moreover, the description of the scene renders an actual conception unlikely. Regarding the question about the identity of Tristram's biological father, Margaret Doody suggests that Yorick is a likely candidate, as he has as conscious presence in the whole novel and she explains, "that Walter's reiterated patriarchal assurance has a shaky base. [...] Tristram himself may insist, with anxious emphasis, on the certainty of that moment of conception, [...]. That 'origin,' however, is deducibly false, and Tristram protests too much" (1996: 446). Meanwhile John Hunter sees "my Uncle Toby" first in line as a possible candidate for Tristram's paternity (Hunter 1989: 184), because he seems to have a much better and intuitive connection to Tristram. Further alternatives include Dr Slop, who Robert Erickson describes as "the technological father of Tristram" (Erickson 1986: 258), Trim, Obadiah, or Jonathan.

While the question about Tristram's illegitimacy is never explicitly articulated, it presents the greatest danger, or rather "a worse alternative than being a carelessly conceived, flat-nosed, misnamed, ill-educated, wounded, and perhaps impotent end-of-the-line Shandy" (Hunter 1989: 182–83). Taking a similar view, Margaret Doody goes as far as to say: "The worst that Roman or English laws regarding marriage, property, and inheritance could imagine has happened in *Tristram Shandy*" (Doody 1997: 446). And therefore the meticulous calculation of Tristram's conception is only a desperate counter-act because it is already too late. Paul Alkon draws attention to the "retrospective calculation of probabilities" (1979: 43) as a persistent pattern in later 18th-century fictions. *Tristram Shandy* is obsessed with retrospection and finding causal connection for past events; as such the novel "pursues lost time" (1979: 45). Critics agree that Tristram's insecurity makes him a typical male character of later 18th-century literature. The staging of an uncertainty of identity at the heart of Sterne's novel mirrors the cultural anxieties and changes within patriarchal society. More

---

[75] An early essay to notice this is John A. Hay's "Rhetoric and Historiography: Tristram Shandy's First Nine Kalendar Months" (1973). Since then many readings have mentioned the possibility, or at least nodded in this direction. See, e. g., Hunter (1990), Doody (1997), and Pesso-Miquel (2004). On the topic of paternal anxiety, see Moglen (2001: 90), Molesworth (2010: 189), and Norton (2006: 414).

specifically, *Tristram Shandy* can be classified among the texts "openly obsessed with bastardy" (Zunshine 2005: 6).[76] Emphasizing the prominence of the topic, Lisa Zunshine writes: "Demographers and historians refer to the eighteenth century as the 'century of illegitimacy,' [....] they all agree that this phenomenon must have touched everyone who lived at that time and played a crucial role in the economic, social, and cultural life of the Enlightenment" (2005: 1). It can be related to a broader crisis of ideology, the crumbling of the feudal system, and questions of lines of tradition, ownership, and property. These are also at the heart of the plot-driving prophecy in Walpole's *The Castle of Otranto* and many other Gothic novels. With regard to Tristram, it is interesting to consider Wolfram Schmidgen's description of the male bastard figure in literature as being permanently "in-between culture and nature, he is with and without an origin" (Schmidgen 2002b: 139). The risk of bastardy places Tristram on a threshold and invites speculation, leaving him and his father with fears of loss and masculinities grounded in anxiety.

Concerning the theme of masculinity and anxiety, many critics see an explicit staging of the fear of sexual deficiency and impotence, which is carried through the text and culminates in Tristram's accident with the window-sash. The incident of a near castration is often taken as a fictionalization of Sterne's own anxieties about his declining health, which rendered him unable to perform sexual intercourse at the time of writing the novel. For example, Patricia Spacks argues for a correspondence between the fear of author/narrator: "Impotence threatens (and overtakes) him; his recurrent worries about the impossibility of completing his literary project reflect among other things, the deeper worry about survival" (Spacks 2006: 257).[77] The topic of potent masculinity at risk is intertwined with a constant malfunctioning of objects in text. Starting with the clock, Molesworth sums up, "just about everything in *Tristram Shandy*, it seems, is either sinking, winding down, running to exhaustion, interrupted, cut short, or dropping off" (2010: 190).

While the novel deals with frustrated ambitions and desires, the narrative focus is exclusively on the male perspective. Men fail at mastery no matter what they do; they combat this by seeking carefully limited and treasured areas of expertise. The discrepancy between a man's aspirations and his actual

---

[76] See Zunshine's *Bastards And Foundlings* (2005) and Schmidgen (2002b).
[77] On the impotence theme and fear of genital damage in the novel, see Spacks (1976: 130–132), Brown (1991: 292), and Parker (1997: 110). Erickson mentions the affair of Toby and Widow Waldman in book 8 and 9 as another example of a relationship, shaped by many delays and abortive attempts, between a sexually active woman with an impaired, possibly impotent man (1986: 239).

accomplishments is a recurring source of tragic humour in the text. Walter Shandy makes vexed attempts at controlling his son's character from the moment of his entrance into the world, yet if anything Walter's risk management and education aims appear comical in their destructiveness. In comparison to the male adult characters, the narrator's paranoia seems more intense and he finds control and liberation only in his own hobbyhorse, writing, and his digressions. Aside from his battle with illness, he suffers from a writer's worst fears: disapproval, insignificance, and rejection. But although Tristram's world, "that inextricable labyrinth of debts, cares, woes, want, grief, discontent, melancholy" (TS 418) is perceived to be full of dangers and sorrows, amidst all chaos and uncertainty intuition and a good heart are shown to be far superior guiding principles than rational calculation and endless sceptical debate: "In the darkest doubts it shall conduct him safer than a thousand casuists, and give the state he lives in a better security for his behaviour than all the clauses and restrictions put together, which law-makers are forced to multiply" (TS 149).

3.4 Overwhelming Fears and Struggles for Authority: *The Castle of Otranto*

Despite the debate about its merits or shortcomings Horace Walpole's *The Castle of Otranto* (1764), subtitled *A Gothic Story*, holds its canonical place as the genre prototype of the Gothic novel.[78] Considering that it is often described as a "hugely improbable tale (even by the loose standards of its genre) of usurpation, supernatural revenge and the workings of a malign providence set in medieval Italy" (Jones 2002: 123), at a first glance at least, Walpole's text presents a challenge to the parameters set in this study. Its characteristic melodramatic plot, providential rhetoric and supernatural events, evoking blind panic and terror, the setting far removed in time and space, and the intensity of emotions, all seemingly combine to oppose the depiction of a calculated, somewhat 'realistic' and rational, perception and management of risk. Besides being slightly tainted with the image of a literary subgenre offering primarily entertainment rather than aesthetic value or didactic-moral instruction, the emergence of the Gothic novel is traditionally seen as counter-movement to Enlightenment rationality and the realist novel, reflecting a desired return of repressed sentimentality

---

[78] For example, H.P. Lovecraft grants *The Castle of Otranto* the status as a founding text of unparalleled influence despite being of mediocre quality, unconvincing, melodramatic, and presenting an artificial and contrived story (1973: 24). On the contemporary reception of Walpole's novel see Sabor (1987).

and imagination, an aesthetic of emotion, escapism, and foreshadowing the development towards Romanticism. Readings of Walpole's novel often comment on the social-political context, the weakening status of the English aristocracy and questions of property, succession and rule of power taken up in the text. Most commonly, however, criticism skips over, or only refers in passing, to the specific and complex fears negotiated in the text and focuses instead on the original formulaic elements of Gothic horror introduced by Walpole.[79]

Yet rather than isolate it as a 'new' beginning, it is interesting to read the text alongside other mid-18th-century fictions. Walpole's comparatively short narrative takes up many concerns discussed in this chapter and shows parallels to the other novels despite the obvious 'generic' differences. Covering only three days and divided into five chapters, a formal set-up corresponding to the rules of classical tragedy, Walpole's novel certainly strives for greater unity than many earlier fictions (see Flint 1998: 269).[80] But it also illustrates why the Gothic aesthetic was appealing to writers and readers of the time. Functioning as a "retreat to a premodern, pre-Enlightenment, world of mystery and suspense" (Molesworth 2010: 228), it possessed a fascination similar to that of gambling and speculation, which allowed a 'safe' play with risk, venturing beyond rational calculations into a realm of hidden dangers and passions.[81]

Leaving an in-depth analysis of the Gothic stock machinery aside, the focus is placed on the text's dealing with many familiar 18th-century fears as well as with those gaining prominence in the 19th century. It engages with anxieties about authority and stability, with a heavy dose of self-conscious irony also found in the other novels discussed in this chapter. One example is the fear about a greater independence and agency of women in public life and in the market place. An "anxious sense of patriarchy" (Hunter 1989: 194) is palpable in Sterne's epic *Tristram Shandy*, as well as in *The Castle of Otranto*; both texts

---

79 For introductory surveys of genre see Botting (1996), Clemens (1999), Kilgour (1995), and Ellis (2000).

80 This is interesting to compare to Eric Rothstein's argument that the "factitious mysteries of Gothic novels" appear as a last attempt to maintain the more hazardous order of 18th-century fiction and resist the causal-linear plot streamlining in the development towards the 19th-century realist novel (1975: 243).

81 See, for instance, Hammond and Ragan's comment: "From a safe vantage point, such novels enable readers to experience delightful pains and dangers, enabling vicarious access to obscurity, darkness, and incarceration, the supernatural and the terrible" (2006: 157); and Walter Kendrick, who says: "In fact, when Walpole's characters flee along labyrinthine passages or recoil from talking skeletons, they are standing in for eighteenth-century readers, who gladly underwent such terrors in the modern safety of a book or the painted gallery of an artificial abbey" (1991: 76).

have plots driven by fears about a male loss of control, mocking them at the same time. Another crucial aspect is the contemporary obsession with rationality, predictability, and empirical observation, so masterfully satirized and subverted in Swift's *Gulliver's Travels*, which brings forth a mounting fear of the opposites of Enlightenment's values: irrationality, coincidence, darkness, superstition and passion. Hence, in the process of replacing the fear of unpredictable forces of nature and unknown 'higher' powers with ideas of regularity and calculability of the world, modernity produced new anxieties rather than unlimited optimism and fearlessness. Matthias Hurst argues in great depth for the intrinsic connection between Enlightenment thought and fear, because anything 'inexplicable' poses a threat to the security provided by the narrow categories of human rationality. Most prominent among the new anxieties produced by Enlightenment paradigms is the fear of a loss of control and the evils springing from within the human mind. Following on the heels of the celebration of human agency and calculation of the future, a reflection of their darker sides gains momentum in mid-18th-century texts.[82] The Gothic novel, full of its own inconsistencies and improbabilities, captures the paradoxical tensions between an increase of fear and sense of being at risk and feelings of greater security, knowledge, and (self-)control. This also includes a new conception of the past as risk, and an altered belief in "History's pattern [which] now appeared malign" (Miles 1991: 41).

Providing a sense of catharsis and restoration of order, the end of Walpole's narrative does not bring full closure by explaining the supernatural events or making sense of the tragedies. What marks the specificity and 'newness' of this novel beyond all the shared contemporary concerns, Jürgen Klein (1975: 273) points out, is that for the first time darkness, uncertainty, and fearful sensations are used as the dominant subjects. While Walpole "brings into play the incongruities most likely to move and terrify the audience of his day" (Clery 2008: xxxii), arguably a main function of the text is to offer an alternative realm of fantasy. Referring to the fact that Gothic fiction came into being at the

---

[82] See Hurst's (2001) excellent study of the tension between rationalism and irrationality in the so-called Age of Enlightenment, Hurst writes: "Als paradoxes Ergebnis ihrer eigenen Absichten erzeugt die Aufklärung allerdings nicht nur existentielle Ängste – Furcht vor der triebhaften Natur des Menschen, Furcht vor der Furcht als irrationaler Kraft, die das Denken und vernünftigen Handeln in einer modernen Welt und einer von bürgerlicher Rationalität geprägten Ökonomie sabotiert – Das Risiko ist konstant spürbar, ja geradezu unvermeidbar, den es scheint so, "als sei mit dem dezidierten Rationalismus eben das stets in Frage stellende Irrationale bis zu dem völligen Umschlagen der Ratio in den Wahnsinn wesentlich verbunden" (2001: 47; referring here also to Wolfgang Promies's *Die Bürger und der Narr oder das Risiko der Phantasie* (1966)).

same time as a new reader response, which had been prepared by the mid-century sentimentalist fictions of Samuel Richardson and others, David Richter states that "it cannot be an accident that both the reader and the protagonist of the Gothic novel share an intense need to escape" (1989: 13). With reading becoming a favoured pastime, for both "imaginative play and escape", Gothic fiction demands from the reader not only a willing suspension of disbelief, but calls "for an empathic participation in the perils and plight of the protagonists" (1989: 8).

In the preface to the first edition, Walpole presents *The Castle of Otranto* as an ancient manuscript, only recently 'discovered', and claims the role of 'translator' for himself. The story is set in medieval Europe, well before any calculus of probability, with a (Catholic) belief in providence and various superstitions still intact. Walpole tells the reader: "Miracles, visions, necromancy, dreams and other preternatural events [...] Belief in every kind of prodigy was so established in those dark ages, that an author would not be faithful to the *manners* of the times who should omit all mention of them" (CO 6). The device of placing the story in the distant past allows a temporary return to older certainties and authorities which are ironically presented as a dark, terrible foil of enslaving superstitions against the enlightened, liberated present. Ann McWhir comments on this aspect, saying: "Walpole invites the reader to have his cake and eat it [...]. The Gothic novel plays at converting us to believe in the supernatural, but it always maintains the level of game" (1989: 38). In other words, Gothic fiction allows for a coexistence of belief and disbelief, for intellectual scepticism alongside emotional indulgence. But Walpole's setting also entails a more political function that puts *The Castle of Otranto* in line with other contemporary sentimental fictions engaging with the tensions between aristocratic and bourgeois ideals of society. Although the Gothic novel, set far away and in the distant past, is often accused of being silent on contemporary social-political issues, it aids the creation of a clear enemy, "a barbarous, past-ridden, superstitious Catholic Europe" (Jones 2002: 124), functioning as a bad Other compared to rationally-enlightened, Protestant England. Whether one wants to see this as a strategy of distraction from the problems at 'home' or as an expression of nostalgia for a rigid feudal society, it remains a reflection of fears of (national) instability and disorder.

Confessing his authorship in the preface to the second edition, Walpole famously described his attempt to write a new kind of story, blending "two kinds of romance, the ancient and the modern" (CO 9). In his narrative, he sought to combine imagination and improbability, characteristics of the older romance-form with "accurate imitation of nature" according to "the rules of probability" (CO 9), hallmarks of the modern novel.[83] The narrative is shaped by this tension between an imaginative use of supernatural events and strange coincidences within a mode of narration, which also ridicules these 'improbabilities' and shows a belief in the paradigms of calculation and the 'laws of nature.' Consequently, Helen Moglen sees the gothic novel as partaking in modernity's "larger deconstructive project, mediating between an older romance tradition, whose metaphysical and social assumptions it cannot share, and an emergent tradition of the fantastic, which is overtly psychological in perspective. From that intermediary location, gothic texts portray the horrifying emptiness of a secularized world" (Moglen 2001: 111). In fact, Walpole's description of the plot of *The Castle of Otranto* sounds all too familiar from today's risk-society-perspective: "Everything tends directly to the catastrophe" (CO 6). Regarding the construction of the plot, it is important to see the string of coincidences, combining to add calamity to calamity, not as a return to the traditional tool of divine design and "as a means of producing the consoling idea of Providence (its traditional function) but rather the disquieting sensation of the uncanny" (Molesworth 2010: 10).[84] In addition, the rise of the Gothic novel, beginning with *The Castle of Otranto*, testifies to the fact that (narrative) causality is motivated increasingly by psychology rather than providence. [85]

The development of 18th-century fiction reflects the changing approach to the constitution of selfhood, and "the painful burden of modern self-awareness" (Moglen 2001: 112), which has been seen in the torments of characters like Crusoe, Roxana, Gulliver, or Tristram. Besides the confrontation with spiritual emptiness, and the fears induced by a lack of orientation and (moral) guidance,

---

[83] How successful this blend turned out in terms of literary style and sophistication is a matter of critical taste and judgment, but it certainly introduced the formula for a new and for a while immensely popular genre.

[84] Although 'coincidence' seems to refer to a rather unscientific, superstitious worldview, it is a modern concept, Molesworth (2010: 229) explains, capturing the phenomenon of perceived causelessness and unintentionality independent of providential design. Strong magical or religious beliefs do not allow for a notion of coincidence, which thus paradoxically unites new and older explanatory frames.

[85] Perhaps even more than prose fiction, in the second half of 18th century poetry takes up the attempt to unite the probable and the marvellous, and seeks new conceptions of the relations between human nature and reality in fiction. Wallace Jackson describes the poets' agenda thus: "The wanted, in sum, a newly marvelous subject not divorced from probability but founded on the probabilities of human nature and justified by the evidence of past literatures" (1978: 5). This idea of testing the "permissible limits of the marvelous consistent with the delineation of probable human action" (1978: 7) underlines the strong turn towards psychological motivations and the workings of the human mind which is so often staged as a source of terror in Gothic fiction.

Walpole's characters are literally overwhelmed by terror, guilt and melancholy. The greatest danger in the novel is Manfred's uncontrolled desires and the imposition of his will at all costs.[86] This epitomizes how human passions and affects are perceived as the dangerous opposites of reason and control, with fear and imagination themselves appearing as disruptive and destructive forces. According to Moglen (2001: 109), later 18th-century fictions highlight the modern subject's individualism and often depict it as being internally torn apart by conflicting instincts suppressed by social rules. Walpole's treatment of this subject matter differs from that by previous writers. For example, in comparison to Laurence Sterne's exploration of modern subjectivity in *Tristram Shandy*, he sought a much more sensational approach and style that involves the reader's emotions. As all theory and criticism of the Gothic novel emphasizes, a main part is the experience of terror and fear, enjoyed from a position of relative safety. The occurrence of "literary fear", i.e. fear in literature as opposed to real-life fear, is tied to the public and private life becoming 'safer' for a large number of people.[87] Although tales of terror have been told since antiquity, the narration of fear gains new prominence at a moment when existential fears begin to disappear (at least from the lives of the reading middle and upper classes), as Horace Walpole himself put it: "A god, or at least a ghost, was necessary to frighten us out of too much sense".[88] This implies that the more rational and stable daily life becomes, the more fear gets banned into the realm of fiction, which answers to people's persisting, if hidden, desire for irrationality (cf. Alewyn 1972: 51). Apart from offering "thrills" in Michael Balint's sense and satisfying the individual's need for affect, other theories stress the possibility of compensating real fears by living through fictional fears in literature.[89] Going beyond a mere cathartic release at the end and new-found enjoyment of one's own safety, Gothic fiction canalizes fear in specific, recognizable forms and renders them, in a sense, manageable (see Hurst 2001: 57; 77–78). Gothic fiction appears in this regard even as

---

86 This suggests another parallel to political texts like Swift's *Gulliver's Travel*. The Gothic elements of *The Castle of Otranto* certainly do not appear only aesthetically motivated. Walpole's novel similarly negotiates notions of civilization and barbarity and stages fears of threats to the power of the old ruling class. Through its main villain-hero, Manfred, it shows the dangers of forms of government, specifically absolutism and tyranny; it exemplifies Gothic fiction's plots which "invest the tyrants with a power so great and so absolute (as seen from within) that no mechanism can be found for circumventing it; it can be evaded only by treating it as a dream of oppression from which one happily wakes up" (Richter 1989: 13).
87 On the concept of 'literary fear' in contrast to 'real' fear, see Alewyn (1972) and Conrad (1974).
88 Walpole in a letter to Élie de Beaumont on March 18, 1765, cited in Morris (1985: 306).
89 See Balint's *Angstlust und Regression* (1976).

a logical continuation of Enlightenment rationality. Although exaggerated feelings of being at risk are turned into entertainment, the thrill is not constituted through the flirt with fortune and the remote chance of winning, as it is in gambling. Yet the threat of a loss of control is similarly at stake. David Morris explains how the Gothic novel "by releasing into fiction images and desires long suppressed, deeply hidden, forced into silence – greatly intensifies the dangers of an uncontrollable release from restraint. Such dangers no doubt help to explain why censorship and swooning were among the most common social responses to Gothic texts. Terror was a liberating – hence dangerous – force" (Morris 1985: 306).

The Castle of Otranto illustrates the coexistence of light and darkness, of rationality and irrational passions and terrors, as one calls forth the other. Though in sensational form, the novel reveals the "anti-superstitious superstition" (McWhir 1989: 32) of radical Enlightenment thought, the fear of coincidence and manipulative trickery. Even before the start of the narrative, the preface identifies the main apparent cause of events, the plot-driving prophecy, that *"the sins of the fathers are visited on their children to the third and fourth generation"* (CO 7; original emphasis), which points towards the danger of the hidden past coming back to haunt the characters in the present. The hidden wrongs from the past are slowly exposed (and eventually set right) through a process perceived by the characters as a mix of coincidences and providential fatalism.[90]

The opening scene presents the disruption of the marriage ceremony between Conrad and Isabella, as Conrad is "dashed to pieces, and almost buried under an enormous helmet, an hundred times more large than any casque every made for human beings" (CO 19), which falls from the sky, leaving the whole wedding party "struck with terror and amazement" (CO 18). The failed marriage and calamity brings forth memories of an ancient prophecy, proclaiming: *"That the castle and lordship of Otranto should pass from the present family, whenever the real owner should be grown too large to inhabit it"* (CO 17; original emphasis). The cruel accident catapults everybody into frightful state of uncertainty, and especially Manfred, current usurping ruler of Otranto, is shaken by the inexplicable event: "The few words he articulated tended solely to inquiries, whether any man knew from whence it could have come? Nobody could give him the

---

[90] See, for instance, Bernstein (1991: 151). Analysing Walpole's elements of horror introduced in the novel from the angle of longevity within the genre, Kendrick concludes that while "Gigantism did not fare well as a trigger of shocks […] The avenging past, however, especially the past that is dead or thought to be, retains the frightening power it had for Walpole's time" (1991: 74–75). The motive of ghosts and the revenge of the past goes, of course, further back than Walpole and can be found, e.g. in Elizabethan drama.

least information" (CO 20). All spectators try to find causal, logical explanations, but these attempts only increase Manfred's fury. Conrad's death leaves him without a male heir and this threat to his supremacy throws him into a state of panic. The following plot action is driven by Manfred's disastrous attempts at managing the risks of losing his illegitimate claim to power, consisting of a series of impulsive decisions mainly made out of sheer rage and desperation. While the scene establishes an important connection of coincidence and the uncanny, the reference to the prophecy introduces an atmosphere of dread. In contrast, for instance, to the opening prophecy in *Roderick Random*, the satire of benevolent providential design is reversed: past crimes will come back to haunt the protagonist, and pride and passion will be Manfred's doom. Instead of assuring the reader that all dangers will be somehow overcome and all will be well in the end, the narrative thus hints at a break with the existing order.

The dramatic, almost surrealist opening scene introduces the recurring motif of "giant things" in the novel. Apart from the enormous helmet adorned with black feathers, the characters later encounter outsized, dissevered body parts and parts of amour. Cynthia Sundberg Wall writes that Walpole's novel "has often seemed to faint under the weight of its own sword – its implausible collection of enormous things. [...]. Their object seems to be terror, but their effect ridiculous" (Wall 2006: 112). A lot in Walpole's narrative appears exaggeratedly out of proportion, be it appearances or emotions. This adds a distinct strangeness to the terror, but also draws attention to the discrepancy between imagination, observation and reality. Although the novel plays with perception like Swift's *Gulliver's Travels*, while Gulliver narrowly escapes all his accidents with giant things in Brobdingnag, Conrad is crushed to death by the helmet. Moreover, instead of detailed descriptions of all strange things and events, all is clouded in obscurity in *The Castle of Otranto*. Arguing therefore for reading the text mainly as a satire of 18th-century literary conventions and the "culture of things" and material descriptions in this context, Sundberg Wall points out that the theme of the deceptiveness of appearances extends well beyond the level of objects: "Every single instance of power, terror, tension, tenderness, love, or poignancy is ruthlessly undercut by a close reading. Neither the moral nor the characters are what they pretend to be" (Wall 2006: 119; 116). This reflects, of course, the basic fear of disorientation and the risks involved in the process of judging by appearances dramatized in the narrative.

Clinging desperately to his role as master of Otranto, Manfred tries to find means to assure the continuance of his family lineage and decides to divorce his wife Hippolita and to marry young Isabella because the latter seems more likely to produce the desired male heir. This plan scares Isabella to such an extent that she immediately tries to flee the castle. From this moment on, she "dreaded nothing so much as Manfred's pursuit of his declaration" (CO 25), while Manfred is in return determined to "use the human means in my power for preserving my race; Isabella shall not escape me" (CO 26). In her fear, Isabella starts to run down the main staircase of the castle, driven by the idea of getting away, but lacking direction. So she pauses to calculate her options:

> There she stopped, not knowing whither to direct her steps, nor how to escape from the impetuosity of the Prince. The gates of the castle, she knew, were locked, and guards placed in the court. Should she, as her heart prompted her, go and prepare Hippolita for the cruel destiny that awaited her, she did not doubt but Manfred would seek her there, and that his violence would incite him to double the injury he meditated, without leaving room for them to avoid the impetuosity of his passions. Delay might give him time to reflect on the horrid measures he had conceived, or produce some circumstance in her favour, if she could—for that night, at least—avoid his odious purpose. Yet where conceal herself? How avoid the pursuit he would infallibly make throughout the castle? (CO 27)

The quote shows Isabella's emotions and feeling of being trapped, but also presents an astute examination of the risks of the situation and Manfred's character. While Isabella clearly perceives Manfred's uncontrolled temper as a danger to her and Hippolita, she also sees it as something momentary that can potentially be deescalated. This aspect is emphasized repeatedly in the narrative. Despite his villainy, Manfred "was not one of those savage tyrants who wanton in cruelty unprovoked. The circumstances of his fortune had given an asperity to his temper, which was naturally humane; and his virtues were ready to operate, when his passion did not obscure his reason" (CO 33). He displays the characteristics of a multi-dimensional villain, of a Byronic hero, who unites wildness and charisma with melancholic grace and a devilish temper. Being "full of anxiety and horror" (CO 24) himself, Manfred's inner good qualities have been overtaken, but not completely erased, by his passions and he is now reigned by jealousy and the thirst for power.[91] This is revealed in the words he chooses to convince Hippolita to agree to the dissolution of their marriage: "Thus you will divert the calamities that are hanging over our heads, and have the merit of saving the principality of Otranto from destruction. [...] though the warmth of my temper betrayed me into some unbecoming expressions, I honour your virtue, and wish to be indebted to you for the repose of my life and the preservation of my family" (CO 50). His pursuit of Isabella is motivated politically, rather than sexually, and a strategic attempt to avert the danger of destruction. To

---

[91] Regardless of whether Walpole was aware of the etymological origin of the name 'Manfred', it appears ironic that it stems from old High German, meaning "man of peace", because peace is the one thing Manfred lacks.

this end, he is ready to risk everything. Embodying the dangers of hubris, he is inevitably punished for his transgression. One can see reactionary tendencies in such an ending, which brings a restoration of 'old', rightful ownership over property rather than change, yet Manfred appears also as a guilty victim of his ancestors and his uncontrolled passions.[92] He is first put at risk by his ancestors seizing power unrightfully, later by his paranoia of discovery which pushes him beyond the recognition of any moral authority: "Heaven nor hell shall impede my designs" (CO 23).

The characterization of Manfred exemplifies the new realism of Walpole's writing, which strives for psychological probability in the sense that characters "respond in recognizably human ways to external events that are themselves implausible and marvellous" (Hammond and Ragan 2006: 159; see Saathoff 2001: 127). Manfred illustrates the complex paranoia induced by the implications of the ancient prophecy; the crisis constructed right at the beginning of the narrative brings out his inner fears and his dark side.[93] The depiction of Manfred as a source of danger builds up in intensity during Isabella's flight through the castle: "Every murmur struck her with new terror; yet more she dreaded to hear the wrathful voice of Manfred urging his domestics to pursue her" (CO 27); "The terror of Manfred soon outweighed every other terror" (CO 28). It eclipses rival fears like being lost and lonely and scared by dark corners and figures. Finally, she manages to hide in the chapel under Friar Jerome's temporary guardianship. This causes a fight for the supremacy of Isabella, who ultimately wants to make her own decision, yet now has both Manfred and Jerome arguing over who has the authority to claim and protect her. Manfred aggressively orders the Friar to make Isabella give up her sanctuary, "and bring the Princess to her duty". But he meets firm rejection: "It is my duty to prevent her return hither", said Jerome. "She is where orphans and virgins are safest from the snares and wiles of this world; and nothing but a parent's authority shall take her thence". "I am her parent", cried Manfred, "and demand her" (CO 49). The friar is very aware of the threats to the stability of the family posed by the turn of events and the

---

[92] Kendrick comments on the array of evil father figures and the frequent incestuous subtexts in Gothic fiction: "Like Gothic castles, they were old, weathered, and psychologically, at least – intricate. They hardly needed sex to make them scary" (1991: 87–88). On the judgment and complexity of Manfred's character see also Saathoff (2001: 122; 130) and Hurst (2001: 282ff).

[93] As in *Roderick Random,* Manfred's male temper is revealed by violent outbursts of passion, rage and fear. He is immune, however, to the calming love of a woman as his saving grace. Regarding the depiction of transgressive behaviour, disorder, and elements of horror and the grotesque, I nonetheless agree with C.J. Rawson that *Roderick Random* appears as a precursor of the Gothic novel (Rawson 1972: 82).

risks Manfred's violence poses for the women. Trying to manage the situation best he can, the quote below underlines the mix of overwhelming emotions and attempts at rational calculation and control in Jerome's reflections, echoing those of Isabella.

> He trembled for Hippolita, whose ruin he saw was determined; and he feared if Manfred had no hope of recovering Isabella, that his impatience for a son would direct him to some other object, who might not be equally proof against the temptation of Manfred's rank. [...] At length, conceiving some hopes from delay, he thought the wisest conduct would be to prevent the Prince from despairing of recovering Isabella. Her the Friar knew he could dispose, from her affection to Hippolita, and from the aversion she had expressed to him for Manfred's addresses, to second his views, till the censures of the church could be fulminated against a divorce. (CO 50–51)

The question of patriarchal authority and its feared reach concerns all female characters in the novel. During a conversation with her maid Bianca, Manfred's daughter Matilda replies to the question "if my Lord Manfred should offer you a handsome young Prince for a bridegroom, you would drop him a curtsey, and tell him you would rather take the veil?", "Thank Heaven! I am in no such danger" (CO 40). In the narrative, Matilda always sees herself being in a state of safety, protected by her status as Manfred's daughter. This illusion is, of course, later shattered ironically by the tragic accident of Manfred stabbing her in a jealous rage, mistaking her in the dark for Isabella on a romantic rendezvous with Theodore. Matilda is characterized by her pragmatic attitude, radically different from Bianca, who is easily sacred and impressed by the supernatural events. On more than one occasion Matilda scolds Bianca: "You resolve every thing into magic" (CO 46). For example, when the two women hear a voice below their bedroom window, Bianca cries out: "This castle is certainly haunted!" (CO 42). Matilda, however, is curious and starts talking to the stranger outside. The ensuing dialogue with Theodore, later revealed to be the son of Frederic, the rightful ruler of Otranto, circles around the risk of secrets and trusting strangers.[94] Matilda displays an openness and fearlessness with clashes with Theodore's caution: "I know not how, I know not if I dare", said the Young stranger, faltering; "yet the humanity with which you have spoken to me emboldens—Lady! dare I trust you?" "Heavens!" said Matilda, "what dost thou mean?

---

94 Cf. Molesworth's argument that Gothic fictions engage with fears caused by urbanization and masses of people living in close proximity. Questions of dealing with strangers and who to trust and who to 'recognize' become urgent matters: "The larger point is that strangers do not exist in Gothic fiction. Rather, strangeness always carries a tinge of the familiar, just as familiarity always carries a tinge of the strange" (2010: 243).

With what wouldst thou trust me? Speak boldly, if thy secret is fit to be entrusted to a virtuous breast" (CO 44). Soon afterwards, Theodore is locked up in a chamber in the castle tower, as punishment for his supposed aid in Isabella's flight. With everybody furiously searching for Isabella, Matilda seizes the chance to free Theodore. Their dialogue, again exclusively concerned with questions of danger and safety also brings the discovery of their romantic feelings for each other. Matilda urges Theodore: "Fly; the doors of thy prison are open [...]. Be gone in safety" He replies: "Let us fly together: the life thou bestowest shall be dedicated to thy defence" (CO 72).[95] She dismisses his chivalrous promises and heroic objections with the fateful assurance: "I am Manfred's daughter, but no dangers await me. [...] I run no risk", said Matilda, "but by thy delay. Depart; it cannot be known that I have assisted thy flight" (CO 72).

Their long conversation shows noticeable, and clearly gendered differences in risk perception, repeated in Theodore's following encounter with Isabella. Theodore is only concerned with the immediate physical risks posed by a confrontation with Manfred, and tries to calm Isabella by assuring his chivalry and protection: "He used every gentle word to dispel her alarms, and assured her that far from injuring, he would defend her at the peril of his life" (CO 75). The girls, however, display the fears, instilled into them by upbringing, of the loss of reputation and virtue – even in a potentially life-threatening situation. Isabella hesitates to follow Theodore deeper into the vault, where he wants to hide her from Manfred, weary that "should we be found together, what would a censorious world think of my conduct?" Theodore, of course, assures her: "I meant to conduct you into the most private cavity of these rocks, and then at the hazard of my life to guard their entrance against every living thing" (CO 76). The novel furthermore contrasts the fears of the two generations. Hippolita, though fearing Manfred's cruelty, "did not doubt that Frederic was destined by heaven to accomplish the fate that seemed to threaten her house" (CO 81–82). She perceives the threat to their family and position triggered by the revelation of the old secret and is only concerned with the "thought of averting our total destruction by the union of our rival houses" (CO 89). For the young generation, the risks of losing power and issues of heritage and lineage are secondary compared to the risky upheavals of romantic love and values like honour, trust, and constancy of feeling. When Matilda confesses her love for Theodore, Isabella says: "Ah! Matilda,

---

95 David Richter interprets the motive of the unguarded prison chamber and the two escapes of Isabella and Theodore as a structural-political allusion to the dwindling power of the ruling class and crisis of aristocracy in England and France at the time. Highlighting the openness of the system and the potential for change, he claims, "the autocratic authority of the prince turns out to conceal a genuine power vacuum" (1989: 12).

your heart is in danger" (CO 88). Her mother reacts with similar concern: "What new calamities has fate in store for us? Thou, a passion! Thou, in this hour of destruction – [...]" (CO 92). Although the narrative presents all these musings in a satirical mode and without going into any depth of characterization, the fears negotiated are the same ones that preoccupy characters in the Victorian novel, the risk of choosing the wrong lover or spouse.

At the beginning of the final chapter, Manfred is still trying to make sense of the events, while his thoughts are dominated by the fear of everybody plotting against him. Although nearly all seems lost, he still desperately tries to find a way to avert a loss of power and the unravelling of his secret:

> Every reflection which Manfred made on the Friar's behaviour, conspired to persuade him that Jerome was privy to an amour between Isabella and Theodore. [...] The Prince even suspected that the Friar depended on some secret support from Frederic, whose arrival coinciding with the novel appearance of Theodore seemed to bespeak a correspondence. Still more was he troubled with the resemblance of Theodore to Alfonso's portrait. The latter he knew had unquestionably died without issue. Frederic had consented to bestow Isabella on him. These contradictions agitated his mind with numberless pangs. He saw but two methods of extricating himself from his difficulties. The one was to resign his dominions to the Marquis —Pride, ambition, and his reliance on ancient prophecies, which had pointed out a possibility of his preserving them to his posterity, combated that thought. The other was to press his marriage with Isabella. (CO 99)

In his increasing panic, as he suspects a romance between Theodore and Isabella threating his marriage plans, he embarks on taking "farther measures for his security" (CO 100) that later lead to the tragic climax of him killing Matilda. But before the prince is pushed into a "frame of mind capable of the most fatal excesses" (CO 108), Walpole's narrative adds another few uncanny sightings and "unaccountable behaviours" (CO 108), which show the very subjective and different attempts of the characters to deal with uncertainty and crisis. Terrified after seeing the giant hand, Bianca "burst into the room with a wildness in her look and gestures that spoke the utmost terror. Oh! my Lord, my Lord! cried she; we are all undone! it is come again! [...]—oh! the hand! the Giant! the hand! —support me! I am terrified out of my senses" (CO 102). In reaction to her plan to leave the castle immediately, Manfred tries to persuade that: "Thou art safe here; be not alarmed" (CO 102). His words have little effect on her panic, but she continues to warn him, full of belief in the supernatural events and providential power of the prophecy. Enraged by this, Manfred tells her to "be gone, and keep these fooleries to frighten thy companions" (CO 102). In contrast to Manfred, who dismisses Bianca's terror as "the delirium of a silly wench, who has heard stories of apparitions until she believes them", Frederic assesses Bianca's fear rationally as being "too natural and too strongly impressed to be the work of imagination" and invites her to share her story: "Tell us, fair maiden, what it is has moved thee thus" (CO 102–103). Earlier in the narrative, Hippolita also had tried to find rational explanations for the uncanny occurrences in the castle, telling Manfred "that the vision of the gigantic leg and foot was all a fable; and no doubt an impression made by fear, and the dark and dismal hour of the night, on the minds of his servants: She and the chaplain had examined the chamber, and found every thing in the usual order" (CO 37). These examples underline how Walpole's Gothic aesthetic plays with a "hybrid mix of epistemological questions" (Molesworth 2010: 237). Throughout, the novel contrasts the characters fears, be it supernatural ones of ghosts, the revenge of demons of the pasts, or 'realistic' ones of being forced into marriage, of betrayal, manipulation, loss of authority or status. Belief is shown to be separable from fact, and becomes more a matter of subjective choice and imagination; the realm of superstition "becomes a vast image for the darkness and mystery of inner experience" (McWhir 1989: 31), which exist alongside rational deductions.

Walpole's narrative is progressive in so far as it does not employ a stereotypical gendered divide between calm rationality (male) and emotional irrationality (female). Especially Manfred appears increasingly hysterical and motivated by passions. Regarding the gender relations in the text, the women do not fare too well. Matilda dies through her father's hands, Hippolita finally resigns to a sterile life in a convent, and Isabella enters into a sombre, dutiful marriage to Theodore, based on shared melancholy rather than love. On the other hand, the men are largely portrayed as good-naturedly, weak and incompetent, or raging madmen. Even Theodore does not fully fit the role of romantic hero, as Sundberg Wall (2006: 120) has argued. For example, when in the vault with Isabella, he fails to open the trap door, and she eventually 'rescues' herself, later it is Matilda who lets Theodore out of the tower. Ultimately, he does not succeed in saving Isabella or Matilda from harm and loss. Manfred's treatment of women is openly cruel, he is indifferent towards Matilda, discards his wife, and only measures female worth on a scale of possible extension of the bloodline and guaranteeing of his dynastic position.[96]

Walpole's novel highlights the precariousness of claims of political and epistemological authority and of a family's social function and stability. The devel-

---

[96] The novel displays similar anxieties about legitimacy as *Tristram Shandy*. See Moglen's feminist argument that *The Castle of Otranto* presents a "melodramatic version of the comic critique of Enlightenment values found in *Tristram Shandy*. [...] Substituting the supernatural for the religious, representing fathers as absent or impotent and the inheritance of power as corrupt, Walpole questions, as does Sterne, the root assumptions of a belief system that upholds patriarchal power and authority" (2001: 117).

opment of the novel genre in the 18th century is generally tied closely to the depiction of family relations and domesticity, the emergence of the nuclear family and questions of obligations of kinship vs. the desires of the individual.[97] Gothic fictions like *The Castle of Otranto* transform family relations into objects of terror and melancholy, in other words, into sites of risk. In fact, this notion runs through 18th-century fiction from Defoe's *Roxana* to Burney's *Camilla*. A motive often repeated in Gothic stories after Walpole's is the interruption of a marriage or courtship set in the fictional present, "complicated by the unexpected appearance of confusing information from the past" (Bernstein 1991: 152). Stephen Bernstein explains further that in the Gothic novel "the establishment of the heterosexual family unit" is often presented in "a sequence fraught with danger; there is no predicting what may surface during courtship" (1991: 152).

To conclude the discussion of the construction of risk, several aspects are decisive. The setting is domestic and limited to a single family and a single location. In contrast to sea-faring adventures and travels between continents in the earlier novels, the location is limited and stable, a characteristic Walpole's novel shares with texts like Sterne's *Tristram Shandy* and which is taken up in Frances Burney's fictions (and, continued in many 19th-century novels). As a consequence, the characters' perception and management of risk is depicted less as productive agency (e.g. Crusoe building his fortress, Moll looking for suitably rich husbands, or Roxana for the best investment for her wealth), but becomes increasingly limited to inner reflections and calculations which can border on despair, paranoia or result in isolation and paralysis. Alternatively, frantic action taken overwhelmed by fear, as in Manfred's case, produces disastrous results. In *The Castle of Otranto*, the past proves to be as unpredictable as the future and influences all characters, be it knowingly or unknowingly. The novel is less concerned with realistic threats, as for example Defoe's *A Journal of the Plague Year*, but it dramatizes various "Bedrohungsverhältnisse" (Saathoff 2001: 11), i.e. subjective relationships between victim and tormentor, which can be concrete (as in the case of Isabella being hunted down by Manfred) or abstract (like Manfred's torment by his guilt and the secret from the past, manifest in outsized things which literally come crushing down on his castle).

---

[97] In *Family Fictions* (1998), Flint argues that in particular the latter half of the 18th century is "marked by an increasing number of narratives that scrutinize the psychological, social, and political consequences of kinship in fundamentally sceptical ways. The anxieties about household government, affective relations, and genealogical imperatives articulated by the mid-century writers become central and disruptive features in the work of Walpole, Sterne, and Wollstonecraft" (1998: 30–31).

Walpole's narrative illustrates the sensational expression of feelings of being at risk, but is still not devoid of calculations and ironically continues the negotiation of human agency, determinism, and the experience of randomness. It establishes a crucial link between family, property, and crime. With the concern with property comes the risk of loss, suggesting why in an age of enlightened speculation and entrepreneurship, tales of feudal order and inheritance make a comeback.[98] With the concern with crime comes the risk of detection and punishment. The novel ends with the re-establishment of social order, the castle being returned to the rightful owner, and the melancholic marriage of Isabella and Theodore. The ordering forces proved to be stronger than the individual's transgression. Fictions like *The Castle of Otranto* aid the institutionalization of the moral that transgressions involve high risks and that there are no lucky escapes. Sooner or later, they will be detected and punished. This also signals the development of bureaucratic modern society and its social surveillance and disciplinary measures as described by Foucault in *Discipline and Punish*. The intersection of risk, surveillance, and courtship are also at the heart of the next novel under scrutiny, Frances Burney's *Camilla*. Meanwhile Walpole's gothic tale leaves its reader with the fearful recognition that the "past is, after all, a truthful representation of the present: that we find our real nature, not in the ideal, but its shadow" (Miles 1991: 51).

---

[98] According to Schmidgen, the discourse about property in the 18th-century cultural imagination sheds light on "the question why the Gothic novel, with its cultivation of feudal fear, should become, in an age of revolution and enlightenment, a genre of delirious popularity" (2002a: 12; 10). He also suggests that the prophecy in *The Castle of Otranto* is an expression of (legal, moral) fears of illegitimacy, showing how one generation can be haunted by the crimes of the previous one. From the 18th to the 19th century, he writes, the problem of illegitimacy takes "on special cultural and literary significance within England" (2002b: 138).

4 Picturing Female Youth at Risk: *Camilla*

Frances Burney's monumental penultimate novel, *Camilla, or A Picture of Youth*, published in serialized form in 1796, runs to almost 1000 pages. Stylistically and generically it combines a traditional marriage plot with elements of dark humour, Gothic thriller, psychological drama, the female Bildungsroman, and traces of Romanticism. It deals with the matrimonial concerns of a group of young people, Camilla Tyrold and her sisters Lavinia and Eugenia, her brother Lionel, their cousin Indiana Lynmere, and the suitable and not-so-suitable love interests of the girls, most importantly among these the relationship between the eponymous heroine and Edgar Mandlebert. After many disasters and misunderstandings, the novel ends, conventionally, with a happy double marriage and a third one on the horizon.

A reading focussing on risk might, at a first superficial glance, seem contradictory, because *Camilla*, George Haggerty writes, "tells of the changes of fortune of a small group of young people who are comfortably installed in the English midlands, with nothing really to menace them but changes in the weather and the irritability of personality" (Haggerty 1998: 137). However, Patricia Spacks notes: "Anxiety dominates the Burney novels, despite their happy endings" (Spacks 1976: 176). Several critics comment on the narrative's atmosphere as being oppressively dark and evoking a feeling of claustrophobia.[1] This creates a paradoxical tension with the events on the plot level because most of the actual complications experienced by the characters seem relatively minor, yet "the anxieties generated by those complications feel exaggeratedly intense" (Henderson 1997: 70). Furthermore, Margaret Doody argues:

> Burney sees the interaction of traditional society and nervously acting individual mind as likely to issue in disaster. The main story of this novel (in which lovers fear they will lose each other while taking courses which would almost assure that loss) is a suitable 'objective correlative' just within the bounds of comedy for expressing anxiety, and exhibiting the perverse activities evoked by pain and fear. (Doody 1988: 263)

The argument that the depiction of anxiety and the mechanism of its construction itself is important, that, in other words, affect takes to some extent priority over incident within the novel, highlights the fictional, subjective element of

---

[1] For instance, Julia Epstein (1989: 125) mentions the particular intensity of the novel which has a distinctly small canvas despite its epic scope; Stephanie Russo speaks of the "claustrophobic, anxious world of Camilla" (2011: 80); Katherine Binhammer (2011: 15), too, speaks of a claustrophobic narrative structure which allows no escape for Camilla.

anticipation, desire, and fear and the importance and struggle of the perception of 'objective' reality, the very duality which characterizes the conception of risk. This aspect and tension are the focus of analysis. The novel touches upon many issues; it can be seen as an illustration of familial structures and constraints, of generational differences, all the while also reflecting the political background and the upheavals and (internal and external) threats preoccupying England at the time: "Conceived amidst the turmoil of the 1790s and dedicated to the Queen of England, *Camilla* is haunted by crises of authority – paternal, political, and literary" (Johnson 1995: 143).[2] At the centre of *Camilla* – and of Burney's other works – as most critics in one way or another acknowledge, are the anxieties about female propriety, about rules of conduct, about marriage, about economic extravagance, debt, and gambling, about the dangers of navigating one's way through society, of making the wrong choices, of keeping up appearances and controlling emotions.[3] Epstein aptly describes *Camilla* and Burney's earlier *Evelina* as fictions which "map the terrain of eighteenth-century social protocols, in relations between the sexes and between youth and age, as a minefield waiting to explode" (Epstein 1989: 91). Moreover, she emphasizes Burney's obsession with violence and hostility (1989: 5), echoing Doody's view of the author as "a student of aggression and obsession" (1988: 3).

A pervasive rhetoric of contemplating danger(s) and safety strikingly shapes the narrative.[4] The opening of the novel reads thus:

> The historian of human life finds less of difficulty and of intricacy to develop, in its accidents and adventures, than the investigator of the human heart in its feelings and its changes. In vain may Fortune wave her many-coloured banner, alternately regaling and dismaying, with hues that seem glowing with all the creation's felicities, or with tints that

---

[2] See Mascha Gemmeke who argues for taking a more general political approach to Burney's writing, rather than a feminist one which focuses on the domestic sphere: "Thus, the violence depicted in Burney's novels has been interpreted almost exclusively as the manifestation of suppressed female aggression, or, alternatively, as a rendering of the more or less open aggression against women throughout the eighteenth century. Yet it is important to keep in mind that Burney lived at a time of constant political turmoil – the American Revolution, the Gordon Riots, the King's madness, the French Revolution, the Reign of Terror, and the Napoleonic Wars followed on each other's heels, and, as Burney repeatedly claimed, permeated private life with insecurity, fear, and horror" (2004: 125).
[3] On the themes of money, commerce, and gambling see, e.g., Burgess (1995), Copeland (1976), Henderson (1997), Lusty (2007), and Lynch (1998: 164–206).
[4] Words like caution, anxiety, fear, alarm, adventure, risk, care, advice, threat, dread, hazard, uncertainty, trust etc. occur on every page and countless examples could be given. Many chapter headings contribute further to this, drawing attention to, e.g., various "computations of self-love", "calculations", "danger of disguise".

> appear stained with ingredients of unmixt horrors; her most rapid vicissitudes, her most unassimilating eccentricities, are mocked, laughed at, and distanced by the wilder wonders of the Heart of man; that amazing assemblage of all possible contrarieties, in which one thing alone is steady – the perverseness of spirit which grafts desire on what is denied. (C 7)

The tone is set right at the beginning, highlighting the focus on the dangers and power of human desire, passion, and choice, causing unsteadiness and defying reasonable warning, calculation and moderation. Emphasizing the connection between passion, youth, and risk-taking, the narrator further specifies this aspect:

> Repose is not more welcome to the worn and to the aged, to the sick and to the unhappy, than danger, difficulty, and toil to the young and adventurous. Danger they encounter but as the forerunner of success; difficulty, as the spur of ingenuity; and toil, as the herald of honour. The experience which teaches the lesson of truth, and the blessings of tranquillity, comes not in the shape of warning or of wisdom; from such they turn aside, defying or disbelieving. (C 7–8)

Although some critics engage insightfully with the discourse of fear in this novel,[5] or the strong motif of surveillance employed in it,[6] and most general discussions of Burney and her fictions sooner or later refer to 'danger', no readings (at least to my knowledge) explicitly apply or conceptualize a notion of 'risk'. My analysis of *Camilla* shows how risk functions as a structuring principle; it links the dominant themes and fruitfully relates to and builds on the existing body of criticism of the novel. [7]

Being "essentially about the pains, perils, and pleasures of courtship" (Kraft 2006: 41), Burney's novel is often classified as a courtesy-novel. Its contemporary purpose was, to a large extent, to function as a warning guide to young people and show the dangers and rewards of right and wrong actions. This is apparent in the view of the text taken by many reviewers,[8] who emphasise its use as a conduct manual for young females.[9] It seems indeed that with *Camilla* Frances

---

5 See Meyer Spacks's chapter "Dynamics of Fear: Fanny Burney" (1976: 158–192).
6 For instance, James Thompson writes: "What sets *Camilla* apart, however, is its regular thematization of surveillance and specularization, for the courtship plot of Edgar and Camilla has been grafted onto a gendered trial" (1996: 163). See also Russo (2011).
7 Good biographical information and introduction to Burney's works are the book-length studies by Doody (1988), Harman (2000), and Epstein (1989). See also Johnson (1995: 140–188), Straub (1987), and Sabor (2007).
8 See Joyce Hemlow's *The History of Fanny Burney* (1958: 249; 270).
9 Yet, as Sarah Salih has argued convincingly, despite, for instance, the inclusion of Mr. Tyrold's famous sermon on female behaviour (Vol. III, Book 5, Chapt. V), the characters are not as two-

Burney did not seek to write a straightforward love story; it presents a curious mix of didactic treatise, sermons, romance, or even Gothic thriller, with most of these elements thrown in strategically to aid the publication and marketability of the text.[10] While one cannot ignore that "the love-tangles of the central group of young people dominate the book" (Harman 2000: 261), the themes of guardianship and protection of youth, the mostly 'absent' parents and the many (unsuitable) mentors trying to take their place, testify that in *Camilla*, "Burney's obsession with unguided or badly-guided youth remains as strong as in *Evelina* and *Cecilia*" (2000: 263). Consequently, showing the young characters at risk is central to the text. Having a palpable presence throughout, risk is manifest in the numerous accidents and catastrophes; its perception and attempts at avoiding it are the plot-driving mechanism between Edgar and Camilla. He, afraid of marrying an 'unfit' wife, monitors and judges Camilla's behaviour and the company she keeps to such an extent as to drive the essentially fearless, if naïve, girl into despair and paranoia. She, on the other hand, embarks on the (impossible) task of avoiding at all costs appearing undesirable to Edgar and potentially losing him. Through all characters, the novel dramatizes risk perception and management gone horribly (if sometimes comically) wrong The climate of suspicion and misunderstanding, as well as all action of risk-taking or avoidance, is shown to have nearly fatal consequences, until the final turn of events brings a restoration of order and safety.

Camilla's father, Mr Tyrold, a clergyman of moderate means, is the brother of Sir Hugh Tyrold, who is the wealthy owner of the Cleaves estate, where he lives with his beautiful, if not too bright, niece Indiana, and her governess Miss Margland. Somewhat starved for company and solace, Sir Hugh is set on keeping his brother's girls close and tries to assume the role of protector and benefactor. As he is particular fond of the sweet and gentle Camilla, he makes her the heiress to his fortune, choosing her over Indiana, who "promises to turn out rather dull" (C 15). So initially, as her uncle's favourite, all fortune seems to be on Camilla's side. The reader is introduced to her as a vivacious,

---

dimensional as common in conduct books (2002: 128). She also comments on the revision of the characters as example of a "feminist editing" (2002: 132) and mentions that Burney, after the book had been accepted as being "instructive" by its first reviewers, could afford to tone down the general didactic mode.

10 On the various publishing decisions made by Burney, the financial considerations and on the writing and editing process see Binhammer (2011) and Gallagher (1994: 203–254). See especially Pink (2006: 55–58) on a description of Burney's attempt to maintain financial control of her own work and Salih (2002) about the editing politics, and the argument that, e.g., the length and the didacticism of the work was determined by financial reasons.

pretty, and carefree young girl, yet gets a hint of the doom which is to come of this: "O blissful state of innocence, purity, and delight, why must it fleet so fast? Why scarcely but by retrospection is its happiness known?" (C 13). Apart from evoking the familiar theme of lost innocence, Sir Hugh's following description of his niece points to a certain recklessness, even if an involuntary one, in her character: "Camilla's a little jewel; she jumps and skips about till she makes my eyes ache with looking after her, for fear of breaking her neck. I must keep a sharp watch, or she'll put poor Indiana's nose quite out of joint, which God forbid" (C 15). This highlights the male desire to protect and control her which is precisely what later leads to Edgar's mistrust of her suitability as a 'steady' wife and to the "blocked romance" (Straub 1987: 185) around which the narrative is constructed. It also introduces the intertwined themes of surveillance and of the dangers and difficulties of interpreting signs of attraction that are central to the narrative.

Within the first few chapters, two accidents occur which drastically change Camilla and Eugenia's future. On the occasion of Camilla's tenth birthday, under the supervision of Sir Hugh, all children attend a fair outside the grounds of Cleves, disobeying the explicit orders of Mrs. Tyrold, who fears that Eugenia might catch smallpox.

> The extreme delicacy of the constitution of Eugenia had hitherto deterred Mrs. Tyrold from innoculating her; she had therefore scrupulously kept her from all miscellaneous intercourse in the neighbourhood: but as the weakness of her infancy was not promising to change into health and strength, she meant to give to that terrible disease its best chance, and the only security it allows from perpetual alarm, immediately after the heats of the present autumn should be over. (C 22)

Clearly showing the novel's typical discourse of danger and safety, its second heroine, Eugenia, and another major realm of risk are introduced, adding the threat of contagion, disease and deformity to the implied dangers of loss of reputation, joy, and innocence. On the fairground, Edgar spots a little boy, apparently "just recovering from smallpox" (C 24), an observation which throws the whole party into a panic and reveals the fear, irrationality and lack of knowledge connected to the question of the spread of diseases and preventive measures at the time.[11]

> Extremely perplexed for them all, and afraid, by going from the sick child, he might himself carry the infection to the coach, he sent a man to Sir Hugh to know what was to be done. Sir

---

[11] On the novel in relation to the contemporary discourse of disease and deformity and of smallpox as a particular risk for women see Haggerty (1998) and Nussbaum (2003).

> Hugh, totally overset by the unexpected accident, and conscience-struck at his own wilful share in risking it, was utterly helpless and could only answer, that he wished young Mr. Edgar would give him his advice. (C 24)

The scene also brings forth the helplessness of Sir Hugh and Edgar's comparative calm and superiority as a guardian of the girls. Nonetheless, all attempts at taking belated precautions are in vain, since the reader learns in the following chapter, tellingly entitled "Consequences", that she has indeed contracted smallpox. But first another accident is brought upon poor Eugenia. Out of fear for her children, Mrs. Tyrold forbids them from leaving the house, where "all was conducted with as much security as gaiety" (C 27). But Lionel, one of the characters whose love of danger and gambling will cause much of the family's distress and disaster, mainly for Camilla, later on, suggests riding on a seesaw in the park. Pondering on the risk of the game of teeter-tooter, Sir Hugh "feared committing the little Eugenia, for whom he was grown very anxious, [...]. The difficulty how to indulge her with safety was, nevertheless, considerable: and, after various experiments, he resolved to trust her to nobody but himself" (C 27). This decision results in Eugenia falling from his arms to the ground, and, "In the agitation of his fright, he stooped forward to save her, but lost his equilibrium; and instead of rescuing, followed her" (C 27). This accident affects Eugenia's growth and she is left permanently crippled. To add to this misfortune, the next day, she displays symptoms of thesmallpox. She survives the disease and eventually, though "scarred by the horrible disorder, was declared out of danger" (C 29). Hence, the novel begins with Eugenia's degeneration from "lovely daughter" into "pock-marked humpback" (Nussbaum 2003: 121); the accidents transform her appearance, her prospects, even her education, while also affecting Camilla in more than one way. The novel, Doody observes, "is from the onset full of pain and loss" (Doody 1988: 263). To compensate for Eugenia's ills and her deformity, and to manage his own guilt, Sir Hugh disinherits Camilla and installs Eugenia as the heiress of his estate and fortune. Furthermore, as Eugenia's beauty is irreparably lost, he decides on a classical education for her, so that she will be able to entertain a future husband with intelligent conversation, and plans to arrange a marriage between her and Clermont Lynmere, who is currently being educated abroad. The episode establishes a crucial association in the narrative between originally 'harmless' activities of pleasure and play with danger, which arises, ironically, from an extreme desire for precaution in combination with a lack of deeper reflection of circumstances. In fact, the whole plot appears to be an elaboration of this theme, and finally near the end, the narrator comments: "It is not very early in life we learn how little is performed, for which no precaution is taken. Care is the offspring of disappointment; and sorrow and repentance commonly hang upon its first lessons" (C 865).

The early scene described above also shows how disaster can be brought on involuntarily, yet not completely unknowingly. One can therefore agree with Julia Epstein who suggests that Burney's narrative seems to advocate that generally "a little calculation [...] is a good thing" (Epstein 1989: 142). In addition to this, apart from illustrating a dominant contemporary fear (of disease, contagion), a gendered distinction is introduced with regard to the encounter and perception of risk. The female characters are either perceived as being at risk by the males, who then rush in to protect them, or the men react to the women as being dangers who they need to protect themselves (or others) from. Either way, the women are caught in this dual risk-perception by the men and suffer the consequences. Felicity Nussbaum comments on this aspect with regard to Eugenia, saying: "Polluted by the public nature of her fall and by the casual inattention of the aristocracy to the hazards of disease and deformity, she embodies the extremes of masculine carelessness perpetrated on a woman, of the deformity produced by contemporary society, and of the pervasive threat of contagion" (Nussbaum 2003: 121). With regard to all characters (i.e. children and adults) the narrative portrays naivety and innocence as being as dangerous and potentially harmful to oneself and to others as deliberate intent or malice. Especially Sir Hugh appears as one of the central "unthinking but allegedly benevolent endangers of women" (Epstein 1989: 142). Without being portrayed as an outright villain, and in contrast to the obvious 'bad' guys, such as the fortune-hunter Alphonso Bellamy who is later to abduct Eugenia, Sir Hugh shows how misguided 'good' intentions of some male characters in the narrative turn out to be even more destructive than the more straightforwardly evil or dangerous ones.

A further love match plotted by Sir Hugh concerns Edgar and Indiana; yet like his plans for Eugenia and Clermont, it will only produce heartache and nearly fatal disaster. When Edgar, after finishing his education, takes over the running of the near-by estate Beech Park, he finds himself drawn to Camilla. Their budding romance and courtship is complicated from the start by the fact that he is considered as being intended for Indiana; further misunderstandings and manipulations are brought on by the ambitious governess Miss Margland, by new acquaintances and potential rivals for Camilla's affection, such as Mr Dubster, Major Cerwood and Sir Sedley Clarendel, and by female friends such as Mrs. Arlbery and Mrs. Berlington. Discussing the decision to marry Camilla and the question of how to obtain certainty about her feelings and character with his mentor Dr. Marchmont, the latter gives Edgar a piece of crucial advice: "'Nothing must escape you; you must view as if you had never seen her before; [...] even justice is insufficient during this period of probation, and instead of inquiring,

'Is this right in her?' you must simply ask, 'Would it be pleasing to me?'" While he grants Edgar with the fact that he has "been very peculiarly situated for obviating all risk upon that first and most important particular" (C 160), and generally does not disapprove of Camilla, he advocates a period of testing and detached surveillance, and above all, no communication of feelings; "to avoid all danger of repentance, you must become positively distrustful'" (C 160). This conversation, intended as well-meant advice, throws Edgar into deep doubts about Camilla's emotions and behaviour; apart from the risk of rejection, he is now conscious of the gravity of the choice and of the dangers of falling for a coquettish woman; "his confidence was gone" (C 162). Thus, at the end of Volume I, a young man excited about love and proposing marriage to his beloved is turned into a suspicious and jealous observer, anxious to 'calculate' his chances and beat the odds in the gamble for marital happiness.

The novel's dominant theme of the "lottery of love" is introduced even before this scene and it is intrinsically tied to the general value-laden discourse on gambling. In chapter V, "A Raffle", during a social gathering everybody enters money into the raffle, the price of which is a locket. At first, "Camilla hung back, totally unused to hazard upon what was unnecessary" (C 93); yet the communal gambling spirit proves hard to resist and she falls prey to "the contagion of example" (C 93). Still, she later asks Edgar to withdraw her money again, so she can give it to the poor family they encounter on the street. Edgar, testing her virtue, asks her if she can be charitable, "yet be content to see your chance for the prize withdrawn?", to which she replies, "my dear father will be so glad to hear I have not spent it so foolishly" (C 99). The episode creates an important bond between the two young people. Satisfied by her answer, Edgar gives her the half guinea, but does not withdraw her entry free, so that the surprised Camilla is later announced as the lucky winner of the locket. When handing her the price, Mrs. Arlbery, an older women living in the neighbourhood, says to Camilla: "Miss Tyrold, I heartily wish you equally brilliant success, in the next, and far more dangerous lottery, in which, I presume, you will try your fate" (C 105), obviously referring to the period of courtship awaiting her. Similarly, Camilla's parents perceive their young girls' unmarried state as precarious, ironically independent of their financial situations. Mr. Tyrold says: "Our two eldest girls are but slightly provided for; and Eugenia is far more dangerously circumstanced, in standing so conspicuously apart, as a prize to some adventurer" (C 120). It becomes clear that he considers Edgar a potentially suitable and lucky choice of husband and protector for his daughter Camilla when he expresses his disappointment that Edgar, at this point in the narrative, does not seem to be interested in her: "With him, however, she would have been the safest, and with him – next alone to her mother, the happiest of her sex"

(C 120). Like Mr. Tyrold, Sir Hugh is constantly anxious when observing the children and their apparently growing or weaning affections, that "he had risked a breach of the marriage he so much desired by his own indiscretion" (C 128).

As these examples show, most of the characters partake in games of some sort, be it cards, raffles, or games of manipulation and match-making and unmaking. Starting with the see-saw in the beginning, games usually bring both joy and danger and, moreover, an "enduring association of game-play-cruelty can be found" (Doody 1988: 237). In fact, the whole constellation of characters and the development of the plot can be related to a financial game in a wider sense, as Deidre Lynch (1998: 171) has suggested. In particular the fates of the three girls appear interlinked and bound to a single system of currency; each time one of the protagonists Camilla, Eugenia, or Indiana loses something (i.e. money, male affection), another wins; thus the narrative resembles a diagram of losses and gains; the stakes and odds are constantly being redistributed. Applying game theory to the reading of the novel, Margaret Doody's analysis, while not employing risk as a category, is illuminating. Doody compares Camilla and Edgar to two players involved in a "courtship game" which can only be won if both break the rules at the same time. The two opposing rules, central to the construction of the plot, Doody explains, are Camilla's principle: "A young woman must never allow her love for a young man to become visible, until he has made an official declaration of marriage", which clashes directly with Edgar's: "A man must never propose to a woman until he knows that she is entirely his own, she must he his exclusively and never have loved anybody else" (1988: 230–231). Doody's reading is interesting because it highlights how both players, although theoretically playing for the same gains, are aware of different risks of loss (love vs. reputation) and how their 'strategies', based on their guardians' advice on how to play the game, operate at cross-purposes. Moreover, both have to be taught these misery-producing rules almost against their intuition, as they were previously unaware of the risks of potential losses. Especially Camilla is instructed to see the dangers of (mis)behaviour by Edgar and her father, while remaining ignorant of many others she has to encounter, such as dealing with money and judging the character of strangers. As the 'game' between Edgar and Camilla shows, Burney's fiction underlines "the absurdity and danger of a system of social relations that locks both male and female subjects in ideologically contradictory positions that disable and thwart human attempts at happiness" (Straub 1987: 183). Yet while the dangers are to some extent applied to both sexes, the motif of having to play a risky game which one cannot really win by one's own control is most strongly connected to Camilla. According to Epstein, she "resides in the no-win territory of the unmarried woman: if she pays too much attention, she is a coquette who transgresses propriety; if she remains heedless of her surroundings, she appears insane" (Epstein 1996: 206). She has to act as if out of having been driven into a corner from where there is no escape. Lionel, Camilla's "bad" brother, who tyrannizes his sister and seeks to manipulate her for his own financial benefit, largely contributes to this situation; her marriage is only another gamble for him, and one from which he intends to profit. He takes all her money and then forces her to borrow 200 pounds from Sir Clarendel, which obliges Camilla to the baronet and causes her break with Edgar. Furthermore, his mounting gambling debts lead to the near bankruptcy of Mr Tyrold. In this way, "Lionel represents the danger and even violence inherent in the family system, which threatens, throughout *Camill*a, to surface and destroy all of the Tyrolds" (Gruner 1994: 28).[12]

In a chapter ironically entitled "Counsels for Conquest", Mrs Arlbery tries to teach Camilla the game of flirtation and advises her on how to win Edgar's affection: "give him cause to fear he will lose you" (C 455). To Camilla's protests the older woman replies:

> Mandlebert has already given the dominion of his to other rulers, who will take more care of his pride, though not of his happiness. Attend to one who has travelled further into life than yourself, and believe me when I assert, that his bane, and yours alike, is his security.' With a colour yet deeper than ever, Camilla resentfully repeated, 'Security!' (C 455–456)

The dialogue underlines the strong association of the game with the opposing poles of danger, i.e. risk of loss, and security. Miraculously, despite all the interferences and clashing strategies, Edgar and Camilla reach an understanding a little bit more than half way through the novel. Edgar has asked Mr Tyrold: "will you trust me your Camilla?" (C 448) and received an affirmative answer. Nonetheless, soon afterwards things start to fall apart. Edgar observes an exchange between Camilla and Sir Sedley, where she tries to thank him for the money he has lent her so that she can repay her brother's gambling debts, and this incident causes Edgar to doubt her feelings all over again. In response to this, Camilla reflects: "And is it, […], for a trifler such as this, so unmeaning, so unfeeling, I have risked my whole of hope and happiness?" (C 560). Meanwhile Edgar consults Dr. Marchmont about his perceived loss of Camilla to Sir Sedley and the conversation proceeds as follows:

> 'The young baronet, probably, has been making his court to her, or she has believed such was his design; but as you first came to the point, she would not hazard rejecting you,

---

[12] On the topic of Burney's depiction of family values see, for instance, Austin (2000).

while uncertain if he were serious. She was, possibly, putting him to the test, by the account of your declaration, at the moment of your unseasonable intrusion.'
'If this, Doctor, is your statement, and if your statement is just, *in how despicable a lottery have I risked the peace of my life!* You suppose then... that, if sure of Sir Sedley... I am discarded?' (C 571–572; my emphasis)

The connection between love and gambling and the element of speculation introduced in the scene of the first raffle is again very apparent here. The motif of the 'lottery' in relation to the 'game' of courtship clearly shows the inevitable element of chance and risk-taking, the raising of stakes and the suffering through speculation, suspense and loss, before both players can obtain the ultimate prize, i.e. marriage and certainty about each other's feelings. It also underlines the importance of the question of (financial) value. Henderson argues that Edgar's behaviour towards Camilla, following the warnings of Dr. Marchmont, resembles more that of him "forever inspecting the merchandise" than of active romantic courtship, because although "he is constantly tormented with the suspense of the gambler; [...] his pursuit of Camilla sometimes takes on the character of mere shopping" (Henderson 1997: 78). Camilla too speculates constantly about Edgar and his intentions and feelings and invests in new clothes and social outings in order to attract and maintain his attention.

Studies of the economic climate and politics of the late 18th century usually describe the historical context as being shaped by an awareness of crisis, causing an increasing intolerance of risk on the one hand and high risk-taking (in business) on the other.[13] The early century's spirit and fascination with adventure, projects, and speculation can by no means seen to have disappeared, but its risk-taking practices had in many ways been absorbed, institutionalized, and pushed further. The time when Frances Burney writes is a period reflecting a higher desire for security, for shielding personal lives and business from the repercussions of the crises brought on by war, politics, and the spirit of industrialization and scientific advance: "Risk-taking had got out of hand and all [...] crises after 1770 can be seen as the growing pains of the first industrializing nation" (Hoppit 1987: 135). Yet, on the other hand, as James Raven explains, in contrast to the beginning of the century "familiarity with the national debt and share investments had eased anxieties, but it is also noticeable that concern was diverted to the use or misuse of wealth rather than to the manner of its accumulation" (Raven 1992: 184). As a result, an ideal of the time, which lived on to shape the whole Victorian era, is economy, while extravagance is condemned. This motif is already foreshadowed in Defoe's writings, especially in *Roxana*.

---

13 See, for example Hoppit (1986; 1987), Raven (1992), and chapter 1.1.

Springing from the fear connected with commercialization and (new) businessmen, from the late 18th century and throughout the 19th century warnings against speculators, stockjobbers, against gambling and high-risk investment frequently appear in public discourse. Raven's argument that a "memorable cast of characters was used by popular writers during this period to spell out the economic threat of extravagance" (Raven 1992: 183), also applies to the 'economic' plot in *Camilla*, which many critics have focused on and see to take priority over the marriage plot,[14] while others see it as constituting a new genre of "economic romance" (Burgess 195: 132).

There was a felt political need to educate the public and fight the persistent fascination with wealth, lotteries and gaming, which the government tried to regulate. "Debate focused upon what was and was not a legitimate risk" (Raven 1992: 195), and fictions of the time naturally participated in these discourses. In this context, gambling appears as the ultimate symbol of condemnable risk: "Gaming now became the shibboleth for unthinking, addictive waste, for illegitimate and profligate risk" (1992: 190). *Camilla* serves as a good example of how social interests and anxieties are taken up in literature, as criticism of gambling, the fear of irresponsible extravagance and ruin feature prominently in the novel. One can agree with Edward Copeland that Burney's fiction offers a female perspective on the topic of women and money which differs radically from the perspective of male writers, e.g. Defoe: "For the male novelists, the world of money, the getting and the spending, was the stage for aggressive action, a world to be manipulated and managed" (Copeland 1976: 24), a statement which holds true even for Defoe's female heroines. With Burney, the fictional fantasies about money become more "frighteningly" real (1976: 25), because the focus is shifted from a primary orientation on financial adventure, spectacular gains and riches to a more sombre balancing of the costs of domestic life, food, clothes, rent, and small debts. James Thompson takes a similar view, emphasizing the difference between Burney and writers like Defoe and Fielding: "Burney's narratives are fundamentally not stories of financial success and accumulation [...] Rather, they are basic tales of financial disaster and retreat, dispossession and disinheritance" (Thompson 1996: 174).[15]

---

14 Cf. Binhammer who argues about *Camilla:* "We are driven through the narrative not by the question 'will she marry Edgar?' but 'how far will she go into debt and how will she pay it?'" (2011: 4–5). Copeland identifies the mix of "a love plot and a plot of hard cash" (1976: 29) as a typical element also in Burney's other novels *Evelina* and *Cecilia.*

15 Thompson also mentions that inheritance is typically an enabling force for male protagonist. An example of her argument would be the ending of *Roderick Random*. In Burney's text, in contrast, Eugenia's inheritance leads to her social isolation and abduction by a fortune-hunter.

While gambling was generally seen as excessive, uncontrollable behaviour, the anxiety about female gamesters reached a height in the 1770s,[16] and was linked to fears of female promiscuity and loss of male control over women's sexuality. With a particular focus on Burney's fictions, Heather Lusty explains how female gambling represented multiple risks; it entailed a rejection of a woman's domestic duties and a challenge of the patriarchal order.

> The usual morality tale detailed the perilous consequences that reckless love of gaming wrought among otherwise noble and upright men. Frances Burney expanded this focus to include women as central figures. Young women entering society without proper guidance also stood in danger of moral degeneracy and ruin, not just in the traditional sense of physical virtue, but through close proximity to gaming and games of chance that were considered entertainment. (Lusty 2007: 136)

Camilla's gambles themselves are pretty half-hearted and harmless; worse is her association with Mrs. Berlinton, who is the main female gambling character in *Camilla*. The older woman also runs hazards with her marriage, flirting with Bellamy, and takes little interest in her domestic duties. Mrs. Berlinton is brought to reason and control at the end of the novel, interestingly by the much younger Camilla, who now assumes the role of warning protector herself, and urges her friend to renounces both the company of Bellamy and gaming: "'Mrs. Berlinton', she emphatically cried, 'if you persist in this unhappy, this perilous intercourse, you risk your reputation, [...], you risk even your own future condemnation!" (C 834); and later; even more passionately: 'O Mrs. Berlinton!' she cried, 'conquer this terrible infatuation, which obscures danger from your sight, and right from your discernment! (C 835). In order to save Mrs. Berlinton, Camilla even writes to her brother Frederic, who is a friend of her own brother Lionel. This letter, in its brevity, contains the main themes and imperatives of the narrative ("watch and save") in a nutshell and shows the characteristic language of risk:

> Retracing, nevertheless, her many amiable qualities, she knew not how, without further effort, to leave her [Mrs. Berlinton] to her threatening fate; and determined, at all risks, to put her into the hands of her brother, whose timely knowledge of her danger might rescue her from public exposure. She wrote therefore the following note:
> To FREDERIC MELMOND, Esq.

---

16 See Russell (2000). Also see Richard (2011: 115–17) for an outline of the often established relation between female sexuality and gambling. As a passion for play was equalled with insatiable sexual appetite, and prostitution, the woman was thus seen to direct her sexual needs into play and 'away' from her husband. Lusty writes: "Wagering and indulging in card play carried a stigma of promiscuity for women unparalleled by any moral censure men's play incurred" (2007: 135).

> *'Watch and save,—or you will lose your sister. CT.'* (C 857; original emphasis)

Regarding the novel's explicit condemnation of gambling on the one hand, it is interesting that the narrative promotes chance and luck on the other. This tension is reflected in the central association between romance and gambling. Jessica Richard, who has focused on this aspect, argues that it shapes the narrative climate of depression, because although the characters have freedom to act and calculate their moves, somehow it is all shown to be beyond their control:

> Representing a world governed by mere luck, the novel celebrates the gambler's wager and critiques paralyzing calculation. [...] In this world, the gambler's wager is shown to be more productive than the endless calculations of those who try to hedge risk on all sides. [...]. Edgar's calculations and efforts at control to minimize his risk offend and alienate Camilla, with the unfortunate consequence of depriving her of his much-needed guidance as she circulates through the economy with Mrs. Berlinton and Mrs. Mitten. (Richard 2011: 123)

It is interesting to consider that while gambling in general, and especially for women, is condemned and portrayed critically in the novel, the narrative still constructs it as a pervasive motive in human relations. As Andrea Henderson puts it, "while gaming and all forms of hazard are derided and termed dangerous, the events of the novel nevertheless suggest their necessity" (Henderson 1997: 80). In this sense, Burney's fiction reflects the development and integration of probability theory and the perception of risk in society.[17] In contrast to the beginning of the century, the 'projecting' spirit shaping Defoe's fictions or the adventures of Roderick and Gulliver, *Camilla* shows a turn towards the more institutionalized and potentially oppressive side of statistical knowledge, risk awareness and probability, especially if seen against a background of a fin-de-siècle atmosphere in a century marked by war and financial crises. Thomas Kavanagh explains how probability theory which had originally functioned as and brought forth "an ethics of the individual freed from the weight of the past", of orientation towards the future and freedom from divine providence, was increasingly subordinated to "the far more oppressive ideologies of the probable and the normal" (1993: 25). Burney's fictions frequently contain episodes of violence, comprising accidents, illness, nightmares, madness, all the while the ordinary is shown to have an explosive, catastrophic potential. All of Burney's novels, Epstein (1986: 133) argues, show struggles against loss of con-

---

[17] Current research on Burney also shows the growing interest in the relation between literature and probability theory and topics such as fortune-telling, gambling and speculation. See, for instance, Jennifer Locke's article "Dangerous Fortune-Telling in Frances Burney's *Camilla*" (2013).

trol and her heroines illustrate ordeals of 18th-century women, i.e. the burden of proper decorum, the protest against limiting situations, and feelings of anger and reduction of autonomy, which cluster around the central dilemma of "how to weigh the risks of rebellion against the humiliations of submission" (1986: 132). The fear of transgression and deviation, which features so prominently later in Victorian fiction, is foreshadowed in Burney's novel.

Most critics agree that Edgar makes for a very "unsatisfactory hero" (Harman 200: 262; cf. Haggerty 1998: 149), and he has even been called "the greatest prig in English literature" (Hemlow 1958: 255). Hemlow describes him further as playing the double part of "monitor-lover" (1958: 255), which makes him – especially to a modern reader – thoroughly unsympathetic as a character. He is always on the lookout for flaws and errors in the behaviour of his beloved Camilla, readily assuming the roles of judge or avenger of her virtue when necessary. As shown above, it is the "arch-monitor" Dr. Marchmont who drives Edgar to his conduct (1958: 260); but as Marchmont himself has two failed marriages behind him, he appears not as an impartial advisor but as a man embittered and frustrated with regard to women. Edgar is a constant presence in the background of all scenes; yet whether this appears in any way reassuring or adds to the atmosphere of Gothic paranoia, in other words, whether he is a risk-reducing presence or rather a constant evocation of risk for Camilla is for the reader to decide.[18] Either way, throughout the narrative Camilla has to "submit to Edgar's moody surveillance" (Lynch 1998: 176) in order to try to secure her love. The only character to voice a strong criticism of Edgar is Mrs. Arlbery, who says to Camilla: "A man who piques himself upon his perfections, finds no mode so convenient and ready for displaying them, as proving all about him to be constantly in the wrong" (C 367); and also describes him as "a pile of accumulated punctilios" (C 375) and as "that frozen composition of premature wisdom" (C 484).

Focusing on the motif of surveillance, Stephanie Russo places Burney's novel in the historical-political context of English anxiety about the French revolution, arguing that the hysteria of the early 1790s, the social fear of rebellion and disorder, and the general air of distrust shape the narrative. Without claiming that Burney expresses any explicit criticism or support of the revolutionary cause, Russo (2011: 82) stresses that the theme of surveillance had deeply political implications at the time; danger and chaos was seen to come from across the channel, like the plague, calling for monitoring and exertion of control.

---

18 Haggerty suggests that Edgar's constant appearance in moments of 'need' "suggests a nightmare of surveillance" (1998: 153), while Doody (1988: 249) argues that the characters appear like detectives in a criminal case, always spying on each other, which places Camilla in the role of a suspect who desperately tries to prove her innocence.

Women featured prominently among the French revolutionaries, and the aspect of female uprising felt especially threatening to many English conservatives: "Women who dared to articulate their own desires, whether sexual or otherwise, were perceived as immensely threatening to social stability at a time when women were believed to be at the center of the upheaval that was the French revolution" (2011: 85). *Camilla* articulates many fears about deviation, about female extravagance, gambling, and generally venturing into spheres beyond (male) control; at the heart, lies, of course, the issue of the control of female sexuality which at the time was deeply tied to the theme of safety and security of the nation, a topic which is also symbolized by the dangerous seductive charms of Defoe's 'Lady Credit'. Aided by Dr. Marchmont, Edgar creates a perception of Camilla as a site of risk, of instability, and volatility. Apart from the potential danger of her being an unsuitable wife, there is the threat of her loss of reputation by association with the 'wrong' people. Therefore Edgar is desperate to control Camilla's female friendships, e.g. with Mrs. Arlbery and Mrs. Berlinton.

In the course of the novel, Camilla internalizes Edgar's guilt-focused gaze on her. She begins to blame herself for all evil befalling her family and her deterioration into a nearly fatal paranoia highlights dramatically the damaging effects of male surveillance on the female psyche. While many, if not all, characters are to some extent controlled by their delusions, and have distorted visions of themselves as well as of others and of reality, the jealousy and wish to control Edgar suffers from is the plot-driving obsession and makes him appear almost a boyish Othello-figure.[19] The surveillance and 'policing' he embarks on only makes things worse, creates confusion instead of clarity, and all his attempts at rational interpretation of "evidence" are clouded by his emotions. On the one hand the narrative thus emphasizes the "dangers of high standards of human beings" (Doody 1988; 227), the inevitable pitfalls in the struggle for perfectionism, the clashing of honour codes and ideals of rigid virtue with human fallibility. On the other hand, "these intellectual processes of decoding and construction" (1988: 249), of observation and reflection are distorted and mainly produce absurd results. In terms of functioning as a guide to (personal, familial) risk-management, the book is a satire. The characters are trapped by their own agency and a circle of false calculations and -speculations. The (mis)representation of risk and danger is especially obvious with regard to the contrast between the 'big' and the little crimes in *Camilla*. The novel ironizes the social weight and panic attached to restraining female behaviour by showing the distortion in com-

---

[19] Several critics have commented on the allusions to Shakespeare's *Othello* in this context. See, e.g., Doody (1988: 224) and Nussbaum (2003: 129).

parison to other threats lurking in the background. In contrast to Camilla's accumulation of minor debts, a few lies, a bit of flirtation, and her naïve ignorance of certain situations, there are her brother Lionel's blackmail and extortion, his and Clermont's huge debts, the swindling money-lender Mrs. Mittin, or the ultimate villain Bellamy, who abducts an under-age girl and finally commits suicide, even if that appears as an accident of sorts. Showing that the risk of compromising oneself is always just around the corner, this almost appears as a counter-mechanism to the 'real' dangers, like bankruptcy or death.

The novel shows the typical late-18th-century turn towards passion and romanticism, in contrast to rational calculation, often one of the highest goal in enlightenment fictions. Especially Edgar can be described as a "hero whose capacity for suspicions about the heroine's worth and integrity defies most of the rules of logic and probability" (Straub 1987: 185) and seems to spring from deep emotions of anxiety. The characters who seemingly represent the credo of calculation, rational guidance and observation are the ultimately damaging 'mentors' in the texts, like Dr Marchmont and Sir Hugh, or curiously absent when they are needed most, like Camilla's mother, or rigidly moralizing like her father. In his letter to Camilla, Mr Tyrold explicitly warns her of the danger of displaying her emotions, arguing that she has to learn self-control, the highest duty of womanhood. While a detailed analysis of Mr Tyrold's well-known sermon[20] is beyond scope, it is relevant in so far that it underlines the connection between risk and individual choice, between passion and the dangers of transgressing gender norms and boundaries, affirming the social constraints of women. Camilla's father speaks of the general "uncertainty of the female fate" (C 357) and of the crucial choice "every modest and reasonable young woman" (C 358) must face, namely between passively waiting to be chosen by a man, or self-destructively bursting out with her feelings and choosing a man for herself. He strongly counsels her against the latter, emphasizing the dangers of showing emotional attachment towards a man:

> Good sense will show you the power of self-conquest, and point out its means. It will instruct you to curb those unguarded movements which lay you open to the strictures of others. It will talk to you of *those boundaries which custom forbids your sex to pass, and the hazard of any individual attempt to transgress them.* It will tell you, that where allowed

---

[20] See Vol. III, Book 5, Chapt. V "A Sermon". Mr. Tyrold's sermon is one of the best-known sections of the novel and has been published and reprinted independently from the rest of the text. Often considered as the educational centerpiece of the novel, it basically contains an exegesis of the theme that (young) women are not be trusted to act independently and that they should practice strict self-abnegation with regard to their desires and passions (see Haggerty 1998: 13; Epstein 1989: 128).

only a negative choice, it is your own best interest to combat against a positive wish. [...] it will soon convince you, that it is not strength of mind which you want, but reflection, to obtain a strict and unremitting control over your passions. (C 358–359; my emphasis)

Apart from the common view of perceiving a loss of self-control and unguarded passions as dangerous, these lines express the male desire to confine women to a particular sphere, and the patriarchal fear of losing control over them. As exemplified by Edgar's neurotic surveillance in the novel, men want to be the unchallenged protectors of female virtue against dangers from the outside, at the same time expecting the women to practice rigid self-restraint, both with regard to finances and emotions. Frances Burney criticizes these restrictions for women through her portrayal of the tormented Camilla while still advocating a contemplation of consequences. The sermon presents the ability of control as a woman's best means of self-protection when making her way through society. It is ironic, though, that all of Camilla's dangers result, in fact, from *not* communicating her emotions clearly. As critics such as Harris and Epstein have noted, *Camilla* tells essentially a story of silencing, and the whole reason why the happy marriage takes so long to achieve is the fact that free communication between Edgar and Camilla is restricted to the extent of being almost impossible (cf. Harris 1998: 151); indeed it often seems that one open word between the young couple could have reduced the whole plot to a few pages: "*Camilla* tells the story of love postponed, thwarted, frustrated, misled, and deliberately unspoken and even disguised" (Epstein 1989: 129). The tension between language and silence, between written or verbal communications of feelings and the constant abortion, suppression of these attempts, or misinterpretation and misdirection of their intent and addressees is important.[21] The theme is again connected to the perceived risks of acting vs. non-acting. Although Camilla makes numerous attempts of writing and speaking,[22] the accumulation of despair and misunderstandings between the characters springs both from the phenomenon of being wrongly "read" by others and the inability to express oneself.[23]

---

[21] For a detailed analysis of the tension between speech, silence and writing in the novel see chapter 4 "Camilla: Silencing the Heroine" in Epstein (1989: 123–150); see also Harris (1998) and Kraft (2006).

[22] Epstein also gives a good analysis of the two abortive interviews between Camilla and Edgar, the longest of which in "six pages of half-finished sentences, unspoken hopes and fears, and surprised facial expressions must bear the entire communication burden" (1989: 138).

[23] Most crucial in this context is Camilla's hallucination at the end of the novel when she imagines herself feverishly writing with an "iron pen" which leaves no mark on the pages. The scene and its symbolic power as a metaphor for the female condition and the painful struggle of the

In many ways, and despite being happily saved in the end, Camilla pays a high price for her silence and comes close to losing her mind. Her sister Lavinia demonstrate a surprising insight into Camilla's fear of detection and exposure of her feelings and tries to console her saying that her imagination of the worst outcome, can only exceed reality: "'This disclosure, my dearest Camilla', she cried, 'can never be so tremendous as *the incessant fear of its discovery*" (C 786; my emphasis). Like Camilla, Eugenia suffers through the majority of the narrative. After being harshly rejected by her intended husband Clermont and having met with openly expressed pity for her appearance by people on the street, Eugenia becomes aware of her deformity and its perception by others. For the first time, she blames her family for "deluding me into utter ignorance of my unhappy defects, and then casting me, all unconscious and unprepared, into the wide world to hear them!" (C 293). Her outburst presents another incident of cautious protection gone horribly wrong. Mr Tyrold steps in to manage Eugenia's situation, explaining Sir Hugh's best intentions behind it, but also admitting that his wife had, in fact, foreseen the potential problems and unhappiness resulting "from the extreme caution used to keep this dear unfortunate child ignorant of her peculiar situation. [...]. *But who should leave any events to the caprices of chance, which the precautions of foresight can determine?*" (C 300; my emphasis). Her father's words show the educational goal of eliminating dangers but also the illusion of complete control and the awareness of the limits of successful risk perception due to the many incalculable variables. Trying to teach his daughter a lesson, Mr Tyrold takes Eugenia, who had earlier exclaimed that she "would purchase a better appearance at any price" (C 308), to see the "mad" girl, who lives in a house nearby and is an imbecile, yet strikingly beautiful. The purpose of the excursion is to teach Eugenia "that beauty, without mind, is more dreadful than any deformity" (C 311). Due to her uncle's management and attempts at compensation for the accidents, Eugenia is, in fact left with a "double deformity – her inferior body and her superior education" (Doody 1988: 242–243) and she now suffers from people's reaction to her both mental and physical alterity. Like Edgar's misguided risk-management of his heart and of Camilla's reputation and safety, Sir Hugh's attempts to protect Eugenia scar her for life, while her bookish education and her sheltered existence leave her ill-prepared to resist the evil charms of Bellamy and render the belated realization about the effect of her appearance to others extremely painful.

---

writing process have been thoroughly analysed by Epstein (1989: 20–21), who sees the "iron pen" as a central metaphor in Burney's life and fiction.

Throughout the novel risk is associated with deviation from the conventional order of things, from customs, norms of behaviour and the unstable ideals of propriety, which also comprises the question of education for women. But it is especially Eugenia's physical deformity which disqualifies her from a 'normal' participation in the marriage game (cf. Salih 2007: 41). Her appearance inspires pity and disgust, a reflection of contemporary fears of illness. In contrast to the plague, which was generally perceived as a disease of the poor, smallpox was seen as being a more noble affliction and especially threatening and ruinous for young women.[24] Disease is one example of the continuities of fear and the perception of risk throughout history. The element of transgression, i.e. pollution, abnormality, harm, and the experienced limits of (medical) knowledge and control of the body is decisive. As a result, confrontation with disease typically causes protective mechanism of separation and attempts at imposing order. Susan Gilman explains:

> Disease, with its seeming randomness, is one aspect of the indeterminable universe that we wish to distance from ourselves. To do so we must construct boundaries between ourselves and those categories of individuals whom we believe (or hope) to be more at risk than ourselves.[...] The construction of the image of the patient is thus always a playing out of this desire for a demarcation between ourselves and the chaos represented in culture by disease. (Gilman 1988: 4)

In *Camilla*, Eugenia's body, marked by disease, violates the perfect picture of youth and deconstructs any notion of having perfect control over the girl's future. The Eugenia-plot illustrates how smallpox haunted particularly the "fear-struck female imagination" (Shuttleton 2007: 3) at the time, David Shuttleton points out, and for writers like Burney, "the trauma of smallpox disfigurement provided a perennial motif for didactic narratives and moral reflections" (2007: 123; 117).[25] He explains further that the social impact of smallpox was most commonly feared by the "young, aspiring, upper-class heiress" (2007: 118); since the disease posed a threat to beauty rather than to life, the risk of disfigurement was directly related to the loss of marketability for young women. While the topic of a woman's self-worth being at risk is introduced by Eugenia's contraction of smallpox but extended later to the other female charac-

---

24 See Shuttleton's *Smallpox and the Literary Imagination* (2007).
25 For further examples and readings of female authors who wrote about smallpox see Shuttleton (2007: 134f). These writers often had personal experience with scarring, like Burney after her mastectomy, or Sara Scott who contracted smallpox herself. Characteristically, smallpox produces abrupt plot turns in 18th century literature, for instance in the beginning of *Camilla* or in Sara Scott's *Millenium Hall*; deformed women also occur in novels by Aphra Behn or Eliza Haywood.

ters; the outing into the world comes at great cost for each of them. Reading Burney's novel alongside Mary Wollstonecraft's *A Vindication of the Rights of Women* (1792), a text which also makes "critical use of the concept of woman as a defective being" (Nussbaum 2003: 109), Nussbaum constructs a more political argument by referring to the 18th-century's perception of scarred and diseased bodies as a fearful representation of the state of national degeneration:

> Anxieties about the nation's health in the face of contamination and disease – in particular the fear of smallpox – are projected onto imperfect bodies, including the excessively feminine and the exotic other, and the irregular and atypical help form a 'normate' identity as they provide the negative measure of the nation's physical and moral health. (Nussbaum 2003: 110)

In the novel, the girls' characters and qualities are constantly compared to each other and can be related to the emerging ideal of the "normal" and ideal femininity. In contrast to Eugenia who embodies deviation in regard to her superior intellectual capacities and her inferior physicality and to Indiana, who displays the opposite extremes – beauty and stupidity –, Camilla is closer to the desirable average, the unblemished norm.[26] She is also the lucky one who miraculously escapes all accidents which could leave her maimed like her sister, for instance the carriage accident. Yet, from the start of the novel, losses and gains are strangely distributed and Eugenia profits from her disease in a bizarre way by gaining financial value through the inheritance bestowed upon her, Nonetheless, Eugenia has to find a new definition of femininity for herself, which reinterprets defect and difference into something valuable and which she achieves in the end. Eugenia has to learn self-love as a strategy of survival in a culture which marginalizes. She steps back from her own romantic feelings and uses her money to make the match of her cousin Indiana and Melmond possible.[27]

---

[26] Patricia Spacks argues: "The ideal woman will be neither too beautiful or too rich; she will be properly humble" (1976: 182). Camilla appears as the perfect embodiment of this construction of femininity. In comparison to her sisters and her cousin, Camilla shows traits of the desirable 'average' with regard to her character, appearance and position. It appears that any tendency to go to or show any extremes (money, beauty, education, deformity) and any deviation from the "norm" is dangerous for the girls in the novel. In a way, Burney's heroine aims exactly for what Robinson Crusoe's father wanted for him, a life of the risk-free middle station, without any adventures and based on adjustment to society's rules and his class.

[27] Eugenia displays generosity and altruism by sharing her fortunes with the pair and gracefully accepts that her own (romantic) love for Melmond is not returned. Interestingly, this kind of decision for a celibate life and giving up one's own love is usually taken by much older, wiser, and male characters, for example Roger in Trollope's *The Way We Live Now*.

Related to the central question of 'normal', i.e. also suitable, female behaviour in the novel, Elizabeth Kraft has stressed the importance of Burney as an author who focuses on "the question of female heroic action, endowing all of her heroines with both an impulse to public service and a natural physical fearlessness – still needed in the world, but rendered increasingly problematic by the conditions of modern life" (Kraft 2006: 38).[28] In fact, we seem to find a curious mix of arguments for 'old' quixotic courage and caution calculations in a risk society. Her fearlessness distinguishes Camilla from the other characters, for instance, she is the only one unafraid of her mother: "Though unaffectedly beloved, Mrs. Tyrold was deeply feared by all her children, Camilla alone excepted" (C 238). There are several instances in the novel where Camilla's courage is highlighted, usually scenes involving animals and accidents, e.g. the episodes with the mad bull, the kicking horse, or the dog. These scenes often bring emotions to the surface. Acute perceptions of other characters being at risk, typically pierce the individual shields of (self-)control. For example, hearing about Edgar's riding accident Camilla "found no sensation so powerful as joy for the safety of Edgar" (C 347). When her father notices her emotional state, he utters again the following warning: "Risk not, my dear girl, to others, those outward marks of sensibility which, to common or unfeeling observers, seem but the effect of an unbecoming remissness in the self-command which should dignify every female who would do herself honour" (C 348). Later, when a butcher boy gives a signal to his bull-dog to attack Sir Hugh's old spaniel, Edgar rushes in to help, while Camilla starts to panic and fear for his life. The perception of risk is, ironically, both what keeps Camilla and Edgar apart and what breaks through boundaries of silence and gives them each an outlet for their emotions. The scene is worth quoting at length:

> Roused at once from her sullen calm to the most agonising sensibility, every thing and every body, herself most of all, were forgotten in the sight of his danger; and, with a piercing shriek, she darted down the bank, and arrived at the tremendous spot, at the same instant that the more useful exhortations of Lavinia, had induced the boy to withdraw the fierce animal; [...] Camilla perceived not if the danger were impending, or over; gasping, pale, and agitated, she caught Mandlebert by the arm, and, in broken accents, half pronounced, 'O Edgar!... are you hurt?' [...] Mandlebert; he could hardly trust his senses, hardly believe he existed; yet he felt the pressure of her hand upon his arm, and saw in her coun-

---

28 Kraft elaborates on the allusions in *Camilla* to epic precursors by Homer and Virgil, e.g. the "female warrior" killed in the Trojan War in Book XI of *The Aeneid* (cf. Kraft 2006: 40). It is interesting to at least consider that Burney names her heroine after an epic "warrior queen", yet it makes her suffering all the more frustrating and makes the final ending appear doubly pessimistic and ironic if seen as a comment on the situation of women at the turn of the century.

tenance terror the most undisguised, and tenderness that went straight to his soul. 'Is it Camilla', he cried, 'who thus speaks to me? ... Is not my safety or my destruction alike indifferent to Camilla?' (C 539)

During a group walk in the countryside, the characters cross a field in which they encounter a bull. The individual characters' behaviour in this scene gives insight into their reactions to danger and perceptions of risk, ranging from impulsive flight and panic to more controlled, rational assessments of the situation. The episode exemplifies the ways in which risk is intrinsic to Burney's characterization and construction of gender roles in the novel, while also showing the distinct comedy which balances out Burney's often darker or even melodramatic style. The description of the characters' detection of the danger while they are resting on a clearing develops as follows:

> [...] their ears received the shock of a prodigious roar from a bull in the field adjoining. Miss Margland screamed, and hid her face with her hands. Indiana, taught by her lessons to nourish every fear as becoming, shriekt still louder, and ran swiftly away, deaf to all that Edgar, who attended her, could urge. Eugenia, to whom Bellamy instantly hastened, seeing the beast furiously make towards the gate, almost unconsciously accepted his assistance, to accelerate her flight from its vicinity; while Dr. Orkborne, intent upon his annotations, calmly wrote on, sensible there was some disturbance, but determined to avoid inquiring whence it arose, [...]. Camilla, the least frightened, because the most enured to such sounds, from the habits and instruction of her rural life and education, adhered firmly to Sir Hugh, who began blessing himself with some alarm; but whom Dr. Marchmont re-assured, by saying the gate was secured, and too high for the bull to leap, even supposing it a vicious animal. (C 132)

The scene, which consciously employs elements of Gothic parody, continues with Indiana's running away, all damsel-in-distress, "her beauty, heightened by her flight", screaming "I shall die! I shall die! – I am pursued by a mad bull!" (C 133). Meanwhile Dr. Marchmont dramatically laments the odds: "Lord help us! What a poor race we are! No safety for us! If we only come out once in a dozen years we must meet with a mad bull!" (C 132). Edgar, reacting rationally and trying to calm and protect the others, "would have explained, that all was safe" (C 133), yet the scene turns into a game of flirtation, as the danger turns out to be non-existent. Melmond is the first to join into Indiana's half-acted fear and exclaims: "give me the ecstasy to protect – to save you!" (C 133). This game of fake risk is dragged out over the next few pages, while the narrative ironically comments on the traditional association of fear, weakness, and femininity which is consciously 'played' out by Indiana and Melmond:

> 'What feminine, what beautiful delicacy! – How sweet in terror! – How soul-piercing in alarm!' These exclamations were nearly enchanting to Indiana, whose only fear was, lest they should not be heard by Edgar; and, whenever they ceased whenever a pause and respectful silence took their place, new starts, fresh palpitations, and designed false steps, again called them forth; [...]. (C 135)

Apart from showing Indiana's strategic use of (acted) fear, the episode strengthens the bound between Edgar and Camilla. In contrast to Melmond, who is attracted to Indiana's vulnerability and sensitivity, he admires Camilla's ability to control herself and singles her out among the other women: "'You can listen, then, even when you are alarmed', said he, expressively, 'to the voice of reason!' (C 136). Meanwhile the episode also brings Eugenia and the fortune-hunter Bellamy closer. In contrast to Indiana, Eugenia, who lacks the outward signs of beautiful femininity and a manipulative nature, has to justify her fear and the acceptance of protection from a man. Due to her exclusively bookish knowledge, she is unable to deal with the realities and dangers of the outward world and lacks the ability to judge character just like Camilla, although she possesses financial independence. Full of fear of being accused of having misbehaved and misjudged the situation, as Edgar declares with authority that "nor has there ever been any danger", Eugenia cries out: "I could not prevail – I could not – this gentleman said the risk was so great – he would not suffer me – but he has sent for a chaise, though I told him I had a thousand times rather hazard my life amongst them [the others], and with them, than save it alone!" (C 137). Reflecting on Edgar's judgment of the situation, Eugenia starts to question Bellamy's actions of forcing a heroic 'rescue' upon her, he "had hurried her from field to field, with an idea that the dreaded animal was in full pursuit" (C 137). Generally, the scene illustrates the strategic construction of risk and the exploitation of fears from both men and women, who utilize it for their ends in the courtship game. The description of the episode and its psychological implications cover pages and pages until Sir Hugh utters a final, and rather ironic, assessment of the situation. His statement illustrates again his cluelessness and the theme of (mis)perception of danger and reality at the heart of the narrative: "we have all been upon the point of being tossed by the mad bull; *which would certainly have happened, but for the lucky chance of its turning out a false alarm*" (C 147; my emphasis).

The sailing excursion in Southampton, another outing of the whole group of young people, similarly highlights how staged and perceived moments of danger and safety are intrinsic to the relationships between the couples. While Eugenia due to her physical impairment really "was in danger of failing every moment" (C 700) when trying to walk on the wobbly wooden plank path of getting into the yacht, and Melmond offers her his hand to steady her, Indiana, who observes the scene, fakes being at risk to attract Melmond's attention; "she gave a shriek at every step, made hazardous by her wilful rejection of assistance, and acted over again the charm of terror" (C 699–700). In response to her theatrics, Melmond, seeing

> Indiana unguarded, unprotected; his imagination painted her immediately in a watery grave; and, seeing Eugenia safe, though not accommodated, he rushed back to the boat, and with trembling respect implored her to accept his aid. Triumphant, now, she conceived herself in her turn, and looking at him with haughty disdain, said, she chose to go alone; and when again he conjured her not to risk her precious safety, added, 'You know you don't care about it; so pray go to your Miss Eugenia Tyrold. (C 700)

The episode also triggers a dramatic worsening of the situation between Camilla and Edgar; she awaits his help, he only stands back to watch, she nearly falls, then at the last minute accepts help from Lord Valhorst, which in turn leads Edgar to take the incidents to be a deliberate exercise of coquettish manipulation; in other words, he accuses her of what Indiana did, while Melmond remains oblivious to all of it.

Soon after this episode and Edgar's apparently final break with Camilla, her psychological decline begins, building towards the gothic climax of the novel. As many critics have noted, Burney's novel displays in parts, a "'Udolphoish' terror" (Bloom and Bloom 1979: 232), and takes a distinctly Gothic turn especially in the final quarter.[29] Camilla is alone, isolated from her family and friends and her despair about her family's financial situation, the loss of Edgar and the abduction of her sister, lead to her mental anguish reaching a point of crisis. After she runs away and seeks shelter in a halfway house, she by chance sees the corpse of Alphonso Bellamy, who is brought there for police investigation. In reaction to this and triggered by her general state of physical and nervous exhaustion, she has a nightmarish vision, from which she is eventually rescued by her mother and Edgar. The following confession of her worries and feelings and the reunion at her bedside mark the beginning of the restoration of order and perceived safety for Camilla and the rest of the girls. As the scene is one of the most frequently analysed in the criticism of the novel, a brief interpretation

---

29 See, e.g. Harman (2000) and Doody (1977). Frances Burney, herself a fan of Anne Radcliffe's writings, referred to her novel as "4 Udolphoish volumes" (cited in Harman 2000: 265), not only with regard to the size of the manuscript but also the use of grotesque elements, violence, and horror.

shall suffice.[30] The scene is decisive for it brings Camilla's state of feeling at risk to a climax; yet she never is in actual danger other than suffering from the feverish hallucinations, in other words, from her own perception of the impossibility of her situation. The narrator reveals later that her "danger was the result of self-neglect, as her sufferings had all flowed from mental anguish" (C 893). Her state develops from the moment she walks through her uncle's deserted house. Although she is on familiar territory, the place inspires only terror, and she desperately searches for people and anyone to talk to. It thus constitutes a change to the fears she harboured before, i.e. her constant keeping of secrets and the fears of being detected and compromised: "The fear of discovery was now combated by an anxiety to see some one, – any one, – and she returned to the passage. All there was still quiet, and she hazarded gliding past the open door, though without daring to look into the room" (C 851). Camilla cannot make sense of the situation and explain the absence of her uncle and the others.

> Nothing was in its wonted order; [...]. She now felt petrified; she sunk on the floor, to ejaculate a prayer for his safety, but knew not how to rise again, for terrour; nor which way next to turn, nor what even to conjecture. Thus she remained, till suspense grew worse than certainty and she forced herself from the room to seek some explanation. (C 851–852)

She leaves the house, and not knowing where to turn, ends up at the halfway house where she sees the dead body of Bellamy; the Gothic atmosphere now reaches its full height:

> It was dark, and she was alone; the corpse she had just quitted seemed still bleeding in full view. [...] She felt nearly stiff with horrour, chilled, frozen, with speechless apprehension. A slumber, feverish nearly to delirium, at length surprised her harassed faculties; but not to afford them rest. Death, in a visible figure, ghastly, pallid, severe, appeared before her, and with its hand, sharp and forked, struck abruptly upon her breast. She screamed-but it was heavy as cold, and she could not remove it. She trembled; she shrunk from its touch; but it had iced her heart-strings. (C 874)

In this fearful, nervous state Camilla sees no other way out than death and starts to compose a goodbye-letter to her parents, a final appeal for help and an attempt to communicate all her pent-up emotions and anxieties. The dark climax brings a reversal of the novel's subtitle, Camilla, the picture of youth and life, is turned into its opposite, when the heroine wonders, "so soon I must represent... a picture of death?" (C 870). In her analysis of female dreams in Gothic

---

30 For an analysis of Camilla's dream ("A Vision", Chapter X) see especially Epstein (1989) and Doody (1977).

novels, Doody considers Camilla's nightmare in a wider contemporary context and describes the dark visions and frightening images as "the necessary and appropriate symbols of the consciousness of unhappy women – imprisoned by social conventions, threatened by slavery, and plagued by loneliness" (Doody 1977: 538–539). Although Doody places *Camilla* in the category of of "comic social novels" (1977: 550), in her discussion of Gothic female dream-scenes she marks Camilla's vision as one of the most horrifying examples, which illustrates how "panic and pain are heightened because of the heroine's growing and intolerable sense of loss, loneliness and guilt" (1977: 548).

Burney's mix of Gothic aesthetic and courtship novel does more than add a bit of drama and heightened emotion; it also offers potential for the heroine. To refer to Botting's apt description of the function of the Gothic: "As well as recasting the nature of social and domestic fears, Gothic fictions presented different, more exciting, worlds in which heroines in particular could encounter not only frightening violence but also adventurous freedom" (Botting 1996: 7). The Gothic here aids the creation of a specific risk environment in which the emotionally distraught characters, especially Camilla, seek to act. The typical blurring between fantasy and reality symbolizes the nature of fear and shows how risk perception, independent of actual danger, can lead to paranoia and overwhelming fear. In this regard, many characteristic elements of the female Gothic can also be seen as structuring principle in *Camilla*, although supernatural elements are more or less toned down completely. Camilla's nightmare is a strong reflection of tension and connected to the narrative's link between religious piousness and worldly (secular) risk. This becomes clear in Claudia Harman's argument, that the scene contains, in fact, Burney's central didactic-moral message: "In this climax to her 'Picture of Youth', [...] she was earnestly attempting to warn the younger generation, so bombarded with impious and revolutionary ideologies, that the consequences of their actions were of the utmost seriousness" (Harman 2000: 267). Such a reading gives credit to the undeniable strong moral orientation of the novel, which is nonetheless far from any firm grounding on providential design. Man awaits higher punishment and judgment, but is clearly left to manage the risks of his life by him/herself.

After her mother and Edgar arrive at Camilla's bedside, her period of isolation and the crisis is over. She falls into a deep sleep, and recovers quickly, because, as the narrator tells us: "The changeful tide of mental spirits from misery to enjoyment, is not more rapid than the transition from personal danger to safety, in the elastic period of youth" (C 889). So all is well again, and when her father arrives back home from debtor's prison, he "welcomed her to the paternal arms – to her home – to peace – to safety – and primaeval joy" (C 893). Nonetheless, this only happens after one more plea to control her emotion and imagination is put to Camilla, this time by her mother; "it is time to conquer this impetuous sensibility, which already, in its effects, has nearly broken all our hearts" (C 882).

Camilla, depicted as emotional, compassionate and ready to act impulsively, experiences the arbitrariness of luck and loss from early childhood through their her sister's accident and her own disinheritance which creates a general feeling of lack of control over the circumstances. It appears plausible for her later to actively partake in the courtship game and make decisions such as going on the trip to Southampton, buying clothes, and to try to solve her financial dilemma without seeking help.[31] To some extent, "Camilla's risk-taking is the only solution to the courtship plot's impasse" (Richard 2011: 125; 126) and the narrative celebrates female willingness to take chances, while caution and calculation are ridiculed. The plot demonstrates on various levels the futility of attempts at control and the inevitability of crisis. It also highlights the dynamics of a social system "against which there is no appeal: one false step and all is lost. The economics are even more terrifying: money is an irrational, uncontrollable force. The smallness of Camilla's offense is no hedge against utter destruction" (Copeland 1976: 34). Considering the analysis above, Burney's novel appears as a harsh criticism of the marriage market and of the triumph of capitalism in England which "saw commerce as a diffuse force that had penetrated into and changed the safest corners of private life" (Burgess 1995: 132). In *Camilla*, the heroine's financial insecurity is paralleled by the uncertainty of her relationship with Edgar who in turn only focuses on the moral suitability of Camilla and the insecurity about her virtue and reputation. In fact, the questions of who to trust, who to turn to, to associate with, who to borrow from, are crucial for all characters. Linked to the continual struggle for credit and credibility, at the centre of the novel lies the illustration of the isolating, destructive force of debt which is again shown as a power which spirals easily beyond human control, or rather especially beyond the management of young women such as Camilla. Fitting this pattern, her problems which culminate in a life-threatening situation are resolved by marriage, which "removes her from the dangerous credit relations in which she was entangled" (Richard 2011: 122). Putting a stop to female economic agency but also guaranteeing safety, the ending is furthermore ambivalent in regard to the link between debt and morality constructed in the narra-

---

[31] Epstein describes her behaviour as typical for the women in Burney's fiction who all "battle strictures on their appearance and dress, their movement, their social skills, and their economic abilities. Literally forced to make a living, they do the only thing respectable young women can do; they market themselves to the most genteel, to the most watchful, and to the highest bidders" (1996: 209).

tive. As Binhammer points out, the fact that Camilla "goes into debt to act selflessly – foregrounds the paradoxical logic in sentimental fiction's narration of commercial life" (Binhammer 2011: 8); yet the reader can also only feel a half-hearted relief when the marriage restores Camilla's financial security "since it comes only after she has literally been reduced to nothing" (2011: 16).

Danger is never only self-afflicted or shown to result from the characters' direct actions. Especially in the financial plot, risk is created by association. This is exemplified by the dangerous "mercenary characters" such as Mrs. Mittin or Mrs. Dubster who corrupt Camilla and enable her downwards slope. Burney's central topic is showing the risk for young women of marriageable age when entering society – "to be aware of the dangers run by Female Youth, when straying from the mother's careful wing" (C 645) – and the ultimate threat is a loss of reputation, a risk run merely by entering society and depicted as being almost absurdly beyond their control. Epstein underlines the riskiness of the prolonged in-between state of a woman's transition from maiden to wife which marks the time when her social identity and a woman's self is at the highest risk:

> This sense of hovering precarious social status is the key to courtship in the later eighteenth-century novel. […] It is this sense of danger that motivates Burney's fictions, danger that emerges from the fine line between 'that innocent desire…which needs not a blush' and the always slippery path of a female sexuality that demands to be policed and controlled before it has even been granted existence. (Epstein 1996: 201).

In many ways, Camilla would have been a lot safer just staying home with her family, yet she tries to take action and "buys into a system of courtship that offers her an elusive and tenous power at the cost of aggravating her economic difficulties" (Straub 1987: 193). The need to dress-up, the expenses of social life are financially ruinous to her, but otherwise she has no chance of a profitable marriage. Her desire, Edgar's love, is portrayed in a predominantly negative way, a motif found in many novels of the late 18th century.[32] Ultimately, it is not Camilla's failure to articulate her desire, but her naïve lack of knowing how to handle her finances and her attempts to conceal the debts from her father and to keep clear accounts that lead to disaster. Repeatedly, the novel draws attention to gender differences. Although both sexes gamble and run up debts, the risk for the young characters, like the numerous warning Camilla receives throughout the novel, are always strongly connected to a control of emotions. James Thomp-

---

[32] Several critics (e.g. Doody, Johnson, Epstein) comment on the frustration inherent in the plot; Henderson (1997: 69–70) takes the argument even further saying that all 'normal' yearning and desire is almost turned into masochism in the novel.

son sums up this point, saying: "Male characters such as Lionel ruin themselves through monetary extravagance, and female characters such as Mrs. Berlinton ruin themselves through emotional extravagance" (Thompson 1996: 35).

Frances Burney herself loathed dependency on men and financial worries as much as social non-conformity and fear is often evoked as a guiding principle in the author's life and fictions. Patricia Meyer Spacks is among the critics who claim that Burney, like many other 18th-century writers, left so much autobiographical material behind that it is possible to judge and draw comparisons between her works and her life.[33] Arguing that Burney's fictions are portraits of the perception and management of female fear at the time, her texts are characterized by a desperate aversion to risk which forms a noticeable contrast to texts by male writers. Spacks's reading of Burney relates usefully to the different constructions of risk in *Tristram Shandy* and *Camilla*. Using Laurence Sterne as foil of contrast to Burney, Spacks says that that the latter writer

> reveals not the chaos of experience but the reiteration of pattern. [...] Tristram Shandy is organized to reveal the pervasiveness of male fear, demonstrating in form and substance how the terror of impotence spreads through every endeavour. The entire mass of Fanny Burney's writings forms itself centrally in relation to female fear – not of the absence of power but of failure of goodness and consequent loss of love. Tristram's fears reduce his life to disorder; Miss Burney's (and her heroines') have ordering force, defending against chaotic possibility. (Spacks 1976: 158)

In her analysis of the "dynamics of fear" in Burney's fiction, Spacks gives an account of Burney's time at the court of Queen Charlotte, where the author was under constant fear of misconduct and losing the appreciation of the people she considered 'loved' authorities.[34] A fictive dialogue from Burney's diary of

---

33 In 1811 Frances Burney underwent a mastectomy, the removal of her right breast, which had pained and worried her for years. See Epstein (1986). Epstein's essay is a good example of the kind of biographical argument made by a number of critics, that Burney thematizes "moments of endured violence in the three novels that predated her mastectomy, and that these moments serve as frameworks for her analyses of female fear and the forced loss of control that constantly lurks beneath society's polite forms and coerces women into self-suppression" (1986: 131–132). The supposed tumour in her breast was probably benign, as Burney lived to the age of 87; however, Burney was an interested patient, actively followed medical research and dramatizes disease and illness it in her fiction, the smallpox episode in *Camilla* being just one example.

34 The element I obviously do not consider is the aspect of writing 'as risk', as a difficult occupation for a woman at the time and all the fears and obstacles related to it, which in Burney's case also plays an important role. However, studies such as Spacks's deal with this issue in detail (1976: 169; 172 ff). Later in life, after marriage and becoming a mother, Burney found new comfort and safety found in her domestic role, which offered a disguise for her unconven-

this time underlinesss this topic being a preoccupation of the author: "What has saved her from misbehaviour? Mr. Turbulent [the name given by Burney to Reverend Charles de Guiffardière, her spiritual guardian in her diaries] suggests prejudice, education, and accident. Miss Burney agrees, but adds fear. *'I run no risks that I can see – I run – but it is always away from all danger that I perceive'*" (cited in Spacks 1976: 160; my emphasis). The obsession with risk-aversion, as the highest goal, and the dangers of emotions and social deviation springs from the clashing of two desires, the want of freedom on the one hand, and the need for compliance, i.e. to avoid offending customs or people, on the other. Seeing Burney's court experience as being dominated by these contradictory needs, the lesson Burney herself learnt at the time also appears as the central moral of Camilla, namely that "only by strict decorum can a woman protect herself" (Spacks 1976: 166). In this sense, Burney's elaborates fears and strategies of risk-avoidance employed by herself. In both Burney's life and fiction there exists a notable contradiction between action and perception, between a lot of drama and fear in a relatively quiet and sheltered life. The emphasis on drama without action is something Burney shares with Sterne; generally her fiction illustrates fiction's moving away from the sensational adventure to more psychological, interior, and domestic drama.

To conclude the analysis it is worth to briefly reflect on Burney's text in the context of the female Bildungsroman tradition.[35] The didacticism of Burney's plot is focussed on the risks for young woman in society, the striving for impossible perfection of self-control and restraint in all areas of life, while at the time showing the dangers of uncontrolled imagination and feelings when rational observation of circumstances fails. Generally, the Bildungsroman takes up many elements of the picaresque novel. Being "concerned with the spiritual and psychological development of the protagonist" (Hardin 1991: ix), it evolved ideas springing logically from preoccupations of Enlightenment thought: cultivation (*Bildung*) of man's faculties (rational, moral, aesthetic) into an ideal of a harmonious, well rounded, and "complete" person (see Martini 1991: 5). In this sense, the Bildungsroman reflects the evolution of the novel, the turn towards the probable and familiar, away from the magical, epic and the fantas-

---

tional desires, i.e. to write. Spacks claims that Burney's later novels are noticeably darker, because she can afford to write them so.
35 Laura Sue Fuderer lists Burney's *Camilla* in her annotated bibliography of the female Bildungsroman in English (cf. 1990: 35). See also Gemmeke (2004) and Tavor Bannet (1991).

tic, towards common life and ordinary people.[36] Apart from shifting the focus on man's agency, probabilities, and the risk of choice and the need for calculation, as the study of 18th-century fiction has shown, the novel thus emerged also as a useful tool for instruction (as moral *Bildung*). As many critical studies have argued, the debate about domesticity, female virtue and conduct were thematic preoccupations of 18th-century literature, gaining importance throughout the century.[37] While in male picaresque novels, such as *Roderick Random*, family life and domesticity are maintained as the idyll of stability and happiness, the female Bildungsroman engages in a critique of family life and this idyll, highlighting the heroines encounter with obstacles, especially to free expression and personal intercourse, while the authors were still seeking to write "exemplar" literature. To achieve this, as Eve Tavor Bannet explains, lady novelists, concerned with the morals of their readers, usually portrayed heroines full of admirable qualities such as patience, control, loyalty, sympathy, beauty, and gentleness. Embodying social, domestic, intellectual and natural perfections, "these perfected heroines serve[d] as the standard against which society is judged" (Tavor Bannet 1991: 205).

Burney's *Camilla* appears typical in this regard; but there remains the question if the characters in the novel really develop, or if the text should rather be considered as negative Bildungsroman. Here, the over-emphasis in the narrative on risk plays a role. Teaching by example involves in *Camilla* showing the dangers of misconduct; arguably the warning aspect, the cautionary tale takes for large parts of the narrative priority over the 'model' character. The narrative seems to replicate also structures of the earlier adventure plots of Defoe and Smollett's fictions. Burney combines a mix of teaching "by example" with what Smollett called teaching "by fear" (cited in Tavor Bannet 1991: 220); *Camilla* shows the awful consequences of wrong behaviour, be it intentional or not. Typically, the reader is made to feel both the virtuousness of the heroine, and shows the evilness of social norms, here especially the 'economic' practices of the courtship game. However claustrophobic the structure and helpless the heroine, she possesses freedom of action and makes her own choices, however misguided they may appear. This aspect rehabilitates the novel from the traditional plot and didacticism and shows its critical potential. One finds the crucial structural development of the isolation of the heroine who needs to be abandoned and put at risk. Although we do not encounter the more common, obvious tropes

---

36 See Karl von Morgenstern's lectures "Über das Wesen des Bildungsromans" (1820), which contain the first official use of the term (Martini 1991: 2; 12–13). On Burney's secular vision see Bloom and Bloom (1979).

37 See Armstrong and Tennenhouse (1987) and Tavor Bannet (1991).

of a heroine who is orphaned or lost in a strange place, Camilla's parents are still absent for most of the narrative and Edgar usually hides in the background. Typical in the Bildungsroman of the time are characters representing either morals or their corruption, and who are either watching the heroine or leading her astray. In *Camilla*, men do the former, while female characters like Mrs. Berlinton and Mrs. Mittin take on the latter function. And the irony of Burney's depiction is that both groups of characters have a, at least in the first degree, destructive influence, since Camilla gets caught in between angry guardians of morality and, on the whole, harmless corruptions. Another characteristic of the genre is interestingly undermined in the novel. According to Tavor Bannet, female novelists were often putting happy relationships on a basis of "a transgressive, composite, hermaphrodictic ideal", meaning that both partners in a relationship, thus ultimately based on equality, possess "both 'masculine' sense and 'feminine' softness", showing that "women can have 'manly' sentiments' of honor, courage, and determination, while men can both fulfil a nurturing role and devote themselves to the good of others" (1991: 216). Yet a lot of the comedy and darker irony in *Camilla* is constructed by showing the sexes having shared qualities and by dissolving clear-but gender binaries; especially a lot of the men appear quite effeminate. It goes, however, beyond comedic effect. The confusion about gender roles and appropriate behaviour leads to many dangerous situations that occur because the men try to 'nurture' and the women try to be courageous and 'independent.' While one may wonder if this, on any level, entails an implicit plea for the 'safety' of clearer roles or just an ironic deconstruction, it in any case reflects the fact that gender roles were never as unambiguously cut or based on a binary masculine/feminine opposition of qualities as critics of the era sometimes want them to be. *Camilla* also signifies the gradual transformation of the female Bildungsroman and conduct literature in another aspect. The idealized heroine, who is usually allowed only one central flaw, and how like Camilla is faulted by an ignorance of the world and that "reigning and radical defect of her character – an imagination that submitted to no control" (C 84), is gradually displaced from the centre. The focus on the second heroine, Eugenia, and her ordeals, as well as on the other women, shows indeed how the discourse becomes polyvocal, and complex, blurring the binaries of right and wrong.

So, what is the moral of this particular story? Other than the fact that Edgar and Camilla should have been more straightforward with each other and could have avoided a lot of suffering, the critical reception of the novel and the ending shows, above all, the ambivalence of Burney's narrative. *Camilla* is both an appeal for maintaining traditional values and social structures *and* a protest against them.[38] Henderson (1997: 84) sees the novel structured around the question how to express desire and sustain human relationships if these are complicated in a world in which financial value, (capitalist) speculation and 'forecasting' dictate everything and the rules of trade are inseparable from romance. But at the same time, Edgar and Camilla's attempts to resist are also noticeable, and both display altruism and emotions, which overrule the attempts at rational profit-loss calculations. The narrative argues both in favour and against the will and need to speculate and to calculate everything; it shows the pros and cons of risk perception and its constitution of subjective imagination as well as of rational measurement.

In many ways, *Camilla* is a transitional novel, foreshadowing the emerging Victorian ideal of virtuous, domestic womanhood. Despite a firm assertion of the split between the private and public spheres, both are shown as dangerous. While venturing out unprotected into the outside world is shown to be risky for Camilla, Eugenia's accident and humiliation happen in her own home. Burney's heroines face the same struggle for survival, marriage and financial security as Defoe's Moll and Roxana, but courtesan life and thievery is clearly not an option for them. In comparison to Defoe's heroines at the beginning of the century, who easily juggled disguises, lies, men, and money, Burney's have less liberty and submit to social restraints. Unlike Smollett's picaro, who survives by relying on his wits, can exist outside society at times and still make a secure comeback into conventional society, Burney's female protagonists are radically different. The minute they enter the world and try to emancipate themselves from paternal protection, disaster strikes, till their future husbands rescue them. Burney appears as an intermediary author, writing between the Augustan satire and adventures of the earlier novel and the domestic interiority of many later writers such as Jane Austen. Her fictions adds a darker touch to the courtship novel, dramatizing the fact that there is no guarantee for safety, either in family or marriage, if one tries to do 'everything right'.

---

38 The debate of whether Burney can be considered as a feminist is grounded in this ambivalence of acceptance and rebellion in the writings. Although the conclusion of *Camilla* is highly conventional, and order is restored on the surface, risk still lurks underneath. Salih shares this opinion, saying that the novel "does not leave the reader with the comforting sense that stability is [...] fully restored, [...] the society in which her [Burney's] characters are inscribed is compromised and profoundly unstable" (2007: 52). The question as to how radical Burney was has been a matter of debate running the gamut from "arch-conservative "to "crypto-proto feminist" (2007: 40; see Gemmeke 2004: 19).

Part II **Out of the Ordinary: The Gamble of Life in the 19th-century Novel**

5 Old and New Concerns

5.1 Cinderella 'At Sea': *Persuasion*

From the Enlightenment onwards philosophers and mathematicians have subscribed to the idea that human beings act with the same degree of regularity and predictability as can be observed in nature. However, as many psychological studies of risk clearly demonstrate, mathematical calculations fail to incorporate and account for the "wild-cart" of human behaviour and circumstances which resist statistical prediction (see Dacunha-Castelle 1996: 143). This phenomenon is starting to be explored with full force in the 19th-century novel. The narrative design of Jane Austen's texts, as Douglas Lane Patey has shown, for instance, on the case of *Emma*, makes them furthermore complex studies of probable judgment, "most completely built up from a fabric rather of accounts of what characters expect, conjecture, guess, and foresee than of what externally they do" (Patey 1984: 218–19). When George Butte argues that something happened to the English novel "around the time of Jane Austen" (Butte 2004: vii), he similarly refers to the introduction of a deep narrative intersubjectivity, i.e. the characters' experience and awareness of each other's mental and emotional states. In comparison to 18th-century literary predecessors, these narratives are newly complex in the sense that characters, for example, make observations about observations, and negotiate multiple layers of perception. This change in storytelling and an altered sense of depicting the discursive relations between self, other, and community, also cause a greater involvement of the reader.[1] Taking Austen's fiction as new archetypes for the treatment of fictional consciousness, Butte's argument has notable influence on the depiction and negotiation of risk; risk management equally becomes more complex and intersubjective, as will be shown on the case of Austen's last finished and most modern of her six canonical novels, *Persuasion* (1818).

Austen's style of writing, often compared to miniature paintings and considered rather conventional or even formulaic, still notably pushes boundaries.[2] According to Ross Hamilton (2007: 220), one innovation is Austen's use of acci-

---

[1] See Zunshine's argument that Austen's narrative pulls the reader "into being profoundly invested emotionally in knowing that Anne knows that Wentworth knows that Elizabeth pretends not to recognize that he wants to be acknowledged as an acquaintance" (2007: 294). Zunshine sees this kind of "multilevel mental embedment" (295) typical for the narrative exploration of deep intersubjectivity pioneered by writers such as Austen.

[2] See Jocelyn Harris's *A Revolution Almost Beyond Expression: Jane Austen's Persuasion* (2007).

dent. It is focused on the domestic and the complicated operations of mind and heart, including unexpected encounters, miss-timings, or overheard remarks, but compared to the 18th century the characters are more rounded, and the narratives allow more room for the depiction of their internal conflicts and different interpretations of accidental events. While Austen's narrative encourages the reader to trace the characters' motivations and actions in detail, much of its tension, as Alan Richardson writes, is due "to the ongoing threat that feelings which can be read only haphazardly, through momentary glimpses, or indirectly, through their bodily manifestations, can always be misread" (Richardson 2002: 152). Arguing that this creates a new dimension of risk, Austen's novels often resemble psychological case studies, e.g. of how one can overcome restrictions created by the social environment, or cope with loss or the threat of it (see Hamilton 2007: 229; Knox-Shaw 2004: 23). As such, one can almost see a pre-Darwinian interest in the texts in mechanisms of adaptation and survival, in prediction and reliability, and in judging the exceptional from the ordinary, topics that increase only in importance throughout the century. They show the complex interrelations of the workings of morality, psyche, and the modalities of social relations. Moreover, the capture the pervasive influence people have on one another and illustrate the individual's and intersubjective perceptions of risk, constructed less through dramatic action but as internal, domestic dramas, which are no less intense and follow the same principles of "strategizing" to conquer the odds.

In literary history Jane Austen's works occupy the transitory terrain between late 18th-century writing and Victorian realism and, as characteristic reflections of their time, point both backwards and forward. *Persuasion* negotiates the tension between the old and emerging new social order and neither fully embraces Romanticism nor rejects Enlightenment values such as rational calculation.[3] The narrative, shaped by a sense of both nostalgia and irony, develops many themes that preoccupy the English novel throughout the 19th century in psychological depth. It has been duly noted that Austen's plots generally intertwine romance and economic concerns to a great extent.[4] While critics like John Vernon consider the theme of money to be "perhaps the most common theme in nineteenth-century fiction" (Vernon 1984: 7), in Austen's novels value, courtship, and calculation are certainly inseparable.[5] As Edward Copeland argues, for Austen as for other female middle-class writers of the time, who had

---

[3] See especially Peter Knox-Shaw's *Jane Austen and the Enlightenment* (2004).
[4] See Copeland (2010), Michie (2011), Vernon (1984), and Scheuermann (1993: 199–238).
[5] On the importance of material wealth in Austen's works see also Sandie Byrne's *Jane Austen's Possessions and Dispossessions* (2014).

begun to write about themselves, the insecurity in their plots is often tied to expressing "the precarious relationship between love and money" (Copeland 1976: 36). Austen's fictions continue the exploration of the topic of wealth, or lack thereof, as limiting or enabling the characters' agency and freedom. Incomes are openly discussed, debt remains a great source of anxiety, and financial mismanagement, as a sign of a questionable, 'bad' character, is often pitted against the 'good' skill of being able to make a fortune. Yet Austen's writing also introduces a new dimension, the negotiation of different forms of wealth and the dichotomy between city and country. As such, *Persuasion* shows the early stirrings of a significant social change and shift towards forms of wealth "beyond the security of the landed estate" (Vernon 1984: 8), fully explored in later novels, for instance, Trollope's *The Way We Live Now*.

In many ways similar to Burney, Austen focuses on the depiction of the dangerous ground of the marriage market in upper and upper-middle class society. Both writers produce fictions which often read like cautionary tales and in which the single heroines are forced – in one form or another – "to pay the price for both the evils of society and for her own at once admirable and foolish errors and aspirations" (Tavor Bannet 1991: 226). This is typically followed by a happy resolution of conflicts and the retreat into marriage and financial safety. The female protagonists, at risk of choosing the wrong partner or letting the right one slip away, are usually lucky in the end and secure a rich and loving husband against all odds. Depicting marriage as a main goal of a woman's life, Austen's fictions suggest that if – and only if – the courtship game is played right, and the necessary little bit of luck comes at the right moment, then all will end well.[6] Financial risk is always the danger on the horizon and drives the plot, but never to the extent that the heroines must actively find other means of making ends meet. In contrast, for instance, to Defoe's novels, money is less connected to survival – or realizing fantastic ambitions of wealth – than to happiness, stability, and upward social movement. From Burney to Austen, one sees a continuation of the obsession with depicting courtship in the novel, yet still a marked silence on what follows afterwards, such as the daily struggle of marriage or a rebellion against the binding force of the legal and moral contract. Austen's texts do not yet allow a questioning of the heroine's happiness beyond

---

6 Cf. Copeland's comment: "In fact, the shadow of the single woman without money, Charlotte Lucas syndrome, continues to haunt her works to the end. [...] Fanny Price, Jane Fairfax, even Anne Elliot, are, in the end, left dependent upon purest chance for their entrance in the moneyed world" (2010: 141).

the marital vows,⁷ although the ending of *Persuasion* presents a change in this regard compared to her previous works.

The overall atmosphere of *Persuasion* is one of loss and risk. Before the beginning of the plot,⁸ the heroine Anne Elliott has already lost her mother and her love interest, the navy Captain Frederick Wentworth, and in the opening chapter she is about to be forced out of her family home, Kellynch Hall, due to her father's mounting debts.⁹ The first paragraph of the narrative famously consists of an accurately recorded loss, the Elliott family's entry in the Baronetage, chronicling the death of Sir Walter Elliot's wife and stillborn son, leaving him with three daughters, Elizabeth, Anne, and Mary, only the latter being safely married. The other two face the risk of spinsterhood. Especially Elizabeth, who is 29 and two years older than Anne, "felt her approach to the years of danger, and would have rejoiced to be certain of being properly solicited by baronet-blood within the next twelve-month or two" (P 8). As for Anne's romantic prospects, her courtship with Captain Wentworth failed eight years ago due to the resistance of the Elliot family and especially Lady Russell, the girls' substitute mother and a woman "able to persuade a person to any thing" (P 96). Her sound reasons for rejecting the Captain as a suitable match for Anne were that he, being a naval officer without a family fortune, "had nothing but himself to recommend him, and no hopes of attaining affluence, but in the chances of a most uncertain profession", and she feared the risk of Anne "sunk by him into a state of most wearing, anxious, youth-killing dependence" (P 27). Yet this effect is in fact produced by Anne's rejection of him against her feelings and, after so many years have gone by, Lady Russell is now full of "anxiety which borders on hopelessness" (P 28) for Anne's ever being tempted by another man. Meanwhile Sir Walter has been caught in a downward spiral after losing his wife, the prudent manger of the family finances. Himself incapable of economizing, he can no longer afford to maintain Kellynch Hall. Although the narrative shows Sir Walter as largely responsible for his situation, the plot of *Persuasion* dramatizes a common fear of the landowner, namely that "the need to raise cash will drive him to mort-

---

7 The precariousness and the tragic potential of the institution of marriage is generally not fully explored until the second half of the century and the advent of writers such as George Eliot and Thomas Hardy.

8 For this reason, *Persuasion* has been called "in effect a second novel" (Tanner 1986: 211; Lynch 1998: 215), because the most significant losses and a whole courtship drama has happened before the plot starts.

9 Anna Sokolsky, drawing on psychoanalytical theories of female melancholia, goes as far as seeing Anne suffering from depression and being dangerously "in love with loss itself" (1994: 129).

gage or sell part of his estate" (Vernon 1984: 42). The first instance of risk-management in the narrative is thus the Elliots' decision to rent out their estate and chose a new place of residence. In the debates largely led by the ever sensible Lady Russell, Bath wins against London because it is considered a cheaper place with less temptations: "It was a much safer place for a gentleman in his predicament" (P 15).

Austen dislocates her heroine – literally as well as figuratively – from the beginning, and links her instability to the loss of the "patriarchal estate, the symbol of inherited security" (Clarkson Holstein 1993: 54). The novel uproots traditionally stable anchors like family homes; in fact, just about all the previous stabilities of Jane Austen's world are called into question, observes Tony Tanner, and describes *Persuasion* as a text of "sadness, [...] deeply shadowed by the passing of things, and the remembrance of things past" (Tanner 1986: 211). Making up for lost time being another major theme, the narrative shows an easily discernible structural pattern of loss and retrieval and illness and recovery. While many readings comment on the novel's "autumnal" feel, mainly portrayed through Anne's fading bloom, Austen, who was already marked by fatal illness during the writing of *Persuasion*, bestows on her heroine the blessing of "a second spring of youth and beauty" (P 115). Despite the pervasive sense of loss and decay, it is thus also a novel about being granted a second chance in life. But, as Jocelyn Harris argues in her biographical study of Jane Austen, the author's personal condition presents but one and not quite sufficient explanation for the narrative's particular atmosphere and the depiction of the heroine's second spring: "The nation's jubilee after the prolonged carnage of the Napoleonic Wars offers a more likely inspiration for the novel's mixed mood of loss and celebration, its intensity of pain and pleasure" (Harris 2007: 90). Although older branches of criticism assumed that Austen was not a political writer, she lived and wrote through the whole length of the Napoleonic wars. Her letters bear ample testimony to the fact that Waterloo and the shadow of Napoleon's return were at the forefront of her mind when writing *Persuasion* (see Deresiewicz 2004: 146 – 7), and it is nowadays rightly seen as her "most profoundly political novel" (Mellor 2002: 122), directly concerned with the effects of war on individual and public consciousness and dwelling on the pains of loss and separation.

As has been frequently noted, the text intertwines a personal drama of love and loss and with the national drama of war and peace. Set in the very recent past, 1814 – 15, *Persuasion* combines two narrative planes, a domestic romance, shaped by poetic imagination and use of language, and a commentary on social and political realities. With the plot ending shortly before Napoleon's escape from Elba and the resumption of the war, Austen sets her narrative inside what Janie Barchas refers to as "a temporary window of false and fragile security" (Barchas 2012: 218). It is also a common argument in the reception of *Persuasion* that it makes multi-layered use of Austen's extensive knowledge of naval culture and the role of the sea for the English nation.[10] According to Brian Southam, the novel, which includes constant references to the dangers and triumphs of the navy, is not only designed to pay homage to it, but also "to show the profession in peacetime" (Southam 2005: 271). Significantly, the most dramatic action in the plot is Louisa's fall on the Cobb in Lyme; all naval adventures are reported by the officers sitting in the drawing room, or, as Southam puts it, "we have to be content with sailors' tales as *sailors safe on shore*" (2005: 3; my emphasis).

But Austen's portrayal of the navy captains still has important implications for the depiction of attitudes towards risk in the narrative and serves as a contrasting foil, especially for forms of masculinity and the old aristocratic order. To some extent, *Persuasion* is indeed a diagnosis of the end of the old land-owning family. In contrast to Sir Walter, who is on his way of running his family – and by extension the nation – to the ground, the navy officers represent the nation's push towards prosperity. Chronicling a time of great change, Austen pits two competing systems of value and tradition – one old and one new – against each other. Her novel captures their different development also literally through the references to the two books, Sir Walter's Baronetage and the Navy List.[11] In the novel, the institution of the navy, which allows for promotions and changes in rank, and in Austen's view blends modernity with respect for tradition, is strongly associated with a new paradigm of masculinity inspired by war and revolution and is based on endurance and risk-taking. Against the background of the Napoleonic Wars, it expresses a new cult of masculine naval heroism and Englishness and Austen arguably models her central male characters, the Captains Wentworth, Croft, and Benwick, on her own navy brothers, and on war heroes such as Lord Nelson or Lord Wellington.[12] The narrative depicts them as masters of strength and self-preservation who come out strong in the fight against the odds of weather, sea, and war. According to Lorrie Clark,

---

10 As studies like Brian Southam's *Jane Austen and the Navy* (2005) have shown in detail, Austen knew a lot about the profession through her two sailor brothers Francis and Charles. On the many details of maritime and imperial history in *Persuasion* see also Harris (2007: 74).
11 In *Matters of Fact in Jane Austen*, Barchas speaks of a "Battle of the Books" in *Persuasion*, one tracking the history of the Elliots, the other the career of Captain Wentworth. Other critics have interpreted especially the opening excerpt from the Baronetage, a chronicle of loss rather than glorification of family lineage, as Austen's symbolic reference to the death of the aristocracy (see Jones 2004: 169; Deresiewicz 2004: 165).
12 See Joseph A. Kestner's essay "Revolutionizing Masculinities" (1994).

they represent a new type of hero, "vigorous, self-made men", "in touch with nature and time and change" (Clark 1996: 35).

In particular the characterization of Wentworth, possibly "Austen's most romantic hero" (Gay 2010: 64), has been closely linked to different risk discourses and new forms of (masculine) entrepreneurship. Having no fortune or family connections to guarantee his rise in society, Wentworth displays an unwavering belief in his own talents and good fortune; "he was confident that he should soon be rich; [...] He had always been lucky; he knew he should be so still" (P 27). Consequently, he takes on the sea, a crucial, multivalent image of risk in the novel, and while coming close to almost going "to the bottom" of it, returns home safely after having made a fortune. Thus he proves wrong Lady Russell, who eight years ago lacked any belief in the chance of Wentworth's character and navy career ever translating into financial success and the ability to secure a stable future. Thinking that her advice to Anne against marrying him was based on prudence and rational caution, she was furthermore weary of his headstrongness and "fearlessness of mind", assessing him altogether as a "dangerous character" (P 27). Ironically what made the Captain dangerous in Lady Russell's eyes were his risk-taking spirit, his self-assured energy, and decisiveness that qualified him to become a prize-winning naval hero in the first place. As Knox-Shaw explains, it is Wentworth's "mind-set that equips him for a profession that is exposed to fatality and hazard at every turn. [...] Though far from blind to risk, he shows that an attitude of self-reliance is of great value where risk exist, whether or not they are taken" (Knox-Shaw 2004: 225–26). This is underlined in his cool, rational estimations of the dangers of running an old navy ship. While the narrative includes many descriptions of the risks at sea, a striking example is Wentworth's telling the story of taking the *Asp*, a ship hardly fit anymore for service, to the West Indies. In retrospect, this hazardous trip turned out to be his lucky break, and he reveals his full awareness of the risk he was taking and his miraculous good luck: "I knew that we should either go to the bottom together, or that she would be the making of me; and I never had two days of foul weather all the time I was at sea in her" (P 61). Wentworth, as any other navy captain, is furthermore completely unfazed by the possible risk to thousands of lives during the capturing of a foreign enemy's ship. Earning his fortune essentially through (state-licensed) piracy and acts of war, he is "he is cavalier about the loss of life" incurred by "such risk-taking acts" (Mellor 2002: 125). After all, this is how navy captains made their money, as they were only paid a comparatively low basic salary: "Prize money was the fairest and most straightforward reward for success, as well as recompensing officers and crew for their risk. Since any admiral in sight of the prize took the biggest share, the really lucky officers were the captains of fast, 'good,' or 'crack' frigates cruising independently within striking distance of the shipping lanes" (Harris 2007: 93). On these grounds, several critics have argued that Wentworth, who began with nothing but makes a rapid fortune with little consideration other than his potential personal profits, resembles "the modern venture capitalist, a speculator who banks upon a small chance at a huge reward" (Barchas 2012: 213); Anne Mellor sees him even as the embodiment of "a rationale for laissez-faire mercantile capitalism: for high-risk investments, aggressive entrepreneurship, and uninsured stock speculation" (Mellor 2002: 126).[13]

The narrative captures English society in transition between the old aristocratic order and the rise of modern professional society with yet uncertain principles and values. But it is difficult to say if it fully supports the argument that caution and old principles should be discarded in favour of an embrace of the new and the risky. Although the plot centrally hinges on Anne's failure to trust and give Wentworth some advance credit – against customary propriety and caution, and although Austen makes a character like Wentworth the hero of *Persuasion*, she does not endorse risk-taking without reservations and the narrative also clearly shows its dangers. Characteristic of many 19th-century fictions, the novel supports the need for financial risks and investments into the future,[14] but condemns risk taking without sufficient consideration or for the mere thrill of it, exemplified by the disastrous ending of Louisa's jumping down the steps of the Cobb. As models for the future rulers of England, men like Wentworth remain fascinating but ambiguous candidates because their flaw is being – however successful, – headstrong risk-takers. Interestingly, Mellor describes Wentworth as "another of the Romantic era's Promethean figures" (2002: 125), with parallels to Mary Shelley's Viktor Frankenstein. Yet this view neglects the crucial economic motivation of Wentworth's risk-taking. It is, however, plausible to see

---

13 Focusing on 'factual' historical references to locations and celebrity families in Austen's works, Barchas argues that Captain Wentworth is one striking case in point because the author names her originally poor sailor after one of England's oldest landholding families. She thus creates a character that "may mitigate his economic risk at sea with the hint of landed wealth, almost as if the name of one of the largest landholders in England stands guarantor for her most entrepreneurial risk-taker" (2012: 220).

14 See Barchas's biographical argument that *Persuasion* reflects the Austen families' own sense of financial insecurities at the time and the belief that it was necessary to diversify mechanisms of wealth creation: "The Austen family, who mixed conservative spending with radical risk-taking, relied in equal measure upon both approaches: the landed income and essential prudence associated with Sir Walter's type of wealth, as well as the naval entrepreneurialism and comfort with risk represented by Wentworth" (2012: 214).

Persuasion as Austen's critical response to (male) Romantic poets' ideals and Jacobin republican politics,

> both of which urged the isolated, risk-taking individual to create his own identity, his own destiny, entirely out of his own strong will and imagination. Such individuals are not safe rulers for the new England. They remain locked within a limited autonomy too willing to risk it all on a gamble, that finds security only in an ethic of justice that demands equal rights for all and in a social contract negotiated among a like-minded band of brothers, a contract that effectively excludes women from the public sphere. (Mellor 2002: 137–138)

The gender aspect is important in this context. As also Knox-Shaw emphasizes, Wentworth's stereotypical ideal of women's steadfastness and passivity is contradictory and clashes with "the virtues of daring and resolution that he so handsomely exemplifies himself" (Knox-Shaw 2004: 229). Anne fails in Wentworth's eyes to take a risk for her love, which is why he still holds a grudge when meeting her again: "She had given him up to oblige others. It had been the effect of over-persuasion. It had been weakness and timidity" (P 57). Instead, Wentworth focuses his attention on Louisa Musgrove, who he considers by contrast a wonderfully firm character: "It is the worst evil of too yielding and indecisive a character, that no influence over it can be depended on. [...] My first wish for all whom I am interested in, is that they should be firm" (P 81).

With the conflict between desire and social conventions being one of the guiding literary themes of the 19th century, Austen's narrative also shows the awareness of gender differences with regard to emotions, and attitudes and opportunities towards risk-taking. In conversation with Captain Harville, Anne vehemently argues for women's stronger and more constant feelings when it comes to love, thus seeking to contradict the common perception of women's dangerous "fickleness" (P 221) that men like Wentworth are so weary of. She offers a pragmatic counter-argument, reasoning that due to women's more restricted and less adventurous lives, they have less distraction from their emotions and little chance of events which can "weaken impressions" (P 218). While admitting that men simply cannot afford to be too emotionally attached, Anne's utterance implicitly suggests that the gender differences are due to opportunities (or lack thereof) in the public sphere rather than "nature": "You have difficulties, and privations, and dangers enough to struggle with. *You are always labouring and toiling, exposed to every risk and hardship.* [...]. It would be too hard [...] if woman's feelings were to be added to all this" (P 219; my emphasis).

Regarding their attitudes towards risk and luck, Captain Wentworth and Anne are shown to be complete opposites. Anne, aware that life itself is already risky enough, is guided by the aim to avoid risk as much as possible. When faced with the decision of accepting or rejecting Wentworth, the 19-year-old Anne was caught in a double bind. She had to respect her elder's advice and place the demands of "proper" behaviour above her own desires. Austen's plot, which emphasizes the socially conditioned "odds against Anne's happiness" (Poovey 1984: 229), implies some of the paradoxes of (female) propriety and caution and suggests that they might be risky to the extent of possibly costing one's personal happiness. At 27, Anne still does neither blame Lady Russell or herself for following her advice, and reminds Wentworth: "If I was wrong in yielding to persuasion once, *remember that it was to persuasion exerted on the side of safety, not of risk*. When I yielded, I thought it was to duty" (P 229; my emphasis). Yet, even before the reunion with Wentworth, Austen's narrative voice expresses the conviction that Anne should have trusted Wentworth's luck – and that she would have been able to cope with a sailor's wife and the insecurities that attended to it, because despite "every anxiety attending his profession, all their probable fears, delays and disappointments, she should yet have been a happier woman in maintaining the engagement than she had been in the sacrifice of it; [...] all his confidence, had been justified" (P 29). Of course, one can also conclude that Anne has simply realized and accepted that in risk and insecurity, in one form or another, is an inevitable part of life. Either way, in the course of the novel, Anne, in direct contrast to the careless Louisa, grows into a well-balanced attitude and acquires "a *cheerful confidence in futurity, against that over-anxious caution* which seems to insult exertion and distrust Providence! She had been forced into prudence in her youth, she learned romance as she grew older" (P 29; my emphasis). This contains *Persuasion*'s whole romantic dilemma and central themes in a nutshell. Debating the question of in how far instincts and emotions should be trusted, the text highlights the impossibility of prediction and precaution, and contrasts the values of determination, spontaneity, and caution.

In her interesting, if not fully convincing, reading of *Persuasion*, Lorrie Clark argues that all characters actively seek "unnecessary risks" and consciously face their consequences based on the general "assumption that one will always be able to pull up short of disaster" (Clark 1996: 37). She specifically relates the emphasis on risk-taking and the text's tragic Romanticism to an aesthetic of the sublime, sustained by the recurrence of events such as shipwrecks, accidents, injuries, and near-death threats. For Clark, Austen's novel deals mainly with pseudo-crises, depending on and creating the aesthetic distance necessary to enjoy the thrilling "*idea* of danger – not actual danger itself" (Clark 1996: 33; original emphasis). Although I do not agree with Clark's generalization that all characters partake in the play with sublime 'risk' – in the sense that the experience of risk generally resolves into a pleasurable feeling of freedom analogous of the sublime – her focus usefully highlights risk as one of the central elements of the text's plot and aesthetics. But the complex depiction of risk in the novel certainly transcends aesthetics. Other critics have also commented on *Persuasion* as being a text that explores Romanticism's aesthetic possibilities through a – for Austen – unusual use of language, depictions of nature, and an affective writing style, which is especially shown in the characterization of Anne.[15] In addition, there is also "a perceptibly new note of emotional volatility and irruptiveness, even excess" (Tanner 1986: 219) in the narrative. The focus on the heroine's inner life and the text's consciousness of the reality of passions and loss has implications for the staging of risk. Meanwhile the abstract title points the reader towards looking for various instances and embodiments of persuasion in the plot, as well as to the critical questioning of character and the motifs for yielding to or resisting it.

Documenting the ongoing and interdisciplinary interest in Austen's work, a recent study by Michael Suk-Young Chwe, *Jane Austen, Game Theorist* (2013), is particularly relevant for the analysis of the construction and perception of risk from this angle and draws attention to *Persuasion*'s psychological realism. Chwe argues that Austen's fictions systematically and soundly explore what becomes later known as core ideas of game theory, and he claims: "Anyone interested in human behavior should read Austen because her research has results" (Chwe 2013: 3). Central aspects in this context are the concept of choice and preferences and the development of strategic thinking in relation to human actions and their possible determining factors. A focus on the psychological mechanisms and conceptions of game theory also includes strategic manipulations (i.e. schemes), the formation of partnerships (i.e. strategizing together), and the depiction of the absence of strategic thinking (i.e. cluelessness) in the texts. Possible explanations for cluelessness (not to be equated with generic foolishness) explored in the narratives include individual character traits, social status and distance (i.e. lack of understanding between the classes or sexes), excessive self-reference and vanity about one's exceptionalism, and, perhaps most importantly and most dangerously, presumptions about another character's 'nature' or thoughts. In the Victorian novel, this is often the cause of great suffering in unhappy relationships, for example the marriage between Rosamond and Lydgate in Eliot's *Middlemarch* ultimately fails due to cluelessness on both sides.

As Chwe's study highlights, choice can be considered a central, even obsessive concern in Austen's writing. The plot of *Persuasion*, revolving around Anne

---

15 See Gay (2010: 66) and Medalie (1999: 165). Regarding the influence of Romanticism, most critical studies of *Persuasion* also draw attention to Austen's intertextual references to contemporary literary works such as Walter Scott's *Marmion* and *The Lady of the Lake* and Lord Byron's *Turkish Tales*. See also Deresiewicz (2004).

overcoming her originally encumbered choice of refusing Wentworth, exemplifies the author's interest in human behaviour and the interaction of different choices. Characters always have to understand the cost of their choices, while a lack of resolution is commonly perceived as a weakness. Yet Austen's fiction also shows how especially women's choices are determined by a lack of economic independence. Due to the greater immobility and enforced passivity it is necessary for them to develop strategic skills and thinking as a means to overcome social constraints (Chwe 2013: 131), and this kind of risk management often drives the plot. Meanwhile all of Austen's texts explore the (often negative) impact of elements determining human choice and action such as instincts and emotions (e.g. envy, pride), habits (e.g. carelessness, selfishness, overconsumption), rules and principles of conduct and propriety (notions of duty, honour, decorum), and wider sociological and ideological factors (i.e. the whole environment in which the individual is making the decision). Although her fictions are concerned with showing how emotions, in combinations with the other factors, can cause bad decisions, Austen's writing is characteristic for the early 19th century in the sense that there is still a largely positive belief in the eventual, final good choice or the option of reversing bad decisions, as is the case in *Persuasion*. The hope of making good choices increasingly vanishes towards the end of the century. The female characters in Hardy or Gissing's novels, for example, are caught in inevitably tragic situations, overwhelmed by either having no choice, or all choices turning bad. Austen's heroines by contrast, even "when overwhelmed by emotions, still make good choices. [...] Their emotions do not hinder as much as drive their decisions" (Chwe 2013: 115). Generally, emotions can present useful agency as well as dangerous obstructing clouds in processes of decision-making. While following or not following 'rational' rules presents itself a matter of choice, Austen's narrative also considers the disadvantages of strategic thinking, which is inseparable from the calculated attempts to management risk. It is no coincidence that it is 'rational' characters like Lady Russell, similar to Sir Hugh in Burney's *Camilla*, who do the most damage and Anne suffers for eight years from a choice against her own emotions.

The implication that Anne should have relied more on intuition and chance in her decision of marriage presents a marked contrast to Austen's earlier heroines (see Hopkins 1987: 149). However, things are even more complex. In the end Anne turns to Lady Russell and says, reassessing the value of her advice in hindsight and still justifying being persuaded by her: "It was, perhaps, one of those cases in which *advice is good or bad only as the event decides*" (P 231; my emphasis). Besides her unwavering sense of duty, she thus, affirms a strong sense of consequentialism and contingency. And even Lady Russell, although she briefly tries to involve Anne in a second marriage plot with her rich cousin

Mr Elliott, admits to "being much *too well aware of the uncertainty of all human events and calculations*", adding somewhat paradoxically that "if you should be disposed to accept him, I think there would be every possibility of your being happy together" (P 149–150, my emphasis).

Several critics to date have pointed to the text's notable affirmation of contingency and Austen's contradictory notion of "moral luck" ruling events (rather than social code).[16] With the place of luck in ethics being generally complicated and puzzling, the term *moral luck* is paradoxical and provocative.[17] Bernard Williams and Thomas Nagel have explained how it challenges the idea that moral value is immune to luck, because "luck" refers to the outcome of actions that often lie outside of human control. It draws attention to the fact that morality is conditioned by circumstance and at the same time made subject to retrospective evaluation. This raises crucial questions of attribution of responsibility (i.e. whether it is possible to be culpable for the outcome of events beyond one's direct control) and suggests the existence of a providential universe whose causal workings are (partially) invisible to the moral agent. Austen's novel projects a deep sense of anxiety about different governing forces and a tension between a sense of moral luck (what *is*, or *has* happened) and benign providence (what *ought* to be).[18] It also underlines the likelihood of error and regret springing from the awareness that one could have acted otherwise; there is always the risk of another outcome. The narrative affirms only one fact, namely that trying to avoid uncertainty equals the avoidance of life itself, and that nonaction is not a viable option. It also shows how easily moral and cognitive judgments of actions are blurred by a fusion of rational reasoning, desires, and emotions, especially with regard to risk-taking.[19]

In his dated but still valid study of *Persuasion*, Paul Zietlow argues for a distinct emphasis on luck and fortuitous circumstances in a plot where the action frequently reaches the brink of disaster. Taking luck to be "the prime instrument for averting disaster" (Zietlow 1965: 189) offers a rather bleak view and seemingly robs the characters of agency. Above all, the happy ending does not result from their original choices, but from accidents and the force of luck or providence

---

16 See Hopkins (1987), Medalie (1999), and Zietlow (1965).
17 On moral luck and responsibility see Kane (1999), Rosebury (1995), Rosenberg (1999), Williams and Nagel (1976), and Zimmerman (1987).
18 Seeking to contradict Hopkins' older argument, Davis (2013) has recently argued for a distinction between providence and luck in the text, and for a greater emphasis on providence as a positive force.
19 On the intersection of risk-taking and emotional judgment regarding processes of decision making see, e.g., Tversky (1990); Tversky and Kahneman (1981).

which seems to justly "reward" the right characters. Although things turn out well in the end, Austen's narrative maintains a constant atmosphere of risk and the reader is left with the distinct feeling that this is a fiction and a perhaps more likely course of events would be a different one (e.g. Captain Wentworth could have drowned on the *Asp*, Luisa could not have survived her fall, Anne could have been left to face life as a spinster). Zietlow considers this to be Austen's strategic use of chance and a means to infuse social comedy with tragic effect; the narrative offers the reader a fearful glance of possible ills while implying "that these 'possibilities' are what in real life would be probabilities – such probabilities as only good fortune or Providence could prevent" (Zietlow 1965: 195). In other words, Austen's fictional depiction and perception of risks is realistic, her staging of the outcome is not always. Refocusing the view on the depiction of moral luck in the novel, Robert Hopkins sees *Persuasion* as an illustration of Austen's struggle "with the problem of moral judgment under uncertainty" (Hopkins 1987: 154). This concerns in particular Lady Russell, who, if she had recognized the full implications of judgment under uncertainty and furthermore "that risk and moral luck are especially inherent in match-making" (1987: 152), would not have dissuaded Anne from marrying Wentworth. Instead, Anne has to pay for not having risked enough first time round and Lady Russell's first estimation of Wentworth, through events brought about by lucky circumstances, is proved to be erroneous. Anne sees her early caution as mistake but decouples it causally from her later accidental happy ending; and for Lady Russell there is nothing left to do other "than to admit that she had been pretty completely wrong, and to take up a new set of opinions and of hopes" (P 233). Thus Austen's narrative, as Medalie has noted, consciously disrupts the customary design of didactic fiction and illustrates the failures in the causal relationship "between conduct and consequence" (Medalie 1999: 164). With courtship being the main realm for dramatizing how moral choices remain uncertain "until proved out consequentially" (Hopkins 1987: 157), Anne's case is used to illustrate that the individual has to shoulder the burden of living with this contingency.[20] This element is decisive and renders the narrative rather unsettling and revolutionary despite its otherwise rather conventional romance plot and the elements of social comedy. Criticizing Enlightenment values of reasoning and moral worth, it challenges linear causality and puts emotion, intuition, and spontaneity over prudential morality and calculation. If only "the event decides" what

---

[20] Matthew Taylor draws attention to an important aspect here, saying that "the narrowly missed unhappiness in Persuasion is not a factor of cruel mischance or 'contingency' (as in a Thomas Hardy novel)" (Taylor 2004: 117), but can be rectified in the end.

is or will be good or bad, the belief in the supremacy of human will is shown as illusionary; it also opens the door for a relativism of principles as moral value is only attributable to choices in retrospect. Emphasizing especially Anne's acceptance of contingency, Medalie argues that *Persuasion* pays tribute of the importance of circumstances and dramatizes to a new degree the notion of the "fallible self" and the subject's "expulsion from certainty" (Medalie 1999: 168; 167). In the novel, the rule of the aleatory certainly fights for supremacy over the schematic, and fortunes, circumstances, and characters are depicted as subject to (often rapid) change. All characters have to consciously grapple with "the uncertainty of all human events and calculations" (P 149–150). They are forced to live with instability and act despite it. Mrs. Croft's comment is telling: "We none of us expect to be in smooth water all our days" (P 70).

The turning point of *Persuasion,* Louisa's fall on the Cobb in Lyme, signifies a dramatic eruption of contingency and presents perhaps the most striking moment of physical violence in all of Austen's work (see Sokolsky 1993: 136; Hamilton 2007: 223–224). The fact that the scene takes place at the seaside underlines its status as a characteristic risk-site for Austen; it is a place of danger as well as liberation and licence.[21] During the Lyme party's walk, Louisa insists on jumping, rather than carefully climbing down the steep steps, into the arms of Captain Wentworth who tries to stop her. But "she smiled and said, 'I am determined I will,' he put out his hands, she was too precipitate by half a second, she fell on the pavement on the Lower Cobb, and was taken up lifeless!" (P 102). The accident changes the course of events and the shock causes various repercussions and reflection of values and emotions in the characters. It leads to Captain Benwick's later engagement to Louisa, and frees Wentworth for Anne. Because while Louis defied caution through her jump, Wentworth was regarded to be almost engaged to Louisa at this point, "he had found too late, in short, that he had entangled himself" (P 227). Even naval officers are seemingly not safe from the danger of being entrapped by appearances and social conventions.

The event's main function in the development of the plot is to make Wentworth's question his belief in the "universal felicity and advantage of firmness of character", and to cause his re-evaluation of Anne's "persuable temper" (P 108). The accident brings out poignantly the contrast between Louisa's wilfulness and Anne's caution. Alan Richardson sees a specific scientific interest

---

[21] See John Mullan's comment: "The sense of the seaside town as a dangerous place is [...] insistent in her fiction. If you were to gather the examples of risky behavior by the sea, you might suppose that the author did have a poor view of the seaside. Louisa Musgrove's self-precipitation from the Cobb in Lyme Regis is but the last of a series of foolish or bad actions" (2012: 90).

in the workings of the brain and the Romanticist era's concern with the emotive and cognitive aspects of mental life reflected in Austen's depiction of Luisa's fall. Austen deliberately links Anne's development with Louisa, who, according to Richardson, is constructed as "an antiheroine, whose character is transformed instead by a severe blow to the head, at a time when brain injury featured centrally in debates on the materiality of mind" (Richardson 2002: 141). The narrator's comment supports such a reading: "The day at Lyme, the fall from the Cobb, might influence her health, her nerves, her courage, her character to the end of her life, as thoroughly as it appeared to have influenced her fate" (P 157).

The event influences Anne by forcing her to take action and break out of her passivity in front of Wentworth. After the first "horror of that moment to all who stood around!" (P 101) has subsided, the only characters who behave "completely rational" (P 103) are Wentworth, Anne, and Charles Musgrove, although both men leave it to Anne to decide what is to be done next.[22] Impressed by her calm handling of the situation, Wentworth declaration of "no one so proper, so capable as Anne!" (P 106) marks the beginning of the rediscovery of his love for her. While it is not until the very end of that narrative that Wentworth openly admits to "the blindness of his own pride, and blunders of his own calculations" (P 228), she starts to wonder not without a certain irony, if faced with the disastrous consequences of the failure to dissuade Louisa from the jump, it now "could scarcely escape him to feel that a persuadable temper might sometimes be as much in favour of happiness as a very resolute character" (P 108). In the end, Wentworth has to acknowledge that it was at Lyme that "he had learnt to distinguish [...] between the darings of heedlessness and the resolution of a collected mind" (P 227). With Louisa's daring as the negative example of risk taking, Anne's triumph is her ability to think strategically under the intense emotional strain of the accident. She furthermore benefits from Louisa's misfortune, Anne Sokolsky points out, because it awakens hope and a new spirit in her, "prompting her to take the further risk of revealing her indispensability [...]. Anne shifts from a fatalistic sense that circumstances are working to thwart her to a more enterprising notion that one makes one's fate" (Sokolsky 1994: 134). A later episode confirms Anne's development towards self-assurance and trust of her own judgment, behaviour, and emotions. She firmly rejects the proposition that she should marry the rich Mr Elliot because her heart still belongs to

---

[22] Cf. Southam's argument that the Captain's reaction to Louisa's fall is in fact not very plausible because "at the mere sight of a girl concussed, Wentworth is made to act like a hysterical civilian" (2005: 279).

Wentworth, and she distrust Mr Elliot's intentions due to rumours about his past and the treatment of his only recently deceased wife. Anne stands by her own opinion and disregards attempts to convince her of the probability of contrary such as the following by Mrs Smith: "Ninety-nine out of a hundred would do the same. [...]. Your peace will not be shipwrecked as mine has been. You are safe in all worldly matters, and safe in his character" (P 185).

Variations of the Cinderella fairy tale, plot patterns concerned with the contrasting fortunes of a group of sisters or cousins, are often at the heart of Austen's novels, and one can also see a use of the motif in *Persuasion*. First of all, Anne takes the role of the undervalued, plain heroine, whose virtues become visible slowly in the course of the narrative by being set off against her siblings (the spoiled Elizabeth and the hypochondriac Mary) and the Musgrove sisters. Especially the flirtatious Louisa is the rival for the affection of Wentworth, but Anne eventually manages to shake off the ashes and reclaim his love. Although Austen maintains the typical equation of virtue with a certain absence of physical beauty in the characterization of her heroine, Anne is made attractive to the reader (and again to Wentworth) through her increasing self-confidence and her kindness. Austen certainly modernizes the familiar story by making the 'prince' "a leader in a profession that requires energy, determination and luck, rather than a good family" (Gay 2010: 67). Meanwhile Anne is a familiar figure in Austen's writing. Representing the "girl on the threshold", no longer child but not yet a wife, who lacks "a secure or defined position in society" (Tanner 1981: 180), she is first introduced to the reader as "only Anne" (P 5), without an effective surname or rank, without being attributed a place or profession. From the beginning, she is in a precarious situation, both financial and emotionally. And although the reunion of the lovers is in typical fashion delayed until the end of the plot, the happiness gained by Anne in the end is much more fragile than that of other female heroines, or as Byrne puts: "*Persuasion* follows the pattern of security, loss, isolation and restitution [....] common to many eighteenth-century narratives, but the security that Anne has is barely secure at all, and the security she gains is of a very different order to that of her former state" (Byrne 2014: 150).

Indeed, although the final union of Anne and Wentworth signifies the triumph of love over calculation and persuasion, the often-quoted final paragraph of *Persuasion* allows for different, not univocally positive readings:

> Anne was tenderness itself, and she had the full worth of it in Captain Wentworth's affection. His profession was all that could ever make her friends wish that tenderness less, *the dread of a future war was all that could dim her sunshine. She gloried in being a sailor's wife, but she must pay the tax of quick alarm for belonging to that profession* which is, if possible,

> more distinguished in its domestic virtues than in its national importance. (P 236; my emphasis)

Austen suggests that her heroine's happiness is as tender as it is precarious and does not come without costs. Anne consciously faces the uncertainties that come with being a naval wife, always dependent on politics and unable to fully retreat into the private sphere. In addition, the union is not grounded in property and thus does not promise local stability. Adhering to convention on the surface, *Persuasion's* ending questions the customary conclusion of Austen's previous fictions, the return to a secure order and domesticity. It highlights uncertainty, not regarding the reciprocated love between Anne and Wentworth, but the circumstances and the world they have to live in. Ending in 1815 with a reference to the "dread of a future war", *Persuasion* dramatizes the continuing risk of war, of separation and loss, even after Waterloo, a threat that lasted till Napoleon's death in 1821 (see Harris 2007: 88; Southam 2005: 303). At the same time it celebrates the patriotic belief in the navy's importance and ability to protect Britain.

The narrative begins with Anne's expulsion from her country home; in the end her future lies literally 'at sea'. It can be read as liberation from old conventions; happiness and domestic virtue can be found beyond a settled household or even permanent location. With the sea being traditionally regarded as the unstable element, established values are now also "'all at sea' – metaphorically (they are in a state of chronic confusion, chaotic flux)" (Tanner 1986: 245; 246). Not restoring paradisiac order or safety, Austen's novel captures a moment of transition and ultimately resolves the struggle between risk-taking and caution, between traditional confinement and personal liberation, "in favour of risk and a larger world" (Wilson cited in Southam 2005: 305).

5.2 The Risk of Our Creation: *Frankenstein, or the Modern Prometheus*

Published the same year as Austen's *Persuasion*, Mary Shelley's *Frankenstein* has been referred to as "the other great political novel of 1818" (Jones 2004: 170), or "the most important minor novel in English" (Levine 1979: 3). Although far exceeding Austen's text in the canonical and mythical status it has acquired over the last two centuries, Shelley's novel also takes up the themes of (moral) sympathy, loss, death, and political upheaval, combining social commentary with a psychological orientation and focus on individual consciousness. But whereas *Persuasion* shows the damaging potential of isolation, loss and uncontrolled or supressed passion as a temporary, reversible state by only delaying the final romantic union of the lovers, Shelley's text, as George Levine notes, ultimately "denies love its triumph", and explores with full force "the powerlessness of love to control the passions that are hidden deep in our being, that are sure to find physical expression, and finally, that are unimaginable without pain or guilt" (Levine 1979: 5; 6). While this bears testimony to the text's affiliation with Romanticism, *Frankenstein* has also been read as a reflection of Enlightenment's criticism of passion and enthusiasm; critics such as Barbara Freeman for example have interpreted it in contrasting correspondence to Kant's third *Critique of Judgment*, because it dramatizes the dangers of an "unbridled imagination", and takes suppressed topics such as "terror, monstrosity, passion, and fanaticism" (Freeman 1987: 22; 23) arguably almost to the level of aesthetic parody.

Despite being an epistolary novel with a rather complex structure of multiple embedded narratives, *Frankenstein*'s popularity proves unbroken and it continues to spark new adaptations and criticism. The novel holds its acclaimed place as a central and founding text both in Gothic and science fiction studies; yet it has been dissected from a myriad of different critical perspectives, comprising (in no particular order and without claiming comprehensiveness) historicist, feminist, Marxist, psychoanalytical, or linguistic approaches, readings focusing on the master-monster relationship, the politics of creation, the depiction of bad vs. good scientific practice, capitalism and commodity culture, class conflict and social criticism, Romanticism and the sublime, genre and literary form, intertextuality, education and the nature vs. culture debate.[23] The survival and popularity of *Frankenstein* is certainly due to the fact that it lends itself as a powerful metaphor for cultural crises and expression of different fears and apocalyptic anxieties.[24] It tells a timeless story, a secular myth of human hubris, echoing the transgression stories of Prometheus or Faust. Mary Shelley famously points out in her introduction to the text how "supremely frightful would be the effect of any human endeavor to mock the stupendous mechanism of the creator of the world" (F 4). *Frankenstein* rejects the fundamental modern myth of the idea that the human condition will improve continually through scientific (and economic) progress. It is also perhaps the first Gothic narrative in which the threatening force assumes an agile mobility and a ubiquity, i.e. it is not confined to a specific locality like Manfred in *The Castle of Otranto*. Instead Frankenstein's creature

---

23 For an overview of criticism see Morton's *A Routledge Sourcebook on Mary Shelley's Frankenstein* (2002), or essay collections such as Levine and Knoepflmacher (1979) and Botting (1995).
24 On the forms and function of fear in *Frankenstein* in the context of Gothic fiction see, e.g., Moretti (2005).

appears as a forerunner in a line of what Frank Moretti sees as modern monsters who "threaten to live forever, and to conquer the world" (Moretti 2005: 85).

As a narrative of risk *Frankenstein* has lost nothing of its urgency and actuality. The perceived risks and fears of what a scientist can create and what happens when the effects of scientific experimentation assume an unpredictable life of their own have not diminished over the course of the past 200 years.[25] As a consequence, *Frankenstein* is nowadays the literary text most commonly evoked in risk-literature in other disciplines. This concerns especially the debates over biotechnology and GMO foods, which are bursting with references to "Frankenfoods" or "Frankenstein", the latter being often utilized as a general short term for modern science and its monstrosities (see MacPherson 2010: 178).[26] Leaving aside the vast body of scholarship on the Gothic elements in *Frankenstein* which, of course, engages with conceptions of danger and fear in the novel, to my knowledge there exists only one reading to date which applies the concept of risk, even if in a narrow economic sense. Charles R. Lewis's (2000) reading usefully supplements the existing Marxist-oriented criticism, which generally does not mention risk. It perceives Victor Frankenstein as an example of an "innovative, risk-taking economic agent" who through creative recombination of 'worthless' elements thrives to produce a new enterprise, beneficial to his himself and society (Lewis 2000: 65). According to Lewis, Shelley's narrative thus closely intertwines economic and non-economic content; it relates aspects "typically associated with romantic notions of individual identity and agency, creativity and risk, personal privacy and revelation, and social triumph and failure" (2000: 65) to the portrayal of Victor as a entrepreneur[27] whose creativity, innovation, and risk-taking is not rewarded by profit. In economic terms, the horrific result of Victor's creation is a classic example of the "unforeseeable", i.e. the inevitable element of risk in capitalist production and highlights loss and disruptions of order as the potential costs of entrepreneurial creativity.

Another interesting angle is offered by ecocriticism, which according to Helena Federer combines many of the important existing critical foci on the text, e.g. the limits of human power, the relations between character and environment, and the cost and consequences of technological production. She argues

---

25 See Jay Clayton's chapter "Frankenstein's Futurity: Replicants and Robots" (2003) and especially Jon Turney's *Frankenstein's Footsteps: Science, Genetics and Popular Culture* (1998).
26 Examples of articles on GMO Foods and (Bio)technology using 'Frankenstein' as a metaphor are: Blanchfield (1999), Campbell (2003), Cooley (2002), and Tait (2001).
27 Lewis refers to the etymology of the term "entrepreneur" from the French "entreprendere", meaning "to embark or to undertake" in the sense of making "choices in the present in order to realize uncertain results in the future" (2000: 69).

that the 'climate' of Frankenstein, while also capturing Shelley's personal memories of the unusually cold and tumultuous weather of the summer of 1816 (see Federer 2014: 72), dramatizes a sense of nature unbound, and questions man's superiority over nature by showing the wild sublime horror of the oceanic or mountain settings. Thus the human terror of nonhuman agency usually focused on the relation between Victor and the creature extends to comprise "culture's terror of nature's agency – the agency of oceans and storms and jagged peaks" (2014: 73). However, it is humankind and not the environment that is at risk in Shelley's novel.

The frame narrative, beginning with mariner Robert Walton's letters to his sister, introduces the reader of a risk context familiar from many travel and adventure tales, that of a long and dangerous sea voyage Walton is about to embark on, "the emergencies of which will demand all my fortitude" (F 15). While seeking to assure his addressee of his prudence and concern for his own safety and those of others, Walton openly admits to his attraction to "the marvellous, intertwined in all my projects, which hurries me out of the common pathway of men, even to the wild sea and unvisited regions I am about to explore" (F 18). Thus, from the beginning the reader is instilled with the strong sense that Walton's journey, his expedition to the North Polar region, despite his all his best resolutions ("I will not rashly encounter danger" (F 19)), will make him face many unpredictable and even 'incredible' situations. One of such is, of course, the encounter with the exhausted, shipwrecked stranger rescued by Walton's ship, the Swiss doctor Victor Frankenstein, who then begins to narrate his life-story. Walton's narrative is important for it suggests an element of human nature shared by all three narrators, namely desire, curiousity and a rebellion against existing borders (in Walton's case geographical, in Frankenstein's ethical-scientific, in the monster's case social and metaphysical). Mary Poovey emphasizes that "if the scientist and the monster lure the reader ever deeper into the heart of ambition", then Walton's function is to remind the reader that "Frankenstein's abortive enthusiasm is not the only possible product of human energy" (Poovey 1984: 131). Out of all three narrators, who appear equally driven by desire, he is the only one we can imagine successfully completing his mission. Concerning the risk personas of the three narrators, Charlotte Sleigh's observation that they are all to some extent "dangerous characters, and all of their testimonies should be treated with caution" (Sleigh 2011: 74) is important. They are furthermore all prone to as well as victims of impulsive behaviour. At the same time, they mask this aspect behind their individual lucid and rational accounts, continuously seeking to back up the causality and probability of events; this makes each narrative strand indeed appear as "epistolary evidence in a scientific case" (2011: 68).

The account of Victor's childhood and education emphasizes two crucial themes: the question of human agency and inevitability of the course of events, and the disastrous consequences of strong passions and ambitions. In addition, it presents the fusion of dread and desire in the key motif of pursuit (of ideas, people etc.) that gains momentum throughout the novel. Victor's affection for his foster sister Elizabeth, who inspires his possessiveness to the extreme that "till death she was to be mine only" (F 29), later causes the fatal, tragic climax of her death on their wedding night and turns Victor's pursuit of the murderous creature he himself brought to life into a manic hunt that finally leads him into the ice of the Artic.

Piecing together the development of his interest in scientific writings, natural philosophy, and specifically the laws of electricity and the 'origin' of life, Victor wonders if there was ever the possibility that the "train of my ideas would never have received the fatal impulse that led to my ruin" (F 32). His narrative reflects the struggle to assign moral and intellectual agency, while acknowledging the power of chance in the development of scientific ideas, the progression through contradictions and accidental turns. It is thus shown to be in many ways beyond the (full) control of the scientist, and he describes himself as "desperately in a very slough of multifarious knowledge, guided by an ardent imagination and childish reasoning, till an accident again changed the current of my ideas" (F 33). This emphasis is repeated in his description of the process of invention, which "it must be humbly admitted does not consist in creating out of void, but out of chaos" (F 8). Out of a chaotic mass of available data, individual parts are combined into something new, complicating the idea of conscious, or pre-structured design and rendering the eventual outcome uncertain. In Victor's case this refers, of course, also literally to the creation of new life out of dead body parts. The risk inherent in the pursuit of scientific knowledge is thus two-fold: To a large extent it is unpredictable – and not only because it entails the venture into the unknown – and it can inspire an insatiable, all-consuming curiousity and ambition. According to Victor's account, his scientific pursuit resembled a powerful pulling he was unable to resist, first in many different directions, and then in the wrong one. Following John Reed's argument that the tension between free will and fate is one of *Frankenstein*'s major themes (Reed 1989: 211), one can identify a contradictory pattern in Victor's tale. He continuously makes his own choices while claiming that they were unavoidable, causing a blurring of the distinction between agency and chance (1989: 214). But Reed also notes: "It is ironic that Frankenstein, often taken as the archetypal scientist, should destroy himself by ignoring the principle of cause and effect, which is the very basis of scientific method" (1989: 216). This statement ignores, of course, the reality of risk and uncertainty in Victor's endeavours that he seeks to grapple with in retrospect. The narrative gives, however, a psychological motivation for Victor's first interest in science and the attempts to usurp control over life and death. The crucial "first misfortune" (F 34) of his life was a serious illness of his beloved Elizabeth, who was "in the greatest danger", suffering from scarlet fever, causing Victor's mother to abandon all caution and fear of infection in taking care of her. As a result, "Elizabeth was saved, but the consequences of this imprudence were fatal to her preserver" (F 34). Losing his mother and the confrontation with a situation beyond his control, as well as witnessing the failure of medicine to save her, makes Victor's later scientific pursuit appear of as a kind of risk-management (of further potential losses of beloved ones) which spirals out of control.

From the moment he leaves his parental home and takes up his studies in Ingolstadt Victor portrays himself as falling under the "omnipotent sway" of "Chance – or rather the evil influence, the Angel of Destruction" (F 36). The fateful influence comes in human form. His professors' words and moments in the medical lecture hall fill Victor's mind henceforth with only "one thought, one conception, one purpose", namely to "explore unknown powers, and unfold to the world the deepest mysteries of creation" (F 38). Still, throughout his narrative Victor seeks to convince the listener/reader of his scientific detachment, of his rationality – or, rather his sanity – for which the summary of his creation process is a good example:

> Remember, I am not recording the vision of a madman. [...] that which I now affirm is true. Some miracle might have produced it, yet the stages of the discovery were distinct and probable. After days and nights of incredible labour and fatigue, I succeeded in discovering the cause of generation and life; nay, more, I became myself capable of bestowing animation upon lifeless matter. (F 41)[28]

While George Levine has rightly claimed that although we as readers recognize "that Victor has stepped over the limits of safe human behaviour, and that his success will be blighted, the rhetoric of scientific probability is never seriously undercut in the book" (Levine 1979: 11), the passage above shows an almost poetic use of oppositions (cause vs. miracle, probable vs. incredible, truth vs. the vision of a madman).

---

28 It needs to be stressed that the later actual 'creation scene' in the novel presents an exception from the attempts at detached description and rationality and is much more emotional. John Sutherland comments on this aspect, and the weight given to repulsion and disgust, saying that Victor "does not make his monster, as one might manufacture a robot – he gives birth to him, as one might to an unwanted child" (Sutherland 1996: 33).

As many critics have noted, Shelley constructs Victor's tale as a warning of how unpredictable and "dangerous is the acquirement of knowledge", and any man's aspiration "to become greater than his nature will allow" (F 42). In addition, Frankenstein's social isolation constitutes a factor increasing the risk. Paul O'Flinn argues that the text illustrates the dangers of acting alone and ignoring the help, or critical intervention, which could be provided by working with or confining in other people (O'Flinn 1995: 28). Yet it is here that the fantastic dimension of Victor's tale creates a preventive boundary, because when faced with the horrific aftermath of his creation Victor has to realize "that he is powerless to explain the monstrous threat and that he must bear his awful burden in silence or risk appearing to be mad" (Hansen 1997: 607–608). Victor's (self-)characterization shows the risky intoxication by passionate ambitions that destroy the safe stability of a calm mind and the capacity to stop oneself from going further.[29] His excitement reaches the state of a feverish nervousness; his inability to stop plays havoc with his physical and mental resources; it also isolates him from his family and he is oblivious to the ways his behaviour might affect them. Shelley's development of Victor's character, Anne K. Mellor points out, therefore presents a "calculated inversion" of a sentimental hero or the 18th century 'man of feeling' (Mellor 1995: 128). He is incapable of empathy and anticipating consequences, which leads to the fateful abandonment of his creature. The brutality of Victor's scientific detachment is also revealed later, when the monster finds Victor's lab journal and reads the outside account of his own creation in which "the whole detail of that series of disgusting circumstances which produced it is set in view; the minutest description of my odious and loathsome person is given'" (F 100).

When two years of manic labour culminate in the successful infusion of life into an assemblage of inanimate body parts, Victor, seeing the product of his ambition, is only left with "breathless horror and disgust" (F 45). He starts to feel disoriented and haunted, a state that only increases in intensity throughout the rest of his story. Judging from his letters to Elizabeth, Victor is continuously on the verge of nervous breakdown. Anything related to science threatens to

---

[29] Interestingly, Shelley inserts here some criticism of imperialist enterprises through an equation with the 'madness' of Victor's scientific pursuits and the crossing of legitimate boundaries: "A human being in perfection ought always to preserve a calm and peaceful mind, and never to allow passion or a transitory desire to disturb his tranquillity. I do not think that the pursuit of knowledge is an exception to this rule. [...] If this rule were always observed; if no man allowed any pursuit whatsoever to interfere with the tranquillity of his domestic affections, Greece had not been enslaved, Caesar would have spared his country; America would have been discovered more gradually; and the empires of Mexico and Peru had not been destroyed" (F 44).

trigger the overwhelming memories of the shocking moment of the monster's creation. In fact, Victor appears to be deeply traumatised: "I had conceived a violent antipathy even to the name of natural philosophy. When I was otherwise quite restored to health, the sight of a chemical instrument would renew all the agony of my nervous symptoms" (F 53). Adding to his burden are the grief and guilt caused by the reports of the murder of his brother William, soon followed by the capital punishment for the creature's crime placed on the innocent Justine. Victor, all-consumed by "remorse, horror, and despair" and the responsibility for the first "hapless victims to my unhallowed arts" (F 70), now faces the task of managing the risk of further deaths through the hands of the creature. It also throws him into ethical conflict. Unable to judge the risk for the general population, he is mainly driven by fear for his loved ones, because it soon becomes clear that the creature's 'evil' mission is a personal one.

The meeting between Victor and the creature high up in the Alps, set against the background of the "awful majesty" of the Mount Blanc (F 76), consists of the famous dialogue in which the creature appeals to Victor's duties as his creator and demands a female companion to relieve his miserable infliction of social isolation. Despite this being an encounter highly charged with emotions and fears, Shelley has both Victor and the creature once again utilize an almost detached scientific rhetoric; one makes claims based on rational arguments, the other assesses their validity, seeking to integrate morality, sentiment, and probability. This does not only negate the question of any difference between their humanity as far as the faculty of reason and the capacity to 'feel' are concerned. For example, Victor says: "I weighed the various arguments that he had used, and determined at least to listen to his tale. I was partly urged by curiosity, and compassion confirmed my resolution. [...] I felt what the duties of a creator towards his creature were, and that I ought to render him happy before I complained of his wickedness" (F 79).

Focusing on the complexity of Victor's "ethical double-entry bookkeeping" (Kaufmann 1995: 31) from an economic vantage point, David Kaufmann emphasizes the element of calculation in Victor's attempts at risk management. Victor is torn between his sense of responsibility for the monster and the awareness that it is an evil and non-human creature. Assuming a utilitarian position, he does not only try to assess whether the creature deserves his sympathy and judgment by human standards but also what should take priority, i.e. if this is a case where "the good of the many requires the misery of this one individual" (Kaufmann 1995: 31). The crucial question of justice hinges on the recognition of the justice of monster's request of having Victor create him a companion weighed against the possible dangers of complying or refusing this request, and of producing a second of his kind. Concerning the latter, the creature repeats his claim with scientific accuracy: "My companion must be of the same species, and have the same defects" (F 111). And although Victor perceives a mortal threat in the creature's words, they are uttered in a calm and logical manner: "I am content to reason with you. I am malicious because I am miserable. [...] if I cannot inspire love, I will cause fear; and chiefly towards you" (F 111–112). Peter Brooks points out how as "a verbal creation", and in striking opposition to his appearance, the creature is eloquent, persuasive, and sympathetic, the very opposite, in fact, of anything monstrous (Brooks 1995: 83).

Adding to the ambivalence of the depiction of the creature, Shelley provides a psychological motivation for his cruelty and mission of revenge. After his education in the human ways and language through his observation of and hidden "co-habitation" with the De Lacey family, the monster becomes aware of his difference and isolation he realizes he cannot overcome through any means of his own. After he feels betrayed and rejected by humankind despair turns into hateful aggression, "from that moment I declared everlasting war against the species, and, more than all, against him who had formed me" (F 105). However, his first murder of little William is accidental, resulting from the desperate search for a human being untainted by prejudice and who will not react with disgust at the sight of him; William, the creature had hoped, "had lived too short a time to have imbibed a horror of deformity. If, therefore, I could seize him, and educate him as my companion and friend" (F 109).

Torn between compassion and hatred, Victor cannot shake his duty to comply, but fear and risk management are the driving forces rather than a desire for compensation, because he says: "His power and threats were not omitted in my calculations" (F 113). The result of these calculations is to conclude that the creature is too dangerous to reject. Victor's imminent marriage with Elizabeth increases his sense of risk, for he knows that the monster will follow through on his threats and find him everywhere. At this stage in the narrative Victor's thoughts are dominated by the wish to "exempt my family from the danger of his machinations" (F 118) and he awaits any letter and sign of safety from home with "feverish impatience: if they were delayed, I was miserable, and overcome by a thousand fears" (F 124).

Arguing from a historicist perspective, Jonathan Grossman (2002) reads *Frankenstein* as a legal-forensic narrative that bears testimony to England's shifting judicial ideology in the early 19th century and explores questions of custody, guardianship, and affective and familial relations. Essentially claiming that judgment is rendered difficult due to a lack of clarity in the judicial context at the time, he draws attention to (the dangers of) a legal vacuum at the heart of the narrative, the unresolved guardian-ward relationship between Frankenstein and the creature. According to Grossman (2002: 69; 82), the haunting power of the novel springs from imagining the horror of the absence of the law, from the experience of a lack of ethical framework. This is useful to consider for the construction of risk and the motif of venturing into unmapped territories and highlights Victor's mounting fear of loss and his isolation from any sort of guiding principles. But Shelley's narrative 'case study' of Victor and his creature raises further related legal-ethical questions. This concerns above all the issue of product liability, i.e. whether Victor is responsible for his creation. Sandra MacPherson, who interprets *Frankenstein* as a text dealing with conceptions of control and responsibility from a legal perspective, emphasizes the significance of the making of the creature as the novel's "most significant accident" (2010: 180). MacPherson's argument draws attention to the gap between a legal and philosophical-ethical understanding of agency. According to the logic of liability, the idea of holding people (agents) responsible for accidents excites discomfort; equally difficult is the notion of nonhuman or machine culpability. A pressing question in this context is what constitutes a 'legal person', because as Leo Wein explains, for example, we presently cannot sue a machine. Although some machines are seemingly beyond our control, we can only hold the operator responsible.[30] The real-life risk–utility or legal analysis of such scenarios as envisioned in *Frankenstein* is certainly complicated. It is, however, important to note that Frankenstein's 'product' meets a crucial requirement for culpability by being able to judge and give a coherent account of events. Technically, Victor appears guilty of negligence, rather than strictly liable for the monster's deeds (MacPherson 2010: 193). Although his behaviour certainly falls in the category of high-risk behaviour, the novel is more concerned with exploring the moral rather than the legal side of liability. Nonetheless, MacPherson demonstrates convincingly how Frankenstein presents a striking illustration of the problem of product liability, in other words of the risk context of harm to humans done by nonhumans:

> Shelley marks this logic in the creature's uncertain ontological status somewhere between human, animal, and thing. [...] But because the creature's tale finally does not absolve him of responsibility for what he has done, it also highlights the insignificance of cherished indices of human personhood (language, self-consciousness, self-justification) to strict liability [...]. (MacPherson 2010: 188)

Responsibility aside, the central question remains whether we can control our creations. While, as Leon Wein claims we have by now certainly unleashed an

---

30 Wein's reference to the historical context is interesting: "The common law of England ascribed criminal culpability to accursed things, inanimate objects called 'deodands', and required that weapons, implements, or instrumentalities that caused a death be forfeited to the Crown. As late as 1842, a railroad locomotive was forfeited as a 'deodand'" (1992: 118–119).

"enormous power of automation" (1992: 103), *Frankenstein* is a symptomatic text for the unease induced by "mankind's ostensible control of science and technology, an anxiety that things – animate things – might get out of hand" (1992: 112). Shelley created a pervasive symbol of this anxiety which has been (re)appearing in different forms and guises ever since the novel's first publication.[31]

With *Frankenstein* typically seen as the parent text of the (Western) genre of science fiction, several critics have noted that the reference to Victor Frankenstein as a "scientist" is anachronistic because the word only entered official language records in the 1830s and 40s (cf. Knight 2009: iix). Whether one considers Frankenstein as an "Enlightenment philosophe" (Sutherland 1996: 25) or scientist *avant la lettre*, Shelley's text reflects the ways in which natural science – even if not yet fully separated into clearly distinctive sub-disciplines (such as chemistry, biology, medicine) became momentous as a practical, intellectual and social activity in the early 19th century. One of the period's many tremendous paradigm shifts in scientific practice was the development of natural history into biology, a term arguably coined around the time *Frankenstein* was composed and introduced in Britain by the surgeon William Lawrence (see Morton 2002: 8; also Butler 1994). The influence of the historical scientific context on Shelley's text is well documented.[32] Especially Marilyn Butler has argued for Mary and Percy Shelley's involvement and knowledge of "radical" science.[33] Among the topics of great interest at the time were electricity, magnetism, polar exploration, or vivisection, as well as many theories which would later lead to evolutionism, in particular Erasmus Darwin's scientific principles and the publicly staged debates about questions on the origin and nature of life, known as the vitalism debate. In this open lecture series, taking place between 1814–19 at London's Royal College of Surgeons, William Lawrence represented the materialist standpoint, arguing against the antagonist surgeon John Abernathy, who claimed the existence of a vitalizing "life-element" analogous to electricity. According to Butler, in *Frankenstein* Shelley plays out this controversy

---

31 Recent examples are TV SF-series like *Humans* (BBC 2015–) and *Orphan Black* (BBC America/Canada 2013–), which feature scientist-father figures who creates 'children', advanced human-like robots and clones respectively, and later commit suicide.

32 Many excerpts of contemporary scientific writings, for example Abernethy and Lawrence's lectures, and Mary Shelley's letters that document her knowledge of these texts are included in Morton (2002).

33 See Butler's essays "The First Frankenstein and Radical Science" (1993) and "The Shelleys and Radical Science" (1994). On *Frankenstein* as a reflection of personal and intellectual connections between Mary Shelley and the radical science in the 1790s and the early 19th century see also Sleigh (2011: 75) and Kaufmann (1995: 57).

in a form close enough for those who knew the debate to recognise. Frankenstein the blundering experimenter, still working with supernatural notions, shadows the intellectual position of Abernethy, who proposes that the superadded life-element is electricity. Lawrence's sceptical commentary on that position finds its echo in Mary Shelley's equally detached, serio-comic representation [...], concerning the over-reacher who gets more than he bargains for. (Butler 1994: xxx-xi)

At the time Shelley was writing, the theories and experiments of the Italian physiologist Luigi Galvani, using electricity to active nerves and muscle of dead tissue, also caused a stir and found many followers. According to Mellor, most notably among them was perhaps Giovanni Aldini of Bologna, whose "most notorious demonstration of galvanic electricity took place on 17 January 1803. On that day he applied galvanic electricity to the corpse of the murderer Thomas Forster. [...] Here is the scientific prototype of Victor Frankenstein, restoring life to dead bodies" (Mellor 1995: 125). Shelley's fictional representation of Frankenstein's attempt to create new life from the body parts of dead criminals by employing chemistry and electricity, thus appears to be directly inspired by some of the most advanced and risky scientific research of her time. [34]

Engaging with science's possibilities, Shelley pits good vs. bad scientific practice against each other and implies that the former is safer in contrast to the latter's potentially incalculable dangers for individual and society. Good scientific research, Mellor explains, is associated in Shelley's novel for example with the works of Erasmus Darwin, which are based on careful description and non-interventionist observations of nature and refrain from attempting to radically change and control the world universe, attitudes embodied, e. g., by Luigi Galvani or the chemist Humphry Davy (Mellor 1995: 108). In addition, Victor's mode of creation, which both denies and reaffirms the power of a single creator, as the result of his creation is monstrous (1995: 120), is set against gradually emerging Darwinian theories of evolutionary theory which understand life as a gradual process rather than momentous creation. This tension is also often linked to the text's reflection of Romanticism's debate of the autonomy of art and the image of the lonely creator, and questions of the freedom of individual in relation to responsibility to the public.

Embodying the archetype of the doctor as a passionate outsider-figure, incapable of balancing his work with his private life, Shelley's Victor Frankenstein is the focus for a cluster of contemporary "anxieties about science, marriage,

---

[34] For a summary of the particular scientific research on which Frankenstein is based see Mellor (1987; 1995). On Aldini's experiments with frogs and executed criminals which sought to demonstrate that electric shock was a life-giving force and that "human life was essentially mechanical", see also Tropp (1990: 31).

female sexuality and violence" (Liggins 2000: 134); he is perceived as a risk to others as well as to himself. His process of experimental creation also has resonances with debates in medicine, in particular anatomy and surgery. It reflects current fears about procedures and "the relationship between surgeon and patient, between anatomist and cadaver" (2000: 129), highlighting their inevitable ties to gender and class differences. As critics such as Emma Liggins (2000) and Tim Marshall (1995) have shown, in the early 19th century dissection was not recognized without controversy as a legitimate method to acquire medical knowledge. Obtaining corpses for anatomical training presented a legal as well as moral problem and was generally considered as a risky business. Up until the 1832 Anatomy Act which established the practices of using corpses of the poor, post-mortal dissection had been a common, much-feared and despised punishment for capital crimes, reinforcing the association with surgery and murder from another angle. As such, Shelley's text illustrates contemporary ethical dilemmas and fears posed by the advances of medical science, dead bodies, and the scientist/surgeon's general disregard of human bodies as ethical subjects.[35] These are, of course, eerily similar to today's debates about the ethics and risks of organ transplantation, stem cell research, or cloning.

Although in the day and age of advanced reproductive technology, AI, and robotics, one is tempted to ask if "Frankenstein's futurity [has] come to pass?" (Clayton 2003: 84), the fact that Shelley set her story in the recent past indicates that she was originally more interested in the science of her own time than prophesizing about the future. However, if one sees *Frankenstein* as one of the first science fiction texts, it certainly contains a dystopian scenario and a cautionary tale, "a warning, not a promise, about the world of tomorrow" (Clayton 2003: 84). At the centre of the tale is Victor's creation of a monster, which if one considers the term's etymological roots from the Latin *monere*, "to warn", as well as *(de)monstrare*, "to show, prove" (cf. Rabkin 1998: 11; Brooks 1995: 81; Freeman 1987: 27), presents a warning and a spectacular realization of an idea which needs to be looked at; it is the personification of a set of risks.

Often read as an allegory about the danger of scientific hubris, this aspect of Shelley's text is also clearly gendered because the issue is undeniably "the disastrous impact of unregulated *male* science" (Hansen 1997: 584; my emphasis). Yet with the dangers of passion and enthusiasm being a generally common theme of Enlightenment thought, infused by Shelley with a critique of Romantic

---

[35] See Liggins (2000: 133; 142) and Marshall (1995: 21). Marshall's study draws attention to Shelley's novel in this context and the problems of legitimizing their practices faced by medical professionals in in the early 19th century.

egotism, it remains a matter of perspective if the inherent criticism of scientific practice takes priority over the denunciation of Romantic male ego in the novel. One can see "the excesses of an overwrought sensibility, not natural philosophy itself" (Clayton 2003: 88) as the main target of criticism, however the text is ultimately about the dangers to control creations *both* in the scientific and the poetic realm, dramatizing the risk of the taking of the "inspirational leap" (Hansen 1997: 582) which can give rise to forces beyond a single individual's control.[36]

Frankenstein continues to allow us to explore conceptions of the self and post-/in-/humanity. In recent literary criticism, the result of Victor's 'leap', has been conceived as an unhappy, failed cyborg *avant la lettre*, only ever referred to in the narrative as the "monster", "creature", "demon", or "miserable wretch", and thus denied individuality (see Haney 2006). It is a patchwork constructed out of inanimate body parts, both completely natural (as collectively assembled only out of natural human ingredients) and unnatural due to his creation (see Brooks 1995: 99). Its struggle to acculturate in human society is due to the creator's failure to provide it with consciousness, a task that to this date "exceeds the power of technology, of whatever paradigm" (Haney 2006: 173). Meanwhile Victor Frankenstein can be taken as an example of an "uncritical posthumanist" (Federer 2014: 51) in a text that highlights anxieties about human/nonhuman identity and agency. Frankenstein's project suggests that both humanity and monstrosity are produced and constructed, rather than miraculously brought to life. His later reaction to the monster and its gradual simultaneous (de-)humanization demonstrates that it is its hybridity and the oscillation between difference and sameness that is perceived as dangerous. Investigating why *Frankenstein* holds such power as a symbolic narrative in the scientific arena of biotechnology, Courtney S. Campell argues that the text, "although obviously not conveying, nor intending to convey, scientific facts, can disclose deeper realities, even 'facts' about the human condition" (Campell 2003: 344). With regard to the question what risks or faults Victor displays (as a scientist) in the novel and which can potentially be transferred to contemporary critiques of real-life science, Campell gives an interesting answer. It is mainly the speed and carelessness of Victor's scientific practice. He is guilty of emotional detachment to his work and failing to care for and support his creation: "Scientific inquiry that proceeds relentlessly without 'pausing to wonder' is a profound form of not caring; it is a science caught up in an intellectual puzzle, devoid of emotional engagement. Thus, [...] [it] will find itself subject to the criticism often directed against

---

[36] On the creation of the monster essentially as a liberation of Frankenstein's egotism and manifestation of his desire and ambition, see also Poovey (1984: 125).

biotechnology – that it is moving too fast" (Campell 2003: 346). In defense of Frankenstein's behaviour in the narrative one can mention his display of many characteristics of a 'good' scientist, including the passionate commitment to his subject of study, seeking the gratification of obtaining knowledge, and a certain objective distance. But the negative aspects of his character, his mania, self-absorption, and carelessness overtake these. He is also isolated from any larger social context and "completely oblivious to the matter of whether this discovery is really for the greatest betterment of humanity" (Campell 2003: 348). While it has been shown time and again that the latter is a difficult criterion to judge medical or biotechnological research practices, Campell's argument illuminates the symbolic meaning of *Frankenstein* in the discursive context of science and risk. A reason why the myth of Frankenstein is invoked in contemporary risk debates does not lie in the disastrous result of the creation but proceeding in the hasty and carelessness that allowed the project to happen in the first place. According to Campell, Frankenstein's tale postulates careful science and restrained aspiration in order to avoid the risk of scientific research which induces horror and revulsion. Nonetheless, there is another important dimension of the mythical legacy of Shelley's novel in contemporary debates about medical or biotechnological advance. The so-called "Frankenstein factor"[37], an irrational, readily invoked bias against new experiments often influences objective risk assessments. Using the example of the risk analysis of 'Frankenstein foods', Joyce Tait argues that this can make it hard to detect what is being criticized or which are the real fear-inducing aspects; because the idea of the Faustian bargain, e.g. in the case of GMO foods putting techno-science and "the industries that increasingly control them in charge of world food production systems" (Tait 2001: 175) is equally scary as the potentially monstrous results of our creations. The perceived risks of usurping power, unleashing rebellion, and creating incalculable dependencies are an integral part of the narrative of *Frankenstein*.

While there is plenty of evidence to suggest the relevance of Shelley's novel in contemporary risk discourse, it is important to continue to read *Frankenstein* as a reflection of the fears springing from its specific historical-scientific context and consider it as a prophetic foreshadowing not just of the future of biotechnology but of social fears of class conflict and rebellion which find their full literary pronunciation in the early Victorian novel and the Industrial fictions of the 1840s. At the time Shelley was writing, the fascination with industrialization had become distinctly tempered with fear. With *Frankenstein* she also captured widespread concerns about working class rebellion in a striking image and fic-

---

37 The term is borrowed from William Gaylin's article "The Frankenstein Factor" (1977).

tionalized popular fears engendered by the factory systems and the nexus of man and machine. Critics such as Martin Tropp emphasize the monster figure's function to represent the dehumanizing effect of new technology on the lower, working classes, as well as the violence-inducing sense of exploitation and abandonment by the patriarchal authorities in this context (see Tropp 1990: 32–37). Frankenstein's creature, a mass of low-class, criminal parts united in one giant monstrous body demanding to be heard and cared for, is legible as a symbol for the ruling classes fear of working class rebellion or "the dangers of mob rule" (1990: 39). Characteristically, the monster's response to injustice is violence and the desire to "tear up the trees, spread havoc and destruction" (F 105).[38] Frankenstein's creature offers a canvas for the projection of fears and feelings of violence, disgust, difference and deformity. Imaginatively it continues the association of radical threats to the traditional social order and monstrosity found in many texts written or set in the aftermath of the French Revolution. Utilizing Gothic motifs of uncanny difference and sameness, Shelley's narrative dramatizes above all the creature's claim of equality that is so shocking to Victor (see Moretti 2005: 87; Botting 1995: 10–11). Being a story of almost constant motion and speed, reflected in the motif of pursuit, Shelley's *Frankenstein* is a timeless tale of modern terrors unbound.

---

[38] Cf. the references to Frankenstein's monster in Elizabeth Gaskell's *Mary Barton* discussed in chapter 6.2.

6 Precariousness, Accidents, and Divisions

6.1 Industrial Novels and the Victorian Risk Society

In relation to the 18th century, Victorian Britain sees an even further growth of the speculative financial drives of capitalism, as well as the development of an entire new industry dedicated to preserving and protecting wealth, property, and commerce against all possible and impossible odds: insurance. Actuarial science is, in fact, an inseparable offspring of the developments in related areas of social and political sciences from the later 18th throughout the 19th century. The scientific and philosophical turn towards empiricism, the calculation of probabilities, and the plain 'numbering' of people, events, and things, leads to the increasing obsession with statistics, which in the course of the Victorian era become institutionalized in various forms and technologies as the basis for constructs of society, the nation, and the life and likes of the average man, *l'homme moyen*. The era's concern with security and norms highlights, in turn, the perceived dangers to life and business, and the discursive construction of deviation and instability as high risks. These developments strongly inform the reading of the mid-century novels in this chapter and the next.

Representative of the portrayal of the Victorian age in most cultural and historical accounts, Joseph W. Childers describes it as an era of "unprecedented material change – steam engines, factories, railroads, urbanization – [which] denoted even grander transformations in the way people thought and acted" (2001: 44). Similarly, Robin Gilmour characterizes Victorian society as consisting of serious people in defiance of "a background of uncertainty, the uncertainty of people who knew they were moving in uncharted waters" (1993: 2). The middle classes, being the main agents and beneficiaries of the scientific and political advancements and reforms of the era, above all the Industrial revolution,[1] try to combat the threats of instability by setting a new 'moral' culture against it, based on the values "hard work, energy, self-help, individualism, earnestness, domesticity" (1993: 14).

Especially from the 1830s onwards, society's increasing social-political insecurities find reflection in a public discourse dominated by threats of disorder, with a strong focus on class conflict and working-class rebellion. While working-class violence and insurgence remain persistent threats throughout the Vic-

---

[1] Arguably, the period from 1780–1830 can be considered "the spring-time of the industrial revolution" (Wrigley 1990: 11). For an informative survey of the developments during this time see also Landes (1969: 41–123).

torian age, they surface very prominently at two junctures, firstly, in the 1830s and 40s and, secondly, the 1880s. In the first instance, particular fears cluster around Chartism, and the formation of trade unions, which to the middle and upper classes, James Eli Adams explains, appeared as "working-class conspiracies bent on the destruction of British society. All of these anxieties converged in the industrial novel, which in many ways might just as aptly be called the insurrection novel" (2005: 63; 62). Significantly, all of the major industrial novels and the four canonical examples under scrutiny in the following, Elizabeth Gaskell's *Mary Barton* and *North and South*, Charles Dickens' *Hard Times*, and Charlotte Brontë's *Shirley* have a riot or related act of violence, motivated by working-class discontent, at the centre of the plot.

As has been thoroughly theorized, the genre of the Industrial, "condition-of-England", or "social problem novel",[2] came into being in the second quarter of the 19th century because prose fiction seemingly offered a suitable vehicle to generate inter-class empathy and educate the majority of middle-class readers about social injustices and the illnesses, dirt, squalor and suffering of the working class. Both in contrast and addition to political essays and other journalistic forms of writing at the time, the novel appeared as an ideal realm to negotiate social tensions and hierarchies, and the anxieties arising from interaction between and within the different classes. With the deplorable working conditions, the child labour, long workdays, and the abusive treatment of workers by their masters being publicized with greater frequency, these issues became subsumed under the label of the "factory question" (Simmons 2002: 338). This formed an integral part of the debates dominating the socio-political climate about urgent reforms and the broader "condition-of-England question" that Thomas Carlyle first raised in his widely received 1840 essay "Chartism".[3] There he expresses clearly the felt distance between the classes and a sense of urgency: "A feeling very generally exists that the condition and disposition of the Working Classes is a rather ominous matter at present; that something ought to be said, something ought to be done, in regard to it" (Carlyle 1840: 1). Carlyle also refers to the rebellious discontent of the working class as "poisonous boils" and "festering ills" (1840: 3), thus portraying Chartism, the first organized working class movement founded in 1838, as a dangerous, feverish delirium. In the middle

---

[2] See, e.g., Childers (2001) and Simmons (2002). For an accessible summary of critical approaches and a reception history of the genre see O'Gorman (2002); particularly influential in criticism have been Catherine Gallagher's new historicist study *The Industrial Reformation of English* Fiction (1985) and Raymond Williams' *Culture and Society 1780–1950* (1958).
[3] Carlyle writes: "The condition of the great body of people in a country is the condition of the country itself" (1840: 5).

class' imagination it posed a threat exceeding the upheaval of previous protests like the "anti-machine" riots of the Luddites two decades before. The rift, however, did not merely run between classes but also geographically severed the country into the richer, predominately agricultural South and the poorer, industrial North. Benjamin Disraeli memorably captured the degree of separation between rich and poor in his metaphor of the "two nations" in his own industrial novel *Sybil, or The Two Nations* (1845).

Commonly thought of as the first industrial city, Manchester rose to become a centre of commerce and distribution in the 1830s and 40s, but also gained a "reputation as the world's shock city" (Hilton 2006: 578). The squalor of the city and its mills and factories has been acknowledged in many contemporary reports, such as William Cooke Taylor's *Notes of a Tour of the Manufacturing District of Lancashire* (1841) and Friedrich Engels's *The Condition of the Working-class in England in 1844*. Not just in Manchester did the significant population growth and urbanization cause severe social problems, such as over-crowding and spread of disease, which lead to drastic negative developments in the working-class population's health, life expectancy and – according to public perception – also their morals. The belief in the prospects of economic growth, while not being really diminished, generally transformed from unconditional optimism into a kind of pessimism with a strong competitive edge, and thus reflected, as Boyd Hilton argues, the "shift from Smithian to Malthusian ways of thinking – from the natural harmony of interests to ecological competition" (2006: 343).[4] Meanwhile, due to the deplorable living conditions in the industrial towns, consumption and other endemic infectious diseases were on the rise, and mortality reached new heights, varying, however, largely with regard to region and class. To borrow a numeric example given by Hilton: "A death rate of eight per thousand in Hereford contrasted with twenty per thousand in Middlesex, while in 1840s Liverpool the gentry and professional classes had an average life expectancy of 35, tradesmen of 22, mechanics, servants, and labourers – the vast majority of whom lived in cellars – only 15" (2006: 574).

Reflecting these conditions, death, illness and fatal accidents are omnipresent in the Industrial novel. Generally, narratives of death gain prominence in the Victorian novel and deaths become central event in the plots. Rather than

---

4 This draws attention to the increasingly perceived danger of an uncontrollable growth of population, which Thomas Robert Malthus first expressed in his *An Essay on the Principle of Population* (1798). Hilton writes further: "The significance of the intervening years from 1783 to 1846, however, is not that England forged ahead into self-sustained growth, but that it just about managed to avoid a demographic catastrophe. [...] Whatever the reasons, more than 60 percent of people were less than 24 years old during the first half of the nineteenth century" (2006: 5).

considering this phenomenon as characteristic of an overly melodramatic or sensational style, the fictions show the reality and continuous presence "of death to the Victorian mind as it tried to keep in bearable view a reality that could never be kept at bay, in any family, for long" (Joseph and Tucker 1999: 115).

As has been frequently noted and also emphasized here, main preoccupations of the Industrial novel are descriptions of the living and working conditions of the poor and the growing hostility between the classes. Besides their didactic-moral ambitions and political agendas, the industrial fictions capture and critically engage with the major fears and perceived risks of the time. They reflect the risk of conditions and conflicts building up into uncontainable eruptions, which reinforce "association of the poor with violence and danger" (Adams 2012: 10). Concerning (middle and upper class) perceptions of the poor as "mad, bad, and dangerous", Hilton notes emphatically:

> Demonization of the poor as potential revolutionaries had been commonplace since the last two decades of the eighteenth century. [...] A vision of a society separated into distinct and hostile groups has replaced the more fluid, ambiguous worlds of Defoe and Hogarth. Such images were symptomatic of polite society's inability to distinguish between poverty and various types of deviance, such as crime, delinquency, lunacy, sexual depravity, and Jacobinism. In their imagination all these horrors merged into one great phantasmagoria of *the mad, bad, and dangerous people, an infectious disease threatening to destroy civilization*. (2006: 580; my emphasis)

The analogy between poverty and infectious diseases Hilton draws attention to here is decisive and often reproduced in public discourse of the time:[5] "Like speculation and disease, poverty seemed capable of being spread through personal contact until it engulfed the whole of society. These phobias affected mainstream thought for as long as revolution seemed a possibility, i.e. until the mid-century" (2006: 581). It is moreover tied to a perception of the workers as a crowd, or mass, gaining uncontrollable force through sheer numbers and ready to overthrow the old order.[6] William Cooke Taylor captures this impression

---

5 "'Pauperism we consider nearly as infectious as smallpox', wrote one official. 'Without constant vigilance it would soon overspread the whole parish'" (*Extracts from the Information received from His Majesty's Commissioners as to the Administration and Operation of the Poor Laws*. 1832. 177; cited in Hilton 2006: 581).
6 See also Herbert Sussman's comment: "This fear of the crowds or mob does much to explain the intense government repression in the early nineteenth century of what the age called 'combination,' the organization of working men into what we would call unions. [...] The fear of workers' becoming organized registered in the bourgeois industrial novels' representation of union organizers and all leaders of the working class as deceptive, bloodthirsty villains" (1999: 251).

in *Notes of a Tour in the Manufacturing Districts of Lancashire* (1841), where he writes:

> The population, like the system to which it belongs, is NEW: but it is hourly increasing its breath, and strength. It is an aggregate of masses, our conceptions of which clothe themselves in terms that express something portentous and fearful. We speak not of them indeed as of sudden convulsions, tempestuous seas or furious hurricanes, but as of the slow rising and gradual swelling of an ocean society afloat upon its bosom, and float them [...]. There are mighty energies slumbering in those masses. (1968: 6)

This fear is illustrated, for example, in the climactic scene in Gaskell's *North and South*, where Margaret Hale watches the workers approach the Thornton family's house like "the slow-surging wave of the dark crowd come, with its threatening crest" (*N&S* 203). According to Deidre David, a reason for the frequent use of these risk metaphors was that it mediated an otherwise unspoken fear by putting it into familiar terms, i.e. natural disasters; in this sense "writing about the apocalyptic moment is one way of fending it off" (1981: 27).

Yet representations of the workers as a threatening mob are also typically counterbalanced in the Industrial novel, Herbert Sussman notes, by the portrayals of "individual workers as sympathetic British subjects" (1999: 250). With regard to the construction of the working-class characters as risk, one therefore has to clearly differentiate between the (typically only vaguely described, unnamed) crowd and individuals singled out to form affective mutual relations with middle-class characters, e.g. the Higgins family in *North and South*, or those praised for their exceptional virtue, e.g. Stephen Blackpool in *Hard Times*.

Many Industrial novels feature a dual plot structure which gives at least as much (if not more) room to courtship and love interests as to the industrial theme. The success or failure of the integration of the two narrative strands has been the subject of much debate in the criticism of these fictions, which will not be repeated in detail here. Relevant, however, in this context is a point stressed by Mary Poovey. Due to the fact, she says, that

> special – and, more specifically, romantic – relationships had become the conventional site of readerly identification by the 1840s, novelists tended to embed stories of individual distress within narratives of affective, often erotic engagement. As a result, practioners of this most feminized of discourses often linked their hopes for 'improvement' not to specific government policies but to the utopian potential culturally ascribed to love. (1995: 153)

Poovey here refers to another aspect frequently criticized about the industrial novel, namely that their authors do not point towards any explicit or politically sound solutions to the conflict between masters and men.[7] While many writers, most strongly perhaps Elizabeth Gaskell, advocate Christian sympathy in their texts, they also show individual altruism and 'true' inter-class understanding as problematic. Finally, one more, sufficiently criticized aspect of the genre deserves a brief mentioning: the 'authenticity' of the depiction of the working classes. Besides seeking to evoke sympathy as a means to overcome social tensions, the industrial fictions produced by middle-class writers function to render the representations of the poor vaguely exotic and remote; they externalize fears, and in the process make poverty and its related risks accessible and 'consumable.' James Eli Adams points out how in the "so-called 'industrial' fiction dealing with working-class characters, the fascination takes on a quasi-ethnographic cast, as if charting the workings of a dangerous alien world" (2012: 10). Similarly, Herbert Sussman compares the attempts of middle-class writers seeking to represent working-class consciousness, to "a journey analogous to colonial exploration" (1999: 249). In any case, the texts entail an engagement with alterity and its fascination and frights on many levels. Yet ultimately the genre, which sought to make visible the 'real' condition of England, was relatively short-lived and became superfluous once the conditions of the factory and mill workers improved through reforms enacted by official legislation. In other words, once society's perception of risk shifted onto different areas, it also found reflection in different kinds of narratives.

Before turning to the novels, the rise of statistics and insurance, and its impact on the construction of risk(s) deserves further contextualization. The 19th century sees a significant reorientation of probability theory and its applications away from rationality, i.e. the calculation of outcome of events, and 'rational' speculation, towards frequency and the analysis of mean values.[8] Many theorists and historians of mathematical probability conceptualise this historical shift as the end of the age of reason and the beginning of the age of the

---

7 The endings of industrial novels are often criticized as unsatisfying or improbable in their dissolution of class animosities because they tend to rely heavily on coincidence. Yet it is perhaps more interesting to interrogate the function of these endings and consider why they had an appeal for the contemporary readership. Also, considering the case of Gaskell, for instance, it is important to keep in mind that, after all, "she was a novelist and not a political economist" (David 1981: 8)

8 Gigerenzer et al note: "It is no accident that during the 1830s and 1840s social statistics and insurance were coming to be seen as the most useful and important applications for a field of mathematics that for more than a century had been trying to escape its association with frivolous games of chance. The frequency interpretation originated as a statistical interpretation of probability" (1989: 45). For a more detailed view on the shift and reorientation of probability theory see also Daston (1987), Hacking (1990), and Porter (1986).

average. According to Reith, "Probabilists turned their attention from 'the rationality of the few to the irrationality of the many'" (1999: 33); Gigerenzer et al. explain this phenomenon further, saying:

> By about 1830, *l'homme éclairé* had given way to *l'homme moyen*. The same awareness of a dynamic and perhaps unstable mass society that superannuated the reasonable man as the most characteristic object of probability theory simultaneously brought into existence a new one. There was, to be sure, some continuity. [...] The reasonable man might still exist, but he did not and could not control public life. Statistics was valued as a way of searching for the larger order that, it was hoped, would prevail nonetheless. [...] The main object of probabilistic analysis became mean values. Its most important and conspicuous filed was now statistics. (1989: 37)

While Hacking speaks in this historical context of the "avalanche of numbers",[9] Porter describes the developments and the transition from late 18th to early 19th century as a furthering of the practical imperative of quantification, an emergence of an ethics of measurement, and an "accounting ideal", which becomes increasingly "crucial agency for managing people and nature" (1995: 50).[10] William Stanley Jevons sums up this characteristic, and morally charged outlook in *The Theory of Political Economy* (1871):

> Previous to the time of Pascal, who would have thought of measuring doubt and belief? [...] Now there can be no doubt that pleasure, pain, labour, utility, value, wealth, money, capital, etc. are all notions admitting of quantity; nay the whole of our actions in industry and trade certainly depend upon comparing quantities of advantage and disadvantage. (cited in Bernstein 1998: 191)

As such, the quest for precision during the Victorian age, if one follows Porter's historical argument further, "has been sustained in science for reasons having more to do with moral economy than theoretical rigor. Precision has been valued as a sign of diligence, skill, and impersonality" (Porter 1995: 50). Narratives of the time reflect this and, especially from the mid-19th century onwards, feature large casts of characters and, furthermore, seek a detailed, realist documentation of society and the ordinary ups and downs of life.

---

9 In *The Taming of Chance*, Hacking repeatedly speaks of an "avalanche of printed numbers" in the period from 1820–1840 (see 1990: 27–34).
10 Excellent historical-theoretical studies of the establishment of statistics are Porter's *Trust in Numbers* (1995) and *The Rise of Statistical Thinking, 1820–1900* (1986). See also Cullen's *The Statistical Movement in Early Victorian Britain* (1975), Glass's *Numbering the People* (1973), Pearson's *The History of Statistics in the 17th and 18th Centuries* (1978), Westergaard's *Contributions to the History of Statistics* (1932), and the chapter "Statistical Probabilities, 1820–1900" in Gigerenzer et al (1989: 37–69).

An important part of the new scientific and political credo of the 19th century is the belief in statistical regularity and a devotion to the acquisition of neutral, descriptive, and thus indubitable knowledge, which excludes all possible counter-arguments.[11] Although the origins of statistics, as the "systematic study of social numbers" can be traced back to the late 17th century, it took almost a century and a half until what was until then known in England as *political arithmetic*[12] becomes an indispensable basis for calculating insurance rates and rational state policy (Porter 1986: 18). From the beginning, statistics are thought of as a strategy of rational government and scientific underpinning of risk management. Promising insight in the internal structure of human society, they form the basis for centralizing bureaucracy. A watershed in the statistical movement in Victorian Britain is the first official census, set up and published in 1801 in order to determine the available manpower in the Napoleonic wars and what supplies were necessary to feed the population (cf. Knights and Vurdubakis 1993: 737; Shaw and Miles 1979: 32). This proved so efficient that population censuses soon became regular events and the 1830s generally saw a burst of official statistical activity, as well as the foundation of the Statistical Society of London, precursor of today's Royal Statistical Society, in March 1834.[13] Generally,

---

[11] This outlook, Gigerenzer et al explain, "reached its zenith in the decision of the London Statistical society to take as its motto *Aliis exterendum* – to be threshed out by others. Statistics, according to the council of that great scientific organization, was not concerned with causes or effects; indeed, its 'first and most essential rule' was 'to exclude all opinions'" (1989: 38; cf. Cullen 1975: 85). Porter puts it similarly: "The first great statistical enthusiasm of the 1820s and 1830s grew out of a commitment to the transparency of numbers. The London statisticians, most notoriously, resolved that the fact should be allowed to speak for themselves, and that there was no room for opinions in the proceedings of a statistical society" (1995: 78).

[12] The term *Political arithmetic* was first used as the title of a book by Sir William Petty in 1690. Later defined by Charles Davenant as "the art of reasoning by figures, upon things relating to government" (cited in Westergaard 1932: 40), it became increasingly part of parliamentary debates in Britain throughout the 18th century. Pioneering studies that used demographic data and prepared the way for the establishment of demographic laws were Richard Price's studies of national debt or John Graunt and Edmund Halley's mathematical analyses of life expectancy. From 1753 onwards, there are records of calls for a programme of social statistics and for a general census (cf. Shaw and Miles 1979: 31f; Johannisson 1990: 349).

[13] The 1801 census, J.H. Plumb explains, exemplified a new approach to political economy, which proved "so successful that the statistical method was rapidly applied to many aspects of English life, so that our knowledge of early nineteenth-century society has a depth and a richness of detail which is totally lacking for eighteenth-century England" (1978: 144). On the first British censuses see also Porter (1995: 35). Door-to-door surveys are another example of new statistical activity that became common practice in the 1830s. These included a wide variety of topics, such as education, public health, or the poor law (see Shaw and Miles 1981: 33).

statistical investigation is considered more and more vital, and supposed to provide sound, rational grounding for necessary reform and information, e.g. on how to relief the poor. In this way, as Porter sums up: "The study of social numbers embodied hope as well as fear, and it is not by chance that statistics became 'the favourite study of the present age' in Great Britain precisely during those years of upheaval that brought forth the Reform Act of 1832, the Factory Act of 1833, and the new Poor Law of 1834" (1986: 31).

Transcending the British context, the development of statistics in Europe at the time shows a strong concern with practical application of numbers and calculation of probabilities in times of crisis, and emerging concepts of the risks of deviation and ideas of normalcy. Especially the situation in Germany, where *Statistik*[14] had been a somewhat nebulous university subject since the mid-18th century, is comparable to England.[15] In both countries it is a sense of national or social crisis – the situation in 1830s' England and the 1848 revolution in Germany, which lent new urgency to the matter of accurately assessing and managing people and social conditions and thus gave a push to the officialising of statistics (cf. Gigerenzer et al. 1989: 49). In other words, the "condition-of-England question" and the perception of the masses at and as risk led to the question of how to measure and control them (– here it is worth remembering that the working class constituted over 70% of the population at the time). Regarding the Industrial novel, Lawrence Poston emphasises the relations between contemporary fictions and the political and scientific context, saying: "It is no accident that the 1830s saw the rise of statistics-gathering, [...] and in general an almost obsessive documentation of 'the condition of England question', which resonates

---

14 "Statistics derives from a German term, *Statistik*, first used as a substantive by the Göttingen professor Gottfried Achenwall in 1749" (Porter 1986: 23). Not until the late 18th century did "political arithmetic" become known as "state-istics" in England. A difference between the German and English understanding and use of statistics is that in Germany it was considered as a method which delivered a systematic, yet static snap-shot of society, typically presented in tabular form, and mainly compiled for comparative analysis of state power. In England, the concern with the collection of data was more dynamic and diachronic, seeking to identify causal regularities and potential for changes and reforms (cf. Shaw and Miles 1979: 31).

15 Although similar developments are observable the rest of Europe at the time, Porter emphasizes the specific role of Britain: "Nowhere else was statistics pursued with quite the level of enthusiasm as in Britain, and numerical statistics developed more slowly outside the politically and economically most advanced states of Western Europe" (1986: 37). Regarding the situation on the British Isles, an early important systematic study was compiled by John Sinclair in *The Statistical Account of Scotland* in ten volumes (Edinburgh, 1791–1798), drawn up from the communications of the ministers of all the different parishes (see Johannisson 1990: 344). On the history of British statistics see also Poovey (1998: 307ff).

in the novels of Disraeli, Gaskell, Charlotte Brontë, and Kingsley in the next decade" (Poston 1999: 9).

While Poovey refers to statistics as "the characteristic form that modern facts took in nineteenth-century Britain" (1998: 306), the statistics of the time only imperfectly compare to present-day practice. Empirical statistical research was born out of particular concern with social reform but still had a long way to go until its firm institutionalization and the formation of the welfare state of the 20th century.[16] Nonetheless, the rise of statistics is inseparable from modernity, the new emerging social-economic order, and highlights the striving against "ontological insecurity" (de Jonge 1975: 14) as a distinctive feature of the development of capitalist society in 19th-century Europe.[17] Thus, the Victorian age sees a gradual acceptance of statistics and of a central "value of statistical inquiry – knowing one's 'risks'" (Choi 2001: 561).

Like financial risk in particular, insurance unites hopes of gain and fears of ruin. By offering an attractive reduction of fears of loss, it provides an incentive for the accumulation of goods and sparks further investments (cf. Pearson 2004: 369). In this way insurance functions as a "productive" procedure within a democratic, capitalist system, as Adam Smith already noted in *Wealth of Nations* (1776): "The trade of insurance gives great security to the fortunes of private people, and by dividing among a great many the loss which would ruin an individual, makes it fall light and easy upon the whole society" (2012: 756).[18] Although the desire for protection and stability grew due to a sense of increased economic insecurity, risk-taking was nonetheless encouraged continuously to boost and support trade, especially in industrial areas. Taking out insurance became a means to mitigate these conflicting impulses and the 1840s saw an

---

[16] See, for instance, Collini (1980), Goldman (1983), and Fraser (1973).
[17] Interestingly, insurance historian Robert Pearson sees the need to "reduce uncertainty for the property-owning classes and to bolster the social order" as the main motivational search behind the scientific search for predictability and "quantifiable patterns in nature" (2004: 3). Meanwhile Shaw and Miles describe statistical inquiry as a quantifying activity, which grows far beyond long-established traditions of "the counting and measuring of things" but is "really specific to the present, capitalist form of industrial society" (1979: 27–28). They write further: "In our time, statistical control has become a major activity in the main institutions which dominate society – the large corporations and the state – as well as in virtually every other sort of organization. Almost all areas of life are subject to one or other sort of bureaucratic control, largely on the basis of statistical knowledge" (1979: 34).
[18] While insurance was relatively uncommon in the late 18th century, Smith's economic ideas were highly influential concerning the establishment of life insurance especially in 19th-century England, Germany, and the US. On the close relations between the growth of capitalism and the insurance business, as well as Smith's *Wealth of Nations*, see Müller-Lutz and Rehnert (1995).

unprecedented growth of insurance business in England.[19] This reflects a crucial change in the 19th-century worldview and shows, as Knights and Vurdubakis point out, the emergence of a new type and demand for security as "the practical accompaniment of the cultural injunction to be in control on one's fate" (1993: 734).[20] Michael Tilby, one of the few literary scholars engaging explicitly with the intrinsic link between insurance and the new 19th-century world picture, argues along the same lines:

> It clearly represented a response to the individual's desire to establish a more settled outlook following the upheaval of Revolution and the Napoleonic wars. If it was no less obviously a reflection of a new emphasis on money that led to a price being placed on everything, it was above all a reflection of a new economic reality […]. It corresponded to a new middle-class desire to control financial risk and, as such, was like Defoe's novels, indissociable form the rise of capitalism. (2011: 113–114)[21]

As such, the practice of insurance is also consistent with the Victorian ideal of "self-help", and taking control of one's life through industry, an idea made popular not least through Samuel Smiles' book *Self-help* (1859). This ideology also informed the political discourse of the poor and critiques of gambling, which are representative of the same spirit, because "insurance provided the symbolic means through which middle-class subjects could distance themselves from the company of gamblers, squanderers, vagabonds and libertines" (Knights and Vurdubakis 1993: 739). The advocacy of insurance sprang from the postulation that everyone should act as rational economic agent and, therefore, "make provisions for the risks and emergencies of life in the form of regular savings and protection

---

19 Pearson even claims: "Only the technologically revolutionized industries such as cotton and iron grew faster after 1815" (2004: 26–7), while Hilton writes: "Insurance selling had been established long before 1783, but there was now an explosion of business amounting to what has been called 'a minor social revolution'" (2006: 153). Informative sources on the development of the insurance system in England are, for instance: Cockerell and Green's *The British Insurance Business* (1976); Pearson's *Insuring the Industrial Revolution* (2004); and the chapter "Experts Against Objectivity: Accountants and Actuaries" in Porter (1995: 89–113). For an interesting transatlantic perspective and a study of insurance in 19th-century American culture see Wertheimer (2006).
20 François Ewald poignantly affirms the link between insurance, social calculation, and secular modernity: "With insurance and its philosophy, one enters a universe where the ills that befall us lose their old providential meaning: a world without God, a laicized world where 'society' becomes the general arbiter for the causes of our destiny" (1991: 208).
21 Tilby offers an analysis of the realist fictions of Balzac in the historical context of the emergence of insurance companies in France after 1815; many of his observations are applicable to the Victorian novel and the English context.

through a friendly society or insurance company" (1993: 746). It is important to note, as Knights and Vurdubakis do, that from their beginnings insurance practices had a strong moral component and have been constituted "within projects directed towards the construction of socially responsible subjects via notions of prudence, forethought and familial responsibility" (1993: 733).[22] In this way, the Protestant spirit of self-help[23] and a new awareness of available forms of risk-management, i.e. security, such as wills, contracts, and different forms of insurance, which function to control the present and future of individuals, also play important roles in the plots of most Victorian novels. This is set against an awareness of new dangers and calamities, as industrialization, e.g. factories and the railway, brought new risks and accidents; meanwhile social crisis and wartime increased the sense of threat to life and property both in life and fictions.

Having to literally deal in and with uncertainty, the young insurance industry, however, faced various problems. [24] On the one hand, it had to calculate diverse and changing risks on a lacking basis of experience and data and assign, for instance, value to individual lives. Generally, statistics and insurance offered an abstract, artificial order but had to struggle for adequate data, reliability and people's trust in numbers. The main task was the search for large-scale order and regularity, beyond the randomness and caprice affecting each individual. Therefore, as Porter points out, 19th century liberals and statisticians were delighted in comparison, "by the uniformity from year to year which was found to characterize not only natural events like births and deaths, but also voluntary acts such as marriages and even seemingly senseless and irrational phenomena like crime and suicide. From this was born Adolphe Quetelet's doctrine of 'statistical law'" (1986: 5).[25] While the regularity of the rates of crime, mar-

---

22 An excellent historical discussion of this aspect is given in Knights and Vurdubakis (1993).
23 It is interesting to note that religion and world view play a decisive role and explain the different development of insurance industry in different parts of the world: e.g. in contrast to Christian and especially Protestant notions of virtue and self-help, Islamic faith is grounded on an idea of chance as fate, which it is diametrically opposed towards an idea of risk-management as a human activity; consequently the insurance business developed comparatively late in Islamic countries (cf. Koch 1995a: 157 ff).
24 According to Baucom, insurance is "a social practice which guaranteed that value was neither inherent in things nor void with their loss but was the secure product of the imagination and agreement" (2005: 95). Baucom's conception of insurance highlights its imaginary, slightly paradoxical nature. Like risk, insurance is detached from reality in the sense of being concerned with a probable event and future temporality.
25 The mathematical formula developed by the Belgian Adolphe Quetelet in the 1830s, formulated in its final version in 1844, was popularized as the 'law of average.' It introduced the ficti-

riage, or suicide conflicts with the idea of human will, agency and randomness, actuarial science and statistics had to invent the stable "average", in others words, "the 'typical' (typical risk, typical life expectancy, typical value of a given commodity)" and superimpose it on "the waywardness of the particular" (Baucom 2005: 40).

Although statistics have proved their longevity, sharp criticism of it arose from the beginning of the science,[26] and there was, in particular, "considerable debate over the possible incompatibility of statistical laws of moral behavior with traditional notions of free will" (Porter 1986: 69–70).[27] These tensions, the questions of human agency vs. (biological) determination and the respective fears connected to each, are negotiated especially in the Victorian fictions in the second half of the 19th century. In this context it is interesting to briefly mention that Arthur Schopenhauer, who is best known for his main work *The World as*

---

tious 'average man', who would live on to become a basic tool of social science. See for instance, Gigerenzer et al. who explain: "The stability of statistical aggregates, and hence of mean values, was the foundation of the science of social physics that Quetelet announced [...]. Its key concept was *l'homme moyen*, the average man. This being was, he realized, a mere abstraction. [...] But the average man can be understood. In the average, everything particular or exceptional balances out, and we are left with a certain penchant for crime characteristic of a given community, and dependent on circumstances which, it is hoped, can be isolated, measured, and then rectified" (1989: 41). One of the leading Victorian scientists and promoters of evolutionary sociology, Herbert Spencer evoked Quetelet's law in his theory of natural selection laid out in his study *Social Statics, Abridged and Revised* (1850), "contending that the death of many is redeemed by the survival 'in the average of cases' of one 'perfect specimen'" (cited in Porter 1986: 68). Later Émile Durkheim also identified an "average type" in his *Rules of Sociological Method* (1895).

26 An early critic of the danger of political arithmetic and the power and potential misuse of numbers was Jonathan Swift, who exposes in *A Modest Proposal* that numbers (especially about the poor) are not the disinterested, neutral quantifiers and expression of scientific facts one might want to take them for. Yet Swift's opinion was an early exception, as Karin Johannisson claims, because: "Only in recent years has this objectivity come under scrutiny, with the recognition that statistics offer no special guarantee of freedom from ideological influences. Numerical data are not collected, they are selected and sorted according to criteria shaped by ideology and politics" (1990: 343). See also especially Porter (1995; 1986).

27 The "law of large numbers", coined by Poisson in 1835, alternatively referred to in the 19th century as "standard deviation", the "error curve", "error law", or "normal law", remained a troubling idea for continental perceptions of free will; especially the British were reluctant to give up the concept of "subjective" probability (cf. Choi 2001: 578; Gigerenzer et al. 1989: 48; Hacking 1990: 115–21, Porter 1986: 87; 13). The issue was also heavily debated in Germany at the time; examples are contemporary studies like Adolph Wagner's *Die Gesetzmässigkeit in den scheinbar willkührlichen menschlichen Handlungen vom Standpunkt der Statistik* (1864), or Moritz Wilhelm Drobisch's *Die moralische Statistik und die menschliche Willensfreiheit* (1867).

Will and Representation (*Die Welt als Wille und Vorstellung*; 1819, 2nd edition 1844), also engaged practically and theoretically with the phenomenon of insurance (cf. Koch 1995b: 261). Schopenhauer's writings, which link ontology, metaphysic and ethics, centre on the notion that the perception and existence of the (material) world depends on human will and imagination. Yet the philosopher also viewed chance and coincidence ('Zufall') as a great danger threatening the security of life. Perceiving chance as such a great force in life, the only rational idea then is to take precaution in the form of insurance. Schopenhauer considers insurance a necessary, rationally justified sacrifice in order to avoid the threats of chance and keep the 'higher powers' friendly; as such it forms a secular, calculated means against risk:

> Unsere Maxime aber sei: Opfere den bösen Dämonen! Das heißt, man soll einen gewissen Aufwand von Mühe, Zeit, Unbequemlichkeit, Weitläufigkeit, Geld oder Entbehrung nicht scheuen, um der Möglichkeit eines Unglücks die Tür zu verschließen: und je größer dieses wäre, desto kleiner, entfernter, unwahrscheinlicher mag jene sein. Die deutlichste Exemplifikation dieser Regel ist die Assekuranzprämie. Sie ist ein öffentlich und von allen auf dem Altar der bösen Dämonen gebrachtes Opfer. (1862. 502–503)[28]

Despite the dramatic metaphor (i.e. chance as the 'bad demon' threatening human riches and security), Schopenhauer expresses the basic idea underlying insurance as a form of collective risk management.

The growing insurance business changed the perceived relationship between individual and community, and, above all, the perception of the state as a "great benefit society or mutual insurance company".[29] Politics and public discourse were preoccupied with distinguishing, for instance, between (necessary, inevitable) poverty and pauperism (self-inflicted through vice, ignorance, or insubordination), and affirmed the belief that it "is a hurtful misuse of money to spend it on assisting the laboring classes to meet emergencies which they should themselves have anticipated and provided for".[30] However, sickness, work-related accidents, and unemployment were still increasingly classified as social risks. According to Knights and Vurdubakis, the project of socialization added a new "vocabulary of welfare, social reform and national efficiency" to its political rep-

---

28 On Schopenhauer and the idea of insurance see also Müller–Lutz and Rehnert (1995: 264).
29 The expression is used by John Stuart Mill in his *Dissertations and Discussions Vol I* ([1867] 2008: 454). See also Sidney Webb's comparison in the tract "Reform of the Poor Law", where he refers to "the State as a vast benefit society, of which the whole body of citizens are necessarily members" (1891: 8).
30 *Eighth Annual Report of the Charity Organisation Society* 1876, Appendix IV, 24–5; cited in Fraser (1973: 249).

ertoire, which gradually came to displace that of progress and improvement (1993: 750). The influence on statistics and insurance on government policies also affected the notions of responsibility and culpability, which slowly found reflection in crucial changes made in legislation. An important factor was that at the beginning of the Victorian era most investment and business ventures were subject to unlimited liability, which added to the endemic insecurity among the upper and middle classes but also invited high-risk speculation. Another aspect is the emerging concept of 'accident' in its legal sense. As Mike Sanders has argued, 'accident' includes the twin notions of the 'accidental', and the negative event, and allowed industrial capitalism to come up with "a compromise formula [...] to accept responsibility for its casualties without having to admit its responsibility in producing those casualties". In this sense, "'accident' effectively de-couples causation and intention" (2000: 321–22), or, as Robert Campbell puts it, accident produces "accountability without culpability" (1997: 30). Throughout the century new laws, such as the Joint Stock Companies Act of 1844 and 1856, slowly introduced limited liability and more employer responsibility. Other examples are the Factory Act of 1844, establishing minimal safety standards in the work place and compensation clauses, which were pushed further in later legislation, like the Employer's Liability Act of 1880 and the Workmen's Compensation Act of 1897.

Generally, the Victorian era and its literature see the emergence of a new concept of risk which differs especially from early 18th-century ideas through a shifted emphasis away from risk as a dare the individual enters into out of his/her own volition, to something which inevitably surrounds the individual and which calls for the taking of precautions. According to Tina Young Choi, the term 'risk' thus underwent a transformation "from a voluntary and chosen state of possibility into an involuntary and inevitable condition of urban life" (2001: 562). The institutionalization of the practice of insurance turns risk in to an important market commodity. It changes the experience of risk, paradoxically, not by neutralizing, or even removing at least the financial consequences, but by heightening the awareness of it; thus it creates a new social ubiquity of risk (see also Tilby 2011: 115). Furthermore, risk becomes closely (but of course not exclusively) tied to urban life. Paralleling actuarial writing, which depends on a minute description of events and predictions and (re)constructions of chains of causality, Victorian literature, both fiction and non-fiction, firmly embrace literary realism.[31]

---

[31] Choi argues along the same lines and draws attention in particular on the emergence of two

Especially in mid-Victorian novels, chance events like sickness or death are contrasted with accidents, such as fires. While the discourse about insurance highlights the intersection of life, death, and money, another crucial part are questions of liability, of business partnerships, trust, and judging personal character, which are negotiated in the texts.[32] Many 19th-century writers mitigate the tension of an idealized desire for safety and increased awareness of risk in their fictions, often presenting change as the main cause of insecurity. The industrial novel illustrates the novelistic range of ambiguous depictions of risk that were stimulated by the growth of the insurance industry. In the following, the aim is to investigate the ways in which the changing experience of risk and a statistical view of society relate to the plot of some of these fictions. In this context, it is also interesting to consider the interdependencies between the strongly emerging realist novel and matters of plot in the sense suggested by Tilby's case study of Balzac and French realism. The turn from Romanticism and Gothic fiction towards literary realism indicates how modern forms of risk assessment in Europe stand increasingly at odds with stereotypical "plots that identified danger with naïve notions of villainy and misfortune" (Tilby 2011: 108); instead writers like Dickens or Gaskell too show a clear awareness of risk in and outside their fictional worlds and create new kinds of plots that break "with Gothic notions of danger and aligned the novel with radically different notions of catastrophe encouraged by the new socio-economic order" (2011: 107). All the while they challenge ironically and emotionally the reader's belief in the idealist tenets of insurance.

6.2 Suffering From Unmanageable Risk: *Mary Barton*

The plot of Elizabeth Gaskell's first Manchester novel *Mary Barton* (1848) is constructed around a case of Chartist violence, the murder of the rich mill owner's son Harry Carson by John Barton.[33] Mary's father is appointed to this deed by his

---

important subgenres of nonfiction prose, literature of urban exploration, and social statistics, in relation to a new nexus of risk, urbanity, and disease in industrial areas.
32 See, for instance, Andrew H. Miller's essay "Subjectivity Ltd: The Discourse of Liability in the Joint Stock Companies Act of 1856 and Gaskell's *Cranford*" (1994). It is one of the few studies explicitly focusing on the contemporary discourse of liability.
33 Due to the influence of Gaskell's publishers at the time, the novel's title, or rather the eponymous heroine came to be not the one the author had originally intended. Still, the heroine's father, John Barton and "the tragedy of a poor man's life" (MB 359) remain central to the text, even if the focus was shifted onto Mary. See Webb (2010: 22ff) for an accessible summary

trade union, as a direct reaction to old Carson's treatment of his men and the starvation of some of the workers' children. Thus Barton, an essentially good-natured and hard-working man, is driven to a capital crime by his circumstances, by the deep poverty, suffering, and rage against the injustices of the factory system. Characteristically, this industrial fiction takes up a felt threat of the middle-class and sets it against the acute risks of the working class. On the one hand, Gaskell dramatizes a fear which in reality showed a high discrepancy between perceived risk and actual danger, as Joseph Childers explains: "Despite the relatively small amount of actual damage the Chartists did to persons and property over the decade of their heyday, for the middle classes, the potential for Chartists violence was very real" (2001: 83). On the other hand, *Mary Barton* presents an excruciating chronicle of working-class life at the time and, in the opinion of Raymond Williams, even holds its place as "the most moving literary response in literature to the industrial suffering of the 1840s" (1958: 87). In her preface to the text, Gaskell acknowledges her

> deep sympathy with the care-worn men, who looked as if doomed to struggle through their lives in strange alternations between work and want; tossed to and fro by circumstances, apparently in even a greater degree than other men. [...] I saw that they were sore and irritable against the rich, the even tenor of those seeming happy lives appeared to increase the anguish caused by the lottery-like nature of their own. (MB 3)

This statement draws attention to important aspects of the narrative: The depiction of the working-class characters as subject to various risks, the differences and the potential of aggression between the classes, and finally, the tension between agency and determinism that complicates moral judgment of individual and collective action. Although most contemporary reviews of the novel, Shirley Forster points out in her introduction to the text, ignored the "important balance in the novel's stance – between arguing for an inevitable unevenness of fortune, and rejecting the notions of laissez-faire and non-interventionism in favour of apportioning responsibility" (MB xv), it is established right from the start. Gaskell's narrative is marked by the inherent concern and the complex perception of life as/at risk. And her narrator reminds the reader with almost ironic detachment that "we are all of us in the same predicament through life; each with a fear and a hope from childhood to death" (MB 273).

Arguably a main strength of the novel, subtitled *A Tale of Manchester Life*, lies in Gaskell's skilful use of melodrama and a mixing of a detailed, almost

---

of the publishing and reception history of *Mary Barton* and the main critical debates surrounding the text.

documentary-style realism with a domestic tale driven by tragic causality.[34] According to Mary Poovey, in her fictions Gaskell typically uses narratives of individual lives and a plethora of details "to engage the reader imaginatively in a quest for what all people (theoretically) want: domestic security" (1995: 146). *Mary Barton* dramatizes the contemporary risks to this security due to poverty and political unrest. The style of the narrative reinforces its effect because the power of the text – in 1848 and today – is not least caused by "its shocking detail" (Webb 2010: 14). Especially the beginning chapters present a portrayal of "a city balanced precariously over disaster" (Lucas 1977: 37). It is strikingly similar to Friedrich Engels' contemporary account of Manchester, which he considers

> far from black enough to convey a true impression of the filth, ruin, and uninhabitableness, the defiance of all considerations of cleanliness, ventilation, and health which characterise the construction of this single district, containing at least twenty to thirty thousand inhabitants. [...] If any one wishes to see in how little space a human being can move, how little air – and *such* air! – he can breathe, how little of civilisation he may share and yet live, it is only necessary to travel hither. Everything which here arouses horror and indignation is of recent origin, belongs to the industrial epoch. (Engels 1892: 53; original emphasis)

Although Mary's existence is to some extent removed from the mill workers' and she is spared the factory life herself because her father sends her to work at a dressmaker's instead, politics and social order break into her world. Her family life is threatened by the political crisis as well as by various accidents and calamities; she very nearly loses all the people she loves. In fact, an extraordinarily high number of deaths occur in *Mary Barton*, as many critical readings have noted. This aligns Gaskell's with Engels' account in so far that "one of the inescapable facts about Manchester life was that it was soon over" (Lucas 1977: 42). In the narrative the deaths are either related as dramatic action, detached or

---

[34] For an analysis of Gaskell's style and the use of melodrama in *Mary Barton* see Gallagher (1985: 75–78), or D'Albertis (1997: 56–58). Despite all 'realist' details, Gaskell openly acknowledged the limits of her knowledge of working-class life in the preface to *Mary Barton*, and also alludes apologetically to her ignorance of the workings of trade and of political economy. However, for writers like Gaskell in particular the novel is a mode of representation superior to the explanatory modes of classical political economy. It allows for dramatizing working-class homes and poverty through simple, haunting images rather than statistics. Mary Poovey expresses this view clearly, saying: "Whereas Kay and Chadwick calculated poverty through tables of whitewashed buildings and diminished life expectancies, Gaskell captures want through citing an insufficiency of teacups and a meal solely made of raw oatmeal" (1995: 145).

sentimental report, or mentioned in flashbacks. But all add up to show the impact of sickness and death among the poor families, the fragility of human life and an "almost universal condition of bereavement" (Lucas 1977: 32).[35] In some cases, like Mary's father or her aunt Esther, death is also a means to relieve a character's (moral) suffering. The death of Mrs Barton in childbirth is the first sudden accident in the narrative and shows the helplessness of the characters: "Nothing could have saved her – there has been some shock to the system" (MB 22). The incident furthermore facilitates the tragic decline of Mary's father and puts him at risk from destructive outside forces: "One of the good influences over John Barton's life had departed that night. One of the ties which bound him down to the gentle humanities of earth was loosened, and henceforward the neighbours all remarked he was a changed man. His gloom and his sternness became habitual instead of occasional" (MB 22). Despite his grief, however, Mr Barton's reaction and the funeral arrangements show how the institutionalization of insurance and risk management has reached the working-class: "He could think on what was to be done, could plan for the funeral, could calculate the necessity of soon returning to his work, as the extravagance of the past night would leave them short of money if he long remained away from the mill. He was in a club, so that money was provided for the burial" (MB 22).

One of the central incidents in the novel that dramatizes a "spectacle of unmanaged risk" (Fyfe 2010: 316) is the burning of Carson's mill in Chapter 5. It is not directly related to the main plot line but significant with regard to the general discourse and staging of collective risk. After first hearing about the fire, John Barton says: "Ay, there is a mill on fire somewhere, sure enough by the light, and it will be a rare blaze, for there's not a drop o' water to be got. And much Carsons will care, for they're well insured, and the machines are a' th' oud-fashioned kind. See if they don't think it a fine thing" (MB 49). Later, his assessment proves indeed to be accurate and underlines the different impact of the accident on the classes: "So this was an excellent opportunity, Messrs. Carson thought, for refitting their factory with first-rate improvements, for which the insurance money would amply pay. They were in no hurry about the business, however. The weekly drain of wages given for labour, useless in the present state of the market, was stopped" (MB 56). In other words, insurance allows the mill owners to profit from the accident, while the closing of the mill brings unemployment for the workers. By placing an industrial accident at

---

35 The following deaths occur or are referred to in the narrative: Mrs Barton, Mary's little brother Tom Barton, Mr Ogden, Davenport, the young Wilson twins, Mr Wilson, Job Legh's daughter, Harry Carson, Alice, Mr Barton, and Esther. See Gravil (2007: 31–32).

the beginning of the narrative, Gaskell's text highlights how class divisions are also played out in terms of risk and relations to uncertainty.

Especially the first part of the novel shows the multifaceted presence of risk for the poor, underlining illness and want. For example, people fear typhoid, which is "brought on by miserable living, filthy neighbourhood, and great depression of mind and body", but lack any means of taking precaution against the highly infectious disease: "But the poor are fatalists with regard to infection! and well for them it is so, for in their crowded dwellings no invalid can be isolated" (MB 59). By relating the episode of how Barton fails to buy food and medicine for his little son, the narrative furthermore suggest the feeling of impotence in the face of potentially manageable risk as a cause for Barton's later crime:

> [...] for weeks Barton was out of work, living on credit. It was during this time that his little son, the apple of his eye, the cynosure of all his strong power of love, fell ill of the scarlet fever. [...] Everything, the doctor said, depended on good nourishment, on generous living, to keep up the little fellow's strength, in the prostration in which the fever had left him. Mocking words! when the commonest food in the house would not furnish one little meal. [...] Hungry himself, almost to an animal pitch of ravenousness, but with the bodily pain swallowed up in anxiety for his little sinking lad, he stood at one of the shop windows where all edible luxuries are displayed; haunches of venison, Stilton cheeses, moulds of jelly – all appetising sights to the common passer-by. [...] Barton returned home with a bitter spirit of wrath in his heart to see his only boy a corpse! (MB 24)

The increasing anxiety and depression of the Barton and Wilson families is directly contrasted with the careless ease of the Carsons. This becomes obvious in Harry Carson's reaction to the impending strike of the workers; for him the conflict is hardly more than a game: "He liked the excitement of the affair. He liked the attitude of resistance. He was brave, and he liked the idea of personal danger" (MB 167–8). Meanwhile for Jem, who is also characterized by courage, risk-taking is motivated by necessity rather than pleasure. To return to the depiction of the burning mill, the scene builds up to a dramatic moment when the crowd of people watches the collapse of the building while Jem dares to rescue the last workers from inside, against the odds of the catastrophe:

> The crowd pressed back from under; firemen's helmets appeared at the window, holding the ladder firm [...]. The multitude did not even whisper while he crossed the perilous bridge, which quivered under him; but when he was across, safe comparatively in the factory, a cheer arose for an instant, checked, however, almost immediately, by the uncertainty of the result, and the desire not in any way to shake the nerves of the brave fellow who had cast his life on such a die. (MB 52–53)

Gaskell's narrative shows the fascination of the onlookers with the dangerous spectacle but also includes reflection on the value of objects and the issue of loss and compensation; "what were magnificent terrible flames – what were falling timbers or tottering walls, in comparison with human life?" (MB 51). However, while one can see interconnections of Gaskell's novel with "the emerging discourse of risk management and fire insurance in particular" (Fyfe 2010: 317), the text displays no interest in investigating the actual cause of the fire: "Unlike writers of loss in the insurance business, Gaskell is less interested in causation than in risk and how we interpret it" (2010: 333). Following the argument of Paul Fyfe, who stresses the shared subject-matter and concerns of insurance and novel writing at the time,[36] a focus on risk management in the Industrial novel allows for a new integration of narrative form and content, offering an "opportunity to elaborate more nuanced histories of novelistic realism in interdisciplinary terms" (2010: 346). Understanding both insurance and industrial writing as being essentially concerned with producing "fictions of loss" adds a useful and specific functionality to realist narrative techniques (like the recording of events, construction of plausible causality and assigning responsibility to the actors involved, collection of details and impressions etc.), which is tied to an awareness of risk and accident.

But Gaskell's fictional negotiation of risk is certainly more complex than any insurance file and encompasses in particular also an important affective domain. In contrast to her father, Mary matures into a morally and socially responsible, action-taking woman in the course of the novel. She has to manage various risks, several related to the men in her life. Initially Mary considers the attractions of a marriage to Harry Carson, before realizing that her heart firmly belongs to Jem Wilson. The decision is motivated by a weighing of the gain of financial security against the prize of denying her true feelings: "What were these hollow vanities to her, now she had discovered the passionate secret of her soul? [...] She had hitherto been walking in grope-light towards a precipice; but in the clear revelation of that past hour she saw her danger, and turned away

---

[36] Fyfe stresses the similarities between insurance and novelistic writing because both genres aim for realistic descriptions in order to make readers/clients accept the representation of risk, event, loss, and compensation. Using Gaskell's text as example, he explains: "The discourse of risk management offers a different way to think about the generic inconsistencies and 'formal paradoxes' for which a novel like *Mary Barton* has received critical attention. [...] By experimenting with descriptive practices and attitudes toward probability, the novel proposes itself as a dedicated domain in which problems of risk can be considered" (2010: 330). See also the chapter "Industrial Accidents and Novel Insurances" in Fyfe's study *By Accident or Design: Writing the Victorian Metropolis* (2015).

resolutely and for ever" (MB 128). Despite John Barton's crime, Harry Carson becomes and remains the true villain in the novel. Mary soon comes to fear him in a sense that even implies the potential of sexual assault from his side: "She was weary of her life for him. From blandishments he had even gone to threats – threats that whether she would or not she should be his" (MB 169). Even after Harry is killed, and thus removed as a threat, Mary continues to suffer from his case. Jem is wrongly arrested for the murder, which causes the dilemma for Mary of wanting to save her lover without incriminating her father. Meanwhile the people who originally set out to protect Mary and manage the risks caused by her father's crime and her situation, Jem and her aunt Esther, each end up in prison. Nonetheless, Mary achieves her goal of saving Jem by making a precarious journey to Liverpool and a boat trip which secures the testimony of Will, Jem's cousin, who can provide his alibi for the night of the murder. She successfully avoids another risk lurking for her in the background, namely sharing the fate of her unhappy aunt Esther, a 'fallen woman', who is forced to make her living as a prostitute on the streets.

Gaskell emphasizes Mary's fragility, but also her strength for surviving the hardship and cunning in times of crisis. Anxieties are continuously mounting for the heroine, reaching a climax halfway through the novel: "Everything seemed going wrong. Will gone; her father gone – [...] Her heart began to despair, too, about Jem. [...] And, as if all this aggregate of sorrowful thoughts was not enough, here was this new woe, of poor Alice's paralytic stroke" (MB 195). The narrative voice asks the reader to empathically consider the psychological burden of the heroine caused as much by realities as by the anticipation of calamity: "But think of Mary and what she was enduring. Picture to yourself (for I cannot tell you) the armies of thoughts that met and clashed in her brain; and then imagine the effort it cost her to be calm, and quiet, and even in a faint way, cheerful and smiling at times" (MB 262). Mary's characterization in particular shows the narrative forging of new links between the social-economic and the political realms and the emergent psychological domain, as Poovey has noted (1995: 150).[37] Furthermore, the narrative underlines the limits (or rather the failure) of rational calculations, with the aim of averting risks, when it comes to human character and behaviour. In one of the final scenes, Job Legh, the wise grandfather of Mary's friend Margaret, says to Mr Carson: "You can never work facts as you would fixed quantities, and say, given two facts, and the product is so and so. God has given men feelings and passions which cannot be

---

[37] See also Adams's argument that Gaskell's main emphasis "falls on the sufferings – physical and psychological – of workers at the mercy of a newly volatile economy" (2012: 105).

worked into the problem, because they are for ever changing and uncertain" (MB 371). The plot of *Mary Barton* is thus shaped by various contingencies and cruelties either man-made or caused by randomness. While the text confirms the unpredictability of providence on the one hand, on the other, Fyfe suggests, "Gaskell offers the novel itself – if not as a substitute for probability thinking, then as a laboratory for the study of its contingencies, limitations, irrationalities, and human quanta" (2010: 343). The text illustrates the contemporary dissatisfaction with the reorientation of probabilistic thinking towards statistical frequency, which has no practical value for the individual's interpretation of single events and, if anything, affirms the experience and threat of random accidents despite the regularities found in large numbers.

Considering Gaskell's treatment of religious faith in the novel, a secular assessment and awareness of risk clash with an unwavering faith in divine providence. For example, after confessing her fears which are precisely caused by the knowledge that prayers will not avert the dangers or miraculously improve Alice's health or her own failing eyesight, Margaret guiltily says to Mary: "An anxious mind is never a holy mind" (MB 46). In a nuanced analysis of Gaskell's writing and the attitude towards causality and free will informed by her Unitarian faith, Catherine Gallagher argues that Gaskell's fictions allow for multiple explanatory modes, for the existence of moral freedom and responsibility alongside inescapable determinism by social circumstances, although her plots are very much shaped by a Christian teleological tradition (Gallagher 1985: 74; 65 ff). Perhaps the best example of Gaskell's complicated depiction of causation and moral ambivalence is the development of John Barton. He epitomizes the view of poor, dissatisfied manual labourer as a threatening yet inevitably tragic figure, driven by a rage against his master, like Frankenstein's monster. It is worth quoting Gaskell's characterization at length:

> John Barton's overpowering thought, [...] the only feeling that remained clear and undisturbed in the tumult of his heart, was hatred to the one class, and keen sympathy with the other. [...] No education had given him wisdom; and without wisdom, even love, with all its effects, too often works but harm. He acted to the best of his judgment, but it was a widely-erring judgment. The actions of the uneducated seem to me typified in those of Frankenstein, that monster of many human qualities, ungifted with a soul, a knowledge of the difference between good and evil. The people rise up to life; they irritate us, they terrify us, and we become their enemies. [...]. Why have we made them what they are; a powerful monster, yet without the inner means for peace and happiness? John Barton became a Chartist, a Communist, all that is commonly called wild and visionary. Ay! but being visionary is something. It shows a soul, a being not altogether sensual; a creature who looks forward for others, if not for himself. (MB 165)

Like a scientific experiment gone wrong and having spiralled out of control, Gaskell here brandishes the egoism inherent in a system that can only produce mutual reproach and harm and tentatively suggests education as the only way out. John Barton's political radicalism appears to be proof that he is in a way corrupted and incapable of moral choice; at the same time he is not devoid of moral agency and responsibility. In the end, he is spared any legal punishment and dies worn down by physical decline and haunted by his crime, but in the arms of Mr Carson, who finally shows some understanding for his motives and the condition of the workers.

The second half of the novel is dominated by speculations about Jem's trial and each of the working-class characters' "consciousness of some great impending calamity" (MB 240). The narrative dedicates much room to speculation about the risks and the probable outcome of the trial,[38] with Mary being the central focalizer.

> All the unfavourable contingencies she had, until now, forbidden herself to dwell upon, came forward to her mind – the possibility, the bare possibility, of Jem being an accomplice in the murder – the still greater possibility that he had not fulfilled his intention of going part of the way with Will, but had been led off by some little accidental occurrence from his original intention; and that he had spent the evening with those, whom it was now too late to bring forward as witnesses. (MB 275)

Driven by the desire to prove Jem's innocence, Mary is no longer able to ignore the evidence of her father's guilt, which makes the balancing of risks impossible: "Monday: that was the day after tomorrow, and on Tuesday, life and death would be tremendous realities to her lover; or else death would be an awful certainty to her father" (MB 256). Due to Mary's perseverance in locating Will, who testifies in court in Jem's favour, the dreaded verdict brings relief and the exculpation of Jem. Moreover, after Mary's court appearance, Jem is finally assured of her feelings for him. Yet there is no immediate happiness for the couple. With regard to risk management, their roles are reversed. It is now Jem who has to fear for Mary's life as she falls dangerously ill with a nervous fever: "He could not hope. The elasticity of his heart had been crushed out of him by early sorrows; and now, especially, the dark side of everything seemed to be presented to him. What if she died, [...]. What if (worse than death) she remained a poor gibbering maniac all her life long [...] terror-distracted as she was now, and no one able to comfort her!" (MB 326). After her recovery and the reunion with Jem, Mary still has one final task to master. She has to return to her family home all the while

---

[38] See, for instance, Jonathan Grossman's article "Telltale Evidence in Mary Barton" (2002).

"the knowledge of her father's capability of guilt seemed to have opened a dark gulf in his character, into the depths of which she trembled to look. [...] she could have cried aloud with terror, at the scenes her fancy conjured up. But her filial duty, nay, her love and gratitude for many deeds of kindness done to her as a little child, conquered all fear" (MB 340). After her father's death soon afterwards, the narrative concludes with the couple escaping the problems of urban industrialization and Jem's tainted reputation in England and starting their life together in Canada. Although it thus ends traditionally with a glimpse of pastoral married bliss of Mary and Jem, and a second union between Will and Margaret on the horizon, Gaskell's humanitarian conclusion is pessimistic, at least with regard to any possibility of resolving conflicts in the present and in England, as many critics have noted (see e.g. Webb 2010: 36). The characters have to be removed to the New World in order to find better economic circumstances and hope of happiness.

Concluding, one can agree with John Lucas who has observed an anarchic energy at work in fiction of Elizabeth Gaskell, arguing that beneath her pious, middle-class air, striving for harmony and reconciliation, lies a constant destructive force, "revealing different patterns of inevitability, of antagonism, misunderstandings, hatred" (Lucas 1977: 13). Moreover he stresses an awareness of change as a disruption of connection and continuity in Gaskell's fiction (1977: 15). This aspect is perhaps even more pronounced in *North and South* and highlights the sense of risk permeating Gaskell's texts. Remarkable in this context is a comment by the narrator at the end of *Mary Barton*. It underlines an inherently secular awareness of risk and the need and possibility of taking precautions in the face of statistically anticipated accidents and crises, which is integral to the intertwined industrial-political and domestic-romantic plot lines:

> There are stages in the contemplation and endurance of great sorrow, which endow men with the same earnestness and clearness of thought that in some of old took the form of Prophecy. To those who have large capability of loving and suffering, united with great power of firm endurance, there comes a time in their woe, when they are lifted out of the contemplation of their individual case into a searching inquiry into the nature of their calamity, and the remedy (if remedy there be) which may prevent its recurrence to others as well as to themselves. (MB 373)

6.3 The Danger of Power Relations: *Shirley*

The plot of Charlotte Brontë's *Shirley* (1849) is also shaped and driven by a sense of life – as the status quo – threatened by class aggression. Written in the significant year of political upheaval, 1848, the narrative describes the industrial depression, the turn against mill owners and Luddite activism in the Yorkshire region in 1811–12, a time when political events where shaking the stable grounds of the middle-classes: "The throes of a sort of moral earthquake were felt heaving under the hills of the northern counties.[...] Misery generates hate" (S 23). In the beginning, Brontë's omniscient narrator warns the reader that nothing but a bleak story awaits him/her: "Do you anticipate sentiment, and poetry, and reverie? Do you expect passion, and stimulus, and melodrama? Calm your expectations; reduce them to a lowly standard. Something real, cool and solid lies before you; something as unromantic as Monday morning" (S 3). The narrator goes on to say that the reader shall still "have a taste of the exiting, perhaps towards the middle and close of the meal" (S 3). This refers to the much criticized climax of the narrative, the depiction of the midnight attack on the mill, which remains a rather briefly described episode and is literally shrouded in darkness.[39] The first part of *Shirley*, however, sketches a developing romance between Caroline Helstone and Robert Moore against the background of a rising threat of an attack on Moore's mill and his new machinery.[40] Another major plotline focuses on the close friendship between Caroline and Shirley Keeldar, a headstrong woman of independent means; later Louis Moore, a language tutor and Robert's brother, is added to the circle of love interests of the two women and the novel ends rather conventionally with a double marriage.

Critics have found fault with Charlotte Brontë for failing to integrate the different narrative strands more fully and for apparently equalling the plight of working-class men and their fear of unemployment with the romantic sorrows of middle-class women and their suffering from a lack of meaningful occupation.[41] Utilizing the industrial setting and the social conflicts as background,

---

39 See especially Eagleton's criticism. He says that "the major protagonist, the working class, is distinguished primarily by its absence", and "wholly invisible" (1975: 49; 47) at the most crucial moment in the narrative.
40 *Shirley* was published in 1849, a year after the official defeat of Chartism. Different opinions exist why Charlotte Brontë chose to date the class-conflict in the text back to the Luddite riots of 1812 rather than deal with present conflicts. According to Eagleton, "when *Shirley* was written the contemporary class-struggle was still too fraught and precarious an issue to render it an ideal context for such an assured outcome. Even so, there can be no doubt that Chartism is the unspoken subject of *Shirley*" (1975: 45). Adding to this, he views Luddism as a strategic foil against which to mediate the current fear of Chartism, because this past period of class-conflict had a comparatively good outcome (147). Alternatively, one can argue that Brontë chose to depict Luddism because she had more personal experience with it (cf. Gezari 1992: 110).
41 Igor Webb writes, "the working-class characters lack typicality. In contrast, the novel's treatment of single women [...] is unsurpassed in English fiction of the Industrial Revolution. Shirley shows what it means to be a woman in a male world" (1981: 146). The question of the authen-

the narrative does show a distinctly feminist streak. According to Janet Gezari, *Shirley* has even "a stronger claim than *Jane Eyre* to be called Brontë's feminist manifesto" (1992: 124). This argument is interesting to consider with regard to the depiction of gender roles and risk-taking in the novel. Though one arguably takes priority over the other, both the industrial-economic and feminist-romantic plotlines are inherently connected to the perception of risk. As the close reading will show, this is reinforced by an explicit rhetoric employed throughout the narrative; in *Shirley*, risk is mainly negotiated through dialogue and is integral to the characterization of the main protagonists.

Tackling class issues, Brontë's text places more importance on gender inequality than Gaskell or Dickens' and highlights the "condition-of-women"-question in the context of the "condition-of-England"-debate. In comparison to *Mary Barton*, there is little description of poverty and the oppressions of working-class life; the focus on conflict is firmly shifted onto the middle-class (Caroline, Robert, Louis) and the upper-class (Shirley). As Penny Boumelha remarks (1990: 99), while *Shirley* constructs an analogy between the invisibility of working-class men and middle-class women, it ignores the issue of working-class women. Ultimately, the portrayal of women's restrictions and need for occupation, which is denied by society, ends up being at least as, if not more, haunting than the industrial conflict.

Similar to Burney or Austen's fiction, Brontë's novel illustrates women's anxieties around the marriage plot. In *Shirley*, the story of the marriage between Reverend Helstone and Mary Cave, which is told early on in the narrative, functions as a warning parable. Being a tale of death from a broken heart, because Mary Cave married Mr Helstone although she truly loved Mr Yorke, it suggests how making the wrong choice of partner, regardless of the reasons, is crippling emotionally as well as physically. In contrast to Defoe's heroines for whom the wrong husband typically brought only financial ruin, Mary Cave's death and later the story of Mrs Pryor signify that marriage can be degrading, dangerous, and even suicidal.[42] It can turn a young, lively woman into a shadow of herself, into "a girl of living marble" (MB 39). Caroline and Shirley discuss the differences between men and women and the state of matrimony several times in the novel; each time the narrative implies that unconventional possibilities, like sisterhood, are in the end "more certain and satisfying than *the dangerous improbability of marriage*" (Webb 1981: 149; my emphasis). For example, during one of their walks

---

ticity or centrality of giving a voice to the working-class is not relevant in the present context, but has, of course, important implications for the specific discourse of risk in the novel.

42 On the function of the story of Mary Cave as a manifestation of the anxieties of the heroines Shirley and Caroline see Gezari (1992: 95–96; 104).

Shirley says to Caroline that she, firstly, does not believe that men are "necessarily and universally different from us", and that she is, secondly, weary of the disappointments of marriage, the risks of loss of love and respect and, above all, her freedom: "I could never be my own mistress more. A terrible thought! It suffocates me! [...] I can comfortably fold my independence round me like a mantle, and drop my pride like a veil, and withdraw to solitude. If married, that could not be" (S 161). While Shirley, being independently rich, has little to gain but much loose by taking a husband, Caroline is devastated when her dreams of marrying Robert seem to slip away and she is uncertain about her future – "What was I created for, I wonder? Where is my place in the world?" (S 133) – and worries about running the risk of joining the "very unhappy race" (S 134) of old maids. However, both Caroline's uncle and Mrs Pryor, who turns out to be her estranged mother, share Shirley's view of the considerable hazards of marriage. Mrs Pryor says: "It is never wholly happy. [...] There is, perhaps, a possibility of content under peculiar circumstances, such as are seldom combined; but it is as well not to run the risk – you may make fatal mistakes" (S 284). And she explains further: "I only wish to warn you, and to prove that the single should not be too anxious to change their state, as they may change for the worse" (S 285). The emphasis is placed on the fact that marriage for women, unlike for men, poses a risk of unhappy imprisonment. Explaining to her daughter why she had to leave her behind as a baby, Mrs Pryor's own life story is revealed as one of desperately trying to escape from an abusive marriage. She describes her feeling at risk to the extent that she took on another identity in order to

> live unmolested. [...] threats were uttered of forcing me to return to bondage. It could not be. [...] My new name sheltered me. I resumed under its screen my old occupation of teaching. At first it scarcely procured me the means of sustaining life; but how [...] safe seemed the darkness and chill of an unkindled hearth when no lurid reflection from terror crimsoned its desolation! (S 324–325)

But entering into matrimony does not only hold potential dangers for the women in the narrative. Robert, burdened by the economic struggles of his business and a lack of cash, explains why he literally cannot afford romance: "I have settled it decidedly that marriage and love are superfluities, intended only for the rich, who live at ease, and have no need to take thought for the morrow; or desperations" (S 125). Like John Thornton in *North and South*, Robert Moore stems from a family-line of merchants, once wealthy, but "disastrous speculations had loosened by degrees the foundations of their credit. [....] he aspired one day to discharge them, and to rebuild the fallen house of Gérard and Moore on a scale at least equal to its former greatness" (S 21). Aside from the usual ups and downs of trade, his position as a merchant of foreign ancestry in Yorkshire is doubly risky, and he becomes the object of hate of the dissatisfied workers who view him as a threat to their jobs and interests: "Hollow's Mill was the place held most abominable; Gérard Moore, in his double character of semi-foreigner and thorough-going progressist, the man most abominated" (S 23).

Although Robert fears the ties of a family – "a nursery full of bairns you can neither clothe nor feed, and very soon an anxious, faded mother; and then bankruptcy, discredit – a life-long struggle" (S 126) – he is portrayed as a determined risk-taker as far as his trade and property are concerned. In the course of the novel, Moore's situation worsens because all Yorkshire manufacturers begin to suffer acutely from the British naval blockade of European ports during the Napoleonic wars, which brings trade temporarily to a standstill; after all, "these, they say, are not safe times, thanks to a bad government" (S 30). Out of desperation Robert ventures to propose marriage to Shirley, as this union could save his mill. But the idea of marriage as a means to avert financial risk is not a successful one in Brontë's novel. After Shirley has turned him down, Robert tells Mr Yorke about his newly found courage and strategy: "never more will I mention marriage to a woman unless I feel love. Henceforth credit and commerce may take care of themselves. Bankruptcy may come when it lists. I have done with slavish fear of disaster. I mean to work diligently, wait patiently, bear steadily. [...] No woman shall ever again look at me as Miss Keeldar looked" (S 399).[43] In general, Robert is characterized as a man who not only exactly knows his dangers and can shrewdly assess risk but who thrives on it in the sense that he "liked a silent, sombre, unsafe solitude" (S 23); and is generally not averse to "the seasoning of a little real peril" (S 13). For instance, "Many a time he rode belated over the moors, moonlit or moonless as the case might be, with feelings far more elate, faculties far better refreshed, than when safety and stagnation environed him in the counting-house" (S 287–288).[44]

From the beginning, the novel introduces a concern for the situation and safety of Robert as the representative mill owner (who, in the end, is shot by a worker, but recovers from his wounds). During their dinner conversation, the assembly of the Yorkshire curates worry that Moore, who is currently alone in

---

[43] Still, the ending of *Shirley* sees a similar idealism and deus-ex-machina solution as *North and South*, where the main characters get both love and financial security.

[44] In the novel Moore is presented as a typical representative of his profession and class. For example, Mr Sykes, a fellow business man, says to Mr Helstone, himself a member of the clergy: "You're a man of peace, sir; but we manufacturers, living in the world, and always in turmoil, get quite belligerent. Really, there's an ardour excited by the thoughts of danger that makes my heart pant" (S 99).

6.3 The Danger of Power Relations: *Shirley*

the dark mill, having sent most of his men away to pick up the new machinery, is unaware of the gravity of the danger he is in. They assess the situation as follows:

> 'But there *is* a chance of a row; [...] it is unlikely this night will pass quite tranquilly. You know Moore has resolved to have new machinery, and he expects two wagon-loads of frames and shears from Stilbro' this evening.' [...]
> 'They will bring them in safely and quietly enough, sir.'
> 'Moore says so, and affirms he wants nobody. [...] I call him very careless. He sits in the counting-house with the shutters unclosed; he goes out here and there after dark, wanders right up the hollow, down Fieldhead Lane, among the plantations, just as if he were the darling of the neighbourhood, [...] He takes no warning from the fate of Pearson, nor from that of Armitage – shot, one in his own house and the other on the moor.' (S 10–11; original emphasis)

This excerpt from the long conversation between the curates suffices to illustrate how Robert's character is introduced and prepares for the main dramatic events. The following chapters contain many dialogues about the risks of the acquisition of machinery and Robert's refusal to buckle in the face of obvious danger. Aware of the attacks on other mill owners, Moore says to Malone: "Let them only pay me a visit and take the consequences;" "What these fellows have done to others they may do to me. There is only this difference: most of the manufacturers seem paralyzed when they are attacked" (S 18). Caroline, who only has a rather abstract notion of the threat the current situation poses to mill owners – "My uncle calls these times dangerous" (S 52) – is, however, highly anxious about nightfall and Robert's behaviour. When he asks her to rationally define the perceived danger, she struggles and has to make light of her feelings: "And what danger is to be apprehended, Caroline, when daylight is gone? What peril do you conceive comes as the companion of darkness for me?' 'I am not sure that I can define my fears, but we all have a certain anxiety at present about our friends'" (S 52). Later on in the novel, Caroline grows a bit more self-assured and understanding of the industrial conflict, and, like Margaret in *North and South*, suggests sympathy as the best cure for deescalating the tensed situation; "you must not be proud to your workpeople; you must not neglect chances of soothing them; and you must not be of an inflexible nature, uttering a request as austerely as if it were a command" (S 70). Yet there is never any doubt that her motivation for seeking to intervene in the matter, in contrast to Shirley's, is always personal rather than political or business-related. Hearing Caroline's pleas, Robert responds by ridiculing her apparent lack of faith in the divine order of things: "'Nothing will happen, Lina. To speak in your own language, there is a Providence above all – is there not?'" (S 93).

The Luddite attack on Robert's mill happens soon afterwards. The scene is told through the eyes of Shirley and Caroline, who sit sheltered in the Helstone's living room and due to the dark night can only hear the noise from outside: "– a dull tramp of marching feet. It drew near. [...] it was the tread of hundreds. They could see nothing" (S 252). In contrast to Caroline, who is overwhelmed by her fear for Robert, Shirley assesses the situation shrewdly and decides that they can make the way over to the mill to check on him. The scene clearly shows the women's different risk personalities, but also how passion interferes with rational calculation. Shirley says, "you would intelligently and gladly die for Moore. But, in truth, there is no question of death to-night; we run no risk at all" (S 254). To save time, the girls take the more difficult way to the mill across the fields.

> Many a wall checked but did not baffle them. Shirley was surefooted and agile; she could spring like a deer when she chose. Caroline, more timid and less dexterous, fell once or twice, and bruised herself; but she rose again directly, saying she was not hurt. [...] At this point a narrow plank formed the only bridge across it. Shirley had trodden the plank successfully and fearlessly many a time before; Caroline had never yet dared to risk the transit. (S 254–255)

The episode is a test of Caroline's composure and strength, and the narrative focuses more on the women's attempt to warn Robert than on the worker's protest march. When the women arrive at the mill, the darkness still hinders the from seeing the tumult clearly, but they hear angry shouting and deduce that "the fighting animal was roused in every one of those men there struggling together, and was for the time quite paramount above the rational human being" (S 259). Thus, although the violence of the scene is not described, it shows the anxiety surrounding uncontrollable outbursts of working-class anger and the literally 'blind' fear of Caroline. The darkness increases the terror for Shirley too; it heightens the sense of loss order and control. For her, as a member of the ruling class, the risk is not directly physical, but an issue of maintaining superiority and control over property and capital.

In the novel, Shirley and Caroline are depicted as opposites; while Caroline fits the part of the typical Victorian woman, Shirley shows many traits traditionally considered as masculine, above all, her "reckless" behaviour (S 374) and love of danger. Caroline says to her: "My uncle, who is not given to speak well of women, say there are not ten thousand men in England as genuinely fearless as you". And Shirley agrees: "I am fearless, physically; I am never nervous about danger" (S 199). Pushing the gender ambiguities further, Shirley is very much in a man's position, even has a man's name, states, "really I feel quite gentleman-like" (S 153), or does not object to the nickname "Captain Keeldar" (S 155). Several times, Brontë employs humour to reveal gender stereotypes and shows Shirley as being more courageous than many of the men. For example, the curate Mr Donne is terrified by Shirley's bulldog Tartar, deeming him an unsuitable animal for a lady: "A very dangerous dog that, Miss Keeldar. [...] purchase in his stead some sweetly pooty pug or poodle – something appropriate to the fair sex. Ladies generally like lap-dogs". Nonchalantly, Shirley replies: "Perhaps I am an exception. [...] Tartar frightened you terribly, Mr. Donne. I hope you won't take any harm" (S 209–10). Throughout the novel, Shirley displays business instincts and a positive outlook despite the political crisis, a standpoint she can afford due to her own safe financial situation: "The neighbourhood seemed to grow calmer. [...] Shirley was sanguine that the evil she wished to avert was almost escaped, that the threatened storm was passing over. With the approach of summer she felt certain that trade would improve" (S 217). Robert, however, is less high-spirited. In the end, it is Shirley who rescues him from his dire straits through her investment in the mill. Generally, she is shown to be extraordinarily resilient in times of crisis, both with regard to her social position and her character. Consequently, she brushes away Robert's concerns in a conversation with Caroline, who says: "'He fears, probably, to occasion your uneasiness.' [Shirley:] 'An unnecessary precaution. I am of elastic materials, not soon crushed'" (S 236).

As the characterization of Shirley, Caroline, and Robert has shown so far, the differences between the main characters are largely captured in their attitude towards risk. Significantly, the two final couples (Shirley-Louis, Caroline-Robert) are mismatched, or rather opposites, with regard to agency, temperament, and economic power.[45] Moreover, in each case a risk-taker is paired with a cautious, risk-averse character. Louis and Caroline are both of little means and constrained by their social position, while Robert and Shirley are more powerful. For Caroline, who feels the limiting bonds of her femininity as well as her financial situation acutely, Shirley is a close friend but also a rival, and she believes she will lose Robert to her: "I am poverty and incapacity; Shirley is wealth and power. And she is beauty too, and love" (S 194). This negative assessment signals Caroline's deterioration into a prolonged serious illness, induced at least partially, the narrative implies, by her tormenting dark thoughts and a lack of hope. She was, "by this time free from illusions: she took a sufficiently grave view of the future" (S 174). Attempting to explain her nervous condition to her mother, Caroline says: "I see things under a darker aspect than I used to do. I have fears I never used to have – not of ghosts, but of omens

---

[45] As several critics have noted, the more logical pairing with regard to economic status and character would have been Shirley-Robert and Caroline-Louis. See especially Eagleton (1975: 58).

and disastrous events; and I have an inexpressible weight on my mind which I would give the world to shake off, and I cannot do it" (S 179–180). Caroline's illness – her nervous breakdown – appears, on the one hand, as an acute identity crisis. With marriage or becoming a governess being her only options, she seemingly can chose only between different forms of imprisonment, disguised as freedom. Furthermore, she suffers from a typically Victorian malaise, lovesickness. As Eagleton argues, Charlotte Brontë's novels "reveal a dangerous 'residue' of potentially uncontrollable emotion" (1992: 86). In *Shirley*, paralleling the threat of the worker's agitation, Caroline's deep, unexpressed passion for Robert appears potentially life threatening, causing her to fade "like any flower in drought" (S 313). As the narrator comments, only by the young, who are unaware of the dangers, "That perilous passion [...] is believed to be an unqualified good" (S 73). While Caroline puts herself at risk by falling deeply in love, the men in turn perceive her as a steady, safe choice for a wife. Therefore, Louis decides she is well suited for Robert, but not for him: "She is certainly pretty [....] all insular grace and purity; but where is there anything to alter, anything to endure, anything to reprimand, to be anxious about?" (S 390). In direct contrast, Shirley "is peculiar, and more dangerous to take as a wife – rashly" (S 448) and Louis is deeply attracted to her daring and strength. Again, depth of feeling is also in this case shown to be inseparable to a sense of precariousness: "I wish there was danger she should lose me, as there is risk I shall lose her. No; final loss I do not fear, but long delay" (S 469).

The relationship between Shirley and Louis is presented as a constant power struggle. Louis is the only one to whom Shirley admits her own weakness. The scene when she confesses to him her fears of dying from a bite by a rabies-infected dog is very telling in this regard. Although the whole chapter 28, "Phoebe" is mostly neglected in the criticism of the novel, it reveals a lot about the Victorian perception of risk, oscillating between grounding on scientific (here medical) knowledge, and irrational fear. It shows the obligation to keep up appearances at all cost, as well as a strikingly modern approach to the risk of death: Essentially, Shirley is convinced that she is dying and asks Louis to assist her with euthanasia before the virus seizes her completely and robs her of control over her faculties. Ultimately, her apprehension, which "hung over her like a cloud which no breeze could stir or disperse" (S 369), is shown to be much more severe than her actual condition. Although she vehemently denies being ill to others, she looks increasingly pale and sickly. Rumours increase when it becomes known that she has apparently taken precautions for the event of her death by making her will. Louis tries to console her: "Your pain is mental.' [...] I believe confession in your case, would be half equivalent to cure.' 'No,' said Shirley abruptly. 'I wish that were at all probable; but I am afraid it is not" (S 377). Finally, she opens up to Louis, shows him the mark on her arm, and admits: "Small as it is, it has taken my sleep away, and made me nervous, thin, and foolish; because, on account of that little mark, I am obliged to look forward to a possibility that has its terrors" (S 378). After informing Louis about the origins of the mark and her having been bitten by Phoebe, a "raging mad" dog (S 379), she explains how the perceived risk of dying has pushed her courage and independence to the limits. Louis reacts seriously but calmly to her story. He inquires: "You apprehend the effects of the virus? You anticipate an indefinitely threatening, dreadful doom? [...] Do you truly expect that you will be seized with hydrophobia, and die raving mad?" After Shirley confirms: "I *expect* it, and have *feared* it", Louis annihilates her fears with rational arguments: "I feel assured it would turn out that there is no danger of your dying at all. [...] I doubt whether the smallest particle of virus mingled with your blood; and if it did, let me assure you that, young, healthy, faultlessly sound as you are, no harm will ensue. For the rest, I shall inquire whether the dog was really mad. I hold she was not mad" (S 380; original emphasis). This scene characterizes the relationship between Shirley and Louis as based on trust and mutual understanding. In addition, like it is the case between Robert and Caroline, or between Margaret and John in *North and South*, the realization and expression of feelings is tied to a perception of the self or the other as being at risk.

Like the other industrial novels, Brontë's fiction notes all the tensions and contradictions but fails to resolve them at all or in a non-conventional manner. The ending of *Shirley* unites the romantic and industrial plot lines and brings a return to safety on all levels. Shirley's business partnership with Robert allows him to look forward to a bright future: "now I shall not give up business; now I shall not leave England; [...] for the first time in my life, I can securely build". And an overjoyed Caroline asks her future husband: "You are saved? Your heavy difficulties are lifted?" (S 477). Meanwhile Shirley's final question, as characteristic of her deep underlying fear as Caroline's, is addressed to Louis: "And are we equal, then, sir? are we equal at last?" (S 464). Ultimately, *Shirley* seeks to occupy a "compromising middle-ground" (Eagleton 1975: 60) and does not envision any radical break or reform. Or one can argue that the radicalism of the text is at least not found in its treatment of class conflict. As far as transgression of conventional gender roles is concerned, it is certainly more progressive. Still, Webb rightly says: "The alternatives to passionate love, as well as its dangers, are not taken in the novel as far as they might be, but neither are they fudged" (1981: 153).

6.4 No Way Out of Coketown: *Hard Times*

According to F.R. Leavis' still valid assessment, Charles Dickens' *Hard Times* (1854) is "a moral fable",[46] written to reveal "a comprehensive vision, one in which the inhumanities of Victorian civilization are seen as fostered and sanctioned by a hard philosophy, the aggressive formulation of an inhumane spirit" (1948: 228; 227). Without arguing in any way that social criticism is absent from Dickens' other novels, as, of course, rather the opposite is true,[47] *Hard Times* is perhaps the one of Dickens' fictions "that asks most clearly to be read not as a mere fictional world but as a commentary on a contemporary crisis" (Schor 2001: 67). The plot acutely illustrates the risk of estrangement stemming from industrial labour, the meaninglessness of statistical inquiry and the despair which comes from a Utilitarian outlook, a rational 'adding up' of facts and a lack of individualism, passion, and sympathy. Unsurprisingly then, Dickens' text is often cited in accounts of the history of probability theory as an "antistatistical tract" (Hacking 1990: 117), or a "bitter anti-statistical novel" (Gigerenzer et al. 1989: 291).[48]

The fact that the text is mainly read and understood as a criticism of Victorian civilization[49] and of industrialization and utilitarianism[50] from a moral-humanist perspective is important especially when comparing Dickens' novel to the industrial fictions of Brontë and Gaskell. A main distinguishing element is that, as Raymond Williams puts it, "*Hard Times* is an analysis of Industrialism, rather than experience of it" (1958: 93). Told from the perspective of a detached, omniscient third-person narrator, it is a bleak portrayal of the ficti-

---

[46] Although Leavis did not include Dickens in his canon of authors of *The Great Tradition*, he did make an exception for *Hard Times* as the only Dickens' novel "controlled throughout to a unifying and organizing significance" (1948: 19), adding though, that this might simply be due to the text's comparative brevity and smaller scale.

[47] Dickens' writings has always engaged with industrial culture, before and after *Hard Times*. Shortly after the serialization of the novel in *Household Words*, in April 1854, Dickens ran an essay, entitled "On Strike", in which he expressed his sympathy with the workers (see Childers 2001: 89). Comparably to the attack on the Utilitarian antipathy towards imagination and an anti-human education dominated by rational inquiry, we find a harsh criticism of governmental incompetence and a neglect of human needs also in *Little Dorrit* (1857).

[48] Examples from the text will be given in the following. For the argument that the novel "expresses a forcefully anti-statistical rhetoric" see also Jordan (2010: 25).

[49] For a summary of reception of the novel from this perspective see, e.g., Amigoni (2011: 19–36).

[50] For a reading of the text with an explicit focus on Dickens and a criticism of Utilitarianism see, e.g., Gallagher, who describes *Hard Times* as an "explicitly Carlylean satire on Benthamism" (2006: 65).

tious Coketown and its citizens. Although "Dickens is as interested in the ruin of the individual as in the tangles of the system" (Schor 2001: 70), the narrative account of Coketown is schematic and satirical rather than dramatic or emotional. It dissects in detail the unhappy states of the characters, each representing a different type or ideology. Thus the characters do not really become individuals in their own right, but function as parts of a system in Dickens' dark satire.

Significantly, the text, which is dedicated to Thomas Carlyle and engages with many issues surrounding the 'condition-of-England' debate, opens not in a factory but the schoolroom of the hard-core utilitarian Thomas Gradgrind. The first scene shows the preoccupation with two main fields of statistical inquiry at the time. Firstly, Victorian education and its proficiency, and secondly, the general obsession with numbers and empirical 'factuality'. Mr Gradgrind, who is easily summed up by his belief that "Facts alone are wanted in life" (HT 3), has only one objective in his teaching and, to his pupils and the outside observer, "seemed a kind of cannon loaded to the muzzle with facts, and prepared to blow them clean out of the regions of childhood at one discharge" (HT 4). A challenge to his teaching method is Sissy Jupe, the little circus girl, who struggles to define a horse according to his exacting standards. Consequently, he advises her to discard all fancy and imagination and to only use "for all these purposes, combinations and modifications [...] of mathematical figures which are susceptible of proof and demonstration" (HT 5). After the departure of Sissy's father, she is taken in by the Gradgrind family and becomes a test case for re-education. However, the girl's optimism, creativity, and empathy prove hard to break. This does not go unnoticed by Gradgrind, who sums up: "You are extremely deficient in your facts. [...] You are altogether backward, and below the mark" (HT 70). Through the character of Gradgrind and his attitude towards Sissy Dickens' narrative reveals a common prejudice of the educated middle-class citizen, who takes extreme pride in rationalism and efficiency. Borrowing the words of J.S. Mill, it indicates a view of poor people as suffering from a "deficiency in the power of reasoning and calculation, which makes then insensible to their own direct personal interests" (Mill 1967: 377–78). However, while Sissy's firm anti-statistical outlook sets her apart from the Gradgrind family, it allows her to cope with the harsh circumstances and not fall into despair. What makes her stay is precisely having hope against all odds; it was "the result of no arithmetical process, was self-imposed in defiance of all calculation, and went dead against any table of probabilities that any Actuary would have drawn up from the premises. The girl believed that her father had not deserted her; she lived in the hope that he would come back" (HT 43). In addition, Sissy reacts with confusion to the lessons imposed on her at school. Dickens' satire repeatedly exposes the inhumanness of a statistical worldview through Sissy, who, for example, expresses her puzzlement about being made to answer questions such as the following she tells Louisa about:

> '[...] and that's another of my mistakes – of accidents upon the sea. And I find (Mr. M'Choakumchild said) that in a given time a hundred thousand persons went to sea on long voyages, and only five hundred of them were drowned or burnt to death. What is the percentage? And I said, [...] it was nothing.'
> 'Nothing, Sissy?' 'Nothing, Miss – to the relations and friends of the people who were killed. I shall never learn [...].' (HT 44–45)

Sissy intuitively identifies the discrepancy between facts and values, between calculable risk of accidents and empirically derived percentages, which clash with realities of loss and measures of grief for the individual. Throughout the novel, Dickens attacks "the machine philosophy" which threatened to permeate the literate public,[51] or, to use one of Thomas Carlyle's memorable phrases, the author depicts the downfall of a society where "men are grown mechanical in head and in heart, as well as in hand" (1899: 63). Gradgrind embodies the negative implications of a statistical worldview as "a shift from all that was alive and human to a frigid absence of all emotions" (Gigerenzer et al. 1989: 291). And even if he comes to admit in the end that "we are all liable to mistakes" (HT 184), which implies some sense of responsibility for the disastrous developments in his own family, his rational principles force his daughter into an unhappy marriage to the much older banker Bounderby and a nervous breakdown, while his son Tom resorts to gambling and blackmail. In contrast to the Gradgrindian sterility, the capitalist greed of Bounderby, and the destructiveness of the industrial spirit of the whole town, Sissy Jupe and the circus represent an alternative sphere of amusement, creativity, joyful deviance, and imagination. Her love of horse riding, a frivolous activity according to Victorian standards of productivity, is symptomatic of her vitality and the ability to find "self-fulfilment in self-forgetfulness – all that is the antithesis of calculating self-interest" (Leavis 1948: 231). She is also the only character capable of non-destructive relationships and positive intervention into other characters' lives,[52] e.g. she later protects Louisa from the swindler James Harthouse and gets him to leave town.

Unlike Sissy, Gradgrind's daughter Louisa is a full-blown victim of her father's education and "never had a child's belief or a child's fear" (HT 79).

---

[51] Cf. Larry Stewart's article "A Meaning for Machines: Modernity, Utility, and the Eighteenth-Century British Public" (1998).
[52] See Gallagher's argument: "Indeed, the book seems suffused with a fear of making connections in a world where relationships are almost without exception destructive" (1985: 159).

Above all, she has internalized the most important lesson: "By means of addition, subtraction, multiplication, and division, settle everything somehow, *and never wonder*" (HT 39; my emphasis). The opposite of wonder, fact, has not only permeated Louisa's character but also the whole town. In the often cited "key-note" of the novel in chapter 5, Dickens describes Coketown as a "triumph of fact" (HT 18), as well as of conformity, routine and ugliness.[53] The hardness of the surroundings is reflected in the hard industrial outlook of its inhabitants. Numerical facts determine all relations, guarantee the order of society, and have as such assumed the status of a new religion: "the relations between master and man were all fact, and everything was fact [...] and what you couldn't state in figures, or show to be purchasable in the cheapest market and saleable in the dearest, was not, and never should be, world without end, Amen" (HT 19). In addition, Coketown is characterized by economic instability and Bounderby's irresponsible capitalist rule: "It had been ruined so often, that it was amazing how it had borne so many shocks" (HT 85). The risks and losses of the frequent over-speculations – be it Mr Harthouse or Tom Gradgrind's gambling, Mr Bounderby's credit schemes – are always carried by others.

In *Hard Times*, all relationships are either shaped by purely rational calculation, exploitation, or suffering; in either case they appear to be suffocating and trap the characters. There is no escape, for instance, for Louisa and Tom, who are united by an almost incestuous bind of sisterly love and brotherly abuse. Tom, having accumulated huge gambling debts, is the incarnate perversion of Gradgrind's educational ideal. He utilizes shrewd calculation to pursue his own interests at all cost and ask his sister to borrow a large sum from her husband, after she has already given him considerable amounts of money. He openly declares the exact nature of his sister's marriage and his own selfishness to Mr Harthouse, saying, "you know she didn't marry old Bounderby for her own sake, or for his sake, but for my sake. Then why doesn't she get what I want, out of him, for my sake?" (HT 135). Louisa can be seen to act of an intense love for her brother, and like Burney's heroine Camilla, she is willing to risk the stability and happiness of her own life to pay the price for her brother's criminal ways and addiction. Apart from the desire to help Tom, indicative of her emotional nature, Louisa enters

---

[53] "It was a town of machinery and tall chimneys, out of which interminable serpents of smoke trailed themselves for ever and ever and never got uncoiled. [...] It contained several large streets all very like one another, and many small streets still more like one another, inhabited by people equally like one another, who all went in and out at the same hours, with the same sound upon the same pavements, to do the same work, and to whom every day was the same as yesterday and tomorrow, and every year the counterpart of the last and the next. These attributes of Coketown were in the main inseparable from the work by which it was sustained [...]" (HT 18).

into the loveless marriage with the rich banker Bounderby after a rational consultation with the father. Hearing about Bounderby's marriage proposal, Gradgrind's advises Louisa to

> to consider this question [...] simply as one of tangible Fact. [...] You are, we will say in round numbers, twenty years of age; Mr. Bounderby is, we will say in round numbers, fifty. There is some disparity in your respective years, but in your means and positions there is none; on the contrary, there is a great suitability. Then the question arises, Is this one disparity sufficient to operate as a bar to such a marriage? In considering this question, it is not unimportant to take into account the statistics of marriage, so far as they have yet been obtained, in England and Wales. I find, on reference to the figures, that a large proportion of these marriages are contracted between parties of very unequal ages, and that the elder of these contracting parties is, in rather more than three-fourths of these instances, the bridegroom. (HT 76)

By setting the huge age difference between Louisa and Bounderby in relation to some abstract notion of the national average ("more than three-fourths of these instances") of the age gap between husband and wife, Gradgrind brushes over Louisa's doubts by 'normalizing' them. Moreover, he fails to listen to the emotional subtext underlying her question and reduces the decision to a simply case of opportunity that only allows for acceptance. The long conversation between father and daughter illustrates Louisa's struggle and Gradgrind's inability to leave the abstract, statistical level behind and get onto to the personal. Gradgrind's responses signify the coldness and unbridgeable gulf between them, springing from his failure to consider an individual's hopes and fears before the quantifiable abstraction of calculable risk and facts:

> 'Father, I have often thought that life is very short.' [...]
> 'It is short, no doubt, my dear. Still, the average duration of human life is proved to have increased of late years. The calculations of various life assurance and annuity offices, among other figures which cannot go wrong, have established the fact.'
> 'I speak of my own life, father.'
> 'O indeed? Still,' said Mr. Gradgrind, 'I need not point out to you, Louisa, that it is governed by the laws which govern lives in the aggregate.' (HT 77)

The scene highlights again the absurdities and risks of applying statistical knowledge and Utilitarian principles without consideration of the feelings of the individual.[54] The aim underlying political economy and Utilitarian theories

---

54 Utilitarianism, as applied in the writings of Jeremy Bentham and John Stuart Mill, is based on the belief that the each action should be measured according to its utility. The idea of 'utility' equals basically a maximizing of pleasure and a minimizing of pain. As a political ethics it is

was to regulate and systematize people's desires and behaviour and thus facilitate government by putting it on 'rational' grounding. Yet obvious flaws, which are alluded to here, are the marked discrepancy between theory and practice and the assumption that all people are psychologically calculable and have exactly identical likes and dislikes. In other words, by assuming that each individual "wants the same ends, and fears the same dangers" (Hilton 2006: 330), no room is allowed, e.g., for differences due to class or gender, or simply personal taste. Dickens' narrator also comments on the irregularity between human character and machines in this context, saying:

> It is known, to the force of a single pound weight, what the engine will do; but, not all the calculators of the National Debt can tell me the capacity for good or evil, for love or hatred, for patriotism or discontent, for the decomposition of virtue into vice, or the reverse, at any single moment in the soul of one of these its quiet servants, with the composed faces and the regulated actions. (HT 54)

Apart from constructing the unpredictability of people (especially here again the masses of working-class people) as a risk, as done so frequently in Industrial fictions, *Hard Times* thoroughly satirizes Bentham's phrase of "the greatest happiness for the greatest number". There is no escape from a system that only produces misery, misunderstanding, and greed. Mr Gradgrind, the rational reformer and educator, and Mr Bounderby, "a rich man: banker, merchant, manufacturer, and what not" (HT 12), are at the centre of the narrative's ideological critique. Both represent different facets of the Utilitarian spirit, and as Childers writes, both "embody twin pillars of industrial discourse in its failure to contribute to increased knowledge, tolerance, and understanding of others, that is, to human and humane progress" (2001: 88).

The estrangement within the Gradgrind family described above is paralleled with the lack of understanding between the middle and the working class in the

---

thus exclusively consequence-, not value-oriented; the guiding principle is often expressed in Bentham's phrase of seeking to achieve the "greatest happiness of the greatest number" of people. As Amigoni sums up: "For Bentham, human subjects were sentient and rational beings who sought the sensation of pleasure, and strove to avoid the sensation of pain: the progress of society could thereby be measured and calculated according to the way in which the greatest happiness would be enjoyed by the greatest number who had achieved the 'pleasure' derived from the accumulated wealth or comfort as a consequence of their (increasingly machine-assisted) labour" (2011: 22). The spirit of Victorian Utilitarianism is therefore closely linked to and characteristic of the "statistical *Lebensgefühl*", a gaze which has shifted "from individuals to averages, [...] from impressions to numbers" (Gigerenzer et al. 1989: 291). For details, context, and criticism of different approaches to Utilitarianism see especially Shirley Robin Letwin's *The Pursuit of Certainty: David Hume, Jeremy Bentham, John Stuart Mill, Beatrice Webb* (1965).

narrative. When Louisa goes to visit Stephen Blackpool, it is her first personal contact with one of the Coketown Hands. Suddenly she finds herself

> face to face with anything like individuality in connection with them. She knew of their existence by hundreds and by thousands. She knew what results in work a given number of them would produce in a given space of time. She knew them in crowds passing to and from their nests, like ants or beetles. [...] Something to be worked so much and paid so much, [...] something that increased at such a rate of percentage, and yielded such another percentage of crime, and such another percentage of pauperism; something wholesale, of which vast fortunes were made; something that occasionally rose like a sea, and did some harm and waste (chiefly to itself), and fell again; this she knew the Coketown Hands to be. But, she had scarcely thought more of separating them into units, than of separating the sea itself into its component drops. (HT 121)

Again, the insufficiency of purely quantitative, descriptive data and its dehumanizing effect in the interaction between people is exposed. Regarding this aspect, Poovey has argued how Dickens' text criticizes the new socio-scientific credo of empirical observation, and the aim to produce knowledge about society and human nature based on the prior generation of abstract, statistically derived notions (i.e. "society", "human nature"). These notions produce what Poovey calls a "structure of anxiety" in the narrative,[55] caused by the repressed discomfort and scepticism about how these abstractions can adequately represent on the large scale what they claim to replace on the individual level. Furthermore, the exclusive focus the average and the law of large numbers poses a cop-out to personal accountability, which is also illustrated, e.g., in the behaviour of Bounderby.

In the novel, the destructive effect of the statistical worldview is reinforced by the mind-numbing routine of industrial labour that eliminates individualism and the capacity for empathy. This bleak diagnosis is later underlined by the indifferent reaction of the Coketown people to the fact that Stephen has been missing for two full days; "the Hard Fact men, abated nothing of their set routine, whatever happened. Day and night again, day and night again. The monotony was unbroken. Even Stephen Blackpool's disappearance was falling into the general way, and becoming as monotonous a wonder as any piece of machinery" (HT 196). Dickens' narrative insinuates that people can no longer distinguish between the value of man and machine. The indifference is also shown to be a result of the people having internalized the ideologies of capitalist lais-

---

[55] Poovey writes: "Dickens, one of political economy's most outspoken critics, insisted, for example, that abstractions like 'the population' threatened to undermine personal responsibility, which could otherwise help keep society intact" (2001: 160).

sez-faire and self-help: "This, again, was among the fictions of Coketown. Any capitalist there, who had made sixty thousand pounds out of sixpence, always professed to wonder why the sixty thousand nearest Hands didn't each make sixty thousand pounds out of sixpence, [...]. What I did you can do. Why don't you go and do it?" (HT 90).

With the dysfunctionality of family relationships mirroring the employer-worker relationships, at the heart of *Hard Times* lays "a crisis of family relations" (Amigoni 2011: 28). Interestingly, the two central plot lines and parallel cases of suffering each involve a marriage. Both Louisa and Stephen Blackpool are trapped in a marriage, forced into or denied exit from by, respectively, Mr Gradgrind and Mr Bounderby. When Stephen comes begging to Mr Bounderby to find a way to release him from the burden of his marriage in order to be free for the love of his life, Rachael, he is met only with the reply that marriage is a risky gamble, which in Stephen's case, has simply been lost. Bounderby tells him: "You didn't take your wife for fast and for loose; but for better for worse. If she has turned out worse – why all we have got to say is, she might have turned out better" (HT 58). While Bounderby and the laws of society keep Stephen locked in his unhappy marriage, Gradgrind leads Louisa into an equally emotionally destructive union.[56] In both cases it is a mix of fatal choice and grim circumstances which is the source of unhappiness. What remains of the Victorian marriage plot here goes beyond negotiating the potential losses and gains of marriage, of obligation and necessity vs. love and freedom. Instead, *Hard Times* depicts how the circumstances are not only "inherently destructive, but its hold on the individual is firmer and somehow more thorough than in Austen" (Webb 1981: 95).

Both Louisa and Stephen are destroyed by their circumstances. Befitting their status as members of the different classes and genders, Stephen dies from his severe injuries after falling into the Old Hell Shaft,[57] while Louisa falls into a deep depression and is denied the fulfilment of motherhood. Stephen is presented as an innocent man, who resists joining the trade union, but for whom all help comes too late. His death comes in the form of a cruel and tragic

---

[56] Regarding the fact that Dickens' text is decidedly pessimistic about family relationships, Gallagher suggests that an important topic that concerns the author here is advocating easier divorce laws (1985: 155).

[57] Dickens' representation of Stephen Blackpool, as the main working class character, has also been criticized as inauthentic, pathetic and reductive. See for instance Schor's comment that Dickens does not go into detail about the Coketown Hands and their political fight and that Stephen ends "in an abandoned mine shaft, brought up only to see the evening star and die" (2001: 68).

accident; he "was on his way to Mr Bounderby's country house after dark, when he fell. He was crossing that dangerous country at such a dangerous time, because he was innocent of what was laid to his charge, and couldn't rest from coming the nearest way to deliver himself up" (HT 207–208). But the narrative dedicates much more room to the description of the downward spiral of Louisa. This is related through the explicit metaphor of the steep staircase in book 2, a projection of Mrs Sparsit's jealous imagination, and telling chapter headings (e.g. "Fading Away", "Lower and Lower", "Down") that suggest an inevitable descent into doom. Mrs Sparsit, Mr Bounderby's loyal housekeeper, is full of hate and suspicion about his young wife and begins to watch her closely, especially after she suspects Louisa of having an affair with James Harthouse. Her surveillance mission is described in comical terms and Dickens' ridicules the common motif of the young woman, whose potential misconduct and virtue become the obsession and main focus of risk in so many novels. After secretly following Louisa, "Mrs Sparsit stood hidden in the density of the shrubbery, considering what next? Lo, Louisa coming out of the house! Hastily cloaked and muffled, and stealing away. She elopes! She falls from the lowermost stair, and is swallowed up in the gulf" (HT 162). The reality of Louisa's behaviour is inseparably entangled with Mrs Sparsit's miscalculations and her bad wishful thinking: "She erected in her mind a mighty Staircase, with a dark pit of shame and ruin at the bottom; [...]. It became the business of Mrs. Sparsit's life, to look up at her staircase, and to watch Louisa coming down" (HT 154); "there Louisa always was, upon it. And always gliding down, down, down!" (HT 157). Finally, she really does hit rock bottom and the unhappiness of her marriage and the shortcomings of her education, which have left her without any access to her own emotions, come crashing down on her. Louisa breaks down in front of her father: "All that I know is, your philosophy and your teaching will not save me. Now, father, you have brought me to this. Save me by some other means!" And Mr Gradgrind, helplessly, watches "the pride of his heart and the triumph of his system, lying, an insensible heap, at his feet" (HT 167).

According to Gallagher, *Hard Times* is marked by an "almost complete lack of narrative hope" (2006: 70). There is no way out of Coketown, neither physically nor spiritually. The novel ends with projections of "futurity" (HT 227) for the characters that affirm the further development towards joyless, barren lives, or death, for all except Sissy, who will be happily surrounded by her children. As with any satire, inherent in what Gallagher calls a "plot about futility" (2006: 72) is a strong appeal to change the status quo. Otherwise, as the telling titles of the three parts of the novel imply, one will reap what one has sown. The notion that circumstance shape character appears as a dark and despairing insight in the text. *Hard Times* stages the risk of industrialization as producing an inhumanity that transcends class conflict and social injustices. The clash between mathematical probability and risk perception is central. While the Coketown citizens can rationally calculate all odds and estimates, they are ignorant of the risk that this outlook poses to them. In comparison to other writers of industrial fiction, Dickens' main fear concerned the idea that industrial culture threatened to turn society into a "large factory, churning out fact while devouring beings who have lost the capacity for feeling and human connection", as Joseph Childers writes. And in this sense, the author is conscious of a risk "beyond a concern about the violence and inequities that industrialism seemed to foster" (Childers 2001: 87). Yet in contrast for instance to writers like Hardy, Dickens also shows industrialism as an inescapable reality, without any nostalgia for rural societies. Like Gaskell, Dickens does not develop any plan for social reform; and the circus is at best a symbolic alternative model of society. The anti-dote lies in "elements of human nature – personal kindness, sympathy, and forbearance" (Williams 1958: 94) and in the dangerous activity which fosters these elements, reading fiction. Ultimately, Dickens' narrator suggests, the citizens need to be made to wonder and take "De Foe to their bosoms, instead of Euclid" (HT 39).

6.5 Dealing with Change and Loss: *North and South*

Out of the four textual examples in this chapter, Gaskell's second Manchester novel *North and South* (1854–55) has received the most critical acclaim.[58] Concerning the depiction of class conflict, however, Raymond Williams considers it less interesting than *Mary Barton* "because the tension is less" (1958: 91),[59] and it has been frequently noted that *North and South* begins with a discussion

---

58 E.g. Joseph Simmons writes: "In literary terms, *North and South* may be the best of all industrial novels. It is neither preachy nor didactic; the factory question is intrinsic to the action of the novel, yet the story can stand on its own; it does not rely entirely on melodrama; and the characters are vividly portrayed rather than stock villains or angels" (2002: 349).
59 Cf. Deidre David's argument: "When Gaskell wrote North and South England had survived the Chartist movement, had coped with the dangerous unrest stemming from the dreadful hunger among the working-class population of the manufacturing districts during the slumps of the 1830s and 1840s […]. Contrary to numerous predictions of anarchy, society had not dissolved. But the working-class remained an irritant force, a force which required containment, a reservoir of passions which needed to be ordered if the middle class was to retain the power it had gradually acquired in the political life of the nation" (1981: 26). So despite the fact that the heyday of the factory question and working-class rebellion were over, social injustice and class conflict were still perceived as dangerous forces and are depicted as such in Gaskell's novel.

of love and marriage, and does not introduce the industrial setting and theme until chapter 7. The narrative opens in the idyllic Southern town of Helstone, the home of the Vicar's daughter Margaret Hale, "a world more stable even than Jane Austen's – the danger would seem to lie only in domestic boredom" (Bodenheimer 1979: 283). In fact, the beginning of *North and South* in many ways resembles a typical novel of manners, but with a distinctly darker twist. Although like in *Mary Barton* a notion of Christian mercy prevails in the text, it also shows that Gaskell despite her Unitarian faith clearly did not believe in the possibility of a risk-free society or that faith can conquer all evils.[60] There is a consistent emphasis on change and a sense of precariousness throughout the narrative. The central plot incidents, the workers' march on Thornton's house, the visit of Margaret's brother Frederick, and the many deaths, are all highly fraught with different risks. Meanwhile the main romantic plot between Margaret and John Thornton is driven by misinterpretations of her conduct according to the era's gender-specific, discriminating standards of judgment.

Early on, Margaret's world is shaken up by her father's decision to break with the Church of England, which means the end of their life in the parish and domestic stability; what follows is a move to the North and a new, rougher life. Mr Hale's decision and its consequences – above all the sense of uncertainty, loss, and newness it brings for Margaret – introduce change as a key theme of the novel.[61] In one of the final chapters, Gaskell's narrator reflects: "There was change everywhere; slight, yet pervading all. Households were changed by absence, or death, or marriage, or the natural mutations brought by days and months and years, which carry us on imperceptibly from childhood to youth, and thence from manhood to age" (N&S 471). Agreeing with Bodenheimer, one can say that besides being a social-problem fiction, *North and South* is a text "about irrevocable change, and about the confused process of response and accommodation that attends it" (1979: 282). Similarly, Terence Wright notes that a "general uncertainty" informs the novel (1995: 102); moreover, he describes it as "a book full of pain – not the pangs of hunger, as in *Mary Barton*, but the pain of stress and disturbance, [...]. It is also the pain of loss, particularly for the heroine" (1995: 105). In the time span of roughly eighteen months covered in the novel Margaret undergoes a process of a steady loss of family and friends, including her mother and father, her friend Bessy Higgins,

---

60 On Gaskell's Unitarianism in relation to the novel see, e.g., Hotz (2000).
61 See Bodenheimer's article "*North and South:* A Permanent State of Change" (1979); also David (1981: 47).

and her guardian Mr Bell. On this subject Gaskell herself comments in a letter to Dickens on December 17th, 1854: "I think a better title than N & S would have been 'Death & Variations. There are 5 deaths, each beautifully suited to the character of the individual" (Gaskell 1997: 324).[62] It is indeed a chronicle of a "fatal year" for Margaret: "No sooner was she fully aware of one loss than another came" (N&S 491). In the end, she is completely overpowered by the "sense of change, of individual nothingness, of perplexity and disappointment [...] [and] this slight, all-pervading instability, had given her greater pain than if all had been too entirely changed for her to recognise it" (N&S 478).

Apart from experiencing in extreme form the precariousness of human life, Margaret struggles to come to terms with less dramatic changes, as even these go very much against her nature. She tells Mr Bell: "I seek heavenly steadfastness in earthly monotony" (N&S 400). Although Margaret takes action in order to manage the risks concerning the people close to her (e.g. she seeks to protect her brother Frederick from being taken by the police, and Thornton from the rage of his workers) the main events are beyond her control.[63] In particular, she has no influence over her parents and over her own reputation, i.e. how her actions are perceived by others. Significantly, despite her proclaimed desire for routine and security, Margaret's efforts and intelligence are never directed towards the domestic (see Mann 1975: 27). In fact, she seemingly lacks female intuition and is, for instance, shocked about the marriage proposal by Henry Lennox, rather than having anticipated his feelings towards her.

The course of the novel closely follows Margaret's growing despair and shows her "heart heavy with various anxieties" (N&S 188), or her being "oppressed with gloom, and seeing no promise of brightness on any side of the horizon" (N&S 128). Jill L. Matus, who reads *North and South* as a "condition-of-consciousness" novel (2009: 61), stresses Gaskell's exploration of the destabilizing effect of strong, overwhelming and potentially traumatizing emotions in the narrative. She writes: "Again and again, North and South explores how people cope with shock and pain" (2009: 62). Furthermore, the many telling chapter titles draw attention to mistakes and dangers and emphasize the lack of human control over actions and consequences, e.g. "Mistakes", "Mischances", "Mistakes Cleared Up", "The

---

[62] In fact, altogether seven deaths occur in the novel (Bessy Higgins, Mrs Hale, Leonards, John Boucher, Mrs Boucher, Mr Hale, Mr Bell). Yet the deaths that affect Margaret the most are her parents and Mr Bell.
[63] This echoes the pattern found in *Mary Barton* where Mary's struggle is to protect Jem and her father.

More Haste The Worse Speed".[64] With the "trance of passion" of the worker's mob (N&S 212) triggering the main climax of the novel and Thornton particularly in the second half being "almost blinded by his baffled passion" (N&S 245) for Margaret, the text intertwines social issues with psychological concerns about the disturbing impact of emotions.

Hit by difficulties and tragedy, Margaret gradually grows in stature. The move to the manufacturing town Milton-Northern forces a new responsibility on her because her mother soon shows signs of fatigue and illness, while her father is robbed of status and professional certainty. Arriving in Milton, Margaret notes how in contrast to the South "everything looked more 'purpose-like' [...] – more enduring, not so gay and pretty" (N&S 65). Thus adjusting to the new location is generally no easy matter: "There was no comfort to be given. They were settled in Milton, and must endure smoke and fogs for a season; indeed, all other life seemed shut out from them by as thick a fog of circumstance" (N&S 75). Although the rough climate and the outspokenness of the Milton people scare her initially, Margaret proves to be quite resilient and in comparison to her parents better equipped to adapt to the North. She is a headstrong woman, marked by a "straight, fearless, dignified presence habitual to her" (N&S 69), and walking through town "with a boundless fearless step" (N&S 80).

After striking up a friendship with the Higgins family, Margaret begins to take an interest in the situation of the poor mill workers. At the same time, she is not free from prejudice towards "the vulgarity of shop-people" (N&S 99) like the Thorntons, the owners of the mill. It is only after her father tells her about John Thornton's past, that Margaret comes to view him in a more positive light. Mr Hale says: "His father speculated wildly, failed, and then killed himself [...]. All his former friends shrunk from the disclosures that had to be made of his dishonest gambling – wild, hopeless struggles, made with other people's money, to regain his own moderate portion of wealth" (N&S 100). Consequently, young Thornton is driven by two conflicting desires; on the one hand regaining his family's position and running a profitable business, one the other, avoiding at all costs to become like his father and engage in any speculations which could puts his creditor's money or his workers' jobs at risk. But the impending strike of the millworkers forces Thornton to take a clear stand and demonstrate strength. His reaction to the threatened attack on his property is the same a Rob-

---

64 See also Mary O'Farrell (1997). She argues that Margaret is characterized to a large extent by her ability to blunder, i.e. to do or say the wrong things at the wrong time. These blunders determine the course of the narrative, often produce injury to others (e.g. John Thornton), or belie her true intentions.

ert Moore's in *Shirley:* "I take the risk. [...] I'm not afraid of anything so bastardly as incendiarism. [...] I can protect myself from any violence that I apprehend. And I will assuredly protect all others who come to me for work" (N&S 195). When Margaret comes to visit the factory and asks him about the growing tension among his men, Thornton warns her: "Milton is not the place for cowards. I have known the time when I have had to thread my way through a crowd of white, angry men, [...] If you live in Milton, you must learn to have a brave heart". Margaret replies: "I do not know whether I am brave or not till I am tried; but I am afraid I should be a coward" (N&S 135–136). This conversation foreshadows the crucial scene when Thornton's house is under siege from an angry mob of workers and it is, in fact, Margaret, who is brave enough to face them.

This scene, which is also a good illustration of the risk rhetoric employed by Gaskell, unfolds as follows: Walking through the streets of Milton, Margaret is lost in her thoughts, contemplating the rapidly declining health of the mother and that she might soon loose her. Thus, she is distracted from the danger right in front of her: "she had got into Marlborough Street before the full conviction forced itself upon her, that there was a restless, oppressive sense of irritation abroad among the people; a thunderous atmosphere" (N&S 203). The marching workers are described as a powerful force of nature; "the first long far-off roll of the tempest; [...] the first slow-surging wave of the dark crowd come, with its threatening crest". The sense of risk is build up further through a focus on the men's eyes – "some fierce with anger, some lowering with relentless threats, some dilated with fear" (N&S 203). Margaret finds shelter inside the Thorntons house and joins the other women, who are all terrified spectators to the chaos outside.[65] The danger increases to the point when they finally hear "the tramp of innumerable steps right under the very wall of the house, and the fierce growl of low deep angry voices [...], more dreadful than their baffled cries not many minutes before" (N&S 208). Margret's reaction to the situation differs from all the other women's. While Mrs Thornton is "white with fear" (N&S 206), Margaret realizes that her dread of faltering like a coward in the face of an emergency was unjustified and that "in this real great time of reasonable fear and nearness of terror, she forgot herself, and felt only an intense sympathy"

---

[65] Similar to the riot scene in *Shirley*, the women are mainly passive spectators, yet in contrast to Shirley and Caroline, Margaret ends up being physically threatened. Nonetheless, in both novels the violent conflict is not told from the perspective of the workers but functions as a backdrop to play out the feelings between the central couples, i.e. Margaret and John and Caroline and Robert. The situation is interesting in so far that emotional risks are negotiated within a different danger scenario.

(N&S 206). Thus, in a state of almost delirious agitation, she shouts at the hesitant Mr Thornton to go outside and "face them like a man" (N&S 209). But the result of Thornton's address to the men is only an increase of their fury and Margret is suddenly aware that he is in acute danger. Acting impulsively, she steps outside: "She only thought how she could save him. She threw her arms around him; she made her body into a shield from the fierce people beyond" (N&S 211–212). In consequence, she is hit by the throw of a stone intended for Thornton and then faints in his arms. While the physical injury proves to be marginal, the situation has deep repercussions for both of them and Margaret's action is complicated by its personal and political symbolism.

The others perceive Margaret's behaviour as reckless: "It was putting your head into the lion's mouth!" (N&S 222), but also view it as a public demonstration of her love for Thornton. She is considered to have made a spectacle of herself and to have openly risked her propriety by showing her passion. John is left, above all, confused by her behaviour: "every pulse beat in him as he remembered how she had come down and placed herself in foremost danger, – could it be to save him? At the time, [...] he had seen nothing but the unnecessary danger she had placed herself in" (N&S 214–215). Influenced by the interpretation of Margaret's behaviour by the others, Thornton is suddenly certain of a reciprocal passion between him and Margaret. Much against his mother's cautioning advice he decides to risk telling her about his feelings: "If it were but one chance in a thousand – or a million – I should do it" (N&S 224). At the same time, Margaret is preoccupied by quite different thoughts. Initially she was both excited by her own courage and feeling responsible for putting John in danger by her provocative words. But reliving the scene in her mind, she is haunted by a deep sense of shame. Still she refuses to accept the public sexualized perception of her action and vehemently defends herself, all the while completely crushing Thornton's romantic hopes. She says, "any woman would have done just the same. *We all feel the sanctity of our sex as a high privilege when we see danger*" (N&S 230; my emphasis); "If I saved one blow, one cruel, angry action that might otherwise have been committed, I did woman's work – Let them insult my maiden pride as they will" (N&S 247); "any woman, worthy of the name of woman, would come forward to shield, with her reverenced helplessness, *a man in danger from the violence of numbers*" (N&S 253; my emphasis). Margaret's utterances reveal the dual awareness of femininity as both limitation and strategic weapon. It is also significant, Deidre David notes, that the angry crowd of men calms down immediately after seeing the bleeding Margaret; thereby Gaskell "shows them to be susceptible to conventional middle-class notions about protection of women", while at the same intensifying "the political threat of the working class by symbolically suggesting sexual attack" (David 1981: 43–44).

In any case, by refusing to see her behaviour as motivated by feelings for John, Margaret turns it into a political act. Through this scene, Mary E. Hotz argues, Gaskell's narrative shows the complications for unmarried women to take on any active role in the public sphere as they always risk being compromised by their sexuality (2000: 178). Margaret openly violates the restriction of passive spectatorship. In Brontë's novel, Shirley stops Caroline from aiding Robert in the attack and making a spectacle of herself. Gaskell, by comparison, has her heroine take the dare of openly suffering the blow meant for Thornton, and thus "does not avoid the consequences that Shirley foresees" (Bodenheimer 1979: 295). In this way, the narrative underlines the crucial risk for women, namely that their reputation and self-presentation are beyond her control and the results of both coincidence and error.[66] Furthermore, it suggests that middle-class women like Margaret have the potential to assert authority and break the cycle of violence between masters and men and acts as mediators in the face of social conflict and injustice.[67]

The second important instance of Margaret's attempt at risk management in the narrative concerns her brother Frederick, who is currently living in Gibraltar. Charged with sparking a mutiny on a navy ship, a return to England for him means facing a court-martial. Although Frederick's function in the plot has been debated as superfluous (see e.g. David 1981: 14), his secret visit is crucial for increasing Margret's crisis and deepening the misconceptions between her and John. Confronted with her mother's wish to see her son one last time, "Margaret felt as if, on Frederick's account as well as on her mother's, she ought to overlook all intermediate chances of danger, and pledge herself to do everything in her power for its realisation" (N&S 242). Discussing the situation with her father, they agree that the potential risk of Frederick is worth taking for Mrs Hale's sake: "I believe it would do her much more good than all the doctor's

---

[66] Deidre David, who reads the scene also with a strong focus on gender and risk, relates it more explicitly to the general class conflict and the threat working-class rebellion presented to middle-class culture: "Woman as the protectress of middle-class ideals, as the centre of family life, is implicitly under attack, and that she can come so close to the threat of physical violence serves as a dramatic indication of how close Gaskell felt the working class could come to violating the system of which woman was the matrilineal guardian" (1981: 42).

[67] See O'Farrell (1997: 67) and also Hotz's comment that Margaret "must step outside the home and into the public arena, [...] This move to contemplation, and the developing capacity to integrate risk in one's life, serves to shape the prophetic role women are to have in society" (2000: 171).

medicine" (N&S 244). Her mother however, once her wish is about to become a reality, reacts with sheer panic: "If he should be taken! If he should be executed, after all these years that he has kept away and lived in safety!" It falls to Margaret to calm her worries: "There will be some risk no doubt; but we will lessen it as much as ever we can. And it is so little! Now, if we were at Helstone, there would be twenty – a hundred times as much. [...]; while here, nobody knows or cares for us enough to notice what we do" (N&S 265). Still, from this moment on Margaret feels solely responsible for summoning Frederick into danger and her anxiety mounts daily during his visit. The terror that a detection of Frederick holds quickly outweighs the joy over his presence. Especially Margaret is weary of tempting their luck even a day or two longer after the passing of Mrs Hale.

After they come up with a plan to safely get Fredrick out of the country, she accompanies him to the train station late at night where there is "less risk of his being seen" (N&S 310). In her parting conversation with her brother, Margaret admits how the last two years have sharpened her sense of contingency and taught her the futility of planning too far ahead: "There have been such strange unexpected changes in my life [...] that I feel more than ever that it is not worth while to calculate too closely what I should do if any future event took place. I try to think only upon the present" (N&S 311). And she immediately has to put her new attitude into practice. On the platform Frederick is recognized by Leonards who threatens to expose him but then stumbles drunkenly down the stairs and dies; furthermore Frederick's narrow escape and Margaret's last embrace of him are witnessed by John Thornton.

This presents Margaret with a dilemma during the following police inquest into Leonards' death. She lies about her presence at the station to protect Frederick's identity, although saving her brother means being seen as liar by John. He, in turn, is tormented by jealousy; at the same time he is still protective of her. He tells her: "At present, believe me, your secret is safe with me. But you run great risks, allow me to say, in being so indiscreet" (N&S 390). Believing that he is saving her reputation by preventing her secret affair from being exposed, Thornton too lies about having seen Margaret at the station, which finally stops the inquest.

Paralleling the scene at Thornton's house, Margaret's action is again motivated solely by the desire to protect a man in a dangerous situation she feels some responsibility for creating. Put differently, each time she tries to manage a risk she has partially foreseen, as well as acting instinctively in a moment of fear. Regarding this aspect Bodenheimer argues: "The unthinking gestures are, in both cases, indirectly successful in averting the danger, but once done, they seem riddled with moral ambiguity, and cause Margaret enormous shame and internal strife. In both cases, too, what she sees as a human action to save another is given a sexual interpretation by others" (Bodenheimer 1979: 295). In this way, the scenes replicate the meta-structure of the whole narrative in which one risk or loss consecutively replaces another. In addition, both scenes reveal her feelings for Thornton she is yet unable to acknowledge.

The final chapters bring a sudden turn to the better and a reconciliation of all conflicts. The reader learns that Thornton has "reviewed his position as a Milton manufacturer", and henceforth the relations between master and men are marked by new humanist insights, the grounding for an "intercourse, which though it might not have the effect of preventing all future clash of opinion and action, [...] would, at any rate, enable both master and man to look upon each other with far more charity and sympathy" (N&S 501–502). Thornton's moral integrity as a businessman is emphasized, especially as far as this attitude towards risk and speculation is concerned. Generally people consider him to be "so prudent with all his daring" (N&S 498–99); and during another period when his business fails and he has to cut his losses, he does "not despair; he exerted himself day and night to foresee and to provide for all emergencies" (N&S 502). Thornton refuses a chance to speculate, which appears as a test of his strength of character, but also means that he is unable to drag himself out of his financial difficulties by his own force. Instead he is finally recued by "money from elsewhere", Margaret's inheritance from Mr Bell. Gaskell here employs "that device of the legacy which solved so many otherwise insoluble problems in the world of the Victorian novel" (Williams 1958: 92). Although she acts as Thornton's saving grace and becomes the main investor of Thornton's mill, Margaret's role in his financial rehabilitation is still passive, as she merely passes on money. But the ending unites John and Margaret, representing North and South, both romantically and financially. After all misunderstandings are cleared up and mutual prejudices overcome, both have also learned in different ways to assume social responsibility and gained self-awareness.

Ultimately, the marriage plot of Gaskell's *North and South* and the geographical metaphor suggest the possibility of healing divisions. At the same time, the deaths in the narrative act as a negative equalizing force between the different classes. Accident and illness, and the emotional upheaval caused by pain, shock and loss, affect the three families and men and women equally. It is also indicative of a statistical worldview because, as the mathematician Émile Borel writes: "Probability theory tells us that even though individuals differ in many ways, they are similar in their liability to accident, to illness, and to death" (cited in Kavanagh 1993: 19; see also Matus 2009: 63). Gaskell counterbalances Margaret's familial losses with three working-class deaths; Leonards' drunken fall, John Boucher's suicide after the failure of the workers' strike fails, and Bessy Higgins' death from lung disease, a result from the hazardous working conditions in the cotton mill: "Anyhow, there's many a one as works in a carding-room, that falls into a waste, coughing and spitting blood, because they're just poisoned by the fluff" (N&S 118). According to Mike Sanders, Gaskell's narrative dramatizes the fact that occupational health became a public issue from the 1830s onwards (2000: 318), while many industrialists continuously fought against the idea that the work environment could directly harm their employees. When Margaret wonders why the bad working conditions that caused Bessy's death are not remedied, Thornton is quick to dismiss her idea and he displays the belief common among industrialists that workers are responsible for their own misfortunes.[68] In any case, like for Stephen Blackpool in *Hard Times*, there is no escape from the destructive factory system for Bessy Higgins and John Boucher. Considering the series of accidents and deaths in the novel, it is furthermore interesting to see it, Mike Sanders suggests, as Gaskell's reflection of the 19th-century's conflicting beliefs in human agency and causality. On the one hand, the narrative places emphasis on "society's capacity to control and thus mitigate (and ultimately perhaps even to remove) the cause of human distress" (2000: 314). On the other, the text illustrates the necessity of managing change and dealing with contingency, which has a constant presence in human experience.

Concluding the discussion of the industrial novel, Gaskell's fiction is also characteristic of the complex negotiation of risk within a morally charged discourse that is taken to even greater depth in the mid-Victorian epical novels of Trollope and Eliot. Continuing the criticism of gambling and financial speculation, these texts see a further development of the discourse of risk and gender and a darkening of the marriage plot, which is shown to be fraught with physical and psychological danger; the greatest one being having to live with one's choices and their consequences.

---

[68] Sanders, in his analysis of the accidents in Gaskell's fiction in relation to the era's public discourse about occupational hazard, explains: "In other words poor physical health is read as a sign of immorality. This attribution of a direct causal link between the moral health of a workman and his physical health persisted throughout the century" (2000: 315). About the triad of working-class deaths in *North and South* he writes: "It is not difficult to see this sequence of narrative events as registering and negotiating the profoundly unsettling insight that middle-class comforts depended on working class suffering" (326–327).

7 Epic Tales of Ambition and Speculation

7.1 New Money and Marriage Plots

With the threats of Chartism and Industrialism no longer immediate, the agitated England, which had been a main concern of the Industrial novel and political writers such as J.S. Mill, was growing sedate by comparison. According to Shirley Letwin, by the middle of the 19th century, it was already "well on the way to the age of Bagehot and Trollope, the time when England seemed to have emerged permanently from dreams and nightmares into a mature, confident serenity. The country was permeated by a sense of satisfaction" (Letwin 1965: 291). Yet this serenity was temporary at best and also gave rise to a set of different anxieties.

The quarter-century from 1848–75, which Eric Hobsbaum referred to the as "the age of capital" (see Hobsbaum 1997) was an important phase of financial globalization and by the 1850s, London had become a centre of global commerce, with the British economy increasingly dependent on foreign investments. With regard to its dominant literary mode, this period of high capitalism is typically described as the "age of realism" (see Brantlinger 1996: 146). In many high-Victorian novels by Dickens, Thackeray, Trollope, Eliot, and Meredith, money and financial issues determine plots, characters, and the relationships between them. Reflecting the ubiquity of monetary discourse and the anxiety about the new scope and expansiveness of Victorian commerce, these texts present affective, fictional responses to pervasive economic and social changes and often explore the ambivalence of the rise of a new monied merchant class and the slow decline of the landed gentry. Generally, Patrick Brantlinger argues, one can see a shift from the social criticism of the industrial novel toward the "'moral currency' of culture", (Brantlinger 1996: 143), a refocusing of the literary gaze away from the working class and industrialization towards personal (and predominately middle and upper class) matters of credit, debt, and speculation. The concern with the class conflict and the condition of England is reshaped into concerns of the individual being affected by economic developments – often beyond one's control – and questions of personal integrity and responsibility.

Following J. Jeffery Franklin's analysis, the plot-shaping circulation of capital in mid-Victorian fictions can be separated into several principal modes of exchange. The modes include marriage, inheritance, charity, work, financial investment, speculation, debt, credit, bankruptcy, gambling, theft, bribery, or blackmail and they are furthermore charged with different moral value, separable into positive and negative, and safer and dangerous forms. Time and speed are important distinguishing factors. Regarding the acquisition of money, rapid forms, such as gambling wins, blackmail, or theft are depicted as harmful to the individual and the social order, in contrast to slower forms such as work. Similarly, past-oriented forms like inheritance are ranked morally superior to future-, and thus risk-oriented forms like speculation and gambling.[1] Interestingly, while there remains a gendered difference between male vs. female speculation – the fictional stock-market villains, bankers, gamblers and spendthrifts are almost exclusively of the male variety – but both sexes continue to partake in the gamble of the marriage market. Marriage and speculative business deals are seen to be equally dependent on "credit" and reputation. The discourse of money and marriage are paired closer than ever and both are fraught with potential gains, dangers, and ruin. The decline of the conventional marriage plot, which gathered momentum from the 1870s onwards, meant that domestic issues and courtship were topics increasingly treated with tragedy, or irony and suspicion. In many fictions matrimony is represented as an unavoidable, but "extremely risky gamble" (Franklin 1994: 905). The risks lie in not knowing till it is too late the outcome of one's hopes, in not really knowing one's partner, and in not being able to fully control or realize one's own desires.

In particular the second half of the 19th century thus appears as "a commercially literate age" in which the "'game of speculation' was played by all" (Russell 1986: 19), yet the state-legislated as well as the public moral opposition to forms of gambling grew.[2] Apart from the risks of addiction and mounting debts, gambling is generally perceived as threatening because it potentially allows for rapid social mobility. The same applies to financial speculation and bankruptcy. Barbara Weiss memorably described the dreaded prospect of financial ruin as the "Hell of the English". She takes it to be indicative of the "very universal Victorian fear of poverty and failure – a fear that appears to have had a compelling foundation in reality", with bankruptcy being its most spectacular expression because it represented the most "sudden, catastrophic, and final" form of economic ruin in Victorian society (Weiss 1986: 15; 14). While the second half of the century saw cyclical financial crises, an intermitted series of speculative bubble ventures, times of prosperity, spectacular crashes and losses of money, and ensuing public panic, bankruptcy was perceived as a symp-

---

[1] See Franklin (2003; 1994).
[2] For example, the 1845 Gaming Act rendered all gambling debts unenforceable and represented an effort to minimize the damaging effect of gambling. See Brenner and Brenner's *Gambling and Speculation* (1990). Their study gives detailed insight into the history of gaming legislation, different types of gamblers, and motivations for gambling (e.g. entertainment, economic pressures, entrepreneurial, criminal motivations).

tom of larger uncertainties. Entailing a rapid reversal of fortune, it highlighted economic vulnerability, fear of change, and the general precariousness of existence. The reality of bankruptcy also challenged and violated Victorian ideas of economic virtue, increasing the public's financial risk perception by making "the threat of failure both more likely and more terrifying than ever before" (Weiss 1986: 23). The fictions of the time negotiate those anxieties, especially the felt rupture of security due to the collapse of a (relatively) safe distance between home and market place. The private sphere becomes invaded by the cash-nexus, by the discourse of commodification, the ideology of possession and accumulation of wealth. Meanwhile bankruptcy signified a complete loss of material wealth as well as of reputation, the latter being an equally valuable asset. Consequently, Jeff Nunokawa says: "Nothing could hurt more in the Victorian novel, where to have property is to settle in life and to lose it a taste of death, a scandal, a terror, a tragedy in which all others gather, a catastrophe where the various meanings of ruin convene, a calamity that causes everything in and out of sight to tremble" (Nunokawa 1994: 7).

The frequency of bankruptcy plots in the grand Victorian novel perverts any sense of security and satisfaction. Although insurance had become an established social practice, in the fictions the characters often experience the opposite of successful precaution or risk management. The large casts of characters and multiple plotlines also reflect the confusing complexity and anonymity of global circulations of money. The era's capitalist economic formations do not only require an increasing trust in abstract entities (schemes, bonds, banks) but also embody the risk of the failure or misconduct of one individual, e. g. overspeculation, taking down many. For example, the crash of the financier Melmotte in Trollope's *The Way We Live Now* affects all characters more or less directly. Questions of whom to trust, what investments and speculations are "safe", and who ends up paying for what assume a new urgency, as do issues of liability, and compensation. Intertwining economic, legal, and moral discourses, these matters are negotiated in many novels via the depiction of financial crimes (such as investment fraud, embezzlement, or blackmail) as signs and tests of a character's moral worth, or the usually disastrous outcomes of risky gambles (both in the domestic and business arena). Whereas characters heavily in debt mostly function as cautionary examples, as a plot pattern, bankruptcy takes the risk of financial ruin to extremes and leaves the characters with usually only exile or suicide as exit strategies.

The Way We Live Now illustrates the evolution of the financial plot – a stock ingredient of the novel from its beginnings – turning from the inheritance plots that dominate the late-18th- and early 19th- century novels to more complex plot patterns that, Poovey points out, "allowed writers to explore matters involving personal agency and individual will, like financial temptation and fiscal responsibility" (Poovey 2002: 33). Similarly, Tamara Wagner argues that the grand Victorian stock-market novels, of which Trollope's is a good example, extricate and modify rather clichéd structures of traditional marital and inheritance plots by relating them instead "to a growing fascination with self-deceived and deceiving speculators" (Wagner, T. 2010: 177). However if one looks at 18th century fictions, this is hardly a new phenomenon. With great frequency, bankruptcy occurs in the Victorian novel, as argued above, as "the perfect structural metaphor for the vulnerability of the individual" (Weiss 1986: 20). In contrast to earlier texts which registered the instability of the emerging credit system, it is only from the in mid-19th century onwards that consequences of financial crises found articulation as "fully fledged stock-market novels" (Wagner, T. 2010: 15). Agreeing with Wagner, the emergence of the stock-market novel signals more than a reflection of financial crises, but presents a "new cultural imaginary expressed changing ideas of moral probity and indeterminate identity, creditworthiness and the management of financial risks" (2010: 3) in an increasingly global market place.

As outlined in chapter 6.1, while the basic groundwork for a national statistical apparatus was laid in the 18th century, the 19th century saw its full implementation and 'society', as well as individual 'case' studies, became important objects of scientific study both in the natural and human sciences. The calculation of averages and standardized norms (and their exceptions) via unified recording methods of data was introduced as a means to master uncertainty, manage risk and facilitate governmental rule. The impact of the debate ensuing around Quetelet's "average man" and the new way of thinking and expressing all matters in terms of likelihoods, comparative analysis, and setting each event or individual in relation to a larger context cannot be overestimated.[3] In the "Morality of the Doctrine of Averages", the philosopher William Cyples claimed that

> this modern notion of averages introduces a habit of thought and a state of feeling which set off the present age from all that have preceded it, and will not fail ever increasingly to modify human experience in the future. The unique feeling which it induces may broadly be stated as something unique in the history of the world; a fresh sentiment, at present confined to Europe, and not before experienced anywhere. (Cyples 1864: 223)

Its relevance and influence on everyday language as well as on fictional plots and characterization becomes obvious also when one considers the conception of averages as what is "between two extremes", calculations of proportionality

---

[3] See Alain Desrosières's *The Politics of Large Numbers: A History of Statistical Reasoning* (1998), especially chapters 3–5.

in relation to other quantities or entities "of the same kind", or notions of "common value". This kind of statistical thinking, as Desrosières explains, was situated in a particular – and very Victorian – "context of political anxiety. Endowed with every virtue, Quetelet's 'average man' was presented as a kind of prudent centrist, who avoided every conceivable form of excess" (Desrosières 1998: 79). The average man also appeared as a persuasive, fictive creation, perfect due to his conforming to the ideals of moderation and normalcy. In many novels this is reflected through notions of "plainness" and "average" vs. "exceptional" as means of characterization. Desrosières's argument further underlines the morally charged dimension of the 19th-century statistical mission and the central tension between determinism and free will. The fact that the idea of the individual being responsible for his/her actions clashes with the stability of macro-social realities like crime or suicide rates is just one example. But the doctrine of averages and the limits of statistical inquiry are also interrogated critically in many fictional and non-fictional texts of the time. It was perceived that a negative result of the focus on the average and the calculation of regularities was the creation of false images of uniformity, which ignore, for instance, the specific circumstances and the moral and mental processes involved in committing a crime. On these grounds, Cyples concludes that "the pushing up of the doctrine of averages into the moral sphere, and thus obliterating the freedom of man, is not justifiable, for that which passes in the conscience is not open to external proof, and can never be collected in a statistical form" (1864: 221). The ambivalent depiction of Grandcourt's death in Eliot's *Daniel Deronda* is a good illustration of the difficulty of extending judgment to human conscience and connecting actions with emotions. In any case, the notion of averages lead to a new mode of thinking, which formed the back-bone of the rapidly growing insurance industry and which thus, as Trotter puts it, "fully acknowledged, while it sought to protect itself against, the force of contingency" (Trotter 2000: 137). In this context Cyples' essay also presents an interesting counter-argument against the development of the national insurance business, viewing the experience of risk as necessary and character-forming. The attempt of insuring and taking precautions against everything is destructive by contrast in the sense that "the dull, level feeling of comfortable and stagnant security to which it leads, is not the best development of human nature. There is at least a show of reason in saying that a man gets nobler thrills from launching an uninsured venture upon stormy seas" (1864: 222–223). In the realm of fiction, although the discourse of gambling and speculation is clearly charged with ethical judgment, the main protagonists are often risk-takers and the plots also affirm dealing with risk and contingency as inevitable parts of life.

The narratives of the time reflect the tensions between individual agency and statistical inevitability and an emerging social consciousness transcending the individual. In particular the multitude of characters in the Victorian novel can be set in relation to the strong influence of statistics and the awareness of the law of large numbers outlined above. When a novel introduces its large number of characters, Tina Choi argues, "it encourages the reader not to consider their believability, but instead to speculate about an already anticipated range of outcomes, like fortune and marriage" (Choi 2001: 580). The reader is thus confronted with texts which offer a "kind of uncertain and contingent space", inviting speculation "about a population, for whom any number of events – disease, marriage, death – exist within the realm of chance, and, by the conclusion, will have assumed the quality of necessity" (2001: 584). In this way the "large, loose, baggy monsters"[4] of Victorian fiction propagate perception of norms, exceptions, and likelihoods, as well as contingency, rather than a sense of miracle or providential 'closure.' They also help to create and perpetuate not just the notion of the average man in general, but also of various 'typical' persons of different ranks and professions, e.g "the typical banker, shopkeeper, suitor, trading partner, or other 'sort' of person whose character and credibility readers were increasingly called on to interpret if they were to transact social life successfully" (Baucom 2005: 70; see Lynch 1998: 5).

The great realist Victorian novel therefore echoes the historical shift described so memorably by Foucault in *Discipline and Punish* as the moment "when the normal took over from the ancestral, and measurement from status, thus *substituting for the individuality of the memorable man that of the calculable man*, that moment when the sciences of man became possible" (Foucault 1995: 193; my emphasis). The evolution of the novel in the course of the 19th century is also a testament of the changing perception of individualization and the emerging administrative bureaucracy supported by statistical methods and the "disciplinary society" in Foucault's sense; the individual becoming (newly) visible as a "fictitious atom of an 'ideological' representation of society" (1995: 194). 19th-century fiction bears testimony to the rising interest in psychology and the study of the relations between human thought and behaviour, while capturing the impact of two parallel developments: The focus on the masses, on averages, and the objective calculation of the human which in turn intensifies the focus on the individual and leads to a new subjectivity. George Levine emphasizes this aspect, relating it to an emerging obsession with scientific observation, measurement, and surveillance reflected in Victorian fiction (Levine 1988: 219). The

---

4 The phrase is, of course, Henry James's (1936: x).

importance of minute observation and the extension of science's authority from natural to human phenomena is a result of both statistical thought and Darwinism. According to Levine, the latter reinforced the idea that all events can be explained causally and gave momentum to the theme of change, and questions of heredity and progress, origins and future. A further parallel between Darwinism and realist Victorian fiction is suggested by the preoccupation with intricate chains of connections, "with multiple and complex social relations, with growth and change, with uniform and minute and inexorable sequences" (1988: 21).[5] With the spirit of observation, measurement, surveillance, and reportage infiltrating the novel, the close scrutiny of characters by others, often causing feelings of hope, dread or guilt, is integral to the plot structures, especially in the works of George Eliot. All these aspects contribute to cementing the importance of risk as a perceptual category for readers and characters alike. Trollope's *The Way We Live Now* and Eliot's *Daniel Deronda* exemplify the characteristics and concerns of Victorian grand multi-plot fictions, dealing with economic threats, and (moral) bankruptcy. They explore the dangers of greed, pride, and narcissism, as well as feelings of dread and denial, Trollope in more satirical, Eliot in more epic and psychological form.

7.2 More Losses than Gains: *The Way We Live Now*

John Vernon referred to Anthony Trollope, perhaps the most prolific writer of the Victorian era, as a "kind of vulgar Jane Austen" (Vernon 1984: 44). His comment emphasizes the centrality of marriage and fortune hunting as themes in Trollope's works, but also draws attention to his much more explicit, sensational treatment of these topics and to his style of writing that oscillates between realist melodrama and dark satire. Trollope's longest novel, *The Way We Live Now* (1875), confronts the vulgarity and corruption of Victorian society and commerce head-on. With its condemnation of speculative finance and the plot centered around August Melmotte, a villainous financier whose own origins are as uncertain and mysterious as those of his wealth and who commits suicide after he runs out of cash and credit, it is representative of many mid- to late-Victorian texts.[6] Further aspects warranting close analysis are the interrelations between risk and gender in the text.

---

[5] See the early seminal studies in the field, George Levine's *Darwin and the Novelists* (1988) and Gillian Beer's *Darwin's Plots* (1984).

[6] The novel is most frequently compared to Dickens's *Little Dorrit* (1857) which includes the story of the fall and suicide of the banker Mr. Merdle.

The figure of the banker in literary representation generally underwent a significant identity change from 1850s to 1870s; the older notion of the banker as somewhat benevolent fatherly figures was replaced by that of ruthless egoists. Above all, there is a perceived change in the sense of social responsibility felt by the bankers, who started to be seen and see themselves as a class of "experts whose main responsibility was to other bankers" (Alborn 1995: 203). Unsurprisingly, while the Victorian novel instigated the alignment of forms of money-making with specific character types, by the second half of the 19th century speculation was top of the list "of unsavoury qualities a villain could be expected to possess" (Jaffe 2010: 54).[7] Many fictions employ bankers as the central villainous, or fallen characters, examples include Mr Merdle in *Little Dorrit*, Mr Bounderby in *Hard Times*, Mr Bulstrode in *Middlemarch* or Mr Melmotte in *The Way We Live Now*. With all characters' fates in one way or another connected to the fall of Melmotte, the novel documents Trollope's interest in capitalism and the workings of the free market society, as well as in the laws and dynamics of social relations. It explores prevalent concerns about the risks of speculation in all areas of society, about collapsing values, and the erosion of certainties and traditions. Speculative business ventures having received new stimulus after limited liability was legally established in 1855, financial instability was as widespread as ever. Many writers and commentators produced vicious attacks of the new legislation for licensing risky speculation, disregarding necessary regulations, and undermining individual responsibility. James Eli Adams notes how from the 1860s onwards dramas and novels dealing with disastrous speculation dominated the Victorian literary scene,[8] modifying earlier sensational plots, that focuses mainly on greed as the cause of financial scandal, to show the vast and opaque complexity of global finance and business ventures. One commonly finds attacks of a system seen to have a destabilizing effect on every aspect of social life, suggesting, as the title of Trollope's novel does, "a more sweeping disaffection: traditional moral norms are giving way on all fronts to a corrosive dishonesty and ruthless self-interest" (Adams 2012: 317).

---

[7] In his analysis of the fears connected with commercialization and new businessmen from the late 18th throughout the 19th century, James Raven argues that negative images of bankers and fictional "representations of the vulgar nouveau riche businessman" (1992: 261; 11–12) are widely adopted in the Victorian novel, connected to warnings against speculation and over-expenditure.

[8] On the boom of financial fictions in the "sensational sixties", see Tamara S. Wagner (2010: 61–88).

The Way We Live Now is written and published in a contradictory climate. It appears after the expansion of the banking industry in the 1860s and 70s and the development of a plutocracy of "great" men of capitalist finance, who claimed they knew how to speculate and handle risk. With the decades of the 1850s–70s being times of immense prosperity, they also saw a disturbing series of spectacular bank failures. Even old established firms began to engaged in 'new' speculation; honourable names were suddenly connected to scandals of fraud, spurred on by the desire to repeat and partake in the "heady if dangerous successes of the railroad-share epoch" (Russell 1986: 69) beginning in the 1840s.[9] Trollope's novel takes up one of the time's "principal fevers of speculation" connected with the "Railway Mania" (Russell 1986: 19; see Michie 2001: 77); it also stages England's fear of America's growing economic power and alludes to the rapid development of the US railroad, realized mainly with British capital. Melmotte's spectacularly grand investment deal consists of shares in the yet to be built South Central Pacific and Mexican railway, stretching over 2000 miles from Salt Lake City to Vera Cruz. It is a scheme with incalculable risks, and all those involved in it have to acknowledge, "that no computation had or perhaps could be made as to the probable cost of the railway" (WWLN 62); nonetheless, "fortunes were to be made [...] before a spadeful of earth had been moved" (WWLN 63). Aside from speculation in railway shares, the plot of The Way We Live Now principally includes another, and much older, form of speculation, the race for the hand of the richest heiress in town, Melmotte's daughter Marie. There is a third, and in Patrick Parrinder's words, "purely wasteful form of speculation, the games of chance played every night by Trollope's young English aristocrats at the Beargarden Club" (Parrinder 2006: 247). Other than Felix Carbury, the main and increasingly desperate suitor for the hand of Marie Melmotte, the group of gambling regulars at the Beargarden Club includes Dolly Longstaffe, Lord Grasslough, and Miles Grendall. All men usually lack ready cash, and IOUs (abbreviated from the phrase "I owe you") are their general, very immaterial, means of money exchange. Like the railway shares, those IOUs are in the end only good on paper. Typically, in the novel the sufferers of losses are also often not identical with the people who caused it. The gambling debts of Felix Carbury and his lot will never be collected, neither will Melmotte's investors see a return of their money.

---

9 Tara McGann notes that readers of Trollope's novel in the 1870s would have directly associated "the fictional railway company with the scandal surrounding the collapse of the venerable London credit house of Overend, Gurney & Company in 1866" (2007: 145).

Geoffrey Baker fittingly describes *The Way We Live Now* as Trollope's "own angry version of the probable bad" (Baker 2009: 151). It is a biting portrait of the state of Victorian society and reveals the consequences of an outlook which puts a price tag on everything and of pursuing material wealth at all costs.[10] The plot development exposes the dangers of unregulated speculation and of money without substance, derived not from land or hard work, "but from a managed combination of speed, public opinion, and risk" (Hensley 2009: 152). The text furthermore evokes a notion of metropolitan danger, taken up in many 18th-century and also especially late-Victorian fictions, such as Gissing's *The Whirlpool*. London, depicted as a changing city and centre of imperial commerce, is swept by a wave of the negative effects of globalization, including the increasing speed and circulation of people and new money, replacing the stable security of land-owned wealth. The plot, at its heart a tale of a criminal, dubious foreigner and a fraudulent overseas investment scheme, reflects the perceived risks of losing national and personal control over England's money.

Various models for Trollope's Melmotte have been suggested, including infamous 19th-century speculators such as the "Railway King" George Hudson, or John Sadleir, who poisoned himself after collapse of the Tipperary Joint-Stock Bank. Melmotte's foreignness and obscure roots have also suggested comparisons to Baron Albert Grant, the American agent of the Rothschild clan and son of a German Jew (see Russell 1986: 160; Swafford 2013: 121). As an outsider to London's high society, Melmotte's embodies the attraction as well as the destructive and criminal forces associated with processes of global expansion and commerce. His implicit statelessness and Jewishness evoke stereotypes of late-Victorian globalizing finance; he symbolizes the "'improperly' international man – subject to no nation, beholden to no forces but the borderless interests of money capital" (Hensley 2009: 155–156; see Baker 2009: 132).[11] Trollope's narrative only offers vague biographical and geographical reference points for the cosmopolitan Melmotte, connecting him to migrations and business ventures across

---

10 On the topic and criticism of commercial interests and the stock-market in Trollope's works see Delany (2002), Jaffe (2010), Lindner (2000), and Michie (2001).

11 On the climate of suspicion and the association of people who are to "good" with money and its mysteries as a breeding ground for literary anti-Semitism see also Delaney (2002: 25). Margaret Anne Doody goes a step further; she underlines the general relation between xenophobia, the imperialist agenda, and the realist Victorian novel, which for her displays stark excluding tendencies. The realist novel "does not on the whole care for ethnic mixing. [...] It hardly seems coincidental that the cult of the 'real' and the 'normal' in fiction should have taken fiercest hold in England and that its rise coincides with [...] the rise of British imperialism" (1996: 292); "The Novel becomes fully 'domestic' – shutting out aliens" (293).

the globe, including New York, Paris, Vienna, Ireland, China, and the Americas. However, Melmotte's national-ethnic identity is ultimately less relevant than the uncertainty he represents. Geoffrey Baker and Paul Delany emphasize the fact that it does not only provides endless fuel for plot development and complication, but that this vagueness "is precisely the point: it corresponds to the opacity of his speculations and the slippery anonymity of finance capital itself" (Delaney 2002: 26–27; see Baker 2009: 141–142). Similarly, Jeffrey Franklin notes that the anxieties evoked by the origins of Melmotte's character parallel the threats posed by new forms of money and the replacement of "signs of origin with anonymity" (Franklin 2003: 506).

Melmotte is first introduced by people's conversations about his ruthlessly ambitious, dubious reputation that extends throughout Europe; "he was regarded in Paris as the most gigantic swindler that had ever lived" (WWLN 25), he was "one who in the dishonest and successful pursuit of wealth had stopped at nothing" (WWLN 55). He represents counterfeit forms of wealth, accumulated by speculation and not heritage. As such, he is always ready to move to another city or country and start anew after a financial crisis following the blow up of a speculative deal: "Such had been his scheme of life" (WWLN 554). Although the public perception of him borders on the criminal, his fantastic wealth eclipses all criticism and does not stop any of the other characters to try and benefit from social association or business deals with Melmotte. A main object of Trollope's satire is the willingness of the members of the upper classes to welcome Melmotte among them and to trust him despite all rumours suggesting the contrary: "who could think of danger in reference to money intrusted to the hands of August Melmotte?" (WWLN 283). In the course of the novel, Melmotte becomes "greater and greater in every direction, – mightier and mightier every day" (WWLN 262), just like the British Empire at the time. He even runs for a seat in Parliament. Through Melmotte Trollope, as he explains in his *Autobiography*, sought to illustrate the phenomenon "that dishonesty, if it can become splendid, will cease to be abominable" (Trollope 1883: 210). In fact, his novel satirizes the modern capitalist insight that: "When a man's frauds have been enormous there is a certain safety in their very diversity and proportions" (WWLN 469).

Melmotte's greatest asset is the power of his name, for the longest time a guarantee for unlimited credit. His case exemplifies a crucial link between financial commitments and the importance of the faith in, as well as the keeping up of, appearances. At the time when Trollope's novel is set, the Victorian public faced the on-going problem to distinguish between legitimate trade and unsafe speculation, a task only complicated by economic relations becoming more complex, distant, and anonymous. Banks, as well as individuals, then as now depend on other people's trust in them and are quickly ruined if their 'credibility is lost. Accordingly, Melmotte explains to Paul Montague: "Gentlemen who don't know the nature of credit, how strong it is – as the air – to buoy you up; how slight it is – as a mere vapour – when roughly touched, can do an amount of mischief of which they themselves don't in the least understand the extent!" (WWLN 307). The quote illustrates the function of the era's fictional literature as a moralizing antidote to the speculative attitudes normalized by economic non-fictional writing, seeking to foster a more critical attitude towards money, as has been described by Poovey (2002). Popularizing and educating the public about finance, the newly emerging genre of financial journalism – as well as realist fictions such as Trollope's – sought to influence the public acceptance of, e.g., speculation and investments. Poovey's implied emphasis that the main function of this kind of writing was risk management is particularly interesting, as she argues that it "sought to depict the financial sector [...] as a law-governed, natural, and – preeminently – *safe sector of modern society*" (2002: 22–23; my emphasis). Following Poovey's argument, the morally charged mission of seeking to rebuke investment and finance was still largely subordinate to the function of financial writing's main aim to normalize workings of financial institutions, seeking to help create clearer-cut distinctions between good and bad forms of speculative finance, rather than condemning it outright.[12] The representation of financial speculation in Trollope as well as in many other fictions is complex and transcends officially advised paradigms of contemporary risk management. The texts refuse reduction to any simple political warning function, but call for caution and regulations of a financial system that threatens to become impossible to oversee and control. While Poovey sees a special "generic proximity" (2002: 19) between realist fiction and journalism at the time, extending her analysis to newspapers, periodicals, and pamphlets, Jane Moody observes interesting similarities to Victorian theatre in this context. Emphasizing how "the growth of the British economy and the empire depended on *the acceptance of risk and uncertainty as the price of growth and expansion*" (Moody 2007: 98; my emphasis), Moody relates this aspect to the era's boom of popular melodramas detailing the consequences of financial speculation.

---

12 Arguing on these grounds, Denise Lovett attempts to turn the existing economic criticism on its head and reads the Trollope's novel not as a warning or the mourning of an old order, but as a forward-looking "argument for how a mature English form of capitalism might develop" (2014: 692). However, several critics have previously commented on the nuanced criticism inherent in Trollope's text which highlights the difficulties to distinguish between legitimate speculative commerce and fraud without suggesting "that commerce is always fraudulent", but that "[t]he marketplace must be cured of rampant borrowing and stock exchange 'gambling' in order to function properly" (Brantlinger 1996: 171).

The discourse of risk, oscillating between acceptance and rejection, impacts the perception of the connections between past, present, and future via the increasing importance of conceptions of liability: "Whereas the language of risk emphasizes the chances involved in taking a stake in the future, the emerging discourse of liability reveals the haunting of the presence by financial obligations made in the past. The consequences of such liabilities – and the psychological confusion they produce – are a recurring theme" (Moody 2007: 103).[13] The latter aspect dominates the second half of Trollope's novel.

Melmotte is ultimately destroyed by the fact that his "speculations had been so great and so wide that he did not really know what he owned, or what he owed" (WWLN 559). Neither is the public opinion undivided on this matter and conflicting newspaper reports document the impossibility to ascertain how much he is, in fact, worth: "One declared that Mr. Melmotte was not in truth possessed of any wealth. The other said that he had derived his wealth from those unfortunate shareholders" (WWLN 412–413). The climate slowly turns against him: "There are a good many who say that Melmotte will burst up" (WWLN 339). Finally, he falls because he fails to raise ready cash after overextending himself during his political campaign and the preparation of the lavish banquet for the Chinese Emperor. Equal measures of arrogance and desperation lead to his fatal mistake, the forging of a signature on the Pickering property deal. Melmotte is ruined by a lack of time and loss of control, although he almost succeeds in maintaining the upper hand in "the very dangerous game which he was playing; but, as crisis heaped itself upon crisis, he became deficient in prudence" (WWLN 414). The narrative details Melmotte's long considerations of all possible circumstances and what-if's scenarios, highlighting his increasing confusion, while he desperately holds on to the illusion of control: "No doubt all danger in that Longstaffe affair might be bought off by payment of the price stipulated for the Pickering property. [...] But the complications were so many!" (WWLN 556).

Dishonesty and the willingness to ignore the truth for as long as possible in order to profit are traits shared by the majority of characters in *The Way We Live Now*. But they are most pronounced in Melmotte. As the story develops, the cracks in his façade of self-assurance become obvious and he reacts with a mixture of laissez-faire and stoic denial to his situation. Showing him overwhelmed

---

13 Examples of Victorian plays dealing explicitly with financial risk are Dion Boucicault's *The Poor of New York* (1857) and *London Assurance* (1841), George Henry Lewes' *The Game of Speculation* (1851), or Edward Bulwer-Lytton's *Money* (1840). These and many other plays saw thousands of performances and adaptation on both sides of the Atlantic, testifying to the popularity of financial emergency as subject for melodrama. See Moody (2007).

by his financial speculations, but very conscious of the risks of his endeavours, Trollope's narrative voice zooms in on Melmotte's thoughts:

> He had always lived with the consciousness that such a burden was on him and might crush him at any time. *He had known that he had to run these risks.* He had told himself a thousand times that when the dangers came, dangers alone should never cow him. [...]. He had studied the criminal laws, so that he might be sure in his reckonings; but *he had always felt that he might be carried by circumstances into deeper waters than he intended to enter.* [...] *the greatness had grown upon him,—and so had the danger.* He could not now be as exact as he had been. [...] as his intellect opened up to him new schemes, and as his ambition got the better of his prudence, he gradually fell from the security which he had preconceived, and became aware that he might have to bear worse than ignominy. (WWLN 468; my emphasis)

The quote exemplifies the risk language and metaphors employed by Trollope throughout the novel, most prominently features the imagery of being "drowned" or carried into "deep waters".[14] The close link of financial and personal risk in the narratives hints at the ethical complexities of capitalist investment culture. Through Melmotte Trollope also shows the reality of cyclic patterns of crisis and prosperity. On more than one occasion he refers to the significance of Melmotte's belief, grown from experience that "life had been made dark by similar clouds before now, and he had lived through the storms which had followed them" (WWLN 475). According to Norman Russell, Victorian bankers and merchants were accustomed to accept precariousness as part of the system and "conditioned to accept at least the possibility of enormous losses consequent on depression and diminishing credit as the crisis of each cycle approached" (Russell 1986: 23). Arguing along similar lines, Tara McGann relates Trollope's narrative specifically to the emerging understanding of business cycle theory in the 1860s and 70s. The mechanism of periodic crises and the quickly fluctuating market becomes apparent in the novel, even without being rationalized in any great, or even plausible depth. It is, for example, never clarified whether Melmotte really possesses the wealth he is credited with, or whether the railway

---

[14] Metaphors connecting risk-taking and water occur countless times in the novel and are used by various characters. To give only a few examples, Lady Carbury claims: "You cannot send a ship to sea without endangering lives" (WWLN 226); "These were deep waters into which Sir Felix was preparing to plunge;" (WWLN 224); after Melmotte's death people say that "the waters around him had become to deep even for him" (WWLN 661); Georgiana Longstaffe reflects on the urgency of finding a husband as follows: "She too must strike out with rapid efforts, unless, indeed, she would abandon herself and let the waters close over her head. [...] That ultimate failure in her matrimonial projects would be the same as drowning she never for a moment doubted" (WWLN 724–725).

scheme is a sham. This is indicative of the plots of what McGann describes as a new kind of financial novel, illustrating the workings of high finance and business cycle theory by developing intricate webs and complex waves instead of singular catastrophes with clear causal connections (see McGann 2007: 155; 136–137).

Melmotte hosts the reception for the Chinese Emperor and London's high society "almost with a rope round his neck" (WWLN 475). Until the very end he tries to keep up appearances. The dinner brings the public collapse of Melmotte's reputation and reinforces the volatileness and rapid movement of credit. The desirability of the dinner party tickets depends exclusively on the social status of Melmotte which is quickly diminished by the rumours about his forgery; the value of the railway shares falls together with the price of the tickets. The public has to weigh the risks of being compromised by being seen at the event, should the rumours prove true, against the chance of missing out on the party of the season. By the time evening comes, however, the tickets are worth no more than the paper they are printed on. Melmotte seeks to manage the risk of further losses by trying to assure his business partners and especially Lord Nidderdale, his desired suitor for Marie's hand, that all is still well and under control. He explains how the rumours surrounding the dinner made the railway shares worthless overnight, trying to divert digress responsibility away from himself: "They persuaded a lot of men to stay away from that infernal dinner, and consequently it was spread about the town that I was ruined. The effect upon shares which I held was instantaneous and tremendous'" (WWLN 563).

Melmotte's last resort of risk management is taking his daughter's money, safely invested in foreign funds in her name. Employing the typical risk rhetoric, Trollope's narrator informs the reader: "This he had done fearing shipwreck in the course which he meant to run [...]. He had sworn to himself solemnly that under no circumstances would he allow this money to go back into the vortex of his speculations [...]. But he had failed to consider various circumstances" (WWLN 554). But Marie bravely refuses to surrender her money to her father, forcing Melmotte to commit another forgery. Outwardly maintaining an arrogant courage until the very end, he is driven into a corner and ruined through losing his calmness and his characteristic cool in handling risky matters of speculation and theft. Particularly the final parts of the narrative are full of endless speculative scenarios from Melmotte about what "might probably" happen. Yet under the mounting pressure, he disregards all those reflections, as a result only increasing rather than managing the risks: "Again he had acted in a hurry, – without giving sufficient thought to the matter in hand. [...] But how is a man to give sufficient thought to his affairs when no step that he takes can be other than ruinous? [...] They might drag him to gaol. They probably would" (WWLN 623). Melmotte's behaviour epitomizes society's moral bankruptcy. It shows how a single individual financier can bring down a whole system by assuming uncontrollable levels of risk, as well as the ruinous attempts of seeking to evade responsibility. While Melmotte embodies a recognizable type of financier of the time, he also displays a risk awareness resembling that of modern day investment bankers, thriving on the precarious edge of audacity. His fall does not come as a surprise to him, yet could apparently neither be anticipated nor controlled when it happened, suggesting in fact little to no difference between 19th- and 21st-century financial crises.

A second important subplot details the struggles and ambitions of the Carbury family. Lady Carbury sacrificed her independence and happiness in order to gain a respected place in society: "To marry and have the command of money [...] had been her ambition" (WWLN 10). It came at the cost of having to keep up appearances and disguise years of domestic abuse. After the ordeal of enduring being "scolded, watched, beaten, and sworn at by a choleric old man" (WWLN 11) and her late husband's death from alcoholism, she is now a single woman again and has a second chance at happiness. She attempts a literary career, venturing into the world of business, self-advertisement, and publicity, now gambling for the success of her novels, one of which is tellingly entitled *The Wheel of Fortune.* Her son, baronet Felix Carbury, embodies the stereotypical member of fallen aristocracy and seems to be set on the course of ruining himself along with his mother and sister Hetta. He is incapable of perceiving risk, be it the ones he is running with his incessant gambling, the family's dire financial circumstances after the death of his father, or any other. This is however not due to bravery or recklessness but ignorance and lack of imagination: "He could not even feel his own misfortunes unless they touched the -outward comforts of the moment" (WWLN 14). His only capital being his title and good looks, and with his debts mounting every day to such an extent that they have assumed a somewhat unreal status, he is used to spending any winnings immediately, incapable of economizing or planning ahead. Although Lady Carbury despises gambling for "being of all pastimes the most dangerous" (WWLN 81), she is lenient towards her son's habit, "almost proud of his vices", and "hardly ventured to say a word to him with the purport of stopping him on his road to ruin" (WWLN 13). Instead, she pins all her hopes on a profitable marriage. Desperate for her own literary success, a reason why she turns a blind eye to her son's activities is that she, at heart, sympathizes with his spirit. To some extent, she is also a fraud and well versed in the art of misrepresentation, denial, and manipulation; like most characters in the novel, she has speculative habits. Annette Van goes as far as saying that Lady Carbury's "scheming self-interest, and self-deceit ally her with Melmotte, [...] the difference between the two seems to be only on the order of magnitude" (Van 2005: 88–89).

With Marie Melmotte being the big prize up for grabs, mother and son agree that this is a gamble worth taking. Felix says, "this is a risky sort of game, I grant, but I am playing it by your advice. If I can marry Miss Melmotte, I suppose all will be right" (WWLN 19). Felix, ironically named the 'lucky one' although he looses constantly, seemingly has struck gold with Marie's romantic interest in him. Yet he soon finds himself in a situation very difficult to control and fraught with numerous conflicting interests and dangers. The urgency of seeing the marriage to Marie come through, does not, however, affect any change of his gambling routine at the Beargarden Club. Hierarchizing the gambles her son is involved in, Lady Carbury says to herself: "Fool, to risk his health, his character, his beauty, the little money which at this moment of time might be so indispensable to his great project, for the chance of winning something which in comparison with Marie Melmotte's money must be despicable!" (WWLN 90).

Sir Felix, though he is heir to the Carbury estate, is not an appropriate suitor for Marie by Melmotte's standards due to his lack of income. Different prejudices are played out between Felix Carbury and Melmotte in the courtship of Marie, an illustration of the historical class struggle of new vs. old money, and snobbery (see Swafford 2013: 122). When Felix plugs up the courage to ask Melmotte for Marie's hand, he is met with violent rejection because he fails to answer the questions about his financial means to Melmotte's satisfaction: "'My daughter, no doubt, will have money, but money expects money'" (WWLN 180). Felix is in truth terribly afraid of offending Melmotte, but greater still is the risk of losing Marie to his rival Lord Nidderdale. He explains to Lady Carbury the delicacy of the affair; if Melmotte disapproves of the match, Marie stands to lose her dowry, the only part of the marriage the Carburys actually want. Not without sarcasm he assesses the risks that make the marriage game more dangerous than the card table: "If a man plays and loses, he can play again and perhaps win; but when a fellow goes in for an heiress, and gets the wife without the money, he feels a little hampered you know" (WWLN 173). The stakes are certainly high, and Lady Carbury contemplates her son's situation, presenting a risk assessment of her own:

> Lady Carbury saw the danger, and turned over the affair on every side in her own mind. [...] As he was, his condition was hopeless. [...] there was nothing coming to Felix in the future. All the goods he would ever have of his own, he had now; – position, a title, and a handsome face. *Surely he could afford to risk something!* [...] And then, though it was possible that old Melmotte should be ruined some day, there could be no doubt as to his present means; and would it not be probable that he would make hay while the sun shone by securing his

daughter's position? [...]. 'I think you should be content to run a little risk,' she said. (WWLN 173–174; my emphasis)

The quote above gives insight into Lady Carbury's shrewd awareness of Melmotte's potential ruin, while weighing the likelihood of him cutting off his daughter against Felix's distinctly "hopeless" condition. Knowing his nature and herself overburdened with debt, Lady Carbury worries about her son's future, which is inseparably tied to her own, to such an extent that she cannot really believe in a happy ending; "she could foresee the nature of the catastrophe which might come. He would go utterly to the dogs and would take her with him" (WWLN 238). Meanwhile Felix, after having won a bit of money at cards and believing himself – as gambler's do – to have a rare lucky streak, is full of hope for the future: "things which heretofore had been troublesome to him, or difficult, or perhaps impossible, were now coming easily within his reach" (WWLN 223). Learning about Miles Grendall's cheating without getting caught, the possibility of making money fast and 'getting away with it' attracts Felix's interest and he displays the characteristic attitude of the criminal speculator. He starts to contemplate various risky schemes to get Marie's money, including robbery or eloping, although the latter entails the high risk of Marie losing her inheritance. When Melmotte offers Felix money in exchange for abandoning the pursuit of his daughter, a further variable is added to Felix's speculative conundrum. It becomes clear, however, that in contrast to the 'unreal' risks Felix routinely runs with his friends at the Beargarden club, amounting debts never to be collected, the reality of the marriage game and its potential consequences scare him: "The game to be played was too full of danger! [...] there was the girl at his elbow, and he no more dared to tell her to her face that he meant to give her up, than he dared to tell Melmotte that he intended to stick to his engagement" (WWLN 311). The narrative continues to parallel Felix and Lady Carbury's risk assessments of their financial situation and the developments in the Melmotte story. Whereas Felix switches between fear, denial, and vague hopes that he will somehow get it all, his mother is desperate to see the marriage come through even after rumours of Melmotte's fraudulent schemes start circulating and damaging the family name. In her eyes, Felix has already fallen so low that a connection with the Melmottes cannot ruin him any further: "To get any niche in the world for him in which he might live with comparative safety would now be to her a heaven-sent comfort" (WWLN 632).

Concerning the pervasive discourse and most characters' obsession with gambling, the novel employs only one clear counter figure, the middle-aged Roger Carbury, the financially secure owner of a country estate. Patrick Brantlinger describes Roger as the only "honorable, creditworthy character" (Brantlinger

1996: 171–72); he symbolizes the old, vanishing value system and displays a firm stance against any form of money made through speculation or gambling. He is in love with his cousin Hetta Carbury, who is, however, in love with Paul Montague. She repeatedly rejects Roger, although she knows and keeps reminding herself "that he was the safest guide that she could have" (WWLN 117), and that "he was a staff on which a woman might safely lean, trusting to it for comfort and protection in life" (WWLN 150). Firm, safe, and constant, Roger lacks any excitement for Hetta, in contrast to Paul, who is involved in Melmotte's railway deal and, more gravely, has been associated with a dubious older American woman, Mrs Hurtle. The narrative, which generally employs classic risk language and metaphors in abundance in the reflections of all characters, shows Roger's futile attempts to convince Hetta to choose safety over danger: "Would she not then see where she could trust her happiness, and where, by so trusting it, she would certainly be shipwrecked!" (WWLN 355). While Trollope's omniscient narrative voice always comments on the characters bravery and cowardice, and judges their fears, hopes, and risk-taking, all romantic relationships appear equally fraught with danger, as do all business deals.

Roger makes several benevolent, yet somewhat passive attempts to warn and save Felix, Paul, or Hetta from their respective dangers, but ultimately ends up losing his own love interest to Paul Montague. Paul Delaney, who describes the tension between landed vs. monied interests as a preoccupation in many of Trollope's later works, argues that the author was aware that "the myth of the land was being threatened not just by the dynamism of commerce, but also by the internal weakness of the landed classes" (Delaney 2002: 21). John Vernon sees the familiar tension between land and money reduced to "a mock battle" in Trollope's fiction because "money has already won, though land is still there" (Vernon 1984: 44). Significantly, Roger, embodying the risk-aversion, security, and tradition associated with the landed estate, is the only male lefts standing alone at the end of the novel. He fails in his romantic pursuits and remains without a family, signalling the extension of his line. But he stays honourable and is neither dead or exiled, the fate of all the gambling male characters.

Paul Montague is the only male character endangered by a woman. Mrs Hurtle comes over from America, chasing him: "Everybody knew that she was very clever and very beautiful, – but everybody also thought that she was very dangerous" (WWLN 197). The subplot involving Mrs Hurtle, a femme fatale with a dubious criminal past, is, of course, full of satire. But concerning the classification of safe vs. dangerous people which runs through the novel, Paul's case is particularly interesting because he is situated somewhere in the middle between voluntary gamblers like Felix Carbury and the risk-averse Roger. A reluctant risk-taker, he always seems to get drawn into dangerous situations against his will. For example, Paul is made director of Melmotte's South Central Pacific and Mexican Railway scheme "with a sorely burdened conscience" (WWLN 167), knowing that the investors have no way of checking its progress or even existence. Nonetheless, he is seduced by the prospect of money. Fully aware of the risks of the projects, Paul "felt that he was standing on ground which might be blown from under his feet at any moment" (WWLN 167). In addition to the burden of the potentially dishonest business deal he is involved in, Paul is caught between two women, having promised marriage to Mrs Hurtle years ago, before meeting Hetta Carbury, and before knowing that Mrs Hurtle was risky womanhood incarnate: "an adventuress, – might never have had a husband, – might at this moment have two or three, – might be overwhelmed with debt, – might be anything bad, dangerous, and abominable" (WWLN 207).

Trollope's railway scheme plot and the story of Paul and Mrs Hurtle have been convincingly interpreted with regard to England's relations with America at the time and notions of globalization. The vast array of foreigners in the novel, concerned with the ways "we" live now, includes a cast of American characters (the railway speculator Mr Hamilton K. Fisker, Mrs Hurtle), the cosmopolitan Melmotte, the Emperor of China, the Canadian delegation at the dinner party, the German Mr Vossner at the Beargarden Club, and many others. Among those, Melmotte, and the American characters are certainly the most important. As Geoffrey Baker has argued, the American characters are shown to possess less scruples when it comes to new speculative business, they remain slightly shifty as their backgrounds are never fully disclosed, and they are more mobile, crossing the Atlantic during and at the end of the plot (see Baker 2009: 144). In the same context Annette Van draws attention to the fact that Trollope's novel generally acknowledges "the necessity of speculation to economy and the nation while warning of its risks", but ameliorates these risks "through its portrayal of America and Americans" (Van 2005: 75). In direct contrast to the English aristocrats Felix Carbury and Miles Grendall who are exposed as scoundrels and finally excludes from respectable society, Mr Fisker, for instance, returns home with hopes for a financially prosperous future and happily engaged to Marie Melmotte. The American characters are more successful navigators of the speculative economy and appear as more competent risk managers, even if, or perhaps due to the fact that they not part of the English scene and system. Whereas Paul has concerns about the railway deal, Mr Fisker is "troubled by no shyness, by no scruples, and by no fears" (WWLN 66) and displays a thoroughly American liberalist attitude to trade and finance, saying that it is important "not to cripple commerce too closely by old-fashioned bandages" (WWLN 68). Similarly, discussing the railway scheme with Mrs Hurtle, Paul admits his scruples about seeking to profit from a deal with a man of Melmotte's character: "It is one of those hazardous things [...]. I fell into it altogether against my will". Mrs Hurtle distracts his fears, viewing it simply as "a golden chance" (WWLN 200). In this way the novel's attitude towards speculation appears indeed complex and transcends again a straightforward critique of speculative finance. It seems to imply that the Americans have somehow already mastered a different attitude to risk, and that different rules and values apply in the vast territory of the American West. The narrative certainly captures a moment of shift towards the acceptance of speculation, perceived and developing differently then on each side of the Atlantic. The novel's negotiation of the new economic frontiers and English-American business relations emphasized by Van, in a way displaces risk, imagining a safer space for speculation elsewhere, "a space on the peripheries yet still within the purview of well-established transatlantic relations" (Van 2005: 92–93).

The Way We Live Now places a strong emphasis on women's status as commodities and marriages as business deals. Felix's pursuit of Marie Melmotte is based purely on the interest in her wealth; her beauty, character, or family origins are more or less irrelevant. In most conversations Marie is never named, but referred to as the "heiress" or "the object of interest". This aspects signals, Paul Delany says, a decrease in importance of class status in comparison to material wealth (Delaney 2002: 3). Whereas the main plot line is focused on the courtship of Marie, the intertwining of romance and money, with the added risk element of foreignness thrown in, is also paralleled in the two relationships between English aristocratic women and Jewish bankers, Lady Julia Start and Lionel Goldsheiner, and Georgiana Longstaffe and Ezekiel Breghert. Generally, courtship is depicted as a risky game most characters are actively involved in; all are aware of the equation summed up by Lady Carbury: "Love is like any other luxury. You have no right to it unless you can afford it. And those who will have it when they can't afford it, will come to the ground" (WWLN 646).

If Melmotte and his riches are stereotyped indeterminacy (cf. Wagner, T. 2010: 167), Madame Melmotte is even more of a blank space than her husband. Her femininity condemns her to a largely silent supporting role. The reader mainly knows that she is mortally afraid of her husband and sees him as a risk to her daughter and herself. She lacks Marie's brave, rebellious spirit, having experienced times of want in the past and a constant sense of risk in her married life:

> She feared Melmotte so thoroughly, and was so timid in regard to her own person, that she could not understand the girl's courage. [...] Her life had been passed in almost daily fear of

destruction. To Marie the last two years of splendour had been so long that they had produced a feeling of security. But to the elder woman the two years had not sufficed to eradicate the remembrance of former reverses, and never for a moment had she felt herself to be secure. (WWLN 591)

Melmotte's role as a domestic risk to his family is largely ignored in criticism, although the narrative clearly depicts him as abusive. For example, despite fearing her father's temper, Marie still dares to refuse the order to marry Lord Nidderdale, choosing Felix instead and willing to risk eloping with him. She tells to Felix on more than one occasion: "I don't think he will beat me, but if he does, I'll bear it, – for your sake" (WWLN 190); "If Papa were to beat me into a mummy I would stick with you" (WWLN 216). Later, Melmotte tries to coerce Marie into signing over her money, which means taking away her last chance of escape. Significantly, the horrific scenes always take place behind close doors in the Melmotte residence, tellingly situated on "Bruton Street" (see Chapter 76 and 77). The narrative voice reveals Marie's feelings and what lies beneath Melmotte's exterior of pathos and fatherly love: "He was always threatening her. All her thoughts respecting him reverted to that inward assertion that he might 'cut her to pieces' if he liked" (WWLN 589–590). Monica Rydygier Smith argues that violence, in particular against women, pervades Trollope's text and is shown as an integral part of the Victorian world in the 1870s. While *The Way We Live Now* is most commonly approached from an economic angle, it can also be read as a chronicle of the violence "endemic to the domestic sphere" (Rydygier Smith 1996: 19). Although this is not Rydygier Smith's focus, her argument sheds light on the rhetoric of violence often ignored in the novel, and adds a dimension to the depiction of risk. Interesting is her implied claim that the narrative shows women to be, in fact, more at risk than the nation's finances and stability. This suggests that Trollope's fiction, usually compared to Dickens', also has distinct parallels to the works of George Eliot, or perhaps even to Gissing or Hardy. The 'national' crisis Trollope diagnosed in *The Way We Live Now* is thus not only financial-moral, but extends far beyond the political. The novel highlights the closeness between male privilege and violent behaviour towards women and the threats to the stability of the nuclear family; it employs the theme of abuse to parallel the ills in the domestic sphere and in the market place.

Whether single or married, and regardless of class or age, for women life is fraught with dangers such as betrayal, physical abuse, sexual assault, exploitation, or dispossession. At the very beginning of the novel, the reader learns about the Carbury family's history of violence. Later, when Lady Carbury receives a marriage proposal from Mr Broune, her publisher, her first impulse is to reject him because from her previous marriage "the remembrance of the tyranny was very clear to her" (WWLN 235). Several other scenes show women at risk from men, e.g. Ruby Ruggels is nearly raped on the streets of London, at home in the country she often faces assault from her drunken grandfather. Indeed, an important part of the novel's bleakness stems from the fact that "female characters cannot anticipate security from physical attack in any enclave; no place in the novel proves to be safe for women;" arguably the novel thus even problematizes the abuse of women "as a key element of social crisis: a risk not only to individual women, but to the whole enterprise of nineteenth-century 'progress'" (Rydygier Smith 1996: 26; 21). Whether it is debatable if Melmotte's worst crimes lie in the domestic or the public-commercial sphere, the narrative creates a parallel between debased character traits, e.g. a lack of integrity and the readiness to abuse others, that is shared by most men except Roger Carbury and, to some extent, Paul Montague.

However, the women in The *Way We Live Now* are not all, or exclusively, presented as victims. Mrs Hurtle, rumoured to have a murder case in her past, is one of the strongest, and fear-inspiring characters. Yet she is also shown to be much more humane, than, for instance Melmotte, who clearly is beyond redemption. Mrs Hurtle "had endured violence, and had been violent. She had been schemed against, and had schemed. [...]. But in regard to money, she had been honest and she had been loving of heart. [...] if she could only escape the wrongs, [...] she could pour forth all the genuine kindness of her woman's nature" (WWLN 363). The female characters are generally more courageous, considerate, and resilient. This applies to Lady Carbury, her vanity and scheming left aside for a moment, but in particular to Marie. The last chapters depict Marie as a strong woman, who had planned her marriage with Felix quite rationally as a way to escape from home. This becomes obvious after the climax of the failed elopement plot. Felix aborts their plan to run away to New York together at the last minute, leaving Marie to board the ship from Southampton by herself, while he, drunk and miserable after having gambled away all his money, is put to bed by his mother. Significantly, Marie later judges Felix's behaviour towards her as worse than her father's: "Papa beats me, but I can bear that. [...] But to think that he was a liar all the time; – that I can't bear" (WWLN 519). She seems disappointed by Felix's lack of honesty, commitment, and courage, rather than by the discovery of his lack of feelings towards her. While neither Marie or her mother show any signs of grief for Melmotte after his death, the event leaves Madame Melmotte full of fears about what is to come and how to face the future without the protection of their once 'great' name; Marie embodies a different strength and hope for the next generation of women to have perhaps a chance of greater freedom and break free – at least temporarily – from a regime of abuse and dependency. For Madame Melmotte: *"There was fear of all things,* fear of solitude, fear of sudden change, fear of terrible revelations, fear of some necessary movement she knew not whither, fear that she might be discovered to be a poor wretched impostor". For Marie, the same fears are present but *"did not conquer her"* (WWLN 655–656; my emphasis); she arises from the catastrophe with firm determination, and "go where she might, she would now be her own mistress" (WWLN 633). Towards the end, the narrative even suggests that Marie has the potential to turn into the better version of her father when it comes to commerce and risk management. Mr Fisker is astonished "how excellent a woman of business she had become" (WWLN 745), and both he and Mr Croll observe that Marie, in direct contrast to her father, is capable of smart economizing and realizing when it is necessary to reign in the desire for profit: "'Ma'me'selle – ah, she is different. She vill never eat too moch, but vill see to eat alvays" (WWLN 746).

In the manner characteristic of the grand Victorian multi-plot novel, the final chapters are dedicated to narrating the fate of each character and resolve all plot strands, typically involving 'punishments' and rewards, and a series of marriages. *The Way We Live Now* ends with the following couples united in matrimony: Marie Melmotte and Mr Fisker, Madame Melmotte and Mr. Croll, Lady Carbury and Mr Bourne, Hetta Carbury and Paul Montague, Ruby Ruggles and John Crumb, and the two Longstaffe daughters with their suitors. There is harmony in the country and in the city, and most of the women get what they want and live on, with an at least momentary happiness on the horizon, if no real emancipation. But it is the end for the members of the Beargarden Club, which is brought down along with Melmotte; Felix Carbury and Miles Grendall are banished to the continent in disgrace. Melmotte, after a final drunken appearance at the House of Commons, commits suicide by swallowing prussic acid. Rather than being put to trial for his crimes, Melmotte thus escapes all responsibilities through death. *The Way We Live Now* presents the story of Melmotte as a bitter moral tale about the rise and fall of an overly confident businessman, exposing in the process "the corruption and spiritual bankruptcy of a world tottering precariously upon an abyss of unreality and chaos" (Weiss 1986: 160). Melmotte's career as a financier satirizes people's "fantasies of easy risk management" (Wagner, T. 2010: 164); moreover the novel is decidedly pessimistic about society's ability to take collective responsibility for large-scale commercial misfortune caused by risks taken by single individuals and reveals flaws in the emerging capitalist-liberalist system. Pointing "forward to twentieth-century individuals' struggles within a network of credit that has grown beyond the bounds of what Victorian novelists could possibly have imagined" (Michie 2001: 94), Trollope produced a risk narrative that still has a lot to tell us about the way we live now.

7.3 Gambling for Self and Happiness: *Daniel Deronda*

In her epic novel *Daniel Deronda* (1876) George Eliot presents a different view of "the way we live now", also turning her literary gaze onto issues of moral integrity, corruption, and vanity. While employing gambling and speculation as dominant themes, in comparison to Trollope, Eliot's focus shifts more distinctly away from the social onto the individual's psyche,[15] and questions of perceptions of self, other, and control over one's destiny. As a writer, Eliot remains within the realm of high-Victorian realism and depicts reality in minute detail, yet reveals the tragedy inherent in common life.[16] Though she is mainly celebrated as a writer capturing English provincial life, in *Daniel Deronda* Eliot maintains a political outlook that transcends England.[17]

Gillian Beer describes *Daniel Deronda* as a text particularly "haunted by the future", situating it in the wake of the publication of Darwin's *The Descent of Man* (1871), which introduced a line of evolutionary thought that caused many traditional topics of the 19th-century novel, such as courtship, (female) beauty, (male) dominance, or inheritance, to become newly fraught with a sense of danger and difficulty (Beer 1984: 181; see 213). These topics are taken up in the two separate plot lines of the novel, the Deronda-plot focusing explicitly of the question of Daniel's origins and the future of the Jewish people. The discovery of his own Jewishness determines and makes possible his desired choice of wife, Mirah, and injects the sense of purpose he has been searching for into Daniel's life. The Gwendolen-Harleth-plot highlights the socio-economic pressures in Gwendolen's struggle for survival, and the feelings of fear and guilt that haunt her from the moment of accepting to marry the rich but evil Grandcourt until after his death by drowning. The novel is largely concerned with the tensions

---

[15] An early essay to focus on this aspect is Sally Shuttelworth's "The Language of Science and Psychology in George Eliot's *Daniel Deronda*" (1981).

[16] See, e.g., Felicia Bonaparte's comment: "Eliot was one of the first writers to wrest tragedy from the stronghold of elitism and concede it to the democratized future of the average man" (1975: xiii).

[17] See John Rignall's *George Eliot, European Novelist* (2011). Rignall's study places focuses on the author's expansive imagination and the references to Europe in her works. After her first journey to Italy, Eliot mentions in one of her journals that a particular kind of consciousness is induced through travel and displacement. "This 'double consciousness'", Rignall explains, "with its dialectical pattern of gain and loss, testifies not only to a characteristic measure of earnest self-scrutiny, but also and more importantly to the mobility of a restlessly questioning mind whose interrogative inclinations European travel did so much to stimulate" (2011: 16). This questioning and patterns of gain and loss also shape *Daniel Deronda*.

between chance, determination, and free will,[18] and with questions of moral responsibility, and chains of cause and effect. Gillian Beer was one of early critics to emphasize in the text the persistent occurrence of words such as "prediction, presentiment, forecasting, preparation, foreboding, foretaste, provision, prevision, anxiety, 'phantom of the future', 'ugly visions', hints, conjecture, calculation, dread" (Beer 1984: 187), which has since inspired many critical readings of Eliot's novel, and which points towards the centrality of conceptions of risk. Several critics have focused on the novel's treatment of chance, contingency,[19] and determinism,[20] and the pervasive motifs of speculation and gambling.[21] Wilfred Stone, for instance, notes that the novel creates a perception "that all of life is a gamble. Beyond the politics and economics and personal morality of the book is *the sense that risk is in the nature of things*" (Stone 1998: 55; my emphasis). Yet no readings of *Daniel Deronda* to date employ risk as the main analytical category. However, it is implicit in the lines of interpretation emphasizing that the exploration of fear and dread[22] are crucial in the novel; equally relevant are the observations of survival and the future as main concerns.[23] My reading takes its cue from the existing views of *Daniel Deronda* as a novel dramatizing the characters' attempts of dealing with "the hazardousness of the unknown future" (Beer 1984: 197), in combination with the distinct rhetoric of gain and loss running through the narrative. Eliot's narrator and characters continuously express their thoughts and actions in terms of risk, including calculations, hopes, fears, and moments of economic or moral-spiritual crisis. While involuntary risks play an important role to trigger the ensuing Gwendolen-plot, the Harleth family being financially ruined by the failure of Grapnell & Co., the narrative's main focus is on the choices and gambles taken voluntarily by the characters, usually under the illusion of full control of their outcome.

Scholarly agreement exists that the novel is divided into a predominately realist and an epic-idealist part, F.R. Leavis famously favouring the first of those, the Gwendolen-plot line, as "the good part of *Daniel Deronda*" (Leavis 1951: 85). Many critics since have stressed the modernity of Eliot's psychological

---

18 On the theme of will and parallels between Eliot's novel and Schopenhauer's writing see, McCobb (1985).
19 See, e.g., Butter (2013).
20 See Levine (1962) and New (1985).
21 See Stone (1998), Franklin (1999), and Wagner (2010).
22 See Beer (1983), Butter (2012), and During (1993).
23 See especially the classic Darwinist-inspired criticism of the novel by Levine (1988: 210–237) and Beer (1984: 181–209).

understanding in the portrayal of Gwendolen Harleth. It is rightly praised as a masterpiece of psychological realism, set against a background entailing a harsh critique of the social and economic practices of patriarchal society limiting female agency. All the while elements of melodrama can be found in both plot lines, the Deronda part is much more tinted with idealism and providential fulfilment, rendering it less suited for an analysis of the perception of risks and sequences of cause and effect. Generally, the frequency of sudden turns of fortune in the whole novel, e.g. Gwendolen's loss of money, Daniel's discovery of his birth, or Grandcourt's drowning, have been criticized as improbable; but one can see Eliot's comparatively greater reliance on coincidence in *Daniel Deronda* as a means to achieve the desired political ends (see Myers 1971: 120). Tellingly, as the epigraph to chapter 41 Eliot choses a quote from Aristotle's *Poetics*: "It is part of probability that many improbable things will happen" (DD 421). Throughout the narrative Eliot explicitly includes chance events in her exploration of human life, although the author is known for condemning chance because it goes against her notion of morality grounded in freely exercised will and sympathy (see Stone 1998: 36; New 1985: 195), and it is at odds with a deterministic worldview. In any case, the tension between determinism and free will lies at the heart of many of her fictions. Referring to Kavanagh's description of the realist novel, Eliot's contains an, in fact, familiar split into two different narratives, which inseparably coexist and shape in particular texts with a strong focus on psychology such as *Daniel Deronda*: "One the one hand, it speaks of a deterministic universe in which actions are followed by reactions. On the other, it tells the story of how, within that predictability, the chance event may at any moment redefine the individual's place within the world's apparently ordered sequences of cause and effect" (Kavanagh 1993 108). Similarly, Stone, who identifies the two clashing belief systems in the text as consequentialism vs. a belief in luck as a governing force (Stone 1998: 39), argues that they are, however, not to be seen to be as mutually exclusive. Eliot's main emphasis is on the recognition that all actions, choices, and events, however motivated, caused or determined, necessarily influence others. Moreover, Eliot – through her characters – clearly seems to favour a selfless, intuitive way of acting, in turn condemning choices which rely on too much calculation or randomness, and viewing an egoistic belief in one's own luck (or lack thereof) as preventing necessary concern for others. The latter is the risk Gwendolen poses to herself and has to master in the course of the novel – with Daniel as her moral-spiritual guide.

Eliot's depicts "the perils of a misguided 'courtship'" (Kaye 2002: 125) in a manner which is stylistically much closer to Hardy's tragedies than to Austen's social comedies or Trollope's satire. The plot hinges on one main ill-conceived choice made by Gwendolen, the decision to marry to the sadist Grandcourt. It is largely motivated by her desire to maintain her social status and financial means, yet involves accepting the liability of wronging Lydia Glasher, Grandcourt's long-term mistress, and her four children. Meanwhile Daniel's plot-driving choice resembles more of a discovery and the acceptance of his Jewishness; for him "the survival of an entire people becomes a messianic mission" (Kaye 2002: 133). Besides the themes of choice and gambling, unity of the two plots is achieved through a concern with inheritance.[24] Gwendolen's conflict is tied to questions of rightful inheritance and ownership; Daniel's task is to assume spiritual leadership by realizing Mordecai's prophecy of taking on "the sacred inheritance of the Jew" (DD 415). Thematically, inheritance also points towards the theme of loss and gains and shows how heredity and circumstances conspire to influence, or even 'create', an individual's self over time.

Gwendolen and Daniel embody two opposite "ethical poles" (McCobb 1985: 541) in the novel, egoism and sympathy. Gwendolen imprisons herself by her commitment to nothing but her own happiness and her desire for power dissociated from responsibility, Daniel is the only one to help her after her bubble of self-centeredness and belief in her ability to control all events has burst. A main contrast between Daniel and Gwendolen lies in their different attitudes to life and risk-taking. This is established right from the beginning, in the famous opening scenes set at the casino in Leubronn. The reflections of Eliot's narrator on the nature of gambling, which dominate the first two chapters, and the introduction to Gwendolen at the roulette table have been analysed extensively. Stone views the opening scene as "a tableau from a risk-taking present – the present of the 1870s – and Gwendolen, like the other risk-takers around the roulette table, is a child of that 'epoch'" (Stone 1998: 29; 25). The crowd gathered around the roulette table epitomizes the democratic, cosmopolitan attraction of the risks of gambling – "Here certainly was a striking admission of human equality" (DD 4) –, but also introduces the reader to Gwendolen, "a winner" (DD 5), who gambles "for the excitement of the play, not the winnings" (DD 6). Yet under Deronda's critical gaze from across the table, she begins to feel judged and insecure. Soon afterwards, her luck changes, foreshadowing the dark developments to come. Though initially, all the power seems to be Gwendolen's; symbolically dressed in a serpent green gown, she is habituated to being admired and considers herself lucky. Her goal is to live a happy and extraordinary existence: "I am not fond of what is likely; it is always dull. [...] My plan is to do

---

24 See Helfer Wajngot (2012).

what pleases me" (DD 55); and it is "her favourite formula, 'not going to do as other women did'" (DD 107).

Directly linked to her credo of doing what pleases her, Gwendolen's gambling functions as a testing ground for "a system of personal teleology, in which the world will succumb to the mastery of her need" (Beer 1984: 231), rather than, for instance, choosing to hope and wait. Gambling unites her strong confidence and feeling of invincibility with the thrill of dealing with uncertainty. It is also metaphor for her desire to advance herself and gain freedom. Specifically, for Gwendolen gambling presents means to escape the Victorian woman's "'risky' predicament" (Wagner, J. 2010: 98). According to Stella Butter, "[t]he opening scene of the novel presents Gwendolen as part of the emerging risk society, intent on breaking free from oppressive gender restrictions by means of her reckless gambling" (Butter 2012: 112). The narrative, Butter argues further, chronicles Gwendolen's development from a speculative into a moral subject, revealing in the process the dangers and difficulties of the female speculative subject's gamble for independence and a stable self.[25] Although Eliot's novel, like Trollope's *The Way We Live Now*, is to some extent concerned with reflecting a time and society in need of "rescue from reckless play" (Stone 1998: 49), narcissistic and egoistic Gwendolen only appears at first glance as a typical gambler. She does not gamble out of compulsion but out of the desire to escape boredom. Like other middle-class heroines of Eliot's, for example Dorothea and Rosamond in *Middlemarch*, Gwendolen desires agency and control over her life to the same degree as material comfort. The risk of gambling is a means to feel intense emotions, interestingly almost akin to pain: "I am bored to death. If I am to leave of play I must break my arm or my collar-bone. I must make something happen" (DD 9). It is also a rebellious assertion of power, a claim made to gender equality, by breaking out of the female sphere into a male dominated realm. Gwendolen at the roulette table is full of confident belief in her own "mastery of life" (DD 31), and she demands the hedonist right for herself to live free from constraints and for her own pleasure: "Such things had been known of male gamblers; why should not a woman have a like supremacy?" (DD 6). Her self-assurance rests on trusting that "no ill luck *would* happen to her" (DD 58; my emphasis). With the conditional "would" underlining the importance of prediction and forecast in the narrative, Gwendolen gets a thrill out of the surrender to uncertainty and generally idealizes risk-taking, aiming to be "daring in speech and reckless in braving danger, both moral and physical" (DD 50). As Gerda Reith points out: "The repetition of gambling derives from the

---

25 Cf. Butter (2012); for a detailed reading of the casino scene, see Butter (2013).

dynamic between fear and faith – gamblers' certainty than they are favoured alongside the simultaneous fear that they are not" (Reith 1999: 179); this attitude is obvious in Gwendolen and the narrative chronicles the process of her fear overtaking her faith. As an activity, gambling intertwines economic interests with particular constructions of self, and it signifies an approach to life which allows greater authority of chance, fate and coincidence than choice and consequence (see Franklin 1999: 9). The beginning of the novel establishes Gwendolen's approach to life; she is shown to determine her actions by calculation of what might happen to her – rather from the result of her actions. As John Reed puts it: "Gwendolyn is a gambler with existence, [...]. She believes in her will but trusts to chance" (Reed 1989: 317). Deronda harshly opposes gambling precisely for this reason, and he tells Gwendolen: "I think it would be better for men not to gamble. [...] There are enough inevitable turns of fortune which force us to see *that our gain is another's loss:* — that is one of the ugly aspects of life" (DD 277; my emphasis). Daniel's words haunt Gwendolen after her marriage as the fact that she has profited from Lydia Glasher's loss starts to weigh heavily on her conscience. In contrast to Daniel's self-control and virtue, Gwendolen is associated with forms of excess, especially regarding her increasingly strong and violent emotions. Forced to act in a world which she perceives to be largely ruled by chance (or 'luck'), Gwendolen is threatened by a loss of self. She has neither deep-reaching familial roots, nor professional ambitions; her selfishness and her aura of extraordinariness have no anchor. Consequently, she fluctuates between fear and insecurities. Meanwhile, in the Deronda parts of the novel, chance is replaced by a sense of destiny as a governing, self-stabilizing force; Daniel's is a counter-world to Gwendolen's 'casino world' ruled by contingency, as Butter shows (see 2012: 116).[26]

Despite Gwendolen's flaws and a distinctly thrill-loving part of her nature, Eliot's narrative voice indicates from the beginning that there are "contrary tendencies" (DD 33) in her character. Untouched by the true "gambler's mania", she

---

[26] On the opening scene revealing Eliot's disdain of gambling and chance as the ultimate refusal of causality and basis of moral behaviour see also McCobb (1985: 537). Arguing that Eliot's own personal ambiguity about gambling shapes the novel, Stone comments on a gendered double standards with regards to Eliot's judgmental depiction of gambling: "When Gwendolen gambles, it is an evil; when Daniel gambles (he risks his whole inheritance for a visionary ideal), he is blessed. [...] Gambling evokes her moral rage, yet it also – when risk-taking is heroically undertaken and wears no taint of the casino – is honoured as the means to a high calling" (Stone 1998: 27). There is certainly a gendered distinction, but it is beside the point. It is hard to call Eliot's treatment of gambling inconsistent, because Daniel's, as well as Mirah's behaviour is not presented as gambling but as the passionate pursuit of a personal, political, or artistic goal and the taking over of responsibility.

has a rational side which prevents her from going too far: "her mind was still sanely capable of picturing balanced probabilities, and while the chance of winning allured her, the chance of losing thrust itself on her with alternate strength" (DD 12). To some extent, this proves to be a fusion of characteristics all the more dangerous, because it puts her under the illusion of being able to predict and control all her gambles. But this rational side of Gwendolen is also clearly revealed in her shrewd assessment of the drastic change of circumstances and her attempts at managing the threat of poverty for her family. Her mother refers to the financial loss as "the will of Providence", and says about Mr Lassman's, the family's investor's, failure: "There were great speculations: he meant to gain. It was all about mines and things of that sort. He risked too much". Gwendolen replies: "I don't call that Providence: it was his improvidence with our money, and he ought to be punished" (DD 193).

The only options for Gwendolen, if she wants to avoid the undesirable fate of becoming a governess, are a profitable marriage or a lucrative professional career. Her ambitions are limited both by the social restraints for women from her class and by a lack of special talent: "she did not wish to lead the same sort of life as ordinary young ladies did; but what she was not clear upon was, how she should set about leading any other" (DD 42). Herr Klesmer, who tells her that her musical talents are mediocre at best, destroys the dreams of a singing career. Besides her lack of natural ability, Klesmer also judges Gwendolen to be unable to handle the uncertainties of an artistic career. While she supposes that she "can put up with the same risks as other people do" (DD 211), Klesmer tries to instil in Gwendolen "a sense of her unfitness for a perilous, difficult course" (DD 212) outside of her sheltered domestic existence. Although his negative appraisal wounds her pride, the narrative emphasizes again the contradictions of Gwendolen's risk personality by affirming furthermore that her "daring was not in the least that of the adventuress" (DD 225). Gwendolen is ruled by a strong sense of propriety; she is increasingly overcome by hopelessness springing from feeling trapped in the social role assigned to her and her own frustrated desires. Struggling to come to grips with various disappointments, she starts to lose her sense of privilege and being "protected and petted, and to have her susceptibilities consulted in every detail;" she moreover fights against the acceptance that she "would never be recognized as anything remarkable, and there was not a single direction in which probability seemed to flatter her wishes" (DD 225–226).

While this suggests reasons for her later accepting Grandcourt's proposal, Gwendolen generally tries to rebel against confining circumstances for as long as she can and while she still has some trust left into her luck to turn things around. In this spirit, she goes horse riding, a typical act of female rebellion and risk-taking in Eliot's fiction. Like Rosamond in *Middlemarch*, who protests against her husband Lydgate's orders by riding while pregnant, Gwendolen is spurred on by prohibition and the argument of impropriety, "her mamma dreading the danger, and her uncle declaring that for his part he held that kind of violent exercise unseemly in a woman" (DD 56–57). Nonetheless, Gwendolen, who on horseback "felt as secure as an immortal goddess" (DD 58) tempts her suitor Rex to a race and taking a leap with the horse, ending with him nearly breaking his neck. In contrast to the doubly unlucky Rex, whose proposal Gwendolen rejects soon after his fall, Baronet Mallinger Grandcourt appears on the scene as man who loves and can handle risks, including Gwendolen's volatile temper. Dismissing rumours about his gambling past, Gwendolen is attracted to his reputation and sees it as proof of his strength of mind and character: "Whatever Grandcourt had done, he had not ruined himself" (DD 75). Significantly, the first official meeting between the couple takes place at an archery contest and picnic, where they bond over a mutual fondness of danger, hunting and horse riding. Provocatively, Gwendolen tells Grandcourt why she, as a woman, should be allowed to make her own decisions: "if I chose to risk breaking my neck, I should like to be at liberty to do it" (DD 108). The scene at the archery picnic also brings the first appearance of Mr Lush, Grandcourt's dark agent, who Gwendolen immediately fears and dislikes. The meeting with Lydia Glasher and her children at the Whispering Stones further increases her sense of unease, leaving her in a state of shock and determined to refuse Grandcourt.

The confrontation with the choice of marrying Grandcourt triggers a crisis for Gwendolen; her dreams of security, domination, and agency are corrupted by a sense of dread and insecurity which proves hard to shake. Starting to feel the burden of choice in the face of the unknown, she contemplates "two likelihoods that presented themselves alternately, [...] as if they were two sides of a boundary-line, and she did not know on which she should fall" (DD 111). She is aware of the risk of projecting her fantasies onto a man she hardly knows, and Eliot's narrator notes how "ignorance gives one a large range of probabilities. [...]. She began to be afraid of herself, and to find out a certain difficulty in doing as she liked" (DD 112). Her mounting distrust of herself and her own luck is shocking to Eliot's heroine. The crucial moment of choice, when she accepts Grandcourt's offer, appears as the desperate attempt to regain control and "a sort of empire over her own life" (DD 241); at the same time she wants to avoid the responsibility of dealing with the risks inherent in her decision.[27]

---

[27] Tellingly, Kaye notes, Eliot entitles the title the chapter detailing Gwendolen courtship with Grandcourt "Gwendolen gets her choice" (2002: 140).

The narrator describes Gwendolen's "contradictory desire to be hastened: hurry would save her from deliberate choice" (DD 242). She desires to escape into her fantasies of happiness and thus sustains her hopeful illusion that in Grandcourt's attraction to her lays her chance of asserting power over him. Peter New says about her acceptance of Grandcourt's proposal: "This is essentially gambling: [...] she has the illusion of freedom, but is actually bound both by the underlying egoism of playing and by causative laws which have no special reference to her desires" (New 1985: 200). Caught in a set of pressurizing circumstances, Gwendolen perceives the union with Grandcourt as risk management for her family, as her chance of "rescue from helpless subjection to an oppressive lot" (DD 249). Her choice can thus be only partially considered a truly free or selfish one. Meanwhile Grandcourt, though he genuinely likes Gwendolen's unpredictability, her being "a girl whom he had not found quite calculable" (DD 248), mostly gets a kick out of the fact that Gwen does not love him but that he owns her due to her family's misfortunes. Eliot's narrative shows risk and power as the main issues at stake between Gwendolen and Grandcourt; both seek to manage different risks through their union and are motivated by their directly opposing desires to "master" the other.

Although Gwendolen achieves money and status through her marriage, they come at a high price. Patricia Ingham even speaks of a Faustian price Gwendolen has to pay for her marriage (Ingham 2000: 81), her dream of ease and happiness being indelibly tainted by the knowledge of Lydia Glasher and Grandcourt's illegitimate children. After receiving Lydia's diamonds, enclosed in a threatening letter on her wedding day, she is increasingly terrorized by the thoughts of her gain made possible by Lydia's loss. While Gwendolen's original pursuit and gamble for pleasure "turns self-destructive" (Wagner, J. 2010: 107) in the course of the novel, as Jodi Wagner notes, later not bearing a child becomes Gwendolen's means to rectify the injustice by asserting the right of Lydia's first born son as Grandcourt's heir through a loss of her own.[28] Gwendolen's suffering is furthermore caused by the crucial of misjudgement of Grandcourt's character and the illusion of her own control over the situation. Initially having imagined "herself an empress of luck" (DD 128), this state is soon replaced for Gwendolen by "her husband's empire of fear" (DD 352). Eliot's narrator employs recurring metaphors of imperial control in the description of her marriage. Regarding Grandcourt's attitude towards his wife, whom he considers his property, the nar-

---

28 Helfer Wajngot draws attention to the fact that Lydia Glasher has also gambled by trusting in Grandcourt's willingness to eventually marry her and legitimize their children. Arguably her stakes have even been "higher than Gwendolen's, since for her, loss has meant life as a 'fallen woman' outside normal social intercourse" (2012: 40).

rator insinuates that he is capable of the force and violence towards her that is necessary and comparable to the colonization of foreign lands: "If this white-handed man with the perpendicular profile had been sent to govern a difficult colony, he might have won reputation among his contemporaries. He had certainly ability, would have understood that it was safer to exterminate than to cajole superseded proprietors, and would not have flinched from making things *safe in that way*" (DD 492; my emphasis). This highlights Grandcourt's desire for absolute control which poses a high risk of suffering for Gwendolen.

During the brief period of her marriage Gwendolen undergoes a transformation into a woman feeling helpless and broken, haunted by a "vague, ever-visiting dread of some horrible calamity" (DD 351). The trigger of her "sense of being blameworthy [...] exaggerated by a dread both definite and vague" (DD 352), the main twin emotions the narrative focuses on, is Lydia's letter cursing Gwendolen for the wrong she has wilfully done her, to which she reacts with utter terror. Perceiving her terror as a bout of female nerves and madness, Grandcourt forces her to wear the diamonds at dinner. From then on, many scenes between them are fraught with risk of violence and Gwendolen's fear of him only increases in intensity: "Grandcourt had become a blank uncertainty to her in everything but this, that he would do just what he willed, and that she had neither devices at her command to determine his will, nor any rational means of escaping it" (DD 353). At the same time she develops an intense hatred of Grandcourt, which in turn causes violent thoughts which scare Gwendolen in their intensity and which the narrative describes as feelings of "self-dread". Grandcourt observes these "threatening moods" (DD 493) in Gwendolen, but is unable to understand them. Instead, he constantly seeks to provoke and punish her. Sometimes the attempts backfire, for example when lets her know that he has made Lydia's son Henleigh his heir in the case that there is to be no son from his marriage to Gwendolen; this intended humiliation is a huge relief for her because she perceives it as offering the possibility of atonement. After realizing that her marriage is, in fact, her "last great gambling loss" (DD 366), Gwendolen considers her options and the idea of leaving Grandcourt; she calculates the risk of staying and living in constant fear against the certainty of the shame and dependence she would bring onto her family. She concludes, typical of a Victorian woman in her position, that the sense of obligation and the need to keep up appearances outweigh the risks of violation and suffering: "If I am to have misery anyhow,' [...] 'I had better have the misery that I can keep to myself" (DD 500).

A certain sign of Gwendolen's depression is that "she trusted neither herself nor her future" (DD 356). She starts to fixate on Daniel as her saving grace, hoping that he can offer her a new, grounding perspective on things, "— *an inward safeguard against possible events which she dreaded*" (DD 356;

my emphasis). Confessing her fears about herself Gwendolen says to Deronda: "When my blood is fired I can do daring things – take any leap [...]". Daniel, aware of the burden of managing Gwendolen's moral risks all the while feeling "as if he were seizing a faint chance of rescuing her from some indefinite danger", replies: "*Take your fear as a safeguard.* [...] It may make consequences passionately present to you" (DD 376; my emphasis). Until the end of novel, Daniel remains the only one Gwendolen turns to for advice on how to act and on how to feel; he is also the one she confesses her dark emotions and mounting anxieties to. Several critics have pointed out that Daniel assumes the role of "ethical coach" (Matus 2009: 157), or has a "therapeutic influence on Gwendolen" (Butter 2012: 119), seeking to guide her towards turning her dread into something enabling and achieving a renunciation of her egoistic impulse at the same time. Weary of her reputation as a coquette, Daniel approaches Gwendolen with a mix of pity and "a self-administered dose of caution" (DD 342). Struggling to avert the risk of Gwendolen's 'spiritual shipwreck', and trying to save her from herself, his reaction especially after her nervous breakdown after Grandcourt's death signals a sense of overburden and points towards the limits of the 'talking cure' as a remedy when confronted with someone in Gwendolen's psychological condition. Employing a classic risk metaphor, Daniel thinks: "Words seemed to have no more rescue in them than if he had been beholding a vessel in peril of wreck [...]. How could he grasp the long-growing process of this young creature's wretchedness? – how arrest and change it with a sentence?" (DD 505–506). Significantly, Daniel later chooses the courageous, exceptionally virtuous and talented Mirah for his wife, who has survived years of hardship and whose nature it is not "to run into planning and devising: only to submit" (DD 185). Mirah, though her characterization remains superficial compared to Gwendolen, is presented as morally superior to 'dangerous' women such as Gwendolen or Daniel's mother.[29]

Through Gwendolen, Eliot's novel presents the capacity for dread and strong fearful emotions as a particularly female experience. Gillian Beer, who argues that anxiety is "the generative emotion" of the whole narrative, emphasizes that it is of all emotions the one "which most takes its life from the future" (Beer 1984: 221; 215). It entails a sense of risk as an overwhelming mental state,

---

[29] One can argue, however, that Daniel's mother, the countess Maria Alcharisi, who Daniel meets for the first time in book 7, shares many characteristics and ambitions with Gwendolen. The reasons she gives Daniel why she abandoned him along with her Jewish identity include selfish choices, attempts at social risk management, and rebellion against the restricted life of a Jewish woman: "I had a right to seek my freedom from a bondage that I hated" (DD 519); "you can never imagine what it is [....] to suffer the slavery of being a girl'" (DD 523).

and the narrator underlines Gwendolen's capacity for dreadful projections; she is described as "a creature with a large discourse of imaginative fears" (DD 351). After she has successfully averted the risk of poverty and loss of social status, Gwendolen's dread, though directed to the future, springs largely from the guilt for her past actions. She dreads the pressure that comes with making choices and feels remorse for some of the wrong one she has made. Above all else, Gwendolen fears moral judgement, exposure, and humiliation. Her anxieties cluster around the potential discovery of her treatment and knowledge of Lydia, Grandcourt, and her own violent feelings towards him. Particularly Gwendolen's self-dread, the risk of herself acting out her wishes, increases towards the end of the novel, culminating in the scene of Grandcourt's fatal boating accident. Although her mental state is never fully explained, Gwendolen displays telling signs such as an instable, threatened sense of identity, nightmarish visions, and a growing self-protective detachment from herself, e.g. she describes an experience of feeling like "leaping away from myself" (DD 696) after Grandcourt's death. Perhaps most crucial is her growing self-perception as risk: "I am frightened at myself" (DD 376). Many critics have perceived Gwendolen's nameless dread in the novel as bordering on hysteria, and Lisa During categorizes it further as "anticipatory repression" (During 1993: 104; 90). Though it is beyond scope to dissect Eliot's depiction of Gwendolen as a portrait of psychic trauma in detail, the narrative certainly dedicates a large part to detailing the heroine's inner conflict and her state of shock, manifesting itself, e.g. in her paleness and punctuated speech after the Grandcourt's death, as for instance Jill Matus has shown. [30] Throughout the novel Eliot portrays the intensity of Gwendolen's emotions and explores the effects of overwhelming fearful experiences on human consciousness and mechanisms of (self-)apprehension. Plagued by the reality of having done harm to another woman, Gwendolen fears "a dark, shadowy self beyond the control of her will", "her own intrusive and uncontrollable unconscious" (Matus 2009: 149). Athena Vrettos, who reads the novel alongside emerging contemporary psycho-medical theories of body and mind, argues that Eliot's novel addresses important social and psychological questions through the vehicle of Gwendolen's implied "nervous disease"

---

[30] Emphasizing the depiction of terror and psychic shock in the novel, Jill Matus reads Gwendolen as a traumatized subject. Although the medical concept of trauma was barely on the horizon when *Daniel Deronda* was written (see 2009: 142), Matus argues that Eliot explores psychic wounding, and the mental processes and effects on memory and emotion, suggesting that mental experiences of fear can have a stronger impact than acute bodily injury. The novel establishes Gwendolen's vulnerability in fact from the very beginning through the haunting impression of Daniel's critical gaze at the roulette table.

(Vrettos 1990: 559). While the pathologization of women as/at risk is a topic that features even more prominently in the fin-de-siècle novels of Hardy and Gissing, Eliot saves her heroine and does not let her go over the edge. Ultimately, Gwendolen survives and is strong enough to resist her despair and dark impulses. The ending suggests a least a glimmer of hope and freedom for her, although the future is shown to firmly belong to Daniel – as it does to Angel Clare in *Tess* or Harvey Rolfe in *The Whirlpool*.

Taking *Daniel Deronda* as an example of the cultural construction of forms of extreme fear (including awe and the sublime which are less relevant here), Stella Butter draws attention to an important element of social criticism inherent in Eliot's characterization of Gwendolen. It reveals, Butter writes, "how a communion with the spiritual inevitably fails in modern market or risk society. Gwendolen's fear is endowed with a positive coding, not only because it is linked to the sublime, but also because her dread serves as a 'moral faculty'" (Butter 2012: 135). Butter's argument usefully refocuses the gaze on the potentially positive outcome, or perhaps even the necessity, of Gwendolen's suffering from fear, charging it with a determining function in the process of subject-formation. In contrast to Daniel, the moral, empathic, courageous subject, Gwendolen, as the speculative one, is characterized by fear and lack of concern for others.

Like Daniel, who seeks to instil feelings of dread as a "safeguard" in Gwendolen, Grandcourt seeks to instil fear in her in order to maintain his power over her. Both men, though in very different ways, thus evoke threats of exposure, judgment, and punishment. Alexander Welsh points out: "The distinction is sometimes hard to discern, since Gwendolen's 'fear' is prevalent throughout" (Welsh 1985: 293). But in stark contrast to Daniel, functioning as the novel's moral conscience, Grandcourt "presents a frightening image of what his culture's values can lead to if unchecked, uncontested by other, rival claims" (During 1993: 109), as During notes. Although Grandcourt's embodies the old order of Englishness, including title and landed wealth, rather than new money and speculation, he emanates the risk of mental and physical violence and abuse women are subjected to in over-confident patriarchy at large. In this regard, he has striking similarities with August Melmotte in *The Way We Live Now*. Another aspect to consider is Nunokawa's argument that *Daniel Deronda* thematizes the danger and catastrophes springing from the obsession with property in various forms (see Nunokawa 1994). The dynamic of the relationship between Gwen and Grandcourt, involving a shift from material ownership towards psychological domination (see Nunokawa 1994: 95), illustrates Foucault's description of the structure of organization characteristic of modern society, and the mechanism of surveillance and control by fear on a micro-level. While Gwendolen suffers in the second half of the narrative from the "continual liability to

Grandcourt's presence and surveillance" (DD 486), many plot-driving scenes in the novel involve characters watching others, or being conscious of being watched themselves; there is also the subplot of blackmail carried out through Mr Lush, who fulfils a role as threatening agent similar to that of Mr Raffles in *Middlemarch*.[31]

The climactic scene of the boating accident and subsequent drowning of Grandcourt, which occurs at an opportune moment and evokes a sense of poetic justice from the reader's side,[32] raises complicated questions of causality and the potential liability of Gwendolen. Numerous and contradictory interpretations exist of the events, which are not actually narrated in detail;[33] instead the focus is placed on Gwendolen's lingering shock and reaction afterwards (cf. Matus 2009). Gwendolen is possibly guilty of not acting immediately when Grandcourt falls over board, passively watching the dark wishes she had been harbouring turn into reality. For in the days prior to the boat trip on the Mediterranean Sea Grandcourt forces her to accompany him on, for Gwendolen, being in "fluctuating stages of despair, gleams of hope came in the form of some possible accident" (DD 558). Torn between her moral dread, "afraid of her own wishes" (DD 565), and the temptation to free herself from Grandcourt, Gwendolen takes a small dagger with her onto the boat, but her accountability for the drowning remains unclear. The narrative explores the question if Gwendolen's feelings and intentions could possibly have influenced exterior events, culminating in her famous confession to Daniel: "I did kill him in my thoughts" (DD 577). His reaction only offers an inconclusive absolution: "*It seemed almost certain that her murderous thought had had no outward effect* – that, quite apart from it, the death was inevitable" (DD 578; my emphasis).

Kathleen McCormack, while emphasizing again the numerous uncertainties which "accompany Eliot's reports of the nautical manoeuver that results in Grandcourt's death" (2015: 88), analyses the fictional accident through what reads, in fact, like a detailed real-life risk assessment taking the specific histor-

---

31 See Alexander Welsh's *George Eliot and Blackmail* (1985).
32 Carol Christ (1976) comments on the generally high number of convenient deaths in Eliot's novels, which often follows marital alienation between the character who dies and the most intimately related survivor. Thus the deaths, Grandcourt's as well as, for example Causabon's in *Middlemarch*, which frees Dorothea, are charged with a sense of providential punishments for personal and moral failings.
33 See Kaye, who aptly describes the accident as an "ethically cloudy [...] spectacle" (2002: 140). Meanwhile Eagleton claims that Eliot's concern with sympathy and tracing the psychological motivation and condition of the characters and their actions generally works against tragic effect in her novels. Weaving intricate chains of causality, though intersected with chance events, she generally lets "explanation take the place of condemnation" (Eagleton 2003: 184).

ical and geographical circumstances (location, sea and weather conditions, the type of boat used etc.) of the scene into consideration. She argues that the accident is largely caused by Grandcourt's imperial arrogance and his ignoring of warnings about "a possible change in breeze" from a local seaman, seeking to assert "his rule over the waves both as the province of the British and as nature subordinate to human will" (2015: 92). He thus enters into a dangerous situation voluntarily, underestimating nature's power and the chance blow of wind shift that leads to his fall, as well as miscalculating the risk of Gwendolen's (possibly negligent) behaviour towards him. Such a reading suggests that Grandcourt's death appears to some extent as another's gambling loss; he is ruined by his arrogant belief into his powers of prediction and control over people and circumstances. Meanwhile Carol Christ, in a more dated but still relevant essay, draws attention to a function of providential deaths in Eliot's novels as an elimination of aggression that is interesting for its implication of accidental death as a form of narrative risk management. The (usually female) character who secretly wishes the other (male) character dead does not actually have to act and commit a criminal act in order to escape a hostile situation, yet, in Gwendolen's case, who – carrying the dagger – is arguably saved by the accident from committing murder, still feels as if she has brought the death about though her wishes (see Christ 1976: 131–133). And though Gwendolen avoids acting out her intention, she still pays for them by being haunted by guilt. Following Christ's argument, Eliot offers Gwendolen a way out, saving her both from her abusive marriage and metaphorically from spiritual 'ship-wreck.'

Sue Zemka underlines the distinct temporal discrepancy between the brevity of the moment of Grandcourt's drowning and the length of the description of Gwendolen's response to it, while her thoughts are narrated as if time stands still.[34] She reads *Daniel Deronda* alongside other Victorian novels that display a fascination with sudden events, accidents, and shocks, in short, with anything that comes in a moment and cannot be anticipated, consequently presenting a threat to ethical agency (Zemka 2012: 1). Her argument about the novel's contrasting of experiences of time, with the two plot strands signifying two different rhythms of life (2012: 147), is relevant with regard to the perception of risk which is closely bound to temporality. In the novel, Gwendolen, originally very

---

34 Significantly, in the other drowning scene of Daniel's rescue of Mirah out of the river Thames, there is no real sense of danger or urgency conveyed; unlike Gwendolen, Daniel is in full control of the situation and seems to have all the time in the world, according to Sue Zemka a deliberate contrast which empathizes Daniel's representation of a transhistorical calmness and stability vs. the chaotic, confusing haste of Gwendolen's reality. See Zemka (2012: 147–173; especially 170–171).

much set on living and enjoying the present, has to suffer through a series of sudden tragedies and shock moments which change her outlook towards only feeling dread of the future and being haunted by her past decisions. Daniel's rhythm by contrast is a slow and constant growth towards finding a long-term, historically and morally charged purpose, with the Zionist concept of life as destiny transcending the ambitions of the individual. He experiences the security of collective time, and a sense of shared history and future; Gwendolen is left with having to deal with her isolation and the cruelty of events beyond her control.

In many ways Gwendolen and Daniel develop in exactly opposite directions throughout the novel. In chapter 3 Eliot's narrator says: "A human life, I think, should be well rooted in some spot of a native land" (DD 15). Underlining a sense of home and belonging as an integral element of the self, Gwendolen loses her family home in the beginning, while Daniel goes out searching for a sense of place and rootedness, ending with him travelling towards his promised homeland, facing the future with a young bride by his side. Gwendolen ends up as a lonely widow. Though she returns to Offendene and now appreciates it as a "restful escape", rather than "a dullness to be fled from" (DD 634), it resembles more a defeat than a romanticized instance of homecoming. After Grandcourt's death, the only risk left for Gwendolen is acting in any way Daniel might disapprove of, and she longs to see and consult him. But he, aware of her dependence on him, detaches himself from the role has her spiritual risk manager. During their last conversation in the drawing room at Offendene he tells her about his Jewishness, the engagement to Mirah, and his devotion of a life to nationalism. Comparing her own small life to Daniel's newly found 'global' purpose, Gwendolen experiences a final shock and humbling moment, triggered by a great sense of alterity. Parting from Deronda, all she can say is: "I will try – try to live" (DD 672).

Chronicling Gwendolen's rebellion against the average and "doing as other women do", the narrative juxtaposes it with the story of Daniel's discovery of his exceptionality and being 'the chosen one.' From the beginning, Daniel has a view for others, for the community, which also guides his perception of risk, Gwendolen focuses mainly on the possible dangers, losses or gains for herself (and her immediate family). Eliot's narrative explicitly contrasts a morally mature ability to look "at calamity as a collective risk", with Gwendolen's initial naïve and selfish "anguish that I and not Thou, He or She, should be just the smitten one" (DD 239). While both protagonists lack orientation in the beginning, the difference between Daniel's and Gwendolen's hopes for the future lies in the fact Daniel's develop from being vague longings towards a clear destiny. And although Jewish life is undoudtely constructed as frail and risky, it appears as precious for Daniel and as a lucky turn of fortune for him that rids him simultaneously of the uncertainty about his past *and* future.[35] Gwendolen, looking for material comfort and the freedom to do "as I please", is as a matter of fact also granted her wishes through her status as Grandcourt's widow, but she does not find a stable sense of self and purpose. This reinforces the ambiguity of Eliot's portrayal of Gwendolen, who does suffer, but does not loose all; her gamble pays off at least financially, and the novel ends with her survival, not death. Nonetheless, as Stone comments: "To say that she 'won' at the end, by inheriting some of Grandcourt's money, is also an ironic measure of how much she lost" (Stone 1998: 52). According to Beer, the final union of Mirah and Daniel facing a journey east together and full of hope for their new life appears as Eliot's "attempt at the end to exorcise the dread of the future" (Beer 1984: 219). Though Eliot's ending is heavy with providential fulfilment for Daniel, the closing image is of a solitary, shattered Gwendolen. The narrative only implies that she will go on living and with the help of the lessons she has learned from Daniel develop further towards a moral understanding of others, and herself. Both protagonists develop towards a different understanding of agency and their attitude towards life, the future, and risk-taking. Patricia Ingham argues, Gwendolen "learns that the future is not controllable, and he [Daniel] learns that it is destined and controlled" (Ingram 2000: 87).

In general, the Deronda-plot is driven by hope and anxieties, which are not presented in depth, while descriptions of dread and frustrated ambitions make up the majority of the Gwendolen story. Daniel's story is narrative full of lucky coincidences (e. g. the reunion of with Mordecai, Mirah's long lost brother); Gwendolen's is full of unlucky, shocking turns of events. Eliot creating Daniel as an exceptional passionate truth-seeker, taking willing to risks for the future of his people, and as a counter-example to the average Englishman. His characterization hinges on the ability to assess risks and their taking in the right manner and for the right reasons. As Deronda says to Mordecai, "the unemotional intellect may carry us *into a mathematical dreamland where nothing is but what is not*" (DD 425; my emphasis). Eliot's *Daniel Deronda* explores danger scenarios of getting lost in selfish wishes disguised as predictions and calculations, condemning gambling and the pursuit of an economy of chance on moral grounds, but not the pursuit of passion or freedom at any risk this might entail. The novel advocates the value of imagination over (ir)rational cal-

---

[35] It has frequently been acknowledged that by finding Judaism Daniel gains a new, distinctly non-English community, an integrated religion and culture, and an almost magic future. Cf. Levine's comment: "What Eliot seeks in Jewish culture might be seen as just that sort of reenchantment" (2001: 65). See also Caron (1983).

culation, suggesting furthermore that any projections of the future should be determined by moral sympathy and concern for consequences, not possible losses or gains, and that there are some risks worth taking, while some only lead to self-destruction.

8 The Dangers of Human Nature and the Struggle Between the Sexes

8.1 The Female Body as Risk: *Tess of the d'Urbervilles*

Thomas Hardy's writing marks an era of transition from late Victorian realism towards modernism, yet also still reveals noticeable traces of influence from older writing traditions, as critics like Pierre D'Exideuil have noted, through the "abuse of coincidence and of other similar forms of procedure" (D'Exideuil, 1970: 152). While life in Hardy's fictions often unfolds as a string of calamities and accidents echoing 18th-century novels, they deviate from the epic scope of mid-19th-century texts like Trollope's *The Way We Live Now* or Eliot's *Daniel Deronda* by employing a much smaller cast of main characters, and achieve a different psychological intensity. Ultimately, the benevolent, omniscient narrator and the Victorian marriage plot, already shaken and satirized by Trollope and Eliot, come to a clear end in Hardy's fiction. In *Tess of the d'Urbervilles* (1891) and *Jude the Obscure* (1895), romantic love and the security of the family are inevitably destroyed by social conventions concerning marriage and sexuality and a brutal ideology, fusing Christian morality and social Darwinism.

All of Hardy's writing is marked by the author's distinct scepticism. *Tess* and *Jude* in particular are concerned with the impact of religion on life and society and the idea that "Christianity is a pervasive hindrance to the fulfilment of human aspiration" (Schweik 1999: 56). Although Hardy does not write about a godless universe, the protagonists in Tess and Jude surely suffer from "the ache of modernism" (T 160). Apart from countless actual losses (of lovers, children, jobs, and housing), there is an acute sense of a loss of security and certainties in the texts. This is reinforced by the recurring ironic commentary of the narrator, which exposes a questioning of authoritative frameworks, and reveals the cruelty of all beliefs, ideals, and the futility of human attempts of control. These include Darwinian theories of sexual selection, heredity, and late-Victorian ideas of "Standardization", with regard to the question of what constitutes 'female' nature and, conversely, deviations from the standard norm.[1] Alongside George

---

[1] Darwinism, especially after *The Descent of Man* (1871), imparted a new momentum to biologically deterministic views of human 'nature', introducing a fixed set of characteristics of the female and male sex and furthermore showing human 'mating' dependent on chance encounters and sexual selection. Part of the new evolutionary discourse, in which the moral and the scientific were closely intertwined, was an idea of the reform of society via 'race' improvement, which perceived uncontrolled breeding as a social threat and placed women's sexuality at the

Eliot, Thomas Hardy is regarded as the main Victorian novelist who has assimilated and reflected Darwin's theory of evolution and natural selection in his writing.[2] The tension between a (loss of) Christian faith and the pessimism about the progress of the human race are palpable in fictions like *Tess*, where "Romantic ideologies, upholding nature's 'holy plan,' clash with a Darwinian notion of nature's randomness and cruelty" (Shires 1999: 156). As a novel, *Tess* dramatizes the ways in which Darwinian lines of inquiry about physical appearance (strength, beauty, race etc.) related to heredity, the choice of mate, and species survival, assume a new urgency in society. Furthermore, there is a new scientific emphasis on diversity, otherness, variability, in other words, to anxiety-inspiring phenomena and processes beyond human control, showing that evolutionary thought is connected to the evocation of fear. In this sense, Hardy's novel illustrates that: "Evolutionary thinking is not a grid; it is a bundle of apprehensions" (Beer 1998: 109). Generally, an anxiety about agency, about a perceived lack of control over events and ideas about heredity and degeneration shapes the late-Victorian age; and while the general belief in progress is fading, certain teleology is provided by evolutionary theory. Yet, as Jil Larson (2001: 37–38) underlines, although autonomy is compromised by ideas of heredity, the power of human agency ('choice') is affirmed at the same time.

In the General Preface to the fifth edition of *Tess of the d'Urbervilles* in 1912, Thomas Hardy refers to his penultimate novel as the fictional rendering of the "shaded side of a well-known catastrophe" (T vii), alluding to the pervasive motif in Victorian literature and culture, that of the fallen woman. Furthermore, Hardy, who is generally taken as an author with many scientific-philosophical-religious interests but lacking any clear, i.e. unambiguously identifiable ideological streak in this writing,[3] famously describes the novel as "an impression, not an argument" (T viii). This highlights one of the most striking qualities of Hardy's writing in general, and of his most iconic novel in particular, namely his visual

---

heart of the discussion. But it is important to note that Hardy also undermines Darwinian gender binaries by assigning stereotypical traits, e.g. tenderness, violence, compassion, self-control, to the opposite sex or to both sexes.
2 The interest in and impact of Darwinian thoughts on Hardy who describes himself as "among the earliest acclaimers of *The Origin of Species*" (cited in Schweik 1999: 55 is well documented in Hardy's letters and notebooks. Relevant sources in this context are Kaye's *The Flirt's* Tragedy (2002: 118–150); Gose jr. (1990); Beer (1984).
3 For an overview of Hardy's widely spread views and the manifold, if unsystematic, ways in which contemporary scientific thought impacted his works see Schweik (1999).

style and the emphasis on perception palpable throughout the text.[4] Regarding this aspect, Hardy's fiction testifies to the transition from Victorianism to Modernism in an exemplary fashion. Virginia Woolf, a self-declared fan of Hardy's works, singled out the author's "moments of vision", "those passages of astonishing beauty and force which are to be found in every book that he wrote" (Woolf 1991: 401). She also identified human love as the central force and catastrophe, "the great fact that moulds human life" (403–404) in all the works of Hardy, whom she concluding called "the greatest tragic writer among English novelists" (405).[5] It is hard to dispute Woolf's description, and *Tess*, although not as dark has Hardy's last novel *Jude the Obscure*, is undoubtedly a tragic tale which continues to move readers and spark critical interest.

The eponymous heroine of *Tess* is a far cry from a stereotypical Victorian "doll";[6] however, the question of her agency and her passivity, about Hardy's representation of womanhood and sexuality, his narrator's gaze on Tess and her body and beauty remain among the many controversially debated issues at the heart of the text.[7] Above all, discussions have clustered around the vexed implications of the novel's subtitle: *A Pure Woman Faithfully Represented*.[8] The present discussion ties in with some of these debates, but shifts the focus

---

[4] Visuality and representation are central themes in the novel, which is perhaps the most visual of all of Hardy's fictions (cf. Widdowson 1993: 1 ff; Shires 1999: 148). For an analysis of visual imagination in Hardy see Bullen's *The Expressive Eye* (1986).

[5] The view of the novel as the greatest prose tragedy since Elizabethan drama was established shortly after its first publication. See, e.g., W.P. Trent's review "The Novels of Thomas Hardy" (1892).

[6] Shortly before completing work on the first edition of *Tess*, Hardy writes in a letter to H.W. Massingham on 31 December 1891: "I have felt that the doll of English fiction must be demolished, if England is to have a school of fiction at all" (Hardy 1978: 250).

[7] Although the author was obviously appalled by the social injustices suffered by women, feminist critics have been divided in their response to Hardy. In the face of the masses of often quite polemic scholarship, one can only agree with Mary Childers remark: "Questions about what Hardy thought about women or whether or not he liked them are, finally, less productive than questions about the function of women in his fiction" (Childers 1981: 325; 320). While Hardy's his treatment of gender has either been either praised or criticized, the author's interest in and sympathy for women and their situation is undeniable. With regard to the much discussed ambiguities in the texts and Hardy's representation of sexuality and Tess's seduction, it is important to keep in mind the various re-writings the text underwent which make judging Hardy's 'original' intentions difficult.

[8] Hardy commented on the subtitle: "It was disputed more than anything else in the book. *Melius fuerat non scribere*. But there it stands" (T xi; original emphasis), acknowledging that it would have perhaps been better not to write it. However, it emphasizes the inevitable problems of judgment the text invites and itself dramatizes, above all the fact, as Patricia Ingham aptly put it, that "Generic 'woman' is up for moral assessment" (1993: 85).

onto a specific discourse in the novel, the presentation of Tess's body as risk both to herself and to the male spectators, notably Alec and Angel. The text is marked by a distinct atmosphere of inevitable catastrophe, and a heroine who is half-aware of being tossed by forces beyond her control, while also possessing remarkable physical strength and a presence, which is corporeal rather than verbal. The prominent risks are, firstly, those of giving in to temptation, of human sexual desire and choice of partner; secondly, the dangers of misreading and misjudging human character, appearance and behaviour by blindly following social norms, ideological convictions, or by chasing ideals.

While Christian notions of purity, transgression, and damnation inform the major ideological backdrop of the narrative, we also find a pronounced tension between discourses of Darwinian determinism of nature and pagan fatalism, which altogether complicates the question of human agency and responsibility in the novel. Relevant in this context appear the alternative titles Hardy considered for *Tess*, including "Too Late, Beloved", "Too Late Beloved", and "The Body and Soul of Sue". The first two highlight the tragic significance of timing and choice, as well as "Hardy's interest in the perversity of circumstances, which often conflict with his characters' desires and intentions" (Brady 1986: 141); the latter emphasizes the split between fleshly desire, emotion, and rationality, and also, as many critics have noted, the fact that in the narrative one man possesses – or seeks to – the heroine's body (Alec), and another her soul (Angel). As Monika Elbert argues, the novel "focuses on man's legal right or natural desire to own and to appropriate woman's body. Much of the controversy in the book revolves around this idea – that Tess belongs to Alec in a biological, 'primitive' sense and to Angel in the legal, 'civilized' sense" (1999: 63). In both cases, however, Tess's body and appearance trigger male projections, fantasies and attempts at appropriation, which, in one way or another, put her at risk. Her body is continuously exposed, to characters and readers, – and arguably made into a spectacle – from the first to the last scenes of the novel. In particular feminist criticism has focused on Tess being turned into a spectacle by Hardy (cf. Sternlieb 2000: 352; Silverman 1993: 142), and much has been written on the relationship between author, narrator, and heroine in a story in which Tess's physicality and virginal body are clear focal points (cf. Henson 2011: 189; Lovesey 2003: 913). While agreement consists that "Everyone is always looking at Tess" (Nunowaka 1992: 72), traditional feminists have been harshly critical of Hardy's male gaze; however, it seems that the text, rather than being complicit with it, criticizes the effects of the public gaze on women and highlights their victimized status.

Rosemarie Morgan rightly argued that Tess is characteristic for Hardy's conception of women as "humanly imperfect, unconventional, strong, sexually vital, risk-taking rebels" (1988: 155), unorthodox heroines according to Victorian standards. Thus attacking gender norms and perceptions, Hardy's fictions reveal how "woman continually risks entrapment by male attitudes" (155), moreover seeking to restore womanhood to a reality which is flawed, i.e. including good and bad characteristics. With Tess running the whole gamut from innocent virgin to murderess, Hardy certainly takes the breaking of binaries to extremes. Tess goes through various phases of womanhood and takes on roles such as daughter, maiden, mother, wife, and mistress, occupying none of them for long, but rather slipping through them. Moreover, the roles are fragmented and separated from each other, denying Tess, for example, the traditional unity of the 'mother-wife' role. It is important to note, though, that Hardy's emphasis is not on weakness but on instability and imperfection, as physical weaknesses is, on the contrary, in many of Hardy's fictions a characteristic of the men, who suffer from break-downs and sickness, like Angel Clare does (cf. Morgan 1988: 160; Higonnet 1990: 207).

While much critical debate exists about Tess's 'passivity' in the novel, Hardy's emphasis from the beginning of the novel is on a physical, active Tess. She is physically strong, resilient and always working or wandering across the country.[9] Yet she does display a complex mix of active and passive impulses throughout the narrative and appears to be either exhausted, asleep, or in a dream-like state of shock or trance in crucial moments. Tess's body, her physical appearance, which certainly "shapes her destiny" (Freeman 1982: 321), is paradoxically powerful on the one hand, yet offers no protection against being violated and appropriated on the other. Throughout the novel, Tess moves constantly, seeking work, escape, or a place to rest and remain 'unseen.' The preoccupation in Hardy's fictions with "walking, travelling, movement of all kinds" (Tanner 1975: 197) is often linked to a sense of uprooting, unrest, and desperate necessity. Especially in *Tess*, it takes on the quality "of hunting or being hunted" (Bullen 1986: 236). Tess's movement is always tied to a sense of risk, while she lacks any sense of safety and stability, i.e. a home or a clear origin. There is no permanence for the tragic heroine anywhere, emphasizing Hardy's belief that "the greatest disaster is for an individual to be rootless" (Harvey 2003: 159*)*.

The narrative deals with the destruction of a female and the various images imposed on her, from which there is no escape for her (other than death). Char-

---

9 See Gussow's comment that: "Surely no 'passive' female protagonist has ever walked so many miles, milked so many cows, threshed so much wheat, harvested so many frozen beets, labored so hard – against the curse of spectacular good looks, above all" (2000: 443).

acteristically for late Victorian society, Tess is "doomed by her physical beauty, by her sexuality, by a body of which she is at first unaware, and subsequently only guiltily and burdensomely aware" (Pykett 1993: 160). Her physical and mental safety and stability is shaken early on, and while Tess grows out of her innocence and into an awareness of the potential risks her beauty and body pose, she struggles to manage them till the end and fails to use it actively to her advantage. Tess's is thus a distinctly female tragedy, her flaw and downfall are her body and looks; "she cannot escape the 'risk' her own appearance constitutes" (Rooney 1991: 97).

According to Margaret Elvy, while in *Tess* "everything fails: love, motherhood, ambition, folklore, custom, history, tradition, education, religion, and matriarchy", in "Hardy's fiction, the most piquant loss is always the loss of love" (Elvy 2012: 103). The novel is surely symptomatic of Hardy's writing as a "literature of loss" (103), yet it appears that a central risk Tess tries to avert and manage throughout the narrative is less her own love than her family's precarious economic situation. As so often the case, class is inseparable from gender in Hardy's fiction. The criticism of the position of women is bound to social issues; the double standards of moral judgment, and all sexual/marital relations are presented in direct reference to economic pressures.[10] In *Tess*, where the heroine presents a prime "example of the worthy and vulnerable woman, who is most at risk in contemporary society" (Harvey 2001: 15), Hardy also engages with several other legal debates of the time and issues of women's right and sexuality, such as the age of consent, rape laws,[11] or the question if a man could marry his deceased wife's sister.[12] These are all placed within a wider discussion of women at risk, either through being tied to the wrong person, the Victorian cult of virginity, feared loss of reputation, financial dependence, or poverty. The text criticizes a socio-moral discourses and a society which perceives in particular the female body as dangerous yet utterly fails to protect women from male gaze and desire.

---

[10] Major critics of Hardy in the realm of gender and feminist studies are Penny Boumelha, Kristin Brady, Margaret Higonnet, Patricia Ingham, and Rosemarie Morgan. For a summary of existing criticism and reception see Brady (1999); for an bibliography of sources see Riquelme (1998: 455–462).
[11] See, for instance, Davis Jr. (1997) and Williams (2001).
[12] In 1907, the British parliament passed the Deceased Wife's Sister's Marriage Act, which allowed a man to legally marry his dead wife's sister, which had previously been forbidden. The ending of *Tess* takes up this topic, with Angel marrying Liza-Lu, the 'pure' virginal image of her older sister.

Consequently, the reader's experience of following Tess is one of "intensity and risk" (Freeman 1982: 312). This is also due to several factors concerning narrative structure and design of the text. The plot of *Tess* enfolds as a string of accidents and coincidences; the heroine's tragic fate is brought on and sealed by one mischance after another.[13] Indeed, as a force, contingency often assumes vast proportions in Hardy's fictions, revealing how his use of accidentalism corresponds to a vision of reality as "chance, mishap, accident, events that affect our lives while they remain far beyond our control" (Van Ghent 1967: 248; see D'Exideuil 1970: 151). In this context, Jil Larson emphasizes the importance of a notion of moral luck which has implications for Hardy's characters' desire for control and highlights the mix of a certain recklessness with and passive acceptance of fate. His writings, she argues, evoke a sense of life "like a game of chance, and therefore suspense, risk, and hope are inevitable for those who play and even for those who would rather sit on the side lines and watch" (Larson 2001: 71). Although parallels between the two writers are rarely drawn, Larson's comment suggests an interesting parallel between Hardy's and the works of Jane Austen. Hardy's accidentalism is similarly reflected in the structural design of his works, highlighting the interdependence of people and events, with chance operating mainly through timing. An example are the many coincidental meetings in *Tess:* Alec intruding on Tess's life, wherever she is, Angel always being tragically too late in 'choosing' Tess, the slipping of her confession letter under the rug, Angel's parents being away from home when Tess comes looking for them for help. Nonetheless, despite the series of little accidents and coincidences, the main episodes and the great crises are also strongly motivated psychologically, i.e. Alec's seduction, Angel's rejection of Tess, and her murder of Alec.

The first view the reader gets of Tess is among a group of "genuine country girls, unaccustomed to many eyes" (T 12) during the ritual May dance. Well-known is the description of the heroine sticking out among them: "She was a fine and handsome girl – not handsomer than some others, possibly – but her mobile peony mouth and large innocent eyes added eloquence to colour and shape. She wore a red ribbon in her hair and was the only one of the white company who could boast of such a pronounced adornment" (T 12). Much has been

---

13 For such as reading see especially Hinde (1976) and Larson (2001: 64–92). Other older studies of Hardy's view of chance and causality are Elliott's *Fatalism in the Works of Thomas Hardy* (1966), Hornback's *The Metaphor of Chance: Vision and Technique in the Works of Thomas Hardy* (1971), and Morrell's *Thomas Hardy: The Will and the Way* (1965).

written about this crucial first scene, the focus on Tess's lips,[14] and the symbolic use of colour,[15] the splash of red which sets her apart from the white mass, marking her as a victim, the chosen virgin in a pagan rite, foreshadowing the later rape, the murder and the final 'sacrifice' on the altar at Stonehenge.[16] The scene also introduces the fatal disconnect between Tess's appearance, "all her bouncing handsome womanliness", and her naïve innocence of mind, as yet "untinctured by experience" (T 13). Angel, who walks by and stops to watch the girls, "took almost the first that came to hand" (T 15), not Tess Durbeyfield. The scene implies that if had he chosen her then, all later tragedy could have been avoided; meanwhile the narrator comments rather sardonically: "Pedigree, ancestral skeletons, monumental record, the d'Urberville lineaments, did not help Tess in her life's battle as yet, even to the extent of attracting to her a dancing-partner over the heads of the commonest peasantry" (T 16). The question of heredity is touched upon here, the issue of the power of genes and Tess's hybrid legacy of both peasant beauty and degenerate criminal aristocracy. Typically, references to Tess' family lineage are rendered ironic by the narrator, who says, e.g., that "the personal charms which Tess could boast of were in main part her mother's gift, and therefore unknightly, unhistorical" (T 20). The scene at the May dance presents sexual selection as a communal, 'naturalistic' ritual, taking place under the eyes of others. Sexual courtship is here neither staged as "meaningless aristocratic game nor as risk-taking social mischief" (Kaye 2002: 143; 145f), like in in so many other 19th-century novels, but for the maids, who outnumber the watching men, there is the high risk of not being chosen.[17] When Angel takes a second look at Tess, he feels "the faintest aspect

---

14 Descriptions of Tess' body are central to the novel, and many critics have noted that the most prominently featured body part is her mouth, yet references to her eyes are, in fact, even more frequent. Tess's body is sexualized from beginning, but in order to avoid censorship, Hardy had to refrain from the description of any explicitly sexual acts in the novel. The focus on Tess's lips is thus explainable through the fact that the mouth was simply a 'safe' part to describe, while also catering to the Victorian fetishization of female body parts (cf. Elvy 2012: 85; Pykett 1993: 159). On the descriptions of Tess' mouth in the text see, e.g., Ingham (2000: 126), Law (1997: 260), Lovesey (2003: 924f), Poole (1991: 478), and Silverman (1993: 131ff).
15 For an analysis of the symbolic pattern of red and white running through the text, see Tanner (1975); also Boumelha (1982: 121), Brady (1986: 134f), Elvy (2012: 92f), and Henson (2011: 191).
16 On the strong references to paganism in the text see Harrington (2005) and Stave (1995). Cf. also Bullen (1986: 204–219), Elvy (2012: 83), Higonnet (1990: 203f), Poole (1991: 474), and Tanner (1975: 194).
17 Sternlieb emphasizes this aspect in her reading, drawing attention to the fact that historically there was a huge surplus of women in Britain at the time. There are, in fact, only two

of reproach that he had not chosen her. He, too, was sorry then that [...] he had not observed her" (T 16). This is a clear foreshadowing of the ending, where Angel is again "too late" in his forgiveness and admittance of his true feelings for Tess.[18] Meanwhile, Tess "instinctively felt that she was hurt by his oversight", "However, it could not be helped" (T 17). From the start, Tess does not assert agency in the selection process, for instance, by flirting with other men, which would have given her greater choice and control. Nature and the ideals of chastity and morality clash from the beginning and the denial of promiscuity has for Tess, as the representative woman of the text, only negative consequences. According to Richard Kaye, "Tess is fixed on a single erotic plot when she should have recognized the advantage sexual selection allowed for the multiplication of opportunities" (2002: 148). The scene also introduces the theme of inevitability and the fatalistic outlook of a heroine, portrayed as a 'play thing' of higher forces, who the narrative follows till the final moment, when "the President of the Immortals, in Aeschylean phrase, had ended his sport with Tess" (T 508).

After the May dance, the narrative moves onto a closer view of Tess's family life and characterization of her parents. Significant is the narrator's extended metaphorical comment on the situation of Tess and her many siblings, comparing them to being on a risky sea voyage with one (or rather two) somewhat careless captains:

> All these young souls were passengers in the Durbeyfield ship – entirely dependent on the judgment of the two Durbeyfield adults for their pleasures, their necessities, their health, even their existence. If the heads of the Durbeyfield household chose to sail into difficulty, disaster, starvation, disease, degradation, death, thither were these half-dozen little captives under their hatches compelled to sail with them – six helpless creatures, who had never been asked if they wished for life on any terms, much less if they wished for it on such hard conditions as were involved [...]. (T 24)

---

men in the novel to accommodate all women, and the choice of one woman ultimately means the rejection of the others. Therefore, Sternlieb says: "One of the last great Victorian novels destroys the nineteenth-century marriage plot by exposing it as a statistical lie" (2000: 351). Hardy's novel also dramatizes the perception of women as easily replaceable; this emphasis is made twice in the plot, when Angel nearly takes Tess's friend Izzie to Brazil, and when he marries her sister Liza-Lu in in the end.

18 Cf. Elizabeth Bronfen's comment: "Angel's not choosing Tess, which she will later read as a metaphor for the fatal belatedness of their love, also signifies that she has already been chosen by the dead, who speak through the father's name, that she has been summoned away from the May Dance of marriage, [...] Indeed, Tess also faces three choices – her ancestors, Angel and Alec – but she is as yet too innocent to choose" (1993: 75). On deferral and belatedness as central themes of the novel see also Higonnet (1990: 213).

The novel leaves no doubt about Tess's precarious family situation, which will, in fact, influence most of her actions and trigger, via various other accidents, the main course of tragic events. The first of these is the carriage accident and the subsequent death of the family horse Prince. Driving through the night and utterly exhausted, Tess is asleep when the accident happens and then "stood helpless looking on" (T 35), pondering on the calamity. Her family's reaction to the misfortune reveals a similar fatalism. The Durbeyfields take on the struggle for survival with a stoic acceptance, rather than with active attempts at risk management, and perceive it as something largely beyond human control. Their attitude shows this certain carelessness and lack of concern largely because

> the very shiftlessness of the household rendered the misfortune a less terrifying one to them than it would have been to a striving family, though in the present case it meant ruin, and in the other it would only have meant inconvenience. In the Durbeyfield countenances there was nothing of the red wrath that would have burnt upon the girl from parents more ambitious for her welfare. Nobody blamed Tess as she blamed herself. (T 37)[19]

Due to the accident, Tess is left in a state of guilty despair, and, foreshadowing the ending, "regarded herself in the light of a murderess" (T 38). However, Tess's self-blame aside, especially her perception of her mother's behaviour is increasingly critical, although Tess retains an ignorance about her own developing sexuality, which puts her at risk soon enough.

> As Tess grew older and began to see how matters stood, she felt quite a Malthusian[20] towards her mother for thoughtlessly giving her so many little sisters and brothers, when it was such a trouble to nurse and provide for them. Her mother's intelligence was that of a happy child: Joan Durbeyfield was simply an additional one, and that not the eldest, to her own long family of waiters on Providence. (T 41)

Consequently, Tess takes over more and more family burdens, and, reluctantly, sets out one day to claim kinship with the d'Urbervilles clan. The first meeting

---

19 Several critics have argued that Hardy associates paganism, fatalism and femininity in the novel. Especially the female characters (Tess, her mother, the other maids and field women) show a pronounced "quality of resignation to one's fate, an acceptance that human beings are fundamentally at the mercy of the forces of the natural world and of destiny itself" (Harrington 2005: 5). Beyond expressing a particular view of life, fatalism appears as a survival strategy in the novel, for example in the women's reaction to Tess's encounter with Alec. It offers an acceptance as well as sense-making strategy of seemingly unalterable circumstances.
20 The reference to Thomas Robert Malthus, who theorized the political-economic risk of population growth, adds another dimension to the debate of the control of human sexuality and social criticism in the novel.

between Tess and Alec has been thoroughly analysed for its eroticism and the foreshadowing of the scene in the Chase and the blurred borderline between seduction and rape.[21] Whatever view one wants to take on this matter, the scene does evoke a clear climate of risk and threat. Tess is unaware of the danger of Alec's obviously sexual interest in her; and she eats the strawberries he feeds her "in a half-pleased, half-reluctant state" (T 47). The narrative emphasizes again the tragic split between her physical appearance and her lack of awareness of its effect:

> Tess Durbeyfield did not divine, as she innocently looked down at the roses in her bosom, that there behind the blue narcotic haze was potentially the 'tragic mischief' of her drama – [...]. She had an attribute which amounted to a disadvantage just now [...], a fullness of growth, which made her appear more of a woman than she really was. (T 47–48)

Hardy's narrator raises again the question of fate and destiny, musing in a half-ironic, half-pitying tone on the accidents of human attraction and sexual selection, which make Tess "doomed to be seen and coveted that day by the wrong man, and not by some other man, the right and desired one in all respects" (T 48), furthermore drawing attention to the dangers and potential suffering this poses, because

> in the present case, as in millions, it was not the two halves of a perfect whole that confronted each other at the perfect moment; a missing counterpart wandered independently about the earth waiting in crass obtuseness till the late time came. Out of which maladroit delay sprang anxieties, disappointments, shocks, catastrophes, and passing-strange destinies. (T 49)

The relationship between Tess and Alec, marked by a distinct notion of force and danger, always hinges on physical proximity and Tess's body. For instance, in the cart with him, she is scared by the speed of Alec's reckless driving. As he refuses to slow down, she is forced to take hold of Alec in order not to fall down. When they reach the bottom of the hill, she exclaims: "Safe, thank God, in spite of your fooling!" (T 63). She is wholly unconscious of the implications of her touch, in contrast to Alec, who replies: "'Well, you need not let go your hold of me so thanklessly the moment you feel yourself out of danger'" (T 64). The situation almost spirals out of control, Alec trying all he can to get in contact with Tess's body, Tess desperately trying to avoid it. She even jumps of the cart, willing to walk all the way back home. Employing a language of risk, the

---

[21] On the extensive debate on rape and seduction and Tess' agency, see: Brady (1986), Heffernan (2005), Morgan (1989), Rooney (1991), Sutherland (1996), and T.R. Wright (2000).

narrative shows Tess's struggle and failure to judge and control the situation as well as being clear about how fear determines her behaviour:

> She might in truth have safely trusted him now; but he had forfeited her confidence for the time, and she kept on the ground progressing thoughtfully, as if wondering whether it would be wiser to return home. Her resolve, however, had been taken, and it seemed vacillating even to childishness to abandon it now, unless for graver reasons. How could she face her parents, get back her box, and disconcert the whole scheme for the rehabilitation of her family on such sentimental grounds? (T 67)

For the next few weeks, Tess grows accustomed to Alec's presence. Yet there remains a felt menace on both sides. Alec constructs Tess as a temptation and risk to his moral restraint; while she fears something from him she does not quite understand.

The fateful night at the Chase, which follows soon after, presents the culmination of the tragic irony of Tess's miscalculations and her attempts at managing the risk she perceives. Tired after a long day's work, Tess is anxiously waiting for the other maids to finish dancing so she can go home in company: "She became restless and uneasy; yet, having waited so long, it was necessary to wait longer; on account of the fair the roads were dotted with roving characters of possibly ill intent; and, though not fearful of measurable dangers, she feared the unknown" (T 78). Finally walking home with the others, Tess joins in the laughter about the one maid having sweet treacle running down her back, which provokes a violent reaction and reveals the other's women's jealousies of her and the male attention she receives. The women all turn threating towards Tess, who "no longer minded the loneliness of the way and the lateness of the hour; her one object was to get away from the whole crew as soon as possible" (T 83). Therefore, she willingly jumps onto Alec's horse when he appears and offers her a ride home, which the other women perceive as a dangerous move rather than a lucky escape, as one comments: "*Out of the frying-pan into the fire!*" (T 84; original emphasis). The following scene in the Chase is literally clouded in "Darkness and silence", with the narrator commenting on the predetermined course of events: "'It was to be.' There lay the pity of it" (T 90–91).

Although Tess is left pregnant after the night in the Chase, she refuses all help and contact with Alec. Her decision is met with the utmost disbelief from her mother, for whom marrying Alec would have been the only sensible management of the situation in which Tess stands to lose her future and reputation. In reply to her mother's accusation of having been careless, Tess blames her for letting her run the risk unprepared: "How could I be expected to know? I was a child when I left this house four months ago. Why didn't you tell me there was danger in men-folk? Why didn't you warn me?" (T 104). Interestingly,

Tess's assessment here is close to Alec's much later, when he tells Tess that "it is a shame for parents to bring up their girls in such dangerous ignorance" (T 402). Inevitably, gossip starts to spread about Tess's precarious situation, and her story, due to the marked class difference between her an Alec, possesses "by its fearsomeness, a far higher fascination that it would have exercised if unhazardous" (T 105). Out of shame and to avoid the preying eyes of others, Tess keeps herself isolated indoors. Her only exercise is taking long solitary walks at night; "her sole idea seemed to be to shun mankind" (T 108). Regarding the public perception of Tess's fate, a conversation between the two field women, who observe Tess nursing her baby, is crucial. It underlines the simple causality established between female beauty and the risk of being violated by a man, as well as the acknowledgment of the physical strength and resilience of her:

> 'Lord, 'tis wonderful what a body can get used to o' that sort in time!' 'A little more than persuading had to do wi' the coming o't, I reckon.' [...] 'Well, a little more, or a little less, 'twas a thousand pities that it should have happened to she, of all others. *But 'tis always the comeliest! The plain ones be as safe as churches* —hey, Jenny?' The speaker turned to one of the group who certainly was not ill-defined as plain. (T 114; my emphasis)

As Ellen Rooney emphasizes, the references to "Tess's beauty and to Jenny's plainness as a source of protection are chilling", but support the persistent portrayal of Tess's sexuality and beauty as "a temptation to men that places her in almost constant danger" (1991: 98). Her difference, obvious from the beginning, is constantly reaffirmed. Paradoxically, despite her exceptional beauty, she is perceived as an "an almost standard woman, but for the slight incautiousness of character inherited from her race" (T 113). This is a crucial description, evoking the tension between the stereotype and the exemplary, which characterizes Tess. Due to her hybrid social status, she presents an anomaly, but has inherited the worst of both worlds, "she is doubly damned because she is [...] a depraved member of the decayed d'Urberville aristocracy as well as an immoral peasant girl" (Elbert 1999: 51). Arguing along similar lines, Jennifer Wicke describes Tess as "an ultimately unstandardizable type", driven to her tragic end by "that mysterious cultural force of Standards" (Wicke 1998: 589; 586), and claims that the novel raises the question who is responsible for setting them. The formation of a notion of "standard" relates back to the influence of Darwinian thought (i.e. the categorization of type, genus, species and the respective mutations and deviations from those categories), and is based on the evaluation of human appearance and performance (behaviour), which occurred across many areas of social life, in economics, science, education, politics, art, and religion at the turn from the 19th to the 20th century. As an on-going process, it stretched over two decades from "1881, when the International Prototype Meter was installed in Paris, to 1891 and Tess's publication, to 1901 and the establishment of the British Standards Institute – a moment wherein the notion of a standard is being crystallized in disparate cultural practices and concretized as a cultural concept" (Wicke 1998: 575). It is reflected in the vocabulary of the narrative, and a frame of categorization based on notions of sameness and difference.

Personifying the threats of deviation and transgression, Tess' story inspires both danger and fasciation and is publicly construed as a typical Victorian risk narrative, of "the maid who went to the merry green wood and came back a changed state. [...] the event which had made of her a social warning had also for the moment made her the most interesting personage in the village to many" (T 116). Meanwhile Tess herself is determined to put her high-flying dreams of a better life behind her. Over the next couple of years, she sets out to avoid exposure to public as well as male interest as much as possible. She finds a new position as a dairymaid at Talbothays; yet while this period is in many ways the happiest section of the account of Tess's life, she is again confronted with her own physical difference. All the other maids are struck by Tess's beauty, which also attracts the attention of Angel Clare. He notices Tess as "a fresh and virginal daughter of Nature", which is, in addition to a vague sense of familiarity she triggers in him, "sufficient to lead him to select Tess in preference to the other pretty milkmaids" (T 155). Tess, herself attracted to Angel, is secretly thrilled about his attention but cannot shake the danger inherent in his misperception of her appearance: "There was, to be sure, hardly a ghost of a chance for either of them" (T 176). As a result, she continues to make contradictory attempts of stirring Angel towards choosing one of the other maids. Yet, she also compares herself to the others and draws the following judgement, which justifies Angel's choice, but also bears the risk of the discovery of the indelible stain of her past: "she who knew herself to be more impassioned in nature, cleverer, more beautiful than they, was in the eyes of propriety far less worthy of him than the homelier ones whom he ignored" (T 189). The choice of Angel, his proposal and Tess's resistance and final agreement, including many aborted attempts at confession, take up the whole middle section of the narrative. For Angel, central are the repeated idealized perceptions of Tess and her being "in sight to choose a mate from unconstrained Nature" (T 222–223). Meanwhile Tess is battling her "fear that her resistance might break down under her own desire" (T 227). Her reflections about answering Angel's proposal underline the sense of the risk involved in her choice, yet hopes that "love's counsel would prevail" (T 228). In a contradictory spirit, the narrative relates her contemplation of confessing to Angel, yet on various occasions her sense of self-preservation wins over her courage. Meanwhile, Joan Durbeyfield urges her daughter not to mention her past troubles, which she refers to in a letter as just a "passing accident" (T 246). But for Tess, this advice clashes with her guilt and desire for honesty.

In the whole decision-making process, which builds up to the final tragic climax on the wedding night, Tess's emotions are inseparably connected to danger, and threatening feelings like shame are only momentarily and barely kept at bay by her love: "*– doubt, fear, moodiness, care, shame. She knew that they were waiting like wolves just outside the circumscribing light, but she had long spells of power to keep them in hungry subjection there*" (T 249; my emphasis). As Morgan observes, most damaging to Hardy's women are usually "defensive acts [...] produced by that socially approved method of subordinating women: the inculcation of guilt" (1988: 157). This applies very much to Tess, who is torn between her conflicting emotions. With the official announcement of her engagement, she is much more in the public eye again and risks being seen; she "paid the penalty of walking about with happiness superadded to beauty on her countenance by being much stared at as she moved amid them on his arm" (T 264). Among the various bad omens connected to Tess's union with Angel is the news of the maid Retty's suicide, out of unrequited love, which reaches the couple on their wedding night. The incident is suggestive of the cruel impact of the sexual selection made by Angel. Yet it is again Tess, who takes on the whole blame for the situation and it triggers her daring decision to confess to Angel, springing from a sense of self-punishment and desperate hope of redemption. However, it is Angel who bursts out first with his own confession of his pre-marital sexual relations. Again, he employs a dramatic rhetoric of risk and danger, explaining to Tess:

> 'I was afraid of endangering my chance of you, darling, the great prize of my life – [...]. Well, *I would not risk it.* I was going to tell you a month ago – at the time you agreed to be mine, but I could not; *I thought it might frighten you away from me.* I put it off; then I thought I would tell you yesterday, to give you a chance at least of escaping me. [...]. I wonder if you will forgive me?' (T 285; my emphasis)

The fifth 'Phase' of the novel, telling entitled "The Woman Pays", opens with the moment after Tess's confession, which is not described to the reader. While the risk Angel has run with his confession appears as best as the standard politeness of a pious man, seeking to keep up appearances, yet well protected by social and sexual norms, Tess's has gambled away all in the hope of Angel's forgiveness. He turns to her, saying: "'O Tess, forgiveness does not apply to the case! [...] the woman I have been loving is not you.' 'But who?' 'Another woman in your shape'" (T 292–293). Tess, although completely broken by Angel's perception of her, sees "in his words the realization of her own apprehensive foreboding in former times" (T 293); again this shows her inconsistent belief in consequence and prediction of chains of events, yet that she was not unaware of the risk of her confession.[22] Without any attempt to fight and change Angel's mind, she accepts being cast-off; now that she has lost Angel's love, she has "nothing more to fear, having scarce anything to hope" (T 299). What is significant in the description of how Tess' tells her story to Angel is her self-control, and apparent absence of emotion, which is, perhaps, what shocks and enrages Angel the most. What appears, from her side, as an act of self-distancing from her past in order not to break down, Angel perceives as cold arrogance. In reaction to her confession, he indulges in anger, panic, even self-pity, an array of emotions Tess' never allows herself openly. From today's perspective, Tess' passively detached, almost trance-like state clearly appears as a protective shield and she shows the characteristic signs of a traumatized victim, accessing her violation as an "'external' memory – socially constructed, skating along the surface of words and engaging the intellect – not the body's re-experience" (Culbertson 1995: 170).[23]

Overcome by the experience of contingency, Angel realizes that his plan of possessing the ideal woman has failed. Yet he continues to be thrown by the contradiction between the appearance of Tess and what he now knows: "Nature, in her fantastic trickery, had set such a seal of maidenhood upon Tess's countenance that he gazed at her with a stupefied air" (T 303–304). This illustrates again how the status of Tess's body is constantly questioned in the narrative. Angel's reading of her body confronts Tess cruelly with a perception of the norm of virtuous womanhood. She struggles to convince him of her 'sameness', or of the fact that her deviation might still be considered to be within the acceptable sexual-moral norm of a wife. Angel's is unaware of his self-deception; while he has idealized her as the epitome of pastoral innocence, he is attracted to her precisely because of her difference and her exceptional beauty. Tess's confession shakes his faith in outward appearances. As he did not see Tess "fall", he is thrown into doubts about his own feelings, perceptions, and judgments based on them. His only solution is to exile himself from the disorienting situation.

The wedding night of Tess and Angel is typical for Hardy's fiction in so far that a classic romantic situation, the union of the people who have chosen

---

[22] Cf. Garson's argument: "It is hard to believe that an adolescent girl brought up by Joan Durbeyfield would be as ignorant as Tess seems to be of the nature of the threat posed by Alec, yet Tess reluctantly surrenders to a number of overtures without any apparent sense of where they are leading. Then, too, despite her obsessive fear of Angel's learning her history, Tess is unrealistically unable to predict his response when he does" (1991: 137).

[23] For a reading of Tess's behaviour through trauma theory see McLaughlin Mitchell (2010).

each other, is portrayed as fraught with anxiety and disaster (see D'Exideuil 1970: 89). To make matters worse, the observing narrative voice implies that, while all seems lost, there might have been a chance to turn the situation around, at least for a woman more experienced and willing to use her sexuality than Tess: "a woman of the world might have conquered him. But Tess did not think of this" (T 307–8). Contrastively, Angel is aware of the power of Tess's body; "she might have used it promisingly" (T 311). However, instead they abstain from all physical contact and Angel confronts Tess with a risk that seems to rule out all chances of marital relations. His words once more reveal the destructive power of Victorian beliefs in social norms, the value attached to female virginity, as well as an evolutionary train of thoughts.

> 'How can we live together while that man lives? – He being your husband in nature, and not I. [...] Think of years to come, and children being born to us, and this past matter getting known [...], think of wretches of our flesh and blood growing up under a taunt which they will gradually get to feel the full force of with their expanding years. [...] Can you honestly say Remain, after contemplating this contingency?' (T 310)

Tess is shaken further by the unexpectedness of this danger described by Angel – her own children one day looking at her in disdain – and accepts it unquestioningly.

Another significant scene in which Tess's nature and beauty is construed as risk occurs shortly after she finds herself married, yet alone and desperate again. In order to find work, Tess sets out to walk through the countryside, aware that "[a]mong the difficulties of her lonely position not the least was the attention she excited by her appearance" (T 351). She decides to avert all eyes from herself through disguise and a striking act of self-mutilation:

> [...] Tess resolved *to run no further risks from her appearance*. As soon as she got out of the village she entered a thicket and took from her basket one of the oldest field-gowns [...]. She also, by a felicitous thought, took a handkerchief from her bundle and tied it round her face under her bonnet, covering her chin and half her cheeks and temples, as if she were suffering from toothache. Then with her little scissors, by the aid of a pocket looking-glass, she mercilessly nipped her eyebrows off, *and thus insured against aggressive admiration*, she went on her uneven way. (T 356; my emphasis)

Obvious in this act is Tess's impulse to "retreat from specularity and the body" (Silverman 1993: 139), and her desire to 'undo' her physical beauty in order to protect herself. Discarding all female vanity, attracting any male attention with her appearance is clearly more liability than pleasure to her. Many critics have noted that in this scene, "[t]he political implications of Tess's self-mutilation are sadly obvious", showing a woman seeking to evade sexual aggression caused by her gendered body (Law 1997: 262). It moreover shows that Tess has come a long way from the innocence of the beginning of the novel. Now knowing the danger springing from her own body, she calculates the risk and tries to take precautions. Similarly, when meeting her new employer, the farmer Groby at Flintcomb-Ash, she is under no illusions regarding the treatment she will receive from him, yet "could read character sufficiently well to know by this time that she had nothing to fear from her employer's gallantry" (T 371).

Still, her bad luck continues. When Tess is on the way home from her unsuccessful mission of going to see and appeal to Angel's parents, she unveils her face, which appears as an act of both careless rebellion and fatal desperation: "Who cares about the looks of a castaway like me!'" (T 384). This decision is tragically important for the course of events in the last part of the narrative. The minute Alec, who is by now a country preacher, sees Tess the "effect upon her old lover was electric" (T 390). Alec's newly found religiosity is portrayed as almost more dangerous than his sexual drive, and it soon becomes obvious that despite Alec's outward conversion, nothing has changed. He still blames Tess's seductive femininity for his moral struggles and trespasses. This is obvious in reoccurring utterances such as: "'it is better that I should not look too often on you. It might be dangerous.' '[...] 'Well, women's faces have had too much power over me already for me not to fear them!' (T 395); 'Tess– don't look at me so – I cannot stand your looks!' (T 404); 'Tess, my girl, I was on the way to, at least, social salvation till I saw you again!' [...] 'You temptress, Tess; you dear damned witch of Babylon – I could not resist you as soon as I met you again!' (T 411); 'Of course you have done nothing except retain your pretty face and shapely figure. [...] – you field-girls should never wear those bonnets if you wish to keep out of danger'" (T 420).

In the face of her family's destitute situation after her father's death, Tess finds herself more and more forced towards accepting Alec's offer of support. Her letter to Angel presents a final outburst of emotion and cry for help. Revealing her acute sense of risk, she still has to disguise the exact nature of her fear. But she refers clearly to the danger her beauty poses to her as a woman without the protection of a husband. Excerpts from her letter read as follows:

> 'I am so exposed to temptation, Angel. I fear to say who it is [...] Can you not come to me now, at once, before anything terrible happens?' [...]
>
> 'People still say that I am rather pretty, [...]. But I do not value my good looks [...]. So much have I felt this, that when I met with annoyance on account of the same, I tied up my face in a bandage as long as people would believe in it. [...]
>
> 'I am in terror as to what an accident might lead to, and I so defenceless on account of my first error. I cannot say more about this – it makes me too miserable. But if I break down

by falling into some fearful snare, my last state will be worse than my first. [...] 'Come to me–come to me, and save me from what threatens me!' (T 428–430)

Trying to resist as long as possible, Tess is vulnerable to Alec's offer because he knows her main anxiety, the burden of care for her siblings. And once again, she has to pay with her body for trying to avert the economic risk from her family.

When Angel finally questions his harsh judgment of Tess and goes to Sandbourne to search for her, he finds a "Mrs d'Urbervilles", who says to him in a ghostly, self-controlled manner that it is all "'Too late, too late!' (T 483). Soon afterwards, when she tells him about killing Alec, her confession is also uncannily devoid of emotion, though she admits that she has long expected to lose control: "'I feared long ago, [...] that I might do it some day for the trap he set for me in my simple youth'" (T 491). In the end, Tess appears almost completely detached from her body and deeply traumatized. Throughout the narrative she is forced to practice a continuous fragmentation of her self, perceiving "herself as separate from those around her, set apart by guilt and experience", "distancing one part of the self from another as a means of survival" (McLaughlin Mitchell 2010: 194). In the end, she lives up to her family inheritance and has become a criminal, violent woman. Tess is ruined by men, survives without them through various hardships, only to be finally killed by them. Characteristically, she seems resigned to her fate, because when the men are closing in on her, her last words are: 'I am ready' (T 505).

Hardy's novel depicts in cultural, social, and historical terms the risks and destructiveness of various misperceptions of his heroine. It highlights the way the male protagonists perceive Tess as a blank, 'virginal' canvas on which to impose their visions and desires, while society's eyes transform her into a spectacle.[24] Her body is undeniably caught up in ideology and politics, clearly gendered and socially constructed. As such it is beyond Tess's control, because she cannot subvert the expectations, and prejudices connected to it. Angle and Alec, while being opposites to some extent, share the misunderstanding and crude violation of Tess. Both act like they are put in danger by Tess – in Alec's case by sexual temptation, in Angel's case through contact with an 'impure' women –, both are attracted and unnerved by her looks. One man destroys Tess out of an excessive 'rational' spirituality, the other out of excessive sensuality. Yet the conclusion drawn by Hardy seems indeed to be that "it is less an illegitimate pregnancy which destroys a woman than the self-righteousness of an attenuated and misapplied Christianity" (Garson 1991: 136). Angel, like the

---

24 On Hardy's ethnographic gaze see, e.g.: Gussow (2000), Elbert (1999), and Nunokawa (1992).

priest who denies Tess's dead baby son the baptism, is brutal in his failure to humanize an ideology, instead perverting Christian values for notions of custom and purity. Ironically, Tess's confession cements her downfall, which shows how Christianity represses women by the emphasis on virginity and chastity. Part of Angel's cruelty is his refusal to accept his natural instincts. Furthermore, by making a split between Tess and his image of her, he denies that she is still the same woman he loves. Several critics have seen this denial as "the most serious crime committed" (Freeman 1982: 320) in the novel and Angel's words on their wedding night as more destructive than anything Alec ever does to Tess. Arguably, his belated return to Tess causes the disastrous ending, while his final union with his child-bride Liza-Lu perpetuates the idealization of woman and appears as the projection of all Tess failed to be. As a gentlemanly hero, Angel is as far from strength and perfection as Tess's is from a Victorian 'doll'. Alec, who epitomizes the war between flesh and spirit, is also shown as loving and helping Tess, which breaks the characterization of him as a villain. In contrast to the classical conception of tragedy dependent on the assumption of inevitability and clearly discernible causal connections, Hardy's novel is famously ambiguous. The reader is given a multiplicity of determinants of risk, which complicate cause-effect explanations.[25]

8.2 'An Irrevocable Oath is Risky': Marriage and Death in *Jude the Obscure*

Both the fictional world of *Tess* and *Jude*, writes William Greenslade, are determined by the effects of laws, customs, and beliefs, and primary among those, "deeply held conventions about the working of ancestry and heredity" (Greenslade 1994: 154). Hardy's final novel, *Jude the Obscure* (1895), holding its unchallenged place as "possibly the grimmest English canonical novel of the nineteenth century" (Stave 1995: 123), takes many of the issues which are hinted at in *Tess* much further and explores the full impact of the contemporary fears of biological determinism, female sexuality, and the emerging moral-medical discourse of normalcy and deviance on the lives of Jude and Sue. Again telling a tragic tale of the war between flesh and spirit, the cruelty of Christian marriage laws, and failed hopes and ambitions, Hardy's narrative is distinctly shaped by fin-de-siècle anxieties; it casts a pessimistic look into the near future,

---

[25] Cf. Shires's comment that "a search for origins proves to be as doomed as Tess herself" (1999: 151). See also Waldoff (1979) and Parker (1992).

leaving characters and readers with a sense of unavoidable doom. In his *Study of Thomas Hardy*, D.H. Lawrence identifies the following as a recurring theme of Hardy's novels: "remain quite within the convention, and you are *good, safe, and happy in the long run*, [...] be passionate, individual, willful, you will die, either of your own lack of strength to bear the isolation and the exposure, or by direct revenge from the community, or from both" (Lawrence 1988: 21; my emphasis). The plot of *Jude* epitomizes the risk and destructiveness of social norms and their transgression, regardless if the violations are caused intentionally by the characters, or by forces of nature and circumstances beyond their control. It shows the dangers of rigid conventions, added to those lurking in one's genes, and the increasingly (self-)alienating conditions of modern life.

There is ample evidence of Hardy's engagement with the contemporary discourse and literature on the new scientific theories of the human mind, of sexuality, heredity, and degeneration (see Greenslade 1994). Above all, these gave new momentum to the anxiety about human agency and rise to the fear that life is uncontrollable and meaningless, foreshadowing the overwhelming sense of the risk of modernity that shapes the 20th century. Apart from the familiar tension between determinism and agency, the ground of investigation turns inwards, focussing on the consciousness and conscience of the individual. Hardy's writing illustrates this turn characteristic of late Victorian writing which, Jil Larson explains, tackles the "very arena the mid-Victorian writers sought to avoid in order not to lose their freedom in morbid introspection, guilt, and confusion" (Larson 2001: 36). But Hardy also shows his characters always engaged in physical action of sorts, typically either manual labour or travel.[26] Like Tess, Jude tries to take accept responsibility for his family's survival and is forced to continually move around in the process. He displays "his form of the modern vice of unrest" (J 85), unable to find stillness, exhausting his spirit of life through perpetual motion and frustrated desires. While *The Whirlpool* focuses on a portrayal of the dangerous vortex of modern city life, London, and its impact on the characters, in *Jude* any sense of rural stability is equally lost and in particular Sue's "townishness" is seen as a ruinous quality and partial cause of her nervous condition (J 111). In the course of the novel Jude moves from Marygreen, to Christminster, Melchester, Shaston, Aldbrickham and back to Christminster again, first drawn to the university city by high hopes of finding entry into academic or clerical life and pursuing a higher 'truth'. He is forced to walk miles and miles to find only provisional employment; later Sue and

---

[26] See Elaine Scarry's article "Work and the Body in Hardy and Other Nineteenth-Century Novelists" (1983).

Jude try to escape vicious rumours about their unlawful union and generally have to navigate a territory in which "any sense of community or love for one's neighbor is all but absent" (Stave 1995: 129). For the couple, the sense of being at risk increases continually throughout the novel; they are perpetually afraid of being watched and judged for their actions. J.S. Mill's words, first written in 1859 and capturing the influence of the Victorian sense of propriety on the individual, still shape the lives of Jude and Sue: "In our times, from the highest class of society down to the lowest, every one lives as under the eye of a hostile and dreaded censorship" (Mill 1946: 54).[27] Typically for Hardy's fictions, the riskscape constructed in the narrative includes urbanized settings or contact with other people; the danger rarely emanates from nature.

Added to the scientific awareness of hereditary risk staged in the text, the narrative also shows the destructive atmosphere created by piousness and the persisting influence of Christian notions of conscience so strongly palpable in the late-Victorian era. Christianity is still the dominant external moral authority people, providing a sense of security and orientation but also a cruel self-denying ethic, in particular regarding female sexuality. According to Levine, the plot of *Jude* "dramatizes *the risk of letting go of governing conventions*" (Levine 1997: 111; my emphasis). This proves to be true especially for Sue, who makes two crucial choices which go against her own principles and which she desperately tries to rectify later. While she seeks to exert control over her body and sexuality for most of the narrative, and is generally more courageous than Jude when it comes to making decisions, Sue becomes depressed and increasingly paralysed by the "terror, of conventions I don't believe in" (J 329). What breaks her in the end is the sense of wrong-doing and shame brought on by violating Christian standards of morality and marriage laws (first by refusing intercourse with and then abandoning her lawful husband Phillotson, next by entering into a sexual relationship outside of matrimony with Jude, finally by feeling responsible for the suicide of their children), as well as the knowledge of having acted against her better instincts and feminist beliefs by getting married in the first place. Sue, as Tess was, is ultimately defeated both by her own choices and outside forces tossing her around.

Hardy's characters literally cannot find a stable place in the world. Jude is always ready to uproot himself and change for the women in his life, turning away from academia for Arabella, and from the clergy for Sue. Written in the tradition of the *Bildungsroman* and dealing with the quest of an ambitious young man, *Jude* is Hardy's adaptation of the genre to accommodate the inherently

---

[27] See Chapter III "Of Individuality" in Mill's *On Liberty* (1946: 49–66).

tragic, George Levine has argued (1997: 110), because in this tale the wanderings of the hero only lead to disenchantment and death, rather than to an enlightened return home. Levine's claim that in the novel the pursuit of "truth in the manner of the Bildungsroman can only lead to pain and loss" (1997: 116) applies, in fact, to both Sue and Jude. Sue fails in her attempt at being a "truthful" mother and lover, her brutal honesty only ever produces suffering; meanwhile Jude does not succeed in becoming "a prophet, however humble", but sinks down to "the barely respectable according to regulation views" (J 217). He frequently drowns his sorrows in alcohol, a means of numbing the pain of living through "'the hell of conscious failure,' both in ambition and love" (J 124).

Originally a stonemason's apprentice with no prospects but high ambitions, Jude possesses a certain juvenile desire for irresponsibility; "He did not want to be a man" (J 18) and a steadily mounting sense of inadequacy. The first crucial experience is the crushing of his hopes at Christminster which lead him "to wish himself out of the world" (J 31); from then on he only grows more "fearful of life" (J 151). Added to this anxiety is his confusion about his own nature, the felt tension between talents, desires and duties. Embodying the crisis of the subject on the verge of modernity, he says: "I am in a chaos of principles – groping in the dark – acting by instinct and not after example. [...] the further I get the less sure I am" (J 327). Throughout the narrative, Francesco Marroni (2010: 167) notes, Jude desperately seeks out values such as community, justice, and belonging that are implicitly negated through his characterization, i.e. a sense of self constituted by solitude, injustice, and non-belonging. Finally, he has to acknowledge that he will remain "an outsider to the end of my days!" (J 328). Jude is depicted as sensitive, effeminate, and never fully in control of his situation, struggling to assume any kind of patriarchal authority. Arguably his only decisive action and assertion of strength in the narrative is his final visit to Sue, which speeds up his demise as he is already weakened by disease: "I have seen her for the last time, and I've finished myself – put an end to a feverish life which ought never to have been begun!" (J 391).

In his fictions Hardy repeatedly attacks the institution of marriage and exposes the social laws and conventions connected to it as bearing a high risk of unhappiness and being intrinsically inhuman. The author clearly expresses this opinion in a letter saying that "a bad marriage is one of the direst things on earth, & one of the cruelest things" (Hardy 1980: 98). In the 'Postscript' to the 1912 edition of *Jude* he consequently postulates "a marriage should be dissoluble, as soon as it becomes a cruelty to either of the parties – being then essentially and morally no marriage" (Appendix I, J 467). The author, however, was not seeking to undermine the institution of marriage all together (see Dutta 2000: 217), but contested the idea of choosing only once, and then having to live with it. Often portraying marriage as a precarious gamble for his characters, Hardy criticized above all the Victorian era's idea of the indissolubility of marriage, which moreover made a wife and her possessions the property of her husband.[28]

The narrative depicts the unhappiness of marriage through various constellations between the four main characters (Jude, Sue, Arabella, Phillotson). Jude gets trapped in marriage early on. After the first passion in his relationship with Arabella has withered, he realizes that Arabella coerced him into the legal commitment by a fake pregnancy and that they have rushed into something "which would cripple him, if not her also, for the rest of a lifetime" (J 62). Meanwhile Arabella views her actions as a justified and well-calculated gamble: "Every woman has a right to do such as that. The risk is hers" (J 67). In a patriarchal society that grants unmarried women no status, Arabella's entrapment is readable as self-defence and the kind of clever risk management some women, such as Tess, fail at. Significantly, Arabella is also the only character who survives relatively unscathed in the end. While tending to the sick Jude, she already makes realistic provisions for her next marriage by flirting with Vilbert, the old physician: "it's well to keep chances open. And I can't pick and choose now as I could when I was younger" (J 401). Jude, however, views their lives as "ruined by the fundamental error of their matrimonial union: that of having based a permanent contract on a temporary feeling" (J 69), expressing Hardy's belief in the high probability of emotions changing with time.

After the separation from Arabella, Jude tries to talk himself out of his budding non-platonic feelings for Sue, due to the threefold obstacle of him being already married, the incestuous nature of a union between cousins, and lastly, the haunting echo of his aunt's warning that the Fawleys as a family are ill-suited for marriage; therefore, a "marriage with a blood-relation would duplicate the adverse conditions, and a tragic sadness might be intensified to a tragic horror" (J 90). This is, of course, exactly what comes to pass. Although he tries to calculate the risks of giving in to his attraction to her, he longs for the possession of Sue and her body, and the temptation is only deepened by "the fearful bliss in doing what was erratic, informal, and unexpected" (J 98).

In the novel, all conversations about marriage are fraught with the language of risk. Sue leaves her much older husband Phillotson for Jude; he lets her go, stunned by the realization "that merely taking a woman to church and putting

---

28 In Britain, the Matrimonial Causes Act of 1857 had made divorce possible, but also prescribed a firm double standard and decreed that in order to obtain a divorce the husband simply had to prove his wife's adultery; the wife, however, had to prove adultery, incest, bigamy, cruelty, or desertion.

a ring upon her finger could by any possibility involve one in such a daily, continuous tragedy as that now shared by her and me!" (J 231). Fleeing from Phillotson and the obligation to consummate the marriage, Sue falls into the arms of Jude, whom she trusts, yet is confronted with even stronger desires and sexual demands, this time comprising the emotional as well as the physical side. According to D.H. Lawrence, Sue is terrified by her inability to connect with her "comrade" in this way and by him discovering her lack of passion: "This was her deepest dread, to see him inevitably disappointed in her" (Lawrence 1988: 155); she has internalized an outside view of herself as somewhat deficient. Jude, despite his feelings for her, denies Sue the expression of her own sexuality – i. e. her proposition of a strictly platonic union – and thus aids her subjugation. Rosemarie Morgan writes, "as elsewhere in Hardy's microcosmic world, the repercussions of this denial are far-reaching and tragic" (Morgan 1988: 199).

Having escaped a loveless union, Sue enters into an even greater risk by living openly "in sin" with Jude. When he asks how she feels about marrying him, she replies: "I have just the same dread lest an iron contract should extinguish your tenderness for me, and mine for you, as it did between our unfortunate parents" (J 259). Paradoxically, the only risk-management for their reputation and social status is legalizing their relationship but in turn entails the high risk of losing their love. Living with Father Time, Jude's son from Arabella, and later their other own children, further increases the moral pressure on the couple because they are outward signs of their sexual union and impossible to hide (see also Faber Oestreich 2013: 141). Yet for Sue, who repeatedly asks, "When shall we have the courage to marry, Jude?" (J 275), the idea of repeating the vows that have made her so unhappy before is unbearably scary: "I feel doubts of – my being proof against the sordid conditions of a business contract again" (J 290). During their cohabitation Jude and Sue refrain from getting married more than once, fearing the alienating effect of the ritualistic and legal procedures: "they had literally not found the courage to repeat it, though they had attempted it two or three times" (J 331). Especially Sue's fear actively constructs marriage as a risk which is the new dimension and ideological standpoint expressed in Hardy's novel. Above all, it points to the fact that times have changed drastically, as Mrs Edlin says: "Nobody thought o'being afread o'matrimony in my time" (J 297). After they realize that their unconventional living arrangements cause rumours wherever they go and make it near impossible to get work or housing, Sue and Jude do their best to keep appearances; they undertake a trip to London in order to make people believe they got married in the city and Sue even adopts the name of Mrs. Fawley. But their "apparent attempt at reparation had come too late to be effective" (J 299), and the only solution is to move again.

One of the main risks of Sue's refusal of marriage is named explicitly in the narrative: "But if people did as you want to do, there'd be a general domestic disintegration. The family would no longer be the social unit" (J 231). Consequently, Sue perceives the hardship and tragedy that follow, the failure to provide for and protect the children, as the punishment for her risk-taking and her unlawful union. Hardy's dramatizes the disintegration of the family unit while also depicting how for Sue "reproduction and the circumstances surrounding it – conception, pregnancy, childbirth, and motherhood" are nothing but "an endless series of hazards and obstacles that must be negotiated at every turn" (Archimedes 2005: 149). Despite her intellectual brilliance, Sue lacks a full understanding of the risks of seeking to defy social norms. She is naive and 'unfit' in comparison to Arabella who is much more aware of the force of convention and thus much better at realizing her desires, navigating her femininity through the hazards of Victorian society and surviving in the world.

Both Sue and Jude continuously seek to rationally explain their fears and emotions to each other in order to gain a sense of control over situations which threaten to overwhelm them. For example, Sue tells Jude how did not fall in love at first sight; instead, she describes her initial feelings for him as a biologically motivated sense of jealousy, which soon gave way to an awareness of the risk inherent in her encouragement of him; "the craving to attract and captivate [...] was in me; and when I found I had caught you, I was frightened" (J 353). Rather than taking this as a valid reason to be angry at her or let Sue go, Jude's sense of being at risk takes priority. Mortally afraid of his weaknesses, he perceives Sue as his saving grace and says to her,

> with a sudden sense of his own danger. [...] 'You know what a weak fellow I am. My two arch-enemies you know – my weakness for womankind and my impulse to strong liquor. [...] They have been kept entirely at a distance since you became my guardian-angel! *Since I have had you I have been able to go into any temptations of the sort, without risk. Isn't my safety worth a little sacrifice of dogmatic principle?*' (J 353; my emphasis)

The couple always oscillates between the perception of different levels of risks, those inherent in their relationship, their individual nature and feelings, and the societal and moral pressures.

The ending of the novel sees all of the four characters once more trapped in a marriage with their original first spouse. Jude's return to Arabella appears as an exhausted collapse into the familiar arms of his first lover after Sue has left him. Sue's second wedding to Phillotson is portrayed as a horrific act of self-sacrifice and "fanatic prostitution" (J 388). In the so-called "New Women" novels of the 1880s and 90s, a loveless marriage was often equated with prostitution. In the frequently cited "Postscript" to the 1912 edition of the novel Hardy describes his heroine Sue Bridehead in this context as

> the first delineation in fiction of the woman who was coming into notice in her thousands every year – the woman of the feminist movement – the slight, pale 'bachelor' girl – the intellectualized, emancipated bundle of nerves that modern conditions were producing, mainly in cities as yet; who does not recognize the necessity for most of her sex to follow marriage as a profession [...]. (Appendix I, J 468)

Henceforth Sue has been seen as Hardy's memorable depiction of the "New Woman",[29] embodying a type of femininity that threatened to erode traditional gender roles, reflecting the negative influence of modern urban life, posing risks to the social order as much as to individual happiness. Sue is the frightening image of womanhood to come, characterized by her "peculiarity" and "queerness", her non-conventional behaviour, her independence and intellectual brilliance. She differs from Victorian ideals of femininity not only through her appearance, but her lack of any sort of deference towards masculine authority. Conversely, she is fearless towards men: "I mean I have not felt about them as most women are taught to feel – to be on their guard against attacks on their virtue" (J 147). Meanwhile Jude perceives her "as innocent as you are unconventional" (J 329), and she is still a virgin when they meet. Although her plainer looks receive less attention and she lacks the cunning of Arabella, Sue is well aware of the dynamics of sexual attraction. Her preference for plain clothing and an almost nun-like appearance can be read as signs of repressed sexuality or the deliberate attempt to avoid making a spectacle out of her body and distract male interest.

Hardy depicts Sue's character and her internal contradictions with even greater complexity than Jude's. The focus is initially placed on her feminine strength and "queer" difference, while the author also employs her character to advocate a change of Victorian marriage laws and the possibility of divorce. After only eight weeks of unhappy life with Phillotson, Sue decides to leave because: "I daresay it happens to lots of women; only they submit, and I kick...;" "I am certain one ought to be allowed to undo what one has done so ignorantly!" (J 215). The contradictory characterization of Sue captures the array of contemporary anxieties surrounding the New Woman and the marriage question. As Kate Faber Oestreich sums up, Sue is puzzling because she is "nei-

---

29 See, e. g., Jurta (1999), Faber Oestreich (2013), and Wilson (1995). For a wider context see Pykett's *The "Improper" Feminine: The Women's Sensation Novel and the New Woman Writing* (1992).

ther asexual nor married nor, oddly enough, a virgin" (Faber Oestreich 2013: 129), and, one might add, bears several children in the novel although all die as infants. Her main flaw, which causes the failure of her first marriage, is being a "bodiless creature", who "has so little animal passion" (J 268). She proposes a sexless union as a way of distancing herself from having to submit at all time to Jude's desire. Yet out of fear of losing Jude again to Arabella, whom he turns to satisfy his needs, Sue then consents to living sexually with him. In reality, Sue is neither sexually responsive nor frigid.[30] Part of her dilemma is how to reconcile the different parts of herself, mature sexual woman and mother, submissive innocent girl, and chaste saintly idol. In Jude's mind she is associated with a complicated blend of eroticism and religion, presenting "a mystery" (J 255) that is hard to solve; she is a "riddle" (J 154), "One lovely conundrum" (J 156), and "puzzling and unstateable" (J 240).[31]

Arabella presents a contrasting version of female sexuality. While Sue's dominant feature is her soul and intellect, Arabella's is her body and confident sexuality; she has an intuitive and emotional understanding of people and is able to use it to her advantage and to survive through hardship. Despite the obvious contrasts, there are interesting parallels between Arabella and Sue, who, as Oestreich notes, do not conform to the typical good/bad girl archetypes: "Instead, both wilfully engage in sex outside marriage. Both are divorced. Both are twice married to the same husband" (Faber Oestreich 2013: 131). Yet both women represent different misogynistic fears: Arabella is the femme fatale who can lure a man into marriage or tempt him into a life of debauchery; Sue personifies the disturbing idea of radical chastity and the horror of free love, a woman choosing to be sexually active with her "comrade" but not her husband. Summing up the anxieties clustering around the figure of the New Woman, Brady argues that these sprang from

> her presumed denial or indulgence of her own sexuality – two strategies that though radically opposed, had the common result of taking the female body out of male control. [...] The New Woman was therefore in an especially perilous position: rejecting masculine control of her body, she fell naturally into the excessive nervousness of the hysteric. (Brady 1993: 95)

In the novel, Sue descends into a form of hysteria after the loss of her children. But Hardy's novel stages the fear of a loss of control from various angles, capturing the general sense of risk and limbo caused by the challenge to "traditional

---

30 See Morgan's comment: "Sexless she is not. Sexually frustrated she may be" (1988: 199).
31 Cf. Dutta (2000: 108–109).

boundaries of gender, labor, and behaviour" (Showalter 2012: 105) coming from New Women-types like Sue and new sensitive men like Jude. The New Women fictions of the turn of the century were so shocking to contemporary readers because they denied any sense of happy closure traditionally provided by marriage plots, Hardy and Gissing's texts discussed in this chapter being examples for this. But it has to be noted that Hardy's novel does not allow for Sue to fully develop into a liberated, rebellious New Woman; instead, Roxanna Jurta points out, her struggle is doomed from the beginning and the narrative resembles "a chronicle of her anticipated downfall" (Jurta 1999: 18). In the end, the reader is not left with an image of emancipated femininity, but a strong sense of "feminine despair, doom, bleakness, and silence" (1999: 20). However accurate this observation, Sue is given a distinct voice in the novel, arguably even assuming the role of its central character. With *Jude* containing the highest proportion of dialogue of all Hardy's works, as J.B. Bullen has noted (1986: 237), it allows for the detailed negotiation of different standpoints and it appears indeed as a political decision that Arabella's remains relatively in the background.

As is also the case in *The Whirlpool,* social and intellectual ambitions in *Jude* are shown to be the cause of nervous disease, and civilized subjects produce their own decline by desiring or being forced to push beyond what mind and body can safely tolerate. Sondra Archimedes puts it thus: "Modern culture in *Jude* is depicted as causing the educated and aspiring classes to become so nervous and depressed that the general population is at risk of decline" (Archimedes 2005: 129).[32] Critics like Elaine Showalter have interpreted Jude's doom as a sign of the laws of nature and heredity according to the warnings of late Victorian physicians and psychiatrists that in particular "working-class men who tried to better themselves were risking madness from a kind of intellectual work their heredity had not prepared them to handle" (Showalter 1986: 107). From the beginning, Jude's difference and obscurity is referred to as a family 'curse', as his great-aunt says, "there is sommat in our blood" (J 69). It renders the Fawleys ill-suited for matrimony and Jude recalls how "it was always impressed upon me [...] that I belonged to an odd and peculiar family – the wrong breed for marriage" (J 168); growing up his cousin Sue has received similar warnings. The narrative dramatizes a dual risk for Jude and Sue. On the one side, the danger lies in their incestuous relationship and shared characteristics, in other words, in their sameness. Sue says to Jude: "You mustn't love me. You are too like me – that's all!" (J 155). Later, Phillotson is struck by the remarkable "similarity between the

---

[32] See Sondra Archimedes' study *Gendered Pathologies* (2005) which places a reading of *Jude* in a wider comparative context.

pair. [...] They seem to be one person split in two!" (J 229). On the other hand, it is their difference and non-conformity to the norms of the time that puts them at risk. With the narrative repeatedly referring to them as a "queer sort of people" (J 286), their deviance lies in their weakness and nervous disposition ("We are horribly sensitive; that's really what's the matter with us"; J 286), as well as in a strong sense of will and independence. The latter forces Jude and Sue to realise that "for us particular two, *an irrevocable oath is risky*" (J 287; my emphasis). The text evokes the hereditary risks that double in the union of Jude and Sue. Both are aware that by being together they create "a terrible intensification of unfitness " (J 187), yet pretend for as long as possible that their family histories are just a matter of bad luck, rather than a rationally calculable danger, i.e. is a disposition in their physical and mental states. The characters' self-deception regarding this matter, as protective mechanism to justify their feelings and sexual relations, becomes increasingly harder to uphold und crumbles completely after the children's suicide.

Besides the marriage question and the debate of free love, Hardy's text reflects a specific historical scientific context. According to Showalter, Hardy's novel is "the consummate literary text of late Victorian psychiatry" and features variations of the theme of degeneracy, i.e. "the ambitious and intemperate working man, the neurasthenic and sexually anxious New Woman, and the morbid and blighted child" (Showalter 1986: 106). The leading figure of psychiatric Darwinism was Henry Maudsley, editor of the *Journal of Mental Medicine* and author of influential texts such as *Body and Mind* (1873), *Responsibility in Mental Disease* (1874), and *The Pathology of Mind* (1879). All his writings are characterized by a distinctly bleak outlook and a pessimism of the future of the human race which pushed the sense of fin-de-siècle gloominess to extremes: "He saw signs of degeneration everywhere – in the irreversibility of mental decline and the genetic multiplication of crime, vice, and mental defect" (Showalter 2012: 119).[33] Maudsley's famous expression of man's biological "tyranny of organization"[34] refers to the powerful

---

[33] On Maudsley's writing and his influence see especially Showalter's *The Female Malady* (2012: 112ff); and Skultans's *Madness and Morals* (1975), which contains many useful excerpts from late-Victorian medical texts. See also Oppenheim's *'Shattered Nerves'* (1991).

[34] Maudsley writes, e.g., in *The Pathology of Mind:* "There is a destiny made for each one by his inheritance; he is the necessary organic consequent of certain organic antecedents; and it is impossible he should escape the tyranny of his organization" (1879: 88); and in *Body and Mind:* "No one can escape the tyranny of his organization; no one can elude the destiny that is innate in him, and which unconsciously and irresistibly shapes his ends, even when he believes that he is determining them with consummate foresight and skill" (1873: 76).

influence of genetic endowment, specifically to mental and physical predispositions for insanity.

The strongly emerging ideas of biological determinism, of these predispositions being inheritable just like wealth or social status, exist side by side with the belief in man's capacity for moral "will" and self-control, the former increasing in significance over the later towards the end of the century. The intellectual and scientific climate of the late-Victorian age is shaped by the tension between a rising spirit of individualism and focus on the individual's psyche, and notions of society, as a body or social organism, constituted by calculable norms and its individual parts measurable according to statistically derived standards of normalcy. The second decisive factor is the on-going tendency to translate social problems and fears into moral terms. The rising discourse of hereditary risk captures the felt threats to the notion of man as a "rational being", and fears of disorder and anti-social behaviour. Vieda Skultans explains how in this regard, especially in contemporary medical and psychiatric thought, "[t]he earlier note of optimism is gone. *Instead, caution and watchfulness are needed to guard against the hidden enemy*" (Skultans 1975: 22; my emphasis). While Henry Maudsley and many other physicians uttered dire warnings about heredity and man's helplessness in the face of the inevitable tragedy of mental illness, in *The History of Sexuality* Foucault argues that "the analysis of heredity was placing sex (sexual relations, venereal diseases, matrimonial alliances, perversions) in a position of *'biological responsibility'* with regard to the species" (Foucault 1990: 118; my emphasis). The rhetoric employed by both Skultans and Foucault draws attention to the emerging sense of heredity as a risk, which can be guarded against, fought, and generally calls for assuming responsibility with regard to sexual relations and reproduction. This is the risk management Jude and Sue so tragically fail at. They try to ignore the idea that choices and action in the present can affect the future, i.e. the next generation, strongly endorsed by what Showalter termed the Victorian "ideology of the hereditary taint" (Showalter 1986: 95). In fact, Hardy's depiction of the life of Jude corresponds to Maudsley's description of "the natural end of a morbidly sensitive nature, with a feeble will, unable to contend with the hard experiences of life. You might as well, in truth, preach moderation to the hurricane as talk philosophy to one whose antecedent life has conducted him to the edge of madness" (Maudsley 1874: 272–273). Jude is unable to control his love of women and, increasingly his drinking, which contributes to this early death.

At the time it was seen as a major scientific as well socio-political task to discover – and thus be able to understand and control – the laws of selection, survival, and deviation (e.g. how potentially 'criminal' anomalies come into being). Maudsley was just one many physicians who contributed to renewed gender imbalance in the construction of insanity, perceiving it as a predominantly "female malady" (see Showalter 2012). Against this background, *Jude* is interesting because the text focuses on the weakness and 'unfitness' of both sexes. Sue is certainly not the only neurotic, partly pathological subject in the novel. For example, the narrator tells us that if Jude "had been a woman he must have screamed under the nervous tension which he was now undergoing. But that relief being denied to his virility, he clenched his teeth in misery" (J 124).[35] Even an early reviewer of the novel, Edmund Gosse, described Jude in 1896 as a "neurotic subject in whom hereditary degeneracy takes an idealist turn" (cited in Archimedes 2005: 130).

Within a framework of social and psychiatric Darwinism, Jude and Sue's actions are construed as high-risk behaviour, triggered by an inability to rationally control their instincts or by making choices against their better judgment. The quote below from Maudsley's *Responsibility and Mental Disease* captures Jude's struggle and failure in a nutshell.

> When one considers the reckless way in which persons, whatever the defects of their mental and bodily constitution, often get married, without sense of responsibility for the miseries which they entail upon those who will be the heirs of their infirmities, without regard, in fact, to anything but their own gratification, one is driven to think that man is not the pre-eminently reasoning and moral animal which he claims to be. (Maudsley 1874: 277)

Darwin's theory of natural selection, and Herbert Spencer's application of it, have frequently been compared as a translation, or rather extension, of 18th-century economic theories and the rising spirit of liberalism and laissez-faire capitalism onto biology and social politics. Social Darwinism, in Spencer's catchy phrase the rule of the "survival of the fittest", becomes a guiding principle in many areas, aiding the perception of class hierarchies and social differences as being underwritten "by nature itself" (Adams 2012: 217; see Archimedes 2005: 17). Biological justifications for opposing government intervention and the notion of nature and society as a self-regulating organism[36] can already be found in Malthus's writing on the politics of population growth. In his *Essay on the Principle of Population* Malthus writes: "[I]f a man chose to marry, without

---

35 See Archimedes (2005: 132ff) for an analysis of Jude's "nervous condition", his sensitivity and constant worrying. Cf. also Levine's comment: "The conventional and probably appropriate reading of the novel emphasizes Sue's extraordinary inconsistency and instability. But [...] [Jude's] actual behavior is almost as inconsistent as Sue's" (1997: 116).
36 Spencer introduces the conception of society as a living organism in his 1860 essay "The Social Organism" (1969: 195–233). It entailed an understanding of the society with an explicit biological referent, based on the metaphorical relation between individual and social body.

8.2 'An Irrevocable Oath is Risky': Marriage and Death in *Jude the Obscure* — 413

a prospect of being able to support a family, he should have the most perfect liberty so to do. [...] nature will govern and punish for us [...]. To the punishment, therefore, of nature he should be left, the punishment of severe want" (Malthus 1804: 121). This is directly applicable as a sinister moral to Hardy's novel; Sue and Jude are punished by nature for bearing children without sufficient means. Furthermore, Caroline Sumpter emphasizes how, in Spencerian terms, Jude and Sue's extreme sensitivity presents a form of 'unfitness' (Sumpter 2011: 674).

It is interesting to remember that Darwin's theories of variation and the role chance in evolutionary processes played an important part in the on-going probabilistic revolution and the development of the understanding of statistical causality. Generally, social Darwinism represented a potent fusion of biology and statistics and had a significant impact on the perception of risk. Francis Galton, the cousin of Charles Darwin, was among the first to apply statistics and utilizes Quetelet's 'normal' curve for the study deviance and variation (see Gigerenzer et al. 1989: 53; 65ff).[37] The idea of indeterministic statistical causation first arose in the 1870s and gained scientific momentum in central Europe in the period up until the 1920s.[38] Although it sounds paradoxical at first, randomness and chance were increasingly conceptualized within a causal frame, as Darwinian theories relied on about chance as causation for evolutionary processes. In fact, chance featured at least twice in the causal chain, including hereditary variants and sexual selection. While biologists with varying attitudes towards chance developed theories of natural selection, a general acceptance existed about its probabilistic base which lead to a "probabilistic shift within the development of causal science, not to any probabilistic rebellion in favour of science without causes" (Hodge 1987: 232).[39] In other words, up to certain point Darwinian theories actually increased awareness of risks and probabilities, not of randomness.

From the 1880s onwards, one frequently finds construction of degenerate types in biology, sociology, and psychiatry, based on notions of "morbid deviation from an original type" (Nordau cited in Amigoni 2011: 149).[40] They all hinge on the notion of the "normal". The mathematical concept of the average

---

37 See Bisset Hawkins and Quetelet's *Comparative Statistics in the 19th Century* (1973) and Klein's *Statistical Visions in Time* (1997; see especially 161–194).
38 See M. Norton Wise's article "How Do Sums Count? On the Cultural Origins of Statistical Causality" (1987).
39 See M.J.S. Hodge's article "Natural Selection as a Causal, Empirical, and Probabilistic Theory" (1987).
40 Nordau's influential study *Degeneration* (1895) was published the same year as *Jude*.

finds its scientific equivalent in medicine and psychiatry in the concept of the norm/normal, a development which is hard to underestimate in its lasting social implications. As such, all categories such as 'normal', 'average', 'deviance', are relational and inseparable from the statistical underpinnings of science, carrying theoretically only probabilistic meanings. In his study *The Normal and the Pathological* (1991) Georges Canguilhem traces in detail the development of the term 'normal' in popular and scientific usage. Originally a neutral statistical category with no connections to the semantic field of health or illness, it became the morally charged opposite of the 'abnormal' or pathological.[41] This echoes the Foucault's diagnosis in *The Birth of the Clinic*, where he described it as a main difference between 18th- and 19th-century medicine that the latter "was regulated more in accordance with normality than with health" (Foucault 1994: 35). The changes in terminology transcended the field of medicine. Social theory underwent a decisive change as social differences became ascribed on a biological basis; in various other fields and in popular discourse notions of (ab)normality were adapted to create stereotypes and fixed beliefs about certain social or ethnic groups.

Many late-Victorian texts show the pervasiveness of the new biometric classifications and the fears of (sexual) deviance.[42] These fears result from the aim for control in the face of various upheavals, changing social and economic conditions, urbanization and scientific advance. They also lead to drastic shifts in gender relations and the perception of codes of behaviour and morality, as Jeffery Weeks explains, assigning sexuality the role of "a symbolic battleground both because it was the focus of many of these changes, and because it was a surrogate medium through which other intractable battles could be fought" (Weeks 1985: 74). Fears of feminism were channelled into moral outrage against perversion and indecency, affirming the crucial fact that in "a significant array of social practices the sexual is discovered as a key to the social" (1985: 74). This phenomenon is very noticeable in the risk discourse of the fin-de-siècle and

---

41 All our chosen norms, Canguilhem writes, "are in fact constants determined by averages. The normal living being is the one who conforms to these norms" (1991: 154). See also Archimedes (2005: 21–22).

42 Cf. Adams's summary of the specific literary climate: "This maelstrom of new sexual visibility, confusion, and danger would profoundly shape the literature of the late 1880s and 1890s. The association of romance with 'primitive' mentalities and desires, states of mind in which the discipline of civilized existence seemed in abeyance, found a new filed within the metropolis, where shocks to decency were increasingly explained in terms of psychological abnormality or deviance" (2012: 371). Adam refers here especially to sensational and Gothic fiction of the fin-de-siècle, a prominent example being Stevenson's *Dr Jekyll and Mr Hyde* (1886).

lies at the heart of Hardy's final novel. The significant shift in the risk perception of the middle and upper classes is the focus away from the poor and the criminal to their own, namely "women, who refused to adjust to the 'inevitable' conditions of their lives, and whose rebellion against their sex roles led to an unprecedented wave of nervous disorders" (Showalter 2012: 120). Thus the female body and the social domain, traditionally seen as sources of domestic and national stability, are associated with a reproductive, physical and/or mental fragility that largely contributed to the perception of the modern "diseased or *at-risk society*" (Archimedes 2005: 14; my emphasis), progressing towards its own extinction.

The tragic climax in Hardy's text is the suicide of the children carried out by Jude's son little Father Time. Sue, unaware of the risk her words pose and wanting to be truthful, tells the boy that it is due to the size of their family that their circumstances are so dire. Shortly afterwards, Sue and Jude are confronted with the horrific scene and the note on the floor: "*Done because we are too menny*". While Sue blames herself, the narrative also offers a medical-scientific reasoning for the tragedy, and Jude reassures her: "It was in his nature to do it. The doctor says [...] it is the beginning of the coming universal wish not to live" (J 336; original emphasis). Further calamity strikes soon in the death of Sue's still-born baby, fully eliminating hope for the future.

The random cruelty of the death of the children, essentially a question of failed risk management, affects Sue and Jude differently. With regards to Sue, it causes a bout of feverish religiosity and the decision to return to Phillotson; her coping strategy is self-punishment and seeking belated atonement. Jude simply views it as another battle they lost fighting against "senseless circumstance" (J 361), freeing himself from responsibility. The event presents the culmination of Sue's anxieties about her union with Jude. It is the moment of irreversible decline and a deeply traumatic event that severs the deep sympathy and understanding between the pair: "Arabella's child killing mine was a judgement – the right slaying the wrong". Jude, verging on tears, replies: "It is monstrous and unnatural for you to be so remorseful when you have done no wrong!" (J 350). Agreeing with Showalter's assessment (1986: 107), little Father Time is perhaps the most troubling character of Hardy's novel, and a sign of the author's modernist experimentation and antirealism. As evoked by his telling name, the child is old beyond his years[43] – "He was Age masquerading as Juvenility" (J 276)

---

43 See Showalter for a reading of Father Time as an example of the "prematurely aged and psychologically disturbed syphilitic child" (1986: 108). She relates his depiction to the specific fear of syphilis as *the* degenerative disease of the turn of the century.

– and shows a strange detachment from the world, devoid of any emotions or curiosity: "The boy seemed to have begun with the generals of life, and never to have concerned himself with the particulars. To him the houses, the willows, the obscure fields beyond, were apparently regarded not as brick residences, pollards, meadows; but as human dwellings in the abstract, vegetation, and the wide dark world" (J 278). This is a significant foreshadowing of the boy's later removal of himself and his half-siblings from the world, appearing as a drastic statistical measure of seeking to correct the problem of over-population and lessen the economic hardship for their parents. The children's suicide is the response to the inability to understand why humans cannot control their numbers (and an indirect criticism of the lack of access and moral support of any kind of birth control). As an event, it takes the discourse of degeneration to extremes and depicts a threat to the entire species. It evokes the widespread political fears of English society becoming weakened from the inside, rendering it vulnerable for attacks from the outside.[44] Yet the focus of Hardy's novel is firmly on domestic tragedies, all causally connected to Sue and Jude's transgression of being together. Throughout the second half of the 19th century, Gillian Beer observes, "topics traditional to the novel – courtship, sensibility, the making of matches, women's beauty, men's dominance, inheritance in all its forms – became charged with new difficulty" (Beer 1984: 213). While Hardy's final novel presents these difficulties in extremely tragic form, their topical ease was never really to return. According to Ariela Freedman, *Jude* is Hardy's attempt "to chart an already doomed modernity" (Freedman 2003: 3), and the text anticipates the depiction of doomed men in the novels of the coming generation of writers such as D.H. Lawrence, Virginia Woolf, E.M. Forster, and Ford Madox Ford.

8.3 Drowning in Modern Life: *The Whirlpool*

The works of George Gissing, who must be considered a neglected writer in comparison to Thomas Hardy, deserve to hold an important place in late 19th-century writing. Offering detailed portraits of London and insights into the psyche of the urban individual, they capture central elements of the intellectual climate of the time and present a moment of aesthetic transition. Although Gissing's novels maintain on the surface a typically mid-Victorian appearance, including

---

[44] Archimedes explains: "One of the many apprehensions evidenced by discourse of racial deterioration was a fear that Britain would not be able to sustain its strength as an imperial and military power" (2005: 140). This sense of the nation being at risk of invasion is, however, nothing new.

a vast cast of characters and intricate plots, they are far from conventional, as John Goode notes (1978: 107), and also show elements characteristic of modernist writing, such as an episodic structure, the focus on individual consciousness, and the move away from narrative omniscience. Still it would go too far to call them revolutionary or experimental. *The Whirlpool* (1897) is in many ways an obvious choice to bring to a close the discussion of the 19th century, foreshadowing the sense of risk and doom carried over into the 20th century, with the specter of mass destruction looming on the horizon. With nothing less at stake again than the survival of the individual in a growingly hostile and unhealthy environment, Gissing's writing has been criticized for being gloomy and favouring a depressing, excessive realism, sometimes bordering on the sensational.[45] *The Whirlpool* takes up the familiar topics of speculation mania, unhappy marriages, hereditary risk, and the link between modern life and nervous disease. Similar to *Jude*, it negotiates the fin-de-siècle discourse of psychiatric Darwinism and psycho-pathological determinism. Degeneracy and reproductive decline play again an important role but the main focus of the narrative is on female neurasthenia as a disease of modern civilization and cause of the decay of Alma Frothingham.[46]

However, Gissing's choice of title signals an important shift away from the individual – after all, the novel is not named after its tragic heroine – to the setting. London is portrayed as the eponymous whirlpool of fashionable metropolitan life in the 1890s; it appears as a place of dynamic tensions and calamities, and, despite being eternally busy and crowded, as a strangely empty terrain. Typical for a fin-de-siècle novel, the text is at its heart a chronicle of futility and highlights the exhaustion of the characters' energies by the city. London is the locus of multiple risks: the epicentre of speculative commerce and corruption, the cause of the pervasive spread of nervous conditions, and of the disruption of domestic stability. To some extent, *The Whirlpool* therefore indeed appears as an "updated version of *The Way We Live Now*" (Goode 1978: 184). Published in the year of Queen Victoria's Diamond Jubilee, the plot is set against the background of the new gambling mania of the 1880s, and the spectacular collapse of the Baring Brothers Bank in 1890, which brought financial scandal into the headlines yet again. It dramatizes the insecurities of a moneyed society in the metropolis and of instability and desperation cutting across moral boundaries. As in *The Way We Live Now*, a central plot event is the suicide of "a great

---

45 See Coustillas and Partridge's *George Gissing: The Critical Heritage* (1972: 1).
46 A number of critical essays have focused on this aspect. See Greenslade (1989), Maltz (2013), Marroni (2010), and Radford (2006).

finance-gambler" (W 38), Bennet Frothingham, after running the "Britannia Loan Assurance, Investment, and Banking Company Limited" into the ground, and thus evading responsibility for his failure and deceits.[47] Yet in contrast to the earlier novel, the suicide occurs within the first few chapters rather than being the climactic event which the narrative builds towards. Gissing's novel opens immediately with ruin, developing its plot from the aftermath and the devastating consequences Frothingsham's crash has for the other characters, especially Hugh Carnaby and his wife Sybil, the Abbott family, and Alma, Frothingham's daughter.

The narrative epitomizes the use of risk as a topic and structuring concept; it is shaped by a persistent sense of insecurity as well as by explicit references to risk. Above all, it shows again how "[s]peculation and risk apply to human relationships as well as money" (Greenslade 1997: xx). Gissing and Hardy are both writers who view relations between the sexes – legal, emotional, physical – as fraught with dangers and critically interrogate the chances of living unhappily ever after. The central tragic union in *The Whirlpool* is the marriage of Alma and Harvey Rolfe: "Only death could part them; but how much better for him and for her if they had never met!" (W 388). Furthermore, the differences which make the couple so ill matched are mainly expressed through their risk personalities and temperaments: "he, with his heart and mind set on grave, quiet, restful things [...], she, her senses crying for the delight of an existence that loses itself in whirl and glare" (W 388).

The underlying concern is again that people, as individuals or couples, can no longer achieve a healthy 'wholeness', a balanced integration of body and mind, desires and societal norms and conditions. As it is also so often the case in Hardy's fictions, the question of "how to live" is closely connected to the question of "where to live", especially for Alma and Harvey Rolfe (see James 1997: 16). Meanwhile contemporary reviews identified the critical reflection of a loss of rootedness and domestic stability as a main theme of the whole narrative: "The malady is restlessness, in money-getting, in pleasure-seek-

---

[47] As many critics have noted, the crash of the Britannia is a historical reference to the collapse of the Baring Brothers merchant bank, the last major financial crash of a century marked by money-madness (see Radford 2006: 15; Baubles 2001: 262). Gissing's narrator comments: "These explosions were periodic, inevitable, wholesome. The Britannia Loan, &c, &c, &c, had run its pestilent course; exciting avarice, perturbing quiet industry with the passion of the gamester, inflating vulgar ambition, now at length scattering wreck and ruin. This is how mankind progresses" (W 44).

ing. [...] homes are growing obsolete".⁴⁸ The confusion and uprooting is also a moral one, and largely results from the debated issue of human agency vs. determinism. John Goode notes how "right action becomes a matter of making the right kind of pact with one's inherited self and one's unalterable circumstances" (Goode 1978: 187). The consequences of making the wrong pact, as Alma does, prove to be fatal.

References to the whirlpool imagery occur scattered throughout the narrative like a constant refrain (see Glover 2005: 85). Although the title undeniably possesses a great metaphoric potential and invites different interpretations, it carried an unambiguous meaning at the time of the novel's first publication. According to Colin Partridge, contemporary readers were directly familiar with the imagery of the whirlpool as a reference to "the destructive force of speculation, which are harder to discern for readers of today" (Partridge 1973: 3). As many critics have notes since, the metaphor refers to the speedy, "groundless circulation of money" (Bowlby 1985: 23), the fluidity of value caused by the capitalist system, and the whirl and frenzy of fashionable city life.⁴⁹ It concentrates on London as an arena of commerce and trade, where "risky speculation is the norm" (1985: 23). The city is described as a vortex of temptation which drags anyone getting too close to the edge into a destructive downward spiral. For example, Rolfe says: "I feel as if we were all being swept into a ghastly whirlpool which roars over the bottomless pit" (W 47); and Carnaby knows that he can longer escape it: "I'm going down, old man – and it looks black as hell"' (W 296–7). Aesthetically and structurally the image evokes entropic forms of energy, and endless repetition and circularity. It foreshadows conceptions of the liquidity and destructive force of modernity: "There's the Whirlpool of the furiously busy. Round and round they go; brains humming till they melt or explode" (W 147). The vortex appears as the quintessential symbol for the condition of modernity, depicting it as a "fast flowing rip-tide, at once deeply trivializing and utterly devastating" (Glover 2005: 84), as constant flux but having only emptiness at its core. This relates to the text's preoccupation with the inevitability of loss (of hopes, money, values, stability, or life). While the vortex becomes a pervasive image in modernist literature and art, e. g. in the poetry of Ezra Pound, Gissing's use of the metaphor appears generally less aesthetically motivated but functions as a bitter ethical critique of the subject's restlessness at the turn of the century. As such, Raymond Baubles argues, it is "emblematic of a larger and

---

48 Anonymous review in *Bookman* (May 1897: 38–39), cited in Coustillas and Partridge (1972: 279).
49 For a detailed interpretation of the title see Bowlby (1985).

debilitating condition: the absence of a sense of responsibility masquerading as liberty" (Baubles 2001: 267), an observation which applies to all characters. This becomes obvious, for instance, in a conversation between Rolfe and Mrs Abbott during which both agree on the dangers of "the whirlpool way of life" (W 147), referring to an irresponsible, self-centred lifestyle that leaves no room for the proper care and education of children.

The title furthermore alludes to the sickening influence and "effect of contemporary civilization, of the vertigo and whirl of our frenzied life" (Nordau 1895: 42) criticized frequently in medical and psychiatric writings of Gissing's time. Especially Alma is drawn to London life like a moth to a flame. Even when she tries to remove herself for a while, she is always quickly "back again within the circle of civilization; or, as she put it [...] 'on the outer edge of the whirlpool'" (W 175). During the marriage to Alma, who is the character most closely associated with the destructiveness of the vortex (see Marroni 2010: 144), Rolfe repeatedly tries to distance his family from city life, first by moving to Wales, and later back to Gunnersbury, which he hopes is just far enough away to stop them from being dragged in again. But in contrast to her husband, who longs for a "tranquil life between the mountains and the sea" (W 201), and who, "if the choice were between rut and whirlpool" (W 306), would always chose the rut, Alma craves the urban excitement. In the narrative, the dichotomy between health and disease is not only gendered but associated with a clear-cut difference between city and country.[50] Increasingly worried about Alma's health and nervousness, and aided by the drama and misfortunes of his friends, Rolfe is very aware that he is losing his customary state of calm and wonders on more than one occasion: "Was he himself to become a victim of this social disease? Was he, resistless, to be drawn into the muddy whirlpool, to spin round and round among gibbering phantoms, [...] clutching in desperation at futile hopes?" (W 201). It is a risk he successfully manages to avoid in the end.

Harvey Rolfe is first introduced in the narrative as a man in his mid-thirties with "no purpose in life, save that of enjoying himself" (W 5). Yet he is not a gambler, hates risk-taking in all forms, and is consequently "very conservative" (W 17) in his finances. He is further characterized by a firm dislike of children, as he "regarded them with apprehension, anxiety, weariness, anything but interest" (W 22). In fact, he initially views marriage and the whole domestic realm as an

---

[50] The novel creates a nexus of the city, the obsession with the money market, and dirt and disease. For example, whenever Rolfe comes home from his club after hours of discussing financial matters, he has to purify himself: "He had to go for a country walk, to bathe and change his clothes, before he was at ease again" (W 194).

avoidable risk and potential source of misery. He even takes pride in his sense of caution and the security of a future as a bachelor laid out for him: "a merciful fate had guarded him [...] and appeared to warrant him in the assurance that a destiny so protective would round the close of his days with tranquillity and content" (W 27). Regarding the next generation and the future of the human race, Rolfe displays a harsh Darwinist attitude, revealed in utterances such as the following: "If a child dies, why, the probabilities are it *ought* to die; if it lives, it lives, and you get survival of the fittest. We don't want to choke the world with people, most of them rickety and wheezing; let us be healthy and have breathing space" (W 15–16; original emphasis). While he undergoes some change through becoming a father and his marriage to Alma, this cautious attitude in financial matters remains firmly the same. Other men, like Hugh Carnaby or Cecil Morphew, generally react with incredulity to Rolfe's aversion of speculation, even after the story of Bennet Frothingham and the ruin of the Britannia breaks. The event causes, amongst others, the bankruptcy of Carnaby and forces him and Sybil to go abroad in order to escape the London gossip and remake themselves. Discussing the catastrophic news with his friend, Rolfe admits that he has had "queer presentiments" (W 43) about Frothingham, to which Carnaby replies. "So had lots of people. But nobody ever does anything till it's too late" (W 43). Gissing's critical diagnosis of people's willingness to ignore signs of financial scandal and take risks against knowing the odds echoes Trollope's in *The Way We Live Now*. Yet the ruin of his friend also makes Rolfe wonder about his own state of security and detachment from the scandal, possibly revealing a lack of feeling, and a sense of him missing out on the anxieties of compassion and the thrills of risk-taking; "this long exemption and security fostered a too exclusive regard of self, an inaptitude for sympathetic emotion, which he recognized as the defect of his character" (W 44). Despite the obvious critique of financial speculation, Harvey's caution is not depicted as a straightforwardly admirable quality.

From the beginning of the novel Alma has to live in the shadow of her father's suicide and face the fact that his name "stood for criminal recklessness, for huge rascality; it would be so for years to come" (W 65). She first seeks to get as far away as possible from any association with the scandal and leaves England for Austria, impatiently driven by only one thought: "I want to be free – I want to break away" (W 59). Her considerable talents as a violinist offer her a chance of an artistic career that she is determined to pursue although she lacks the true makings of a musician; rather "her emotions responded to almost any kind of excitement sooner than to the musical" (W 228). As Gissing's telling surname of his heroine implies, it is all about superficial appearances for Alma, who desires to float like froth on a wave of male admiration and comfort, save from all duties except to herself. She justifies her attitude by viewing her family disaster as the price she had to pay to earn her independence and "gloried in a new intoxicating sense of irresponsibility" (W 63), first signs that she really is her father's daughter. But her social status and upbringing leave her ill prepared to fend for herself in the world. She is soon caught between various suitors, toys with the idea of either marrying Cyril Redgrave or Felix Dymes, and, as a single woman, puts herself at risk of rumours and giving wrong impressions: "She dreaded the observation of women [...]. The only retreat was her bedroom" (W 81). After rejecting Redgrave's proposal of becoming his mistress, although he promises to help advance her musical career, she eventually marries Harvey Rolfe, a union motivated on both sides less by passion than by sensible calculation and a sense of not wasting an opportunity before it might be too late.

Following the birth of their son Hughie, the Rolfes' marriage deteriorates steadily due to a lack of trust, understanding, and honesty of feeling. Harvey is guilty of keeping his arrangement with Mary Abbott secret from Alma – he funds the education of the two Abbott children, abandoned after the suicide of their father following the crash of the Britannia. He also idealizes Mrs Abbott's natural 'fitness' as a mother in comparison to Alma, especially after the death of their second child. He gets caught in a gendered, stereotypical perception of Alma and her condition. Although Rolfe constantly worries about his wife, who "seemed fallen so far from her better self that he could only look forward with anxiety to new developments of her character", (W 307) and fears "the peril of estrangement" (W 313) in their marriage, he is never interested in the cause of Alma's condition; he only seeks to manage the risks he perceives for him and his son. Rolfe is critical but helpless in the face of Alma's lack of motherly and domestic instincts and skills, and he is also worried about his son having inherited her nervous disposition. This makes Rolfe for better or worse principally responsible for the child's future; he must "use his weary knowledge to cast the horoscope of this dawning life" (W 135).

For Alma, marriage and motherhood are generally a disappointment. With the birth of Hughie meaning the end of her dreams of fame and a bohemian life, and her only getting conventional domesticity in return, she painfully realizes that she has falsely calculated "the social benefits and risks of performing as 'Mrs. Harvey Rolfe'" (Maltz 2013: 184). The deterioration in the relationship with Rolfe takes place in various stages, often paralleled by a change of environment. For a long time Alma is tormented by "a morbid jealousy – a symptom, no doubt, of the disorder of the nerves which was growing upon her" (W 337), while she assumes Mrs Abbott's children to be Harvey's illegitimate offspring. Harvey's admittance of his secret arrangement only brings temporary relief. She soon replaces her jealousy and suspicion of Mary Abbott with a passionate hatred of Sybil Carnaby's relationship with Cyril Redgrave because she is desperate for his attention and support of her solo recital. She steadily descends into an illness, with symptoms such as insomnia, nervous breakdowns, and paranoia suggesting her suffering from neurasthenia. For example, Alma is described as "pallid and shaking" (W 148), her "nerves upset" (W 150), especially the second half of the narrative is full of references to "her morbid condition [...] she fell repeatedly into fits of silent weeping; she had lost all strength, and her flesh had begun to waste" (W 294). Significantly though, her initial descent into illness occurs after her first pregnancy, while still living in the countryside. Alma rebels against the domestic boredom, social isolation, and confinement by going for a perilous drive which ends in a nervous collapse.

Neurasthenia was among *the* diseases of the time, first introduced by George Miller Beard to describe the "American nervousness" in the late 1860s as a response to the living conditions in the rapidly growing cities after the Civil War. It was based on a perceived correlation between nervous illness and modern social organization, including industrial progress and all technological innovations increasing the speed of life, such as the steam engine or the telegraph. Showalter explains how "American nervousness was alarmingly frequent among the well-to-do and the intellectual, and especially among those in the professions and in the higher walks of business life, who are in deadly earnest in the race for place and power" (Showalter 1985: 135). The metaphor of the race implies the danger of unhealthy ambition. This was, of course, most commonly tied to women and the emerging feminism, seen as the desire for a life beyond the confinement of their traditional roles (1985: 144). The psychiatric literature of the time often presented case studies of hysteria and degeneration, typically of female patients who aspired sexual independence and professional freedom. It was put in causal connection with a violation of their "natural" female roles as mothers and wives, exposing them to dangerous energies, further aided by the general idea that nerves were strained and overtaxed by the speed of urban life and that society's fatigue resulted from the continuous pursuit of wealth. It is easy to see Gissing's plot as a reflection of this historical context.

A medical text typically mentioned in passing in most critical studies of Gissing's novel is T.C. Albutt's "Nervous Disease and Modern Life" (1895) because it employs the contemporary whirlpool metaphor. In the essay, the physician Albutt attributes the individual's sense of unrest "to living at high pressure, to the whirl of the railway, [...] the decay of those controlling ethics handed down from statelier and more steadfast generations" and asks, "surely at any rate, these maladies and these causes of maladies are more rife than they were in the days of our fathers?" (Albutt 1895: 214–15). Albutt's argument and his description of the fin-de-siècle risk society deserve a closer reading.

He sets out to inquire into the allegation "that the nervous energy of our race is being exhausted, that worries and cares are killing us" (1895: 211). Taking the rising fear of insanity as "gravest apprehension of the moment" (211), Albutt seeks to give a rational answer and counteract the poplar risk discourse by taking all statistical variables into account when investigating if mental illness is factually on the rise. He deduces that a general longer life expectancy and increase of total number of people are the reason behind the increase of the total number of lunatics. He then offers a provocative argument for the modern risk society creating itself through fears which have a factual base but are perpetuated and blown into fictional disproportions in public discourse. In other words, "history does not seem to indicate that the most civilised States are the maddest" (214), but public knowledge and media coverage create an appearance of ubiquity, "sharpening our apprehensions in these matters" (215). Rather than reflecting a statistically significant increase – and thus risk – it is caused by the fact "that we know more of morbid processes; we talk more of them, read more of them" (216). Finally, the essay entails the very modern insight into the phenomenon of 'fashionable' diseases, because "what was 'liver' fifty years ago has become 'nerves' today" (217). More interesting than simply being another contemporary text dealing with the topic of modern urban life as breeding ground for nervous diseases, Albutt's writing bears testimony to the pervasiveness of the risk discourse in an almost satirical mode. Gissing takes up this aspect with great poignancy in his fiction.

Although Gissing's narrative chronicles the decay of Alma's physical and mental health in detail, William Greenslade rightly notes that the reader is denied access to Alma's perspective and her emotions, which are mainly depicted through the perception of others, and never rationalized or explained. The narrative voice never questions the outside assessment of Alma, and no "counter-diagnosis is made available" (Greenslade 1994: 140). Consequently she is reduced to the function of a – however central – "type" or symbol in the novel. It ultimately remains up to the reader to tear away the layers of Gissing's social satire and decide what finally destroys Alma, a series of ill-conceived choices and irresponsible behaviour, her genetic disposition, the rat race of modern life and a 'heartless' society, or tragic accidents. However, there are two strong suggestions made for the reasons behind Alma's condition, one being that it is the price she has to pay for gambling away her energies in the public sphere; the other main causal factor for her demise is a gendered conception of pathology and hereditary influences.

As has been frequently noted, Gissing includes explicit references to emerging theories of female hysteria and inherited mental disorders in the novel; for example Rolfe and Mrs Abbott discuss Robot's *L'Hérédité Psychologi-*

que (W 29). When Rolfe first notices Alma's nervous temper he immediately starts to makes inquiries into the death of her mother (W 136), rather than ask Ama what upset her. According to Greenslade, in the portrayal of Alma the author heavily drew on public opinion and "contemporary anti-feminist discourses which underscored a conservative and passive view of woman as victim of her own 'nature'" (Greenslade 1989: 522). Alma seemingly suffers from a fusion of negative character traits, combining a disposition for dangerous speculation and insincerity from her father's, and nervous excitability from her mother's side. Her son Hughie continues the embodiment of the risk of heredity even more clearly. Andrew Radford notes in this context: "Both Hardy and Gissing suggest that the son bears the physical traces of spoiled or tainted fertility" (Radford 2006: 14). Similar to Hardy's little Father Time, Hughie is a pale and pensive boy. Although the degenerative influence here only comes from his mother's side, "He had no colour in his cheeks, and showed the nervous tendencies which were to be expected in a child of such parentage" (W 383). But unlike Jude and Sue, Rolfe recognizes the danger before it is too late. Seeing education as the only possible risk management in order to give the boy the tools to survive in an increasingly threatening and unpredictable world, Rolfe is weary about making him in turn too insensitive. His reflections show the difficulty of achieving a 'safe' balance: "that's what we shall aim at – to cultivate his sympathetic emotions, [...] try to make of him a healthy ruffian, with just enough conscience to keep him from crime" (W 319). While her son lives on beyond the last page of the novel, Alma does not and fails in both the domestic and the professional sphere, paralleling her father's end. Part of her pathologized character profile is the inability to ever be content and settle; she is too deeply caught in the net of petty jealousies of the beau monde. As a result she over-exhausts herself without consideration of the risk she carries in her body. Yet this line of argument is thrown into question at least once in the narrative, in Alma's final self-assessment of her life choices. She contemplates how different her life could been if she had, years ago, dared to choose to be an artist and Redgrave's mistress, instead of choosing a conventional marriage which only led to "a baffled ambition, a life of envy, hatred, fear, suffered in secret" (W 388). In hindsight, Gissing's narrative voice suggests – with the usual hint of irony – that Alma sees it as her only mistake to not have risked enough and thus having gone against her nature and rejected her father's legacy. After all, she was the

> [d]aughter of a man who had set all on a great hazard; who had played for the world's reward, and, losing, flung away his life. [...] Could it but come over again, she would accept the challenge of circumstance, which she had failed to understand; accept the scandal and

the hereditary shame; welcome the lot cast for her, and, like her father, play boldly for the great stakes. (W 388)

This underlines the complexity of Gissing's satire and risk discourse and the treatment of the intertwined topics of financial speculation and biological determinism. Regarding the author's attitude to feminism, this novel shows him neither as a champion of women's rights, nor as a conservative misogynist, as Greenslade emphasizes in his introduction to the text: "Gissing allows his women to think beyond the domestic space to which they were too often consigned, yet requires them to suffer the consequences of venturing into what was still, for the period, the hazardous space – socially and morally – between public and private life. *To become visible, in this novel, is to risk it all*" (W xxiv; my emphasis).

The narrative also engages with the discourse of the New Woman as a threat to the 'natural' social order of things. Alma, like Hardy's Sue, is caught in the paradoxical perception of the new woman. She is both cold and "mannish" due to her lack of interest in all matters domestic and for failing to embrace the mother role. One the other, she is portrayed as hyperfeminine, marked by a weak constitution and an excess of emotions, including extreme sensibility and nervousness. These signs of deviance from the implied norm of healthy womanhood make her an unfit mother in Rolfe's eyes.[51] Alma's unfitness is further underlined by her dependence on narcotics, her inability to take care of domestic affairs, and the death of her second child after only two weeks. She is also judged against rival images of ideal motherhood and domesticity,[52] and she is the only female character who undergoes moral and physical collapse. Besides the healthy mother-figures, Mary Abbott and Mrs Morton, Sybil Carnaby depicts another counter example of femininity, a vain, narcissistic woman only interested in social status, but still able to navigate the whirlpool and survive in the city.

In her reading of Gissing's text Lydia Pykett draws attention to the parallel between the hysterized New Woman in fin-de-siècle literary representations and the female hysteric in Freud's psychoanalytical case studies. Both in the 'factual' and fictional writings of the time, "woman became the embodiment of a danger

---

[51] See Pykett (1992: 140–142) and Rothfield's study *Vital Signs* (1992).
[52] See also Greenslade's comment: "Gissing offers a comfortable and comforting version of family life – the sort of family life from which Rolfe feels his son is excluded, due to Alma's neurosis and the crisis in their marriage. Inscribed within this organic ideal of a stable, unchanging backwater – unruffled by the whirlpool – is the reconstituted ideal of late-Victorian motherhood, a standard by which Alma's maternal unfitness is to be judged" (1989: 520).

which had to be controlled" (Pykett 1992: 164), implying that the control of hysteria offered a means of containing traditional domestic ideology. This aspect is also indicative of the general way bodies were increasingly perceived as "dubious or even failed mechanisms" (Greenslade 1994: 135), systems prone to accident and malfunction and thus calling for medical risk management. In the novel, Alma is not prescribed a 'talking cure' but sleeping-medication that will kill her in the end.[53]

In addition to the nexus of feminism, hysteria, and degeneration, a "devastating rumour mill" (Maltz 2013: 178) is at work in the novel. There is a general atmosphere of malicious suspicion from spouses, friends, and neighbours, motivated by jealousies, fears of betrayal and becoming the topic of social ridicule. For example, Harvey is always conscious about the outside appearance of this marriage and being at least partly to "blame for allowing his wife a freedom of which she threatened to make absurd use" (W 226); meanwhile Alma's fears and distrust of people take on such dimensions that she is "suspicious of any relation between man and woman which might suggest, however remotely, dubious possibilities. Innocence appeared to her the exception, lawlessness the rule" (W 234). The relations between male and female characters are infused with a sense of traditionally gendered risk. While financial speculation is a male preoccupation, the women are closely associated with the whirlpool in the sense that the fashionable, 'empty' life is more attractive to them; furthermore women themselves are an integral part of the idle temptations which can bring a man to ruin (see Bowlby 1985: 26). In return, the fall of women like Alma and Sybil is instigated by their desperate pursuit of male attention and flirtation as a means to obtain money, in Alma's case she desperately tries to obtain financial support for her solo concert. Thus she enters a dangerous game of exploiting Redgrave's feelings for her and opens herself to the risks of debts, dishonesty, and blackmail.

Though it seems initially as if the reigniting of her musical ambition presents a saving grace from losing herself completely in "brooding over mysteries and jealousies" (W 212) and channelling her energies in a different direction. But she soon realizes she needs money to promote the event, and, lacking the support of her husband who basically forbids her from pursuing her career, she seeks to strike dangerous bargains with her old suitors Dymes and Redgrave: "She was playing with fire; knew it; enjoyed the excitement of it; trusted herself

---

53 Gissing and Freud were writing at the same time; e. g. Freud's *Studies on Hysteria* (1895) was published while Gissing was already working on *The Whirlpool*. Although psychoanalysis does not plays a role in the novel, it depicts an in-depth study of hysteria and degeneration. See Glover's chapter "Sex and the City: Gissing, Helmholtz, Freud" (2005).

with the completest confidence to come out of the game unscorched" (W 210). Her gamble ultimately does not pay off, although the concert is a success, and her striving for fame produces disastrous results on a grand scale.

Especially leading up to the dramatic climax, Gissing employs a language of risk, focussing on Alma's loss of perspective and deterioration into paranoia. She dramatizes her solo performance to be an event of life-or-death importance and is consumed by jealousy of Sybil to such an extent that she can "no longer balance probabilities" (W 250). In contrast to Rolfe, who even in the face of great anxieties or crisis remains capable of rational detachment and calculation of the likely outcome of events, Alma is too absorbed by her fears and the thrills of the possibility of winning against all odds, "up to the fatal moment she was still holding her own in the game which had become to her a passion" (W 337). In the end, she accidentally ruins the Carnabys socially, just as her father had ruined them financially, but the causal connections are complicated: Alma's jealousy of Sybil's alleged relationship with Redgrave leads her to go to his house seeking to confront him and Sybil in a compromising situation, instead she finds him alone and they are surprised by Hugh Carnaby, who assumes the woman with Redgrave to be Sybil and strikes him down in the dark. Carnaby's accidental manslaughter of Redgrave, which sends him to jail for several years, presents the eruption of the brooding jealousies triggered by the nexus of money, vanity, and sexual relations.

Similar to Gwendolen's accidental participation in and reaction to Grandcourt's death in *Daniel Deronda*, Redgrave's death means Alma's relief of her fears from him and the ruin of her reputation, as well being haunted by a sense of guilty responsibility. At first, in the feverish last moments before her concert, the narrator tells us,

> it became the realization of a hope which she had entertained without knowing it. [...] She gave no thought to wider consequences: she saw the event only as it affected herself [...]. She had feared him; she had feared herself; now all danger was at an end. Now – now she could find courage to front the crowd of people and play to them. (W 287)

Although her concert is a triumph, it is eclipsed by the scandal of Cyril's death and it does not see the end of her fears. Initiated by Mrs Strangeways, rumours start to circulate that Alma was so jealous of Sybil that she plotted with Redgrave's housekeeper to tell Carnaby lies about Sibyl to provoke the murder. Felix Dymes also uses the rumours to rattle Alma further and threaten her with the knowledge of her debts. In return, Alma tries to discredit Sybil's reputation; in a showdown on the street both women accuse each other of spreading malicious gossip about each other. All characters typically resort to lies and deception in order to protect themselves or to seek personal gains. Their risk management consists of primarily of secrecy, retreat, games of manipulation, or even outright blackmail. The fact that communication between the characters is largely conducted via letters creates further opportunity for misunderstandings and false assumptions. Honesty or direct communication never seems to be the first option. Alma in particular gets caught in a web of lies and secrecy. Haunted by Redgrave's voice in her dreams, she reconstructs over and over the course of events in her head. Although she barely remembers her state of mind before going to his house on the fatal night other than as being caught in a "a vortex of wretchedness" (W 345), she is aware she could have acted differently, revealed her identity, and thus saved Hugh from committing the crime. She dares to confess her motives for her actions to Rolfe only weeks later: "I knew all I was risking; but I felt I could give my life to detect that woman and have her in my power" (W 412). Regarding the depiction of the circumstances leading up to Redgrave's death, the narrative highlights the destructive power of human pride and power as well as how, Rachel Bowlby argues, "the prevailing sexual and marital mores work against any approach to individual security" (Bowlby 1985: 26), and negatively impact personal freedom and agency.

After the feverish nightmare of preparing for her solo performance and its scandalous aftermath has come to an end, Alma makes one final attempt to settle into a quiet suburban existence at Gunnersbury. It is her last attempt at a stable, ordinary life without extremes; for a fleeting moment she takes pleasure in taking "lessons in domestic economy" and the discovery of "this *calm, secure, and graceful middle-way*" (W 335; my emphasis). Yet when Alma tries thus to rectify her situation and conform to social expectations out of sheer desperation, it is all too late, just like it was for Hardy's Sue Bridehead. The plot progresses with tragic inevitability. Alma is already in the throws of a drug addiction, the risks of which she is unaware of: "Insomnia began to trouble her again, and presently she had recourse to the forbidden sleeping-draught. [...] In the spring her health would improve, as usual, and then she would give up the habit" (W 389). Instead, as she continues to be overcome by feelings of panic and dread and can only find drug-induced rest at night, the morphine habit leads to her accidental death from an overdose: "The doctor could only say, 'We warned her'" (W 415).

Throughout the narrative Rolfe's habitual tranquillity is threatened by the worries about his wife's neurotic condition and later by mounting financial pressures (see Maltz 2013: 174), because their living expenses increase drastically after the return to the city. While Rolfe tries to reign in the costs and avoid "that tendency to extravagance of living which nowadays universal" (W 202), Alma's death relieves him from all dangers and restores his peace of mind.

The final paragraph is set two years later and brings the plot to a close with an image of stable domesticity and familial harmony. Rolfe and his son, "[h]and in hand, each thinking his own thoughts, [...] walked homeward through the evening sunshine" (W 419). Francesco Marroni argues that Gissing's ending implies that masculinity is the solution to the destruction and disharmony of the world and the antidote to women's pathological self-destructive impulses. The final moment of pastoral stillness appears indeed as "an improbable construction that can only be interpreted as an escape from the whirlpool of modernity" (Marroni 2010: 158), and women are clearly excluded from it. Nonetheless, Gissing's text casts a dark glance into the future of the next generation of young men and it is doubtful that he envisions a chance of survival for the majority them. *The Whirlpool* adds a new dimension of bleakness to the Darwinist struggle for existence and the awareness that only the strongest will survive ("As it is, our little crabs must grow their hard shell, or they've no chance"; W 319). Gissing includes what reads like a dark prophecy of a mentality and a war that would kill the author's own son in July 1916: "We must look to our physique, and make ourselves ready. [...] We may reasonably hope, old man, to see our boys blown into small bits by the explosive that hasn't got its name yet" (W 416). He shows a whole society at the brink of disintegration, chronicling "the bankruptcies of the nation on the threshold of the twentieth century" (Baubles 2001: 262). And the condition extends to all spheres – social, political, economic, and moral. *The Whirlpool* captures a particular atmosphere and its pervasive metaphor of the endless roundabout shows rationality and the ability to act itself as being under threat. Due to the demoralising, corrupting influence of civilization, as one reviewer writes, "It seems dangerous to take any step in any direction; there is nowhere any simplicity; it is as though a rational human existence were no longer possible".[54] Meanwhile, this condition is entirely man-made.

---

[54] Unsigned Review, *Academy* (15 May 1897: 516–517); cited in Coustillas and Partridge (1972: 283).

Part III **Crisis and Contingency: Threats to Humanity in the 20th- and 21st-century Novel**

9 A Sense of Endings

9.1 'Madness or Despair': *The Secret Agent*

In many ways Joseph Conrad's *The Secret Agent. A Simple Tale* (1907) is the quintessential narrative for beginning the study of risk and society in the 20th century, which Albert Camus describes as "the century of fear".[1] *The Secret Agent*, a full-blown expression of "the sense of disaster that licks at the edge of every major Conrad novel" (Karl 1979: 627), is situated in a historical-scientific context ripe with perceived dangers and fears of decay which where the subject of much popular journalism and many fictions of the time. Within Conrad's literary oeuvre, this novel in particular has been interpreted as a reflection of the author's personal fears, the precarious state of his own family, his illness, and his status as a foreigner living in Britain.[2] Yet far transcending the author's personal sense of risk at the time of writing, the novel channels many fin-de-siècle anxieties and future danger scenarios, including anarchist terror, foreign invasion, scientific theories applied to propagating the degeneration of the human race or the exhaustion of energy resources, as well as the loss of British imperial control and the disintegration of the nuclear family. With regard to genre, Conrad's novel testifies to the boom of popular revolutionary conspiracy narratives at the turn of the century,[3] fusing it with a satirical stance and an experimental aesthetics, and points the way from Edwardian realism to modernist 'high-brow' fiction.

Set in late-Victorian London, the plot develops around Adolf Verloc, the eponymous "famous and trusty secret agent" (SA 31), who has infiltrated an international anarchist group while working for a dubious foreign embassy and keeping up a domestic disguise-existence as "a seller of shady wares"

---

[1] Camus ties this perception of the 20th century specifically to secular man's loss of hope in the future through the disillusionment with scientific advancement as a form of progress, as well as to the political exploitation of risk: "Our twentieth century is the century of fear. [...] science is no doubt involved, for its latest advances have brought it to the point of negating itself, while its perfected technology threatens the entire world with destruction. Moreover, if fear itself cannot be considered a science, it is certainly a technique. What is indeed most striking about our world is that most men (with the exception of true believers) are cut off from the future. Life has no validity unless it projects itself toward the future, unless it promises growth and progress" (Camus 1991: 117).
[2] See Frederick R. Karl's biography *Joseph Conrad. The Three Lives* (1979).
[3] For a survey of the period's conspiracy fiction see Arnett Melchiori's *Terrorism in the Late Victorian Novel* (1985).

(SA 13). When he receives the order to conduct a spectacular terrorist act with the aim of giving the British public "a jolly good scare" (SA 33), he fatefully delegates the deed of blowing up the Greenwich Royal Observatory to his mentally retarded brother-in-law, Stevie, who accidentally gets killed in the attempt. Narrating the events around the cruel catastrophe in a non-linear fashion, the novel's dramatic climax is Verloc's murder at the hands of his wife Winnie, who stabs him after she learns that he is responsible for Stevie's death. Commonly seen to fulfil the role as the novel's 'true' anarchist, Winnie commits suicide in the end, jumping off a ship while crossing the Channel to France, thus adding a final "*act of madness or despair*" (SA 265; original emphasis) to Conrad's in fact anything but "simple tale".

Many of the topical issues and debates surrounding Conrad's novel – political as well as aesthetically – bring a strong sense of *déjà vu* to a 21st-century reader and critic. It is hard to find a 20th-century text that rivals the mass of (re-)readings and interest *The Secret Agent* has sparked nearly a hundred years and onwards after its first publication. Considering the critical wave of the study of terror(ism) triggered in and outside of academia[4] in the aftermath of the 9/11 attacks, it is hardly surprising that the majority of 21st-century approaches to Conrad's novel pivots around its literary treatment of terrorism.[5] Having been assigned global "cult status as the classic novel for the post-9/11 age" (Reiss 2005),[6] Terry Eagleton names it as "the first suicide-bomber novel of English literature" and a striking dramatization of bombing as an action whose effects are "in principle incalculable" (Eagleton 2005: 126). Recent essays have also proposed reading *The Secret Agent* as a "novel of crisis" (Haines 2012: 89) in the context of biopolitics, or as Michael Jonik (2014) does, in relation to the conception of systemic risk at the turn of the century. Although I do not agree with Jonik's rather superficial sketch of the development of probabilistic thinking and the claim of its first emergence at the turn from the 19th to the 20th century, the general direction of his approach is relevant. Jonik suggests that Conrad's text registers "the 'atmospheric pressure' of risk in a variety of cultural formations" (2014: 22). These deserve closer analysis. While the novel gives prominence to uncertainty and

---

4 See, e.g., Houen (2004), Lacquer (2003), Ward (2008), Zulaika and Douglass (1996).
5 See Houen (2002), Mallios (2005), and Scanlan's *Plotting Terror* (2001).
6 Ward writes: "*The Secret Agent* is commonly presented as the first literary account of terrorism; or at least the first to be found in what we can loosely term canonic literature. And it is equally often credited with being one of the most perceptive and nuanced" (2008: 273). However, others have voted for Conrad's *Under Western Eyes* being the 'true classic' of literary terrorism, because it gives an inside perspective, while *The Secret Agent* presents a more detached, outside-view (see Reiss 2005).

risk in various forms and guises, the domestic drama is rendered almost undistinguishable from the political anarchist plot, causing – and herein lies an important novelty of Conrad's narrative – reflection on the contingency of the notion of plot itself. The narrative is fragmented in design, "as if unbound from the necessary ordering of events" (2014: 30), and constructs both chaos and the modern experience of temporality as risks. Through its emplotments of failed plans and the futility of efforts, either due to incompetence, ignorance, madness, or mere randomness, the narrative offers insight into contemporary perceptions of the future as fragile and incalculable yet without any clear alternatives or nostalgia for the past. Developing further than writers before him "the threat of personal annihilation" (Levine 1988: 268), Conrad engages with the risk of lives being ended prematurely at any moment, the suffering of ordinary, innocent people due to misguided political actions and the heading of Western civilization towards destruction and chaos. The significance of Conrad's vision of breakdown, Frederick Karl emphazises, lies in the fact that it coincides with the widely held perception of the Edwardian era as a period of national "confidence in the future, of relative prosperity, [...] and an egalitarian society. Conrad was the sole novelist of stature and breadth to tell the English that their goals as well as the texture of their lives were melancholy matters, not reasons for celebration" (Karl 1979: 626–627).

In *The Secret Agent* modern life is rendered essentially unknowable and unpredictable. London is a disorienting metropolitan space of social and moral fragmentation and isolation, shrouded in darkness ("choked, and suffocated by the blackness" (SA 134), "sullen, brooding, and sinister" (SA 136)), consisting of "monotonous streets with unknown names where the dust of humanity settles inert and hopeless out of the stream of life" (SA 260). Aside from the setting, several other forces aid the distortion of perception and security, operating as "antitheses of knowledge" (Fleishman 1967: 194). They include ignorance, foolishness, madness and overwhelming emotions. The pervasive symbolism of fragmentation and explosion in the novel, that Avron Fleishman (1967: 188) has noted, highlights the obstruction of linearity and clarity. The central and most literal example is the starting point of Inspector Heat's investigation, finding Stevie reduced to "a heap of nameless fragments" (SA 82). In general, Conrad's London is filled with alienated citizens, appearing as obscure to others as they do to themselves. Watching people in an Italian restaurant, the Assistant Police Commissioner considers them "as denationalised as the dishes set before them [...]. Neither was their personality stamped in any way, professionally, socially or racially. [...] It was impossible to form a precise idea what occupations they followed by day and where they went to bed at night" (SA 134). As a result the means of surveillance and struggle to maintain the social order becoming equally inefficient or even directly destructive as the means of subversion or inducing change. Mark Conroy, for instance, emphasizes that the narrative shows all surveillance and traditional control mechanisms of late Victorian society "doomed to failure" (Conroy 1985: 143), revealing in turn the increase of anonymity and lack of contact between people in modern society as a breeding ground for suspicion and uncertainty.[7] The series of events leading up to Verloc's failed terrorist plot and Stevie's accident present police and anarchists alike with a reality they can only describe as "rather unaccountable" (SA 94). Focusing on the absurd and destructive results of all characters' struggle for secrecy and the realization of hidden agendas,[8] the novel also poses questions about the public distortion of narratives for certain political ends, and about the clash of terrorism and counter-terrorism measures, practices of surveillance and governmental control with British ideals of liberalism.[9] Mr Vladimir and the other foreign Embassy officials voice their criticism of "the utter absence of all repressive measures" (SA 23), seeing Britain endangered by "its sentimental regard for individual liberty" (SA 33). Discarding all spying and surveillance activities as ineffectual, Mr Vladimir tells Mr Verloc that more actions rather than more bureaucracy are needed: "Don't you be too English. [...] We don't want prevention – we want cure" (SA 30). Although the violent act Verloc seeks to commit and Stevie's death do not affect the social order but trigger the destruction of his whole family,[10] Inspector Heat later still decides that the incident offers him a "starting-point for a crusade" (SA 195), facilitating the implementation of more coercive measures with the aim of "clearing out of this country of all the foreign political spies, police, [...] a ghastly nuisance; also an element of danger" (SA 199).

From beginning to end the novel evokes an atmosphere of anonymity, secrecy and distrust that is mirrored in the intertwined political and domestic plot lines. It reflects a social-political climate on the rise since the mid-19th century marked by heightened anxiety about the growth of the foreign immigrant population, British asylum and law enforcement policies, and the Irish struggle

---

7 See also Conroy (1983) and Moseley (1997).
8 Avron Fleishman has noted the striking frequency of the use of the word "secrecy" which occurs more than 50 times in the text (Fleishman 1967: 190).
9 See Mallios's argument that "*The Secret Agent's* special 'contemporary' feel for us today" (2005: 156) derives from representations and responses to how media responds and seeks to control people's responses to terrorism.
10 Stephen Bernstein argues that *The Secret Agent* is essentially a novel about the shattering of a family situation, revealing the diseased condition of the nuclear family through presenting a "travesty of gothic domesticity" (2003: 292). On Conrad's own sense of familial destruction, his son's illness, their financial worries and his wife's breakdown see Karl (1979: 591–592).

for independence. Adding to the sense of social upheaval caused by the Fenian dynamite outrages of the 1880s come the increase of European espionage activities and the rise of the anarchist movement.[11] The latter shared roots and concerns with socialist thought and the working-class rebellion from the first half of the 19th-century onwards.[12] Spreading its explosive "propaganda of the deed"[13] throughout continental Europe, it reached international proportions during the 1890s following the successful assassinations of six different heads of states.[14] Despite the fact that anarchist attacks on British soil remained few, London became known as "the greatest safe haven for terrorists and revolutionaries" (Webb 2012: 21) during this period. The felt presence of foreign anarchist and other revolutionary groups caused confusion among British police and public, largely obfuscated by the media. Adrian Wisnicki stresses the great difficulty to identify and differentiate the terrorist movements and their actual aims (Wisnicki 2008: 147), and Conrad's novel picks up on this confusion and muddled sense of political risk. Although the fear of porous borders has been dominant throughout history, and terrorist activity has certainly been part of life in the British capital for much longer than a century, a fact Simon Webb rightfully draws attention to, terrorism gained new currency towards the end of the 19th-century. Nowadays perceived as the time when the conceptual origins of modern terrorist campaigns were formed, the most threatening aspect lies in their randomness of direction and choice of target/victim, creating a different sense of risk for the individual and the public, "a general fear or apprehension, which is, of course, precisely the aim of modern-day acts of terrorism" (Webb 2012: 12).

Strong evidence exists to sustain the ties of Conrad's narrative to actual historical events, centrally the 'Greenwich bomb outrage', the attempted attack on the Royal Observatory on 15 February 1894 by the French anarchist Martial Bour-

---

[11] See Webb's *Dynamite, Treason & Plot* (2012), Wisnicki's *Conspiracy, Revolution, and Terrorism from Victorian Fiction to the Modern Novel* (2008), and O'Donghaile's *Blasted Literature* (2010).
[12] For introductions see, e.g., Oliver's *The International Anarchist Movement in Late Victorian London* (1983) and Woodcock's *Anarchism: A History of Libertarian Movements and Ideas* (1963).
[13] The expression of "propaganda by the deed" was coined by the French terrorist Paul Brousse and commonly used in anarchist campaigns during the 1880s in Europe and North America. It is often evoked in context with "the philosophy of the bomb", the title of an 1881 book by the Bavarian anarchist, Johann Most, who was later offered asylum in Britain (see Webb 2012: 14). Conrad's anarchists refer to both terms in the novel.
[14] See Reiss: "Conrad began writing during the first great terrorist wave of modern times. From 1881 to 1901, the death toll from anarchist attacks included two American presidents (Garfield and McKinley), one French president (Carnot), a Spanish prime minister (Canovas), an Austrian empress (Elizabeth) and an Italian king (Umberto I)" (Reiss 2005). See also Bright (2015: 192), Houen (2002: 35), O'Donghaile (2010: 97), Tuchman (1966: 63), and Wisnicki (2008: 147).

din, who was found mutilated in the park on the hill near the Observatory after the premature detonation of his bomb.[15] In the often-cited "Author's Note" to the novel Conrad, who had been living in London at the time, claims that the tale came to him during "a casual conversation about anarchists" (SA 3) with a friend; as further inspirational clues he adds recalling "the already old story of the attempt to blow up the Greenwich Conservatory; a blood-stained inanity of so fatuous a kind that it was impossible to fathom its origin", a friend's remark about Bourdin being "half an idiot" (SA 3) and his sister later committing suicide, and having come across "summary recollections of an Assistant Commissioner of Police, [...] who was appointed to his post at the time of the dynamite outrages in London, away back in the eighties" (SA 4).[16] While the extent of Conrad's knowledge of and sympathy with anarchist thought have been subject to much debate, the novel demonstrates an understanding of the dynamics of anarchist violence and highlights its futility. Conrad simultaneously places emphasis on showing "every act as an act of disorder – every attempt at control a move toward chaos" (Karl 1979: 597), an effect hard to separate in hindsight from the looming mass-destruction in the shape of WWI.

According to David Mulry, the extensive contemporary press coverage of the Greenwich bomb outrage was symptomatic of the felt risk of foreign terror and anarchy.[17] It functioned in two different ways. It sought to exorcize fears by focusing the reporting of the Bourdin affair away from political motivation to the depiction of Bourdin as a lonely sociopath, thus diminishing the political threat. At the same time, the press emphasized Bourdin's foreignness, fostering the risk image of "the enemy within" und fuelling the fear of a "social revolution that crosses borders" (Mulry 2000: 46–47). The incident can generally be tied to a shift in risk perception, suggesting the acceptance of the British public of a reality of domestic threat, as for example *The Times*'s reporting of the incident

---

[15] For an early and detailed study of the historical background of the plot see Sherry (1971: 228–247).

[16] While Conrad stresses his fascination with "the absurd cruelty of the Greenwich Park explosion" (SA 5), some critics argue that the novel is closely inspired by the author's observations of the Fenian situation, because the "summary recollections" refer to the memoirs of Assistant Commissioner of Police Robert Anderson, who worked against the Fenian dynamite outrages in the 1880s, and the novel's setting is around this time, earlier than the Greenwich bombing (see Karl 1979: 595; Wisnicki 2008: 162). Conrad's attitude toward terrorism is also discussed in relation to his family background, e.g. his father's arrest as a revolutionary with alleged ties to the Russian anarchist Mikhail Bakunin in 1861 (see Reiss 2005).

[17] See Mulry (2000). Cf. also the Appendix D "The Greenwich mystery!" (a pamphlet written and published by David Nicholl in 1897) included in Sherry (1971: 379–394) and Knapp Hay (1963: 221–228).

documents (see O'Donghaile 2010: 118). Reacting to public fears, an increasing number of fictions took up the threat of anarchist terrorism. Examples featuring opaque conspiracy plots, solitary 'mad' protagonists threatening the lives of many, and terrorists shown to be equally as incompetent as the policemen include novel such as Edward Douglas Fawcett's *Hartman, the Anarchist: or the Doom of the Great City* (1893), Henry James's *The Princess Casamassima* (1886),[18] H.G. Wells's *Invisible Man* (1897), his short story "The Stolen Bacillus" (1895) whose protagonist plans to infect London's water supply with a super virus, and G.K. Chesterton's *The Man Who Was Thursday* (1909). Especially writers like Wells, Chesterton, and Conrad, as Deaglan O'Donghaile argues, produced texts that parody the political threat of radicalism and feed into popular constructions of "anarchism as morbid irrationality" (O'Donghaile 2010: 109). In *The Secret Agent*, slipping generically between espionage thriller, satire, and domestic melodrama, the parody assumes distinctly tragic dimensions. Crossing the boundary between high brow and popular culture, Conrad's employs the theme of anarchism to show how it lends itself – apart from the envisioning of risk scenarios – to the reflection of the politics of individual agency, and to fictionalizing the breakdown of political, social, as well as literary order.

Conrad's literary treatment of the Greenwich bomb outrage reveals a fascination with the discrepancy between the ordinariness of people and extraordinary events. As a secret agent, Mr Verloc is about as far from Ian Fleming's James Bond as one can possibly imagine: "His is not the thrilling life of the glamorous spy or the liberator of the masses" (Ward 2008: 258). He rather seems to loathe danger and activity; after he is given the deadline to realize the dynamite outrage by Mr Vladimir he feels threatened "in what is dearest to him – his repose and his security" (SA 52). Due to his unspecified foreign roots, Mr Verloc is also perceived as shifty; "He came and went without any apparent reason", arriving "in London (like the influenza) from the Continent" (SA 14). Ironizing the long-standing British fear of contagion spreading from across the channel, the novel contains several metaphorical references to the anarchists as a modern sort of "pest". Although Mr Verloc is portrayed as good-natured at heart, his main characteristics are mediocrity, passivity and ignorance, "his mission in life being the protection of the social mechanism, not its perfectionment or even its criticism" (SA 21). Thus he strives to avert any risks to the ruling classes, the capitalist system and the existing social order apparently unreflectively. For example, walking

---

18 *The Secret Agent* is often read in comparison with James' *The Princess Casamassima*, e.g. by Jonik (2014) and Stinga (2012).

through London, the sight of luxurious town houses calls forth his desire to safeguard the people living inside them:

> All these people had to *be protected*. *Protection* is the first necessity of opulence and luxury. They had to be *protected*; and their horses, carriages, houses, servants had to be *protected*; and the source of their wealth had to be *protected* in the heart of the city and the heart of the country; the whole social order favourable to their hygienic idleness had to be *protected* against the shallow enviousness of unhygienic labour. (SA 18–19; my emphasis)

Verloc's bodily features reflect his mental (in)capacities, he is "burly in a fat-pig style" (SA 19), and Mr Vladimir considers him "the embodiment of fraudulent laziness and incompetency" (SA 31). The other members of Verloc's anarchist group (Comrade Ossipon, Michaelis, Karl Yundt, the Professor) seem equally ill equipped to carry out a revolutionary secret attack; they "appeared hopelessly futile" (SA 52) and remind the Assistant Police Commissioner of "nasty little children" (SA 125). Although Conrad depicts the anarchists as immature, corpulent, ineffectual, and motivated by egotism or amorous games rather than by political ideology, they are still frightening.[19] In the course of the novel, ignorance and foolishness become menacing spectres equal to fanaticism in their essentially random destructiveness. While this applies also in particular to Stevie and Winnie, the anarchists each display in different forms, Ian Ward points out, "a grotesque immaturity born out of a failure to empathize. […] The fanatic and the deluded; both fail to anticipate the misery that their haphazard violence will cause to real people, that spectacular public acts can only lead to devastatingly private consequences" (Ward 2008: 263).[20] Though none of the self-proclaimed anarchists actually commits an act of violence, the only one appearing truly dangerous among them is the Professor. On his lonely walks around the city he has always one hand in his pocket placed on the trigger of the bomb strapped around his body, "the supreme guarantee of his sinister freedom" (SA 77). Embracing anonymity, speed and danger, the Professor manages his own risk of being apprehended by the police by becoming a walking risk to others. The danger is increased through its randomness and instantaneity as the bomb detonator can go off in a flash, like the shatter of a camera (cf. Sleigh 2011: 169).

---

19 There is, of course, an inherent paradox in Anarchist thought that rendered the movement (partially) unproductive: In order to instigate a revolution one needs the very ideas rejected by Anarchism, organization, authority and discipline; George Bernard Shaw, for instance, details this aspect in his Fabian tract *The Impossibilities of Anarchism* (1893). See Tuchman (1966: 65–66).

20 Ian McEwan draws a similar conclusion in his post-9/11 diagnosis of the terrorist mind-set being caused by a failure of imagination and empathy (see McEwan 2001a; 2001b).

The Professor also underlines the importance of (irrational) belief and public perception for the construction of risk, which is in his case a means of self-protection: "I have the means to make myself deadly, but that by itself, you understand, is absolutely nothing in the way of protection. What is effective is the belief those people have in my will to use the means" (SA 65). Conrad's characterization of the Professor reflects the symbolic transference of the risk of violence and revolutionary power away from the mob of the urban working-class masses onto the 'mad' individual and away from on-going riots to the singular momentous destructive event which was the topic of many of the era's popular dynamite fictions (see O'Donghaile 2010: 102). Epitomizing mad subjectivity seeking to oppose the masses, in the Professor's opinion the greatest risk is the stupor of the public. He is painfully aware of his own agitated singularity being blown out by the multitude of people "pushing on blind and orderly and absorbed, *impervious to sentiment, to logic, to terror too perhaps*. [...] What if nothing could move them?" (SA 77; my emphasis). He is haunted by the fear of the ineffectuality of his own methods and beliefs crushed by the "resisting power of numbers, the unattackable stolidity of a great multitude" (SA 89). Interestingly, both police and anarchists assert the importance and risk of the unpredictability of "that strange emotional phenomenon called public opinion", alarming through "its irrational nature" (SA 92). Ultimately, Comrade Ossipon says: "There is no law and no certainty. [...] The only thing that matters to us is the emotional state of the masses" (SA 51).

The question of how to implant a sense of risk into the masses is also at the forefront of Mr Vladimir's debate of the most effective target for Verloc's attack. Discarding churches or any other representative buildings which would lend an ideological explanation to the destructive act, he postulates that it must "be purely destructive" (SA 35). Randomness is the only guarantee of inducing lasting threat because the press is already well versed into safely digesting terrorist events into existing narratives: "Every newspaper has ready-made phrases to explain such manifestations away" (SA 35). Although the chosen target is anything but free from symbolic and ideological value even if of a distinctly secular nature, the decision to target the Greenwich Royal Observatory is made because it houses science, the "sacrosanct fetish of to-day" (SA 34). Aside from Mr Vladimir's dream of throwing "a bomb into pure mathematics" (SA 36), blowing up Greenwich means an attack against the order of modernity, science, time management, and capitalist imperial power, because the controlling, organizing power of the standard time system and the first meridian extend from the heart of the metropolis throughout Europe and Britain's empire.[21]

Several studies have convincingly situated *The Secret Agent* in the context of persisting late-Victorian and newly emerging scientific thought and its popular pseudo-scientific mediations. A brief survey shall suffice to point explicitly towards the risk discourse inherent in these theories and their dissemination in Conrad's novel. The relevant critical approaches can be divided into two fields, the focus on degeneration and hereditary criminal abnormalities of character, and the advent of thermodynamics,[22] which are connected through their application to fostering apocalyptic thought by creating risk scenarios. Charlotte Sleigh explains the popular scientific doctrine that "everything in the universe was inclined to decay, become disordered and wear out. The technical terms for these phenomena were 'entropy' and 'degeneration', ideas that also had a counterpart in biological theories about evolution slipping backwards" (Sleigh 2011: 167). In the novel, Conrad has Winnie's mother reflect "stoically that everything decays, wears out, in this world' (SA 145), while Winnie's firm belief that "things did not stand much looking into" (SA 158), arguably a leitmotif of the narrative, captures a profound insecurity. It can be related to advances in fields of physics and thermodynamics at the time which were seemingly threatening the stability of the physical world, as Alex Houen has argued. Both Houen and Michael Whitworth base their analyses of the novel, focussing on the second law of thermodynamics and the principles of entropy and dissipation, on the fact that in the early 20th-century scientific thought and social ills become intertwined to a great extent. According to the second law of thermodynamics, the universe is moving towards a maximum state of entropy in terms of energy flow, thus striving towards flux and chaos. Meanwhile the definition of "dissipation" as the "wasteful expenditure or consumption" of power and resources highlights the inherent moral reproach (Whitworth 2001: 64). The widespread applicability of thermodynamic theory produced various scientifically only half-digested risk discourses. One great fear was solar decay, the idea that the sun would eventually cool down and leave the earth in darkness.[23] For example,

---

[21] In the post-9/11 context the Greenwich Observatory has been described as a terrorist target analogous to the Twin Towers and the Pentagon (see Lütticken 2006: 100). On the significance of Greenwich during Conrad's time see Barrows (2010).
[22] See Whitworth (2001); also Clark (2004); Houen (1998; 2002); MacDuffie (2009); and Sleigh (2011: 166–169).
[23] On fears of the sun's extinctions disseminated in the press see also MacDuffie (2009: 75–76). Whitworth (2001: 59) suggests that Conrad alludes to this idea through the gloomy setting and the use of a thermodynamic rhetoric. Examples are descriptions such as the "bloodshot", "pecu-

Winnie's state after hearing of Stevie's death is compared to the way "the population of half the globe would keep still in astonishment and despair, were the sun suddenly put out in the summer sky" (SA 213). Another aspect is an emerging global focus on energy resources and the destructive effects of industrial civilization. Allen MacDuffie suggests that the narrative contains an implicit call for economizing with resources through showing (Western) civilization as a risk to the earth; he also draws attention to the links between thermodynamic and capitalist economic rhetoric with both discursive fields employing terms such as "efficiency", "productivity", "waste", and "energy" (see MacDuffie 2009: 80). Yet more important is the argument about the narrative's display of the risk of systemic inefficiency through a plot fused "with a pervasive sense of the absolute futility and waste of characters' actions" (2009: 91), and the view of it evoking a sense of general "thermodynamic degeneracy" (Clark 2004: 20) that has all action inevitably aspire to the point of nothingness, culminating in the deaths of Stevie and Winnie.

In its fearful popular perception, the notion of entropy was furthermore used to support and express threats of degeneration of the nation/race, especially against the background of the Boer War. The prediction of an increase of "slower, weaker bodies that might reduce the average level of energy" (Whitworth 2001: 78–79) shows parallels between thermodynamic and eugenic thought. They can be found in many contemporary pamphlets and reports and are closely related to political fears of the empire having expanded beyond its limits and the metropolitan centre being unable to hold in the future (2001: 80). Although *The Secret Agent* is a Conradian novel that contains only implicit references to imperialism, the author shows the inhabitants of the metropolis at risk of literally living in the heart of perpetual darkness. Moreover, the characters – with few exceptions – are depicted as "grown fat and spiritually exhausted from sloth, dependency, and purposeless effort" (MacDuffie 2009: 93).[24] The dwindling physical and mental strength of the individual and, by extension, the national 'body' of citizens is a topic that is carried over from the fictions of Hardy and Gissing to Conrad and Forster. In Conrad's text one also detects the idea that humanity develops steadily towards the worst, producing its own risk society,

---

liar London sun" (SA 18) and Mr Verloc feeling like the "last particle of his nervous force had been expended" (SA 225).

24 Most critical studies comment on the prevalence of fat bodies and physical apathy in the novel, especially in relation to the satirical description on the incompetency of the anarchists and the police agents. James English lists recurring key words such as "idleness, indolence, gluttony, lethargy, immobility, inertness, complacence, and domesticity" (English 1992: 619); see also Fleishman (1967: 196).

while the thrill of risk-taking and the calculation of potential gains is completely absent.

Arguably, Conrad is bleaker even than Hardy in his general evolutionary outlook (see O'Hanlon 1984: 1),[25] and several critics have traced the influence of Nordau's and Lombroso's theories on Conrad's character psychology in *The Secret Agent*. Though Conrad's knowledge of degeneration theory is well documented, he was not necessarily sympathetic of it.[26] It is rather one of the most obvious objects of satire in the narrative. Similar to Nordau's theories (see chapters 3.4.2 and 3.4.3), the Italian criminologist Cesare Lombroso proposed the idea of "delinquent types", seeking to account for the appearance of extreme and criminal personalities in society. He based his theory on the correlation of psychic and physical manifestations, e.g. abnormalities being reflected in specific facial structures or shapes of skull.[27] As many have noted, Comrade Ossipon, the spokesman for science among Conrad's anarchists, diagnoses Winnie and Stevie as "perfect types" and Conrad employs descriptions suggestive of Lombroso's theories on several occasions. When first examining Stevie's physique, Ossipon says: "Very good type, too, altogether, of that sort of degenerate. It's enough to glance at the lobes of his ears. If you read Lombroso..." (SA 47); later he looks at Winnie "and invoked Lombroso [...]. He gazed at her cheeks, at her nose, at her eyes, at her ears. ... Bad! ... Fatal!" (SA 257–258). Especially ironic is Ossipon's attribution of Winnie's increasing panic of being caught by the police and her traumatic state of shock after killing her husband to progress-

---

25 On evolutionary thought in Conrad's writing see O'Hanlon's *Joseph Conrad and Charles Darwin* (1984) and Hunter's *Joseph Conrad and the Ethics of Darwinism* (1983).

26 On the author's familiarity with Nordau and Lombroso's writing see Karl (1979: 626; 728) and Moseley (1997: 69–70); see the essays by Ray, "Conrad, Nordau, and Other Degenerates: The Psychology of The Secret Agent" (1984), and Jacobs, "Comrade Ossipon's Favorite Saint: Lombroso and Conrad" (1968). Jacobs's essay, however, sees Conrad endorsing rather than criticizing Lombrosian theory.

27 On Conrad's suffering from neurasthenic illnesses throughout his writing career see Ray (1984: 136–137), who suggests that the narrative is the author's way to explore his condition as a "degenerate" artistic type, fictionalizing his own sense of being at risk of deviance and mental illness. A similar argument is given by Jacobs, although he also admits that it remains conjectural: "In one sense, it was Conrad's device for working out his own fears about the relationship between genius, insanity, idiocy, and epilepsy in order to understand his family's 'sickness' in Lombrosian terms. There is no written record of that effort; it would be surprising to find one. His struggle as an artist was to be 'normal,' or to be accepted as 'normal,' fearing all the while the evidence of his family history and his experience of epileptic seizures. That is not an anxiety easily confessed in public, and, as the Prefaces to the collected works indicate, it was Conrad's posture to appear to be the chatty retailer of glamorous adventure stories, normal in all respects, the 'happy sailor'" (Jacobs 1968: 83).

ing hereditary insanity. Forced by Winnie's appeals to his male support – "Save me. Hide me. Don't let them have me" (SA 245) – Ossipon suddenly finds himself at risk through the proximity with "the sister of the degenerate – a degenerate herself of a murdering type;" this leaves him "terrified scientifically in addition to all other kinds of fear" (SA 252). After abandoning Winnie on the train, he is filled with a great sense of relief, yet the newspaper report of her suicide soon afterwards renews his acute sense of risk. Despite feeling saved by his foresight of leaving Winnie to her fate, he is more than ever "scientifically afraid of insanity" (SA 267).

Although Stevie's involuntary suicide mission is obviously motivated by his loyalty to Verloc instilled into him by Winnie, he is characterized from the beginning by his capacity for excitement that easily crosses into violence, he also enjoyed playing with fireworks as a child, oblivious to the panic his "reckless naughtiness" (SA 16) caused his family. In his ignorance, he reacts violently to all cruelty and injustice; his temper erupts, for example, in the scene when their cabman beats his horse: "In the face of anything which affected directly or indirectly his morbid dread of pain, Stevie ended by turning vicious. [...] Supremely wise in knowing his own powerlessness, Stevie was not wise enough to restrain his passions" (SA 151). Thus, Jill Clark argues (2004: 16; 26), Stevie is shown to be incapable of moderation and control of his behaviour as well as of foresight, let alone perceiving risk. Though being of age, he is infantilized by the exclusive reference to him in the narrative as the "peculiar" or "the poor boy" (see Mageean 1996: 243); thus he is denied agency and shown to be in need of protection. Ossipon's 'scientific' assessment of Stevie is pregnant with doom, "his thin neck, sunk into a deep hollow at the base of the skull, seemed ready to snap" (SA 47). Stevie, however, looks with unconditional love upon his sister as his protector; Winnie in turn watches over him "with maternal vigilance" (SA 17). Ultimately, Stevie is killed due to his fierce devotion to Mr Verloc and his inability to be suspicious of ulterior motifs and of perceiving danger. In terms of the Professor's risk psychology, postulating that "it is character alone that makes for one's safety" (SA 65), Stevie's death is the tragic result of a lack of character. Jill Clark aptly describes Stevie in this sense as a "human zero" who has "no such force of personality, so safety and protection are not considerations for him" (Clark 2004: 18). Yet, in terms of plot causality or, rather randomness, equally important are the female characters' attempts at risk management that produce results completely perverting good intentions.

Stevie's both dangerously innocent and unpredictable behaviour is a source of anxiety to his mother and sister. Right up until the final chapters, their actions consist solely of managing the perceived risks for Stevie. It becomes clear that Winnie only became Mrs Verloc to extend the protection of the marital home over him and the reader suspects from the beginning that the exaggerated statements of felt security by the two women can only signal destruction to come; "the poor boy was pretty safe in this rough world;" Mr Verloc's "heavy good nature inspired her with *a sense of absolute safety*" (SA 15; my emphasis). However, it is the very act of leaving Stevie in Verloc's care that destroys him and both women fail at controlling their domestic life. The move of Winnie's mother out of Mr Verloc's house into other far less convenient lodgings is another step of supposedly efficient risk management that only leads to disintegration. The old woman rationally calculates that Stevie "had not a sufficient standing" and that abandoning him is the only way to assure his safety at the price of her own discomfort: "The first sense of security following on Winnie's marriage wore off in time (for nothing lasts), [...] the less strain put on Mr Verloc's kindness the longer its effects were likely to last" (SA 145). Enforcing the narrative's climate of suspicion and opacity, no character has at any point the same knowledge or perception of a situation or people's motifs and behaviour as another. While Winnie is still grieving for her mother's departure, Mr Verloc's interpretation of events is heavily influenced by his own fears of what is to come out of the bomb outrage he has to organize, "a peculiar aptness in circumstances [...] made him think of rats leaving a doomed ship" (SA 159). Another precaution taken by Winnie in case Stevie gets lost, carefully sewing his name and address inside his coat collar turns into evidence – in fact the only shrapnel of evidence – revealing the supposed terrorist's identity to the police and leading them directly to Verloc's house. Being shown the torn label from her brother's coat by Inspector Heat triggers Winnie's step-by-step realization of Stevie's death and Verloc's involvement. It painfully robs her of her illusion of being able to control and protect herself and her brother through paying her dues in wifely loyalty. Suddenly "her married life appeared to her as lonely and unsafe as though it had been situated in the midst of a forest" (SA 177), a drastic change from the "absolute safety" she used to feel in her husband's presence in the beginning. As a reaction to the shock and a terribly belated sense of risk awareness, Winnie transcends into a trance-like state. Her emotions oscillate between passionate rage due to the sense of betrayal that despite all her efforts of protection failed and the exhilarating feeling of liberation after realizing that she is relieved from all domestic obligations: "no need for her now to stay there, in that kitchen, in that house, with that man – [...] Mrs Verloc began to look upon herself as released from all earthly ties" (SA 219).

The novel omits describing the Greenwich incident and Stevie's death, but details the struggle of the characters to construct what happened and assign responsibility. The police as well as Verloc and the other anarchists are shocked and puzzled by the event. They each experience a lack of control by being confronted with the reality of a danger they failed to anticipate. Eventually, everybody arrives at the conclusion that Stevie was victimized through his own foolishness and the force of accident. At once victim and perpetrator, for the police Stevie's death represents the human and mechanical unpredictability that resists all risk calculations: "The system's worked perfectly. [...] But there are more kinds of fools than one can guard against" (SA 72). Similarly, discussing the course of events with the Professor, who had minutely calculated the time of the bomb's detonation, Mr Verloc realizes that they had foreseen anything but Stevie's falling; instead he had prepared for eventualities such as getting arrested or Stevie getting lost or distracted. The second accident, in Verloc's perception equally crucial and damaging to his mission, is Winnie's completely differently motivated precaution of sewing Stevie's address inside his overcoat. Thus Verloc, the secret agent who "had calculated with correct insight" (SA 205) so many odds, is brought down by two domestic agents, a random fall, and failing to imagine the reach of Winnie's protective measures. He accepts it with fatalist stoicism, comparing it to "slipping on a bit of orange peel in the dark and breaking your leg" (SA 206). This allows him to avoid taking responsibility and to relieve his guilt, at least to himself as well as towards Winnie. Ironically, when it comes to facing the legal consequences of his action, which he considers unavoidable, he views a prison sentence as an escape from the muddled espionage world and his regular domestic existence rather than as a punishment. To Verloc, a prison appears "a place as safe [...] as the grave, with this advantage, that in a prison there is room for hope" (SA 205). Prison is attractive – at least temporarily – because it offers the individual everything that seems lost in the world (of the novel, i.e. security, a clear order, and the ability to plan the future even if being confined and stripped of all power.

The Assistant Police Commissioner and the Professor, who describes terrorists and policemen as coming "from the same basket" (SA 67), still possess the illusion of control over themselves and each other. They conceive of their actions as moves and counter moves in a game, which implies shared rules, predictability, and of course, the chance to eventually win against the other. Inspector Heat, for example, believes he has the upper hand against the Professor, and he plans "to get hold of him in his own time, [...] according to the rules of the game" (SA 112). Yet it becomes clear that the only thing terrorists and anarchists share is the capacity for mutual deception, isolation, and lack of organization. Heat, the novel's detective figure "armed with the defensive mandate of a menaced society" (SA 79), tries to follow the rules and thinks he knows them. Yet he completely fails to predict Verloc's move of bombing and has to admit that the anarchists the police had been monitoring had nothing to do with it. Ellen Burton Harrington reads Conrad's novel therefore as a negation of traditional detective fiction because it perverts ideals such as truth and justice (Harrington 1999: 114; 117–18). Another relevant argument is made by Alex Houen who observes that the innovative aspect of Conrad's plot lies in the suggestion that individual events are simultaneously inseparable from wider plots, yet "the possibility that an episode might *not* be connected to a general scheme is precisely what threatens the efficacy of surveillance and control. [...] this also threatens governmental and legislative stability" (Houen 2002: 50; original emphasis).

There is, however, one character who, at least in one scene, proceeds with icy efficiency and the sharpness of a detective mind: Winnie. After Verloc returns home, she minutely observes his behaviour, noticing small deviations from his routine and the prolonged scene builds suspense towards the murder of Verloc. Unlike in traditional detective fiction, in the novel the focus is not the police discovering the truth about Stevie's death and the political plot surrounding it, but Winnie's shocking realization about her husband's true nature and the loss of her brother. Significantly, after the discovery of Verloc's secret identity, Inspector Heat and Verloc only contemplate the risks a full disclosure poses to the system, treating Stevie's death as a tragic casualty. They agree that it is impossible to clear up the affair by letting the public in on the "full story" and that Verloc's confession would be counterproductive by "laying waste of fields of knowledge, which, cultivated by a capable man, had a distinct value for the individual and for the society" (SA 185–186). With the men thus occupied with their on-going games of alleged terror-risk management, they make the fatal mistake of ignoring Winnie, who silently "expressed the agitation of rage and despair, all the potential violence of tragic passions" (SA 187).

It is commonly observed that Stevie and Winnie are the story's real anarchists and Conrad underlines the focus on Winnie in the "Author's Note" to the text. However, the implications this has for the novel's risk discourse have not been fully explored. Winnie possesses the very strength of conviction lacked by the anarchists. Her commitment to her cause, the protection of Stevie, is absolute because "he was connected with what there was of the salt of passion in her tasteless life – the passion of indignation, of courage, of pity, and even of self-sacrifice" (SA 155). It gives her a singleness of purpose that is described as largely instinctual; consequently she rejects partaking in the anarchist's favourite pastime in the novel, i.e. "barren speculation", and lives according to the belief "that things did not stand being looked into" (SA 159). By having the anarchist story reside essentially with Winnie, *The Secret Agent*, Ian Ward notes, acknowledges the phenomenon that a rather striking number of Russian anarchist terrorists at the time were female, "a gendered fact that "caused special consternation amongst the terrified and the thrilled" (Ward 2008: 261). More crucially perhaps, the novel alludes to the persisting association of women with madness and criminal destructiveness. Winnie's turn to violence also evokes the timely spectre of suffragette violence, representing the force of unpredictable, infuriated women, who demand freedom to act after years of peaceful struggle for their rights. But above all, the terror emanating from Conrad's telling of "Winnie Verloc's story to its anarchistic end of utter desolation, madness and despair" (SA 7), is not due to gender, but her embodiment as a general unpredictability of ordinary individuals turning violent. It is the terror of the risk of destructive powers lying dormant within people who escape surveillance, as the whole development of the murder scene shows. In terms of causality, in Conrad's text there are also traces of the sense of mismatch and estrangement between spouses as a source of tragedy so prevalent in the writing of Eliot, Hardy, and Gissing. There is a marked lack of "sincerity of feeling and openness of statement" (SA 225) between Winnie and Mr Verloc, who also "refrained from going to the bottom of facts and motives" (SA 214). In a way, the couple is destroyed through their marriage and failing to know each other. Aided by cruel randomness, death springs from the alienation between them.

In the final scene, all of Verloc's explanations and excuses come too late and only infuriate Winnie further. Worse than his defence that he kept her in the dark out of the desire to protect her are his attempts to justify how he came to choose Steve to carry the bomb out of mere desperation: "I couldn't find anyone crazy enough or hungry enough" (SA 224). Verloc realizes his wife's murdering intentions too late. Although the narrative develops in tune with Winnie's movements as in slow motion, Verloc glimpses only for a cruel instant the danger he is in. Winnie's movement "were leisurely enough for Mr Verloc to elaborate a plan of defence involving a dash behind the table [...]. But they were not leisurely enough to allow Mr Verloc the time to move either hand or foot. The knife was already planted in his breast" (SA 228–29). Like Hardy's Tess, Winnie is driven by the overwhelming desire to protect her family and the murderous act appears in reaction to feeling a deep betrayal and despair after recognizing the futility of her sacrifice. Afterwards, the sound of Verloc's dripping blood wakes Mrs Verloc out of her passive, almost corpse-like state (SA 229), another description echoing Tess's murder of Alec. Winnie immediately starts to fear the capital punishment for her crime and seeks to escape.[28] On her initially aimless flight, she stumbles upon Ossipon and finds in him "a sensation of support, of security" (SA 236). Before his fear of Winnie's madness takes over,

---

[28] According to Mallios, as a direct "consequence of the internalized terror and authority of newspapers, Winnie pronounces sentence on herself and commits suicide" (2005: 164). While his argument underlines the crucial role of the press for the individual's risk perception, the chain of causality is more complicated.

Ossipon agrees to help, half-flattered by her attention and clueless that Winnie has not just left, but killed Verloc. Continuing the pattern running through the whole narrative, both characters are unaware of events and the other's thoughts and aim to manage different risk.

Just like Stevie's death, Winnie's suicide is not narrated directly but conveyed through the characters' readings of an inconclusive newspaper report that provokes terror and confusion rather than deliver information: "*An impenetrable mystery seems destined to hang for ever over this act of madness or despair*" (SA 265; original emphasis). Fittingly, the narrative ends shortly afterwards with two men walking through the city, one desperate and one mad. Ossipon walks away, broken by his fears and seeking solace in beginning to drink his way towards ruin. The Professor continues on walking, "terrible in the simplicity of his idea calling madness and despair to the regeneration of the world. [...] *He passed on unsuspected and deadly, like a pest in the street full of men*" (SA 269; my emphasis). He is the only character whose illusion of control over his own life (and death) is left intact. As a closing image which denies the reader any reassurance of order and safety, he is the personified risk of destruction and unpredictability.

The narrative satirizes fears of invasion and ridicules the terror/counter-terror plotting, but portrays the alienation between people as an imminent danger resulting from modern life. Paradoxically, depending on the circumstances and aiding the characters' helplessness and confusion both ignorance and knowledge about one's environment and the wider world constitute risks. If for Winnie an "uninquiring acceptance of facts" is initially her "force and her safeguard in life" (SA 138), once the safe veil of ignorance is ruptured, her knowledge about the incident triggers a chain of events that leads her to suicide. If there is one certainty in the novel, it is the belief that "Madness alone is truly terrifying" (SA 36).[29] Though ironized in Ossipon's "scientific" fear of degenerative insanity, madness and despair are also the only forces to shake people out of their stupor and achieve change. While Conrad apparently had very mixed feelings about the social order Mr Verloc wishes to protect, the status quo ultimately remains intact. In a narrative exposing "the poor expedients devised by a mediocre mankind for preserving an imperfect society from the dangers of moral and physical corruption" (SA 225), risk, as a category of perception, is completely devoid of hope, gains, or thrill. If life seemingly does not follow any predictable rules, risks

---

29 See also A.N. Monkhouse's 1907 review of *The Secret Agent* in which he asserts the relation between terrorism, randomness, and the sense of danger for innocent individuals: "Attacks on crowned heads and even malignant attacks on the crowd are intelligible, if not calculable, and it is madness alone that really terrifies a community" (cited in Sherry 1973: 182).

become impossible to manage; instead they are instead associated with negative unavoidability and a sudden, random forcefulness. To vary Karl Marx's famous phrase, Conrad's novel depicts a modernity in which "all that's solid" blows up rather than "melts into air" (cf. Berman 1982). Dealing with alienation at home as well as in society, *The Secret Agent* is a testimony of Conrad's power as a novelist who wants to make us see the risks of apathy as well as of rebellion. This, at least, was the view on Conrad by one of his contemporaries, John Galsworthy: "If, at the bottom of our hearts, below our network of defences, we did not feel uncertainty, we should expire – suffocated in the swaddling bands of safety [...]" (Galsworthy cited in Sherry 1973: 204).

9.2 'Panic and Emptiness': *Howards End*

The fictions of all three writers discussed in this chapter share an underlying concern with fragmented modern society replacing the traditional, coherent patterns and stability of English life. This is very pronounced in E.M. Forster's *Howards End* (1910). Dealing with the relations between three families – the wealthy and materialist Wilcoxes, the artsy-liberal Schlegels, and the aspiring but poor Basts – it is commonly read as a classic Edwardian "condition-of-England" novel. Though Forster's text has shared the fate of most 19th-century predecessors in this category and has been critiqued for being slightly flawed and contradictory in terms of political vision and artistic style, and for its escapist ending,[30] it indisputably captures the atmosphere of anxiety that the majority of literary and cultural historians view as a keynote of the period. John Batchelor notably characterizes it as the "age of anxiety", fuelled by the progressing erosion of old certainties which left the Edwardians and their writers with the sense of an ever increasing void of values and full of scepticism about the future of progress and the aims of the individual and society.[31] Undeniably "a consciously political book" (Batchelor 1982: 226), *Howards End* presents a quiet but haunting response to a gamut of early 20th-century fears. It is a novel about the loss of values that Forster cherished and whose survival he saw at stake, a narrative symptomatic of a particular cultural moment, of

---

[30] See, e.g., Duckworth (1997).
[31] See especially chapter 1 in Batchelor's *The Edwardian Novelists* (1982); see also Nowell-Smith's *Edwardian England 1901–1914* (1965), Kemp, Mitchel and Trotter's *The Oxford Companion to Edwardian Fiction* (2002a), and Trotter's *The English Novel in History, 1895–1920* (1993). For an introduction to the period from a historical viewpoint see Tuchman's *The Proud Tower: A Portrait of the World Before the War 1890–1914* (1966).

"that Indian summer of Victorian liberal-humanist culture" (Widdowson 1977: 7) before WWI.[32] But despite transporting a sense of imminent breakdown, Peter Widdowson argues (1977: 12), Forster's novel affirms a vision of "hope this side of the grave" (HE 282), of "the earth beating time (HE 290). It is a hope, however, which remains bound to the fact that money is the ultimate cushion of risks surrounding the individual. This is perhaps the most crucially realist and very Edwardian aspect of the narrative pinned against any modernist sense of instability. Nonetheless, economic-physical as well as spiritual risks are negotiated in the two major plotlines, focussed on Leonard Bast and Margaret Schlegel respectively.

C.F.G. Masterman's assessment of instabilities and anxieties in *The Condition of England* (1909), an inevitable touchstone for any analyses of the era (see Kaplan and Simpson 1996: ix) as well as of Forster's novel, alongside Masterman's study *In Peril of Change* (1919) provides a frame of references for reading *Howards End* as a portrayal of Edwardian risk society. In the concluding chapter of *The Condition of England*, tellingly entitled "The Illusion of Security", Masterman dramatically describes the challenge for anyone seeking social reform as a high-risk rescue mission, because one is confronted with "a society beyond measure complex, baffling and uncertain in its energies and aims. [...] *Humanity 'at best' appears but as a shipwrecked crew which has taken refuge on a narrow ledge of rock*, beaten by wind and wave; which cannot tell how many, if any at all, will survive when the long night gives place to morning" (1909: 302–303; my emphasis).

The call for "connection" inherent in *Howards End*'s famous epigraph and the negotiation of the theme in the novel involves an ambivalent discourse of risk and debate of the appropriate means to rescue humanity from shipwreck. "Only connect…" is usually interpreted as the author's plea for extending ties of sympathy according to liberal humanist ideals. The epigraph readdresses the Victorian question of the possibility of peaceful connections across class lines, of bridging gaps of money, status and education.[33] Forster himself wrote: "'Only connect…' is not an optative, it is a declarative [...], a formula for survival'" (cited in Stone 1996:

---

[32] Peter Widdowson's study *Howards End: Fiction as History* offers a still valid and comprehensive evaluation of *Howards End* as writing "history from within" (1977: 11); despite many shortcomings, e.g. Forster's pronounced country nostalgia and the exclusion of the realities of London and its poor, the vast majority of criticism considers the novel as a realist portrayal of a particular moment in history.

[33] Delany (1988: 288) argues that the phrase "Only connect" also applies to economic links between the characters, alluding to the ways in which all members of society are connected for better or worse to the same workings of capital.

174); thus he sought to affirm the urgency of people either treating each other with kindness or risking to perish. Yet in terms of language and due to its focus on the life of the middle classes, the narrative's emphasis is on maintaining safety rather than danger and risk-taking. The novel thus explores the schizophrenia which we have come to perceive as the characteristic condition of the Edwardian age because there are, to some extent, equal grounds for arguing for the dominance of change and insecurity as there are for prosperity and security.[34] Although it is necessary to acknowledge that the popular image of the Edwardian era tends to be somewhat reductive and mythologized in socio-economic terms (see Kemp, Mitchell, and Trotter 2002b: xi), and one may legitimately doubt whether the dualism of "all glitter for the rich, all tight-rope walking on the poverty-line for the poor" (Nowell-Smith 1965: viii) holds up, especially if one moves the focus away from London, Forster's novel reinforces rather than deconstructs such an image. It thematizes various middle-class anxieties at the end of a long century of British political and economic pre-eminence, as well as realties of expanding wealth and the persisting terror of the increasingly dispossessed lower classes. The threat of the abyss, a risk metaphor which occurs several times in *Howards End*, is a pervasive image of the time employed to express the nightmarish vision of falling over the edge into a bottomless pit of poverty. This fear reverberates through contemporary fictions, pamphlets, and sociological texts such as C.F.G. Masterman's *From the Abyss* (1902), Jack London's *The People of the Abyss* (1903), and H.G. Wells's "In the Abyss" (1897), to name but a few. Aside from the fear of economic downfall, David Medalie argues, the fear of the abyss is symptomatic for the era's sense of stable ground becoming "insecure beneath one's feet" (Medalie 2002: 9). Many anxieties come from the feeling that the forces of modernity intruded into the individual's life and rendered it powerless. With the abyss symbolizing an incalculable, bottomless vastness, "the same lack of control is expressed in relation to social phenomena such as overpopulation, unemployment, urbanisation, the growth of the suburbs and the consequential whittling away of the countryside" (2002: 9), which are all threats of modernity referred to in *Howards End*. However, the threats of the time do not only come from below or within, but also from abroad. Seen against the background of the mounting industrial and

---

34 Tuchman describes the period as "culmination of a century of the most accelerated rate of change in man's record. [...] [Man] entered the Twentieth with his capacities in transportation, communication, production, manufacture and weaponry multiplied a thousandfold by the energy of machines. [...] By the time he left the Nineteenth Century he had as much new unease as ease" (1966: xiv–xv).

military rivalry between Germany and England, the Schlegel sisters with their half-German ancestry, who end up inheriting and living at Howards End, the symbolic English country house, arguably function as a vague representation of the 'German' threat. Although this foreign invasion anxiety is treated with the same sense of distance as the risks of racial degeneration, mass culture, socialism or the suffragette movement,[35] *Howards End*, as Elizabeth Bowen contends, "for all its Edwardian surface, is a violent novel" (Bowen 1962: 132). While far from reaching the dark intensity and the despair that shapes Conrad's *The Secret Agent*, it shows the explosive potential springing from opposing views of life and a lack of mutual understanding, the frailty of liberal values, and the destructive force of the 'flux' of modernity.

Evoking the 19th-century novel of manners in its opening chapters, from the beginning the text raises questions about differences between people and the risks of being hurt or abused. With an ironic undertone, Forster's narrative voice introduces the Schlegel's safe financial situation and their traits of character that predestine them for getting into trouble, namely impulsiveness and a naïve trust in the world. These might cause a lack of caution and lead to risky associations with the wrong kind of people; "it was dangerous and disaster was bound to come" (HE 12). In this spirit, Margaret, always anxious for her sister, leaps without a moment's hesitation into trying to manage the "crisis" of Helen's briefest of engagements to Paul. Affirming the importance of money, Margaret announces her income to the reader as follows: "You and I and the Wilcoxes stand upon money as upon islands. [...] I stand each year upon six hundred pounds, and Helen upon the same [...] as fast as our pounds crumble away into the sea they are renewed – from the sea" (HE 52). A clear statement of their financial security, the metaphor of insularity does not signal isolation but a safe ground of privilege. Through the depiction of the Schlegels and their awareness that "there's never any great risks as long as you have money" (HE 51), the novel negotiates the indeed "brutal premise that only a small section of the population will ever be able to find a place on terra firma" (Medalie 2002: 11). Like the Schlegel siblings, Forster himself did not have to work for a living and was part of the English rentier class.[36] Worries about money concerned the author throughout his life, not about either getting or losing it, but, Wilfred Stone points out, about "how to possess it, how to be

---

35 See Widdowson, who writes that in the novel "[m]any of the insistent realities of Edwardian life [...] hang in the air, but they are not allowed to obtrude" (1977: 93).

36 Forster's family background and childhood inheritance of 8000 pounds made him a member of the English rentier class, those who could afford to live exclusively off their wealth, freed from the responsibility for an estate or having to earn a living through work. See Delany (1988).

an honourable have in a world of have-nots" (Stone 1979: 69).[37] Accordingly, *Howards End* only hints at the topic of financial speculation and it works out as a no-risk activity with gains for the middle-class characters, e.g. when Helen Schlegel reinvests the money from selling her shares in the Nottingham and Derby Railway, and "owing to the good advice of her stockbrokers", becomes "rather richer than she had been before" (HE 219).

Meanwhile Leonard Bast is introduced as the character standing "at the extreme verge of gentility. He was not in the abyss, but he could see it, and at times people whom he knew had dropped in, and counted no more" (HE 38). At the heart of the Helen-Leonard plot lays, in fact, a case study of the destructive effects of capitalist modernity on the urban poor and failed risk management, the later triggered in equal parts by the Wilcoxes's lack of concern and the Schlegels's misguided philanthropism. Following a snap remark by Henry Wilcox about the momentarily uncertain future of the Porphyrion Fire Insurance Company, the Schlegel sisters urge Mr Bast to give up his secure position as a clerk there. This advice proves ruinous to Leonard who is soon afterwards made redundant at his new, much lower paid job at a bank. At the same time the Porphyrion, as Mr Wilcox casually mentions, is again "safe as houses – safer" (HE 161). While Leonard's fall is also presented in eugenic terms in the narrative, he cannot be rescued by Helen's charitable endeavours which only endanger him further. After the disastrous excursion to Oniton where Helen drags the exhausted Basts in order to appeal to Henry's social conscience, Helen's plan of compensation is to send Leonard a cheque over the fantastic sum of five thousand pounds, half of her total wealth. She acts with the aim to properly help raise "one person from the abyss; not these puny gifts of shillings and blankets" (HE 216). The repercussions of Leonard's rejection of Helen's help are of a tragic irony. The Basts are evicted for not paying their rent and thus officially fall into the abyss, Helen makes a huge financial profit through reinvesting the money she deemed dispensable in the first place. Leonard refuses the cheque out of pride, or possibly, Wilfred Stone argues, because he has through his involvement with the Schlegel sisters at this point "already suffered too much at the hands of outrageous fortune to risk any more" (Stone 1969: 115). Helen's failed support plan of the Basts and its implications are not pursued in any detail in the narrative but serve to show contrasting opinions about what forms philanthropy should take and whether it can be effective or harmful. In the social Darwinist view of the matter, embodied by Henry Wilcox, Helen's pity and felt responsibility for the poor Basts is an instinct that needs strong

---

37 See Stone (1969; 1979).

guidance by reason. Henry rejects the idea of financial burdens or other risks being imposed upon efficient members of society through "thoughtless" reformers such as Helen and their "obsessive pursuit of worthwhile 'causes'" (Widdowson 1977: 29). Both Schlegel sisters demonstrate a sense of duty to aid less fortunate members of society, yet Helen's dramatic behaviour, her temporary break with her family over the Basts' case, and the ultimate failure to rescue Leonard, only supports Henry's dismissal, characteristic of popular eugenic views of much philanthropy "as a cowardly escape from harsh reality" (Searle 1981: 49). Even Margaret worries about Helen's behaviour, although she sees it more as a manifestation of her aggression against Henry and the Wilcoxes' way of life: "Reaction against the Wilcoxes had eaten into her life until she was scarcely sane. At twenty-five she had an idée fixe. What hope was there for her as an old woman?" (HE 237).

In *Howards End*, the English capital is again the prime locus of showing modernity as overwhelming and destructive to the individual, as in *The Secret Agent*. Though the setting is generally much less dark, alienating and obscure, especially Margaret, who dreads change and dislikes speed, feels continually threatened by the "flux of London. [...] all the qualities, good, bad and different, streaming away – streaming, streaming forever" (HE 156). Her sense of flux culminates when the Schlegels are uprooted from the stability of their family home. Regina Martin relates this plot event to the era's transition from industrial to finance capitalism and increasing real estate speculation, which "unmoors the Schlegels and sets them adrift in the sea of London" (Martin 2013: 452). The negative influence of the city's real estate developments aside, Forster's disaffection for modern London is obvious in the emphasis of it being a health risk. The city is described as hectic and overcrowded, "exhaling her exhausted air" (HE 92); even Mrs Wilcox's death is attributed to London having "done the mischief" (HE 75). Forster's diagnosis of ills echoes Masterman's, who claimed "without a shadow of uncertainty, great London itself will become but a vast tomb for all its busy people" (Masterman 1909: 288). A handful of critical accounts in the late 1990s have suggested that Forster's unease with the transformation of modernity in the novel even reveals a sense of environmental risk and ecological consciousness *avant la lettre*.[38] Stone for example argues that *Howards End* captures the movements of change and impact of capitalism also "on 'nature,' or what be called the environment or the ecosystem" (Stone 1996: 172). It is certainly plausible to consider *Howards End* as an examination of

---

[38] Royle reads *Howards End* as "first modern ecological novel in English" (1999: 49); see also Stone (1996) and Duckworth (1997: 5).

Forster's lament for the death of a green England in the face of rapid industrialization and in relation to the question if the machinery of progress is compatible with human survival. The novel relates the increasing presence of motor cars not only to a new and dizzying speed of transportation but to a growth of air pollution and negative impact of the emissions on the environment: "And month by month the roads smelt more strongly of petrol, and were more difficult to cross, and human beings heard each other speak with greater difficulty, breathed less of the air, and saw less of the sky. Nature withdrew: the leaves were falling by mid-summer; the sun shone through dirt with an admired obscurity" (HE 92). Elsewhere, Forster also comments nostalgically on the destruction of nature: "I am glad to have known our countryside before its roads were too dangerous to walk on and its rivers too dirty to bathe in, before its butterflies and wild flowers were decimated by arsenical spray, before Shakespeare's Avon frothed with detergents and the fish floated belly-up in the Cam" (Forster 1960: 1230). Still, it would be far stretched to view Forster as a 'environmentalist' in our contemporary sense, as Wilfred Stone has to admit, because the author's "lament for a despoiled nature is essentially the voicing of a personal fear and grief [...] and only incidentally a moral argument for the health and welfare of the planet" (1996: 183). Forster's concerns about urbanization and technological advances threatening the environment nonetheless remain of interest. Even though the ecological is not the main risk scenario depicted in the novel, it is part of early 20th-century anxieties and the text hints at an awareness that the developments of modernity entail speculation "with a priceless inheritance and flirting with catastrophe" (Stone 1996: 172).

Apart from depicting modern urban life as damaging to nature as well as to people's health, Forster engages with contemporary fears of race degeneration, though in a different way than Conrad does in *The Secret Agent*. The focus is on eugenic thought that found expression in a mushrooming volume of popular and scientific literature on the topic in the decade before WWI. With apocalyptical fears having customarily intensified at the fin-de-siècle, new sustaining fuel comes from medical science and a "biologizing of social theory" (Trotter 1993: 114). The theme of pessimism and degeneration in literature and art at the fin- de-siècle is a very familiar one. Yet, as sociologist Richard Soloway emphasizes, "the intense relationship of these often emotional ideas to the dry, dull population statistics of the twentieth century, which preoccupied a significant segment of the educated British public for decades" (Soloway 1990: xi) has received much less attention. Rooted in Victorian ideas about biological determinism and the debate about nature vs. nurture,[39] Eugenics and its evaluation of classes, ethnic and cultural groups, sprang from a line of tradition stretching from Charles Darwin to Francis Galton. The theory of natural selection provided the base work for the growing climate of degeneration anxieties and projections of "a new 'dark age'" (Searle 1981: 32).[40] The debate of racial decline and the eugenic movement gain momentum against the political background of the Boer War because the pessimistic assessment of English national physique and project of race improvement relate directly to seeking to manage the risk of losing control of the Empire. There is a distinctly sensational quality to Eugenic thought but its popular mediations based on frightening prognostics about "what would happen if present trends were allowed to proceed unchecked" (Searle 1918: 28–29) are also a testimony to the further implementation of statistics in numerous domains and popular discourse.[41] Eugenics, which basically sought to stop the hereditary spreading of 'unfitness' via selective breeding, appears as a politicized and sensationalized method of risk assessment via prognostics and the calculation of probabilities rather than a science in its own right. Forster's novel reflects this climate of scientifically-backed fears perpetuated through popular tracts such as Everard Dingby's "The Extinction of the Londoner" (1904), Sidney Webb's *The Decline in the Birth-Rate* (1907), and Ethel Elderton's *Report on the English Birth Rate* (1914), which all claim the statistical soundness of their gloomy assessments.[42] The factual absence of reliable data and the, in fact, rather contradictory statistics did not stop cries of doom disguised as scientific analyses.[43] Even reputable medical journals

---

39 Like terrorism, eugenics is a risk discourse that relates to 21st-century debates in the risk society. This becomes clear, for example, when one considers Dan Stone's argument about the ongoing concern with hereditary risk: "Indeed, many discussions of genes today – often involving the reduction of real people to their genes, and hence the dangerous abstraction and reification of human beings – mirror exactly the discussions about heredity of a century ago" (2002: 137).
40 Francis Galton, Charles Darwin's cousin, is credited with the coinage of the term 'eugenics', which he defined as "'the study of agencies under social control that may improve or impair the racial qualities of future generations, either physically or mentally'" (Galton 1908: 321). On the origins and development of Eugenics in Britain see Searle's *Eugenics and Politics in Britain: 1900–1914.* (1981), Soloway's *Demography and Degeneration: Eugenics and the Declining Birthrate in Twentieth-century Britain* (1990), D. Stone's *Breeding Superman: Nietzsche, Race and Eugenics in Edwardian and Inter-war Britain* (2002), and Bradshaw (2003).
41 See Desrosières's account (1998: 104 ff).
42 Galton, who gave a series of lectures on "Probability – the Foundation of Eugenics" in 1907, contends: "Skilful and cautious statistical treatment is needed in most of the many inquiries upon whose results the methods of Eugenics will rest" (1908: 321). See also Searle (1981: 7).
43 Soloway sees the fall in the birth-rate as the main catalyst that turned eugenics "from a relatively obscure, neo-Darwinist, statistically based science into an organized propagandist move-

like the *Lancet* published articles on the falling birth-rate, and Sidney Webb, for example, proclaimed that nothing less was at stake than "race degeneration, if not race suicide" (1907: 19). In the novel, Margaret remarks that "our race is degenerating" (HE 135), and the declining of the birth-rate is the topic of casual small talk on the street between Mr Cunningham and Mr Bast: "'If this kind of thing goes on the population of England will be stationary in 1960" (HE 40). Showing the preoccupation with the future of the English nation and its potential rulers, Forster's narrative also echoes contemporary socialist ideas that the change and revolution must take place within the human species and not come from the outside, i.e. in the form of social organization (cf. Taylor 1965: 299). This becomes obvious, for instance, when Forster's narrative voice, as so often using Margaret as a focalizer, asks: "The population still rose, but what was the quality of the men born?" (HE 93).

With all ideas and proposed measures of eugenics in Britain resting on an analysis of society being in need of rescue from decline, it is important to note that it had an equal concern with class as it had with race. It allowed the upper and middle classes to justify contempt for the lower classes with the belief that they were superior "in all those attributes to which humans attached value: health, sturdy physique, and intelligence" (Searle 1981: 51; see also Stone 2002: 95; 6). Engaging critically yet from a distinctly class-biased perspective with this discourse, Forster's narrator describes Leonard's inferiority in economic, physical, moral, cultural terms in negative statistical comparison: "He was not as courteous as the average rich man, nor as intelligent, nor as healthy, nor as lovable. His mind and his body had been alike underfed" (HE 39). It is hard to see the main function of Leonard's character as anything other than the representation of the dysgenic effects of modern urban life; David Bradshaw underlines this aspect saying that his "feeble, deformed, and undernourished body is the incarnation of all that dread" (Bradshaw 2007: 161). Leonard exemplifies the mass of pale young men of the urban working classes confined to lowly desk jobs and

---

ment and, more important, into a credible biological way of explaining social, economic, political and cultural change" (1990: 18) and thus into to a legitimate public risk discourse. While many proclaimed a general decline of fertility due to "progressive 'urbanization'" (Webb 1907: 4), a particular additional concern was the uneven development of the birth-rate, declining among upper classes but teamed with a by comparison excessive fertility identified by demographers among the poorest people in London. For example, much enduring alarm about the potential survival of the unfittest was caused by the prognosis made in 1887 by mathematician Karl Pearson that more than half of the next generation would be bred by no more than 15–20 percent of the present generation of married couples (see Soloway 1990: 12–13; Searle 1981: 26–27).

unhealthy living conditions in grey, unaired block of flats who were the main subjects of the popular charge of 'unfitness' – always by implication for military service. The description of the Basts's dinner, consisting mostly of different jelly cubes dissolved in water, aids the impression of mass culture reinforcing any weaknesses induced by heredity or the environment, diminishing value and substance rather than providing nutrition.⁴⁴ In contrast to Leonard, who ends up depending on his family's charity for survival rather than defending the nation, the Wilcox men epitomize a robust and healthy masculinity, well suited for ruling the world. They "keep England going" and reassuringly "breed like rabbits" (HE 233) – Henry's son Charles fathers four kids – and about Paul Wilcox, stationed in Nigeria, people say: "A nation who can produce men of that sort may well be proud" (HE 95). Through this opposition, the narrative highlights how middle-class worries about the physical unfitness of the lower classes were pinned against on-going dreams of imperial greatness.⁴⁵ The Wilcoxes clearly are England's future. But as avid lovers of all the facets of modernity, they are also unable to see Howards End as anything other than a country house past its prime and inconveniently located.

In the view of each of the main characters, Leonard is associated with a different risk. Helen, who is the only one actively trying to manage Leonard's situation and to connect with him emotionally, worries that he is ill suited to fight his way through life: "One is so afraid that circumstances will be too strong for him and that he will sink" (HE 113). Judging Leonard from a more rational perspective, Margret thinks him a third generation member of a family who has never left London,⁴⁶ all potential and vitality drained by the city. Her description, while not without a certain sympathy, also reveals a view of Leonard, as a living reminder of the risk of evolutionary failure: "Hints of robustness survived in him, [...] the spine that might have been straight, and the chest that might have broadened" (HE 98). To Henry Wilcox, who does not take enough interest in Leonard to scrutinize him in any depth, he is merely a "type" (HE 125) that the Schlegel sisters, as yet both without husbands, need protection from. Leonard's case also illustrates attitudes towards class and social welfare hinging

---

44 On the eating habits of the urban poor and their food often barely reaching nutritional minimum see Fraser (1981). See also Hegglund (1997: 412).
45 See, e. g., studies such as Arnold White's *Efficiency and Empire* (1901).
46 This echoes Galton's calculations that London-born parents transmit a certain lower degree of fertility to their children and the scientific observation cited by Everard Dingby that "during the whole of his experience he had never discovered a family completely London in birth and living, which had survived into the third generation" (1904: 15). In the novel, however, Leonard's genes survive into the next generation.

on notions of the "unfit", identified with men who "whose distinguishing feature was their inability to maintain an independent existence" (Searle 1981: 60). Forster's narrator tells the reader that Leonard after his death "would figure at length in a newspaper report", but he generally seems "not a man, but a cause" (HE 266). The father of Helen's child appears almost as a statistical abstraction in the end, his struggle with anonymity coming full circle. In the beginning, the sisters identify themselves to Leonard by their calling card; he, however, after his first visit to them "has left no address behind him, and no name" (HE 38).

Determined to prove his worth and his equality not just to the Schlegels but the world, Leonard is set on improving himself through culture, e.g. by playing the piano and reading Ruskin. Despite his strong sense of precarity surrounding him and spending most of his energies, rather aimlessly and ineffectively on "defending himself against the unknown" (HE 31), Leonard initially still shows a belief in instigating positive economic change for him and Jacky, well aware that he is her only chance to escape the abyss. Knowing deep down that trusting people, especially members of the bourgeoisie like the Schlegels, is a risk he should not take and that can only lead to disappointment, if not disaster, Leonard's contact with the Schlegels is a chance to break out of the greyness of his world. However, Leonard's aspiration and his love of adventure do not serve to individualize him, but are representative of what was perceived as another statistical truism about class differences. Comparing the current condition of the working classes to the 1840s, C.F.G. Masterman states the common perception that the reality of the poor had bettered, at least for a new majority; as a result a "longing for pleasure and excitement are common to all classes" (Masterman 1909: 209). Leonard's longing is crushed by the harsh reality of unemployment. When Helen ambushes the Wilcoxes at Oniton, acting out of anger, guilt, and her middle-class optimism that any ill can be remedied, Leonard knows that her hopes do not apply to him: "If rich people fail at one profession, they can try another. Not I. [...]. I have seen it happen to others. [...] in the end they fall over the edge" (HE 193–194). When Leonard falls, there is no network, either official or underground, to catch him. Regardless of her good intentions, Helen's interference only produces disaster. The Shropshire expedition accelerates the Basts downfall; in her agitation Helen carelessly leaves them in the hotel unable to pay the bill and without return tickets to the city. The only option for Leonard is to go begging to his family; even when his sister's family later offers him a job he is no longer capable of re-joining the work force, "too much anxiety had shattered him" (HE 271). Helen, who solely blames Henry for ruining the Basts, both through his extra-marital affair with Jackie and the damaging advice to Leonard, is as much astonished as enraged by Leonard's acceptance of the course of things. She fails to grasp that she can rebel against the Wilcoxes and what she perceives as unjust circumstances because she does so from a position of security; she possesses the physical strength and economic standing Leonard lacks.

The child, the classic symbol of hope for the next generation in the tradition of the realist novel, presents a turning point for Helen who changes towards more stability, conquers her flightiness, and grows to forgive Henry. Crushed by guilt and anxieties, Leonard is denied being able to see Helen's pregnancy as something hopeful even for a moment; in the end he is denied a future all together.[47] He dies after his already weakened heart gives way after a blow from Charles Wilcox who mistakes him for an intruder at Howards End. With the tragic irony characteristic of Forster's novel, Leonard thus dies violently from a moment of shock and a physical weakness, aided through the strong hands of a Wilcox striking him with the flat side of the Schlegel family sword and burying him under a bookcase. It is a climactic accident and links the different risk discourses running through the novel. Though Forster's own position on the subject remains ambivalent, David Bradshaw for instance, reads Charles's role in causing the death of Leonard from heart failure an enactment of "the eugenicists' most cherished fantasy, the eradication of the unfit by the fit" (Bradshaw 2007: 162). It is also interesting to consider Medalie's argument about Forster's engagement with eugenics as an intrinsic part of "the liberals' understanding of social advancement and personal betterment" (Medalie 2002: 18). He emphasizes that eugenics was attractive to liberal thought because it offered a way of control and "of minimising the power of contingency in human life" (2002: 19). However, Leonard's death in the novel is both charged with social-biological determinism and the arbitrary force of randomness. The duality is underlined by Margaret's reflections on the course of events. Although she cannot imagine how "healthy life should re-emerge" (HE 281), she is at the same time paradoxically comforted by the thought that "the future was certainly inevitable; cause and effect would go jangling forward to some goal doubtless, but to none that she could imagine" (HE 283). Showing an acceptance of chance

---

47 In *Death, Men, and Modernism*, Ariel Freedman argues that disaster in literature of "the early twentieth-century wears a male face. The face of the disaster is the face of a young, dead, man" (2003: 3), i.e. typically a soldier or lower-class ingénue. Hardy's Jude Fawley can be seen as a forerunner for the depiction of a fatally vulnerable masculinity which influenced later writers such as Woolf, Forster and Ford Madox Ford. One might add Conrad to the examples given by Freedman. The focus on the quintessentially modern figure of the young dead man, and the plotting of his death as a climactic moment, links *Howards End* (Leonard Bast) and *The Secret Agent* (Stevie Verloc).

and chaos, Forster's narrative once again echoes Masterman's diagnosis of the condition of society and people being confronted with changes "they can neither comprehend nor control" (Masterman 1919: 313). In addition, it ironizes eugenic hopes.

Despite the reflections on the uncertainty of the future and the dramatic depiction of the risk of extinction, Leonard's child is endowed with all the opportunities denied to his father. The fact that he has escaped the city seems to guarantee his survival; there is hope for Leonard's son if only he grows up at Howards End. According to David Trotter, the mismatched pairing of Helen and Leonard in Forster's novel is symptomatic of a new kind of "decline plots" which differ from the pairing of different types of degeneracy that features prominently in New Women fictions, e.g. in *Jude the Obscure*. A motif already tentatively found in Gissing's writing and in later novels by writers such as Forster and D.H. Lawrence, degeneracy is paired with the hope of regeneration (see Trotter 1993: 124). Helen embodies this hope in *Howards End*. Yet it is hard to argue that this pairing across the wide economic and cultural divide between Helen and Leonard implies a conscious strategy of biological risk management, although their child survives.

The opposition between the Schlegels and the marriage plot between Margaret and Henry offers an exploration of risks much less material and physical. After a brief moment of infatuation, Helen's opinion of the whole Wilcox family turns into a firm dislike of their façade of strength, finding "nothing behind it *but panic and emptiness*" (HE 22; my emphasis). In direct opposition to Margaret's belief that the world as long as men like the Wilcoxes will govern it will "never be a bad one" (HE 233), Helen sees them as part of a new race of empire-building supermen (there is an explicit reference to Nietzsche in the narrative), strong on the outside but hollow on the inside. I agree with Bradshaw's suggestion that the phrase "panic and emptiness", applied several times in the narrative to describe the Wilcoxes, would make an equally if not more fitting epigraph to the text (Bradshaw 2007: 170). It draws attention to the text's concern with change, vacuous energy, and fear, modifying the theme of connection by highlighting the aspect of risk inherent in following the imperative as well as in seeking to avoid it. Another recurring phrase is that of "having the hands on the ropes", a metaphor the characters use to describe those they admire for their alterity and their seemingly safe grip on life – always in perceived contrast to their own sense of slippery precariousness. For example, the Schlegels are drawn to the Wilcoxes because they "have their hands on all ropes" (HE 23); meanwhile Leonard thinks the same of the Schlegels (HE 43). The question of survival concerns all characters except Henry Wilcox. He is the only one who actually considers himself to have his hands "on all the ropes of life"

(HE 112), at least until his break-down due to the tragic events surrounding Leonard's death and Charles's imprisonment. An integral part of the Wilcoxes's materialist approach to life is outsourcing protection and compensation for risk-taking to insurance companies; e.g. Evie nonchalantly tells the story of her car accident saying "we're insured against third-party risks, it won't so much matter" (HE 74); Charles similarly reacts to the incident with the dog on the street that made Margaret jump out of the driving car: "The insurance company will see to that" (HE 181). The second form of typical Wilcox' behaviour is more important in the narrative. Full of faith in their own survival skills, it becomes clear that the one risk in particular the Wilcox men can only manage trough strict avoidance is that of the emotional entanglements that come with personal relations. Detachment is a strategy for Henry and Charles to minimize affection and stop themselves from seeing and making any connections by compartmentalizing all occurrences. As a result they are able "to voyage for a little past the emotions" like Ulysses past the Sirens (HE 87). For this reason, Henry is for instance only able to comprehend Margaret's worry about Helen's behaviour and her flight abroad when he starts to consider her "madness" as a medical condition: "Henry began to grow serious. Ill-health was to him something perfectly definite" (HE 241). On several occasions the narrative underlines the Wilcoxes' fear of "the personal note in life" (HE 79) which equals emptiness and compares to a sort of "panic". It does, however, show both positive and negative aspects of pragmatism and emotional involvement. In fact, the opposition between the Wilcoxes and the Schlegels' view, although both can to afford to manage a lot of risks through financial control, is played out in their different attitudes concerning emotional risk-taking and the potential vulnerability of others. The steadiness of the Wilcoxes and the ability to detach themselves from people and events is much admired by Margaret, who sees it as an antidote to her and Helen's emotional temperament. Her acceptance of Henry's marriage proposal is as much motivated by the desire to protect Henry from himself and his deficiencies as it is a means to assure his protective guidance on practical matters she feels ill-equipped to handle: "Henry was the only hope. [...] He might know some paths in the chaos that were hidden from them" (HE 239).

But in the end, it is Margaret who possesses the strength to save everything from falling apart. Throughout the narrative, she functions as the manager of domestic and, in a sense, spiritual risk for both families. And while she recognizes the practicality of the Wilcoxes' view of life and desires steadiness herself, Margaret firmly dislikes preparing for all emergencies. Through Margaret's character, Forster's mouthpiece in the novel, the narrative emphasizes the need to embrace the risk of the unknown and show a certain blind faith in others, of holding on to the hope of influencing them through love and kindness against all odds. It also includes a reflection on the energy wasted by worrying about and seeking to manage risks that never materialize into danger that is worth quoting at length:

> Margaret realized the chaotic nature of our daily life, and its difference from the orderly sequence that has been fabricated by historians. Actual life is full of false clues and signposts that lead nowhere. *With infinite effort we nerve ourselves for a crisis that never comes.* [...] On a tragedy of that kind our national morality is duly silent. It assumes that preparation against danger is in itself a good, and that men, like nations, are the better for staggering through life fully armed. *The tragedy of preparedness* has scarcely been handled [...]. *Life is indeed dangerous,* but not in the way morality would have us believe. *It is indeed unmanageable,* but the essence of it is not a battle. It is unmanageable because it is a romance, and its essence is romantic beauty. (HE 91; my emphasis)

The passage contains a romanticization of instability and a call for embracing the unpredictability of life that appears only convincing if uttered from a position of relative safety, i.e. when one's existence is not threatened in its core. Still, it serves well to demonstrate the specific risk language employed by Forster all through *Howards End* and shows the emphasis placed on risk as an inescapable, essential part of the human outlook on life.

Margaret's approach to risk and human relationships is treated in equal if not greater depth than the Bast-plot. Interestingly, her conception of kindness and the "the inner life" as an investment that will pay off in the end slightly contradicts the underlying argument about the need to free human relations from being guided by rational calculation and to "only connect". Though Margaret does loyally – and perhaps irrationally – stand by Henry and Helen and is able to disregard their flaws, her feelings towards them are often described with phrases and metaphors borrowed from economic or actuarial assessments. For example, faced with the fact that her sister will always disagree with her on the opinion of the Wilcoxes, Margaret feels that "[t]heir inner life was so safe that they could bargain over externals" and that she was "assured against estrangement" (HE 167). In her marriage, Margaret has to tread more carefully; she conforms to the role as loyal wife and tries to manage Henry in order to avoid rows and achieve her ends with a mix of tactics and instincts. Her caution backfires, however, when Henry discovers the identity of Jacky and perceives it all as a female manoeuvre to humiliate him. Margaret brings herself to forgive Henry his angry outburst and past transgression, significantly through finding solace in statistics: "He was a good average Englishmen, who had slipped" (HE 210). After the Oniton incident Margaret assesses the risk of getting seriously hurt in her marriage, and considers it minimal; she is, however anxious about having "mismanaged" (HE 211) her sister and the situation with the Basts.

Always striving for diplomatic, affectionate control over her family, as losing that is the highest risk to Margaret, she succeeds in the end. The novel's final pastoral scene is a tentative triumph of restored harmony and safety, set over a year after the tragic events. Margaret has managed to pull the family together and settle at Howards End. Read pessimistically, Forster's narrative suggests that connections between the classes remain utopian and that the condition of England, the development of mass consumer culture aside, has improved little since the Industrial novel. Contact with the other still bears the risk of upheaval and contamination for all, but the actual losses are distributed unevenly and fall exclusively on the lower class characters; e.g. Jacky's chances in life are twice ruined by Henry, Helen does not 'fall' despite conceiving a child out of wedlock. And the image of safety restored in the end is largely made possible through the – however accidental – eradication of the threats from below; Leonard dies and Jacky is never mentioned again. Depicting harmonious connections as difficult enough to establish between men and women and between the members of one class, the ending suggests that distance is a saving grace. The removal from the city offers an at least temporary escape from the risks of urban modernity. Yet the invasion of the countryside by the city suburbs looms on the horizon, a sign of changes on a global scale: "London's creeping [...] Life's going to be melted down, all over the world" (HE 289–290). Margaret can only set the illogical wish that the old permanence, represented by their old country house, will survive against the odds of these unstoppable developments: "they had no right to be alive. One's hope was in the weakness of logic" (HE 290). In this spirit, the ending restores a sense of order and continuity. Margaret takes on the material and spiritual legacy of the late Mrs Wilcox, as she was the only one to recognize the value of Howards End, which will be passed on to Helen and Leonard's son. Arguing that Forster's novel commodifies a nostalgic sense of loss and endangerment, Elizabeth Outka reads the ending as an "ambivalent gesture towards purification" revealing the author's "nostalgic desire to preserve a space [...] away from the commercial 'taint' of urban life" (2003: 331; 346). Several readings see the retreat to Howards End as Forster's attempt to 'purify' the present by preserving the past and save both from contamination by the onrush of the chaos of modernity. Hegglund (1997: 400) and Delany (2002: 139–140) emphasize the symbolic paralleling of the domestic and the nation and the old country house's function as a promise of safety from any exterior threats and infection by 'unhealthy' mass culture. Stone writes that in the end: "The elect are saved not by connection, but by quarantine" (Stone 1979:

77). The rhetoric shared by these arguments reveals the underlying preoccupation with danger, potential loss and contamination crucial to any risk discourse.

As a novel concerned with a projection of England's future, in contrast, for instance, to Gaskell's *North and South,* opposition and class conflict are not resolved into complementarity. Mediation is only achieved between the Schlegels and the Wilcoxes; the Basts are removed from the picture. Two further aspects are of importance. *Howards End* negotiates Forster's belief that personal relationships offer "something comparatively solid in a world full of violence and cruelty" (Forster 1951: 77), a view that differs radically from the Victorian novels discussed in this study. Neither does Helen 'fall' through her involvement with Leonard, nor does marriage cause danger and misery to Margaret or Henry. Secondly, the novel testifies to Forster's struggle with the fact "that values cannot survive without secure financial support" (Widdowson 1977: 19). The ending reinforces the impression that the most secure means of risk management are money and distance – although sympathy and mediation are helpful. Closing with a scenic depiction of hope overcoming fear and dissonance, *Howards End* still leaves the reader questioning the longevity of what Masterman viewed as the most remarkable illusion at the beginning of the 20th century, that of security.

9.3 Ordinary Apocalypse: *Coming Up For Air*

If Conrad and Forster's novels present modernity "as a crisis and even as an apocalypse; something which must be opposed" (Medalie 2002: 7), George Orwell's *Coming Up For Air* (1939), continues the theme but with a marked difference that is rooted in its time of production. As the text is written in the inter-war period and published just a few months before the outbreak of WW2, illusions of safety are clearly no longer tenable and fears of decline and destruction have taken on an unprecedented reality. Orwell's fourth novel is commonly perceived as a transitional text, summing up the themes of the author's 'poverty books' of the 1930s and anticipating his cultural-political satires and essays of the 1940s. Although *Coming Up For Air* is regarded as a 'minor' novel in comparison to works such as *Homage to Catalonia, Animal Farm* and *1984,*[48] it foreshadows many of the topics of Orwell's later famous

---

48 Though equally if not better known for his non-fictional journalistic writing during the 1930s Orwell also published four novels, *Burmese Days* (1934), *A Clergyman's Daughter* (1935), *Keep the Aspidistra Flying* (1936), and *Coming Up For Air* (1939), which all more or less explicitly address social and political issues. A particular and influential branch of Orwell criticism unjustly sees the author's fictional works of the decade flawed artistically by a sense of political urgency that

political and dystopian fictions, including the advent and effects of totalitarianism and the concern with language as an instrument to control society, history, and identity.[49] The plot is structured around the first-person narrator George Bowling's desire to return to the past, to his pre-war childhood in the Oxfordshire town of Lower Binfield, a rural, less industrialized society, and thus more 'securely' in touch with the continuities offered by provincial life, tradition and history. Yet in contrast to *Howards End*, the pastoral idyll is no longer available as an escape from the risks of modern life. Like most of Orwell's fictional works, it raises questions about preservation and survival pinned against gloomy anticipations of the future, suggesting that the effects of consumer mass culture, a loss of individual agency, a paralysing disillusionment and, ultimately, self-destruction constitute the risks faced by individual and society at this particular historical moment.[50] Orwell biographer George Bowker describes the author's state of mind while writing thus:

> Many of the acute fears he felt at this time permeate *Coming Up For Air* – a repetition of 1914 and the abolition of truth, the bombing of towns and the threat of the concentration camp. Isolation in Morocco had distanced him from the daily ebb and flow of news and prevailing air of crisis [...], he was able to achieve a novel that was both highly personal and yet politically and socially perceptive [...]. (Bowker 2003: 249)[51]

One frequently finds the biographical argument that Orwell wrote *Coming Up For Air* in Marrakech during a period of detachment from the events in England and after having reread his favourite Dickens's novels which inspired the imaginative return to his own schooldays when war still seemed unthinkable.[52] Nonetheless,

---

culminates in *Coming Up For Air*. Cf. Eagleton's assessment: "The sense of social reality is still alive [...] but it has taken the form of rambling, unstructured social-documentary observation which cannot be significantly related in feeling or quality to contemporary life" (1974: 24).

49 On Orwell's concern for language and its misuse and ideas for its reform that remained with the writer throughout his career see Woodcock (1987). For a detailed study of Orwell's life and writing and the intensifying alarm at the political-moral state of the world progressing from *Coming Up For Air* to *1984*, see Woodcock's *The Crystal Spirit* (1984: esp. 255)

50 See Levenson's argument that Orwell's novels of the 1930s "could only have been written in that decade", for they all recognize a sense of imminent catastrophe and are pervaded by a "double sense" of literary belatedness and social emergency (2007: 59).

51 For biographical background information on Orwell's works see Bowker (2003).

52 Meyers points out the Dickensian passage in the narrative, detailing "cozy and mindless domestic dullness would be used satirically by most modern writers, but Orwell portrays the scene from *the point of view of a secure and protected child*" (1975: 71; my emphasis). The aim is to reveal the irretrievable loss of this security; but Orwell does so in a nuanced way that far transcends nostalgia. On Dickens' influence on Orwell and English culture during the 1930s see also Mechie (2015: 193).

Orwell's use of domestic realism and the description of Bowling's childhood is less sentimental than strategic in terms of interrogating available modes of survival, presenting, as will be shown, only one possible option.[53]

Haunted by the nightmarish vision of WW1 about to repeat itself on an even greater scale, the protagonist's monologue – addressing the reader dialogically – resonates with early 20th-century warnings "that modern civilisation carries within itself the seeds of its own destruction" (Masterman 1909: 289). Utilizing the past as a contrasting foil to the present, juxtaposing an – however idealized and essentially irretrievable – tranquillity with the imminence of destructive chaos,[54] the novel explores the question of personal liberty focussing on the life of Bowling, a 45-year old travelling insurance salesman and a typical member of the suburban lower middle-class, whose main distinguishing characteristic is his ordinariness, "you know fifty others exactly like it" (CUA 9). A comic embodiment of the common man on the one hand,[55] vainly trying to restore from the past a feeling of innocence and continuity and scheming to achieve a brief moment of freedom from his nagging wife, in the midst of his mundane domestic frustrations Bowling is acutely aware of what C.F.G. Masterman pre-WWI described as "that present danger: the instability which of necessity must prevail when vast implements of destruction are placed in the hands of a civilisation imperfectly self-controlled, and subject to panic fears and hatreds" (1909: 289). A main, hardly concealed function of Bowling's character is being the mouthpiece of the author.[56] Resembling a dire "prophet of doom" (Fink 1973: 56), Bowling repeatedly proclaims:

> '*It's all going to happen.* […] the things you're terrified of, the things you tell yourself are just a nightmare or only happen in foreign countries. The bombs, the food-queues, the rubber

---

[53] According to Levenson, realism and the focus on the ordinary can also be considered as an expression of Orwell's conviction that it is the appropriate mode of writing at the time and forms a necessary aesthetic bulwark in an era of self-delusion (see 2007: 60).

[54] Meyers (1975; 1987) has argued that the novel is predominately concerned with the apocalyptic vision of the destruction of a nostalgic dream of childhood, with the protagonist caught in a brief window of security before a destructive future.

[55] See especially Calum Mechie, who reads the novel's comedic aspects as a deliberate stylistic choice from Orwell's side, creating a "comedic counterpoint to the polemic patriotically socialist tracts of the war years" (2015: 199).

[56] Cf. Woodcock's apt description of on Bowling's character: "Sometimes he seems intended as a type of his class and period, at other times he is little more than his creator's voice […] like Don Quixote, he soon wins his way into our minds as a kind of probable improbability, and once we have made that acceptance, his monologue immediately takes on a consistency of its own" (1984: 147).

truncheons, the barbed wire, the coloured shirts, the slogans, the enormous faces, the machine-guns squirting out of bedroom windows. [...] There's no escape.' (CUA 238)

It is also obvious that the narrator is at least equally, if not more, concerned with the political regime that potentially comes *after* the war than war itself, which is frightening yet familiar and which he has, by contrast, survived once before. The scene when Bowling attends the anti-Fascist lecture organized by the Left Book Club of West Bletchley reveals Orwell's concerns with the risk of sloganizing and the manipulation of words, be it for political and commercial purposes (see Woodcock 1987: 124; 126–127). Bowling reacts with shock to the speaker's agitated warnings of Hitler: "The world we're going down into,' 'the kind of hate-world, slogan-world. [...] It was all in the sound of the little lecturer's voice" (CUA 157). For the narrator, the risk is inherent in the rhetoric of hate itself, regardless of the ideological content. At the same time he recognizes fearful projections of the very near future as the main motivation behind the lecture: "This is merely a chap who's got sufficient foresight to be a little more frightened than the others" (CUA 157). Through Bowling's reflections Orwell shows the 'average man' to be able to exceed intellectually superior men like the lecturer in the Left Book Club or the Oxford educated school-master Porteous through his almost intuitive understanding of political risk. He grants Bowling with the ability of detached analysis, e.g. when the narrator sees Porteous's learned arguments as an escape from the present "into Oxford wisdom about antiquity, [...] it soothes you, somehow" (CUA 164).

What makes *Coming Up For Air*, in Orwellian fashion, distinctly dystopian and what links it to common anxieties prevalent in late-Victorian and Edwardian fictions is that it induces the belief that Western civilization is at the verge of "blowing up" or "dying out": "Wherever we're going, we're going downwards. Into the grave, into the cesspool" (CUA 177); "everything you've ever known is going down, down into the muck" (CUA 239). The eponymous metaphor is that of suffocation, of humankind not being able to "come up for air". The fear of a certain social class of people at risk of falling into the abyss depicted in *Howard End* now concerns all of society; in fact, it seems to be already at the bottom of a pit full of rubbish. Near the end of the novel, Bowling concludes: "Coming up for air! But there isn't any air. The dustbin we're in reaches up to the stratosphere" (CUA 230). While working on the novel, Orwell admitted to Cyril Connolly: "Everything one writes now is overshadowed by this ghastly feeling that *we are rushing towards a precipice and, though we shan't actually prevent ourselves or anyone else from going over, must put up some sort of fight*" (cited in Woodcock 1984: 145; my emphasis). The author's comment captures the preoccupation of *Coming Up For Air* in a nutshell: how is one supposed to act in the face of perceived risks that seem to have assumed the status of unpreventable dangers; in particular, what options of resistance and personal as well as political risk management are viable for the common "little man",[57] epitomized by George Bowling. Besides the eponymous imagery of suffocation, the narrative includes other risk metaphors, e.g. that of drowning, of too many men being trapped on board of a burning or a sinking ship. Walking around London after picking up his new set of false teeth, Bowling is overcome by such a vision: "We're all on the burning deck and nobody knows it except me. [...] It was as if I'd got X-rays in my eyes and could see the skeletons walking" (CUA 26). Later Bowling compares the risks induced by capitalist economic competition, one of the destructive "realities of modern life" at the heart of Orwell's criticism, to "an everlasting, frantic struggle to sell things. [...] It's like on a sinking ship when there are nineteen survivors and fourteen lifebelts" (CUA 132). This is always juxtaposed with the half-intuitive, half politically well-informed foresight that Orwell credits his archetypal common man with: "There are millions of others like me. Ordinary chaps that I meet everywhere [...] have got a feeling that the world's gone wrong. They can feel things cracking and collapsing under their feet" (CUA 166).

A risk specific to average men like Bowling, born at the end of the 19th century and thus able to remember a different world, is the constant disillusionment through the confrontation with the artificiality and absurd realities of the present. In a famous scene, Bowling bites into a fake Frankfurter sausage which literally fills him with disgust of modern Ersatz-culture: "I'd bitten into the modern world and discovered what it was really made of. [...] Everything slick and streamlined, everything made out of something else. [...] Rotten fish in a rubber skin. Bombs of filth bursting inside your mouth" (CUA 24). In the last part of the narrative, when Bowling travels to Lower Binfield to regain a sense of calm, authenticity and stability, re-entry into the 'golden age' of his past is undoubtedly and unceremoniously denied. Upon arrival in Lower Binfield disillusioning discoveries follow in quick succession: George generally finds the place and its people changed beyond recognition; nobody remembers his family name, the town is an enormous, unfamiliar maze of streets: "It might have been anywhere" (CUA 189). Walking through the streets, he describes a ghostly feeling of disorientation, not insubstantially aided by the fact that he is mostly heavily inebriated. Drinking is Bowling's stubborn attempt to enjoy himself as well as a coping

---

[57] Cf. a contemporary review of the novel in the *Times* (23 June, 1939: 2) which praised it for presenting an answer to "'one of the age's puzzles' – 'the cult of the 'little man'"" (cited in Bowker 2003: 251); for a more recent perspective, see also Mechie (2015).

mechanism for his disappointment. The only familiar face he encounters belongs to his childhood sweetheart, of whom he has fond memories of leisurely summer days and first sex which are shattered by now seeing Elsie as a haggard middle-aged woman, an experience Bowling can only describe as "horrible" and "frightening" (CUA 217); the whole quiet market town has disappeared into an anonymous city of factories and sprawling housing projects; in the place of his father's corner seed store he finds an arty tea shop; hardest of all is discovering a garbage dump in the place of his secret pool swarming with giant fish; the adjoining grand manor house has been turned into a mental asylum.

While in many ways Bowling's past is hence indeed "lost even before the bombs start to fall" (Lowe 2009: 246), the climax of disillusionment is reached when the government accidentally drops a bomb on Lower Binfield during a training mission. Although the incident highlights the insignificance of Lower Binfield as a locality, and the event is generally rather anti-climactic in terms of the actual damage it causes – destroying half a house and a leg, splattering a little blood and marmalade on the high street, otherwise "it hadn't really made much impression" (CUA 237) – it epitomizes randomness, the fallibility of modern technology, as well as the fact that there is no safety for the individual even in a place with little relevance to world politics. The falling bomb, the symbol of the war to come, is ironized as a random accident, as a greater plan gone wrong that victimizes only innocent people like Stevie's fall does in *The Secret Agent*. However, hearing the bomb drop Bowling says: "A noise like the Day of Judgment, [...] it's terrible, and it's real" (CUA 233). The emphasis is on the suddenness of the attack and the inescapable yet unpredictable reality of the risk of destruction.

Orwell's narrative constitutes the present moment through a contrast of the nostalgic sense of security associated with the per-war past set against the danger of an imminent future that can come crushing down on the individual at any second. The main counter-activity – fulfilling a function similar to Howards End in Forster's novel – is fishing, the beloved pastime that dominates Bowling's teenage memories.[58] Fishing is employed as the antithesis, as "the opposite of war" (CUA 85), representing a lost civilization, a time of innocence, closely tied to nature and tradition: "As soon as you think of fishing you think of things that don't belong to the modern world. The very idea of sitting all day under a willow tree beside a quiet pool – and being able to find a quiet pool

---

58 Federico suggests that Orwell uses the novel to satisfy his desire to write about commonplace activities such as fishing and to celebrate the ordinary in his preferred style of reportage in a fictional narrative; this also serves as a deliberate counter narrative to the grand political-ideological battles of Europe at the time (see 2005: 50).

to sit beside, belongs to the time before the war" (CUA 76). Aside from the wonderful secrecy of the hidden pool in the woods, which as George Woodcock has noted, gives Bowling "the focus of personal myth" (Woodcock 1984: 149), fishing symbolizes a peaceful, reflective way of spending time that is directly opposed to the aimless hassle and terror of modern life. It evokes a crucial lost feeling "of not being in a hurry and not being frightened" (CUA 107) which Orwell not only idealizes nostalgically but its recovery is postulated as a form of risk management through 'slowing down' in order to instigate change towards a better – and, by implication, safer – future: "Stop firing that machine-gun! Stop chasing whatever you're chasing! Calm down, get your breath back, let a bit of peace seep into your bones" (CUA 173). Similar to Forster's pastoral vision, Orwell's novel suggests that seeking a life closer to nature, and, if not the present life then at least the memories of it, can function as a saving grace against the alienation of man in the technocratic age and reduce the likelihood of the advent of totalitarianism and fascism. As the author writes elsewhere:

> I think that by retaining one's childhood love of such things as trees, fishes, butterflies, [...] *one makes a peaceful and decent future a little more probable*, and by preaching the doctrine that nothing is to be admired except steel and concrete, one merely makes it a little surer that human beings will have no outlet for their surplus energy except in hatred and leader worship. (Orwell 2000: 363; my emphasis)

Thus the protagonist's desire to return to the life and locale of his childhood is less escapist and nostalgic than expressive of a (utopian) vision for the future based on the necessity to recover a sense of past security in the face of an increasingly chaotic present.[59] According to Orwell, at stake is nothing less than the survival of civilization as a whole. His narrator, therefore, does not, or at least not primarily, seek out the past out of a bourgeois mid-life crisis but out of an urgent need to guarantee his survival: "I don't even want to be young again. I only want to be alive" (CUA 172).

Bowling's opposition thus lies, as also Jeffery Meyers argues, in "this preservation of the past in the free minds of the helpless yet resisting men" (1987: 96). During his time as an officer during WW1, reading is another activity Bowling likes to engage in and which functions as a countermeasure against the erosive effects of the present. As is the case with fishing, reading allows for 'slowing

---

59 Stressing the idealistic, utopian aspect of the depiction of childhood in the narrative, Howard Fink has read *Coming Up For* Air as a "parody utopia" (1973: 58) of H.G. Wells's fictions and Wellsian socio-political idealism. However, this completely sidesteps the question of risk management and the moral, as well as aesthetic, emphasis on realism and ordinariness in the novel.

down', internal retreat and stationary, quiet reflection. It also allows for the development of critical consciousness and independent thought: "If the war didn't happen to kill you it was bound to start you thinking" (CUA 127). Annette Federico emphasizes the importance of the qualities shared by fishing and reading in Bowling's "project of survival" (Federico 2005: 60). Both are passive rather than active, solitary rather than communal, both require protection from outside disturbances, and, lastly, both can be considered "affirmative activities that may be said to constitute an ethics of hope" (2005: 60). Orwell's narrative also resonates with a critical diagnosis of fin-de-siècle fears of exhaustion and decay of the human race, the erosion of energy, inner substance and value, a perceived risk that has only increased since the war: "It's a kind of vital juice that we've squirted away until there's nothing left. All this rushing to and fro! [...] Nerves worn all to bits, empty places in our bones where the marrow ought to be" (CUA 177). Orwell was certainly not alone in perceiving the turn of the century and WW1 as watershed moments rupturing society's sense of security as well as crucially affecting people's sense of agency and capacity to affect social change. And other writers similarly conceived of the turn to the recent past as an inevitable reaction and attempt of (self-)preservation. For example, Virginia Woolf's words, written in the inter-war period, seem to directly describe the almost childish desires and the struggle of Orwell's protagonist: "It is a barren and exhausted age, [...] we must look back with envy to the past" (Woolf 1988: 356); the war "has shaken the fabric from top to bottom, alienated us from the past and made us perhaps to vividly conscious of the present. [...] We feel ourselves indeed driven to them [our predecessors; the past], impelled not by calm judgment but by some imperious need to anchor our instability upon their security" (1988: 357). It is important to note, however, that although Orwell takes 1900 as a moment in time where "[e]verything is safe, solid and unquestionable" (cited in Meyers 1975: 74), the evaluation arises only out of a favourable comparison with the present. I thus agree with Woodcock's emphasis that Orwell never contended that the late Victorian era was "an ideal age" (Woodcock 1984: 189) or a risk-free society. Yet clear-cut moral concepts and a belief in the continuity of civilization against all odds were still intact to a greater extent. In the novel, the experiences of George Bowling as a soldier during the war highlight war's effect – in addition to its direct threat to human lives – to shatter security on all levels, rob the individual of agency and instil a deep sense of futility and absurdity in its place. The narrator says: "The war did extraordinary things to people. [...] It was like a great flood rushing you along to death, and suddenly it would shoot you up some backwater where you'd find yourself doing incredible and pointless things" (CUA 120). The incredible, pointless way Bowling spends the war, after a brief spell at the frontline and a minor injury, is by guarding for two years a stack of tins of bully beef in a forgotten seaside town, regularly filling out forms on behalf of the West Coast Defence Force, but otherwise left to his own devices and boredom.

His memories of Lower Binfield, told in detailed flashbacks, paint an image of a rural, class-ridden and rather poor society, of a life devoid of modern luxuries. The crucial difference between his parents' lives, their harsh economic struggle and intellectual impoverishment, is that they were able to deal with the precarity of the present because it was firmly separated from an unbroken hope in the continuity of established patterns of life and the future. Yet the basis for this felt security that Bowling envies in retrospect is ignorance and the ability to abstain from making predictions and seeking causalities. He remembers his father's reaction to his slow demise into illness and bankruptcy: "Father had had a bad year and lost money, but was he really frightened by the future? I don't think so. This was 1909, remember. He didn't know what was happening to him [...]. All he knew was that times were bad" (CUA 96–97). Accordingly, George also does not recall himself feeling responsible to help his parents but only being a passive spectator of their inevitable decline: "It was a race between death and bankruptcy and, thank God, death got Father first, and Mother too" (CUA 105). The past meant acceptance of a by no-means comfortable existence, full of short-term personal risks ("People on the whole worked harder, lived less comfortably and died more painfully"; CUA 109), but an absence of the risk of losing (faith in) the future, and of the illusion to look at it without terror. This does not only mean a blissful ignorance about political events, but, for example, his mother's death from cancer without her ever having known about her illness. Orwell's narrator places the emphasis on the previous generation's possession of the paradoxical *"feeling of security,* even when they weren't secure" (CUA 110; my emphasis). Moreover, while the life described bears little resemblance to the standard of absolute safety of existence that is the implicit measure behind late 20th-century conceptions of the (Western) risk society, Orwell diagnoses a change of world view that hinges on a radically different experience of risk and security that Bowling's parents do not live to see: "Individually they were finished, but their way of life would continue. [...] They didn't feel the ground they stood on shifting under their feet" (CUA 111). This feeling of the ground shifting beneath captures the sense of epistemological uprooting caused by the war, the risk of losing, or having already lost, any reliable measure for good and evil. While the impeding war, and the threat of the invasion of England by German troops colours the whole narrative, according to Terry Eagleton, Bowling is also particularly disturbed by the imminent yet still somewhat incredible intrusion of politics into private lives, in other words by the idea that a known world of domestic routine "is likely to be brought into destructive collision with an abstract world of political strategy and theory" (Eagleton 1974: 32). Regarding the perception of risk, it is precisely *"this connection of the domestically known and the abstractly feared"* (1974: 32; my emphasis) described by Eagleton that constitutes the paradigm shift between the present and the prewar past, between Bowling and his parents, although their domestic lives were in many ways much less secure.[60]

George, "Fatty Bowling" (CUA 4), is in all regards the average level of his suburban environment; "I'm the middling type, the type that gravitates by a kind of natural law toward the five-pound-a-week-level" (CUA 132–133). Describing himself as "neither a go-getter nor a down-and-out" (CUA 136), he is also professionally invested in risk-aversion, working for the insurance company the Flying Salamander, "Life, fire, burglary twins, shipwreck – everything" (CUA 5). The narrative opens by showing his boredom with being a good father, husband, and employee. Although he is not the gambling type ("I don't bet as a general rule. [...] I forget the exact odds, but my share worked out as seventeen quid"; CUA 5), a little stroke of luck at the races enables him to start fantasising about taking a trip somewhere. Walking along the Strand, a poster triggers a flood of memories from "before the War", "it was as though it was back in 1900 that I'd been breathing real air" (CUA 31).[61] This settles the plan to spent the money obtained by small-scale risk-taking on another such activity, namely going back to Lower Binfield without telling his family about his plan. The mere thought of his illicit solitary trip revitalizes Bowling. He then starts schem-

---

[60] Cf. Leonard Woolf's observation that "by 1918 one had unconsciously accepted a perpetual public menace and darkness and had admitted in the privacy of one's mind or soul an iron fatalistic acquiescence in insecurity and barbarism" (1968: 9).

[61] Several critics have commented on the intertextual references between Orwell's novel and modernist classics such as Joyce's *Ulysses* or Proust's *Search For Lost Time*. Considering the plot's concentration on the protagonist's venturing out in search of an almost forgotten past, Orwell's literary treatment of visual and physical sensations as triggers of memories, the employment of trains of association and stream-of-consciousness-like reflections about man's relationship with the past and civilization of verge of disintegration, these arguments are not without plausibility (see, e.g., Meyers (1975: 79)). Arguably the most Proustian scene in the narrative is Bowling's reflection: "The past is a curious thing. It's with you all the time. I suppose an hour never passes without your thinking of things that happened ten or twenty years ago, and yet most of the time it's got no reality [...]. Then some chance sight or sound or smell, especially smell, sets you going, and then the past doesn't merely come back to you, you're actually *in* the past" (CUA 27; original emphasis). However, analyses of Orwell's style of writing have also provoked direct counter arguments, for instance by Woodcock, who contends "while *Coming Up For Air* derives a great deal from Proustian time-juggling and Proust's theories of memory, there is little sign of influence of the French writer on the actual style of this or any other Orwell book" (1984: 56).

ing in order to deceive his ever-suspicious wife, involving a complicated lie about taking a business trip to Birmingham and getting a colleague to post a false postcard from a hotel there. Ironically, he feels the need to plan his harmless time-out like an act of crime or adultery due to the lack of understanding between him and Hilda. In fact, he goes to absurd lengths to deceive his wife, which resemble, as Annette Federico notes, "the tactical moves of the person nobody notices" (Federico 2005: 52). From the moment he puts his plan in motion and leaves Ellesmere Road for Lower Binfield in his old car, he feels haunted by the ghosts of his bad conscience: "It was as if a huge army were streaming up the road behind me. [...] Hilda was in front, of course, with the kids tagging after her" (CUA 182). The narrative humorously depicts Bowling's attempts at managing the risk of discovery for an action that only involves a break from his routine and no betrayal or putting his family in financial danger. And the only real danger Bowling faces is the rage of Hilda.

In terms of their risk personalities, although Bowling is far from adventurous, his wife Hilda, stemming from a decaying Anglo-Indian family, far exceeds him in pessimism; moreover, her constant worrying about money despite living in relative lower-middle class comfort renders her oblivious to any wider political context than her immediate surroundings. She has cultivated the anticipation of financial disaster into a constant view of life; this is both a draining and sustaining force for her. George describes her as "one of those people who get their main kick in life out of foreseeing disasters. [...] The funny thing is that if we ever do get to the workhouse Hilda won't mind it a quarter as much as I shall, in fact she'll probably rather enjoy the feeling of security" (CUA 7). Hilda is not able 'to make do' as George is and her attitude does not change with an improvement of her circumstances: "What really shocks her is the fact that I refuse to worry. [...] She loves getting into a panic because something or other is 'serious'" (CUA 142). George does not share Hilda's incessant worrying about the price of butter going up, and ironizes her fears because they are exclusively tied to consumerism. At the same time, his life choices reveal a paradoxical longing for both safety and personal freedom. After the war, he had no desire to return to his previous static existence as a grocer's assistant, choosing instead a job as a salesmen on a on-commission contract travelling the country. However, he is first attracted to the insurance business because it is "fairly safe, you know. People have got to have insurance, same as they've got to eat" (CUA 134), "It's a beautifully simple method of increasing your sales and advertising your stuff without taking any risks, and it always flourishes when times are bad" (CUA 130). For this reason, Bowling joins the Flying Salamander and stays there for 18 years; in the same spirit he enters at the age of 23 into his marriage, from the beginning a predictable and joyless accelerated journey into middle-age decay and suburban life. Bowling is controlled by his marital ties to Hilda, as well as by other conventional demands of society, which are all presented as 'naturalized': "Hilda is part of the order of things. [...] Besides there were the kids" (CUA 144). With similar passive acceptance, Bowling refers to the inevitable direction of politics, i.e. the war, controlled by authorities beyond his control, "1941 *they* say it's booked for" (CUA 26; my emphasis). The forces that infringe on the narrator's freedom and sense safety come in various manifestations. For example, with the other homeowners on Ellesmere Street the Bowlings share "the ghastly fear" (CUA 13) of losing their house before they can pay off the mortgage. But Orwell always makes his narrator step back from the realistic descriptions of his domestic life through abstract reflections on the function of risk perception as a means of controlling society: "Fear! We swim in it. It's our element. Everyone who isn't scared stiff of losing his job is scared stiff of war, or Fascism, or Communism, or something" (CUA 15–16).

The above already points to the ways *Coming Up For Air* explores the themes and central image of one of Orwell's longest and best known essays, "Inside the Whale" (1940). Containing a survey of 1930s fictional writing and dealing with the question of its engagement with or rather, avoidance of, politics, the essay is mainly a critical response to Henry Miller's literary attitude of conscious passivism. Having met Miller in Paris in 1936, and studied his novels, such as *Tropic of Cancer*, Orwell was fascinated by Miller's stance of philosophic irresponsibility in the face of coming disaster and he notes: "Our civilization was destined to be swept away and replaced by something so different that we should scarcely regard it as human – a prospect that did not bother him" (cited in Woodcock 1984: 144). He compares the contemporary author's position to that of Jonah inside the whale, looking out from the inside, aware of social ills and the risks of violent atrocities in the name of politics, but rendered impotent to achieve any effects in the outside world both by the inability to be heard from inside the womb-like space and the escapist, immature desire to remain in this space of safe detachment. While Orwell explores the implications of the "Jonah in the whale"-metaphor in many of his texts, he also criticizes the fact that in the 1930s literature has inevitably become so caught up with world politics, that it struggles to give attention to the lives of ordinary men. *Coming Up For Air* presents the attempt to reconcile both aspects. By employing Bowling's "comedic, dialectical and, indeed, maverick modern voice", as Mechie points out, Orwell tries to identify and speak "to and for an imagined community of ordinary English chaps" (2015: 186). At the same time, as Woodcock argues, Orwell's narrator, "although he puts forward many Orwellian ideas, differs from his creator in being a kind of natural Millerite [...], conscious of what is happening in the world but resolutely refusing to become engaged" (Woodcock 1984: 146).

All the characters either live or seek to remain "inside the whale", by actively or unconsciously avoiding being 'in touch' with the present. This includes, for example, schoolmaster Porteous who firmly lives in the past worlds of his books and Hilda, who "even when the bombs are dropping" will be "thinking about the price of butter" (CUA 204). The characterization of Bowling's wife is representative of the ways in which consumerism – to Orwell – appears as a dangerous numbing of the population, of the risk of missing political developments and empathically engaging with the people close to oneself by being instead so fully caught up in petty domestic issues that no time remains for critical reflection. The narrator is distinguished in this regard from Hilda as well as from all the people he sees in London: "I felt as if I was the only person awake in a city of sleep-walkers" (CUA 25). So although Orwell's narrator criticizes and distances himself from the rest of English society which he perceived to be in a sleep-like state of ignorance or denial, the narrative also probes the limits of Bowling's own options for survival and depicts his attitude, necessitated by the socio-historical conditions, as an ambivalent mix of an overwhelming sense of powerlessness,[62] passive acceptance, and the firm commitment to personal survival.

Using Bowling's voice, Orwell contrasts the past the narrator longs to return to, the 1900s in Lower Binfield, when "Jonah's in the whale", and when "it was a good world to live in" (CUA 31), to the ending, when after his failed attempt to escape the present he concludes: "The old life's finished, [...] you can't put Jonah back into the whale" (CUA 237). Bowling self-consciously employs the Jonah-figure as a metaphor for his own relationship with the world, finding himself exposed and unable to return to inside the protection of the cushioning whale-belly. However, the attitude of Orwell's narrator has provoked various and contradictory readings with regard to what solution or 'moral' is implied by this realization. Put differently, the question is what options, if any, of personal and political risk management for the ordinary individual still seem to be tenable. Several critics have commented on George Bowling's role as the fictional embodiment of Orwell's Jonah in this context. Levenson argues that the protagonist, constrained from every side in his capacity to act by the prospect of the looming war and the confines of his marriage and domestic existence, "neither comprehends the political world nor tries to change it" (Levenson 2007: 72); others have seen him has a typical central figure in an Orwell novel, depicted with a "wry sense of 'realistic' impotence" (Eagleton 1974: 13), and

---

[62] On the political climate of the 30s and 40s and the strong reflection of a feeling of impotence in the novel, see Van Dellen (1975).

after some attempt at rebellion, doomed to failure, destruction or enslavement (see Woodcock 1984: 53). It is more constructive, I think, to emphasize, as for instance Richard Van Dellen has done, that what makes Bowling unique in his 'ordinariness' is precisely this paradoxical struggle of modern man (inside the whale), simultaneously trying to expose the ills of society and probing the limits of his own social confinement within (see Van Dellen 1975: 65–66). Concerning this aspect, Terry Eagleton rightly underlines the significance of the first-person narrative perspective allowing Orwell "to project a criticism of society which is the more convincing because it emerges, not from the contemptible 'abstractions' of the ideologists, but from a man trapped within its limits" (1974: 31). He situates Bowling's stance furthermore within the tradition of the typical "lower middle-class hero" in English fiction, oscillating between passive withdrawal while being caught in the middle of things, situated somewhere between fool and intellectual and between radical and law-abiding citizen.

From the beginning, the novel complicates an unambiguous view of the protagonist as passive. Rather the suggestion, though not without Orwell's characteristic irony, is that Bowling's present self resembles, in a way, both Jonah and the whale; his corpulent, aging body engages the more hopeful and rebellious agility of his past. His thinner self is literally trapped inside his bulging body, which has significantly expanded only in the decade since the first war, struggling to be remembered and heard. Bowling tells the reader:

> Mind you, I haven't always been fat. I've been fat for eight or nine years, and I suppose I've developed most of the characteristic. But it's also a fact that internally, mentally, I'm not altogether fat. No! Don't mistake me. [....] I've got something else inside me, chiefly a hangover from the past. [...] I'm fat, but I'm thin inside. Has it ever struck you that there's a thin man inside every fat man [...]? (CUA 20)

Nonetheless, the restoration of the rural peace of Lower Binfield is rendered as unlikely as that of Bowling's younger body. Thus Orwell puts forth the argument that a physical as well mental apathy of the average majority of the population would need to be shaken in order to induce change of an apocalyptic future. At the same time, Bowling is also aware that fatness, real as well as metaphorical, "prevents you from taking things too hard" (CUA 18). The fact remains, however, that the figure of an ordinary, ultimately passively accepting man, be he as committed as he might to taking some petty risks in order to obtain what little pleasures are available, is the very opposition of rebellion and political engagement. It remains up to the reader to interpret Bowling's behaviour and his dark prognostications as a call for action. Alternatively, the narrative suggests that at this point in time, with war looming so close, passive endurance and nostalgic escape form the individual's best, as most realistic, strategies for survival.

Annette Federico sums up, George Bowling "is too old to risk the kind of pointless rebellion [...] And he's too practical to imagine that people could actually return to nature or innocence or some imagined ideal past. [...] Orwell's man must make do with intense nostalgia, delinquency, and daydreams" (Federico 2005: 52). Orwell's narrator is depicted (– or rather, depicts himself to the reader), largely but not exclusively, as the victim of larger structures of society and its demands of conformity. Endurance and passive submission are the necessary modes to guarantee survival for the ordinary man, who somewhat cynically accepts his fate but refuses to let it crush him (cf. van Dellen 1975: 66; Mechie 2015: 189).

The argument that Bowling's provinciality, corpulence, and averageness give him hope for survival, hinges on the idea, expressed for instance in Levenson's reading of Orwell's fictions of the 1930s, that the author places all his faith in the decency and the conduct of the ordinary person "as the one integrity amid unavailing alternatives" (Levenson 2007: 64–65). As such, Orwell's narrative postulates and develops no major challenge to the system but the preservation of a recognizable humanism retrievable from "a notion of ordinariness not as "a state of mind, but a social practice" (2007: 70). Emphasizing that Orwell maintains faith in the pursuits and humanist and political skills of the individual, Federico concludes: "It's not revolution, but it will have to do" (2005: 62). While the personal and political spheres thus appear inseparably intertwined, the narrative is indeed motivated by the proposition that "the logic of disaster" (Levenson 2007: 74) that determines the present can only be broken by seeking out the past, through recognition and rediscovery of moral standards and ways of life. However, Bowling's nostalgic mission is a complete failure.

Considering the ending and overall atmosphere of the book, *Coming Up For Air* has therefore been criticized for being (too) apocalyptic and defeatist (see, e.g., Eagleton 1974: 30); yet especially in more recent criticism one finds justified counterarguments that such conclusive readings of the novel miss "the ethical importance of both the excessively engaging mode of its narration and the survival tactics it determinedly describes" (Federico 2005: 54).[63] The latter in particular inform my reading. If Bowling left West Bletchley in a spirit of hopeful excitement momentarily masking his anxiety, on his way home he is filled only with the overwhelming feeling that his whole trip was meaningless: "Why had I bothered about the future and the past, seeing that the future and

---

[63] See also Lowe's claim that despite its mode of anxiety and apocalyptic vision the novel shows that Orwell "had not lost his belief in the need for lasting social change and economic equality, and hoped that war and domestic revolution would be inherently connected" (2009: 245–246).

the past don't matter? [...] Nothing remained except a vulgar low-down row in a smell of old mackintoshes" (CUA 247). Having been forced to discard the past, Bowling's grim conclusion is that it will also make no difference – for "chaps like you and me" (CUA 240) what the future holds. As Harold Fink observes, at this point the narrator's "only prophesy for the future consists, ironically, of several weeks of nagging quarrels" (Fink 1973: 59). His return journey is further spurred on by a radio SOS message that he believes has been send by his wife. Adding to his already guilty conscience and the dread of the expected spousal rage, he is now overcome by fearful imaginations of actually losing Hilda. But ultimately, he recovers a sense of safety in the return to the present and resigning to his domestic routine, although he is greeted at the door by Hilda, who is very much alive and furious after the deconstruction of George's alibi. After some failed, half-hearted attempts to tell her the truth he choses passive acceptance in order to ensure the easiest and most probable return to life as he knows it, presenting any other option as futile: "She'd found me guilty [...] All I wanted was the line of least resistance" (CUA 246). The narrative thus ends with Bowling's ironic calculation of domestic risk management: He considers three possibilities, discarding (A) honesty (because Hilda is not empathic enough to listen and believe him) and (B) a fantastic excuse about amnesia (because Hilda is not stupid enough to fall for it); he thus settles for (C), the acceptance of the charge with adultery (not least because it pushes his ordinary male ego). The hope inherent in the ending of Orwell's novel and its dark prophetic warning lies in Bowling's behaviour, in the resilience of ordinary men, who have no illusion about a risk-free existence or their ability to avert risks by making them not materialize into danger, but by loyalty, mere stubbornness and survival instincts. As the author has his narrator say: "In almost all circumstance I'd make a living – always a living, and never a fortune – and even in war, revolution, plague and famine I'd back myself to stay alive longer than most people. I'm that type" (CUA 20).

10 Gendered Routines of Risk-Taking

10.1 'If You Don't Weaken': *Saturday Night and Sunday Morning*

Published at the tail end of the 'Angry Young Men' movement and coinciding with the rise of the field of British Cultural studies, Alan Sillitoe's novel *Saturday Night and Sunday Morning* (1958) is usually perceived as a classic social realist study of working-class life[1] offering insight into constructions of urban masculine identity set against the background of the post-war era and an emerging working-class consumer culture. If criticism traditionally focuses on the text's documentary qualities,[2] its capturing of what Raymond Williams (1977) influentially termed the "structures of feeling" of a generation, recent studies have argued for a more nuanced approach to Sillitoe's complex depiction of masculine consciousness and temporality, emphasizing the experimental use of narrative techniques, and the depiction of gender roles which necessitate transcending a narrow focus on class conflict and the realist frame work.[3] These aspects can be linked through an analysis of the protagonist's contradictory attitude and risk behaviour. Structured by the strict split between work and leisure time, the narrative contrasts 21-year old Arthur Seaton's numbing and backbreaking weekday routine as a lathe worker in a Nottingham bicycle factory with weekends filled with drinking, pub brawls, and adultery, that eventually cause serious consequences such as illness, an abortion, and a fight with a couple of swaddies, ordered by one of the cuckolded husbands. It ends with Arthur's plan to get married, though still assuring the reader that he will be "fighting every day until I die" (SNSM 219).

While the plot action consists of various distinctly gendered risk activities, at the heart of the narrative lays a tension between recklessness and the desire of safety and stability. For Sillitoe's protagonist and narrator, risk-taking – as thrill seeking – is a means to assert agency and to puncture routine by breaking with fixed, imposed structures of temporality and deny futurity and consequentiality. At the same time, Arthur is an unreliable narrator; aided by the text's episodic structure, the reader is lead to doubt his reiterations of irresponsibility

---

[1] The most comprehensive study of Sillitoe is still Stanley S. Atherton's *Alan Sillitoe* (1979).
[2] For an analysis of the cultural signifiers of working-class life in the text (e.g. vernacular language, typical settings like factory, home, pub) see Peter Hitchcock's *Working-class Fiction in Theory and Practice* (1989: esp. 63ff).
[3] On Sillitoe's specific use of realism see Bentley (2010) and Minogue and Palmer (2002).

which appear as desperate attempts to mask social-critical concerns and personal fears: "I couldn't care less if the world did blow up tomorrow, as long as I'm blown up with it" (SNSM 40).

The title *Saturday Night and Sunday Morning* shifts the focus away from the hero to the experience and division of time. However, Sillitoe's original title for the novel, "The Adventures of Arthur Seaton", which the publisher rejected, draws attention to the narrative's picaresque elements and suggests another line of literary tradition; it links the rebellion of the male protagonist, the (anti)hero characteristic of 'Angry Young Men'-fiction, to the Industrial novel. Both have implications for the depiction of risk. Although Arthur's exuberant masculine energy and reckless behaviour and the plot ending in marriage show parallels to older picaresque narratives like Smollett's *Roderick Random*, Arthur is not a true lover of adventure and is content to stay where he is, as long as he can guarantee temporary escapes from his work routine and social conventions. His attitude and ordinary struggle for survival, oscillating between defeatism and opportunism, as Andrea Ochsner has shown,[4] also echoes George Bowling's in Orwell's *Coming Up For Air*.

However, with regard to social and economic security WW2 is a firm dividing line. The late 1950s, having seen the rise of the British welfare state, are typically described as a time of affluence, a perception that culminates in the catchphrase uttered by PM Harold Macmillan in 1957 that a majority of people "have never had it so good". The new prosperity and greater general job security emancipated the working-classes from austerity and contributed to a changed sense of social identity that, Sally Munt points out, "promised to destroy the Victorian imaginary of the lumpen, threatening masses who lurked on the edges of British society like a savage breed" (Munt 2000: 1). Though having to work hard for his money, Arthur does not have to struggle for economic survival like his parents before the war. Still, Sillitoe's narrator is not merely an emblem of working-class affluence but always measures his experiences and riches through an inter-generational lens, a point stressed by John Brannigan, and displays a deep scepticism towards the notion that "history is unfolding towards a classless utopia" (Brannigan 2003: 60). Emphasizing the validity of reading Sillitoe's novel as a key literary-sociological text of the post-war period, Brannigan speaks of a "kind of time-lag" (2003: 57) in the narrative, as memories and fear of pre-war poverty and unemployment continually intrude into the present, throwing

---

4 In contrast to other 'Angry Young Men'-protagonists such as Joe Lampton in John Braine's *Room at the Top*, Arthur has no desire or opportunity for social mobility and mainly short-term aspirations focused on instant gratification of his desires. See Ochsner (2011).

any sense of linear progression off balance. In contrast to the time before the war, Arthur is aware of the fact that his father now has money for a holiday in Blackpool, a TV set, "all the Woodbines he could smoke, money for a pint if he wanted one" (SNSM 27). And he takes great pride in his own disposable income that allows him to spent money at the weekend and buy a collection of expensive suits. The Seatons do not live "below the telly-line, as well as below the bread-line" (Sillitoe 1964: 124) which Sillitoe elsewhere describes as the borderlines of poverty. Yet their world still allows little to no social mobility and is firmly conditioned by the factory work that guarantees their economic status. Brian Jackson contends: "The truth is that working-class life has always been changing, but also that the relative economic position of that class has altered little. At certain times it may be poorer or richer, but it is always the base of the pyramid" (Jackson 2002: 160). One might add that neither has the health risk posed by the factory as work environment been reduced significantly. Arthur describes the bicycle factory and its oily fumes as a place with "a smell all day that turns your guts" (SNSM 30), where he works "with rotten guts and an aching spine" (SNSM 219), returning home every evening "feeling as though your arms and legs had been stretched to breaking point on a torture-rack" (SNSM 39). Aside from these descriptions of the hazardous working conditions, the narrative implicitly refers to the high risks of accidents because lathe workers like Arthur are forced to manually operate machines at an incredible speed and with extreme precision; "you were cutting and boring and rough-threading to within limits of only five-thousandths of an inch" (SNSM 39). But not only memories of pre-war austerity and his working conditions impact on Arthur's perception of risk and his desire to maintain security and stability. His present is structured around the experience of a system of risk-taking he can control – always either leading to reward or punishment and the stakes being bodily harm or limitations of freedom. But the risks of mass destruction through another war loom in the background. The hope of lasting security thus coexists with an awareness of the destructive randomness of world politics the individual cannot escape, because "you never knew when the Yanks were going to do something daft like dropping the H-bomb on Moscow" (SNSM 27).

If one situates Sillitoe's text in the tradition of the Industrial novel, the risk discourse has shifted distinctly. Poverty is not a present threat, although Arthur's first-person narration frequently draws comparisons between his situation and his father's life in the 1930s. In addition, the class conflicts seems no longer agitated enough to inspire any sort of communal action. Nonetheless, the felt sense of alterity and injustice of the balance of power and material circumstances between the classes is affirmed by the frequently employed rhetoric of "us vs. them", a binary introduced in one of the (still) most influential sociological studies of the cultural formation and changes of working-class life published a year before *Saturday Night and Sunday Morning*, Richard Hoggart's *The Uses of Literacy* (1957). According to Hoggart, the collective noun 'they' refers to anyone with the power to infringe on the (political, social, personal) freedom of the workers ('us'), i.e. government representatives, policemen, landlords, and factory bosses: "'They' are 'the people at the top', 'the higher ups', the people who give you your dole, call you up, tell you to go to war, fine you [...]" (Hoggart 1957: 62). Sillitoe echoes this description when he writes: "The poor know of only two classes in society. [...] *There are them and us*. Them are those who tell you what to do, [...]. Them are those who robbed you of your innocence, live on your backs, buy the house from over your head, eat you up, or tread you down" (Sillitoe 1964: 127; my emphasis). Hoggart explains further that the working-class's sense of oppression from above is typically accompanied by a severe mistrust of authorities and a lack of illusion of "what 'They' will do for one" (Hoggart 1957: 63). In the novel the depths of the sense of alterity between Arthur and the factory foreman Robboe is expressed in hostile encounters resembling "different species met beneath white flags, with wage-packets as mediators" (SNSM 61).

This binary structure is met with passive acceptance rather than rebellion for two reasons: The new affluence and ability to partake in consumer culture causes the feeling that despite everything things are "alright up to a point;" furthermore there is noticeable feeling that it is impossible to induce any significant, lasting changes (Hoggart 1957: 79; 77). Arthur's final address to the reader epitomizes this attitude: "Well, it's a good life and a good world, all said and done, *if you don't weaken*" (SNSM 219; my emphasis). Throughout the narrative, he reiterates this motto; he also says: "Don't let the bastards grind you down" (SNSM 40). Arthur's conviction that things will turn out alright as long as one does not "weaken" is readable as an imperative to keep on fighting against social injustice, but, more importantly, it sums up his existential view of life as a "jungle",[5] full of threats, which requires continual fight for survival. As Stanley Atherton has noted, for the characters' in many of Sillitoe's fictions life consists of seeking coping mechanisms for real or imagined threats to their freedom or well-being (Atherton 1979: 77). For Arthur, this mechanism is above all a hedonistically oriented escapism (violent or pleasant fantasies, drinking, sex, and fishing) as a means of resistance against the authority of temporal structures and activities imposed on him, primarily the numbing work routine but also the

---

5 The word 'jungle' is used several times in the novel to describe Arthur's view of the streets, people's behaviour, and the world in general. Cf. also Gindin's essay "Alan Sillitoe's Jungle" (1976).

weeks of mandatory military service he has to endure.⁶ Feeling threatened, Arthur is also often physically or verbally evasive, e. g. he escapes to the nearest pub, dives into the crowd, disappears into the darkness of the streets, or tells lies to Doreen. Another strategy is physical violence, though he never crosses over into doing real damage (e. g. when tipping over a man's car or shooting a gossiping neighbour with an air rifle).

While Sillitoe's writing can be traced back to the Industrial fiction of the 1840s and 50s as well as to the social realist novels of the 1930s, Dominic Head argues that in British post-war writing class identities resting on binary oppositions (us/them) become increasingly insecure (see Head 2002: 53).⁷ In the novel, Arthur and his brother experience a moment of rage and insecurity about the boundaries between "us" and "them" when they try to help a man who has smashed a shop window to get away. Appalled by the behaviour of the crowd of onlookers who want to inform the police, Arthur perceives the lack of communal solidarity as a factor that increases the risk for the individual: "*You might as well live in a jungle with wild animals.* You'd be better off, in fact. [...] At least you knew you had to be on your guard. You could always fend for yourself there" (SNSM 113; my emphasis).

Arthur's felt need and belief in his ability to 'fend for himself' is characteristic of the shift towards individualism induced by consumer culture and greater social stability that also lead to the often-lamented decrease of political consciousness and group dynamic among the working classes. John Kirk, for instance, describes the prevalent (male) attitude of the age of affluence as an "'I'm alright, Jack' individualism" (Kirk 2003: 54). Sillitoe's protagonist moreover embodies the force of masculine youth challenging the force of class in society (2003: 55). In Sillitoe's working-class picaresque, Arthur's freedom is framed by the factory and the social system he chooses to comply to because the pursuit of his hedonistic ends ultimately depends on money. However, as many critics have noted, like other "Angry Young Men" fictions,⁸ Sillitoe's novel also explores "the

---

6 Only Karel Reisz's 1960 film version of *Saturday Night and Sunday Morning*, starring Albert Finney in the role of Arthur, brought lasting popularity to Sillitoe's novel. The film strengthens the aspect of hedonism in Arthur's protagonist; it begins with a shot of Arthur standing behind his lathe, while we hear him say in voice-over: "What I'm out for is a good time. All the rest is propaganda". See Hitchcock (1989: 85).
7 See also Ian Haywood's *Working-Class Fiction from Chartism to Trainspotting* (1997).
8 Despite the fact that writers like John Osborne, John Braine, Kinsley Amis, and Alan Sillitoe publicly rejected being part of a literary group sharing political (and even aesthetic) allegiance, their writings are subsumed under the label of the "Angry Young Men". And Ochsner rightly draws attention to the fact that "though they are often referred to as a consistent and coherent literary group, their anger was not uniform or homogenous, less political than cultural, and their

contradictions within the working class's anxious historical movement from 'austerity' to 'affluence' (Haywood 1997: 95). With the real battlegrounds of the war a not too distant memory, the fights left to fight mainly concern forces of conformity, e.g. domestic institutions such as marriage, that impose limits on male individualism, and a paradoxical criticism of society's consumerist complacency. Yet conversely, for young single workers like Arthur, consumption is also directly linked to the assertion of masculine power (see Brook 2007: 85); therefore any serious threat or even slight worsening of his spending power is also a threat to his identity, which he seeks to protect at all costs.

In Arthur's opinion, factories and insurance companies are institutions that "keep us alive and kicking – so they say – *but they're booby-traps and will suck you under like sinking-sands if you aren't careful*" (SNSM 202; my emphasis). In the contradictory manner characteristic of his narrative – always oscillating between rebellious, incendiary rants and appeals to individual caution in order to maintain the status quo, he immediately adds that "there ain't much you can do about it unless you start making dynamite to blow their four-eyed clocks to bits" (SNSM 202). This underlines the felt lack of political agency as well as the spirit of anarchist rejection directed in particular against the control over worker's time imposed by the capitalist system. And while a sense of class-based injustice translates into a belligerent attitude, e.g. Arthur's fantasies of blowing up the factory or his aversion to army duty, there is an overwhelming sense that rebellion against the system is not really worth it. Arthur remains an ambivalent, incipient rebel, conscious of the need for political and social reform but lacking the drive – that only comes from a clear sense of purpose – and the ability and desire to commit to a cause other than his individualistic goals of pleasure, stability, and survival. Like other characters in Sillitoe's fiction, Atherton argues, Arthur thus contends himself "with small triumphs, with temporary and individual successes" (Atherton 1979: 89), a phenomenon readable both as defeatism and egoism.[9]

Aside from the opposition of 'us vs. them', another binary that remains naturalized in Sillitoe's novel, as it was in the 19th-century Industrial novel, is the difference between men and women. Particularly with regard to risk, it is productive to take up the impetus given by gender-critical studies, which emphasize the nexus

---

political impact should not be overrated as their main concern was with culture" (2011: 180). Nonetheless, there are similarities between their fictions that are hard to ignore.

9 Sawkins underlines the significance of Arthur's paradoxical stance between rebellion and conformism saying that this "midway position" makes him "representative of a class, and therefore a society, caught, as it were, in just such a position, in an enduring crisis that can only be solved by moving decisively one way or the other" (2001: 95).

of anger and masculinity in fictions by 'Angry Young Men' writers,[10] and to shift the focus from class rebellion onto anxieties about gender roles rooted in shared socio-political changes of the time and the tension between anxieties and contradictory desires. These are at the core of Sillitoe's novel. Sharing Susan Brook's argument that it is necessary to guard against conflating (white heterosexual male) individualistic rebellion with political left-wing rebellion in readings of post-war writing by male authors (see Brook 2003: 23), many fictions of the 'Angries' romanticize alienated young men as (anti-)heroes and represent masculinity either as a "great white hope" or as "cautionary tale", as also Alice Ferrebe notes (2005: 3); both conceptions are fraught with positive or negative associations of risk behaviour.[11] Despite the fact that it is undoubtedly important to situate 'Angry Young Men' fictions in a context of relative prosperity and security, male anger and anxiety are the result of the increasing collapse between male and female spheres and traditionally fixed gender roles. In many of these texts risk-taking is an integral part of the performance of male "working-class identity – rugged, robust, and aggressively heterosexual" (Brook 2007: 5), and the characters resort to the domestic realm as a battleground on which they can assert their agency. In *Saturday Night and Sunday Morning*, the resistance of the protagonist, Brook says, "does not translate into active rebellion against the class system; rather, Arthur's rebellion and authenticity are shown by his aggressive heterosexuality and his affairs with other men's wives" (2003: 29). Choosing women and pubs is one of the freedoms Arthur seemingly has left because everything else is decided for him, and, Daniel Lewis adds, whereas the war offered young men of the previous generation a conventional method of asserting their masculinity through partaking in collective fighting and risk-taking for a cause, Arthur firmly rejects his role in the army "because he was forced to enlist and did not chose to do so of his own free will" (Lewis 2012: 98). Just like his attitude towards politics, Arthur is deeply ambivalent in his view of women and marriage. Deep down, he seemingly desires what he detests; for example, forced to leave the warm comfort Brenda's bed before Jack returns, he reflects: "It must be good to live all the time with a woman, [...] and sleep in a bed with her that belonged to both of you, that no one could turn you out of if they caught you there" (SNSM 128–129). He does not challenge the idea of the husband as the head of the nuclear family; moreover the perpetuation of the stereotypical role of the working-class man is a means to provide orienting security as well as giving him license to enjoy himself.

---

10 See Brook (2003) and Kalliney (2001).
11 See Brook (2007), Ferrebe (2005), and Lewis (2012).

Throughout the narrative Arthur is caught in contradictions. The overarching structure of meaning he imposes to retrieve a sense of agency in the face of forces beyond his control is a conception of life as a game of chance, in which possibilities and limitations are equally cast. In order to continue playing and to stand a chance of 'winning', in Arthur's opinion, man needs "cunning", a key word in his inner monologues. Cunning means strategic risk taking and avoidance, not in the sense of careful and rational calculation of probabilities but through a quick, more intuitive assessment of people and circumstances teamed with an optimistic belief in one's own luck and survival skills. In the eternal fight against "them", here including "the vast crushing power of government" (SNSM 203), other authorities, as well as women, he concludes:

> the only tolerable rule that would serve as a weapon was [...] *the exuberant cunning of a man who worked all day in a factory* and was left with fourteen quid a week to squander as best he could at the weekend [...] *a man could rarely play for safety if he was to win in the end* [...] To win meant to survive; to survive with some life left in you meant to win. (SNSM 203–204; my emphasis)

Arthur's concept of cunning depends on speed and calculation of the right timing, be it by getting out of Brenda's bed just minutes before Jack returns, or at work where he tries to exploit the piecework system to his best advantage, avoiding going too slow or falling into in a "Knuckle-knocking undiplomatic speed of four hundred for a week" (SNSM 32) which both would lead to a reduction of his wage through the factory owners. The goal is always to cheat conformity to the rules and to maximise his personal sexual or financial gains. He refuses to get beaten by the system whose authority he, however, does not question and he accepts punishment for getting caught in his transgressions (see Ochsner 2011: 192).

It is obvious that Arthur, despite his frequent affirmations of the contrary, is not careless. However, his attitude towards risk switches between deliberate denial, fatalistic acceptance, and head-on confrontation. With regard to the later, Sawkins says: "Arthur's cunning is more the result of what we call 'high spirits', and there the danger lies. There is an elemental recklessness in it'" (Sawkins 2001: 132). While he is almost incredulous at his ability to deceive Jack for as long as he does, this does not impact on his behaviour, which only happens after the probable risk of getting caught has been transformed into an actual danger after his encounter with the swaddies. Generally, dating married women is a game with clear rules for Arthur, the most important one being carefully picking the woman depending on the "slowness" of the husband, i.e. his good-natured ignorance, incapacity to look after and keep watch over his wife, assessed "by a blind and passionate method that weighed their more basic worth" (SNSM 42) or lack thereof. Reversely, "with the strong men's [wives] you have too much fear, [...] Arthur [...] yet relied on the accuracy of his total 'weighings-up' from meetings with Jack and the reports of Brenda. But you could never be sure" (SNSM 53).

One may, however, wonder in how far Arthur is really in charge of his actions because a lot of his risk-taking mostly takes place when he is heavily inebriated. In any case, he is usually saved by "an ever-ready instinct of self-preservation" (SNSM 14), or so his narrative presents it to the reader. The whole narrative deals with the success or failing of this instinct, whose function is not the avoidance of danger, but to go right to the edge and then make a precarious escape by a hair's breath just before there are any consequences. Often this takes on almost farcical form, e.g. when he manages to exit Brenda's house through the back door while Jack enters through the front, or when he after vomiting on a woman in the pub quickly disappears, "impelled by a strong sense of survival towards the street-door, to take himself away from a scene of ridicule, disaster, and certain retribution" (SNSM 16).

Aside from cunning, luck is the second key component of Arthur's risk-taking. While Arthur considers himself privileged in comparison to his parents, his belief in his own good fortune goes far beyond the temporal comparison of belonging to a 'luckier' generation, but constitutes an integral part of his world view and masculine identity. It creates the basis of justification for his reckless behaviour and his hedonist attitude and sets him apart from other men: "'I'm just too lucky for this world,' Arthur told himself [...], 'so I'd better enjoy it while I can'" (SNSM 37); "Mostly I'm lucky and all. But sometimes I get a smack between the eyes. Not often though" (SNSM 35). The opening scene of the novel introduces Arthur's typical risk behaviour on a Saturday night: he seeks pleasurable oblivion and escape from his work routine in ritualized communal activity, i.e. drinking at the pub, and the assertion of his strength and individuality through his luck and cunning. It presents the precarious situation of Arthur unsteadily walking towards a flight of stairs in a pub, with nobody stepping in to stop him, "though they all must have known that he was dead drunk, and seen the danger he would soon be in" (SNSM 9). Although Arthur is dangerously drunk and could have hurt himself badly, the focus is placed on his double luck, first having won free booze in the drinking competition against a sailor, with makes him happily laugh "to himself as he rolled down the stairs" (SNSM 11) and then arriving unharmed at the bottom in a blissfully drowsy state.

Arthur takes great pride in his ability to cheat the system as well as "slow" husbands like Jack. At the same time, he is conscious that his winning streak in the game will end eventually: "Luck was always changing. It thumped you with knuckle-dusters on the back of the neck in one minute, and stuffed your gob with sugar the next. The thing was: not to weaken" (SNSM 100); this highlights the dualism between agency and determinism by random forces in Arthur's narration. The superstitious belief in luck and the perception of life as a game of chance enables Arthur to accept risks, random events and defeats as intrinsic, inevitable parts of human existence. Viewing life as a cycle of rewards and punishments, helps manage disappointments; it also offers a means to defer control and responsibility. For example, the downside of Arthur's secret relationship with Brenda is that he is sometimes stood up; he copes by betting with himself on the odds of her arrival while waiting at the bus stop: "Sometimes he won, and sometimes he didn't" (SNSM 49). Through Arthur's eyes the narrative evaluates the belief in luck and the acceptance of life's randomness as paradoxically more positive than the rejection of superstition and gambling of older men, like Jack, which demonstrates "a mistrust in any ordering of events beyond one's control or understanding" (Sawkins 2001: 134). In opposition to strength and cunning, rational calculation and the acceptance of (con-)sequentiality equal weakness and bear the risk of being cheated on; Lewis MacLeod even argues that Arthur expresses a social Darwinist view of "slow" men as being unfit for survival in the jungle (MacLeod 2012: 118–119).

Always trying to counteract the deadening routine of factory life, the main value of Arthur's risky pranks, sexual escapades and drinking bouts is revitalization as well as assuring himself that he is able to maintain his freedom just a little while longer. He is, however, conscious of the dangers involved. As Anna Ryan Nardella explains, these risks are "proving his existence. He can for a time control the risks and balance the forces, but he knows that 'the winner takes nothing'" (Nardella 1973: 472). Nardella as well as Gillian Hanson suggest to consider Sillitoe's novel in the tradition of existentialist fiction because main concerns are man's attempt to define himself in a "universe where life and identity are constantly threatened by personal and/or impersonal forces – where man faces the chasm of nothingness, sapped of his vitality by monotonous ritualistic routine and meaningless institutions" (Nardella 1973: 469), and the protagonist's experience of "existential escape" from all what threatens his possibility of choice (see Hanson 1999: 26; 29). From this perspective, Arthur's life, despite all affluence, appears neither safe nor secure, he is constantly at risk from suffering a loss of self through a loss of agency.

The sense of existential risk is also inherent in the opposition of the recurrent metaphor of the world as "jungle" and the symbolism of the "Big Wheel" that man cannot escape.[12] According to Gindin, the world constructed in Silli-

---

[12] Most critical studies comment on the recurrent circular imagery in the text (e.g. the bicycle

toe's text is governed by chance as well as by "unjust and inhumane restrictions" (Gindin 1976: 23; 26), but it is also a world beyond change: "A man may win or lose, depending on the wheel of chance, but he cannot control the wheel or change his position" (1976: 33). The imagery needs to be understood against the lingering memory of the war as an event that shattered the world beyond comprehension and control. It is important to note that the jungle is not only a space associated negatively with the individual's disorientation and fight for survival, but it is the direct other of the big wheel, i.e. the fixed, eternally moving, circular structure of work and socially conditioned time. As such it is less mechanical and alienating; it is dynamic and offers the opportunity to feel alive. An example is Arthur's shooting of his neighbour, Mrs. Bull, with an air rifle because he wants to punish her for gossiping about his adulterous affairs; this act of childishness and archaic self-justice greatly revives his spirits and restores a sense of control, counterbalancing his mounting dread of being attacked by the swaddies.

The construction of time in the novel affirms both circularity and binary opposition. The beginning of the narrative asserts the often-cited contrast between weekdays and weekends, specifically between the excesses of "Saturday night, the best and bingiest glad-time of the week", and all the other non-holidays in "the slow-turning Big Wheel of the year" (SNSM 9). While Saturday is associated with community and violence, a time when "passions were exploded" and necessary relief is granted from "a week's monotonous graft in the factory" (SNSM 9), Sunday morning offers a different, more quiet and reflective kind of escape; it is the only time when Arthur gets to be outside and enjoy fishing or walks through the countryside. During the week, any contact with nature and thus also with the experience of 'natural' time, e.g. the changing of the seasons, is reduced to "a brief glimpse of sky at midday and evening" (SNSM 130); "Living in a town and working in a factory, only a calendar gave any real indication of passing time" (SNSM 129).

As a result of the experience of life as a "relentless cycle of work and play" (Haywood 1997: 103), there is little incentive to plan ahead or take any sort of precaution. As Hanson emphazises, Arthur's life is circumscribed by a gruelling work routine and temporarily liberating, yet essentially equally repetitive weekends "of routine boozing and lovemaking" (Hanson 1999: 33). The protagonist's commitment to living in the present and not caring about the future springs from

---

wheels, fishing reels, "the slow-turning Big Wheel of the year"; SNSM 9). Daniels and Rycroft view the metaphor of the wheel even as a "driving structure of the novel" (1998: 274), arguing that each episode as well as the whole text has a circular structure.

an alienated sense of naturally progressing time and the inability to make decisions outside a fixed and mostly restrictive socio-temporal structure.[13] In addition, he distrusts the political climate and does not rule out the possibility of another war or recession. Both aspects impact on his attitude towards risk, intrinsically dependent on calculating future events and probable consequences of actions. Arthur, carefully and ably calculating and managing his speed at work and his weekly wages, refuses to plan ahead, out of a vague conviction that it might be futile. For example, he considers saving money pointless, prefers living with his parents to the long-term obligations of owning one's own place, and he tells Doreen that he might not live to the age of sixty. Though he continually focuses on the present and the immediate future, he simultaneously tries to live outside of real time, an impression reinforced by the episodic structure of the narrative that prioritises the description of Saturday nights as an elastic, extended time slot; clock-time only operates before and after these in reality brief episodes and the majority of actual life-time and routine disappears in compressed gaps of time that are not narrated. His physical escapes at the weekends also provide the material for mental escape – Arthur's "pipe-dreams" (SNSM 39) while he is standing at the lathe. The minute he has clocked in at seven-thirty am, "as on every morning since he was fifteen" (SNSM 29), Arthur detaches himself from the factory time he has to obey, and retreats into his own rhythm. While at work, Arthur is never in the present, revelling either in pleasant memories or "things that you hoped would happen to you in the future", "memory and imagination ran free and did acrobatic tricks with your past and with what might be your future, an amok that produced all sorts of agreeable visions" (SNSM 39). Paradoxically, Arthur perceives his sobriety at work as an isolated, "drugged life" (SNSM 170), a perpetual stupor which he has to pierce with the reality, anticipation, or memory of sex and drink, his preferred means of numbing (or, in his view, activating his senses); he always aches "for the noise of a public house, wanting to lose himself in a waterfall of ale and laughter" (SNSM 146).

Sociological studies of working-class attitudes towards drinking affirm its distinctly gendered nature and the link to ritualized social occasions like weekend nights at the pub, holidays, or celebrations. On the latter occasions, Hoggart points out, everybody is expected to consume a lot of alcohol, but drinking is especially accepted as part of "the normal man's life, like smoking. [...] if one can't have a bit of pleasure like that, then what is there to live for?" (Hoggart

---

[13] Several critics describe Arthur's transgressive behaviour as a rebellion against "the arbitrary structure of existence which is enforced by capitalist working practices" (Bentley 2010: 195), or as attempted liberation from mechanisation of time (see Wilson 1981: 415; Brannigan 2003: 57).

1957: 80). Craig MacAndrew and Robert Edgerton similarly describe drinking as a socially conditioned activity for men (1970: 165). In their anthropological study of drunkenness they also develop the notion of "time out", as an alcohol-induced, socially licensed state of freedom from "the otherwise enforceable demands that persons comply with conventional proprieties. For a while [...] the drunkard finds himself, if not beyond good and evil, at least partially removed from the accountability nexus in which he normally operates" (MacAndrew and Edgerton 1970: 89–90). Accepted in many, if not most cultures in one form or another, drunken "time out" features largely in Sillitoe's novel, as Lewis Macleod (2012) argues in his analysis of drunkenness in relation to Arthur's experience of time. A majority of the plot takes place during ceremonial episodes of "time out" (weekends, the Goose Fair, Christmas). The difference between time drunk ('out') and time sober ('in') correlates to the opposition between weekend and weekday, i.e. between leisure and work. In contrast to the week, dictated by the rhythm of the factory, 'time out' is a discontinuous space, where demands and rules are suspended. But it is by no means risk-free. Applying MacAndrew and Edgerton's definition of 'time out' to Arthur's behaviour, the main appeal of drunkenness is being temporarily absolved from guilt and accountability; it allows for a suspension of causality through a specific experience of temporality which reduces chains of events to episodic happenings and allows for a telescopic extension or compression of time outside of 'clock-time.' The implications of Arthur's experience and preference of 'time-out' for his perception and taking of risks is obvious. Generally, drunkenness makes Arthur oblivious to risk: all of his illicit sexual conquests take place during 'time out', and arriving at Brenda's house after the pub, he can hardly remember how he got there and only has "a vague memory of [...] voices of anger and the hard unsympathetic stones of houses and pavements" (SNSM 17).

MacLeod goes as far as to suggest that Arthur tries "to make 'time out' a permanent condition, to extend the limited and socially sanctioned freedoms of temporary drunken irresponsibility to every aspect of his life, to treat the suspended, commitment-free conditions of Saturday night as a steady state rather than a tolerated aberration" (MacLeod 2012: 116); as such he refuses submission to the fact that no culture allows 'time out' to endure permanently. But in the narrative Arthur is ultimately not allowed to suspend liability and time indefinitely. Attending the Goose Fair with Winnie and Brenda on a Saturday night, an illustration of ceremonial, communal 'time out' and licensed excess, he constantly has to be on his guard. He has to deceive Doreen and later only makes a narrow escape from the swaddies who wait for him in the crowd; the scene presents the culmination of his delusion of being able to extend time out and is his first contact with the swaddies, who embody the reality of the consequences of his actions catching up with him.

In the novel sleep and alcohol fulfil a similar function for Arthur; both allow him to escape into oblivion and a different experience of time passing. During the obligatory military training, he drinks every night in reaction to his hatred of the army and the deviation from his work-leisure routine forced upon him. He experiences the two weeks as an eternity: "The days and nights did not pass quickly enough" (SNSM 138). He sneaks out of the camp at night to get drunk with a mate helps them to forget everything except "their own existence, the now, the this minute" (SNSM 139). Then, after gets caught by an officer for missing a parade and is tied up in bed, he happily accepts the confinement because he is free to escape into sleep, "the hours passing with such pleasant speed [...] he could think of no better way to spend his fifteen days" (SNSM 142). The positive associations of Arthur's drunkenness aside, it is also important to note that Arthur, as is it the case with his sexual affairs, is at least partially conscious about the risk posed by his alcohol consumption. He is also aware that his habit – however temporarily licensed by social convention – limits his choice of women because "if a woman didn't like a man who drank, then it was going to be touch-and-go, whichever way you looked at it. Which is my big trouble, and *why I'm not so cocksure about everything, in the end, and why I have to be careful* and find the most loving woman of all" (SNSM 45; my emphasis). Underneath Arthur's openly expressed aversion of marriage intimacy thus lays the perceived risk of being controlled and reigned in further than he already is, with regard to his drinking and how he spends his time and money.

According to Lynne Segal, Arthur's attitude and behaviour in the novel are characteristic of 'Angry Young Men' fiction because they show masculinity and promiscuous male sexuality as a strategy of resistance to the nuclear family and its restrictions; they also spring from the belief that "women are never to be trusted. They are part of the system trying to trap, tame and emasculate men" (Segal 2007: 11). In Arthur's perception, this belief is not at odds with his rejection of authority; the male authority over women is never questioned[14] and he harshly judges female adultery with a moral double standard: "If ever I get married, he thought, and have a wife that carries on like Brenda and Winnie [...] I'd kill her" (SNSM 145). Meanwhile his choice of older married women reflects his characteristic denial of futurity as these relationships cannot progress and can only be conducted in secret gaps of time. The reflex to distance himself from inti-

---

[14] Several critics comment on Sillitoe's depiction of an "aggressive, misogynistic" masculinity in the text, see Daniels and Rycroft (1998: 273; 280); Segal (2007: 11).

macy, perceived as a largely restrictive force, is also obvious in Arthur's behaviour after witnessing Brenda's abortion when he ends up getting drunk and spending the night with Brenda's married sister Winnie. The scene takes what Macleod refers to as the protagonist's "commitment to discontinuity at all costs" (Macleod 2012: 117) to extremes.

19-year old Doreen, afraid "of being 'left on the shelf'" (SNSM 155), is driven by the directly opposing desire to ascertain continuity in her relationship with Arthur from the first moment; it is her first serious chance to avoid the old female risk of ending up as a spinster. He, by contrast, partakes reluctantly in their courtship because it feels too boringly safe in the short-term and entails the long-term risk of permanent entrapment. Walking out with Doreen, he enjoys the absence of the risk of being discovered by an angry husband at the turn of every corner, but also knows that he faces the real possibility that he might "unwittingly and of course disastrously – find himself on the dizzy and undesired brink of the hell that older men called marriage" (SNSM 156). At this point, he is not ready to stay with Doreen on "the safe and rosy path" (SNSM 156) to domesticity, still drawn to the thrill of the affair with two married women. Though his carefree attitude and commitment to discontinuous pleasure is increasingly darkened by the possibility of being beaten up by the swaddies, he yet sees no reason to alter his behaviour because he has no evidence of a reality of danger derived from his subjective experience; "*so far the tight-rope neither sagged nor weakened nor even threatened to throw him off balance*" (SNSM 156; my emphasis).

Brenda's pregnancy is what begins to throw Arthur off balance; he reacts to the news with his typical paradoxical mix of avoiding responsibility and asserting his risk-agency: "It's an act of God, like a pit disaster. I should have been careful, I suppose, but what's th good o' going wi' a married woman if you've got to use a frenchie?" (SNSM 69). Nonetheless, he tries to help Brenda by getting advice from his aunt, who tells him that there are no safe and legal means to get an abortion.[15] The only available method is to try to abort the pregnancy by consuming a large quantity of hot gin while sitting in a hot bath, a painful and dangerous procedure for Brenda, described in the narrative only through Arthur's perspective as a passive, helpless spectator. While Brenda is assisted by her friend Em'ler, Arthur appears twice removed from the scene due to the fact that he runs a fever and feels the discomfort of a man intruding on a scene of secret, female risk management. The incident strongly affects Arthur: "No more bubble-baths for Brenda.

---

15 Hitchcock has noted the absence of the word 'abortion' in the novel; only euphemism (such as "getting rid of it") are used; the act is also neither directly named nor shown in the film version (see 1989: 71).

Never again. I'd rather cut me throat" (SNSM 89). Yet though the reader feels that he is clearly shaken by the ordeal Brenda has to undergo, he reacts with his usual escapism and immediately tries to distance himself from the event, unwilling to let it ruin his leisure time, "a major tragedy or a ton of dynamite was needed to blast him out of it" (SNSM 69). His hankering for pleasure takes on a distinctly desperate quality in this scene and his customary "couldn't care less"-attitude is hardly credible. He appears trapped in the performance of a stereotypical performance of masculinity, unable to express his emotions and always needing greater risks to compensate the feeling of being reigned by circumstances and the consequences of his choices. Going to bed with Winnie, a married woman, means a form of risk-taking he is familiar with, but in his feverish, agitated state he misjudges the character of Bill, who is not a 'slow' husband like Jack, and thus violates his own rule. This moment of recklessness teamed with carelessness is a turning point in the novel.

Meeting Doreen is the second main plot event that initiates a change in Arthur's pattern of behaviour. Although he initially continues to see Brenda and Winnie and thus only ups the risk of his sexual affairs, he also for the first time begins and conducts a relationship with a woman comparatively sober and on time 'in' (he meets Doreen on a Sunday night, their first date takes place on a Monday night, he later takes her to the Goose Fair on a Thursday night, keeping her separated from the excesses of Saturday nights reserved for his other affairs; he is also "stone-cold sober" (SNSM 215) when proposing marriage to her). Another crucial episode is Arthur's witnessing of the fight between Jane and Jim during a drunken family Christmas party. Once he begins to recognize that marriage entails fight rather than submission it becomes more compatible with his worldview. The same way Arthur loathes routine but also finds orientation and pleasure in it, he rejects marriage's association with containment but values it as "a secure space in which to ritualise commitment and love" (Minogue and Palmer 2002: 139). Doreen, the 'good', virginal woman, appears as the traditional saving grace in the narrative after Arthur's risky hedonism is reduced to a façade and clashes with unpleasant realities (after Brenda falls pregnant and he is beaten by the swaddies); he now realizes "with a strange feeling of frustration mixed with relief that an avenue of safety lay before him" (SNSM 204). But she also offers him a way to unite his love of rebellious resistance with social convention. Significantly, the moment of deciding to get married entails relief and panic for both of them; Sillitoe's narration implies that their future together will mean ongoing fight rather than surrender: "Arthur held her murderously tight, as if to vanquish her spirit even in the first short contest. But she responded to him as if she would break him first" (SNSM 214–5). Arthur thus less renounces fighting and risk-taking than settles for a different kind. As Sawkins puts it, Arthur decides that with Doreen "he is on 'better' but also on safer ground; but in thus calculating he finds that with Doreen he has to be not less but more on his guard" (Sawkins 2001: 114). And only after experiencing real-time danger does Arthur allow himself to get caught by Doreen, also aware that it might be time to quit the game while he is ahead: "he had juggled Brenda, Winnie and Doreen crazily, like a man on the stage, throwing himself up into the air as well each time and always landing safely in one soft bed or another" (SNSM 170).

To further explore the ambivalence of Sillitoe's characterization of masculinity in the novel, despite his in many ways stereotypical belligerence and transgressive escapades, Arthur detests physical violence: "He did not like to fight, and would avoid it by all means possible: only the stupid fought with their fists" (SNSM 100).[16] While this is another reason for his dislike of the army, he nonetheless accepts violence – domestic as well as political – as a necessary, unchangeable part of reality. This acceptance episodically takes on an invigorating quality and renews his desire for thrill seeking. After tipping the man's car over, who had shouted at Arthur and his brother for drunkenly crossing the road, Arthur is again alert and capable of anticipating seeing Brenda again. Witnessing his cousin Jim get struck in the face with a beer bottle by his wife Jane he similarly feels "strangely and joyfully alive" (SNSM 201). Rather than being shocked by this act of domestic violence,[17] it renews his sense of rebellion, "now he was awake once more, ready to tackle all obstacles, to break any man, or woman, that came for him" (SNSM 201).

This episode follows the climactic encounter with the swaddies, the first truly negative and destructive event Arthur experiences on a Friday night. When he is attacked, he is alone on a dark street, and although he has not anticipated the precise moment, he experiences the attack as consequential. Arthur's behaviour, in his extreme drunkenness, is marked by passivity, he accepts the punishment that he has sought to escape for so long; the narrative voice emphasizes his trance-like state: "The way was open to run, but for some reason that he could never bring himself to understand, he did not run. [...] he felt as though he were in a dream" (SNSM 174). The narrative suggests that resistance is no longer an option, both due to Arthur's mental state and the physical realities of the sit-

---

16 According to MacLeod, Arthur's "impulse for stillness over rowdiness" (2012: 123) is repeatedly affirmed in the narrative and epitomized by his love of fishing.
17 Sillitoe elsewhere describes violence as "part of the world I grew up in" (cited in Hanson 1999: 37). Verbal and physical violence are usually seen as inevitable realities of working-class life as a result of physical and economic pressures and living conditions shaped by constant proximity and noise (see Atherton 1979: 65).

uation. Sociologist Joyce Canaan, in a study of the relations between drinking and fighting in the construction of male working-class identity, explains that both activities provide a chance to affirm one's place in society, and often originate in a felt pessimism about the future and felt intrusion of authoritative policies intruding into one's private life and constraint of personal freedom (Canaan 1996: 117). Yet due to the fact that drinking falsely expands one's sense of power and control, while fighting requires the exactness of psychological awareness and physical control that drunkenness destroys, these activities, though both seeking to affirm masculinity, are "at best contradictory" (1996: 123; 119). This is a battle even Arthur does not win, though he is usually able to subsume contradictions into coherence in his subjective narrative.

Although Arthur remains unwavering in his determination to fight for what he considers his rightful pleasures and freedom until the end, the feeling of his luck running out progresses from one episode to the next and culminates in him getting beaten up. Afterwards he stays in bed at home for three days. This relatively short period is experienced as sober, stretched out time, similar to him laying strapped to his bed during the weeks of army training: "They seemed like a hundred years" (SNSM 179). It triggers a change in Arthur that is expressed in classic risk language. Although this is not the first time that he has been on the losing side of a fight, the experience makes him feel "like a ship that had never left its slipway suddenly floundering in mid-ocean" (SNSM 182). Forced to acknowledge a sense of his own fragility, he announces a felt sudden lack of security – comparable to Crusoe's reaction to seeing the single footprint in the sand. Arthur is suddenly 'outside the whale', realizing that

> [...] there had never been any such thing as safety, and never would be, the difference being that now he knew it as a fact, whereas before it was natural unconscious state. If you lived in a cave in the middle of a dark wood you weren't safe, not by a long way, he thought, and you had to sleep always with one eye open and a pile of sharp stones by your side [...]. Life was like that, [...] one day you hit the bottom without knowing it, like a bubble bursting when it touches something solid [...]. (SNSM 183)

The encounter with the swaddies marks the protagonist's transference out of a "natural unconscious state" of safety and belief in his invincibility into full risk consciousness and thus, into 'real' time. As Macleod puts it, Arthur cannot shake the realization that "the timer has been switched on" (MacLeod 2012: 122).

The last episode shows Arthur sitting by the canal on Sunday morning, lost in quiet reflection about his impeding transition into married life with Doreen. His final inner monologue is consistent with his contradictory attitude towards risk explored throughout the narrative. Utilizing the metaphor of fishing, he envisions marriage and the life in general as an ongoing wrestle between 'catching' and 'being caught'. In his characteristic manner he embraces "taking the bait" as a choice he takes willingly because it promises safety from getting stuck in routine and the thrill of new risks and fights. Arthur knows "that he had really only licked the bait [...], that he could still disengage his mouth from the nibble morsel. But he did not want to do so. [...] Life would be as dull as ditchwater. You could kill yourself by too much cunning" (SNSM 217). While Sillitoe's ending to *Saturday Night and Sunday Morning* is often interpreted as Arthur's surrender to conformity, I rather agree with MacLeod's suggestion that the narrator, at least to himself, views his decision as way of continuing the fight and perhaps even as "one of his most daring and risky manoeuvres" (MacLeod 2012: 130). While the emphasis of self-determined choice is crucial, it is equally significant that Arthur clearly affirms his desire for domestic safety; he looks forward to a happy future which seems possible only "as long as a war didn't start, or trade slump [...]. As long as there wasn't a famine, a plague to sweep over England, an Earthquake to crack it in two and collapse the city around them, or a bomb to drop and end the world with a big bang" (SNSM 218). Concluding that one's only chance is to ignore the risk man is helpless to control in order to remain capable of action, Arthur dares to hope, while being aware of the limitations of his agency to change any circumstances beyond the local. Due to the fact that he has more to lose than his parents had at his age, and with a sense of existential risk undermining his sense of having a good life, Arthur chooses a comfortable, limited existence over an unknown freedom or an endless cycle of rebellion. In the end, Sillitoe's narrator appears to be able to reconcile the conflicting interests of risk-taking and security after realizing that his choice of giving up his freedom as a single man and thus "to live with his feet on the ground did not demand [...] that he go against his own strong grain of recklessness [...] but also accepting some of the sweet and agreeable things of life" (SNSM 203–204).

10.2 Illusions of Safe Space: *The Swimming-Pool Library*

Alan Hollinghurst's *The Swimming-Pool Library* (1988) has been reviewed as "the first major novel in Britain to put gay life in its modern place and context".[18] Set in 1983, and thus right before public consciousness about the AIDS crisis hit Britain, it deals with a London summer filled with swimming and casual sex in the

---

18 See Nicholas de Jongh's review in *The Guardian*, "The Deep End" (25 February 1988: 25), which is no longer available online; here cited from Liggins (2003: 164).

life of 25-year-old Will Beckwith, whose upper-class family background allows him to lead a life dedicated exclusively to leisure and hedonistic pursuits. The first-person narrator Will is eventually shaken out of his carefree existence and oblivion about his personal implication in gay history and politics[19] through an affair with a Black British youth, Arthur, a violent encounter with a group of skinheads, and through meeting Lord Charles Nantwich, an 83-year old philanthropist who served as a colonial commissioner in Sudan and was incarcerated for gross indecency in London in the 1950s. The painful discovery awaiting the narrator is that his grandfather Sir Denis Beckwith and the financial enabler of his lifestyle, then serving as Director of Public Prosecutions, was the driving force behind Nantwich's imprisonment during which his beloved Sudanese manservant Taha was killed in a racist attack.

The novel's depiction of masculinity in relation to routines of leisure and risk-taking offers interesting points of comparison with Sillitoe's *Saturday Night and Sunday Morning*. Although employing a protagonist firmly situated at the other end of the class hierarchy, Hollinghurst's debut novel also explores a specific male subculture in sociological detail and works through a juxtaposition of generational difference. In the course of the novel, the young narrator's present is contrasted with the past through Nantwich's journals, covering the time span from the 1920s to the 1950s, which Will reads after reluctantly taking on the task of writing the old man's biography. Like Sillitoe's narrator, Will has to confront pre-war history from his own position of comparably much greater safety; yet whereas Arthur Seaton knows from the beginning that his generation has it better than his parents', Will takes his freedom and material comfort for granted and is forced to undergo a process of re-evaluation of his own historically contingent privilege and vulnerability. The narrative's focus is firmly placed on white upper-class homosexual identity and life prior to the AIDS crisis, and thus removed from depicting economic precarity, health risks, or engaging with the double marginality of Black gay men. It uncovers a sense of historical continuity of gay identity, including stereotypes such as promiscuity, athleticism, or the sexual attraction to racial otherness, as well as that of values such as community and friendship and, most importantly, the inescapable risks of loss, emotional attachment, isolation, and homophobic discrimination.

---

19 Alan Sinfield identifies the narrator's "discovery that he is deeply implicated in gay history and not, as he has supposed, free from responsibility and social process" (1998: 106) as one of the novel's major themes.

10.2 Illusions of Safe Space: *The Swimming-Pool Library*

The reception of the novel shows that the text has proved difficult if not impossible to separate from its time of publication. The fact that Hollinghurst chooses a protagonist who only vaguely perceives of his sexual freedom, inseparable from years of struggle against discrimination and criminalization, as a recent privilege has provoked critical responses which question the legitimation of presenting the present through the eyes of an elitist protagonist.[20] Moreover, assessments of a 'gay' novel published in the late 1980s that does not once mention AIDS but depicts a carefree promiscuous and hyper-sexualized masculinity obsessed with youth, sports, and beauty, range from seeing the text itself as "risky" in its escapist nostalgia, to cautious acknowledgments of Hollinghurst's attempt to free the literary portrayal of gay desire from the proximity to disease and death and to celebrate survival instead.[21] A discussion of the political-historical dimension or of the 'authenticity' of gay consciousness in relation to the novel is certainly beyond scope. However, it needs to be stressed that the text engages with the vulnerability of gay identity in its historicity and evokes a sense of risk and of "this cannot last" from the first page onwards. Though it does not openly thematize fears of infection and illness, it highlights the mechanisms and motivation of casual sex, raises questions about risks of trusting and engaging with strangers, and explores the tension between public and private spaces and their perceptions as locales of safety or danger.

The opening paragraphs set the tone of the novel by conveying a strong sense of nostalgia, looming danger and loss.[22] At the same time Will is introduced as a narrator filled with a sense of his own privilege and exceptionalism. It was, he says,

> [...] the last summer of its kind there was ever to be. I *was riding high on sex and self-esteem* – it was my time, my *belle époque* – but all the while with *a faint flicker of calamity*, like flames around a photograph, something seen out of the corner of the eye. I wasn't in work – oh, not a tale of hardship, or a victim of recession, not even, I hope, a part of a statistic. [...] I belonged to that tiny proportion of the populace that indeed owns almost every-

---

20 One of the few unconditional appraisals of Hollinghurst's debut novel is Colin Tóibín's review "The Comedy of Being English" (2005). A political contextualization of the novel is given in Sinfield (2000).
21 AIDS arrived the moment there seemed some chance to disrupt the long-established association between homosexuality, disease, and death, in public consciousness and literary representations alike, and it threatened to reverse the previous two decades' happier outlook and focus on gay liberation (see Woods 1998: 359; Sinfield 1998: 82; Yebra 2011: 116).
22 Most critical studies and reviews emphasize the novel's "aura of sadness and nostalgia" (Tóibín 2005: 6); it is also often seen as a troubling work of fiction due to its mourning for a lost period of (comparably) carefree gay existence (Bristow 1995: 172). On the Hollinghurst's elegiac style of writing see especially Alderson (2000).

thing. I'd surrendered to the prospect of doing nothing, though it kept me busy enough. (SPL 3; my emphasis)

Like the Schlegel siblings in Forster's *Howards End*, Will is standing on a protective 'island' of family money that raises him above economic concerns; his superiority is also further sustained by the possession of the physical values of youth, health, and attractiveness. Like Sillitoe's Arthur Seaton, being sexually confident – i.e. being better than other men at the game of seduction – is an important part of his masculine identity and motivates his risk-taking. Also consciously aiming to avoid the responsibility of a committed relationship, in the beginning he only vaguely fears that outside forces will eventually infringe on his freedom and the ways he spends his leisure time – in Will's case a constant state of being. He is conscious, however, that other characters, such as his best friend James, a hard-working doctor, or his old Oxford tutor, perceive a directly opposing risk for him and worry about his "drifting unopposed into the routine of bars and clubs, [...] swamped with unwholesome leisure" (SPL 3) after he has voluntarily quit an editorial job at an architectural magazine.

Most criticism of Hollinghurst's protagonist focuses on his lack of purpose, social responsibility and his taking of his liberties for granted.[23] Yet there is also an underlying sense of threat that is less frequently acknowledged in his characterization. Will's sense of danger transcends the half-prophetic, half-nostalgic mourning of "the last summer of its kind there was ever to be", a statement typically related to the implicit historical frame of the brief window of time before the AIDS epidemic destroyed fantasies of endless sexual freedom. Perhaps more crucial in the novel is the narrator's risk of disillusionment and the perceived threat of a sort of inevitable punishment and expulsion from the state of innocence and ignorance he seeks to maintain; "*the threat too of some realisation about life, something obscurely disagreeable and perhaps deserved*" (SPL 4; my emphasis). From the beginning the narrator confronts the discrepancy between the critical outside perception of his "empty months" (SPL 5) and the protective function the established routine of leisure has for himself. He describes "the sex-sharp little circuits of discos and pubs and cottages" as laying at the heart of what he calls "the 'romance of myself'" (SPL 5), his ability to drown himself in "the sexed immediacy of London life" and to cover "all these mundanities with a protective glow" (SPL 5). For Will, his leisure assumes an "urgent, all-consuming quality" (SPL 81) and appears as such as something he is paradoxically

---

23 See, e.g., Ross Chambers's (1993) reading of the narrator's devotion to techniques of idleness and his "parasite-like" existence.

forced into as a means of self-protection against overwhelming emotions. His two affairs with Arthur and Phil threaten to disrupt the consecutive string of casual, non-strings attached sexual encounters and bring Will repeatedly to the verge of feeling like he is losing control. The other disturbance and threat to the clarity of his summer days "of nothing but exercise and sun" (SPL 189) is the task of reading Nantwich's diaries which he initially rejects. It becomes clear that the narrator desires living in the moment not merely out of hedonism but out of a – however childish – self-protective urge to perceive himself removed from the consequentiality of being bound to the past or the future and avoid the reality of gay identity as being inevitably precarious and politically charged.

Depending on Will's mood, moments of recklessness thus either originate or result from the 'pure' desire of pleasure or a sense of needing to escape overwhelming feelings of fear and concern for others; his hedonism often appears as a psychological necessity. Another aspect that renders Hollinghurst's narrator more complex than being a shallow seeker of short-term pleasure (cf. Sinfield 2000: 92–93) is his felt need "of an ever-intensifying privacy" (SPL 98). Despite the fact that his privileged background and his looks theoretically enable him to pursue any activity and keep any company he desires, he leads a rather isolated existence: "There were people I was glad to see, but almost no one I would seek out, or invite for a meal or a drink" (SPL 123). With the exception of James he has no friends and the contact to his family is reduced to occasional phone calls and visits from his little nephew Rupert.

Therefore largely filling his time with "chance encounters" (Tóibín 2005: 6), Will displays a half-intuitive and half-risky, provocative trust of strangers. In the case of Arthur, after a week of blissful intimacy hidden away his flat, Will's fascination with the alterity between them (Arthur is 17 and comes from a West Indian family living in an East London council estate), soon gives way to the realization that Arthur's clinging to him "as if in danger" (SPL 3) springs from actual fear for his life and having nowhere else to go. When Arthur, who is involved in drug-related gang crime and the killing of a friend of his older brother, disappears and later shows up bleeding at Will's doorstep, the outside world intrudes for the first time into the narrator's life. With intimate seclusion turning into confinement, the encounter with Arthur marks the beginning of the end of Will's feeling of safety, although he is conscious of the difference in the degree of danger between him and his lover: "Then we had stayed in for pleasure; now we could not risk going out. I was free, but Arthur did not dare go out, and was nervous to be left alone" (SPL 30). Will begins to have violent nightmares in addition to being haunted by a lingering sense of threat that transforms his day-time perception of his surroundings and establishes a link between public space and risk: "The neighbourhood seemed eerily impregnated with it" (SPL 33).

Will's attraction to Arthur overrides his rational judgment, and although he starts to imagine danger scenarios involving the police or Arthur's family, he is never frightened of his "strange" lover (SPL 13) and feels bound to him by "a rare, unjustified trust" (SPL 33). The possessiveness he feels towards Arthur – and later for Phil – make him afraid of losing him; he also develops a strong urge to protect and "save" Arthur: "It was a strange conviction I had, that I could somehow make these boys' lives better, as by a kind of patronage" (SPL 284). These feelings transform and darken the carefree affair and Will's superiority forces him into a role "as protector mined by *the morbid emotion of protectiveness*" (SPL 31; my emphasis). His half-hearted struggle to overcome the alterity to Arthur and to risk-manage the situation echoes Helen Schlegel's difficulty to find a way to help the poor Basts in *Howards End*. Haunted by feelings of guilt, of having "fallen short in helping Arthur" (SPL 131), he briefly considers giving money to Arthur's family but never takes any action. A telling sign of Will's isolation and discomfort, his nephew Rupert is the only person Will feels safe enough with to confine his fears about Arthur's wellbeing to and he asks him to look out for Arthur on the street.

But despite the fact that Will is loyal to and apparently also willing to risk something to protect the men he is emotionally attached to (James, Arthur, and Phil), he regularly needs spatial separation from them and his customary antidotes of alcohol, sex, and swimming, whenever anything disturbing happens, or when the burden of intimacy and concern becomes too great. Will seeks escape, for example, from the intensity of Arthur's care imposed on him, and from the responsibility that comes from the involvement in Charles' life. In his study of gay masculinity and sexuality, Tim Edwards argues that the pressure that comes through constructing and maintaining an 'outside', or public, gay identity frequently puts relationships at risk of failure from the beginning and can be avoided through the momentariness of casual sex; furthermore, he says "gay existence is often dominated with a sense of distance and difference that can potentially create a psyche so convinced of its isolation that relationships are put under particular stress and intensity" (Edwards 1994: 112–113). With his felt isolation (from the world) being revealed as an illusion, Will's behaviour in the novel is an illustration of this phenomenon which reoccurs in the two affairs with Arthur and Phil.

There are several moments in the narrative when the narrator fights against the sudden feeling of not being "in control of myself" (SPL 30). The scene at the Shaft, the gay club he visits with Phil, demonstrates the reality of Will's fear of being overcome by a sudden rush of emotion he cannot explain and only seek to manage through his usual outlet, sexual contact. Consequently, his reaction to seeing Arthur is to push him into the toilet, in a desperate attempt to establish closeness; at the same time he is afraid of his urge to hurt him: "I felt angry – I didn't know why – and frightened at my own lack of control. Over and over, under my breath, [...] I said, 'He's alive, he's alive.' [...] I had almost no idea what I was doing" (SPL 202–203). Hollinghurst's description of their encounter epitomizes the emotional complexity and the darkness – or irony – of many of the explicit the sex scenes in the novel and complicates reading them as pornographic.

However, it is hard to ignore the distinct racialization of the majority of male desire depicted in the narrative, as is the colonial set-up of pairings determined by marked differences in class, education, or age.[24] Choosing lovers exclusively for their innocence, in-experience, beauty, and race, in other words reducing them to predominantly physical qualities out of a position of power, forms one of the parallels revealed between Lord Nantwich and Will in the course of the novel. The reason for the narrator's attraction to men like Arthur, as he unapologetically admits, is their "youngness and blackness" (SPL 31); further examples include Will's encounter with the Argentinian guy and with Abdul, the chef at Nantwich's club; meanwhile Nantwich's diary is a detailed testimony of his attraction to black African men.[25] All these encounters or relationships formed between 'unequals' are fraught with risks of exploitation and suffering for both sides; Charles spends decades pinning for his (straight) African servant Taha and his almost broken by his death; Will is devastated when losing Phil, a waiter, who choses another man over him. The impact of these losses is partic-

---

24 On the text's concern with "the residues of empire" see Sinfield (2000: 96) and Dukes (1996). Christopher Lane briefly refers to *The Swimming-Pool Library* in the epilogue to his study *The Ruling Passion* and suggests that part of the difficult message of Hollinghurst's novel is showing the inseparable link between homosexuality and colonial splendour (Lane 1995: 231).

25 While not creating a parallel between gay and black oppression, the novel reveals a persistence of the "search of exotic pleasures" (Alderson 2000: 32), and the stereotypical eroticisation of black men. Certain to cause the uneasiness of many readers, it is debatable if the narrative aims to historicizes these depictions or, more disturbingly, suggests and even aids their replication in the present. According to Sinfield, the text lends itself to interpretations that view "it as a setting up objectified stereotypes so that readers will place them historically and reject them as an infringement of humanity", alternatively, he argues, parts of "*The Swimming-Pool Library* may revitalise stereotypical motifs; they may give them new plausibility; they may make them available, in fact, to a pornographic reading" (Sinfield 2000: 97–98). However, I agree with the arguments made by Lane and Bristow that the novel's unapologetic and multi-faceted engagement with patterns of inter-racial and cross-class gay desire is a strength rather than a flaw: "The subtlety and strength of Hollinghurst's novel lies in its ability to implicate every character in this invidious economy of racism without banalizing the complexity (and often the simplicity) of their sexual encounters or drawing pious conclusions about the need to transform or eradicate their thoughts" (Lane 1995: 230; see Bristow 1995: 177).

ularly crushing because they are perceived as random and unpredictable by men who thought of themselves as superior and being in control.

Through the juxtaposition of the lives of Charles and Will the novel touches on many aspects of gay culture and history. Born in 1900, Charles is "as old as the century" (SPL 224), whereas Will is born in 1957, the year of the Wolfenden report, which formed the basis for the legalisation of male homosexuality in the 1967 British Sexual Offences Act. Therefore, as John Bristow notes, the two characters serve indeed "as representative figures for larger political shifts as they affected homosexual men, decade by decade, from 1900 to the moment just before the acronym AIDS was invented" (1995: 175). Nantwich's diaries offer the reader and the narrator a view of a world where Will's uninhibited sexuality would have been impossibly dangerous. But the narrative also brings into sharp focus the continuity of homophobia which puts gay men at risk. Chronicling the impact of shifts in the official policing of homosexual men, the narrative parallels past and present through the arrests of Charles and James. Similarly, the incidents of Taha's death at the hands of a racist gang and Will's assault by a group of right-wing extremists for being a "Fuckin' nigger-fucker" (SPL 173) shows the persistence of homophobia and racist sentiments being translated into violence. But while all male characters in the novel suffer aggressions, the effects for James and Will's generation are less fatal: James can await trial rather than being incarcerated and Will's broken nose and ego heal, whereas Taha dies from his injuries. It is part of the complexity of Hollinghurst's narrative that it maintains an ambivalent 'risk discourse' of male sexuality that is complicated by questions of agency and responsibility and avoids straightforward victimization. It also draws attention to historical ironies in this context. For example, Nantwich recalls in his diary that a country like Sudan was a more liberal and safer place than Britain for upper-class homosexual men in the 1930s and that the authorities often chose them deliberately for jobs as colonial officers: "*Quite unlike all this modern nonsense about how we're security risks* and what have-you. They had the wit to see that we were prone to immense idealism and dedication" (SPL 241; my emphasis).

In addition to gay policing, racial relations, and colonialism, *The Swimming-Pool Library* engages with pop culture myths and constructions of gay masculinity, especially the rise of liberal gay subculture and its commercialization in the 1970s and 80s (see Alderson 2000: 36; also Liggins 2003). These are closely tied to specific risk behaviour. The characterization of Hollinghurst's protagonist illustrates what Tim Edwards describes as the metropolitan gay community's overt "emphasis placed upon promiscuity and the positivity of sexuality and sexual pleasure *per se*", teamed, in turn, with a neglect of "areas of concern to the gay community including the continuity of its inequality, discrimination and oppression in society" (1994: 154). Without explicit critical commentary on the downsides of the celebration of casual, and often public, sex as the ultimate expression of masculinity, it still reveals how the resistance to engage with these issues can be motivated by individual self-protection rather than a political attitude and moreover fails to develop an alternative support system, that of intimacy and private, monogamous love (1994: 154).

The narrative explores other stereotypes of urban gay identities, e. g. the cruising *flâneur* (Will, Charles)[26] or the endangered foreign lover (Arthur, Taha), as Sinfield (1998: 96) and Liggins (2003: 170) have noted. A main function of James, who is "full of caution and common sense" (SPL 2) and who lacks Will's athleticism and confidence in his looks, is the embodiment of a different risk personality and a masculinity which struggles to confirm to the predominant model of what Liggins calls the "super-stud", thriving on promiscuity (see Liggins 2003). James' reaction to Will's success when it comes to the game of sexual pick-ups is highly ambivalent; he is torn between admiration and jealousy, knowing that he himself lacks both the confidence and recklessness necessary to manoeuvre public sex scenarios. He knows that Will succeeds because he does not get discouraged by fears of rejection or by calculating possible dangers, e. g. of getting caught or of taking virtual strangers into his home. Tim Edwards explains that the gay male "pick-up system" is usually viewed in economic terms by maximising efficiency in terms of invested time and effort and return (i.e. sexual gratification and thrill) and minimising the risks of emotional investment and rejection (Edwards 1994: 94). Whereas this rationalised system is liberating for Will, it does not work for James. This is highlighted through the direct contrast of the two characters' individual encounters with the policeman Colin. Will picks up Colin on the tube and enjoys some "efficient sex" (SPL 94), although he is not really attracted to him. For James, who actually fancies Colin and tries to pick him out outside a gay bar, one of his rare attempts at initiating casual sex, the situation ends with his arrest, ironically by Colin, for solicitation. The narrative demonstrates how the search for 'public'[27] casual sex for gay men was and remains "essentially socially and structurally 'risk-taking'" (Edwards 1994:

---

26 For the most part, Will appears like the epitome of Frank Mort's description of the late 20th-century gay *flâneur*, who "cruised the streets with a clear agenda. Casual sex between men, desacrilised and uncoupled from the context of romantic love or long-term relationships, was a high priority. It was a sexual perspective which paralleled other liberationist ideologies of the 1960s and 1970s [...]" (1996: 176).
27 Edwards suggests that it would be more appropriate, in fact, to speak of "non-private" rather than "public sex" in this context because it is an activity that then still takes place in hidden spaces and essentially seeks protection from sight and state surveillance (1994: 91).

108). The paralleling of Will and James's encounters with Colin and Will's experiences at The Shaft demonstrates how this kind of risk-taking can either pay off or lead to humiliation and disaster. Emphasizing the link between risk and space, the narrative shows how typical locations like gay bars resemble grounds shifting between "safe space" (Liggins 2003: 168) and danger-zones of the criminalization of sexuality. It also continuously affirms the suggestion that in his sexual risk-taking Will is protected by his experience and skill, as well as by his age and looks. On various occasions Hollinghurst's novel thus appears as a realist staging of findings of sociological studies of gay subculture and sexuality. The depiction of Will's risk-taking demonstrates the discriminating fact that, Stephen Whittle explains, "beautiful young people don't need safe and tolerant places – because sex is always going to be easy for them; [...] Able bodied, white, beautiful young men have always had power and freedom" (Whittle 1994: 38). While James feels excluded and inadequate with regard to openly expressing his sexuality and consequently appears vulnerable, Will's confidence and risk-taking, paradoxically, go a long way in protecting him from harm.

It is obvious that for the narrator thrill and a feeling of control are the main reasons for seeking casual sex: "I loved the nerve with which I'd done all this, and like most random sex it gave me the feeling that I could achieve anything I wanted" (SPL 53). Casual sex and swimming being the chosen constants in his life, Will's favourite place he frequents almost daily, the men's club The Corinthian ("the Corrie"), allows him to combine both. The Corrie's pool and changing rooms,[28] "a gloomy and functional underworld full of life, purpose and sexuality" (SPL 9), offer opportunities for reckless voyeurism and cruising in a protected space. Although he enjoys the safe familiarity offered by the Corrie, Will occasion-

---

[28] The eponymous swimming-pool library has several meanings in the text. It refers to a nostalgically treasured memory of the origins of Will's love of swimming during his public school days where prefects were called 'librarians' and he was in charge of overseeing the pool and the changing-rooms, the latter providing a hidden realm of male contact and sexual exploration, "a notion fitting to the double lives we led" (SPL 141). There is also a mosaic of a Roman bath, showing naked men swimming together, hidden in the basement at Lord Nantwich's house, adding another layer to the image of the swimming-pool as an archive of gay culture. In the present, Will also assembles a library of men, his collection of sexual conquests. The metaphor also applies more literally to the access to another 'library' offered in the novel through the intertextual web of references to the history of gay writing (e. g. to works of L.P. Hartley, E.M. Forster, and Ronald Firbank). According to John Bristow, "allusions to a longstanding queer history [...] are, in fact, so numerous that the novel becomes an archive of gay literary history, one especially resonant for those who, like Hollinghurst, have undertaken graduate research into the lives and work of homosexual writers from William Beckford to W.H. Auden" (Bristow 1995: 175), On the myriad of literary references in the novel see also Sinfield (2000: 95).

ally searches ways of "heightening the drama of the pick-up" (SPL 93). Banned from driving after a DUI, Will makes the most of being forced to ride the tube, finding that it brings him in contact with all different sorts of men, "sexy and strange, like a gigantic game of chance" (SPL 47). Like Arthur Seaton in *Saturday Night and Sunday Morning*, Will also perceives himself as exceptionally "lucky" (SPL 101) when it comes to pursuing his sexual affairs. This is particularly crucial considering that the pick-up system largely rests on instantaneous, intuitive judgment made under uncertainty. In a way, the scenarios simultaneously depend on and defy the calculation of risk. The narrator explains how:

> it was strangers who by their very strangeness quickened my pulse and made me feel I was alive – that and *the irrational sense of absolute security* that came from the conspiracy of sex with men I had never seen before and might never see again. Yet those daring instincts were by no means infallible: their exhilaration was sharpened by the courted risk of rejection, misunderstanding, abuse. (SPL 132; my emphasis)

In Will's case, the certainty and safety inherent in brief intimate encounters with strangers, which for him contain only minimal chance of rejection, is only disturbed and compromised once he becomes emotionally attached. Meeting Phil triggers the same desire to care for and protect felt with Arthur; emotions the narrator experiences as a prolonged sense of risk opposed to the "brief certainties of casual sex;" "I had let something dangerous happen, a roundabout, slow insinuation into my feeling. [...] more protective and caressing" (SPL 101).

Will's "irrational sense of absolute security" described above corresponds to findings of contemporary sociological studies of sexual behaviour and risk perception. Only the narrator's homosexuality and his forced recognition of sense of communal gay identity compromise the characteristic sense of superiority and fearlessness referred to as the "white male effect".[29] It is based on the assumption that risk attitudes, i.e. the selective acceptance or dismissal of certain dangers, are dependent on culture-specific worldviews determined by the interdependencies between gender and ethnicity and that individuals (or groups of people) are less inclined to feel vulnerable the more (politically) empowered they feel. Finucane et al. (2000) argue that due to their felt sense of power and control white men therefore tend to have comparatively lower risk perceptions and that the phenomenon is increased among those who endorse hierarchical, individualistic and anti-egalitarian worldviews. On these grounds, in a later study Kahan et al. describe the "insensitivity to risk reflected in the white-

---

29 See Flynn, Slovic and Mertz (1994), Finucane et al.(2000), Kahan et al. (2007), and Palmer (2003).

male effect" (Kahan et al 2007: 467) as a defensive mechanism in response to any form of threat to their cultural identity manifested in specific kinds of behaviour. This means that the formation of risk attitudes proceeds in a manner that deliberately "protects from interference the activities on which their identities depends" (2007: 498). In Will Beckwith's case, perceptions of danger related to the activities of freely and leisurely moving around the city and of public and casual gay sex are overridden by the perceived threats any interference with these activities would mean to a personal sense of liberty.[30]

It is interesting to consider in a bit more depth the relation between an increasing egocentricity and the wide-spread phenomenon of casual sex and unsafe sex practices among young white males, as identified by Skidmore and Hayter.[31] With explicit reference to Beck's risk society thesis, they argue that by placing himself firmly at the centre of his world, the individual fails to perceive the alterity of the unknown other. Instead he imposes his own standards of behaviour and criteria of judgment onto the other which can lead – illustrated in the novel, for example, through the figure of Colin – to remaining ignorant of a person's profession or (sexual, health, criminal etc.) history. The risks inherent in sexual encounters are increased by the erection of a temporary emotional shield of irrational trust between strangers which, Skidmore and Hayter explain, "in effect, allows the individual to negate risk and feel protected from physical danger" (Skidmore and Hayter 2000: 30; 24–25). One of the major themes identified in their study is the tendency to ascribe qualities to strangers without rational or experiential grounding. The sexual encounter proceeds through a dual ignorance maintained by the fascination with alterity and a sense of familiarity achieved through projection: "In the ego-centric world imposing one's own values on an encounter can make it seem all too familiar and, hence, less risky" (2000: 32; 31).[32] The nexus opened in Skidmore and Hayter's study between risk-

---

[30] This also applies to the boozing and womanizing of Arthur Seaton in *Saturday Night and Sunday Morning*, although the white-male effect is here impacted by the protagonist's class identity.

[31] See Skidmore and Hayter's case study "Risk and Sex: Ego-Centricity and Sexual Behavior in Young Adults" (2000). Although their focus is on heterosexual male behaviour, the findings suggest in my opinion that the underlying psychological principles apply to and occur equally (if not in magnified form) in the gay community.

[32] The underlying question for Skidmore and Hayter is how people's sexual risk perception can be changed, in particular with the aim of reducing the risk of sexually transmitted diseases. The results of their (though hardly comprehensive) study suggest that explanations of mechanisms of disease transmission will never be efficient; rather the individual's behaviour and worldview need to become the points of focus because risk-taking behaviour within sexual encounters can only be changed by influencing the ways 'others' are perceived (Skidmore and Hayter

taking and egocentric identity and between ignorance/knowledge and trust/suspicion of oneself and others is explored throughout *The Swimming-Pool Library*. But perhaps the most striking and controversial scene in this regard is Will's reaction to the group of skinheads in the minutes prior to being attacked. He is distracted from perceiving the danger he is in by sexual attraction to the men and further put at risk by thinking he can control the situation intellectually like his other chance encounters with strangers: "the sexy one tossed my arm away from him, I gave a nervous gasp of a laugh, and decided I was in control of things" (SPL 172). The fascination with the skinheads' alterity remains intact even while the reality of the horror of the situation begins to dawn on him: "Cretinously simplified to booted feet, bum and bullet head, they had some, if not all, of the things one was looking for" (SPL 172).

As J. Stephen Murphy notes, the narrator spends his time "going from one gay space to another, indeed transforming all spaces into sexualized zones of potential encounter" (Murphy 2004: 70). The novel opens with an episode of Will entering a classic, yet for him unfamiliar gay space. Wandering aimlessly through the city he impulsively decides to follow an Arab boy into a public lavatory; the thrill induced by the situation is just strong enough to overcome the awareness that he enters a risk space designated, in his eyes, to the needs of older or less attractive men and causes a vague "fear of one day being like that" (SPL 6). In the narrative, any time Will ventures into territory that dislocates him from the spatial axis of his routine the results are unexpected, unsettling or downright harmful, like when he goes to visit Arthur in East London which ends with him getting beat up by the group of National Front-supporters. This shows how his superiority and sense of safety only operate within the confines of relatively narrow boundaries. The surprise awaiting both reader and narrator in the beginning scene is that the expectations of a scene of "cottaging" are ironically reversed. Will enters the very space that he will later discover was the place of Charles Nantwich's arrest in the 1950s. At this point, Will is, however, equally unaware of Charles' identity as he is of the long and often tragic history of policing that haunts the space he is in. Protected by his usual armour of good looks, confidence, and the greater sexual freedom of the present day, Lisa Avery point out, the danger of entering the lavatories and risking identification "as someone who cruises for men in these places" (2007: 138) is not a real threat but a tacit acknowledgment of a stereotypical space of cruising that is simultaneously dangerous and safe. Instead of the risk of exposure or the pleasurable sexual encounter the narrator (or the reader) might expect, the space

---

2000: 31). Although the novel, as argued above, is not explicitly concerned with sexual health risks, one might consider this idea with regard to Will's character and the historical context.

becomes the setting for a near-death scenario. Will stumbles across Charles Nantwich collapsed on the floor in cardiac arrest; his instinctual duty to help takes over and he performs CPR on the old man – instead of performing oral sex on the young Arab guy, the behaviour implied by the initial set-up of the scene.

From the beginning, the novel evokes histories of gay contact in relation to a specific perception of space. Stephen Whittle's sociological argument about the "illusion of safe space" (Whittle 1994: 31) as a characteristic feature of contemporary urban gay culture is relevant particularly with regard to Will's characterization and his ignorance for most of the narrative of his capitalist complicity with the power that oppresses and sustains him (see Chambers 1993: 216). Will, who believes liberal society to be a reality, is forced to discover a risk subculture in its historicity, the vulnerability of his own privileged class, as well as his personal risk of unwilling complicity in profit from forces violating 'his' culture. Hollinghurst's novel thus explores how being gay, according to Whittle,

> has moved from being dangerous to being safe, not just for the gay man or lesbian but also for the state. Alternatively, if we take the view of 'battles fought and won', being gay has not become safe in itself. Gay men and lesbians [...] have gained ground, both geographically and ethically, but none of it is safe. The geographical space gained is under constant threat from the forces of the state including the supposedly 'gay' activity of gentrification [...]. (Whittle 1994: 31)

Aside from the risk of unwilling collaboration with the state, the narrative reveals the illusion of safe space for all characters as they move in and out of designated gay "safe places" and "walk out into a dangerous world of queer bashers and sadistic policemen" (Whittle 1994: 39). For Will, the illusion is shattered by the attack of the gang of NF-supporters which brings the realization that "his wealth and indifference do not protect him" (Sinfield 2000: 93) from assault for being gay. The scene of him getting beat-up serves a similar function as Arthur Seaton's encounter with the swaddies in *Saturday Night and Sunday Morning*. It also occurs towards the end of the narrative, and although it similarly does not trigger a significant change in the protagonist's behaviour, the experience of becoming a victim of violence destroys his sense of invincibility and unlimited freedom. Both Will' and Arthur Seaton's sexual activities are not criminal in a legal sense but they are met with social reprimand and hatred from others they share communal space with. Whereas the sense of injustice and on-going discrimination is clearly greater in Will's case, the episode also results from a moment of careless transgression. Driven by the wish to check on Arthur, Will is attacked after entering ground where he should not have trod; venturing far beyond his usual territory ("I was amazed to think it was in the city where I lived"; SPL 169); he puts him-

10.2 Illusions of Safe Space: *The Swimming-Pool Library* — 515

self at risk by failing to predict that his security, based on class privilege, will not extend to a realm outside of designated 'gay' space and the realm of the inner city wealth. His confidence wavers with the spatial displacement and nearly deserts him outside the Hope's flat's door, consequently he is almost relieved when no one answers the doorbell; "It is horrible to be cowed by circumstances. [...] Oh, the relief as the seconds pounded by... and nothing happened" (SPL 171). However, he quickly regains a (false) sense of safety and control which leads to him approaching the group of skinheads without the caution appropriate to the danger he is in.

The description of Will's feelings and behaviour during the attack, eerily similar to Arthur Seaton's, is marked by passivity once he realizes that he is "completely helpless and exposed" (SPL 173); there is also a strong sense of dissociation from reality of the events; before boots and broken bottles smash his face and break his nose and a few ribs, his last thoughts are that he can hardly believe that this "was actually happening to me" (SPL 174). Afterwards, though he tries to make light of his mainly superficial injuries and self-mockingly notes how "[f]or a while I became the sort of person that someone like me would never look at" (SPL 176), Will is deeply in shock. While his beauty is soon restored, the more lasting change caused by the incident concerns his perception of risk once he dares to leave the safety of his home again:

> The pavements were normal, the passers-by had preoccupied, harmless expressions. Yet to me *it was a glaring world, treacherous with lurking alarm*. A universal violence had been disclosed to me, and I saw it everywhere [...]. I understood for the first time the vulnerability of the old, unfortified by good luck or inexperience. (SPL 176–177; my emphasis)[33]

According to Lisa Avery, as Will "comes to terms with his brutal beating, his relationship to the landscape changes" (Avery 2007: 142) and his once safe London becomes vulnerable. Through the first-hand experience of being at risk the attack also has a democratizing effect. Realizing the non-permanence and permeability of his own protective guards enables Will for the first time to identify with men like Charles or James. At least while the effects are clearly palpable, he is no longer able to detach himself from past and present as he desires. Thomas Dukes argues: "The novel by this time is a story of Will's progression out of the safety of social class; the novel has become a *Bildungsroman* not of a young man grow-

---

[33] See Burton's autobiographical interpretation of the scene: "His world will never again be quite so safe. Hollinghurst, who had a similar experience while at Oxford, agrees that once a previously unperceived threat is made apparent, one's view of the world is for ever changed" (1991: 49–50).

ing up but of a young man getting smart about his culture – and his own role in its corruption" (1996: 101–102). The attack by the skinheads is followed by a series of developments that further challenge and compromise Will's sense of safety and control over events. The first is the arrest of James; the second the discovery in the final pages of Charles' journal that his own grandfather was responsible for the "*crusade to eradicate male vice*" (SPL 260; original emphasis) Nantwich fell victim to; finally, seeking to purge himself from the feeling of being surrounded by danger, betrayal, and corruption, Will visits Phil, "the only true, pure, simple thing I could see in my life at the moment" (SPL 271). Walking into his room unannounced, he finds him in bed with Bill, a scene that shocks Will due to the intimacy he witnesses rather than the sexual act. All these events reveal to Will that his knowledge of people and the connections between them is not only limited, but in fact, far inferior to everyone around him. Aside form the shock of his grandfather's past which forces an re-evaluation of the present onto him, and the awareness that it is "really not another world, [...] it's going on in London now almost every day" (SPL 265), the narrator is unsettled by the fact that everyone except himself knew about Nantwich's history and his grandfather's role in it. In addition, Will, who from the start mainly felt with pity for Charles' vulnerability due to his old age, has to transform his view of him into that of a cunning, "dangerous man, a fixer and favouritiser" (SPL 245). Will realizes he has put himself at risk of disillusionment by falsely projecting his own isolation and lack of connection onto others.

Will is brought to an at least temporary change of his self-perception through being exposed in his ignorance and selfishness by others; significantly it is after reading the 'secret' diaries of two men, Charles and James, that he admits "the delectable blond super-stud I loved so much was really a selfish little rich boy, vain, spoilt" (SPL 216); "I had unthinkingly been raised" (SPL 268). As a consequence, he is determined to help James by testifying in court against Colin, a task he also sees as a belated symbolic gesture of reparation "for Charles, and for Lord B.'s other victims;" at the same time Will anxiously perceives the whole series of events as a kind of "test" (SPL 280) of his political stance and courage he does not want to take. Chambers argues, as the gay grandson redeeming the homophobic grandfather's victims Will certainly lacks the necessary dose of altruism and heroism (Chambers 1993: 216). Even though he is in the end lead to feel an "an urge to solidarity with my kind I wasn't used to in our liberal times", he still appears to be at the verge of detaching himself again from a collective gay identity from a vantage point of almost colonial superiority: "I looked at the others [...], with a kind of foreboding, as an exotic species menaced by brutal predators" (SPL 223). It is furthermore debatable whether there is any change in the protagonist because the novel ends with him strolling around the Corrie pool, apparently having reassumed his routine: "going into the showers I saw a suntanned young lad in pale blue trunks that I rather liked the look of" (SPL 288). As several critics have noted, the novel ends on a note of moral indeterminacy; the narrator does not awake to any sort of political activism or lets the experience of injustice and discrimination change his behaviour (see Dukes 1996: 104).[34] One can see Will's escapist behaviour at least partially as defeatist. He is (admittedly rather easily) discouraged by the difficulties he encounters in his rescue mission of James when he finds that the incriminating nude pictures of Colin have been disappeared by Charles and his group, who treat him as an outsider although he is from the same class. The experience of exclusion from a group set on protecting their own aids robbing Will of any budding sense of communal identity and he returns, perhaps disappointed and relieved in equal measures, to his leisurely aimlessness.

Generally, Hollinghurst's novel resists the reestablishment of the link between homosexuality, disease, and death without ignoring the depiction of gay men as a "high-risk" group.[35] Revealing "a history fraught with calamities", Stephen Murphy argues, "it is ultimately about survival and survivors who have moved beyond the catastrophe" (Murphy 2004: 66–67). The ending underlines the function of sex as an integral means of self-affirmation for gay men and a sign of 'survival' frequently employed in literature of and about the era of AIDS (see Woods 1998: 366; 368). As mentioned in the beginning, a recurring point of critical debate in the reception of the novel is that fact that the text nostalgically celebrates a moment condemned to the past, and that it violates an implied obligatory agenda of gay fiction at the time by not mentioning AIDS.[36] Various possible justifications have been given for this elision. These responses reflect the expectations resulting from the novel's distinct labelling as a "gay" text, as well as the difficulty to accept and make sense of the implied ethical-political stance (or rather, the evasion of one)[37] of a text in which the characters

---

34 I agree with positive readings of the novel's ambivalence and indeterminate ending as given by Dukes (1996: 107) and Bristow (1995: 178), as these draw attention the text's complex exploration of risk, refusing to condemn erotic pleasure in an era overshadowed by the danger of unsafe sex but highlighting mechanisms and behaviour (by the individual and the state) that render gay identity and sexuality vulnerable.
35 See Edward King's study *Safety in Numbers. Safer Sex and Gay Men* (1993).
36 On the different stages in the historical development of AIDS and literary responses to the disease, see Edwards (Chapter 7: "The Aids Dialectic;" 1994: 118–133), Sinfield ("Aids, Art, and Subcultural Myth;" 1998: 80–94), and Woods (Chapter 31: "The AIDS Epidemic;" 1998: 359–374).
37 On the novel's avoidance of political consciousness see Alderson (2000: 42) and Sinfield (2000).

apparently have a different knowledge and awareness of the risks and sense of impending disaster inherent in a promiscuous lifestyle and sexual risk-taking than the reader and – by implication – the author. While it is, of course plausible, to read the novel as trauma fiction[38] and argue that it is in some ways temporally too close to the shocking impact of AIDS to narrate it,[39] it is, I argue, useful to shift the focus onto the ways in which Hollinghurst's narrative allows critical insight and explores precisely the risk-behaviour which facilitated the spread of the disease among the gay metropolitan community. The novel does not simply celebrate a time of carelessness gone but chronicles a time of unconsciousness about risk.[40] And it is debatable whether AIDS ought to be considered the most crucial one in the text; rather, the narrator awakens to a general sense of the vulnerability of gay identity, which connects past and present. Sidestepping the issue of sexual health risks, this concerns the danger of physical harm, and risks of/to personal liberty, intimacy, and the inhabitation of private as well as public space. Another historical argument can be applied to the novel and suggest why the text, as a piece of realist fiction, is silent about AIDS. The AIDS crisis commonly invokes imagery and responses from the US that simply do not compare to Britain; particularly not at the time when the novel is set. In Britain, the disease did not develop with the same force and the losses did not reach the same scale, Alan Sinfield explains: "*as a community*, North-west European gay men have not lived with AIDS in the way US people have lived with it – and represented it" (Sinfield 1998: 91; original emphasis). Accordingly, Tim Edwards describes Britain's sense of distance to America when the crisis hit as a vague notion "of something threatening like a gathering storm (it was over here)" (Edwards 1994: 121) and underlines that

---

38 See, e. g., Yebra (2011), Murphy (2004), and Dellamora (1994).

39 Cf. Yebra's claim that "[a]lthough the novel never makes direct reference to AIDS, the disease lies behind Will's discourse and story" (2011: 123). According to Dellamora, who, views AIDS as a traumatic sign of the threat of annihilation of an entire community that equals that of nuclear destruction (1994: 28), the absence of the word AIDS from Hollinghurst's narrative parallels the absence of any detailed descriptions of the prosecution of homosexuals in the 1950s and he takes both as signifiers of "the traumatic structure of the history that the novel adumbrates" (1994: 173).

40 When asked in an interview why he did not address AIDS explicitly in his first novel, Hollinghurst explained that although the disease changed from a distant threat into a more imminent reality during the writing process, he "wanted to retain an element of celebration in the novel". Even if, or perhaps because, he said, "the party about which he was writing was already over" (Stimpson 1988).

10.2 Illusions of Safe Space: *The Swimming-Pool Library* — 519

> AIDS was barely conceived of in Britain before 1983 or 1985. The few cases of AIDS in 1983 crept in under a shadow of doubt and uncertainty and national attention was not drawn to the issue until 1986 when the Conservative Government became concerned [....]. The number of AIDS cases in Britain remains relatively small compared with other infections or causes of death such as heart attacks, cancer, or accidents. (1994: 123).

The recurrence to statistics makes the depiction of deaths and physical harm appear realistic rather than evasive, considering, for example, the heart attack of Lord Nantwich which is the incident that triggers the whole plot, and the absence of the topic of contagious disease. Yet this lack of public awareness due to comparatively small numbers, Sinfield argues further, in turn increased the risk of a lack of caution due to an illusionary sense of safety and a premature celebration of survival: "Thus people may start to believe they will be all right whatever they do" (Sinfield 1998: 91). The novel captures this illusion through the portrayal of the protagonist's ignorance and detachment from his surroundings and his trust of strangers. Considering the question raised Liggins whether it is "brave" to write a text that allows identification with a promiscuous character such as Will Beckwith in the post-AIDS era, "despite, or perhaps because of, greater public awareness of the risks of unsafe and/or casual sex" (Liggins 2003: 164), rather than to perceive Hollinghurst's text in itself as 'risky', it should be appreciated for its exploration of a particular time and behaviour that works through contradictions. Will's lifestyle is offered as an alternative to conventional ideals of monogamy, political engagement, and caution, but not uncritically. It is ultimately disputable that Hollinghurst should be obliged to produce a gay 'condition-of-England' novel and write only about the 'now' in a moment of public crisis; moreover, no fictional text should be burdened with having to function as an explicit safe-sex manual. Hollinghurst's depiction of the narrator in *The Swimming-Pool Library* contains a celebration of and commitment to survival as well a warning: it reveals historically continuous patterns of sexual desire that put men at risk while resisting to be reduced to pushing what is considered the most important gay agenda at the time of the text's publication.[41]

---

[41] This argument is in line with Hollinghurst's explanation of the ending: "At one point I'd intended writing an epilogue which would have made it clear that William was 'writing' the book practically on his death-bed with AIDS – but I forgot that idea because it was too much of a cliché. It would have been too near and turned the novel into a moral fable" (cited in Burton 1991: 48).

11 Running Out of Time

11.1 Posthumans Coming of Age: *Never Let Me Go*

In this chapter, the risk discourse turns towards two of the most prevalent topics in 21st-century Anglophone literature and popular cultural and scientific discourse which are typically negotiated with a strong sense of crisis - of humanity and its living environment as we know it running out of time. Risk assumes overwhelmingly negative connotations; there is little to gain in the present but all of the past and future to lose. This concerns, firstly, the impact of developments in the field of biotechnology on the human race and society, and, secondly, the hazards posed by climate change and environmental destruction.[1] Thus, the questions about the survival of the individual and humanity in general assume new urgency and are, as ever, closely tied to ethical issues and perceptions of agency. In the two exemplary texts under scrutiny, Kazuo Ishiguro's *Never Let Me Go* (2005) and Ian McEwan's *Solar* (2010), there is also a characteristic focus on the vulnerability of the human body and psyche as reflections of the precarious state of humanity and the globe.

The term posthumanism, which has gained prominence in literary studies and across a number of academic fields over the last two decades,[2] is commonly employed to designate a complex, entangled set of attempts to reframe conceptions of the relationship between biotechnology, human identity and embodiment. The frightening and fascinating possibilities of technological enhancement and human manipulations of nature possess an imaginative appeal that

---

[1] In accordance with critical voices who see genetic engineering as one of the most enduring themes and risk narratives of 20th-century science fiction, another, more short-lived genre, which has produced mainly (post)apocalyptic narratives which fall outside the 'realist' mode that functions as the overarching frame for this study of risk and the novel, is excluded here, namely nuclear fiction. Jimena Escudero Pérez, for example, argues: "The dangers of genetic manipulation seem to have, in fact, displaced those of nuclear power in the shaping of a common suspicion of science which reached its zenith after the Second World War. [...] Altering the natural order of things is unavoidably and intrinsically wrong, a discourse that prevailed in the depiction of nuclear power and that has now [...] been assimilated by biomedical praxis" (2014: 2).

[2] Undoubtedly, posthumanist scholarship has come of age since N. Katherine Hayles' (1999) claim that we already *are* posthuman. Other early studies in this rapidly growing field are: Badmington (2000), Fukuyama (2002), Graham (2002). More recent studies include: Bartosch and Hoydis (2019), Braidotti (2013), Clarke and Rossini (2016), Hauskeller, Carbonell and Philbeck (2015), Herbrechter (2013), Lippert-Rasmussen, Rosendahl Thomsen and Wamberg (2012), Nayar (2014b), Roden (2014), Snaza, and Weaver (2015), and Wolfe (2010).

https://doi.org/10.1515/9783110615418-012

can, of course, be traced much further back in time, Mary Shelley's *Frankenstein* being the most obvious historical point of reference.³ Yet since the late 20th-century, 'posthumans', in particular clones, populate with increasing frequency novels such as Fay Weldon's *The Cloning of Joanna May* (1989), Margaret Atwood's *Oryx and Crake* (2003), films (e.g. *The Boys from Brazil* (1978), *Island* (2005)), and TV-series (e.g. *Orphan Black* (2013–), *Humans* (2015–)). Focusing on the symbiotic interdependencies between human/animal/machine and ethically charged ontological distinctions between human/nonhuman/inhuman, the general preoccupation of posthumanism is seeking a redefinition of the category of the human. This undertaking is intrinsically motivated by and captures the perceived risk of losing the traits of the 'essential' human, which Francis Fukuyama, for lack of a better term, has called "Factor X" (2002: 149). These issues, centrally the question of what constitutes human subjectivity and originality, lie at the heart of Ishiguro's novel *Never Let Me Go*, a text that has rapidly acquired canonical status because it presents a to date exceptional haunting and nuanced engagement with the depiction of (post)human identity, telling the story of a group of clone children, brought up at a boarding school tucked away in a "lost corner" of North England in the 1990s with the sole purpose of donating their vital organs soon after they reach early adulthood. The narrative is presented through the voice of 31-year-old Kathy H., who revisits her memories of growing up at Hailsham while trying to deal with the traumatic loss of her two closest friends, Ruth and Tommy, and her own soon-to-end life.

Ishiguro's novel raises various questions about our (post)human condition and about sameness and difference: the crucial one, shaping the whole fictional set-up, is about what constitutes acceptable risk management for humans in the face of death and disease; in a broader sense, the narrative takes up the negotiation of what kind of risk-taking is acceptable in the name of inevitable scientific progress. In the end, when literally coming face to face with the cruel results of the Hailsham project, all that Madame, who functions as the text's main representative of the opinions and authority of late 20th-century British society, can offer as justification to Kathy and Tommy is this: "Suddenly there were all these new possibilities laid before us, all these ways to cure so many previously incurable conditions. [...] how can you ask such a world to put away that cure, go back to the dark days?" (NLMG 257). Ishiguro's narrative therefore entails a critique of anthropocentrism, Rebecca Walkowitz argues, of "the idea that it is ethical or acceptable to sacrifice nonhuman animals to the needs and desires

---

3 Ishiguro's *Never Let Me Go* has been compared to, or even seen as an explicit rewriting of, Shelley's *Frankenstein*. See, e.g., McDonald (2007: 75), Caryn James (2005), De Boever (2013: 68).

of human life" (Walkowitz 2015: 103). Emphasizing the Utilitarian logic underlying the argument made by Madame, Margaret Atwood puts it even more bluntly in her review of the novel: "The children of Hailsham are human sacrifices, offered up on the altar of improved health for the population at large" (Atwood 2005).

In their survey of the treatment of cloning in fiction Nerlich, Clarke and Dingwall sum up the dominantly negative perception "according to which CLONES ARE COPIES that have inferior value, CLONES ARE PLANTS/ANIMALS that can be farmed and harvested, CLONES ARE PRODUCTS, CLONES ARE MACHINES, BODY PARTS OF CLONES ARE SPARE SPARTS that can be bought and sold, exchanged for better ones [...]" (Nerlich, Clarke, and Dingwall 2001: 45; original emphasis). As a result, they explain further, clones are perceived as less-than-human, even monstrous, creatures, making it "difficult to see them 'just as babies' that would grow up in the normal way" (2001: 49). Ishiguro engages precisely with this question of the education and coming of age of clone children.[4] The outside perception of them as repulsive, slightly threatening sub-human others is shown in Madame's reaction during one of her regular visits to Hailsham. Kathy notes: "I can still see it now, the shudder she seemed to be suppressing, the real dread that one of us would accidentally brush against her. [...] she was afraid of us in the same way someone might be afraid of spiders" (NLMG 35). Madame's shudder cements the awareness of their identity as other; "the moment when you realise that you really are different to *them*" (NLMG 36; my emphasis). Further typical features of clone narratives found in the novel include the negotiation of the clones as a threat to the subjectivity and originality of the individual, one of the fundamental concepts of Western culture, and the creation of an alternative society which works through the strict separation of victims and beneficiaries, as well as the deprivation and manipulation of knowledge available to the clones; these aspects will be discussed in more detail.

Although the novel clearly adheres to most characteristics of contemporary clone narratives,[5] there has been much debate about Ishiguro's use of other generic conventions. Most central is the observation that the text which due to its subject matter falls into the realm of speculative science fiction, is, however, set in the recent past, in the 1990s, and contains little to none "actual" science, i.e.

---

[4] For the argument that fictions such as *Never Let Me Go* expand the ethical biotechnological controversy surrounding cloning into the social-educational realm, see also Griffin (2009).
[5] See Nerlich, Clarke and Dingwall (2001); Marcus (2012); Escudero Pérez (2014).

detailed descriptions of scientific processes or terminology.[6] However, it undeniably provokes "cognitive estrangement" (Sawyer 2011: 236)[7] not least due to the fact that the reader knows that cloning humans neither was a reality in the 1990s nor is now. The author himself explains that he never intended to write science fiction and has no interest in futuristic technology except as a metaphor that offers a contemporary lens on the great old questions about the meaning and purpose of 'being human' and the existence of the human soul. Novelists, Ishiguro says, "have struggled to find an appropriate vocabulary [...] to discuss these questions without sounding pompous or archaic. The introduction of clones [...] as main characters can reawaken these questions for modern readers in a natural and economic way. [...] It's a futuristic way of going ancient" (Ishiguro 2006).

With regards to the depiction of cloning in fiction measured against the real-life scientific context, one generally has to distinguish between therapeutic and reproductive cloning, i.e. between the cloning of tissue cells or individual body parts and that of full human beings. The first is usually seen as beneficial and the second, by contrast, as unpredictably dangerous, yet also as being a still very unrealistic scenario. In clone narratives, one of the most common types of contemporary science fiction novels and films, Amit Marcus explains, therapeutic cloning or the scientific risks and problems of reproductive cloning are neglected because they are "not narratively appealing" (Marcus 2012: 406). While typically only rather "perfunctory remarks on the technique of cloning" (2012: 406) are provided, or the topic is avoided completely, the focus is placed instead on the psychology of the clones – as human characters – and on the exploration of the sociology of a community of clones. Accordingly, as a new type of posthuman Bildungsroman,[8] *Never Let Me Go* dramatizes, Matthew Eatough argues, "the circumstances that produce communality" (Eatough 2011: 140). It is crucial to take Ishiguro's emphasis on the metaphorical function of the clones into consideration. Marcus explains that, as fictional characters, "Clones tackle similar problems of those of 'normal' human beings (e.g., constituting an autonomous self, developing a loving relationship with a significant other, negotiating the desire for immortality), but as clones they face *a whole*

---

6 See reviewer John Harrison's often-cited observation: "But there's no science here" (Harrison 2005). In her reading of the novel as critical science fiction Griffin (2009) emphasizes the absence of "acute science" in the text; on scientific discourse in *Never Let Me Go* see also Lochner (2011).
7 Cf. Sawyer's reading of the novel as, "outsider science fiction" (2011); another reviewer referred to the text as a "quasi-science-fiction novel" (Menand 2005).
8 On this still under-explored variation of the genre see, e.g., Rollo (2012).

gamut of new possibilities and risks" (Marcus 2012: 430; my emphasis). Presenting a risk narrative that can be read on many levels, within the cluster of interrelated biotechnological and bioethical issues *Never Let Me Go* also engages specifically with the psychological risk posed to the clones by being brought up with no future. As will be shown, the main function – and cruelty – of the 'exclusive' educational system (Hailsham and the Cottages), is to install "care" and a belief in values such as love and art as coping mechanisms that minimize not only the risks of the clones' rebellion against the oppressive system but that guarantee their mental stability through a trained detachment from their own bodies in order to maintain a healthy, calm balance between body and psyche for as long as possible (– until "they switch you off" –) in the face of a reality of hopelessness and suffering that can only be described as "horror movie stuff" (NLMO 274).

The bodies of humans and clones are intrinsically bound together through a process aiming at risk management; one is violated in order to save and sustain the other.[9] Referring to Agamben's conception of "bare life",[10] the clone characters are assigned the status of subhuman life, raised to be more than pure biological substance, but existing solely to be exploited and eventually killed by humans. Their perceived otherness, comparable to the status often given to animals, is a source of slight fear and disgust, as well as necessary prerequisite to justify their treatment.[11] Having been created to forestall human death as living resources of health risk management through human organ and tissue transplantation, in turn, any risks to the children's bodies need to be diminished. Unsurprisingly then, the only apparently openly enforced rule at Hailsham is a strict ban of smoking. Kathy recalls how guardians "made sure to give us some sort of lecture each time any reference to cigarettes came along" (NLMG 67), and how Miss Lucy tells them: "You're ... *special*. So keeping yourselves well, keeping yourselves very healthy inside, that's much more important for each of you than it is for me" (NLMG 68; original emphasis). Through their socialization, the children have internalized a view of themselves as different from the human adults and a notion of their bodies as precious commodities

---

9 On the representation of posthumanism in the novel see especially Nayar (2014a). He argues that through the process of transplantation the donated clone organs live on in the bodies of the 'normal' humans, creating, in fact, a new hybrid kind of (post)humanity through assimilation of an Other into a Self, a process of mutual dependency and exploitation that evokes comparisons to colonialism.
10 See Giorgio Agamben's *Homo Sacer* (1998).
11 On the parallels between the perception of clones and animals, which similarly challenge traditional conceptions of the fully human, see Summers-Bremner (2006).

they need to protect. But, as yet, they have only a vague idea what their future as donors entails and so Tommy worries, for example, about his body accidentally 'unzipping' during the night and his organs spilling out; he also tells Kathy: "We should never take chances with our health" (NLMG 84). While the narration omits all technicalities of the process of organ donation and largely avoids detailed descriptions of the pain and suffering of the clones, for the characters also notions about the outside world are "kept deliberately hazy" (NLMG 120), including sex, relationships, and the health risks faced by real humans. It is apparently known to them, however, that they face a high chance of completing, i.e. dying, after their first donation and that they generally never survive more than four. The odds of life and death are thus, in contrast to other humans, strikingly clear to them. Part of the uncanny effect of Kathy's narration on the reader is the absence of the characters' fear of death which is replaced by a rational acceptance and concept of duty. Ruth says: "I was pretty much ready when I became a donor. It felt right. After all, it's what we're *supposed* to be doing, isn't it?" (NLMG 223; original emphasis). A question at the heart of the novel is about how it is possible to install a sense of moral responsibility in the clones that makes them not only accept but feel obliged to donate their organs to humans they have little to no contact with. Bruce Jennings notes: "This sense of responsibility is based at least in part on deception. It is also fostered through emotional support during childhood, which allows a sense of conscience and empathy to develop" (Jennings 2010: 19).

In *Never Let Me Go*, the characters lack agency and any inclination for rebellion or trying to escape, a fact that has disturbed many critics and readers to the degree of "intense outrage" (Black 2009: 791).[12] There are no emotional outbursts from the clones, let alone any rumours of a carer plotting to rescue a donor; the only exceptions are "Tommy's tantrums" (NLMG 9) which, however, culminate in nothing more than him screaming against the wind on a deserted country roadside. Generally, the clones in Ishiguro's text are as far removed as can possibly be from a renegade group of superhumans threatening to take over the world; they seem resigned to their status as the precious risk-management property of others, forced into obedience and acceptance of their lives by the outwardly benevolent means of a system based on rigid control through

---

12 See Tomoiagă's comment: "The feeling the reader has is overwhelming anger at [...] the characters, themselves, for not being more daring, more courageous and just run away" (2012: 258); Harrison says: "*Never Let Me Go* makes you want to have sex, take drugs, run a marathon, dance – anything to convince yourself that you're more alive, more determined, more conscious, more dangerous than any of these characters" (Harrison 2005).

the soft violence of 'sheltered' education and exclusion.[13] The epitome of the clones' lack of control over their own future is the image of Kathy, Ruth, and Tommy, the latter at this point already severely weakened by several donations, climbing into a boat stranded on a Norfolk beach that literally cannot take them anywhere.

If Ishiguro's novel does not quite fit into the generic confines of science fiction, a first-time reader of *Never Let Me Go*, as John Mullan (2010: 104) points out, will also notice that it evades some of the expectations of classical dystopian fiction, primarily the lack of rebellion of a single character against the system. It also lacks the fully-fledged development of an alternative society with oppressive laws and the 'evil' authorities in power, "there is no indication to an articulate political, economical or cultural system" (Tomoiagă 2012: 264).[14] Still, it contains many distinctly Orwellian elements, including – however hazily depicted – mechanisms of surveillance and restrictions of personal freedom and expression. Furthermore, the clones are corrupted into complicity through careful control of language and emotions, through the use of euphemisms disguising harsh, fearful realities (see Jennings 2010: 19), and through fostering illusions and myths that sustain hope and a sense of privilege. These strategies form part of the experimental 'humane' cloning project, which Miss Emily and Madame are forced to explain to Kathy and Tommy in the end: "You were lucky pawns. There was a certain climate and now it's gone" (NLMG 261). But they are also readable as strategies of systemic risk management guided towards avoiding rebellion of the clones and their falling into despair which could potentially compromise their health.[15]

The novel opens with the narrator Kathy H. revealing to the reader startling factors about her life and character. It only becomes clear later how these are intrinsically connected to managing risk and terror connected to a breakdown of self and social order. The opening chapter also introduces the array of euphe-

---

13 Several critics have noted the obvious parallels evoked in the narrative between slavery and racial discrimination and the clones' oppression and their perception as inferior being, more akin to animals than 'full' humans; see Atwood (2005), Black (2009), and Gill (2014).

14 Concerning warning function typical of endings of dystopian fictions, Ishiguro reiterates his concern with the present and human condition in general, cautioning against reductive readings of his text: "'I didn't want,' he explains, 'to imply that this was in any way a prophecy or a warning. I wanted the story to have clear metaphorical links with the way we all live as human beings" (cited in Patterson 2005).

15 See De Boever's argument that *Never Let Me Go* illustrates how the novel as a genre reflects Foucault's theory of governmentality and biopolitics, revealing modern government's interest in the biological life of the citizens, including health, reproduction, emotional regulation etc. (2013: 63; 67).

misms running through the narrative, i.e. words such as "guardians, training, students, carers, donations, deferrals, completion", which, Mark Currie says, serve to obscure "a brutal reality more properly named as captors, socialization, clones, prefects, enforced organ donations, false hope, and death" (Currie 2010: 103). Kathy is full of pride about her job, which apparently requires great efficiency and the ability to stay calm and cope with loneliness; her second main source of pride is her privileged upbringing at Hailsham and she repeatedly considers "just how lucky we'd been – Tommy, Ruth, me, all the rest of us" (NLMG 6). Presenting the children's actually rigidly regulated and limited life as full and complex, Kathy's narration reveals what Currie refers to as the paradoxical concept of "privileged deprivation" instilled in the Hailsham pupils during their secluded upbringing, "an entirely internal economy of privilege and deprivation, where comparisons are not relative to the general population or standards in the outside world" (Currie 2013: 159).

The narration contains many direct addresses of the reader: "I don't know how it was where you were" (NLMG 13). While the appeal to general childhood memories and the boarding school setting allow for empathy,[16] distance is created by the detailed description of banal memories, which seem of special importance only to the characters, and of bizarre activities, e.g. at Hailsham the students are encouraged to treasure "exchanges", and their own art works to an absurdly high degree. The exchanges, a circulation of worthless knick-knacks and self-made art works are the children's only chance to built a collection of personal belongings and a measure of their popularity and self-worth according to "how good you were at 'creating'" (NLMG 16). The criterion of (artistic) "originality" presents an almost perverse test for clones as human copies;[17]

---

[16] Although the plot exclusively focuses on the clones, the reader is brought to empathize with the posthuman narrator and challenged to recognize the fuzzy borders between sameness and difference with regards to the humanity and lives of the clone characters. Several critics have noted how the reader, through being directly addressed by Kathy and through being made to share the struggle for comprehension, is made to share a frame of reference; see Black (2009: 790), Robbins (2007: 293), and Sawyer (2011: 241). This can be described as a strategy of evoking "reverse sympathy", as Kathy assumes likeness with the implied reader, who is then lead to question the assumed similarity (see Puchner 2008: 47), but in the end left with a strong sense of the narrator's humanity. Escudero Pérez sums up this process of creating narrative empathy in clone narratives as follows: "Clone characters draw the audience into a three-stage process of identification: they first have to be textually recognised as human – or almost human –, then their artificiality has to be stressed and finally, from that objectified position they reclaim their personhood thus gaining subjectivity" (2014: 17).

[17] Walkowitz stresses Ishiguro's topical engagement with the disdain for things "copied" and with originality and authenticity as values for humanity in the novel. She argues that the nar-

moreover this "recycling of personal possessions", Rosemary Rizq points out, "foreshadows the future recycling of their own body parts" (Rizq 2014: 520). Aside from strengthening communal bonds among the students, it encourages an economy of exchange and an instrumental perception of themselves that is a crucial stabilizing pillar of the clones' socialization. The students have several other obsessions such as the myth of "deferrals", allowing a stalling of the imminent slope towards death: "You could ask for your donations to be put back by three, even four years. [...] So long as you *qualified*" (NLMG 150; original emphasis). According to rumours, qualification is measured by the ability to prove that a couple is "properly in love" (NLMG 151); meanwhile the capacity for love seems to be hinging on the value of one's art work – as a dubious indicator of one's ability to 'feel.' The judge ruling over the value of love and art, as the only temporary saving graces imagined to be available to the characters, is Madame, who regularly selects the best art works for her 'Gallery'. Unwavering in their belief in the possibility of deferrals and the purpose of the gallery till near the end of the narrative when Tommy and Ruth's hope is shattered during their visit to Madame and Miss Emily, the characters' utopian idea of "living happily ever after" is thus limited to a span of three to four years. Another obsession, which similarly inspires a lot of conversation and imaginations among the characters, but little action, is the rumour of being able to find one's "possible". Aware that they are genetic copies, "One big idea behind finding your model was that when you did, you'd glimpse your future" (NLMG 137). For the children, who have no control over their futures, the confrontation with their possible is the only option of imagining an alternative course of life and of discovering what "your life held in store" (NLMG 138). But during their stay at the Cottages – a sort of in-between place where the clones are put after Hailsham in order to await the beginning of their short professional lives as donors and carers –, they only make one half-hearted attempt to find Ruth's possible. Filled with disappointment after the failed mission, Ruth angrily reveals the characters' knowledge about their origins which they normally do not dare to mention: "We're modelled from trash. Junkies, prostitutes, winos, tramps. Convicts, maybe, just so long as they aren't psychos" (NLMG 164).

Kathy's narrative is apparently driven by a sense of urgency to remember her past – to 'never let go' of her memories – that the reader at this point still struggles to understand. According to Keith McDonald, the novel is written as

---

rative explores concepts of uniqueness, the "capacity for genuine love, authentic expressivity, and artistic originality" with cruel consequences: "In *Never Let Me Go*, valuing uniqueness leads to killing clones and preserving people" (2015: 121; 105).

a kind of "speculative memoir" (McDonald 2007: 82) which differs from the generic convention of autobiographical writing, or rather, which presents them with the customary emotional intensity but in a very reduced form, eliminating, for instance, dramatic life events and all information about the narrator's birth and parentage:[18] "The result is an autobiography drained of its usual depth and acknowledgement of a fuller life outside of the textual boundaries, but fixated instead on what little experience the protagonist holds. This poverty of experience can also be seen in the social events, rituals, and artifacts presented in the novel" (2007: 78). The purpose of her narration, it seems, is to stop herself from losing memories but also to gain an understanding of what happened; it is a struggle for causality and clarity. Uncertainty, vagueness and opacity are reflected in her use of language riddled with conjunctive constructions and words such as "baffling", "hazy", "perhaps", "maybe", and "somehow" (see Kemp 2005). While critical readings have emphasized Kathy's role as an unreliable narrator (cf. Mieth 2015: 228), I agree with John Mullan's observation that in her struggle for recollection Kathy is "not so much an unreliable narrator, as an inadequate narrator. [...] Much that she recalls is puzzling, as if her past were a tissue of mysteries" (Mullan 2010: 111). The mysteries comprise, for instance, the rumours surrounding Madame's gallery or the behaviour of the guardians which, in Kathy's memory, "remained in a hazy realm" (NLMG 32). Nonetheless, she continually tries to recollect what utterances, things and events meant and why her and the other students' younger selves acted and felt the way she remembers it. Concerning the depiction of consciousness and risk perception, it is significant that the narrator's frequent references to difficulties of recollection cluster around questions of knowledge and anticipation: "It's hard now to remember just how much we knew by then. [...] we perhaps even knew that a long way down the line there were donations waiting for us" (NLMG 69). Though not considering the issue of risk perception, Mark Currie usefully identifies Kathy's paradoxical struggle for remembered anticipation and the memories of false hopes as lying at the core of the novel (Currie 2010: 97; 99). The attempt to remember what one thought the future would be like, what one hoped for or was fearful about, in the past requires the (impossible) return to a remembered state of knowing or not-knowing measured against one's currents state of experience. Therefore, Currie argues, "the very idea of dread develops an irony produced in the chasm between Kathy's remembered anticipations, and

---

18 With Kathy H., John Mullan argues, "Ishiguro has invented a person who is related to no one. [...] She has no possibility or fantasy of a biological relationship with another person" (2010: 113). As such, the clone child as first-person narrator presents the figure of the orphan, recurrent throughout Ishiguro's fictions, in its most extreme form (see Puchner 2008: 44).

the anticipations made by a reader of the more extreme horrors which lie in wait. Many of the novel's remembered anticipations work in this way, as ironic failures to anticipate the really awful thing around the corner" (Currie 2013: 155). While there are no explicit calculations for risks from the side of clone characters and all references to perceived dangers and transgression remain vague, it also becomes clear that this evasion of risk perception, of consequences and probabilities, is the central foundation of the Hailsham system and the characters' conditioning.

It is, however, not entirely successful in eliminating the children's ability of risk perception despite controlling and limiting the children's understanding about themselves and the outside world. Kathy reflects: "Maybe all of us at Hailsham had little secrets like that – little private nooks created out of thin air *where we could go off alone with our fears and longings*. But the very fact that we had such needs would have felt wrong to us at the time – like somehow we were letting the side down" (NLMG 73; my emphasis). Another episode illustrates how the clones are capable of perceiving risk and making predictions, if in a strangely detached manner though equally based on emotional and rational experiences. Aware that Madame is "scared of us" (NLMG 33), the children experimentally force her into close proximity with them by blocking the door, for them a small act of disobedience that requires great courage. The result, Madame's "shudder" of disgust, is deeply unsettling, and Kathy remembers how up until this moment, "it had been a pretty light-hearted matter, *with a bit of a dare element to it*. And it wasn't as though Madame did anything other than what we predicted she'd do: she just froze and waited for us to pass by" (NLMG 35; my emphasis).

In the novel, hope and a sense of privilege and purpose largely depend on not knowing or not admitting certain knowledge; the second important means of sustaining hope is through rumours and stories fuelled by imagination. When Kathy, remembering a particular story they used to make up about one of their favourite guardians, Miss Geraldine, admits that "we must have had an idea of how precarious the foundations of our fantasy were, because we always avoided any confrontation" (NLMG 51), this confession applies, in fact, to her whole narrative. It highlights the precarious balance of the Hailsham system between keeping the children in a state of 'secure' belief and, Arne De Boever argues, "the risk of them being unsettled. [...] Hailsham life is in fact so scripted that it risks to collapse under any kind of critique. It is a world that can only exists on the condition that one does not ask too many questions" (De Boever 2013: 63). Indeed, in her struggle to recollect – and also somehow justify – why they refrained, for instance, from pressing the guardians to tell them more about their future when they had the chance, Kathy affirms the perception of asking certain questions as bearing the risk of emotional discomfort and feelings of instability for both sides: *"we knew just enough to make as wary of that whole territory.* [...] It unnerved us to see them change like that" (NLMG 69; my emphasis).

Aside from this, the consequences of risking transgression are never clearly articulated in the narrative. There is apparently a strong attachment to following the rules that stifles any curiosity or attempts to escape and is fuelled by a fear of what lies beyond the "Hailsham boundaries" (NLMG 50). Puchner argues: "The power of indoctrination is confirmed through the absence of external enforcement mechanisms; no patrols or police forces are mentioned anywhere in the novel" (Puchner 2008: 38). The whole system instead seemingly works through "unspoken agreements" and the upholding of the "mystery dimension" (NLMG 121) of the outside world as being fraught with danger. At Hailsham, while Kathy even remembers certain paths through the garden being "out of bounds" (NLMG 198), the main frontier is made up by the woods surrounding the school grounds, "a dark fringe of trees" (NLMG 49), the children do not even dare to look at: "Safest was the front of the main house, because you couldn't see them from any of the windows. [...] There were all kinds of horrible stories about the woods" (NLMG 50). These stories, ghostly tales of people running off into the woods and ending up dead, capture fears of punishment for violating the rules as well as a general fear of the unknown, disorienting territory of the real world which the children seem set to avoid. Even after leaving Hailsham and living in the Cottage, an environment which allows them the comparatively greater freedom of taking trips into Norfolk towns, the characters rarely take advantage of this and Kathy underlines how "there was definitely an understanding" (NLMG 130) of what one did or did not do.

This lack of curiosity and desire to venture beyond boundaries is commonly taken as one of the main signs of the characters' posthuman difference. Tomoiagă explains how this "strikes the reader as mostly uncommon: pre-teens and teenagers are known to be willing to cross boundaries and dare each in this respect" (Tomoiagă 2012: 257). Affirming risk-taking as an intrinsically human ability, in the novel the depiction of the clones' passivity has raised the difficult question if they are creatures "designed with certain limitations, including [...] a lack of rebelliousness that makes their policing unnecessary" (Puchner 2008: 41). As the clones are undoubtedly capable of strong emotions and developing fierce loyalties, which cause fears of loss or harm of the people they care for, what is hard to bear for the reader is Kathy's confession of her own reluctance to act. At Hailsham, Ruth and Kathy make a pact to be "secret guards" (NLMG 49) for Miss Geraldine, because they have a vague sense that the guardian's open communication with the students puts her at risk (and she is later indeed removed from her position). But typically, their plot of protecting Miss Geraldine consists only of conversations and gathering "evidence": "For some reason, we were satisfied this would keep any immediate danger at bay" (NLMG 51). For Kathy, a sense of safety is not only upheld by treasured fantasies, avoiding transgressing into the outside world or asking too many questions, but by limiting contact and trust largely to her relationships with Ruth and Tommy. When another girl, Moira, seeks to intrude into the close-knit group, it is obvious how any change or crossing into new territory frightens her, highlighting the fact that the fear of their unacknowledged future is a constant presence: "What it was, I suppose, is that Moira was suggesting she and I cross some line together, and I wasn't prepared for that yet. I think I sensed how beyond that line, there was something harder and darker and I didn't want that. Not for me, not for any of us" (NLMG 55). There is, however, one a brief moment, when the characters dare to and actually enjoy venturing beyond their set routines and known world, and, at least, talk about their hopes and desires. At the cottages, "just for those few months, we somehow managed to live in this cosy state of suspension in which we could ponder our lives without the usual boundaries. [...] lost in conversation about our plans for the future" (NLMG 140).

Several critics have suggested that Ishiguro's exploration of the characters' reluctance to break through the confines of the system transcends the question of the clones' humanity and extends to the reasons and circumstances in which humans in general "might not only accept but actually beseech our own confinement" (Currie 2010: 91). For Currie, the title already draws attention to a complicated "request for everlasting captivity" (Currie 2013: 14), while, in the opinion of John Harrison, the text "isn't about cloning, or being a clone, at all" (Harrison 2005). Rather, it engages critically with the passive acceptance of disappointed ambitions and highlights the human capacity for denial and the unquestioning acceptance of authorities instilled through processes of socialization (see Harrison 2005; also Sawyer 2011: 243).[19] However, two aspects need to be stressed: The characters' behaviour is motivated by fear at least to the same degree as conditioned acceptance. Though offering glimpses of self-critical reflection of their lack of action, Kathy's narration underlines that it springs from a deep fear of the future and a desire to hold onto the present – in other words, it reveals nothing but the very human desire to avoid thinking about the inevitability of death and hold onto life. After moving to the Cottages, she tells the reader, "a part of us

---

19 See the author's own comment on the subject: "With *Never Let Me Go* I knew from the start that I didn't want to write a story about an enslaved, exploited class that would then rebel. [...] I was interested in the human capacity to accept what must seem like a limited and cruel fate" (Ishiguro in Moore and Sontheimer 2005).

stayed like that: fearful of the world around us, and – no matter how much we despised ourselves for it – unable quite to let each other go" (NLMG 118). In a broader sense, the novel explores the intrinsic connection between risk perceptions, the instillation of fear and governmentality in the Foucauldian sense. The clones, as a part of the population, become easily manageable and the risks of rebellion and deviation are minimized. To be specific: the mechanisms of holding onto soothing memories and illusions, detachment from their bodies and denial combine to form a psychological safety net that assures the steadiness through the painful process of organ donation.

With their education designed to occupy the clone characters until their organs have grown up and they are taught just enough humanist values to create strong bonds of communality, love and friendship and to make the later process of 'care-taking' possible, the politics of Hailsham are based on a deliberate "*sheltering*" (NLMG 263; original emphasis) of the clone children from the outside world. It allows them to focus their attention and energies exclusively onto their lessons and art works, giving them a sense of purpose and value without destabilizing disruptions. Miss Emily, and Madame explain in the end: "You wouldn't be who you are today if we'd not protected you [...] you wouldn't have lost yourselves in your art and your writing" (NLMG 263). The concept of "care", usually involving empathy and concern and aiming for the protection and development of a loved other, is generally a highly complicated one in the novel. The characters are first taken care of from the side of the school and later through a system of professional "carers" from their own ranks which keep them calm and quiet during the slow, painful process of dying. This care, Arne De Boever writes, "dulls the pain of their existence, and it might be that if it were not for this care, their pain would develop into something more explosive that would overthrow the dubious biopolitical system" (De Boever 2013: 60). In the novel, education and 'care-taking' are presented as means to eliminate anger and minimize risks of psychological trauma, yet seemingly also to impede critical thinking and the striving for independence and freedom. On more than one occasion the reader is made to wonder if these versions of sheltering and care taking resemble acts of cruelty rather than risk management. In turn, one may ask what actually constitutes kindness towards others in the face of a limited life and horrific fate. For example, Tommy, who contests the system to a much greater degree than any of the other characters, is repeatedly told by thee guardians as well as by his fellow students, and later even by Kathy, that his art is "rubbish", and as a result struggles nearly until the end of his life with his supposedly creative inadequacy. While this can be seen as a way to channel his rage towards himself, I also agree with Bruce Robbins' suggestion that it appears as a way of protection: "If there is no way out for him, then perhaps better to leave him in a state of self-delusive aspiration" (Robbins 2007: 299).

In the last part of the narrative, after Ruth's death, Kathy becomes Tommy's carer; this marks also the beginning of their briefest of love stories. There is a terrible sense of belatedness all around. In her roles as Tommy's lover and carer, which appear complicit with the system and almost congruent at this point, Kathy's task is to calm Tommy down and to grant him the his wish of the visit to Madame. It is unclear to what extent Kathy can recollect the extent of her own remaining belief in the myth of deferrals at this point; she certainly cannot shake the feeling "that we were doing all of this too late" (NLMG 237). Tommy, however, is still fully caught in the story. Despite being physically depleted, he prepares for the visit with all the energy he has left, making new art in order to compensate up for the material that was not chosen for Madame's Gallery while at Hailsham. With death being imminent, he clings to the hope of borrowed time more than ever. Madame and Emily react with shock when they are confronted with the deep seriousness of Tommy and Kathy's belief and hope of a deferral: "Poor creatures. What did we do to you?" (NLMG 249). The visit epitomizes the feeling of discomfort of the human characters when they are made to witness, as Jimena Escudero Pérez puts it, "the clash between the very humane hopes of the clones with their inhuman fate and *purpose*" (Escudero Pérez 2014: 12; original emphasis). The other crucial scene in this regard, is, of course, when Madame watches Kathy dancing with a pillow in her arms to the tape recording of Judy Bridgewater's "Never Let Me Go", imagining it to be a song about a mother's wish for a child.

With what appears as more than slightly cruel irony at the end, Miss Emily explains to Kathy the belief underlying long since abandoned government policies that "a little fantasy", as well as liberal arts education would do no harm to the clone children but give them hope (NLMG 253); she also asks her to try and see it "historically" (NLMG 257), alluding to the British post-war scientific context in which Hailsham was founded as an experiment to test and disprove the clones' their perception by the public as "less than fully human" (NLMG 256). Ultimately, the employment of creative artwork as the main, and only, measure of the character's humanity and means to prove the existence of their 'souls', is revealed to be nothing more than an illusion and pointless experiment. However much the reader may struggle with the flatness of Kathy's narration and the absence of rebellion, it becomes blatantly obvious that the clone children truly humane characteristics go unnoticed by the system. Agreeing with Robbins (2007: 294) and Rizq (2014: 529), these lie in the characters' abilities of story-telling and holding onto stories, reworking memories, participating in rumours and myth-making, and experiencing love and loss, which are, in fact, the main preoccupations of Kathy's narration. The scene of Kathy dancing alone in her room to "Never let me go" demonstrates her imagination, desire and subjectivity; all the clone characters' fascination with the search for their "possibles" shows their desire to create a personal identity, to engage in fantasies of origin and the future. Instances of intrinsically human emotions, desires and (inter)actions are revealed in particular in the final chapters. Shortly before her death, Ruth is desperate to settle her affairs and apologizes to Kathy, confessing her selfishness and guilt for keeping her and Tommy apart despite knowing about their feeling for each other. For Ruth, dying is made easier through the hope that Kathy and Tommy can finally prove their love to Madame: "If it's you two, there's got to be a chance. A real chance" (NLMG 228). Later, Kathy is shown to be capable of spite, wishing that Ruth had not died with the hope of atoning her selfishness by believing in an illusion that is painfully shattered for the remaining couple.

In comparison to Shelley's *Frankenstein*, the 'creatures' in *Never Let Mo Go* likewise suffer from the treatment and "traumatic education at the hands of a world that will not recognize" (McDonald 2007: 81) them. But though they are, like Frankenstein's monster, confined to a shadow existence, after their reasoned appeal to their 'makers' and subsequent disillusionment, they do not seek revenge. Instead, Kathy H. dedicates her energy to her job and what Keith MacDonald describes as a "life writing project that will preserve the memory of dead and dying loved ones" (McDonald 2007: 80). Resistance in the narrative is ultimately not directed against the system that denies the characters their humanity, but against the risk of loss and time running out. Determinedly, Kathy says: "I lost Ruth, then I lost Tommy, but I won't lose my memories of them" (NLMG 280); "I'll have Hailsham with me, safely in my head, and that'll be something no one can take away" (NLMG 281). Her motivation for becoming Ruth's carer and the reunion with Tommy largely springs from seeking to counteract her shock after hearing of the closing of Hailsham, for her, a definite ending intrinsically connected to her sense of continuity and safety: "It's not that I started to panic, exactly. But it definitely felt like Hailsham's going away had shifted everything around us" (NLMG 209). She seeks to renew her closeness to Ruth and Tommy as a means to protect and to hold onto a sense of her self, based on the reality of her past, which is harder to sustain without being surrounded by people with whom she shares memories.

The final chapters deal with Kathy's reality as a carer, the lonely, long hours she spends driving through the country from one completion centre to another, and those spent at the bedside of dying donors. Proudly efficient because she can cope with these circumstances and lend detached support to others, she still confesses to the reader: "I don't claim I've been immune to all of this, but I've learnt to live with it" (NLMG 203). With haunting sadness the final scene underlines how Kathy is rationally able to control her imagination and feelings of longing and loss and avoid the risk of being overwhelmed by them. Conjuring up the image of Tommy waving at her from a distance, she says: "The fantasy never got beyond that – I didn't let it – [...]. I just waited a bit, then turned back to the car, to drive off to wherever it was I was supposed to be" (NLMG 282). Reading *Never Let Me Go* as a coming-of-age narrative alongside biomedical studies of patients' subjective experience of quality of life, Matthew Eatough (2011) argues that Ishiguro's depiction of the Hailsham students reveals a conjunction of a particular affective indifference and vocational proficiency that is comparable to patients, who during prolonged illness experience the body as somehow removed from the self. To a large extent, the system presented in the novel seems to succeed in inducing indifference towards bodies; in the end, all clone characters seemingly care more about their professional duty than their lives. With Kathy's job as a carer mainly involving regulating the negative emotions "that trouble donors and transforming them into malleable indifference" (Eatough 2011: 147), her professional duty is the manipulation of affect towards indifference to the body (and thus also towards death). Diverting all her attention towards other bodies is also a way for her to safely channel her own affect. Agreeing with Eatough's argument, it needs to be stressed that the main function of this indifference towards the body is guarding against a risk that is never fully articulated in the narrative. One can only imagine what the undeniably even more inhumane alternative to the care-taking system would look like. Ishiguro's posthuman narrator shows no sign of the emotional impact the witnessing of the suffering of others has on her; this lack of emotional response is typically interpreted as a sign of her deficient humanity. But rather than viewing Kathy's monologue as "evasive narration, which only peripherally registers the morally and politically contentious nature of the issues" (Eatough 2011: 135), the non-engagement with these issues and her own body form conditioned strategies to guarantee survival (as long as necessary) and the stability of the system. The Hailsham children are able to cope with a reality of suffering beyond relief and compensation by being trained to carry on with what they are supposed to do and seeking refuge in storytelling, illusions, and memories. Aside from the bioethical context, what makes the narrative dystopian is the deconstruction of two great myths of humankind, the immortality of love and the possibility to survive through artistic creation; but, as Ligia Tomoiagă puts it, "finitude is 'round the corner', and there is no escape" (Tomoiagă 2012: 266). While the title of Ishiguro's novel already contains the imperative to guard against the risk of letting go of the other, in the end, time runs out for all human creatures.

11.2 The Ticking Bomb of Denial and Inertia: *Solar*

Anthropogenic climate change is widely conceived to be among the top global risks humanity faces today (see Beck 2006; 2007; Mayer 2016: 207), and thus comes, as Anthony Giddens notes, attached "with a doomsday literature" (2009: 28). Ian McEwan's novel *Solar* (2010) has been received as the first work by a "leading literary novelist" that tackles climate change and the risks of global warming as its "explicit and central subject" (Kerridge 2010; original emphasis). But rather than developing a dark apocalyptic scenario in the speculative, dystopian fashion typical of contemporary "cli-fi" novels,[20] it presents a satirical and allegorical narrative about greed, denial and inertia, suggesting that these intrinsically human qualities contribute to the mounting of environmental risks and hinder the taking of urgently required counter-measures.

The critical responses to McEwan's novel and the author's choice of genre transcended the question of literary quality even before the text was published, raising the question whether a realist satire should be considered an appropriate treatment of the morally and politically charged subject matter.[21] As such, *Solar*'s initial "shocking surprise" was not its topic, the fact that it is a "global warming novel" (Sutcliffe 2010), but that it uses comedy for its literary variation of the dooms-day motif which seems to prescribe a certain seriousness[22] or invoke a "new catastrophism".[23] The text also engages self-critically with the question of art, specifically fictional literature's power to impact on real-life politics. Whereas many critics' reaction to the novel seems motivated by the belief that the novel ought to do more with regards to being *engagé*, depicting the threat of global warming and suggesting potential remedies, the author himself

---

[20] By now already canonical "cli-fi" novels include Maggie Gee's *The Flood* (2004), Kim Stanley Robinson's *The Science in the Capital* trilogy (2004–2007), Cormac McCarthy's *The Road* (2006), Margaret Atwood's *Year of the Flood* (2009), and Barbara Kingsolver's *Flight Behavior* (2012). Further examples are Susan M. Gaines *Carbon Dreams* (2001), and Paolo Bacigalupi *The Windup Girl* (2009). For a survey of climate change as a dominant theme in literature and literary studies and on the overlap of climate change fiction, science fiction, dystopia, and post-apocalyptic scenarios, see, e.g., Goodbody and Johns-Putra (2018), Irr (2015), Johns-Putra (2016), S. Mayer (2016), Trexler (2015), and Tuhus-Dubrow (2013); on climate change fictions and the Anthropocene see Bartosch (2015).
[21] See Kellish (2013) and Kerridge (2010).
[22] Cf. Heather Houser's comment: "*Solar* is not the novel of climate change that environmentally conscious and curious readers have awaited" (2010: 10).
[23] See John Urry on "this new catastrophism in social and scientific thought" (2011: 38) that is also reflected in the increasing occurrence of doomsday scenarios in novels and films in the last two decades.

declares that "it is not the job of novelists to save the world. No. But I am as keen that it should be saved as anybody'" (in Brown 2010). Thus McEwan explicitly rejects the role of literary risk manager while his novel presents a haunting diagnosis of the human condition that causes the ongoing progressive decline of the globe by establishing allegorical parallels between the protagonist Michael Beard's 'sickening' body and behaviour and the state of the earth.

The differences and relations between literature and science are a topical preoccupation in McEwan's works, which often feature protagonists who are scientists, e. g. in *Enduring Love* or *Saturday*, as is the exploration of the causality of (potentially) catastrophic events and the question of human agency. Evi Zemanek, who explicitly engages with Beck's risk society thesis[24] in her reading of *Solar*, argues: "For many years, McEwan has focused in his writing on the differences between risks (as consequences of human decisions and as factors that can be reduced), dangers (of contingent disasters that cannot be prevented), and disaster itself (as the actual event of damage), and [in *Solar*] he skilfully stages the turning point from anticipation to catastrophe" (Zemanek 2012: 52).[25] To some extent McEwan, whom Daniel Zalewski refers to as a "connoisseur of dread" how has mastered the "art of unease" by "performing the literary equivalent of turning on the tub faucet and leaving the room" (Zalewski 2009), is well-accustomed when it comes to dealing with potentially (un)controllable risks and disasters in his fictions.[26] But the literary depiction of global warming presents a challenge even to a writer of McEwan's calibre and he feels forced to acknowledge that in spite of "all the reading that I've done around climate change, none of it suggests anything useful in the way of approaching this novelistically"

---

[24] There is a discernible trend in recent critical studies to view climate change in relation to the increasingly dominant concept of risk, following Beck's "risk society" thesis, and Heise's pioneering application of Beck's theory to literary criticism (see Heise 2008; Johns-Putra 2016). See also Mayer and Weik von Mossner's *The Anticipation of Catastrophe* (2014), which focuses on climate change as risk narrative in selected case studies of North American literature and culture. In this volume, see especially the essays by Mayer (2014: 21–37), Mehnert (2014: 59–78), and Goodbody (2014: 39–58).

[25] Cf. Mayer (2014) who distinguishes between two types of risk narratives in contemporary novels which deal with climate change: "narratives of catastrophe" which are set after the disaster has happened and focus on the consequences and "narratives of anticipation" that engage with the discourses of uncertainty about current environmental problems. McEwan's *Solar* would fall into the latter of Mayer's categories; however, in my opinion Zemanek's argument rightly draws attention to the dramatic development of the narrative, although the final catastrophe is not narrated in detail.

[26] In fact, the prominence of the topic of risk perception and management in McEwan's literary oeuvre would warrant a detailed study in its own right, though *Solar* and *Saturday* can be seen as representative examples.

(Tonkin 2007). Trying to avoid dystopia and didacticism in his "global warming novel" by employing a generic fusion of dark satire, slapstick humour, and thriller elements, McEwan's *Solar* bears testimony to the limits of artistic production which inevitably falls short of advancing the technology or government regulations that could productively tackle environmental threats, but also challenges the belief in the capacities of science and politics to deal with them adequately. Bearing in mind Garrard's argument that the phenomenon of climate change generally tests our convictions "that science and liberal democracy can steer us clear of catastrophe" (Garrard 2013: 135), *Solar*, as a fictional text that fuses laughter and a celebration of life with humanist pessimism, suggests that potential risk management in this context can only be found in a deepening of the self-awareness of humans as (intrinsically selfish) individuals and, as one of the central moral parables in the novel, the Arctic boot room episode shows, in stricter and better government laws which serve as a corrective to the human inability 'to stop'[27] and act collaboratively towards the achievement of a long-term goal of risk-management.

In addition to the use of humour and (supposed lack of) political engagement, critics have taken issue with McEwan's detached narrative voice and almost exclusive focus on the "anti-hero protagonist" (Kerridge 2010) Michael Beard, a deeply flawed character and, arguably, "a joyfully monstrous creation" (Brown 2010). Professionally, Beard is an aging Nobel-prize winning physicist who in the last part of the narrative embarks on a new solar energy project using artificial photosynthesis only in order to revitalize his stagnant scientific career, plagiarizing a younger colleague's research in the process, and an exemplary egoist and womanizer fighting a lost battle against his self-destructive appetites in his private life. Through Beard's character, the novel highlights the contradictory tension between knowledge and (conscious) ignorance with regards to the danger of global warming. Climate scientist Stefan Rahmstorf describes the latter as "an existential threat that is well-understood by its scientists, but largely ignored by a population who prefers to delude itself in creative ways about the gradually unfolding disaster" (Rahmstorf 2010). Despite being a scientist, Beard epitomizes this attitude of the general public. Fulfilling his role as head of the National Renewable Energy Centre with hardly more than disinterested reluctance, Beard's opinion of climate change consists of scepticism and

---

[27] In 2005, McEwan joined the interdisciplinary Cape Farewell project, a trip to the Svalbard archipelago in the Arctic led by the artist David Buckland, which aimed to raise cultural awareness of the issues of global warming. This expedition marked the beginning of the author's public engagement with the topic of climate change. In an interview, he says: "How do we stop? That really does become a matter of human nature" (Tonkin 2007).

a felt lack of relevance of the issue, viewing it largely as public scare-mongering perpetuated through the usual media channels,[28] only loosely backed-up by scientific facts. The narration repeatedly details Beard's detached view and his refusal to see climate change as risk. To give an example:

> It was one in a list of issues, of looming sorrows, that comprised the background to the news, and he read about it, vaguely deplored it and expected governments to meet and take action. [...] And he was unimpressed by some of the wild commentary that suggested the world was in 'peril', that humankind was drifting towards calamity, when coastlines would disappear under the waves, crops fail, and hundreds of millions of refugees surge from one country, one continent, to another [...]. (S 15–16)

Using the threat of nuclear destruction during the Cold War era as comparison for a similarly apocalyptic scenario that failed to materialize, Beard cynically perceives climate change simply as the intentionally created risk *du jour*; "in the absence of any other overwhelming concern [...] the apocalyptic tendency had conjured yet another beast" (S 16). Beard's reaction to the news reports exemplifies the phenomenon of "attention fatigue" (Giddens 2009: 33) and draws attention to the difficulty that the real-life political mediation and management of climate change risk faces.[29] Giddens, for example, emphasizes that it is hard to keep any given risk, but global warming in particular, "in the public consciousness in the context of other perceived dangers that come and go" (Giddens 2009: 33). Moreover, Beard's mocking defamation of both scientific and public media risk discourses (see Zemanek 2012: 53), reveals an indifference and habitation to risk without, however, being able to factually negate its specific shapes in this context. As far as "the familiar litany of shrinking glaciers, encroaching deserts, [...] disappearing this and that" (S 36) is concerned, as the narrator sums up, "Beard had heard these predictions before and believed none of them. And if he had, he would not have been alarmed" (S 75).[30]

Consequently, he also has no professional interest in climate science and technology and fiercely dislikes Tom Aldous, one of the Centre's most promising

---

28 On the role of the media in *Solar* see Nicklas (2010).
29 In addition, climate science faces the problem that S. Mayer sums up: " [It] has to come to terms with the fact that the communication of its results always occurs in a by now highly politicized context that is characterized by a wide spectrum of stances on the issue of global climate change, a spectrum that runs from acute fear and concern through apathy and indifference to the denial that there is a problem in the first place" (2016: 210).
30 On the reality of climate change and its negotiation in scientific and popular discourse see, Foster (2015), Mike Hulme's seminal book *Why We Disagree About Climate Change* (2009), Giddens's *The Politics of Climate Change* (2009), and Urry's *Climate Change and Society* (2011).

post-docs, both for his campaigning for solar energy and for challenging his own scientific authority. But Aldous, who just wants "to do what's right by the planet" (S 34) and the only character in the novel seriously concerned with climate change is denied the role of the eco-hero. Instead, he dies early on in the novel in an accident at Beard's house, after his affair with Beard's wife Patrice has been discovered. Though the incident appears almost farcically improbable – Aldous slips on a polar bear rug on a polished wooden floor and sustains a fatal head injury – the situation is brought about by his personal desires and sexual risk-taking, creating a characteristic parallel between the young and the old scientist.

From the beginning *Solar* is a narrative of endings and decline (see Houser 2010: 10). Part 1, set in the year 2000 (the other two parts are set in 2005 and 2009 respectively), opens with 53-year old Michael Beard's fifth marriage being at the point of disintegration. He is also past his professional prime, living of the reputation build during his early career. This continual cashing-in on glories past is not only the symptom of laziness but of a lack of new ideas. Beard counteracts his vague sense of professional failure, mixed with feelings of safe stagnation, through his womanizing which gives him a sense of agency and pleasant thrill: "All the excitement and unpredictability was in the private life" (S 14). Despite the fact that he has had a string of affairs throughout his marriages and does no longer seem overtly interested in his current wife, he is shaken to the point of panic by the perceived risk of losing Patrice to her lover, the builder Tarpin. Beard's behaviour generally serves as a satirical illustration of humanity (always in allegorical relation to the subject of climate change) and highlights why it is nearly impossible to induce change in the present, when no current discomfort is felt, in order to avoid risks of destruction in the future. Johns-Putra therefore describes Beard's function as that of "*an everyman* (a representative of humankind)" who "represents us at our selfish worst" (Johns-Putra 2016; my emphasis).

The novel's beginning reveals McEwan's scepticism about humans' ability to change and the inclination towards greed and self-interest in addition to another fact utterly disastrous in its allegorical global dimensions: even intelligent individuals like Beard, theoretically capable of assessing values and calculating consequences, need to reach the point of almost losing something before recognizing its value. Regarding the case of Patrice, Beard "was convinced that just as he was about to lose her he had found the perfect wife" (S 6). Out of panic and jealousy he then embarks on a disastrous course of impulsive actions, ending with him covering up his own involvement in the accidental death of Aldous and tampering with the evidence so that the innocent Tarpin is sent to prison. Hence the ensuing plot, pushed forward by the protagonist's string of bad choices, quickly satirizes his initial vow, made after the realization that he has missed any clues about his wife's affair, namely from now on to "act conservatively, passively, honestly, and break no rule, do nothing extreme" (S 10). In the following, Beard does nothing but violate this decision, breaking rules, devising schemes, and going to extreme length to secure his own advantage. In the process he proves time and again his aptitude to miscalculate and disregard certain risks, and a disastrous mismanagement of the ones he does perceive.[31]

Beard makes the mistake of not only misjudging but also compartmentalizing people, events and temporalities, leading to him missing inevitable chains of connection. He has a particular misogynistic tendency to underestimate the agency and determination of the women in his life and is unpleasantly taken off guard by Patrice's affair or by Melissa's pregnancy. The later forces the responsibility of becoming a father onto him, a risk he has avoided for a long time, until "meaning and consequences [...] clicked into alignment like a steel bolt. His cell door had been open for months, years, and he could have walked free. Too late" (S 173).[32] Right up until the final scenes, when all his choices and actions combine in one disastrous climax, he is able to simultaneously ignore his past, which increasingly resembles "a mess, [...] a ripe, odorous cheese oozing into or over his present" (S 260) and to hold onto the illusion that he is somehow exempt from suffering any bad consequences. He also maintains a significant split in his professional, rational perception of the outside world and his private life, shaped by chaos and an irrational approach to disorder: "The material world simply could not be so complicated. But the domestic world could" (S 21).

Both spheres are brought together in a crucial turning point in the plot when Beard returns home from his trip to the Arctic and is shocked to find Aldous sit-

---

31 See Zemanek's (2012) reading focused on Beard's disastrous personal risk management and its allegorical dimensions which, in her opinion, are what renders the text interesting to Ecocritics. She writes: "Thanks to the many comic and humorous elements, the taking of individual, voluntary, familiar and often trivial risks is apparently quite pleasurable for Beard. But read allegorically with reference to the collective, involuntary and unfamiliar ecological risk, this satirical portrait demonstrates the consequences of inadequate risk perception and disastrous risk management'" (2012: 58). Though I agree with Zemanek's interpretation of *Solar* as a complex risk narrative, which shall not be replicated here, I hesitate to subscribe to her argument that in the novel "[...] all faces of risk allegorically refer to that of climate change, the only one truly relevant for the reader" (2012: 56). McEwan's exploration of human risk behaviour is relevant beyond the specific environmental context.

32 There is a striking preoccupation with the topic of parenthood in many climate change novels and plays (see Johns-Putra 2016); the metaphorical link between familial responsibility, emotional response and global warming is worth pursuing in more detail.

ting in his living room in his own dressing gown. In this scene both men fail to extend their professional rationality to their private life and the confrontation quickly spirals out of control. Aldous completely misjudges the situation and the humiliation his presence means to Beard and tries again to get his boss interested in artificial photosynthesis, reasoning that it is "the whole world's future that's at stake, and that's why we can't afford to be enemies" (S 87). His following accident triggers a case of selfish, misguided risk management from Beard's side. Though briefly stunned by the improbability of the event, he decides to erase any signs of his presence at the scene and, instead of calling the authorities, tries to create evidence that incriminates Tarpin. Beard's risk management appears paradoxically both instinctual and calmly reflective, affirming, in any case, his almost infinite capacity for self-deception: "*His body had a plan*. And he walked through, as though experimentally, believing at every stage he could undo it, go back to the beginning, with nothing lost or compromised. Everything he was doing now merely served a *precautionary principle*" (S 91; my emphasis). Bear's actions are solely aimed at averting the short-term danger of being associated with the accident and also at eliminating Tarpin as a rival – two goals he successfully achieves. He fails, however, to consider the long-term consequences which he will have to face in the final climax, namely what will happen after Tarpin is released from prison.

This scene epitomizes how Beard is mainly interested in thinking about the present and the immediate future. Despite his once prize-winning scientific brilliance, he has little interest in intellectual pursuits left and derives satisfaction not only from instant, but above all, sensual gratification of his desires through food and sex. According to Kerridge, the protagonist is the quintessential "*L'homme moyen sensuel*" (Kerridge 2010; original emphasis), though he is possibly even below average in his ability to order his private affairs and sensibly control his appetites. Typically, his risk management behaviour is short-sighted and exclusively oriented towards the personal, illustrating the crux of taking effective risk-management action against climate change which would require the exact opposite strategy of putting the collective and long-term consequences above self-interest and present needs.

Meanwhile Beard's behaviour and especially his lifestyle equal a form of prolonged form of self-endangerment. Tuhus-Dubrow points out: "As an extremely intelligent creature who exploits those around him and is ultimately self-destructive, he seems to stand in for the entire human species" (Tuhus-Dubrow 2013: 60). Though he lacks self-discipline and exploits others, his monstrosity does not lie in a truly criminal or malevolent nature – although his behaviour takes on both qualities at times –, rather, his slowly decaying, ever-expanding body becomes a metaphorical stand-in for the risks of greed and the damage it poses to individual, society, and environment. The novel chronicles his immoderate indulgences and denial of all warnings of his body as a form of self-abuse that is enjoyable until it is too late. His failure to restraint himself, the inability to control appetites in the present for the benefit of well being in the future, is a depiction of a failing of humanity in general, but specifically of affluent (Western) consumers, to change behaviour if it is connected to a reduction of pleasure. For example, after giving into buying yet another bag of crisps, his drug of choice, Beard reflects: "What defeated him was always the present, the moment of vivid confrontation with the affirming tidbit [...]" (S 118). His health, though rapidly deteriorating, does only cause him mild, occasional discomforts and thus not any motivation to change. The same principle applies to his surroundings. The decaying London flat Beard moves into after his fifth divorce mirrors the state of his body. He avoids tiding up, fixing originally small problems, and dealing with the landlord up to the point that the whole place becomes uninhabitable. As such, the apartment reflects "his worst, fattest self, incapable of translating a decent plan into a course of action. [...] there was always something he would far rather do – read, drink, eat, talk on the phone" (S 222). Unable to create an ordered liveable home environment for himself, Beard relies solely on other people to take care of everything and creates internal as well as external sides of ignored decay slowly building up into full collapse.

Even when noticing a problem, Beard never wants to spoil the present by worrying about the future and his risk-taking always results from acting instinctually and improvising out of desperation but not from a love of adventure. He also displays the firm belief that his habitual denial to dwell on things in all realms of his life will ultimately pay off: "The past had shown him many times that the future would be its own solution" (S 247). And this attitude shapes his standard response to all risks and problems until the end: "Was he really going to deal with this now [...]? He thought it unlikely. It would take care of itself" (S 278). Again, Beard's behaviour illustrates the crux at the heart of the problematic public perception of climate change as risk. A major part of its lack of affect lies in its futurity and abstraction, as Giddens notes. Due to the "gulf between the familiar preoccupations of everyday life" and the "apocalyptic, future of climate chaos [...] the vast majority are doing very little, if anything at all, to alter their daily habits, even though those habits are the source of the dangers that climate change has in store for us" (Giddens 2009: 1). Aside from Beard's frequent air travelling and the rest of his consumer lifestyle which directly contributes to global warming, his denial of his own deteriorating health – in particular the cancerous mole on the back of his hand – make McEwan's novel appear like a literal case study of "'Giddens's paradox'", which argues that "since the dangers posed by global warming aren't tangible, immediate or visible in the course of day-to-day life, [...] many will sit on their hands and do nothing of a concrete nature about them. Yet waiting until they become visible and acute before being stirred to serious action will, by definition, be too late" (Giddens 2009: 2). As such, Beard's attitude also typifies a complex form of denial that fuses "literal" denial, i.e. knowing the dangers involved but choosing to pretend they will not materialize (in one's lifetime) and "implicatory" denial, which involves refusing the consequential change of behaviour that should follow from the facts one is aware of.[33] Till the end, Beard's attitude towards his own health and body thus remain based to what John Foster refers to as "forms of double-think" (Foster 2015: 26), deployed to preserve the ways of life undoubtedly known to be the on-going cause of the damage. Beard's case is an individual 'embodiment' of this denial which is a typical collaborative reaction to anthropogenic climate change.[34]

In alignment with his dismissal of apocalyptic environmental disaster scenarios that fail to materialize into actual dangers, Beard believes in his own (and, by allegorical extension, the globe's) capacity to survive unscathed, though he knows he is prone to accidents which are typically described with slapstick humour, like him having to vomit behind the curtain after his conference speech or his penis freezing stuck to his snowsuit during his trip to the Arctic. The narrator observes that "Beard possessed the gift, or curse, of recklessness" (S 44), which he demonstrates in several episodes of impulsive behaviour with potentially harmful consequences, for example, when he goes to confront Tarpin, a physically much stronger man, at his home. He also makes the professionally damaging mistake to publicly declare his misogynistic belief in essential gender differences: "Men and women had different priorities in life, different attitudes to risk" (S 134). This leads to him being attacked by feminist scientists; the situation is made worse by his insult of a Jewish lecturer that earns him the reputation of the "'neo-Nazi' Professor", and his impulsive throwing of a rotten tomato into the crowd and hitting an old woman. While these events cause Beard's forced resignation from his post at the Renewable Energy Centre, he quickly bounces back from the media scandal, having his slate wiped clean by "fresh scandals, sporting events, confessions, war, celebrity gossip and the tsunami" (S 128). He also creates a new business venture for himself by using Tom Aldous's research material, left years ago at his house after the accident, to develop an Artificial Photosynthesis Plant in Lordsburg, New Mexico.

---

33 See the chapter "Varieties of Denial" in Foster (2015: 23–45); borrowing the framework by Stanley Cohen, Foster distinguishes between literal, interpretive, and implicatory denial.
34 Cf. Norgaard's *Living in Denial. Climate Change, Emotions and Everyday Life* (2011).

This is one of the most cynical developments in the plot. In the third part, Beard is actively engaged in working against climate change and cultivates a new self-image as a scientific rescuer of "humankind from self-destruction" (S 223), based on the work of Aldous which, and that is another one of his crucial miscalculations, he assumes is "long forgotten by the rest of the world" (S 185). Without having altered his sceptical opinion about the reality of global warming Beard now sees the risk discourse surrounding it as something he can profit from. When his business partner Hammer anxiously asks him about the latest statistiscal evidence which suggests that "the planet's getting cooler" (S 215), Beard assures him: "Here's the good news. The UN estimates that already a third of a million people a year are dying from climate change. [...] It's a catastrophe. Relax!" (S 216–217).

Nonetheless, however much he might violate the expectations of a main character in an eco-disaster novel (see Zemanek 2012: 58), McEwan's flawed and clumsy protagonist is by no means an unfamiliar character in the history of fiction,[35] especially with regards to his risk behaviour. Referring to the narrative techniques described in Joseph Meeker's study of comedy and the picaresque, *The Comedy of Survival* (1997), Kerridge argues, "the way in which characters in a comedy do not react to threatening events with the emotional vulnerability displayed by those in tragedy or realistic fiction – is a basic survival mechanism" (Kerridge 2010). In *Solar*, the protagonist – as picaresque hero – is indeed characterized by his survival skills and a defensive and opportunistic confrontation of the present that resembles an instinctual, even animalistic struggle and hope to keep himself alive from-day-to-day (see Meeker 1997: 72), rather than rationally trying to plan ahead. Beard seeks to navigate "the spectacular mess of his personal life" (Kerridge 2010) only reactively and by relying on improvisation and instinctual behaviour. Pushed forth by circumstances and accidents, he survives through a mix of luck and cunning, while the ending of the novel also refuses closure and the restoration of moral certainties in the manner typical of the picaresque, as Kerridge and also Goodbody (2010: 139) have noted.

Beard's trip to the Arctic circle, modelled on McEwan's participation in the 2005 Cape Farewell project, an international expedition of journalists, artists and scientists to view first-hand the melting of the polar caps, is one of the text's satirical highlights. The expedition, in which Beard has no interest other

---

35 Acknowledging the parallels between his protagonist and Shakespeare's Falstaff, one of the great clumsy scoundrels of English literature, McEwan says in an interview: "The difficult task, and I know I haven't succeeded with all readers, is to somehow make the reader both dislike this man and yet be prepared to travel with him" (in Medley 2010); see also Nicklas (2010: 97).

than its media glamour, highlights the protagonist's self-centeredness and his physical clumsiness. In the Arctic setting, the narrative also begins to develop the strong link between Beard's slow decay and climate change, paralleling an inner and outer risk narrative. The implicit question, raised on both levels, is about the determinism of change leading towards destruction and its potential reversibility. The narrator muses rhetorically about Beard's ballooning weight: "Surely, it was not inevitable that he should get heavier by the month until he dropped dead?" (S 73). In another scene, which once again comically shows how Beard is consumed by his physical needs rather than rational calculations, he leaves the snowmobile, against the vehement warnings of the guard, and tries to relief himself outside. The result is severe frostbite on his penis, an injury to which Beard reacts with childish panic. It stops him from bedding any of the women present on the expedition, but he compensates the loss of pleasure through an increased intake of food and alcohol. Another mishap of Beard is described as a pseudo-adventure, underlining his opportunistic nature and the general sense of 'safe' risk-tourism the privileged group of spectators enjoys at this site of environmental risk. During an excursion onto a glacier Beard underestimates the speed with which a polar bear is approaching and is too slow getting back into the snowmobile. Saved by hair's breath by the guard, Beard delights in the experience of wildlife and danger, a thrilling change from his safe und civilized existence. He glances back "hoping to catch sight, for anecdote's sake, of the animal he was about to outpace. [...] How liberating to discover in the modern age that he, a city-dweller [...] could be tracked and ravaged and be an entire meal, a source of nourishment to others" (S 71).

One more episode of comic chaos and helplessness deserves mentioning. Beard's snow clothes keep disappearing from the boot room. Every day the disorder increases while people apparently start to grab whatever items they can without concern for the others' belongings. McEwan employs the boot room as a metaphorical microcosm of the planet put into disarray by human selfish behaviour: "Only good laws would save the boot room" (S 80). In his essay "A Boot Room in The Frozen North" (2005), written prior to *Solar*, the authors sums up the moral implications of the episode and utters a criticism that foreshadows the depiction of his protagonist, saying that "it is not evil that undoes the world, but small errors prompting tiny weaknesses [...] gathering in rivulets, the cascades of consequences. In the golden age of yesterday, the boot room had finite resources, equally shared – [...] the paradise we are about to lose". And therefore, he concludes, "All boot rooms need good systems so that flawed creatures can use them well" (McEwan 2005). This frequently-cited scene contains McEwan's most explicit political commentary and suggestion of environmental risk management strategies: a call for strong regulations and cooperation necessary to correct the potentially self-defeating tendencies of human nature and to maintain a functioning, 'safe' community and habitable environment.[36]

The second part of the novel opens with the narrator's prophetic statement: "He was running out of time. Everyone was, it was the general condition" (S 107). The protagonist is, of course, only concerned with his personal sense of time running out on this day because he is late to arrive for his climate change conference speech at the Savoy. Nonetheless, before going on stage Beard finds time to stuff himself with salmon sandwiches out of fear of missing them if he waits until later, then proceeds to open his speech with the emotional proclamation: "The planet [...] is sick" (S 148). These words refer to his own more than to the ecological condition, and Zemanek points out further: "While fighting his increasing nausea, he automatically unwinds an argument on how to solve the energy crisis, in which he still does not believe any more than before, but from which he now knows he can profit" (Zemanek 2012: 55). With literally nauseating hypocrisy Beard argues: "For humanity en masse, greed triumphs virtue. So we have to welcome into our solutions the ordinary compulsions of self-interest [...]" (S 149). The speech also incorporates the anecdote of Beard accidentally eating the crisps belonging to a man sitting across from him on the train and blaming the stranger for stealing his own, until he discovers his mistake. Retold as a variation of the well-known tale of the "Unwitting Thief"[37] as a fellow scientist points out to him later, Beard employs the – in his eyes original – story to illustrate how the assessment of a situation can change when new information is revealed, concluding how in "a crisis, we understand, sometimes too late", that the problem lies in "our own follies and unexamined assumptions" (S 155).

Despite Beard's customary denial of risks personal and collective, he cannot always suppress the "usual bundle of congealed anxieties" (S 184), including work, his relationships and his health, in particular the darkening mole on the back of his hand, and these concerns overwhelm him late at night. Through the protagonist's reflections about what worries keep him awake at 4am, the nar-

---

36 For this reason Robert P. Marzec (2015), who situates the novel in the American post-9/11 war-on-terror discourse, reads the implied moral of the boot room episode critically, arguing that it perpetuates anthropocentric fantasies of security that counteract social chaos, "turning the concept of order and the government of order into a fundamental paradigm" (2015: 94; 80 ff). Though I do not find Marzec's transference of the novel into the American context fully convincing, his reading emphasizes the discursive construction of climate change as a high risk and draws on Foucault's (2010) theorizations of biopolitics and the emergence of the security state that inform Beck's thesis of world risk society in the 21st-century.

37 According to Garrard (2013: 132–133) both the boot room episode and the crisps incident are half-humorous, secular anecdotes but presented in the narrative loaded with significance in the style of religious parables.

rative offers a comment on the nature of human risk perception which is presented as largely beyond the individual's control and determined by emotions, irrational fears and desires: "Even in daylight, in optimal conditions, *one rarely exercises a free choice over what to fret about*. What needled him now, hours before the winter dawn, as much as health, money, work, an imminent abortion, or an accidental death, was that lecturer, [...] outrageously accusing him of being inauthentic, a fraud, a plagiariser" (S 187; my emphasis). Beard only feels his optimism resurge after engaging into violent fantasies of physically hurting the lecturer as a means to reassert his superiority. Telling in this scene is also Beard's outrage at the charge of (intellectual) theft while being oblivious to the similar crimes he commits. The motif of the risks of theft, of taking possession of something (accidentally or deliberately) without having the right to do so, or fully being able to understand the consequences, runs through the whole narrative and includes, in Beard's case adultery, scientific plagiarism and an environmentally unconscious and hazardous lifestyle.

In the final part of the narrative, building up to the momentous climax of the failed launch of the solar energy plant in Lordsburg, the sense of mounting dangers increases and affects Beard to the uncharacteristic extent of him rejecting food during brunch with his business partner. With a tragic timing suggestive of a Thomas Hardy-novel, as Kerridge argues, the protagonist's "reckless personal life [thus] ripens to its catastrophic crisis [...]" (Kerridge 2010). All of Beard's past bad decisions catch up with him and there seems to be no escape from the accumulation of disastrous events which are all consequences he could have anticipated, but either chose to ignore or thought too improbable due to the belief in his own invincibility. They include the serious legal trouble he faces due to the theft of Aldous's research, Tarpin's destruction of the solar panels out of revenge for Beard's refusal to help him financially after he is released from prison, Melissa's discovery of his affair with the trailer park waitress Darlene, and her determination to force him to honour his responsibilities to her and his little daughter, and, perhaps the most frightening threat of them all, his diagnosis with a bad general health condition and malignant skin cancer, *the* disease related to global warming.

Yet Beard refuses to come out of his denial about the seriousness of his condition. Doctor Parks warns Beard that his body resembles a fast ticking time bomb and recommends not to delay starting radiation therapy for his melanoma: "No time to lose, [...]." "This won't go away just because you don't want it or are not thinking about it" (S 238). While the doctor's words also serve as an ethical imperative for the public's approach to climate change, even at this point, Beard chooses to reject the idea and is instead even glad that he managed to hide further crucial symptoms from the doctor – "the occasional sensation of tightness around his chest" (S 240) –, a classic warning sign of a heart attack that foreshadows the soon-to-follow dual end of Beard and the narrative. Having avoided medical check-ups for years out of fear, Beard displays an irrational and cowardly approach to dealing with health risks which is reflected in his quasi-religious rhetoric: he perceives his symptoms as punishments and "crimes" he should "confess'" to a doctor (S 185), and a diagnosis as "a kind of modern curse" (S 214). With a logic owing more to superstition than to rational calculation he even justifies not having taken any remedies or faced up to the problem sooner: "If you didn't go and see these people, you wouldn't get whatever it is they want you to have" (S 214). In a similarly irrational assessment of risk, Beard lets any concern about the impeding patent lawsuit, which in all likelihood means the end of his career and the whole project, as well as financial ruin for himself and his business partner, fade into the background when he is confronted with the immediate, personal risk of facing an angry Melissa and perhaps losing her and his daughter Catriona. Stoically awaiting their arrival, he sits down in the diner for yet another fat-laden meal, the same he always eats there. This final action of Beard – as the narrative ends with his daughter running towards him while he suffers a (probably fatal) heart attack – sums up his whole life, his habituation to risk, denial of consequentiality, and his focus on survival as muddling through the present moment. As usual, "he had no need to reflect on choices [...]. Everything was terrible, but he was not feeling so bad" (S 275). The ambivalent – though not improbable – ending of *Solar* either suggests that Beard, the picaresque anti-hero, makes one final lucky escape before he has to suffer the more painful consequences from his decisions and behaviour (i.e. hospitalization, imprisonment, abandonment) or that he, the quintessential human profit-and-pleasure-seeking creature, is finally destroyed by his own nature and prevented from living on.

In his non-fiction book *The Great Derangement* (2016), Indian novelist Amitav Ghosh addresses the imaginative and technical challenges that climate change poses for the contemporary writer and argues that the extreme nature of climate events and natural disasters makes them resistant to the depiction in serious, i.e. realist literary fiction because they feel too improbable.[38] As a result the topic of climate change is usually confined to being treated exclusively in popular science fiction or non-fiction writing. While not writing the great novel of global warming himself, Ghosh identifies several reasons for contempo-

---

[38] Ghosh writes: "And it appears that we are now in an era that will be defined precisely by events that appear, by our current standards of normalcy, highly improbable: flash floods, hundred-year storms, persistent droughts, spells of unprecedented heat, sudden landslides, raging torrents pouring down from breached glacial lakes, and, yes, freakish tornados" (2016: 24).

rary fiction's silence about climate change which are useful to apply to reading McEwan's *Solar* and also have implications for the relation between the evolution of the realist novel and risk perception in general. Interrogating contemporary literature's silence about the reality of the life-changing threat of climate change,[39] noting how to date only a handful of writers, such as Margaret Atwood, Ian McEwan, Cormac McCarthy, and Barbara Kingsolver, have dared to tackle the topic in their fictional works, and mostly as speculative disaster stories set in the future, Ghosh postulates that the disastrous, uncanny, and improbable needs to be incorporated into writing about our present reality. This echoes both Ishiguro and McEwan's rejection of writing in the classic dystopian mode.[40] It also draws attention to the difference between climate change and the improbability of events in speculative or fantastic fiction because the former is "happening on this earth, at this time" (Ghosh 2016: 27).[41] At the same time these events possess an uncanny quality. They are "the mysterious work of our hands returning to haunt us in unthinkable shapes and forms" (32) in the sense that humans have collectively and individually caused these improbable, disastrous events and failed to predict them. This is literally illustrated in the ending of *Solar* where the darkening, cancerous mark on the protagonist's hand that has been haunting him for a long time has turned deadly and all his deeds, long forgotten or repressed, return to crush him with combined vehemence.

According to Ghosh, aside from the fact that climate change events present a challenge to the (spatial, temporal) scale of the modern realist novel and its customary rejection of nonhuman agency, main reasons why the trajectory of the novel opposes the depiction of climate change include what John Updike identified as the focus on "individual moral adventure" (see Ghosh 2016: 127), which

---

39 Therefore, Ghosh suggests, it is possible that "this era, which so congratulates itself on its self-awareness, will come to be known as the time of the Great Derangement" (2016: 11). It has to be noted, though, that while Ghosh's own literary oeuvre testifies to a preoccupation with the moral obligation of "remembering the stories we have not written" (Ghosh 2005: 203; see Hoydis 2011: 11), he resorts to writing non-fiction when it comes to the carbon economy and the novel in non-fiction. Considering this far from uncommon mismatch between a contemporary writer's concern and his/her fictional works, as many chose to write about climate change 'elsewhere' (see Ghosh 2016: 9), McEwan's novel does present an exceptional case to date.
40 In an interview McEwan explains why he is not only not interested in writing in that mode but also does not consider it effective: "We've had so many dystopias that we're brain-dead in that direction" (in Tonkin 2007).
41 Tuhus-Dubrow sees this awareness as the main reason that despite a felt delay novelists are now taking up the subject of climate change for "the threat seems to have become too pressing to ignore, and less abstract" (2013: 59).

caused the banishment of the collective from the realm of fictional imagination. With the individual typically triumphing over the collective in the novel, writers and readers alike struggle to imagine global warming as a shared predicament (see 80). *Solar* is no exception to these rules. As Zemanek argues, McEwan's novel does not "develop an apocalyptic ecological scenario that culminates in a gigantic *collective* disaster. [...] Nevertheless, it fits well into an issue on 'writing catastrophes', since it takes a disastrous course and ends in a *personal* [...] catastrophe for its protagonist" (Zemanek 2012: 51; my emphasis). Thus, the plot of *Solar* renders the topic manageable in the scope of the realist novel, yet through its use of allegory and satire suggests a wider social – possibly even global – dimension and transports a sense of collective risk and disaster via a focus on Beard's individual (im)moral adventures.

Interestingly, Ghosh bases his argument on some scholarship on the coinciding of probability theory and the modern novel (Hacking 1975) that also forms the point of departure for my study. The concealment of the dramatic unlikeliness of climate change events appears as a result of the development of the realist novel which reflects from its beginnings the end of the delight in the extraordinary and the unlikely and which especially during the course of the 19th century, its coming-of-age period, centres on a worldview oriented toward progress and the human control of nature that perceives the very idea of uncontrollable interference of nature as improbable and characterizes "catastrophism as un-modern" (Ghosh 2016: 22).[42] While humans have always been unable to prepare for rare, improbable events, the fundamental 'modern' patterns of thought hinge on the belief in the regularity of society and the measurability of life leads to the perception that we are unfit for dealing with climate change risks, which 'should not exist' and thus threaten to overwhelm us with their improbable reality. Ghosh sums up this suggestion:

> [...] human beings were generally catastrophists at heart until their instinctive awareness of the earth's unpredictability was gradually supplanted by a belief in uniformitarianism – a regime of ideas that was supported by scientific theories [...] and also by a range of governmental practices that were informed by statistics and probability. (25)

Due to the fact that climate change events tend to defy current statistical prediction models – i.e. the scientific calculation of risk –, they are routinely underestimated as threats and potential counter-measures are delayed. But another factor appears possibly even more crucial. As risk, climate change is disre-

---

[42] This echoes the often pro-claimed backlash (Western) societies are feeling now and Bruno Latour's famous diagnosis that 'we have never been modern' (Latour 1991).

garded, or rather deliberately graded down in a hierarchy of threats, because trying to mange it would mean facing a much greater and more immediate fear, namely that of moving backwards and losing the competitive capitalist race towards progress. Because, according to Ghosh, "for modern man, terror is exactly what is evoked by the fear of being left behind" (2016: 124), or, in Giddens's terms, by the fear of acting against the "development imperative" (Giddens 2009: 9). Ghosh rightly cautions against assuming denialist attitudes only to be a symptom of capitalism and (media) manipulation, rather their existence in abundance suggests that the crisis of global warming "threatens to unravel something deeper, without which large numbers of people would be at a loss to find meaning in their history and indeed their existence in the world" (2016: 138). The climate crisis appears as a result of human capitalist culture and it needs acknowledging that any risks whose management would pose a threat to capitalist progression as we know it, one of the grand narratives of Western civilization, are likely to be underestimated in comparison to other risks.

Though a longer discussion of these aspects is beyond scope, Ghosh's book draws attention to the necessity to look at climate change through the prism of empire and to also consider Asia's belated but increasingly central role when it comes to the nexus of capitalism and global warming; Asia is also home to the majority of people at risk from climate change. There is, however, another side to the uneven distribution of environmental risk between first and third world countries that is relevant here. McEwan's protagonist, a representation of the privileged metropolitan subject, demonstrates how Western civilization not only produces the damage itself but turns the potential discomforting consequences of the behaviour of the capitalist consumer into high risks of full breakdown. By contrast, a novel such as Hari Kunzru's *Transmission* (2005) assumes a much more 'global' scope and focuses on the uneven flows (of capital, people, cultural goods, technology etc.) between Asia and the West. With equal, if not stronger, satirical bite it stages how the risk of immediate systemic stress is intensified by Western high-industrialized societies' lack of tolerance for malfunction and extreme conditions of any kind. In contrast to poor countries where, Ghosh points out, "even the middle classes are accustomed to coping with shortages and discomforts of all sorts; in the West, wealth, and habits based upon efficient infrastructures, may have narrowed the threshold of bearable pain" (Ghosh 2016: 147), and thus not only climate change events but other globally perceived risks such as (cyber) terrorism lead to systemic breakdown and chaos. Before tackling the particular 21st-century risk narratives that have emerged after the 9/11 attacks, one final point from Ghosh's insightful study of the relation between literature and climate change deserves mentioning for it echoes the argument at the heart of McEwan's novel. Ghosh admits that even his own (private) reaction to climate change is partially shaped by inaction and denial; for example he finds himself reluctant to force his mother out of the house in Kolkata, one of the cities most at risk from climate change, or to take any other drastic action which involve a change of behaviour. His confessional words underline why McEwan's choice of the flawed and passive Michael Beard, rather than the activist Tom Aldous as protagonist for his global warming novel is one based on the probability of human behaviour in the face of this particular risk. Ghosh says,

> [...] contrary to what I might like to think, my life is not guided by reason; it is ruled, rather, by the inertia of habitual motion. This is indeed the condition of the vast majority of human beings, which is why very few of us will be able to adapt to global warming if it is left to us as individuals, to make the necessary changes; those who will uproot themselves and make the right preparations are precisely those obsessed monomaniacs who appear to be on the borderline of lunacy. (54)

12 Domestic (In)securities

12.1 'Or you can be happy if you dare': *Saturday*

It is hard to find a volume on contemporary fictional writing[1] that does not include chapters on terrorism and globalization, topics typically charged with ethical-cultural criticism and risk discourse.[2] Ian McEwan's novel *Saturday* (2005), which contains an ambivalent exploration of private and public risk perception and management, has become one of the most critically acclaimed and debated texts of the new millennium. It is an already canonical example of one of the most productive and steadily theorized genres of 21st century Anglophone fiction to date,[3] the post-9/11 novel.[4] Although terrorism is hardly a new, i.e. 21st-century phenomenon,[5] the events and aftermath of the 9/11 attacks have globalised the fears and risk discourse surrounding terrorism and rekindled the debate about the power of literature and the role of writers in times of crisis (see Hoydis 2015: 6). *Saturday*, and its reception, exemplifies this, as well as contemporary

---

[1] See, e.g., Adiseshiah and Hildyard (2013), Boxall (2013), Head (2008), Ribbat and Linke (2005).
[2] See, e.g., Amoore and de Goede's *Risk and the War on Terror* (2008); Beck's essays "Terror and Solidarity" (2002a) and "The Terrorist Threat: World Risk Society Revisited" (2002b); see also Holland (2009), and Mythen and Walklate (2008).
[3] The body of theory and criticism of books on post-9/11 literature and terror is too substantial to offer a comprehensive survey here: See, e.g., DeRosa (2011), Spahr (2012), and Araújo (2007). For a predominantly American focus, see Gray (2011); for more comparative, transatlantic perspectives, see Cilano (2009; 2014), Kenniston and Quinn (2008), and Henningfeld (2014); for an inclusion of genres beyond the novel, see Bragard, Dony and Rosenberg (2011), and McAlary (2012). For monographs focusing on the experimentalism and diversity of the genre, see Michael (2014) and Randall (2011). For perspectives from postcolonial studies, see Boehmer and Morton (2010), and Scanlan (2010). Hardly any of these contributions theorize risk explicitly, an exception is Banita (2010) who focuses on the relations between race, risk, and terror in contemporary fiction, but does not discuss *Saturday*.
[4] Examples of Anglophone fictions dealing directly with the events of the 9/11 attacks or their aftermath, the lasting political effects and the impact of (Islamic) terrorism on the socio-cultural imagination include: Don DeLillo's *Falling Man*, Jonathan Safran Foer's *Extremely Loud and Incredibly Close*, Kamila Shamsie's *Burning Shadows*, Richard Flanagan's *The Unknown Terrorist*, Mohsin Hamid's *The Reluctant Fundamentalist*, Salman Rushdie's *Shalimar the Clown*, Joseph O'Neill's *Netherland*, Claire Messud's *The Emperor's Children*, and John Updike's *The Terrorist*.
[5] See the discussion of Joseph Conrad's *Secret Agent* in chapter 9.1. From a diachronic perspective modern terrorism and its treatment as a literary topic can be traced back at least until the second half of the 19th century, though it has gained new momentum toward the end of the 20th century. See, e.g., Appelbaum and Paknadel (2008).

fiction's resurfacing concern with temporality, with bearing witness and capturing consciousness and experience through narrative. Recalling the tradition of the modernist circadian novel,[6] *Saturday* chronicles a single day in the life of Henry Perowne, a 48-year-old neurosurgeon, loving husband and father of two grown-up children. He spends the day leisurely preparing for a family dinner party in the evening which is violently interrupted by Baxter and his gang, lower-class thugs Henry encountered earlier in the day, intruding into the Perownes's luxurious home in the heart of London. Set on Saturday, February 15, 2003, eighteen months after the attack on the Twin Towers and the day of huge anti-Iraq war demonstrations, the narrative rewrites canonical modernist texts such as *Mrs Dalloway* by exploring individual consciousness and the ordinariness of domestic routine set against wider social and political issues. Aside from various other structural and stylistic intertextual relations, Monica Latham argues, McEwan's novel adapts the trauma of WWI that haunts society in Virginia Woolf's text to the post-9/11 context (Latham 2015: 140).[7] A difference lies in the stronger anticipatory (and thus imaginative) orientation of trauma with regards to the kind of terror evoked by the events of 9/11 that *Saturday* seeks to capture.[8] It is a fusion of the memory of events past and the anticipation of disaster yet to come in the sense described by Barbara Arizti, borrowing Lyndsey Stonebridge's term, as a pervasive "spirit of 'dreading forward'" (Arizti 2014: 238), or by Jacques Derrida as the symptomatic of traumatism in the 'globalized' post-9/11 world: "Traumatism is produced by the *future*, by the *to come*, by the threat of the worst *to come*, rather than by an aggression that is 'over and done with'" (Derrida and Borradori 2003: 96–97; original emphasis). The reference to trauma asserts how the conception of risk is central to McEwan's works and this novel in particular. According to Laura Marcus, aside from the temporal setting of the fictions, a concern with time and experienced temporality, i.e. "narrative duration, the looping backwards and forwards" (Marcus 2013: 83), is at the heart of McEwan's novels. The experience of temporality, memory and anticipation form the basis for any narrative construction of risk which is in *Saturday* furthermore focussed on the contrasts and dependencies of public-collective experiences of risk pinned against those of the individual.[9]

---

6 On aspects of modernist narration in *Saturday* see Groes (2013) and Marcus (2013).
7 On the parallels between *Saturday* and *Mrs Dalloway* see especially Latham (2013; 2015) and Adams (2012); also Michael (2007), Foley (2010), and Brown (2008).
8 On the thematic and aesthetic exploration of private and public trauma in *Saturday*, see Arizti (2014) and Ganteau (2015; 2017); also Bentley (2013).
9 In the substantial body of criticism of the novel, (to my knowledge) only a couple of critics essays to date engage explicitly with the concept of risk: Ganteau (2015; 2017) reads the texts

Although *Saturday* "communicate[s] the sense of living with an ongoing threat of a large-scale disaster from its very first pages" (Latham 2015: 141) by making use of the iconic 'terrorist' imagery of a burning plane descending over the city, the plot, echoing *Mrs Dalloway*, is mainly structured around no-risk, everyday events (e.g. Henry shopping for a dinner party, playing a game of squash, reflecting on the past, politics, life and death). However, these are shattered, Andrew Foley notes, "by a moment of crisis involving insanity and violence" (Foley 2010: 140). Personified by Baxter, the random and violent intrusions into the realm of domestic security are perceived as being beyond rational calculation and control, the pillars of Henry Perowne's professional ego. For from his days as a young doctor Henry has experienced his medical life and skills, the ability (up to a point) to control life and death and the habitual diagnosing and close observation of people and situations as a "superhuman capacity, more like a craving" (S 11). While the highly charged atmosphere of the operating theatre stimulates him, he is dulled by the comparative safety of office paper work. Yet, however much he craves thrill in his professional life, he seeks routine and stability in his private life and, after over two decades of marriage, still only thinks of his wife when he thinks of sex: "This is what he has to have: possession, belonging, repetition" (S 40). As a result of Henry's love of order, routine and his belief in his diagnostic and predictive skills, any experience of feeling at risk, for him, derives from a felt lack of control over the course of actions and events. His sense of human exposure to the risks of sudden change or endings is also partially derived from his profession, because he has scientific experience of the random fickleness of nature, e.g. during surgery. This awareness feeds into the weariness and fear of forces he cannot control in his private life, e.g. attacks on his home and person by terrorists or others people less fortunate than him in the capitalist system and the general "lottery" of life. In the narrative, Henry, a convinced biological and social Darwinist, repeatedly reflects on the arbitrariness of life, e.g. "the accidents of character and circumstance" (S 65) that separate him and his family from the poor addicts on the square: "It troubles him to consider the powerful currents and fine-tuning that alter fates" (S 65). Considering this it is hardly surprising that *Saturday* also employs a formula typical of other McEwan novels. As does, for example, the

---

through the lens of trauma theory and emphasizes the protagonist's passivity (in crucial moments in the plot) and the sense of vulnerability conveyed in the narrative; De Michelis, with reference to sociological theories of risk (Beck, Douglas), describes *Saturday* as "an impressive exploration of the human 'imagining' of risk" in which "the encroaching of private and public risks, of bordering and intruding, progressively delineates a battlefield where humanity itself is out to the test" (De Michelis 2011: 139–140).

beginning of *Enduring Love* with the meeting of Jed and Joe during the balloon accident, a chance incident, here Henry's encounter with Baxter, in a closed-off street he normally never drives through, sparks off the destructive part of the plot, culminating in the later home invasion. Therefore, Dominic Head argues, in *Saturday*, on various occasions chance is shown to have a determining effect on life, functioning as an arresting counterpoint to any sense of idyll or perfection (2007: 194).

The protagonist's main strategies of risk – and chance – management spring from his professional and private background. The first consists of Henry's habitual "intellectual game of diagnosis" (S 91), which he employs, for example, in the first encounter with Baxter in order to avoid the risk of physical harm. Discovering Baxter's trembling right hand, he speculates about the cause of the tremor, which immediately takes on a soothing quality and restores his faith in his own powers. It allows him to simultaneously despise, pity and ridicule Baxter and to distract himself from the potentially seriously dangerous reality of the situation. In his head, he begins to run through an imagined patient history for Baxter, teamed with a medical risk assessment for Huntington's disease: "If a parent has it, you have a fifty-fifty chance of going down too. Chromosome four. The misfortune lies within a single gene, [...]. More than forty repeats of that one little codon, and you're doomed" (S 93). Through the certainty and determinism inherent in this diagnosis, Henry regains a sense of control. He protects himself – both, in fact, from the risks of being harmed and of losing his superior position – by reverting to his professional knowledge and habitual lack of pity for a human other at risk from suffering and decline. Thus he manages to momentarily distract Baxter from attacking him by sparking false hope for a cure for his condition. Similarly, when later facing Baxter again, who is apparently set on hurting his wife and daughter, Henry offers the intruder a drink. Weighing the risks of increasing inhibition against reducing Baxter's physical coordination and strength is "a calculation Perowne in his terror finds he can make" (S 212).

Also based on a form of detachment, the protagonist's second strategy of risk management consists of seeking spatial as well as emotional separation from the menacing outside world. Aside from the fact that the narrative focuses on the immersion in routine and planning ahead as means of maintaining a sense of self and security, Henry, Clemens Spahr points out, tries to keep "a safe distance from this world [...]. He withdraws into an imagined isolation that he sees constantly threatened" (Spahr 2012: 232). Henry is unwilling to tolerate the constant intrusion of news about world events into his home, rejecting "this infection from the public domain" (S 108). In particular, although he cannot fully resist or escape partaking in the general post-9/11 climate, he refuses to join what he calls "a community of anxiety" (S 176). Assessing the condition of the times as a global community united by the threat of terrorism, Perowne tries to distance himself from this abstract risk society, which transcends his felt realm of control, and he consequently only becomes involved once his personal safety is directly threatened. His son Theo displays a similar strategy of shutting out an overwhelming sense of global risk (– "the political situation, global warming, world poverty, it all looks really terrible" (S 34)) by thinking "small", i.e. by focussing on the local and on the immediate future. According to Foley, who reads *Saturday* as a case study of an individual's right to the pursuit of happiness and the threats posed to liberalism in the new millennium, the novel shows Perowne's attempt to isolate himself from the outside world as not only ethically irresponsible but dangerous (Foley 2010: 139; 137). To some extent, at least, Perowne really is endangered by his lack of imaginative empathy for the less fortunate (see 149–150). But the novel ends with Perowne's security and boundaries well restored.

If Perowne's social-emotional detachment and his Darwinist-inspired attitude that "the key to human success and domination, is to be selective in your mercies" (S 127) might already be hard to accept, the narrative moreover, as Migali Cornier Michael argues, forces the uneasy recognition onto the reader that "holding on to and reconsolidating power is a survival mechanism for those in positions of power" (2009: 46). In other words, the narrative illustrates the principle of the survival of the fittest, however threatened they may (temporarily) be; meanwhile the unfit stand no chance of escaping their biologically predetermined futures of doom. In Baxter's case, Henry clearly foresees a life span of up to two decades "to complete the course, from the first small alterations of character" to "total loss of muscular control [...], nightmarish hallucinations and a meaningless end" (S 94). The implications of his genetic and social disposition are naturalized and appear unchangeable by culture: "*It is written*. No amount of love, drugs, Bible classes or prison sentencing can cure Baxter or shift him from his course" (S 210; original emphasis). The belief in genetic determinism of human life in all its qualities (moral, mental, physical), though based on the randomness of evolution generates a new principle of order, hierarchy and responsibility, as Head argues (2007: 195) and, as such, presents both a source of risk and a possible means of predicting and controlling it through the ever-advancing process of scientific knowledge.

The whole narrative is filtered through the firmly secular and scientifically oriented mind of a character who accepts chance as a condition of life because "the pickiness of pure chance and physical laws seemed like freedom from the scheming of a gloomy god" (S 128). With the protagonist's scientific view of life being his "only kind of faith", summed up in the well known citation from the closing paragraph of *On the Origins of Species* ("There's grandeur in this view of life"; S 255), Darwinian theory of evolution is invested with an almost mythical sense of awe and purpose (see Beattie 2007: 23). For this reason, *Saturday* in addition to McEwan's essayistic oeuvre has earned the author the reputation as a New Atheist writer,[10] a movement of militant atheism promoted in Britain by writers such as Richard Dawkins, Christopher Hitchens, Martin Amis and Philip Pullman. Aiming to bring scientific objectivity to the forefront, part and parcel of the New Atheist agenda is the ideological affirmation of self-help and risk management as falling in the realm of human agency. Though informing the exploration of risk and terror(ism) in *Saturday*, this becomes strikingly clear, for instance, in McEwan's essay "The Day of Judgment" (2008) in which he reveals the inherent contradiction of popular contemporary lamentations of nearing disaster. Either, McEwan argues, the "recent secular apocalyptic beliefs – the certainty that the world is inevitably doomed through nuclear exchange, viral epidemics, meteorites, population growth or environmental degradation" are to be understood as calls for action (akin to Ulrich Beck's conception of the dynamics of the global risk society) because they are essentially avoidable and manageable risks, which would deconstruct them as threats. Or, these fearful lamentations are expressions of fatalistic beliefs based on leaving control over the world to forces beyond human authority, an idea the author firmly rejects. Ultimately, he writes, humans are left with having to deal with the future as radical uncertainty: "We may yet destroy ourselves; we might scrape through. Confronting that uncertainty is the obligation of our maturity and our only spur to wise action. [...] it is highly improbable that there is anyone up there at all. [...] – *there will be no one to save us but ourselves*" (McEwan 2008; my emphasis).

Interestingly, *Saturday* features a protagonist characterized by his inability and refraining from voluntary risk-taking ("He simply doesn't know how to be reckless"; S 214) who generally struggles to act and to judge actions made in the face of uncertainty. This functions as the wider comparative lens employed in the novel to critically assess the uncertainty of measures in the proclaimed war against terror. During several conversation with his children about the protest march and the pros and cons of going to war in Iraq, Henry rejects being forced to take sides and act on vague probabilities in ways which for him only resemble "guesses about the future" (S 193). Trying to argue rationally about the uncertainty of risk assessments in this context, e.g. the fact that risking the lives of soldiers only offers a vague guarantee of more safety and in turn cre-

---

10 On *Saturday* and the ideas preoccupying the new Atheist movement see Beattie (2007), Bradley and Tate (2010), and Wally (2012).

ates the added risk of increasing hatred of the West in the Arab world, he offers the following reason for not taking a clearer anti-war stance: "it could be a disaster. But it could be the end of a disaster and the beginning of something better. It's all about outcomes, and no one knows what they'll be" (S 187). It becomes clear that Henry is less disinterested in politics than that he dislikes the lack of clarity of decisions and opinions in the political realm. In contrast to the safe clarity of his world of medical science, he experiences the unpredictability of events and his own indecisions regarding matters of anti-terror policy as a dizzying "form of vertigo" (S 141). In another scene, containing an intertextual reference to Arnold's "Dover Beach" foreshadowing of the climactic scene near the end of the novel, Henry's argument with Daisy, who vehemently defends the protest marchers, is compared to an intellectual fight "over *armies they will never see, about which they know almost nothing*" (S 190; my emphasis). While Henry questions the rationality of the motives of the masses and the supposed certainty of their decisions ("Opinions are a roll of the dice; by definition"; S 73), another one of his beliefs – and a strong influence on his risk management behaviour – is perhaps more troubling: though he admits the validity of fearing for one's own safety as a strong motif for action, he rejects an overt concern for suffering one has not experienced or cannot fully assess first-hand. In other words, acting out of risk for oneself or loved ones is legitimate, but not out of a felt sense of risk to unknown others, at least not in a way that transcends the protagonist's professional sense of duty.

Saturday exemplifies the recurrent interest in McEwan's writing in exploring the relations between certainty and uncertainty (see Brown 2008: 92) by offering extended insight into the protagonist's cognitive process of risk perception. A close reading of two passages shall illustrate this in the following. The opening scene of Henry Perowne, watching a burning plane descend over the city from his bedroom window in the early morning hours, is commonly seen as a classic reflection of contemporary risk consciousness. The cultural trauma and sense of risk haunting Western society post 9/11 is epitomized by the burning plane in the sky, an image that, Tim Gauthier writes, "hijacks the already edgy post-9/11 reader into a heightened state of anxiety" (2003: 11). Henry's reaction to what he observes show how the anxieties triggered by disaster and terror images made familiar through the media override other possible explanations than an attack on the Western metropolis by (Islamic) terrorist forces. The long inner monologue reveals how risk perception is constituted through a rapid process of observation, calculation and recalculation – one that takes seconds in reality but much longer to narrate, taking the reader through a detailed struggle between ratio and fear and mutually exclusive explanatory scenarios in Henry's mind which are only resolved with reference to the paradoxical scientific thought experiment of Schrödinger's Cat. Henry first mistakes the plane for a meteor, then reflects on the contingency of terror acts, but also briefly considers the option of "simple, secular mechanical failure" (S 18). His risk assessment undeniably influenced by recent events, he notes how "airliners look different in the sky these days, predatory or doomed" (S 16), i.e., either way, they are publically perceived as risks. Henry's thoughts also circle around the general, non-terrorism related risks of air travel and highlight the intrinsic link between risk calculations and capitalism:

> Looked at a certain way – deaths per passenger mile – the statistics are consoling. And how else attend a conference in Southern California? Air travel is a stock market, a trick of mirrored perceptions, a fragile alliance of pooled belief; so long as nerves hold steady and no bombs or wreckers are on board, everybody prospers. When there's failure, there will be no half measures. Seen another way – death per journey – the figures aren't so good. (S 15)

Always filtered through Henry's mind, from the beginning the narrative explores the divide between subjective and objective risk perception, and the fact that a sense of risk even if based on statistics and probabilities and empirically derived from observation, is still an informant of decision-making highly dependent on opinion and belief.

The scene also explores the question of active involvements vs. passive spectatorship when it comes to (potentially) catastrophic events. Watching the plane triggers Henry's sense of professional responsibility because as a doctor he could be at the scene of the crash to help minimize the extent of the casualties. Yet he remains immobile, waiting to see what happens: "Culpable in his helplessness. [...] His crime was to stand in the safety of his bedroom, [...] as he watched people die" (S 22–23). The protagonist's passivity during crucial moments in the plot (e.g. in the beginning he watches the burning plane, in the final climactic scene he watches Baxter threatening to rape his daughter Daisy) has caused critical commentary. Henry's "onlooker status" in the middle of a crisis has been attributed to his habitual detachment from individual human lives and destinies in favour of observing a larger natural order of the world (Root 2011: 66). Alternatively, Cornier Michael argues, his behaviour can be seen as a characteristic response in the post-9/11 context where people are confined to repeatedly watch traumatic events they cannot stop from a distance, which not only causes feelings of terror and anxiety but leads to a felt lack of agency (Cornier Michael 2009: 33). While in my opinion Henry's individual risk personality explains his behaviour and relative non-involvement in these scenes, it is also important to note that the novel in general is undeniably concerned with what Robert Young describes as "a First World form of terror", feared by a majority of people but remaining "thankfully, always a Burkean remove"; it is focussed more on an aesthetic affect generated by terror, in contrast to other, more real and "immediate forms of fear, to the state of living in apprehension" (Young 2010: 323). Young also argues that this kind of first world terror(ism), hinging on the experience of traumatic events perpetuated via media channels, "moves you into a state of producing fiction: it makes you live imaginatively on the borderlines of the real" (2010: 309). This "logic of an anticipated repetition" (309) creates a distance from reality which is illustrated in the opening of *Saturday* and Henry's behaviour throughout the narrative. Later, when Henry learns the truth behind "his story" from the news – an engine fire in a Russian cargo plane – his first response, tellingly, is not relief because no people have been hurt, but a questioning of the reality and the implications of his own nightly panic. It now leaves him with a slight sense of embarrassment: "Have his anxieties been making a fool of him?" (S 180). According to Cécile Leupolt, McEwan's narrative draws attention to the extent with which media images of traumatic catastrophes feed the fundamental human fascination with apocalyptic fantasies (Leupolt 2010: 57). In the opening scene, Henry's "readiness to be persuaded that the world has changed beyond recall, that harmless streets like this and the tolerant life they embody can be destroyed by the new enemy" (S 76) demonstrates people's habitual imaginative manipulation through the media images. In addition, it reveals the "consoling element" (Leupolt 2010: 59) of first world terrorism by giving a reassuring purpose and clearly identifiable source of "evil" to casualties and accidents which are easier to accept than randomness. However, the beginning of the novel explores another idea that transcends the immediate post 9/11-context and is linked to the Darwinian theme of natural order and selection. Henry's reflections suggest that the human capacities for imaging the worst, for risk perception and fear are, in fact, results of the evolutionary process: "*there must have been survival advantage in dreaming up bad outcomes* and scheming to avoid them. The trick of dark imagining is one legacy of natural selection in a dangerous world" (S 39; my emphasis). With this recourse to science Henry seeks an explanation and justification for his nightly bout of fear and misinterpretation of an event the details of which "he half-ignored in order to nourish his fears […] he should have sensed it straight away – a simple accident in the making. Not an attack on our whole way of life then" (S 39).

Henry's first confrontation with Baxter contains an equally detailed narration of the complexities and contradictions of subjective risk perception and management as the beginning scene, but here the protagonist has to manage a slower and inconsistently increasing sense of danger which is much more immediate and personal. Eager to get to his game of squash, at first Henry is only annoyed by the inevitable delay in having to sort out the details of the accident after the run in with Baxter's car. When he sees three guys approaching, his annoyance becomes intermingled with fear, though he does not yet anticipate any physical harm to himself or his car. But he is determined to maintain his superiority and throughout the scene his male ego struggles against the rational call for caution. He tries to perceive the situation like a game, not merely out of arrogance but because watching menacing events as if they would happen on a stage offers security through intellectual and emotional detachment. At this particular moment, Henry feels like he is trapped in an "urban drama", as if a bit of "play-acting is about to begin" (S 86). This is quickly followed by the realization that the experience of some sort of physical violence is probable and inevitable. Consequently, Henry proceeds by rationally assessing his physical fitness and the odds of winning a fight against three guys. Discarding this option as too risky – ("it's a ridiculous thought; he hasn't been in a hand-to-hand fight since he was eight"; S 88) – Henry promises himself not to fight back, or, if he does, to at least avoid at all cost to fall and hit his head on the ground. Throughout the scene Henry's thoughts gallop forward to anticipations of the consequences of possible courses of events: "As with the insurance claims [for the car], he sees the dreary future ahead. Weeks of painful convalescence" (S 93). After his professional attention has discovered Baxter's tremor, he resorts to the strategy outlined above which allows him to avoid the risk of physical harm altogether. Though he successfully regains the control over the situation by 'diagnosing' Baxter, Henry misjudges the effects of the humiliation of Baxter and the risk which springs from exploiting the other's desperation for these cause the later much more serious attack on his and his family's safety. In summary, Henry is able to aptly stun Baxter with his knowledge and to correctly assess the other's physical appearance and the situation from the outside, but misreads the significance of the encounter in emotional-psychological terms for all those involved. The question that haunts him later is whether his treatment of Baxter was justified as a means of self-preservation, whether using his medical knowledge to his own advantage was a legitimate strategy of risk aversion. But when Baxter holds a knife to Rosalind's throat, he blames himself for not foreseeing the risk of his earlier action, to him now a clear case of failed risk management: "Why could he not see that it's dangerous to humble a man as emotionally labile as Baxter? [...] He used or misused his authority to avoid one crisis, and his actions have steered him into another, far worse" (S 211).

At the same time, during both encounters Henry is intrigued by Baxter and takes an almost voyeuristic interest in him, perceiving him as "a special case – a man who believes he has no future and is therefore free of consequences" (S 210). Functioning as a symbol of contingency and irrationality, Baxter, as many critical voices have noted, is presented as a biological rather than social problem and denied a voice, real motivation or storyline in the novel. Gauthier, for example, argues that he is "simply cast as someone to whom life has dealt a bad hand, quite randomly and without human implication" (Gauthier 2003: 15). He is also confined to being "a rather impotent threat who is humiliated, vanquished, and ultimately rendered unconscious" (2003: 16). Thus the reader, along with the protagonist, eventually wonders if Baxter should be pitied rather than feared (– a typical effect of narrative 'othering' of the subaltern –) and this leaves, either way, only limited room for empathy in an ethical sense (2003: 25). Perowne's main concern is to risk-manage Baxter, but from a medical rather than ethical-social perspective. He only reflects superficially on the psychological motivations of Baxter's violence, reducing him to the causes of his genetic make-up and judging all his reactions according to his (impaired) physical condition. As a consequence, Perowne does not factor in how they are through being part in an inherently unequal social system. As Gauthier emphasizes, when Baxter lets Daisy go instead of raping her, Henry attributes the change of mind as well as the previous threat of violence to Baxter's 'diseased' mind rather than "to the possible affront a disadvantaged individual might feel when confronted with the affluence and good luck embodied by the Perowne family" (Gauthier 2003: 19).

Though McEwan's protagonist is haunted throughout the day by a sense of dread and looming threats, the novel, focussing on protected upper-middle class life, is predominately concerned with security. It reveals, as one reviewer points out, McEwan's ongoing fascination with "sinister, chaotic, violent forces" (Tait 2005: 21) that disrupt stable domestic lives. The forces destabilizing Henry Perowne's routine, his certainty, and his family's safe and comfortable existence include allusions to the iconic 9/11 attacks through the story of the burning cargo plane, debates of the pros and cons of the US military intervention in Iraq, the confrontation with Baxter's gang, and they culminate in the home invasion. All are observed by the protagonist with varying degrees of distance and detachment; moreover, the risks never fully materialize into dangers or are rather quickly averted. While his earlier works have earned the author the nickname "Ian Macabre" (see Impastato 2009: 14), in *Saturday*, where the author's preoccupation with security, Tait writes, "has become *the* great obsession" (Tait 2005: 21; original emphasis), the dominant public mood and McEwan's fictional world seem to resemble each other with particular closeness. The text captures a climate of uncertainty, anxiety and risk among an educated upper middle-class living in a Western metropolis in which terrorism is cast as a main threat due to the perceived irrationality of a hostile agent who has little to lose. Comparable to the anarchists in *The Secret Agent*, Baxter's character personifies this nightmarish threat of lower class agency and irrationality. Like Stevie and the other 'terrorists' in Conrad's novel, the Basts' in *Howards End*, or Septimus Smith in *Mrs*

Dalloway, in *Saturday* Baxter, the threat to the domestic security of the upper middle-class characters, is represented as dually subaltern because he is socially as well as physically and mentally inferior. The confrontation between Baxter and Perowne is very much one of class opposition, full of intrinsic stereotypes such as lower-class physical aggression which is met with 'rational' attempts to defuse the situation out of a position of material and educational superiority. It is also charged with the strong link between low class, disease and degeneration originating in the Victorian era. Baxter's threatening and dis-abling difference is pathologized due to his he suffering from a hereditary degenerative brain disorder. Significantly, in the end, Daisy's pregnancy signals the continuation of the (healthy) Perowne family line, while Baxter's is 'saved' by Henry on the operating table, condemning him to live on but without a cure.

As several other post-9/11 novels, e. g. Salman Rushdie's *Shalimar the Clown*, Richard Flanagan's *The Unknown Terrorist* and Mohsin Hamid's *The Reluctant Fundamentalist*, McEwan's novel does not depict religious fanaticism as the main risk to society and individual but irrationality and insanity, social inequality, and, most centrally perhaps, violent emotions such as humiliation, jealousy, and fears of loss which are canalized into violence. Thus, in *Saturday*, though better described as a security than as a risk novel in terms of its plot and protagonist, contemporary anxieties are intertwined with persisting risk discourses that can be traced back to the middle of the 19th century. The setting, however, presents a similarly ambivalent case and allows arguments for both increased danger and security. While Sebastian Groes observes that in contrast to the darkness and dangerousness of Victorian (and even more pronounced, one might add, 18th-century) London "Perowne's city is a clean, light and sanitized Eden" (Groes 2013: 108), the capital is still depicted as a place full of "junkies and beggars" (S 77) lurking in the square outside Henry's home, with foreign terrorists more far away also posing threats to the city and its inhabitants. Fusing public and private concerns, through the two encounters with Baxter and the home invasion plot, Henry, the representative of a privileged class removed far from economic precarity, is forced to reconsider his ideas about the risk of violence to the safety of the city and his own home and privilege. This, Andrew Foley notes, unsettles "his belief in the indestructibility of his own well-being" (Foley 2010: 151). The narrative details Perowne's "padded privacy" (S 121), his fragile sense of security upheld by the guarded walls of his home. A 21st-century upper-middle class version of Crusoe's fortress on the island, the elaborate security measures (– "two black iron bolts as old as the house, two tempered steel security chains, a spyhole with a brass cover, the box of electronics that works the Entryphone system, the red panic button, the alarm pad with its softly gleaming digits"; S 36–37), are designed to keep the risk of intruders at bay, "the fear of being eaten. Resolved at last, by central locking" (S 121). From within, he can safely watch the people on the square, the likes of Baxter, "the city's poor, the drug-addicted, the downright bad" (S 37).

Perowne's risk narrative, or rather, his "cautionary refrain" (Hillard 2008: 193) of the threatening agency of the physically and morally debilitated masses outside his protected realm of privilege, echoes, Molly Clarke Hillard observes, the pseudo-scientific discourse of Victorian social theorists like Thomas Carlyle or Matthew Arnold. Ross (2008) and Ganteau (2015) also focus their readings on how *Saturday* appears as an updated version of the "condition-of-England" novel. McEwan's text evokes the Victorian model of the genre in terms of risk through the focus on the vulnerability of the white English middle class[11] and the fact that the protection of privacy and property plays an important role. According to Ganteau, the condition of England depicted in *Saturday* is one of precarity and inescapable interdependence, of "a nation of frail supermen and superwomen" (Ganteau 2015: 151; 150). This particular risk narrative has strong Victorian as well as Edwardian undertones. There are noticeable parallels to *Howards End,* a text which similarly propagates liberal values while probing "the question of the survival of English civilization in a time of crisis" (Ross 2008: 79). However, the risk discourse is different in its intensity and, as far as contact between the classes is concerned, the issues of violent confrontation and the question of philanthropy are negotiated with a different outcome: In the end Henry saves Baxter, while Leonard Bast dies at the hands of Charles Wilcox (however aided by his weakened heart); in *Saturday* the intruder does not struggle for acceptance by the Perownes as Leonard does by the Schlegels; instead he seeks revenge for humiliation and demands help. Thus one can agree with Ross's assessment that the risk discourse is intensified into the underclass now – or rather, I might add, once again – posing a distinct threat, rather than a problem, for the elite (Ross 2008: 85).

It is generally hard to dispute descriptions of *Saturday* as a fictional "study in homeland insecurity" (Ross 2008: 82), for it deals literally and metaphorically with the threat of home intrusion and border transgressions. It is a text saturated with debates of war and reflections of uncertainties and unease, highlighting "a new darkness" (Groes 2013: 111) of life in the post-9/11 metropolis and struggling to represent the vague sense of how everything is now somehow perceptibly more uncertain and dangerous. Yet the narrative also contains many satirical

---

11 This aspect has been harshly criticized, for example by Lars Eckstein, who sees *Saturday* as a text which ignores "the postcolonial realities of contemporary British culture" (2011: 2) and in which moral agency is "almost exclusively reserved for the cultured and affluent elite" (5).

comments on the ubiquity of contemporary risk and disaster discourses in the media, in academia, or in the work place. In fact, the object of risk here being terrorism instead of climate change, McEwan has his protagonist in *Saturday* express opinions that are eerily similar to those of Michael Beard in *Solar*. Perowne shows a certain habituation bordering on denial with regard to the medial representation of the contemporary risk society in Beck's sense. He says: "Islamic terrorism will settle into place, alongside recent wars, climate change, the politics of international trade, land and fresh water shortages, hunger, poverty and the rest" (S 77). This habituation applies even more to the younger generation. Theo, having come of age during the era of the 9/11 attacks, has perfected means to screen the news and public terror discourses: "As long as there's nothing new, his mind is free. International terror, security cordons, preparations for war – these represent the steady state, the weather" (S 32). Henry's professionally conditioned scientific view of the world also shapes an optimism in the values and progress of Western civilization and the conviction that life, in many ways, is continuously being made safer than ever before: "The world should take note: not everything is getting worse" (S 69). On several occasions he identifies the numbing – instead of change-inducing – effect of the constant confrontation with a public rhetoric and imagination that indulges in danger scenarios, e.g. he notes how "words like 'catastrophe' and 'mass fatalities', 'chemical and biological warfare' and 'major attack' have recently become bland through repetition" (S 11–12). Specifically he discards the gloomy perspective prevailing in the humanities, exemplified by his daughter Daisy's college lecturers and their keenness "to dramatise modern life as a sequence of calamities" (S 77).[12] And concerning the debate about the Iraq war, he is weary about public opinion being based on uncertain risk probabilities ("worst-case guesses"; S 186) that assume the status of facts through mere repetition.

Proclaimed to offer an image of Western society at the beginning of the 21st century, *Saturday* has proved to be nothing but a polarizing novel and has attracted a mass of critical praise as well as hatred.[13] This is due to the climactic

---

[12] In this passage, McEwan has his narrator add: "for the humanities generally, misery is more amendable to analysis: happiness is a harder nut to crack" (S 78). In my opinion McEwan's narrative is full of self-irony here and anticipates a lot of the negative reactions a thoroughly "happy" and perfect protagonist as Henry Perowne was bound to inspire in literary critics.

[13] Cf. Banville's remark: "*Saturday* has the feel of a neoliberal polemic gone badly wrong; if Tony Blair [...] were to appoint a committee to produce a 'novel for our time,' the result would surely be something like this" (2005: 14). Among the harshest critics of the novel and in particular McEwan's reference to Victorian liberal values are Hadley (2005) and Eckstein (2011).

ending and the nothing short of miraculous power credited to Matthew Arnold's poem "Dover Beach", which, when recited by Daisy, moves Baxter to the extent that he forgets his intention of raping her, transforming him "from lord of terror to amazed admirer" (S 223). In line with McEwan's non-fictional responses immediately after 9/11 in which he identifies a failure of imagination as the cause of terrorism,[14] the scene contains a strong emphasis of the power of literature, empathy, and emotion as means of managing the risk of violence.[15] In addition to these hardly uncontroversial suggestions, the characterization of Henry – as the epitome of white male class privilege – has been a source of outrage and many critics have expressed difficulty in liking *Saturday* for these reasons (see Hillard 2008: 185–186). It is certainly important to note, as Louisa Hadley has done with particular critical vehemence, that Perowne's thoughts and anxieties are representative of an educated white middle-class "trying to function on the darkling plain of global terrorism, a nightmare vision of social alterity that exceeds only in technological scale and cultural alienation the threat posed by the working-class masses" (Hadley 2005: 96).[16] However, though undoubtedly belonging to the upper stratum of society in terms of education and material wealth, Henry Perowne has also been described as a kind of "everyman of the post-9/11 world" (Root 2011: 61), a "quintessential home moyen sensual" (Banville 2005: 12). Lacking any extra-ordinary courage, political activism, or altruism, the central character has maddened many readers due to his complacency. He is, Tina Beattie argues, "*too secure in his environment. Perowne is a man of certainty and* [...] *he comes across as a rather dull and unadventurous Englishman* who experiences no existential dread about his place in the universe and no real thirst for knowledge beyond the closed horizons of his own scientific world" (Beattie 2007: 159–160; my emphasis). On one level, Henry's continual risk assessment in the narrative is indeed exclusively self-centred. Being "a habitual observer of his own moods'" (S 4) he is always taking stock of his physical

---

14 See McEwan's essays in *The Guardian*, "Only Love and then Oblivion" (2001a) and "Beyond Belief" (2001b).
15 Cf. Bradley and Tate, who write: "If McEwan's almost Victorian faith in the ameliorative power of the novel will strike many readers as even more naïve than his explanation of terrorism – does he believe that the September 11 attacks would not have happened if Mohammed Atta had only put down the Qur'an and read *Middlemarch* instead? – it is a testament to the sophistication of his fiction that this credo is continually tested, challenged and problematized in the works that follow" (2010: 23).
16 Hadley even admits her personal sympathy with Perowne's liberal fantasies and the pride and comfort found in his nuclear family idyll and his profession, but rejects the supposedly uncritical embrace of it in the narrative (see 2005: 97).

and mental state. Resembling internal "diagnostic tests on himself" (Ferguson 2007: 47), Perowne employs this empirically deduced 'data' in order to assess his own (middle to long-term) risks of decline and (short-term) risks of injury and discomfort. For example, he reflects that he should refrain from his habit of taking the stairs two steps at a time because the probability of injuring himself is greater now that he is approaching the age of fifty (S 150) and he insists on taking regular breaks when playing squash for similar reasons.[17] The visit to his mother confronts Henry with the inevitable risk of human decline in another form; tellingly, his mother, an Alzheimer's patient, suffers from a disease that robs her of her mental faculties, including the abilities to anticipate and calculate actions and events. On some occasions during the day, however, Henry's professional ego and competitive nature clash with his instincts of self-protection and caution, rationally fuelled by the awareness of his own physical limitations. Shaken and exhausted after the car accident and the encounter with Baxter, he contemplates ending his squash game earlier than usual: "His heart will be all the more vulnerable after that punch. [...] *he mustn't endanger his own life for a mere game*" (S 102; my emphasis). But he plays till the end, driven by "the irreducible urge to win, as biological as thirst" (S 113).

The powerful effect credited to poetry in the novel aligns *Saturday* with the recurrent staging of the relationship between literature and science as different, and, according to the two-cultures-debate, radically opposed types of knowledge in many of McEwan's fictions (see Sleigh 2011). If several critics have disputed the unapologetic centrality the novel gives to literature's humanizing power to give access to aspects of reality which defy rational scientific explanation and as a tool of risk management that fosters empathy and averts violence – according to Hadley a distinctly "Victorian fantasy that still entices us" (Hadley 2005: 93)[18] –, in my opinion Charlotte Sleigh rightly draws attention to the fact that Arnold's poem works as a momentary emotional seduction, but that the battle against the threat of violence is ultimately won by cunning, scientific knowledge, and physical violence. Under the pretence of showing him evidence about a successful clinical trial of a cure against Huntington's disease Henry manages to lure Baxter into his study and then, with the help of Theo, knocks him unconscious by throwing him down the stairs. The decision to later operate on Baxter's

---

17 For the argument that the text is focussed on Perowne's aging, vulnerable body see also Ganteau (2015: 153).
18 According to Eckstein, McEwan's "infatuation" with Matthew Arnold is deeply ideological and problematic because it propagates Eurocentric civilizing values prior to postcolonialism, "Arnoldian Culture with a capital C as a remedy against the contingencies of the Western world after 9/11" (2011: 7).

head injury himself offers him a familiar stabilizing form of closure: "Revenge enough. And here is one area where Henry can exercise authority and shape events" (S 278). Seemingly, Henry saves Baxter's life and transcends hatred and otherness through professionalism, but the surgery is only made necessary by Baxter's non-accidental fall. Cecile Leupolt rightly notes: "This can hardly be considered a peaceful resolution of conflict, however comprehensible Henry's act of self-defence in a life-threatening situation might be" (Leupolt 2010: 63). The risk management proposed in the novel firmly rests on Western Enlightenment values, individual agency and responsibility, knowledge, and art and science. It ends with a sense of danger averted and domestic security restored, and with a triumph of the powerful and privileged over the socially inferior and powerless, an ending which aligns *Saturday* with the tradition of the condition-of-England novel. The Perownes have suffered a traumatising incident, but it could have been much worse. The threat to them is ultimately weak and meaningless; still it affirms both hope of lasting safety – or rather, a risk-free state, as well as fears of how easily it can be destroyed. In the end, Henry stands again at this bedroom window, looking out over the nightly city: "All he feels now is fear. He's weak and ignorant, scared of the way consequences of an action leap away from your control [...], until you're led to a place you never dreamed of and would never choose – a knife at the throat" (S 277). The reader is left with McEwan's protagonist standing there in the safety of his luxurious home in his nightgown, ignorantly envious of his imaginary Edwardian predecessor for supposedly having a view of the future as being safer and more predictable. Critics like Foley emphasise that although Perowne does not undergo any change concerning this his fundamental beliefs in the novel, he is left feeling more worried about the future, "uncertain and more vulnerable", "[l]ike the post-9/11 liberal world in general" (Foley 2010: 157). But perhaps one ought to read the fearful reflections of having to face "a horizon indistinct with possibilities" (S 276) alongside the lyrics of the blues song written by Theo Perowne, *"Baby, you can choose despair, Or you can be happy if you dare"* (S 170; original emphasis), which contain an almost ironic appeal to deny being overwhelmed by risk – against the odds.

12.2 'The bullet of an ordinary life': *Arlington Park*

McEwan's *Saturday* offers a "contemporary version of a domestic narrative" (Cornier Michael 2009: 27), which owns a debt to modernist aesthetics and centrally deals with the perception of risk, time, and agency. As does Rachel Cusk's novel *Arlington Park* (2006). It is also an even more obvious variation of Woolf's

Mrs Dalloway. While both novels can be categorized as "neomodernist glocal novels", which respond to and reflect how "[o]n or about 9/11 human nature changed" (Latham 2015: 137), in comparison to the steadily growing body of criticism on McEwan's writing and *Saturday's* canonicity in the field of post-9/11 fiction, Cusk still belongs to "a new generation of pre-canonical writers whose work has so far received very little attention" (Schoene 2010: 33). Not just arguing that *Arlington Park* is a text worthy of critical attention, in many regards it allows the analysis of the primary texts in this study to come full circle. With Rachel Cusk herself describing *Arlington Park* as the "book of repetition" (Cusk 2009), referring to the reiterative experience of femininity and ordinary domestic life still commonly marginalized as the 'improper stuff' of serious fiction, her novel appears doubly suited to serve as a final example because it deals explicitly with the nexus between risk and gender, femininity and motherhood that is already opened up in Defoe's *Moll Flanders* (– though Moll's does, of course, hardly qualify as an in any way *ordinary* life story –) and reverberates through many of the Victorian novels.

The setting adds another dimension because it removes the focus from the dangers of the metropolis, London, and turns it onto its suburban surroundings, specifically to the leafy suburb Arlington Park where the main characters, all wives and mothers residing in spacious homes, lead lives sheltered from any economic or social risks. Instead, Cusk's bleak if at times darkly humorous depiction of female life in suburbia, in vivid sketches of five women in their mid-thirties (Juliet Randall, Amanda Clapp, Maisie Carrington, Solly Kerr-Leigh and Christine Lanham), is saturated with a daily struggle of mental and emotional survival against thoughts about cruelty and violence, frustration, loneliness and depression. The effect is a revelation of bodily and mental vulnerability characteristic of contemporary fiction, theorized in several recent studies as the 'turn to precarity'.[19] The novel exemplifies female-oriented responses to the 9/11 attacks in the sense described by Childs, Colebrook and Groes (2014) in the introduction to one of the rare book-length studies of contemporary women's writing in this context. They draw attention to the persistently highly gendered nature of risk and violence in the early 21st century and argue that while female fictions often connect with the political only peripherally, they are "explicitly contextualized by the atmosphere of the aftermath" of the events (Childs, Colebrook and Groes 2014: 19; 15). The engagement with the effects of the threatening realities of war and global terrorism is captured predominantly at the formal, symbolic,

---

19 A foundational book in this context is Judith Butler's *Precarious Life* (2004); see also Botha (2014), Morrison (2014), Korte and Regard (2014), and Ganteau (2015; 2017).

and stylistic level, with the fictions demonstrating the use of a modified realist aesthetic, and "a renewed exploration of emotion and affect, a search for consolation in a time of precarity" (2014: 7), "a new emotional climate seared with the reality or anticipation of fear and loss [...] an acknowledgment of a new uncertainty confronting us with the vulnerability and complexity of human society in a post-9/11 world" (2014: 20). The re-emergence of feminist thinking, the return to realism, the return of affect and emotion, are all subsumable under a focus on precariousness that, in this way reflects and accommodates the perception of a world full of risk, unpredictable and insecure and of the individual as essentially vulnerable. Cusk's writing furthermore illustrates another 'turn', which differentiates it, for instance, from other post-9/11 novels by male writers such as McEwan's *Saturday* that also push understandings of domestic fiction beyond its traditional boundaries. Her novel is more firmly committed to what Childs, Colebrook and Groes describe as "the turn to the 'anti-spectacular' [...] a deliberate move away from the celebration of Spectacle" (2014: 17). *Arlington Park* situates and negotiates distinctly gendered risk at the level of the spectacularly ordinary – which Peter Child refers to as the "ordinary sublime" (Childs 2014) in Cusk's fiction – in the realm of the middle-class nuclear family. This is summed up in the following quotation which exemplifies the text's abundant use of risk metaphors from the semantic fields of nautics, sea and weather, especially storm and rain. It reveals the characteristic undercurrent of violence and the concern with meaninglessness, disorienting ambivalences and questions of judgment and scale.

> It was a dangerous place to live in, a family: it was tumultuous as the open sea beneath a treacherous sky, the shifting allegiances, the flurries of cruelty and virtue, the great battering waves of mood and mortality, the endless alternation of storm and calm. [...] in the end you didn't know what the difference was, what it all meant, what it added up to, when set against the necessity for just surviving and getting through. (AP 186–187)

But in a sense, Cusk's novel, bordering on dark satire, also turns the perception of risk on its head. The female characters all show "an unstable level of dissatisfaction" (AP 179) and suffer from having to live with their past choices. Faced with the unpredictability of their own emotions and reactions, the women's pronounced fear of loss of control and order, and of contact with or simply acknowledging the general unpredictability of life, continually clashes with the paradoxical realization that, quite possibly, one has "taken excessive pains to seclude oneself from what was actually harmless and even have been fruitful" (AP 79); and that generally, regardless of location, "life should tend less towards a killing orderliness and more in the fruitful direction of risk and whimsicality" (AP 60). The latter is caused by a felt lack of subjective distinctiveness and a sense of isolation and feeling that "life that was being lived elsewhere" (AP 115). The narrative explores the question of the risks and price of choosing ordinariness over adventure, in other words, it deals with the risks that come with choosing the very "middle station" that is so firmly rejected in the beginning of Defoe's *Robinson Crusoe* and also the plight of the protagonist in Orwell's *Coming Up For Air*.

In her essay "Shakespeare's Daughters" (2009), Cusk argues that as far as women's writing is concerned the same value system prevails and not much has changed since the publication of Virginia Woolf's *A Room of One's Own* and Simone de Beauvoir's *The Second Sex*, for Cusk the two most important texts to shape the discourse of 20th-century women's writing. What persists to compromise women and women writers is their inescapable physicality – dramatized as the "crisis of the flesh" (AP 121) in *Arlington Park*. Various scenes depict the women's struggle against their own heaviness and fleshiness tied directly to motherhood and biological functions such as eating and pregnancy: Amanda Clapp is overcome with a general disgust when buying minced meat at the butchers with her little son, something she feels no man or single woman would be forced to do. Solly Kerr-Leigh, pregnant with her fourth child, longs "to expel from her this great, mounting force of debris, to clarify herself" (AP 132), and notes, by envious comparison, her Italian au pair Paola's "unsullied distance from this crude business of reproduction" (AP 137). Incidentally, Paola is also a vegetarian. Cusk's depiction of maternal bodies and the expression of female self-hatred through images such as bloody meat and recurring thoughts about physical violence and fears of uncontrollable physical expansion and dissolution, fit into a wider context of cultural representations of the maternal body as abject (see Hanson 2015: 96). They are also connected to fears and rage against inequalities determined by biological sex. With pregnancy and its aftermath – nursing, childcare – women risk a loss of physical autonomy and inevitable alteration of their bodies that men are spared. Thus Solly envies her husband who is able to remain "continuous with his child self" (AP 121) and "harden into a lean, vertical masculinity" (AP 113) while she turns into "into a great, expectant precariousness", soon to be "diffused entirely into fleshy relatedness" (AP 114). According to Clare Hanson, a persistent theme that emerges with startling clarity when comparing literary and other artistic depictions of maternal bodies over the last two centuries is their construction in terms of physical and emotional instability: "Such anxious constructions of the maternal body are surely an index of the inchoate fears that continue to surround reproduction and the lease on the future which it represents" (2015: 98). In *Arlington Park*, this is expressed as "*the worst kind of terror really, to live in a body and yet it offered you no protection*" (AP 133; my emphasis).

The experience of motherhood – and trying to write about it – is for Cusk the worst hazard of femininity.[20] And while there have been significant changes in women's lives in other respects, these realities remain unaltered: "She can look at her own body: if a woman's body signifies anything, it is that repetition is more powerful than change. [...] 'Women's writing' might be another name for the book of repetition" (Cusk 2009). The oppression of women in general and the one specific to female writers can never be fully resolved due to the felt pressure to produce "women's writing", to engage with pre-conditioned topics typically dismissed because of their political insignificance and thus limiting the fictions' reception and criticism. With reference to Fredrika Scarth's work on Simone de Beauvoir, Maria Tang reads Cusk's novel as rehearsing the old paradigm of sexual difference and consciously running the risk of getting trapped in it. Cusk dares to embrace "the immanent 'Other' of patriarchy" (Tang 2013) by writing about themes traditionally coded as female and suggests analogous risks exist for the female writer and female subjectivity in general. The tension between politics and the personal, between the effects of war and the conflicted feelings of a woman in the drawing-room that so masterfully shapes *Mrs Dalloway*, is, for Cusk, one laden with value judgment and signifying a persistent, hierarchical view of fictional content according to which "[a] scene in a battle-field is more important than a scene in a shop" (Cusk 2009).

In this context the author clearly postulates the need for women writers to break through the "fog around iterative female experience" (Cusk 2009), and to tackle taboo subjects, such as the feeling of regret after having had children and the high risks of a loss of freedom and self-worth that are inherent to the choices of marriage, motherhood and domesticity. For she sees the silence about these issues as only intensified by a lack of sisterhood solidarity after the peak of feminism at the end of the 20th-century: "If a woman feels suffocated and grounded and bewildered by her womanhood, she feels these things alone, as an individual: there is currently no public unity among women" (Cusk 2009). Where Defoe's Moll finds cunning help and shelter during and after her pregnancy, supplied by Mother Midnight and other women and a temporary alternative to living with a man, Cusk's characters in *Arlington Park* struggle alone

---

20 Cusk has also been outspoken about her personal trauma after the birth of her first daughter in 1999. See her essay "I was only being honest" (2008), a response to the many critical reactions to her book *A Life's Work* (2001) that deals with her difficult experience of becoming a mother. Arguing biographically, Childs (2014) identifies a paralleling of crisis in Cusk's writing post-2001, relating the author's struggle to come to terms with motherhood to the fictional depictions of the world as bleak and insecure.

through the risk management of their choices, while keeping up a façade of domestic contentment.

Rachel Cusk who reads *Mrs Dalloway* as a fictional text "about its author's fear of her own ordinariness and triviality" (Cusk 2009), seemingly grapples with the same anxiety as Virginia Woolf in her writing. At the same time, Cusk, wanting to write about the "ordinary experience of sorrow, of doubt, of morality, of time" (Cusk 2005), pursues an aesthetic and political aim similar to the one Woolf formulated so memorably in her essay "Modern Fiction" (1925), seeking to capture the "ordinary mind on an ordinary day" and its "myriad impressions – trivial, fantastic, evanescent, or engraved with the sharpness of steel" (Woolf 1984: 160). Thus, as Monica Latham argues, both writers employ the triviality of the non-spectacular and the everyday and microscopic observations of their characters psychological experiences and of time in order to write against the grain of contemporary fiction from a feminist vantage point (see Latham 2015: 182; 194). Without analysing the intertextual relations between *Arlington Park* and *Mrs Dalloway* in great depth,[21] there are many parallels, which will strike any reader familiar with Woolf's novel, such as the circadian time-frame, the preoccupation with a minute dissection of life and the passing of time, the awareness of individual fleeting moments, and the questioning of past choices and relationships. Moreover, according to Latham, Cusk's five main female characters each have different features of Clarissa Dalloway – "Dallowayisms" (Latham 2015: 207; 168) – and function to represent "a collective female self" (2015: 169), united in the sense of feeling trapped and burdened by time and their femininity. As also Armelle Parey (2013) notes, the five individual portraits blend into one large picture of a contemporary suburban upper-middle-class housewife, more importantly, Cusk thus conveys a sense of the interchangeability of female identity in what Claire Wrobel describes as the author's "visions of *the hazards of the female experience*" (Wrobel 2013; my emphasis).

For example, Juliet, a 36-year old teacher at Arlington High School for Girls and mother of two, feels overwhelmed by a demeaning, crushing sense of ordinariness,[22] a result of her domestic existence which allows her little contact with the outside world, and drains all her energy into keeping the family running,

---

[21] This has been done by Latham (2013; 2015).
[22] Child describes Cusk's envisioned state of domesticity fittingly with the oxymoronic concept of an "ordinary sublime" which lends a bit of pathos to "the sense of a life's lack of permanence, its repetitiveness, and its frequent banality", in either case it captures the overwhelming quality of the mundane, "whether it brings fleeting exultation or near-permanent exhaustion" (2014: 114; 112).

leaving her husband to do the extra-ordinary things in the outside world; all women struggle to detach themselves, feel morphed into symbiotic physical existence with their children, their houses, their surroundings, which leaves them no room of their own. All women struggle with a sense of their own unreality and nothingness, failing to be seen; Juliet feels like her pupils see her only as a "carved figure that symbolized human attributes" (AP 20), devoid of passion, desires, ambitions of her own, identity crisis, feels invisible: "The window wouldn't reflect her properly. She was just a shape, an amorphous shape with water running down her" (AP 37). What marks the characters' subjective worlds and Cusk's depiction of the contemporary female (white, middle-class) condition is a shared experience of a mundane nothingness, which is intensely felt as a crisis and brings each woman close to the point of collapse or explosion. Even their nightmares only serve to enrage them next morning with memories of disgust and haunt them with their nothingness, e.g. Juliet's dream of a cockroach embedded in her scalp "almost infuriated her in its non-existence" (AP 7). One day, Christine Lanham confesses, she is "going to have to do something desperate" (AP 92), whereas Maisie Carrington harbours "violent feelings [...] that came as though from some geological past, like lava" (AP 173); Amanda's violent thoughts often gather focus on her son Eddie who at least twice a day puts her close to "failure and meaninglessness" (AP 45). The narrative frequently employs a rhetoric of aggression and risk, and even metaphors of archaic warfare to describe the tumultuous inner life of the women and perception of life in the close-knit community of Arlington Park, e.g. Juliet feels "at one minute that she and Benedict might be eaten, or enslaved" (AP 12). Amanda compares the women waiting outside the school ground to "a demoralised troop of soldiers" in which she discerns "an unusual vulnerability, an exposure of flank" (AP 57). Standing in her own perfectly remodelled kitchen, she feels temporarily secure but still "to be at the front line of the possibility that things might not turn out for the best" (AP 50); "the prospect of fresh sieges remained a possibility" (AP 53). There is a constant sense of risk assessment, of doom, non-belonging and insufficiency. Suburban domestic routine is depicted as a battlefield where survival is constantly at stake. Looking after children, houses and gardens, all daily chores are perceived as things that need to "mastered", "subjugated", "penetrated", with "sanitary force" (AP 56–57), but still leave the women after each small victory feeling defeated and wondering if they seek to assert control over the right battleground in the first place.

Every ordinary situation and all relationships are fraught with the risk of violence, such as a dinner party conversation during which Juliet dares to contradict one of the men's opinions: "She saw how close she was to his hatred: it was like a nerve she was within a millimetre of touching" (AP 17). While this violent tension underlying the relationships between the sexes culminates in the female perception of marriage as a form of slow violence and of all men as "murderers" (AP 18), it also extends to the interactions the women have with each other and their children. In particular the latter is a source of ambiguous emotions and the continued references in the narrative to the news story of Betsy Miller, a little girl who has disappeared and is later found dead, adds to the sense of horror lurking in the background and, as Wrobel (2013) points out, sustains the thematic emphasis on violence against children. It certainly adds a layer of risk, even if it is never translated into actual danger of harm. For example, outwardly maintaining a polite smile to the mother whose son has ruined her expensive white sofa with finger paint, Amanda bottles up her murderous thoughts and only whispers a few harsh words into Owen's ears: "He was like a seedling she could have torn up, [...] and dashed to the ground" (AP 71).

As Childs argues, typical for Cusk's fiction is the exploration of opposite forces and ideals in the domestic realm, such as security and freedom, novelty and familiarity (2014: 114), longing for intimacy and rejection of emotional bonds. The tensions between these irreconcilable desires are the cause of unhappiness for the women who literally suffer from the daily realization that they cannot have it all. Family life, the sought-after bulwark against the instabilities and isolation of contemporary life, is depicted as an entrapment which instils a slow-building sense of failure and insecurity. Asserting the frailty of human bonds in the 21st century, Zygmunt Bauman sums up the paradoxical tension between the "yearning for the security of togetherness" which makes men and women – and Cusk's characters – "so desperate to 'relate'; yet wary of the state of 'being related' and particularly of being related 'for good', not to mention forever – since they fear that such a state may bring burdens and cause strains they neither feel able nor are willing to bear, and so may severely limit the freedom they need" (Bauman 2003: viii).[23]

The same way that coupledom instils a paradoxical sense of suffocation and security in the women, they all seem to want to see other women break free and achieve the things they feel they themselves have no chance in achieving, teamed with an equally strong, jealous longing to see the other also bound and dragged down by marriage and motherhood. It seems to spring from the desire to minimize the risk of being confronted with a version of a different life that might contaminate one's own chosen version of happiness, the same

---

[23] Schoene (2011: 162) also refers to this passage from Bauman's *Liquid Love* in his reading of *Arlington Park*.

way a bit of dirt might contaminate a clean kitchen surface; telling words used to describe these emotional impulses are the desire to "secure" and "neutralise" (e.g. AP 85; 57). Of all the women, Solly Kerr-Leigh has the most contact with other versions of femininity from outside of Arlington Park and England through her series of international au-pairs from Taiwan, Japan and continental Europe, who get to stay in her spare room. This otherwise empty guest room, untouched by the mess of family life which swallows the rest of the house, is Solly's place of projection for her escape fantasies and contemplating what once "her intentions had been" (AP 113). When secretly looking through Paola's small array of pretty and delicate possessions (a few clothes, accessories and bath oils), Solly suddenly sees herself as monstrously large and out of control by comparison. Thinking of her cupboards stuffed with family-size value packs and belongings shared with her husband and children she feels she has lost everything that is exclusively feminine and her own. All these possessions, accumulated to guarantee comfort and security, now only weigh her down: "Why had she required such bulk, so much heaviness? What was she afraid of?" (AP 133). But Solly also knows that she will not dare to change anything. In addition to the motif of the experience of time as a painful burden or disorienting onrush – bearing the risk of getting crushed by "the oncoming stream of minutes and hours [which] broke its banks and flooded sideways, on and on, until she seemed to be disgorging a force of pure catastrophe" (AP 42) – the narrative employs various metaphors of captivity, immobility, heaviness, and the risk of falling, drowning etc., to express the women's state of self-alienation and dissatisfaction; "she was heavy, full of lead. She sank like a stone through the onrush of time" (AP 36). Domestic female existence is compared to being precariously exposed to the elementary force of nature. Solly "clung on, as though to the deck of a ship in a storm [...] to the solid matter of her life" (AP 135); to Amanda her day resembles walking on "a single wire on which she maintained an unpredictable balance" (AP 42).

Consequently, there are different kinds of risk management strategies and protective façades employed by each of the women. For Amanda Clapp, her car is the space where she feels shielded and removed from the outside world but which still allows her a spectator position. Christine Lanham, the character who perhaps most closely resembles Clarissa Dalloway in her determination to keep a happy façade and maintain a rational outlook, repeats the belief that "We're all actually very lucky" (AP 93) like a mantra in order to fend off any possibility of discontent or worry. Her personal risk philosophy that guarantees survival in the stormy sea of life, once again expressed by nautical metaphors, consists of a clear assessment of one's limits and properties teamed with deliberate blocking out of unproductive concern for others: "You had to protect what was worthwhile, [...] it never did any good worrying about things that had nothing to do with you. You had *to steer a course* and get what you could, never forgetting what the limitations were" (AP 237); "That's all you can do really, *steer your own through it and not think too much*" (AP 224; my emphasis); "We're all so lucky – wouldn't it be a waste if we spoiled it by worrying all the time about the people who are less lucky than us?" (AP 66). Cusk's satire depicts Christine as the most vocal, volatile and certainly most unlikeable of the female characters. What allows her to sail around cliffs of potentially unsettling concern for the condition of others, the environment, or the world at large is apparently based on a radical self-centred, class-conscious social Darwinism. She is also deeply afraid of any contact with otherness – social, ethnic, ideological, a fear which is revealed, for instance, in her openly racist comments about the school's black lunch lady, or her attitude towards the neighbouring, ethnically much more diverse suburbs, Redbourne and Firley, she has to drive through on her way to the Merrywood Mall: "Its presence was a constant hazard, in that it sustained a distinction in the face of which she could never feel entirely safe" (AP 81). Venturing outside the security of Arlington Park furthermore triggers in Christine an irrational sense of anxiety less, about any physical harm than about the exposure of herself as inauthentic, as an insufficient, non-belonging fraudulent existence. Of these other places she has "a black, private fear, [...] from which the plain unlikelihood of its realisation could not protect her. It [...] seemed to reveal to her the vulnerability of her grasp on the real, the authentic life" (AP 80 – 81).[24] Generally, Christine is the most risk-averse character and this includes the public display or even slight admittance of any sort of worry or panic. Behind this attitude lies a desperate attempt to maintain control of her life which she feels slipping through her hands. She compensates by verbalizing the belief in the duty of self-help of the socially inferior which removes the privileged from responsibility, mind the exception of natural disasters: "If an earthquake razed your house to the ground, you'd have my full sympathy. No, what I can't stand is the guilt we're all made to feel about people who have as much control over their lives as we do" (AP 107).

In marked contrast to Christine's armour of detachment and denial, Juliet dedicates her Friday afternoons to running a book club where she preferably

---

[24] On the anxious relation between identity and space, see also Parey (2013). All female characters harbour deep anxieties about the blurring or complete loss of boundaries, between inside and outside, between their selves and others, e.g. Solly fears a loss of control over contours of her body and dissolution into her maternity, Amanda anxiously feels that the tearing down of all walls in her house in order to create a bigger kitchen space has only produced monstrous results: "they had created not space but emptiness. They had gone too far" (AP 63).

teaches 19th-century novels about unhappy, passionate women, such as Madame Bovary, Anna Karenina and Catherine Earnshaw, intending them to serve as cautionary tales to her pupils not to pin all their ambitions on love and marriage.[25] She fears the girls' instinctual desire to attract men, knowing that it can easily override all her protective efforts as well as the girls' professional goals. Characteristic of the deep ambivalence at the heart of Cusk's novel and the female characters, Juliet, who is both disappointed and surprised by her own under-achievement of her once promising talents as a student, has a deterministic view of women's lives. But she still hopes to influence their limited agency and protect them from making the wrong choices: "they would meet a man [...] and little by little he would murder her. [...] Juliet tried to stave off this inevitability, in whatever limited way she could. She tried to acquaint them with the nature of the beast" (AP 154). For the same reason, Juliet fears for her daughter in a much different way than she does for her son, who, she beliefs, will not risk putting his ambitions on hold for anything and then be painfully disillusioned once "you realise that there isn't a next stage. This is all there is" (AP 166). Looking at her daughter Katherine, whom she perceives as an extension of her own self, Juliet desperately wants to shield her from "the bullet of an ordinary life" (AP 28). According to Juliet's – like Christine's, a privileged, self-centred – outlook, getting hit by this bullet is the greatest risk a woman can face. It has wounded her in the form of failed ambitions which have only led her back to school where once she used to be "the exceptional one" (AP 22). Through Juliet's character Cusk's narrative also illustrates the perception which, according to Deborah Philips is typical of each new generation of contemporary women writers from the mid-20th-century onwards,[26] namely a lingering sense that "the world could be better for women", but also a deferral of freedom and revenge which is left to the next generation to achieve, "there is a hope that the world will be better for their daughters; there is also perpetual displacement of the hope for women's equality" (Philips 2007: 17). Juliet's mission to protect the girls from dangers they do not want rescuing from, is largely also a means to alleviate her own sense of metaphorical 'murder' through the confinement to a dissatisfying domestic and professional life.

By casting the female characters in *Arlington Park* as "'bodies at risk'" (Tang 2013) but also as potential risks to people close to them, Cusk's narrative dram-

---

25 19th-century fiction is a dominant point of reference throughout the novel. As Parey notes, *Arlington Park* also employs the tradition of Victorian women's writing of being named after a setting like, for instance, Gaskell's *Cranford*, Eliot's *Middlemarch*, or Brontë's *Wuthering Heights* (Parey 2013).

26 See Deborah Philips's *Women's Fiction 1945–2005* (2007).

atizes the experience of femininity and motherhood as being full of physical as well as ontological risks, revealing the (im)possibilities of enduring life. Only occasionally, the characters are relieved by small epiphanic moments, when they suddenly see the beauty of the world "not filtered through her veil of anger, but as it was" (AP 167); one such moment comes when Juliet pauses to watch a pair of swans taking flight: "Side by side they flew, beautiful and alive, exulting" (AP 168), and it is epitomized in Christine's Dallowayesque outburst in the last chapter: "'You've got to love just – being alive" (AP 238).[27] But despite these lyrical moments and the poetic and stylized use of language throughout the narrative, in its aggressive intensity the novel transcends the echoes of Woolf and comes to resemble, as one reviewer puts it, "an angry, state-of-the-nation book, an elegy to metropolitan decline" (Ratcliffe 2006), which arguably shares as much with the darkness of mid-Victorian novels as it does with early 20th-century modernist fiction.[28]

The novel's ten untitled chapters, with one exception each focussing on one of the characters, are linked through the depiction on individual, domestic space and shared suburban living space. As Parey (2013) emphasises, Cusk's narrative treatment of space resembles the separation and clear gendering of public and domestic sphere in the Victorian era. Firmly confined to the domestic sphere, the female characters all suffer from a felt lack of private space as a place of escape from their household responsibilities. But, in contrast to their Victorian predecessors, the women of Arlington Park feel trapped and weighed down by the consequences of their choices. Although these backstories are mostly only hinted at and not narrated in detail, all have received an education and once had careers or professional opportunities they voluntarily gave up in order to exclusively pursue the role of wife and mother. The dimension of risk perception here comes in with a sense of belatedness,[29] after the realization that they have miscalculated the consequences and the reality of their life choices and wrongly measures losses against gains. For Maisie, "There was nothing in their situation in Arlington Park she could say hadn't chosen, except to actually live it" (S 183). Now she feels cheated by the burden of suburban domesticity, "strangulated, almost overcome by the fear of falsity and death" (AP 190).

---

27 On the use of Woolf-inspired epiphanies in the novel see Latham (2015: 172).
28 Or, as Childs and Schoene suggest, it should be read as a satire that fuses black comedy with a shrewd analysis of contemporary middle-class life (Childs 2014: 116; Schoene 2011: 177).
29 Standing at the window, Juliet feels a sense of belated dread, both very different from and eerily similar to Henry Perowne's anticipation of uncertainty and unrest in the first and last scene of *Saturday*. It is a sense of irrevocable loss of stability, "a fear of something it was too late to prevent, something that had already occurred" (AP 8).

She regrets having "gone too far" (AP 192) by having left her job and London behind, motivated once by wanting "to cash in luck and love and see what she got for them" (AP 193). Meanwhile Juliet, who in the course of the narrative decides to chop off her Rapunzel-long hair, remembers her youthful lack of risk consciousness and the courtship with her husband Benedict as a mix of game and fairy-tale romance: "When he came climbing up her hair, she didn't detect him as a threat, not at all. She saw him as a prize, her first, in the strange new field of endeavour known as human relationships" (AP 36). All women revisit the particular decision for their husbands, assessing it in terms of risk – then and now. Christine recalls her once desperate wish to escape economic instability and feeling adrift like "a piece of litter blowing in the wind" (AP 216) through marriage: "Somehow, her life had become contingent on this one chance, this opportunity of Joe" (AP 215). There is the shared sense of aimless risk management having gone wrong. Looking at her unmarried self, Juliet recalls, above all, her sense of risk and disorientation: "She didn't know exactly where she was going, just that it was necessary to remain in motion while avoiding outright disaster" (AP 183).

Covering the span of one day, to which the incessantly falling rain, Childs writes, "provides a soundtrack to the lives of characters eternally seeking shelter" (Childs 2014: 115) the narrative probes into the lives of five women who all regret choices they willingly made, and which now appear as the culprits of their unhappy existences – oscillating between frustration, rage, and despair. Aside from leaving their professional lives behind, this includes above all, motherhood, "with its relentless cycle of petty, ego-obliterating chores" (Lasdun 2006) and, tellingly, the only seemingly happy female character is Paola, Sally's live-in au-pair who has left her child behind in Italy with its father. All five women feel equally haunted and constrained by their former and possible future selves, by what might have been, as they are by present personal, familial and social obligations. Their homes in Arlington Park represent both minefields of risk – of dissolution into space and possession that only alienates them further from their selves, as well as too safe and stable havens that imprison them with the absence of any hope of self-enabling change or adventure. Maisie notes how: "The room, the house, even Arlington Park itself, increasingly wore the lineaments of a lived past into which future possibilities were unable to intrude" (AP 175).

To some extent, Cusk's female characters suffer from the same paradoxical female 'risk and no-risk' syndrome as Austen's do in *Persuasion*. While the men venture out into the world and engage in risk-taking as a means of asserting their subjectivity and agency, transcending their immediate and familiar surroundings and stifling ordinariness – in the novel this is expressed as the "separation" and "thought". In contrast to Juliet, her husband Benedict "thought, in order to be extraordinary. [...] he separated himself and thought" (AP 11). The women are confined to the safe space of home and thus denied the positive rewards of risk-taking in the sense it has been conceptualised by feminist writers such as Simone de Beauvoir. Scarth explains: "Beauvoir writes infamously that 'it is not in giving life, but in risking life' that man asserts himself as subject, and woman was doomed because she was excluded from the warlike forays of the men [...] she equates subjectivity with the risk of death: becoming a subject requires risk" (Scarth 2004: 106). The domestic realm is thus fraught with an exclusively negative kind of risk and vulnerability which is, as Tang (2013) argues, physical and ontological. Solly Kerr-Leigh, weary of being subsumed under her husband's existence with her own hyphenated surname being pronounced as a single syllable by most people, longs for separation from her husband in both these senses in order to safeguard her sense of self; "she felt merged with him, unshielded, indistinct. [...] She had no protection from him (AP 132–133). Meanwhile the narrative also satirizes the women's version of (no) risk-taking, e. g. in Christine Lanham's ruminations in the mall about whether or not she should dare to buy a risqué top and show a little more cleavage than usual at her dinner party.

Reaffirming the ambivalence at the centre of Cusk's narrative, the women each battle with the violent frustration springing from a sense of imprisonment and lack of authorial control over their own lives captured in evocative metaphors such as the following: "She was like a boat in a harbour where the tide has gone out, lying helplessly on her side" (AP 184). At the same time they are united by their strategic choice of risk-aversion and, despite all, still choose to remain exactly where they are. The reader is left wondering if they do so out of fear, depression, or a felt lack of alternative and unwillingness to give to comfort and face uncertainty. In chapter 5, a short interlude which gives a panoramic outside view of the women standing huddled together in the park, watching their children play, once more shows the awareness of a lack of agency – "nothing could be fundamentally changed" (AP 145) – but this passive, risk-averse attitude also seems to suit their present state of mind: "They weren't interested any more in things you could lose, in time or love [...]. *What they wanted to avoid was destruction. Like politicians, they were interested in survival*" (AP 148; my emphasis). However, as far as politics and an awareness of the world risk society in Beck's sense is concerned, the female characters appear strangely lethargic, as if they were living "in some secluded, securely safeguarded, parallel variant" of the world (Schoene 2010: 166), in which outside risks do not intrude, except as almost pleasantly horrifying topics of conversation. The safety of their chosen living space is discussed in a highly satirical scene that also reveals the pattern of denial and misunderstanding the women show about each other's feelings, and the underlying fear of failing under the constant scrutiny of their neighbours:

> 'Everybody's leaving London now,' Christine said [...] It's the pollution and the crime and the drugs. And terrorism! [...] *That's one thing you're safe from here.* I mean, why would anyone bother to drop a bomb on Arlington Park? Why would they?'
> *'I'm more frightened here than I was in London,'* said Maisie.
> Christine stopped chewing in astonishment. 'What of?' Maisie did not reply.
> 'Are you worried you'll go to seed?' Stephanie said, *as though this were a hazard she'd once heard of.* (AP 103; my emphasis)

In *Arlington Park*, ordinariness is both sought-after value and curse; it is the epitome of the average life of the well-to-do middle class families who seek out the suburb for the very "solid, bourgeois, profitable ordinariness of life" (AP 12) they later come to resent. While deviation from it is both threat and hidden desire, the female characters display an almost manic need for clarity, order, stability, closure; they want certainties instead of probabilities. As Schoene put it, they "do not appreciate the contingency of nature and other extraneous uncontrollabilities as these must inevitably exacerbate their already-severe performance anxiety" (Schoene 2010: 176). Cusk's women feel the weight of outside judgment and ponder on the same questions about choices in life and what makes happiness as many heroines of 19th-century fictions. They take pride in the "certainty" of their husbands (AP 234) and consider an unmarried woman in her thirties without children to be "the greatest failure of all" (AP 129). While other women's ability to live differently, beyond the confines of the traditional feminine role of housewife and mother, inspires envy, as well as fear, it is only one facet of a general dislike of uncertainty and open-endedness: "It was a kind of unstoppable need for resolution that grew from her like ivy over the prospect of freedom and tried to strangle it. She couldn't bear the idea of loose threads, [...] of stories without endings" (AP 129).

In Cusk's exploration of the contemporary female psyche in the realm of the nuclear family in suburbia, it is depicted as a volatile and vulnerable entity, as familial love and intimacy provide dangerously exposing and draining outlets rather than shelter. As Schoene argues further, Cusk's picture of post-feminist womanhood is bleak and defeatist. In Cusk's contemporary suburbia, half a century after the sexual revolution and the second wave of feminism one thus finds "the sexes locked in a primordial battle that, both systematically and biologically, women are doomed to lose" (Schoene 2010: 162; 161), trapped by an all too familiar reality of traditional structures and gendered discourses of propriety and possibility.[30] Similarly, the suggestion of Cusk's novel, "that there is evil lurking beyond the surface" (Wrobel 2013) is not an original one. *Arlington Park* reads like a satire of belated risk awareness, with suburban married life turning into a site of danger and uncertainty: "Anything could happen up there: it was a place of unpredictable danger and occasional savagery" (AP 47). All women have escape fantasies, from their own bodies, "where bitterness lay like lead in the veins" (AP 31); the streets of Arlington Park where car lights "glowed like devilish pars of eyes" (AP 32), and more generally, the whole civilised bourgeois way of being that equals a kind of warfare: "it seemed uncivilised to the core. [...] it lacked any conception of justice" (AP 33). Here they are seemingly stuck. Jane Smiley notes how Cusk's bleak depiction of suburbia excludes any diagnostics or cures. In this regard differing radically from early 20th-century novels such as *Howards End* and *Coming Up For Air* in which the pastoral remains an escape and ideal of risk-free existence, here, "old alternatives of English life – London and the countryside – are either chaotic or depopulated" (Smiley 2006). Cusk, Smiley goes on to argue, seems to suggest that "Arlington Park may be comfortable, maddening, deracinating, alienating nothingness, but it is the only choice" (Smiley 2006).[31] The novel's ending affirms this view. After the cracks in Christine's protective façade of exclusive, optimistic cheerfulness are revealed when she gets recklessly drunk at her own dinner party, she stumbles towards her husband Joe, who calls her into his arms – "Come here" (AP 240). One can read this final gesture either as a threat of loss of independence or as rescue from falling. Maintaining ambivalence throughout, Cusk's *Arlington Park* unmasks the emotional contradictions and dissatisfactions the reader feels privileged 21st-century women might or should not feel, living removed as far as one could possibly imagine from economic and physical precariousness, only with the "ordinary terror" (AP 76) of domesticity.

---

30 With the narrative pervaded by the women's own sense of the prescriptedness and unoriginality of their sorrows, their passivity and inability to change and how they remain, as Parey puts it, "angrily entombed in the sphere allotted to them" (Parey 2013), might be hard to bear and understand, especially for female readers.

31 The recital of a stanza from Philip Larkin's poem "Going, going" (1972) in the last chapter of *Arlington Park* creates a parallel to *Saturday* and the use of "Dover Beach". Although the significance of the poem in relation to the novel has not been acknowledged in criticism and detailed analysis is beyond scope here, it draws attention to the value of art and the risks of environmental destruction, the loss of nature and the beauty of 'old' England: "And that will be England gone,/ The shadows, the meadows, the lanes,/ The guildhalls, the carved choirs./ There'll be books; it will linger on/ In galleries; but all that remains/ For us will be concrete and tyres" (AP 236).

Epilogue

Taking the cue from the contemporary preoccupation with risk in popular and academic, especially sociological, discourse, the aim of this study has been to develop and show it as a viable category for literary analysis, arguing for the necessity to historicize, and also broaden the understanding and application of the concept in an interdisciplinary context, claiming the relevance of fictional narratives in risk discourses and research. As risk is always conceptualised in relation to the future and deals with fictitious scenarios and outcomes, any study of risk is by definition not concerned with 'realities', but with "possibilities, potentialities, projections, predictions, speculations, fictions, fantasies, myths" (Crosthwaite 2011b: 4). These imagined causalities, communicated through narratives, reflect illusions of and struggles for control and agency. Tied to crucial issues of knowledge, power, choice and responsibility, risk discourses illustrate the paradoxical coexistence of imaginations or retrospective experiences of causality and contingency, fears of loss and hopes of gain. G.K. Chesterton describes the conundrum of the modern view of the world in a way that also aptly captures it in regards to the ambivalent nature of risk: "it is nearly reasonable, but not quite. [...] It looks just a little more mathematical and regular than it is; its exactitude is obvious, but its inexactitude is hidden; *its wildness lies in wait*" (Chesterton 1909: 146; my emphasis).

Fictional literature, and the novel as a genre in particular, presents a ground of negotiation for the ways in which the perception and management of risk shape depictions of human character, relationships, and society. Connected to the endeavour to illustrate how prose fictions serve to disclose the workings of risk as one of the major narratives of modernity and identity construction from a representational and conceptual perspective, is the appeal to identify the values determining and determined by the way in which the language of risk is used to depict social life (cf. Capeola Gil 2013: 260; Wilkinson 2010: 9). A narrative concept of risk as employed in this study combines aspects from sociological theories, especially governmentality and cultural-anthropological approaches, and is centered on ethical aspects. Conceiving of risk essentially as being "based on a discourse of uncertainty that mediates between the subject's own beliefs and the uncertain odds of the natural and social worlds" (Capeola Gil 2013: 241), it furthermore draws attention to choice, which, Isabel Capeola Gil argues, is generally "a risky endeavor as risk selection incurs moral, social and political implications" (241). By relating the analysis of narrative forms and themes to the reflection of risk, it appears as an intrinsic part of the experience and evolution of modernity and the novel. The coinciding of the histories of risk and the English novel is the picture that emerges from reading the chapters in chronological order. Without summarizing these again in detail, this study furthermore yielded the following results: The close readings make visible the dominance of risk rhetoric in the novels on the level of language, i.e. of words and metaphors belonging to the semantic realm of risk; they demonstrate the significance of risk as a category of causal experience that shapes narratives, drives plots, motivates or prevents actions, defines and distinguishes characters and values. As such, risk presents a narrative concept that usefully supplements and refocuses existing interpretations of canonical fictions, in many cases without adding a completely new analytical direction or meaning, but rather by bringing together concerns with a wide array of anxieties and instabilities, with uncertainties and chances, struggles for survival and control, fears of decline and transgression. From its earliest scientific origins a neutral term, risk comprises both positive and negative associations but has been subject to semantic shifts and inconsistencies, e.g. the one from individual adventure to collective danger, or the only rather oblique nod to scientific rationality inherent in the use of risk in everyday language which mostly does not raise questions of mathematical probability but concerns emotionally charged perceptions of dread and danger (see Wilkinson 2010: 23). The protagonists in all the novels demonstrate the internalization of a predominately secular, calculative attitude to life which leaves the individual to deal with decisions in the face of uncertainty. As David Trotter puts it, the characters "accept risk as risk; they know the 'choice of life' [...] can be a dangerous as well as a rewarding business, and that they may not get all that much help in making it. The options they choose are often those provided by modernity's abstract systems" (Trotter 2000: 329), e.g. the capitalist market system. Meanwhile, tracing the history of the novel from Defoe over the Victorian era to the fictions of McEwan also reveals crucial shifts in changing perception of individualization which are connected to risk, above all the substitution of what Foucault describes as the change from "memorable man [into] [...] *calculable man*" (Foucault 1995: 193; my emphasis); these emerging discourses of normalcy and predictability remain grounds of on-going negotiation in the novel.

Without arguing in any way that the contemporary Anglophone "risk novel" of environmental destruction and climate change, which slowly emerges as a genre in its own right, does not warrant critical attention, my study demonstrates the need to remove risk from the narrow analytical focus on contemporary fictions dealing with the unmanageable, global risks of Beck's world risk society. What needs acknowledging, and undoubtedly calls for further studies, is the implementation of risk, shaped by probability theory and statistics in different forms and guises, in our worldview and its historicity. Due to its complexity and heterogeneity, this undertaking necessarily resists drawing up any sort of comprehensive history. The best one can hope for, as the present study does, is to reveal processes and strategies – social, cultural, discursive – governing the human attempts to rule over the "empire of chance" in the sense Gigerenzer et al. describe it:

> Probability and statistics have transformed explanation and reasoning in the sciences, and views of contingency and risk in the wide world beyond. These transformations are too varied and vast to sum up into a coherent picture of the world [...]. Yet we who have been born into the empire of chance hardly notice its dominion over us; over the way we parse our world, make up our minds, argue our points, and judge our fellows. Our statistical way of life is too much a way of life to catch the eye. (1989: 289)

Finally, one more general question needs addressing: Even if the majority of sociologists trace "the beginning of Western countries' obsession with risk and safety to the 1970s" (Gardner 2008: 60), seeing that humanity has always faced threats, Dan Gardner asks: "Why should we worry more than previous generations?" (2008: 7). Faced with the ubiquity of risk discourses, do we indeed witness an increase of risks beyond control, as Beck and others contend? Or are 'we' (as the imagined collective of bourgeois individuals living in the Western hemisphere) in fact safer than ever before, living in a society obsessed with insurance,[1] security and risk-management, which in turn lowers the general tolerance for risk and sees us striving for an impossible ideal of a "no-risk society"[2]? Reasons for the undeniable increase in risk communication can be sought either in fundamental changes in the dangers we face, or in a new sensitivity to and awareness of risk, largely created by the media (see Zinn 2008: 10). Comparing the occurrence of the word 'risk' in UK newspapers between 1994–2000 which indicates an expotentially growing usage, Frank Furedi reads it as a symp-

---

[1] See poet and accountant Wallace Stevens, who writes: "The objective of all of us is to live in a world where nothing unpleasant can happen. Our prime instinct is to go on indefinitely like the wax flowers on the mantelpiece. [...]. The truth is that we may well be entering an insurance era" (Stevens 1980: 37). Regarding insurance, it is also important to remember that it only "became possible not when the world had become a more dangerous place, but rather when it became sufficiently less hazardous that the hazards that existed were newly sortable into particular packages and defined as discrete risks" (O'Brien 2011: 290).

[2] See Yair Aharoni's *The No-Risk Society* (1981). According to Aharoni, the development of the capitalist welfare state leads to the formation of a 'no-risk society' because risks are regarded as problems the government continuously aims at reducing for the individual. While the welfare state is turned into insurance state, the ideal of a "no-risk society" remains impossible to achieve, as, for instance, new kinds of risk management create new risks (1981: 12; see also O'Malley 1996: 203).

tomatic tendency to regard situations as threats (Furedi 2005: xiii). He claims that our current public imagination is dominated by a "culture of fear", based on an obsessive preoccupation with safety and risk-aversion (2005: 7). Along the same lines argues Didier Dacunha-Castelle, who sees the media largely responsible for creating a new culture of intolerance towards risk in the late 20th century that leads, for example, to the presentation of 'normal' seasonal weather in predominantly catastrophic terms (Dacunha-Castelle 1996: 150). This is just one aspect contributing to the seeming fact that life is becoming filled with more and more risks. However, while many of these insecurities are new, it is important to remember that various others are "endemic to human life in general" (Reith 1999: 183). This has been shown in the readings of narratives covering a time span of over three hundred years.

To take just three examples that are heralded as primary global and unmanageable threats of the contemporary moment, but which are in fact 'old' risks: disasters caused by financial speculation,[3] terrorism, and environmental destruction. Financial crises, debts, speculations, and bankruptcy haunt the literary imagination at least from the 18th century onwards. By the Victorian era, at the latest, as Barbara Weiss sums up, there was no escape from the "recognition that industrial capitalism had transformed the collective social life beyond the power of the individual to control his own fate or affect the destiny of his community"; and we can turn to the novels as testimonies of "an age not unlike our own in which transition and mutability seem to have become the permanent condition of human life" (Weiss 1986: 175). The same applies in the case of terrorism, although one finds arguments that it is a phenomenon that dates much further back with much less frequency. Simon Webb is among those who emphasize that terrorism has been an intermittent feature of British life at least since the mid-19th century and that perceived risks of porous borders and of society being overrun by potentially dangerous foreigners "are not new. They are simply the latest manifestation of a very British phenomenon. [...] The focus of fears about terrorism has varied from decade to decade. At one time it was Indians and Irishmen, at others women or Jews" (Webb 2012: 8; 7). In fact, the contemporary 'risk' debates

---

[3] For a study of contemporary British fiction and financial risk see Marsh (2007) and (2011). For the historical argument see Reith, who writes: "Since the speculative boom of the seventeenth century and the disastrous bursting of the South Sea Bubble, the economic history of the west has been littered with such gambling losing runs [....]. Despite its failed bets, the capitalist economic system seems to be both driven by the risking of money on uncertain future events and limitlessly able to cope when the risk fails. For these reasons it always appears slightly disingenuous of commentators to feign surprise when the gambling-speculation equation is highlighted by a spectacular loss" (Reith 1999: 90).

about immigration and terrorism seem eerily familiar when compared to London newspapers reports from a hundred years ago (see 2012: 8–9). While new technologies of surveillance and risk profiling surely allow for attempts of risk management on an unprecedented scale, the fear of terrorism bears undeniable traces of colonial paranoia and the "white fear factor" which refers back to other historical legacies in which, Vron Ware explains, the gap "between rich and poor, white and black, becomes further naturalized by being made racialized" (Ware 2010: 108).[4] Lastly, even an awareness of environmental risk can be traced back to 18th-century writings on natural history which contain beginnings of ideas of nature and the environment as a primordial, complex balance "which civilized man interferes with at his own risk" (Glacken 1990: 657).[5] From the Enlightenment era onwards one finds serious criticism of technological growth and advancement, also reflected in fictional narratives, and, upon closer scrutiny, eerily similar to today's debates about the reach of science, e.g. in biotechnological engineering. Even climate change, a risk, perhaps indeed without real precedent, which in recent years forced human beings to rethink their place in the world, and, as Ghosh in *The Great Derangement* (2016) has argued, presents one of the greatest challenges for contemporary writers to depict in realist fiction, allows for another perspective. According to Tuhus-Dubrow, when reading, for instance, a novel like McEwan's *Solar* and looking at the narrative depiction of causes and repercussions of climate change, one also inevitably finds older themes: "There have always been disasters; there has always been loss; there has always been change" (Tuhus-Dubrow 2013: 61). In this sense, a focus on risk in the English novel can reveal "some enduring truths of the human condition. Like Michael Beard, we've always screwed up; and [...] we've always been afraid. And in the ends, as ever, we survive the storm, or drown" (61).

However, while one can argue that, one the one hand, our 21st-century present hardly confronts humanity with risks and problems that are more complex than those in previous centuries (cf. Postman 2003: 19), there is, on the other hand, a wide consensus that risks "such as the nuclear threat, the dangers of genetic engineering, or anthropogenic global warming are marked by an unprecedented degree of complexity and, in their causes and effects, by an ultimately global scale" (Mayer 2016: 208; see Beck 2009: 9). In addition, in particular terrorism is conceived of as a "risk beyond risk" because it defies knowledge and measure (Aradau and van Muster 2007: 23; Furedi 2007: 63; 64–65). Like environ-

---

4 Cf. also Aradau and van Muster (2007: 26–27).
5 See also Glacken (1990: 659f). This topic would certainly deserve a study in its own right.

mental risk, terrorism is perceived as incalculable and, with probability theory being insufficient to 'manage' it or make it 'known', as a threat beyond the original realm of risk. Nonetheless, these supposedly 'incalculable' threats do not differ all that much from how, for instance, the plague or other natural disasters were perceived in the 17th century. Only because we nowadays consider a vast number of risks as 'manageable' does not mean that they were always seen as such. For example, it is hard to imagine how terrorism in the late Victorian era would have been perceived as 'calculable;' the bomb-carrying 'sleeper' Professor in Conrad's *The Secret Agent* is nothing but the embodiment of randomness. Furthermore, looking at fictional narratives also supports the view that probability theory has always been a lose stepping stone, at best, for public and individual 'lay' perceptions of risk, refuting the general claim that the current climate dominated by apprehension about uncertainty challenges "the use of probability theory *to make sense of risks*" (Furedi 2007: 62; my emphasis). From the risk computations of the first individual in the English novel, Defoe's Robinson Crusoe, risk has never been assessed with any kind of purely, rational, scientific consistency.

Still, theorists such as Furedi see in 21st-century responses to terrorism and climate change a conception of risk which is radically new because it entails a far-reaching apprehension of the future as essentially unknowable (Furedi 2007: 49; 53).[6] The prevalence of risk discourse in the last three decades is part of a wider discursive net, including precarity and vulnerability which gained ascendancy since the 1990s and momentum after the 9/11 attacks.[7] According to Giddens: "We have become preoccupied with safety and therefore tend to see threats everywhere – which translate into feelings of apprehension and powerlessness" (Giddens 2009: 31). But Stephen Haller, stressing a connection between the early 18th century and the modern perception of risk, asks if we have, in fact, any means of telling current fears and anticipations of catastrophe apart from the apocalyptic visions of the Laputians satirized in Swift's *Gulliver's*

---

[6] Referring to Homer-Dixon's argument about the rise of so-called "complex terrorism", these risks present "unknown unknowns" (Homer-Dixon 2002: 61; see Furedi 2007: 57), an argument based on the perceived vulnerability of high-tech first World societies to terrorism, due to their dependence on technology and an infrastructure concentrated on certain crucial nodes. The systems are vulnerable due to their complexity and replete with dangers that are impossible to anticipate, but exploitable by terrorists (see Homer-Dixon 2002: 55).

[7] According to Furedi, "This cultural narrative of vulnerability stands in sharp contrast to the way that people in previous decades were encouraged to perceive their engagement with adversity" (2007: 119). See Korte and Regard (2014) on the turn to "precariousness", Morrison (2013) and Botha (2014) on "precarity", and Ganteau (2015; 2017) on "vulnerability" in contemporary fiction; see also chapter 12, and Hoydis (2015).

Travels; "we risk being paralyzed with fear, like the Laputians, because we do not know how to assess the accuracy of these visions" (Haller 2000: 176). In this context it is interesting to consider the difference between *probabilist* and *possibilist* thinking introduced by sociologist Lee Clarke (2006). Taking probabilistic thinking to be the hallmark of modern scientific thought, Clarke argues that though we are safer than ever before, there is a current focus on worst-case-thinking, i.e. possibilist thinking of the worst that can possibly happen, instead of what would be the most likely. Probabilistic thinking, in turn, would lead to the realization that "disasters are normal parts of life – [...] All that is special about them is the searchlight they throw upon power, politics, and imagination" (Clarke 2006: 24). These worst-case anxieties (Clarke) shape the contemporary culture of fear (Furedi) and are seen to mark the advent of a "new age of superstition" (Giddens 2009: 24),[8] in which the discomfort with uncertainty and risk are paramount. While in such a culture of security even comparatively minor events and acts of disruption can cause feelings of terror charged with a great significance, as for instance depicted in the plot of McEwan's *Saturday*, it remains a cognitive challenge to objectively explain why a sense of vulnerability should overwhelm Western societies despite their factual safety (see Furedi 2007: 133–134; 73). The question of the measure and, also historical comparability of risks remains a valid and difficult one. Ultimately, it is futile to try and assess if, for example, contemporary fears about terrorism are on any scale more 'real' or severe than others about personal and political security in the past. It might be useful here, however, to recall Frank Kermode's nuanced description of apocalyptic thinking and crisis as a general "way of thinking about one's moment, and not inherent in the moment itself" (Kermode 2000: 101). In the updated edition of *The Sense of an Ending* (2000), based on a series of lectures originally given in the 1960s, he comments on the in retrospect rather quick lessening of apocalyptic anxiety (2000: 181) after the nuclear threats of the cold war era and suggests that as far as this particular risk of extinction is concerned: "Perhaps we have simply grown accustomed to the idea" (183). Once again, it appears that perceived knowledge and/or uncertainty, as well as circumstances, determine the human sense of risk more than the 'reality' of danger. Kermode also points towards the almost domestic, unexceptional quality apocalyptic thinking: "The possibility of personal disaster is, after all, never quite absent from our lives, and if anything is needed to give additional substance to our anxieties, the world, at whatever period, will surely provide it" (2000: 182). This is nothing but an argument for the centrality of risk perception. With

---

8 See also Booker and North's *Scared to Death. From BSE to Global* Warming (2013).

risks always being imagined, fabricated, narrated, often quite independently from actual estimations of threats (see 181) – who is to decide whose are or were worse?

Another insight can be drawn from the contemporary accounts of the obsession with risk and safety. Considering risk one of the most important categories and shaping forces of modernity, what is new is not the salience of risk but the expectation that risk should be (completely) managed (see Garland 2003: 71; Luhmann 1993: 215). Part and parcel of the proclaimed culture of fear and security is the illusion that man should have complete control, which runs counter to the experince of overwhelming, unmangeable, unknowable risks. Ironically, at the point when (as upheld in a majority of popular and academic Western thought), "man has attained a breathtaking anthropocentrism, based on his power over nature, unmatched by anything in the past" (Glacken 1990: 494), s/he becomes also more than ever afraid of nature and of losing control over it.[9] One can therefore agree with the critical positions that see a difference in contemporary Western societies' increased consciousness of rather than in 'real', physical exposure to risk (Ericson and Doyle 2003: 71; Szerszynski, Lash and Wynne 1996: 12). Gerda Reith says: "This perception should be seen as the product, not of a society that has suddenly become full of risks, but of a long historical process that gave ontological status to chance, and to us a probabilistic Lebensgefühl" (Reith 1999: 43). This view shapes the perspective of the present study of fictional narratives, with all texts negotiating what Wolfgang Bonß calls risk orientations ("Risikoorientierungen") (Bonß 1996: 176), employed in order to judge and guide individual and collective actions. They impact on and find shapes in different narrative patterns in genres such as the picaresque, the Gothic, the Bildungsroman, they drive money-and-marriage-plots as well as adventure- and decline-plots; and in particular the 'condition-of-England' novel, from the Industrial fictions of the 19th-century over *Howards End* to *Saturday* and *Arlington Park*, presents narratives that express contemporary horizons of risk perception.

Risk is a characteristic of human behaviour and a measure of subjectivity in the sense that seeking *ad*-venture forms a way to ascertain agency. The desire to 'know' the future and the encounter and management of dangers can be consid-

---

9 This interrelation of power and perceived risk is, of course, also not without historical precedent. Cf. also Giddens's argument: "We are currently living in a civilization that, as far as we can determine, looks unsustainable. It isn't surprising that the past few years have seen the emergence of a doomsday literature, centred on the likelihood of catastrophe. Other civilizations have come and gone; why should ours be sacrosanct? Yet risk is risk – the other side of danger is always opportunity" (2009: 10).

ered as a human universal, although those encounters, of course, remain bound to particular cultural and historical circumstances as well as to constraints and time specific experiences of class, race and gender. While it is a human survival instinct to minimize risk, the striving for security is one of the most basic desires of humankind (see Delumeau 1985: 20) – a fact reflected in the vast body of risk research and literature for the majority concerned with the reduction of risk and the ficticious subject of homo prudens. But people, as John Adams emphazises, also "willingly take risks. [...] Zero-risk man is a figment of the imagination of the safety profession. *Homo prudens* is but one aspect of the human character. *Homo aleatorius* – dice man, gambling man, risk-taking man – also lurks within every one of us" (Adams 1995: 16). This dualistic nature of risk and different risk personalities is shown in all the novels, as is risk's long-established function not only as a scientifically-based approach to uncertainty but as a response to social problems, above all economic, and typically dependent on the categorisation of certain risk groups or pathologies. Consequently, we have been living in the risk society for centuries.

Tracing junctures and shifts in the history of risk narratives, one can either emphasize that every age has its own terrors, or the recurrence of the same anxieties about 'the way we live now' in different specific guises: "Each era of history had its own fears which set it apart from other epochs; or, rather, each gave the fears known to all epochs names of its creation" (Bauman 1995: 105). The English novel gives examples of both. The workings of risk and the human mind are reflected in new narratives as well as in some of the most treasured ones, in the ones we keep reading and teaching. Meanwhile, the tendency to conceptualize events and temporalities (past, present and future) in imagined causalities in the name of risk forms a main reason why we narrate fictions in general, in the sense that Cavell notes:

> Epistemology will demonstrate that we cannot know, cannot be certain of, the future; but we don't believe it. [...] Even when what we anticipate comes to pass we get the wrong idea of our powers and of what our safety depends upon, for we imagine that we knew this would happen, and take it either as an occasion for congratulations or for punishments, of ourselves or others. Instead of acting as we can and remaining equal to the consequences. (Cavell 2003: 322)

The history and future of the novel is shaped by this obsession with anticipation and consequentiality, and with danger and safety. And while humans are perhaps no closer to dealing 'rationally' with risk than Defoe's Crusoe was three hundred years ago, the genre reflects the evolution of a complex concept and the on-going negotiation of perceived risks – in and outside of fiction.

Works Cited

Primary Works

Atwood, Margaret. (2003) 2009. *Oryx and Crake*. London: Virago.
Atwood, Margaret. (2009) 2010. *The Year of the Flood*. London, Virago.
Austen, Jane. (1817) 2003. *Persuasion*. Introduction and Notes by Gillian Beer (ed.). London: Penguin.
Bacigalupi, Paolo. 2009. *The Windup Girl*. London: Orbit.
Boucicault, Dion. 1857. *The Poor of New York*. New York, Samuel French. *openlibrary.org*. ID: OL23509822M. [accessed 1 March 2019].
Boucicault, Dion. (1841) 2001. "London Assurance". In: Klaus Stiersdorfer (ed.). *London Assurance and Other Victorian Comedies*. Oxford: Oxford University Press. 74–144.
Braine, John. (1957) 2002. *Room at the Top*. London: Arrow.
Brontë, Charlotte. (1850) 2009. *Shirley*. With an Introduction by Sally Minogue. Ware, Hertfordshire: Wordsworth.
Bulwer-Lytton, Edward. (1840) 2001. "Money". In: Klaus Stiersdorfer (ed.). *London Assurance and Other Victorian Comedies*. Oxford: Oxford University Press. 1–74.
Burney, Fanny. (1794) 1999. *Camilla, or A Picture of Youth*. Introduction and Notes by Edward A. Bloom and Lillian D. Bloom (eds.). Oxford: Oxford University Press.
Chesterton, G.K. (1909) 2001. *The Man Who Was Thursday. A Nightmare*. Introduction by Jonathan Lethem. New York: Modern Library.
Conrad, Joseph. (1907) 1993. *The Secret Agent. A Simple Tale*. Ware, Hertfordshire: Wordsworth.
Conrad, Joseph. 1921. "Autocracy and War". *Notes on Life and Letters*. London: J.M. Dent. 83–114.
Conrad, Joseph 2015. *The Selected Letters of Joseph Conrad*. Lawrence Davies (ed.). Cambridge: Cambridge University Press.
Cusk, Rachel. 2001. *A Life's Work: On Becoming a Mother*. London: Fourth Estate.
Cusk, Rachel. (2006) 2007. *Arlington Park*. London: Faber and Faber.
Cusk, Rachel. 2008. "I was only being honest". *The Guardian* March 21. <https://www.theguardian.com/books/2008/mar/21/biography.women> [accessed 1 March 2019].
Cusk, Rachel. 2005. "The Outsider". *The Observer Sunday* August 20. <https://www.theguardian.com/books/2005/aug/20/featuresreviews.guardianreview2> [accessed 1 March 2019].
Cusk, Rachel. 2009. "Shakespeare's Daughters". *The Guardian* December 12. <https://www.theguardian.com/books/2009/dec/12/rachel-cusk-women-writing-review> [accessed 1 March 2019].
Defoe, Daniel. (1697) 2008. *Essay on Projects*. Charleston, SC.: Biblio Bazaar.
Defoe, Daniel. 1701. *The Villainy of Stock-jobbers Detected, and the Causes of the Late Run upon the Bank and Bankers Discovered and Considered*. London. Eighteenth Century Collections Online, Gale. Document No.: CW105445267. [accessed 1 March 2019].
Defoe, Daniel. (1704) 2005. *The Storm*. Introduction and Notes by Richard Hamblyn (ed.). London: Penguin.
Defoe, Daniel. (1710) 1840. "Essay Upon Public Credit". *The Works of Daniel De Foe. Vol. II*. W. Hazlitt (ed.). London: Clements and Pulteney Library. 69–98.

Defoe, Daniel. (1719) 2009. *The Life and Strange Surprising Adventures of Robinson Crusoe of York, Mariner.* London: Arcturus.

Defoe, Daniel. (1722) 1993. *The Fortunes and Misfortunes of the Famous Moll Flanders.* Introduction and Notes by R.T. Jones. Ware, Hertfordshire: Wordsworth.

Defoe, Daniel. (1722) 1966. *A Journal of the Plague Year.* Introduction by David J. Johnson. London: Dent and Sons.

Defoe, Daniel. 1722. *Due Preparations for the Plague, as well for Soul as Body.* London. Eighteenth Century Collections Online, Gale. Document No.: CW117399741. [accessed 1 March 2019].

Defoe, Daniel. (1724) 1982. *Roxana: The Fortunate Mistress.* 1724. Introduction by David Blewett (ed.). London: Penguin.

Defoe, Daniel. (1726–1727) 2007. *The Complete English Tradesman.* Charleston, SC.: Biblio Bazaar.

Defoe, Daniel. 1727. *Conjugal Lewdness: or, Matrimonial Whoredom.* London. Eighteenth Century Collections Online, Gale. Document No.: CW117689771. [accessed 1 March 2019].

Defoe, Daniel. (1715–1718) 1800. *The Complete Family Instructor: In Five Parts.* Liverpool: H. Forshaw. Eighteenth Century Collections Online. Gale Document No.: CW117169513. accessed 1 March 2019

Defoe, Daniel. (1729) 1890. *The Compleat English Gentleman.* Ed. for the first time from the author's autograph manuscript in the British Museum, with introduction, notes, and index by Karl D. Bülbring. London: David Nutt.

Defoe, Daniel. 1719. *The Anatomy of Exchange-Alley: or, A System of Stock-jobbing.* London. Eighteenth Century Collections Online, Gale. Gale Document Number: CW106555224. [accessed 1 March 2019].

Defoe, Daniel. (1723) 1840. *The Life of Colonel Jack: And, a True Relation of the Apparition of One Mrs. Veal.* Oxford: Tolboys.

DeLillo, Don. (2007) 2011. *Falling Man.* Berlin: Cornelsen.

Dickens, Charles. (1857) 1996. *Little Dorrit.* Introduction and Notes by Peter Preston. Ware, Hertfordshire: Wordsworth.

Dickens, Charles. (1854) 1995. *Hard Times.* Ware, Hertfordshire: Wordsworth.

Disraeli, Benjamin. (1845) 1995. *Sybil, or, The Two Nations.* Ware, Hertfordshire: Wordsworth.

Dostoevsky, Fyodor M. (1867) 1997. *The Gambler.* Trans. and with an Introduction by Andrew R. MacAndrew. London and New York: W.W. Norton and Company.

Eliot, George. (1869–1871) 2000. *Middlemarch.* With an Introduction and Notes by Doreen Roberts. Ware, Hertfordshire: Wordsworth.

Eliot, George. (1876) 1996. *Daniel Deronda.* With an Introduction and Notes by Carole Jones. Ware, Hertfordshire: Wordsworth.

Fawcett, Edward Douglas. (1893) 2009. *Hartman, the Anarchist: or the Doom of the Great City.* Revised ed. Bristol: Tangent.

Fielding, Henry. (1732) 1785. *The Lottery. A Farce.* Glasgow. Eighteenth Century Collections Online, Gale. Document Number: CW110156440. [accessed 1 March 2019].

Fielding, Henry. (1743) 1997. *A Journey from this World to the Next and The Journal of a Voyage to Lisbon.* 1743. Ian A. Bell and Andrea Varney (eds.). Oxford: Oxford University Press.

Fielding, Henry. (1749) 1999. *The History of Tom Jones A Foundling.* With an Introduction and Notes by Doreen Roberts. Ware, Hertfordshire: Wordsworth.

Flanagan, Richard. 2007. *Unknown Terrorist*. London: Atlantic.
Forster, Edward Morgan. (1910) 2000. *Howards End*. Introduction and Notes by David Lodge. New York: Penguin.
Forster, Edward Morgan. 1960. "Aspect of a Novel". *The Bookseller* September 10: 1228–1230.
Forster, Edward Morgan. (1951) 1962. *Two Cheers For Democracy*. London: Edward Arnold.
Gaines, Susan M. 2001. *Carbon Dreams*. Berkeley, CA: Creative Arts Book Company.
Gaskell, Elizabeth. (1848) 2006. *Mary Barton*. Introduction and Notes by Shirley Foster (ed.). Oxford: Oxford University Press.
Gaskell, Elizabeth. (1854–1855) 1994. *North and South*. London: Penguin Popular Classics.
Gaskell, Elizabeth. 1997. *The Letters of Mrs Gaskell*. J.A.V. Chapple and Arthur Pollard (eds.). Manchester: Manchester University Press.
Gee, Maggie. 2004. *The Flood*. London: Saqi.
Gissing, George. (1897) 1997. *The Whirlpool*. Introduction by William Greenslade (ed.). London: Everyman.
Hamid, Mohsin. 2007. *The Reluctant Fundamentalist*. London: Penguin.
Hardy, Thomas. 1978. *The Collected Letters of Thomas Hardy: Vol. One 1840–1892*. Richard Little Purdy and Michael Millgate (eds.). Oxford: Claredon.
Hardy, Thomas. 1980. *The Collected Letters of Thomas Hardy. Vol. Two 1893–1901*. Richard Little Purdy and Michael Millgate (eds.). Oxford: Claredon.
Hardy, Thomas. (1891) 1994. *Tess of the D' Urbervilles*. London: Penguin.
Hardy, Thomas. (1895) 1998. *Jude the Obscure*. Introduction and Notes by Dennis Taylor (ed.). London: Penguin.
Haywood, Eliza. (1725) 2000. *Love in Excess, Or the Fatal Enquiry*. David Oakleaf (ed.). 2nd ed. Peterborough, Ontario: Broadview.
Hollinghurst, Alan. (1988) 1989. *The Swimming-Pool Library*. London: Penguin.
Humans. 2015–. Created by Sam Vincent and Jonathan Brackley. Kudos Film and Television, Channel 4, AMC Studios. UK/USA/Sweden.
Ishiguro, Kazuo. 2005. *Never Let Me Go*. London: Faber and Faber.
Ishiguro, Kazuo. 2006. "Future Imperfect". *The Guardian* March 25. <https://www.theguardian.com/books/2006/mar/25/featuresreviews.guardianreview36> [accessed 1 March 2019].
James, Henry. (1908) 1936. "Preface". *The Tragic Muse*. Vol. I. New York: Charles Scribner's Sons. v–xxii.
James, Henry. (1886) 1987. *The Princess Casamassima*. Introduction by Derek Brewer (ed.). Notes by Patricia Crick. London: Penguin.
Joyce, James. (1922) 1998. *Ulysses*. Introduction and Notes by Jeri Johnson (ed.). Oxford: Oxford University Press.
Kingsolver, Barbara. 2012. *Flight Behavior*. London: Faber and Faber.
Kunzru, Hari. (2004) 2005. *Transmission*. London: Penguin.
Lewes, George Henry. (1851) 1995. *The Game of Speculation*. Lyceum. Reprinted in: Michael R. Booth (ed.). *The Lights O' London and Other Victorian Plays*. Oxford: Oxford World's Classics. 49–102.
London, Jack. (1903) 2013. *The People of the Abyss*. Cambridge: Cambridge University Press.
McCarthy, Cormac. (2006) 2010. *The Road*. London: Picador.

McEwan, Ian. 2001a. "Only Love and then Oblivion". *The Guardian* September 15. <https://www.theguardian.com/world/2001/sep/15/september11.politicsphilosophyandsociety2> [accessed 1 March 2019].
McEwan, Ian. 2001b. "Beyond Belief". *The Guardian* September 12. <https://www.theguardian.com/world/2001/sep/12/september11.politicsphilosophyandsociety> [accessed 1 March 2019].
McEwan, Ian. (1997) 2004. *Enduring Love*. London: Vintage.
McEwan, Ian. 2005. "A Boot Room in the Frozen North". *capefarewell.com*. <https://capefarewell.com/explore/215-a-boot-room-in-the-frozen-north.html> [accessed 1 March 2019].
McEwan, Ian. (2005) 2006. *Saturday*. London: Vintage.
McEwan, Ian. 2008. "The Day of Judgment". *The Guardian* May 31. <https://www.theguardian.com/books/2008/may/31/fiction.philosophy> [accessed 1 March 2019].
McEwan, Ian. 2010. *Solar*. London: Jonathan Cape.
Messud, Claire. (2006) 2015. *The Emperor's Children*. London: Picador.
O'Neill, Joseph. (2008) 2009. *Netherland*. London: Harper Perennial.
Orphan Black. 2013–. Created by John Fawcett and Graeme Manson. BBC America/Canada.
Orwell, George. (1939) 1990. *Coming Up For Air*. London: Penguin.
Orwell, George. (1940) 2000. "Inside the Whale". In: Sonia Orwell and Ian Angus (eds.). *George Orwell: Essays*. London: Penguin. 101–132.
Orwell, George. (1946) 2000. "Some Thoughts on the Common Toad". In: Sonia Orwell and Ian Angus (eds.). *George Orwell: Essays*. London: Penguin. 360–363.
Pope, Alexander. (1744) 2007. *Epistles to Several Persons*. Ann Arbor, MI: University of Michigan Library.
Proust, Marcel. (1922) 2003. *In Search of Lost Time. Vol 1: The Way by Swann's*. Christopher Prendergast (ed.). Trans. Lydia Davis. London: Penguin Modern Classics.
Richardson, Samuel. (1747–1748) 2004. *Clarissa, or the History of a Yong Lady*. Introduction and Notes by Angus Ross (ed.). London: Penguin Classics.
Richardson, Samuel. (1753) 1986. *The History of Sir Charles Grandison*. Introduction by Jocelyn Harris (ed.). Oxford: Oxford University Press.
Robinson, Kim Stanley. 2015. *Green Earth*. (The Science in the Capital). London: Del Rey.
Rushdie, Salman. 2005. *Shalimar the Clown*. New York: Random House.
Safran Foer, Jonathan. (2005) 2011. *Extremely Loud and Incredibly Close*. London: Penguin.
Saturday Night and Sunday Morning. 1960. Dir. Karel Reisz, written by Alan Sillitoe. Woodfall Film Productions. UK.
Scott, Sarah. (1726) 2009. *A Description of Millenium Hall*. Campaign, IL: Book Jungle.
Shamsie, Kamila. 2009. *Burning Shadows*. London: Bloomsbury.
Shelley, Mary. (1818) 1999. *Frankenstein, or, The Modern Prometheus*. Introduction and Notes by Siv Jansson. Ware, Hertfordshire: Wordsworth.
Sillitoe, Alan. (1958) 1994. *Saturday Night and Sunday Morning*. London: Flamingo.
Sillitoe, Alan. 1964. "Poor People". *Anarchy* 38 (April): 124–28.
Sillitoe, Alan. 1975. "The Long Piece". *Mountains and Caverns. Selected Essays*. London: W.H. Allen. 9–40.
Smollett, Tobias G. (1748) 1964. *Roderick Random*. Introduction by H.W. Hodges. London: Dent, Everyman's Library.
Sterne, Laurence. (1759–1767) 1967. *The Life and Opinions of Tristram Shandy, Gentleman*. Graham Petrie (ed.), with an Introduction by Christopher Ricks. London: Penguin.

Sterne, Laurence. (1768) "Time and Chance". *The Sermons of Mr. Yorick. Vol. 2.* 9th ed. London. Eighteenth Century Collections Online, Gale. 4–22. [accessed 1 March 2019].
Sterne, Laurence. (1768) 2005. *A Sentimental Journey*. London: Penguin Classics.
Stevenson, Robert Louis. (1886) 2010. *The Strange Case of Dr Jekyll and Mr Hyde*. London: Collins Classics.
Swift, Jonathan. *Gulliver's Travels*. (1726) 1994. London: Penguin Popular Classics.
Swift, Jonathan. (1729) 1996. *A Modest Proposal and Other Satirical Works*. New York: Dover Publications.
The Boys from Brazil. 1978. Dir. Franklin J. Schaffner, written by Ira Levin (novel) and Heywood Gould (screenplay). UK/USA.
The Island. 2005. Dir. Michael Bay, screenplay by Caspian Tredwell-Owen and Alex Kurtzman. DreamWorks, Warner Brothers. USA.
Trollope, Anthony. (1874) 1995. *The Way We Live Now*. Ware, Hertfordshire: Wordsworth.
Trollope, Anthony. 1883. *An Autobiography. Vol. II*. Edinburgh and London: William Blackwood, 1883.
Updike, John. (2006) 2007. *The Terrorist*. London: Penguin.
Walpole, Horace. (1764) 2008. *The Castle of Otranto. A Gothic Story*. W.S. Lewis (ed.), with a New Introduction and Notes by E.J. Clery. Oxford: Oxford University Press.
Weldon, Fay. 1989. *The Cloning of Joanna May*. Glasgow: Fontana/Collins.
Wells, H.G. (1897) 1900. "In the Abyss". *The Plattner Story, and Others*. Leipzig: Bernhard Tauchnitz. 76–97.
Wells, H.G. (1895) 1913. "The Stolen Bacillus". *The Country of the Blind and Other Stories*. London and Edinburgh: Nelson. 41–49.
Wells, H.G. 1934. *Experiment in Autobiography*. Vol. II. London: Victor Gollancz.
Wells, H.G. 1958. "The Contemporary Novel, 1911". *Henry James and H.G. Wells: A Record of Their Friendship, Their Debate on the Art of Fiction, and Their Quarrel*. In: Leon Edel and Gordon N. Ray (eds.). London: Rupert Hart-Davis. 131–155.
Wells, H.G. (1897) 2012. *Invisible Man*. London: Penguin.
Woolf, Leonard. 1968. *Downhill all the Way. An Autobiography of the Years 1919–1939*. London: Hogarth Press.
Woolf, Virginia. (1923) 1988. "How it Strikes a Contemporary". *The Common Reader. Vol. III 1919–1924*. London: The Hogarth Press. 353–360.
Woolf, Virginia. (1925) 1996. *Mrs Dalloway*. London: Penguin Popular Classics.
Woolf, Virginia. 1984. "Modern Fiction". In: Andrew McNeille (ed.). *The Essays of Virginia Woolf. Volume IV: 1925 to 1928*. London: The Hogarth Press. 157–165.
Woolf, Virginia. (1928) 2004. *A Room of One's Own*. London: Penguin.

Secondary Sources

Adam, Barbara, Ulrich Beck and Joost Van Loon (eds.). 2000. *The Risk Society and Beyond: Critical Issues for Social Theory*. London: Sage.
Adams, Ann Marie. 2012. "Mr. McEwan and Mrs. Woolf: How a Saturday in February Follows 'This Moment in June'". *Contemporary Literature* 53.3: 548–572.

Adams, James Eli. 2005. "'The Boundaries of Social Intercourse': Class in the Victorian Novel". In: Francis O'Gorman (ed.). *A Concise Companion to the Victorian Novel*. Oxford: Blackwell. 47–70.
Adams, James Eli. 2012. *A History of Victorian Literature*. Oxford: Wiley-Blackwell.
Adams, John. 1995. *Risk*. London: UCL Press.
Adamson, William Robert. 1989. *Cadences of Unreason: A Study of Pride and Madness in the Novels of Tobias Smollett*. Frankfurt a/Main: Peter Lang.
Adiseshiah, Sian and Rupert Hildyard (eds.). 2013. *Twenty-First Century Fiction. What Happens Now*. Basingstoke: Palgrave Macmillan.
Agamben, Giorgio. 1998. *Homo Sacer: Sovereign Power and Bare Life*. Trans. Daniel Heller-Roazen. Stanford, CA: Stanford University Press.
Aharoni, Yair. 1981. *The No-Risk Society*. Chatham, NJ: Chatham House.
Alber, Jan. 2014. "Unnatural Narrative". In: Peter Hühn, John Pier, Wolf Schmid and Jörg Schönert (eds.). *The Handbook of Narratology. Vol. II*. Berlin and Boston, MA: De Gruyter. 887–895.
Alborn, Timothy L. (1995). "The Moral of the Failed Bank: Professional Plots in the Victorian Money Market". *Victorian Studies* 38.2: 199–226.
Albutt, T.C. (1895). "Nervous Disease and Modern Life". *Contemporary Review* 67: 210–231.
Alderson, David. (2000). "Desire as Nostalgia: The Novels of Alan Hollinghurst". In: David Alderson and Linda Anderson (eds.). *Territories of Desire in Queer Culture: Refiguring Contemporary Boundaries*. Manchester: Manchester University Press. 29–48.
Alexander, Jeffery C. (1996). "Critical Reflections on 'Reflexive Modernization'". *Theory, Culture and Society* 13.4: 133–138.
Alexander, Jeffery C. and Philip Smith. (1996). "Social Science and Salvation: 'Risk Society' as Mythical Discourse". *Zeitschrift für Soziologie* 25.4: 251–262.
Alewyn, Richard. (1972). "Die literarische Angst". In: Hoimar von Ditfurth (ed.). *Aspekte der Angst*. München: Kindler. 38–60.
Alkon, Paul K. (1979). "The Odds Against Friday: Defoe, Bayes, and Inverse Probability". In: Paula R. Backscheider (ed.). *Probability, Time, and Space in Eighteenth-Century Literature*. New York: AMS Press. 29–61.
Allen, Dennis W. (1985). "Sexuality and Textuality in *Tristram Shandy*". *Studies in English Literature, 1500–1900* 25.3: 651–670.
Alter, Robert. 1968. "*Tristram Shandy* and the Game of Love". *American Scholar* 37: 316–323.
Altham, J.E.J. 1984. "Ethics of Risk". *Proceedings of the Aristotelian Society* 84: 15–29.
Amigoni, David. 2011. Victorian Literature. Edinburgh: Edinburgh University Press.
Amoore, Louise and Marieke de Goede (eds.). 2008. *Risk and the War on Terror*. London: Routledge.
Appadurai, Arjun. 1996. *Modernity at Large. Cultural Dimensions of Globalization*. Minneapolis, MN: University of Minnesota Press.
Appelbaum, Robert and Alexis Paknadel. 2008. "Terrorism and the Novel, 1970–2001". *Poetics Today* 29.3: 387–436.
Aradau, Claudia and Rens van Munster. 2007. "Governing Terrorism Through Risk: Taking Precautions, (Un)knowing the Future". *European Journal of International Relations* 13.1: 89–115.

Araújo, Susana. 2007. "Images of Terror, Narratives of Captivity: The Visual Spectacle of 9/11 and Its Transatlantic Projections". *Symbiosis: A Journal of Anglo-American Literary Relations* 11.2: 27–46.
Aravamudan, Srinivas. 2009. "The Secret History of the Eighteenth-century Novel". In: Paula R. Backscheider and Catherine Ingrassia (eds.). *A Companion to the Eighteenth-Century English Novel and Culture*. Oxford: Wiley-Blackwell. 48–74.
Archimedes, Sondra. 2005. *Gendered Pathologies. The Female Body and Biomedical Discourse in the Nineteenth-Century Novel*. New York et al: Routledge.
Arizti, Barbara. 2014. "'Welcome to Contemporary Trauma Culture': Foreshadowing, Sideshadowing and Trauma in Ian McEwan's *Saturday*". In: Marita Nadal and Monica Calvo (eds.). *Trauma in Contemporary Literature: Narrative and Representation*. New York: Routledge. 237–48.
Armstrong, Nancy. 1987. *Desire and Domestic Fiction: A Political History of the Novel*. New York and Oxford: Oxford University Press.
Armstrong, Nancy and Leonard Tennenhouse. 1987. *The Ideology of Conduct: Essays on Literature and the History of Sexuality*. London: Methuen.
Arnauld, Antoine and Pierre Nicole. (1662) 1850. *Logic, or, The Art of Thinking Being the Port-Royal Logic*. Trans. from the French; with an introduction by Thomas Spencer Bayes. Edinburgh: Sutherland and Knox. Library of Congress BC62.A7 E5. *open library.org* Id: OL7083029M [accessed 1 March 2019].
Arnoldi, Jakob. 2009. *Risk: An Introduction*. Cambridge: Polity.
Atherton, Stanley S. 1979. *Alan Sillitoe. A Critical Assessment*. London: W.H. Allen.
Atwood, Margaret. 2005. "Brave New World: Kazuo Ishiguro's Novel Really Is Chilling". *slate.com* April 1. <https://slate.com/culture/2005/04/kazuo-ishiguro-s-creepy-clones.html> [accessed 1 March 2019].
Austin, Sara K. 2000. "All Wove into One": *Camilla*, the Prose Epic, and Family Values". *Studies in Eighteenth Century Culture* 29: 273–298.
Avery, Lisa Katherine. 2007. *Vulnerable London, Narratives of Space and Affect in a Twentieth-Century Imperial Capital*. Dissertation. Ann Arbor, MI: University of Texas at Austin. UMS Microform 3277881. <https://repositories.lib.utexas.edu/handle/2152/3232> [accessed 1 March 2019].
Ayto, John. 1990. *Bloomsbury Dictionary of Word Origins*. London: Bloomsbury.
Babrow, Austin S., Kimberly N. Kline and William K. Rawlins. 2005. "Narrating Problems and Problematizing Narratives: Linking Problematic Integration and Narrative Theory in Telling Stories about our Health". In: L.M. Harter, P.M. Japp and C.S. Beck (eds.). *Narratives, Health, and Healing: Communication Theory, Research, and Practice*. Mahwah, NJ: Erlbaum. 31–59.
Backscheider, Paula R. (ed.). 1979. *Probability, Time, and Space in Eighteenth-Century Literature*. New York: AMS Press.
Backscheider, Paula R. 1981. "Defoe's Lady Credit". *Huntington Library Quarterly* 44.2: 89–100.
Badmington, Neil. 2000. *Posthumanism*. New York: Palgrave.
Baines, Paul. 2007. *Daniel Defoe. Robinson Crusoe/ Moll Flanders. A Reader's Guide to Essential Criticism*. London: Palgrave Macmillan.

Baker, Geoffrey. 2009. "Global London and *The Way We Live Now*". *Realism's Empire: Empiricism and Enchantment in the Nineteenth-Century Novel*. Columbus, OH: Ohio State University Press. 131–154.
Baker, Tom and Jonathan Simon. 2002. "Embracing Risk". In: Tom Baker and Jonathan Simon (eds.). *Embracing Risk. The Changing Culture of Insurance and Responsibility*. Chicago and London: University of Chicago Press. 1–25.
Balint, Michael. 1976. *Angstlust und Regression*. (Thrills and Regression, London, 1959). Trans. Konrad Wolff. Stuttgart: Klett.
Banita, Georgiana. 2010. "Race, Risk, and Fiction in the War on Terror: Laila Halaby, Gayle Brandeis, and Michael Cunningham". *Literature Interpretation Theory* 21: 242–268.
Banse, Georg, (ed.). 1996. *Risikoforschung zwischen Disziplinarität und Interdisziplinarität: Von der Illusion der Sicherheit zum Umgang mit Unsicherheit*. Berlin: edition sigma.
Banville, John. 2005. "A Day in the Life". Rev. of *Saturday* by Ian McEwan. *New York Review of Books* May 26. 52.9: 12–14.
Barchas, Janine. 2012. *Matters of Fact in Jane Austen*. Baltimore, MD: Johns Hopkins University Press.
Barrows, Adam. 2010. "'The Shortcomings of Timetables': Greenwich, Modernism, and the Limits of Modernity". *Modern Fiction Studies* 56.2: 262–89.
Bartosch, Roman. 2015. "The Climate of Literature: English Studies in the Anthropocene". *Anglistik* 26.2: 59–70. <https://angl.winter-verlag.de/data/article/3239/pdf/91502006.pdf> [accessed 1 March 2019].
Bartosch, Roman and Julia Hoydis (eds.). 2019. *Teaching the Posthuman*. A&E Series Bd. 89. Heidelberg: Winter.
Bataille, Georges. 2011. "The Attraction of Gambling". *Guilty (Le Coupable)*. Trans. Stuart Kendall. Albany, NY: Suny Press. 61–78.
Batchelor, John. 1982. *The Edwardian Novelists*. London: Duckworth.
Baubles, Raymond L., Jr. 2001. "At Our Millennium Fables from Their Time: The Bankruptcies of the Nation in Meredith's *One of Our Conquerors* and Gissing's *The Whirlpool*". In: Bouwe Postmus (ed.). *A Garland for Gissing*. Amsterdam: Rodopi. 261–270.
Baucom, Ian. 2005. *Specters of the Atlantic. Finance Capital, Slavery, and the Philosophy of History*. Durham and London: Duke University Press.
Bauman, Zygmunt. 1991. *Modernity and Ambivalence*. Cambridge: Polity Press.
Bauman, Zygmunt. 1995. *Life in Fragments: Essays in Postmodern Morality*. Oxford: Blackwell.
Bauman, Zygmunt. 2000. *Liquid Modernity*. Cambridge: Polity Press.
Bauman, Zygmunt. 2003. *Liquid Love. On the Frailty of Human Bonds*. Cambridge: Polity Press.
Bauman, Zygmunt. 2007. *Liquid Times. Living in an Age of Uncertainty*. Cambridge: Polity Press.
Beasley, Jerry C. 1998. *Tobias Smollett. Novelist*. Athens, GA: University of Georgia Press.
Beattie, Tina. 2007. *The New Atheists: The Twilight of Reason and the War on Religion*. London: Darton Longman and Todd,.
Beck, Ulrich. (1986) 1992. *Risk Society: Towards a New Modernity*. Trans. Mark Ritter. London: Sage.
Beck, Ulrich. 1994. "The Reinvention of Politics: Towards a Theory of Reflexive Modernization". In: Ulrich Beck, Anthony Giddens and Scott Lash (eds.). *Reflexive*

Modernization: Politics, Tradition and Aesthetics in the Modern Social Order. Cambridge: Polity Press. 1–55.

Beck, Ulrich. 1998. "Politics of Risk Society". In: J. Franklin (ed.). *The Politics of Risk Society*. Cambridge: Polity Press. 9–22.

Beck, Ulrich. 2002a. "Terror and Solidarity". In: Mark Leonard (ed.). *Re-ordering the World*. London: The Foreign Policy Centre. 112–118.

Beck, Ulrich. 2002b. "The Terrorist Threat: World Risk Society Revisited". *Theory, Culture and Society* 19.4: 39–56.

Beck, Ulrich. 2002c. "The Cosmopolitan Society and its Enemies". *Theory, Culture and Society* 19.1–2: 17–44.

Beck, Ulrich. 2006. "Living in the World Risk Society". *Economy and Society* 35.3: 329–345.

Beck, Ulrich. 2007. *Weltrisikogesellschaft. Auf der Suche nach der verlorenen Sicherheit*. Frankfurt a/Main: Suhrkamp.

Beck, Ulrich, Wolfgang Bonß and Christoph Lau. 2003. "The Theory of Reflexive Modernization: Problematic, Hypotheses and Research Programme". *Theory Culture Society* 20.2: 1–33.

Beer, Gillian. 1983. "Anxiety and Interchange: Daniel Deronda and the Implications of Darwin's Writing". *Journal of the History of the Behavioral Sciences* 19.1: 31–44.

Beer, Gillian. *1984. Darwin's Plots. Evolutionary Narrative in Darwin, George Eliot and Nineteenth-Century Fiction*. London: Routledge and Kegan Paul.

Beer, Gillian. 1998. "Evolution of the Novel". In: Andrew Fabian (ed.). *Evolution: Society, Science and the Universe*. Cambridge: Cambridge University Press. 100–117.

Beggs, Courtney Beth. 2010. *Risky Business: The Discourse of Credit and Early Modern Female Playwrights before Defoe*. Dissertation, Texas A&M University. <https://oaktrust.library.tamu.edu/handle/1969.1/ETD-TAMU-2010-08-8287> [accessed 1 March 2019].

Bender, John. 1987. *Imagining the Penitentiary: Fiction and the Architecture of Mind in Eighteenth-Century England*. Chicago and London: University of Chicago Press.

Bender, John. 1998. "Enlightenment Fiction and the Scientific Hypothesis". *Representations* 61 (Winter): 6–28.

Benjamin, Walter. 1999. "Notes on a Theory of Gambling". *Walter Benjamin: Selected Writings, Vol. 2, 1927–1934*. Trans. Rodney Livingstone. Cambridge, MA: Belknap Press. 297–298.

Bennett, Jane. 2001. *The Enchantment of Modern Life: Attachments, Crossings, and Ethics*. Princeton, NJ, and Oxford: Princeton University Press.

Bentley, Nick. 2013. "Mind and Brain: the Representation of Trauma in Martin Amis' *Yellow Dog* and Ian McEwan's *Saturday*". In: T.J. Lustig and James Peacock (eds.). *Diseases and Disorders in Contemporary Fiction. The Syndrome Syndrome*. New York and London: Routledge. 115–129.

Bentley, Nick. 2010. "Alan Sillitoe: Realism and the (Ir)responsibility of Writing". *Realism's Other*. In: Geoffrey Baker and Eva Aldea (eds.). Newcastle-upon-Tyne: Cambridge Scholars. 189–207.

Berman, Marshall. 1982. *All That is Solid Melts Into Air: The Experience of Modernity*. New York: Simon and Schuster.

Bernstein, Peter L. 1998. *Against the Gods: The Remarkable Story of Risk*. New York: John Wiley and Sons.

Bernstein, Stephen. 1991. "Form and Ideology in the Gothic Novel". *Essays in Literature* 18: 151–165.
Bernstein, Stephen. 2003. "Politics, Modernity, and Domesticity: The Gothicism of Conrad's *The Secret Agent*". *CLIO* 32.3: 285–301.
Binhammer, Katherine. 2011. "The Economics of Plot in Burney's *Camilla*". *Studies in the Novel* 43.1: 1–20.
Black, Shameen. 2009. "Ishiguro's Inhuman Aesthetics". *MFS* 55.4: 785–807.
Blanchfield, J. R. 1999. "Enough of Frankenstein". *Food and Science Technology Today* 13.4: 179–181.
Blewett, David. 1981. "Changing Attitudes Towards Marriage in the Time of Defoe: The Case of *Moll Flanders*". *Huntington Library Quarterly* 44.2: 77–87.
Blewett, David. 1982. "Introduction". In: David Blewett (ed.). *Daniel Defoe. Roxana, The Fortunate Mistress*. London: Penguin. 9–25.
Bloom, Lillian D. and Edward A. Bloom. 1979. "Fanny Burney's Novels: The Retreat from Wonder". *NOVEL: A Forum on Fiction* 12.3: 215–235.
Bloom, Lillian D. and Edward A. Bloom. 1988. "Hostage to Fortune: Time, Chance, and Laurence Sterne". *Modern Philology* 85.4: 499–513.
Boehmer, Elleke and Stephen Morton (eds.). 2010. *Terror and the Postcolonial*. Oxford: Wiley-Blackwell.
Boholm, Asa. 2003. "The Cultural Nature of Risk: Can there be an Anthropology of Uncertainty?" *Ethos: Journal of Anthropology* 68.2: 159–178.
Bodenheimer, Rosemarie. 1979. "*North and South:* A Permanent State of Change". *Nineteenth-Century Fiction* 34.1: 281–301.
Bonaparte, Felicia. 1975. *Will and Destiny: Morality and Tragedy in George Eliot's Novels*. New York: New York University Press.
Bonß, Wolfgang. 1995. *Vom Risiko: Unsicherheit und Ungewissheit in der Moderne*. Hamburg: Hamburger Edition.
Bonß, Wolfgang. 1996. "Die Rückkehr der Unisicherheit. Zur gesellschaftstheoretischen Bedeutung des Risikobegriffs". In: Georg Banse *(ed.). Risikoforschung zwischen Disziplinarität und Interdisziplinarität: Von der Illusion der Sicherheit zum Umgang mit Unsicherheit*. Berlin: edition sigma. 165–184.
Booker, Christopher and Richard North. 2007. *Scared to Death. From BSE to Global Warming: Why Scares are Costing Us the Earth*. London: Bloomsbury.
Booth, Wayne C. 1961. *Rhetoric of Fiction*. Chicago and London: University of Chicago Press.
Bord, Richard J. and Robert E. O'Connor. 1997. "The Gender Gap in Environmental Attitudes: The Case of Perceived Vulnerability to Risk". *Social Science Quarterly* 78.4: 830–840.
Boswell, James and Marshall Waingrow. (1791) 1994. *James Boswell's Life of Johnson: An Edition of the Original Manuscript in Four Volumes*. Edinburgh: Edinburgh University Press; Yale University Press. <https://boswelleditions.yale.edu/james-boswells-life-johnson-edition-original-manuscript-four-volumes-volume-1-1709-1765> [accessed 1 March 2019].
Botha, Marc. 2014. "Precarious Present, Fragile Future: Literature and Uncertainty in the Early Twenty-First Century". *English Academy Review* 31.2: 1–19.
Botting, Fred. 1995. "Introduction". *Frankenstein: Mary Shelley. Contemporary Critical Essays*. In: Fred Botting (ed.). Basingstoke: Macmillan. 1–20.
Botting, Fred. 1996. *Gothic*. London and New York: Routledge.

Boucé, Paul-Gabriel. 1976. *The Novels of Tobias Smollett*. Trans. Antonia White. London and New York: Longman.
Boumelha, Penny. 1982. *Thomas Hardy and Women: Sexual Ideology and Narrative Form*. Brighton: The Harvester Press.
Boumelha, Penny. 1990. *Charlotte Brontë*. Hemel Hempstead: Harvester Wheatsheaf.
Bowen, Elizabeth. 1962. "Truth and Fiction". *Afterthought; Pieces About Writing*. London: Longmans. 114–143.
Bowker, Gordon. 2003. *George Orwell*. London: Little Brown.
Bowlby, Rachel. 1985. "Review Article on Gissing, George. *The Whirlpool*, edited with a new introduction and notes by Patrick Parrinder, Brighton: The Harvester Press, 1984". *The Gissing Newsletter* 21.2: 22–29.
Boxall, Peter. 2013. *Twenty-First Century Fiction. A Critical Introduction*. Cambridge: Cambridge University Press.
Boyne, Roy. 2003. Buckingham: Open University Press.
Brack, O.M. (ed.). 2007. *Tobias Smollett, Scotland's First Novelist: New Essays in Memory of Paul-Gabriel Boucé*. Newark, DE: University of Delaware Press.
Bradley, Arthur and Andrew Tate. 2010. "Ian McEwan's End of the World Blues". *The New Atheist Novel: Fiction, Philosophy and Polemic after 9/11*. London: Continuum. 16–35.
Bradshaw, David. 2007. "*Howards End*". In: David Bradshaw (ed.). *The Cambridge Companion to E.M. Forster*. Cambridge: Cambridge University Press. 151–172.
Bradshaw, David. 2003. "Eugenics: They Should Certainly Be Killed". In: David Bradshaw (ed.). *A Concise Companion to Modernism*. Oxford: Blackwell. 34–55.
Brady, Kristin. 1986. "Tess and Alec: Rape or Seduction?" In: Norman Page (ed.). *Thomas Hardy Annual No. 4*. Houndmills: Macmillan. 127–147.
Brady, Kristin. 1993. "Textual Hysteria: Hardy's Narrator on Women". In: Margaret Higonnet (ed.). *The Sense of Sex: Feminist Perspectives on Hardy*. Urbana and Chicago: University of Illinois Press. 87–106.
Brady, Kristin. 1999. "Hardy and Matters of Gender". In: Dale Kramer (ed.). *The Cambridge Companion to Thomas Hardy*. Cambridge: Cambridge University Press. 93–111.
Bragard, Veronique, Christophe Dony and Warren Rosenberg (eds.). 2011. *Portraying 9/11: Essays on Representations in Comics, Literature, Film and Theatre*. Jefferson, NC: McFarland.
Braidotti, Rosi. 2013. *The Posthuman*. Cambridge: Polity Press.
Brannigan, John. 2003. "After History: Memory and Time in Postwar Writing". *Orwell to the Present: Literature in England, 1945–2000*. Basingstoke: Palgrave Macmillan. 39–72.
Brantlinger, Patrick. 1996. *Fictions of State: Culture and Credit in Britain, 1694–1994*. Ithaca, NY, and London: Cornell University.
Braudy, Leo. 1981. "Providence, Paranoia, and the Novel". *ELH* 48.3: 619–637.
Brenner, Reuven and Gabriele A. Brenner. 1990. *Gambling and Speculation*. Cambridge: Cambridge University Press.
Brewer, John. 1982. "Commercialization and Politics". In: Neil MacKendrick, John Brewer and J.H. Plumb (eds.). *The Birth of a Consumer Society. The Commercialization of Eighteenth-Century England*. London: Europa Publications. 197–264.
Bright, Gillian. 2015. "Paper, Ink, and the 'Blood-Stained Inanity': The Aesthetics of Terrorist Violence in Joseph Conrad's *The Secret Agent*, Paul Theroux's *The Family Arsenal*, and

Doris Lessing's *The Good Terrorist*". *Critique: Studies in Contemporary Fiction* 56.2: 190–206.

Bristow, Joseph. 1995. *Effeminate England. Homoerotic Writing After 1885*. Buckingham: Open University Press.

Broberg, Gunnar. 1990. "The Broken Circle". In: Tore Frängsmyr, J.L. Heilbron and Robin E. Rider (eds.). *The Quantifying Spirit in the 18th Century*. Berkeley and Los Angeles, CA: University of California Press. 45–71.

Brodsley, Laurel. 1992. "Defoe's *The Journal of the Plague Year:* A Model for Stories of Plagues". In: Emmanuel S. Nelson (ed.). *AIDS: The Literary Response*. New York: Twayne. 1–22.

Bronfen, Elisabeth. 1993. "Pay As You Go: On the Exchange of Bodies and Signs". In: Margaret Higonnet (ed.). *The Sense of Sex: Feminist Perspectives on Hardy*. Urbana and Chicago: University of Illinois Press. 66–86.

Brook, Susan. 2003. "Engendering Rebellion: The Angry Young Men". In: Daniel Lea and Berthold Schoene (eds.). *Posting the Male: Masculinities in Post-war and Contemporary British Literature*. Rodopi: Amsterdam. 19–34.

Brook, Susan. 2007. *Literature and Cultural Criticism in the 1950's: The Feeling Male Body*. Basingstoke: Palgrave Macmillan.

Brooks, David. 1992. "Daniel Defoe's *Journal of the Plague Year*". In: Peter Hinton (ed.). *Disasters: Image and Context*. Sydney, NSW: Sydney Association for the Study of Literature and Culture. 167–185.

Brooks, Peter. 1995. "What is a Monster (According to Frankenstein)". In: Fred Botting (ed.). *Frankenstein: Mary Shelley. Contemporary Critical Essays*. Basingstoke: Macmillan. 81–106.

Brown, Laura. 2001. *Fables of Modernity: Literature and Culture in the English Eighteenth-Century*. Ithaca, NY, and London: Cornell University Press.

Brown, Marshall. 1991. "Sterne's Stories". *Preromanticism*. Stanford, CA.: Stanford University Press. 261–300.

Brown, Mick. 2010. "Warming to the Topic of Climate Change". Interview with Ian McEwan. *The Telegraph* March 11. <https://www.telegraph.co.uk/culture/books/7412584/Ian-McEwan-interview-warming-to-the-topic-of-climate-change.html> [accessed 1 March 2019].

Brown, Richard. 2008. "Politics, the Domestic and the Uncanny Effects of the Everyday in Ian McEwan's *Saturday*". *Critical Survey* 20.1: 80–93.

Buell, Lawrence. 2001. *Writing for an Endangered World: Literature and Culture, and the Environment in the U.S. and Beyond*. Cambridge, MA: Belknap Press of Harvard University Press.

Bullen, J.B. 1986. *The Expressive Eye: Fiction and Perception in the Work of Thomas Hardy*. Oxford: Claredon Press.

Bunge, Mario. 1951. "What is Chance?" *Science & Society* 15.3: 209–231.

Bunn, James H. 1981. "Signs of Randomness in *Roderick Random*". *Eighteenth-Century Studies* 14.4: 452–469.

Burchell, Graham, Colin Gordon and Peter Miller (eds.). 1991. *The Foucault Effect: Studies in Governmentality*. London: Harvester Wheatsheaf.

Burckhardt, Sigurd. 1961. "Tristram Shandy's Law of Gravity". *ELH* 28.1: 70–88.

Burgess, Miranda J. 1995. "Courting Ruin: The Economic Romances of Frances Burney". *NOVEL: A Forum on Fiction* 28.2: 131–153.
Burton, Peter. 1991. "Alan Hollinghurst". *Talking to ... Writers Writing on Gay Themes*. Exeter: Third House. 47–50.
Butler, Judith. 2004. *Precarious Life. The Powers of Mourning and Violence*. New York and London: Verso.
Butler, Marilyn. 1993. "The First Frankenstein and Radical Science". *Times Literary Supplement* April 9: 12.
Butler, Marilyn. 1994. "The Shelleys and Radical Science". *Frankenstein or the Modern Prometheus: The 1818 Text*. Oxford: Oxford University Press. iv–xxi.
Butte, George. 2004. I *Know That You Know That I Know. Narrating Subjects from Moll Flanders to Marnie*. Columbus, OH: Ohio State University Press.
Butter, Stella. 2012. "Cultural Constructions of Fear and Empathy: The Emotional Structure of Relationships in George Eliot's *Daniel Deronda* (1876) and Jonathan Nasaw's *Fear Itself* (2003)". In: Marion Gymnich (ed.). *Who's afraid of ...?: Facets of Fear in Anglophone Literature and Film*. Göttingen: V&R Unipress. 109–139.
Butter, Stella. 2013. *Kontingenz und Literatur im Prozess der Modernisierung. Diagnosen und Umgangsstrategien im britischen Roman des 19.–21. Jahrhunderts*. Tübingen: Narr.
Byrne, Sandie. 2014. *Jane Austen's Possessions and Dispossessions. The Significance of Objects*. Basingstoke. Palgrave Macmillan.
Callois, Roger. 2001. *Man, Plays and Games*. (*Les jeux et les hommes*. 1958). Trans. Meyer Barash. Urbana and Chicago: University of Illinois Press.
Campbell, Courtney S. 2003. "Biotechnology and the Fear of Frankenstein". *Cambridge Quarterly of Healthcare Ethics* 12.4: 342–352.
Campbell, Robert. 1997. "Philosophy and the Accident". In: Roger Cooter and Bill Luckin (eds.). *Accidents in History: Injuries, Fatalities and Social Relations*. Amsterdam: Rodopi. 17–34.
Campell, Scott and Greg Currie. 2006. "Against Beck: In Defence of Risk Analysis". *Philosophy of the Social Sciences* 36: 149–179.
Campe, Rüdiger. (2002) 2012. *The Game of Probability. Literature and Calculation From Pascal to Kleist*. Trans. Ellwood H. Wiggins, Jr. Stanford, CA: Stanford University Press.
Camus, Albert. 1991. *Between Hell and Reason. Essays from the Resistance Newspaper Combat, 1944–1947*. Trans. Alexandre de Gramont. Foreword by Elisabeth Young-Bruehl. Hanover, NH: Wesleyan University Press.
Canaan, J. 1996. "'One Thing Leads to Another': Drinking, Fighting and Working-Class Masculinities". In: Mairtin Mac an Ghaill (ed.). *Understanding Masculinities*. Buckingham: Open University Press. 114–125.
Canguilhem, Georges. 1991. *The Normal and the Pathological*. With an Introduction by Michel Foucault. Trans. Carolyn R. Fawcett and Robert S. Cohen. New York: Zone.
Capeloa Gil, Isabel. 2013. "The Risk Doctrine". In: Monika Schmitz-Emans et al. *Literatur als Wagnis/ Literature as a Risk* (eds.). Berlin: de Gruyter. 239–263.
Capeloa Gil, Isabel and Christoph Wulf (eds.). 2015. *Hazardous Future: Disaster, Representation and the Assessment of Risk*. Berlin: De Gruyter.
Carey, Daniel. 2009. "Reading Contrapuntally: *Robinson Crusoe*, Slavery, and Postcolonial Theory". In: Daniel Carey and Lynn Festa (eds.). *The Postcolonial Enlightenment*.

Eighteenth-Century Colonialism and Postcolonial Theory. Oxford: Oxford University Press. 105–136.

Carlyle, Thomas. 1840. *Chartism*. 2nd ed. London: Fraser.

Carlyle, Thomas. (1897) 1969. *Past and Present. In One Volume*. (London: Chapman and Hall). New York: AMS Press.

Carlyle, Thomas. (1829) 1899. "Signs of the Times". (*Edinburgh Review* XCVIII). *Critical and Miscellaneous Essays. Vol. II*. London: Chapman and Hall. 56–82.

Caron, James. 1983. "The Rhetoric of Magic in *Daniel Deronda*". *Studies in the Novel* 15.1: 1–9.

Carr, David. 1986. *Time, Narrative, and History*. Bloomington, IN: Indiana University Press.

Carswell, John. 1960. *The South Sea Bubble*. London: Cresset Press.

Case. Arthur E. 1958. *Four Essays on Gulliver's Travels*. 1945. Gloucester, MA: Peter Smith.

Castel, Robert. 1991. "From Dangerousness to Risk". In: Graham Burchell, Colin Gordon and Peter Millers (eds.). *The Foucault Effect: Studies in Governmentality*. London: Harvester Wheatsheaf. 281–298.

Castle, Terry. 1995. "Amy Who Knew My Disease: A Psychosexual Pattern in Defoe's *Roxana*". *The Female Thermometer: Eighteenth-Century Culture and the Invention of the Uncanny*. Oxford and New York: Oxford University Press. 44–55.

Cavell, Stanley. 2002. "The Avoidance of Love: A Reading of *King Lear*". *Must We Mean What We Say? A Book of Essays*. Updated ed. Cambridge: Cambridge University Press. 267–353.

Chaber, Lois A. 1982. "Matriarchal Mirror: Women and Capital in *Moll Flanders*". *PMLA* 97.2: 212–226.

Chambers, Ross. 1993. "Messing Around: Gayness and Loiterature in Alan Hollinghurst's *The Swimming-Pool Library*". In: Judith Still and Michael Worton (eds.). *Textuality and Sexuality: Reading Theories and Practices*. Manchester: Manchester University Press. 207–217.

Chan, Wendy and Rigakos, George S. 2002. "Risk, Crime and Gender". *British Journal of Criminology* 42.4: 743–761.

Chandler, James. 1998. *England in 1819: The Politics of Literary Culture and the Case of Romantic History*. Chicago: University of Chicago Press.

Chesterton, G.K. 1931. *Orthodoxy*. London: John Lane The Bodley Head.

Childers, Joseph V. 2001. "Industrial Culture and the Victorian Novel". In: Deidre David (ed.). *The Cambridge Companion to the Victorian Novel*. Cambridge: Cambridge University Press. 77–96.

Childers, Mary. 1981. "Thomas Hardy, the Man Who 'Liked' Women". *Criticism* 23.4: 317–334.

Childs, Peter. 2014. "Ordinary Sublime: The Frustration of Life and Art in Rachel Cusk's Domestic Novels". In: Peter Childs, Claire Colebrook and Sebastian Groes (eds.). *Women's Fiction and Post-9/11 Contexts*. Lanham, MD: Lexington. 112–122.

Childs, Peter, Claire Colebrook and Sebastian Groes. 2014. "Introduction". In: Peter Childs, Claire Colebrook and Sebastian Groes (eds.). *Women's Fiction and Post-9/11 Contexts*. Lanham, MD: Lexington. 7–22.

Chilton, Leslie A. 2011. Smollett, the Picaresque, and Two Medical Satires". In: Christopher D. Johnson (ed.). *New Contexts for Eighteenth-Century Fiction*. "*Hearts Resolved and Hands*

Prepared": Essays in Honor of Jerry C. Beasley. Newark, DE: University of Delaware Press. 219–237.

Choi, Tina Young. 2001. "Writing the Victorian City: Discourses of Risk, Connection, and Inevitability". *Victorian Studies* 43.4: 561–589.

Chwe, Michael Suk-Young. 2013. *Jane Austen, Game Theorist*. Princeton, NJ, and Oxford: Princeton University Press.

Cilano, Cara. 2014. *Post-9/11 Espionage Fiction in the US and Pakistan. Spies and 'Terrorists'*. London: Routledge.

Cilano, Cara (ed.). 2009. *From Solidarity to Schisms: 9/11 and After in Fiction and Film from Outside the US*. Amsterdam, Rodopi.

Cisney, Vernon W. and Nicolae Morar (eds.). 2016. *Biopower: Foucault and Beyond*. Chicago and London: University of Chicago Press.

Clark, Jill. 2004. "A Tale Told by Stevie: From Thermodynamics to Informational Energy in *The Secret Agent*". *Conradia: A Journal of Joseph Conrad Studies* 36: 1–31.

Clark, Lorrie. 1996. "Transfiguring the Romantic Sublime in *Persuasion*". In: Juliet McMaster and Bruce Stovel (eds.). *Jane Austen's Business*. London: Macmillan. 30–41.

Clark, T.J. 1999. "Introduction". *Farewell to an Idea: Episodes from a History of Modernism*. New Haven, CT: Yale University Press. 1–13.

Clark, William C. 1980. "Witches, Floods, and Wonder Drugs: Historical Perspectives on Risk Management". In: Richard C. Schwing and Walter A. Albers (eds.). *Societal Risk Assessment: How Safe is Safe Enough?* New York: Plenum. 287–318.

Clarke, Bruce and Manuela Rossini (eds.). 2016. *The Cambridge Companion to Literature and the Posthuman*. Cambridge: Cambridge University Press.

Clarke, Geoffrey. 1999. *Betting on Lives. The Culture of Life Insurance in England, 1695–1775*. Manchester: Manchester University Press.

Clarke, Lee. 2006. *Worst Cases: Terror and Catastrophe in the Popular Imagination*. Chicago and London: University of Chicago Press.

Clarkson Holstein, Suzy. 1993. "Out of the Estate and into the Rescue Boat". *Persuasions* 15: 53–56.

Clayton, Jay. 2003. "Frankenstein's Futurity: Replicants and Robots". In: Esther Schor (ed.). *The Cambridge Companion to Mary Shelley*. Cambridge: Cambridge University Press. 84–100.

Clemens, Valdine. 1999. *The Return of the Repressed. Gothic Horror from 'The Castle of Otranto' to 'Alien'*. New York: State University of New York Press.

Clery, E.J. 2008. "Introduction". In: W.S. Lewis (ed.). *Horace Walpole. The Castle of Otranto. A Gothic Story*. Oxford: Oxford University Press. vii–xxxiii.

Clifford, James L. 1974. "Gulliver's Fourth Voyage: 'Hard' and 'Soft' Schools of Interpretation". In: Larry S. Champion (ed.). *Quick Springs of Sense: Studies in the Eighteenth Century*. Athens, GA: University of Georgia Press. 33–49.

Cockerell, H. A. L. and Edwin Green. 1994. *The British Insurance Business. A Guide to Its History and Records*. Sheffield: Sheffield Academic Press.

Cohen, Maurie J. 1999. "Science and Society in Historical Perspective: Implications for Social Theories of Risk". *Environmental Values* 8.2: 153–176.

Cohen, Margaret. 2010. *The Novel and the Sea*. Princeton, NJ: Princeton University Press.

Collini, Stefan. 1980. "Political Theory and the Science of Society in Victorian Britain". *Historical Journal* 23.1: 203–231.

Cone, Carl B. 1952. *Torchbearer of Freedom: The Influence of Richard Price on Eighteenth-Century Thought*. Lexington, KY: University of Kentucky Press.
Conroy, Mark. 1983. "The Panoptical City: The Structure of Suspicion in *The Secret Agent*". *Conradiana* 15.3: 203–217.
Cooley, D. R. 2002. "So Who's Afraid of Frankenstein Food?" *Journal of Social Philosophy* 33.3: 442–463.
Copeland, Edward W. 1976. "Money in the Novels of Fanny Burney". *Studies in the Novel* 8.1: 24–37.
Copeland, Edward W. 2010. "Money". In: Edward Copeland and Juliet McMaster (eds.). *The Cambridge Companion to Jane Austen*. Cambridge: Cambridge University Press. 127–143.
Corbin, Alain. 1994. *The Lure of the Sea: The Discovery of the Seaside in the Western World 1750–1840*. Trans. Jocelyn Phelps. Cambridge: Polity Press.
Cornier Michael, Magali. 2009. "Writing Fiction in the Post-9/11 World: Ian McEwan's *Saturday*". In: Cara Cilano (ed.). *From Solidarity to Schisms. 9/11 and After in Fiction and Film from Outside the US*. New York: Rodopi. 25–52
Cornier Michael, Magali. 2014. *Narrative Innovation in 9/11 Fiction*. Amsterdam: Rodopi.
Coustillas, Pierre and Colin Partridge (eds.). 1972. *George Gissing: The Critical Heritage*. London and New York: Routledge.
Christ, Carol. 1976. "Aggression and Providential Death in George Eliot's Fiction". *Novel: A Forum of Fiction* 9.2: 130–140.
Conrad, Horst. 1974. *Die literarische Angst. Das Schreckliche in Schauerromantik und Detektivgeschichte*. Düsseldorf: Bertelsmann.
Crosthwaite, Paul (ed.). 2011a. *Criticism, Crisis, and Contemporary Narrative: Textual Horizons in an Age of Global Risk*. New York: Routledge.
Crosthwaite, Paul. 2011b. "Introduction". In: Paul Crosthwaite (ed.). *Criticism, Crisis, and Contemporary Narrative: Textual Horizons in an Age of Global Risk*. New York: Routledge. 1–14.
Crosthwaite, Paul. 2010. "Anticipations of the Accident: Modernist Fiction and Systemic Risk". *Textual Practice* 24.2: 331–52.
Culbertson, Roberta. 1995. "Embodied Memory, Transcendence, and Telling: Recounting Trauma, Re-establishing the Self". *New Literary History* 26.1: 169–95.
Cullen, Michael J. 1975. *The Statistical Movement in Early Victorian Britain. The Foundations of Empirical Social Research*. Hassocks: Harvester Press.
Currie, Mark. 2010. "Controlling Time: Kazuo Ishiguro's *Never Let Me Go*". In: Sean Matthews and Sebastian Groes (eds.). *Kazuo Ishiguro*. London: Continuum. 91–103.
Currie, Mark. 2013. "Freedom and the Inescapable Future". *The Unexpected: Narrative Temporality and the Philosophy of Surprise*. Edinburgh: Edinburgh University Press. 148–162.
Cutter, Susan L., John Tiefenbacher and William. D. Solecki. 1992. "Engendered Fears: Femininity and Technological Risk Perception". *Industrial Crisis Quarterly* 6: 5–22.
Cyples, William. 1864. "Morality of the Doctrine of Averages". *The Cornhill Magazine* 10: 218–224.
Dacunha-Castelle, Didier. 1997. *Spiele des Zufalls. Instrumente zum Umgang mit Risiken*. Trans. Bernd Wilczek. München: Gerling Akademie.

D'Albertis, Deidre. 1997. "'Wild Night Wanderings': Getting out of the House in Gaskell's Industrial Fictions". *Dissembling Fictions: Elizabeth Gaskell and the Victorian Social Text*. Basingstoke: Macmillan. 45–71

Dake, Karl. 1991. "Orienting Dispositions in the Perception of Risk – An Analysis of Contemporary Worldviews and Cultural Biases". *Journal of Cross-Cultural Psychology* 22.1: 61–82.

Dake, Karl. 1992. "Myths of Nature: Culture and the Social Construction of Risk". *Journal of Social Issues* 48.4: 21–37.

Dake, Karl and Aaron Wildavsky. 1990. "Theories of Risk Perception: Who Fears What and Why?" *Daedalus: Journal of the American Academy of Arts and Sciences* 119 (Fall): 41–60.

Damrosch, Leopold Jr. 1985. *God's Plot and Man's Stories: Studies in the Fictional Imagination from Milton to Fielding*. Chicago and London: University of Chicago Press.

Dandeker, Christopher. 1990. *Surveillance, Power and Modernity: Bureaucracy and Discipline from 1700 to the Present Day*. Cambridge: Polity Press.

Daniels, Stephen and Simon Rycroft. 1998. "Mapping the Modern City: Alan Sillitoe's Nottingham Novels". In: K.D.M. Snell (ed.). *The Regional Novel in Britain and Ireland: 1800–1990*. Cambridge: Cambridge University Press. 257–289.

Darwin, Charles. (1859) 1998. *The Origin of Species*. Introduction by Jeff Wallace. Ware, Hertfordshire: Wordsworth.

Darwin, Charles. 1890. *The Descent of Man and Selection in Relation to Sex*. 2nd ed., revised and augmented. London: John Murray.

Daston, Lorraine J. 1987. "The Domestication of Risk: Mathematical Probability and Insurance, 1650–1830". In: Lorenz Krüger, Lorraine Daston and Michael Heidelberger (eds.). *The Probabilistic Revolution Vol I: Ideas in History*. Cambridge, MA: MIT Press. 237–260.

Daston, Lorraine J. 1988. *Classical Probability in the Enlightenment*. Princeton, NJ: Princeton University Press.

Daston, Lorraine J. 1994a. "Enlightenment Calculations". *Critical Inquiry* 21: 182–202.

Daston, Lorraine J. 1994b. "Fortuna and the Passions". In: Thomas M. Kavanagh (ed.). *Chance, Culture, and the Literary Text*. Ann Arbor, MI: University of Michigan Press. 25–47.

David, Deidre. 1981. *Fictions of Resolution in Three Victorian Novels: North and South, Our Mutual Friend, Daniel Deronda*. New York: Columbia University Press.

David, Florence Nightingale. 1998. *Games, Gods and Gambling: A History of Probability and Statistical Ideas*. Mineola, NY: Dover Publications.

David, Marjorie S. (ed.). 1973. *The Sermons of Mr. Yorick by Laurence Sterne Selected by Marjorie David*. Cheadle Hulme: Carcanet Press.

Davidson, Debra. J. and William R. Freudenburg. 1996. "Gender and Environmental Risk Concerns: A Review and Analysis of Available Research". *Environment & Behavior* 28.3: 302–339.

Davis, Kathryn. 2013. "Austen's 'Providence' in *Persuasion*". *Persuasions: The Jane Austen Journal* 35: 212–224.

Davis, Lennard J. 1983. *Factual Fictions. The Origins of the English Novel*. New York: Columbia University Press.

Davis, Philip J. and Reuben Hersh. 1986. "The Stochastized World: A Matter of Style?" *Descartes' Dream: The World According to Mathematics*. San Diego, CA: Harcourt Brace Jovanovich. 18–32.

Davis, Jr., William A. 1997. "The Rape of Tess: Hardy, English Law, and the Case for Sexual Assault". *Nineteenth-Century Literature* 52.2: 221–231.

De Boever, Arne. 2013. *Narrative Care: Biopolitics and the Novel*. London: Bloomsbury.

de Jonge, Alex. 1975. *Dostoevsky and the Age of Intensity*. London: Secker and Warburg.

De Michelis, Lidia. 2011. "Risk and Morality in Ian McEwan's *Saturday*". In: Paul Crosthwaite (ed.). *Criticism, Crisis, and Contemporary Narrative: Textual Horizons in an Age of Global Risk*. New York: Routledge. 127–144.

Dean, Mitchell. 1999. "Risk, Calculable and Incalculable". In: Deborah Lupton (ed.). *Risk and Sociocultural Theory*. Cambridge: Cambridge University Press. 131–159.

Delany, Paul. 1988. "Islands of Money: Rentier Culture in E.M. Forster's *Howards End*". *English Literature in Transition, 1880–1920* 31.3: 285–296.

Delany, Paul. 2002. *Literature, Money and the Market: From Trollope to Amis*. Basingstoke: Palgrave.

Delumeau, Jean. (1978) 1985. *Angst im Abendland. Die Geschichte kollektiver Ängste im Europa des 14. bis 18. Jahrhunderts*. Bd. 1. Trans. Monika Hübner, Gabriele Konder und Martina Roters-Burck. Reinbek bei Hamburg: Rowohlt.

Dellamora, Richard. 1994. *Apocalyptic Overtures: Sexual Politics and the Sense of an Ending*. New Brunswick, NJ: Rutgers University Press.

Deporte, Michael V. 1977. *Nightmares and Hobbyhorses: Swift, Sterne, and Augustan Ideas of Madness*. San Marino, CA: The Huntington Library.

Deresiewicz, William. 2004. *Jane Austen and the Romantic Poets*. New York: Columbia University Press.

DeRosa, Aaron. 2011. "Analyzing Literature after 9/11". *Modern Fiction Studies* 57.3: 607–618.

Derrida, Jacques and Giovanna Borradori. 2003. "Autoimmunity: Real and Symbolic Suicides – A Dialogue With Jacques Derrida". In: Giovanna Borradori (ed.). *Philosophy in a Time of Terror: Dialogues with Jürgen Habermas and Jacques Derrida*. Trans. Pascale-Anne Brault and Michael Naas. Chicago and London: University of Chicago Press. 85–136.

Desrosières, Alain. 1998. *The Politics of Large Numbers: A History of Statistical Reasoning*. Trans. Camille Naish. Cambridge, MA: Harvard University Press.

Devlin, Keith. 2008. *The Unfinished Game: Pascal, Fermat, and the Seventeenth-Century Letter that Made the World Modern (A Tale of How Mathematics is Really Done)*. New York: Basic.

D'Exideuil, Pierre. (1930) 1970. *The Human Pair in the Work of Thomas Hardy: An Essay on the Sexual Problem As Treated in the Wessex Novels, Tales, and Poems*. Trans. Felix W. Crosse with an Introduction by Havelock Ellis. Port Washington, NY: Kennikat Press.

Dharwadker, Aparna. 1998. "Nation, Race, and the Ideology of Commerce in Defoe". *The Eighteenth Century: Theory and Interpretation* 39.1: 63–84.

Dickson, P.G.M. 1967. *The Financial Revolution in England: A Study in the Development of Public Credit, 1688–1756*. London: Macmillan.

Dingby, Everard. 1904. "The Extinction of the Londoner". *Contemporary Review* 86 (July): 115–126.

Dijsktra, Bram. 1987. *Defoe and Economics: The Fortunes of Roxana in the History of Interpretation*. London: Macmillan.
Dingwall, Robert. 1999. "'Risk Society': the Cult of Theory and the New Millennium?" *Social Policy & Administration* 33.4: 474–494.
Doody, Margaret Anne. 1977. "Deserts, Ruins and Troubled Waters: Female Dreams in Fiction and the Development of the Gothic Novel". *Genre* 10: 529–572.
Doody, Margaret Anne. 1988. *Frances Burney: The Life in the Works*. Cambridge and New York: Cambridge University Press.
Doody, Margaret Anne. 1997. *The True Story of the Novel*. London: HarperCollins.
Douglas, Mary. 1990. "Risk as a Forensic Resource". *Daedalus* 119.4: 1–16.
Douglas, Mary. 1992. *Risk and Blame: Essays in Cultural Theory*. London: Routledge.
Douglas, Mary. (1966) 2002. *Purity and Danger: An Analysis of the Concept of Pollution and Taboo*. London: Routledge.
Douglas, Mary and Aaron B. Wildavsky. (1980) 1983. *Risk and Culture: An Essay on the Selection of Technical and Environmental Dangers*. Berkeley and Los Angeles, CA: University of California Press.
Drobisch, M.W. 1867. *Die moralische Statistik und die menschliche Willensfreiheit: Eine Untersuchung*. Leipzig.
Duckworth, Alistair M. 1997. "A Critical History of *Howards End*". In: Alistair M. Duckworth (ed.). *Howards End. Complete, Authoritative Text with Biographical and Historical Contexts, Critical History, and Essays From Five Contemporary Critical Perspectives*. Boston, MA: Bedford. 295–312.
Duncan, Fiona. 2012. "Swift's Anxiety Regarding Economic Change and the Ascent of the Moneyed Interest". *Stirling International Journal of Postgraduate Research* 1.1: 1–18
Dukes, Thomas. 1996. "Mappings of Secrecy and Disclosure". *Journal of Homosexuality* 31.3: 95–107.
During, Lisbeth. 1993. "The Concept of Dread: Sympathy and Ethics in *Daniel Deronda*". *Critical Review* 33: 88–111.
Dutta, Shanta. 2000. *Ambivalence in Hardy: A Study of His Attitude to Women*. London: Anthem.
Eagleton, Terry. 1974. "Orwell and the Lower-Middle-Class Novel". In: Raymond Williams (ed.). *George Orwell: A Collection of Critical Essays*. Englewood Cliffs, NJ: Prentice-Hall. 10–33.
Eagleton, Terry. 1975. *Myths of Power. A Marxist Study of the Brontës*. London and Basingstoke. Macmillan.
Eagleton, Terry. 2003. "Tragedy and the Novel". *Sweet Violence: The Idea of the Tragic*. Oxford: Blackwell. 178–201.
Eagleton, Terry. 2005. *Holy Terror*. Oxford: Oxford University Press.
Eatough, Matthew. 2011. "The Time that Remains: Organ Donation, Temporal Duration, and Bildung in Kazuo Ishiguro's *Never Let Me Go*". *Literature and Medicine* 29.1: 132–160.
Eckstein, Lars. 2011. "Saturday on Dover Beach: Ian McEwan, Matthew Arnold, and post-9/11 Melancholia". *Hard Times* 89.1: 6–10.
Edwards, Tim. 1994. *Erotics and Politics. Gay Male Sexuality, Masculinity and Feminism*. London and New York: Routledge.
Ehlers, Leigh A. 1981. "Mrs Shandy's 'Lint and Basilicon': The Importance of Women in *Tristram Shandy*". *South Atlantic Review* 46.1 (1): 61–75.

Ehrenpreis, Irvin. 1964–1983. *Swift. The Man, His Works, and the Age.* Vol. I–III. London: Methuen.
Elbert, Monika. 1999. "Malinowski's Reading List: Tess a Field Guide to Woman". *Colby Quarterly* 35.1: 49–67.
Elderton, Ethel Mary. 1914. *Report on the English Birth Rate.* (University of London, Francis Galton Laboratory for National Eugenics. Eugenics Laboratory Memoirs 19–20). London: Dulau.
Elliott, Albert Pettigrew. (1935) 1966. *Fatalism in the Works of Thomas Hardy.* New York: Russell and Russell.
Elliott, Anthony. 2002. "Beck's Sociology of Risk: A Critical Assessment". *Sociology* 36.2: 293–315.
Ellis, Markman. 1996. "Crusoe, Cannibalism, and Empire". In: Lieve Spaas and Brian Stimpson (eds.). *Robinson Crusoe, Myths and Metamorphoses.* London: Macmillan. 45–61.
Ellis, Markman. 2000. *The History of Gothic Fiction.* Edinburg: Edinburgh University Press.
Elvy, Margaret. 2012. *Thomas Hardy's Tess of the d'Urbervilles: A Critical Study.* 3rd ed. Maidstone: Crescent Moon.
Engels, Friedrich. 1892. *The Condition of the Working-Class in England in 1844. With a Preface Written in 1892.* Trans. Florence Kelley Wischnewetzky. London: Swan Sonnenschein.
English, James F. 1992. "Anarchy in the Flesh: Conrad's Counterrevolutionary Modernism and the Witz of the Political Unconscious". *Modern Fiction Studies* 38.3: 615–30.
Epstein, Julia L. 1986. "Writing the Unspeakable: Fanny Burney's Mastectomy and the Fictive Body". *Representations* 16: 131–166.
Epstein, Julia L. 1989. *The Iron Pen: France Burney and the Politics of Women's Writing.* Madison, WI: University of Wisconsin Press.
Epstein, Julia L. 1996. "Marginality in Frances Burney's Novels". In: John Richetti (ed.). *The Cambridge Companion to the Eighteenth-Century Novel.* Cambridge: Cambridge University Press. 198–211.
Erickson, Robert A. 1986. *Mother Midnight: Birth, Sex, and Fate in Eighteenth-Century Fiction (Defoe, Richardson, Sterne).* New York: AMS Press.
Ericson, Richard V. and Aaron Doyle (eds.). 2003. *Risk and Morality.* Toronto: University of Toronto Press.
Ermath, Elizabeth. 1981. "Realism, Perspective, and the Novel". *Critical Inquiry* 7.3: 499–520.
Escudero Pérez, Jimena. 2014. "Sympathy for the Clone: (Post)Human Identities Enhanced by the 'Evil Science' Construct and its Commodifying Practices in Contemporary Clone Fiction". *Between* IV.8: 1–24.
Ewald, Francois. 1991. "Insurance and Risk" In: Graham Burchell, Colin Gordon and Peter Millers (eds.). *The Foucault Effect: Studies in Governmentality.* London: Harvester Wheatsheaf. 197–210.
Ewald, Francois. 1993. "Two Infinities of Risk". In: Brian Massumi (ed.). *The Politics of Everyday Fear.* Minneapolis, MN: University of Minnesota Press. 221–228.
Ewald, Francois. 2002. "The Return of Descartes Malicious Demon: An Outline of a Philosophy of Precaution". In: Tom Baker and Jonathan Simon (eds.). *Embracing Risk. The Changing Culture of Insurance and Responsibility.* Chicago and London: University of Chicago Press. 273–301.

Faber Oestreich, Kate. 2013. "Sue's Desires: Sexuality and Reform Fashion in *Jude the Obscure*". *Victorian Institute Journal* 41: 128–154.
Faller, Lincoln B. 1993. *Crime and Defoe. A New Kind of Writing*. Cambridge: Cambridge University Press.
Faurot, Ruth Marie. 1970. "Mrs Shandy Observed". *Studies in English Literature, 1500–1900* 10: 579–589.
Federer, Helena. 2014. "Ecocriticism and the Production of Monstrosity in Frankenstein" *Ecocriticism and the Idea of Culture Biology and the Bildungsroman*. Farnham: Ashgate. 49–74.
Federico, Annette. 2005. "Making Do: George Orwell's *Coming Up For Air*". *Studies in the Novel* 37.1: 50–63.
Ferguson, Frances. 2007. "The Way We Love Now: Ian McEwan, *Saturday*, and Personal Affection in the Information Age". *Representations* 100 (Fall): 42–52.
Ferrebe, Alice. 2005. *Masculinity in Male-authored Fiction 1950–2000: Keeping it Up*. Basingstoke: Palgrave Macmillan.
Figlio, Karl. 1985. "What is an Accident?" In: Paul Weindling (ed.) *The Social History of Occupational Health*. London: Croom Helm. 180–206.
Fink, Howard. 1973. "*Coming Up For Air:* Orwell's Ambiguous Satire on the Wellsian Utopia". *Studies in the Literary Imagination* 6.2: 51–60.
Finucane, Melissa L., Paul Slovic, C.K. Mertz, James Flynn and Theresa A. Satterfield. 2000. "Gender, Race, and Perceived Risk: The White Male' Effect". *Health, Risk & Society* 2.2: 111–172.
Fitzgerald, Robert P. 1988. "Science and Politics in Swift's Voyage to Laputa". *The Journal of English and Germanic Philology* 87.2: 213–229.
Fleishman, Avron. 1967. *Conrad's Politics: Community and Anarchy in the Fiction of Joseph Conrad*. Baltimore, MD: Johns Hopkins.
Flint, Christopher. 1998. *Family Fictions. Narrative and Domestic Relations in Britain, 1688–1798*. Stanford, CA: Stanford University Press.
Fluck, Winfried. 1999. "Henry James's *Washington Square:* The Female Self at Risk". In: Gudrun M. Grabher and Sonja Bahn-Coblans (eds.). *The Self at Risk in English Literatures and Other Landscapes*. Innsbruck: Innsbrucker Beiträge zur Kulturwissenschaft. 75–94.
Flynn, Carol Houlihan. 1987. "Defoe's Idea of Conduct: Ideological Fictions and Fictional Reality". In: Nancy Armstrong and Leonard Tennenhouse (eds.). *The Ideology of Conduct*. New York and London: Methuen. 73–95.
Flynn, Christopher. 2000. "Nationalism, Commerce, and Imperial Anxiety in Defoe's Later Works". *Rocky Mountain Review of Language and Literature* 54.2: 11–24.
Flynn, James, Paul Slovic and C.K. Mertz. 1994. "Gender, Race and Perception of Environmental Health Risks". *Risk Analysis* 14: 1101–1108.
Foley, Andrew. 2010. "Liberalism in the New Millennium: Ian McEwan's *Saturday*". *Journal of Literary Studies* 26.1: 135–162.
Forster, Shirley. 2006. "Introduction". In: Shirley Forster (ed.). *Mary Barton*. Oxford: Oxford University Press. vii–xxvi.
Foster, John. *After Sustainability: Denial, Hope, Retrieval*. London and New York: Routledge/Earthscan, 2015.

Foucault, Michel. (1976) 1990. *The History of Sexuality: Volume 1, An Introduction*. Trans. Robert Hurley. New York: Vintage.
Foucault, Michel. 1991. "Governmentality". In: Graham Burchell, Colin Gordon and Peter Millers (eds.). *The Foucault Effect: Studies in Governmentality*. London: Harvester Wheatsheaf. 87–104
Foucault, Michel. (1973) 1994. *The Birth of the Clinic: An Archaeology of Medical Perception*. Trans. Alan M. Sheridan Smith. New York: Vintage,.
Foucault, Michel. (1977) 1995. *Discipline and Punish. The Birth of the Prison*. Trans. Alan Sheridan. New York: Vintage.
Foucault, Michel. 2007. *Security, Territory, Population. Lectures at the Collège de France, 1977–78*. Michel Senellart (ed.). Trans. Graham Burchell. New York: Palgrave Macmillan.
Foucault, Michel. 2010. *The Birth of Biopolitics. Lectures at the Collège de France 1978–1979*. Michel Senellart (ed.). Trans. Graham Burchell. New York: Palgrave Macmillan.
Fox, Christopher. 1998. "Swift and the Spectacle of Human Science". In: Herman Real (ed.). *Reading Swift: Papers from the Third Münster Symposium on Jonathan Swift*. München: Fink. 199–212.
Frängsmyr, Tore, J.L. Heilbron and Robin E. Rider (eds.). 1990. *The Quantifying Spirit of the 18th Century*. Berkeley and Los Angeles, CA: University of California Press.
Franklin, J. Jeffrey. 1994. "The Victorian Discourse of Gambling: Speculations on *Middlemarch* and *The Duke's Children*". *ELH* 61.4: 899–921.
Franklin, J. Jeffrey. 1999. *Serious Play: The Cultural Form of the Nineteenth-Century Realist Novel*. Philadelphia, PA: University of Pennsylvania Press.
Franklin, J. Jeffrey. 2003. "Anthony Trollope Meets Pierre Bourdieu: The Conversion of Capital as Plot in the Mid-Victorian British Novel". *Victorian Literature and Culture* 31.2: 501–521.
Fraser, Derek. 1973. *The Evolution of the British Welfare State*. London: Macmillan.
Fraser, W. Hamish. 1981. *The Coming of the Mass Market, 1850–1914*. London and Basingstoke: Macmillan.
Freedgood, Elaine. 2000. *Victorian Writing about Risk: Imagining a Safe England in a Dangerous World*. Cambridge: Cambridge University Press.
Freedman, Ariela. 2003. *Death, Men, and Modernism. Trauma and Narrative in British Fiction from Hardy to Woolf*. New York and London: Routledge.
Freeman, Barbara. 1987. "*Frankenstein* with Kant: A Theory of Monstrosity, or the Monstrosity of Theory". *SubStance* 16.1 Issue 52: 21–31.
Freeman, Janet. 1982. "Ways of Looking at Tess". *Studies in Philology* 79.3: 311–323.
Freudenburg, William R. 1996. "Risky Thinking: Irrational Fears About Risk and Society". *The Annals of the American Academy of Political and Social Science* 545 (May): 44–53.
Frick, Werner. 1988. *Providenz und Kontingenz: Untersuchungen zur Schicksalssemantik im deutschen und europäischen Roman des 17. und 18. Jahrhunderts*. Band 1. Tübingen: Max Niemeyer.
Fuderer, Laura Sue. 1990. *The Female Bildungsroman in English. An Annotated Bibliography of Criticism*. New York: The Modern Language Association of America.
Fücker, Sonja and Uwe Schimank. 2015. "Gesellschaftliche Risikodiskurse durch die Linse der Literatur". In: Stephan Lessenich (ed.). *Routinen der Krise – Krise der Routinen: Verhandlungen des 37. Kongresses der Deutschen Gesellschaft für Soziologie in Trier 2014*. 1343–1352.

Fukuyama, Francis. 2002. *Our Posthuman Future*. New York: Farrar, Straus and Giroux.
Furedi, Frank. 2005. *Culture of Fear. Risk-Taking and the Morality of Low Expectation*. Revised ed. New York and London: Continuum.
Furedi, Frank. 2007. *Invitation to Terror. The Expanding Empire of the Unknown*. London: Continuum.
Fyfe, Paul. 2010. "Accidents of a Novel Trade: Industrial Catastrophe, Fire Insurance, and *Mary Barton*". *Nineteenth-Century Literature* 65.3: 315–346.
Fyfe, Paul. 2015. *By Accident or Design: Writing the Victorian Metropolis*. Oxford Scholarship Online.
Gallagher, Catherine. 1985. *The Industrial Reformation of English Fiction: Social Discourse and Narrative Form, 1832–1867*. Chicago and London: University of Chicago Press.
Gallagher, Catherine. 1994. "Nobody's Debt: Frances Burney's Universal Obligation". *Nobody's Story: The Vanishing Acts of Women Writers in the Marketplace, 1670–1820*. Berkeley, CA: University of California Press. 203–254.
Gallagher, Catherine. 2006. "*Hard Times* and the Somaeconomics of the Early Victorians". *The Body Economic Life Death and Sensation in Political Economy and the Victorian Novel*. Princeton, NJ: Princeton University Press. 62–85.
Gallant, Thomas. 1991. *Risk and Survival in Ancient Greece: Reconstructing the Rural Domestic Economy*. Cambridge: Polity Press.
Galton, Francis. 1908. *Memoirs of My Life*. London: Methuen.
Ganteau, Jean-Michel. 2015. *The Ethics and Aesthetics of Vulnerability in Contemporary British Fiction*. New York: Routledge.
Ganteau, Jean-Michel. 2017. "The Powers of Exposure: Risk and Vulnerability in Contemporary British Fiction". *Textual Practice* 31.3: 443–455.
Gardner, Daniel. 2008. *Risk: The Science and Politics of Fear*. London: Virgin
Garland, David. 2003. "The Rise of Risk". In: Richard V. Ericson and Aaron Doyle (eds.). *Risk and Morality*. Toronto: University of Toronto Press. 48–86.
Garrard, Greg. 2013. "*Solar*: Apocalypse Not". In: Sebastian Groes (ed.). *Ian McEwan. Contemporary Perspectives*. 2nd ed. London: Bloomsbury. 123–136.
Garson, Marjorie. 1991. *Hardy's Fables of Integrity: Woman, Body, Text*. Oxford: Clarendon Press.
Gauthier, Tim S. 2013. "Privilege, Vulnerability, and the Limits of Empathy in Ian McEwan's *Saturday*". *College Literature* 40.2: 7–30.
Gay, Penny. 2010. "*Emma* and *Persuasion*". In: Edward Copeland and Juliet McMaster (eds.). *The Cambridge Companion to Jane Austen*. Cambridge: Cambridge University Press. 55–71.
Gaylin, William. 1977. "The Frankenstein Factor". *New England Journal of Medicine* 297: 665–667.
Gemmeke, Mascha. 2004. *Frances Burney and the Female Bildungsroman. An Interpretation of The Wanderer: or, Female Difficulties*. Frankfurt a/Main: Peter Lang.
Germain, Gilbert G. 1993. *A Discourse on Disenchantment. Reflections on Politics and Technology*. Albany, NY: State University of New York Press.
Gezari, Janet. 1992. *Charlotte Brontë and Defensive Conduct: The Author and the Body at Risk*. Philadelphia, PA: University of Pennsylvania Press.
Ghosh, Amitav. 2016. *The Great Derangement. Climate Change and the Unthinkable*. Chicago and London: University of Chicago Press.

Ghosh, Amitav. 2005. *Incendiary Circumstances. A Chronicle of the Turmoil of Our Time*. New York: Houghton Mifflin Company.
Gibbard, Alan. 1985. "Risk and Value". In: Douglas MacLean (ed.). *Values at Risk*. Totowa, NJ: Rowman and Allanheld. 94–112.
Giddens, Anthony. 1991. *Modernity and Self-Identity*. Cambridge: Polity Press.
Giddens, Anthony. 1998. "Risk Society: The Context of British Politics". In: J. Franklin (ed.). *The Politics of Risk Society*. Cambridge: Polity Press. 23–34.
Giddens, Anthony. 1999. "Risk and Responsibility". *The Modern Law Review* 62.1: 1–10.
Giddens, Anthony. 2000. "Risk". *Runaway World: How Globalization Is Reshaping Our Lives*. New York: Routledge. 38–53.
Giddens, Anthony. 2009. *The Politics of Climate Change*. London: Polity Press.
Gigerenzer, Gerd, Zeno Swijtink, Theodore Porter, Lorraine Daston, John Beatty, Lorenz Krüger (eds.). 1989. *The Empire of Chance: How Probability Changed Science and Everyday Life*. Cambridge: Cambridge University Press.
Gill, Josie. 2014. "Written on the Face: Race and Expression in Kazuo Ishiguro's *Never Let Me Go*". *Modern Fiction Studies* 60.4: 844–862.
Gilman, Susan. 1988. *Disease and Representation. Images of Illness From Madness to AIDS*. Ithaca, NY, and London: Cornell University Press.
Gilmour, Robin. 1993. *The Victorian Period: The Intellectual and Cultural Context of English Literature, 1830–1890*. London: Longman.
Gindin, James. 1976. *Postwar British Fiction: New Accents and Attitudes*. Westport, CT: Greenwood.
Glacken, Clarence J. (1967) 1990. *Traces on the Rhodian Shore: Nature and Culture in Western Thought from Ancient Times to the End of the Eighteenth Century*. Berkeley, CA: University of California Press.
Glass, D.V. 1973. *Numbering the People. The Eighteenth-century Population Controversy and the Development of Census and Vital Statistics in Britain*. Farnborough, Hants: Saxon House.
Glover, David. 2005. "Sex and the City: Gissing, Helmholtz, Freud". In: Martin Ryle and Jenny Bourne Taylor (eds.). *George Gissing: Voices of the Unclassed*. Aldershot, Hants: Ashgate. 77–91.
Goldman, Lawrence. 1983. "The Origins of British 'Social Science': Political Economy, Natural Science and Statistics, 1830–1835". *Historical Journal* 26.3: 587–616.
Goodbody, Axel. 2010. "*Die Ringe des Saturn* und *Solar*. Sinnbilder und Schreibstrategen in literarischen Stellungnahmen zur ökologischen Krise von W.G. Sebald und Ian McEwan". In: Maren Ermisch, Ulrike Krise and Urte Stobbe (eds.). *Ökologische Transformationen und literarische Repräsentationen*. Göttingen: Universitätsverlag. 131–148.
Goodbody, Axel. 2014. "Risk, Denial and Narrative Form in Climate Change Fiction: Barbara Kingsolver's *Flight Behavior* and Iljia Trojanow's *Melting Ice*". In: Sylvia Mayer and Alexa Weik von Mossener (eds.). *The Anticipation of Catastrophe. Environmental Risk in North American Literature and Culture*. Heidelberg: Winter. 39–58.
Goodbody, Axel and Adeline Johns-Putra. 2018. *Cli-Fi. A Companion*. Oxford: Peter Lang.
Goode, John. 1978. *George Gissing. Ideology and Fiction*. London: Vision.
Gordon, Colin. 1991. "Governmental Rationality: An Introduction". In: Graham Burchell, Colin Gordon and Peter Millers (eds.). *The Foucault Effect: Studies in Governmentality*. London: Harvester Wheatsheaf. 1–52.

Gose Jr., Elliott B. 1990. "Psychic Evolution: Darwinism and Initiation in *Tess of the d'Urbervilles*". In: Dale Kramer (ed.). *Critical Essays on Thomas Hardy: The Novels*. Boston, MA: G.K. Hall. 219–228.

Gottlieb, Evan. 2007. "'Fools of Prejudice': Smollett and the Novelization of National Identity". *Feeling British: Sympathy and National Identity in Scottish and English Writing, 1707–1832*. Lewisburg, PA: Bucknell University Press. 61–98.

Grabher, Gudrun M. and Sonja Bahn-Coblans (eds.). 1999. *The Self at Risk in English Literatures and Other Landscapes*. Honoring Brigitte Scheer-Schäzler on the Occasion of her 60th Birthday. (Das Risiko Selbst in der englischen Literatur und anderen Bereichen. Zu Ehren von Brigitte Scheer-Schäzler anlässlich ihres 60. Geburtstages). Innsbruck: Innsbrucker Beiträge zur Kulturwissenschaft.

Graham, Elaine. 2002. *Representations of the Post/human. Monsters, Aliens and Others in Popular Culture*. New Brunswick, NJ: Rutgers University Press.

Gravil, Richard. 2007. *Elizabeth Gaskell: Mary Barton*. Penrith: Humanities E-books.

Gray, Richard. 2011. *After the Fall. American Literature Since 9/11*. Oxford: Wiley-Blackwell.

Gregg, Stephen H. 1999. "Godly Manliness: Defoe's Good Men in Bad Times". In: Andrew P. Williams (ed.). *The Image of Manhood in Early Modern Literature: Viewing the Male*. Westport, CT: Greenwood. 141–159.

Gregg, Stephen H. 2009. "*Journal of the Plague Year*: Godly Manliness Under Stress". *Defoe's Writings and Manliness: Contrary Men*. Farnham, Surrey: Ashgate. 91–112.

Greenslade, William. 1989. "Women and the Disease of Civilization: George Gissing's *The Whirlpool*". *Victorian Studies* 32.4: 507–523.

Greenslade, William. 1994. *Degeneration, Culture and the Novel, 1880–1940*. Cambridge: Cambridge University Press.

Greenslade, William. 1997. "Introduction". In: William Greenslade (ed.). *George Gissing. The Whirlpool*. London: J.M. Dent. xvii–xxx.

Griffin, Gabriele. 2009. "Science and the Cultural Imaginary: The Case of Kazuo Ishiguro's *Never Let Me Go*". *Textual Practice* 23.4: 645–663.

Groes, Sebastian. 2013. "Ian McEwan and the Modernist Consciousness of the City in *Saturday*". In: Sebastian Groes (ed.). *Ian McEwan. Contemporary Perspectives*. 2nd ed. London: Bloomsbury. 99–114.

Grossman, Jonathan. 2002. *The Art of the Alibi. English Law Courts and the Novel*. Baltimore, MD: John Hopkins University Press.

Gruner, Elisabeth Rose. 1994. "The Bullfinch and the Brother: Marriage and Family in Frances Burney's *Camilla*". *The Journal of English and Germanic Philology* 93.1: 18–34.

Gussow, Adam. 2000. "Dreaming Holmberry-Lipped Tess: Aboriginal Reverie and Spectatorial Desire in Tess of the D'Urbervilles". *Studies in the Novel* 32.4: 442–463.

Hacking, Ian. 1975. *The Emergence of Probability: A Philosophical Study of Early Ideas about Probability, Induction and Statistical Inference*. Cambridge: Cambridge University Press.

Hacking, Ian. 1990. *The Taming of Chance*. Cambridge: Cambridge University Press.

Hacking, Ian. 2016. "Biopower and the Avalanche of Printed Numbers". In: Vernon W Cisney and Nicolae Morar (eds.). *Biopower: Foucault and Beyond*. Chicago and London: University of Chicago Press. 65–81.

Hadley, Elaine. 2005. "On a Darkling Plane: Victorian Liberalism and the Fantasy of Agency". *Victorian Studies*: 92–102.

Haggerty, George E. 1998. "Defects and Deformity in *Camilla*". *Unnatural Affections: Women and Fiction in the later 18th Century*. Bloomington, IN: Indiana University Press. 137–157.

Haines, Christian. 2012. "Life in Crisis: The Biopolitical Ambivalence of Joseph Conrad's *The Secret Agent*". *Criticism* 54.1: 85–115.

Haller, Stephen. 2000. "A Prudential Argument for Precaution under Uncertainty and High Risk". *Ethics and Environment* 5.2: 175–189.

Haltaufderheide, Joschka. 2015. *Zur Risikoethik. Analysen im Problemfeld zwischen Normativität und unsicherer Zukunft*. Würzburg: Königshausen and Neumann.

Hamilton, Ross. 2007. *Accident: A Philosophical and Literary History*. Chicago and London: University of Chicago Press.

Hammond, Brean and Shaun Regan. 2006. *Making the Novel: Fiction and Society in Britain, 1600–1789*. New York: Palgrave Macmillan.

Haney, William S. Haney. 2006. *Cyberculture, Cyborgs and Science Fiction: Consciousness and the Posthuman*. Amsterdam and New York: Rodopi.

Hannah-Moffat, Kelly and Pat O'Malley. 2007. "Gendered Risks: An Introduction". *Gendered Risks*. In: Kelly Hannah-Moffat and Pat O'Malley (eds.). Abingdon: Routledge-Cavendish. 1–29.

Hansen, Mark. 1997. "Not Thus, After All, Would Life be Given: Technesis, Technology and the Parody of Romantic Poetics in *Frankenstein*". *Studies in Romanticism* 36.4: 575–609.

Hanson, Gillian Mary. 1999. *Understanding Alan Sillitoe*. Columbia, SC: University of South Carolina Press.

Hanson, Clare. 2015. "The Maternal Body". In: David Hillman and Ulrika Maude (eds.). *The Cambridge Companion to the Body in Literature*. Cambridge: Cambridge University Press. 87–100.

Hansson, Sven Ove. 1989. "Dimensions of Risk". *Risk Analysis* 9: 107–112.

Hansson, Sven Ove. 1999. "A Philosophical Perspective on Risk". *Ambio* 28.6: 539–542.

Hansson, Sven Ove. 2011. "Risk". *In:* Edward N. Zalta (ed.). *The Stanford Encyclopaedia of Philosophy* (Fall 2011 ed.). <https://plato.stanford.edu/archives/fall2011/entries/risk/> [accessed 1 March 2019].

Hansson, Sven Ove. 2013. *Ethics of Risk. Ethical Analysis in an Uncertain World*. Basingstoke: Palgrave Macmillan.

Hardin, James (ed.). 1991. *Reflection and Action: Essays on the Bildungsroman*. Columbia, SC: University of South Carolina Press.

Harman, Claire. 2000. *Fanny Burney. A Biography*. London: Harper Collins.

Harrington, Ellen Burton. 1999. "That 'Blood Stained Inanity': Detection, Repression, and Conrad's *The Secret Agent*". *Conradiana* 31.2: 114–19.

Harrington, Ralph. 2005. "The Shadow of Stonehenge: Paganism, Fate and Redemption in Thomas Hardy's Tess of the D'Urbervilles". *artificialhorizon.org*. 1–11. [available at <https://studylib.net/doc/8349692/the-shadow-of-stonehenge–paganism–fate-and-redemption-in> accessed 1 March 2019].

Harris, Diane. 1998. "Eugenia's Escape: The Written Word in Frances Burney's *Camilla*". *Lumen: Selected Proceedings from the Canadian Society for Eighteenth-Century Studies/ Lumen: travaux choisis de la Société canadienne d'étude du dix-huitième siècle* 17: 151–164.

Harris, Jocelyn. 2007. *A Revolution Almost Beyond Expression: Jane Austen's Persuasion*. Newark, DE: University of Delaware Press.

Harrison, John M. 2005. "Clone Alone". *The Guardian* February 26. <https://www.theguardian.com/books/2005/feb/26/bookerprize2005.bookerprize> [accessed 1 March 2019].
Harvey, Geoffrey (ed.). 2001. *Thomas Hardy: Tess of the d'Urbervilles*. Basingstoke: Palgrave Macmillan.
Harvey, Geoffrey. 2003. *The Complete Critical Guide to Thomas Hardy*. London and New York: Routledge.
Hauskeller, Michael, Curtis D. Carbonell and Thomas D. Philbeck (eds.). 2015. *Palgrave Handbook of Posthumanism in Film and Television*. Basingstoke: Palgrave Macmillan.
Hawes, Clement. 1991. "Three Times Round the Globe: Gulliver and Colonial Discourse". *Cultural Critique* 18: 187–214.
Hawkins, Francis Bisset and Adolphe Quetelet. 1973. *Comparative Statistics in the 19th Century*. Introduction by Richard Wall. Farnborough: Gregg International.
Hay, Eloise Knapp. 1963. *The Political Novels of Joseph Conrad*. Chicago and London: University of Chicago Press.
Hay, John A. 1973. "Rhetoric and Historiography: Tristram Shandy's First Nine Kalendar Months". In: R. F. Brissenden (ed.). *Studies in the Eighteenth Century II: Papers Presented at the Second David Nichol Smith Memorial Seminar, Canberra 1970*. Toronto: University of Toronto Press. 73–91.
Hayles, N. Katherine. 1999. *How We Became Posthuman: Virtual Bodies in Cybernetics, Literature and Informatics*. Chicago and London: University of Chicago Press.
Haywood, Ian. 1997. *Working-Class Fiction from Chartism to Trainspotting*. Plymouth: Northcote House.
Head, Dominic. 2002. *The Cambridge Introduction to Modern British Fiction. 1950–2000*. Cambridge: Cambridge University Press.
Head, Dominic. 2007. *Ian McEwan*. Contemporary British Novelists Series. Manchester and New York: Manchester University Press.
Head, Dominic. 2008. *The State of the Novel. Britain and Beyond*. Chichester, and Malden, MA: Wiley-Blackwell.
Healy, Margaret. 2001. *Fictions of Disease in Early Modern England. Bodies, Plagues and Politics*. New York: Palgrave.
Heffernan, James A. W. 2005. "'Cruel Persuasion': Seduction, Temptation, and Agency in Hardy's *Tess*". *Thomas Hardy Yearbook* 35: 5–18.
Hegglund, Jon. 1997. "Defending the Realm: Domestic Space and Mass Cultural Contamination in *Howards End* and *An Englishman's Home*". *English Literature in Transition, 1880–1920* 40.4: 398–423.
Heilbron, J.L. 1990. "Introductory Essay". In: Tore Frängsmyr, J.L. Heilbron and Robin E. Rider (eds.). *The Quantifying Spirit in the 18th Century*. Berkeley and Los Angeles, CA: University of California Press. 1–25.
Heise, Ursula K. 2002a. "Risk and Narrative at Love Canal". In: Marion Gymnich, Vera Nünning and Ansgar Nünning (eds.). *Literature and Linguistics: Approaches, Models, and Applications. Essays in Honor of Jon Erickson*. Trier: Wissenschaftlicher Verlag. 77–99.
Heise, Ursula K. 2002b. "Toxins, Drugs, and Global Systems: Risk and Narrative in the Contemporary Novel". *American Literature* 74.4: 747–778.
Heise, Ursula K. 2002c. "Die Zeitlichkeit des Risikos im amerikanischen Roman der Postmoderne". In: Martin Middeke (ed.). *Zeit und Roman: Zeiterfahrung im historischen*

Wandel und ästhetischen Paradigmenwechsel vom achtzehnten Jahrhundert bis zur Postmoderne. Würzburg: Königshausen and Neumann. 373–394.
Heise, Ursula K. 2008. "Narrative in the World Risk Society". *Sense of Place and Sense of Planet: The Environmental Imagination of the Global*. Oxford: Oxford University Press. 119–159.
Heise, Ursula K. 2009. "Cultures of Risk and the Aesthetic of Uncertainty". In: Klaus Benesch and Meike Zwingenberger (eds.). *Scientific Cultures – Technological Challenges. A Transatlantic Perspective*. Heidelberg: Winter. 17–44.
Helfer Wajngot, Marion. 2012. "Victorian Fiction and the 'What if?': Theory, Heritage and Inheritance in *Daniel Deronda*". *Partial Answers: Journal of Literature and the History of Ideas*. 10.1: 29–47.
Hemlow, Joyce. 1958. *The History of Fanny Burney*. Oxford: Claredon.
Henderson, Andrea. 1997. "Commerce and Masochistic Desire in the 1790s: Frances Burney's Camilla". *Eighteenth-Century Studies* 31.1: 69–86.
Henningfeld, Ursula (ed.). 2014. *Poetiken des Terrors. Narrative des 11. September 2001 im interkulturellen Vergleich*. Heidelberg: Winter.
Henry, John. 1992. "Scientific Revolution in England". In: Roy Porter and Mikulas Teich (eds.). *The Scientific Revolution in National Context*. Cambridge: Cambridge University Press. 178–209.
Hensley, Nathan K. 2009. "Mister Trollope, Lady Credit, and *The Way We Live Now*". In: Margaret Markwick, Deborah Denenholz Morse and Regenia Gagnier (eds.). *The Politics of Gender in Anthony Trollope's Novels: New Readings for the Twenty-First Century*. Farnham: Ashgate. 147–160.
Henson, Eithne. 2011. *Landscape and Gender in the Novels of Charlotte Brontë, George Eliot, and Thomas Hardy: The Body of Nature*. Aldershot: Ashgate.
Hentzi, Gary. 1991. "Holes in the Heart: *Moll Flanders, Roxana*, and "Agreeable Crime". *boundary 2* 18.1: 174–200.
Hentzi, Gary. 1993a. "Sublime Moments and Social Authority in *Robinson Crusoe* and *A Journal of the Plague Year*". *Eighteenth-Century Studies* 26.3: 419–434.
Hentzi, Gary. 1993b. "An Itch of Gaming: The South Sea Bubble and the Novels of Daniel Defoe". *Eighteenth-Century Life* 17.1: 32–45.
Herbrechter, Stefan. 2013. *Posthumanism. A Critical Analysis*. London: Bloomsbury.
Heyman, Bob. 2012. "Risk and Culture". In: Jaan Valsiner (ed.). *The Oxford Handbook of Culture and Psychology*. Oxford: Oxford University Press. 602–624.
Higonnet, Margaret R. 1990. "Fictions of Feminine Voice: Antiphony and Silence in Hardy's *Tess of the D'Urbervilles*". In: Laura Claridge and Elizabeth Langland (eds.). *Out of Bounds: Male Writers and Gender(ed) Criticism*. Amherst, MA: University of Massachusetts Press. 197–218.
Hilton, Boyd. 2006. *A Mad, Bad, and Dangerous People? England 1783–1846*. Oxford: Clarendon.
Hillard, Molly Clarke. 2008. "'When Desert Armies Stand Ready to Fight': Re-reading McEwan's Saturday and Arnold's 'Dover Beach.'" *Partial Answers* 6.1: 181–206.
Hinde, Thomas. 1976. "Accident and Coincidence in *Tess of the d'Urbervilles*". In: Margaret Drabble (ed.). *The Genius of Thomas Hardy*. London: Weidenfeld and Nicholson. 74–79.
Hitchcock, Peter. 1989. *Working-class Fiction in Theory and Practice. A Reading of Alan Sillitoe*. Ann Arbor, MI, and London: UMI.

Hobbes, Thomas. (1651) 2003. *Leviathan*. With an Introduction by C.B. Macpherson (ed.). London: Penguin.
Hobsbaum, E.J. 1975. *The Age of Capital: 1848–1875*. New York: New York American Library.
Hodge, M.J.S. 1987. "Natural Selection as a Causal, Empirical, and Probabilistic Theory". In: Lorenz Krüger, Gerd Gigerenzer and Mary S. Morgan (eds.). *The Probabilistic Revolution. Vol II: Ideas in the Sciences*. Cambridge, MA: MIT Press. 233–270.
Hodges, W.H. 1964. "Introduction". In: W.H. Hodges (ed.). *Roderick Random*. London: Dent, Everyman's Library.
Hoggart, Richard. 1957. *The Uses of Literacy*. London: Chatto and Windus.
Holland, Jack. 2009. "From September 11th, 2001 to 9/11: From Void to Crisis". *International Political Sociology* 3.3: 275–92.
Hopkins, Robert. 1987. "Moral Luck and Judgment in Jane Austen's *Persuasion*". *Nineteenth-Century Literature* 42.2: 143–158.
Hoppit, Julian. 1986. "Financial Crises in Eighteenth-Century England". *The Economic History Review* 39.1: 39–58.
Hoppit, Julian. 1987. *Risk and Failure in English Business 1700–1800*. Cambridge: Cambridge University Press.
Hoppit, Julian. 1990. "Attitudes to Credit in Britain, 1680–1790". *The Historical Journal* 33.2: 305–322.
Hornback, Bert G. 1971. *The Metaphor of Chance: Vision and Technique in the Works of Thomas Hardy*. Athens, OH: Ohio University Press.
Hotz, Mary Elizabeth. 2000. "'Taught by Death What Life Should Be': Elizabeth Gaskell's Representation of Death in *North and South*". *Studies in the Novel* 32.2: 165–184.
Houen, Alex. 1998. "*The Secret Agent*: Anarchism and the Thermodynamics of Law". *ELH* 65: 99–106.
Houen, Alex. 2002. "Joseph Conrad: Entropolitics and the Sense of Terror". *Terrorism and Modern Literature, From Joseph Conrad to Ciaran Carson*. Oxford: Oxford University Press. 34–92.
Houen, Alex. 2004. "Novel Spaces and Taking Place(s) in the Wake of September 11". *Studies in the Novel* 36.3: 419–437.
Houser, Heather. 2010. "Comic Crisis". Rev. of Ian McEwan's *Solar*. *American Book Review* 32.1: 10.
Howes, Alan B. (ed.). 1974. *Sterne: The Critical Heritage*. London and Boston, MA: Routledge and Kegan Paul.
Hoydis, Julia. 2011. *Tackling the Morality of History. Ethics and Storytelling in the Works of Amitav Ghosh*. Heidelberg: Winter.
Hoydis, Julia. 2015. "Introduction". Special Issue "Focus on 21st Century Studies". Julia Hoydis (ed.). *Anglistik* 26.2: 5–13. <https://angl.winter-verlag.de/data/article/3231/pdf/91502002.pdf> [accessed 1 March 2019].
Huizinga, Johan. 1956. *Homo Ludens. Vom Ursprung der Kultur im Spiel*. Hamburg: Rowohlt.
Hulme, Mike. 2009. *Why We Disagree About Climate Change. Understanding Controversy, Inaction and Opportunity*. Cambridge: Cambridge University Press.
Hulme, Peter. 1992. "Robinson and Friday". *Colonial Encounters*. London and New York: Routledge. 175–222.
Hume, David. (1739–1740) 2003. *A Treatise of Human Nature*. Mineola, NY: Dover Philosophical Classics.

Hume, Robert D. 1982. "The Conclusion of Defoe's *Roxana:* Fiasco or Tour de Force?" In: Regina und Helmut Heidenreich (eds.). *Daniel Defoe: Schriften zum Erzählwerk.* Darmstadt: Wissenschaftliche Buchgesellschaft. 374–391.

Hunter, Alan. 1983. *Joseph Conrad and the Ethics of Darwinism.* London: Croom Helm.

Hunter, John Paul. 1989. "Clocks, Calendars, and Names: The Troubles of Tristram and the Aesthetics of Uncertainty". In: John Paul Hunter and Douglas J. Canfield (eds.). *Rhetorics of Order, Ordering Rhetorics in English Neoclassical Literature.* Newark, DE: University of Delaware Press. 173–198.

Hunter, John Paul. 1990a. *Before Novels. The Cultural Context of Eighteenth-Century English Fiction.* New York: W.W. Norton.

Hunter, John Paul. 1990b. "*Gulliver's Travels* and the Novel". In: Fredrick N. Smith (ed.). *The Genres of Gulliver's Travels.* London and Toronto: Associated University Press. 56–74.

Hunter, John Paul. 2003. "*Gulliver's Travels* and the Later Writings". In: Christopher Fox (ed.). *The Cambridge Companion to Jonathan Swift.* Cambridge: Cambridge University Press. 216–440.

Hurst, Matthias. 2001. *Im Spannungsfeld der Aufklärung: von Schillers Geisterseher zur TV-Serie The x-files: Rationalismus und Irrationalismus in Literatur, Film.* Heidelberg: Winter.

Impastato, David. 2009. "Secular Sabbath: Unbelief in Ian McEwan's Fiction". *Commonwealth Magazine* 136.18: 14–19.

Ingham, Patricia. 1993. "Fallen Woman as Sign, and Narrative Syntax in *Tess of the d'Urbervilles*". In: Peter Widdowson (ed.). *Tess of the D'Urbervilles: Thomas Hardy.* Houndsmills: Macmillan. 80–89.

Ingham, Patricia. 2000. *Invisible Writing and the Victorian Novel. Readings in Language and Ideology.* Manchester and New York: Manchester University Press.

Ingram, Allan. 2012. "Introduction". In: Allan Ingram (ed.). *Gulliver's Travels. Jonathan Swift.* Peterborough, Ontario: Broadview Press. 13–40.

Ingram, Allan. 2013. "Doctor at Sea: Gulliver and Medical Perception". In: Kirsten Juhas, Hermann J. Real and Sandra Simon (eds.). *Reading Swift: Papers from The Sixth Münster Symposium on Jonathan Swift.* München: Fink. 497–506.

Ingrassia, Catherine. 1998. *Authorship, Commerce and Gender in Eighteenth-Century England.* Cambridge: Cambridge University Press.

Ingrassia, Catherine. 2009. "Introduction". In: Paula R. Backscheider and Catherine Ingrassia (eds.). *A Companion to the Eighteenth-Century English Novel and Culture.* Oxford: Wiley-Blackwell. 1–17.

Inkster, Ian. 1983. "Introduction: Aspects of the History of Science and Science Culture in Britain, 1780–1850". In: Ian Inkster and Jack Morrell (eds.). *Metropolis and Providence: Science in British Culture, 1780–1850.* London: Hutchinson. 11–54.

Irr, Caren. 2015. "The Space of Genre in the New Green Novel". *Studia Neophilologica* 87: 82–96.

Jackson, Brian. (1968) 2002. *Working Class Community.* London: Routledge.

Jackson, Wallace. 1978. *The Probable and the Marvelous.* Athens, GA: University of Georgia Press.

Jacobs, Robert G. 1968. "Comrade Ossipon's Favorite Saint: Lombroso and Conrad". *Nineteenth-Century Literature* 23.1: 74–84.

Jaffe, Audrey. 2010. *The Affective Life of the Average Man: The Victorian Novel and the Stock-Market Graph*. Columbus, OH: Ohio State University Press.

James, Caryn. 2005. "Duplicates That Can Beat the Real Thing". *The New York Times* April 22. <https://www.nytimes.com/2005/04/22/movies/MoviesFeatures/duplicates-that-can-beat-the-real-thing.html> [accessed 1 March 2019].

James, Simon. 1997. "Negotiating 'The Whirlpool'". *The Gissing Journal* 33.2: 15–24.

Japp, Klaus P. and Isabel Kusche. 2008. "Systems Theory and Risk". In: Jens O. Zinn (ed.). *Social Theories of Risk and Uncertainty: An Introduction*. Oxford: Blackwell. 76–105.

Jennings, Bruce. 2010. "Biopower and the Liberationist Romance". *Hastings Center Report* 40.4: 16–20.

Johannisson, Karin. 1990. "Society in Numbers: The Debate over Quantification in 18th Century Political Economy". In: Tore Frängsmyr, J.L. Heilbron and Robin E. Rider (eds.). *The Quantifying Spirit in the 18th Century*. Berkeley and Los Angeles, CA: University of California Press. 343–362.

Johnson, Christopher D. 2011. "Rescuing Narcissa: Monstrous Vision, Imagination, and Redemption in *Roderick Random*". In: Christopher D. Johnson (ed.). *New Contexts for Eighteenth-Century Fiction. "Hearts Resolved and Hands Prepared": Essays in Honor of Jerry C. Beasley*. Newark, DE: University of Delaware Press. 201–218.

Johnson, Claudia L. 1995. *Equivocal Beings: Politics, Gender, and Sentimentality in the 1790s. Wollstonecraft, Radcliffe, Burney, Austen*. Chicago: University of Chicago Press.

Johns-Putra, Adeline. 2016. "Climate Change in Literature and Literary Studies: From Cli-fi, Climate Change Theatre and Ecopoetry to Ecocriticism and Climate Change Criticism". *WIREs Climate change* 7.2: 266–282. <https://doi.org/10.1002/wcc.385> [accessed 1 March 2919].

Jones, Darryl. 2002. *Horror. A Thematic History in Fiction and Film*. London: Arnold.

Jones, Darryl. 2004. *Jane Austen*. Houndmills: Palgrave Macmillan.

Jones, R.T. 2001. "Introduction". In: R.T. Jones (ed.). *Daniel Defoe. Moll Flanders*. Ware, Hertfordshire: Wordsworth Classics. v–xvi.

Jones, Richard J. 2011. *Tobias Smollett in the Enlightenment: Travels Through France, Italy, and Scotland*. Bucknell University Press.

Jonik, Michael. 2014. "'The Péripéties of the Contest': Risk, Love, and Anarchism in James's *The Princess Casamassima* and Conrad's *The Secret Agent*". *The English Academy Review* 31.2: 20–34.

Jordan, Julia. 2010. *Chance and the Modern British Novel. From Henry Green to Iris Murdoch*. London: Continuum.

Joseph, Gerhard and Herbert F. Tucker. 1999. "Passing On: Death". In: Herbert F. Tucker (ed.). *A New Companion to Victorian Literature and Culture*. Oxford: Wiley-Blackwell. 110–123.

Juengel, Scott J. 1995. "Writing Decomposition: Defoe and the Corpse". *Journal of Narrative Technique* 25.2: 139–153.

Jurta, Roxanne. 1999. "'Not-So-New' Sue: The Myth of *Jude the Obscure* as a New Woman Novel". *Journal of the Eighteen Nineties Society* 26: 13–21.

Kalliney, Peter. 2001. "Cities of Affluence: Masculinity, Class, and The Angry Young Men". *MFS Modern Fiction Studies* 47.1: 92–117.

Kalpakgian, Mitchell. 1981. *The Marvellous in Fielding's Novels*. Washington, D.C.: University Press of America.

Kahan, Dan M., Donald Braman, John Gastil, Paul Slovic and C.K. Mertz. 2007. "Culture and Identity-Protective Cognition: Explaining the White-Male Effect in Risk Perception". *Journal of Empirical Legal Studies* 4: 465–505.

Kane, Robert. 1999. "Responsibility, Luck, and Chance: Reflections on Free Will and Indeterminism". *Journal of Philosophy* 96: 217–40.

Kaplan, Carola M. and Anne B. Simpson. 1996. "Edwardians and Modernists: Literary History and the Problem of Evaluation". In: Carola M. Kaplan and Anne B. Simpson (eds.). *Seeing Double. Revisioning Edwardian and Modernist Literature.* Basingstoke: Macmillan. vii –xxi.

Karl, Frederick Robert. 1979. *Joseph Conrad. The Three Lives. A Biography.* London: Faber and Faber.

Karremann, Isabel. 2008. *Männlichkeit und Körper.* Sulzbach: Ulrike Helmer. 55–98.

Karremann, Isabel. 2011. "Found and Lost in Mediation. Manly Identity in Defoe's *A Journal of the Plague Year*". In: Isabel Karremann and Anja Müller (eds.). *Mediating Identities in Eighteenth-Century England.* Farnham, Surrey: Ashgate. 31–44.

Kasperson, Jeanne X., Roger E. Kasperson, Nick Pidgeon and Paul Slovic. 2003. "The Social Amplification of Risk: Assessing Fifteen Years of Research and Theory". In: Nick Pidgeon, Roger E. Kasperson and Paul Slovic (eds.). *The Social Amplification of Risk.* Cambridge: Cambridge University Press. 13–46.

Kasperson, Roger E., et al. 1988. "The Social Amplification of Risk: A Conceptual Framework". *Risk Analysis* 8 (April): 177–187.

Kaufmann, David. 1995. *The Business of Common Life. Novels and Classical Economics between Revolution and Reform.* Baltimore, MD: Johns Hopkins University Press.

Kavanagh, Thomas M. 1993. *Enlightenment and the Shadows of Chance: The Novel and the Culture of Gambling in Eighteenth Century France.* Baltimore and London: Johns Hopkins University Press.

Kaye, Richard. 2002. *The Flirt's Tragedy: Desire Without End in Victorian and Edwardian Fiction.* Charlottesville, VA, and London: University Press of Virginia.

Kelly, Lionel (ed.). 1995. *Tobias Smollett: The Critical Heritage.* London: Routledge.

Kelly, Patrick. 2003. "Swift on Money and Economics". In: Christopher Fox (ed.). *The Cambridge Companion to Jonathan Swift.* Cambridge: Cambridge University Press. 128–135.

Kelly, Veronica. 1993. "The Paranormal Roxana". In: Bill Readings and Bennet Schaber (eds.). *Postmodernism Across the Ages.* Syracuse, NY: Syracuse University Press. 138–149.

Kemp, Peter. 2005. "*Never Let Me Go* by Kazuo Ishiguro". *The Sunday Times* February 20. <https://www.thetimes.co.uk/article/never-let-me-go-by-kazuo-ishiguro-0v9mbp99jmh> [accessed 1 March 2019].

Kemp, Sandra, Charlotte Mitchel and David Trotter (eds.). 2002a. *The Oxford Companion to Edwardian Fiction.* Oxford: Oxford University Press.

Kemp, Sandra, Charlotte Mitchel and David Trotter. 2002b. "Introduction". In: Sandra Kemp, Charlotte Mitchel and David Trotter (eds.). *The Oxford Companion to Edwardian Fiction.* Oxford: Oxford University Press. ix–xviii.

Kendall, Maurice G. and R. L. Plackett (eds.). 1978. *Studies in the History of Statistics and Probability. Vol. II.* London and High Wycombe: Charles Griffin and Company.

Kendrick, Walter. 1991. *The Thrill of Fear. 250 Years of Scary Entertainment.* New York: Grove Weidenfeld.

Kenniston, Ann and Jeanne Folansbee Quinn (eds.). 2008. *Literature After 9/11*. New York: Routledge.
Kermode, Frank. (1967) 2000. *The Sense of an Ending*. Oxford: Oxford University Press.
Kerridge, Richard. 2010. "The Single Source". *Ecozon@* 1.1: 155–161.
 <http://ecozona.eu/article/view/334/310>. (accessed 1 March 2019).
Kestner, Joseph. 1994. "Revolutionizing Masculinities". *Persuasions* 16: 147–160.
 <http://www.jasna.org/assets/Persuasions/No.–16/kestner.pdf> (accessed 1 March 2019).
Keymer, Thomas. (2002) 2010. *Sterne, the Moderns and the Novel*. Oxford: Oxford Scholarship Online. DOI:10.1093/acprof:oso/9780199245925.001.0001 [accessed 1 March 2019].
Keynes, John Maynard. 1921. *A Treatise on Probability*. London: Macmillan.
Kibbie, Ann Louise. 1995. "Monstrous Generation: The Birth of Capital in Defoe's *Moll Flanders* and *Roxana*". *PMLA* 110.5: 1023–1034.
Kilgour, Maggie. 1995. *The Rise of the Gothic Novel*. London and New York: Routledge.
King, Edward. 1993. *Safety in Numbers. Safer Sex and Gay Men*. New York: Routledge.
Kirk, John. 2003. *Twentieth Century Writing and the British Working Class*. Cardiff: University of Wales.
Klein, Ernest. 1967. *A Comprehensive Etymological Dictionary of the English Language*. Vol. II. Amsterdam et al.: Elsevier Publishing.
Klein, Judy L. 1997. *Statistical Visions in Time. A History of Time Series Analysis, 1662–1938*. Cambridge: Cambridge University Press.
Klein, Jürgen. 1995. *Der gotische Roman und die Ästhetik des Bösen*. Darmstadt: Wissenschaftliche Buchgesellschaft.
Knight, Frank H. (1921) 2002. *Risk, Uncertainty and Profit*. Washington, D.C: Beard.
Knight, David. 2009. *The Making of Modern Science. Science, Technology, Medicine and Modernity: 1789–1914*. Cambridge: Polity Press.
Knights, David and Theodore Vurdubakis. 1993. "Calculations of Risk: Towards an Understanding of Insurance as a Moral and Political Technology". *Accounting Organizations and Society* 18 7/8: 729–764.
Knights, Mark. 2005. "History and Literature in the Age of Defoe and Swift". *History Compass* 3.1: 1–20.
Knox-Shaw, Peter. 2004. *Jane Austen and the Enlightenment*. Cambridge: Cambridge University Press.
Koch, Peter. 1995a. "*Der geistesgeschichtliche Hintergrund der Versicherungswirtschaft*". In: Heinz Leo Müller-Lutz und Karl-Heinz Rehnert (eds.). *Beiträge zur Geschichte des deutschen Versicherungswesens. Aus Anlaß des 60. Geburtstags von Peter Koch*. Karlsruhe: Verlag Versicherungswirtschaft e.V. 151–163.
Koch, Peter. 1995b. "'Opfere den bösen Dämonen!' Arthur Schopenhauers Vorstellung vom Versicherungsgedanken". In: Heinz Leo Müller-Lutz und Karl-Heinz Rehnert (eds.). *Beiträge zur Geschichte des deutschen Versicherungswesens. Aus Anlaß des 60. Geburtstags von Peter Koch*. Karlsruhe: Verlag Versicherungswirtschaft e.V. 261–267.
Koselleck, Reinhart. 1979. *Vergangene Zeiten: Zur Semantik geschichtlicher Zeiten*. Frankfurt a/Main: Suhrkamp.

Korshin, Paul J. 1979. "Probability and Character in the Eighteenth Century". In: Paula R. Backscheider (ed.). *Probability, Time, and Space in Eighteenth-Century Literature*. New York: AMS Press. 63–77.
Korte, Barbara and Frédéric Regard (eds.). 2014. *Narrating "Precariousness". Modes, Media, Ethics*. Heidelberg: Winter.
Kraft, Elizabeth. 2006. "Female Heroic Action in Frances Burney's *Camilla*". In: Bernhard Schweitzer (ed.). *Approaches to the Anglo and American Female Epic, 1621–1982*. Aldershot: Ashgate. 37–54.
Krüger, Lorenz, Lorraine Daston and Michael Heidelberger (eds.). 1987. *The Probabilistic Revolution Vol I: Ideas in History*. Cambridge, MA: MIT Press.
Krüger, Lorenz, Gerd Gigerenzer and Mary S. Morgan (eds.). 1987. *The Probabilistic Revolution. Vol II: Ideas in the Sciences*. Cambridge, MA: MIT Press.
Kunreuther, Howard and Paul Slovic. 1996. "Science, Values, and Risk". *The Annals of the American Academy of Political and Social Science* 545 (May): 116–125.
Lacquer, Walter. 2003. *No End to War. Terrorism in the Twenty-First Century*. New York and London: Continuum.
Lacy, Mark. 2002. "Deconstructing Risk Society". *Environmental Politics* 11.4: 42–62.
Landa, Louis A. 1963. "The *Shandean Homunculus:* The Background of Sterne's 'Little Gentleman'". In: Carrol Camden (ed.). *Restoration and Eighteenth-Century Literature: Essays in Honour of Alan Dugald McKillop*. Chicago: University of Chicago Press. 49–68.
Lane, Christopher. 1995. *The Ruling Passion. British Colonial Allegory and the Paradox of Homosexual Desire*. Durham and London: Duke University Press.
Landes, David S. 1969. *The Unbound Prometheus: Technological Change and Industrial Development in Western Europe from 1750 to the Present*. Cambridge: Cambridge University Press.
Lanham, Richard. 1973. *Tristram Shandy: Games of Pleasure*. Berkeley, CA: University of California Press.
Larson, Jil. 2001. *Ethics and Narrative in the English Novel, 1880–1914*. Cambridge: Cambridge University Press.
Lasdun, James. 2006. "Disparate Housewives. Review of *Arlington Park* by Rachel Cusk". *The Guardian* September 16. <https://www.theguardian.com/books/2006/sep/16/featuresreviews.guardianreview6> [accessed 1 March 2019].
Lash, Scott. 2000. "Risk Culture". In: Barbara Adam, Ulrich Beck and Joost Van Loon (eds.). *The Risk Society and Beyond: Critical Issues for Social Theory*. London: Sage. 47–62
Lash, Scott, Bronislaw Szerszynski and Brian Wynne (eds.). 1996. *Risk, Environment and Modernity: Towards a New Ecology*. London: Sage.
Latham, Monica. 2013. "Variations on *Mrs. Dalloway*: Rachel Cusk's *Arlington Park*". *Woolf Studies Annual* 19: 195–215.
Latham, Monica. 2015. *A Poetics of Postmodernism and Neomodernism: Rewriting Mrs Dalloway*. Basingstoke: Palgrave Macmillan.
Latour, Bruno. 1991. *We Have Never Been Modern*. Trans. Catherine Porter. Hemel Hempstead: Harvester Wheatsheaf.
Law, Jules. 1997. "A 'Passing Corporeal Blight': Political Bodies in *Tess of the d'Urbervilles*". *Victorian Studies* 40.2: 245–270.
Lawrence, D.H. 1988. *Study of Thomas Hardy and Other Essays*. Brice Steele (ed.). Cambridge: Cambridge University Press.

Leavis, Frank R. 1948. *The Great Tradition: George Eliot, Henry James, Joseph Conrad*. London: Chatto and Windus.

Leavy, Barbara Fass. 1992. *To Blight with Plague: Studies in a Literary Theme*. New York: New York University Press.

Letwin, Shirley Robin. 1965. *The Pursuit of Certainty: David Hume, Jeremy Bentham, John Stuart Mill, Beatrice Webb*. London: Cambridge University Press.

Leupolt, Cécile. 2010. "Resisting Media Manipulation: Ian McEwan's Politics of Scepticism in *Saturday*". *Anglistik* 21.2: 57–68.

Levenson, Michael. 2007. "The Fictional Realist: Novels of the 1930s". In: John Rodden (ed.). *The Cambridge Companion to George Orwell*. Cambridge: Cambridge University Press. 59–75

Levine, George. 1962. "Determinism and Responsibility in the Works of George Eliot". PMLA 77.3: 268–279.

Levine, George. 1988. *Darwin and the Novelists. Patterns of Science in Victorian Fiction*. Cambridge, MA: Harvard University Press.

Levine, George. 1997. "The Cartesian Hardy: I Think Therefore I'm Doomed". *Nineteenth-Century Studies* 11.1: 109–132.

Levine, George. 1979. "The Ambiguous Heritage of *Frankenstein*". In: George Levine and U.C. Knoepflmacher (eds.). *The Endurance of Frankenstein*. Berkeley, CA: University of California Press. 3–30.

Levine, George and U.C. Knoepflmacher (eds.). 1979. *The Endurance of Frankenstein*. Berkeley, CA: University of California Press.

Lewens, Tim (ed.). 2007. *Risk: Philosophical Perspectives*. London and New York: Routledge.

Lewis, Charles R. 2000. *A Coincidence of Wants: The Novel and Neoclassical Economics*. New York: Garland.

Lewis, Daniel. 2012. "'Say it, don't do it': Male Speech and Male Action in *Saturday Night and Sunday Morning*". *The Journal of Men's Studies* 20.2: 91–107.

Lewis, Jeremy. 2003. *Tobias Smollett*. London: Jonathan Cape.

Liggins, Emma. 2000. "The Medical Gaze and the Female Corpse: Looking at Bodies in Mary Shelley's *Frankenstein*". *Studies in the Novel* 32.2: 129–146.

Liggins, Emma. 2003. "Alan Hollinghurst and Metropolitan Gay Identity". In: Daniel Lea and Berthold Schoene (eds.). *Posting the Male Masculinities in Post-war and Contemporary British Literature*. Rodopi: Amsterdam. 159–170.

Lindner, Christoph. 2000. "Sexual Commerce in Trollope's Phineas Novels". *Philological Quart*erly 73.9: 343–363.

Lindner, Oliver. 2010. *Matters of Blood. Defoe and the Cultures of Violence*. Heidelberg: Winter.

Lippert-Rasmussen, Kasper, Mads Rosendahl Thomsen and Jacob Wamberg (eds.). 2012. *The Posthuman Condition: Ethics, Aesthetics and Politics of Biotechnological Challenges*. Aarhus: Aarhus University Press.

Lochner, Liani. 2011. "'This is What We're Supposed to be Doing, Isn't It?': Scientific Discourse in Kazuo Ishiguro's *Never Let Me Go*". In: Sebastian Groes and Barry Lewis (eds.). *Kazuo Ishiguro. New Critical Visions of the Novels*. Basingstoke: Palgrave Macmillan. 225–235.

Lock, Frederic P. 1980. *The Politics of Gulliver's Travels*. Oxford: Claredon.

Locke, Jennifer. 2013. "Dangerous Fortune-Telling in Frances Burney's *Camilla*". *Eighteenth-Century Fiction* 25.4: 701–720.
Locke, John. (1689) 2008. *An Essay Concerning Human Understanding*. Oxford: Oxford University Press.
Löfstedt, Ragnar and Lynn Frewer (eds.). 1998. *The Earthscan Reader in Risk and Modern Society*. London: Earthscan.
Loewenstein, George F., Elke U. Weber, Christopher K. Hsee and Ned Welch. 2001. "Risk as Feelings". *Psychological Bulletin* 127.2: 267–286.
Lovecraft, Howard Phillips. 1973. *Supernatural Horror in Literature*. With a New Introduction by E.F. Bleiler. Mineola, NY: Dover Publications.
Lovesey, Oliver. 2003. "Reconstructing *Tess*". *SEL: Studies in English Literature, 1500–1900* 43.4: 913–938.
Lovett, Denise. 2014. "The Socially-Embedded Market and the Future of English Capitalism in Anthony Trollope's *The Way We Live Now*". *Victorian Literature and Culture* 42: 691–707.
Lowe, Peter. 2009. "Englishness in a Time of Crisis: George Orwell, John Betjeman, and the Second World War". *The Cambridge Quarterly*: 243–263.
Lütticken, Sven. 2006. "Suspense and Surprise". *New Left Review* 40: 95–109.
Luhmann, Niklas. 1993. *Risk: A Sociological Theory*. Trans. Rhodes Barrett. New York: de Gruyter.
Lukács, George. 1971. *The Theory of the Novel: A Historico-Philosophical Essay on the Great Epic Literature*. London: Merlin Press.
Lucas, John. 1977. *The Literature of Change. Studies in the Nineteenth-Century Provincial Novel*. Sussex: Harvester Press.
Lupton, Deborah. 1999a. *Risk*. London: Routledge.
Lupton, Deborah. 1999b. "Introduction". In: Deborah Lupton (ed.). *Risk and Sociocultural Theory: New Directions and Perspectives*. Cambridge: Cambridge University Press. 1–11.
Lupton, Deborah and John Tulloch. 2002. "Life would be pretty dull without Risk: Voluntary Risk-taking and its Pleasures". *Health, Risk & Society* 4: 113–124.
Lupton, Christina. 2003. "*Tristram Shandy*, David Hume, and Epistemological Fiction". *Philosophy and Literature* 27.1: 98–115.
Lusty, Heather. 2007. "Gambling with Virtue: Female Gaming in the Novels of Frances Burney". *The Burney Journal* 7: 135–158.
Lynch, Deidre Shauna. 1998. *The Economy of Character. Novels, Market Culture, and the Business of Inner Meaning*. Chicago and London: University of Chicago Press.
Lyng, Stephen. 1990. "Edgework: A Social Psychological Analysis of Voluntary Risk Taking". *American Journal of Sociology* 95.4: 851–886.
Lyng, Stephen and Rick Matthews. 2007. "Risk, Edgework, and Masculinities". In: Kelly Hannah-Moffat and Pat O'Malley (eds.). *Gendered Risks*. Abingdon: Routledge-Cavendish. 75–98.
MacAndrew, Craig and Robert B. Edgerton. 1970. *Drunken Comportment. A Social Explanation*. London: Nelson.
MacDuffie, Allen. 2009. "Joseph Conrad's Geographies of Energy". *EHL* 76 (Spring): 75–98.
MacLean, Douglas. 1985. "Risk and Consent: Philosophical Issues for Centralised Decisions". In: Douglas MacLean (ed.). *Values at Risk*. Totowa, NJ: Rowman and Allanheld. 17–30.
MacLeod, Lewis. 2012. "'Various pubs gave signs of life': Of Drink and Time in Alan Sillitoe's *Saturday Night and Sunday Morning*". *Yearbook of English Studies* 42: 113–131.

Macpherson, Sandra. 2010. *Harm's Way: Tragic Responsibility and the Novel Form*. Baltimore, MD: Johns Hopkins University Press.

Mäkikalli, Aino. 2007. *From Eternity to Time. Conceptions of Time in Daniel Defoe's Novels*. Bern: Peter Lang.

Mageean, Michael. 1996. "*The Secret Agent's* (T)extimacies: A Traumatic Reading Beyond Rhetoric". In: Carola M. Kaplan and Anne B. Simpson (eds.). *Seeing Double. Revisioning Edwardian and Modernist Literature*. Basingstoke: Macmillan. 235–258.

Mallios, Peter Lancelot. 2005. "Reading *The Secret Agent* Now: The Press, the Police, the Premonition of Simulation". In: Carola M. Kaplan, Peter Lancelot Mallios and Andrea White (eds.). *Conrad in the Twenty-First Century: Contemporary Approaches and Perspectives*. New York: Routledge. 155–175.

Malthus, Robert. 1804. "Malthus Essay on the Principle of Population". *The Imperial Review: Or, London and Dublin Literary Journal Vol. 1* (January–April): 111–132.

Maltz, Diana. 2013. "The Solipsistic Heroine in 1897: George Gissing's *The Whirlpool* and May Sinclair's *Audrey Craven*". In: Christine Huguet and Simon J. James (eds.). *George Gissing and the Woman Question: Convention and Dissent*. Farnham: Ashgate. 169–184.

Mann, Nancy. D. 1975. "Intelligence and Self-Awareness in *North and South*: A Matter of Sex and Class". *Rocky Mountain Review of Language and Literature* 29.1: 24–38.

Marcus, Amit. 2012. "The Ethics of Human Cloning in Narrative Fiction". *Comparative Literary Studies* 49.3: 405–433.

Marcus, Laura. 2013. "Ian McEwan's Modernist Time: *Atonement* and *Saturday*". *Ian McEwan. Contemporary Perspectives*. London: Bloomsbury, 2nd ed. 83–98.

Marroni, Francesco. 2010. *Victorian Disharmonies: A Reconsideration of Nineteenth-century English Fiction*. Rome: John Cabot University Press.

Martin, John. 2006. *Beyond Belief. The Real Life of Daniel Defoe*. Pembrock Dock: Accent Press.

Martin, Regina. 2013. "Finance Capitalism and the Creeping London of *Howards End* and *Tono-Bungay*". *Criticism* 55.3: 447–469.

Martini, Fritz. 1991. "Bildungsroman: Term and Theory". In: James Hardin (ed.). *Reflection and Action: Essays on the Bildungsroman*. Columbia, SC: University of South Carolina Press.

Marsh, Nicky. 2007. *Money, Speculation, and Finance in Contemporary British Fiction*. London Continuum.

Marsh, Nicky. 2011. "The Corporation of Terror: Risk and the Fictions of the 'Financial War'". In: Paul Crosthwaite (ed.). *Criticism, Crisis, and Contemporary Narrative: Textual Horizons in an Age of Global Risk*. New York: Routledge. 145–160.

Marshall, Tim. 1995. *Murdering to Dissect: Graverobbing, Frankenstein, and the Anatomy Literature*. Manchester: Manchester University Press.

Marzec, Robert P. 2015. "Climate Change and the Evolution of the 9/11 Security State: The Fantasy of Adaptation and Ian McEwan's *Solar*". In: John N. Duvall and Robert P. Marzec (eds.). *Narrating 9/11: Fantasies of State, Security, and Terrorism*. Baltimore, MD: Johns Hopkins University Press. 70–97.

Masterman, Charles Frederick Gurney. 1905. *In Peril of Change: Essays Written in Times of Tranquillity*. London: T. Fisher Unwin.

Masterman, Charles Frederick Gurney. (1902) 1980. *From the Abyss: Of Its Inhabitants, by One of Them*. Reprinted from the ed. by R. Brimley Johnson, London. New York: Garland.

Masterman, Charles Frederick Gurney. (1909) 2012. *The Condition of England*. London: Methuen. Classic Reprint Series, Forgotten Books.

Mathias, Peter (ed.). 1972. *Science and Society, 1600–1900*. Cambridge: Cambridge University Press.

Matus, Jill. 2009. *Shock, Memory and the Unconscious in Victorian Fiction*. Cambridge: Cambridge University Press.

Maudsley, Henry. 1873. *Body and Mind. An Inquiry into their Connection and Mutual Influence, Specially in Reference to Mental Disorders*. London: Macmillan.

Maudsley, Henry. 1874. *Responsibility in Mental Disease*, London: Henry S. King.

Maudsley, Henry. 1879. *The Pathology of the Mind*. London: Macmillan.

Mayer, Sylvia. 2014. "Explorations of the Controversially Real: Risk, the Climate Change Novel, and the Narrative of Anticipation". In: Sylvia Mayer and Alexa Weik von Mossner (eds.). *The Anticipation of Catastrophe. Environmental Risk in North American Literature and Culture*. Heidelberg: Winter. 21–37.

Mayer, Sylvia. 2016. "Science in the World Risk Society: Risk, the Novel, and Global Climate Change". *Zeitschrift für Anglistik und Amerikanistik* 64.2: 207–221.

Mayer, Sylvia and Alexa Weik von Mossner (eds.). (2014). *The Anticipation of Catastrophe. Environmental Risk in North American Literature and Culture*. Heidelberg: Winter.

Mayer, Robert. 1990. "The Reception of *A Journal of the Plague Year* and the Nexus of Fiction and History in the Novel". *ELH* 57.3: 529–555.

Mayer, Robert. 1997. *History and the Early English Novel. Matters of Fact From Bacon to Defoe*. Cambridge: Cambridge University Press, 1997.

Mazella, David. 1999. "'Be wary, sir, when you imitate him': The Perils of Didacticism in *Tristram Shandy*". *Studies in the Novel* 31.2: 152–177.

McAlary, Katy. 2012. *Extremely Visual & Incredibly Communal: Trauma, Multimodality, and 9/11 Literature*. Saarbrücken: LAP Lambert Academic Publishing.

McCobb, E.A. 1985. "*Daniel Deronda* as Will and Representation". *The Modern Language Review* 80.3: 533–549.

McCormack, Kathleen. 2015. "Yachting with Grandcourt: Gwendolen's Mutiny in *Daniel Deronda*". *Victorian Literature and Culture* 43: 83–95.

McDonald, Keith. 2007. "'Days of Past Futures: Kazuo Ishiguro's *Never Let Me Go* as 'Speculative Memoir'". *Biography* 30.1: 74–83.

McDowell, Paula. 2006. "Defoe and the Contagion of the Oral: Modeling Media Shift in *A Journal of the Plague Year*". *PMLA* 121.1: 87–106

McGann, Tara. 2007. "Literary Realism in the Wake of the Business Cycle Theory: *The Way We Live Now*". In: Francis O'Gorman (ed.). *Victorian Literature and Finance*. Oxford: Oxford University Press. 133–156.

McGurl, Mark. 2010. "Ordinary Doom: Literary Studies in the Waste Land of the Present". *New Literary History* 41.2: 329–349.

McKeon, Michael. 1987. *The Origins of the English Novel 1600–1740*. Baltimore, MD: Johns Hopkins University Press.

McLaughlin Mitchell, Brooke. 2010. "Silence, and the Fractured Self: Hardy's *Tess of the d'Urbervilles*". In: Albert D. Pionke and Denise Tischler Millstein (eds.). *Victorian Secrecy: Economies of Knowledge and Concealment*. Farnham et al: Ashgate. 193–204.

McMaster, Juliet. 1989. "Walter Shandy, Sterne and Gender: A Feminist Foray". *English Studies in Canada* 15.4: 441–458.

McNeil, David. 1990. *The Grotesque Depiction of War and the Military in Eighteenth-Century English Fiction*. London and Toronto: Associated University Presses.

McWhir, Ann. 1989. "The Gothic Transgression of Disbelief: Walpole, Radcliffe and Lewis". In: Kenneth Wayne Graham (ed.). *Gothic Fictions: Prohibition – Transgression*. New York: AMS Press. 29–47.

Mechie, Calum. 2015. "Funny Old Fatty Bowling: *Coming Up for Air* and George Orwell's Comedic Common Man". In: Anthony Patterson and Yoonjoung Choi (eds.). *We Speak a Different Tongue: Maverick Voices and Modernity 1890–1939*. Newcastle-upon-Tyne: Cambridge Scholars. 185–199.

Medalie, David. 1999. "Only-as-the-event-decides': Contingency in *Persuasion*". *Essays in Criticism* 49.2: 152–169.

Medalie, David. 2002. *E.M. Forster's Modernism*. Basingstoke: Palgrave.

Medley, Mark. 2010. "Ian McEwan: Sometime Skeptic". *National Post* April 16. <https://nationalpost.com/news/ian-mcewan-sometime-skeptic/wcm/3f912c44-4e47-4dcd-99d4-e61f2cbaedbd> [accessed 1 March 2019].

Meeker, Joseph. 1997. *The Comedy of Survival: Literary Ecology and a Play Ethic*. Tuscon, AZ: University of Arizona Press.

Mehnert, Antonia. 2014. "*Things We Didn't See Coming* – Riskscapes in Climate Change Fiction". In: Sylvia Mayer and Alexa Weik von Mossner (eds.). *The Anticipation of Catastrophe. Environmental Risk in North American Literature and Culture*. Heidelberg: Winter. 59–78.

Melchiori, Barbara Arnett. 1985. *Terrorism in the Late Victorian Novel*. Dover, NH: Croom Helm.

Mellor, Anne K. 1995. "A Feminist Critique of Science". In: Fred Botting (ed.). *Frankenstein: Mary Shelley. Contemporary Critical Essays*. Basingstoke: Macmillan. 107–139.

Mellor, Anne K. 2002. *Mothers of the Nation: Women's Political Writing in England, 1780–1830*. Bloomington, IN: Indiana University Press.

Menand, Louis. 2005. "Something About Kathy. Ishiguro's Quasi-science-fiction novel". *The New Yorker* March 28. <https://www.newyorker.com/magazine/2005/03/28/something-about-kathy> [accessed 1 March 2019].

Meyer Spacks, Patricia. 1976. *Imagining a Self: Autobiography and Novel in Eighteenth-Century England*. Cambridge, MA: Harvard University Press.

Meyer Spacks, Patricia. 2006. *Novel Beginnings: Experiments in Eighteenth-Century English Fiction*. New Haven, CT, and London: Yale University Press.

Meyers, Jeffery. 1975. "Orwell's Apocalypse: *Coming Up for Air*". *Modern Fiction Studies* 21.1: 69–80.

Meyers, Jeffery. 1987. "Orwell's Apocalypse: *Coming Up for Air*". In: Harold Bloom (ed.). *George Orwell*. New York and Philadelphia: Chelsea House. 85–96.

Michie, Elsie B. 2001. "Buying Brains: Trollope, Oliphant, and Vulgar Victorian Commerce". *Victorian Studies* 44.1: 77–97.

Michie, Elsie B. 2011. *The Vulgar Question of Money. Heiresses, Materialism, and the Novel of Manners from Jane Austen to Henry James*. Baltimore, MD: Johns Hopkins University Press.

Miers, David. 1989. "A Social and Legal History of Gaming from the Restoration to the Gaming Act of 1845". In: Thomas Watkin (ed.). *Legal Record and Historical Reality:*

Proceedings of the Eighth British Legal History Conference. London: Hambledon Press. 107–120.
Mieth, Dietmar. 2015. "Narrative Ethik am Beispiel des Romans *Never Let Me Go* von Kazuo Ishiguro und weitere Überlegungen". In: Monika Fludernik, Nicole Falkenhayner and Julia Steiner (eds.). *Faktuales und fiktionales Erzählen: Interdisziplinäre Perspektiven*. Würzburg: Ergon. 219–240.
Miles, Robert. 1991. "The Gothic Aesthetic: The Gothic as Discourse". *The Eighteenth Century: Theory and Interpretation* 32.1: 39–57.
Miller, Andrew H. 1994. "Subjective Ltd: The Discourse of Liability in the Joint Stock Companies Act of 1856 and Gaskell's *Cranford*". *ELH* 61.1: 139–157.
Mill, John Stuart. (1867) 2008. *Dissertations and Discussions Vol I*. New York: Cosimo.
Mill, John Stuart. (1845) 1967. "The Claims of Labour". In: John M. Robson (ed.). *The Collected Works of J. S. Mill. Vol. IV*. Toronto: University of Toronto Press. 363–389.
Mill, John Stuart. 1946. "Of Individuality". Mill's *On Liberty, and Considerations on Representative Government*. With an Introduction by R.B. McCallum (ed.). Oxford: Basil Blackwell. 49–66.
Minogue, Sally and Andrew Palmer. 2002. "Helter skelter, topsy-turvy and 'loonycolour': Carnivalesque Realism in *Saturday Night and Sunday Morning*". *English* 51.200: 127–143.
Mizruchi, Susan L. 2010. "Risk Theory and the Contemporary American Novel". *American Literary History* 22.1: 109–135.
Moglen, Helen. 2001. *The Trauma of Gender: A Feminist Theory of the English Novel*. Berkeley, CA: University of California Press.
Molesworth, Jesse. 2010. *Chance and the Eighteenth-Century Novel: Realism, Probability Magic*. Cambridge: Cambridge University Press.
Monk, Leland. 1993. *Standard Deviations: Chance and the Modern British Novel*. Stanford, CA: Stanford University Press.
Moody, Jane. 2007. "The Drama of Capital: Risk, Belief, and Liability on the Victorian Stage". In: Francis O'Gorman (ed.). *Victorian Literature and Finance*. Oxford: Oxford University Press. 91–109.
Moore, Wendy. 2011. "Medical Classics: *The Adventures of Roderick Random*". *BMJ: British Medical Journal* 343 Issue 7823: 591.
Moretti, Frank. 2005. "Dialectic of Fear". *Signs Taken for Wonders: On the Sociology of Literary Forms*. London: Verso. 83–108.
Morgan, Rosemarie. 1988. *Women and Sexuality in the Novels of Thomas Hardy*. London and New York: Routledge.
Morgan, Rosemarie. 1989. "Passive Victim? *Tess of the D'Urbervilles*". *Thomas Hardy Journal* 5.1: 31–54.
Morgenstern, Karl von. 1820. "Über das Wesen des Bildungsromans". *Inländisches Museum* 1: 46–61.
Morrell, Roy. 1965. *Thomas Hardy: The Will and the Way*. Kuala Lumpur: University of Malaysia Press.
Morris, David B. 1985. "Gothic Sublimity". *New Literary History* 16.2: 299–319.
Morrison, Jago. 2014. "The Turn to Precarity in Twenty-First Century Fiction". *American, British and Canadian Studies Journal* 21.1: 10–29.

Mort, Frank. 1996. *Cultures of Consumption. Masculinities and Social Space in Late Twentieth-Century Britain*. London and New York: Routledge.

Morton, Stephen and Stephen Bygrave. 2008. *Foucault in an Age of Terror. Essays on Biopolitics and the Defence of Society*. Houndmills, Basingstoke: Palgrave Macmillan.

Morton, Timothy. 2002. *A Routledge Sourcebook on Mary Shelley's Frankenstein*. London: Routledge.

Moseley, William W. 1997. "The Vigilant Society: *The Secret Agent* and Victorian Panopticism". *Conradiana* 29.1: 59–78.

Motooka, Wendy. 1998. *The Age of Reasons: Quixotism, Sentimentalism and Political Economy in Eighteenth Century Britain*. London: Routledge.

Müller-Lutz, Heinz Leo und Karl-Heinz Rehnert. 1995. *Beiträge zur Geschichte des deutschen Versicherungswesens. Aus Anlaß des 60. Geburtstags von Peter Koch*. Karlsruhe: Verlag Versicherungswirtschaft e.V.

Münkler, Herfried. 2010. "Strategien der Sicherung: Welten der Sicherheit und Kulturen des Risikos. Theoretische Perspektiven". In: Herfried Münkler, Matthias Bohlender Sabine Meurer (eds.). *Sicherheit und Risiko: Über den Umgang mit Gefahr im 21. Jahrhundert*. Bielefeld: transcript. 11–34.

Mullan, John. 2010. "Afterword: On First Reading *Never Let me Go*". In: Sean Matthews and Sebastian Groes (eds.). *Kazuo Ishiguro*. London: Continuum. 104–113.

Mullan, John. 2012. *What Matters in Jane Austen?* London: Bloomsbury.

Mulry, David. 2000. "Popular Accounts of the Greenwich Bombing and Conrad's *The Secret Agent*". *Rocky Mountain Review of Language and Literature* 54.2: 43–64.

Munt, Sally (ed.). 2000. "Introduction". *Cultural Studies and the Working Class: Subject to Change*. London and New York: Cassell. 1–16.

Murphy, J. Stephen. 2004. "Past Irony: Trauma and the Historical Turn in *Fragments* and *The Swimming-Pool Library*". *Literary & History* 13.1: 58–75.

Myers, William. 1971. "George Eliot: Politics and Personality". In: John Lucas (ed.). *Literature and Politics in the Nineteenth Century*. London: Methuen. 105–130.

Mythen, Gabe and Sandra Walklate. 2006. "Introduction: Thinking Beyond the Risk Society". In: Gabe Mythen and Sandra Walklate (eds.). *Beyond the Risk Society. Critical Reflections on Risk and Human Security*. Maidenhead: Open University Press. 1–7.

Mythen, Gabe and Sandra Walklate. 2008. "Terrorism, Risk and International Security: The Perils of Asking 'What If?'" *Security Dialogue* 39.2–3: 221–242. <https://doi.org/10.1177/0967010608088776> [accessed 1 March 2019].

Nardella, Anna Ryan. 1973. "The Existential Dilemmas of Alan Sillitoe's Working-Class Heroes". *Studies in the Novel* 5.4: 469–482.

Nayar, Pramod K. 2014a. "The Fiction of Bioethics: Posthumanism in Kazuo Ishiguro's *Never Let Me Go*". *Notes on Contemporary Literature* 44.3: 9–12.

Nayar, Pramod K. 2014b. *Posthumanism*. Cambridge: Polity Press.

Nechtman, Tillman W. 2010. "Introduction: An Imperial Footprint". *Nabobs: Empire and Identity in Eighteenth-Century Britain*. Cambridge: Cambridge University Press. 1–21.

Nerlich, Brigitte, David D. Clarke and Robert Dingwall. 2001. "Fictions, Fantasies, and Fears: The Literary Foundations of the Cloning Debate". *Journal of Literary Studies* 30: 37–52.

Nerlich, Michael. 1997. *Abenteuer oder das verlorene Selbstverständnis der Moderne. Von der Unaufhebbarkeit experimentalen Handelns*. München: Gerling Akademie.

New, Melvyn. 1976. "'The Grease of God': The Form of Eighteenth-Century English Fiction". *PMLA* 91.2: 235–244.
New, Peter. 1985. "Chance, Providence and Destiny in George Eliot's Fiction". *English. The Journal of the English Association* 34.150: 191–208.
Newsom, Robert. 1988. *A Likely Story: Probability and Play in Fiction*. New Brunswick and London: Rutgers University Press.
Nicholson, Colin. 1994. "'Some very bad effect': The Strange Case of *Gulliver's Travels*". *Writing and the Rise of Finance: Capital Satires of the Early Eighteenth Century*. Cambridge: Cambridge University Press. 91–122.
Nicolson, Marjorie and Nora M. Mohler. 1937. "The Scientific Background of Swift's 'Voyage to Laputa'". *Annals of Science* 2: 299–334.
Nicklas, Pascal. 2010. "The Media Persona of Ian McEwan and the Mediation of the Media in *Solar*". *Anglistik* 21.2: 93–103.
Nordau, Max. 1895. *Degeneration*. New York: Appleton.
Norgaard, Kari Marie. 2011. *Living in Denial. Climate Change, Emotions and Everyday Life*. Cambridge, MA: MIT Press.
Norton, Brian Michael. 2006. "The Moral in Phutatorius's Breeches: *Tristram Shandy* and the Limits of Stoic Ethics". *Eighteenth-Century Fiction* 18.4: 405–423.
Novak, Maximilian E. 1966. "Crime and Punishment in Defoe's *Roxana*". *Journal of English and Germanic Philology* 65: 445–465.
Novak, Maximilian E. 1976. *Economics and the Fiction of Daniel Defoe*. New York: Russell and Russell.
Novak, Maximilian E. 1977. "Defoe and the Disordered City". *PMLA* 92.2: 241–252.
Novak, Maximilian E. 1990. "*Gulliver's Travels* and the Picaresque Voyage: Some Reflections on the Hazards of Genre Criticism". In: Fredrick N. Smith (ed.). *The Genres of Gulliver's Travels*. London and Toronto: Associated University Press. 23–38.
Novak, Maximilian E. 2001. *Daniel Defoe. Master of Fictions. His Life and Ideas*. Oxford: Oxford University Press.
Nowell-Smith, Simon (ed.). 1965. *Edwardian England 1901–1914*. London: Oxford University Press.
Nowotny, Helge. 2016. *The Cunning of Uncertainty*. Cambridge: Polity.
Nunokawa, Jeff. 1994. *The Afterlife of Property: Domestic Security and the Victorian Novel*. Princeton, NJ: Princeton University Press.
Nunokawa, Jeff. 1992. "*Tess*, Tourism, and the Spectacle of the Woman". In: Linda M. Shires (ed.). *Rewriting the Victorians: Theory, History and the Politics of Gender*. New York: Routledge. 70–86.
Nussbaum, Felicity. 2003. "Scarred Women: Frances Burney and Smallpox". *The Limits of the Human: Fictions of Anomaly, Race and Gender in the Long Eighteenth Century*. Cambridge: Cambridge University Press. 109–132.
O'Brien, John F. 1996. "The Character of Credit: Defoe's 'Lady Credit,' 'The Fortunate Mistress,' and the Resources of Inconsistency in Early Eighteenth-Century Britain". *ELH* 63.3: 603–631.
O'Brien, John F. 2011. "Insurance, Risk and the Limits of Sentimental Representation". *Journal of Cultural Economy* 4.3: 285–299.
Ochsner, Andrea. 2011. "Opportunism versus Defeatism in *Room at the Top* and *Saturday Night and Sunday Morning*: A Literary Analysis from a Cultural Studies Perspective". In:

Gabriele Linke (ed.). *Teaching Cultural Studies. Methods–Matters–Models*. Heidelberg: Winter. 175–198.

O'Donghaile, Deaglan. 2010. *Blasted Literature: Victorian Political Fiction and the Shock of Modernism*. Edinburgh: Edinburgh University Press.

O'Farrell, Mary Ann. 1997. "Gaskell's Blunders: *North and South*". *Telling Complexions: The Nineteenth Century English Novel and the Blush*. Durham: Dukes University Press. 58–81.

O'Flinn, Paul. 1995. "Production and Reproduction: The Case of *Frankenstein*". In: Fred Botting (ed.). *Frankenstein: Mary Shelley. Contemporary Critical Essays*. Basingstoke: Macmillan. 21–47.

O'Gorman, Francis. 2002. "Social Problem Fiction: Historicism and Feminism". *The Victorian Novel: A Guide to Criticism*. Oxford: Blackwell. 149–195.

O'Gorman, Francis (ed.). 2007. *Victorian Literature and Finance*. Oxford: Oxford University Press.

O'Hanlon, Redmond. 1984. *Joseph Conrad and Charles Darwin*. Edinburgh: Salamander Press.

Oliver, Hermia. 1983. *The International Anarchist Movement in Late Victorian London*. London: Croom Helm.

O'Malley, Pat. 1996. "Risk and Responsibility". In: Andrew Barry, T. Osborne and N. Rose (eds.). *Foucault and Political Reason: Liberalism, Neo-Liberalism and Rationalities of Government*. London: University of London Press. 189–207.

Oppenheim, Janet. 1991. *'Shattered Nerves': Doctors, Patients and Depression in Victorian England*. Oxford: Oxford University Press.

Outka, Elizabeth. 2003. "Buying Time: *Howards End* and Commodified Nostalgia". *NOVEL: A Forum on Fiction*. 36.3: 330–350.

Palmer, Christina G.S. 2003. "Risk Perception: Another Look at the White Male Effect". *Health, Risk & Society* 5.1: 71.

Parey, Armelle. 2013. "Space Matters in Rachel Cusk's *Arlington Park*." *E-rea* 10.2. <https://journals.openedition.org/erea/3192> [accessed 1 March 2019].

Parker, Fred. 2010. Scepticism and Literature: An Essay on Pope, Hume, Sterne, and Johnson. Oxford Scholarship Online. DOI:10.1093/acprof:oso/9780199253180.001.0001 [accessed 1 March 2019].

Parker, Jo Alyson. 1997. "Spiralling Down the Gutter of Time: *Tristram Shandy* and the Strange Attractor of Death". *Weber Studies* 14: 102–114.

Parker, Lynn. 1992. "'Pure Woman' and Tragic Heroine? Conflicting Myths in Hardy's *Tess of the D'Urbervilles*". *Studies in the Novel* 24.3: 273–281.

Parnell, J. T. 1994. "Swift, Sterne, and the Skeptical Tradition". *Studies in Eighteenth Century Culture* 23: 221–242.

Parrinder, Patrick. 2006. *Nation and Novel: The English Novel from its Origins to the Present*. Oxford: Oxford University Press.

Partridge, Colin. 1973. "The Human Center: George Gissing's *The Whirlpool*". *The Gissing Newsletter* 9.3: 1–10.

Patey, Douglas Lane. 1984. *Probability and Literary Form: Philosophical Theory and Literary Practice in the Augustan Age*. Cambridge: Cambridge University Press.

Patterson, Christina. 2005. "(Interview) Kazuo Ishiguro: The Samurai of Suburbia". *The Independent* March 4. <https://www.independent.co.uk/arts-entertainment/books/features/kazuo-ishiguro-the-samurai-of-suburbia-527080.html> [accessed 1 March 2019].

Pearson, Karl. 1978. *The History of Statistics in the 17th and 18th Centuries Against the Changing Background of Intellectual, Scientific, and Religious Thought.* E.S. Pearson (ed.). London: Charles Griffin.
Pearson, Robin. 2002. "Moral Hazard and the Assessment of Insurance Risk in Eighteenth and Early-Nineteenth-Century Britain". *Business History Review* 76.1: 1–35.
Pearson, Robin. 2004. *Insuring the Industrial Revolution: Fire Insurance in Great Britain, 1700–1850.* Aldershot: Ashgate.
Perrow, Charles. 1984. *Normal Accidents. Living with High-Risk Technologies.* New York: Basic.
Pesso-Miquel, Catherine. 2004. "Clock-ridden Births: Creative Bastardy in Sterne's *Tristram Shandy* and Rushdie's *Midnight's Children*". In: Susana Onega and Christian Gutleben (eds.). *Refracting the Canon in Contemporary British Literature and Film.* Amsterdam and New York: Rodopi. 17–52.
Philips, Deborah. 2007. *Women's Fiction 1945–2005. Writing Romance.* London: Continuum.
Pink, Emma E. 2006. "Frances Burney's *Camilla*: 'to print my Grand Work…by subscription'". *Eighteenth-Century Studies* 40.1: 51–68.
Plumb, John Herbert. (1950) 1978. *England in the Eighteenth Century.* London: Penguin.
Plumb, John Herbert. 1982. "The Acceptance of Modernity". In: Neil MacKendrick, John Brewer and J.H. Plumb (eds.). *The Birth of a Consumer Society. The Commercialization of Eighteenth-Century England.* London: Europa Publications. 316–334.
Pocock, John Greville Agard. 1985. *Virtue, Commerce, and History: Essays on Political Thought and History, Chiefly in the Eighteenth Century.* Cambridge: Cambridge University Press.
Pollak, Ellen. 1989. "*Moll Flanders*, Incest, and the Structure of Exchange". *The Eighteenth Century: Theory and Interpretation* 30.1: 3–21.
Pollard, William Grosvenor. 1960. *Zufall und Vorsehung. (Chance and Providence).* München: Claudius.
Poole, Adrian. 1991. "'Men's Words' and Hardy's Women". In: Scott Elledge (ed.). *Tess of the d'Urbervilles: An Authoritative Text, Backgrounds and Sources, Criticism.* New York: Norton. 471–484.
Poovey, Mary. 1976. "Journeys from this World to the Next: The Providential Promise in *Clarissa* and *Tom Jones*". *ELH* 43.3: 300–315.
Poovey, Mary. 1984. *The Proper Lady and the Woman Writer: Ideology as Style in the Works of Mary Wollstonecraft, Mary Shelley and Jane Austen.* Chicago and London: University of Chicago Press.
Poovey, Mary. 1995. *Making a Social Body: British Cultural Formation 1830–1864.* Chicago: University of Chicago Press.
Poovey, Mary. 1998. *A History of the Modern Fact: Problems of Knowledge in the Sciences of Wealth and Society.* Chicago: University of Chicago Press.
Poovey, Mary. 2001. "The Structure of Anxiety in Political Economy and *Hard Times*". In: Suzy Anger (ed.). *Knowing the Past: Victorian Literature and Culture.* Ithaca: Cornell University Press. 151–171.
Poovey, Mary. 2002. "Writing about Finance in Victorian England: Disclosure and Secrecy in the Culture of Investment". *Victorian Studies* 45.1: 17–41.
Poovey, Mary. 2008. *Genres of the Credit Economy. Mediating Value in Eighteenth- and Nineteenth-Century Britain.* Chicago and London: University of Chicago Press.

Popper, Karl R. *Conjectures and Refutations*. 1963. *The Growth of Scientific Knowledge.* London: Routledge.
Porter, Roy. 1989. "'The Whole Secret of Health': Mind, Body and Medicine in *Tristram Shandy*". In: John Christie and Sally Shuttleworth (eds.). *Nature Transfigured: Science and Literature, 1700–1900*. Manchester and New York: Manchester University Press. 61–84.
Porter, Theodore M. 1995. *Trust in Numbers. The Pursuit of Objectivity in Science and Public Life*. Princeton, NJ: Princeton University Press.
Porter, Theodore M. 1986. *The Rise of Statistical Thinking, 1820–1900*. Princeton, NJ: Princeton University Press.
Postman, Neil. 2003. "Building a Bridge to the Eighteenth Century". In: Marleen S. Barr (ed.). *Envisioning the Future: Science Fiction and the Next Millennium*. Middletown, CT: Wesleyan University Press. 19–28.
Poston, Lawrence. 1999. "1832". In: Herbert F. Tucker (ed.). *A New Companion to Victorian Literature and Culture*. Oxford: Wiley-Blackwell. 3–18.
Powell, Melanie and David Ansic. 1997. "Gender Differences in Risk Behavior in Financial Decision-Making: An Experimental Analysis". *Journal of Economic Psychology* 18.6: 605–628.
Promies, Wolfang. 1966. *Die Bürger und der Narr oder das Risiko der Phantasie. Sechs Kapitel über das Irrationale in der Literatur des Rationalismus*. München: Carl Hanser.
Puchner, Martin. (2008) "When We Were Clones". *Raritan* 27.4: 34–39.
Pykett, Lyn. 1992. *The "Improper" Feminine: The Women's Sensation Novel and the New Woman Writing*. London and New York: Routledge.
Pykett, Lyn. 1993. "Ruinous Bodies: Women and Sexuality in Hardy's Late Fiction". *Critical Survey* 5.2: 157–166.
Rabinow, Paul and Nikolas Rose. 2016. "Biopower Today". In: Vernon W Cisney and Nicolae Morar (eds.). *Biopower: Foucault and Beyond*. Chicago and London: University of Chicago Press. 297–325.
Rabkin, Eric. 1998. "Imagination and Survival: The Case of Fantastic Literature". In: Brett Cooke, George E. Slusser and Jaume Mart-Olivella (eds.). *The Fantastic Other. An Interface of Perspectives*. Rodopi: Amsterdam. 1–20.
Radford, Andrew. 2006. "Unmanned by Marriage and the Metropolis in Gissing's *The Whirlpool*". *Victorian Newsletter* 110: 10–18.
Rahmstorf, Stefan. 2010. "*Solar*". Review. realclimate.org. May 4. <http://www.realclimate.org/index.php/archives/2010/05/solar/> [accessed 1 March 2019].
Rambuss, Richard. 1989. "'A Complicated Distress': Narrativizing the Plague in Defoe's *A Journal of the Plague Year*". *Prose Studies* 12.2: 115–131.
Randall, Martin. 2011. *9/11 and the Literature of Terror*. Edinburgh: Edinburgh University Press.
Ratcliffe, Sophie. 2006. "Under the Microscope: *Arlington Park* by Rachel Cusk". *New Statesman* October 9: 57–58.
Raven, James. 1992. *Judging New Wealth. Popular Publishing and Responses to Commerce in England, 1750–1800*. Oxford: Clarendon Press.
Ray, Martin. 1984. "Conrad, Nordau, and Other Degenerates: The Psychology of *The Secret Agent*". *Conradiana* 16.2: 125–140.

Rayner, Steve. 1992. "Cultural Theory and Risk Analysis". In: Sheldon Krimsky and Dominic Goldin (eds.). *Social Theories of Risk*. Westport, CT: Praeger. 83–116.
Rayner, Steve and Robin Cantor. 1987. "How Fair is Safe Enough? The Cultural Approach to Societal Technology Choice". *Risk Analysis* 7: 3–9.
Rawson, C. J. 1972. *Henry Fielding and the Augustan Ideal under Stress*. London and Boston, MA: Routledge and Kegan Paul.
Real, Hermann J. 2001a. "Allegorical Adventure and Adventurous Allegory: Gulliver's Several Ridiculous and Troublesome Accidents' in Brobdingnag". *Qwerty* 11: 81–87.
Real, Hermann J. 2001b. "Voyages to Nowhere: Moore's Utopia and Swift's *Gulliver's Travels*". In: Howard D. Weinbrot, Peter J. Schakel and Stephen E. Karian (eds.). *Eighteenth Century Contexts Historical Inquiries in Honor of Phillip Harth*. Madison, WI: University of Wisconsin Press. 96–113.
Reed, John R. 1989. *Victorian Will*. Athens, OH: Ohio University Press.
Rehmann-Sutter, Christoph. 1998. "Toward an Ethical Concept of Risk". *Risk: Health, Safety & Environment 9* 119: 119–136.
Reith, Gerda. 1999. *The Age of Chance: Gambling in Western Culture*. London and New York: Routledge.
Reiss, Tom. 2005. "The True Classic of Terrorism". *The New York Times* September 11. <https://www.nytimes.com/2005/09/11/books/review/the-true-classic-of-terrorism.html> [accessed 1 March 2019].
Renn, Ortwin. 1992. "Concepts of Risk: A Classification". In: Sheldon Krimsky and Dominic Goldin (eds.). *Social Theories of Risk*. Westport, CT: Praeger. 53–82.
Rescher, Nikolas. 1983. *Risk. A Philosophical Introduction to the Theory of Risk Evaluation and Management*. Lanham, MD: University Press of America.
Ribbat, Christoph and Gabriele Linke (eds.). 2005. *Twenty-First Century Fiction: Readings, Essays, Conversations*. Heidelberg: Winter.
Richard, Jessica. 2011. *The Romance of Gambling in the Eighteenth-Century British Novel*. Basingstoke: Palgrave Macmillan.
Richardson, Alan. 2002. "Of Heartache and Head Injury: Reading Minds in *Persuasion*". *Poetics Today* 23.1: 141–160.
Richardson, Brian. 1997. *Unlikely Stories: Causality and the Nature of Modern Narrative*. Newark, DE: University of Delaware Press.
Richetti, John A. 1982. "The Family, Sex, and Marriage in Defoe's *Moll Flanders* and *Roxana*". *Studies in the Literary Imagination* 15.2: 19–36.
Richetti, John A. 1988. "The Novel and Society: The Case of Daniel Defoe". In: Robert W. Uphaus (ed.). *The Idea of the Novel in the Eighteenth Century*. East Lansing: Colleagues Press. 47–66.
Richetti, John A. 1993. "Epilogue: *A Journal of the Plague Year* as Epitome". In: Paula Backscheider (ed.). *Daniel Defoe: A Journal of the Plague Year*. New York: Norton. 295–301.
Richetti, John A. 2005. *The Life of Daniel Defoe. A Critical Biography*. Oxford: Blackwell.
Richter, David. H. 1989. "The Unguarded Prison: Reception, Theory, Structural Marxism, and the History the Gothic Novel". *The Eighteenth Century: Theory and Interpretation* 30.3: 3–17.
Ricks, Christopher. 1985. "Introduction". In: Graham Petrie (ed.). *Laurence Sterne: The Life and Opinions of Tristram Shandy. 1759–1767*. London: Penguin. 7–28.

Rider, Robin E. 1990. "Bibliographical Afterword". In: Tore Frängsmyr, J.L. Heilbron and Robin E. Rider (eds.). *The Quantifying Spirit in the 18th Century.* Berkeley and Los Angeles, CA: University of California Press. 381–397.
Rigakos, George S. and Alexandra Law. 2009. "Risk, Realism and the Politics of Resistance". *Critical Sociology* 35.1: 79–103.
Rigakos, George S. and Richard W. Hadden. 2001. "Crime, Capitalism and the Risk Society: Towards the Same Olde Modernity?" *Theoretical Criminology* 5.1: 61–84.
Rignall, John. 2011. *George Eliot, European Novelist.* Farnham: Ashgate.
Riquelme, John Paul (ed.). 1998. *Thomas Hardy: Tess of the d'Urbervilles. Case Studies in Contemporary Criticism.* Boston, MA: Bedford.
Rizq, Rosemary. 2014. "Copying, Cloning and Creativity: Reading Kazuo Ishiguro's *Never Let Me Go*". *British Journal of Psychotherapy* 30.4: 517–532.
Robbins, Bruce. 2007. "Cruelty is Bad. Banality and Proximity in *Never Let Me Go*". *Novel* 40.3: 289–302.
Roden, David. 2014. *Posthuman Life: Philosophy at the Edge of the Human.* London and New York: Routledge.
Rogers, Pat. 1985. *Eighteenth Century Encounters: Studies in Literature and Society in the Age of Walpole.* Brighton, Sussex: Harvester Press.
Rollo, Katherine. 2012. "The Posthuman Bildungsroman: The Clone as Authentic Subject". Paper. 'Authenticity': Centre for Modern Studies Second Annual Symposium. University of York. May 31. <https://docplayer.net/64269400-The-posthuman-bildungsroman-the-clone-as-authentic-subject.html> [accessed 1 March 2019].
Rooney, Ellen. 1991. "'A Little More than Persuading': *Tess* and the Subject of Sexual Violence". In: Lynn Higgins and Brenda R. Silver (eds.). *Rape and Representation.* New York: Columbia University Press. 87–114.
Root, Christina. 2011. "A Melodiousness at Odds with Pessimism: Ian McEwan's *Saturday*". *Journal of Modern Literature* 35.1: 60–78.
Rosa, Hartmut. 2012. *Weltbeziehungen im Zeitalter der Beschleunigung.* Berlin: Suhrkamp.
Rose, Nikolas. 1998. *Inventing Our Selves. Psychology, Power, and Personhood.* Cambridge: Cambridge University Press.
Rose, Nikolas. 1999. *Governing the Soul. The Shaping of the Private Self.* 2nd ed. London and New York: Free Association.
Rosebury, Brian. 1995. "Moral Responsibility and 'Moral Luck'". *The Philosophical Review* 104.4: 499–524.
Rosenberg, Shapir. 1999. "Luck and Responsibility". *Dialogue* 41 (April): 38–44.
Rosenblum, Michael. 1977. "Shandean Geometry and the Challenge of Contingency". *Novel: A Forum of Fiction* 10.3: 237–247.
Rosengarten, Richard A. 2000. "Principled Diffidence: Religion, the Narration of Providence, and the Novels of Henry Fielding". *Henry Fielding and the Narration of Providence: Divine Design and the Incursions of Evil.* New York: Basingstoke. 1–20.
Roser, Sanine, Rafaela Hillerbrand, Per Sandin and Martin Peterson (eds.). 2012. *Handbook of Risk Theory.* Heidelberg: Springer Science + Business Media B.V.
Ross, Ian Campell. 2001. *Laurence Sterne: A Life.* Oxford: Oxford University Press.
Ross, Michael L. 2008. "On a Darkling Planet: Ian McEwan's *Saturday* and the Condition of England". *Twentieth-Century Literature* 54.1: 75–96.

Rousseau, G.S. and Roy Porter (eds.). 1980. *The Ferment of Knowledge: Studies in the Historiography of 18th Century Science*. Cambridge: Cambridge University Press.

Rothfield, Lawrence. 1992. *Vital Signs: Medical Realism in Nineteenth-Century Fiction*. Princeton, NJ: Princeton University Press.

Rothstein, Eric. 1975. *Systems of Order and Inquiry in Later Eighteenth Century Fiction*. Berkeley, CA: University of California Press.

Royle, Nicholas. 1999. "Posthumous Bustle: *Howards End*". *E.M. Forster*. Plymouth: Northcote House. 46–59.

Russell, Gillian. 2000. "'Faro's Daughters': Female Gamesters, Politics, and the Discourse of Finance in 1790s Britain". *Eighteenth-Century Studies* 33.4: 481–504.

Russell, Laura D. and Austin S. Babrow. 2011. "Risk in the Making: Narrative, Problematic Integration, and the Social Construction of Risk". *Communication Theory* 21.3: 239–260.

Russell, Norman. 1986. *The Novelist and the Mammon: Literary Responses to the World of Commerce in the Nineteenth Century*. Oxford: Clarendon.

Russo, Stephanie. 2011. "Would it be Pleasing To Me? Sexuality and Surveillance in Frances Burney's *Camilla*". *The Burney Journal* 11: 80–93.

Rydygier Smith, Monika. 1996. "Trollope's Dark Vision: Domestic Violence in *The Way We Live Now*". *Victorian Review* 22.1: 13–31.

Saathoff, Jens. 2001. *Motive krisenhafter Subjektivität. Eine vergleichende Studie zu deutscher und englischer Schauerliteratur des 18. und 19. Jahrhunderts*. Frankfurt a/Main: Peter Lang.

Sabor, Peter. 1987. *Horace Walpole. The Critical Heritage*. London and New York: Routledge and Kegan Paul.

Sabor, Peter (ed.). 2007. *The Cambridge Companion to Frances Burney*. Cambridge: Cambridge University Press.

Said, Edward. 1994. *Culture and Imperialism*. London: Vintage.

Salih, Sarah. 2002. "Camilla in the Marketplace: Moral Marketing and Feminist Editing in 1796 and 1802". In: E.J. Clery, Caroline Franklin and Peter Garside (eds.). *Authorship, Commerce and the Public: Scenes of Writing, 1750–1850*. Basingstoke: Palgrave Macmillan. 120–135.

Salih, Sarah. 2007. "*Camilla* and *The Wanderer*". In: Peter Sabor (ed.). *The Cambridge Companion to Frances Burney*. Cambridge: Cambridge University Press. 39–54.

Sanders, Mike. 2000. "Manufacturing Accident: Industrialism and the Worker's Body in Early Victorian Fiction". *Victorian Literature and Culture* 28.2 (2000): 313–329.

Sawkins, John. 2001. *The Long Apprenticeship: Alienation in the Early Work of Alan Sillitoe*. Oxford et al.: Peter Lang, 2001.

Sawyer, Andy. 2011. "Kazuo Ishiguro's *Never Let Me Go* and 'Outsider Science Fiction'". In: Sebastian Groes and Barry Lewis (eds.). *Kazuo Ishiguro. New Critical Visions of the Novels*. Basingstoke: Palgrave Macmillan. 236–246.

Scanlan, Margaret. 2001. *Plotting Terror: Novelists and Terrorists in Contemporary Fiction*. Charlottesville, VA: University Press of Virginia.

Scanlan, Margaret. 2010. "Migrating from Terror: The Postcolonial Novel after September 11". *Journal of Postcolonial Writing* 46.3: 266–278.

Scarth, Fredrika. 2004. *The Other Within. Ethics, Politics, and the Body in Simone de Beauvoir*. Lanham, MD: Rowman and Littlefield.

Scarry, Elaine. 1983. "Work and the Body in Hardy and Other Nineteenth-Century Novelists". *Representations* 3: 90–123.
Schaffer, Simon. 1989. "Defoe's Natural Philosophy and the Worlds of Credit". In: John Christie and Sally Shuttleworth (eds.). *Nature Transfigured: Science and Literature, 1700–1900*. Manchester and New York: Manchester University Press. 13–44.
Scheuermann, Mona. 1987. "Women and Money in Eighteenth-Century Fiction". *Studies in the Novel* 19.3: 311–22.
Scheuermann, Mona. 1993. *Her Bread to Earn: Women, Money, and Society from Defoe to Austen*. Lexington, KY: University Press of Kentucky.
Schmidgen, Wolfram. 2002a. *Eighteenth-Century Fiction and the Law of Property*. Cambridge: Cambridge University Press.
Schmidgen, Wolfram. 2002b. "Illegitimacy and Social Observation: The Bastard in the Eighteenth Century Novel". *ELH* 69.1: 133–166.
Schmitz-Emans, Monika. 2013. "Wagnis "und "Risiko". In: Monika Schmitz-Emans et al. (eds.). *Literatur als Wagnis/ Literature as a Risk*. Berlin: de Gruyter. 835–870.
Schmitz-Emans, Monika, with Georg Braungart, Achim Geisenhanslüke and Christine Lubkoll (eds.). 2013. *Literatur als Wagnis/ Literature as a Risk*. DFG Symposium 2011. Berlin: de Gruyter.
Schoene, Berthold. 2010. *The Cosmopolitan Novel*. 2nd ed. Edinburg: Edinburg University Press.
Schopenhauer, Arthur. 1862. *Parerga und Paralipomena: kleine philosophische Schriften*. Band 1. Julius Frauenstädt (ed.). Berlin: A.W. Hahn.
Schor, Hilary. 2001. "Novels of the 1850s: *Hard Times*, *Little Dorrit*, and *A Tale of Two Cities*". In: John O. Jordan (ed.). *The Cambridge Companion to Charles Dickens*. Cambridge: Cambridge University Press. 64–77.
Schweik, Robert. 1999. "The Influence of Religion, Science, and Philosophy on Hardy's Writing". In: Dale Kramer (ed.). *The Cambridge Companion to Thomas Hardy*. Cambridge: Cambridge University Press. 54–72.
Scott Moore, Michael and Michael Sontheimer. 2005. "Spiegel Interview with Kazuo Ishiguro: 'I Remain Fascinated by Memory.'" *SPIEGEL Online* May 10. <http://www.spiegel.de/international/spiegel-interview-with-kazuo-ishiguro-i-remain-fascinated-by-memory-a-378173.html> [accessed 1 March 2019].
Searle, Geoffrey R. 1981. *Eugenics and Politics in Britain: 1900–1914*. Leyden: Noordhoff.
Segal, Lynne. 2007. *Slow Motion. Changing Masculinities, Changing Men*. 3rd ed. Basingstoke: Palgrave Macmillan.
Sen, Amartya. 1985. "The Right to Take Personal Risks". In: Douglas MacLean (ed.). *Values at Risk*. Totowa, NJ: Rowman and Allanheld. 155–170.
Shapin, Steven. 1994. *A Social History of Truth: Civility and Science in Seventeenth Century England*. Chicago and London: University of Chicago Press.
Shapin, Steven and Simon Schaffer. 1985. *Leviathan and the Air-Pump. Hobbes, Boyle, and the Experimental Life*. Princeton, NJ: Princeton University Press.
Shapiro, Barbara J. 1983. *Probability and Certainty in Seventeenth Century England: A Study of the Relationships between Natural Science, Religion, History, Law, and Literature*. Princeton, NJ: Princeton University Press.
Shaw, George Bernard. 1893. *The Impossibilities of Anarchism*. Fabian Tract No 45. London: Fabian Society.

Shaw, Martin and Ian Miles. 1979. "The Social Roots of Statistical Knowledge". In: John Irvine, Ian Miles and Jeff Evans (eds.). *Demystifying Social Statistics*. London: Pluto Press. 27–38.

Sherry, Norman. 1973. *Joseph Conrad. The Critical Heritage*. London and Boston, MA: Routledge and Kegan Paul.

Sherry, Norman. 1971. *Conrad's Western World*. Cambridge: Cambridge University Press.

Sherman, Sandra. 1996. *Finance and Fictionality in the Early Eighteenth Century: Accounting for Defoe*. Cambridge: Cambridge University Press.

Shires, Linda M. 1999. "The Radical Aesthetic of *Tess of the d'Urbervilles*". In: Dale Kramer (ed.). *The Cambridge Companion to Thomas Hardy*. Cambridge: Cambridge University Press. 145–163.

Shklovsky, Victor. 1968. "A Parodying Novel: Laurence Sterne's *Tristram Shandy*". In: John Traugott (ed.). *Laurence Sterne: A Collection of Critical Essays*. Englewood Cliffs, NJ: Prentice Hall. 66–89.

Showalter, Elaine. 1986. "Syphilis, Sexuality and the Fiction of the Fin de Siècle". In: Ruth B. Yeazell (ed.). *Sex, Politics and Science in the Nineteenth-Century Novel*. Baltimore and London: Johns Hopkins University Press. 88–115.

Showalter, Elaine. 2012. *The Female Malady. Women, Madness, and English Culture, 1830–1980*. New York: Virago.

Shuttleton, David E. 2007. *Smallpox and the Literary Imagination: 1660–1820*. Cambridge: Cambridge University Press.

Shuttleworth, Sally. 1981. "The Language of Science and Psychology in George Eliot's *Daniel Deronda*". In: James Paradis and Thomas Postlewait (eds.). *Victorian Science and Victorian Values: Literary Perspectives*. New York: New York Academy of Sciences. 269–298.

Sill, Geoffrey. 2000. "Roxana's Susan: Whose Daughter is She Anyway?" *Studies in Eighteenth-Century Culture* 29: 261–272.

Silverman, Kaja. 1993. "History, Figuration and Female Subjectivity". In: Peter Widdowson (ed.). *Tess of the D'Urbervilles: Thomas Hardy*. Houndsmills: Macmillan. 129–146.

Sim, Stuart. 1996. "'All that Exists are Islands of Determinism': Shandean Sentiment and the Dilemma of Postmodern Physics". In: David Pierce and Peter de Voogd (eds.). *Laurence Sterne in Modernism and Postmodernism*. Amsterdam: Rodopi. 109–121.

Simmons, James Richard. 2002. "Industrial and 'Condition of England' Novels". In: Patrick Brantlinger and William B. Thesing (eds.). *A Companion to the Victorian Novel*. Oxford: Blackwell. 336–352.

Sinfield, Alan. 1998. *Gay and After*. London: Serpent's Tail.

Sinfield, Alan. 2000. "Culture, Consensus, Difference: Angus Wilson to Alan Hollinghurst". In: Alistair Davies and Alan Sinfield (eds.). *British Culture of the Postwar: An Introduction to Literature and Society 1945–1999*. London and New York: Routledge. 83–102.

Skeat, Walter W. (1879–1882) 1963. *An Etymological Dictionary of the English Language*. Oxford: Claredon.

Skidmore, D. and E. Hayter. 2000. "Risk and Sex: Ego-Centricity and Sexual Behavior in Young Adults". *Health, Risk & Society* 2.1: 23–32.

Skinner, John. 1996. *Constructions of Smollett: A Study of Gender and Genre*. Newark, DE: University of Delaware Press.

Skultans, Vieda. 1975. *Madness and Morals. Ideas on Insanity in the Nineteenth Century*. London and Boston, MA: Routledge and Kegan Paul.
Skwire, Daniel D. 2008. "The Castaway Actuary: The Financial Projects of Daniel Defoe". *Contingencies* (Jan/Feb): 22–26.
Sleigh, Charlotte. 2011. *Literature and Science*. London: Palgrave Macmillan.
Slovic, Paul. 1987. "Perception of Risk". *Science* (New Series) 236 No. 4799 (17 April): 280–285.
Slovic, Paul. 1997. "Trust, Emotion, Sex, Politics and Science: Surveying the Risk Assessment Battlefield". In: M.H. Bazerman, D.M. Messick, A.E. Tenbrunsel and K.A. Wade-Benzoni (eds.). *Environment, Ethics and Behavior*. San Francisco, CA: New Lexington. 277–313.
Slovic, Paul (ed.). 2010. *The Feeling of Risk. New Perspectives on Risk Perception*. London and Washington, D.C.: Earthscan.
Slovic, Paul, Melissa L. Finucane, Ellen Peters and Donald G. MacGregor. 2010. "Risk as Analysis and Risk as Feelings: Some Thoughts about Affect, Reason, Risk and Rationality". In: Paul Slovic (ed.). *The Feeling of Risk*. London and Washington, D.C.: Earthscan. 21–36
Smiles, Samuel. (1859) 1967. *Self-Help*. London: Sphere.
Smiley, Jane. 2006. "Trapped in English Suburbia". Rev. of *Arlington Park* by Rachel Cusk. *Los Angeles Times* December 31. <http://articles.latimes.com/2006/dec/31> [accessed 1 March 2019].
Smith, Adam. (1776) 2012. *An Inquiry into the Nature and Causes of the Wealth of Nations*. With an Introduction by Mark G. Spencer. Ware, Hertfordshire: Wordsworth.
Smith, Frederik N. 1990a. "Afterword: Style, Swift's Reader, and the Genres of *Gulliver's Travels*". In: Fredrick N. Smith (ed.). *The Genres of Gulliver's Travels*. London and Toronto: Associated University Press. 246–260.
Smith, Frederik N. 1990b. "Scientific Discourse: *Gulliver's Travels* and the Philosophical Transactions". In: Fredrick N. Smith (ed.). *The Genres of Gulliver's Travels*. London and Toronto: Associated University Press. 139–162.
Snaza, Nathan and John Weaver. 2015. *Posthumanism and Educational Research*. London and New York: Routledge.
Snow, Malinda. 1976. "Diabolic Intervention in Defoe's *Roxana*". *Essays in Literature* 3: 52–60.
Sokolsky, Anna. 2014. "The Melancholy Persuasion". In: Maud Ellmann (ed.). *Psychoanalytic Literary Criticism*. London: Routledge. 128–142.
Soloway, Richard A. 1990. *Demography and Degeneration: Eugenics and the Declining Birthrate in Twentieth-century Britain*. Chapel Hill, NC, and London: University of North Carolina Press.
Sontag, Susan. 1973. "The Third World of Women". *Partisan Review* 40.2: 181–206.
Southam, Brian C. 2005. *Jane Austen and the Navy*. London: National Maritime Museum Publishing.
Spahr, Clemens. 2012. "Prolonged Suspension: Don DeLillo, Ian McEwan, and the Literary Imagination after 9/11". *Novel: A Forum on Fiction* 45.2: 221–237.
Spencer, Herbert. (1860) 1969. "The Social Organism". In: Donald Macrae and Donald Gunn (eds.). *The Man Versus the State: With Four Essays on Politics and Society*. Harmondsworth: Penguin. 195–233.

Stafford, Barbara Maria. 1995. "The Eighteenth Century at the End of Modernity: Towards the Re-Enlightenment". In: Carla H. Hay (ed.). *The Past as Prologue: Essays to Celebrate the Twenty-Fifth Anniversary of ASECS* . New York: AMS Press. 403–416.

Starr, Chauncey. 1969. "Social Benefit versus Technological Risk". *Science* (New Series) 165 No. 3899 (19 September): 1232–1238.

Starr, George Alexander. 1971. *Defoe and Casuistry*. Princeton, NJ: Princeton University Press.

Stave, Shirley A. 1995. *The Decline of the Goddess: Nature, Culture, and Women in Thomas Hardy's Fiction*. Westport, CT: Greenwood Press.

Steel, David. 1981. "Plague Writing from Boccaccio to Camus". *Journal of European Studies* 11.3: 88–110.

Sternlieb, Lisa. 2000. "'Three Leahs to Get One Rachel': Redundant Women in *Tess of the d'Urbervilles*". *Dickens Studies Annual* 29: 351–365.

Stevick, Peter. 1969. "Miniaturization in Eighteenth-Century English Literature". *University of Toronto Quarterly* 38.2: 159–173.

Stevick, Peter. 1971. "Smollett's Picaresque Games". In: Georges S. Rousseau and Paul Gabriel Boucé (eds.). *Tobias Smollett: Bicentennial Essays Presented to Lewis M. Knapp*. New York: Oxford University Press. 111–130.

Stewart, Larry. 1998. "A Meaning for Machines: Modernity, Utility, and the Eighteenth-Century British Public". *Journal of Modern History* 70.2: 259–294.

Stimpson, Catherine. R. 1988. "Not Every Age Has Its Pleasures". *The New York Times* October 9. <https://www.nytimes.com/1988/10/09/books/not-every-age-has-its-pleasures.html> [accessed 1 March 2019].

Stinga, Valentina. 2012. "Literary Imagination and Late Nineteenth-Century Terrorism: Joseph Conrad's *The Secret Agent* and Henry James's *The Princess Casamassima*". *Language and Literature: European Landmarks of Identity* 1: 172–180.

Stone, Dan. 2002. *Breeding Superman: Nietzsche, Race and Eugenics in Edwardian and Inter-war Britain*. Liverpool: Liverpool University Press.

Stone, Wilfred H. 1969. "Forster on Love and Money". In: John Arlott (ed.). *Aspects of E.M. Forster*. London: Edward Arnold. 107–122.

Stone, Wilfred H. 1979. "Forster on Profit and Loss". In: G.K. Das and Jon Beer (eds.). *E.M. Forster, A Human Exploration. Centenary Essays*. London and Basingstoke: Macmillan. 69–78.

Stone, Wilfred H. 1996. "Forster, the Environmentalist". In: Carola M. Kaplan and Anne B. Simpson (eds.). *Seeing Double. Revisioning Edwardian and Modernist Literature*. Basingstoke: Macmillan. 171–192.

Stone, Wilfred H. 1998. "The Play of Chance and Ego in *Daniel Deronda*". *Nineteenth-Century Literature* 53.1: 25–55.

Straub, Kristina. 1987. *Divided Fictions: Fanny Burney and Feminine Strategy*. Lexington, KN: University of Kentucky Press.

Strydom, Piet. 2002. *Risk, Environment and Society*. Buckingham and Philadelphia, PA: Open University Press.

Summers-Bremner, Eluned. 2006. "'Poor Creatures': Ishiguro's and Coetzee's Imaginary Animals". *Mosaic* 39.4: 145–60.

Sumpter, Caroline. 2011. "On Suffering and Sympathy. *Jude the Obscure*". *Victorian Studies* 53.4: 665–687.

Sussman, Charlotte. 2000. *Consuming Anxieties. Consumer Protest, Gender, and British Slavery, 1713–1833*. Stanford, CA: Stanford University Press.
Sussman, Charlotte. 2012. *Eighteenth-Century English Literature. 1660–1789*. Cambridge: Polity Press.
Sussman, Herbert. 1999. "Industrial". In: Herbert F. Tucker (ed.). *Victorian Literature & Culture*. Oxford: Wiley-Blackwell. 244–257.
Sutcliffe, William. 2010. "Ian McEwan's Climate-Change Comedy". *Financial Times* March 5. <https://www.ft.com/content/db777db4-27e0-11df-9598-00144feabdc0> [accessed 1 March 2019].
Sutherland, John. 1996. *Is Heathcliff a Murderer—Puzzles in Nineteenth-Century Fiction*. Oxford: Oxford University Press.
Swafford, Kevin. 2013. "'False From Head to Foot': Social Performance and the Ideology of Recognition in *The Way We Live Now*". *Victorians: A Journal of Culture and Literature* 123: 113–125.
Swaminathan, Srividhya. 2003. "Defoe's Alternative Conduct Manual: Survival Strategies and Female Networks in *Moll Flanders*". *Eighteenth-Century Fiction* 15.2: 185–206.
Swenson, Rivka. 2011. "Revising the Scottish Plot in Tobias Smollett's *Roderick Random*". In: Christopher D. Johnson (ed.). *New Contexts for Eighteenth-Century Fiction. "Hearts Resolved and Hands Prepared": Essays in Honor of Jerry C. Beasley*. Newark, DE: University of Delaware Press. 201–218.
Szerszynski, Bronislaw, Scott Lash and Brian Wynne. 1996. "Introduction: Ecology, Realism, and the Social Sciences". In: Scott Lash, Bronislaw Szerszynski and Brian Wynne (eds.). *Risk, Environment and Modernity*. London: Sage. 1–26.
Tait, Joyce. 2001. "More Faust than Frankenstein: The European Debate about the Precautionary Principle and Risk Regulation for Genetically Modified Crops". *Journal of Risk Research* 4.2: 175–189.
Tait, Theo. 2005. "A Rational Diagnosis". Rev. of *Saturday* by Ian McEwan. *TLS* 5315: 21–22.
Tang, Marie. 2013. "Bodies at Risk: Ambiguous Subjectivities in *Arlington Park*. A Beauvoirean Perspective". *E-rea* 10.2. <https://journals.openedition.org/erea/3200> [accessed 1 March 2019].
Tanner, Tony. 1975. "Colour and Movement in *Tess of the d'Urbervilles*". In: R.P. Draper (ed.). *Thomas Hardy: The Tragic Novels*. London: Macmillan. 182–208.
Tanner, Tony. 1981. "In Between – Anne Elliot Marries a Sailor and Charlotte Heywood Goes to the Seaside". In: David Monaghan (ed.). *Jane Austen in a Social Context*. London: Macmillan. 180–194.
Tanner, Tony. 1986. *Jane Austen*. Houndsmills: Macmillan.
Tavor Bannet, Eve. 1991. "Rewriting the Social Text: The Female Bildungsroman in Eighteenth-Century England". In: James Hardin (ed.). *Reflection and Action: Essays on the Bildungsroman*. Columbia, SC: University of South Carolina Press. 195–227.
Taylor, Anthony J. 1965. "The Economy". In: Simon Nowell-Smith (ed.). *Edwardian England 1901–1914*. London: Oxford University Press. 103–138.
Taylor, Matthew. 2004. "What Persuasion Really Means in *Persuasion*: A Mimetic Reading of Jane Austen". *Contagion: Journal of Violence, Mimesis, and Culture* 11: 105–123.
Taylor, William Cooke. (1841) 1968. *Notes of a Tour in the Manufacturing Districts of Lancashire*. 3rd ed. with a new Introduction by W.H. Chaloner. New York: A.M. Kelley.

Taylor-Gooby, Peter and Jens O. Zinn. 2006. "The Current Significance of Risk". In: Peter Taylor-Gooby and Jens O. Zinn (eds.). *Risk in Social Science*. Oxford: Oxford University Press. 1–19.
Teuber Andrea. 1990. "Justifying Risk". *Daedalus* 119: 235–54.
Thomas, Keith. (1971) 1991. *Religion and the Decline of Magic. Studies in Popular Beliefs in Sixteenth- and Seventeenth-century England*. Reprinted ed. London: Penguin.
Thompson, James. 1996. *Models of Value: Eighteenth-century Political Economy and the Novel*. Durham and London: Duke University Press.
Thompson, Judith Jarvis. 1985. "Imposing Risks". In: Mary Gibson (ed.). *To Breathe Freely. Risk, Consent, and Air*. Totowa, NJ: Rowman and Allanheld. 124–140.
Thompson, Paul B. 1986. "The Philosophical Foundations of Risk". *Southern Journal of Philosophy* 24.2: 273–286.
Thorne, Christian. 2003. "Providence in the Early Novel, or Accident If You Please". *Modern Language Quarterly* 64.3: 323–347.
Tilby, Michael. 2011. "Playing with Risk: Balzac, the Insurance Industry and the Creation of Fiction". *Journal of European Studies* 41 (June): 107–122.
Todd, Dennis. 2003. "Crusoe's and Gulliver's 'Natural' Aversion to Savagery and the Idea of Human Nature". In: Herrmann J. Real and Helgard Stöver-Leidig (eds.). *Reading Swift: Papers from the Fourth Münster Symposium on Jonathan Swift*. München: Fink. 363–376.
Todhunter, Isaac. 1865. *A History of the Mathematical Theory of Probability from the Time of Pascal to that of Laplace*. Cambridge and London: Macmillan.
Tóibín, Colm. 2005. "The Comedy of Being English". *The New York Review*: 6–10.
Tomoiagă, Ligia. 2012. "Kazuo Ishiguro's *Never Let Me Go*: A Non-Scientific View on a Dystopian World of Clones". In: Ligia Tomoiagă, Minodora Barbul and Ramona Demarcsek (eds.). *From Francis Bacon to William Golding: Utopias and Dystopias Today and of Yore*. Newcastle-upon-Tyne: Cambridge Scholars. 255–266.
Tonkin, Boyd. 2007. "Ian McEwan: I Hang on to Hope in a Tide of Fear". *The Independent* April 6. <https://www.edge.org/images/Independent_McEwan.pdf> [accessed 1 March 2019].
Trent, W.P. 1892. "The Novels of Thomas Hardy". *Sewanee Review* 1: 20.
Trexler, Adam. 2015. *Anthropocene Fictions. The Novel in a Time of Climate Change*. Charlottesville, VA, and London: University of Virginia Press.
Tropp, Martin. 1990. *Images of Fear: How Horror Stories Helped Shape Modern Culture (1818–1918)*. Jefferson, NC: McFarland.
Trotter, David. 1993. *The English Novel in History, 1895–1920*. London and New York: Routledge.
Trotter, David. 2000. *Cooking with Mud. The Idea of Mess in Nineteenth-Century Art and Fiction*. Oxford: Oxford University Press.
Tuchman, Barbara W. 1966. *The Proud Tower: A Portrait of the World Before the War 1890–1914*. London: Hamish Hamilton.
Tuhus-Dubrow, Rebecca. (2013). "Cli-Fi: Birth of a Genre". *Dissent* 60.3: 58–61.
Tulloch, John. 2008. "Culture and Risk". In: Jens O. Zinn (ed.). *Social Theories of Risk and Uncertainty: An Introduction*. Oxford: Blackwell. 138–167.
Tulloch, John and Deborah Lupton. 2003. *Risk and Everyday Life*. London: Sage.

Turley, Hans. 2004. "Protestant Evangelism, British Imperialism, and Crusonian Identity". *New Imperial History: Culture; Identity, and Modernity in Britain and the Empire, 1660–1840.* Cambridge: Cambridge University Press. 176–193.
Turner, Bryan S. 1994. *Orientalism, Postmodernism and Globalism.* London and New York: Routledge.
Turney, Jon. 1998. *Frankenstein's Footsteps: Science, Genetics and Popular Culture.* New Haven, CT: Yale University Press.
Tversky, Amos. 1990. "The Psychology of Risk". In: William F. Sharpe and Katrina F. Sherrerd (eds.). *Quantifying the Market Risk Premium Phenomenon for Investment Decision Making.* New York: Institute of Chartered Financial Analysts. 73–77.
Tversky, Amos and Daniel Kahneman. 1981. "The Framing of Decisions and the Psychology of Choice". *Science* (New Series) 211 No. 4481: 453–458.
Urry, John. 2011. *Climate Change and Society.* Cambridge: Polity Press.
Van, Annette. 2005. "Ambivalent Speculations: America as England's Future in *The Way We Live Now*". *NOVEL: A Forum on Fiction* 39.1: 75–96
Van Dellen, R.J. 1975. "George Orwell's *Coming Up For Air:* The Politics of Powerlessness". *Modern Fiction Studies* 21.1: 57–68.
Van Ghent, Dorothy. 1967. "On *Tess of the D'Urbervilles*". *The English Novel: Form and Function.* New York: Harper and Row. 237–255.
Vanderbeke, Dirk. 2006. "Winding Up the Clock: The Conception and Birth of Tristram Shandy". In: Anja Müller (ed.). *Fashioning Childhood in the Eighteenth Century: Age and Identity.* Burlington, VT: Ashgate. 179–188.
Vernon, John. 1984. *Money and Fiction. Literary Realism in the Nineteenth and Early Twentieth Century.* Ithaca, NY, and London: Cornell University Press.
Vickers, Ilse. 1996. *Defoe and the New Sciences.* Cambridge: Cambridge University Press.
Vrettos, Athena. 1990. "From Neurosis to Narrative: The Private Life of the Nerves in *Villette* and *Daniel Deronda*". *Victorian Studies* 33.4: 551–579.
Wagner, Adolph. 1864. *Die Gesetzmässigkeit in den scheinbar willkührlichen menschlichen Handlungen vom Standpunkt der Statistik.* Hamburg: Boyes and Geisler.
Wagner, Jodi. 2010. "Gambling as Simulation in *Daniel Deronda*". *George Eliot –George Henry Lewes Studies* 58–59: 95–110.
Wagner, Tamara S. 2010. *Financial Speculation in Victorian Fiction. Plotting Money and the Novel Genre, 1815–1901.* Columbus, OH: Ohio State University Press.
Waldoff, Leon. 1979. "Psychological Determinism in Tess of the d'Urbervilles". In: Dale Kramer (ed.). *Critical Approaches to the Fiction of Thomas Hardy.* London and Basingstoke: Macmillan. 135–154.
Wally, Johannes. 2012. "Ian McEwan's *Saturday* as a New Atheist Novel? A Claim Revisited". *ANGLIA* 130.1: 95–119.
Wahrman, Dror. 2004. *The Making of the Modern Self: Identity and Culture in Eighteenth-Century England.* New Haven, CT, and London: Yale University Press.
Walkowitz, Rebecca L. 2015. *Born Translated. The Contemporary Novel in an Age of World Literature.* New York: Columbia University Press.
Wall Sundberg, Cynthia. 2006. *The Prose of Things: Transformations of Description in the Eighteenth Century.* Chicago and London: University of Chicago Press.
Wallace, Stevens. 1980. "Insurance and Social Change". *Wallace Stevens Journal* 4.3/4: 37–39.

Ward, Ian. 2008. "Towards a Poethics of Terror". *Law, Culture and the Humanities* 4.2: 248–279.

Ware, Vron. 2010. "The White Fear Factor". In: Elleke Boehmer and Stephen Morton (eds.). *Terror and the Postcolonial*. Oxford: Wiley-Blackwell. 99–112.

Watt, Ian. (1957) 1987. *The Rise of the Novel. Studies in Defoe, Richardson and Fielding*. London: Hogarth.

Webb, Igor. 1981. *From Custom to Capital: The English Novel and the Industrial Revolution*. Ithaca, NY, and London: Cornell University Press.

Webb, Igor. 2010. *Rereading the Nineteenth Century. Studies in the Old Criticism from Austen to Lawrence*. New York: Palgrave Macmillan.

Webb, Sidney. (1891) 1969. "The Reform of the Poor Law". *Fabian Tracts. Nos. 1–47. 1884–1893*. 3–19. Nendeln, Liechtenstein: Kraus Reprint. 223–239.

Webb, Sidney. 1907. *The Decline in the Birth-Rate*. Fabian Tract No. 131. London: Fabian Society.

Webb, Simon. 2012. *Dynamite, Treason & Plot: Terrorism in Victorian & Edwardian London*. Stroud: The History Press.

Weeks, Jeffrey. 1985. *Sexuality and its Discontents*. London: Routledge and Kegan Paul.

Wegener, Susanne. 2014. *Restless Subjects in Rigid Systems. Risk and Speculation in Millennial Fictions of the North American Pacific Rim*. Bielefeld: transcript.

Wein, Leon. 1992. "The Responsibility of Intelligent Artifacts: Toward an Automation Jurisprudence". *Harvard Journal of Law and Technology* 6.1: 103–154.

Weiss, Barbara. 1968. *The Hell of the English: Bankruptcy and the Victorian Novel*. Lewisburg, PA: Bucknell University Press.

Weiss, Eric A. 1985. "Jonathan Swift's Computing Invention". *Annals of the History of Computing* 7.2: 164–165.

Welsh, Alexander. 1985. *George Eliot and Blackmail*. Cambridge, MA: Harvard University Press.

Wertheimer, Eric. 2006. *Underwriting: The Poetics of Insurance in America, 1722–1872*. Stanford, CA: Stanford University Press.

Westergaard, Harald. 1932. *Contributions to the History of Statistics*. London: P.S. King and Son.

White, Arnold. 1901. *Efficiency and Empire*. London: Methuen.

Whitworth, Michael. 2001. "Things Fall Apart: *The Secret Agent* and Literary Entropy". *Einstein's Wake: Relativity, Metaphor, and Modernist Literature*. Oxford: Oxford University Press. 58–82.

Whittle, Stephen. 1994. "Consuming Differences: The Collaboration of the Gay Body with the Cultural State". In: Stephen Whittle (ed.). *The Margins of the City. Gay Men's Urban Lives*. Aldershot: Arena. 27–41.

Wicke, Jennifer. 1998. "The Same and the Different: Standards and Standardization in Thomas Hardy's *Tess of the d'Urbervilles*". In: John Paul Riquelme (ed.). *Thomas Hardy: Tess of the d'Urbervilles. Case Studies in Contemporary Criticism*. Boston, MA: Bedford. 571–589.

Widdowson, Peter. 1977. *E.M. Forster's Howards End: Fiction as History*. London: Chatto and Windus.

Widdowson, Peter. 1993. "Introduction: *'Tess of the d'Urbervilles'* Faithfully Presented By Peter Widdowson". In: Peter Widdowson (ed.). *Tess of the D'Urbervilles: Thomas Hardy*. Basingstoke: Macmillan. 1–23.
Williams, Bernard. 1993. "Recognising Responsibility". *Shame and Necessity*. Berkeley, CA: University of California Press. 50–75.
Williams, Bernard and Thomas Nagel. 1976. "Moral Luck". *Proceedings of the Aristotelian Society Supplementary Volumes* 50: 115–135.
Williams, Melanie. 2001. "'Sensitive as Gossamer': Law and Sexual Encounter in *Tess of the D'Urbervilles*". *Thomas Hardy Journal* 17.1: 54–60.
Williams, Raymond. 1958. *Culture and Society 1780–1950*. London: Chatto and Windus.
Williams, Raymond. 1977. *Marxism and Literature*. Oxford and New York: Oxford University Press.
Wilkinson, Iain. 2001. "Social Theories of Risk Perception: At Once Indispensable and Insufficient". *Current Sociology* 49.1: 1–22.
Wilkinson, Iain. 2006. "The Psychology of Risk". In: Gabe Mythen and Sandra Walklate (eds.). *Beyond the Risk Society. Critical Reflections on Risk and Human Security*. Maidenhead: Open University Press. 25–42.
Wilkinson, Iain. 2010. *Risk, Vulnerability and Everyday Life*. London and New York: Routledge.
Wilson, Martin. 1995. "'Lovely Conundrums and Locus for Conflict: The Figure of Sue Bridehead in Hardy's *Jude the Obscure*". *The Thomas Hardy Journal* 11.3: 90–101.
Wilson, Keith. 1981. "Arthur Seaton Twenty Years On: A Reappraisal of Sillitoe's *Saturday Night and Sunday Morning*". *English Studies in Canada* 7.4: 414–425.
Wise, M. Norton. 1987. "How Do Sums Count? On the Cultural Origins of Statistical Causality". In: Lorenz Krüger, Lorraine Daston and Michael Heidelberger (eds.). *The Probabilistic Revolution Vol I: Ideas in History*. Cambridge, MA: MIT Press. 395–425.
Wisnicki, Adrian S. 2008. *Conspiracy, Revolution, and Terrorism from Victorian Fiction to the Modern Novel*. New York and London: Routledge.
Wolf, Burkhardt. 2010. "Riskante Partnerschaft. Shakespeares *Merchant of Venice* und die Geburt der Versicherung aus dem Meer". In: Herfried Münkler, Matthias Bohlender and Sabine Meurer (eds.). *Sicherheit und Risiko: Über den Umgang mit Gefahr im 21. Jahrhundert*. Bielefeld: transcript. 53–72.
Wolfe, Cary. 2010. *What Is Posthumanism?* Minneapolis, MN, and London: University of Minnesota Press.
Womersley, David. 2005. "Confessional Politics in Defoe's *Journal of the Plague Year*". In: David Womersley, Paddy Bullard and Abigail Williams (eds.). *"Cultures of Whiggism": New Essays on English Literature and Culture in the Long Eighteenth Century*. Newark, DE: University of Delaware Press. 237–256.
Woodcock, George. 1963. *Anarchism: A History of Libertarian Movements and Ideas*. Harmondsworth: Penguin.
Woodcock, George. (1966) 1984. *The Crystal Spirit: A Study of George Orwell*. London: Fourth Estate.
Woodcock, George. 1987. "George Orwell and the Living Word". In: Harold Bloom (ed.). *George Orwell*. New York and Philadelphia: Chelsea House. 121–138.
Woods, Gregory. 1998. *A History of Gay Literature: The Male Tradition*. New Haven, CT, and London: Yale University Press.

Woolf, Virginia. 1991. "Hardy's Moments of Vision". In: Scott Elledge (ed.). *Tess of the d'Urbervilles: An Authoritative Text, Backgrounds and Sources, Criticism*. New York: Norton. 400–406.

Wrigley, E.A. 1990. *Continuity, Chance and Change: The Character of the Industrial Revolution in England*. Cambridge: Cambridge University Press.

Wright, Terence R. 1995. "Women, Death and Integrity 3: *North and South*". *Elizabeth Gaskell, "We are not angels": Realism, Gender, Values*. Basingstoke: Palgrave Macmillan. 97–118.

Wright, Terence R. 2000. "Tess is a Victim of Men". In: Bonnie Szumski (ed.). *Readings on Tess of the d'Urbervilles*. San Diego, CA: Greenhaven Press. 128–141.

Wrobel, Claire. 2013. "Haunted Houses, Haunted Bodies: Spectral Presence in *Arlington Park*". *E-rea* 10.2. <https://journals.openedition.org/erea/3222> [accessed 1 March 2019].

Wynne, Brian. 1996. "May the Sheep Safely Graze? A Reflexive View of the Expert-Lay Knowledge Divide". In: Scott Lash, Bronislaw Szerszynski and Brian Wynne (eds.). *Risk, Environment and Modernity*. London: Sage. 44–83.

Yebra, José M. 2011. "The Belated Trauma of Aids in Alan Hollinghurst's *The Swimming-Pool Library*". In: Dolores Herrero and Sonia Baelo-Allué (eds.). *Between the Urge to Know and the Need to Deny: Trauma and Ethics in Contemporary British and American Literature*. Heidelberg: Winter. 113–125.

Young, Robert J.C. 2010. "Terror Effects". In: Elleke Boehmer and Stephen Morton (eds.). *Terror and the Postcolonial*. Oxford: Wiley-Blackwell. 307–328.

Zach, Wolfgang. 1993. "Jonathan Swift and Colonialism". In: Richard H. Rodino and Hermann J. Real (eds.). *Reading Swift: Papers from The Second Münster Symposium on Jonathan Swift*. München: Fink. 91–99.

Zalewski, Daniel. 2009. "The Background Hum: Ian McEwan's Art of Unease". *The New Yorker* 23 February. <https://www.newyorker.com/magazine/2009/02/23/the-background-hum> [accessed 1 March 2019].

Zemanek, Evi. 2012. "A Dirty Hero's fight for Clean Energy: Satire, Allegory and Risk Narrative in Ian McEwan's *Solar*". *Ecozon@* 3.1: 51–60. <http://ecozona.eu/article/view/450/472> [accessed 1 March 2019].

Zemka, Sue. *Time and the Moment in Victorian Literature and Society*. Cambridge: Cambridge University Press, 2012.

Zietlow, Paul N. "Luck and Fortuitous Circumstance in *Persuasion*: Two Interpretations". *ELH* 32.2 (1965): 179–195.

Zimmermann, Everett. 1992. "H.F.'s Meditations". In: Paula Backscheider (ed.). *A Journal of the Plague Year: Authoritative Text, Backgrounds, Contexts, Criticism*. New York: Norton. 285–295.

Zimmerman, Michael J. 1987. "Luck and Moral Responsibility". *Ethics* 97.2: 374–386.

Zinn, Jens O. (ed.). 2008a. *Social Theories of Risk and Uncertainty: An Introduction*. Oxford: Blackwell.

Zinn, Jens O. 2008b. "Introduction: The Contribution of Sociology to the Discourse on Risk and Uncertainty". In: Jens O. Zinn (ed.). *Social Theories of Risk and Uncertainty: An Introduction*. Oxford: Blackwell. 1–17.

Zinn, Jens O. 2010. "Risk as Discourse: Interdisciplinary Perspectives". *Critical Approaches to Discourse Analysis Across the Disciplines* 4.2: 106–124.

Zinn, Jens O. and Peter Taylor-Gooby. 2006a. "Risk as an Interdisciplinary Research Area". In: Peter Taylor-Gooby and Jens O. Zinn (eds.). *Risk in Social Science*. Oxford: Oxford University Press. 20–53.

Zinn, Jens O. and Peter Taylor-Gooby. 2006b. "The Challenge of (Managing) New Risks". In: Peter Taylor-Gooby and Jens O. Zinn (eds.). *Risk in Social Science*. Oxford: Oxford University Press. 54–75.

Žižek, Slavoj. 2008. "The Risk Society and Its Enemies". *The Ticklish Subject: the Absent Centre of Political Ontology*. London: Verso. 404–446.

Zulaika, Joseba and William A. Douglass. 1996. *Terror and Taboo: The Follies, Fables, and Faces of Terrorism*. New York and London: Routledge.

Zunshine, Lisa. 2005. *Bastards And Foundlings: Illegitimacy in Eighteenth-Century England*. Columbus, OH: Ohio State University Press.

Zunshine, Lisa. 2007. "Why Jane Austen Was Different and Why We May Need Cognitive Science to See it". *Style* 41: 275–298.

Subject Index

accidental   144, 163, 186, 188, 191, 193, 195, 254, 266, 274, 278, 300, 309, 377, 428 f., 466, 541, 549, 571
actuarial   300, 465
– actuarial science   54, 74, 286, 298
– actuary   50, 74, 321
adventure   1, 29, 31 f., 34, 37, 39, 43 f., 65, 68, 76–81, 98, 127 f., 132, 134, 149, 151, 154, 160, 163, 165, 168 f., 171 f., 178, 190, 215, 218, 224, 227 f., 230, 237, 247 f., 250, 258, 273, 444, 461, 484, 544, 547, 551 f., 574, 583, 588, 594
– ad-ventura   44
– ad-venture   594
AIDS   108, 114, 503, 508, 517–519
– AIDS crisis   35, 501 f., 518
– AIDS epidemic   117, 504, 517
A Journal of the Plague Year   30, 49, 73, 76 f., 84, 91, 98–118, 133, 144, 159, 215
A Journey from this World to the Next   109
aleatory   43, 165, 267
– homo aleatorius   595
A Modest Proposal   150, 298
anarchist   433–441, 443 f., 446–448, 488, 565
– anarchism   437, 439 f.
Angry Young Men   484, 487, 489, 496
annuities   48 f., 77
anticipation   5, 25, 69, 96, 218, 307, 468, 477, 494, 529 f., 538, 556, 564, 573, 582, 592, 595
apocalypse   467
– apocalyptic   9, 35, 37, 98, 156, 271, 290, 442, 469, 480 f., 520, 537, 540, 544 f., 552, 560, 563, 592 f.
– post-apocalyptic   537
Arlington Park   36, 39, 571–583, 585 f., 594
Ars conjectandi   49, 62
A Sentimental Journey   193
average   51, 53, 63, 237, 288, 292, 298, 324, 326, 343, 378 f., 413 f., 443, 459, 465, 471, 476, 480, 543, 585

– average man   286, 298, 342–344, 363, 470
– averages   325, 342–344, 414
– law of average   297
– l'homme moyen   286, 292, 298, 543
bankrupt   120
– bankruptcy   30, 32, 74 f., 121, 136, 226, 233, 314, 339–342, 345, 354, 362, 421, 475, 590
Bildungsroman   26, 37, 217, 247–249, 402 f., 515, 523, 594
biopolitics   13, 434, 526, 548
biotechnology   272, 283 f., 520
blackmail   233, 322, 339–341, 376, 427, 429
calculable   5, 45, 105, 322, 324 f., 344, 371, 410 f., 450, 588, 592
– calculability   12, 51, 62, 108, 203
– calculations   5, 49, 52, 71, 74, 79 f., 85 f., 92, 95, 101, 114, 117, 121 f., 128, 140, 142 f., 153, 156, 159, 175, 179, 188, 196, 198, 202, 215 f., 218, 230, 232, 238, 250, 253, 265, 267 f., 278, 307, 324, 342, 364, 379, 460, 530, 547
– incalculable   7, 12, 30, 64, 235, 281, 284, 347, 434 f., 453, 592
Camilla   31 f., 58, 70, 124, 181, 215–250, 264, 323
catastrophe   18, 25, 28, 30, 61, 77, 106, 181 f., 197, 205, 220, 288, 301, 305, 341, 353, 356, 362, 375, 382–384, 391, 434, 457, 468, 517, 538 f., 546, 552, 563, 568, 579, 592, 594
– catastrophic   9, 36, 60, 64, 157, 186, 230, 340, 421, 538, 549, 562, 590
– catastrophism   537, 552
– catastrophists   552
Chartism   287, 311, 339, 487
– Chartist   301 f., 308, 329
Clarissa   68 f., 123, 576, 579

climate change 25, 36, 39, 520, 537–554, 568, 588, 591f.
– global warming 10, 537–540, 542, 544, 546, 549f., 552–554, 559, 591, 593
clone 280, 521–536
– clone narrative 522f., 527
– cloning 36, 282, 521–523, 526, 532
coincidence 22f., 30, 64, 67f., 72, 87, 124, 130, 144, 163f., 181, 192, 203, 205, 207f., 264, 291, 299, 335, 365, 368, 379, 381, 387
coincidental 45, 348, 387
Coming Up For Air 35, 467f., 470, 473, 476, 478, 481, 484, 574, 586
condition of England 36, 291, 294, 339, 452, 466, 567
– condition-of-England novel 37, 571
– condition-of-England question 287, 294
consequentialism 264, 365
contagion 91, 99, 101, 107–110, 112, 221, 223f., 439
contingency 2, 20, 23, 31, 34, 38, 56, 61, 69, 86f., 95, 131, 164, 192–194, 196f., 264–267, 336, 338, 343f., 364, 368, 387, 396f., 435, 462, 562, 564, 585, 587, 589
– contingencies 120, 192f., 308f., 570
– contingent 75, 88, 193f., 344, 502, 538, 583
courtesy-novel 219
courtship game 225, 240, 244, 248, 255
courtship novel 243, 250
Cranford 301, 581
credit 10, 28, 30, 53–59, 63, 74f., 107, 123, 132–135, 150, 162, 243f., 260, 305, 313f., 323, 339f., 342, 345, 347, 349f., 352f., 362, 471
– Lady Credit 55f., 132, 232
crisis 9, 11, 24, 34, 53, 56, 66, 73, 86, 98f., 102, 106f., 109–111, 116, 118, 179, 200, 210, 212f., 227, 241, 243f., 294, 297, 303, 307, 317f., 320, 327, 335, 351f., 360f., 364, 370, 403, 426, 428, 434, 454, 465, 467f., 473, 488, 518–520, 548f., 553, 555, 557, 562, 564, 567, 574f., 577, 593
Cultural Theory 16f., 20

dangerousness 39, 130, 566
Daniel Deronda 33, 144, 343, 345, 363–365, 374f., 377, 379, 381, 428
debt 30, 53–56, 59, 68, 74f., 121, 149, 201, 218, 226–228, 233, 244f., 255f., 293, 323, 325, 339–341, 347, 354, 356, 358, 427f., 571, 590
decline 35, 47f., 52, 107, 241, 304, 309, 339f., 409f., 415, 417, 458f., 467, 475, 538, 541, 558, 570, 582, 588, 594
– decline plots 39, 463
degeneration 222, 237, 382, 401, 410, 413, 416, 423, 427, 433, 442–444, 454, 457–459, 566
– degenerate 388, 413, 444f.
determinism 21f., 31, 88, 164, 185, 216, 302, 308, 343, 364f., 384, 400f., 411, 417, 419, 426, 458, 462, 492, 547, 558f.
– deterministic 62, 185f., 192, 365, 381, 581
deviance 289, 322, 400, 410, 413f., 426, 444
– deviation 24, 32f., 50, 231f., 236f., 247, 286, 294, 298, 381, 393f., 396, 411, 413, 448, 496, 533, 585
Discipline and Punish 216
disease 16, 30f., 33, 47, 49, 53, 67, 73, 75f., 84, 98–101, 103–114, 116, 135, 158, 161, 172, 175, 179, 221–223, 236f., 246, 288f., 301, 305, 337, 344, 374, 389, 403, 409–412, 415, 417, 420, 423f., 503, 512, 517–519, 521, 549, 558, 566, 570
Doctrine of Chances 47, 49f., 62, 84, 95, 185

ecocriticism 25f., 272
Enduring Love 538, 558
Enlightenment 23, 27f., 45f., 51f., 60, 62, 68, 77, 96, 152, 189, 200–203, 207, 214, 216, 233, 247, 253f., 266, 271, 280, 282, 571, 591
empire of chance 29, 589
environmental 9f., 24–26, 29, 38, 520, 538f., 542, 560, 586, 588, 590
– environmental disaster 7, 37, 157, 545
environmental risk 25, 38f., 456, 537, 547, 553, 591f.

Subject Index — 657

epidemic 30, 50, 73, 99, 101, 112, 560
eugenics 458f., 462
Evelina 218, 220, 228
evolution 14, 27, 37, 44, 54, 86, 114, 178, 247, 341, 344, 382, 442, 551, 559f., 587, 595
– evolutionary 33, 71, 281, 298, 363, 381f., 397, 413, 444, 460, 563
existential risk 30, 492, 501

fate 22, 28, 44, 58, 60, 63, 69, 81, 102, 113, 122, 130, 166f., 171f., 181, 188, 196, 212f., 224f., 229, 233, 268, 274, 296f., 307, 315, 346, 357, 362, 368f., 387, 390f., 393, 399, 421, 445, 451, 481, 532–534, 557, 590
feminine 132, 177, 237, 240, 249, 407, 409, 579, 585
femininity 31, 36, 39, 56, 110, 123, 132, 145, 177, 237, 239f., 317, 334, 359, 390, 398, 406f., 409, 426, 572, 575f., 579, 582
feminist 36, 62, 65, 71, 123, 182, 214, 218, 220, 250, 271, 312, 383f., 386, 402, 407, 425, 545, 573, 576, 584f.
financial crisis 75, 123, 349
financial risk 54, 69, 75, 255, 260, 295f., 314, 341f., 351, 590
financial speculation 30, 53, 56, 61, 74, 76, 79, 131, 338, 340, 350, 352, 421, 426f., 455, 590
fortunate 88, 131f., 456, 557, 559
fortune 22, 28–30, 44, 48, 51f., 58f., 63, 69, 74, 76, 82, 97, 106, 113, 119, 123, 125, 127, 130–132, 135, 138, 143, 149, 161–166, 168, 171, 177f., 187, 195, 207, 209, 217f., 220, 222f., 228, 230, 237, 240, 255f., 259f., 266f., 269, 295, 302, 326, 341, 344f., 347, 354, 365, 368, 379, 455, 482, 491
Frankenstein 32, 37, 260, 270–274, 276, 278–285, 308, 521, 535

gambling 23f., 28, 30, 39, 43, 47f., 51, 53, 57–61, 63, 68–70, 74f., 79f., 150, 164, 170, 202, 207, 218, 222, 224, 226–230, 232, 296, 322f., 332, 338–340, 343, 347, 350, 354–357, 363f., 366–368, 370–372, 377, 379, 417, 424, 476, 492, 590, 595
– gambler 59–61, 227, 230, 296, 340, 356f., 367f., 418, 420
– gamester 59f., 162, 171, 229, 418
– gaming 49f., 59, 170f., 178, 228–230, 340
– game of chance 43, 47, 49, 60, 69, 77, 121, 170, 198, 229, 291, 347, 387, 490, 492, 511
game theory 225, 263
gender 10, 13, 33, 35, 38f., 55f., 62, 70, 110f., 123, 126, 134, 136, 141, 156, 177, 214, 233, 239, 245, 249, 261, 282, 312, 316f., 319, 325, 327, 330, 335, 338, 345, 367, 382f., 385f., 407, 409, 412, 414, 449, 483, 488f., 511, 545, 572, 595
– gendered risk 427, 483, 573
genetic 410f., 424, 520, 528, 559, 565, 591
– genes 388, 401, 458, 460
– genetics 272
globalization 8, 12, 339, 348, 358, 555
Goodbye to Berlin 101
Gothic 26, 31, 201f., 205–207, 210, 214–217, 220, 231, 239, 241–243, 271f., 285, 301, 436, 594
– Gothic fiction 203–206, 210f., 215, 243, 271, 301, 414
– Gothic novel 194, 200–207, 210, 215f., 243
governmentality 2, 7, 13–15, 17, 33, 526, 533, 587
– governmental 15, 320, 342, 436, 448, 552
Greenwich bomb outrage 437–439
Gulliver's Travels 23, 31, 37, 96, 102, 147–151, 153, 159, 183, 203, 208, 593

Hard Times. 33, 287, 290, 320–328
harm 15, 65, 71, 121, 124, 144, 177, 193, 198, 214, 236, 279, 308f., 317, 319, 326, 338, 374, 485, 510, 518f., 531, 534, 558, 564, 578, 580
hazard 1–3, 11, 14, 16, 25, 29f., 39, 43, 49, 51, 78, 82, 95, 97, 104f., 113, 118, 121f., 124, 127, 130, 134, 140–142, 153, 160f., 163, 173f., 187, 212, 218, 223f.,

226, 229f., 233, 240, 259, 313, 338, 406, 425, 520, 575f., 580, 585, 589
– hazardous   5, 24, 39, 55, 87, 111, 202, 241, 259, 337, 359, 426, 485, 549, 589
health   6f., 13, 32, 50f., 87, 103f., 117, 127, 138, 156, 162, 178f., 183, 200, 221, 237, 268, 277, 288, 293, 303, 308, 333, 338, 355, 389, 414, 420, 424, 429, 456f., 459, 464, 485, 504, 512, 522, 524–526, 544f., 548f.
– health risks   38f., 172, 502, 513, 518, 525, 550
heredity   13, 345, 366, 381f., 388, 400f., 409, 411, 425, 458, 460
– hereditary disease   36
– hereditary risk   34, 402, 410f., 417, 458
homo economicus   61, 78, 86
Howards End   35, 451–456, 460, 462f., 465–468, 472, 504, 506, 565, 567, 586, 594

illness   26, 107–109, 125, 140, 165, 172, 179, 197, 201, 230, 236, 246, 257, 275, 287f., 305, 317f., 332, 337, 411, 414, 423f., 433, 436, 444, 475, 483, 503, 536
Industrial fiction   284, 289, 291, 302, 320, 325, 329, 487, 594
Industrial novel   32f., 130, 286–291, 294, 301, 306, 319, 329, 338f., 466, 484f., 488
inheritance   136, 199, 214, 216, 228, 237, 337, 339–342, 356, 363, 366, 368, 399, 410, 416, 454, 457
insurance   1f., 13f., 28–30, 32f., 44, 48–51, 54f., 65, 73f., 77, 114, 286, 291, 293, 295–297, 299–301, 304, 306, 341, 343, 464, 469, 476f., 488, 564, 589
– fire insurance   306, 455
– insurance industry   54, 297, 301, 343
– life insurance   50, 295
irrationality   20f., 61, 93, 110, 123, 167, 188, 203, 206, 214, 221, 292, 439, 564–566
– irrational   16, 20, 39, 52, 60, 80, 91, 101, 160f., 191, 203, 207, 244, 284, 297, 318, 441, 511f., 542, 549f., 580

Jude the Obscure   33, 381, 383, 400–415, 463

liability   6, 65, 74, 104, 127, 144, 279, 300f., 337, 341, 346, 351, 366, 375f., 397, 495
– liabilities   351
– product liability   279
likelihood   106, 265, 342, 344, 356, 370, 473, 550, 594
– unlikelihood   580
Little Dorrit   320, 345f.
lottery   58f., 84, 106, 121, 195, 224, 227, 302, 557
– lotteries   30, 59, 74, 228
luck   22, 35, 44, 48, 60, 84, 129, 131f., 164, 166, 230, 244, 255, 259, 261f., 265, 269, 336, 365–371, 398, 410, 476, 490–492, 500, 515, 546, 565, 583
– lucky   31, 58, 72, 76, 95, 118, 129–131, 170, 175, 193, 195, 216, 224, 237, 240, 255, 259, 266, 355f., 366, 379, 392, 491, 511, 526f., 550, 579f.
– moral luck   265f., 387
Luddism   311
– Luddite   288, 311, 316

marriage market   31, 121, 244, 255, 340
marriage plot   33, 217, 228, 264, 312, 327, 337–340, 381, 389, 409, 463
Mary Barton   33, 130, 285, 287, 301–303, 306, 308–310, 312, 329–331
masculinity   31, 35, 39, 70, 111, 123, 147, 182, 198, 200, 258, 430, 460, 462, 489, 496, 498–500, 502f., 506, 508f., 574
mathematic   53
– mathematical probability   29, 47f., 60, 84f., 291, 329, 588
– mathematics   29, 47–50, 52, 58, 62, 155, 186, 189, 291, 441
mean value   291f., 298
Middlemarch   263, 346, 367, 370, 376, 569, 581
misfortune   17, 76, 78, 81, 84, 94, 120, 126, 138, 152, 154f., 164, 171, 184,

186f., 222, 268, 275, 301, 338, 354, 362, 371, 390, 420, 558
Moll Flanders 30f., 39, 73, 106, 116, 118f., 122–125, 127f., 131, 133, 136, 146, 572
motherhood 31, 36, 39, 327, 386, 406, 422, 426, 572, 574f., 578, 582f.
Mrs Dalloway 36, 556f., 566, 572, 575f.

neurasthenia 417, 423
Never Let Me Go 23, 36f., 520–526, 528, 532, 534–536
– New Atheist 560
New Woman 407–410, 426
– New Women fiction 409, 463
normal 32, 50f., 85, 192, 196, 230, 236–238, 245, 298, 344, 348, 371, 413f., 444, 494, 515, 522–524, 590, 593
– normal curve 50
– normalcy 32f., 50, 294, 343, 400, 411, 550, 588
– normalities 14
North and South 11, 33, 287, 290, 310, 313–315, 319, 329–331, 337f., 467

orientation 3, 5, 9, 21, 28, 45, 48, 66, 69, 72f., 77, 83, 85, 88, 95, 99, 131, 162, 205, 228, 230, 243, 270, 378, 402, 498, 556, 594
– disorientation 208, 471, 493, 583
Oryx and Crake 521

Pascal's wager 87
Persuasion 15, 32, 198, 253–258, 260–267, 269f., 583
picaresque 31, 37, 68, 78, 149, 164, 170, 247f., 484, 487, 546, 550, 594
political arithmetic 293f., 298
Port-Royal *Logic* 49, 66
possibilist 593
post-9/11 36, 434, 440, 442, 548, 555f., 558, 561f., 566f., 569, 571–573
– 9/11 434, 553, 555f., 561, 563, 565, 568–570, 572, 592
posthuman 32, 36, 520f., 523, 527, 531, 536
– posthumanism 520f., 524
– posthumanist 283, 520

precarious 3, 31f., 68, 74, 111, 119, 121, 123, 127, 133, 135f., 142, 168, 174, 197, 224, 245, 255, 269f., 307, 311, 354, 386, 390, 393, 404, 433, 491, 505, 520, 530, 572
– precariousness 33, 108, 122, 137, 154, 182, 214, 256, 286, 318, 330f., 341, 352, 463, 573f., 586, 592
precarity 1, 34, 461, 475, 502, 566f., 572f., 592
precaution 13, 15, 32, 38, 82, 88, 91, 112, 138, 153, 157, 175, 189, 193, 222, 235, 262, 299f., 305, 310, 317f., 341, 343, 398, 446f., 493
– precautionary principle 543
predict 45, 48, 113, 185, 369, 396, 447, 515, 551
– predictability 3, 7, 22, 51, 62, 185, 203, 253, 295, 365, 447, 588
– prediction 2, 14, 16, 23, 48f., 60, 67, 140, 157, 159–161, 185, 253f., 262, 300, 329, 364, 367, 377, 379, 396, 443, 475, 530, 540, 552, 587
pregnancy 124, 126, 138, 166, 178, 399, 404, 406, 423, 462, 497, 542, 566, 574f.
probability 1, 6, 12f., 22–24, 28f., 32, 34, 43f., 47–53, 57, 59f., 62f., 66f., 69, 80, 84–86, 95, 114, 130, 164, 190, 204f., 210, 230, 233, 269, 273, 275, 277, 291, 298, 306, 308, 365, 369, 404, 458, 552, 554, 570, 589
– probabilist 49, 292, 593
– probabilities 4, 15–17, 22, 29, 49f., 53, 61, 67, 84f., 90, 97, 105, 122, 142, 165, 184, 190, 195, 199, 205, 248, 266, 286, 292, 294, 321, 369f., 413, 421, 428, 458, 490, 530, 560, 562, 568, 585
– probability theory 23f., 29, 32, 43f., 47–51, 53, 60, 62, 66, 73f., 77, 80, 84, 115, 164, 185, 198, 230, 291f., 320, 337, 552, 588, 592
– probable 4, 29, 32, 51f., 64, 205, 230, 247, 253, 262, 275, 297, 309, 318, 347f., 355, 469, 473, 482, 490, 494, 564
prognosis 45, 459

prognostication   480
project   22, 28, 30, 58, 71, 74, 79, 112, 144, 158 f., 188, 200, 205, 227, 265, 273, 283 f., 297, 299, 352, 355, 358, 433, 458, 472, 474, 480, 521, 526, 535, 539, 546, 550
projecting   5, 30, 37, 53, 144, 148, 159, 230, 370, 516
projection   5, 37, 86, 107, 176, 285, 328, 374, 380, 384, 400, 458, 467, 470, 512, 579, 587
providence   22, 28 f., 47 f., 64, 68 f., 72, 77, 81, 86 f., 96, 107, 132, 144, 153 f., 167, 185, 195, 201, 204 f., 230, 262, 265 f., 308, 315, 369, 390
– providential   48, 64, 68 f., 72, 87, 95, 100, 102, 144, 178, 187, 201, 205, 207 f., 213, 243, 265, 296, 344, 365, 376 f., 379
prudence   63, 111, 259 f., 262, 273, 297, 351 f.
– homo prudens   595
– prudentialism   14

quantification   32, 43, 50, 189, 292
quantifiable   43, 295, 324

randomness   21, 38, 45, 49, 51, 60, 62, 108, 113, 121, 130 f., 163 f., 167, 178, 187, 192, 216, 236, 297 f., 308, 365, 382, 413, 435, 437, 440 f., 445, 449 f., 462, 472, 485, 492, 559, 563, 592
rape   123, 386, 388, 391, 562
rationality   5 f., 13 f., 20 f., 32 f., 48, 51, 61 f., 67, 87, 104, 110 f., 123, 160, 162, 201, 203, 207, 214, 275, 291 f., 384, 430, 543, 561, 588
realism   20, 23, 61, 63–67, 79, 93, 97, 100, 148 f., 210, 254, 263, 300 f., 303, 306, 339, 363, 365, 381, 417, 433, 469, 473, 483, 573
reflexive modernization   8, 10
responsibility   9, 14, 17, 28, 33, 65 f., 73, 81, 129, 136, 144, 194, 265, 277, 279, 281, 297, 300, 302, 306, 308 f., 322, 326, 332, 336 f., 339, 342, 346, 353 f., 362, 364, 366, 368, 370, 384, 401, 410–412, 415, 418, 420, 428, 446 f., 454 f., 492, 497, 502, 504, 506, 508, 525, 542, 559, 562, 571, 580, 587
Risikogesellschaft   8
risk as feeling   16, 19
risk-avers   19, 70, 89 f., 104, 128, 317, 357, 580, 584
risk behaviour   16, 34–38, 116, 279, 412, 483, 489, 491, 508, 542, 546
risk calculations   31, 447, 562
risk consciousness   11, 38, 500, 561, 583
risk management   7, 14, 29 f., 35 f., 86, 98 f., 110, 112, 116, 119, 124, 141 f., 170, 201, 253, 264, 277 f., 293, 299, 304, 306, 309, 335, 341, 350, 353, 362, 371, 373, 377, 390, 404, 411, 415, 425, 427, 429, 445 f., 448, 455, 463, 467, 471, 473, 479, 482, 497, 521, 524, 526, 533, 539, 542 f., 558, 560 f., 564, 570 f., 576, 579, 583, 589, 591
risk perception   6, 11, 13, 16–21, 26 f., 29, 34 f., 37–39, 52, 73, 79, 90, 96, 101, 117, 119, 156, 158, 182, 212, 220, 235, 243, 250, 329, 415, 438, 449, 478, 511, 529 f., 533, 538, 542, 549, 551, 555, 561–563, 582, 593 f.
risk personality   369, 509, 562
risk personalities   316, 418, 477, 595
risk research   4, 7, 16, 19 f., 35, 192, 595
riskscape   39
risk society   2–5, 7–12, 14, 22 f., 25, 27, 30, 33, 36, 38, 67, 71, 76, 111, 146, 157, 238, 286, 367, 375, 415, 423 f., 443, 452, 458, 475, 512, 538, 559, 568, 589, 595
– global risk society   8, 10, 25 f., 560
– no-risk society   589
– world risk society   8 f., 25, 548, 555, 584, 588
risk theory   1, 4, 10, 17, 25 f.
Robinson Crusoe   15, 30, 32, 34, 60, 67 f., 71 f., 75–80, 84 f., 88, 92 f., 95, 97, 102, 105 f., 118, 125, 128, 132 f., 135, 149, 169, 237, 574, 592
Roderick Random   31, 127, 130, 149, 162–165, 171 f., 177 f., 182, 208, 210, 228, 248, 484

Romanticism 202, 217, 233, 254, 262f., 271, 281, 301
Roxana, The Fortunate Mistress 30f., 39, 58, 68, 72, 74, 76, 91, 94, 97, 102, 106, 116, 118f., 123f., 127, 131–146, 205, 215, 227

safety 5–7, 15, 18, 28, 34, 39, 44, 67, 74, 81–84, 87f., 91, 96f., 104f., 110, 116, 120f., 126, 128f., 131, 134f., 141–143, 145, 149, 178, 202, 206, 211f., 218, 220–222, 232, 235, 238–244, 246, 249f., 255, 262, 270, 273, 278, 300f., 314, 319, 336, 349, 356f., 385f., 406, 445f., 450f., 453, 465–467, 472, 475, 477f., 482f., 490, 498, 500–503, 505, 511, 513, 515–517, 519, 532f., 535, 557, 559–562, 564, 566, 571, 584, 589f., 592–595
satire 26, 33, 37, 59, 68, 109, 149, 157, 159f., 164, 167, 176, 178, 180, 198, 208, 232, 250, 320f., 328, 345, 349, 357, 365, 424, 426, 439, 444, 467, 537, 539, 552, 573, 580, 582, 586
Saturday 36, 491, 493–495, 498, 538, 555–561, 563, 565–573, 582, 586, 593f.
Saturday Night and Sunday Morning 35f., 483f., 486f., 489, 501f., 511f., 514
science fiction 37, 271, 280, 282, 520, 522f., 526, 537, 550
sexual risk 510, 512, 518, 541
Shirley 33, 287, 302, 310–319, 325, 333, 335, 339
Solar 26, 36, 442, 520, 537–542, 546f., 549–552, 568, 591
South Sea Bubble 30, 56, 59, 74f., 78f., 149f., 590
South Sea Company 54, 75, 150
speculation 1, 23, 25, 28f., 33f., 39, 48, 53–61, 74–76, 78, 80, 84, 90, 98, 109, 123, 134, 145, 147, 149f., 155f., 159f., 162, 165, 183f., 188, 198, 200, 202, 216, 227, 230, 232, 250, 260, 289, 291, 300, 309, 313, 323, 332, 337, 339–341, 343f., 346–351, 353, 357–359, 363f., 369, 375, 417, 419, 421, 425, 448, 456f., 587, 590
– speculative 3, 24, 28, 54, 56, 66, 118, 123, 148, 158f., 188, 286, 340, 345f., 349f., 353f., 356, 358f., 367, 375, 417, 522, 529, 537, 551, 590
– speculative fiction 23, 37
standard 24f., 33, 36, 49–51, 80, 137, 145, 152, 163, 201, 232, 248, 277, 298, 300, 311, 321f., 330, 355, 368, 381, 385f., 393–395, 402, 404, 411, 426, 442, 475, 481, 496, 512, 527, 544, 550
– standardization 381
– standardized norms 342
statistic 53, 503
– statistical 4, 6, 14, 33, 47f., 76f., 84, 87, 103, 106f., 114f., 164, 190, 230, 253, 291–295, 297f., 301, 308, 320–322, 324–326, 337, 342–345, 389, 413f., 416, 424, 458f., 461, 552, 589
– statistics 4, 29, 33f., 48–50, 62, 98, 102, 110, 114f., 188, 286, 291–295, 297f., 300f., 303, 324, 344, 413, 457f., 465, 519, 552, 562, 588f.
– Statistik 294, 298
stochastic 51
– stochastized 32, 51
stock-market 59, 340, 342, 348
– Joint Stock Companies Act 300f.
– stock-jobbing 59, 74
– stock-trading 29
stoicism 197, 447
– stoic 197, 351, 390
surveillance 13f., 34, 101, 112, 130–132, 139, 157, 176, 216, 219, 221, 224, 231f., 234, 328, 344f., 375f., 435f., 448f., 509, 526, 591
systems theory 7, 13, 15

table of mortality 76, 114
terror 13, 29, 46, 81, 90, 93, 109, 138, 174, 197, 201f., 205–208, 210, 213, 215, 218, 239–242, 246, 271, 273, 285, 309f., 313, 316, 319, 333, 336, 341, 372, 374, 398, 402, 433f., 438, 441, 448–450, 453, 473, 475, 526, 548, 553,

555f., 558, 560–563, 568f., 574, 586, 593, 595
- terrorism 7, 16, 35f., 433f., 436–439, 450, 458, 553, 555, 559, 562f., 565, 568f., 572, 585, 590–593
- terrorist 10, 26, 434, 436f., 439–442, 446–448, 555, 557, 561, 565f., 592
Tess of the d'Urbervilles 33, 39, 375, 381–400, 404, 449
The Birth of the Clinic 13, 414
The Castle of Otranto 31, 37, 200–202, 204–208, 214–216, 271
The Great Derangement 550f., 591
The History of Sir Charles Grandison 69
The Lottery. A Farce 59
The Princess Casamassima 439
thermodynamics 442
The Secret Agent 27, 35, 433–436, 439, 442–444, 447f., 450f., 454, 456f., 462, 472, 565, 592
The Swimming-Pool Library 35f., 501, 507f., 513, 519
The Way We Live Now 33f., 237, 255, 341, 345–348, 351, 359–363, 367, 375, 381, 417, 421, 595
The Whirlpool 33, 348, 375, 401, 409, 416–420, 426f., 430
The Year of the Flood 537
Tom Jones 68f., 163, 193
trauma 62, 236, 374, 518, 533, 556, 561, 575
- trauma theory 396, 557
- traumatism 556
travel narrative 31, 37, 63, 148
Tristram Shandy 31, 68, 160, 163, 168, 178–181, 183, 185f., 189–193, 196–200, 202, 206, 214f., 246
trust 5, 13, 16, 19, 31, 35, 56–58, 63, 66, 68, 97, 103f., 125, 129, 134, 140, 143, 169, 171, 173, 211f., 218, 222, 226, 238, 244, 260, 268, 292, 297, 301, 319, 341, 349, 357, 368f., 405, 422, 454, 505f., 512f., 519, 532

uncertainty 1–3, 5–9, 12, 14f., 21, 25, 28f., 37, 45, 52f., 56, 59f., 67, 76, 90, 94, 100, 104, 114f., 132, 142, 149, 186, 194, 196, 199, 201, 203, 207, 213, 218, 233, 244, 265–267, 270, 274, 286, 295, 297, 305, 330, 342, 349f., 367, 372, 379, 434, 436, 451, 456, 463, 511, 519, 529, 538, 560f., 565, 573, 582, 584–588, 592f., 595
utilitarian 277, 320f., 324f., 522
- Utilitarianism 320, 324f.

Victorian 24, 33, 39, 227, 231, 250, 254, 286f., 289, 292f., 295f., 298, 300, 306, 316, 318, 320–322, 325, 327, 338–346, 348–352, 360, 362f., 367, 372, 381–383, 385f., 388, 394, 397, 400–402, 404, 406f., 409–411, 414, 416, 426, 433, 436f., 442, 452, 457, 470, 474, 484, 566–570, 581f., 588, 590, 592
- Victorian novel 32f., 70, 122, 127, 213, 263, 284, 288, 296f., 301, 337, 339, 341f., 344, 346, 348, 377, 389, 433, 467, 572, 582
vulnerable 94, 170, 182, 386, 399, 416, 462, 510f., 515, 517, 570f., 573, 585, 592
- vulnerability 240, 341f., 374, 464, 502f., 514–516, 518, 520, 546, 557, 567, 572f., 577, 580, 584, 592f.

white male effect 35, 511

Index of Persons

Abernathy, John   280
Agamben, Giorgio   524
Albutt, T.C.   423f.
Aldini, Giovanni   281
Amis, Martin   487, 560
Appadurai, Arjun   39
Arnauld, Antoine   49
Arnold, Matthew   460, 561, 567, 569f.
Atwood, Margaret   521f., 526, 537, 551
Austen, Jane   32, 55, 250, 253–255, 257–270, 312, 327, 330, 345, 365, 387, 583

Bacigalupi, Paolo   537
Bacon, Francis   46, 72, 95, 103
Bataille, Georges   61
Bauman, Zygmunt   7f., 45, 578, 595
Bayes, Thomas   24, 80, 95
Beauvoir, Simone de   574f., 584
Beck, Ulrich   2, 4, 7–12, 15, 17, 20, 22f., 25, 36, 38, 111, 512, 537f., 548, 555, 557, 560, 568, 584, 588f., 591
Behn, Aphra   68, 71, 236
Benjamin, Walter   61
Bentham, Jeremy   320, 324f.
Bernoulli, Jacob   24, 49f., 76
Bernstein, Peter L.   1, 21, 27f., 43f., 47, 49f., 55, 207, 215, 292, 436
Boswell, James   180
Boucicault, Dion   351
Bourdin, Martial   438
Braine, John   484, 487
Brontë, Charlotte   33, 287, 295, 310–312, 314, 317–320, 335, 581
Bulwer-Lytton, Edward   351
Burney, Frances   31f., 58, 70, 124, 181, 194, 215–220, 223, 225–231, 234–239, 241, 243–250, 255, 264, 312, 323
Butler, Judith   280f., 572

Camus, Albert   114, 433
Canguilhem, Georges   414
Carlyle, Thomas   287, 321f., 567
Chesterton, G.K.   439, 587

Conrad, Joseph   35, 65, 206–208, 433–444, 447–451, 454, 457, 462, 467, 555, 565, 592
Cromwell, Thomas   50
Cusk, Rachel   36, 571–578, 580–586
Cyples, William   342f.

Darwin, Charles   33, 35, 254, 281, 345, 364, 381f., 384, 393, 410, 412f., 417, 421, 430, 444, 455, 458, 492, 557, 559f., 563, 580
Darwin, Erasmus   280f., 345, 363, 382, 412f.
Daston, Lorraine J.   29, 48–53, 59f., 115, 291
David, Florence Nightingale   43, 45, 47–50,
Davy, Humphry   281
Defoe, Daniel   1, 30–32, 34, 39, 49, 53, 55–60, 62f., 67–69, 71–81, 84f., 88, 90f., 93–104, 106–111, 113–119, 121–124, 126–137, 139, 141, 143–146, 148–151, 159, 162, 164, 170f., 181–183, 194, 215, 227f., 230, 232, 248, 250, 255, 289, 296, 312, 572, 574f., 588, 592, 595
DeLillo, Don   25f., 555
Derrida, Jacques   556
Dickens, Charles   33f., 287, 301, 312, 320–323, 325–329, 331, 339, 345, 360, 468
Dingby, Everard   458, 460
Disraeli, Benjamin   288, 295
Dostoevsky, Fyodor M.   61
Douglas, Mary   4, 7, 17f., 22, 109f., 253, 434, 557

Eagleton, Terry   64f., 181, 311, 317–319, 376, 434, 468, 475f., 479–481
Eliot, George   33f., 144, 256, 263, 338f., 343, 345, 360, 363–368, 370f., 373–379, 381f., 449, 581
Engels, Friedrich   288, 303
Ewald, Francois   5, 13–15, 29, 44, 296

Fawcett, Edward Douglas   439
Fermat, Pierre de   28, 47, 49

Fielding, Henry   59, 68f., 109, 162–164, 193, 228
Flanagan, Richard   555, 566
Ford, Ford Maddox   416, 462
Forster, Edward Morgan   35, 180, 281, 302, 416, 443, 451–454, 456–459, 461–467, 472f., 504, 510
Foucault, Michel   2, 7, 13, 15, 22, 33, 110, 112, 157, 216, 344, 375, 411, 414, 526, 533, 548, 588
Freud, Sigmund   426f.
Fukuyama, Francis   520f.

Gaines, Susan M.   537
Galsworthy, John   451
Galton, Francis   413, 458, 460
Galvani, Luigi   281
Gaskell, Elizabeth   33, 130, 285, 287, 290f., 295, 301–303, 305–310, 312, 320, 329–331, 333–335, 337f., 467, 581
Gee, Maggie   537
Ghosh, Amitav   550–554, 591
Giddens, Anthony   7–9, 537, 540, 544f., 553, 592–594
Gigerenzer, Gerd   29f., 44, 47f., 51, 53, 59, 291–294, 298, 320, 322, 325, 413, 589
Gissing, George   33, 264, 348, 360, 375, 409, 416–421, 423–428, 430, 443, 449, 463
Graunt, John   49f., 114, 293

Hacking, Ian   13, 22, 28f., 34, 48f., 51, 62, 185, 190, 291f., 298, 320, 552
Halley, Edmund   50, 158, 293
Hamid, Mohsin   555, 566
Hardy, Thomas   33f., 39, 65, 256, 264, 266, 329, 360, 365, 375, 381–391, 395f., 399–411, 413, 415f., 418, 425f., 429, 443f., 449, 462, 549
Haywood, Eliza   68, 71, 236, 487f., 493
Heise, Ursula K.   17, 25f., 37, 39, 538
Hobbes, Thomas   102, 157
Hobsbaum, E.J.   339
Hogarth, William   59, 289
Hollinghurst, Alan   35, 39, 501–505, 507f., 510, 514f., 517–519
Hoyle, Edmund   24

Hume, David   52, 95, 143, 164, 185, 189–191, 325
Huygens, Christiaan   49

Isherwood, Christopher   101, 104
Ishiguro, Kazuo   23, 36, 520–523, 525–527, 529, 532, 536, 551

James, Henry   65, 344, 439
Jevons, William Stanley   292
Joyce, James   219, 284, 476, 500

Kavanagh, Thomas M.   23, 29, 32, 43, 51, 57, 59, 62f., 66, 115, 186f., 230, 337, 365
Kermode, Frank   194, 593
Keynes, John Maynard   49, 51
Kingsley, Charles   295
Kingsolver, Barbara   537, 551
Knight, Frank H.   2f.,
Koselleck, Reinhart   45f.
Kunzru, Hari   553

Larkin, Philip   586
Lash, Scott   10, 17, 25, 594
Latour, Bruno   67, 102, 552
Lawrence, D.H.   401, 405, 416, 463
Lawrence, William   280
Leibniz, Gottfried Wilhelm   48
Levine, George   270f., 275, 344f., 364, 379, 402f., 412, 435
Lewes, George Henry   351
Locke, John   52, 95, 189–191, 230
Lombroso, Cesare   444
London, Jack   453
Lovecraft, H.P.   201
Luhmann, Niklas   3, 7, 15f., 594
Lukács, George   65
Lupton, Deborah   4f., 10f., 17, 20f., 37–39, 189, 191

Malthus, Thomas Robert   288, 390, 412f.
Marx, Karl   451
Masterman, C.F.G.   452f., 456, 461, 463, 467, 469
Maudsley, Henry   410–412
McCarthy, Cormac   26, 537, 551

Index of Persons

McEwan, Ian   1, 26, 36, 39, 440, 520, 537–539, 541f., 544, 546f., 551–557, 560f., 563, 565–573, 588, 591, 593
Méré, Chevalier de   47
Meredith, George   339
Messud, Claire   555
Mill, John Stuart   299, 314, 321, 324f., 339, 402
Miller, Henry   301, 423, 478, 578
Moivre, Abraham de   24, 47, 49f., 84

Newton, Isaac   58, 158
Nietzsche, Friedrich   458, 463
Nordau, Max   413, 420, 444

O'Neill, Joseph   555
Orwell, George   35, 467–476, 478–482, 484, 526, 574

Pascal, Blaise   24, 28, 47–49, 87, 292
Poovey, Mary   55, 57, 63, 69, 86, 102, 114, 262, 273, 283, 290, 294f., 303, 307, 326, 341f., 350
Pope, Alexander   57
Popper, Karl R.   43
Porter, Theodore M.   31, 33f., 179, 192, 291–294, 296–298
Pound, Ezra   419
Price, Richard   50, 255, 293
Proust, Marcel   476

Quetelet, Adolphe   297f., 342f., 413

Reith, Gerda   28, 43, 48–51, 55, 59–61, 186, 193, 292, 367f., 590, 594
Richardson, Samuel   22, 68–70, 123, 162, 204, 254, 267f.
Robinson, Kim Stanley   537
Rose, Nikolas   4, 13, 34
Rushdie, Salman   555, 566

Safran Foer, Jonathan   555
Said, Edward   77, 92
Schopenhauer, Arthur   298f., 364
Scott, Sarah   69, 236, 263
Shamsie, Kamila   555
Shaw, George Bernard   440

Shelley, Mary   32, 260, 270–273, 276–282, 284f., 521, 535
Shelley, Percy   280
Shklovsky, Victor   180
Sillitoe, Alan   35, 39, 483–489, 492f., 495f., 498f., 501f., 504
Slovic, Paul   3, 7, 19, 38, 511
Smiles, Samuel   296
Smith, Adam   77, 295
Smollett, Tobias G.   31, 39, 69, 127, 130, 147, 149, 162–165, 167–176, 178, 181, 198, 248, 250, 484
Sontag, Susan   123
Spencer, Herbert   298, 412
Sterne, Laurence   31, 39, 68f., 147, 151, 160, 163, 168, 178–200, 202, 206, 214f., 246f.
Stevens, Wallace   589
Stevenson, Robert Louis   414
Swift, Jonathan   23, 31, 39, 63, 68, 78, 95, 102, 147–154, 156–160, 162, 164, 179, 183, 191, 198, 203, 206, 208, 298, 592

Taylor, William Cooke   288f.
Thackeray, William   339
Todhunter, Isaac   48
Trollope, Anthony   33f., 237, 255, 338f., 341f., 345–353, 357f., 360, 362f., 365, 367, 381, 421
Tversky, Amos   19, 265

Updike, John.   551, 555

Walpole, Horace   31, 39, 75, 147, 178, 200–210, 213–216
Weber, Max   19, 88
Weldon, Fay   521
Wells, H.G.   439, 453, 473
Wildavsky, Aaron B.   7, 17–19
Williams, Raymond   287, 302, 320, 329, 483
Wollstonecraft, Mary   123, 215, 237
Woolf, Leonard   476
Woolf, Virginia   36, 383, 416, 462, 474, 556, 571, 574, 576, 582

Žižek, Slavoj   11